Collins
German
Dictionary

D0067915

BEGINNER'S

GERMAN

DICTIONARY

 HarperResource

An Imprint of HarperCollins*Publishers*

Collins

Collins
German
Dictionary

HarperCollins Publishers
Westerhill Road
Bishopbriggs
Glasgow
G64 2QT
Great Britain

Fourth Edition 2007

Reprint 10 9 8 7 6 5 4 3 2 1 0

ISBN-13 978-0-00-725352-4
ISBN-10 0-00-725352-4

www.collins.co.uk

A catalogue record for this book is available from the British Library

HarperCollins Publishers,
10 East 53rd Street, New York, NY 10022

COLLINS BEGINNER'S GERMAN DICTIONARY.
Third US Edition 2007

ISBN-13 978-0-06-134963-8
ISBN-10 0-06-134963-1

Library of Congress Cataloging-in-Publication Data has been applied for

www.harpercollins.com

Typeset by Morton Word Processing Ltd, Scarborough, Thomas Callan and Davidson's Prepress, Glasgow

Printed in Italy by Rotolito Lombarda S.p.A.

Acknowledgements
We would like to thank those authors and publishers who kindly gave permission for copyright material to be used in the Collins Word Web. We would also like to thank Times Newspapers Ltd for providing valuable data.

EDITORS
Horst Kopleck
Veronika Schnorr
Christine Bahr
Elizabeth Morris
Philip Mann
Martin Crellin
Elspeth Anderson

EDITORIAL COORDINATION
Maree Airlie
Joyce Littlejohn
Susie Beattie

ILLUSTRATIONS
Richard Anderson

CONCEPT DEVELOPMENT
Michela Clari
Ray Carrick

SERIES EDITOR
Lorna Knight

William Collins' dream of knowledge for all began with the publication of his first book in 1819. A self-educated mill worker, he not only enriched millions of lives, but also founded a flourishing publishing house. Today, staying true to this spirit, Collins books are packed with inspiration, innovation, and practical expertise. They place you at the centre of a world of possibility and give you exactly what you need to explore it.

Language is the key to this exploration, and at the heart of Collins Dictionaries is language as it is really used. New words, phrases, and meanings spring up every day, and all of them are captured and analysed by the Collins Word Web. Constantly updated, and with over 2.5 billion entries, this living language resource is unique to our dictionaries.

Words are tools for life. And a Collins Dictionary makes them work for you.

Collins. Do more.

CONTENTS

INTRODUCTION

Collins Easy Learning German Dictionary is an innovative dictionary designed specifically for anyone starting to learn German. We are grateful to everyone who has contributed to the development of the Easy Learning series, and acknowledge the help of the examining boards in providing us with word lists and exam papers, which we carefully studied when compiling this dictionary.

Note on trademarks
Words which we have reason to believe constitute trademarks have been designated as such. However, neither the presence nor the absence of such designation should be regarded as affecting the legal status of any trademark.

DICTIONARY SKILLS

Using a dictionary is a skill you can improve with practice and by following some basic guidelines. This section gives you a detailed explanation of how to use the dictionary to ensure you get the most out of it.

The answers to all the checks in this section are on page 16.

▶ MAKE SURE YOU LOOK IN THE RIGHT SIDE OF THE DICTIONARY

The German-English side comes first, followed by the English-German. The middle pages of the book have a blue border so that you can see where one side finishes and the other starts.

> 1   Which side of the dictionary would you look up to translate "das Fahrrad"?

▶ FINDING THE WORD YOU WANT

When you are looking for a word, for example **froh**, look at the first letter – **f** – and find the **F** section in the German-English side. At the top of each page, you'll find the first and last words on that page. When you find the page with the words starting with **fr**, scan down the page until you find the word you want. Remember that even if a word has an umlaut on it, for example *für*, it makes no difference to the alphabetical order.

> 2   On which page will you find the word – "gestern"?
> 3   Which comes first – "Bruder" or "Brötchen"?

▶ MAKE SURE YOU LOOK AT THE RIGHT ENTRY

An entry is made up of a **word**, its <u>translations</u> and, often, example phrases to show you how to use the translations. If there is more than one entry for the same word, then there is an information box to tell you so. Look at the following example entries:

flat ADJECTIVE

> see also **flat** NOUN
> [1] flach ◊ *flat shoes* flache Schuhe
> ♦ **a flat roof** ein Flachdach NEUT
> [2] platt *(tyre)* ◊ *I've got a flat tyre.* Ich habe einen platten Reifen.

flat NOUN

> see also **flat** ADJECTIVE
> die Wohnung ◊ *She lives in a flat.* Sie wohnt in einer Wohnung.

4 Which entry for "*flat*" should you look at if you want to translate the phrase "*My car has a flat tyre*"?

Always pay attention to information boxes – they tell you if there is more than one entry for the same word, give you guidance on grammatical points, or tell you about differences between German and British life.

▶ CHOOSING THE RIGHT TRANSLATION

The main translation of a word is shown on a new line and is underlined to make it stand out from the rest of the entry. If there is more than one main translation for a word, each one is numbered. If an entry continues over the page there is a signpost to indicate this ☞.

Often you will see phrases in *italics*, preceded by a white diamond ◊. These help you choose the translation you want because they show how the translation they follow can be used.

5 Use the phrases given at the entry "*hard*" to help you translate: "*This bread is hard*".

Words often have more than one meaning and more than one translation, for example, a **pool** can be a puddle, a pond or a swimming pool; **pool** can also be a game. When you are translating from English into German, be careful to choose the German word that has the particular meaning you want. The dictionary offers you a lot of help with this. Look at the following entry:

pool NOUN
1 (*puddle*)
die Pfütze
2 (*pond*)
der Teich (PL die Teiche)
3 (*for swimming*)
das Schwimmbecken (PL die
Schwimmbecken)
4 (*game*)
das Poolbillard ◊ *Shall we have a game of
pool?* Sollen wir eine Partie Poolbillard spielen?
◆ **the pools** (*football*) das Toto ◊ *to do the pools*
Toto spielen

The underlining points out all the main translations, the numbers tell you that
there is more than one possible translation and the words in brackets in *italics*
help you choose which translation you want.

> 6 How would you translate "*I like playing pool*"?

**Never take the first translation you see without looking at the others.
Always look to see if there is more than one translation underlined.**

Phrases in **bold type** preceded by a black diamond ◆ are phrases which are
particularly common or important. Sometimes these phrases have a completely
different translation from the main translation; sometimes the translation is the
same. For example:

cancer NOUN
der Krebs (GEN des Krebses) ◊ *He's got
cancer.* Er hat Krebs.
◆ **I'm Cancer.** Ich bin Krebs.

abgemacht ADJECTIVE
agreed ◊ *Wir trafen uns zur abgemachten
Zeit.* We met at the agreed time.
◆ **Abgemacht!** OK!

When you look up a word, make sure you look beyond the main translations to
see if the entry includes any **bold phrases**.

> 7 Look up "*fahren*" to help you translate the sentence "*Ich werde
> morgen mit dem Zug fahren*".

▶ MAKING USE OF THE PHRASES IN THE DICTIONARY

Sometimes when you look up a word you will find not only the word, but the
exact phrase you want. For example, you might want to say "*What's the date
today?*" Look up **date** and you will find the exact phrase and its translation.

Sometimes you have to adapt what you find in the dictionary. If you want to say
"*I play darts*" and look up **dart** you will find:

dart NOUN
der Pfeil (PL die Pfeile)
◆ **to play darts** Darts spielen

You have to substitute *ich spiele* for the infinitive form *spielen*. You will often have to adapt the infinitive in this way, adding the correct ending to the verb for **ich**, **du**, **er** etc and choosing the present, future or past form. For help with this, look at the German verb tables in the middle of the dictionary. **Spielen** is a regular verb so it follows the same pattern as **machen**, which is set out on page 344.

8 How would you say *"We played football"*?

Phrases containing nouns and adjectives may also need to be adapted. You may need to make the noun genitive, plural or dative plural, or the adjective feminine, neuter or plural. Remember that some nouns have irregular genitive or plural forms and that this information is shown in the entry.

9 How would you say *"The red flowers are beautiful"*?

▶ DON'T OVERUSE THE DICTIONARY

It takes time to look up words so try to avoid using the dictionary unnecessarily, especially in exams. Think carefully about what you want to say and see if you can put it another way, using the words you already know. To rephrase things you can:

　◇Use a word with a similar meaning. This is particularly easy with adjectives, as there are a lot of words which mean *good, bad, big* etc and you're sure to know at least one.

　◇Use negatives: if the cake you made was a total disaster, you could just say that it wasn't very good.

　◇Use particular examples instead of general terms. If you are asked to describe the sports facilities in your area, and time is short, you could say something like "In our town there is a swimming pool and a football ground."

10 How could you say *"The Black Forest is huge"* without looking up the word "huge"?

You can also guess the meaning of a German word by using others to give you a clue. If you see the sentence *"ich lese ein gutes Buch"*, you may not know the meaning of the word **lese**, but you know it's a verb because it's preceded by **ich**. Therefore it must be something you can do to a book: **read**. So the translation is: *I'm reading a good book.*

11 Try NOT to use your dictionary to work out the meaning of the sentence *"Das Mädchen schreibt ihrer Brieffreundin einen Brief auf Deutsch"*.

PARTS OF SPEECH

If you look up the word **flat**, you will see that there are two entries for this word as it can be a noun or an adjective. It helps to choose correctly between the entries if you know how to recognize these different types of words.

▶ NOUNS

Nouns often appear with words like *a, the, this, that, my, your* and *his*.
They can be singular (abbreviated to SING in the dictionary):

his **dog**   *her* **cat**   *a* **street**

or plural (abbreviated to PL in the dictionary):

the **facts**   *those* **people**   *his* **shoes**   *our* **holidays**

They can be the subject of a verb:

Vegetables are good for you

or the object of a verb:

I play **tennis**

> *I bought my mother a box of chocolates.*
>
> **12 Which three words in this sentence are nouns?**
> **13 Which of the nouns is plural?**

German nouns all start with a capital letter and can be either masculine, feminine or neuter (abbreviated to MASC, FEM or NEUT in the dictionary).
Masculine nouns are shown by **der**:

der Hund   ***der*** Zug   ***der*** Arm

feminine nouns are shown by **die**:

die Katze   *die* Milch   *die* Tür

neuter nouns are shown by **das**:

das Auto   *das* Kind   *das* Sofa

The plural form of **der**, **die** and **das** is **die**. The plural of most feminine German nouns is made by adding **en** or **n**:

die Katzen   *die* Türen   *die* Familien

Many German nouns, however, do not add **en** or **n** in the plural, so the plural of these nouns is shown in the entry:

die Hunde   *die* Häuser   *die* Autos   *die* Wagen   *die* Mütter

In German **der**, **die** and **das** (and also **ein** and **eine**) may change when the noun they precede is used in another case, for example in the accusative, genitive or dative case (abbreviated to ACC, GEN and DAT in the dictionary). It is important to learn when you should use each case in German.

The **nominative** case is used to show the subject of a sentence – *the* **dog** is chasing the cat. All German nouns are shown in the nominative case in the dictionary:

Ich esse ein Eis.   *Die Katze* schläft.   *Der Ball* ist im Garten.

The **accusative** case is used to show the direct object of a sentence – I love *chocolate* – and after certain prepositions e.g. durch, ohne:

Ich sehe **den Hund.**   Sie liebt **mich.**   Wir gingen durch **den Wald.**

The **genitive** case is used to show that something belongs to somebody – my *father's* hat – and after certain prepositions e.g. wegen:

das Auto **des Mannes**   der Hund **meiner Mutter**   wegen **des** schlechten **Wetters**

The **dative** case is used to show the indirect object of a sentence – she told *me* the news – and after certain prepositions e.g. mit, aus:

Ich gebe **dem Lehrer** das Heft.   Er schreibt **mir** einen Brief.   Sie spielen mit **dem Ball.**

The rules for the changes to **der**, **die**, **das**, **ein** and **eine** are shown here:

	MASC SING	FEM SING	NEUT SING	PL
NOM	der	die	das	die
ACC	den	die	das	die
GEN	des	der	des	der
DAT	dem	der	dem	den

	MASC SING	FEM SING	NEUT SING
NOM	ein	eine	ein
ACC	einen	eine	ein
GEN	eines	einer	eines
DAT	einem	einer	einem

Masculine and neuter singular German nouns usually add **es** or **s** when they are used in the genitive case:

des Vaters   des Hundes   des Autos

feminine and plural German nouns do not change in the genitive:

der Mutter   der Tür   der Katzen   der Männer

Sometimes, however, the genitive form is irregular, and this is shown in the entry:

des Jazz   des Herrn   des Abiturienten

An **n** is added to the plural form of German nouns in the dative case, unless the plural form already ends in **n**:

den Kindern   den Häusern   den Katzen   den Lehrerinnen

> *Ich gebe meinem Bruder ein Buch.*
>
> 14 Which two words in the sentence are nouns – are they singular or plural?
> 15 What is the genitive form of "*Bruder*"?
> 16 Use your dictionary to find the plural form of "*Buch*". Then work out the dative plural form.

▶ PRONOUNS

Words like *I, me, you, he, she, him, her* and *they* are pronouns. They can be used instead of nouns. You can refer to a person as *he* or *she* or to a thing as *it*.

> *I showed him the new computer.*
>
> 17 Which words are pronouns in this sentence?

▶ ADJECTIVES

Flat can be an adjective as well as a noun. Adjectives describe nouns: your tyre can be **flat**, you can have a pair of **flat** shoes.

> *I'm afraid of the dark.*
> *The girl has dark hair.*
>
> 18 In which sentence is "*dark*" an adjective?

German adjectives can be masculine, feminine or neuter, singular or plural. The ending of the adjective may also change depending on whether the noun is preceded by **ein**, **eine** etc or by **der**, **die** or **das**:

der **kleine** Hund
kleine Kinder

ein **kleines** Kind
die **kleinen** Katzen

Adjectives are also affected by the case i.e. **nominative**, **accusative** etc of the noun they describe:

des **kleinen** Hundes
einem **kleinen** Mädchen

der **kleinen** Katze
den **kleinen** Kindern

The endings of German adjectives follow the rules shown here:

	MASC SING(der)	FEM SING(die)	NEUT SING(das)	PL(die)
NOM	kleine	kleine	kleine	kleinen
ACC	kleinen	kleine	kleine	kleinen
GEN	kleinen	kleinen	kleinen	kleinen
DAT	kleinen	kleinen	kleinen	kleinen

	MASC SING(ein)	FEM SING(eine)	NEUT SING(ein)	PL
NOM	kleiner	kleine	kleines	kleine
ACC	kleinen	kleine	kleines	kleine
GEN	kleinen	kleinen	kleinen	kleiner
DAT	kleinen	kleinen	kleinen	kleinen

Only the basic form of the adjective is shown in the dictionary. So, if you want to find out what kind of girls **die schönen Mädchen** are, look under **schön**.

Some adjectives, called **invariable adjectives**, don't change whether they are masculine, feminine, neuter or plural or describing a noun in a different case. This is shown in the dictionary:

pink ADJECTIVE
rosa
rosa is invariable.
◊ a pink shirt ein rosa Hemd

19 What is the feminine accusative singular form of "schwarz"?
20 What is the basic form of the adjective in the sentence "Peter ist ein braves Kind"?

▶ VERBS

She's going to record the programme for me.
His time in the race was a new world record.

Record is a verb in the first sentence, and a noun in the second.

One way to recognize a verb is that it frequently comes with a pronoun such as **I**, **you** or **she**, or with somebody's name. Verbs can relate to the present, the past or the future. They have a number of different forms to show this: **I'm going** (present), **he will go** (future), and **Nicola went** (past). Often verbs appear with **to**: **they promised to go**. This basic form of the verb is called the infinitive.

In this dictionary verbs are preceded by "to", so you can identify them at a glance. No matter which of the four previous examples you want to translate, you should look up to **go**, not **going** or **went**. If you want to translate I **thought**, look up to **think**.

I came	she's crying	they've done it	he's out

21 What would you look up to translate the verbs in these phrases?

Verbs have different endings in German, depending on whether you are talking about **ich**, **du**, **wir** etc: **ich mache**, **du machst**, **wir machen** etc. They also have different forms for the present, past (imperfect and perfect tenses), future etc; **wir machen** (*we do* = present), **wir machten** (*we did* = imperfect), **wir haben gemacht** (*we have done* = perfect), **wir werden machen** (*we will do* = future). **machen** is the infinitive and is the form that appears in the dictionary.

Sometimes the verb changes completely between the infinitive form and the **ich**, **du**, **er** etc form. For example, *to give* is **geben**, but *he gives* is **er gibt**, and *ich bin gegangen* comes from the verb **gehen** (*to go*).

On pages 344-356 of the dictionary, you will find tables of the most important forms of German verbs. And on pages 357-360 you will find a list of the most important forms of other German irregular verbs. Any irregular forms of verbs are also shown in the entry.

to **bowl** VERB
    see also **bowl** NOUN
  (*in cricket*)
  werfen (PRESENT **wirft**, IMPERFECT **warf**, PERFECT hat geworfen)

heben VERB (IMPERFECT **hob**, PERFECT **hat gehoben**)
to lift

22 Look up the dictionary to find the imperfect and perfect tenses of "laufen".

▶ ADVERBS

An adverb is a word which describes a verb or an adjective:

> Write **soon**.
> The film was **very** good.

> Check your work **carefully**.

In the sentence "*The swimming pool is open daily*", **daily** is an adverb describing the adjective **open**. In the phrase "*my daily routine*", **daily** is an adjective describing the noun **routine**. We use the same word in English for both adjective and adverb forms, and the same word is used in German too. In many cases the same German word is used to translate an adjective and an adverb in English. Sometimes, however, the translations are different and you will need to know the difference between an adjective and an adverb to be able to choose the correct German translation.

Take the sentence "The menu changes daily".

23 Is "*daily*" an adverb or an adjective here?

▶ PREPOSITIONS

Prepositions are words like **for**, **with** and **across**, which are followed by nouns or pronouns:

> I've got a present **for** David.   Come **with** me.   He ran **across** the road.

In German, all prepositions are followed by nouns or pronouns in a certain case, for example, **mit** is followed by nouns or pronouns in the dative case. The case which follows a preposition is shown in the entry:

ab PREPOSITION, ADVERB
*The preposition **ab** takes the dative.*
[1] from ◇ *Kinder ab zwölf Jahren* children from the age of twelve ◇ *ab morgen* from tomorrow
[2] off ◇ *Die Straße geht nach links ab.* The road goes off to the left. ◇ *Der Knopf ist ab.* The button has come off. ◇ *Ab nach Hause!* Off you go home!
♦ **ab sofort** as of now
♦ **ab und zu** now and then

above PREPOSITION, ADVERB
über ◇ *above forty degrees* über vierzig Grad
Use the accusative to express movement or a change of place. Use the dative when there is no change of place.
◇ *He put his hands above his head.* Er hielt die Hände über den Kopf. ◇ *The lamp is hanging above the table.* Die Lampe hängt über dem Tisch.
♦ **the flat above** die Wohnung darüber
♦ **mentioned above** oben erwähnt
♦ **above all** vor allem

The party's over.
The shop's just over the road.

24 Which sentence shows a preposition followed by a noun?
25 What case does the preposition "*durch*" take?
26 Use your dictionary to help you translate "*He is going into the garden*".

▶ ANSWERS

1 the German side

2 on page 123

3 **Brötchen** comes first

4 the first (ADJECTIVE) entry

5 **Dieses Brot ist hart.**

6 **Ich spiele gern Poolbillard.**

7 **I'm going by train tomorrow.**

8 **Wir spielten Fußball.**

9 **Die roten Blumen sind schön.**

10 **Der Schwarzwald ist sehr groß.**

11 **The girl is writing a letter to her pen friend in German.**

12 **mother**, **box** and **chocolates** are nouns

13 **chocolates** is plural

14 **Bruder** and **Buch** are nouns – they are both singular

15 **Bruders**

16 **Bücher** – **Büchern** is the dative plural form

17 **I** and **him** are pronouns

18 in the second sentence

19 **schwarze**

20 **brav**

21 to **come**, to **cry**, to **do**, to **be**

22 the imperfect tense is **lief**, the perfect tense is **ist gelaufen**

23 **daily** is an adverb

24 the second sentence

25 **durch** takes the accusative case

26 **Er geht in den Garten.**

A

der **Aal** NOUN (PL die **Aale**)
eel

ab PREPOSITION, ADVERB
*The preposition **ab** takes the dative.*
[1] from ◊ *Kinder ab zwölf Jahren*
children from the age of twelve ◊ *ab morgen* from tomorrow
[2] off ◊ *Die Straße geht nach links ab.*
The road goes off to the left. ◊ *Der Knopf ist ab.* The button has come off. ◊ *Ab nach Hause!* Off you go home!
♦ **ab sofort** as of now
♦ **ab und zu** now and then

abbiegen VERB (IMPERFECT **bog ab**, PERFECT **ist abgebogen**)
[1] to turn off ◊ *Sie bog an der Kreuzung nach links ab.* At the crossroads she turned off to the left.
[2] to bend ◊ *Die Hauptstraße biegt nach rechts ab.* The main road bends to the right.

die **Abbildung** NOUN
illustration

abbrechen VERB (PRESENT **bricht ab**, IMPERFECT **brach ab**, PERFECT **hat abgebrochen**)
[1] to break off ◊ *Sie brach einen blühenden Zweig ab.* She broke off a flowering branch.
[2] to pull down ◊ *Das alte Gebäude muss abgebrochen werden.* The old building will have to be pulled down.
[3] to stop ◊ *Es ist schon spät, wir sollten abbrechen.* It's late now; we ought to stop.
[4] to abort ◊ *Das dauert zu lang, du solltest das Programm abbrechen.* It's taking too long; you should abort the program.

abbuchen VERB (PERFECT **hat abgebucht**)
to debit ◊ *Der Betrag wird von Ihrem Konto abgebucht.* The amount will be debited from your account.

der **Abend** NOUN (PL die **Abende**)
evening ◊ *Sie macht jeden Abend einen Spaziergang.* She goes for a walk every evening. ◊ *guten Abend* good evening
♦ **zu Abend essen** to have dinner
♦ **heute Abend** this evening

das **Abendbrot** NOUN
supper

das **Abendessen** NOUN (PL die **Abendessen**)
dinner ◊ *Zum Abendessen gibt es Spaghetti.* There's spaghetti for dinner.

abends ADVERB
in the evening

das **Abenteuer** NOUN (PL die **Abenteuer**)
adventure

der **Abenteuerfilm** NOUN
adventure film

aber CONJUNCTION, ADVERB
[1] but ◊ *Er wollte mit uns mitkommen, aber seine Eltern haben es nicht erlaubt.* He wanted to come with us, but his parents wouldn't let him.
[2] however ◊ *Ich möchte nach Ägypten reisen. Ich habe aber kein Geld.* I'd like to go to Egypt. However, I haven't got any money.
♦ **Das ist aber schön!** That's really nice.
♦ **Nun ist aber Schluss!** Now that's enough!

abfahren VERB (PRESENT **fährt ab**, IMPERFECT **fuhr ab**, PERFECT **ist abgefahren**)
to leave ◊ *Wir fahren morgen sehr früh ab.* We're leaving very early tomorrow.
◊ *Wann fährt dein Zug ab?* When does your train leave?

die **Abfahrt** NOUN
departure

der **Abfall** NOUN (PL die **Abfälle**)
rubbish

der **Abfalleimer** NOUN (PL die **Abfalleimer**)
rubbish bin

abfällig ADJECTIVE
disparaging

abfliegen VERB (IMPERFECT **flog ab**, PERFECT **ist abgeflogen**)
to take off ◊ *Die Maschine ist mit Verspätung abgeflogen.* The plane was late taking off.
♦ **Um wie viel Uhr fliegt ihr ab?** What time does your plane leave?

der **Abflug** NOUN (PL die **Abflüge**)
[1] departure ◊ *Wir müssen eine Stunde vor Abflug am Flughafen sein.* We have to be at the airport one hour before departure.
[2] takeoff ◊ *Die Maschine stürzte kurz nach dem Abflug ab.* The plane crashed shortly after takeoff.

abfragen VERB (PERFECT **hat abgefragt**)
[1] to test orally ◊ *die Vokabeln abfragen* to give an oral vocabulary test
[2] to call up ◊ *Sie können die Abfahrtszeiten am Computer abfragen.* You can call up departure times on the computer.

das **Abgas** NOUN (GEN des **Abgases**, PL die **Abgase**)
exhaust fumes

abgeben VERB (PRESENT **gibt ab**, IMPERFECT **gab ab**, PERFECT **hat abgegeben**)
[1] to hand in ◊ *Die Klassenarbeiten müssen am Ende der Stunde abgegeben werden.* Tests must be handed in at the end of the lesson.

2 to pass ◊ *Er gab den Ball an den Mittelstürmer ab.* He passed the ball to the centre-forward.
♦ **sich mit jemandem abgeben** to associate with somebody
♦ **sich mit etwas abgeben** to bother with something ◊ *Mit solch dummen Fragen will ich mich nicht abgeben.* I don't want to bother with such stupid questions.
♦ **jemandem etwas abgeben** to let somebody have something
♦ **Du würdest eine wunderbare Lehrerin abgeben.** You would make a wonderful teacher.

abgelegen ADJECTIVE
remote

abgemacht ADJECTIVE
agreed ◊ *Wir trafen uns zur abgemachten Zeit.* We met at the agreed time.
♦ **Abgemacht!** OK!

abgeneigt ADJECTIVE
disinclined

abgesehen ADJECTIVE
♦ **es auf jemanden abgesehen haben** to be out to get somebody
♦ **es auf etwas abgesehen haben** to be after something
♦ **abgesehen von ...** apart from ...
◊ *Abgesehen von ein paar Fehlern war der Aufsatz sehr gut.* The essay was very good, apart from a few mistakes.

abgewöhnen VERB (PERFECT **hat abgewöhnt**)
♦ **sich etwas abgewöhnen** to give something up ◊ *Ich will mir das Rauchen abgewöhnen.* I want to give up smoking.

der **Abhang** NOUN (PL die **Abhänge**)
slope

abhängen (1) VERB (PERFECT **hat abgehängt**)
1 to take down ◊ *Weil ihr das Bild nicht mehr gefiel, hängte sie es ab.* She took the picture down because she didn't like it any more.
2 to unhitch ◊ *Er hängte den Wohnwagen ab, bevor er in die Stadt fuhr.* He unhitched the caravan before he drove into town.
3 to shake off ◊ *Den Räubern gelang es, die Polizei abzuhängen.* The robbers managed to shake off the police.

abhängen (2) VERB (IMPERFECT **hing ab**, PERFECT **hat abgehangen**)
♦ **von jemandem abhängen** to depend on somebody
♦ **von etwas abhängen** to depend on something ◊ *Es hängt vom Wetter ab, ob das Fußballspiel stattfindet.* Whether or not the football match goes ahead depends on the weather.

abhängig ADJECTIVE
♦ **abhängig von** dependent on

abheben VERB (IMPERFECT **hob ab**, PERFECT **hat abgehoben**)
1 to answer ◊ *Es scheint niemand zu Hause zu sein, es hebt nämlich keiner ab.* There doesn't seem to be anyone at home as nobody's answering the phone.
2 to withdraw ◊ *Ich muss Geld vom Sparbuch abheben.* I'll have to withdraw some money from my savings account.
3 to take off ◊ *Wir sahen zu, wie das Flugzeug abhob.* We watched the plane take off.
4 to lift off ◊ *Die Rakete hob senkrecht ab.* The rocket lifted off vertically.
♦ **sich von etwas abheben** to stand out against something ◊ *Das Muster hebt sich gut vom Hintergrund ab.* The pattern stands out well against this background.

abholen VERB (PERFECT **hat abgeholt**)
1 to collect ◊ *Der Müll wird einmal in der Woche abgeholt.* Rubbish is collected once a week.
2 to pick up ◊ *Ich hole dich um sieben ab.* I'll pick you up at seven. ◊ *Der Krankenwagen hat den Verletzten abgeholt.* The ambulance picked up the injured man.

das **Abitur** NOUN
A levels

der **Abiturient** NOUN (GEN des **Abiturienten**, PL die **Abiturienten**)
A level student

die **Abiturientin** NOUN
A level student

abkürzen VERB (PERFECT **hat abgekürzt**)
to abbreviate ◊ *Man kann "bitte wenden" mit b. w. abkürzen.* You can abbreviate "please turn over" to PTO.
♦ **den Weg abkürzen** to take a short cut

die **Abkürzung** NOUN
1 abbreviation ◊ *Die Abkürzung für Europäische Union ist EU.* The abbreviation for European Union is EU.
2 short cut ◊ *Wir haben eine Abkürzung genommen.* We took a short cut.

abladen VERB (PRESENT **lädt ab**, IMPERFECT **lud ab**, PERFECT **hat abgeladen**)
to unload

ablaufen VERB (PRESENT **läuft ab**, IMPERFECT **lief ab**, PERFECT **ist abgelaufen**)
1 to expire ◊ *Ihr Pass ist leider abgelaufen.* Unfortunately, your passport has expired.
2 to drain away ◊ *Der Abfluss ist verstopft, und deshalb läuft das Wasser nicht ab.* The waste pipe is blocked, and that's why the water won't drain away.
♦ **Erzähl mir, wie der Abend abgelaufen ist.** Tell me how the evening went.

ablehnen VERB (PERFECT **hat abgelehnt**)
1 to turn down ◊ *Sie hat das Amt der Klassensprecherin abgelehnt.* She turned down being class representative. ◊ *Mein*

A

Antrag auf ein Stipendium wurde abgelehnt. My application for a grant was turned down.
[2] to disapprove of ◊ *Ich lehne eine solche Arbeitseinstellung ab.* I disapprove of such an attitude to work.

ablenken VERB (PERFECT **hat abgelenkt**)
to distract ◊ *Lenk ihn nicht von seiner Arbeit ab.* Don't distract him from his work.
♦ **Sie hat in letzter Zeit viel Sorgen. Versuch mal, sie etwas abzulenken.** She's had a lot of worries recently. Try to take her mind off things.
♦ **vom Thema ablenken** to change the subject

abliefern VERB (PERFECT **hat abgeliefert**)
[1] to drop off ◊ *Wir haben die Kinder wieder wohlbehalten zu Hause abgeliefert.* We dropped the children off at home safe and sound.
[2] to hand in ◊ *Bis wann musst du das Referat abliefern?* When do you have to hand your assignment in by?
♦ **etwas bei jemandem abliefern** to take something to somebody ◊ *Wir haben die gefundene Uhr beim Fundbüro abgeliefert.* We took the watch we found to the lost property office.

abmachen VERB (PERFECT **hat abgemacht**)
[1] to take off ◊ *Weißt du, wie man den Deckel abmacht?* Do you know how to take the lid off?
[2] to agree ◊ *Wir haben abgemacht, dass wir uns um sieben Uhr treffen.* We agreed to meet at seven.
[3] to sort out ◊ *Ihr solltet das untereinander abmachen, wer heute aufräumt.* Sort out amongst yourselves who's going to clear up today.

die **Abmachung** NOUN
agreement

die **Abnahme** NOUN
decrease ◊ *eine weitere Abnahme der Teilnehmerzahlen* a further decrease in attendance

abnehmen VERB (PRESENT **nimmt ab**, IMPERFECT **nahm ab**, PERFECT **hat abgenommen**)
[1] to remove ◊ *Bei diesem Auto kann man das Verdeck abnehmen.* You can remove the hood on this car.
♦ **Als das Telefon klingelte, nahm sie ab.** When the telephone rang, she answered it.
♦ **jemandem etwas abnehmen** to take something away from somebody ◊ *Ihr wurde der Führerschein abgenommen.* They took away her driving licence.
[2] to decrease ◊ *Die Zahl der Teilnehmer hat stark abgenommen.* The number of participants has decreased dramatically.

[3] to lose weight ◊ *Ich muss dringend abnehmen.* I really must lose weight. ◊ *Ich habe schon zwei Kilo abgenommen.* I've already lost two kilos.
[4] to buy ◊ *Wenn Sie mehr als zehn Stück abnehmen, bekommen Sie einen Rabatt.* If you buy more than ten you get a discount.
♦ **Hat sie dir diese Geschichte wirklich abgenommen?** Did she really buy that story?

das **Abonnement** NOUN (PL die **Abonnements**)
subscription

abonnieren VERB (PERFECT **hat abonniert**)
to subscribe to

abräumen VERB (PERFECT **hat abgeräumt**)
to clear away ◊ *Sie räumte die Teller ab.* She cleared away the plates.
♦ **den Tisch abräumen** to clear the table

abreagieren VERB (PERFECT **hat abreagiert**)
♦ **etwas an jemandem abreagieren** to take something out on somebody
♦ **sich abreagieren** to calm down

die **Abreise** NOUN
departure

abreisen VERB (PERFECT **ist abgereist**)
to leave

Abs. ABBREVIATION (= *Absender*)
sender

die **Absage** NOUN
refusal

absagen VERB (PERFECT **hat abgesagt**)
[1] to call off ◊ *Die Vorstellung wurde abgesagt.* The performance was called off.
[2] to turn down ◊ *eine Einladung absagen* to turn down an invitation

der **Absatz** NOUN (GEN des **Absatzes**, PL die **Absätze**)
[1] heel ◊ *Die Absätze von deinen Schuhen sind ganz schief.* The heels of your shoes are worn down.
[2] paragraph ◊ *Hier solltest du einen Absatz machen.* You need to start a new paragraph here.
[3] sales ◊ *Der Absatz an elektrischen Geräten ist gestiegen.* Sales of electrical appliances have risen.

abschaffen VERB (PERFECT **hat abgeschafft**)
[1] to abolish ◊ *Wann wurde in Deutschland die Todesstrafe abgeschafft?* When was the death sentence abolished in Germany?
[2] to get rid of ◊ *Ich werde mein Auto abschaffen.* I'm going to get rid of my car.

abscheulich ADJECTIVE
abominable

abschicken VERB (PERFECT **hat abgeschickt**)
to send off

der **Abschied** NOUN (PL die **Abschiede**)
parting

☞

♦ **von jemandem Abschied nehmen** to say goodbye to somebody

der **Abschleppdienst** NOUN (PL die **Abschleppdienste**)
breakdown service

abschleppen VERB (PERFECT **hat abgeschleppt**)
to tow ◊ *ein Auto abschleppen* to tow a car

♦ **jemanden abschleppen** to pick somebody up ◊ *Paul hat auf der Party versucht, Petra abzuschleppen.* Paul tried to pick Petra up at the party.

abschließen VERB (IMPERFECT **schloss ab,** PERFECT **hat abgeschlossen**)

[1] to lock ◊ *Ich schließe meinen Schreibtisch immer ab.* I always lock my desk.

♦ **Bist du sicher, dass du abgeschlossen hast?** Are you sure you locked up?

[2] to conclude ◊ *einen Vertrag abschließen* to conclude a contract

abschließend ADJECTIVE, ADVERB
in conclusion ◊ *Abschließend möchte ich noch Folgendes sagen: ...* In conclusion I would like to say this: ...

die **Abschlussprüfung** NOUN
final exam

abschneiden VERB (IMPERFECT **schnitt ab,** PERFECT **hat abgeschnitten**)

[1] to cut ◊ *Kannst du mir bitte eine Scheibe Brot abschneiden?* Can you cut me a slice of bread, please?

[2] to do ◊ *Sie hat in der Prüfung sehr gut abgeschnitten.* She did very well in the exam.

abschrecken VERB (PERFECT **hat abgeschreckt**)
to deter ◊ *Diese Maßnahmen sollen Jugendliche davon abschrecken, Drogen zu nehmen.* These measures are intended to deter young people from taking drugs.

abschreiben VERB (IMPERFECT **schrieb ab,** PERFECT **hat abgeschrieben**)
to copy ◊ *Er wurde dabei erwischt, wie er von seinem Nachbarn abgeschrieben hat.* He was caught copying from his neighbour. ◊ *Schreibt diesen Satz bitte in eure Hefte ab.* Please copy this sentence into your exercise books.

absehbar ADJECTIVE
foreseeable ◊ *in absehbarer Zeit* in the foreseeable future

♦ **Das Ende ist absehbar.** The end is in sight.

abseits ADVERB
apart ◊ *Sie stand etwas abseits von den anderen.* She was standing somewhat apart from the others.

der **Absender** NOUN (PL die **Absender**)
sender

absetzen VERB (PERFECT **hat abgesetzt**)

[1] to drop off ◊ *Ich setze dich am Bahnhof ab.* I'll drop you off at the station.

[2] to take off ◊ *Willst du nicht deinen Motorradhelm absetzen?* Don't you want to take your helmet off?

[3] to drop ◊ *Dieser Sprachkurs musste vom Programm abgesetzt werden.* This language course has had to be dropped from the syllabus.

♦ **die Pille absetzen** to stop taking the pill

die **Absicht** NOUN
intention ◊ *Das war nicht meine Absicht.* That was not my intention.

♦ **mit Absicht** on purpose

absichtlich ADJECTIVE, ADVERB
deliberate ◊ *eine absichtliche Beleidigung* a deliberate insult

♦ **etwas absichtlich tun** to do something deliberately

absolut ADJECTIVE, ADVERB
absolute

♦ **Das ist absolut unmöglich.** That's absolutely impossible.

♦ **Ich habe absolut keine Lust.** I really don't feel like it.

abspülen VERB (PERFECT **hat abgespült**)
to rinse ◊ *Er spülte die Teller ab.* He rinsed the plates.

♦ **Geschirr abspülen** to wash up

der **Abstand** NOUN (PL die **Abstände**)
distance ◊ *Abstand halten* to keep one's distance

abstellen VERB (PERFECT **hat abgestellt**)

[1] to put down ◊ *Der Koffer ist so schwer, ich muss ihn kurz abstellen.* The case is so heavy that I'll have to put it down for a moment.

[2] to park ◊ *Wir haben das Auto am Stadtrand abgestellt.* We parked the car on the outskirts of town.

[3] to switch off ◊ *Kannst du bitte das Radio abstellen?* Can you switch the radio off, please?

die **Abstimmung** NOUN
vote

abstrakt ADJECTIVE, ADVERB

[1] abstract ◊ *abstrakte Kunst* abstract art

[2] in an abstract way ◊ *Er drückt sich sehr abstrakt aus.* He expresses himself in a very abstract way.

abstreiten VERB (IMPERFECT **stritt ab,** PERFECT **hat abgestritten**)
to deny

abstürzen VERB (PERFECT **ist abgestürzt**)

[1] to fall ◊ *Mathis ist beim Klettern abgestürzt.* Mathis fell while climbing.

[2] to crash ◊ *Die Maschine ist kurz nach dem Start abgestürzt.* The plane crashed shortly after takeoff.

das **Abteil** NOUN (PL die **Abteile**)
compartment

die **Abteilung** NOUN

[1] department ◊ *Sie wurde in eine andere Abteilung versetzt.* She was transferred to another department.
[2] ward ◊ *In welcher Abteilung liegt Mathis?* Which ward is Mathis in?

die **Abtreibung** NOUN
abortion

abtrocknen VERB (PERFECT **hat abgetrocknet**)
to dry

abwärts ADVERB
down

der **Abwasch** NOUN
washing-up ◊ *den Abwasch machen* to do the washing-up

abwaschen VERB (PRESENT **wäscht ab**, IMPERFECT **wusch ab**, PERFECT **hat abgewaschen**)
[1] to wash ◊ *Du solltest dir das Gesicht abwaschen!* You ought to wash your face. ◊ *Wer muss heute das Geschirr abwaschen?* Whose turn is it to wash the dishes today?
♦ **Ich muss noch schnell abwaschen, dann können wir gehen.** I'll just have to wash up, then we can go.
[2] to wash off ◊ *Wasch dir mal die Soße vom Gesicht ab!* Wash that gravy off your face.

das **Abwasser** NOUN (PL die **Abwässer**)
sewage

die **Abwechslung** NOUN
change ◊ *zur Abwechslung* for a change

abwerten VERB (PERFECT **hat abgewertet**)
to devalue

abwertend ADJECTIVE, ADVERB
derogatory ◊ *sich abwertend über etwas äußern* to talk in a derogatory way about something

abwesend ADJECTIVE
absent

die **Abwesenheit** NOUN
absence

abwischen VERB (PERFECT **hat abgewischt**)
to wipe ◊ *Er wischte die Tafel ab.* He wiped the board.

abzählen VERB (PERFECT **hat abgezählt**)
to count

das **Abzeichen** NOUN (PL die **Abzeichen**)
badge

abziehen VERB (IMPERFECT **zog ab**, PERFECT **hat/ist abgezogen**)
*For the perfect tense use **haben** when the verb has an object and **sein** when there is no object.*
[1] to take out ◊ *Er zog den Zündschlüssel ab.* He took out the ignition key.
[2] to withdraw ◊ *Sie haben ihre Truppen aus der Stadt abgezogen.* They have withdrawn their troops from the town.
[3] to deduct ◊ *Die Steuer wird*

vom Gehalt abgezogen. Tax is deducted from earnings.
♦ **Er ist beleidigt abgezogen.** He went away in a huff.

abzüglich PREPOSITION
*The preposition **abzüglich** takes the genitive.*
less ◊ *das Gehalt abzüglich der Steuern* earnings less tax

die **Achsel** NOUN
shoulder

acht NUMBER
see also **die Acht** NOUN
eight
♦ **acht Tage** a week

die **Acht** NOUN
see also **acht** NUMBER
eight ◊ *Schreibe eine Acht.* Write the figure eight.
♦ **sich in Acht nehmen** to beware ◊ *Du solltest dich vor ihr in Acht nehmen!* You should beware of her.
♦ **etwas außer Acht lassen** to disregard something
♦ **Acht geben** see **achtgeben**

achte ADJECTIVE
eighth ◊ *Sie wiederholte den Satz ein achtes Mal.* She repeated the sentence for an eighth time. ◊ *Er kam als Achter.* He was the eighth to arrive.

achten VERB
to respect ◊ *Ich achte deine Meinung.* I respect your opinion. ◊ *Sie ist sehr geachtet.* She's highly respected.
♦ **auf etwas achten** to pay attention to something ◊ *Du solltest auf die Verkehrsschilder achten.* You should pay attention to the road signs.
♦ **auf jemanden achten** to take notice of somebody ◊ *Achte nicht auf ihn!* Don't take any notice of him!

die **Achterbahn** NOUN
roller coaster

achtgeben VERB
to pay attention ◊ *Du solltest etwas mehr auf die Rechtschreibung achtgeben!* You should pay a bit more attention to spelling.
♦ **auf jemanden achtgeben** to keep an eye on somebody ◊ *Würden Sie mal bitte auf meinen Sohn achtgeben?* Would you keep an eye on my son for a minute, please?
♦ **Gib acht, da kommt uns ein Auto entgegen!** Look out, there's a car coming towards us.

achthundert NUMBER
eight hundred

achtmal ADVERB
eight times

die **Achtung** NOUN
respect ◊ *Ich habe große Achtung vor ihr.* I've great respect for her.
♦ **Achtung!** Look out!

☞

♦ **Achtung Stufe!** Mind the step.

♦ **Achtung, Achtung, hier eine Durchsage!** Your attention, please. Here is an announcement.

♦ **Alle Achtung!** Well done!

achtzehn NUMBER
eighteen

achtzig NUMBER
eighty

der **Acker** NOUN (PL die **Äcker**)
field

der **ADAC** NOUN (GEN des **ADAC**) (= *Allgemeiner Deutscher Automobil-Club*)
AA (*motoring organization*)

addieren VERB (PERFECT **hat addiert**)
to add

der **Adel** NOUN
nobility

die **Ader** NOUN
vein

das **Adjektiv** NOUN (PL die **Adjektive**)
adjective

der **Adler** NOUN (PL die **Adler**)
eagle

adlig ADJECTIVE
noble

adoptieren VERB (PERFECT **hat adoptiert**)
to adopt

die **Adoption** NOUN
adoption

die **Adoptiveltern** PL NOUN
adoptive parents

das **Adoptivkind** NOUN (PL die **Adoptivkinder**)
adopted child

die **Adresse** NOUN
address

adressieren VERB (PERFECT **hat adressiert**)
to address ◊ *An wen soll ich den Brief adressieren?* To whom should I address the letter?

die **Adria** NOUN
the Adriatic

der **Advent** NOUN
Advent

der **Adventskalender** NOUN (PL die **Adventskalender**)
Advent calendar

der **Adventskranz** NOUN (PL die **Adventskränze**)
Advent wreath

das **Adverb** NOUN (PL die **Adverbien**)
adverb

das **Aerobic** NOUN
aerobics

der **Affe** NOUN (GEN des **Affen**, PL die **Affen**)
monkey

Afrika NEUT NOUN
Africa

♦ **aus Afrika** from Africa

♦ **nach Afrika** to Africa

der **Afrikaner** NOUN (PL die **Afrikaner**)
African

die **Afrikanerin** NOUN
African

afrikanisch ADJECTIVE
African

AG ABBREVIATION (= *Aktiengesellschaft*)
plc

Ägypten NEUT NOUN
Egypt ◊ *nach Ägypten* to Egypt

der **Ägypter** NOUN (PL die **Ägypter**)
Egyptian

die **Ägypterin** NOUN
Egyptian

ägyptisch ADJECTIVE
Egyptian

ähneln VERB

♦ **jemandem ähneln** to resemble somebody ◊ *Sie ähnelt ihrer Mutter.* She resembles her mother.

♦ **Sie ähneln sich.** They are alike.

ahnen VERB

[1] to know ◊ *Ich habe geahnt, dass er nicht kommen würde.* I knew he wouldn't come. ◊ *Das konnte ich doch nicht ahnen!* How was I supposed to know that?

[2] to sense ◊ *Das Tier hat die Gefahr geahnt und ist schnell verschwunden.* The animal sensed the danger and quickly disappeared.

ähnlich ADJECTIVE
similar ◊ *Unsere Kleider sind sehr ähnlich.* Our dresses are very similar.

♦ **Er ist seinem Vater sehr ähnlich.** He's very like his father.

♦ **Das sieht ihr ähnlich!** That's typical of her.

die **Ähnlichkeit** NOUN
similarity

die **Ahnung** NOUN

[1] idea ◊ *Ich habe keine Ahnung, ob er kommt.* I've no idea whether he's coming.

♦ **Er hat von Computern keine Ahnung.** He doesn't know the first thing about computers.

[2] hunch ◊ *Er hatte eine Ahnung, dass etwas Schlimmes geschehen würde.* He had a hunch that something terrible would happen.

ahnungslos ADJECTIVE
unsuspecting

der **Ahorn** NOUN (PL die **Ahorne**)
maple

das **Aids** NOUN (GEN des **Aids**)
AIDS (= Acquired Immune Deficiency Syndrome) ◊ *Gerd ist an Aids gestorben.* Gerd died of AIDS.

der **Akademiker** NOUN (PL die **Akademiker**)
university graduate

die **Akademikerin** NOUN
university graduate

akademisch ADJECTIVE

academic

der **Akkusativ** NOUN (PL die **Akkusative**)
accusative

die **Akne** NOUN
acne ◊ *Sie hat Akne.* She's got acne.

die **Akte** NOUN
file
♦ **etwas zu den Akten legen** to file
something away

die **Aktentasche** NOUN
briefcase

die **Aktie** NOUN
share ◊ *in Aktien investieren* to invest in
shares

die **Aktiengesellschaft** NOUN
public limited company

die **Aktion** NOUN
1 campaign ◊ *eine Aktion für den
Frieden* a campaign for peace
2 operation ◊ *Wir alle nahmen an der
Aktion teil.* We all took part in the
operation.
♦ **in Aktion treten** to go into action ◊ *In
solchen Fällen tritt die Feuerwehr in
Aktion.* In cases like these, the fire
brigade goes into action.

aktiv ADJECTIVE
active

die **Aktivität** NOUN
activity

aktuell ADJECTIVE
1 topical ◊ *ein aktuelles Thema* a topical
issue
2 up-to-date ◊ *ein aktueller Fahrplan* an
up-to-date timetable
Be careful! aktuell does not mean actual.

der **Akzent** NOUN (PL die **Akzente**)
1 accent ◊ *Sie spricht mit einem
amerikanischen Akzent.* She speaks with
an American accent.
2 emphasis ◊ *Der Akzent unserer
Ausstellung liegt auf
Benutzerfreundlichkeit.* The emphasis in
our exhibition is on user-friendliness.

albern ADJECTIVE
silly
♦ **sich albern benehmen** to act silly

der **Albtraum** NOUN (PL die **Albträume**)
nightmare

das **Album** NOUN (PL die **Alben**)
album

die **Algebra** NOUN
algebra

der **Alkohol** NOUN
alcohol

alkoholfrei ADJECTIVE
nonalcoholic

der **Alkoholiker** NOUN (PL die **Alkoholiker**)
alcoholic

die **Alkoholikerin** NOUN
alcoholic

alkoholisch ADJECTIVE
alcoholic

das **All** NOUN
space ◊ *Sie haben eine Rakete ins All
geschossen.* They've sent a rocket into
space.

alle ADJECTIVE, PRONOUN
see also **alles** PRONOUN
1 all the ◊ *Alle Schüler sollten kommen.*
All the pupils should come.
2 all ◊ *Nicht alle Afrikaner sind schwarz.*
Not all Africans are black.
3 all of them ◊ *Wir haben alle gesehen.*
We saw all of them.
♦ **Sie kamen alle.** They all came.
♦ **wir alle** all of us
♦ **Ich habe alle beide eingeladen.** I've
invited both of them.
4 every ◊ *alle vier Jahre* every four
years ◊ *alle fünf Meter* every five metres
♦ **Die Milch ist alle.** The milk's all gone.
♦ **etwas alle machen** to finish something up

die **Allee** NOUN (PL die **Alleen**)
avenue

allein ADJECTIVE, ADVERB, CONJUNCTION
1 alone ◊ *Sie lebt allein.* She lives alone.
◊ *Du allein kannst das entscheiden.* You
alone can decide.
2 on one's own ◊ *Sie hat das ganz
allein geschrieben.* She wrote that all on
her own. ◊ *Seit ich allein bin, habe ich
mehr Zeit.* Since I've been on my own,
I've had more time.
♦ **Er fühlt sich allein.** He feels lonely.
♦ **nicht allein** not only

alleinstehend ADJECTIVE
single

allerbeste ADJECTIVE
very best ◊ *Felix ist mein allerbester
Schüler.* Felix is my very best pupil.

allerdings ADVERB
1 though ◊ *Der Urlaub war schön,
allerdings etwas kurz.* The holiday was
nice, though it was rather short. ◊ *Ich
werde kommen, kann allerdings nicht
lange bleiben.* I'll come. I can't stay long,
though.
2 certainly ◊ *Das ist allerdings
schwierig.* That's certainly difficult.

die **Allergie** NOUN
allergy

allergisch ADJECTIVE
allergic ◊ *Sie ist allergisch gegen Katzen.*
She's allergic to cats.

das **Allerheiligen** NOUN
All Saints' Day

> ⓘ *Allerheiligen (November 1st) is a
> public holiday in those parts of
> Germany where most of the population
> are Roman Catholics.*

allerhöchstens ADVERB
at the very most

allerlei ADJECTIVE
all sorts of ◊ *allerlei Sachen* all sorts of things
allerletzte ADJECTIVE
very last ◊ *zum allerletzten Mal* for the very last time
allerseits ADVERB
on all sides ◊ *Dieser Vorschlag fand allerseits Zustimmung.* This suggestion met with approval on all sides.
♦ **Prost allerseits!** Cheers, everyone!
alles PRONOUN

see also **alle** ADJECTIVE, PRONOUN

everything ◊ *Sie haben alles aufgegessen.* They've eaten everything up.
♦ **alles, was er sagt** everything he says
♦ **alles in Allem** all in all
♦ **Alles Gute!** All the best!
allgemein ADJECTIVE
general
♦ **im Allgemeinen** in general
allmählich ADJECTIVE, ADVERB
① gradual ◊ *eine allmähliche Besserung* a gradual improvement
② gradually ◊ *Es wird allmählich wärmer.* It's gradually getting warmer.
♦ **Allmählich solltest du das wissen.** You should know that by now.
der **Alltag** NOUN
everyday life
allzu ADVERB
all too ◊ *allzu oft* all too often
♦ **allzu viel** far too much
die **Alm** NOUN
alpine pasture
die **Alpen** PL NOUN
Alps
das **Alphabet** NOUN (PL die **Alphabete**)
alphabet
alphabetisch ADJECTIVE
alphabetical ◊ *alphabetisch geordnet* arranged in alphabetical order
der **Alptraum** NOUN (PL die **Alpträume**)
nightmare
als CONJUNCTION
① when ◊ *Als ich ein Kind war ...* When I was a child ...
② as ◊ *Sie kam, als ich gerade gehen wollte.* She arrived as I was about to leave. ◊ *Ich als Lehrerin weiß, ...* As a teacher, I know ...
♦ **gerade, als ...** just as ...
♦ **als ob** as if ◊ *Er tat, als ob er nichts bemerkt hätte.* He acted as if he hadn't noticed anything.
③ than ◊ *Sie ist älter als ich.* She's older than me. ◊ *Ich kam später als er.* I came later than he did.
♦ **lieber als ...** rather than ... ◊ *Ich mag Süßes lieber als Salziges.* I like sweet things rather than savoury things.
♦ **nichts als Ärger** nothing but trouble

also ADVERB, CONJUNCTION, EXCLAMATION
① then ◊ *Was sollen wir also tun?* What shall we do, then? ◊ *Du willst also nicht mit.* You don't want to come along, then. ◊ *Du hast es also gewusst.* You did know then.
② so ◊ *Es war schon spät, also bin ich nach Hause gegangen.* It had got late, so I went home.
③ well ◊ *Also ich gehe jetzt!* Well, I'm off now. ◊ *Also, Sie fahren immer geradeaus ...* Well, keep going straight on ...
♦ **Also gut!** Okay then.
♦ **Also, so was!** Well really!
♦ **Na also!** There you are then!
*Be careful! The German word **also** does not mean **also**.*
alt ADJECTIVE
old ◊ *Wie alt bist du?* How old are you? ◊ *Felix ist zehn Jahre alt.* Felix is ten years old. ◊ *Sein Auto ist älter als unseres.* His car is older than ours. ◊ *Das ist meine ältere Schwester.* That's my elder sister. ◊ *Mein ältester Bruder heißt Thomas.* My eldest brother's called Thomas.
♦ **alles beim Alten lassen** to leave everything as it was
der **Altar** NOUN (PL die **Altäre**)
altar
das **Alter** NOUN (PL die **Alter**)
① age ◊ *In deinem Alter sollte man das wissen.* You ought to know that at your age.
② old age ◊ *Im Alter sind die Menschen oft einsam.* People are often lonely in old age.
♦ **im Alter von** at the age of
die **Altersgrenze** NOUN
age limit
das **Altglas** NOUN (GEN des **Altglases**)
used glass
der **Altglascontainer** NOUN (PL die **Altglascontainer**)
bottle bank
altmodisch ADJECTIVE
old-fashioned
das **Altpapier** NOUN
waste paper
die **Altstadt** NOUN (PL die **Altstädte**)
old town
die **Alufolie** NOUN
tinfoil
das **Aluminium** NOUN
aluminium
der **Alzheimer** NOUN
Alzheimer's ◊ *Sie hat Alzheimer.* She's got Alzheimer's.
am = an dem
♦ **am fünften März** on the fifth of March
♦ **am höchsten** the highest
♦ **am schönsten** the most beautiful

die **Ameise** NOUN
  ant
Amerika NEUT NOUN
  America
  ♦ **aus Amerika** from America
  ♦ **in Amerika** in America
  ♦ **nach Amerika** to America
der **Amerikaner** NOUN (PL die **Amerikaner**)
  American
die **Amerikanerin** NOUN
  American
amerikanisch ADJECTIVE
  American
die **Ampel** NOUN
  traffic lights ◊ *Die Ampel ist grün.* The
  traffic lights are at green.
die **Amsel** NOUN
  blackbird
das **Amt** NOUN (PL die **Ämter**)
  office ◊ *Welches Amt ist für Kindergeld
  zuständig?* Which office deals with child
  benefit?
amtlich ADJECTIVE
  official
amüsant ADJECTIVE
  amusing
amüsieren VERB (PERFECT **hat amüsiert**)
  to amuse ◊ *Diese Geschichte hat uns
  sehr amüsiert.* The story amused us very
  much.
  ♦ **sich amüsieren** to enjoy oneself ◊ *Wir
  haben uns blendend amüsiert.* We
  enjoyed ourselves immensely.
an PREPOSITION, ADVERB
  see also **am**

  *Use the accusative to express movement
  or a change of place. Use the dative
  when there is no change of place.*

  [1] on ◊ *Das Wort stand an der Tafel.* The
  word was written on the blackboard.
  ◊ *Der Lehrer schrieb das Wort an die
  Tafel.* The teacher wrote the word on the
  blackboard.
  [2] to ◊ *Er ging ans Fenster.* He went to
  the window. ◊ *Wir waren gestern am
  Meer.* We went to the seaside yesterday.
  ◊ *Wir wollen morgen ans Meer fahren.*
  We want to go to the seaside tomorrow.
  ◊ *Ich habe einen Brief an meine Mutter
  geschrieben.* I've written a letter to my
  mother.
  ♦ **eine Frage an dich** a question for you
  ♦ **an diesem Ort** in this place
  ♦ **unten am Fluss** down by the river
  [3] by ◊ *Ihr Haus liegt an der Autobahn.*
  Their house is by the motorway.
  ♦ **Köln liegt am Rhein.** Cologne is on the
  Rhine.
  ♦ **am neunten November** on the ninth of
  November
  ♦ **an diesem Tag** on this day
  ♦ **an Ostern** at Easter
  ♦ **an etwas denken** to think of something

  ♦ **reich an Nährstoffen** rich in nutrients
  ♦ **an etwas sterben** to die of something
  ♦ **an und für sich** actually ◊ *Das ist an und
  für sich ganz einfach.* Actually, it's quite
  simple.
  ♦ **an die hundert** about a hundred
  ♦ **von heute an** from today onwards
  ♦ **Das Licht ist an.** The light's on.
  ♦ **ohne etwas an** with nothing on
die **Ananas** NOUN (PL die **Ananas**)
  pineapple
anbauen VERB (PERFECT **hat angebaut**)
  [1] to build on ◊ *eine Garage ans Haus
  anbauen* to build a garage onto the
  house
  [2] to cultivate ◊ *Reis anbauen* to
  cultivate rice
anbei ADVERB
  enclosed
anbieten VERB (IMPERFECT **bot an**, PERFECT **hat
  angeboten**)
  to offer ◊ *Ich bot ihr eine Tasse Kaffee
  an.* I offered her a cup of coffee.
  ♦ **Kann ich dir etwas zum Trinken
  anbieten?** Can I get you something to
  drink?
  ♦ **anbieten, etwas zu tun** to volunteer to
  do something ◊ *Er hat angeboten, mir
  beim Umzug zu helfen.* He volunteered
  to help me move house.
der **Anblick** NOUN (PL die **Anblicke**)
  sight
anbrechen VERB (PRESENT **bricht an**, IMPERFECT
  brach an, PERFECT **ist/hat angebrochen**)

  *For the perfect tense use **haben** when
  the verb has an object and **sein** when
  there is no object.*

  [1] to break into ◊ *Für den Kauf müsste
  ich meine Ersparnisse anbrechen.* To buy
  it, I'd have to break into my savings.
  [2] to dawn ◊ *Ein neues Zeitalter ist
  angebrochen.* A new age has dawned.
  [3] to break ◊ *wenn der Tag anbricht*
  when day breaks
anbrennen VERB (IMPERFECT **brannte an**,
  PERFECT **ist angebrannt**)
  to burn ◊ *Der Kuchen ist angebrannt.*
  The cake's burnt.
andauernd ADJECTIVE, ADVERB
  [1] continual ◊ *diese andauernden
  Unterbrechungen* these continual
  interruptions
  [2] constantly ◊ *Er stört andauernd.* He's
  constantly interrupting.
das **Andenken** NOUN (PL die **Andenken**)
  [1] memory ◊ *Zum Andenken an eine
  schöne Zeit.* In memory of a wonderful
  time.
  [2] souvenir ◊ *Ich habe mir aus dem
  Urlaub einige Andenken mitgebracht.* I
  brought a few souvenirs back from my
  holiday.
andere ADJECTIVE, PRONOUN

1 other ◊ *Nein, nicht dieses Buch, gib mir das andere.* No, not that book, please give me the other one.

2 different ◊ *Er hat jetzt eine andere Freundin.* He's got a different girlfriend now.

3 another ◊ *ein anderes Mal* another time ◊ *Wir werden das an einem anderen Tag machen.* We'll do that another day.

♦ **kein anderer** nobody else

♦ **die anderen** the others ◊ *Martin ist noch da, die anderen sind schon gegangen.* Martin's still here, the others have already left.

♦ **andere** other ones ◊ *Wenn Ihnen dieses Kleid nicht gefällt, haben wir auch andere.* If you don't like this dress, we also have other ones.

♦ **etwas anderes** something else ◊ *von etwas anderem sprechen* to talk about something else

andererseits ADVERB
on the other hand ◊ *Einerseits ..., andererseits ...* On the one hand ..., on the other hand ...

andermal ADVERB
♦ **ein andermal** some other time

ändern VERB
to alter ◊ *Ich habe das Kleid ändern lassen.* I've had the dress altered.

♦ **So ist das nun mal, ich kann's nicht ändern.** That's the way it is. I can't do anything about it.

♦ **sich ändern** to change ◊ *Sie hat sich in letzter Zeit sehr geändert.* She's changed a lot recently. ◊ *Wenn sich die Lage nicht ändert ...* If the situation doesn't change ...

anders ADVERB
differently ◊ *So geht das nicht, du musst das anders machen.* Not like that – you have to do it differently.

♦ **anders als** different from ◊ *Sie ist ganz anders als ihr Bruder.* She's quite different from her brother. ◊ *Sie hat das anders als ich übersetzt.* She translated it differently from me.

♦ **Wer anders?** Who else?

♦ **jemand anders** somebody else

♦ **irgendwo anders** somewhere else

♦ **anders aussehen** to look different

anderthalb ADJECTIVE
one and a half

die **Änderung** NOUN
alteration

andeuten VERB (PERFECT **hat angedeutet**)
to hint ◊ *Sie hat angedeutet, dass sie weiß, wer es war.* She's hinted that she knows who it was.

die **Andeutung** NOUN
hint ◊ *Sie hat eine Andeutung gemacht, dass sie es weiß.* She hinted that she knew.

anerkennend ADJECTIVE, ADVERB
appreciative

♦ **Sie sprach sehr anerkennend von seiner Leistung.** She spoke very appreciatively of his work.

die **Anerkennung** NOUN
1 appreciation ◊ *Ihre Leistung fand nicht die entsprechende Anerkennung.* Her work didn't get the appreciation it deserved.

2 recognition ◊ *Dieser neue Staat hofft auf Anerkennung durch die Bundesrepublik.* This new country is hoping for recognition by the Federal Republic.

anfahren VERB (PRESENT **fährt an,** IMPERFECT **fuhr an,** PERFECT **hat/ist angefahren**)
1 to hit ◊ *Er hat einen Fußgänger angefahren.* He hit a pedestrian.

2 to start up ◊ *beim Anfahren* when starting up

der **Anfall** NOUN (PL die **Anfälle**)
fit ◊ *Sie hatte einen epileptischen Anfall.* She had an epileptic fit. ◊ *Wenn er das erfährt, bekommt er einen Anfall.* If he finds out, he'll have a fit.

der **Anfang** NOUN (PL die **Anfänge**)
beginning ◊ *von Anfang an* right from the beginning

♦ **am Anfang** at the beginning

♦ **zu Anfang** first

♦ **Anfang Mai** at the beginning of May

anfangen VERB (PRESENT **fängt an,** IMPERFECT **fing an,** PERFECT **hat angefangen**)
1 to begin ◊ *Es fängt an zu regnen.* It's beginning to rain. ◊ *Märchen fangen mit dem Satz an: "Es war einmal".* Fairy tales begin with the words: "Once upon a time".

2 to start ◊ *Der Film hat schon angefangen.* The film's already started. ◊ *Hast du den Aufsatz schon angefangen?* Have you already started your essay?

♦ **Damit kann ich nichts anfangen.** It doesn't mean anything to me.

♦ **Das fängt ja gut an!** That's a good start!

der **Anfänger** NOUN (PL die **Anfänger**)
beginner

anfassen VERB (PERFECT **hat angefasst**)
1 to touch ◊ *Fass den Hund besser nicht an!* You'd better not touch the dog.

2 to treat ◊ *Du solltest die Kinder nicht immer so rau anfassen!* You shouldn't treat the children so roughly.

♦ **mit anfassen** to lend a hand ◊ *Kannst du mal mit anfassen, den Schrank wegzuschieben?* Can you lend a hand shifting this cupboard to one side?

♦ **sich anfassen** to feel ◊ *Samt fühlt sich weich an.* Velvet feels soft.

sich **anfreunden** VERB (PERFECT **hat sich angefreundet**)

1 to make friends ◊ *Ich habe mich in den Ferien mit einer Engländerin angefreundet.* I made friends with an English girl during the holidays.
2 to become friends ◊ *Die beiden haben sich angefreundet.* The two of them have become friends.

anfühlen VERB (PERFECT **hat angefühlt**)
to feel ◊ *Fühl mal meine Stirn an, ich glaube, ich habe Fieber.* Feel my forehead, I think I've got a temperature. ◊ *Der Stoff fühlt sich weich an.* The material feels soft.

die **Anführungszeichen** NEUT PL NOUN
inverted commas

die **Angabe** NOUN
1 information ◊ *Die Angaben waren falsch.* The information was wrong.
2 serve (*tennis*) ◊ *Wer hat Angabe?* Whose serve is it?
♦ **Das ist doch alles nur Angabe!** That's nothing but show.

angeben VERB (PRESENT **gibt an**, IMPERFECT **gab an**, PERFECT **hat angegeben**)
1 to give ◊ *Geben Sie bitte Ihre Personalien an.* Please give your personal details.
2 to state ◊ *Sie hat angegeben, dass sie zu dem Zeitpunkt zu Hause war.* She stated that she was at home at the time.
3 to indicate ◊ *Alle Raststätten sind auf der Karte angegeben.* All service areas are indicated on the map.
4 to show off ◊ *Glaub ihm kein Wort, er gibt nur an.* Don't believe a word he says – he's just showing off.

der **Angeber** NOUN (PL die **Angeber**)
show-off

angeblich ADJECTIVE, ADVERB
1 alleged ◊ *Sie ist die angebliche Täterin.* She's the alleged culprit.
2 allegedly ◊ *Angeblich hat sie es getan.* Allegedly, she did it.

das **Angebot** NOUN (PL die **Angebote**)
offer ◊ *Ich nehme dein Angebot an.* I accept your offer.
♦ **ein Angebot an etwas** a selection of something ◊ *Das Kaufhaus hat ein großes Angebot an Kleidern.* The department store has a large selection of dresses.
♦ **Angebot und Nachfrage** supply and demand

angeheitert ADJECTIVE
tipsy

angehen VERB (IMPERFECT **ging an**, PERFECT **hat/ist angegangen**)
*For the perfect tense use **haben** when the verb has an object and **sein** when there is no object.*
1 to concern ◊ *Diese Angelegenheit geht mich nichts an.* This matter doesn't concern me.

♦ **Was geht dich das an?** What business is it of yours?
2 to tackle ◊ *Ich weiß noch nicht so richtig, wie ich das Thema angehen soll.* I'm not really sure how to tackle the subject.
3 to light ◊ *Das Holz war zu nass, also ist das Feuer nicht angegangen.* The wood was too wet, so the fire wouldn't light.
4 to go on ◊ *Das Licht ging an.* The light went on.
♦ **was ... angeht** as regards ... ◊ *Was die Ferien angeht, haben wir noch nichts entschieden.* As regards the holidays, we still haven't decided anything.

angehend ADJECTIVE
prospective

der **Angehörige** NOUN (GEN des/der
die **Angehörigen**, PL die **Angehörigen**)
relative ◊ *Er ist ein Angehöriger von mir.* He's a relative of mine.

die **Angel** NOUN
1 fishing rod
2 hinge (*Türangel*)
*Be careful! The German word **Angel** does not mean **angel**.*

die **Angelegenheit** NOUN
1 matter ◊ *Ich werde diese Angelegenheit prüfen.* I'll look into the matter.
2 affair ◊ *Das ist meine Angelegenheit.* That's my affair.

angeln VERB
1 to catch ◊ *Er hat eine große Forelle geangelt.* He caught a large trout.
2 to fish ◊ *Sonntags geht Alex immer angeln.* Alex always goes fishing on Sundays.

die **Angelrute** NOUN
fishing rod

angenehm ADJECTIVE, ADVERB
pleasant
♦ **Der Motor ist angenehm leise.** The engine is pleasantly quiet.
♦ **Angenehm!** Pleased to meet you.

angesehen ADJECTIVE
respected

der **Angestellte** NOUN (GEN des/der
die **Angestellten**, PL die **Angestellten**)
employee ◊ *Er ist nur ein kleiner Angestellter.* He's just a lowly employee.
♦ **Sie ist Angestellte bei der Firma Boll & Co.** She works at Boll & Co.

angewiesen ADJECTIVE
♦ **auf jemanden angewiesen sein** to be dependent on somebody
♦ **auf etwas angewiesen sein** to be dependent on something

angewöhnen VERB (PERFECT **hat angewöhnt**)
♦ **jemandem etwas angewöhnen** to teach somebody something ◊ *Sie sollten Ihrem*

☞

Sohn bessere Manieren angewöhnen. You ought to teach your son better manners.

♦ **sich etwas angewöhnen** to get into the habit of doing something ◊ *Ich habe es mir angewöhnt, jeden Morgen um sieben Uhr aufzustehen.* I've got into the habit of getting up at seven every morning.

die **Angewohnheit** NOUN
habit ◊ *Das ist so eine Angewohnheit von ihr.* That's a habit of hers.

angreifen VERB (IMPERFECT **griff an,** PERFECT **hat angegriffen**)
[1] to attack ◊ *Ich wurde von einem Hund angegriffen.* I was attacked by a dog.
[2] to criticize ◊ *Sie wurde wegen dieser Aussage von ihren Freunden angegriffen.* She was criticized by her friends for what she said.

der **Angriff** NOUN (PL die **Angriffe**)
attack
♦ **etwas in Angriff nehmen** to make a start on something

die **Angst** NOUN (PL die **Ängste**)
fear
♦ **vor jemandem Angst haben** to be afraid of somebody
♦ **vor etwas Angst haben** to be afraid of something
♦ **Ich habe Angst vor der Prüfung.** I'm worried about the exam.
♦ **Angst um jemanden haben** to be worried about somebody
♦ **Mir ist angst.** I'm afraid.
♦ **jemandem Angst machen** to scare somebody

ängstlich ADJECTIVE, ADVERB
[1] scared ◊ *Nun sei doch nicht so ängstlich, der Hund tut dir nichts!* There's no need to be scared, the dog won't harm you.
[2] anxious ◊ *"Wird er wieder gesund?", fragte sie ängstlich.* "Will he get well again?", she asked anxiously.

anhaben VERB (PRESENT **hat an,** IMPERFECT **hatte an,** PERFECT **hat angehabt**)
to have on ◊ *Sie hatte heute das rote Kleid an.* She had her red dress on today.
♦ **jemandem nichts anhaben können** to have nothing on somebody ◊ *Ich bin unschuldig, die Polizei kann mir nichts anhaben.* I'm innocent, the police have got nothing on me.

anhalten VERB (PRESENT **hält an,** IMPERFECT **hielt an,** PERFECT **hat angehalten**)
[1] to stop ◊ *Können wir bitte anhalten, mir ist schlecht.* Can we stop please? I feel sick. ◊ *Kannst du bitte das Auto anhalten?* Can you stop the car please?
[2] to last ◊ *Das wird nicht lange anhalten.* It won't last long.
♦ **die Luft anhalten** to hold one's breath

der **Anhalter** NOUN (PL die **Anhalter**)
hitchhiker
♦ **per Anhalter fahren** to hitchhike

anhand PREPOSITION
*The preposition **anhand** takes the genitive.*
with the help of ◊ *Wir werden das anhand der Unterlagen prüfen.* We'll check that with the help of the documents.

der **Anhang** NOUN (PL die **Anhänge**)
appendix

der **Anhänger** NOUN (PL die **Anhänger**)
[1] supporter ◊ *Er ist Anhänger von Borussia Dortmund.* He's a Borussia Dortmund supporter.
[2] trailer (*on car*)
[3] label ◊ *Mach einen Anhänger mit deinem Namen und deiner Adresse an deinen Koffer.* Put a label with your name and address on your case.
[4] pendant ◊ *Sie trug eine Kette mit Anhänger.* She was wearing a chain with a pendant.

die **Anhängerin** NOUN
supporter ◊ *Sie ist Anhängerin von Borussia Dortmund.* She's a Borussia Dortmund supporter.

anhören VERB (PERFECT **hat angehört**)
to listen to ◊ *Wir haben CDs angehört.* We listened to CDs.
♦ **jemandem etwas anhören** to hear something in somebody's voice ◊ *Man hat ihr ihre Aufregung angehört.* You could hear the excitement in her voice.
♦ **sich anhören** to sound ◊ *Der Vorschlag hört sich gut an.* That sounds a good suggestion.

der **Anker** NOUN (PL die **Anker**)
anchor

der **Anklang** NOUN
♦ **bei jemandem Anklang finden** to meet with somebody's approval

die **Ankleidekabine** NOUN
changing cubicle

anklicken VERB (PERFECT **hat angeklickt**)
to click on (*computer*) ◊ *ein Icon anklicken* to click on an icon

ankommen VERB (IMPERFECT **kam an,** PERFECT **ist angekommen**)
to arrive ◊ *Wir kommen morgen Nachmittag an.* We'll arrive tomorrow afternoon. ◊ *Ist der Brief schon angekommen?* Has the letter arrived yet?
♦ **bei jemandem gut ankommen** to go down well with somebody ◊ *Das Stück ist bei den Zuschauern gut angekommen.* The play went down well with the audience.
♦ **bei jemandem schlecht ankommen** to go down badly with somebody ◊ *Der Witz ist offensichtlich schlecht angekommen.* The joke clearly went down badly.

◆ **es kommt darauf an** it depends ◊ *Es kommt darauf an, wie das Wetter ist.* It depends what the weather's like.

◆ **Es kommt auf jeden einzelnen von uns an.** It depends on each and every one of us.

◆ **wenn es darauf ankommt ...** when it really matters ...

◆ **Bei diesem Beruf kommt es auf Genauigkeit an.** What matters in this job is accuracy.

◆ **es darauf ankommen lassen** to wait and see

ankreuzen VERB (PERFECT **hat angekreuzt**)
to mark with a cross

ankündigen VERB (PERFECT **hat angekündigt**)
to announce

die **Ankunft** NOUN (PL die **Ankünfte**)
arrival

die **Ankunftszeit** NOUN
arrival time

die **Anlage** NOUN
[1] gardens ◊ *Wir sind in der Anlage spazieren gegangen.* We went for a walk in the gardens.
[2] plant ◊ *Das ist eine neuartige Anlage zum Recycling von Kunststoff.* That's a new plastics recycling plant.
[3] investment ◊ *Wir raten zu einer Anlage in Immobilien.* We would advise investment in real estate.

der **Anlass** NOUN (GEN des **Anlasses**, PL die **Anlässe**)
occasion ◊ *ein festlicher Anlass* a festive occasion

◆ **ein Anlass zu etwas** cause for something ◊ *Das ist ein Anlass zum Feiern.* That's cause for celebration.

◆ **aus Anlass** on the occasion of ◊ *Aus Anlass ihres fünfzigsten Geburtstags ...* On the occasion of her fiftieth birthday ...

◆ **Anlass zu etwas geben** to give cause for something ◊ *Ihr Sohn gibt keinen Anlass zu Klagen.* Your son doesn't give cause for complaint.

der **Anlasser** NOUN (PL die **Anlasser**)
starter (*of car*)

die **Anleitung** NOUN
instructions

der **Anlieger** NOUN (PL die **Anlieger**)
resident ◊ *"Anlieger frei"* "residents only"

anmachen VERB (PERFECT **hat angemacht**)
[1] to put on ◊ *Mach bitte das Licht an.* Please put the light on.
[2] to light ◊ *Wir haben ein Feuer angemacht.* We lit a fire.
[3] to dress ◊ *Sie macht den Salat immer mit Zitrone an.* She always dresses her salads with lemon.
[4] to chat up ◊ *Ich glaube, der Typ versucht, dich anzumachen.*

I think that bloke is trying to chat you up.

das **Anmeldeformular** NOUN (PL die **Anmeldeformulare**)
registration form

anmelden VERB (PERFECT **hat angemeldet**)
to announce ◊ *Sie hat für morgen ihren Besuch angemeldet.* She's announced that she'll visit us tomorrow.

◆ **jemanden anmelden (1)** to make an appointment for somebody ◊ *Er hat seinen Sohn für morgen beim Zahnarzt angemeldet.* He's made a dental appointment for his son for tomorrow.

◆ **jemanden anmelden (2)** to put somebody's name down ◊ *Habt ihr Maximilian schon im Gymnasium angemeldet?* Have you already put Maximilian's name down for grammar school?

◆ **sich anmelden (1)** to make an appointment ◊ *Ich muss mich beim Zahnarzt anmelden.* I must make an appointment with the dentist.

◆ **sich anmelden (2)** to put one's name down ◊ *Sie hat sich für einen Judokurs angemeldet.* She's put her name down for a judo course.

◆ **Alle Besucher müssen sich beim Pförtner anmelden.** All visitors must report to the gatehouse.

◆ **Haben Sie sich schon beim Einwohnermeldeamt angemeldet?** Have you already registered with the residents' registration office?

> ❶ *Anyone moving to a new address in Germany is required by law to register (**sich anmelden**) at the residents' registration office (**Einwohner-meldeamt**).*

die **Anmeldung** NOUN
registration ◊ *Schluss für Anmeldungen ist der erste Mai.* The deadline for registrations is the first of May.

annehmen VERB (PRESENT **nimmt an**, IMPERFECT **nahm an**, PERFECT **hat angenommen**)
[1] to accept ◊ *Sie wollte das Geschenk nicht annehmen.* She didn't want to accept the present. ◊ *Danke für die Einladung, ich nehme gerne an.* Thank you for the invitation, which I'm happy to accept.
[2] to take ◊ *Er hat den Namen seiner Frau angenommen.* He took his wife's name.

◆ **ein Kind annehmen** to adopt a child
[3] to believe ◊ *Die Polizei nimmt an, dass er der Täter war.* The police believe he did it.

☞

4 to suppose ◊ *Nehmen wir einmal an, es wäre so.* Let's suppose that was the case.

♦ **angenommen ... supposing ...** ◊ *Angenommen, er kommt nicht.* Supposing he doesn't come.

anordnen VERB (PERFECT **hat angeordnet**)
1 to arrange ◊ *Er ordnete die Blumen zu einem hübschen Gesteck an.* He arranged the flowers into a pretty bouquet.
2 to order ◊ *Wer hat das angeordnet?* Who ordered that?

anprobieren VERB (PERFECT **hat anprobiert**)
to try on

die **Anrede** NOUN
form of address ◊ *Für verheiratete und unverheiratete Frauen benutzt man die Anrede "Frau".* "Frau" is the form of address used for married and unmarried women.

der **Anruf** NOUN (PL die **Anrufe**)
phone call

der **Anrufbeantworter** NOUN (PL die **Anrufbeantworter**)
answering machine

anrufen VERB (IMPERFECT **rief an**, PERFECT **hat angerufen**)
to phone ◊ *Hat jemand angerufen?* Did anyone phone? ◊ *Ich muss mal eben meine Eltern anrufen.* I must just phone my parents. ◊ *Ruf mal bei Wengels an, vielleicht ist sie dort.* Phone the Wengels; perhaps she's there.

ans = **an das**

anschalten VERB (PERFECT **hat angeschaltet**)
to switch on

anschauen VERB (PERFECT **hat angeschaut**)
to look at ◊ *Schau mich an!* Look at me.
♦ **Willst du dir mal die Fotos anschauen?** Do you want to have a look at the photos?
♦ **Den Film will ich mir unbedingt anschauen.** I must go and see that film.

anscheinend ADVERB
apparently

der **Anschlag** NOUN (PL die **Anschläge**)
1 notice ◊ *Sie machte einen Anschlag am Schwarzen Brett.* She put a notice on the notice board.
2 attack ◊ *Es gab einen Anschlag auf den Präsidenten.* There's been an attack on the President.

anschließen VERB (IMPERFECT **schloss an**, PERFECT **hat angeschlossen**)
1 to connect ◊ *Das Telefon ist noch nicht angeschlossen.* The telephone hasn't been connected yet.
2 to follow ◊ *Wir können an den Vortrag gern noch eine Diskussion anschließen.* We can of course follow the lecture with a discussion.

♦ **sich jemandem anschließen** to join somebody ◊ *Wir gehen ins Kino, willst du dich uns nicht anschließen?* We're going to the cinema. Won't you join us?
♦ **Ich schließe mich dieser Meinung an.** I endorse this view.

anschließend ADJECTIVE, ADVERB
1 subsequent ◊ *die daran anschließende Diskussion* the subsequent discussion
2 adjacent ◊ *das anschließende Grundstück* the adjacent plot of land
3 afterwards ◊ *Wir waren essen, und anschließend sind wir ins Kino gegangen.* We had a meal and afterwards went to the cinema.

der **Anschluss** NOUN (GEN des **Anschlusses**, PL die **Anschlüsse**)
connection ◊ *Sie haben Anschluss an einen Zug nach Paris.* You have a connection with a train to Paris.
♦ **im Anschluss an** following ◊ *Im Anschluss an die Ansprache findet ein Empfang statt.* Following the speech there will be a reception.
♦ **Anschluss finden** to make friends ◊ *Sie hat in der neuen Klasse schnell Anschluss gefunden.* She quickly made friends in her new class.

sich **anschnallen** VERB (PERFECT **hat sich angeschnallt**)
to fasten one's seat belt

die **Anschrift** NOUN
address

ansehen VERB (PRESENT **sieht an**, IMPERFECT **sah an**, PERFECT **hat angesehen**)
see also **das Ansehen** NOUN
1 to look at ◊ *Sieh mich an!* Look at me.
♦ **Willst du dir mal die Fotos ansehen?** Do you want to have a look at the photos?
♦ **Den Film will ich mir unbedingt ansehen.** I must go and see that film.
♦ **Man hat ihr ihre Enttäuschung angesehen.** You could see the disappointment in her face.
2 to regard ◊ *Sie wird als eine Expertin auf diesem Gebiet angesehen.* She's regarded as an expert in this field.
♦ **Sieh mal einer an!** Well, fancy that!

das **Ansehen** NOUN
see also **ansehen** VERB
1 respect ◊ *Sie genießt großes Ansehen bei ihren Kollegen.* She enjoys great respect among her colleagues.
2 reputation ◊ *Ein solches Benehmen könnte unserem Ansehen schaden.* Behaviour like that could damage our reputation.

die **Ansicht** NOUN
view ◊ *eine Postkarte mit der Ansicht des Matterhorns* a postcard with a view of the Matterhorn ◊ *Wenn Sie meine Ansicht in dieser Sache hören wollen ...* If

you want to hear my view on this business ...
♦ **zur Ansicht** on approval
♦ **meiner Ansicht nach** in my view

die **Ansichtskarte** NOUN
picture postcard

die **Ansichtssache** NOUN
matter of opinion

ansprechen VERB (PRESENT **spricht an,** IMPERFECT **sprach an,** PERFECT **hat angesprochen**)
1 to approach ◊ *Mich hat ein wildfremder Mann angesprochen.* I was approached by a complete stranger.
2 to appeal to ◊ *Diese Art von Malerei spricht mich nicht an.* This style of painting doesn't appeal to me.
3 to ask ◊ *Ich werde Herrn Arnold ansprechen, ob er uns vielleicht hilft.* I'll ask Mr Arnold if he'll maybe help us.
4 to mention ◊ *Sie hat dieses Problem bis jetzt noch nicht angesprochen.* She hasn't mentioned this problem yet.
♦ **auf etwas ansprechen** to respond to something ◊ *Der Patient spricht auf die Medikamente nicht an.* The patient isn't responding to the drugs.

der **Anspruch** NOUN (PL die **Ansprüche**)
demand ◊ *Sie war den Ansprüchen ihres Berufs nicht gewachsen.* She wasn't up to the demands of her job.
♦ **hohe Ansprüche haben** to demand a lot
♦ **hohe Ansprüche an jemanden stellen** to demand a lot of somebody
♦ **Anspruch auf etwas haben** to be entitled to something ◊ *Ich habe Anspruch auf eine Erklärung.* I'm entitled to an explanation.
♦ **etwas in Anspruch nehmen** to take advantage of something ◊ *Wir sollten dieses Angebot in Anspruch nehmen.* We should take advantage of this offer.
♦ **Ihr Beruf nimmt sie sehr in Anspruch.** Her job's very demanding.

anständig ADJECTIVE
decent ◊ *ein anständiges Essen* a decent meal
♦ **Ich bin eine anständige Frau!** I'm a respectable woman.
♦ **sich anständig benehmen** to behave oneself

anstarren VERB (PERFECT **hat angestarrt**)
to stare at

anstatt PREPOSITION, CONJUNCTION
The preposition **anstatt** takes the genitive.
instead of ◊ *Sie kam anstatt ihres Bruders.* She came instead of her brother.
♦ **anstatt etwas zu tun** instead of doing something

anstecken VERB (PERFECT **hat angesteckt**)

♦ **Er hat die halbe Klasse mit seiner Grippe angesteckt.** He gave half the class his flu.
♦ **Lachen steckt an.** Laughter is infectious.
♦ **sich anstecken** to catch something ◊ *Pass auf, dass du dich nicht ansteckst.* Be careful you don't catch anything. ◊ *Ich habe mich bei ihm angesteckt.* I caught it from him.
♦ **sich etwas anstecken** to pin something on ◊ *Ich habe mir das Abzeichen des Sportvereins angesteckt.* I pinned my sports club badge on.

ansteckend ADJECTIVE
infectious ◊ *eine ansteckende Krankheit* an infectious disease
♦ **Herpes ist ansteckend.** Herpes is contagious.

anstelle PREPOSITION
The preposition **anstelle** takes the genitive.
instead of ◊ *Anstelle der Mutter hat seine Tante unterschrieben.* His aunt has signed instead of his mother.
♦ **Pralinen anstelle von Blumen** chocolates instead of flowers

anstellen VERB (PERFECT **hat angestellt**)
1 to turn on ◊ *Kannst du mal bitte den Fernseher anstellen?* Can you turn the television on, please?
2 to employ ◊ *Sie ist bei einem Versandhaus angestellt.* She's employed by a mail-order company.
3 to do ◊ *Wie soll ich es bloß anstellen, dass er es erlaubt?* What can I do to get him to allow it? ◊ *Was stellen wir denn heute Nachmittag an?* What shall we do this afternoon?
4 to be up to ◊ *Was hat der Lümmel denn schon wieder angestellt?* What has that rascal been up to this time?
♦ **sich anstellen (1)** to queue ◊ *Musstet ihr euch für die Karten lange anstellen?* Did you have to queue for long for the tickets?
♦ **sich anstellen (2)** to act ◊ *Sie hat sich wirklich dumm angestellt.* She acted really stupidly.
♦ **Stell dich nicht so an, natürlich kannst du das.** Don't make such a fuss. Of course you can do it.

anstrengen VERB (PERFECT **hat angestrengt**)
♦ **Die Reise hat mich sehr angestrengt.** The journey took a lot out of me.
♦ **Streng deinen Kopf an!** Use your head!
♦ **sich anstrengen** to make an effort

anstrengend ADJECTIVE
tiring

die **Anstrengung** NOUN
effort

die **Antarktis** NOUN
the Antarctic ◊ *in der Antarktis* in the Antarctic

der Anteil NOUN (PL die **Anteile**)
share ◊ *Ich möchte meinen Anteil am Gewinn haben.* I would like to have my share of the profit.
♦ **Anteil nehmen an (1)** to sympathize with ◊ *Ich nehme Anteil an deinem Pech.* I sympathize with you in your bad luck.
♦ **Anteil nehmen an (2)** to take an interest in ◊ *Der Patient nimmt keinen Anteil an seiner Umgebung.* The patient takes no interest in his surroundings.

die Antenne NOUN
aerial

Anti- PREFIX
anti-

antiautoritär ADJECTIVE
anti-authoritarian

das Antibiotikum NOUN (PL die **Antibiotika**)
antibiotic

antik ADJECTIVE
antique

die Antiquitäten FEM PL NOUN
antiques

der Antrag NOUN (PL die **Anträge**)
1 application ◊ *Sie stellte einen Antrag auf Arbeitslosenunterstützung.* She put in an application for unemployment benefit.
2 motion ◊ *der Antrag der Opposition* the motion put by the opposition
♦ **Ich stelle den Antrag, dass wir diesen Punkt erst später behandeln.** I move that we deal with this point later.

antun VERB (IMPERFECT **tat an,** PERFECT **hat angetan**)
♦ **jemandem etwas antun** to do something to somebody ◊ *Das kannst du deinen Eltern nicht antun!* You can't do that to your parents.
♦ **jemandem ein Unrecht antun** to wrong somebody ◊ *Uns ist ein großes Unrecht angetan worden.* We've been cruelly wronged.
♦ **sich Zwang antun** to force oneself ◊ *Tu dir keinen Zwang an!* Don't force yourself!
♦ **sich etwas antun** to kill oneself ◊ *Wenn ich durchfalle, dann tue ich mir was an.* If I fail, I'll kill myself.

die Antwort NOUN
answer ◊ *jemandem eine Antwort geben* to give somebody an answer

antworten VERB
to answer ◊ *Antworte bitte!* Please answer.
♦ **auf etwas antworten** to answer something ◊ *Sie konnte auf diese Frage nicht antworten.* She couldn't answer the question.
♦ **jemandem antworten** to answer somebody ◊ *Wo warst du? Antworte mir gefälligst!* Where have you been? Answer me, will you!

der Antwortschein NOUN (PL die **Antwortscheine**)
reply coupon

der Anwalt NOUN (PL die **Anwälte**)
lawyer

die Anwältin NOUN
lawyer

die Anweisung NOUN
instruction ◊ *Folgen Sie bitte den Anweisungen Ihres Führers.* Please follow your guide's instructions.
♦ **Anweisung haben, etwas zu tun** to have instructions to do something

anwenden VERB (IMPERFECT **wendete** or **wandte an,** PERFECT **hat angewendet** or **angewandt**)
1 to use ◊ *Welche Software wenden Sie an?* What software do you use? ◊ *Sie wenden eine neue Technik zum Recycling von Kunststoff an.* They use a new recycling technique for plastic.
2 (*law, rule*)
to apply
♦ **Gewalt anwenden** to use violence

anwesend ADJECTIVE
present

die Anwesenheit NOUN
presence

die Anzahl NOUN
number ◊ *je nach Anzahl der Teilnehmer* according to the number of participants ◊ *eine große Anzahl an Fehlern* a large number of mistakes

anzahlen VERB (PERFECT **hat angezahlt**)
♦ **fünfzig Euro anzahlen** to pay fifty euros deposit
♦ **ein Auto anzahlen** to put down a deposit on a car

die Anzahlung NOUN
deposit ◊ *eine Anzahlung leisten* to pay a deposit

das Anzeichen NOUN (PL die **Anzeichen**)
sign

die Anzeige NOUN
advertisement ◊ *Ich habe ihn über eine Anzeige kennengelernt.* I met him through an advertisement.
♦ **Anzeige gegen jemanden erstatten** to report somebody to the police
♦ **Ich möchte Anzeige wegen Diebstahls erstatten.** I wish to report a theft.

anzeigen VERB (PERFECT **hat angezeigt**)
1 to show ◊ *Der Tachometer zeigt die Geschwindigkeit an.* The speedometer shows the speed.
2 to report ◊ *Ich werde Sie wegen Ruhestörung anzeigen!* I'll report you for breach of the peace. ◊ *Ich habe einen Diebstahl anzuzeigen.* I wish to report a theft.

anziehen VERB (IMPERFECT **zog an,** PERFECT **hat angezogen**)

1 to put on ◊ *Ich muss mir nur noch die Schuhe anziehen.* I just have to put my shoes on.

2 to dress ◊ *Kannst du bitte die Kinder anziehen?* Can you dress the children, please? ◊ *Er war sehr schick angezogen.* He was dressed very elegantly.

♦ **sich anziehen** to get dressed

3 to attract ◊ *Der Zoo zieht viele Besucher an.* The zoo attracts a lot of visitors.

♦ **sich von jemandem angezogen fühlen** to feel attracted to somebody

♦ **sich von etwas angezogen fühlen** to feel attracted to something

4 to tighten (*screw*)

der **Anzug** NOUN (PL die **Anzüge**)
suit

anzünden VERB (PERFECT **hat angezündet**)
to light ◊ *Ich habe mir eine Zigarette angezündet.* I lit a cigarette.

die **AOK** NOUN (= *Allgemeine Ortskrankenkasse*)
German health insurance

der **Apfel** NOUN (PL die **Äpfel**)
apple

das **Apfelmus** NOUN (GEN des **Apfelmuses**)
apple purée

der **Apfelsaft** NOUN (PL die **Apfelsäfte**)
apple juice

die **Apfelsine** NOUN
orange

die **Apotheke** NOUN
chemist's ◊ *in der Apotheke* at the chemist's

der **Apotheker** NOUN (PL die **Apotheker**)
pharmacist ◊ *Er ist Apotheker.* He's a pharmacist.

der **Apparat** NOUN (PL die **Apparate**)
1 gadget ◊ *Mit diesem Apparat kann man Dosen zerkleinern.* You can crush tins with this gadget.

2 camera

3 telephone ◊ *Wer war am Apparat?* Who was on the telephone?

♦ **Am Apparat!** Speaking!

♦ **Bleiben Sie bitte am Apparat.** Please stay on the line.

4 set

das **Appartement** NOUN (PL die **Appartements**)
flat

der **Appetit** NOUN
appetite

♦ **Ich habe keinen Appetit.** I'm not hungry.

♦ **Guten Appetit!** Enjoy your meal!

die **Aprikose** NOUN
apricot

der **April** NOUN (GEN des **April** or **Aprils**, PL die **Aprile**)
April ◊ *im April* in April ◊ *am dritten April* on the third of April ◊ *Ulm, den 3. April 2001* Ulm, 3 April 2001 ◊ *Heute ist*

der dritte April. Today is the third of April.

♦ **April, April!** April Fool!

der **Araber** NOUN (PL die **Araber**)
Arab

die **Araberin** NOUN
Arab

arabisch ADJECTIVE

♦ **arabische Länder** Arab countries

♦ **die arabische Sprache** Arabic

die **Arbeit** NOUN
1 job ◊ *Das ist eine sehr anstrengende Arbeit.* That's a very tiring job. ◊ *Er sucht eine Arbeit auf dem Bau.* He's looking for a job on a building site.

2 work ◊ *Ich habe im Moment viel Arbeit.* I've got a lot of work at the moment. ◊ *Die Arbeiten an unserem neuen Haus gehen gut voran.* Work on our new house is progressing well.

♦ **Sie hat keine Arbeit.** She's out of work.

♦ **Das war eine Arbeit!** That was hard work.

3 dissertation ◊ *Sie schreibt eine Arbeit über englische Ortsnamen.* She's writing a dissertation on English place names.

4 test ◊ *Ich habe in der Arbeit eine Fünf geschrieben.* I got an "E" in the test. ◊ *Morgen schreiben wir in Mathe eine Arbeit.* We've got a maths test tomorrow.

♦ **in Arbeit sein** to be in hand ◊ *Ihre Reparatur ist in Arbeit.* Your repair work is in hand.

arbeiten VERB
to work ◊ *Sie arbeitet hart.* She works hard. ◊ *Er arbeitet als Elektriker bei der Firma Müller.* He works as an electrician for Müller's. ◊ *Seine Nieren arbeiten nicht richtig.* His kidneys don't work properly.

♦ **sich durch etwas arbeiten** to work one's way through something ◊ *Nach dem Urlaub musste ich mich durch Berge von Post arbeiten.* After my holiday I had to work my way through piles of mail.

der **Arbeiter** NOUN (PL die **Arbeiter**)
worker

die **Arbeiterin** NOUN
worker

der **Arbeitgeber** NOUN (PL die **Arbeitgeber**)
employer

der **Arbeitnehmer** NOUN (PL die **Arbeitnehmer**)
employee ◊ *Als Arbeitnehmer hat man gewisse Rechte.* As an employee you have certain rights.

das **Arbeitsamt** NOUN (PL die **Arbeitsämter**)
job centre

die **Arbeitsbedingungen** PL NOUN
working conditions

die **Arbeitserlaubnis** NOUN (PL die **Arbeitserlaubnisse**)
work permit

arbeitslos ADJECTIVE

☞

unemployed

der **Arbeitslose** NOUN (GEN des/der
die **Arbeitslosen**, PL die **Arbeitslosen**)
unemployed person ◊ *Ein Arbeitsloser
hat die Stelle bekommen.* An
unemployed person got the job.
  ✦ **die Arbeitslosen** the unemployed

die **Arbeitslosigkeit** NOUN
unemployment

die **Arbeitslosenhilfe** NOUN
unemployment benefit

der **Arbeitsort** NOUN (PL die **Arbeitsorte**)
place of work

der **Arbeitsplatz** NOUN (GEN des
Arbeitsplatzes, PL die **Arbeitsplätze**)
[1] job ◊ *Suchen Sie einen neuen
Arbeitsplatz?* Are you looking for a new
job?
[2] desk ◊ *Frau Marr ist im Moment nicht
an ihrem Arbeitsplatz.* Ms Marr isn't at
her desk at the moment.

das **Arbeitspraktikum** NOUN (GEN des
Arbeitspraktikums, PL die **Arbeitspraktika**)
work experience ◊ *Sie absolviert gerade
ihr Arbeitspraktikum.* She's doing work
experience.

die **Arbeitszeit** NOUN
working hours
  ✦ **gleitende Arbeitszeit** flexitime

das **Arbeitszimmer** NOUN (PL die
Arbeitszimmer)
study

der **Architekt** NOUN (GEN des **Architekten**, PL die
Architekten)
architect ◊ *Er ist Architekt.* He's an
architect.

die **Architektur** NOUN
architecture

die **ARD** ABBREVIATION (= *Arbeitsgemeinschaft
der Rundfunkanstalten Deutschlands*)
German TV channel

Argentinien NEUT NOUN
Argentina ◊ *nach Argentinien* to
Argentina

der **Ärger** NOUN
[1] anger ◊ *Er hat seinen Ärger über die
Verspätung an mir ausgelassen.* He took
out his anger at the delay on me.
[2] trouble ◊ *Wenn du das machst,
bekommst du Ärger.* If you do that, you'll
get into trouble.
  ✦ **Ärger mit etwas haben** to have trouble
with something ◊ *Hast du wieder Ärger
mit deinem Computer?* Are you having
trouble with your computer again?

ärgerlich ADJECTIVE
[1] annoying ◊ *Diese dauernden
Störungen sind sehr ärgerlich.* These
constant interruptions are very annoying.
[2] angry ◊ *Ich bin auf ihn ärgerlich.* I'm
angry with him. ◊ *Er ist über die
Verzögerung ärgerlich.* He's angry at the
delay.

  ✦ **jemanden ärgerlich machen** to annoy
somebody

ärgern VERB
to annoy ◊ *Du sollst deine Schwester
nicht immer ärgern!* Don't keep annoying
your sister.
  ✦ **sich ärgern** to be annoyed ◊ *Ich habe
mich über diesen Fehler sehr geärgert.* I
was very annoyed about that mistake.

die **Arktis** NOUN
the Arctic ◊ *in der Arktis* in the Arctic

der **Arm** NOUN (PL die **Arme**)
  [see also **arm** ADJECTIVE]
arm
  ✦ **jemanden auf den Arm nehmen** to pull
somebody's leg ◊ *Du willst mich wohl
auf den Arm nehmen?* You're pulling my
leg.

arm ADJECTIVE
  [see also **der Arm** NOUN]
poor ◊ *Er ist ärmer als ich.* He's poorer
than me.

das **Armband** NOUN (PL die **Armbänder**)
bracelet

die **Armbanduhr** NOUN
wristwatch

die **Armee** NOUN
army

der **Ärmel** NOUN (PL die **Ärmel**)
sleeve

der **Ärmelkanal** NOUN
the English Channel

die **Armut** NOUN
poverty

arrangieren VERB (PERFECT **hat arrangiert**)
to arrange ◊ *Sie hat ein Treffen der
beiden arrangiert.* She arranged for them
both to meet.

die **Art** NOUN (PL die **Arten**)
[1] way ◊ *Ich mache das auf meine Art.* I
do that my way.
[2] kind ◊ *Ich mag diese Art Obst nicht.* I
don't like this kind of fruit. ◊ *Häuser aller
Art* all kinds of houses
[3] species ◊ *Diese Art ist vom
Aussterben bedroht.* This species is in
danger of extinction.
  ✦ **Es ist nicht seine Art, das zu tun.** It's not
like him to do that.

der **Artikel** NOUN (PL die **Artikel**)
article

die **Arznei** NOUN
medicine

das **Arzneimittel** NOUN (PL die **Arzneimittel**)
drug

der **Arzt** NOUN (PL die **Ärzte**)
doctor ◊ *Helmut ist Arzt.* Helmut's a
doctor.

die **Ärztin** NOUN
doctor ◊ *Jutta ist Ärztin.* Jutta's a doctor.

ärztlich ADJECTIVE
medical

A

♦ **Die Wunde muss ärztlich behandelt werden.** The wound will have to be treated by a doctor.

das **As** NOUN *see* **Ass**

die **Asche** NOUN (PL die **Aschen**)
ash

der **Aschenbecher** NOUN (PL die **Aschenbecher**)
ashtray

der **Aschermittwoch** NOUN
Ash Wednesday ◊ *am Aschermittwoch* on Ash Wednesday

der **Asiat** NOUN (GEN des **Asiaten**, PL die **Asiaten**)
Asian

die **Asiatin** NOUN
Asian

asiatisch ADJECTIVE
Asian

Asien NEUT NOUN
Asia
♦ **aus Asien** from Asia
♦ **nach Asien** to Asia

aß VERB *see* **essen**

das **Ass** NOUN (GEN des **Asses**, PL die **Asse**)
ace ◊ *das Herzass* the ace of hearts

der **Assistent** NOUN (GEN des **Assistenten**, PL die **Assistenten**)
assistant

die **Assistentin** NOUN
assistant

der **Ast** NOUN (PL die **Äste**)
branch

das **Asthma** NOUN
asthma ◊ *Sie hat Asthma.* She's got asthma.

die **Astrologie** NOUN
astrology

der **Astronaut** NOUN (GEN des **Astronauten**, PL die **Astronauten**)
astronaut ◊ *Er ist Astronaut.* He's an astronaut.

die **Astronomie** NOUN
astronomy

das **Asyl** NOUN (PL die **Asyle**)
asylum ◊ *um Asyl bitten* to ask for asylum
♦ **ein Obdachlosenasyl** a hostel for the homeless

der **Asylbewerber** NOUN (PL die **Asylbewerber**)
asylum-seeker

die **Asylbewerberin** NOUN
asylum-seeker

der **Atem** NOUN
breath ◊ *außer Atem* out of breath

atemlos ADJECTIVE
breathless

die **Athletik** NOUN
athletics

der **Atlantik** NOUN
the Atlantic

der **Atlas** NOUN (GEN des **Atlasses**, PL die **Atlasse**

or **Atlanten**)
atlas

atmen VERB
to breathe

die **Atmosphäre** NOUN
atmosphere

das **Atom** NOUN (PL die **Atome**)
atom

atomar ADJECTIVE
atomic

die **Atombombe** NOUN
atom bomb

die **Atomwaffen** FEM PL NOUN
atomic weapons

atomwaffenfrei ADJECTIVE
nuclear-free

attraktiv ADJECTIVE
attractive ◊ *attraktiv aussehen* to look attractive

das **At-Zeichen** NOUN (PL die **At-Zeichen**)
@ symbol

ätzend ADJECTIVE
1 rubbish ◊ *Die Musik ist ätzend.* The music's rubbish.
2 corrosive
3 caustic

au! EXCLAMATION
ouch!
♦ **Au ja!** Oh yes!

auch ADVERB
1 also ◊ *Gummienten verkaufen wir auch.* We also sell rubber ducks.
2 too ◊ *Das ist auch schön.* That's nice, too.
♦ **Ich auch.** Me too.
♦ **Ich auch nicht.** Me neither.
♦ **Er kommt. – Sie auch.** He's coming. – So is she.
♦ **auch nicht** not ... either ◊ *Nein, das Kleid gefällt mir auch nicht.* No, I don't like that dress either.
♦ **Auch das noch!** That's all we needed!
3 even ◊ *Auch wenn das Wetter schlecht ist.* Even if the weather's bad. ◊ *ohne auch nur zu fragen* without even asking
♦ **Du siehst müde aus. – Bin ich auch.** You look tired. – I am.
♦ **wer auch** whoever ◊ *Wer das auch gesagt hat, ich glaube es nicht.* I don't believe it, whoever said it.
♦ **was auch** whatever ◊ *Was du auch sagst, ich finde es schön.* Whatever you say, I think it's nice.
♦ **wie dem auch sei** be that as it may ◊ *Wie dem auch sei, ich gehe jetzt trotzdem.* Be that as it may, I'm still going.
♦ **wie sehr er sich auch bemühte** however much he tried

auf PREPOSITION, ADVERB
1 on
Use the accusative to express movement or a change of place. Use the dative when there is no change of place.

☞

◊ *Stell die Suppe bitte auf den Tisch.*
Please put the soup on the table. ◊ *Die
Suppe steht auf dem Tisch.* The soup's
on the table.
♦ **Auf dem Land ist die Luft besser.** The air
is better in the country.
♦ **Wir fahren morgen aufs Land.** We're
going to the country tomorrow.
♦ **auf der ganzen Welt** in the whole world
♦ **auf Deutsch** in German
♦ **bis auf ihn** except for him
♦ **auf einmal** at once
♦ **auf seinen Vorschlag hin** at his
suggestion
[2] open ◊ *Das Fenster ist auf.* The
window's open. ◊ *Die Geschäfte sind am
Sonntag nicht auf.* The shops aren't open
on Sunday.
[3] up ◊ *Ist er schon auf?* Is he up yet?
◊ *Ich bin schon seit sieben Uhr auf.* I've
been up since seven.
♦ **auf und ab** up and down
♦ **auf und davon** up and away

aufatmen VERB (PERFECT **hat aufgeatmet**)
to heave a sigh of relief

aufbauen VERB (PERFECT **hat aufgebaut**)
to build up

aufbekommen VERB (IMPERFECT **bekam auf,**
PERFECT **hat aufbekommen**)
[1] to get open ◊ *Ich bekomme das
Fenster nicht auf.* I can't get the window
open.
[2] to be given homework ◊ *Wir haben
heute nichts aufbekommen.* We weren't
given any homework today.

aufbewahren VERB (PERFECT **hat
aufbewahrt**)
to keep ◊ *Sie bewahrt ihre Ersparnisse in
einer Blechdose auf.* She keeps her
savings in a tin.

aufblasen VERB (PRESENT **bläst auf,** IMPERFECT
blies auf, PERFECT **hat aufgeblasen**)
to inflate

aufbleiben VERB (IMPERFECT **blieb auf,** PERFECT
ist aufgeblieben)
[1] to stay open ◊ *Donnerstags bleiben
die Geschäfte länger auf.* The shops stay
open longer on Thursdays.
[2] to stay up ◊ *Heute dürft ihr
ausnahmsweise länger aufbleiben.*
Today you can stay up late for once.

aufbrechen VERB (PRESENT **bricht auf,**
IMPERFECT **brach auf,** PERFECT **hat/ist
aufgebrochen**)
*For the perfect tense use **haben** when
the verb has an object and **sein** when
there is no object.*
[1] to break open ◊ *Die Diebe haben den
Safe aufgebrochen.* The thieves broke
the safe open.
[2] to open up ◊ *Die Wunde ist wieder
aufgebrochen.* The wound has opened
up again.

[3] to set off ◊ *Wann seid ihr
aufgebrochen?* When did you set off?

aufbringen VERB (IMPERFECT **brachte auf,**
PERFECT **hat aufgebracht**)
[1] to open ◊ *Ich bringe das
Konservenglas nicht auf.* I can't open the
jar.
[2] to raise ◊ *Wie soll ich nur das Geld für
die Reparatur aufbringen?* However am I
going raise the money for the repairs?
♦ **Verständnis für etwas aufbringen** to be
able to understand something

aufeinander ADVERB
on top of each other ◊ *Leg die
Handtücher aufeinander.* Put the towels
on top of each other.
♦ **aufeinander schießen** to shoot at one
another
♦ **aufeinander vertrauen** to trust each
other

der **Aufenthalt** NOUN (PL die **Aufenthalte**)
[1] stay ◊ *Während unseres Aufenthalts
in London ...* During our stay in
London ...
[2] stop ◊ *Der Zug hat fünf Minuten
Aufenthalt in Ulm.* The train has a five-
minute stop in Ulm.

aufessen VERB (PRESENT **isst auf,** IMPERFECT **aß
auf,** PERFECT **hat aufgegessen**)
to eat up

auffallen VERB (PRESENT **fällt auf,** IMPERFECT **fiel
auf,** PERFECT **ist aufgefallen**)
to be conspicuous
♦ **jemandem auffallen** to strike somebody
◊ *Es fiel mir auf, dass sie sich recht
seltsam benahm.* It struck me that she
was behaving rather strangely.

auffällig ADJECTIVE
conspicuous
♦ **auffällig gekleidet sein** to be dressed
strikingly

auffangen VERB (PRESENT **fängt auf,** IMPERFECT
fing auf, PERFECT **hat aufgefangen**)
to catch

aufführen VERB (PERFECT **hat aufgeführt**)
[1] to perform ◊ *ein Stück aufführen* to
perform a play
[2] to list ◊ *Alle Fachausdrücke sind im
Anhang aufgeführt.* All technical terms
are listed in the appendix.
♦ **sich aufführen** to behave

die **Aufführung** NOUN
performance

die **Aufgabe** NOUN
[1] task ◊ *Vier Kinder zu erziehen ist eine
schwierige Aufgabe.* Bringing up four
children is a difficult task.
[2] question ◊ *Ich konnte die zweite
Aufgabe in der Mathearbeit nicht lösen.* I
couldn't solve the second question in the
maths test.

A

3 homework ◊ *Hast du deine Aufgaben schon gemacht?* Have you done your homework yet?

aufgeben VERB (PRESENT **gibt auf,** IMPERFECT **gab auf,** PERFECT **hat aufgegeben**)

1 to give up ◊ *Du solltest das Rauchen aufgeben.* You should give up smoking.

2 to post ◊ *Ich habe das Paket an dich vor drei Tagen aufgegeben.* I posted the parcel to you three days ago.

3 to check in ◊ *Du kannst den Koffer ja vor der Reise aufgeben.* You can check in your suitcase before you travel.

◆ **eine Anzeige aufgeben** to place an advertisement

◆ **Ich gebe auf!** I give up.

aufgehen VERB (IMPERFECT **ging auf,** PERFECT **ist aufgegangen**)

1 to rise ◊ *Der Mond ist aufgegangen.* The moon has risen.

2 to open ◊ *Die Tür ging auf, und Christoph kam herein.* The door opened and Christoph came in.

3 to become clear ◊ *Mir ist inzwischen aufgegangen, warum sie das gesagt hat.* It has since become clear to me why she said that.

◆ **Zwanzig durch sechs geht nicht auf.** Six into twenty doesn't go.

aufgelegt ADJECTIVE

◆ **gut aufgelegt sein** to be in a good mood

◆ **schlecht aufgelegt sein** to be in a bad mood

◆ **zu etwas aufgelegt sein** to feel like something ◊ *Ich bin zu einem Spaziergang aufgelegt.* I feel like a walk.

aufgeregt ADJECTIVE
excited

aufgeschlossen ADJECTIVE
open-minded

aufgrund PREPOSITION

*The preposition **aufgrund** takes the genitive.*

1 because of ◊ *Das Spiel ist aufgrund des schlechten Wetters ausgefallen.* The game was cancelled because of the bad weather.

2 on the basis of ◊ *Sie wurde aufgrund von Indizien überführt.* She was convicted on the basis of circumstantial evidence.

aufhaben VERB (PRESENT **hat auf,** IMPERFECT **hatte auf,** PERFECT **hat aufgehabt**)

1 to have on ◊ *Sie hatte einen roten Hut auf.* She had a red hat on.

2 to have homework to do ◊ *Wir haben heute in Englisch nichts auf.* We haven't got any English homework to do today.

aufhalten VERB (PRESENT **hält auf,** IMPERFECT **hielt auf,** PERFECT **hat aufgehalten**)

1 to detain ◊ *Ich möchte dich nicht aufhalten.* I don't want to detain you.

2 to check ◊ *Wie kann die Vergrößerung des Ozonlochs aufgehalten werden?* How can the growth of the ozone hole be checked?

3 to hold open ◊ *Kannst du mir bitte die Tür aufhalten?* Can you hold the door open for me, please?

◆ **Sie hielt die Hand auf.** She held out her hand.

◆ **Halt die Augen auf, ob du sie sehen kannst.** Keep your eyes peeled. You might see them.

◆ **sich aufhalten (1)** to live ◊ *Sie hat sich lange im Ausland aufgehalten.* She lived abroad for a long time.

◆ **sich aufhalten (2)** to stay ◊ *Ich möchte mich nicht lange aufhalten.* I don't want to stay long.

◆ **sich mit etwas aufhalten** to waste time over something ◊ *Mit solchen Kinderspielen halte ich mich doch nicht auf.* I'm not wasting my time over such childish games.

aufhängen VERB (PERFECT **hat aufgehängt**)
to hang up (*washing*)

◆ **sich aufhängen** to hang oneself ◊ *Er hat gedroht, sich aufzuhängen.* He's threatened to hang himself.

aufheben VERB (IMPERFECT **hob auf,** PERFECT **hat aufgehoben**)

1 to pick up ◊ *Sie hob das Heft, das auf den Boden gefallen war, auf.* She picked up the exercise book which had fallen on the floor.

2 to keep ◊ *Sie hat alle seine Briefe aufgehoben.* She's kept all his letters.

◆ **gut aufgehoben sein** to be well looked after ◊ *Unsere Tochter ist bei ihrer Oma gut aufgehoben.* Our daughter's being well looked after at her granny's.

aufheitern VERB (PERFECT **hat aufgeheitert**)

◆ **jemanden aufheitern** to cheer somebody up ◊ *Versuch, sie etwas aufzuheitern.* Try to cheer her up a bit.

aufhören VERB (PERFECT **hat aufgehört**)
to stop ◊ *Der Regen hat aufgehört.* The rain's stopped.

◆ **aufhören, etwas zu tun** to stop doing something ◊ *Hör endlich auf, dich dauernd zu beklagen.* Will you stop complaining all the time!

aufklären VERB (PERFECT **hat aufgeklärt**)
to solve ◊ *Die Polizei hat den Mord aufgeklärt.* The police have solved the murder.

◆ **jemanden aufklären (1)** to explain to somebody ◊ *Kannst du mich bitte aufklären, wie man das machen muss.* Can you please explain to me how this should be done.

◆ **jemanden aufklären (2)** to tell somebody the facts of life ◊ *Meine Eltern haben mich aufgeklärt, als ich zehn war.* My

☞

parents told me the facts of life when I
was ten.

♦ **sich aufklären** to clear up ◊ *Das Wetter
klärt sich auf.* The weather's clearing up.

♦ **Das Rätsel hat sich aufgeklärt.** The
mystery has been solved.

der **Aufkleber** NOUN (PL die **Aufkleber**)
sticker

auflassen VERB (PRESENT **lässt auf**, IMPERFECT
ließ auf, PERFECT **hat aufgelassen**)
1 to leave open ◊ *Lass bitte das Fenster
auf.* Please leave the window open.
2 to keep on ◊ *Kann ich meine Mütze
auflassen?* Can I keep my hat on?

auflegen VERB (PERFECT **hat aufgelegt**)
to hang up ◊ *Sie hat einfach aufgelegt.*
She simply hung up.

auflesen VERB (PRESENT **liest auf**, IMPERFECT **las
auf**, PERFECT **hat aufgelesen**)
to pick up ◊ *etwas von der Straße
auflesen* to pick something up off the
street

auflösen VERB (PERFECT **hat aufgelöst**)
1 to dissolve ◊ *Du solltest die Tablette
in Wasser auflösen.* You should dissolve
the tablet in water.
2 to break up ◊ *Die Polizei hat die
Demonstration aufgelöst.* The police
broke up the demonstration.

♦ **sich auflösen** to dissolve ◊ *Der Zucker
hatte sich schnell im Tee aufgelöst.* The
sugar had quickly dissolved in the tea.

♦ **wenn sich der Nebel aufgelöst hat** when
the fog has lifted

♦ **Die Menschenmenge löste sich auf.** The
crowd dispersed.

♦ **in Tränen aufgelöst sein** to be in tears

aufmachen VERB (PERFECT **hat aufgemacht**)
1 to open ◊ *Kannst du bitte die Tür
aufmachen?* Can you open the door,
please? ◊ *Wann machen die Geschäfte
auf?* When do the shops open?
2 to undo ◊ *Ich schaffe es nicht, den
Reißverschluss aufzumachen.* I can't
undo the zip.

♦ **sich aufmachen** to set out ◊ *Wir machten
uns nach London auf.* We set out for
London.

aufmerksam ADJECTIVE
attentive

♦ **jemanden auf etwas aufmerksam
machen** to point something out to
somebody ◊ *Ich habe ihn auf das
Schloss aufmerksam gemacht.* I pointed
the castle out to him.

die **Aufmerksamkeit** NOUN
attention ◊ *Darf ich um Ihre
Aufmerksamkeit bitten!* May I have your
attention?

♦ **Wir sollten ihnen eine kleine
Aufmerksamkeit mitbringen.** We ought
to take them a little something.

aufmuntern VERB (PERFECT **hat
aufgemuntert**)
to cheer up

die **Aufnahme** NOUN
1 welcome ◊ *Wir fanden eine sehr
freundliche Aufnahme in unserer
Partnerstadt.* We were given a very
friendly welcome in our twin town.
2 recording ◊ *Wir haben uns die
Aufnahme des Konzerts angehört.* We
listened to a recording of the concert.
3 photograph ◊ *Möchtest du die
Aufnahmen sehen, die ich in den Ferien
gemacht habe?* Would you like to see the
photographs I took on holiday?

die **Aufnahmeprüfung** NOUN
entrance test

aufnehmen VERB (PRESENT **nimmt auf**,
IMPERFECT **nahm auf**, PERFECT **hat
aufgenommen**)
1 to take ◊ *Wie hat sie die Nachricht
aufgenommen?* How did she take the
news?
2 to record ◊ *Wenn das Lied im Radio
kommt, muss ich es unbedingt
aufnehmen.* If they play the song on the
radio, I really must record it.
3 to photograph ◊ *Diesen tollen
Sonnenuntergang muss ich aufnehmen.* I
must photograph this wonderful sunset.
4 to admit ◊ *Was muss man tun, um in
den Tennisklub aufgenommen zu
werden?* What do you have to do to be
admitted to the tennis club?

♦ **es mit jemandem aufnehmen können** to
be able to compete with somebody

aufpassen VERB (PERFECT **hat aufgepasst**)
to pay attention ◊ *Ich habe heute im
Unterricht nicht aufgepasst.* I didn't pay
attention in class today.

♦ **auf jemanden aufpassen** to look after
somebody ◊ *Ich muss auf meinen
kleinen Bruder aufpassen.* I have to look
after my little brother.

♦ **auf etwas aufpassen** to look after
something ◊ *Kannst du mal eben auf
meinen Koffer aufpassen?* Can you look
after my suitcase for a moment?

♦ **Aufgepasst!** Look out!

aufpumpen VERB (PERFECT **hat aufgepumpt**)
to pump up

aufräumen VERB (PERFECT **hat aufgeräumt**)
to tidy up ◊ *Ich darf erst raus, wenn ich
mein Zimmer aufgeräumt habe.* I can't
go out until I've tidied up my room.

aufrecht ADJECTIVE
upright

aufrechterhalten VERB (PRESENT **erhält
aufrecht**, IMPERFECT **erhielt aufrecht**, PERFECT
hat aufrechterhalten)
to maintain

aufregen VERB (PERFECT **hat aufgeregt**)
to excite

A

♦ **sich aufregen** to get excited

aufregend ADJECTIVE
exciting

aufs = **auf das**

der **Aufsatz** NOUN (GEN des **Aufsatzes**, PL die **Aufsätze**)
essay ◊ *Wir haben heute in Deutsch einen Aufsatz geschrieben.* We wrote an essay in today's German lesson.

aufschieben VERB (IMPERFECT **schob auf**, PERFECT **hat aufgeschoben**)
[1] to push open ◊ *Man kann diese Tür aufschieben.* You can push this door open.
[2] to put off ◊ *Wir haben unsere Abreise noch einmal aufgeschoben.* We put off our departure once again.

aufschlagen VERB (PRESENT **schlägt auf**, IMPERFECT **schlug auf**, PERFECT **hat aufgeschlagen**)
[1] to open ◊ *ein Buch aufschlagen* to open a book ◊ *Schlagt Seite 111 auf.* Open your books at page 111.
[2] to pitch ◊ *Sie schlugen ihre Zelte auf.* They pitched their tents.
[3] (*prices*)
to go up ◊ *Butter ist wieder aufgeschlagen.* The price of butter has gone up again.
[4] (*tennis*)
to serve ◊ *Du schlägst auf.* It's your turn to serve.

aufschließen VERB (IMPERFECT **schloss auf**, PERFECT **hat aufgeschlossen**)
to unlock ◊ *Schließ bitte die Tür auf!* Please unlock the door. ◊ *Sie schloss auf und ging hinein.* She unlocked the door and went in.

aufschlussreich ADJECTIVE
informative

der **Aufschnitt** NOUN (PL die **Aufschnitte**)
cold meat

aufschreiben VERB (IMPERFECT **schrieb auf**, PERFECT **hat aufgeschrieben**)
to write down

aufsehen VERB (PRESENT **sieht auf**, IMPERFECT **sah auf**, PERFECT **hat aufgesehen**)
see also **das Aufsehen** NOUN
to look up ◊ *Als die Tür aufging, sah sie von ihrer Arbeit auf.* When the door opened she looked up from her work.

das **Aufsehen** NOUN
see also **aufsehen** VERB
stir ◊ *Ihre Kleidung hat Aufsehen erregt.* Her outfit caused a stir.

aufsehenerregend ADJECTIVE
sensational

aufsein VERB *see* **auf**

aufsetzen VERB (PERFECT **hat aufgesetzt**)
to put on ◊ *Setz dir eine Mütze auf!* Put a hat on.
♦ **Ich setze das Teewasser auf.** I'll put the kettle on.
♦ **sich aufsetzen** to sit up ◊ *Der Patient setzte sich auf.* The patient sat up.

die **Aufsicht** NOUN
supervision
♦ **die Aufsicht haben** to be in charge

aufstehen VERB (IMPERFECT **stand auf**, PERFECT **ist/hat aufgestanden**)
*Use **sein** for **to get up** and **haben** for **to be open**.*
[1] to get up ◊ *Wann bist du heute Morgen aufgestanden?* When did you get up this morning? ◊ *Sie stand auf und ging.* She got up and left.
[2] to be open ◊ *Die Tür hat aufgestanden, also ging ich hinein.* The door was open, so I went in.

aufstellen VERB (PERFECT **hat aufgestellt**)
[1] to pitch ◊ *Wir haben unser Zelt am Waldrand aufgestellt.* We pitched our tent at the edge of the woods.
[2] to stand up ◊ *Der Sonnenschirm ist umgefallen, ich muss ihn wieder aufstellen.* The sunshade has fallen over. I'll have to stand it up again.
[3] to set up ◊ *Sie stellte die Schachfiguren auf.* She set up the chess pieces.
♦ **eine Liste aufstellen** to draw up a list
♦ **einen Rekord aufstellen** to set a record
♦ **die Mannschaft aufstellen** to pick the team
♦ **jemanden für ein Spiel aufstellen** to pick somebody for a game
♦ **sich aufstellen** to line up ◊ *Stellt euch bitte in Zweierreihen auf!* Please line up in twos.

auftauchen VERB (PERFECT **ist aufgetaucht**)
to appear

auftauen VERB (PERFECT **hat/ist aufgetaut**)
*For the perfect tense use **haben** when the verb has an object and **sein** when there is no object.*
[1] to thaw ◊ *Der Schnee taute auf.* The snow thawed.
[2] to defrost ◊ *Ich habe die Pizza im Mikrowellenherd aufgetaut.* I've defrosted the pizza in the microwave. ◊ *Sobald das Fleisch aufgetaut ist, kann ich es zubereiten.* As soon as the meat has defrosted I can cook it.

aufteilen VERB (PERFECT **hat aufgeteilt**)
to divide up ◊ *Wir wurden in drei Gruppen aufgeteilt.* We were divided up into three groups.

der **Auftrag** NOUN (PL die **Aufträge**)
orders ◊ *Ich habe den Auftrag, Sie davon zu unterrichten, dass ...* I have orders to inform you that ...
♦ **Wir haben dem Architekten den Auftrag erteilt, einen Bauplan zu zeichnen.** We instructed the architect to draw up some building plans.

♦ im Auftrag von on behalf of ◊ *Ich komme im Auftrag der Firma Haehnle & Co.* I'm here on behalf of Haehnle and Co.

auftreten VERB (PRESENT **tritt auf,** IMPERFECT **trat auf,** PERFECT **ist aufgetreten)**

⓵ to appear ◊ *Dieser Schauspieler tritt erst im dritten Akt auf.* This actor doesn't appear until the third act.

⓶ to occur ◊ *Sollten Probleme auftreten, wende dich an uns.* If any problems occur, get in touch with us.

⓷ to behave ◊ *Er ist ziemlich unbeliebt, weil er immer so überheblich auftritt.* He's quite unpopular because he always behaves so arrogantly.

aufwachen VERB (PERFECT **ist aufgewacht)**
to wake up

aufwachsen VERB (PRESENT **wächst auf,** IMPERFECT **wuchs auf,** PERFECT **ist aufgewachsen)**
to grow up

aufwecken VERB (PERFECT **hat aufgeweckt)**
to wake up

aufzählen VERB (PERFECT **hat aufgezählt)**
to list

aufziehen VERB (IMPERFECT **zog auf,** PERFECT **hat aufgezogen)**

⓵ to draw ◊ *Zieh die Vorhänge auf und lass das Licht herein!* Draw the curtains and let some light in.

⓶ to wind ◊ *Ich habe vergessen, die Uhr aufzuziehen.* I forgot to wind the clock.

♦ jemanden aufziehen to tease somebody ◊ *Sie haben mich wegen meiner roten Haare aufgezogen.* They teased me about my red hair.

♦ Kinder aufziehen to bring up children

der **Aufzug** NOUN (PL die **Aufzüge)**
lift ◊ *Wir sind mit dem Aufzug nach oben gefahren.* We went up in the lift.

das **Auge** NOUN (PL die **Augen)**
eye ◊ *Sie hat dunkle Augen.* She's got dark eyes.

♦ unter vier Augen in private

der **Augenblick** NOUN (PL die **Augenblicke)**
moment

♦ im Augenblick at the moment

die **Augenbraue** NOUN
eyebrow

der **August** NOUN (GEN des **Augustes** or **August,** PL die **Auguste)**
August ◊ *im August* in August ◊ *am fünften August* on 5 August ◊ *Ulm, den 5. August 2000* Ulm, 5 August 2000 ◊ *Heute ist der fünfte August.* Today is the fifth of August.

die **Aula** NOUN (PL die **Aulen)**
assembly hall

aus PREPOSITION, ADVERB

*The preposition **aus** takes the dative.*

⓵ out of ◊ *Sie nahm ein Bonbon aus der Tüte.* She took a sweet out of the bag. ◊ *aus dem Fenster* out of the window

⓶ from ◊ *Wenn er aus der Schule kommt, ist er immer sehr müde.* When he comes home from school he's always very tired. ◊ *Ich komme aus Deutschland.* I come from Germany. ◊ *Er ist aus Berlin.* He's from Berlin.

⓷ made of ◊ *Die Vase ist aus Porzellan.* The vase is made of china.

♦ aus Erfahrung from experience

♦ aus Spaß for fun

♦ Ich habe ihr aus Freundschaft geholfen. I helped her out of a sense of friendship.

♦ Aus ihr wird nie etwas. She'll never get anywhere.

⓸ finished ◊ *wenn das Kino aus ist* when the film's finished ◊ *Komm sofort nach Hause, wenn die Schule aus ist.* Come straight home when school has finished.

♦ Wann ist die Schule aus? When does school finish?

⓹ off ◊ *Der Fernseher ist aus.* The television's off.

♦ Licht aus! Lights out!

♦ Sie können meinen Mann nicht sprechen, er ist aus. You can't speak to my husband. He's out.

♦ von sich aus of one's own accord

♦ von ihm aus as far as he's concerned

ausatmen VERB (PERFECT **hat ausgeatmet)**
to breathe out

ausbeuten VERB (PERFECT **hat ausgebeutet)**
to exploit

ausbilden VERB (PERFECT **hat ausgebildet)**
to train ◊ *Er bildet Lehrlinge aus.* He trains apprentices. ◊ *Sie ist ausgebildete Krankenschwester.* She's a qualified nurse.

die **Ausbildung** NOUN
training ◊ *eine solide Ausbildung* a decent training

der **Ausbildungsplatz** NOUN (GEN des **Ausbildungsplatzes,** PL die **Ausbildungsplätze)**
training job

die **Ausdauer** NOUN
stamina

ausdenken VERB (IMPERFECT **dachte aus,** PERFECT **hat ausgedacht)**

♦ sich etwas ausdenken to think something up ◊ *Da hast du dir aber was Witziges ausgedacht.* You've certainly thought up something imaginative.

der **Ausdruck (1)** NOUN (PL die **Ausdrücke)**
expression ◊ *Sie hat in der Schule ein paar schlimme Ausdrücke gelernt.* She's learned a few nasty expressions at school. ◊ *Als Ausdruck meiner Dankbarkeit habe ich ihr Blumen geschenkt.* I gave her flowers as an expression of my gratitude. ◊ *Ich kann am Ausdruck in deinem Gesicht sehen,*

dass dir das nicht passt. I can see by your expression that it doesn't suit you.

der **Ausdruck (2)** NOUN (PL die **Ausdrucke**)
  printout ◊ *Kannst du mir von der Datei einen Ausdruck machen?* Can you do me a printout of the file?

  ausdrucken VERB (PERFECT **hat ausgedruckt**)
  to print out ◊ *Soll ich dir die Namen ausdrucken?* Shall I print out the names for you?

  ausdrücken VERB (PERFECT **hat ausgedrückt**)
  to express ◊ *Ich weiß nicht, wie man das auf Englisch ausdrückt.* I don't know how to express it in English.

  ausdrücklich ADJECTIVE
  explicit

  auseinander ADVERB
  apart ◊ *weit auseinander* far apart
  ♦ **Auseinander, ihr beiden!** Break it up, you two!

  auseinanderhalten VERB (PRESENT **hält auseinander,** IMPERFECT **hielt auseinander,** PERFECT **hat auseinandergehalten**)
  to distinguish

  auseinandernehmen VERB (PRESENT **nimmt auseinander,** IMPERFECT **nahm auseinander,** PERFECT **hat auseinandergenommen**)
  to take to pieces

  auseinanderschreiben VERB (IMPERFECT **schrieb auseinander,** PERFECT **hat auseinandergeschrieben**)
  to write separately

die **Ausfahrt** NOUN
  exit ◊ *Wir müssen an der nächsten Ausfahrt raus.* We have to take the next exit.

  ausfallen VERB (PRESENT **fällt aus,** IMPERFECT **fiel aus,** PERFECT **ist ausgefallen**)
  1 to be cancelled ◊ *Der Sportunterricht fällt heute aus.* PE has been cancelled today.
  2 to break down ◊ *Die Heizung ist mal wieder ausgefallen.* The heating has broken down again.
  ♦ **Wenn der Strom ausfällt, dann sind alle Dateien weg.** If there's a power cut all the files are lost.
  ♦ **Die Mathearbeit ist furchtbar schlecht ausgefallen.** The results of the maths test were really awful.
  3 to fall out ◊ *Ihm sind die Haare ausgefallen, als er noch ziemlich jung war.* His hair fell out when he was still quite young.

der **Ausflug** NOUN (PL die **Ausflüge**)
  outing ◊ *einen Ausflug machen* to go on an outing

  ausfragen VERB (PERFECT **hat ausgefragt**)
  to question

die **Ausfuhr** NOUN
  export

  ausführen VERB (PERFECT **hat ausgeführt**)

to carry out ◊ *Sie hat ihren Plan ausgeführt.* She carried out her plan.
  ♦ **jemanden ausführen** to take somebody out ◊ *Er hat mich zum Essen ausgeführt.* He took me out for a meal.
  ♦ **einen Hund ausführen** to take a dog for a walk
  ♦ **Waren ausführen** to export goods

  ausführlich ADJECTIVE, ADVERB
  1 detailed ◊ *ein ausführlicher Bericht* a detailed report
  2 in detail ◊ *Sie hat mir ausführlich erzählt, wie es in den Ferien war.* She told me in detail about her holidays.

  ausfüllen VERB (PERFECT **hat ausgefüllt**)
  to fill in ◊ *Hast du den Antrag schon ausgefüllt?* Have you filled in the application form yet?
  ♦ **Mein Beruf füllt mich nicht aus.** My job doesn't satisfy me.

die **Ausgabe** NOUN
  1 expenditure ◊ *Wir hatten in der letzten Zeit viele Ausgaben.* We've had a lot of expenditure recently.
  2 edition ◊ *Sie hat eine sehr alte Ausgabe von Goethes Werken.* She's got a very old edition of Goethe's works.
  3 issue ◊ *Ich habe das in der letzten Ausgabe meines Computermagazins gelesen.* I read it in the last issue of my computer magazine.

der **Ausgang** NOUN (PL die **Ausgänge**)
  1 exit ◊ *Ich warte dann am Ausgang auf euch.* I'll wait for you at the exit, then.
  ♦ **"Kein Ausgang"** "No exit"
  2 ending ◊ *Der Film hat einen sehr traurigen Ausgang.* The film has a very sad ending.
  3 result ◊ *Welchen Ausgang hatte das Spiel?* What was the result of the match?

  ausgeben VERB (PRESENT **gibt aus,** IMPERFECT **gab aus,** PERFECT **hat ausgegeben**)
  1 to spend ◊ *Wir haben auf dem Volksfest hundert Euro ausgegeben.* We spent a hundred euros at the fair.
  2 to distribute ◊ *Da werden die Karten ausgegeben.* That's where the tickets are being distributed.
  ♦ **einen ausgeben** to stand a round ◊ *Ich habe heute Geburtstag, darum gebe ich einen aus.* It's my birthday today, so I'm standing a round.
  ♦ **sich für jemanden ausgeben** to pass oneself off as somebody ◊ *Sie hat sich für meine Schwester ausgegeben.* She passed herself off as my sister.
  ♦ **sich als etwas ausgeben** to pretend to be something ◊ *Er hat sich als Computerfachmann ausgegeben.* He pretended to be a computer expert.

  ausgebucht ADJECTIVE
  fully booked

  ausgehen VERB (IMPERFECT **ging aus,** PERFECT **ist ausgegangen**)

1 to go out ◊ *Sollen wir heute Abend ausgehen?* Shall we go out this evening? ◊ *Fritz will mit dir ausgehen.* Fritz wants to go out with you. ◊ *Plötzlich ging das Licht aus.* Suddenly the light went out.

2 to run out ◊ *Wir sollten tanken, bevor das Benzin ausgeht.* We ought to fill up before we run out of petrol.

♦ **Mir ging das Benzin aus.** I ran out of petrol.

♦ **Wie ist das Spiel ausgegangen?** How did the game end?

♦ **schlecht ausgehen** to turn out badly

♦ **wir können davon ausgehen, dass ...** we can assume that ...

ausgelassen ADJECTIVE
exuberant

ausgenommen CONJUNCTION
except ◊ *Alle kamen, ausgenommen Günter.* Everyone came except Günter.

♦ **Anwesende sind ausgenommen.** Present company excepted.

ausgerechnet ADVERB

♦ **ausgerechnet heute** today of all days

♦ **ausgerechnet du** you of all people

ausgeschlossen ADJECTIVE
impossible ◊ *Ich halte das für ausgeschlossen.* I think that's impossible.

ausgezeichnet ADJECTIVE, ADVERB
1 excellent ◊ *Werner ist ein ausgezeichneter Koch.* Werner's an excellent cook.

2 excellently ◊ *Sie hat es ausgezeichnet gemacht.* She did it excellently.

ausgiebig ADJECTIVE
substantial ◊ *Das Frühstück war sehr ausgiebig.* Breakfast was very substantial.

♦ **ausgiebig schlafen** to have a good sleep

♦ **sich ausgiebig erholen** to have a good long rest

aushalten VERB (PRESENT **hält aus,** IMPERFECT **hielt aus,** PERFECT **hat ausgehalten**)

♦ **Ich halte diese Hitze nicht aus!** I can't stand this heat.

♦ **Wie hast du es in dieser Stadt nur ausgehalten?** How could you stand living in this town?

♦ **Das ist nicht zum Aushalten.** It's unbearable.

sich **auskennen** VERB (IMPERFECT **kannte sich aus,** PERFECT **hat sich ausgekannt**)
1 to know about ◊ *Sie kennt sich mit Kindern gut aus.* She knows a lot about children.

2 to know one's way around ◊ *Er kennt sich in Stuttgart aus.* He knows his way around Stuttgart.

auskommen VERB (IMPERFECT **kam aus,** PERFECT **ist ausgekommen**)

♦ **mit jemandem auskommen** to get on with somebody ◊ *Ich komme mit meinen Eltern gut aus.* I get on well with my parents.

♦ **mit etwas auskommen** to manage on something ◊ *Ich muss mit siebzig Euro in der Woche auskommen.* I have to manage on seventy euros a week.

die **Auskunft** NOUN (PL die **Auskünfte**)
1 information ◊ *Nähere Auskunft erhalten Sie unter der folgenden Nummer.* For further information ring the following number.

2 information office ◊ *Fragen Sie bei der Auskunft, wann der nächste Zug nach Bremen geht.* Ask at the information office when the next train leaves for Bremen.

♦ **Telefonauskunft** directory inquiries ◊ *Ruf doch die Auskunft an!* Ring directory inquiries.

auslachen VERB (PERFECT **hat ausgelacht**)
to laugh at ◊ *Sie hat mich nur ausgelacht.* She just laughed at me.

ausladen VERB (PRESENT **lädt aus,** IMPERFECT **lud aus,** PERFECT **hat ausgeladen**)
to unload ◊ *Wir müssen noch das Auto ausladen.* We still have to unload the car.

♦ **jemanden ausladen** to tell somebody not to come

das **Ausland** NOUN

♦ **im Ausland** abroad ◊ *Er lebt im Ausland.* He lives abroad.

♦ **ins Ausland** abroad ◊ *Nach dem Examen möchte sie ins Ausland gehen.* After the exams she wants to go abroad.

der **Ausländer** NOUN (PL die **Ausländer**)
foreigner ◊ *Ihr Mann ist Ausländer.* Her husband's a foreigner.

die **Ausländerin** NOUN
foreigner ◊ *Seine Frau ist Ausländerin.* His wife's a foreigner.

ausländisch ADJECTIVE
foreign

das **Auslandsgespräch** NOUN (PL die **Auslandsgespräche**)
international call

auslassen VERB (PRESENT **lässt aus,** IMPERFECT **ließ aus,** PERFECT **hat ausgelassen**)
1 to leave out ◊ *Die nächste Übung können wir auslassen.* We can leave out the next exercise.

♦ **Ich lasse heute das Mittagessen aus.** I'm skipping lunch today.

2 to leave off ◊ *Heute lass ich den Fernseher aus.* I'm leaving the television off today. ◊ *Bei der Hitze kannst du die Jacke auslassen.* You can leave your jacket off in this heat.

♦ **seine Wut an jemandem auslassen** to take one's anger out on somebody

ausleeren VERB (PERFECT **hat ausgeleert**)
to empty

ausleihen VERB (IMPERFECT **lieh aus,** PERFECT **hat ausgeliehen**) to lend ◊ *Kannst du mir dein Moped ausleihen?* Can you lend me your moped?

♦ **sich etwas ausleihen** to borrow something ◊ *Ich habe mir das Wörterbuch meines Bruders ausgeliehen.* I've borrowed my brother's dictionary.

ausloggen VERB (PERFECT **hat ausgeloggt**)
to log off (*computer*)

ausmachen VERB (PERFECT **hat ausgemacht**)
1 to turn off ◊ *Mach bitte das Radio aus, die Musik stört mich.* Please turn the radio off. The music's disturbing me.
♦ **das Licht ausmachen** to switch off the light
2 to put out ◊ *Du solltest deine Zigarette ausmachen, bevor du hineingehst.* You should put your cigarette out before you go in.
3 to arrange ◊ *Habt ihr schon einen Termin für das Fest ausgemacht?* Have you arranged a date for the party yet? ◊ *Ich habe mit ihr ausgemacht, dass wir uns um fünf Uhr treffen.* I've arranged to meet her at five.
4 to settle ◊ *Macht das unter euch aus.* Settle the matter between you.
5 to mind ◊ *Es macht mir nichts aus, wenn ich allein gehen muss.* I don't mind having to go alone. ◊ *Macht es Ihnen etwas aus, wenn ...?* Would you mind if ...?

die **Ausnahme** NOUN
exception

ausnahmsweise ADVERB
for once

ausnützen VERB (PERFECT **hat ausgenützt**)
to use

auspacken VERB (PERFECT **hat ausgepackt**)
to unpack

ausprobieren VERB (PERFECT **hat ausprobiert**)
to try out

der **Auspuff** NOUN (PL die **Auspuffe**)
exhaust

der **Auspufftopf** NOUN (PL die **Auspufftöpfe**)
silencer

ausrechnen VERB (PERFECT **hat ausgerechnet**)
to calculate

die **Ausrede** NOUN
excuse

ausreichend ADJECTIVE
1 sufficient ◊ *ausreichend Geld* sufficient money
2 adequate

> ❶ German marks range from one (**sehr gut**) to six (**ungenügend**).

die **Ausreise** NOUN
departure

♦ **bei der Ausreise** when leaving the country

ausrichten VERB (PERFECT **hat ausgerichtet**)
1 to tell ◊ *Ich werde es ihm ausrichten.* I'll tell him.
♦ **Richte bitte an deine Eltern schöne Grüße aus.** Please give my regards to your parents.
2 to gear to ◊ *Wir müssen unser Veranstaltungsangebot mehr auf Jugendliche ausrichten.* We must gear our events more to young people.

ausrufen VERB (IMPERFECT **rief aus**, PERFECT **hat ausgerufen**)
to cry out
♦ **jemanden ausrufen lassen** to page somebody

das **Ausrufezeichen** NOUN (PL die **Ausrufezeichen**)
exclamation mark

sich **ausruhen** VERB (PERFECT **hat sich ausgeruht**)
to rest

ausrüsten VERB (PERFECT **hat ausgerüstet**)
to equip

die **Ausrüstung** NOUN
equipment

ausschalten VERB (PERFECT **hat ausgeschaltet**)
to switch off

ausschlafen VERB (PRESENT **schläft aus**, IMPERFECT **schlief aus**, PERFECT **hat ausgeschlafen**)
to have a good sleep
♦ **Morgen kann ich ausschlafen.** I can have a lie-in tomorrow.
♦ **Ich bin nicht ausgeschlafen.** I didn't get enough sleep.

ausschließlich ADVERB, PREPOSITION
1 exclusively ◊ *Der Schulhof ist ausschließlich für Schüler dieser Schule.* The school yard is exclusively for pupils of this school.
2 except ◊ *Wir haben jeden Tag geöffnet ausschließlich Sonntag.* We're open every day except Sunday.

ausschneiden VERB (IMPERFECT **schnitt aus**, PERFECT **hat ausgeschnitten**)
to cut out

der **Ausschuss** NOUN (GEN des **Ausschusses**, PL die **Ausschüsse**)
committee

aussehen VERB (PRESENT **sieht aus**, IMPERFECT **sah aus**, PERFECT **hat ausgesehen**)
see also **das Aussehen** NOUN
to look ◊ *Sie sieht sehr hübsch aus.* She looks very pretty. ◊ *Wie siehst du denn aus?* What do you look like! ◊ *Es sieht nach Regen aus.* It looks like rain. ◊ *Es sieht schlecht aus.* Things look bad.

das **Aussehen** NOUN
see also **aussehen** VERB
appearance

aussein VERB see **aus**

außen ADVERB
on the outside ◊ *Außen ist es rot.* It's red on the outside.

das **Außenministerium** NOUN (PL die **Außenministerien**)
foreign office

die **Außenpolitik** NOUN
foreign policy

der **Außenseiter** NOUN (PL die **Außenseiter**)
outsider

außer PREPOSITION, CONJUNCTION

> The preposition **außer** takes the dative.

[1] apart from ◊ *Außer dir haben das alle verstanden.* Everyone has understood apart from you. ◊ *Wer war noch da außer Horst?* Apart from Horst, who was there?

♦ **außer Haus** out ◊ *Er ist heute den ganzen Tag außer Haus.* He's out all day today.
♦ **außer Landes** abroad
♦ **außer Gefahr** out of danger
♦ **außer Betrieb** out of order
♦ **außer sich sein** to be beside oneself ◊ *Sie war außer sich vor Wut.* She was beside herself with rage.

[2] if ... not ◊ *Wir machen morgen ein Picknick, außer es regnet.* We're having a picnic tomorrow if it doesn't rain.
♦ **nicht ... außer** not ... unless ◊ *Wir können sie nicht mitnehmen, außer sie ist schon reisefertig.* We can't take her with us unless she's all packed and ready to go.

außerdem CONJUNCTION
in addition

äußere ADJECTIVE
[1] outer ◊ *Sie bildeten einen äußeren und einen inneren Kreis.* They formed an outer and an inner circle.
[2] external ◊ *Nur zur äußeren Anwendung.* For external use only.
♦ **Der äußere Eindruck trügt manchmal.** Appearances are sometimes deceptive.

außergewöhnlich ADJECTIVE
unusual

außerhalb PREPOSITION, ADVERB

> The preposition **außerhalb** takes the genitive.

[1] outside ◊ *Es liegt außerhalb der Stadt.* It's outside the town.
[2] out of town ◊ *Sie wohnt nicht in Ulm, sondern ziemlich weit außerhalb.* She doesn't live in Ulm, but quite a way out of town.
♦ **außerhalb der Saison** out of season

äußern VERB
to express ◊ *Sie hat den Wunsch geäußert, allein in die Ferien fahren zu dürfen.* She's expressed the wish to be allowed to go on holiday alone.
♦ **eine Meinung äußern** to give an opinion ◊ *Willst du nicht auch deine Meinung äußern?* Don't you want to give your opinion, too?

♦ **sich äußern** to comment ◊ *Sie wollte sich zu dem Vorwurf nicht äußern.* She didn't wish to comment on the accusation.

außerordentlich ADJECTIVE, ADVERB
exceptional ◊ *Sie hat eine außerordentliche Begabung.* She's exceptionally gifted.
♦ **Sie ist außerordentlich intelligent.** She's exceptionally intelligent.

äußerst ADVERB

> see also **äußerste** ADJECTIVE

extremely

äußerste ADJECTIVE

> see also **äußerst** ADVERB

utmost ◊ *Diese Sache ist von äußerster Wichtigkeit.* This matter is of the utmost importance.
♦ **Tausend Euro sind der äußerste Preis, den ich für den Computer bezahlen kann.** One thousand euros is the most I can pay for the computer.

die **Äußerung** NOUN
remark

die **Aussicht** NOUN
[1] view ◊ *Vom Hotel aus hat man eine schöne Aussicht aufs Meer.* You have a wonderful view of the sea from the hotel.
[2] prospect ◊ *Die Aussicht auf diese Stelle hat ihr neuen Mut gegeben.* The prospect of this job gave her new hope.
♦ **Das sind ja schöne Aussichten!** What a prospect!
♦ **etwas in Aussicht haben** to have the prospect of something ◊ *Sie hat eine Stelle bei Collins in Aussicht.* She has the prospect of a job with Collins.

ausspannen VERB (PERFECT hat **ausgespannt**)
to relax

die **Aussprache** NOUN
[1] pronunciation ◊ *Die Aussprache der Wörter ist mit phonetischen Zeichen angegeben.* The pronunciation of the words is shown by phonetic symbols.
[2] frank discussion ◊ *Ich hatte gestern eine lange Aussprache mit ihm.* I had a long, frank discussion with him yesterday.

aussprechen VERB (PRESENT **spricht aus**, IMPERFECT **sprach aus**, PERFECT hat **ausgesprochen**)
to pronounce ◊ *Wie spricht man dieses Wort aus?* How do you pronounce this word?
♦ **sich mit jemandem aussprechen** to talk things out with somebody ◊ *Meinst du nicht, wir sollten uns einmal aussprechen?* Don't you think we ought to talk things out?
♦ **sich gegen etwas aussprechen** to speak out against something ◊ *Die Mehrheit hat sich gegen eine Klassenfahrt nach*

Helgoland ausgesprochen. The majority spoke out against a school trip to Heligoland.

♦ **sich für etwas aussprechen** to speak out in favour of something ◊ *Die Lehrer haben sich für eine Verlängerung der Pausenzeiten ausgesprochen.* The teachers spoke out in favour of longer breaks.

♦ **Lass ihn doch aussprechen!** Let him finish.

aussteigen VERB (IMPERFECT **stieg aus,** PERFECT **ist ausgestiegen)**
to get off ◊ *Ich sah, wie sie aus der Straßenbahn ausstieg.* I saw her get off the tram.

ausstellen VERB (PERFECT **hat ausgestellt)**
1 to exhibit ◊ *Im Museum werden zurzeit Bilder von Chagall ausgestellt.* Pictures by Chagall are currently being exhibited in the museum.
2 to be on display ◊ *Im Schaufenster war exotisches Obst ausgestellt.* Exotic fruit was on display in the window.
3 to switch off ◊ *Die Heizung wird im Mai ausgestellt.* The heating's switched off in May.
4 to write ◊ *Die Lehrerin hat ihm ein gutes Zeugnis ausgestellt.* The teacher wrote him a good report.
5 to issue ◊ *Auf welchem Amt werden Pässe ausgestellt?* Which office issues passports?

die **Ausstellung** NOUN
exhibition

aussterben VERB (PRESENT **stirbt aus,** IMPERFECT **starb aus,** PERFECT **ist ausgestorben)**
to die out

der **Ausstieg** NOUN
1 exit ◊ *Der Ausstieg ist hinten.* The exit is at the back.
2 abandonment ◊ *der Ausstieg aus der Atomenergie* abandonment of nuclear energy

ausstreichen VERB (IMPERFECT **strich aus,** PERFECT **hat ausgestrichen)**
to cross out

aussuchen VERB (PERFECT **hat ausgesucht)**
to choose ◊ *Such dir ein Eis aus.* Choose yourself an ice cream.

der **Austausch** NOUN (GEN des **Austausches)**
exchange ◊ *ein Schüleraustausch* a school exchange

austauschen VERB (PERFECT **hat ausgetauscht)**
1 to replace ◊ *Ich habe die Festplatte ausgetauscht.* I've replaced the hard disk.
◊ *Wir müssen die Winterreifen gegen die Sommerreifen austauschen.* We'll have to replace our winter tyres with summer tyres.

2 to substitute ◊ *Der Mittelstürmer wurde in der zweiten Halbzeit ausgetauscht.* The centre-forward was substituted in the second half.

♦ **Unsere Schule tauscht jedes Jahr Schüler mit einer Schule aus Cardiff aus.** Every year, our school has a student exchange with a school in Cardiff.

♦ **Wir tauschen seit ein paar Jahren Briefe aus.** We've been writing to each other for a few years.

austeilen VERB (PERFECT **hat ausgeteilt)**
to give out

die **Auster** NOUN
oyster

austragen VERB (PRESENT **trägt aus,** IMPERFECT **trug aus,** PERFECT **hat ausgetragen)**
1 to deliver ◊ *Morgens trägt er immer die Post aus.* In the morning he always delivers the post.
2 to hold ◊ *Der Wettkampf wird im Olympiastadion ausgetragen.* The competition will be held in the Olympic stadium.

♦ **Sie will das Kind austragen.** She wants to have the baby.

Australien NEUT NOUN
Australia
♦ **aus Australien** from Australia
♦ **in Australien** in Australia
♦ **nach Australien** to Australia

der **Australier** NOUN (PL die **Australier)**
Australian

die **Australierin** NOUN
Australian

australisch ADJECTIVE
Australian

austreten VERB (PRESENT **tritt aus,** IMPERFECT **trat aus,** PERFECT **ist ausgetreten)**
♦ **aus etwas austreten** to leave something ◊ *Sie ist aus dem Verein ausgetreten.* She's left the club.
♦ **Ich muss mal austreten.** I need to go to the loo.

austrinken VERB (IMPERFECT **trank aus,** PERFECT **hat ausgetrunken)**
to drink up ◊ *Er trank aus und ging.* He drank up and left.
♦ **Lass mich noch schnell meinen Saft austrinken.** Let me just quickly finish my juice.

der **Ausverkauf** NOUN (PL die **Ausverkäufe)**
clearance sale

ausverkauft ADJECTIVE
1 sold out ◊ *Die Vorstellung ist leider ausverkauft.* The performance is sold out, I'm afraid.
2 full ◊ *Das Kino war ausverkauft.* The cinema was full.

die **Auswahl** NOUN
selection ◊ *Sie haben eine große Auswahl an Schuhen.* They have a large selection of shoes.

auswählen VERB (PERFECT **hat ausgewählt**)
to select

auswandern VERB (PERFECT **ist ausgewandert**)
to emigrate ◊ *Sie sind nach Australien ausgewandert.* They emigrated to Australia.

auswärts ADVERB
1 in another town ◊ *Sie wohnt in Calw, arbeitet aber auswärts.* She lives in Calw but works in another town.
2 away ◊ *Unsere Mannschaft spielt nächste Woche auswärts.* Our team's playing away next week.
 ♦ **auswärts essen** to eat out

das **Auswärtsspiel** NOUN (PL die **Auswärtsspiele**)
away game

der **Ausweg** NOUN (PL die **Auswege**)
way out

ausweichend ADJECTIVE
evasive

der **Ausweis** NOUN (PL die **Ausweise**)
1 identity card ◊ *Der Polizist wollte meinen Ausweis sehen.* The policeman wanted to see my identity card.
2 card ◊ *Wenn du Schüler bist und deinen Ausweis zeigst, bekommst du Ermäßigung.* If you're a student and show them your card, you get a reduction.

auswendig ADVERB
by heart ◊ *etwas auswendig lernen* to learn something by heart

auswerten VERB (PERFECT **hat ausgewertet**)
to evaluate

die **Auswertung** NOUN
evaluation

ausziehen VERB (IMPERFECT **zog aus**, PERFECT **hat/ist ausgezogen**)
*For the perfect tense use **haben** when the verb has an object and **sein** when there is no object.*
1 to take off ◊ *Sie hat ihren Mantel nicht ausgezogen.* She didn't take off her coat.
2 to undress ◊ *Kannst du bitte die Kinder ausziehen und ins Bett bringen?* Can you undress the children and put them to bed, please?
 ♦ **sich ausziehen** to undress ◊ *Haben die Kinder sich schon ausgezogen?* Have the children undressed yet?
3 to pull out ◊ *Der Zahnarzt hat mir zwei Zähne ausgezogen.* The dentist pulled out two of my teeth.
4 to move out ◊ *Meine Nachbarn sind*

letzte Woche ausgezogen. My neighbours moved out last week.

der **Auszubildende** NOUN (GEN des/der
die **Auszubildenden**, PL die **Auszubildenden**)
trainee

das **Auto** NOUN (PL die **Autos**)
car
 ♦ **Auto fahren** to drive

die **Autobahn** NOUN
motorway

das **Autobahndreieck** NOUN (PL die **Autobahndreiecke**)
motorway junction

das **Autobahnkreuz** NOUN (GEN des **Autobahnkreuzes**, PL die **Autobahnkreuze**)
motorway intersection

der **Autobus** NOUN (GEN des **Autobusses**, PL die **Autobusse**)
bus

der **Autofahrer** NOUN (PL die **Autofahrer**)
motorist

das **Autogramm** NOUN (PL die **Autogramme**)
autograph

das **Autokennzeichen** NOUN (PL die **Autokennzeichen**)
registration number

der **Automat** NOUN (GEN des **Automaten**, PL die **Automaten**)
machine

automatisch ADJECTIVE
automatic ◊ *Die Türen schließen automatisch.* The doors close automatically.

der **Autor** NOUN (PL die **Autoren**)
author

das **Autoradio** NOUN (PL die **Autoradios**)
car radio

das **Autorennen** NOUN (PL die **Autorennen**)
motor racing

die **Autorin** NOUN
author

autoritär ADJECTIVE
authoritarian

die **Autorität** NOUN
authority

der **Autostopp** NOUN
 ♦ **per Autostopp fahren** to hitchhike

das **Autotelefon** NOUN (PL die **Autotelefone**)
car phone

der **Autounfall** NOUN (PL die **Autounfälle**)
car accident

die **Autowäsche** NOUN
car wash

die **Axt** NOUN (PL die **Äxte**)
axe

B

das **Baby** NOUN (PL die **Babys**)
baby

babysitten VERB (PERFECT **hat gebabysittet**)
to babysit

der **Babysitter** NOUN (PL die **Babysitter**)
babysitter

die **Babysitterin** NOUN
babysitter

der **Bach** NOUN (PL die **Bäche**)
stream

die **Backe** NOUN
cheek

backen VERB (PRESENT **bäckt**, IMPERFECT **backte**
or **buk,** PERFECT **hat gebacken**)
to bake

der **Bäcker** NOUN (PL die **Bäcker**)
baker ◊ *beim Bäcker* at the baker's ◊ *zum Bäcker* to the baker's

die **Bäckerei** NOUN
baker's

der **Backofen** NOUN (PL die **Backöfen**)
oven

das **Bad** NOUN (PL die **Bäder**)
bath
♦ **ein Bad im Meer** a swim in the sea

der **Badeanzug** NOUN (PL die **Badeanzüge**)
bathing suit

die **Badehose** NOUN
swimming trunks

die **Bademütze** NOUN
bathing cap

baden VERB
to have a bath
♦ **jemanden baden** to bath somebody
◊ *Das Baby muss noch gebadet werden.*
The baby still has to be bathed.
♦ **sich baden** to have a bath

Baden-Württemberg NEUT NOUN
Baden-Württemberg

> *ⓘ* **Baden-Württemberg** is one of the 16 **Länder.** Its capital is Stuttgart. Baden-Württemberg is home to the cuckoo clock and to Mercedes-Benz and Porsche.

der **Badeort** NOUN
spa

das **Badetuch** NOUN (PL die **Badetücher**)
bath towel

die **Badewanne** NOUN
bath (*tub*)

das **Badezimmer** NOUN (PL die **Badezimmer**)
bathroom

das **Badminton** NOUN (GEN des **Badminton**)
badminton

die **Bahn** NOUN (PL die **Bahnen**)

[1] railway ◊ *Er arbeitet bei der Bahn.* He works for the railway.
♦ **Wir sind mit der Bahn gefahren.** We went by rail.
[2] tram
[3] lane ◊ *Die Schwimmerin auf Bahn drei liegt in Führung.* The swimmer in lane three is in the lead.
♦ **auf die schiefe Bahn geraten** to go off the rails

die **Bahnfahrt** NOUN
railway journey

der **Bahnhof** NOUN (PL die **Bahnhöfe**)
station ◊ *auf dem Bahnhof* at the station

die **Bahnhofshalle** NOUN
station concourse

der **Bahnsteig** NOUN (PL die **Bahnsteige**)
platform

der **Bahnübergang** NOUN (PL die **Bahnübergänge**)
level crossing

bald ADVERB
[1] soon ◊ *Es wird bald Frühling.* It'll soon be spring.
♦ **Bis bald!** See you later.
[2] almost ◊ *Ich hätte bald was gesagt.* I almost said something.
♦ **Wird's bald!** Get a move on!

der **Balkan** NOUN
Balkans
♦ **auf dem Balkan** in the Balkans

der **Balken** NOUN (PL die **Balken**)
beam

der **Balkon** NOUN (PL die **Balkons** or **Balkone**)
balcony

der **Ball** NOUN (PL die **Bälle**)
ball ◊ *Die Kinder spielen mit dem Ball.*
The children are playing with the ball.
◊ *Mit wem kommst du zum Ball?* Who are you going to the ball with?

das **Ballett** NOUN (PL die **Ballette**)
ballet

der **Ballon** NOUN (PL die **Ballons** or **Ballone**)
balloon

der **Bambus** NOUN (GEN des **Bambusses,** PL die **Bambusse**)
bamboo

die **Banane** NOUN
banana

der **Band** NOUN (PL die **Bände**)
[see also **die Band** NOUN, **das Band** NOUN]
volume ◊ *ein Lexikon in fünf Bänden* an encyclopaedia in five volumes

die **Band** NOUN (PL die **Bands**)
[see also **der Band** NOUN, **das Band** NOUN]
band ◊ *Er spielt Gitarre in einer Band.* He plays the guitar in a band.

das **Band** NOUN (PL die **Bänder**)

☞

see also **der Band** NOUN, **die Band** NOUN

[1] ribbon ◊ *Sie hatte ein rotes Band im Haar.* She had a red ribbon in her hair.

[2] production line ◊ *Mein Vater arbeitet am Band.* My father works on the production line.

[3] tape ◊ *Ich habe diesen Song auf Band.* I've got this song on tape.

♦ **etwas auf Band aufnehmen** to tape something

♦ **am laufenden Band** nonstop

band VERB see **binden**

die **Bank (1)** NOUN (PL die **Bänke**)
bench ◊ *Sie saß auf einer Bank im Park.* She was sitting on a park bench.

die **Bank (2)** NOUN (PL die **Banken**)
bank ◊ *Ich muss Geld von der Bank holen.* I'll have to get money from the bank.

der **Bankkonto** NOUN (PL die **Bankkonten**)
bank account

die **Bankleitzahl** NOUN
bank sort code

die **Banknote** NOUN
banknote

bankrott ADJECTIVE
bankrupt ◊ *Die Firma ist bankrott.* The firm is bankrupt.

♦ **Bankrott machen** to go bankrupt

die **Bar** NOUN (PL die **Bars**)
see also **bar** ADJECTIVE
bar

bar ADJECTIVE
see also **die Bar** NOUN

♦ **bares Geld** cash

♦ **etwas bar bezahlen** to pay cash for something

der **Bär** NOUN (GEN des **Bären**, PL die **Bären**)
bear

barfuß ADJECTIVE
barefoot

das **Bargeld** NOUN
cash

der **Barren** NOUN (PL die **Barren**)
parallel bars

der **Bart** NOUN (PL die **Bärte**)
beard

bärtig ADJECTIVE
bearded

Basel NEUT NOUN
Basle

♦ **nach Basel** to Basle

die **Basis** NOUN (PL die **Basen**)
basis

der **Bass** NOUN (GEN des **Basses**, PL die **Bässe**)
bass

basteln VERB
to make things ◊ *Ich bastle gern.* I like making things.

♦ **etwas basteln** to make something ◊ *Ich habe einen Untersetzer gebastelt.* I've made a coaster.

der **Bastler** NOUN (PL die **Bastler**)
do-it-yourselfer

♦ **Er ist ein guter Bastler.** He is good at making things.

bat VERB see **bitten**

die **Batterie** NOUN
battery

der **Bau** NOUN (PL die **Bauten**)
[1] construction ◊ *Das Haus ist noch im Bau befindlich.* The house is still under construction.

[2] building ◊ *In New York gibt es viele beeindruckende Bauten.* There are many impressive buildings in New York.

[3] building site ◊ *In den Ferien arbeitet er auf dem Bau.* He works on a building site in the holidays.

der **Bauarbeiter** NOUN (PL die **Bauarbeiter**)
building worker

der **Bauch** NOUN (PL die **Bäuche**)
stomach ◊ *Mir tut der Bauch weh.* My stomach's sore.

der **Bauchnabel** NOUN (PL die **Bauchnabel**)
belly button

die **Bauchschmerzen** MASC PL NOUN
stomachache

bauen VERB
to build ◊ *Meine Eltern haben das Haus gebaut, in dem wir wohnen.* My parents built the house we live in.

der **Bauer** NOUN (GEN des **Bauern**, PL die **Bauern**)
[1] farmer ◊ *Friedas Vater ist Bauer.* Frieda's father is a farmer.

[2] pawn ◊ *Sie zog mit dem Bauer.* She moved the pawn.

die **Bäuerin** NOUN
[1] farmer ◊ *Sie möchte Bäuerin werden.* She would like to be a farmer.

[2] farmer's wife ◊ *Die Bäuerin melkt die Kühe, während der Bauer aufs Feld fährt.* The farmer's wife milks the cows while the farmer drives out to the fields.

der **Bauernhof** NOUN (PL die **Bauernhöfe**)
farm

baufällig ADJECTIVE
dilapidated

der **Baum** NOUN (PL die **Bäume**)
tree

die **Baumwolle** NOUN
cotton ◊ *eine Tischdecke aus Baumwolle* a cotton tablecloth

die **Baustelle** NOUN
building site

die **Bauten** PL NOUN see **Bau**

der **Bauunternehmer** NOUN (PL die **Bauunternehmer**)
building contractor

der **Bayer** NOUN (GEN des **Bayern**, PL die **Bayern**)
Bavarian

die **Bayerin** NOUN
Bavarian

Bayern NEUT NOUN

Bavaria

> ❶ **Bayern** is one of the 16 **Länder**. Its capital is München (Munich). It has the longest political tradition of any of the Länder, and since 1945 has developed into an important industrial region.

bayrisch ADJECTIVE
Bavarian
beabsichtigen VERB (PERFECT **hat beabsichtigt**)
to intend ◊ *Ich beabsichtige, ins Ausland zu fahren.* I intend to go abroad.
beachten VERB (PERFECT **hat beachtet**)
1 to pay attention to ◊ *Beachte ihn nicht!* Don't pay any attention to him. ◊ *Du solltest den Hinweis auf der Packung beachten.* You should pay attention to the instructions on the packet.
2 to obey ◊ *Man muss die Verkehrsregeln beachten.* You have to obey the traffic regulations.
3 to observe ◊ *Sie hat die Vorfahrt nicht beachtet.* She didn't observe the right of way.
beachtlich ADJECTIVE
considerable
der **Beamte** NOUN (GEN des **Beamten,** PL die **Beamten**)
1 official ◊ *Der Beamte stempelte meinen Pass ab.* The official stamped my passport.
2 civil servant

> ❶ In Germany, traditionally all public employees are civil servants. They enjoy many privileges.

◊ *Er ist Beamter.* He is a civil servant.
◊ *Deutsche Lehrer sind Beamte.* German teachers are civil servants.
die **Beamtin** NOUN
civil servant ◊ *Meine Mutter ist Beamtin.* My mother's a civil servant.
beängstigend ADJECTIVE, ADVERB
alarming
♦ **Sie ist beängstigend schnell gefahren.** She drove alarmingly fast.
beanspruchen VERB (PERFECT **hat beansprucht**)
1 to claim ◊ *Bei fünf Kindern können Sie Kindergeld beanspruchen.* You can claim child benefit if you have five children.
2 to take up ◊ *Die Kinder beanspruchen meine ganze Zeit und Kraft.* The children take up all my time and energy.
♦ **jemanden beanspruchen** to take up somebody's time ◊ *Ich möchte Sie nicht länger beanspruchen.* I don't want to take up any more of your time.

3 to take advantage of ◊ *Wir haben eure Gastfreundschaft lange genug beansprucht.* We've taken advantage of your hospitality for long enough.
beantragen VERB (PERFECT **hat beantragt**)
to apply for
beantworten VERB (PERFECT **hat beantwortet**)
to answer
bearbeiten VERB (PERFECT **hat bearbeitet**)
1 to deal with ◊ *Welches Thema hat sie in ihrer Diplomarbeit bearbeitet?* What subject did she deal with in her dissertation?
2 to process ◊ *Wir haben Ihren Antrag noch nicht bearbeitet.* We haven't processed your application yet.
3 to treat ◊ *Sie hat den Fleck mit Fleckenmittel bearbeitet.* She treated the stain with stain remover.
♦ **jemanden bearbeiten** to work on somebody ◊ *Ich werde meine Mutter bearbeiten, dass sie mich gehen lässt.* I'll work on my mother and get her to let me go.
der **Becher** NOUN (PL die **Becher**)
1 mug ◊ *Auf ihrem Schreibtisch stand ein Becher mit Kaffee.* There was a mug of coffee on her desk.
2 carton
3 tub
das **Becken** NOUN (PL die **Becken**)
1 sink ◊ *Er ließ Wasser ins Becken laufen.* He ran water into the sink.
2 pool
♦ **Sie hat ein breites Becken.** She has broad hips.
sich **bedanken** VERB (PERFECT **hat sich bedankt**)
to say thank you ◊ *Hast du dich auch bedankt?* Did you say thank you?
♦ **Ich bedanke mich für Ihre Gastfreundschaft.** Thank you for your hospitality.
♦ **sich bei jemandem bedanken** to say thank you to somebody
der **Bedarf** NOUN
demand ◊ *je nach Bedarf* according to demand
♦ **bei Bedarf** if necessary
♦ **Bedarf an etwas haben** to be in need of something ◊ *Wir haben Bedarf an Aushilfskräften.* We're in need of temporary workers.
bedauerlich ADJECTIVE
regrettable
bedauern VERB (PERFECT **hat bedauert**)
1 to be sorry for ◊ *Wir bedauern es sehr, dass wir nicht kommen können.* We're very sorry that we can't come.
♦ **Ich bedaure!** I'm sorry!
♦ **Ich bedaure kein Wort.** I don't regret a single word!

2 to pity ◊ *Ich bedaure dich wirklich! I really pity you!*

bedeckt ADJECTIVE

1 covered ◊ *Die Erde war mit Laub bedeckt.* The ground was covered with leaves.

2 overcast ◊ *Heute ist es bedeckt.* It's overcast today.

die **Bedenken** NEUT PL NOUN

doubts ◊ *Ich habe Bedenken, ob das klappt.* I have my doubts as to whether it'll work.

♦ **Hast du keine Bedenken, wenn du deine Eltern so anlügst?** Don't you feel bad about lying to your parents like that?

bedenklich ADJECTIVE

1 dubious ◊ *Das sind sehr bedenkliche Methoden.* These are very dubious methods.

2 dangerous ◊ *Die Lage ist bedenklich.* The situation is dangerous.

♦ **Ihr Gesundheitszustand ist bedenklich.** Her state of health is giving cause for concern.

bedeuten VERB (PERFECT **hat bedeutet**)

to mean ◊ *Was bedeutet dieser Ausdruck?* What does this expression mean? ◊ *Was hat das zu bedeuten?* What's that supposed to mean? ◊ *Er bedeutet mir sehr viel.* He means a lot to me.

bedeutend ADJECTIVE

1 important ◊ *Er ist ein bedeutender Wissenschaftler.* He's an important scientist.

2 considerable ◊ *Sie haben eine bedeutende Summe dafür bezahlt.* They paid a considerable sum for it.

♦ **bedeutend besser** considerably better

♦ **bedeutend schlechter** considerably worse

die **Bedeutung** NOUN

1 meaning ◊ *die Bedeutung eines Worts* the meaning of a word

2 importance ◊ *eine Erfindung von großer Bedeutung* an invention of great importance

bedienen VERB (PERFECT **hat bedient**)

1 to serve ◊ *Wir wurden sehr schnell bedient.* We were served very quickly.

2 to operate ◊ *Er bedient die Druckmaschine.* He operates the printing press.

♦ **Kannst du einen Computer bedienen?** Can you use a computer?

♦ **sich bedienen** to help oneself ◊ *Bitte bedien dich!* Please help yourself.

die **Bedienung** NOUN

1 service ◊ *In diesem Geschäft ist die Bedienung schlecht.* The service is very poor in this shop.

2 waiter
waitress

◊ *Wir haben bei der Bedienung ein Bier bestellt.* We ordered a beer from the waitress.

3 shop assistant ◊ *Die Bedienung im Kaufhaus war äußerst unfreundlich.* The shop assistant in the department store was extremely unfriendly.

4 service charge ◊ *Die Bedienung ist im Preis enthalten.* The service charge is included in the price.

die **Bedingung** NOUN

condition ◊ *unter der Bedingung, dass ...* on condition that ...

bedrohen VERB (PERFECT **hat bedroht**)
to threaten

das **Bedürfnis** NOUN (GEN des **Bedürfnisses**, PL die **Bedürfnisse**)
need

das **Beefsteak** NOUN (PL die **Beefsteaks**)
steak

♦ **deutsches Beefsteak** hamburger

sich **beeilen** VERB (PERFECT **hat sich beeilt**)
to hurry

beeindrucken VERB (PERFECT **hat beeindruckt**)
to impress

beeindruckend ADJECTIVE
impressive

beeinflussen VERB (PRESENT **beeinflusst**, IMPERFECT **beeinflusste**, PERFECT **hat beeinflusst**)
to influence

beenden VERB (PERFECT **hat beendet**)
to end

die **Beerdigung** NOUN
funeral

die **Beere** NOUN

1 berry

2 grape

das **Beet** NOUN (PL die **Beete**)
bed ◊ *ein Blumenbeet* a flowerbed

sich **befassen** VERB (PERFECT **hat sich befasst**)

♦ **sich mit etwas befassen** to deal with something

der **Befehl** NOUN (PL die **Befehle**)
command

befehlen VERB (PRESENT **befiehlt**, IMPERFECT **befahl**, PERFECT **hat befohlen**)

1 to order ◊ *Der General hat den Rückzug befohlen.* The general ordered his men to retreat.

2 to give orders ◊ *Du hast hier nicht zu befehlen!* You're not the one who gives the orders here!

♦ **jemandem etwas befehlen** to order somebody to do something

befestigen VERB (PERFECT **hat befestigt**)
to fix ◊ *Die Regalbretter sind mit Schrauben an der Wand befestigt.* The shelves are fixed to the wall with screws.

sich **befinden** VERB (IMPERFECT **befand sich**, PERFECT **hat sich befunden**) to be ◊ *Er befindet sich zur Zeit im Ausland.* He's abroad at the moment.

befolgen VERB (PERFECT **hat befolgt**)
to obey

befördern VERB (PERFECT **hat befördert**)
1 to carry ◊ *Die städtischen Busse befördern täglich viele Menschen.* The municipal buses carry many people every day.
2 to promote ◊ *Sie ist zur Abteilungsleiterin befördert worden.* She's been promoted to head of department.

die **Beförderung** NOUN
1 transport ◊ *Das Rote Kreuz übernimmt die Beförderung der Hilfsgüter.* The Red Cross undertakes the transport of emergency supplies.
2 promotion ◊ *Bei einer Beförderung bekommt man auch mehr Geld.* Promotion also means more money.

befragen VERB (PERFECT **hat befragt**)
to question

befreien VERB (PERFECT **hat befreit**)
1 to set free ◊ *Die Geiseln sind noch nicht befreit.* The hostages haven't been set free yet.
2 to exempt ◊ *Sie ist vom Sportunterricht befreit.* She's exempt from PE lessons.

befreundet ADJECTIVE
♦ **mit jemandem befreundet sein** to be friends with somebody ◊ *Ich bin mit Petra seit Jahren befreundet.* I've been friends with Petra for years.

befriedigen VERB (PERFECT **hat befriedigt**)
to satisfy

befriedigend ADJECTIVE
satisfactory

> ❶ German marks range from one (**sehr gut**) to six (**ungenügend**).

befristet ADJECTIVE
limited

befürchten VERB (PERFECT **hat befürchtet**)
to fear

befürworten VERB (PERFECT **hat befürwortet**)
to support

begabt ADJECTIVE
talented

die **Begabung** NOUN
talent

begann VERB *see* **beginnen**

begegnen VERB (PERFECT **ist begegnet**)
♦ **jemandem begegnen** to meet somebody ◊ *Ich bin ihr heute schon einmal begegnet.* I've met her once today already. ◊ *Wir sind uns das erste Mal in London begegnet.* The first time we met was in London. ◊ *Eine solche Frechheit*

ist mir noch nie begegnet. I've never met such cheek.

die **Begegnung** NOUN
meeting

begehen VERB (IMPERFECT **beging**, PERFECT **hat begangen**)
to commit ◊ *Er hat einen Mord begangen.* He committed a murder.

begehren VERB (PERFECT **hat begehrt**)
to desire

begehrt ADJECTIVE
1 in demand
2 eligible

begeistern VERB (PERFECT **hat begeistert**)
to thrill ◊ *Der Film hat mich begeistert.* I was thrilled with the film.
♦ **sich für etwas begeistern** to get enthusiastic about something

begeistert ADJECTIVE
enthusiastic

begießen VERB (IMPERFECT **begoss**, PERFECT **hat begossen**)
to water ◊ *Sie begoss ihre Rosen.* She watered her roses.
♦ **das muss begossen werden!** that calls for a drink!

der **Beginn** NOUN
beginning ◊ *zu Beginn* at the beginning

beginnen VERB (IMPERFECT **begann**, PERFECT **hat begonnen**)
to start

begleiten VERB (PERFECT **hat begleitet**)
to accompany ◊ *Er hat mich zum Ball begleitet.* He accompanied me to the ball.

beglückwünschen VERB (PERFECT **hat beglückwünscht**)
to congratulate ◊ *Alle meine Freunde haben mich zur bestandenen Prüfung beglückwünscht.* All my friends congratulated me on passing the exam.

begonnen VERB *see* **beginnen**

begraben VERB (PRESENT **begräbt**, IMPERFECT **begrub**, PERFECT **hat begraben**)
to bury

begreifen VERB (IMPERFECT **begriff**, PERFECT **hat begriffen**)
to understand

der **Begriff** NOUN (PL die **Begriffe**)
term ◊ *Das ist ein Begriff aus der Architektur.* That is an architectural term.
♦ **im Begriff sein, etwas zu tun** to be about to do something ◊ *Ich war im Begriff zu gehen.* I was about to go.
♦ **schwer von Begriff** slow on the uptake
♦ **sich einen Begriff von etwas machen** to imagine something ◊ *Du machst dir keinen Begriff, wie schwierig das war.* You can't imagine how difficult it was.

begriffsstutzig ADJECTIVE
dense

begründen VERB (PERFECT **hat begründet**)

☞

to justify

die **Begründung** NOUN
justification

begrüßen VERB (PERFECT **hat begrüßt**)
to welcome ◊ *Ich begrüße diese Änderung sehr.* I very much welcome this change.
♦ **Wir wurden sehr herzlich begrüßt.** We received a very warm welcome.

die **Begrüßung** NOUN
welcome

behaglich ADJECTIVE
cosy

behalten VERB (PRESENT **behält,** IMPERFECT **behielt,** PERFECT **hat behalten**)
[1] to keep ◊ *Kann ich das Buch noch ein paar Tage behalten?* Can I keep the book for another couple of days?
[2] to remember ◊ *Ich kann mir ihren Namen nie behalten.* I can never remember her name.

der **Behälter** NOUN (PL die **Behälter**)
container

behandeln VERB (PERFECT **hat behandelt**)
[1] to treat ◊ *Wir wurden sehr freundlich behandelt.* We were treated in a very friendly manner. ◊ *Die Wunde muss behandelt werden.* The wound will have to be treated. ◊ *Welcher Arzt behandelt Sie?* Which doctor is treating you?
[2] to deal with ◊ *Der Film behandelt das Thema Jugendkriminalität.* The film deals with the subject of juvenile delinquency.
♦ **Das Passiv haben wir in Englisch noch nicht behandelt.** We haven't done the passive in English yet.

die **Behandlung** NOUN
treatment

behaupten VERB (PERFECT **hat behauptet**)
to claim

beherrschen VERB (PERFECT **hat beherrscht**)
[1] to master ◊ *Ich beherrsche diese Technik noch nicht.* I haven't mastered this technique yet.
[2] to control ◊ *Er konnte seine Wut nicht mehr beherrschen.* He couldn't control his anger any longer.
♦ **sich beherrschen** to control oneself

behilflich ADJECTIVE
helpful
♦ **jemandem bei etwas behilflich sein** to help somebody with something

behindern VERB (PERFECT **hat behindert**)
to hinder

behindert ADJECTIVE
disabled

der **Behinderte** NOUN (GEN des/der
die **Behinderten,** PL die **Behinderten**)
disabled person
♦ **die Behinderten** the disabled

die **Behinderung** NOUN

[1] obstruction ◊ *Das Fahrzeug stellt eine Behinderung des Verkehrs dar.* The vehicle is an obstruction to traffic.
[2] handicap ◊ *Sie hat gelernt, mit ihrer Behinderung zu leben.* She's learned to live with her handicap.

die **Behörde** NOUN
authorities

bei PREPOSITION
*The preposition **bei** takes the dative.*
[1] near ◊ *Unser Haus ist beim Bahnhof.* Our house is near the station. ◊ *bei München* near Munich
[2] at ◊ *Felix ist zur Zeit bei seiner Großmutter.* Felix is at his grandmother's at the moment. ◊ *Wenn man bei fremden Leuten zu Besuch ist ...* When you're at other people's houses ... ◊ *beim Friseur* at the hairdresser's ◊ *bei Nacht* at night
♦ **bei uns** at our place
♦ **bei uns in Deutschland** in Germany
♦ **bei seinen Eltern wohnen** to live with one's parents
♦ **Ich habe kein Geld bei mir.** I don't have any money on me.
♦ **Ich habe zur Zeit meine Mutter bei mir.** My mother's staying with me at the moment.
♦ **Wenn du bei mir bist, habe ich keine Angst.** When you're with me, I'm not afraid.
♦ **bei einer Firma arbeiten** to work for a firm ◊ *Sie arbeitet bei der Post.* She works for the post office.
♦ **beim Militär** in the army
[3] on ◊ *bei meiner Ankunft* on my arrival ◊ *bei der Abreise* on departure
[4] during ◊ *beim Abendessen* during dinner
♦ **Bei der Arbeit höre ich gern Musik.** I like listening to music when I'm working.
♦ **beim Fahren** while driving
♦ **bei solcher Hitze** in such heat
♦ **bei Nebel** in fog
♦ **bei Regen** if it rains

beibringen VERB (IMPERFECT **brachte bei,** PERFECT **hat beigebracht**)
♦ **jemandem etwas beibringen** to teach somebody something ◊ *Sie hat mir Schwimmen beigebracht.* She taught me to swim.

die **Beichte** NOUN
confession

beichten VERB
♦ **etwas beichten** to confess something ◊ *Ich muss dir beichten, dass ich dein Fahrrad benutzt habe.* I have to confess that I used your bike.

beide ADJECTIVE, PRONOUN
see also **beides** PRONOUN
both ◊ *Ich habe beide Bücher gelesen.* I've read both books. ◊ *Ich will beide.* I

want both of them. ◊ *jeder der beiden* both of them
◆ **Meine Eltern haben das beide verboten.** Both my parents have forbidden it.
◆ **meine beiden Brüder** both my brothers
◆ **die ersten beiden** the first two
◆ **wir beide** we two
◆ **einer von beiden** one of the two

beides PRONOUN

see also **beide** ADJECTIVE

both ◊ *Ich möchte beides.* I want both of them. ◊ *Beides ist schön.* Both of them are lovely.
◆ **alles beides** both of them

beieinander ADVERB
together

der **Beifahrer** NOUN (PL die **Beifahrer**)
passenger

der **Beifall** NOUN
applause
◆ **Beifall spenden** to applaud

beige ADJECTIVE
beige

das **Beil** NOUN (PL die **Beile**)
axe

die **Beilage** NOUN
1 supplement ◊ *eine Beilage zur Samstagszeitung* a supplement in Saturday's paper
2 side dish
◆ **Wir hatten Lamm und als Beilage Pommes frites und Brokkoli.** We had lamb with chips and broccoli.

beilegen VERB (PERFECT **hat beigelegt**)
1 to enclose ◊ *Ich lege einen Scheck bei.* I enclose a cheque.
2 to settle ◊ *Der Streit war schnell beigelegt.* The argument was quickly settled.

das **Beileid** NOUN
sympathy ◊ *Wir haben ihr unser Beileid ausgesprochen.* We offered her our sympathy.
◆ **herzliches Beileid** deepest sympathy

beiliegend ADVERB
enclosed

beim = **bei dem**

das **Bein** NOUN (PL die **Beine**)
leg

beinahe ADVERB
almost

der **Beinbruch** NOUN (PL die **Beinbrüche**)
broken leg ◊ *Sie wurde mit einem Beinbruch ins Krankenhaus eingeliefert.* She was taken to hospital with a broken leg.

beisammen ADVERB
together

das **Beisammensein** NOUN
get-together

beiseite ADVERB

to one side ◊ *Sie schob ihren Teller beiseite.* She pushed her plate to one side.

beiseitelegen VERB
to put by ◊ *Ich habe ein paar Hundert Euro beiseitegelegt.* I've got a few hundred euros put by.

beiseitelassen VERB (PRESENT **lässt beiseite**, IMPERFECT **ließ beiseite**, PERFECT **hat beiseitegelassen**)
to leave ◊ *Diese Frage sollten wir im Moment beiseitelassen.* We should leave this question for the moment.

beiseiteschaffen VERB
to put by ◊ *Er hat sehr viel Geld beiseitegeschafft.* He's put a lot of money by.

das **Beispiel** NOUN (PL die **Beispiele**)
example
◆ **sich an jemandem ein Beispiel nehmen** to take a leaf out of somebody's book ◊ *Du solltest dir an deinem Bruder ein Beispiel nehmen.* You should take a leaf out of your brother's book.
◆ **zum Beispiel** for example

beispielsweise ADVERB
for example

beißen VERB (IMPERFECT **biss**, PERFECT **hat gebissen**)
1 to bite ◊ *Mein Hund beißt nicht.* My dog doesn't bite. ◊ *Sie biss in den Apfel.* She bit into the apple.
2 to burn ◊ *Der Rauch beißt mich in den Augen.* The smoke's burning my eyes.
◆ **sich beißen** to clash ◊ *Rosa beißt sich mit Orange.* Pink clashes with orange.

der **Beitrag** NOUN (PL die **Beiträge**)
1 contribution ◊ *einen Beitrag zu etwas leisten* to make a contribution to something
◆ **Er schreibt Beiträge für die Zeitung.** He writes articles for the newspaper.
2 membership fee ◊ *Der Beitrag für den Klub wird am Monatsanfang fällig.* Membership fees for the club are due at the beginning of the month.
3 premium ◊ *die Beiträge zur Krankenversicherung* the health insurance premiums

beitragen VERB (PRESENT **trägt bei**, IMPERFECT **trug bei**, PERFECT **hat beigetragen**)
◆ **zu etwas beitragen** to contribute to something ◊ *Er trägt selten etwas zum Unterricht bei.* He seldom contributes anything to the lesson.

beitreten VERB (PRESENT **tritt bei**, IMPERFECT **trat bei**, PERFECT **ist beigetreten**)
to join ◊ *einem Verein beitreten* to join a club

bekämpfen VERB (PERFECT **hat bekämpft**)
to fight ◊ *ein Feuer bekämpfen* to fight a fire
◆ **sich bekämpfen** to fight ◊ *Diese beiden Parteien bekämpfen sich seit Jahren.* These two parties have been fighting for years.

bekannt ADJECTIVE

☞

1 well-known ◊ *Sie ist eine bekannte Schauspielerin.* She's a well-known actress.

2 familiar ◊ *Bekannte Wörter brauche ich nicht nachzuschlagen.* I don't have to look up familiar words.

♦ **Sie kommt mir bekannt vor.** She seems familiar.

♦ **Das kommt mir bekannt vor.** That sounds familiar.

♦ **mit jemandem bekannt sein** to know somebody ◊ *Wir sind seit Jahren mit den Bauers bekannt.* We've known the Bauers for years.

♦ **für etwas bekannt sein** to be known for something ◊ *Sie ist für ihren Witz bekannt.* She's known for her humour.

♦ **Das ist mir bekannt.** I know that.

♦ **etwas bekannt geben** to announce something publicly

♦ **etwas bekannt machen** to announce something

der **Bekannte** NOUN (GEN des/der **Bekannten**, PL
die die **Bekannten**)

1 friend ◊ *Ein Bekannter von mir hat mir das erzählt.* A friend of mine told me.

2 acquaintance ◊ *Sie hat viele Bekannte, aber wenig Freunde.* She has a lot of acquaintances but few friends.

bekanntgeben VERB *see* **bekannt**

bekanntlich ADVERB

as you know ◊ *Rauchen macht bekanntlich süchtig.* As you know, smoking is addictive.

bekanntmachen VERB *see* **bekannt**

sich **beklagen** VERB (PERFECT **hat sich beklagt**)

to complain ◊ *Die Schüler haben sich darüber beklagt, dass sie Hausaufgaben aufbekommen haben.* The pupils complained about being given homework.

die **Bekleidung** NOUN

clothing

bekommen VERB (IMPERFECT **bekam,** PERFECT **hat bekommen**)

1 to get ◊ *Was hast du zum Geburtstag bekommen?* What did you get for your birthday? ◊ *Sie hat in Englisch eine schlechte Note bekommen.* She got bad marks in English. ◊ *Wir haben nichts zu essen bekommen.* We didn't get anything to eat.

♦ **Hunger bekommen** to feel hungry

♦ **Durst bekommen** to feel thirsty

♦ **Angst bekommen** to become afraid

♦ **ein Kind bekommen** to have a baby ◊ *Unsere Deutschlehrerin bekommt ein Kind.* Our German teacher's having a baby.

2 to catch ◊ *Ich habe den letzten Bus gerade noch bekommen.* I just caught the last bus.

♦ **Das fette Essen ist ihm nicht bekommen.** The fatty food didn't agree with him.

♦ **Was bekommen Sie?** What would you like?

♦ **Bekommen Sie schon?** Are you being served?

♦ **Was bekommen Sie dafür?** How much do I owe you?

Be careful! **bekommen** *does not mean* **to become.**

belasten VERB (PERFECT **hat belastet**)

1 to burden ◊ *Ich möchte dich nicht mit meinen Problemen belasten.* I don't want to burden you with my problems.

2 to load ◊ *Der Aufzug darf mit maximal zehn Personen belastet werden.* The lift's maximum load is ten people.

♦ **Unsere Umwelt ist mit zu vielen Schadstoffen belastet.** Too many harmful substances pollute our environment.

3 to debit ◊ *Wir werden Ihr Konto mit diesem Betrag belasten.* We will debit this amount from your account.

4 to incriminate ◊ *Die Zeugin hat den Angeklagten belastet.* The witness incriminated the accused.

belästigen VERB (PERFECT **hat belästigt**)

to pester

♦ **jemanden sexuell belästigen** to sexually harass somebody

die **Belastung** NOUN

1 burden ◊ *Kinder sind eine große Belastung.* Children are a great burden.

2 strain ◊ *Die Hitze stellt eine Belastung des Kreislaufs dar.* The heat puts a strain on the circulation.

♦ **die Belastung unserer Umwelt mit Schadstoffen** the pollution of our environment by harmful substances

belegen VERB (PERFECT **hat belegt**)

to register for ◊ *Ich habe einen Volkshochschulkurs für Spanisch belegt.* I've registered for an adult education course in Spanish.

♦ **Ist der Platz belegt?** Is this seat taken?

♦ **Das Hotel ist belegt.** The hotel's full.

♦ **den ersten Platz belegen** to come first

♦ **Womit soll ich dein Brot belegen?** What shall I put on your sandwich?

belegt ADJECTIVE

♦ **ein belegtes Brot** an open sandwich

♦ **Es ist belegt.** It's engaged. ◊ *Die Nummer ist belegt.* The number's engaged.

beleidigen VERB (PERFECT **hat beleidigt**)

to insult

die **Beleidigung** NOUN

insult

Belgien NEUT NOUN

Belgium

♦ **aus Belgien** from Belgium

♦ **in Belgien** in Belgium

♦ **nach Belgien** to Belgium

der **Belgier** NOUN (PL die **Belgier**)
Belgian

die **Belgierin** NOUN
Belgian

belgisch ADJECTIVE
Belgian

die **Belichtung** NOUN
exposure

der **Belichtungsmesser** NOUN (PL die **Belichtungsmesser**)
exposure meter

beliebig ADJECTIVE, ADVERB

1 any you like ◊ *in beliebiger Reihenfolge* in any order you like ◊ *eine beliebige Anzahl* any number you like ◊ *Du kannst jeden beliebigen Schüler unserer Klasse fragen.* You can ask any pupil you like in our class.

2 as you like ◊ *beliebig oft* as often as you like ◊ *beliebig viel* as much as you like ◊ *beliebig viele* as many as you like

beliebt ADJECTIVE
popular ◊ *sich bei jemandem beliebt machen* to make oneself popular with somebody

die **Beliebtheit** NOUN
popularity

bellen VERB
to bark

belohnen VERB (PERFECT **hat belohnt**)
to reward

die **Belohnung** NOUN
reward ◊ *zur Belohnung* as a reward

belügen VERB (IMPERFECT **belog**, PERFECT **hat belogen**)
to lie to

belustigen VERB (PERFECT **hat belustigt**)
to amuse

bemerken VERB (PERFECT **hat bemerkt**)
to notice ◊ *Ich habe keine Änderung bemerkt.* I haven't noticed any change.

die **Bemerkung** NOUN
remark

bemitleiden VERB (PERFECT **hat bemitleidet**)
to pity

sich **bemühen** VERB (PERFECT **hat sich bemüht**)
to make an effort ◊ *Er hat sich bemüht, höflich zu bleiben.* He made an effort to remain polite.

♦ **Bemühen Sie sich nicht, ich finde schon allein hinaus.** Don't trouble yourself, I'll show myself out.

♦ **Er hat sich sehr um seine Gäste bemüht.** He went to a lot of trouble for his guests.

♦ **Rudi muss sich um eine neue Arbeit bemühen.** Rudi's got to try and find a new job.

♦ **Ich werde mich bemühen!** I'll do my best!

benachrichtigen VERB (PERFECT **hat benachrichtigt**)
to inform

die **Benachrichtigung** NOUN
notification

benachteiligt ADJECTIVE
disadvantaged

sich **benehmen** VERB (PRESENT **benimmt sich**, IMPERFECT **benahm sich**, PERFECT **hat sich benommen**)

see also **das Benehmen** NOUN

to behave ◊ *sich anständig benehmen* to behave properly ◊ *Sie haben sich furchtbar benommen.* They behaved terribly. ◊ *Benimm dich!* Behave yourself!

das **Benehmen** NOUN

see also **sich benehmen** VERB

behaviour

beneiden VERB (PERFECT **hat beneidet**)
to envy

♦ **jemanden um etwas beneiden** to envy somebody something ◊ *Ich beneide dich um deine schöne Wohnung.* I envy you your lovely flat.

♦ **Er ist nicht zu beneiden.** I don't envy him.

beneidenswert ADJECTIVE
enviable

♦ **Sie ist beneidenswert reich.** She's enviably rich.

benoten VERB (PERFECT **hat benotet**)
to mark

benutzen VERB (PERFECT **hat benutzt**)
to use

der **Benutzer** NOUN (PL die **Benutzer**)
user

benutzerfreundlich ADJECTIVE
user-friendly

die **Benutzung** NOUN
use

das **Benzin** NOUN
petrol

der **Benzinkanister** NOUN (PL die **Benzinkanister**)
petrol can

beobachten VERB (PERFECT **hat beobachtet**)
to observe

bequem ADJECTIVE

1 comfortable ◊ *ein bequemer Stuhl* a comfortable chair

♦ **eine bequeme Ausrede** a convenient excuse

2 lazy ◊ *Er ist zu bequem, sich selbst etwas zu kochen.* He's too lazy to cook himself something.

beraten VERB (PRESENT **berät**, IMPERFECT **beriet**, PERFECT **hat beraten**)

1 to give advice ◊ *Der Mann vom Arbeitsamt hat mich gut beraten.* The man at the job centre gave me good advice.

B

☞

♦ **Lassen Sie sich von Ihrem Arzt beraten.** Consult your doctor.

  2 to discuss ◊ *Wir müssen das weitere Vorgehen beraten.* We have to discuss further action.

♦ **gut beraten sein** to be well advised

♦ **schlecht beraten sein** to be ill advised

berauben VERB (PERFECT **hat beraubt**)
to rob

berechnen VERB (PERFECT **hat berechnet**)
to charge ◊ *Was berechnen Sie für eine Beratung?* What do you charge for a consultation?

der **Bereich** NOUN (PL die **Bereiche**)

  1 field ◊ *In diesem Bereich kennt sie sich sehr gut aus.* She's very knowledgable in this field.

♦ **Er ist für den Bereich Kundendienst zuständig.** He's responsible for after-sales service.

  2 area ◊ *im Bereich der Innenstadt* in the city centre area

bereit ADJECTIVE
ready ◊ *Wir sind bereit abzufahren.* We're ready to leave. ◊ *Das Essen ist bereit.* Dinner's ready.

♦ **bereit sein, etwas zu tun** to be prepared to do something ◊ *Ich bin nicht bereit, noch länger zu warten.* I'm not prepared to wait any longer.

♦ **etwas bereit haben** to have something ready ◊ *Sie hat immer eine Ausrede bereit.* She always has an excuse ready.

bereiten VERB (PERFECT **hat bereitet**)
to cause ◊ *Das hat mir einige Schwierigkeiten bereitet.* That caused me some problems.

♦ **Die Kinder bereiten mir sehr viel Freude.** The children give me a great deal of pleasure.

bereits ADVERB
already

bereuen VERB (PERFECT **hat bereut**)
to regret

der **Berg** NOUN (PL die **Berge**)

  1 mountain ◊ *Im Winter fahren wir in die Berge zum Skifahren.* In winter we go skiing in the mountains.

  2 hill ◊ *Hinter unserem Haus ist ein kleiner Berg.* There's a small hill behind our house.

der **Bergarbeiter** NOUN (PL die **Bergarbeiter**)
miner

die **Bergbahn** NOUN (PL die **Bergbahnen**)
mountain railway

der **Bergbau** NOUN
mining

das **Bergsteigen** NOUN
mountaineering ◊ *Bergsteigen ist ihr Hobby.* Her hobby's mountaineering. ◊ *Sie ist beim Bergsteigen verunglückt.* She had a mountaineering accident.

der **Bergsteiger** NOUN (PL die **Bergsteiger**)

mountaineer

die **Bergwacht** NOUN
mountain rescue service

der **Bericht** NOUN (PL die **Berichte**)
report

berichten VERB (PERFECT **hat berichtet**)
to report ◊ *Die Zeitungen haben nichts über diesen Zwischenfall berichtet.* The newspapers didn't report anything about this incident.

Berlin NEUT NOUN
Berlin

> ❶ **Berlin** is one of the 16 **Länder**. It is a "city-state" like Bremen and Hamburg. From 1963 to 1989 it was divided by the Berlin Wall. Now it is again the German capital.

berücksichtigen VERB (PERFECT **hat berücksichtigt**)
to bear in mind

der **Beruf** NOUN (PL die **Berufe**)
occupation ◊ *Welchen Beruf hat dein Vater?* What's your father's occupation?

♦ **Sie ist Lehrerin von Beruf.** She's a teacher by profession.

beruflich ADJECTIVE
professional

♦ **beruflich unterwegs sein** to be away on business

der **Berufsberater** NOUN (PL die **Berufsberater**)
careers adviser

die **Berufsberatung** NOUN
careers advice

das **Berufspraktikum** NOUN (GEN des **Berufspraktikums**, PL die **Berufspraktika**)
work experience ◊ *Sie absolviert gerade ihr Berufspraktikum.* She's doing work experience.

die **Berufsschule** NOUN
technical college

berufstätig ADJECTIVE
working ◊ *Seit wann ist deine Mutter wieder berufstätig?* When did your mother start working again?

der **Berufsverkehr** NOUN
rush-hour traffic

beruhigen VERB (PERFECT **hat beruhigt**)
to calm down ◊ *Dem Lehrer gelang es nicht, die Klasse zu beruhigen.* The teacher didn't manage to calm the class down.

♦ **sich beruhigen** to calm down ◊ *Die Lage hat sich beruhigt.* Things have calmed down.

♦ **Beruhige dich doch!** Calm down!

das **Beruhigungsmittel** NOUN (PL die **Beruhigungsmittel**)
tranquillizer

berühmt ADJECTIVE
famous

berühren VERB (PERFECT **hat berührt**)

[1] to touch ◊ *Er berührte meinen Arm.* He touched my arm.

[2] to affect ◊ *Die Armut der Menschen hat mich sehr berührt.* The poverty of the people affected me deeply.

[3] to touch on ◊ *Ich kann diese Frage heute nur berühren.* I can only touch on this question today.

♦ **sich berühren** to touch ◊ *Die beiden Drähte berührten sich.* The two wires touched.

die **Berührung** NOUN

contact ◊ *mit etwas in Berührung kommen* to come into contact with something

beschädigen VERB (PERFECT **hat beschädigt**)

to damage

beschaffen VERB (PERFECT **hat beschafft**)

to get ◊ *Ich muss mir ein Visum beschaffen.* I have to get a visa. ◊ *Können Sie mir nicht einen Job beschaffen?* Can't you get me a job?

beschäftigen VERB (PERFECT **hat beschäftigt**)

[1] to occupy ◊ *Kannst du nicht irgendwie die Kinder beschäftigen?* Can't you occupy the children somehow? ◊ *Diese Frage beschäftigt mich seit Langem.* This question has been occupying me for a long time.

[2] to employ ◊ *Unsere Firma beschäftigt zweihundert Leute.* Our company employs two hundred people.

♦ **sich beschäftigen** to occupy oneself ◊ *Sebastian hat Mühe, sich allein zu beschäftigen.* Sebastian has difficulty occupying himself.

♦ **Kannst du dich mit den Kindern beschäftigen?** Can you keep the children occupied?

♦ **Der Artikel beschäftigt sich mit Jugendarbeitslosigkeit.** The article deals with youth unemployment.

beschäftigt ADJECTIVE

busy

die **Beschäftigung** NOUN

work ◊ *Er sucht eine Beschäftigung.* He's looking for work.

♦ **Sie ist zur Zeit ohne Beschäftigung.** She is unemployed at the moment.

der **Bescheid** NOUN (PL die **Bescheide**)

information ◊ *Ich warte auf den Bescheid des Konsulats.* I'm waiting for information from the consulate.

♦ **Bescheid wissen** to know ◊ *Weiß deine Mutter Bescheid, dass du hier bist?* Does your mother know that you're here? ◊ *Ich weiß Bescheid.* I know.

♦ **über etwas Bescheid wissen** to know a lot about something ◊ *Sie weiß über Grammatik gut Bescheid.* She knows a lot about grammar.

♦ **jemandem Bescheid sagen** to let somebody know

bescheiden ADJECTIVE

modest

die **Bescheinigung** NOUN

certificate ◊ *Du brauchst eine Bescheinigung über die Teilnahme am Kurs.* You need a certificate showing that you attended the course. ◊ *eine Bescheinigung des Arztes* a doctor's certificate

beschenken VERB (PERFECT **hat beschenkt**)

♦ **jemanden mit etwas beschenken** to give somebody something as a present

♦ **beschenkt werden** to receive a present ◊ *Wir sind reichlich beschenkt worden.* We received lots of presents.

die **Bescherung** NOUN

giving out of Christmas presents

♦ **Da haben wir die Bescherung!** What did I tell you!

beschimpfen VERB (PERFECT **hat beschimpft**)

to swear at

beschleunigen VERB (PERFECT **hat beschleunigt**)

[1] to increase ◊ *Wir müssen das Arbeitstempo beschleunigen.* We have to increase our work rate.

[2] to accelerate ◊ *Das Auto vor mir beschleunigte.* The car in front of me accelerated.

beschließen VERB (IMPERFECT **beschloss**, PERFECT **hat beschlossen**)

to decide ◊ *Wir haben beschlossen, nach Spanien zu fahren.* We decided to go to Spain.

der **Beschluss** NOUN (GEN des **Beschlusses**, PL die **Beschlüsse**)

decision

beschränken VERB (PERFECT **hat beschränkt**)

to limit ◊ *Wir müssen unsere Ausgaben beschränken.* We have to limit our spending.

♦ **sich auf etwas beschränken** to restrict oneself to something ◊ *Ich werde mich auf ein paar Worte beschränken.* I'll restrict myself to a few words.

beschränkt ADJECTIVE

[1] limited ◊ *Diese Regel hat nur beschränkte Gültigkeit.* This regulation only has limited validity.

[2] stupid ◊ *Wie kann man nur so beschränkt sein?* How can anyone be so stupid?

beschreiben VERB (IMPERFECT **beschrieb**, PERFECT **hat beschrieben**)

to describe ◊ *Können Sie den Täter beschreiben?* Can you describe the culprit?

die **Beschreibung** NOUN

description

beschützen VERB (PERFECT **hat beschützt**)

☞

to protect ◊ *Ich möchte euch vor diesen Gefahren beschützen.* I want to protect you from these dangers.

die **Beschwerde** NOUN

complaint ◊ *Wenn Sie eine Beschwerde haben, dann wenden Sie sich an den Geschäftsführer.* If you have a complaint, then please contact the manager.

♦ **Beschwerden** trouble ◊ *Mein Knie macht mir immer noch Beschwerden.* My knee's still giving me trouble.

sich **beschweren** VERB (PERFECT **hat beschwert**)

to complain ◊ *Deine Lehrerin hat sich über dich beschwert.* Your teacher has complained about you.

beschwipst ADJECTIVE

tipsy

beseitigen VERB (PERFECT **hat beseitigt**)

to remove

der **Besen** NOUN (PL die **Besen**)

broom

besetzen VERB (PERFECT **hat besetzt**)

[1] to occupy ◊ *Napoleons Truppen haben weite Teile Deutschlands besetzt.* Napoleon's troops occupied large areas of Germany.

♦ **Studenten haben dieses Haus besetzt.** Students are squatting in this house.

[2] to keep ◊ *Kannst du den Platz bitte für mich besetzen?* Can you keep this seat for me?

[3] to fill ◊ *Der Posten soll mit einer Frau besetzt werden.* The position is to be filled by a woman. ◊ *Die Stelle ist noch nicht besetzt.* The position hasn't been filled yet.

besetzt ADJECTIVE

[1] full ◊ *Der Zug war voll besetzt.* The train was full.

[2] engaged ◊ *Es ist besetzt.* It's engaged.

[3] taken ◊ *Ist der Platz hier besetzt?* Is this seat taken?

das **Besetztzeichen** NOUN (PL die **Besetztzeichen**)

engaged tone

besichtigen VERB (PERFECT **hat besichtigt**)

to visit

die **Besichtigung** NOUN

visit

besitzen VERB (IMPERFECT **besaß**, PERFECT **hat besessen**)

[1] to own ◊ *Sie besitzen ein Haus am Meer.* They own a house by the seaside.

[2] to have ◊ *Sie besitzt das Talent, sich mit allen zu zerstreiten.* She has the talent of quarrelling with everyone.

der **Besitzer** NOUN (PL die **Besitzer**)

owner

besoffen ADJECTIVE

plastered

besondere ADJECTIVE

special ◊ *Das sind besondere Umstände.* Those are special circumstances.

♦ **keine besonderen Kennzeichen** no distinguishing features

die **Besonderheit** NOUN

peculiarity

besonders ADVERB

particularly ◊ *Es hat mir nicht besonders gefallen.* I didn't particularly like it.

besorgen VERB (PERFECT **hat besorgt**)

to get ◊ *Kannst du mir nicht einen Ferienjob besorgen?* Can't you get me a holiday job? ◊ *Soll ich dir ein Taxi besorgen?* Shall I get you a taxi? ◊ *Ich muss Milch und Eier besorgen.* I'll have to get milk and eggs.

besorgt ADJECTIVE

worried ◊ *Sie ist sehr besorgt um dich.* She's very worried about you.

besprechen VERB (PRESENT **bespricht**, IMPERFECT **besprach**, PERFECT **hat besprochen**)

to discuss ◊ *Das muss ich mit deiner Mutter besprechen.* I'll have to discuss it with your mother.

die **Besprechung** NOUN

[1] meeting ◊ *Frau Airlie ist in einer Besprechung.* Ms Airlie is in a meeting.

[2] review ◊ *Hast du die Besprechung dieses Films gelesen?* Have you read the review of this film?

besser ADJECTIVE, ADVERB

better ◊ *eine bessere Note* a better mark ◊ *Du gehst jetzt besser nach Hause.* You'd better go home now.

♦ **Es geht ihm besser.** He's feeling better.

♦ **je schneller, desto besser** the quicker the better

sich **bessern** VERB

to improve ◊ *Das Wetter hat sich gebessert.* The weather's improved.

die **Besserung** NOUN

improvement

♦ **Gute Besserung!** Get well soon!

der **Bestandteil** NOUN (PL die **Bestandteile**)

[1] component ◊ *Hier werden die einzelnen Bestandteile der Maschine zusammengesetzt.* The individual components of the machine are assembled here.

[2] ingredient ◊ *Die Bestandteile sind in Gramm angegeben.* The ingredients are given in grams.

♦ **sich in seine Bestandteile auflösen** to fall to pieces

bestätigen VERB (PERFECT **hat bestätigt**)

to confirm ◊ *Ich kann bestätigen, dass sie die Wahrheit gesagt hat.* I can confirm that she told the truth.

♦ **Hiermit bestätigen wir den Erhalt Ihres Briefes.** We hereby acknowledge receipt of your letter.

♦ **sich bestätigen** to prove to be true ◊ *Mein Verdacht hat sich bestätigt.* My suspicion proved to be true.

beste ADJECTIVE

best ◊ *Sie ist die beste Schülerin der Klasse.* She's the best pupil in the class.
♦ **So ist es am besten.** It's best that way.
♦ **Am besten gehst du gleich.** You'd better go at once.
♦ **jemanden zum Besten haben** to pull somebody's leg
♦ **einen Witz zum Besten geben** to tell a joke
♦ **Es ist nur zu deinem Besten.** It's for your own good.

bestechen VERB (PRESENT **besticht**, IMPERFECT **bestach**, PERFECT **hat bestochen**)
to bribe

die **Bestechung** NOUN
bribery

das **Besteck** NOUN (PL die **Bestecke**)
cutlery

bestehen VERB (IMPERFECT **bestand**, PERFECT **hat bestanden**)
[1] to be ◊ *Es besteht die Möglichkeit, einen Sprachkurs zu belegen.* There's the chance of registering for a language course. ◊ *Es besteht keine Hoffnung mehr, sie jemals wiederzusehen.* There's no more hope of ever seeing her again.
[2] to exist ◊ *Die Firma besteht seit hundert Jahren.* The firm has existed for a hundred years.
♦ **etwas bestehen** to pass something ◊ *Ich hoffe, dass ich die Prüfung bestehe.* I hope I pass the exam.
♦ **Sie hat in Mathe mit "gut" bestanden.** She got a "B" in maths.
♦ **auf etwas bestehen** to insist on something ◊ *Wir bestehen auf sofortiger Bezahlung.* We insist on immediate payment.
♦ **bestehen aus** to consist of ◊ *Eine Fußballmannschaft besteht aus elf Spielern.* A football team consists of eleven players.

bestehlen VERB (PRESENT **bestiehlt**, IMPERFECT **bestahl**, PERFECT **hat bestohlen**)
♦ **jemanden bestehlen** to rob somebody

bestellen VERB (PERFECT **hat bestellt**)
[1] to order ◊ *Ich habe im Versandhaus ein Kleid bestellt.* I've ordered a dress from a mail-order company. ◊ *Haben Sie schon bestellt?* Have you ordered yet? ◊ *Wir sollten ein Taxi bestellen.* We should order a taxi.
[2] to reserve ◊ *Ich habe einen Tisch beim Chinesen bestellt.* I've reserved a table at the Chinese restaurant.
[3] to send for ◊ *Der Direktor hat mich zu sich bestellt.* The headmaster sent for me.
♦ **Bestell deiner Mutter schöne Grüße.** Give my regards to your mother.
♦ **Soll ich ihr etwas von dir bestellen?** Shall I give her a message from you?

♦ **Ich soll dir von Martin bestellen, dass er nicht mitkommen kann.** Martin says to tell you that he can't come.

die **Bestellung** NOUN
order
♦ **auf Bestellung** to order

bestenfalls ADVERB
at best

bestens ADVERB
very well ◊ *Die Geschäfte gehen bestens.* Business is going very well.

bestimmen VERB (PERFECT **hat bestimmt**)
to decide ◊ *Du kannst bestimmen, wer mitkommen soll.* You can decide who's coming. ◊ *Wer bestimmt hier, was gemacht werden muss?* Who decides what has to be done?
♦ **Du hast hier nichts zu bestimmen!** You're not the one who decides here!
♦ **für jemanden bestimmt sein** to be meant for somebody ◊ *Diese Bemerkung war für mich bestimmt.* This comment was meant for me.
♦ **Das Geschenk ist für meine Freundin bestimmt.** The present's for my girlfriend.
♦ **für etwas bestimmt sein** to be intended for something ◊ *Dieses Geld ist für die Anschaffung von Computern bestimmt.* This money's intended for the purchase of computers.

bestimmt ADJECTIVE, ADVERB
[1] certain ◊ *Wir treffen uns immer zu einer bestimmten Zeit.* We always meet at a certain time. ◊ *Die Teilnehmer sollten eine bestimmte Anzahl nicht überschreiten.* The participants shouldn't exceed a certain number.
[2] particular ◊ *Ich suche ein ganz bestimmtes Buch.* I'm looking for a particular book.
♦ **Suchen Sie etwas Bestimmtes?** Are you looking for something in particular?
♦ **der bestimmte Artikel** the definite article
♦ **Ich habe ihn bestimmt gesehen.** I'm sure I've seen him.
♦ **Das hat er bestimmt nicht so gemeint.** I'm sure that's not how he meant it.
♦ **Hast du auch bestimmt keine Hausaufgaben auf?** Are you sure you don't have any homework?
♦ **Das hat sie bestimmt vergessen.** She's bound to have forgotten.

die **Bestimmung** NOUN
regulation ◊ *neue Sicherheitsbestimmungen* new safety regulations

bestrafen VERB (PERFECT **hat bestraft**)
to punish

die **Bestrahlung** NOUN
radiotherapy

der **Besuch** NOUN (PL die **Besuche**)

B

[1] visit ◊ *Deutschland bereitet sich auf den Besuch der Königin vor.* Germany's preparing for the Queen's visit. ◊ *bei unserem Besuch in London* during our visit to London
♦ **Der Schulbesuch ist Pflicht.** School attendance is compulsory.
[2] visitor ◊ *Ist euer Besuch noch da?* Is your visitor still there?
♦ **bei jemandem einen Besuch machen** to pay somebody a visit
♦ **Besuch haben** to have visitors
♦ **bei jemandem zu Besuch sein** to be visiting somebody
♦ **zu Besuch kommen** to be visiting ◊ *Nächste Woche kommt Onja zu Besuch.* Onja's visiting us next week.

besuchen VERB (PERFECT **hat besucht**)
[1] to visit ◊ *Hast du schon das Planetarium besucht?* Have you visited the planetarium yet?
♦ **Besuch uns mal wieder!** Come again!
[2] to attend ◊ *Sie besucht das Gymnasium.* She attends grammar school.
♦ **Der Vortrag war sehr gut besucht.** The lecture was very well-attended.
♦ **Wir haben ein Konzert besucht.** We went to a concert.

der **Besucher** NOUN (PL die **Besucher**)
visitor

betätigen VERB (PERFECT **hat betätigt**)
♦ **die Hupe betätigen** to sound the horn
♦ **einen Schalter betätigen** to press a switch
♦ **die Bremse betätigen** to apply the brakes
♦ **Du solltest dich sportlich betätigen.** You should do some sport.
♦ **Mein Vater betätigt sich politisch.** My father's involved in politics.

betäuben VERB (PERFECT **hat betäubt**)
[1] to stun ◊ *Der Schlag hat ihn betäubt.* The blow stunned him.
[2] to anaesthetize ◊ *Der Patient muss betäubt werden.* The patient has to be anaesthetized.

das **Betäubungsmittel** NOUN (PL die **Betäubungsmittel**)
anaesthetic

die **Bete** NOUN
♦ **Rote Bete** beetroot

beteiligen VERB (PERFECT **hat beteiligt**)
♦ **sich an etwas beteiligen** to take part in something ◊ *Franz beteiligte sich nicht an der Diskussion.* Franz didn't take part in the discussion.
♦ **Kann ich mich an eurem Spiel beteiligen?** Can I join in your game?
♦ **Ich habe mich mit zwanzig Euro an seinem Geschenk beteiligt.** I gave twenty euros towards his present.
♦ **Alle werden am Gewinn beteiligt.** Everyone will share in the winnings.

beten VERB
to pray

der **Beton** NOUN (PL die **Betons**)
concrete

betonen VERB (PERFECT **hat betont**)
to stress

die **Betonung** NOUN
stress ◊ *Wo liegt die Betonung bei diesem Wort?* Where's the stress in this word?

beträchtlich ADJECTIVE, ADVERB
[1] considerable ◊ *eine beträchtliche Summe* a considerable amount
[2] considerably ◊ *Es hat beträchtlich länger gedauert.* It took considerably longer.

der **Betrag** NOUN (PL die **Beträge**)
amount

betragen VERB (PRESENT **beträgt**, IMPERFECT **betrug**, PERFECT **hat betragen**)
see also **das Betragen** NOUN
to come to ◊ *Die Reparatur betrug dreihundert Euro.* The repair came to three hundred euros.
♦ **sich betragen** to behave ◊ *Ich hoffe, die Kinder haben sich ordentlich betragen.* I hope the children behaved well.

das **Betragen** NOUN
see also **betragen** VERB
behaviour ◊ *Ich werde mich über dein schlechtes Betragen beschweren.* I'm going to complain about your bad behaviour.

betreffen VERB (PRESENT **betrifft**, IMPERFECT **betraf**, PERFECT **hat betroffen**)
to concern
♦ **was mich betrifft** as far as I'm concerned

betreten VERB (PRESENT **betritt**, IMPERFECT **betrat**, PERFECT **hat betreten**)
to enter ◊ *Sie klopfte, bevor sie das Zimmer betrat.* She knocked before entering the room.
♦ **"Betreten verboten"** "Keep out"

der **Betrieb** NOUN (PL die **Betriebe**)
[1] firm ◊ *Unser Betrieb beschäftigt dreihundert Menschen.* Our firm employs three hundred people.
[2] operation ◊ *Die Maschine ist jetzt in Betrieb.* The machine is now in operation.
♦ **In der Stadt war heute viel Betrieb.** It was really busy in town today.
♦ **außer Betrieb sein** to be out of order ◊ *Der Fahrstuhl ist außer Betrieb.* The lift's out of order.

die **Betriebsferien** PL NOUN
company holidays

der **Betriebsleiter** NOUN (PL die **Betriebsleiter**)
manager

sich **betrinken** VERB (IMPERFECT **betrank sich**, PERFECT **hat sich betrunken**)
to get drunk

betroffen ADJECTIVE

full of concern ◊ *Sie machte ein betroffenes Gesicht.* Her face was full of concern.

♦ **Wir sind über diese Nachricht zutiefst betroffen.** We are deeply affected by the news.

♦ **von etwas betroffen sein** to be affected by something

betrügen VERB (IMPERFECT **betrog**, PERFECT **hat betrogen**)
1 to cheat ◊ *Der Händler hat dich betrogen.* The dealer's cheated you.
2 to defraud ◊ *Er hat seinen Arbeitgeber um Millionen betrogen.* He defrauded his employer of millions.

♦ **Hast du deine Freundin schon mal betrogen?** Have you ever been unfaithful to your girlfriend?

betrunken ADJECTIVE
drunk

das **Bett** NOUN (PL die **Betten**)
bed ◊ *ins Bett gehen* to go to bed ◊ *im Bett bleiben* to stay in bed ◊ *das Bett machen* to make the bed

der **Bettbezug** NOUN (PL die **Bettbezüge**)
duvet cover

die **Bettdecke** NOUN
blanket

betteln VERB
to beg

das **Bettlaken** NOUN (PL die **Bettlaken**)
sheet

der **Bettler** NOUN (PL die **Bettler**)
beggar

das **Betttuch** NOUN (PL die **Betttücher**)
sheet

die **Bettwäsche** NOUN
bed linen

das **Bettzeug** NOUN
bedding

beugen VERB
to bend ◊ *Ich kann den Arm nicht beugen.* I can't bend my arm.

♦ **sich beugen** to bow ◊ *Ich beuge mich der Mehrheit.* I bow to the majority.

♦ **Sie beugte sich über das Bett des Kindes.** She bent over the child's bed.

die **Beule** NOUN
1 bump ◊ *eine Beule am Kopf* a bump on the head
2 dent ◊ *Das Auto hat eine Beule.* The car has a dent in it.

beunruhigen VERB (PERFECT **hat beunruhigt**)
to alarm

beurteilen VERB (PERFECT **hat beurteilt**)
to judge ◊ *Ich beurteile die Leute nicht nach ihrem Aussehen.* I don't judge people on their appearance.

der **Beutel** NOUN (PL die **Beutel**)
1 bag ◊ *Sie tat die Einkäufe in den Beutel.* She put the shopping in the bag.
2 purse ◊ *Er nahm einen Euro aus dem Beutel.* He took a euro from the purse.

die **Bevölkerung** NOUN
population

bevor CONJUNCTION
before ◊ *Sie war gegangen, bevor ich es ihr sagen konnte.* She left before I could tell her.

bevorstehen VERB (IMPERFECT **stand bevor**, PERFECT **hat bevorgestanden**)
to be imminent ◊ *Die Prüfung steht bevor.* The exam's imminent.

♦ **jemandem bevorstehen** to be in store for somebody ◊ *Da steht uns ja einiger Ärger bevor.* There's trouble in store for us.

bevorzugen VERB (PERFECT **hat bevorzugt**)
to prefer

sich **bewähren** VERB (PERFECT **hat sich bewährt**)
to prove oneself ◊ *Er hat sich als mein Freund bewährt.* He proved himself to be my friend. ◊ *Diese Methode hat sich bewährt.* This method has proved itself.

bewährt ADJECTIVE
tried and tested ◊ *Das ist eine bewährte Methode.* That's a tried and tested method.

♦ **Sie ist eine bewährte Mitarbeiterin.** She's a reliable colleague.

bewegen VERB (PERFECT **hat bewegt**)
to move

♦ **sich bewegen** to move

♦ **jemanden zu etwas bewegen** to persuade somebody to do something

beweglich ADJECTIVE
1 movable ◊ *Die Puppe hat bewegliche Beine.* The doll has movable legs.
2 agile ◊ *Sie ist trotz ihres Alters noch sehr beweglich.* She's still very agile despite her age.

bewegt ADJECTIVE
1 eventful ◊ *Sie hatte ein bewegtes Leben.* She had an eventful life.
2 touched ◊ *Wir waren von seinen Worten sehr bewegt.* We were very touched by his words.

die **Bewegung** NOUN
1 movement ◊ *Mir fällt jede Bewegung schwer.* Every movement is difficult for me.
2 motion ◊ *Er setzte das Fahrzeug in Bewegung.* He set the vehicle in motion.
3 exercise ◊ *Du brauchst mehr Bewegung.* You need more exercise.

der **Beweis** NOUN (PL die **Beweise**)
1 proof ◊ *Die Polizei hat keine Beweise.* The police don't have any proof.
2 sign ◊ *als Beweis meiner Freundschaft* as a sign of my friendship

beweisen VERB (IMPERFECT **bewies**, PERFECT **hat bewiesen**)

1 to prove ◊ *Ich kann nicht beweisen, dass sie das gesagt hat.* I can't prove that she said it. ◊ *Die Polizei kann nichts beweisen.* The police can't prove anything.

2 to show ◊ *Er hat sehr viel Mut bewiesen.* He showed great courage.

sich bewerben VERB (PRESENT **bewirbt sich**, IMPERFECT **bewarb sich**, PERFECT **hat sich beworben**)
to apply ◊ *Es haben sich dreißig Kandidaten beworben.* Thirty candidates have applied. ◊ *Sie hat sich bei Siemens um einen Ausbildungsplatz beworben.* She applied to Siemens for an apprenticeship.

der **Bewerber** NOUN (PL die **Bewerber**)
applicant

die **Bewerbung** NOUN
application

das **Bewerbungsformular** NOUN (PL die **Bewerbungsformulare**)
application form

das **Bewerbungsgespräch** NOUN (PL die **Bewerbungsgespräche**)
job interview

bewerten VERB (PERFECT **hat bewertet**)
to assess ◊ *Der Lehrer hat unsere Aufsätze zu bewerten.* The teacher has to assess our essays.

bewirken VERB (PERFECT **hat bewirkt**)
to bring about ◊ *Dieses Medikament wird eine schnelle Besserung bewirken.* This medicine will bring about a rapid improvement.
♦ **Meine Bitte hat nichts bewirkt.** My request didn't achieve anything.
♦ **Ich konnte bei ihm nichts bewirken.** I couldn't get anywhere with him.

bewohnen VERB (PERFECT **hat bewohnt**)
to live in ◊ *Das Haus wird von drei Familien bewohnt.* Three families live in the house.

der **Bewohner** NOUN (PL die **Bewohner**)
1 inhabitant ◊ *die Bewohner des Landes* the inhabitants of the country
2 resident ◊ *die Bewohner des Hauses* the residents of the house

bewölkt ADJECTIVE
cloudy

die **Bewölkung** NOUN
clouds

bewundern VERB (PERFECT **hat bewundert**)
to admire

die **Bewunderung** NOUN
admiration

bewusst ADJECTIVE
1 conscious ◊ *umweltbewusst* environmentally conscious
2 deliberate ◊ *Das war eine bewusste Beleidigung.* That was a deliberate insult.
♦ **Er hat ganz bewusst gelogen.** He lied quite deliberately.
♦ **sich einer Sache bewusst sein** to be aware of something ◊ *Ich bin mir der Konsequenzen bewusst.* I'm aware of the consequences.
♦ **Ihr wurde plötzlich bewusst, welche Folgen das haben könnte.** She suddenly realized the consequences this could have.

bewusstlos ADJECTIVE
unconscious
♦ **bewusstlos werden** to lose consciousness

die **Bewusstlosigkeit** NOUN
unconsciousness

das **Bewusstsein** NOUN
consciousness
♦ **bei Bewusstsein** conscious

bezahlen VERB (PERFECT **hat bezahlt**)
to pay ◊ *Er bezahlte die Rechnung.* He paid the bill.

die **Bezahlung** NOUN
payment

bezeichnen VERB (PERFECT **hat bezeichnet**)
1 to mark ◊ *Bezeichnen Sie die Stelle mit einem Kreuz.* Mark the spot with a cross.
2 to call ◊ *Sie hat mich als Lügnerin bezeichnet.* She called me a liar.

bezeichnend ADJECTIVE
typical ◊ *Das ist bezeichnend für sie!* That's typical of her!

beziehen VERB (IMPERFECT **bezog**, PERFECT **hat bezogen**)
1 to cover ◊ *Sie beschloss, alle Kissen zu beziehen.* She decided to cover all the cushions.
♦ **das Bett beziehen** to change the bed
2 to move into ◊ *Wann könnt ihr euer neues Haus beziehen?* When can you move into your new house?
3 to get ◊ *Wir beziehen unsere Kartoffeln direkt vom Bauern.* We get our potatoes straight from the farm. ◊ *Sie beziehen Arbeitslosenhilfe.* They get unemployment benefit.
4 to subscribe to ◊ *Ich beziehe eine Tageszeitung.* I subscribe to a daily newspaper.
♦ **sich beziehen** to cloud over ◊ *Der Himmel bezieht sich.* It's clouding over.
♦ **sich auf etwas beziehen** to refer to something ◊ *Sein Beispiel bezog sich auf das Tierreich.* His example referred to the animal kingdom.

die **Beziehung** NOUN
1 relationship ◊ *Er hat eine Beziehung mit einer verheirateten Frau.* He has a relationship with a married woman.
2 relations ◊ *unsere Beziehungen zu dieser Firma* our relations with this company ◊ *diplomatische Beziehungen* diplomatic relations

B

③ connection ◊ *Es besteht eine Beziehung zwischen den beiden Straftaten.* There's a connection between the two crimes.

♦ **in dieser Beziehung** in this respect

♦ **Beziehungen haben** to have contacts ◊ *Er kann bestimmt etwas für dich tun, er hat Beziehungen.* I'm sure he can do something for you, he has contacts.

♦ **eine Beziehung zu etwas haben** to be able to relate to something ◊ *Ich habe keine Beziehung zu moderner Kunst.* I can't relate to modern art.

der **Bezirk** NOUN (PL die **Bezirke**)
district

der **Bezug** NOUN (PL die **Bezüge**)
cover ◊ *Das Sofa hatte einen bunten Bezug.* The sofa had a brightly-coloured cover.

♦ **Zu dieser Musik habe ich keinen Bezug.** I can't relate to this kind of music.

♦ **in Bezug auf** regarding ◊ *in Bezug auf Kinder* regarding children

♦ **Bezug nehmen auf** to refer to ◊ *Sie hat in ihrer Rede mehrfach Bezug auf ihren Vorredner genommen.* In her speech she referred several times to the previous speaker.

bezüglich PREPOSITION

*The preposition **bezüglich** takes the genitive.*

with reference to ◊ *Bezüglich Ihrer Anfrage können wir Ihnen mitteilen ...* With reference to your inquiry we can inform you that ...

bezweifeln VERB (PERFECT **hat bezweifelt**)
to doubt ◊ *Ich bezweifle das.* I doubt it.

der **BH** NOUN (PL die **BHs**) (= Büstenhalter)
bra

Bhf. ABBREVIATION (= Bahnhof)
station

die **Bibel** NOUN
Bible

die **Bibliothek** NOUN (PL die **Bibliotheken**)
library

biegen VERB (IMPERFECT **bog**, PERFECT **hat gebogen**)
to bend ◊ *Sie bog den Draht zur Seite.* She bent the wire to one side.

♦ **Ein Auto bog um die Kurve.** A car came round the corner.

♦ **Du musst an der Ampel rechts in die Seitenstraße biegen.** You'll have to turn right into the side street at the traffic lights.

♦ **sich biegen** to bend ◊ *Die Bäume bogen sich im Wind.* The trees were bending in the wind.

die **Biene** NOUN
bee

der **Bienenstich** NOUN (PL die **Bienenstiche**)
① bee sting
② cream-filled cake

das **Bier** NOUN (PL die **Biere** or **Bier**)
beer ◊ *Zwei Bier, bitte!* Two beers, please!

die **Bierhalle** NOUN
beer hall

der **Bierkeller** NOUN (PL die **Bierkeller**)
beer cellar

das **Bierzelt** NOUN
beer tent

bieten VERB (IMPERFECT **bot**, PERFECT **hat geboten**)
① to offer ◊ *Dieser Job bietet mir die Möglichkeit, meine Englischkenntnisse anzuwenden.* This job offers me the chance to use my knowledge of English.
② to bid ◊ *Sie hat zweihundert Euro für den Stuhl geboten.* She bid two hundred euros for the chair. ◊ *Wer bietet mehr?* Any more bids?

♦ **Ich will ins Ausland, sobald sich die Gelegenheit bietet.** I want to go abroad as soon as the opportunity arises.

♦ **sich etwas bieten lassen** to put up with something ◊ *Eine solche Frechheit lasse ich mir nicht bieten.* I won't put up with such cheek.

der **Bikini** NOUN (PL die **Bikinis**)
bikini

das **Bild** NOUN (PL die **Bilder**)
① picture ◊ *ein Bild von Picasso* a picture by Picasso

♦ **ein Bild der Verwüstung** a scene of destruction
② photo ◊ *Hast du ein Bild von deinem Freund?* Have you got a photo of your boyfriend?

bilden VERB
① to form ◊ *Bildet einen Kreis.* Form a circle. ◊ *Wie wird der Plural dieses Worts gebildet?* How do you form the plural of this word?
② to set up ◊ *Sie haben einen Ausschuss gebildet.* They set up a committee.

♦ **sich eine Meinung bilden** to form an opinion ◊ *In dieser Frage habe ich mir noch keine Meinung gebildet.* I haven't formed an opinion on this question yet.

♦ **Reisen bildet.** Travel broadens the mind.

♦ **sich bilden (1)** to form ◊ *Am Himmel bildeten sich dunkle Wolken.* Dark clouds formed in the sky.

♦ **sich bilden (2)** to educate oneself ◊ *Sie macht Kurse, um sich zu bilden.* She attends courses in order to educate herself.

der **Bildschirm** NOUN (PL die **Bildschirme**)
screen

der **Bildschirmschoner** NOUN (PL die **Bildschirmschoner**)
screen saver

die **Bildung** NOUN

☞

[1] education ◊ *Sie hat eine gute Bildung.* She has a good education.
[2] formation ◊ *Die Bildung des Plurals im Englischen ist ziemlich regelmäßig.* The formation of the plural in English is quite regular.

billig ADJECTIVE
cheap

der **Billigflieger** NOUN (PL die **Billigflieger**)
low-cost airline

die **Binde** NOUN
[1] bandage ◊ *eine elastische Binde* an elastic bandage
[2] sanitary towel ◊ *Sie benützt lieber Binden als Tampons.* She prefers sanitary towels to tampons.

binden VERB (IMPERFECT **band**, PERFECT **hat gebunden**)
to tie ◊ *Die Tomaten werden an einen Stock gebunden.* The tomatoes are tied to a cane. ◊ *Sie band die Haare zu einem Pferdeschwanz.* She tied her hair back into a ponytail.
◆ **ein Buch binden** to bind a book
◆ **sich binden** to get involved ◊ *Sie möchte sich in ihrem Alter noch nicht binden.* She doesn't want to get involved at her age.

der **Bindestrich** NOUN (PL die **Bindestriche**)
hyphen

der **Bindfaden** NOUN (PL die **Bindfäden**)
string

die **Bindung** NOUN
[1] tie ◊ *Meine emotionale Bindung an meine Eltern ...* My emotional ties to my parents ...
[2] bindings ◊ *Bei einem Sturz müsste die Bindung aufgehen.* When you fall the bindings should come open.

Bio- PREFIX
organic ◊ *der Biomüll* organic waste

die **Biologie** NOUN
biology

biologisch ADJECTIVE
biological

die **Birke** NOUN
birch

die **Birne** NOUN
[1] pear ◊ *Zum Nachtisch gab es Birnen mit Schokoladensoße.* There were pears with chocolate sauce for dessert.
[2] bulb ◊ *Die Lampe funktioniert nicht, weil die Birne kaputt ist.* The lamp isn't working because the bulb's gone.

bis PREPOSITION, CONJUNCTION
*The preposition **bis** takes the accusative.*
[1] until ◊ *Sie bleibt bis Ende August in England.* She's staying in England until the end of August. ◊ *Du hast bis Montag Zeit.* You have until Monday. ◊ *bis es dunkel wird* until it gets dark
◆ **bis auf weiteres** until further notice
[2] by ◊ *Das Referat muss bis nächsten Montag fertig sein.* The assignment must be finished by next Monday.
◆ **bis in die Nacht** into the night
◆ **bis bald** see you later
◆ **bis gleich** see you soon
[3] as far as ◊ *Ich fahre bis Köln.* I'm going as far as Cologne.
◆ **bis hierher** this far
◆ **von ... bis ...** from ... to ... ◊ *von Köln bis Bonn* from Cologne to Bonn ◊ *von Anfang Mai bis Ende Juni* from the beginning of May to the end of June
[4] up to ◊ *Kinder bis drei fahren umsonst.* Children up to three travel free. ◊ *bis zu dreißig Grad* up to thirty degrees
◆ **zehn bis zwanzig** ten to twenty
◆ **bis zu** up to ◊ *Ich kann bis zu drei Personen mitnehmen.* I can take up to three people.
◆ **bis auf** apart from ◊ *Bis auf Jan sind alle mitgekommen.* Everybody came along apart from Jan.

bisher ADVERB
up to now

bisherig ADJECTIVE
previous

der **Biss** NOUN (GEN des **Bisses**, PL die **Bisse**)
bite

biss VERB see **beißen**

bisschen ADJECTIVE, ADVERB
bit ◊ *ein bisschen* a bit

bissig ADJECTIVE
[1] vicious
◆ **Vorsicht, bissiger Hund!** Beware of the dog!
[2] cutting ◊ *Er machte eine bissige Bemerkung.* He made a cutting remark.

bist VERB see **sein**

das **Bit** NOUN (PL die **Bits**)
bit ◊ *Bits und Bytes* bits and bytes

die **Bitte** NOUN
*see also **bitte** EXCLAMATION*
request ◊ *Ich habe eine Bitte.* I have a request. ◊ *auf seine Bitte hin* at his request

bitte EXCLAMATION
*see also **die Bitte** NOUN*
[1] please ◊ *Kann ich bitte noch etwas Saft haben?* Can I have some more juice, please? ◊ *Könnten Sie mir bitte sagen, wie ich zum Bahnhof komme?* Could you please tell me how to get to the station?
◆ **Wie bitte?** Pardon?
◆ **Hier bitte!** Here you are.
◆ **Bitte warten.** Please hold the line. (phone)
[2] don't mention it ◊ *Vielen Dank für die Hilfe! – Bitte!* Many thanks for your help! – Don't mention it!
◆ **Bitte schön!** It was a pleasure.
◆ **Bitte sehr!** You're welcome.
◆ **Darf ich? – Aber bitte!** May I? – Please do.

bitten VERB (IMPERFECT **bat**, PERFECT **hat gebeten**)

♦ **jemanden um etwas bitten** to ask somebody for something

bitter ADJECTIVE
bitter

blamieren VERB (PERFECT **hat blamiert**)
♦ **sich blamieren** to make a fool of oneself
♦ **jemanden blamieren** to let somebody down

die **Blase** NOUN
[1] bubble ◊ *Die Blase platzte.* The bubble burst.
[2] blister ◊ *Ich habe Blasen an den Füßen.* I've got blisters on my feet.
[3] bladder ◊ *Sie hat eine schwache Blase.* She has a weak bladder.

blasen VERB (PRESENT **bläst**, IMPERFECT **blies**, PERFECT **hat geblasen**)
to blow

das **Blasinstrument** NOUN (PL die **Blasinstrumente**)
wind instrument

die **Blaskapelle** NOUN
brass band

die **Blasmusik** NOUN
brass band music

blass ADJECTIVE
pale ◊ *Als sie das hörte, wurde sie blass.* When she heard that, she turned pale.

das **Blatt** NOUN (PL die **Blätter**)
[1] leaf ◊ *Im Herbst fallen die Blätter von den Bäumen.* In autumn, the leaves fall from the trees.
[2] sheet ◊ *ein Blatt Papier* a sheet of paper
[3] newspaper ◊ *In welchem Blatt hast du die Anzeige aufgegeben?* Which newspaper did you place the advertisement in?

blau ADJECTIVE
[1] blue ◊ *Er hat blaue Augen.* He has blue eyes.
[2] sloshed ◊ *Gestern Abend warst du ganz schön blau.* You were absolutely sloshed yesterday evening.
♦ **ein blaues Auge** a black eye
♦ **ein blauer Fleck** a bruise
♦ **eine Fahrt ins Blaue** a mystery tour

das **Blech** NOUN (PL die **Bleche**)
[1] sheet metal
[2] baking tray

das **Blei** NOUN
lead

bleiben VERB (IMPERFECT **blieb**, PERFECT **ist geblieben**)
[1] to stay ◊ *Wie lange bleiben Sie hier?* How long are you staying here?
◊ *Hoffentlich bleibt das Wetter schön.* I hope the weather will stay fine.
♦ **bei etwas bleiben** to stick to something ◊ *Ich bleibe bei meiner Meinung.* I'm sticking to my opinion.

[2] to be left ◊ *Vom Kuchen war nur noch ein Stück für mich geblieben.* There was only one piece of cake left for me.
♦ **Es bleibt abzuwarten, was passiert.** We'll have to wait and see what happens.
♦ **Bleibt es bei morgen zehn Uhr?** Is ten o'clock tomorrow morning still on?
♦ **Wo bleibt sie denn?** Where's she got to?

bleich ADJECTIVE
pale ◊ *Als er das hörte, wurde er bleich.* When he heard that, he turned pale.

bleifrei ADJECTIVE
unleaded

der **Bleistift** NOUN (PL die **Bleistifte**)
pencil

der **Bleistiftspitzer** NOUN (PL die **Bleistiftspitzer**)
pencil sharpener

blenden VERB
to blind ◊ *Das entgegenkommende Auto hat mich geblendet.* The approaching car blinded me.

blendend ADJECTIVE
marvellous
♦ **Du siehst blendend aus.** You look marvellous.
♦ **sich blendend amüsieren** to have a wonderful time
♦ **Mir geht's blendend.** I'm feeling great.

der **Blick** NOUN (PL die **Blicke**)
[1] glance ◊ *Ich habe mit einem Blick gesehen, dass das nicht gut gehen kann.* I saw at a glance that it couldn't work.
♦ **Er warf einen Blick auf die Uhr.** He glanced at the clock.
[2] look ◊ *Sie warf mir einen verzweifelten Blick zu.* She gave me a desperate look.
[3] view ◊ *Das Zimmer hat einen herrlichen Blick auf die Berge.* The room has a wonderful view of the mountains.
♦ **auf den ersten Blick** at first glance

blicken VERB
to look ◊ *Sie blickte zur Seite.* She looked to one side.
♦ **sich blicken lassen** to show one's face ◊ *Er hat sich hier nie wieder blicken lassen.* He's never shown his face here again.
♦ **Das lässt tief blicken!** That's very revealing!

blieb VERB *see* **bleiben**

blind ADJECTIVE
[1] blind ◊ *Er ist auf einem Auge blind.* He's blind in one eye.
[2] tarnished ◊ *Der Spiegel war blind geworden.* The mirror had become tarnished.
♦ **ein blinder Passagier** a stowaway

der **Blinddarm** NOUN (PL die **Blinddärme**)
appendix ◊ *Er wurde am Blinddarm operiert.* He had his appendix out.

B

die **Blinddarmentzündung** NOUN
appendicitis
blinzeln VERB
to blink
der **Blitz** NOUN (PL die **Blitze**)
lightning ◊ *Der Blitz schlug in den Baum ein.* The tree was struck by lightning.
blitzen VERB
♦ **Es blitzt.** There's a flash of lightning.
das **Blitzlicht** NOUN (PL die **Blitzlichter**)
flashlight
der **Block** NOUN (PL die **Blöcke**)
1 block ◊ *Unsere Nachbarn aus dem nächsten Block haben uns gestern besucht.* Our neighbours from the next block visited us yesterday.
2 pad ◊ *Er riss ein Blatt vom Block und fing an zu schreiben.* He tore a sheet from the pad and began to write.
die **Blockflöte** NOUN
recorder
blöd ADJECTIVE
stupid ◊ *Du bist blöd!* You're stupid!
♦ **blöd fragen** to ask stupid questions ◊ *Wer blöd fragt, bekommt auch eine blöde Antwort.* If you ask a stupid question, then you get a stupid answer.
der **Blödsinn** NOUN
nonsense
blond ADJECTIVE
1 blond ◊ *Er hat blonde Haare.* He has blond hair.
2 blonde ◊ *Meine Schwester ist blond.* My sister's blonde. ◊ *Sie hat ihre Haare blond gefärbt.* She dyed her hair blonde.
bloß ADVERB, ADJECTIVE
only ◊ *Er hat bloß einen Fehler gemacht.* He only made one mistake. ◊ *Wenn das bloß schon fertig wäre!* If only it was finished. ◊ *Das Konzert war ganz nett, bloß ein bisschen laut.* The concert was quite nice, only a little loud.
♦ **Lass das bloß!** Don't do that!
♦ **Wie ist das bloß passiert?** How on earth did that happen?
♦ **Wo ist er bloß?** Where's he got to?
♦ **mit bloßem Auge** with the naked eye
♦ **der bloße Gedanke** the very thought
♦ **bloßer Neid** sheer envy
blühen VERB
to be in bloom ◊ *Zurzeit blüht der Flieder.* The lilac's in bloom at the moment.
die **Blume** NOUN
flower ◊ *Sie hat mir einen Strauß Blumen mitgebracht.* She brought me a bunch of flowers.
das **Blumenbeet** NOUN (PL die **Blumenbeete**)
flowerbed
der **Blumenkohl** NOUN (PL die **Blumenkohle**)
cauliflower
die **Bluse** NOUN
blouse
das **Blut** NOUN
blood
der **Blutdruck** NOUN
blood pressure
die **Blüte** NOUN
blossom
bluten VERB
to bleed ◊ *Meine Nase blutet.* My nose is bleeding.
die **Blutprobe** NOUN
blood test
der **Blutspender** NOUN (PL die **Blutspender**)
blood donor
die **Blutvergiftung** NOUN
blood poisoning
der **Bock** NOUN
♦ **Bock haben, etwas zu tun** to fancy doing something ◊ *Hast du Bock, mit ins Kino zu kommen?* Do you feel like coming to the cinema? ◊ *Ich habe heute überhaupt keinen Bock auf die Schule.* I don't fancy school today at all.
die **Bockwurst** NOUN (PL die **Bockwürste**)
frankfurter
der **Boden** NOUN (PL die **Böden**)
1 soil ◊ *Der Boden ist in dieser Gegend sehr fruchtbar.* The soil in this area is very fertile. ◊ *auf deutschem Boden* on German soil
2 floor ◊ *Wir haben auf dem Boden gesessen.* We sat on the floor.
3 bottom ◊ *Das Schiff sank auf den Boden des Meers.* The ship sank to the bottom of the sea. ◊ *Das Fass hat einen hölzernen Boden.* The barrel has a wooden bottom.
4 attic ◊ *Wir haben die alten Möbel auf den Boden gebracht.* We put the old furniture into the attic.
die **Bodenschätze** MASC PL NOUN
mineral resources
der **Bodensee** NOUN
Lake Constance ◊ *eine Stadt am Bodensee* a town on Lake Constance
die **Bohne** NOUN
bean
bohren VERB
to bore ◊ *Sie bohrte ein Loch in das Brett.* She bored a hole in the shelf.
♦ **Der Zahnarzt musste nicht bohren.** The dentist didn't have to drill.
♦ **nach etwas bohren** to drill for something ◊ *In der Nordsee wird nach Erdöl gebohrt.* They're drilling for oil in the North Sea.
♦ **in der Nase bohren** to pick one's nose
der **Bohrer** NOUN (PL die **Bohrer**)
drill
die **Bohrinsel** NOUN
oil rig
die **Bohrmaschine** NOUN

drill

der **Bohrturm** NOUN (PL die **Bohrtürme**)
derrick

die **Bombe** NOUN
bomb

der **Bonbon** NOUN (PL die **Bonbons**)
sweet

das **Boot** NOUN (PL die **Boote**)
boat

der **Bord** NOUN
see also **das Bord** NOUN
♦**an Bord** on board

das **Bord** NOUN (PL die **Borde**)
see also **der Bord** NOUN
shelf ◊ *Er brachte über dem Schreibtisch ein Bord für seine Bücher an.* He put up a shelf over his desk for his books.

borgen VERB
to borrow ◊ *Das gehört nicht mir, das habe ich mir geborgt.* That doesn't belong to me, I borrowed it.
♦**jemandem etwas borgen** to lend somebody something ◊ *Meine Schwester hat mir ihr Rennrad geborgt.* My sister lent me her racing bike.

die **Börse** NOUN
1 purse ◊ *Sie nahm zehn Euro aus ihrer Börse.* She took ten euros out of her purse.
2 stock exchange ◊ *Diese Aktien werden an der Börse gehandelt.* These shares are traded on the stock exchange.

böse ADJECTIVE
1 bad ◊ *Er ist ein böser Mensch.* He's a bad man. ◊ *Die Kinder waren böse.* The children were bad. ◊ *Sie hat eine böse Erkältung.* She has a bad cold.
♦**Er hat sich böse verletzt.** He's injured himself badly.
2 angry ◊ *Ich habe ihm einen bösen Brief geschrieben.* I wrote him an angry letter.
♦**böse werden** to get angry ◊ *Wenn du das noch einmal tust, werde ich böse.* If you do that again, I'll get angry.
♦**auf jemanden böse sein** to be angry with somebody ◊ *Ich bin böse auf Martin, weil er nicht gekommen ist.* I'm angry with Martin because he didn't come.
♦**Bist du mir noch böse?** Are you still angry with me?
♦**Das war eine böse Überraschung.** That was a nasty shock.
♦**Mit ihm sieht es böse aus.** It doesn't look too good for him.

Bosnien NEUT NOUN
Bosnia

Bosnien-Herzegowina NEUT NOUN
Bosnia-Herzegovina

bot VERB see **bieten**

die **Botschaft** NOUN

1 message ◊ *Kannst du ihm eine Botschaft übermitteln?* Can you give him a message?
2 embassy ◊ *Sie müssen das Visum auf der Botschaft beantragen.* You have to apply to the embassy for a visa.

boxen VERB
to box

der **Boxer** NOUN (PL die **Boxer**)
boxer

brach VERB see **brechen**

brachte VERB see **bringen**

der **Brand** NOUN (PL die **Brände**)
fire

Brandenburg NEUT NOUN
Brandenburg

> ℹ **Brandenburg** is one of the 16 **Länder.** Its capital is Potsdam, which is famous as Frederick the Great's residence. Agriculture and forestry are still important parts of the economy.

Brasilien NEUT NOUN
Brazil
♦**aus Brasilien** from Brazil
♦**nach Brasilien** to Brazil

braten VERB (PRESENT **brät,** IMPERFECT **briet,** PERFECT **hat gebraten**)
see also **der Braten** NOUN
1 to roast ◊ *Wir haben das Hähnchen im Backofen gebraten.* We roasted the chicken in the oven.
2 to fry ◊ *Sie briet die Kartoffeln in der Pfanne.* She fried the potatoes in the frying pan.

der **Braten** NOUN (PL die **Braten**)
see also **braten** VERB
roast

das **Brathähnchen** NOUN (PL die **Brathähnchen**)
roast chicken

die **Bratkartoffeln** FEM PL NOUN
fried potatoes

die **Bratpfanne** NOUN
frying pan

die **Bratwurst** NOUN (PL die **Bratwürste**)
fried sausage

der **Brauch** NOUN (PL die **Bräuche**)
custom

brauchbar ADJECTIVE
1 usable ◊ *Dieses alte Gerät ist nicht mehr brauchbar.* The old appliance is no longer usable.
2 capable ◊ *Sie ist eine sehr brauchbare Mitarbeiterin.* She's a very capable colleague.

brauchen VERB
1 to need ◊ *Wir brauchen noch Brot und Butter.* We still need bread and butter. ◊ *Dazu brauche ich mindestens zwei Tage.* I'll need at least two days.

2 to have to ◇ *Du brauchst heute nicht kommen.* You don't have to come today. ◇ *Du brauchst nur Bescheid zu sagen, dann helfe ich dir.* You only have to let me know and I'll help you.

♦ **Das kann ich gut brauchen.** I could really do with that.

die **Brauerei** NOUN
brewery

braun ADJECTIVE
1 brown ◇ *Sie hat braune Haare.* She has brown hair.
2 tanned ◇ *Wir kamen ganz braun aus den Ferien zurück.* We came back all tanned from our holidays.

die **Braut** NOUN (PL die **Bräute**)
bride

der **Bräutigam** NOUN (PL die **Bräutigame**)
bridegroom

das **Brautpaar** NOUN (PL die **Brautpaare**)
bride and groom

brav ADJECTIVE
good ◇ *Die Kinder waren brav.* The children were good.
Be careful! **brav** *does not mean* **brave**.

bravo! EXCLAMATION
well done!

die **BRD** NOUN (= *Bundesrepublik Deutschland*)
Federal Republic of Germany

brechen VERB (PRESENT **bricht,** IMPERFECT **brach,** PERFECT **hat/ist gebrochen**)
For the perfect tense use **haben** *when the verb has an object and* **sein** *when there is no object. Use* **haben** *for to vomit.*
1 to break ◇ *Der Zweig ist gebrochen.* The branch broke. ◇ *Ich habe den Stock in zwei Teile gebrochen.* I broke the stick in two. ◇ *Ich habe mir den rechten Arm gebrochen.* I've broken my right arm. ◇ *Sie hat ihr Versprechen gebrochen.* She broke her promise. ◇ *einen Rekord brechen* to break a record
2 to vomit ◇ *Ihm wurde schlecht, und er musste brechen.* He felt ill and had to vomit.

breit ADJECTIVE
wide ◇ *Das Brett ist fünfzehn Zentimeter breit.* The plank is fifteen centimetres wide.

der **Breitbandanschluss** NOUN (PL die **Breitbandanschlüsse**)
broadband connection

die **Breite** NOUN
width ◇ *die Breite des Tisches* the width of the table

Bremen NEUT NOUN
Bremen

ⓘ The "Free Hanseatic City of Bremen" is one of the 16 **Länder**. It is a "city-state" like Berlin and Hamburg, and is made up of the cities Bremen and Bremerhaven.

die **Bremse** NOUN
1 brake ◇ *Sie trat auf die Bremsen.* She stepped on the brakes.
2 horsefly ◇ *Wir sind von Bremsen gestochen worden.* We were bitten by horseflies.

bremsen VERB
to brake ◇ *Als er das Kind sah, bremste er.* When he saw the child, he braked.

♦ **Sie versuchte, das Auto zu bremsen.** She tried to stop the car.

♦ **Wenn sie erst einmal angefangen hat, dann ist sie nicht mehr zu bremsen.** Once she's started, there's no stopping her.

das **Bremslicht** NOUN (PL die **Bremslichter**)
brake light

das **Bremspedal** NOUN (PL die **Bremspedale**)
brake pedal

brennen VERB (IMPERFECT **brannte,** PERFECT **hat gebrannt**)
to burn ◇ *Das Holz ist zu nass, es brennt nicht.* The wood's too wet, it won't burn. ◇ *Im Wohnzimmer brennt Licht.* There's a light burning in the living room. ◇ *Der Schnaps brennt auf der Zunge.* The schnapps burns your tongue. ◇ *ein Loch in etwas brennen* to burn a hole in something

♦ **Das Haus brannte.** The house was on fire.

♦ **sich brennen** to burn oneself ◇ *Ich habe mich an der heißen Platte gebrannt.* I've burned myself on the hot plate.

♦ **darauf brennen, etwas zu tun** to be dying to do something ◇ *Ich brenne darauf, deinen Freund kennenzulernen.* I'm dying to meet your boyfriend.

die **Brennnessel** NOUN
stinging nettle

der **Brennstoff** NOUN (PL die **Brennstoffe**)
fuel

das **Brett** NOUN (PL die **Bretter**)
1 board ◇ *Die Hütte bestand aus ein paar zusammengenagelten Brettern.* The hut consisted of a few boards nailed together. ◇ *Sie stellte die Schachfiguren aufs Brett.* She set up the chessmen on the board.
2 shelf ◇ *Die Gewürze stehen auf einem Brett über dem Herd.* The spices are on a shelf above the cooker.

♦ **das Schwarze Brett** the notice board

♦ **Ich hatte ein Brett vor dem Kopf.** My mind went blank.

die **Brezel** NOUN
pretzel

bricht VERB *see* **brechen**

der **Brief** NOUN (PL die **Briefe**)
letter

der **Brieffreund** NOUN (PL die **Brieffreunde**)
  pen friend

die **Brieffreundin** NOUN
  pen friend

die **Brieffreundschaft** NOUN
  ♦ **Ich habe eine Brieffreundschaft mit ihm.** He's my pen friend.

der **Briefkasten** NOUN (PL die **Briefkästen**)
  ⓵ letterbox
  ⓶ postbox

die **Briefmarke** NOUN
  stamp

die **Brieftasche** NOUN
  wallet

der **Briefträger** NOUN (PL die **Briefträger**)
  postman ◊ *Günter ist Briefträger.* Günter's a postman.

die **Briefträgerin** NOUN
  postwoman ◊ *Meine Tante ist Briefträgerin.* My aunt's a postwoman.

der **Briefumschlag** NOUN (PL die **Briefumschläge**)
  envelope

der **Briefwechsel** NOUN (PL die **Briefwechsel**)
  correspondence

brief VERB *see* **braten**

die **Brille** NOUN
  ⓵ glasses ◊ *Lesley trägt eine Brille.* Lesley wears glasses. ◊ *eine Brille* a pair of glasses
  ⓶ goggles ◊ *Beim Schweißen sollte man eine Brille tragen.* You should wear goggles when welding.
  ⓷ toilet seat ◊ *Ich hasse es, wenn Männer die Brille oben lassen.* I hate it when men leave the seat up.

bringen VERB (IMPERFECT **brachte,** PERFECT **hat gebracht**)
  ⓵ to bring ◊ *Unsere Gäste haben uns einen schönen Blumenstrauß gebracht.* Our guests have brought us a lovely bunch of flowers. ◊ *Kann ich meine Schwester mit zur Party bringen?* Can I bring my sister to the party?
  ⓶ to take ◊ *Meine Freunde haben mich zum Flughafen gebracht.* My friends took me to the airport. ◊ *jemanden nach Hause bringen* to take somebody home
  ⓷ to bring in ◊ *Diese Anlage bringt fünf Prozent Zinsen.* This investment brings in five per cent interest.
  ⓸ to publish ◊ *Alle Zeitungen brachten diese Geschichte auf der ersten Seite.* All the newspapers published this story on the first page.
  ⓹ to be on ◊ *Sieh mal in der Zeitung nach, was das Theater bringt.* Look in the paper to see what's on at the theatre.
  ♦ **jemanden zu etwas bringen** to make somebody do something ◊ *Sie hat mich zum Lachen gebracht.* She made me laugh. ◊ *Du bringst mich noch zur Verzweiflung.* You make me despair.
  ♦ **jemanden dazu bringen, etwas zu tun** to get somebody to do something ◊ *Wie hast du deine Eltern dazu gebracht, dass sie das erlaubt haben?* How did you get your parents to let you do that?
  ♦ **es über sich bringen, etwas zu tun** to bring oneself to do something ◊ *Ich habe es nicht über mich gebracht, ihr das zu sagen.* I couldn't bring myself to tell her.
  ♦ **Der Betrüger hat die alte Frau um ihre ganzen Ersparnisse gebracht.** The swindler cheated the old lady out of all her savings.
  ♦ **jemanden auf eine Idee bringen** to give somebody an idea
  ♦ **jemanden in Gefahr bringen** to put somebody in danger
  ♦ **Unser Computer bringt's nicht.** Our computer's rubbish.
  ♦ **Das bringt nichts!** That's no use!

der **Brite** NOUN (GEN des **Briten,** PL die **Briten**)
  Briton
  ♦ **die Briten** the British

die **Britin** NOUN
  Briton

britisch ADJECTIVE
  British

die **Brokkoli** PL NOUN
  broccoli

die **Brombeere** NOUN
  blackberry

die **Broschüre** NOUN
  brochure

das **Brot** NOUN (PL die **Brote**)
  ⓵ bread ◊ *Haben wir noch Brot im Haus?* Do we still have some bread in the house?
  ⓶ loaf ◊ *Kannst du für die Party drei Brote holen?* Can you get three loaves for the party?

das **Brötchen** NOUN (PL die **Brötchen**)
  roll

browsen VERB (PERFECT **hat gebrowst**)
  to browse

der **Browser** NOUN (PL die **Browser**)
  web browser

der **Bruch** NOUN (PL die **Brüche**)
  ⓵ fracture ◊ *Sie wurde mit einem Bruch ins Krankenhaus eingeliefert.* She was taken to hospital with a fracture.
  ♦ **zu Bruch gehen** to get broken ◊ *Die ganzen Teller sind zu Bruch gegangen.* All the plates got broken.
  ⓶ hernia ◊ *Trag das nicht allein, du hebst dir sonst einen Bruch!* Don't carry that on your own, you'll give yourself a hernia!
  ⓷ fraction ◊ *Das Rechnen mit Brüchen haben wir noch nicht gelernt.* We haven't learned fractions yet.

die **Brücke** NOUN
bridge

der **Bruder** NOUN (PL die **Brüder**)
brother

der **Brühwürfel** NOUN (PL die **Brühwürfel**)
stock cube

brüllen VERB
to roar ◊ *Der Löwe brüllte.* The lion roared.
♦ **Er brüllte vor Schmerz.** He screamed with pain.

brummen VERB
1 to growl ◊ *Der Bär brummte.* The bear growled.
2 to buzz ◊ *Eine dicke Fliege brummte durchs Zimmer.* A huge fly buzzed around the room.
♦ **etwas brummen** to mumble something ◊ *Er hat irgendetwas Unfreundliches gebrummt.* He mumbled something unfriendly.

der **Brunnen** NOUN (PL die **Brunnen**)
1 fountain ◊ *Am Marktplatz steht ein Brunnen.* There's a fountain in the market square.
2 well ◊ *Die Burgbewohner bekamen ihr Wasser aus diesem Brunnen.* The inhabitants of the castle got their water from this well.

die **Brust** NOUN (PL die **Brüste**)
breast ◊ *Sie hat kleine Brüste.* She has small breasts.

der **Brustkasten** NOUN
chest

das **Brustschwimmen** NOUN
breaststroke

brutal ADJECTIVE
brutal

die **Brutalität** NOUN
brutality

brutto ADVERB
gross

das **BSE** NOUN
BSE (= bovine spongiform encephalopathy) ◊ *Nicht alle Kühe haben BSE.* Not all cows have got BSE.

das **Buch** NOUN (PL die **Bücher**)
book

die **Buche** NOUN
beech tree

buchen VERB
to book ◊ *Wir haben eine Reise nach Kreta gebucht.* We've booked a trip to Crete.

die **Bücherei** NOUN
library

das **Bücherregal** NOUN (PL die **Bücherregale**)
bookcase

der **Buchhalter** NOUN (PL die **Buchhalter**)
accountant

die **Buchhandlung** NOUN
bookshop

der **Buchladen** NOUN (PL die **Buchläden**)
bookshop

die **Büchse** NOUN
tin ◊ *Sie bewahrt den Tee in einer Büchse auf.* She keeps her tea in a tin.

der **Büchsenöffner** NOUN (PL die **Büchsenöffner**)
tin opener

der **Buchstabe** NOUN (GEN des **Buchstabens**, PL die **Buchstaben**)
letter of the alphabet

buchstabieren VERB (PERFECT **hat buchstabiert**)
to spell

buchstäblich ADVERB
literally ◊ *Sie kam buchstäblich in der letzten Minute.* She arrived at literally the last minute.

sich **bücken** VERB
to bend down

die **Bude** NOUN
stall ◊ *die Buden auf dem Jahrmarkt* the stalls at the fair
♦ **Kommt ihr noch mit auf meine Bude?** Do you want to come back to my place?

das **Büfett** NOUN (PL die **Büfetts**)
sideboard
♦ **kaltes Büfett** cold buffet

der **Bügel** NOUN (PL die **Bügel**)
hanger

das **Bügeleisen** NOUN (PL die **Bügeleisen**)
iron ◊ *Ich habe mir die Hand am Bügeleisen verbrannt.* I burnt my hand on the iron.

bügeln VERB
to iron

die **Bühne** NOUN
stage ◊ *auf der Bühne stehen* to be on stage

buk VERB see **backen**

Bulgarien NEUT NOUN
Bulgaria
♦ **aus Bulgarien** from Bulgaria
♦ **nach Bulgarien** to Bulgaria

der **Bummel** NOUN (PL die **Bummel**)
1 stroll ◊ *Wir machten einen Bummel an der Donau entlang.* We went for a stroll along the Danube.
2 window-shopping ◊ *Bei meinem Bummel durch die Innenstadt habe ich eine tolle Hose gesehen.* I saw a fantastic pair of trousers while I was window-shopping in the city centre.

bummeln VERB

Use sein to form the perfect tense for to stroll and haben for to dawdle.

1 to stroll ◊ *Wir sind durch die Stadt gebummelt.* We strolled through the town.
2 to dawdle ◊ *Heute hast du auf dem Heimweg aber gebummelt.* You've really been dawdling on your way home today.

der **Bund** NOUN (PL die **Bünde**)
1 association ◊ *Die Bauern schlossen sich zu einem Bund zusammen.* The farmers formed an association.
♦ **Bund und Länder** the Federal Government and the Länder
2 waistband ◊ *Die Hose ist am Bund zu eng.* The trousers are too tight at the waistband.

Bundes- PREFIX
Federal

der **Bundesbürger** NOUN (PL die **Bundesbürger**)
German citizen

der **Bundeskanzler** NOUN (PL die **Bundeskanzler**)
Federal Chancellor

das **Bundesland** NOUN (PL die **Bundesländer**)
state

die **Bundesliga** NOUN
Premier League

> *ℹ The **Bundesliga** was founded in 1963, and consists of 18 teams. At the end of the season, play-offs between the bottom 3 clubs of the **Bundesliga** and the top 3 of the **zweite Bundesliga** decide who is relegated and who is promoted.*

der **Bundespräsident** NOUN (GEN des **Bundespräsidenten**, PL die **Bundespräsidenten**)
Federal President

der **Bundesrat** NOUN
upper chamber of the German Parliament

> *ℹ The **Bundesrat** is not directly elected, but is made up of representatives of the 16 **Länder**. In many cases, **Bundesrat** approval is required before laws (particularly amendments to the constitution) can be passed.*

die **Bundesregierung** NOUN
Federal government

die **Bundesrepublik** NOUN
Federal Republic ◊ *die Bundesrepublik Deutschland* the Federal Republic of Germany

die **Bundesstraße** NOUN
federal road

der **Bundestag** NOUN
German Parliament

> *ℹ The **Bundestag** is the German parliamentary assembly, elected every four years.*

die **Bundeswehr** NOUN
German Armed Forces

> *ℹ The **Bundeswehr** is based on conscription for men, but there are also career servicemen. The basic period of military service is 10 months.*

der **Bungalow** NOUN (GEN des **Bungalows**, PL die **Bungalows**)
bungalow

bunt ADJECTIVE
1 brightly-coloured ◊ *Sie hatte ein buntes Kleid an.* She was wearing a brightly-coloured dress.
2 mixed ◊ *Unsere Klasse ist ein buntes Häufchen.* Our class is a mixed bunch.
♦ **Mir wird es zu bunt.** It's getting too much for me.

der **Buntstift** NOUN (PL die **Buntstifte**)
coloured pencil

die **Burg** NOUN (PL die **Burgen**)
castle

der **Bürger** NOUN (PL die **Bürger**)
citizen

bürgerlich ADJECTIVE
1 civil ◊ *bürgerliche Rechte* civil rights
2 middle-class ◊ *eine gute bürgerliche Familie* a good middle-class family

der **Bürgermeister** NOUN (PL die **Bürgermeister**)
mayor

der **Bürgersteig** NOUN (PL die **Bürgersteige**)
pavement

das **Büro** NOUN (PL die **Büros**)
office

die **Büroklammer** NOUN
paper clip

die **Bürste** NOUN
brush

bürsten VERB (PERFECT **hat gebürstet**)
to brush

der **Bus** NOUN (GEN des **Busses**, PL die **Busse**)
bus ◊ *mit dem Bus fahren* to go by bus

der **Busbahnhof** NOUN (PL die **Busbahnhöfe**)
bus station

der **Busch** NOUN (PL die **Büsche**)
bush

der **Busen** NOUN (PL die **Busen**)
bosom

der **Busfahrer** NOUN (PL die **Busfahrer**)
bus driver

die **Bushaltestelle** NOUN
bus stop

die **Buslinie** NOUN
bus route

das **Bußgeld** NOUN (PL die **Bußgelder**)
fine

der **Büstenhalter** NOUN (PL die **Büstenhalter**)
bra

die **Butter** NOUN
butter

das **Butterbrot** NOUN (PL die **Butterbrote**)
bread and butter

B

C

ca. ABBREVIATION (= *circa*)
approx.

die **Cabin Crew** NOUN
cabin crew

das **Café** NOUN (PL die **Cafés**)
café ◊ *Sonntags gehen wir immer ins Café.* On Sundays we always go to a café.

die **Cafeteria** NOUN (PL die **Cafeterias**)
cafeteria

campen VERB
to camp

das **Camping** NOUN
camping

der **Campingkocher** NOUN (PL die **Campingkocher**)
camping stove

der **Campingplatz** NOUN (GEN des **Campingplatzes**, PL die **Campingplätze**)
campsite

die **CD** NOUN (PL die **CDs**)
CD

die **CD-ROM** NOUN (PL die **CD-ROMs**)
CD-ROM

der **CD-Spieler** NOUN (PL die **CD-Spieler**)
CD player

das **Cello** NOUN (PL die **Cellos** or **Celli**)
cello ◊ *Ich spiele Cello.* I play the cello.

der **Cent** NOUN (PL die **Cents**)
cent

der **Champignon** NOUN (PL die **Champignons**)
button mushroom

die **Chance** NOUN
chance

das **Chaos** NOUN (GEN des **Chaos**)
chaos

chaotisch ADJECTIVE
chaotic

der **Charakter** NOUN (PL die **Charakter**)
character

charmant ADJECTIVE
charming

der **Charterflug** NOUN (PL die **Charterflüge**)
charter flight

der **Chatroom** NOUN (PL die **Chatrooms**)
chat room

chatten VERB
to chat ◊ *Wir haben im Internet gechattet.* We chatted on the Net.

der **Chauvinist** NOUN (GEN des **Chauvinisten**, PL die **Chauvinisten**)
chauvinist
◆ **männlicher Chauvinist** male chauvinist pig

der **Chef** NOUN (PL die **Chefs**)
1 head ◊ *Er ist Chef einer großen Firma.* He's the head of a large company.
2 boss ◊ *Da muss ich den Chef fragen.*

I'll have to ask my boss.

die **Chefin** NOUN
boss

die **Chemie** NOUN
chemistry

der **Chemiker** NOUN (PL die **Chemiker**)
industrial chemist

chemisch ADJECTIVE
chemical
◆ **chemische Reinigung** dry cleaning

der **Chicorée** NOUN
chicory

Chile NEUT NOUN
Chile
◆ **aus Chile** from Chile
◆ **nach Chile** to Chile

China NEUT NOUN
China
◆ **aus China** from China
◆ **nach China** to China

der **Chinese** NOUN (GEN des **Chinesen**, PL die **Chinesen**)
Chinese
◆ **die Chinesen** the Chinese

die **Chinesin** NOUN
Chinese

chinesisch ADJECTIVE
Chinese

die **Chips** PL NOUN
crisps
*Be careful! The German word **Chips** does not mean **chips**.*

der **Chirurg** NOUN (GEN des **Chirurgen**, PL die **Chirurgen**)
surgeon

die **Chirurgie** NOUN
surgery

das **Chlor** NOUN
chlorine

der **Chor** NOUN (PL die **Chöre**)
choir ◊ *Sie singt im Chor.* She sings in a choir.

der **Christ** NOUN (GEN des **Christen**, PL die **Christen**)
Christian ◊ *Er ist Christ.* He's a Christian.

die **Christin** NOUN
Christian ◊ *Sie ist Christin.* She's a Christian.

christlich ADJECTIVE
Christian

circa ADVERB
approximately

cm ABBREVIATION (= *Zentimeter*)
cm

die **Cola** NOUN (PL die **Colas**)
Coke®

der **Computer** NOUN (PL die **Computer**)
computer

das **Computerspiel** NOUN (PL die **Computerspiele**)
computer game

cool ADJECTIVE
cool

der **Cousin** NOUN (PL die **Cousins**)
cousin

die **Cousine** NOUN
cousin

die **Creme** NOUN (PL die **Cremes**)
1 cream ◊ *eine Handcreme* a hand cream

2 polish ◊ *Hast du schwarze Schuhcreme?* Do you have any black shoe polish?

3 mousse ◊ *eine Zitronencreme* a lemon mousse

der **Curry** NOUN
curry powder

die **Currywurst** NOUN (PL die **Currywürste**)
curried sausage

der **Cursor** NOUN (PL die **Cursors**)
cursor

C

D

da ADVERB, CONJUNCTION

1 there ◇ *Da ist es schön.* It's beautiful there.
+ **da draußen** out there
+ **Da haben wir Glück gehabt.** We were lucky there.
+ **da sein** to be there

2 here ◇ *Da liegt meine Brille ja.* Here are my glasses. ◇ *Da bin ich.* Here I am.
+ **Ist noch Milch da?** Is there any milk left?
+ **Da kann man nichts machen.** It can't be helped.

3 since ◇ *Da du gerade hier bist ...* Since you're here ...

dabehalten VERB (PRESENT **behält da,** IMPERFECT **behielt da,** PERFECT **hat dabehalten**)
to keep

dabei ADVERB

+ **nahe dabei** close by ◇ *Er stand nahe dabei, als die Bombe explodierte.* When the bomb exploded he was standing close by.
+ **Sie hatten ihren Hund dabei.** They had their dog with them.
+ **Was ist schon dabei?** What of it?
+ **es ist doch nichts dabei, wenn ...** it doesn't matter if ...
+ **Bleiben wir dabei.** Let's leave it at that.
+ **Es bleibt dabei.** That's settled.
+ **dabei sein** to be there ◇ *Ich bin dabei gewesen.* I was there.
+ **Er war gerade dabei, zu gehen.** He was just about to leave.
+ **Er hat es doch gemacht, dabei hatte ich ihn ausdrücklich gewarnt.** He did it even though I expressly warned him.

das **Dach** NOUN (PL die **Dächer**)
roof

der **Dachboden** NOUN (PL die **Dachböden**)
attic

dachte VERB *see* **denken**

der **Dackel** NOUN (PL die **Dackel**)
dachshund

dadurch ADVERB, CONJUNCTION

1 through it ◇ *Er muss dadurch gekrochen sein.* He must have crawled through it.

2 that's why ◇ *Dadurch habe ich mich verspätet.* That's why I was late.

3 as a result ◇ *Der Zug hatte Verspätung, dadurch haben wir unseren Anschluss verpasst.* The train was late, and as a result we missed our connection.

+ **dadurch, dass** because ◇ *Dadurch, dass sie kein Englisch kann ...* Because she doesn't speak any English ...

dafür ADVERB

1 for it ◇ *Was hast du dafür bezahlt?* What did you pay for it? ◇ *Was bekomme ich dafür?* What will I get for it?
+ **Er ist bekannt dafür.** He's well-known for that.

2 instead ◇ *Wenn du nicht mit ins Schwimmbad kannst, dann komm dafür doch mit ins Kino.* If you can't come with us to the swimming pool, then come along to the cinema instead.
+ **Er kann nichts dafür.** He can't help it.

dagegen ADVERB, CONJUNCTION

1 against it ◇ *Was hast du dagegen?* What have you got against it? ◇ *Ich war dagegen.* I was against it.
+ **Ich habe nichts dagegen.** I don't mind.
+ **Dagegen kann man nichts tun.** You can't do anything against it.

2 into it ◇ *Er sah den Baum nicht und rannte dagegen.* He didn't see the tree and ran into it.

3 for it ◇ *Das ist jetzt mein Ball, ich habe meine Murmeln dagegen getauscht.* This is my ball now – I swapped my marbles for it.

4 by comparison ◇ *Dagegen ist unser Haus klein.* Our house is small by comparison.

5 however ◇ *Sie wollte gehen, er dagegen wollte bleiben.* She wanted to leave, however he wanted to stay.

daheim ADVERB
at home

daher ADVERB, CONJUNCTION

1 from there ◇ *Daher komme ich gerade.* I've just come from there.

2 that's where ◇ *Das war ein schwerer Unfall; daher hat er sein kaputtes Bein.* It was a serious accident – that's where he got his bad leg.

3 that's why ◇ *Sie war krank und konnte daher nicht mitkommen.* She was ill, and that's why she couldn't come.

dahin ADVERB
there ◇ *Dahin gehe ich jetzt.* I'm going there now.

dahinten ADVERB
over there

dahinter ADVERB
behind it ◇ *Er versteckte sich dahinter.* He hid behind it.

dahinterkommen VERB (IMPERFECT **kam dahinter,** PERFECT **ist dahintergekommen**)
to find out ◇ *Meine Mutter ist dahintergekommen, dass ich gestern nicht bei dir war.* My mother has found out that I wasn't at your place yesterday.

damals ADVERB
in those days

die **Dame** NOUN
  [1] lady
  [2] (*chess, cards*)
  queen
  [3] draughts ◊ *Dame ist mein Lieblingsspiel.* Draughts is my favourite game.

damit ADVERB, CONJUNCTION
  [1] with it ◊ *Wisch damit den Tisch ab.* Wipe the table with it.
  [2] by that ◊ *Was meint er damit?* What does he mean by that?
  ◆ **Was willst du damit sagen?** What are you getting at?
  ◆ **Genug damit!** That's enough of that!
  ◆ **Damit eilt es nicht.** There's no hurry.
  [3] so that ◊ *Ich sage dir das, damit du das weißt.* I'm telling you so that you know.

der **Dampf** NOUN
  steam

der **Dampfer** NOUN (PL die **Dampfer**)
  steamer ◊ *mit dem Dampfer fahren* to go by steamer
  ◆ **Du bist auf dem falschen Dampfer.** You've got the wrong idea.

danach ADVERB
  [1] afterwards ◊ *Ich habe etwas getrunken, und danach fühlte ich mich besser.* I had something to drink and afterwards felt much better.
  [2] accordingly ◊ *Verhalte dich bitte danach.* Please behave accordingly.

der **Däne** NOUN (GEN des **Dänen**, PL die **Dänen**)
  Dane

daneben ADVERB
  [1] beside it ◊ *Sein Stuhl stand daneben.* His chair was beside it.
  [2] by comparison ◊ *Er ist sehr klug, daneben wirkt sie ziemlich dumm.* He's very clever, and she seems rather stupid by comparison.

sich **danebenbenehmen** VERB (PRESENT **benimmt sich daneben**, IMPERFECT **benahm sich daneben**, PERFECT **hat sich danebenbenommen**)
  to misbehave

Dänemark NEUT NOUN
  Denmark
  ◆ **aus Dänemark** from Denmark
  ◆ **nach Dänemark** to Denmark

die **Dänin** NOUN
  Dane

dänisch ADJECTIVE
  Danish

der **Dank** NOUN
  see also **dank** PREPOSITION
  thanks ◊ *Unser Dank gilt vor allem Herrn Morris.* Our thanks to Mr Morris in particular.
  ◆ **Vielen Dank!** Many thanks.

dank PREPOSITION
  see also **der Dank** NOUN

dank takes the genitive or dative.
  thanks to ◊ *Dank meiner Schwester habe ich noch rechtzeitig davon erfahren.* Thanks to my sister I found out about it in time.

dankbar ADJECTIVE
  grateful ◊ *Ich bin dir sehr dankbar.* I'm very grateful to you.
  ◆ **eine dankbare Aufgabe** a rewarding task

danke EXCLAMATION
  thank you
  ◆ **Danke sehr!** Thank you.
  ◆ **Danke schön!** Thank you very much.
  ◆ **Nein, danke!** No, thanks.

danken VERB
  to thank ◊ *Ich möchte dir dafür danken.* I'd like to thank you for that.
  ◆ **nichts zu danken!** don't mention it!

dann ADVERB
  then
  ◆ **dann und wann** now and then

daran ADVERB
  on it ◊ *ein Päckchen mit einem Zettel daran* a parcel with a label on it
  ◆ **Ich habe nicht daran gedacht.** I didn't think of that.
  ◆ **Er ist daran gestorben.** He died of it.
  ◆ **Es liegt daran, dass ...** This is because ...
  ◆ **das Beste daran** the best thing about it
  ◆ **Ich war nahe daran, zu gehen.** I was on the point of going.

darauf ADVERB
  [1] on it ◊ *Nimm einen Untersetzer und stelle den Topf darauf.* Take a mat and put the pan on it.
  [2] afterwards ◊ *kurz darauf* shortly afterwards
  ◆ **die Tage darauf** the following days
  ◆ **am Tag darauf** the next day
  ◆ **Er ging darauf zu.** He walked towards it.
  ◆ **es kommt ganz darauf an, ob ...** it all depends whether ...

daraus ADVERB
  out of it ◊ *Sie nahm einen Keks daraus.* She took a biscuit out of it.
  ◆ **Was ist daraus geworden?** What became of it?
  ◆ **daraus geht hervor, dass ...** this means that ...

darf VERB see **dürfen**

darin ADVERB
  in it ◊ *eine Dose mit Keksen darin* a tin with biscuits in it
  ◆ **Darin sehe ich kein Problem.** I don't see any problem there.

der **Darm** NOUN (PL die **Därme**)
  intestine

darstellen VERB (PERFECT **hat dargestellt**)
  [1] to portray ◊ *etwas in einem günstigen Licht darstellen* to portray something in a good light

D

☞

2 to describe ◊ *So wie er es dargestellt hat, war alles ihre Schuld.* The way he described it, it was all her fault.

darüber ADVERB

1 over it ◊ *ein Tisch mit einer Lampe darüber* a table with a light over it ◊ *Da war eine Brücke, wir sind aber nicht darüber gefahren.* There was a bridge, but we didn't drive over it.

2 about it ◊ *Wir haben darüber gesprochen.* We talked about it. ◊ *Denk mal darüber nach.* Think about it.

3 more ◊ *Sie verdient fünftausend oder vielleicht sogar darüber.* She earns five thousand or maybe even more.

darum ADVERB, CONJUNCTION

1 round it ◊ *Sie machte ein rotes Band darum.* She put a red ribbon round it.

♦ **es geht darum, dass ...** the important thing is to ...

♦ **er würde viel darum geben, wenn ...** he would give a lot to ...

2 that's why ◊ *Darum bin ich nicht gekommen.* That's why I didn't come.

♦ **Ich tue es darum, weil ...** I'm doing it because ...

darunter ADVERB

1 under it ◊ *Der Topf ist heiß, leg einen Untersetzer darunter.* The pot's hot, put a mat under it.

♦ **ein Stockwerk darunter** one floor below

♦ **viele Jungen und zwei Mädchen darunter** a lot of boys and two girls

2 less ◊ *Er verdient nur dreitausend Euro oder vielleicht sogar darunter.* He earns only three thousand euros or maybe even less.

♦ **Was verstehst du darunter?** What do you understand by that?

das ARTICLE, PRONOUN

das is the definite neuter article.

1 the ◊ *das Auto* the car

♦ **das Leben** life

♦ **Er hat sich das Knie verletzt.** He's hurt his knee.

2 who ◊ *das Kind, das dir das gesagt hat* the child who told you

♦ **das Kind, das du gesehen hast** the child you saw

3 which ◊ *das Fahrrad, das du da siehst* the bike which you can see over there

♦ **das mit dem roten Sattel** the one with the red saddle

4 that ◊ *Das habe ich nicht gehört.* I didn't hear that.

♦ **das da** that one

dasein VERB *see* **da**

dass CONJUNCTION

that ◊ *Ich bin böse, dass er nicht gekommen ist.* I'm annoyed that he didn't come. ◊ *Ich weiß, dass du besser in Mathe bist als ich.* I know you're better at maths than me.

dasselbe PRONOUN

the same ◊ *dasselbe Kind* the same child

dastehen VERB (IMPERFECT **stand da,** PERFECT **hat dagestanden**)

to stand there

die **Datei** NOUN

file

die **Daten** NEUT PL NOUN

data

die **Datenbank** NOUN (PL die **Datenbanken**)

data base

die **Datenverarbeitung** NOUN

data processing

der **Dativ** NOUN (PL die **Dative**)

dative

das **Datum** NOUN (PL die **Daten**)

date

die **Dauer** NOUN

1 duration ◊ *für die Dauer meines Aufenthalts* for the duration of my stay

2 length ◊ *die Dauer einer Reise* the length of a journey ◊ *die Dauer eines Anrufs* the length of a call

♦ **von Dauer sein** to be permanent

♦ **Ihr Glück war nur von kurzer Dauer.** Their happiness was only short-lived.

♦ **auf die Dauer (1)** in the long run ◊ *Auf die Dauer wird ihm das langweilig werden.* He'll get bored with it in the long run.

♦ **auf die Dauer (2)** indefinitely ◊ *Auf die Dauer geht das aber nicht.* That can't go on indefinitely.

die **Dauerkarte** NOUN

season ticket

dauern VERB

to last ◊ *Der Krieg hat zehn Jahre gedauert.* The war lasted ten years.

♦ **lange dauern** to take a long time ◊ *Das hat lange gedauert.* That took a long time. ◊ *Es hat sehr lang gedauert, bis er ...* It took him a long time to ...

♦ **Wie lange dauert das denn noch?** How much longer is this going to take?

dauernd ADJECTIVE, ADVERB

constant ◊ *Ich konnte sein dauerndes Stöhnen nicht ertragen.* I couldn't stand his constant moaning.

♦ **Musst du mich dauernd stören?** Do you have to constantly interrupt me?

die **Dauerwelle** NOUN

perm

der **Daumen** NOUN (PL die **Daumen**)

thumb

♦ **Ich drücke dir die Daumen.** I'll keep my fingers crossed for you.

davon ADVERB

1 of them ◊ *Sie nahm zwei davon.* She took two of them.

♦ **Sie nahm hundert Gramm davon.** She took a hundred grams.

2 away ◊ *Er lief davon.* He ran away.

③ from it ◊ *Sie hat den Knopf davon abgetrennt.* She removed the button from it.
♦ **Sie bekommt Kopfschmerzen davon.** It gives her a headache.
♦ **davon abgesehen** apart from that
♦ **davon sprechen** to talk about it
♦ **Sie weiß nichts davon.** She doesn't know anything about it.
♦ **Was habe ich davon?** What's the point?
♦ **Das kommt davon!** That's what you get.

davonkommen VERB (IMPERFECT **kam davon,** PERFECT **ist davongekommen**)
to escape ◊ *Wir sind noch einmal davongekommen.* We've had a lucky escape.

davor ADVERB
① in front of it ◊ *Ich stellte mich davor.* I stood in front of it.
② first ◊ *Du solltest davor aber noch zum Friseur.* You ought to go to the hairdresser's first.
♦ **Ich habe dich davor gewarnt.** I warned you about it.

dazu ADVERB
with it ◊ *Was sollen wir dazu trinken?* What shall we drink with it?
♦ **ein Beispiel dazu** an example of this
♦ **seine Gedanken dazu** his thoughts on this
♦ **Möchtest du dich dazu äußern?** Do you wish to comment on it?
♦ **dazu fähig sein** to be capable of it
♦ **und dazu noch** and in addition

dazwischen ADVERB
① in between ◊ *Wir können dazwischen ja eine Pause machen.* We can have a break in between.
② between them ◊ *Siehst du die beiden Pfosten, stell dich dazwischen.* You see the two posts? Go and stand between them. ◊ *der Unterschied dazwischen* the difference between them

dazwischenkommen VERB (IMPERFECT **kam dazwischen,** PERFECT **ist dazwischengekommen**)
♦ **Es ist etwas dazwischengekommen.** Something's cropped up.

DB ABBREVIATION (= *Deutsche Bahn*)
German railways

die **DDR** NOUN (GEN der **DDR**)
(= *Deutsche Demokratische Republik*)
GDR ◊ *die ehemalige DDR* the former GDR

die **Decke** NOUN
① ceiling ◊ *Wir haben die Decke des Kinderzimmers gestrichen.* We've painted the ceiling of the children's room.
② blanket ◊ *eine Wolldecke* a woollen blanket
♦ **eine Tischdecke** a tablecloth

der **Deckel** NOUN (PL die **Deckel**)
lid

decken VERB
to cover ◊ *Er deckte die Hand über seine Augen.* He covered his eyes with his hand.
♦ **den Tisch decken** to lay the table

dehnen VERB
to stretch
♦ **Er dehnte sich und gähnte.** He stretched and yawned.

dein ADJECTIVE
① your ◊ *Dein Englischlehrer ist nett.* Your English teacher's nice. ◊ *Hat deine Mutter das erlaubt?* Did your mother let you? ◊ *Ist das dein Buch?* Is that your book? ◊ *Wo sind deine Eltern?* Where are your parents?
② yours ◊ *Der Bleistift hier, ist das deiner?* Is this pencil yours? ◊ *Meine Mutter heißt Ulla, wie heißt deine?* My mother's called Ulla, what's yours called? ◊ *Mein Fahrrad ist kaputt, kann ich deins benutzen?* My bike's broken, can I use yours? ◊ *Meine Noten waren nicht gut, wie waren deine?* My marks weren't good, what were yours like?

deinetwegen ADVERB
① for your sake ◊ *Ich habe deinetwegen darauf verzichtet.* I did without for your sake.
② on your account ◊ *Er hat sich deinetwegen aufgeregt.* He got upset on your account.

die **Deklination** NOUN
declension

deklinieren VERB (PERFECT **hat dekliniert**)
to decline

der **Delfin** NOUN (PL die **Delfine**)
dolphin

dem ARTICLE
dem is the dative of der and das.
the ◊ *auf dem Tisch* on the table
♦ **Gib es dem Mann.** Give it to the man.
♦ **der Mann, dem ich es gegeben habe** the man I gave it to

demnächst ADVERB
shortly

die **Demokratie** NOUN
democracy

demokratisch ADJECTIVE
democratic

die **Demonstration** NOUN
demonstration

demonstrieren VERB (PERFECT **hat demonstriert**)
to demonstrate

den ARTICLE
den is the accusative of der.
the ◊ *Ich sehe den Mann.* I can see the man. ◊ *durch den Wald* through the wood
♦ **Er hat sich den Fuß verletzt.** He's hurt his foot.

D

♦ **der Mann, den ich gesehen habe** the man I saw

denen PRONOUN

denen is the dative of die (plural).

[1] whom
♦ **die Leute, denen ich die Bücher gegeben habe** the people I gave the books to
♦ **die Leute, denen ich helfen wollte** the people I wanted to help
[2] which ◊ *Probleme, denen wir nicht gewachsen sind* problems which we can't cope with

denkbar ADJECTIVE
conceivable

denken VERB (IMPERFECT **dachte,** PERFECT **hat gedacht**)
to think

das **Denkmal** NOUN (PL die **Denkmäler**)
monument

denn CONJUNCTION, ADVERB
[1] because ◊ *Ich habe sie nicht gesehen, denn sie war schon weg.* I didn't see her because she had already left.
[2] than ◊ *besser denn je* better than ever
♦ **es sei denn ...** unless ...
♦ **Warum denn?** But why?

dennoch CONJUNCTION
nevertheless

deprimiert ADJECTIVE
depressed

der ARTICLE, PRONOUN

der is the definite masculine article and genitive and dative of die.

[1] the ◊ *der Mann* the man
♦ **der Tod** death
♦ **das Auto der Frau** the woman's car
♦ **Gib es der Frau.** Give it to the woman.
[2] who ◊ *der, der dir das gesagt hat* the person who told you that
♦ **die Frau, der ich es gegeben habe** the woman I gave it to
[3] which ◊ *der Computer, der mir gehört* the computer which belongs to me
♦ **der mit der Brille** the one with glasses
♦ **der da** that one

derselbe PRONOUN
the same ◊ *derselbe Mann* the same man

deshalb ADVERB
that's why

dessen PRONOUN

dessen is the genitive of der and das.

whose ◊ *mein Freund, dessen Schwester krank ist* my friend whose sister is ill

desto ADVERB
all the ◊ *desto besser* all the better
♦ **je ... desto ...** the ... the ... ◊ *Je mehr er sagte, desto wütender wurde sie.* The more he said, the angrier she became. ◊ *je eher, desto besser* the earlier the better

deswegen CONJUNCTION

that's why ◊ *Hat er deswegen so geschimpft?* Is that why he was so mad?
♦ **Es ist spät, deswegen gehen wir jetzt.** It's late, so we're leaving.
♦ **Ich sage das deswegen, weil das alle wissen müssen.** The reason I'm saying this is that everybody should know.

deutlich ADJECTIVE, ADVERB
[1] clear ◊ *mit klarer Stimme* in a clear voice
[2] clearly ◊ *Drück dich bitte deutlicher aus.* Please speak more clearly.
♦ **ein deutlicher Unterschied** a distinct difference

das **Deutsch** NOUN (GEN des **Deutschen**)

see also **deutsch** ADJECTIVE

German ◊ *Er lernt Deutsch in der Schule.* He's learning German at school.
♦ **auf Deutsch** in German

deutsch ADJECTIVE

see also **das Deutsch** NOUN

German

der **Deutsche** NOUN (GEN des/der **Deutschen,** PL
die die **Deutschen**)
German
♦ **Ich bin Deutscher.** I'm German.

Deutschland NEUT NOUN
Germany
♦ **aus Deutschland** from Germany
♦ **in Deutschland** in Germany
♦ **nach Deutschland** to Germany

der **Dezember** NOUN (GEN des **Dezember** or **Dezembers,** PL die **Dezember**)
December ◊ *im Dezember* in December ◊ *am vierten Dezember* on the fourth of December ◊ *Ulm, den 5. Dezember 2003* Ulm, 5 December 2003 ◊ *Heute ist der sechste Dezember.* Today is the sixth of December.

das **Dezimalsystem** NOUN
decimal system

DGB ABBREVIATION (= *Deutscher Gewerkschaftsbund*)
German trade union federation

d. h. ABBREVIATION (= *das heißt*)
i.e.

das **Dia** NOUN (PL die **Dias**)
slide

diagonal ADJECTIVE
diagonal

der **Dialekt** NOUN (PL die **Dialekte**)
dialect

der **Diamant** NOUN (GEN des **Diamanten,** PL die **Diamanten**)
diamond

die **Diät** NOUN
diet ◊ *Sie muss Diät halten.* She has to stick to a strict diet.

dich PRONOUN
[1] you ◊ *Ich habe dich gesehen.* I saw you.

[2] yourself ◇ *Sieh dich mal im Spiegel an.* Look at yourself in the mirror.

dicht ADJECTIVE, ADVERB
[1] dense ◇ *dichte Wälder* dense woods
[2] thick ◇ *dichter Nebel* thick fog
[3] watertight ◇ *Ist der Behälter dicht?* Is the container watertight?
♦ **Die Gasleitung war nicht dicht.** There was a leak in the gas pipe.
♦ **dichter Verkehr** heavy traffic
♦ **dicht an** close to ◇ *Geh nicht zu dicht ans Feuer.* Don't go too close to the fire.

der **Dichter** NOUN (PL die **Dichter**)
poet

dick ADJECTIVE
[1] thick ◇ *Das Brett ist drei Zentimeter dick.* The plank's three centimetres thick.
[2] fat ◇ *Ich bin zu dick.* I'm too fat.

der **Dickkopf** NOUN (PL die **Dickköpfe**)
♦ **einen Dickkopf haben** to be stubborn

die **Dickmilch** NOUN
soured milk

die ARTICLE, PRONOUN

die is the definite feminine article and the definite article plural.

[1] the ◇ *die Frau* the woman ◇ *die Kinder* the children
♦ **die Liebe** love
♦ **Er hat sich die Hand verletzt.** He's hurt his hand.
[2] who ◇ *die, die dir das gesagt hat* the person who told you that
♦ **die Frau, die du gesehen hast** the woman you saw
[3] which ◇ *die Uhr, die mir gehört* the watch which belongs to me
♦ **die mit der Brille** the one with glasses
♦ **die da** that one

der **Dieb** NOUN (PL die **Diebe**)
thief

der **Diebstahl** NOUN (PL die **Diebstähle**)
theft

die **Diele** NOUN
hall ◇ *Sie stand vor dem Spiegel in der Diele.* She stood in front of the mirror in the hall.

dienen VERB (PERFECT **hat gedient**)
to serve ◇ *Es dient einem guten Zweck.* It serves a useful purpose.
♦ **womit kann ich Ihnen dienen?** what can I do for you?

der **Dienst** NOUN (PL die **Dienste**)
service
♦ **Dienst haben** to be on duty

der **Dienstag** NOUN (PL die **Dienstage**)
Tuesday ◇ *am Dienstag* on Tuesday

dienstags ADVERB
on Tuesdays

dies PRONOUN
[1] this ◇ *Dies ist unser Haus.* This is our house.
[2] these ◇ *Dies sind meine Bücher.* These are my books.

diese PRONOUN
[1] this ◇ *Dieses Kleid gefällt mir besonders gut.* I particularly like this dress.
[2] these ◇ *diese Bücher* these books
[3] this one ◇ *Ich möchte diesen hier.* I'd like this one.
[4] these ones ◇ *Ich suche ein Paar Sandalen, kann ich diese anprobieren?* I'm looking for a pair of sandals, can I try these ones on?

der **Diesel** NOUN
diesel

dieselbe PRONOUN
the same ◇ *dieselbe Frau* the same woman

diesmal ADVERB
this time

digital ADJECTIVE
digital ◇ *die digitale Revolution* the digital revolution

das **Digitalfernsehen** NOUN
digital television

das **Diktat** NOUN (PL die **Diktate**)
dictation

diktieren VERB (PERFECT **hat diktiert**)
to dictate

das **Ding** NOUN (PL die **Dinge**)
thing

das **Diplom** NOUN (PL die **Diplome**)
diploma

die **Diplomatie** NOUN
diplomacy

diplomatisch ADJECTIVE
diplomatic

dir PRONOUN

dir is the dative of du.

[1] you ◇ *Ich habe es dir doch gesagt.* I told you so.
[2] to you ◇ *Ich habe es dir gestern gegeben.* I gave it to you yesterday.

direkt ADJECTIVE
direct ◇ *Der Flug geht direkt.* It's a direct flight.

der **Direktor** NOUN (PL die **Direktoren**)
[1] director ◇ *der Direktor der Firma* the director of the company
[2] headmaster ◇ *Mein Bruder musste gestern zum Direktor.* My brother was sent to the headmaster yesterday.

die **Direktübertragung** NOUN
live broadcast

der **Dirigent** NOUN (GEN des **Dirigenten,** PL die **Dirigenten**)
conductor (of orchestra)

dirigieren VERB (PERFECT **hat dirigiert**)
to conduct ◇ *Wer dirigiert das Orchester?* Who's conducting the orchestra?

die **Disco** NOUN (PL die **Discos**)
disco

die **Diskette** NOUN

diskette

die **Diskothek** NOUN
disco

die **Diskussion** NOUN
discussion
♦ **zur Diskussion stehen** to be under
discussion

das **Diskuswerfen** NOUN
throwing the discus

diskutieren VERB (PERFECT **hat diskutiert**)
to discuss ◊ *Wir haben über Politik
diskutiert.* We discussed politics.

DJH ABBREVIATION (= *Deutsches
Jugendherbergswerk*)
German Youth Hostel Association

DM ABBREVIATION (= *Deutsche Mark*)
Deutschmark

die **D-Mark** NOUN (PL die **D-Mark**)
Deutschmark

doch ADVERB, CONJUNCTION
⓵ after all ◊ *Sie ist doch noch
gekommen.* She came after all.
⓶ anyway ◊ *Du machst ja doch, was du
willst.* You do what you want anyway.
⓷ but ◊ *Ich habe ihn eingeladen, doch er
hatte keine Lust.* I invited him, but he
didn't feel like it. ◊ *Sie ist doch noch so
jung.* But she's still so young.
⓸ yes

doch is used to contradict a negative
statement.

◊ *Du magst doch keine Süßigkeiten. –
Doch!* You don't like sweets. – Yes I do.
◊ *Er ist sicher kein Österreicher. – Doch.*
I'm sure he's not an Austrian. – Yes he is.
◊ *Das ist nicht wahr. – Doch!* That's not
true. – Yes it is!
♦ **Komm doch.** Do come.
♦ **Lass ihn doch.** Just leave him.

der **Doktor** NOUN (PL die **Doktoren**)
doctor ◊ *Er ist Doktor der Philosophie.*
He's a doctor of philosophy.

das **Dokument** NOUN
document

der **Dokumentarfilm** NOUN (PL die
Dokumentarfilme)
documentary

die **Dokumentation** NOUN
documentation

dolmetschen VERB
to interpret

der **Dolmetscher** NOUN (PL die **Dolmetscher**)
interpreter

der **Dom** NOUN (PL die **Dome**)
cathedral

die **Donau** NOUN
Danube

der **Donner** NOUN (PL die **Donner**)
thunder

donnern VERB
to thunder ◊ *Es donnerte.* It was
thundering.

der **Donnerstag** NOUN (PL die **Donnerstage**)
Thursday ◊ *am Donnerstag* on Thursday

donnerstags ADVERB
on Thursdays

doof ADJECTIVE
thick

das **Doppelbett** NOUN (PL die **Doppelbetten**)
double bed

die **Doppelfenster** NEUT PL NOUN
double glazing

das **Doppelhaus** NOUN (GEN des **Doppelhauses**,
PL die **Doppelhäuser**)
semidetached house

der **Doppelpunkt** NOUN (PL die **Doppelpunkte**)
colon

die **Doppelstunde** NOUN
double period

doppelt ADJECTIVE
⓵ double ◊ *die doppelte Menge* double
the amount
⓶ twice the ◊ *der doppelte Preis* twice
the price ◊ *die doppelte Geschwindigkeit*
twice the speed
♦ **doppelt so viel** twice as much
♦ **in doppelter Ausführung** in duplicate

das **Doppelzimmer** NOUN (PL die
Doppelzimmer)
double room

das **Dorf** NOUN (PL die **Dörfer**)
village

dort ADVERB
there
♦ **dort drüben** over there

dorther ADVERB
from there

dorthin ADVERB
there ◊ *Wir gehen jetzt dorthin.* We're
going there now.

die **Dose** NOUN
tin

der **Dosenöffner** NOUN (PL die **Dosenöffner**)
tin opener

der **Dotter** NOUN (PL die **Dotter**)
yolk

der **Drache** NOUN (GEN des **Drachen**, PL die
Drachen)
dragon ◊ *Ein Drache bewacht den
Schatz.* A dragon guards the treasure.

der **Drachen** NOUN (PL die **Drachen**)
kite ◊ *Wir haben Drachen fliegen lassen.*
We've been flying our kites.

das **Drachenfliegen** NOUN
hang-gliding ◊ *Er ist beim
Drachenfliegen verunglückt.* He had a
hang-gliding accident.

der **Draht** NOUN (PL die **Drähte**)
wire
♦ **auf Draht sein** to be on the ball

das **Drama** NOUN (PL die **Dramen**)
drama

dran ADVERB
♦ **Jetzt bin ich dran!** It's my turn now.

♦ **Wer ist dran?** Whose turn is it?
♦ **gut dran sein** to be well-off
♦ **schlecht dran sein** to be in a bad way

drauf ADVERB see **darauf**

draußen ADVERB
outside

der **Dreck** NOUN
dirt

dreckig ADJECTIVE
dirty ◊ *Mach deine Kleider nicht dreckig.*
Don't get your clothes dirty.

drehen VERB
to turn ◊ *Dreh mal deinen Kopf zur Seite.*
Turn your head to one side.
♦ **eine Zigarette drehen** to roll a cigarette
♦ **einen Film drehen** to shoot a film
♦ **sich drehen** to turn
♦ **es dreht sich um ...** it's about ...

drei NUMBER
see also **die Drei** NOUN
three

die **Drei** NOUN
see also **drei** NUMBER
1 three
2 satisfactory

*ⓘ German marks range from one (**sehr gut**) to six (**ungenügend**).*

das **Dreieck** NOUN (PL die **Dreiecke**)
triangle

dreieckig ADJECTIVE
triangular

dreihundert NUMBER
three hundred

dreimal ADVERB
three times

dreißig NUMBER
thirty

dreiviertel NUMBER
three-quarters

die **Dreiviertelstunde** NOUN
three-quarters of an hour ◊ *Eine Dreiviertelstunde war vergangen.* Three-quarters of an hour had passed.

dreizehn NUMBER
thirteen

drin ADVERB see **darin**

dringend ADJECTIVE
urgent

drinnen ADVERB
inside

dritte ADJECTIVE
third ◊ *Sie nahm beim dritten Klingeln ab.* She answered on the third ring. ◊ *Er kam als Dritter.* He was the third to arrive.
♦ **die Dritte Welt** the Third World
♦ **das Dritte Reich** the Third Reich

das **Drittel** NOUN (PL die **Drittel**)
third

drittens ADVERB
thirdly

die **Droge** NOUN
drug

drogenabhängig ADJECTIVE
addicted to drugs

die **Drogerie** NOUN
chemist's shop

der **Drogist** NOUN (GEN des **Drogisten,** PL die **Drogisten**)
pharmacist

die **Drogistin** NOUN
pharmacist

drohen VERB
to threaten ◊ *jemandem drohen* to threaten somebody

drüben ADVERB
over there

der **Druck** NOUN (PL die **Drucke**)
1 pressure ◊ *Der Behälter muss viel Druck aushalten.* The container has to withstand a lot of pressure.
♦ **jemanden unter Druck setzen** to put pressure on somebody
2 printing ◊ *der Druck eines Buches* the printing of a book
3 print ◊ *An der Wand hingen Drucke.* There were prints on the wall.

drücken VERB
1 to press ◊ *Er drückte auf den Knopf.* He pressed the button.
♦ **Sie drückte ihm die Hand.** She squeezed his hand.
2 to pinch ◊ *Meine Schuhe drücken.* My shoes pinch.
♦ **sich vor etwas drücken** to get out of something ◊ *Du willst dich bloß wieder vor dem Abwasch drücken.* You just want to get out of washing up again.

der **Drucker** NOUN (PL die **Drucker**)
printer

der **Druckknopf** NOUN (PL die **Druckknöpfe**)
press stud

die **Drucksache** NOUN
printed matter

die **Druckschrift** NOUN
block letters

die **Drüse** NOUN
gland

der **Dschungel** NOUN (PL die **Dschungel**)
jungle

DTP ABBREVIATION (= *Desktop-Publishing*)
DTP

du PRONOUN
you ◊ *Hast du das gesehen?* Did you see that?
♦ **du sagen** to use the "du" form of address

*ⓘ The familiar form of address **du** (plural **ihr**) is used when addressing family members, friends, children under 16 and pets.*

sich **ducken** VERB
　　to duck

der **Dudelsack** NOUN (PL die **Dudelsäcke**)
　　bagpipes ◊ *Er spielt Dudelsack.* He
　　plays the bagpipes.

der **Duft** NOUN (PL die **Düfte**)
　　scent

duften VERB
　　to smell ◊ *Hier duftet es nach Kaffee.* It
　　smells of coffee here.

dumm ADJECTIVE
　　[1] stupid ◊ *Das ist die dümmste
　　Ausrede, die ich je gehört habe.*
　　That's the stupidest excuse I've ever
　　heard.
　　[2] bad ◊ *Es ist wirklich zu dumm, dass
　　du nicht gekommen bist.* It's really too
　　bad that you didn't come.
　　♦ **der Dumme sein** to draw the short straw

dummerweise ADVERB
　　stupidly

die **Dummheit** NOUN
　　[1] stupidity ◊ *Deine Dummheit ist
　　wirklich grenzenlos.* Your stupidity really
　　knows no bounds.
　　[2] stupid mistake ◊ *Es war eine
　　Dummheit, ihr das zu erzählen.* It was a
　　stupid mistake telling her that.
　　♦ **Dummheiten machen** to do
　　something stupid ◊ *Macht bloß keine
　　Dummheiten!* Don't do anything
　　stupid.

der **Dummkopf** NOUN (PL die **Dummköpfe**)
　　idiot

der **Dünger** NOUN (PL die **Dünger**)
　　fertilizer

dunkel ADJECTIVE
　　dark ◊ *Im Zimmer war es dunkel.* It was
　　dark in the room.
　　♦ **eine dunkle Stimme** a deep voice
　　♦ **eine dunkle Ahnung** a vague idea
　　♦ **dunkle Gestalten** sinister figures
　　♦ **dunkle Geschäfte** shady dealings
　　♦ **im Dunkeln tappen** to grope about in the
　　dark
　　♦ **ein Dunkles** a dark beer

die **Dunkelheit** NOUN
　　dark ◊ *Er hat Angst vor der Dunkelheit.*
　　He's afraid of the dark.

dünn ADJECTIVE
　　thin

der **Dunst** NOUN (PL die **Dünste**)
　　haze

durch PREPOSITION, ADVERB
　　*The preposition **durch** takes the
　　accusative.*
　　[1] through ◊ *durch den Wald* through
　　the wood ◊ *Ich habe die Stelle durch
　　meinen Onkel bekommen.* I got the job
　　through my uncle. ◊ *durch seine
　　Bemühungen* through his efforts
　　[2] throughout ◊ *die ganze Nacht durch*
　　throughout the night ◊ *den Sommer*

durch throughout the summer
　　[3] owing to ◊ *Durch die Verspätung
　　haben wir den Anschluss verpasst.*
　　Owing to the delay we missed our
　　connection.
　　♦ **Tod durch Herzschlag** death from a heart
　　attack
　　♦ **durch die Post** by post
　　♦ **durch und durch** completely ◊ *Wir waren
　　durch und durch nass.* We were
　　completely soaked.

durcharbeiten VERB (PERFECT **hat
　　durchgearbeitet**)
　　to work without a break

durchblättern VERB (PERFECT **hat
　　durchgeblättert**)
　　to leaf through

der **Durchblick** NOUN (PL die **Durchblicke**)
　　♦ **Der hat den Durchblick.** He knows what's
　　what.

durchblicken VERB (PERFECT **hat
　　durchgeblickt**)
　　to understand
　　♦ **Bei Computern blickt Tobias durch.**
　　Tobias knows his stuff with
　　computers.
　　♦ **etwas durchblicken lassen** to hint at
　　something

durchdrehen VERB (PERFECT **ist
　　durchgedreht**)
　　to crack up

durcheinander ADVERB
　　see also **das Durcheinander** NOUN
　　[1] in a mess ◊ *Warum ist dein Zimmer
　　so durcheinander?* Why is your room in
　　such a mess?
　　[2] confused ◊ *Ich war völlig
　　durcheinander.* I was completely
　　confused.
　　♦ **Du bringst mich ganz durcheinander.**
　　You completely confuse me.

das **Durcheinander** NOUN
　　see also **durcheinander** ADVERB
　　[1] mess ◊ *In ihrem Zimmer war ein
　　völliges Durcheinander.* Her room was in
　　a complete mess.
　　[2] confusion ◊ *Im Durcheinander des
　　Aufbruchs habe ich das ganz vergessen.*
　　In the confusion of leaving I completely
　　forgot it.

durcheinandertrinken VERB (IMPERFECT **trank
　　durcheinander,** PERFECT **hat durcheinandergetrunken**)
　　♦ **alles durcheinandertrinken** to mix one's
　　drinks

durchfahren VERB (PRESENT **fährt durch,**
　　IMPERFECT **fuhr durch,** PERFECT **ist
　　durchgefahren**)
　　[1] to drive through ◊ *Wir sind durch
　　einen Tunnel durchgefahren.* We drove
　　through a tunnel.
　　[2] to drive without a break ◊ *Wir sind
　　die ganze Nacht durchgefahren.* We
　　drove all night without a break.

◆ **Der Zug fährt bis Hamburg durch.** The train runs direct to Hamburg.

die **Durchfahrt** NOUN (PL die **Durchfahrten**)
way through ◊ *auf unserer Durchfahrt durch Frankreich* on our way through France

◆ **"Durchfahrt verboten"** "no through road"

der **Durchfall** NOUN
diarrhoea

durchfallen VERB (PRESENT **fällt durch**, IMPERFECT **fiel durch**, PERFECT **ist durchgefallen**)
1 to fall through ◊ *Die Münze ist durch dieses Gitter durchgefallen.* The coin fell through this grating.
2 to fail ◊ *Sie ist in der Prüfung durchgefallen.* She failed the exam.

durchführen VERB (PERFECT **hat durchgeführt**)
to carry out

der **Durchgang** NOUN (PL die **Durchgänge**)
passageway ◊ *Zwischen den Häusern ist ein schmaler Durchgang.* There's a narrow passageway between the houses.

der **Durchgangsverkehr** NOUN
through traffic

durchgehen VERB (IMPERFECT **ging durch**, PERFECT **ist durchgegangen**)
1 to go through ◊ *durch einen Tunnel durchgehen* to go through a tunnel
2 to break loose ◊ *Das Pferd ist durchgegangen.* The horse has broken loose.

◆ **jemandem etwas durchgehen lassen** to let somebody get away with something

◆ **ein durchgehender Zug** a through train

durchkommen VERB (IMPERFECT **kam durch**, PERFECT **ist durchgekommen**)
1 to get through ◊ *Obwohl die Öffnung sehr schmal war, sind wir durchgekommen.* Although the opening was very narrow, we got through.
2 to pass ◊ *Es war knapp, aber ich bin durchgekommen.* It was a close shave, but I passed.
3 to pull through ◊ *Er war schwer verletzt, ist aber durchgekommen.* He was seriously injured, but he pulled through.

durchlassen VERB (PRESENT **lässt durch**, IMPERFECT **ließ durch**, PERFECT **hat durchgelassen**)
to let through ◊ *Der Ordner wollte uns nicht durchlassen.* The steward didn't want to let us through.

◆ **Der Behälter lässt Wasser durch.** The container isn't watertight.

durchlesen VERB (PRESENT **liest durch**, IMPERFECT **las durch**, PERFECT **hat durchgelesen**)
to read through

durchmachen VERB (PERFECT **hat durchgemacht**)
to go through ◊ *Sie hat viel durchgemacht in ihrem Leben.* She's been through a lot in her life.

◆ **die Nacht durchmachen** to make a night of it

der **Durchmesser** NOUN (PL die **Durchmesser**)
diameter

durchnehmen VERB (PRESENT **nimmt durch**, IMPERFECT **nahm durch**, PERFECT **hat durchgenommen**)
to do ◊ *Wir nehmen gerade Shakespeare durch.* We're doing Shakespeare just now.

die **Durchreise** NOUN
journey through ◊ *die Durchreise durch die Schweiz* the journey through Switzerland

◆ **Ich bin nur auf der Durchreise.** I'm just passing through.

durchs = **durch das**

der **Durchschnitt** NOUN
average ◊ *Mein Notendurchschnitt liegt bei zwei.* My average mark is a "B".
◊ *über dem Durchschnitt* above average
◊ *unter dem Durchschnitt* below average
◊ *im Durchschnitt* on average

durchschnittlich ADJECTIVE, ADVERB
1 average ◊ *Ich habe durchschnittliche Noten.* My marks are average.
2 on average ◊ *Durchschnittlich brauche ich eine Stunde für die Hausaufgaben.* On average, my homework takes me an hour.

durchsehen VERB (PRESENT **sieht durch**, IMPERFECT **sah durch**, PERFECT **hat durchgesehen**)
to look through

durchsetzen VERB (PERFECT **hat durchgesetzt**)

◆ **sich durchsetzen** to assert oneself ◊ *Er kann sich nicht durchsetzen.* He doesn't know how to assert himself.

◆ **Du solltest dich mehr durchsetzen.** You should be more assertive.

◆ **Sie muss immer ihren Willen durchsetzen.** She always has to have her own way.

◆ **seinen Kopf durchsetzen** to get one's way

durchsichtig ADJECTIVE
transparent

durchsprechen VERB (PRESENT **spricht durch**, IMPERFECT **sprach durch**, PERFECT **hat durchgesprochen**)
to talk over

durchsuchen VERB (PERFECT **hat durchsucht**)
to search

dürfen VERB (PRESENT **darf**, IMPERFECT **durfte**, PERFECT **hat gedurft** or **dürfen**)
to be allowed to ◊ *Ich darf das.* I'm allowed to do that. ◊ *Er darf das nicht.* He's not allowed to do that. ◊ *Ich habe*

D

leider nicht gedurft. Unfortunately, I wasn't allowed.

◆ **Darf ich?** May I?

◆ **Darf ich ins Kino?** Can I go to the cinema?

> The past participle **dürfen** is used when **dürfen** is a modal auxiliary.

◆ **etwas tun dürfen** to be allowed to do something ◊ *Die Kinder haben gestern länger aufbleiben dürfen.* The children were allowed to stay up late yesterday.

◆ **Es darf geraucht werden.** You may smoke.

◆ **darf nicht** must not ◊ *Das darf nicht geschehen.* That must not happen.

◆ **Da darf sie sich nicht wundern.** That shouldn't surprise her.

◆ **Das darf nicht wahr sein!** I don't believe it!

◆ **Darf ich Sie bitten, das zu tun?** Could I ask you to do that?

◆ **Was darf es sein?** What can I do for you?

◆ **Das dürfen Sie mir glauben.** You can take my word for it.

◆ **Das dürfte genug sein.** That should be enough.

◆ **Es dürfte Ihnen bekannt sein, dass ...** As you will probably know ...

die **Dürre** NOUN

drought ◊ *In Äthiopien hat es eine Dürre gegeben.* There was a drought in Ethiopia.

der **Durst** NOUN

thirst

◆ **Durst haben** to be thirsty

durstig ADJECTIVE

thirsty

die **Dusche** NOUN

shower

duschen VERB

to have a shower

◆ **sich duschen** to have a shower

das **Düsenflugzeug** NOUN (PL die **Düsenflugzeuge**)

jet (*plane*)

düster ADJECTIVE

1 dark ◊ *Hier drin ist es so düster.* It's so dark in here.

2 gloomy

das **Dutzend** NOUN (PL die **Dutzende** or **Dutzend**)

dozen ◊ *zwei Dutzend Bücher* two dozen books

duzen VERB

to address sb as "du"

> ℹ The familiar form of address **du** (plural **ihr**) is used when addressing family members, friends, children under 16 and pets.

dynamisch ADJECTIVE

dynamic

der **D-Zug** NOUN (PL die **D-Züge**)

through train

E

die **Ebbe** NOUN
　　low tide ◊ *bei Ebbe* at low tide
eben ADJECTIVE, ADVERB
　　1 flat ◊ *eine ebene Fläche* a flat surface
　　2 just ◊ *Er ist eben erst gegangen.* He's just gone.
　　3 exactly ◊ *Eben, das sage ich ja.* That's exactly what I'm saying.
　　◆ **eben deswegen** that's precisely why
die **Ebene** NOUN
　　1 plain ◊ *Wir sahen auf die Ebene hinunter.* We looked down onto the plain.
　　2 level ◊ *Das muss auf höherer Ebene entschieden werden.* That has to be decided at a higher level.
ebenfalls ADVERB
　　likewise
ebenso ADVERB
　　just as ◊ *Sie ist ebenso groß wie ihr Bruder.* She's just as tall as her brother.
das **Echo** NOUN (PL die **Echos**)
　　echo
echt ADJECTIVE, ADVERB
　　1 real ◊ *echtes Gold* real gold
　　◆ **Der Geldschein ist nicht echt.** That banknote's a fake.
　　2 really ◊ *Die Party war echt gut.* The party was really good.
　　◆ **Echt?** Really?
die **Ecke** NOUN
　　corner ◊ *um die Ecke* round the corner
der **Edelstein** NOUN (PL die **Edelsteine**)
　　precious stone
die **EDV** NOUN (= *elektronische Datenverarbeitung*)
　　electronic data processing
die **EG** NOUN (= *Europäische Gemeinschaft*)
　　EC
egal ADJECTIVE
　　all the same ◊ *Das ist mir egal.* It's all the same to me.
　　◆ **Das ist egal.** That makes no difference.
　　◆ **Egal, ob er das gesagt hat oder nicht.** It doesn't matter whether he said it or not.
egoistisch ADJECTIVE
　　selfish
die **Ehe** NOUN
　　| see also **ehe** CONJUNCTION |
　　marriage
ehe CONJUNCTION
　　| see also **die Ehe** NOUN |
　　before ◊ *Ehe ich es vergesse, ...* Before I forget, ...
die **Ehefrau** NOUN
　　wife
ehemalig ADJECTIVE
　　former

der **Ehemann** NOUN (PL die **Ehemänner**)
　　husband
das **Ehepaar** NOUN (PL die **Ehepaare**)
　　married couple
eher ADVERB
　　sooner ◊ *Das hättest du eher sagen müssen.* You should have said that sooner.
　　◆ **Das kommt schon eher der Wahrheit nahe.** That's more like the truth.
die **Ehre** NOUN
　　honour
ehrgeizig ADJECTIVE
　　ambitious
ehrlich ADJECTIVE
　　honest
die **Ehrlichkeit** NOUN
　　honesty
das **Ei** NOUN (PL die **Eier**)
　　egg
die **Eiche** NOUN
　　oak
das **Eichhörnchen** NOUN (PL die **Eichhörnchen**)
　　squirrel
der **Eid** NOUN (PL die **Eide**)
　　oath ◊ *einen Eid schwören* to swear an oath
die **Eidechse** NOUN
　　lizard
der **Eierbecher** NOUN (PL die **Eierbecher**)
　　egg cup
der **Eifer** NOUN
　　enthusiasm
die **Eifersucht** NOUN
　　jealousy
eifersüchtig ADJECTIVE
　　jealous ◊ *Er ist eifersüchtig auf seine Schwester.* He's jealous of his sister.
eifrig ADJECTIVE
　　eager
das **Eigelb** NOUN (PL die **Eigelb**)
　　egg yolk
eigen ADJECTIVE
　　own ◊ *meine eigene Meinung* my own opinion
die **Eigenart** NOUN
　　peculiarity ◊ *Wir haben alle unsere Eigenarten.* We all have our own peculiarities.
eigenartig ADJECTIVE
　　peculiar
die **Eigenschaft** NOUN
　　quality
eigensinnig ADJECTIVE
　　obstinate
eigentlich ADJECTIVE, ADVERB

1 actual ◊ *Er ist der eigentliche Besitzer.* He's the actual owner.

2 actually ◊ *Eigentlich wollte ich heute nicht weggehen.* Actually I didn't want to go out today.

♦ **Eigentlich nicht.** Not really.

das **Eigentum** NOUN
property

der **Eigentümer** NOUN (PL die **Eigentümer**)
owner

sich **eignen** VERB
to be suited ◊ *Er eignet sich nicht für diese Stelle.* He's not suited to this position.

eilen VERB
to be urgent ◊ *Das eilt nicht.* It's not urgent.

eilig ADJECTIVE
urgent ◊ *Ich muss zuerst die eiligen Dinge erledigen.* I'll have to do the urgent things first.

♦ **es eilig haben** to be in a hurry

der **Eilzug** NOUN (PL die **Eilzüge**)
fast stopping train

der **Eimer** NOUN (PL die **Eimer**)
bucket

ein NUMBER, ARTICLE

see also **eins** NUMBER, die **Eins** NOUN

1 one ◊ *Es war nur ein Kind da.* There was only one child there. ◊ *Ich möchte nur einen.* I only want one.

2 somebody ◊ *Wenn einer dir das sagt, glaube es nicht.* If somebody tells you that, don't believe it.

3 you ◊ *Da kann einem die Lust vergehen.* It's enough to put you off.

4 a ◊ *ein Mann* a man ◊ *eine Frau* a woman ◊ *ein Kind* a child

an ◊ *ein Ei* an egg ◊ *eine Stunde* an hour

einander PRONOUN
each other

einatmen VERB (PERFECT **hat eingeatmet**)
to breathe in

die **Einbahnstraße** NOUN
one-way street

einbiegen VERB (IMPERFECT **bog ein,** PERFECT **ist eingebogen**)
to turn ◊ *Er ist in die zweite Seitenstraße eingebogen.* He turned down the second side street.

einbilden VERB (PERFECT **hat eingebildet**)
♦ **sich etwas einbilden** to imagine something ◊ *Das bildest du dir nur ein.* You're imagining it.

einbrechen VERB (PRESENT **bricht ein,** IMPERFECT **brach ein,** PERFECT **ist eingebrochen**)
to break in ◊ *Bei ihnen wurde eingebrochen.* Their house has been broken into. ◊ *Er ist in das Haus eingebrochen.* He broke into the house.

der **Einbrecher** NOUN (PL die **Einbrecher**)
burglar

der **Einbruch** NOUN (PL die **Einbrüche**)
break-in ◊ *In dieser Gegend gibt es häufiger Einbrüche.* There are a lot of break-ins in this area.

♦ **bei Einbruch der Nacht** at nightfall
♦ **vor Einbruch der Nacht** before nightfall

eincremen VERB (PERFECT **hat eingecremt**)
to put cream on

eindeutig ADJECTIVE
clear ◊ *eine eindeutige Antwort geben* to give a clear answer

der **Eindruck** NOUN (PL die **Eindrücke**)
impression

eindrucksvoll ADJECTIVE
impressive

eine see **ein**

eineinhalb NUMBER
one and a half

einer see **ein**

einerseits ADVERB
on the one hand ◊ *Einerseits ..., andererseits ...* On the one hand ..., on the other hand ...

eines see **ein**

einfach ADJECTIVE, ADVERB

1 easy ◊ *Das war eine einfache Frage.* That was an easy question. ◊ *Das ist nicht einfach.* That isn't easy.

2 simple ◊ *aus dem einfachen Grund ...* for the simple reason ... ◊ *Sie leben in sehr einfachen Verhältnissen.* They live very simple lives.

3 single ◊ *eine einfache Fahrkarte* a single ticket

4 simply ◊ *Ich will das einfach nicht.* I simply don't want it. ◊ *Er wollte einfach nicht begreifen.* He simply didn't want to understand.

die **Einfachheit** NOUN
simplicity

die **Einfahrt** NOUN
entrance

der **Einfall** NOUN (PL die **Einfälle**)
idea ◊ *Das war so ein Einfall von mir.* It was just an idea. ◊ *Du hast manchmal Einfälle!* You do come up with strange ideas sometimes!

einfallen VERB (PRESENT **fällt ein,** IMPERFECT **fiel ein,** PERFECT **ist eingefallen**)
♦ **jemandem einfallen** to occur to somebody ◊ *Mir ist das Wort nicht eingefallen.* The word didn't occur to me.

♦ **Das fällt mir gar nicht ein.** I wouldn't dream of it.

♦ **sich etwas einfallen lassen** to come up with a good idea ◊ *Meine Freunde haben sich zu meinem Geburtstag etwas Tolles einfallen lassen.* My friends came up with a really great idea for my birthday.

◆ **Lass dir was einfallen.** See if you can think of something.

das **Einfamilienhaus** NOUN (GEN des **Einfamilienhauses**, PL die **Einfamilienhäuser**)
detached family house

einfarbig ADJECTIVE
plain

der **Einfluss** NOUN (GEN des **Einflusses**, PL die **Einflüsse**)
influence ◊ *Er hat einen schlechten Einfluss auf dich.* He has a bad influence on you.

einfrieren VERB (IMPERFECT **fror ein**, PERFECT **hat/ist eingefroren**)

*For the perfect tense use **haben** when the verb has an object and **sein** when there is no object.*

to freeze ◊ *Wir haben die Reste eingefroren.* We've frozen the left-overs. ◊ *Die Leitung ist eingefroren.* The pipe has frozen.

die **Einfuhr** NOUN
import

die **Eingabe** NOUN
input ◊ *die Eingabe von Daten* data input

der **Eingang** NOUN (PL die **Eingänge**)
entrance

eingeben VERB (PRESENT **gibt ein**, IMPERFECT **gab ein**, PERFECT **hat eingegeben**)
to enter ◊ *Beate hat den Text in den Computer eingegeben.* Beate entered the text into the computer.

eingebildet ADJECTIVE
conceited ◊ *Sie ist furchtbar eingebildet.* She's terribly conceited.
◆ **Ihre Krankheit ist nur eingebildet.** Her illness is all in the imagination.

der **Eingeborene** NOUN (GEN des/der
die **Eingeborenen**, PL die **Eingeborenen**)
native

eingehen VERB (IMPERFECT **ging ein**, PERFECT **ist eingegangen**)
1 to die ◊ *Mir ist schon wieder eine Pflanze eingegangen.* Another of my plants has died.
2 to shrink ◊ *Der Pulli ist in der Wäsche eingegangen.* The pullover shrank in the wash.
◆ **auf etwas eingehen** to comment on something ◊ *Er ist auf meinen Vorschlag nicht eingegangen.* He didn't comment on my suggestion.

eingenommen ADJECTIVE
◆ **eingenommen von** taken with ◊ *Ich war sofort von dem Plan eingenommen.* I was immediately taken with the plan.
◆ **Du bist ja ziemlich von dir eingenommen.** You really fancy yourself.

eingeschrieben ADJECTIVE
registered ◊ *ein eingeschriebener Brief* a registered letter

eingestellt ADJECTIVE

◆ **auf etwas eingestellt sein** to be prepared for something ◊ *Ich war nicht auf Ihren Besuch eingestellt.* I wasn't prepared for your visit.

eingießen VERB (IMPERFECT **goss ein**, PERFECT **hat eingegossen**)
to pour ◊ *Darf ich Ihnen noch Kaffee eingießen?* Can I pour you some more coffee?

sich **eingewöhnen** VERB (PERFECT **hat sich eingewöhnt**)
◆ **sich eingewöhnen in** to settle down in ◊ *Sie hat sich gut in der neuen Schule eingewöhnt.* She's settled down very well in her new school.

eingreifen VERB (IMPERFECT **griff ein**, PERFECT **hat eingegriffen**)
to intervene

einheimisch ADJECTIVE
native

der **Einheimische** NOUN (GEN des/der
die **Einheimischen**, PL die **Einheimischen**)
local ◊ *Wir sollten einen Einheimischen fragen.* We should ask a local.

einholen VERB (PERFECT **hat eingeholt**)
1 to catch up with ◊ *Wir werden euch sicher bald einholen.* We'll soon catch up with you.
2 to make up ◊ *Wir haben die Verspätung nicht mehr eingeholt.* We didn't make up the delay.

einhundert NUMBER
a hundred

einig ADJECTIVE
◆ **sich einig sein** to be in agreement
◆ **einig werden** to reach an agreement

einige ADJECTIVE, PRONOUN
1 some ◊ *einige Bücher* some books ◊ *einige von uns* some of us
◆ **einiges** quite a lot of things ◊ *Wir haben einiges gesehen.* We saw quite a lot of things.
2 several ◊ *Wir sind dort einige Tage geblieben.* We stayed there several days. ◊ *Bei dem Konzert sind einige früher gegangen.* Several people left the concert early.

sich **einigen** VERB
to agree ◊ *Wir haben uns auf diesen Termin geeinigt.* We agreed on this date.

einigermaßen ADVERB
1 somewhat ◊ *Ich war einigermaßen erstaunt.* I was somewhat surprised.
2 reasonably ◊ *Diesmal hast du dich wenigstens einigermaßen angestrengt.* At least this time you've tried reasonably hard. ◊ *Das Wetter war einigermaßen trocken.* The weather was reasonably dry.

die **Einigung** NOUN
agreement

der **Einkauf** NOUN (PL die **Einkäufe**)
purchase

E

♦ **Einkäufe machen** to go shopping

einkaufen VERB (PERFECT **hat eingekauft**)

[1] to buy ◇ *Wir müssen Brot einkaufen.* We'll have to buy bread.

[2] to shop ◇ *Wir kaufen meist samstags ein.* We usually shop on Saturdays.

♦ **einkaufen gehen** to go shopping

der **Einkaufsbummel** NOUN (PL die **Einkaufsbummel**)

shopping spree

die **Einkaufsliste** NOUN

shopping list

die **Einkaufspassage** NOUN

shopping arcade

der **Einkaufswagen** NOUN (PL die **Einkaufswagen**)

shopping trolley

das **Einkaufszentrum** NOUN (PL die **Einkaufszentren**)

shopping centre

der **Einkaufszettel** NOUN (PL die **Einkaufszettel**)

shopping list

einklammern VERB (PERFECT **hat eingeklammert**)

to put in brackets

das **Einkommen** NOUN (PL die **Einkommen**)

income

einladen VERB (PRESENT **lädt ein**, IMPERFECT **lud ein**, PERFECT **hat eingeladen**)

[1] to invite ◇ *Sie hat mich zu ihrer Party eingeladen.* She's invited me to her party.

♦ **jemanden ins Kino einladen** to take somebody to the cinema

♦ **Ich lade dich ein.** I'll treat you.

[2] to load ◇ *Kannst du bitte die Koffer ins Auto einladen?* Can you load the cases into the car, please?

die **Einladung** NOUN

invitation

einlaufen VERB (PRESENT **läuft ein**, IMPERFECT **lief ein**, PERFECT **ist eingelaufen**)

[1] to come in ◇ *Das Schiff läuft in den Hafen ein.* The ship is coming into the harbour.

[2] to shrink ◇ *Mein Pullover ist eingelaufen.* My jumper has shrunk.

sich **einleben** VERB (PERFECT **hat sich eingelebt**)

to settle down ◇ *Wir haben uns in unserer neuen Schule gut eingelebt.* We've settled down well in our new school.

die **Einleitung** NOUN

introduction

einleuchten VERB (PERFECT **hat eingeleuchtet**)

♦ **jemandem einleuchten** to make sense to somebody ◇ *Das leuchtet mir nicht ein.* That doesn't make sense to me.

einleuchtend ADJECTIVE

clear

einloggen VERB (PERFECT **hat eingeloggt**)

to log on (*computer*)

einlösen VERB

to cash ◇ *Kann ich diesen Scheck einlösen?* Can I cash this cheque?

♦ **ein Versprechen einlösen** to keep a promise

einmal ADVERB

[1] once ◇ *Wenn du das erst einmal begriffen hast ...* Once you've understood it ...

♦ **Es war einmal ...** Once upon a time there was ...

♦ **noch einmal** once more

♦ **auf einmal** all at once ◇ *Auf einmal waren alle weg.* All at once they were all gone.

[2] one day ◇ *Das wirst du schon einmal begreifen.* You'll understand it one day.

♦ **Nehmen wir einmal an: ...** Let's just suppose: ...

♦ **nicht einmal** not even

einmalig ADJECTIVE

[1] unique ◇ *Das ist eine einmalige Gelegenheit.* This is a unique opportunity.

[2] single ◇ *Das erfordert nur eine einmalige Überprüfung.* That requires only a single check.

[3] fantastic ◇ *Das war eine einmalige Party.* That was a fantastic party.

sich **einmischen** VERB (PERFECT **hat sich eingemischt**)

to interfere ◇ *Ich will mich nicht in deine Angelegenheiten einmischen.* I don't want to interfere in your affairs.

sich **einordnen** VERB (PERFECT **hat sich eingeordnet**)

[1] to fit in ◇ *Du musst lernen, dich einzuordnen.* You'll have to learn to fit in.

[2] to get into lane ◇ *Du musst dich in die linke Spur einordnen.* You'll have to get into the left-hand lane.

einpacken VERB (PERFECT **hat eingepackt**)

to pack ◇ *Hast du deine Zahnbürste eingepackt?* Have you packed your toothbrush?

einplanen VERB (PERFECT **hat eingeplant**)

to plan for

einprägen VERB (PERFECT **hat eingeprägt**)

♦ **sich etwas einprägen** to memorize something ◇ *Diesen Namen kann ich mir leicht einprägen.* I can easily memorize this name.

einreiben VERB (IMPERFECT **rieb ein**, PERFECT **hat eingerieben**)

to rub in ◇ *Sie rieb sich das Gesicht mit Creme ein.* She rubbed cream into her face.

einreichen VERB (PERFECT **hat eingereicht**)

to hand in

die **Einreise** NOUN

entry

♦ **bei der Einreise** when entering the country

einreisen VERB (PERFECT **ist eingereist**)

♦ **in ein Land einreisen** to enter a country

einrichten VERB (PERFECT **hat eingerichtet**)

  1 to furnish ◇ *Sie haben ihr Haus antik eingerichtet.* They've furnished their house with antiques.

  2 to set up ◇ *Die Stadt hat eine Beratungsstelle eingerichtet.* The town has set up an advice bureau.

  3 to manage ◇ *Komm früher, wenn du es einrichten kannst.* Come earlier if you can manage.

♦ **sich auf etwas einrichten** to prepare for something ◇ *Wir hatten uns auf mehr Besucher eingerichtet.* We had prepared for more visitors.

die **Einrichtung** NOUN

  1 furnishings ◇ *Die moderne Einrichtung gefiel mir gut.* I liked the modern furnishings.

  2 facility ◇ *städtische Einrichtungen* municipal facilities

einrosten VERB (PERFECT **ist eingerostet**)
to get rusty

die **Eins** NOUN (PL die **Einsen**)

  see also **eins** NUMBER

  1 one

  2 very good

  🛈 German marks range from one (**sehr gut**) to six (**ungenügend**).

eins NUMBER

  see also **die Eins** NOUN, **ein** NUMBER, ARTICLE

one ◇ *Ich habe nur eins bekommen.* I only got one.

♦ **Es ist mir alles eins.** It's all the same to me.

einsam ADJECTIVE

  1 lonely ◇ *Ich fühle mich einsam.* I'm feeling lonely.

  2 remote ◇ *eine einsame Gegend* a remote area

einsammeln VERB (PERFECT **hat eingesammelt**)
to collect

einschalten VERB (PERFECT **hat eingeschaltet**)
to switch on ◇ *Schalt mal das Radio ein.* Switch the radio on.

einschl. ABBREVIATION (= *einschließlich*)
incl.

einschlafen VERB (PRESENT **schläft ein**, IMPERFECT **schlief ein**, PERFECT **ist eingeschlafen**)
to fall asleep

einschließen VERB (IMPERFECT **schloss ein**, PERFECT **hat eingeschlossen**)

  1 to lock in ◇ *Sie hat mich im Badezimmer eingeschlossen.* She locked me in the bathroom.

  2 to lock away ◇ *Du solltest die Wertsachen einschließen.* You should lock away the valuables.

  3 to include ◇ *Der Preis schließt die Verpflegung ein.* The price includes all meals.

♦ **sich einschließen** to lock oneself in ◇ *Sie hat sich in ihrem Zimmer eingeschlossen.* She locked herself in her room.

einschließlich ADVERB, PREPOSITION

  *The preposition **einschließlich** takes the genitive.*

  1 inclusive ◇ *Wir sind vom zehnten bis einschließlich fünfzehnten Juni weg.* We're away from the tenth to the fifteenth of June inclusive.

  2 including ◇ *Das macht zwanzig Euro einschließlich Bedienung.* That's twenty euros including service.

einschränken VERB (PERFECT **hat eingeschränkt**)

  1 to restrict ◇ *Dadurch wurde unsere Freiheit eingeschränkt.* This restricted our freedom.

  2 to reduce ◇ *Wir müssen die Kosten einschränken.* We'll have to reduce costs.

♦ **sich einschränken** to cut down

sich **einschreiben** VERB (IMPERFECT **schrieb sich ein**, PERFECT **hat sich eingeschrieben**)

  see also **das Einschreiben** NOUN

to register ◇ *Hast du dich für den Kurs eingeschrieben?* Have you registered for the course?

♦ **sich an der Universität einschreiben** to enrol at university

das **Einschreiben** NOUN (PL die **Einschreiben**)

  see also **einschreiben** VERB

recorded delivery

einschüchtern VERB (PERFECT **hat eingeschüchtert**)
to intimidate

einsehen VERB (PRESENT **sieht ein**, IMPERFECT **sah ein**, PERFECT **hat eingesehen**)
to see ◇ *Siehst du das nicht ein?* Don't you see that?

einseitig ADJECTIVE
one-sided

einsenden VERB (IMPERFECT **sendete ein** or **sandte ein**, PERFECT **hat eingesendet** or **hat eingesandt**)
to send in

einsetzen VERB (PERFECT **hat eingesetzt**)

  1 to put in ◇ *Setzt das richtige Wort ein.* Put in the correct word.

  2 to bet ◇ *Wie viel Geld hast du eingesetzt?* How much money did you bet?

  3 to use ◇ *An den Schulen werden immer mehr Computer eingesetzt.* More and more computers are being used in schools.

E

4 **to set in** ◊ *Wenn der Winter einsetzt ...* When winter sets in ...

♦ **sich einsetzen** to work hard ◊ *Du solltest dich in der Schule etwas mehr einsetzen.* You should work harder at school.

♦ **sich für jemanden einsetzen** to support somebody

die **Einsicht** NOUN

♦ **zu der Einsicht kommen, dass ...** to come to the conclusion that ...

einsilbig ADJECTIVE

1 monosyllabic ◊ *ein einsilbiges Wort* a monosyllabic word

2 uncommunicative ◊ *Er war sehr einsilbig.* He was very uncommunicative.

einsperren VERB (PERFECT **hat eingesperrt**)

to lock up

einsprachig ADJECTIVE

monolingual

der **Einspruch** NOUN (PL die **Einsprüche**)

objection

einstecken VERB (PERFECT **hat eingesteckt**)

1 to insert ◊ *Du musst zuerst eine Münze einstecken.* You have to insert a coin first.

♦ **einen Brief einstecken** to post a letter

♦ **ein Gerät einstecken** to plug in an appliance

2 to take ◊ *Hast du genügend Geld eingesteckt?* Have you taken enough money?

einsteigen VERB (IMPERFECT **stieg ein,** PERFECT **ist eingestiegen**)

1 to get on ◊ *Wir sind in den Bus eingestiegen.* We got on the bus.

♦ **Bitte einsteigen!** All aboard!

2 to climb in ◊ *Wir sind durchs Kellerfenster ins Haus eingestiegen.* We climbed into the house through the cellar window.

einstellen VERB (PERFECT **hat eingestellt**)

1 to adjust ◊ *den Spiegel einstellen* to adjust the mirror

♦ **eine Kamera einstellen** to focus a camera

2 to tune in to ◊ *Welchen Sender hast du da eingestellt?* Which station have you tuned in to?

3 to stop ◊ *Sie haben die Produktion eingestellt.* They've stopped production.

4 to employ ◊ *Sie wurde als Sekretärin eingestellt.* She was employed as a secretary.

♦ **sich auf etwas einstellen** to prepare oneself for something ◊ *Stell dich besser auf eine lange Warterei ein.* You'd better prepare yourself for a long wait.

die **Einstellung** NOUN

attitude ◊ *Ich mag deine Einstellung nicht.* I don't like your attitude.

der **Einstieg** NOUN

entrance ◊ *Der Einstieg ist vorn.* The entrance is at the front.

einstimmen VERB (PERFECT **hat eingestimmt**)

to join in ◊ *Alle stimmten in das Lied ein.* Everyone joined in the singing.

♦ **sich auf etwas einstimmen** to get oneself in the right mood for something

eintägig ADJECTIVE

one-day

eintausend NUMBER

a thousand

eintönig ADJECTIVE

monotonous

der **Eintopf** NOUN (PL die **Eintöpfe**)

stew

der **Eintrag** NOUN (PL die **Einträge**)

entry ◊ *ein Eintrag im Wörterbuch* a dictionary entry

eintragen VERB (PRESENT **trägt ein,** IMPERFECT **trug ein,** PERFECT **hat eingetragen**)

to write ◊ *Tragt die Vokabeln in euer Heft.* Write the vocabulary in your exercise book.

♦ **sich eintragen** to put one's name down ◊ *Hast du dich schon in die Liste eingetragen?* Have you put your name down on the list yet?

einträglich ADJECTIVE

profitable

eintreffen VERB (PRESENT **trifft ein,** IMPERFECT **traf ein,** PERFECT **ist eingetroffen**)

1 to arrive ◊ *Sobald die Gäste eintreffen ...* As soon as the guests arrive ...

2 to come true ◊ *Die Prophezeiung ist tatsächlich eingetroffen.* The prophecy actually came true.

eintreten VERB (PRESENT **tritt ein,** IMPERFECT **trat ein,** PERFECT **ist eingetreten**)

♦ **eintreten in (1)** to enter ◊ *Er ist ins Zimmer eingetreten.* He entered the room.

♦ **eintreten in (2)** to join ◊ *Wann bist du in den Tennisklub eingetreten?* When did you join the tennis club?

♦ **Es ist eine Verzögerung eingetreten.** There has been a delay.

der **Eintritt** NOUN (PL die **Eintritte**)

admission ◊ *Wie viel kostet der Eintritt?* How much does the admission cost?

♦ **"Eintritt frei"** "Admission free"

das **Eintrittsgeld** NOUN (PL die **Eintrittsgelder**)

admission charge

die **Eintrittskarte** NOUN

admission ticket

der **Eintrittspreis** NOUN (PL die **Eintrittspreise**)

admission charge

einverstanden ADJECTIVE

♦ **einverstanden sein** to agree ◊ *Bist du mit dem Vorschlag einverstanden?* Do you agree to the suggestion?

♦ **Einverstanden!** Okay!

der **Einwanderer** NOUN (PL die **Einwanderer**)

immigrant

einwandern VERB (PERFECT **ist eingewandert**)
to immigrate

die **Einwegflasche** NOUN
nonreturnable bottle

die **Einwegspritze** NOUN
disposable syringe

einweihen VERB (PERFECT **hat eingeweiht**)
to open ◊ *Morgen wird die neue Brücke eingeweiht.* The new bridge is being opened tomorrow.
♦ **jemanden in etwas einweihen** to initiate somebody into something ◊ *Wir haben die Neue in unseren Klub eingeweiht.* We've initiated the newcomer into our club.
♦ **Willst du mich nicht in dein Geheimnis einweihen?** Won't you let me in on your secret?

einwerfen VERB (PRESENT **wirft ein**, IMPERFECT **warf ein**, PERFECT **hat eingeworfen**)
to smash ◊ *Ich habe eine Scheibe eingeworfen.* I've smashed a pane.
♦ **einen Brief einwerfen** to post a letter
♦ **Geld einwerfen** to insert money

der **Einwohner** NOUN (PL die **Einwohner**)
inhabitant

das **Einwohnermeldeamt** NOUN (PL die **Einwohnermeldeämter**)
registration office

> ⓘ *Anyone moving to a new address in Germany is required by law to register (**sich anmelden**) at the residents' registration office (**Einwohnermeldeamt**).*

der **Einwurf** NOUN (PL die **Einwürfe**)
1 slot ◊ *Sie steckte den Brief in den Einwurf.* She put the letter through the slot.
2 throw-in (*sport*) ◊ *Der Schiedsrichter gab einen Einwurf.* The referee gave a throw-in.

die **Einzahl** NOUN
singular

einzahlen VERB (PERFECT **hat eingezahlt**)
to pay

das **Einzelbett** NOUN (PL die **Einzelbetten**)
single bed

der **Einzelfahrschein** NOUN (PL die **Einzelfahrscheine**)
single ticket

die **Einzelheit** NOUN
detail

das **Einzelkind** NOUN (PL die **Einzelkinder**)
only child

einzeln ADJECTIVE, ADVERB
1 single ◊ *Jeder einzelne Schüler wurde befragt.* Every single pupil was asked.
2 odd ◊ *Ich habe ein paar einzelne Socken.* I've got a couple of odd socks.
3 one at a time ◊ *Bitte einzeln eintreten.* Please come in one at a time.
♦ **einzeln angeben** to specify
♦ **der Einzelne** the individual
♦ **ins Einzelne gehen** to go into details

das **Einzelteil** NOUN (PL die **Einzelteile**)
component

das **Einzelzimmer** NOUN (PL die **Einzelzimmer**)
single room

einziehen VERB (IMPERFECT **zog ein**, PERFECT **ist/hat eingezogen**)
> *For the perfect tense use **haben** when the verb has an object and **sein** when there is no object.*

1 to retract
♦ **den Kopf einziehen** to duck one's head
2 to collect
3 to move in ◊ *Wann sind die neuen Nachbarn eingezogen?* When did the new neighbours move in?

einzig ADJECTIVE
only ◊ *Er ist unser einziges Kind.* He's our only child.
♦ **das Einzige** the only thing
♦ **der Einzige** the only one

einzigartig ADJECTIVE
unique

das **Eis** NOUN (PL die **Eis**)
1 ice ◊ *Es war Eis auf dem See.* There was ice on the lake.
2 ice cream ◊ *Möchtest du ein Eis?* Would you like an ice cream?

der **Eisbär** NOUN (GEN des **Eisbären**, PL die **Eisbären**)
polar bear

der **Eisbecher** NOUN (PL die **Eisbecher**)
sundae

der **Eisberg** NOUN (PL die **Eisberge**)
iceberg

die **Eisdiele** NOUN
ice-cream parlour

das **Eisen** NOUN (PL die **Eisen**)
iron ◊ *Die Brücke ist aus Eisen.* The bridge is made of iron.

die **Eisenbahn** NOUN
railway

eisern ADJECTIVE
iron ◊ *eine eiserne Stange* an iron rod
♦ **die eiserne Reserve** emergency reserves

das **Eishockey** NOUN
ice hockey

eisig ADJECTIVE
icy

eiskalt ADJECTIVE
1 ice-cold ◊ *ein eiskaltes Getränk* an ice-cold drink
2 icy cold ◊ *In diesem Zimmer ist es eiskalt.* This room's icy cold.

der **Eiswürfel** NOUN (PL die **Eiswürfel**)
ice cube

der **Eiszapfen** NOUN (PL die **Eiszapfen**)
icicle

eitel ADJECTIVE
vain

der **Eiter** NOUN
pus

das **Eiweiß** NOUN (PL die **Eiweiße**)
[1] egg white ◊ *Das Eiweiß zu Schnee schlagen.* Whisk the egg whites until stiff.
[2] protein ◊ *eine eiweißreiche Diät* a diet rich in protein

der **Ekel** NOUN
disgust
ekelhaft ADJECTIVE
disgusting

sich **ekeln** VERB
to disgust
♦ **sich vor etwas ekeln** to find something disgusting ◊ *Ich ekle mich vor diesem Dreck.* I find this dirt disgusting.

der **Elch** NOUN (PL die **Elche**)
elk

der **Elefant** NOUN (GEN des **Elefanten**, PL die **Elefanten**)
elephant
elegant ADJECTIVE
elegant

der **Elektriker** NOUN (PL die **Elektriker**)
electrician
elektrisch ADJECTIVE
electric

die **Elektrizität** NOUN
electricity

das **Elektrogerät** NOUN
electrical appliance

der **Elektroherd** NOUN (PL die **Elektroherde**)
electric cooker

die **Elektronik** NOUN
electronics ◊ *Er studiert Elektronik.* He's studying electronics. ◊ *Die Elektronik am Auto ist kaputt.* There's something wrong with the electronics in the car.
elektronisch ADJECTIVE
electronic ◊ *elektronische Post* electronic mail ◊ *elektronischer Briefkasten* electronic mailbox

der **Elektrorasierer** NOUN (PL die **Elektrorasierer**)
electric razor

das **Element** NOUN (PL die **Elemente**)
element

das **Elend** NOUN
see also **elend** ADJECTIVE
misery
elend ADJECTIVE
see also **das Elend** NOUN
miserable ◊ *Ich fühle mich so elend.* I feel so miserable.

elf NUMBER
eleven ◊ *Sie ist elf.* She's eleven.

der **Elfmeter** NOUN (PL die **Elfmeter**)
penalty ◊ *einen Elfmeter schießen* to take a penalty

der **Ellbogen** NOUN (PL die **Ellbogen**)
elbow

die **Eltern** PL NOUN
parents

der **Elternteil** NOUN (PL die **Elternteile**)
parent ◊ *beide Elternteile* both parents

die **E-Mail** NOUN (PL die **E-Mails**)
e-Mail ◊ *Meine E-Mail-Adresse ist ...* My e-mail address is ...

das **Emoticon** NOUN (PL die **Emoticons**)
smiley

der **Empfang** NOUN (PL die **Empfänge**)
[1] reception ◊ *Wart ihr auch bei dem Empfang?* Were you at the reception too?
[2] receipt ◊ *Bitte bestätigen Sie den Empfang der Ware.* Please acknowledge receipt of the goods.
♦ **in Empfang nehmen** to receive

empfangen VERB (PRESENT **empfängt**, IMPERFECT **empfing**, PERFECT **hat empfangen**)
to receive

der **Empfänger** NOUN (PL die **Empfänger**)
receiver
empfänglich ADJECTIVE
susceptible ◊ *Sie ist für Schmeicheleien sehr empfänglich.* She's very susceptible to flattery.

die **Empfängnisverhütung** NOUN
contraception

die **Empfangsbestätigung** NOUN
acknowledgement

die **Empfangsdame** NOUN
receptionist

empfehlen VERB (PRESENT **empfiehlt**, IMPERFECT **empfahl**, PERFECT **hat empfohlen**)
to recommend ◊ *Dieses Restaurant ist zu empfehlen.* This restaurant is to be recommended.

empfinden VERB (IMPERFECT **empfand**, PERFECT **hat empfunden**)
to feel ◊ *Ich empfinde nichts für sie.* I don't feel anything for her.
empfindlich ADJECTIVE
[1] sensitive ◊ *Er ist ein sehr empfindlicher Mensch.* He's very sensitive.
[2] touchy ◊ *Sie ist schrecklich empfindlich.* She's terribly touchy.

empfohlen VERB see **empfehlen**

das **Ende** NOUN (PL die **Enden**)
end
♦ **am Ende (1)** at the end ◊ *am Ende des Zuges* at the end of the train
♦ **am Ende (2)** in the end ◊ *Am Ende ist er dann doch mitgekommen.* He came in the end.
♦ **zu Ende gehen** to come to an end
♦ **zu Ende sein** to be finished
♦ **Ende Dezember** at the end of December

enden VERB
to end

endgültig ADJECTIVE
definite

die **Endivie** NOUN
endive

endlich ADVERB
finally ◊ *Ich bin endlich fertig.* I've finally finished. ◊ *Hast du das endlich begriffen?* Have you finally understood it?
♦ **Endlich!** At last!
♦ **Komm endlich!** Come on!

endlos ADJECTIVE
endless

das **Endspiel** NOUN (PL die **Endspiele**)
final

die **Endstation** NOUN
terminus

die **Endung** NOUN
ending

die **Energie** NOUN
energy ◊ *seine ganze Energie für etwas einsetzen* to devote all one's energies to something

energisch ADJECTIVE
energetic

eng ADJECTIVE
[1] narrow ◊ *ein enger Durchgang* a narrow passageway
[2] tight ◊ *Die Hose ist mir zu eng.* The trousers are too tight for me.
[3] close ◊ *Wir sind eng befreundet.* We are close friends.

die **Enge** NOUN
narrowness
♦ **jemanden in die Enge treiben** to drive somebody into a corner

der **Engel** NOUN (PL die **Engel**)
angel

England NEUT NOUN
England
♦ **aus England** from England
♦ **in England** in England
♦ **nach England** to England

der **Engländer** NOUN (PL die **Engländer**)
Englishman
♦ **Er ist Engländer.** He's English.
♦ **die Engländer** the English

die **Engländerin** NOUN
Englishwoman
♦ **Sie ist Engländerin.** She's English.

das **Englisch** NOUN (GEN des **Englischen**)
see also **englisch** ADJECTIVE
English ◊ *Er lernt Englisch in der Schule.* He's learning English at school.

englisch ADJECTIVE
English

der **Engpass** NOUN (GEN des **Engpasses**, PL die **Engpässe**)
bottleneck

der **Enkel** NOUN (PL die **Enkel**)
grandson
♦ **alle ihre Enkel** all her grandchildren

die **Enkelin** NOUN
granddaughter

das **Enkelkind** NOUN (PL die **Enkelkinder**)
grandchild

enorm ADJECTIVE
enormous ◊ *Er verdient enorm viel Geld.* He earns an enormous amount of money.

entdecken VERB (PERFECT **hat entdeckt**)
to discover

die **Ente** NOUN
duck

entfernen VERB (PERFECT **hat entfernt**)
to remove

entfernt ADJECTIVE
distant ◊ *ein entfernter Verwandter* a distant relative
♦ **weit entfernt** far away
♦ **weit davon entfernt sein, etwas zu tun** to be far from doing something
♦ **nicht im Entferntesten** not in the slightest

die **Entfernung** NOUN
distance

entführen VERB (PERFECT **hat entführt**)
to kidnap

entgegen PREPOSITION
entgegen takes the dative.
contrary to ◊ *entgegen meinen Anweisungen* contrary to my instructions

entgegengesetzt ADJECTIVE
[1] opposite ◊ *die entgegengesetzte Richtung* the opposite direction
[2] opposing ◊ *Er vertrat die entgegengesetzte Meinung.* He represented the opposing view.

entgegenkommen VERB (IMPERFECT **kam entgegen**, PERFECT **ist entgegengekommen**)
[1] to come towards ◊ *Uns kam ein Lastwagen entgegen.* A lorry came towards us.
[2] to meet half way ◊ *Ich werde Ihnen entgegenkommen, sagen wir zwanzig Euro.* I'll meet you half way, let's say twenty euros.

entgegenkommend ADJECTIVE
obliging

entgehen VERB (IMPERFECT **entging**, PERFECT **ist entgangen**)
♦ **jemandem entgehen** to escape somebody's attention ◊ *Dieser Fehler ist mir entgangen.* That mistake escaped my attention.
♦ **sich etwas entgehen lassen** to miss something ◊ *Das Konzert will ich mir nicht entgehen lassen.* I'm not going to miss the concert.

enthalten VERB (PRESENT **enthält**, IMPERFECT **enthielt**, PERFECT **hat enthalten**)
to contain ◊ *Dieses Fass enthält radioaktiven Müll.* This drum contains radioactive waste.

♦ **sich enthalten** to abstain ◊ *Sie hat sich bei der Abstimmung enthalten.* She abstained from voting.

entkommen VERB (IMPERFECT **entkam,** PERFECT **ist entkommen**)
to escape

entlang PREPOSITION

> *entlang takes the accusative or the dative.*

along ◊ *Entlang der Mauer wuchs Efeu.* Ivy was growing along the wall. ◊ *Wir gingen den Fluss entlang.* We walked along the river.

entlassen VERB (PRESENT **entlässt,** IMPERFECT **entließ,** PERFECT **hat entlassen**)
1 to release ◊ *Er wurde aus dem Gefängnis entlassen.* He was released from prison.
2 to make redundant ◊ *500 Arbeiter mussten entlassen werden.* 500 workers had to be made redundant.

entmutigen VERB (PERFECT **hat entmutigt**)
to discourage

entrüstet ADJECTIVE
outraged

entschädigen VERB (PERFECT **hat entschädigt**)
to compensate ◊ *jemanden für etwas entschädigen* to compensate somebody for something

entscheiden VERB (IMPERFECT **entschied,** PERFECT **hat entschieden**)
to decide
♦ **sich entscheiden** to make up one's mind

entscheidend ADJECTIVE
decisive

die **Entscheidung** NOUN
decision

entschieden ADJECTIVE
1 decided ◊ *Es ist entschieden, wir fahren nach Rom.* It's been decided that we're going to Rome.
2 resolute ◊ *ein sehr entschiedener Mensch* a very resolute person

sich **entschließen** VERB (IMPERFECT **entschloss sich,** PERFECT **hat sich entschlossen**)
to decide

entschlossen ADJECTIVE
determined

der **Entschluss** NOUN (GEN des **Entschlusses,** PL die **Entschlüsse**)
decision

entschuldigen VERB (PERFECT **hat entschuldigt**)
1 to excuse ◊ *Entschuldige bitte die Verspätung.* Please excuse the delay.
2 to apologize ◊ *Du solltest dich besser bei ihm entschuldigen.* You'd better apologize to him.

die **Entschuldigung** NOUN

1 apology ◊ *Hat er deine Entschuldigung angenommen?* Did he accept your apology?
♦ **jemanden um Entschuldigung bitten** to apologize to somebody
2 excuse ◊ *Krankheit ist keine Entschuldigung.* Illness is no excuse.
♦ **Mein Vater hat mir eine Entschuldigung geschrieben.** My father wrote me a note for the teacher.
♦ **Entschuldigung!** Sorry.
♦ **Entschuldigung ...** Excuse me ... ◊ *Entschuldigung, können Sie mir sagen, wie spät es ist?* Excuse me, could you tell me what time it is?

entsetzlich ADJECTIVE
dreadful

entsetzt ADJECTIVE, ADVERB
horrified

die **Entsorgung** NOUN
waste disposal

sich **entspannen** VERB (PERFECT **hat sich entspannt**)
1 to relax ◊ *Entspann dich!* Relax!
2 to ease ◊ *Die Lage hat sich entspannt.* The situation has eased.

entsprechen VERB (PRESENT **entspricht,** IMPERFECT **entsprach,** PERFECT **hat entsprochen**)
to meet ◊ *Sie hat den Anforderungen nicht entsprochen.* She didn't meet the requirements.
♦ **Dieses Gerät entspricht nicht den Normen.** This appliance doesn't comply with the standards.

entsprechend ADJECTIVE, ADVERB
1 appropriate ◊ *Die entsprechende Antwort ankreuzen.* Tick the appropriate answer.
2 accordingly ◊ *Benimm dich entsprechend.* Behave accordingly.

enttäuschen VERB (PERFECT **hat enttäuscht**)
to disappoint

enttäuschend ADJECTIVE
disappointing

die **Enttäuschung** NOUN
disappointment

entweder CONJUNCTION
either
♦ **entweder ... oder ...** either ... or ...

entwerten VERB
to cancel ◊ *Du musst die Fahrkarte erst entwerten.* You have to cancel your ticket first.

der **Entwerter** NOUN (PL die **Entwerter**)
ticket stamping machine

> 🛈 *When you travel by train or tram (and sometimes by bus) you have to stamp your ticket in an **Entwerter**. The machines are either on the platforms or inside the vehicles.*

entwickeln VERB (PERFECT **hat entwickelt**)
  1 to develop ◊ *Fähigkeiten entwickeln*
to develop skills ◊ *einen Film entwickeln*
to develop a film
  2 to show ◊ *Sie hat eine enorme
Energie entwickelt.* She showed terrific
energy.
  ♦ **sich entwickeln** to develop ◊ *Das
Geschäft entwickelt sich gut.* The
business is developing well.
  ♦ **Sie hat sich zu einem hübschen
Mädchen entwickelt.** She's turned into a
pretty girl.

die **Entwicklung** NOUN
  development

die **Entwicklungshilfe** NOUN
  development aid

das **Entwicklungsland** NOUN (PL die
Entwicklungsländer)
  developing country

entwürdigend ADJECTIVE
  degrading

entzückend ADJECTIVE
  delightful

sich **entzünden** VERB (PERFECT **hat sich
entzündet**)
  to become inflamed ◊ *Die Wunde hat
sich entzündet.* The wound has become
inflamed.

die **Entzündung** NOUN
  inflammation

entzwei ADVERB
  broken ◊ *Die Vase ist entzwei.* The vase
is broken.

der **Enzian** NOUN (PL die **Enziane**)
  gentian

er PRONOUN
  1 he ◊ *Er ist größer als ich.* He's taller
than me.
  2 it ◊ *Schöner Ring, ist er neu?* Lovely
ring, is it new?
  3 him ◊ *Er ist es.* It's him. ◊ *Er war es
nicht, ich war's.* It wasn't him, it was me.

erben VERB
  to inherit

erblich ADJECTIVE
  hereditary

erbrechen VERB (PRESENT **erbricht**, IMPERFECT
erbrach, PERFECT **hat erbrochen**)
  to vomit

die **Erbschaft** NOUN
  inheritance

die **Erbse** NOUN
  pea

das **Erdbeben** NOUN (PL die **Erdbeben**)
  earthquake

die **Erdbeere** NOUN
  strawberry

die **Erde** NOUN
  earth
  ♦ **zu ebener Erde** at ground level
  ♦ **auf der ganzen Erde** all over the world

das **Erdgas** NOUN (GEN des **Erdgases**)
  natural gas

das **Erdgeschoss** NOUN (GEN des
Erdgeschosses, PL die **Erdgeschosse**)
  ground floor ◊ *im Erdgeschoss* on the
ground floor

die **Erdkunde** NOUN
  geography

die **Erdnuss** NOUN (PL die **Erdnüsse**)
  peanut

das **Erdöl** NOUN
  mineral oil

sich **ereignen** VERB (PERFECT **hat sich ereignet**)
  to happen

das **Ereignis** NOUN (GEN des **Ereignisses**, PL die
Ereignisse)
  event

erfahren VERB (PRESENT **erfährt**, IMPERFECT
erfuhr, PERFECT **hat erfahren**)
  see also **erfahren** ADJECTIVE
  1 to hear ◊ *Ich habe erfahren, dass du
heiraten willst.* I've heard that you want
to get married.
  2 to experience ◊ *Sie hat im Leben viel
Gutes erfahren.* She's experienced a lot
of good things in her life.

erfahren ADJECTIVE
  see also **erfahren** VERB
  experienced ◊ *Er ist ein erfahrener
Lehrer.* He's an experienced teacher.

die **Erfahrung** NOUN
  experience

erfassen VERB (PERFECT **hat erfasst**)
  1 to understand ◊ *Ich habe den Text
noch nicht erfasst.* I haven't understood
the text yet.
  2 to register ◊ *Alle Aidsfälle
werden erfasst.* All AIDS cases are
registered.

erfinden VERB (IMPERFECT **erfand**, PERFECT **hat
erfunden**)
  to invent

der **Erfinder** NOUN (PL die **Erfinder**)
  inventor

erfinderisch ADJECTIVE
  inventive

die **Erfindung** NOUN
  invention

der **Erfolg** NOUN (PL die **Erfolge**)
  success
  ♦ **Erfolg versprechend** promising
  ♦ **Viel Erfolg!** Good luck!

erfolglos ADJECTIVE
  unsuccessful

erfolgreich ADJECTIVE
  successful

erforderlich ADJECTIVE
  necessary

erfreulicherweise ADVERB
  happily

erfreut ADJECTIVE

E

pleased ◊ *Über mein gutes Zeugnis war ich sehr erfreut.* I was very pleased with my good report.

erfrieren VERB (IMPERFECT **erfror,** PERFECT **ist erfroren)**
to freeze to death ◊ *Er ist erfroren.* He froze to death.

♦ **Die Pflanze ist erfroren.** The plant was killed by frost.

♦ **Er hat sich bei der Bergtour einen Zeh erfroren.** He got a frostbitten toe on his mountaineering trip.

die **Erfrischung** NOUN
refreshment

der **Erfrischungsstand** NOUN (PL die **Erfrischungsstände)**
refreshment stand

erfüllen VERB (PERFECT **hat erfüllt)**
to fulfil ◊ *Er hat ihr den Wunsch erfüllt.* He fulfilled her wish.

♦ **sich erfüllen** to come true ◊ *Die Prophezeiung hat sich erfüllt.* The prophecy came true.

ergänzen VERB (PERFECT **hat ergänzt)**
to complete ◊ *Ergänzt den Satz.* Complete the sentence.

♦ **sich ergänzen** to complement one another

das **Ergebnis** NOUN (GEN des **Ergebnisses,** PL die **Ergebnisse)**
result

die **Ergonomie** NOUN
ergonomics

ergreifen VERB (IMPERFECT **ergriff,** PERFECT **hat ergriffen)**
[1] to seize ◊ *Er ergriff meine Hand.* He seized my hand. ◊ *die Gelegenheit ergreifen* to seize the opportunity

♦ **einen Beruf ergreifen** to take up a profession

♦ **Maßnahmen gegen etwas ergreifen** to take measures against something
[2] to move ◊ *Ihr Schicksal hat uns sehr ergriffen.* Her fate moved us deeply.

ergreifend ADJECTIVE
moving

ergriffen ADJECTIVE
deeply moved

erhalten VERB (PRESENT **erhält,** IMPERFECT **erhielt,** PERFECT **hat erhalten)**
[1] to receive ◊ *Sie hat den ersten Preis erhalten.* She received first prize.
[2] to preserve ◊ *Das Gebäude sollte erhalten werden.* The building should be preserved.

♦ **gut erhalten** in good condition

erhältlich ADJECTIVE
obtainable

erheitern VERB (PERFECT **hat erheitert)**
to amuse

erhitzen VERB (PERFECT **hat erhitzt)**
to heat

sich **erholen** VERB (PERFECT **hat sich erholt)**
[1] to recover ◊ *Der Patient muss sich nach der Operation erholen.* The patient needs to recover after the operation.
[2] to have a rest ◊ *Wir haben uns in den Ferien gut erholt.* We had a good rest when we were on holiday.

erholsam ADJECTIVE
restful

die **Erholung** NOUN
rest ◊ *Wir fahren zur Erholung ans Meer.* We're going to the sea for a rest.

erinnern VERB (PERFECT **hat erinnert)**
♦ **erinnern an** to remind of ◊ *Du erinnerst mich an meine Schwester.* You remind me of my sister. ◊ *Erinnere mich bitte daran, dass wir noch Eier brauchen.* Remind me that we still need eggs.

♦ **sich erinnern** to remember ◊ *Ich kann mich nicht erinnern.* I can't remember. ◊ *Erinnerst du dich noch an unser Abenteuer in Erlangen?* Can you still remember our adventure in Erlangen?

die **Erinnerung** NOUN
[1] memory ◊ *Wir haben Erinnerungen ausgetauscht.* We swapped memories.
[2] souvenir ◊ *eine Erinnerung an meinen Russlandaufenthalt* a souvenir of my stay in Russia

sich **erkälten** VERB (PERFECT **hat sich erkältet)**
to catch a cold

erkältet ADJECTIVE
♦ **erkältet sein** to have a cold

die **Erkältung** NOUN
cold

erkennbar ADJECTIVE
recognizable

erkennen VERB (IMPERFECT **erkannte,** PERFECT **hat erkannt)**
[1] to recognize ◊ *Ich hätte dich nicht erkannt.* I wouldn't have recognized you.
[2] to see ◊ *Jetzt erkenne ich, dass das ein Fehler war.* I see now that it was a mistake.

erklären VERB (PERFECT **hat erklärt)**
to explain

die **Erklärung** NOUN
explanation

♦ **eine Liebeserklärung** a declaration of love

sich **erkundigen** VERB (PERFECT **hat sich erkundigt)**
♦ **sich erkundigen nach** to inquire about ◊ *Wir sollten uns nach den Abfahrtszeiten erkundigen.* We should inquire about departure times.

♦ **Er hat sich nach dir erkundigt.** He was asking about you.

erlauben VERB (PERFECT **hat erlaubt)**
♦ **jemandem etwas erlauben** to allow somebody to do something ◊ *Mein Vater hat mir erlaubt auszugehen.* My father allowed me to go out.

E

♦ **sich etwas erlauben** to allow oneself something ◊ *Ich erlaube mir jetzt ein Bier.* Now I'm going to allow myself a beer.

♦ **Was erlaubst du dir denn eigentlich?** How dare you!

die **Erlaubnis** NOUN (PL die **Erlaubnisse**)
  permission

erleben VERB (PERFECT **hat erlebt**)
  ⊡ to experience ◊ *Eine solche Frechheit habe ich selten erlebt.* I've seldom experienced such cheek.

♦ **Wir haben in den Ferien viel Schönes erlebt.** We had a lovely time on holiday.

♦ **Sie hat viel Schlimmes erlebt.** She's had a lot of bad experiences.

  ⊡ to live through ◊ *Mein Opa hat den Zweiten Weltkrieg erlebt.* My grandpa lived through the Second World War.

  ⊡ to live to see ◊ *Ich möchte die Geburt deines Kindes noch erleben.* I would like to live to see the birth of your child.

das **Erlebnis** NOUN (GEN des **Erlebnisses**, PL die **Erlebnisse**)
  experience

erledigen VERB (PERFECT **hat erledigt**)
  ⊡ to see to ◊ *Ich habe heute noch viel zu erledigen.* I've a lot to see to today.

♦ **Hast du deine Hausaufgaben schon erledigt?** Have you done your homework already?

  ⊡ to wear out ◊ *Die Wanderung hat mich ziemlich erledigt.* The hike's really worn me out.

die **Erleichterung** NOUN
  relief ◊ *Das war eine Erleichterung!* That was a relief!

der **Erlös** NOUN (GEN des **Erlöses**, PL die **Erlöse**)
  proceeds ◊ *Der Erlös kommt Kindern in Rumänien zugute.* The proceeds will go to children in Romania.

erlösen VERB (PERFECT **hat erlöst**)
  to save ◊ *Sie erlöste ihn aus einer gefährlichen Lage.* She saved him from a dangerous situation.

die **Ermahnung** NOUN
  admonition

ermäßigen VERB (PERFECT **hat ermäßigt**)
  to reduce

die **Ermäßigung** NOUN
  reduction

ermöglichen VERB (PERFECT **hat ermöglicht**)
♦ **jemandem etwas ermöglichen** to make something possible for somebody

ermorden VERB (PERFECT **hat ermordet**)
  to murder

ermüdend ADJECTIVE
  tiring

ermutigen VERB (PERFECT **hat ermutigt**)
  to encourage

ernähren VERB (PERFECT **hat ernährt**)
  to support ◊ *Er hat eine Familie zu ernähren.* He has a family to support.

♦ **sich von etwas ernähren** to live on something ◊ *Sie ernähren sich hauptsächlich von Reis.* They live mainly on rice.

♦ **Du ernährst dich ungesund.** Your diet's unhealthy.

ernennen VERB (IMPERFECT **ernannte**, PERFECT **hat ernannt**)
  to appoint

erneuern VERB (PERFECT **hat erneuert**)
  to renew

ernst ADJECTIVE
  │ *see also* **der Ernst** NOUN │
  serious

der **Ernst** NOUN
  │ *see also* **ernst** ADJECTIVE │
  seriousness

♦ **Das ist mein Ernst.** I'm quite serious.

♦ **im Ernst** in earnest

ernsthaft ADJECTIVE
  serious ◊ *ein ernsthaftes Gespräch* a serious talk ◊ *Glaubst du das ernsthaft?* Do you seriously believe that?

ernstlich ADJECTIVE, ADVERB
  serious

♦ **ernstlich besorgt** seriously concerned

die **Ernte** NOUN
  harvest

ernten VERB
  to harvest ◊ *Es ist Zeit, die Kirschen zu ernten.* It's time to harvest the cherries.

♦ **Lob ernten** to earn praise

erobern VERB (PERFECT **hat erobert**)
  to conquer

die **Eroberung** NOUN
  conquest

erotisch ADJECTIVE
  erotic

erpressen VERB (PERFECT **hat erpresst**)
  ⊡ to blackmail ◊ *Du willst mich wohl erpressen?* Are you trying to blackmail me?

  ⊡ to extort ◊ *Er hat von ihm Geld erpresst.* He extorted money from him.

erraten VERB (PRESENT **errät**, IMPERFECT **erriet**, PERFECT **hat erraten**)
  to guess

die **Erregung** NOUN
  excitement

erreichen VERB (PERFECT **hat erreicht**)
  ⊡ to reach ◊ *Wir haben Hamburg am späten Nachmittag erreicht.* We reached Hamburg in the late afternoon.

  ⊡ to catch ◊ *Wir haben den Zug nicht mehr erreicht.* We didn't manage to catch the train.

  ⊡ to achieve ◊ *seinen Zweck erreichen* to achieve one's purpose ◊ *Was willst du damit erreichen?* What do you aim to achieve by this?

☞

♦ **So erreichst du bei mir gar nichts.** You won't get anywhere with me by doing that.

der **Ersatzreifen** NOUN (PL die **Ersatzreifen**)
spare tyre

das **Ersatzteil** NOUN (PL die **Ersatzteile**)
spare part

erschaffen VERB (IMPERFECT **erschuf**, PERFECT **hat erschaffen**)
to create

erscheinen VERB (IMPERFECT **erschien**, PERFECT **ist erschienen**)
to appear

erschießen VERB (IMPERFECT **erschoss**, PERFECT **hat erschossen**)
to shoot dead

erschöpft ADJECTIVE
exhausted

die **Erschöpfung** NOUN
exhaustion

erschrecken (1) VERB (PERFECT **hat erschreckt**)
to frighten ◊ *Hast du mich erschreckt!* You really frightened me!

erschrecken (2) VERB (PRESENT **erschrickt**, IMPERFECT **erschrak**, PERFECT **ist erschrocken**)
to be frightened ◊ *Ich bin furchtbar erschrocken, als plötzlich das Licht ausging.* I was terribly frightened when the light suddenly went out.

♦ **Erschrick nicht, wenn du ihn siehst.** Don't be shocked when you see him.

erschreckend ADJECTIVE
alarming

erschrocken ADJECTIVE
frightened

ersetzen VERB (PERFECT **hat ersetzt**)
to replace ◊ *Du musst die Vase ersetzen.* You'll have to replace that vase.

♦ **jemandem die Unkosten ersetzen** to pay somebody's expenses

die **Ersparnisse** FEM PL NOUN
savings

erst ADVERB
1 first ◊ *Erst will ich wissen, was das kostet.* First I want to know what it costs. ◊ *Mach erst mal die Arbeit fertig.* Finish your work first.

♦ **Wenn du das erst mal hinter dir hast, ...** Once you've got that behind you, ...
2 only ◊ *Das ist erst gestern passiert.* That happened only yesterday. ◊ *Er ist gerade erst angekommen.* He's only just arrived.

♦ **erst als** not until ◊ *Er hat es erst gemacht, als ich es ihm befohlen habe.* He didn't do it until I told him.
♦ **erst morgen** not until tomorrow
♦ **erst um 5 Uhr** not until 5 o'clock
♦ **Wir fahren erst später.** We're not going until later.

erstaunlich ADJECTIVE
astonishing

erstaunt ADJECTIVE
astonished

erstbeste ADJECTIVE
first that comes along ◊ *Du kannst doch nicht den erstbesten Mann heiraten.* But you can't marry the first man that comes along.

erste ADJECTIVE
first ◊ *Ich habe gerade mein erstes Auto gekauft.* I've just bought my first car. ◊ *Er kam als Erster.* He was the first to arrive.

♦ **Erste Hilfe** first aid

erstechen VERB (PRESENT **ersticht**, IMPERFECT **erstach**, PERFECT **hat erstochen**)
to stab to death

erstens ADVERB
firstly

ersticken VERB (PERFECT **ist erstickt**)
to suffocate ◊ *Ich bin fast erstickt.* I almost suffocated.

♦ **Er versuchte, die Flammen zu ersticken.** He tried to smother the flames.
♦ **in Arbeit ersticken** to be snowed under with work

erstklassig ADJECTIVE
first-class

erstmals ADVERB
for the first time

ertragen VERB (PRESENT **erträgt**, IMPERFECT **ertrug**, PERFECT **hat ertragen**)
to stand ◊ *Ich kann die Schmerzen kaum ertragen.* I can hardly stand the pain. ◊ *Sie erträgt es nicht, wenn man ihr widerspricht.* She can't stand being contradicted.

erträglich ADJECTIVE
bearable

ertrinken VERB (IMPERFECT **ertrank**, PERFECT **ist ertrunken**)
to drown

erwachsen ADJECTIVE
grown-up

der **Erwachsene** NOUN (GEN des/der
die **Erwachsenen**, PL die **Erwachsenen**)
adult ◊ *Erwachsene können das nicht verstehen.* Adults can't understand that.

die **Erwachsenenbildung** NOUN
adult education

erwähnen VERB (PERFECT **hat erwähnt**)
to mention

erwarten VERB (PERFECT **hat erwartet**)
to expect ◊ *Er erwartet zu viel von uns.* He's expecting too much of us.

♦ **Wir können es kaum erwarten, dass die Ferien beginnen.** We can hardly wait for the holidays to begin.

erwartungsgemäß ADVERB
as expected

erweisen VERB (IMPERFECT **erwies**, PERFECT **hat erwiesen**)

E

♦ **sich erweisen als** to prove to be ◊ *Er erwies sich als guter Schüler.* He proved to be a good pupil.

erwerben VERB (PRESENT **erwirbt**, IMPERFECT **erwarb**, PERFECT **hat erworben**)
to acquire

das **Erz** NOUN (GEN des **Erzes**, PL die **Erze**)
ore

erzählen VERB (PERFECT **hat erzählt**)
to tell

die **Erzählung** NOUN
story

erzeugen VERB (PERFECT **hat erzeugt**)
to produce ◊ *In dieser Gegend wird Wein erzeugt.* Wine is produced in this region.

♦ **Strom erzeugen** to generate electricity

das **Erzeugnis** NOUN (GEN des **Erzeugnisses**, PL die **Erzeugnisse**)
produce ◊ *ausländische Erzeugnisse* foreign produce

erziehen VERB (IMPERFECT **erzog**, PERFECT **hat erzogen**)
to bring up ◊ *Sie hat fünf Kinder erzogen.* She brought up five children. ◊ *Sie sollte ihre Kinder zu etwas mehr Höflichkeit erziehen.* She should bring her children up to be more polite.

die **Erziehung** NOUN
education

der **Erziehungsberechtigte** NOUN (GEN des/
die der **Erziehungsberechtigten**, PL die **Erziehungsberechtigten**)
parent or guardian ◊ *Du brauchst dafür die Unterschrift eines Erziehungsberechtigten.* You need the signature of your parent or guardian for this.

es PRONOUN
it ◊ *Es ist rot.* It's red. ◊ *Ich habe es nicht gesehen.* I didn't see it. ◊ *Es schneit.* It's snowing.

der **Esel** NOUN (PL die **Esel**)
donkey

der **Eskimo** NOUN (PL die **Eskimos**)
Eskimo

essbar ADJECTIVE
edible

essen VERB (PRESENT **isst**, IMPERFECT **aß**, PERFECT **hat gegessen**)
see also **das Essen** NOUN
to eat

das **Essen** NOUN (PL die **Essen**)
see also **essen** VERB
[1] meal ◊ *Komm doch am Freitag zum Essen.* Why don't you come for a meal on Friday?
[2] food ◊ *Das Essen war lecker.* The food was delicious.

der **Essig** NOUN (PL die **Essige**)
vinegar

die **Essiggurke** NOUN
gherkin

die **Esskastanie** NOUN
sweet chestnut

das **Esszimmer** NOUN (PL die **Esszimmer**)
dining room

die **Etage** NOUN
floor ◊ *Wir wohnen in der dritten Etage.* We live on the third floor.

die **Etagenbetten** NEUT PL NOUN
bunk beds

das **E-ticket** NOUN (PL die **E-tickets**)
e-ticket

das **Etikett** NOUN (PL die **Etikette** or **Etiketten**)
label ◊ *Lies mal, was auf dem Etikett steht.* Read what's on the label.

etliche PL PRONOUN
quite a few ◊ *etliche Leute* quite a few people

das **Etui** NOUN (PL die **Etuis**)
case ◊ *ein Brillenetui* a glasses case

etwa ADVERB
[1] about ◊ *Es waren etwa zwanzig.* There were about twenty.
[2] for instance ◊ *Leute wie etwa Hans wissen das eben nicht.* People like Hans, for instance, just don't know that.

♦ **Soll das etwa heißen, dass du nicht mitkommst?** Is that supposed to mean that you're not coming?

♦ **Hat er das etwa wirklich gesagt?** Did he really say that?

♦ **Du willst doch nicht etwa schon gehen.** You're not going already, are you?

etwaig ADJECTIVE
possible

etwas PRONOUN, ADVERB
[1] something ◊ *Wir sollten ihr etwas schenken.* We should give her something.
[2] anything ◊ *Hast du nicht etwas gehört?* Haven't you heard anything?
[3] a little ◊ *Wir sollten uns etwas ausruhen.* We should have a little rest. ◊ *Nur etwas Milch bitte.* Just a little milk, please.

die **EU** NOUN (= *Europäische Union*)
EU (= European Union)

euch PRONOUN
*euch is the accusative and dative of **ihr**.*
[1] you ◊ *Ich habe euch gesehen.* I saw you. ◊ *Ich komme mit euch.* I'll come with you.
[2] yourselves ◊ *Seht euch mal im Spiegel an.* Look at yourselves in the mirror.
[3] to you ◊ *Sie hat es euch gegeben.* She gave it to you.

euer PRONOUN, ADJECTIVE
[1] your ◊ *Euer Deutschlehrer ist nett.* Your German teacher is nice. ◊ *Wenn das eure Mutter erlaubt.* If your mother lets you. ◊ *Ist das euer Haus?* Is that your house? ◊ *Wir haben eure Bücher mitgebracht.* We've brought your books.

☞

2 yours ◊ *Das ist nicht unser Computer, das ist eurer.* That's not our computer, that's yours. ◊ *Unsere Mutter heißt Ulla, wie heißt eure?* Our mother's called Ulla, what's yours called? ◊ *Wenn es in unserem Haus nicht geht, feiern wir in eurem.* If it's not OK in our house, then we'll celebrate in yours. ◊ *Wir holen unsere Karten, sollen wir eure mitbringen?* We're picking up our tickets, shall we get yours too?

die **Eule** NOUN
owl

eure *see* **euer**

eures *see* **euer**

euretwegen ADVERB
1 for your sakes ◊ *Wir sind euretwegen nicht in Urlaub gefahren.* We didn't go on holiday for your sakes.
2 on your account ◊ *Er hat sich euretwegen aufgeregt.* He got upset on your account.

der **Euro** NOUN (PL die **Euros**)
euro ◊ *Das kostet fünf Euro.* It costs five euros.

der **Eurocheque** NOUN (PL die **Eurocheques**)
Eurocheque

Europa NEUT NOUN
Europe
♦ **aus Europa** from Europe
♦ **in Europa** in Europe
♦ **nach Europa** to Europe

der **Europäer** NOUN (PL die **Europäer**)
European

die **Europäerin** NOUN
European

europäisch ADJECTIVE
European

e. V. ABBREVIATION (= *eingetragener Verein*)
registered society

evangelisch ADJECTIVE
Protestant

eventuell ADVERB, ADJECTIVE
perhaps ◊ *Eventuell komme ich später nach.* Perhaps I'll come on later.
♦ **Eventuelle Fragen wird mein Kollege gerne beantworten.** My colleague will be pleased to answer any questions you may have.

Be careful! **eventuell** *does not mean* **eventual**.

ewig ADJECTIVE
eternal

die **Ewigkeit** NOUN
eternity

das **Examen** NOUN (PL die **Examen**)
exam

das **Exemplar** NOUN (PL die **Exemplare**)
1 copy ◊ *Von dem Buch habe ich zwei Exemplare.* I've got two copies of the book.
2 specimen ◊ *Er hat ein ganz seltenes Exemplar gefangen.* He caught a very rare specimen.

explodieren VERB (PERFECT **ist explodiert**)
to explode

die **Explosion** NOUN
explosion

der **Export** NOUN (PL die **Exporte**)
export

exportieren VERB (PERFECT **hat exportiert**)
to export

extra ADVERB, ADJECTIVE
see also **das Extra** NOUN
1 separately ◊ *Schicke die Diskette lieber extra.* It'd be better to send the diskette separately.
2 specially ◊ *Das wurde extra für sie angefertigt.* That was made specially for her. ◊ *Ich bin extra wegen dir gekommen.* I came specially because of you.
3 on purpose ◊ *Das hat er extra gemacht.* He did that on purpose.
4 extra ◊ *Ich habe das extra schnell gemacht.* I did it extra quickly. ◊ *Das sind extra starke Pfefferminzbonbons.* These are extra strong peppermints.
5 another ◊ *Stell noch einen extra Teller auf den Tisch.* Put another plate on the table.

das **Extra** NOUN (PL die **Extras**)
see also **extra** ADVERB
extra ◊ *ein Auto mit vielen Extras* a car with lots of extras

extrem ADJECTIVE
extreme

F

fabelhaft ADJECTIVE
fabulous

die **Fabrik** NOUN
factory
Be careful! Fabrik does not mean fabric.

der **Fabrikarbeiter** NOUN (PL die **Fabrikarbeiter**)
factory worker

die **Fabrikarbeiterin** NOUN
factory worker

das **Fach** NOUN (PL die **Fächer**)
1 shelf ◊ *Das ist mein Fach im Schrank.* This is my shelf in the cupboard.
2 pigeonhole ◊ *Jeder Lehrer hat im Lehrerzimmer ein Fach.* Every teacher has a pigeonhole in the staff room.
3 subject ◊ *In welchem Fach bist du am besten?* What subject are you best at?

der **Facharzt** NOUN (GEN des **Facharztes**, PL die **Fachärzte**)
specialist (*doctor*)

die **Fachärztin** NOUN
specialist (*doctor*)

der **Fachausdruck** NOUN (PL die **Fachausdrücke**)
technical term

die **Fachfrau** NOUN
expert

die **Fachhochschule** NOUN
college

die **Fachschule** NOUN
technical college

der **Fachmann** NOUN (PL die **Fachleute**)
expert

das **Fachwerkhaus** NOUN (GEN des **Fachwerkhauses**, PL die **Fachwerkhäuser**)
half-timbered house

die **Fackel** NOUN
torch

der **Faden** NOUN (PL die **Fäden**)
thread

fähig ADJECTIVE
capable ◊ *Sie ist eine sehr fähige Lehrerin.* She's a very capable teacher.
♦ **fähig sein, etwas zu tun** to be capable of doing something ◊ *Bist du fähig, diesen Text zu übersetzen?* Are you capable of translating this text?

die **Fähigkeit** NOUN
ability

die **Fahne** NOUN
flag
♦ **eine Fahne haben** to stink of booze

der **Fahrausweis** NOUN (GEN des **Fahrausweises**, PL die **Fahrausweise**)
ticket ◊ *Die Fahrausweise, bitte.* Tickets, please.

die **Fahrbahn** NOUN
carriageway

die **Fähre** NOUN
ferry

fahren VERB (PRESENT **fährt**, IMPERFECT **fuhr**, PERFECT **ist/hat gefahren**)
*For the perfect tense use **haben** when the verb has an object and **sein** when there is no object.*
1 to drive ◊ *Er hat mich nach Hause gefahren.* He drove me home. ◊ *Er ist sehr schnell gefahren.* He drove very fast.
♦ **ein Rennen fahren** to drive in a race
2 to go ◊ *Der Intercity fährt stündlich.* The Intercity train goes every hour.
3 to leave ◊ *Wann seid ihr gefahren?* When did you leave?
4 to sail ◊ *Das Schiff fährt nach Amerika.* The ship's sailing to America. ◊ *Wir sind mit dem Schiff nach Amerika gefahren.* We sailed to America.
♦ **Rad fahren** to cycle ◊ *Früher bin ich viel Rad gefahren.* I used to cycle a lot.
♦ **mit dem Auto fahren** to go by car
♦ **mit dem Zug fahren** to go by train ◊ *Seid ihr mit dem Zug gefahren?* Did you go by train?
♦ **Sie fuhr mit der Hand über sein Haar.** She ran her hand through his hair.

der **Fahrer** NOUN (PL die **Fahrer**)
driver

die **Fahrerflucht** NOUN
hit-and-run accident

die **Fahrerin** NOUN
driver

der **Fahrgast** NOUN (PL die **Fahrgäste**)
passenger

das **Fahrgeld** NOUN (PL die **Fahrgelder**)
fare ◊ *Bitte das Fahrgeld abgezählt bereithalten.* Please have exact fare ready.

die **Fahrkarte** NOUN
ticket ◊ *Die Fahrkarten, bitte.* Tickets, please.

die **Fahrkartenausgabe** NOUN
ticket office

der **Fahrkartenautomat** NOUN (GEN des **Fahrkartenautomaten**, PL die **Fahrkartenautomaten**)
ticket machine

der **Fahrkartenschalter** NOUN (PL die **Fahrkartenschalter**)
ticket office

fahrlässig ADJECTIVE
negligent

der **Fahrlehrer** NOUN (PL die **Fahrlehrer**)
driving instructor

der **Fahrplan** NOUN (PL die **Fahrpläne**)

☞

fahrplanmäßig ADJECTIVE
scheduled

der **Fahrpreis** NOUN (GEN des **Fahrpreises**, PL die **Fahrpreise**)
fare

die **Fahrprüfung** NOUN
driving test

das **Fahrrad** NOUN (PL die **Fahrräder**)
bicycle

der **Fahrradweg** NOUN (PL die **Fahrradwege**)
cycle lane

der **Fahrschein** NOUN (PL die **Fahrscheine**)
ticket ◊ *Die Fahrscheine, bitte.* Tickets, please.

der **Fahrscheinentwerter** NOUN (PL die **Fahrscheinentwerter**)
ticket stamping machine

> ❶ When you travel by train or tram (and sometimes by bus) you have to stamp your ticket in a **Fahrscheinentwerter**. The machines are either on the platforms or inside the vehicles.

die **Fahrschule** NOUN
driving school

der **Fahrstuhl** NOUN (PL die **Fahrstühle**)
lift

die **Fahrt** NOUN

⟦1⟧ journey ◊ *Die Fahrt nach Hamburg war lang.* It was a long journey to Hamburg.

⟦2⟧ trip ◊ *Am Wochenende haben wir eine Fahrt in den Schwarzwald gemacht.* We went on a trip to the Black Forest at the weekend.

♦ **Gute Fahrt!** Have a good journey.

die **Fahrtkosten** PL NOUN
travelling expenses

das **Fahrzeug** NOUN (PL die **Fahrzeuge**)
vehicle

der **Fahrzeugbrief** NOUN (PL die **Fahrzeugbriefe**)
log book

fair ADJECTIVE
fair ◊ *Das ist nicht fair!* That's not fair!

der **Faktor** NOUN (PL die **Faktoren**)
factor

die **Fakultät** NOUN
faculty

der **Falke** NOUN (GEN des **Falken**, PL die **Falken**)
falcon

der **Fall** NOUN (PL die **Fälle**)
case ◊ *Die Polizei untersucht den Fall.* The police are investigating the case. ◊ *In diesem Fall mache ich eine Ausnahme.* I'll make an exception in this case. ◊ *Welcher Fall steht nach "außer"?* Which case does "außer" take?

♦ **auf jeden Fall** definitely ◊ *Ich komme auf jeden Fall.* I'll definitely come.

♦ **für alle Fälle** just in case ◊ *Nimm für alle Fälle einen Schirm mit.* Take an umbrella, just in case.

♦ **Auf keinen Fall!** No way!

die **Falle** NOUN
trap

fallen VERB (PRESENT **fällt**, IMPERFECT **fiel**, PERFECT **ist gefallen**)
to fall

♦ **etwas fallen lassen (1)** to drop something ◊ *Lass es nicht fallen!* Don't drop it!

♦ **etwas fallen lassen (2)** to abandon something ◊ *Wir haben die Idee, in Frankreich Ferien zu machen, wieder fallen lassen.* We've abandoned the idea of spending our holidays in France.

♦ **eine Bemerkung fallen lassen** to make a remark

fällen VERB

♦ **einen Baum fällen** to fell a tree

♦ **ein Urteil fällen** to pronounce judgement

fallenlassen VERB *see* **fallen**

fällig ADJECTIVE
due

falls ADVERB
if

der **Fallschirm** NOUN (PL die **Fallschirme**)
parachute

falsch ADJECTIVE

⟦1⟧ wrong ◊ *Die Antwort war falsch.* The answer was wrong.

♦ **jemanden falsch verstehen** to get somebody wrong

⟦2⟧ false ◊ *falsche Zähne* false teeth

fälschen VERB
to forge

fälschlicherweise ADVERB
mistakenly

die **Fälschung** NOUN
forgery

die **Falte** NOUN

⟦1⟧ fold ◊ *eine Falte im Papier* a fold in the paper

⟦2⟧ crease ◊ *Die Hose ist voller Falten.* The trousers are all creased.

⟦3⟧ wrinkle ◊ *Ihr Gesicht ist voller Falten.* Her face is all wrinkled.

⟦4⟧ pleat ◊ *eine Rockfalte* a pleat in a skirt

falten VERB
to fold

faltig ADJECTIVE

⟦1⟧ wrinkled ◊ *Er hat ein faltiges Gesicht.* He's got a wrinkled face.

⟦2⟧ creased ◊ *Deine Hose ist ganz faltig.* Your trousers are all creased.

familiär ADJECTIVE
familiar

die **Familie** NOUN
family

der **Familienname** NOUN (GEN des **Familiennamens**, PL die **Familiennamen**)
surname

der **Familienstand** NOUN (PL die **Familienstände**)
marital status

der **Fan** NOUN (PL die **Fans**)
fan ◊ *Sie ist ein Fan von Sting.* She's a Sting fan.

fand VERB *see* **finden**

fangen VERB (PRESENT **fängt**, IMPERFECT **fing**, PERFECT **hat gefangen**)
to catch

die **Fantasie** NOUN
imagination

fantasielos ADJECTIVE
unimaginative

fantasieren VERB (PERFECT **hat fantasiert**)
to fantasize ◊ *Er fantasierte von einem Lottogewinn.* He fantasized about a win on the lottery.

fantasievoll ADJECTIVE
imaginative

fantastisch ADJECTIVE
fantastic

die **Farbe** NOUN
1 colour ◊ *Rosa ist Beates Lieblingsfarbe.* Pink is Beate's favourite colour.
2 paint ◊ *Hast du Farben, ich möchte was malen?* I'd like to do some painting, have you got any paints?

farbecht ADJECTIVE
colourfast

färben VERB
to dye ◊ *Sie hat ihre Haare gefärbt.* She's dyed her hair.

farbenblind ADJECTIVE
colour-blind

das **Farbfernsehen** NOUN
colour television

der **Farbfilm** NOUN (PL die **Farbfilme**)
colour film

das **Farbfoto** NOUN (PL die **Farbfotos**)
colour photograph

farbig ADJECTIVE
coloured

farblos ADJECTIVE
colourless

der **Farbstift** NOUN (PL die **Farbstifte**)
coloured pencil

der **Farbstoff** NOUN (PL die **Farbstoffe**)
dye

der **Farbton** NOUN (PL die **Farbtöne**)
shade

der **Fasan** NOUN (PL die **Fasane** or **Fasanen**)
pheasant

der **Fasching** NOUN (PL die **Faschinge**)
carnival

> ❶ The German carnival season lasts from 11 November to Shrove Tuesday but most events, fancy-dress processions and parties take place in the week leading up to Ash Wednesday.

der **Faschingsdienstag** NOUN
Shrove Tuesday

die **Faser** NOUN
fibre

das **Fass** NOUN (GEN des **Fasses**, PL die **Fässer**)
barrel ◊ *ein Weinfass* a wine barrel
♦ **Bier vom Fass** draught beer

fassen VERB (PERFECT **hat gefasst**)
1 to grasp ◊ *Er fasste mich am Arm.* He grasped my arm.
2 to hold ◊ *Der Behälter fasst zwanzig Liter.* The container holds twenty litres.
3 to understand ◊ *Ich kann es nicht fassen, dass du das noch immer nicht gemacht hast.* I can't understand why you still haven't done it.
♦ **nicht zu fassen** unbelievable
♦ **sich fassen** to calm down

die **Fassung** NOUN
1 composure ◊ *Sie hat die Fassung verloren.* She lost her composure.
♦ **jemanden aus der Fassung bringen** to upset somebody
2 version ◊ *der Text in einer neuen Fassung* the text in a new version

fassungslos ADJECTIVE
speechless

fast ADVERB
almost

> Be careful! The German word **fast** does not mean **fast**.

fasten VERB
to fast

die **Fastenzeit** NOUN
Lent

das **FastFood** NOUN (PL die **FastFoods**)
fast food

die **Fastnacht** NOUN
carnival

> ❶ The German carnival season lasts from 11 November to Shrove Tuesday but most events, fancy-dress processions and parties take place in the week leading up to Ash Wednesday.

faul ADJECTIVE
1 rotten ◊ *Der Apfel ist faul.* The apple's rotten.
2 lazy ◊ *Er ist der faulste Schüler.* He's our laziest pupil.
♦ **eine faule Ausrede** a lame excuse
♦ **Daran ist etwas faul.** There's something fishy about it.

faulen VERB
to rot

F

faulenzen VERB
to laze about

die **Faust** NOUN (PL die **Fäuste**)
fist
◆ **auf eigene Faust** off one's own bat

das **Fax** NOUN (GEN des **Faxes**, PL die **Faxe**)
fax

faxen VERB
to fax ◊ *jemandem etwas faxen* to fax something to somebody

das **Faxgerät** NOUN (PL die **Faxgeräte**)
fax machine

die **Faxnummer** NOUN
fax number

der **FCKW** NOUN (= *Fluorchlorkohlen-wasserstoff*)
CFC (= chlorofluorocarbon)

der **Februar** NOUN (GEN des **Februar** or **Februars**, PL die **Februare**)
February ◊ *im Februar* in February ◊ *am dritten Februar* on the third of February ◊ *Bonn, den 3. Februar 2005* Bonn, 3 February 2005 ◊ *Heute ist der zweite Februar.* Today is the second of February.

fechten VERB (PRESENT **ficht**, IMPERFECT **focht**, PERFECT **hat gefochten**)
to fence

die **Feder** NOUN
1 feather ◊ *Er hatte eine Feder am Hut.* He had a feather in his hat.
2 spring ◊ *Die Federn des Betts sind ausgeleiert.* The bed springs have worn out.

der **Federball** NOUN (PL die **Federbälle**)
shuttlecock

das **Federbett** NOUN (PL die **Federbetten**)
continental quilt

die **Federung** NOUN
suspension (*in car*)

die **Fee** NOUN
fairy

fegen VERB
to sweep

fehl ADJECTIVE
◆ **fehl am Platz** out of place

fehlen VERB
1 to be absent ◊ *Er hat gestern in der Schule gefehlt.* He was absent from school yesterday.
2 to be missing ◊ *Da fehlt ein Knopf.* There's a button missing.
◆ **Wer fehlt?** Is anyone missing?
◆ **Mir fehlt das nötige Geld.** I haven't got the money.
◆ **Du fehlst mir.** I miss you.
◆ **Was fehlt ihm?** What's wrong with him?

der **Fehler** NOUN (PL die **Fehler**)
1 mistake ◊ *Wie viele Fehler hast du gemacht?* How many mistakes did you make?
2 fault ◊ *Sein einziger Fehler ist, dass er den Mund nicht halten kann.* His only fault is that he can't keep his mouth shut.

die **Feier** NOUN
celebration

der **Feierabend** NOUN (PL die **Feierabende**)
clocking-off time
◆ **Feierabend machen** to clock off
◆ **Wann hat dein Vater Feierabend?** When does your father finish work?
◆ **Schönen Feierabend!** Have a nice evening.

feierlich ADJECTIVE
solemn

die **Feierlichkeit** NOUN
festivity (PL

feiern VERB
to celebrate

der **Feiertag** NOUN (PL die **Feiertage**)
holiday ◊ *ein öffentlicher Feiertag* a public holiday

feige ADJECTIVE
see also **die Feige** NOUN
cowardly

die **Feige** NOUN
see also **feige** ADJECTIVE
fig

der **Feigling** NOUN (PL die **Feiglinge**)
coward

die **Feile** NOUN
file ◊ *eine Nagelfeile* a nailfile

feilschen VERB
to haggle

fein ADJECTIVE
1 fine ◊ *feiner Sand* fine sand
2 refined ◊ *feine Leute* refined people
◆ **Fein!** Great!

der **Feind** NOUN (PL die **Feinde**)
enemy

feindlich ADJECTIVE
hostile

die **Feindschaft** NOUN
hostility

das **Feld** NOUN (PL die **Felder**)
1 field ◊ *Auf diesem Feld wächst Hafer.* There are oats growing in this field.
2 pitch ◊ *ein Fußballfeld* a football pitch
3 square ◊ *Er rückte mit seinem Bauern ein Feld vor.* He moved his pawn forward one square.

der **Fels** NOUN (GEN des **Felsen**, PL die **Felsen**)
rock
◆ **die weißen Felsen von Dover** the white cliffs of Dover

feminin ADJECTIVE
feminine

das **Fenster** NOUN (PL die **Fenster**)
window

der **Fensterladen** NOUN (PL die **Fensterläden**)
shutter

die **Fensterscheibe** NOUN
windowpane

die **Ferien** PL NOUN
  holidays
  ♦ **Ferien haben** to be on holiday
der **Ferienjob** NOUN (PL die **Ferienjobs**)
  holiday job
der **Ferienkurs** NOUN (GEN des **Ferienkurses**, PL
  die **Ferienkurse**)
  vacation course
das **Ferienlager** NOUN (PL die **Ferienlager**)
  holiday camp
  fern ADJECTIVE, ADVERB
  distant ◊ *in ferner Zukunft* in the distant
  future
  ♦ **fern von hier** a long way from here
  ♦ **der Ferne Osten** the Far East
die **Fernbedienung** NOUN
  remote control
das **Ferngespräch** NOUN (PL die
  Ferngespräche)
  long-distance call
das **Fernglas** NOUN (GEN des **Fernglases**, PL die
  Ferngläser)
  binoculars ◊ *ein Fernglas* a pair of
  binoculars
der **Fernsehapparat** NOUN (PL die
  Fernsehapparate)
  television set
das **Fernsehen** NOUN
  see also **fernsehen** VERB
  television ◊ *im Fernsehen* on television
  fernsehen VERB (PRESENT **sieht fern**, IMPERFECT
  sah fern, PERFECT **hat ferngesehen**)
  see also **das Fernsehen** NOUN
  to watch television
der **Fernseher** NOUN (PL die **Fernseher**)
  television set
der **Fernsehfilm** NOUN (PL die **Fernsehfilme**)
  TV film
die **Fernsehsendung** NOUN
  TV programme
die **Fernsehserie** NOUN
  TV series
der **Fernsprecher** NOUN (PL die **Fernsprecher**)
  telephone
die **Fernsteuerung** NOUN
  remote control
die **Ferse** NOUN
  heel ◊ *Ich habe eine Blase an der Ferse.*
  I've got a blister on my heel.
  fertig ADJECTIVE
  1 ready ◊ *Das Essen ist fertig.* Dinner's
  ready.
  2 finished ◊ *Der Aufsatz ist fertig.* The
  essay's finished. ◊ *Bist du mit deinen
  Hausaufgaben fertig?* Have you finished
  your homework?
  ♦ **etwas fertig machen** to finish something
  ◊ *Ich muss noch die Matheaufgaben
  fertig machen.* I've just got to finish my
  maths homework.
  ♦ **sich fertig machen** to get ready
  fertigbringen VERB (IMPERFECT **brachte fertig**,

PERFECT **hat fertiggebracht**)
  ♦ **es fertigbringen, etwas zu tun** to bring
  oneself to do something ◊ *Ich bringe es
  nicht fertig, ihr das zu sagen.* I can't bring
  myself to tell her.
das **Fertiggericht** NOUN (PL die **Fertiggerichte**)
  ready meal
  fertigmachen VERB
  ♦ **jemanden fertigmachen (1)** to wear
  somebody out ◊ *Die Radtour hat mich
  fertiggemacht.* The cycling trip wore me out.
  ♦ **jemanden fertigmachen (2)** to tear
  somebody off a strip ◊ *Meine
  Englischlehrerin hat mich heute
  fertiggemacht.* My English teacher tore
  me off a strip today.
  fesselnd ADJECTIVE
  captivating
das **Fest** NOUN (PL die **Feste**)
  see also **fest** ADJECTIVE
  1 party ◊ *Fritz macht am Samstag ein
  Fest.* Fritz is having a party on Saturday.
  2 festival ◊ *das Backnanger Straßenfest*
  the Backnang Street Festival
  ♦ **Frohes Fest!** Happy Christmas!
  fest ADJECTIVE, ADVERB
  see also **das Fest** NOUN
  firm ◊ *Er hielt sie mit festem Griff.* He
  had a firm grip of her. ◊ *Er hat einen
  festen Händedruck.* He has a firm
  handshake.
  ♦ **ein festes Einkommen** a regular income
  ♦ **fest schlafen** to sleep soundly
  ♦ **feste Nahrung** solids
  festbinden VERB (IMPERFECT **band fest**, PERFECT
  hat festgebunden)
  to tie ◊ *Sie hat ihren Hund am Baum
  festgebunden.* She tied her dog to the
  tree.
  festhalten VERB (PRESENT **hält fest**, IMPERFECT
  hielt fest, PERFECT **hat festgehalten**)
  to keep hold of ◊ *Du musst das Steuer
  festhalten.* You must keep hold of the
  wheel.
  ♦ **sich festhalten an** to hold on to ◊ *Sie
  hielt sich am Geländer fest.* She held on
  to the banister.
  festigen VERB
  to strengthen
die **Festigkeit** NOUN
  strength
das **Festland** NOUN
  mainland
  festlegen VERB (PERFECT **hat festgelegt**)
  to fix ◊ *einen Termin festlegen* to fix a
  date
  ♦ **sich festlegen** to commit oneself
  festlich ADJECTIVE
  festive
  festmachen VERB (PERFECT **hat festgemacht**)
  1 to fix ◊ *Habt ihr den Termin schon
  festgemacht?* Have you fixed the date yet?

F

☞

2 to moor ◊ *Wir haben das Boot im Hafen festgemacht.* We moored the boat in the harbour.

die **Festnahme** NOUN
arrest

festnehmen VERB (PRESENT **nimmt fest,** IMPERFECT **nahm fest,** PERFECT **hat festgenommen**)
to arrest

die **Festplatte** NOUN
hard disk

die **Festspiele** NEUT PL NOUN
festival

feststehen VERB (IMPERFECT **stand fest,** PERFECT **hat festgestanden**)
to be certain ◊ *So viel steht fest: ...* This much is certain: ...

feststellen VERB (PERFECT **hat festgestellt**)
1 to establish ◊ *Wir konnten nicht feststellen, wer das geschrieben hatte.* We couldn't establish who'd written it.
2 to see ◊ *Ich stelle fest, dass du schon wieder nicht aufgepasst hast.* I see that you haven't been paying attention again.
♦ **Wir haben da einen Fehler festgestellt.** We've detected an error.

der **Festtag** NOUN
special day

das **Fett** NOUN (PL die **Fette**)
see also **fett** ADJECTIVE
fat

fett ADJECTIVE
see also **das Fett** NOUN
fat ◊ *Er ist zu fett.* He's too fat.
♦ **fettes Essen** greasy food
♦ **fette Schrift** bold type

fettarm ADJECTIVE
low-fat

fettig ADJECTIVE
greasy

der **Fetzen** NOUN (PL die **Fetzen**)
scrap ◊ *ein Fetzen Papier* a scrap of paper

feucht ADJECTIVE
1 damp ◊ *etwas mit einem feuchten Tuch abwischen* to wipe something with a damp cloth
2 humid ◊ *Das Klima ist sehr feucht.* The climate's very humid.

die **Feuchtigkeit** NOUN
1 moisture ◊ *Salz zieht Feuchtigkeit an.* Salt attracts moisture.
2 humidity ◊ *hohe Luftfeuchtigkeit* high humidity

das **Feuer** NOUN (PL die **Feuer**)
fire
♦ **Haben Sie Feuer?** Have you got a light?

der **Feuerlöscher** NOUN (PL die **Feuerlöscher**)
fire extinguisher

die **Feuerwehr** NOUN (PL die **Feuerwehren**)
fire brigade

das **Feuerwehrauto** NOUN (PL die **Feuerwehrautos**)
fire engine

die **Feuerwehrfrau** NOUN
firewoman

der **Feuerwehrmann** NOUN (PL die **Feuerwehrleute** or **Feuerwehrmänner**)
fireman

das **Feuerwerk** NOUN (PL die **Feuerwerke**)
fireworks ◊ *Wir waren beim Feuerwerk.* We went to the fireworks.

das **Feuerzeug** NOUN (PL die **Feuerzeuge**)
lighter

das **Fieber** NOUN (PL die **Fieber**)
1 fever ◊ *Das Fieber wird sich in ein paar Tagen senken.* The fever will pass in a couple of days.
2 temperature ◊ *Hast du Fieber?* Have you got a temperature?

fiel VERB see **fallen**

fies ADJECTIVE
nasty

die **Figur** NOUN
figure ◊ *Sie hat eine gute Figur.* She's got a good figure.
♦ **eine Schachfigur** a chessman

die **Filiale** NOUN
branch

der **Film** NOUN (PL die **Filme**)
film

filmen VERB
to film

die **Filmkomödie** NOUN
comedy film

die **Filterzigarette** NOUN
tipped cigarette

der **Filzstift** NOUN (PL die **Filzstifte**)
felt-tip pen

das **Finanzamt** NOUN (PL die **Finanzämter**)
Inland Revenue Office

finanziell ADJECTIVE
financial

finanzieren VERB (PERFECT **hat finanziert**)
to finance

finden VERB (IMPERFECT **fand,** PERFECT **hat gefunden**)
1 to find ◊ *Hast du deinen Radiergummi gefunden?* Have you found your rubber?
2 to think ◊ *Ich finde, er sieht gut aus.* I think he's good-looking. ◊ *Ich finde sie nicht attraktiv.* I don't think she's attractive.
♦ **Ich finde nichts dabei, wenn ...** I don't see what's wrong with ... ◊ *Ich finde nichts dabei, wenn man mal einen Tag faulenzt.* I don't see what's wrong with lazing about for one day.
♦ **Das wird sich finden.** Things will work out.

fing VERB see **fangen**

der **Finger** NOUN (PL die **Finger**)
finger

der **Fingerabdruck** NOUN (PL die **Fingerabdrücke**)
fingerprint
♦ **genetische Fingerabdrücke** genetic fingerprinting

der **Fingernagel** NOUN (PL die **Fingernägel**)
fingernail

der **Finne** NOUN (GEN des **Finnen,** PL die **Finnen**)
Finn

die **Finnin** NOUN
Finn

finnisch ADJECTIVE
Finnish

Finnland NEUT NOUN
Finland
♦ **aus Finnland** from Finland
♦ **nach Finnland** to Finland

finster ADJECTIVE
[1] dark ◊ *Hier ist es aber finster.* It's dark in here.
[2] sinister ◊ *finstere Gestalten* sinister figures
♦ **ein finsteres Gesicht** a grim face

die **Finsternis** NOUN
darkness

die **Firma** NOUN (PL die **Firmen**)
firm

der **Fisch** NOUN (PL die **Fische**)
fish
♦ **Fische** Pisces ◊ *Adelheid ist Fisch.* Adelheid's Pisces.

fischen VERB
to fish ◊ *Sonntags geht Alex immer fischen.* Alex always goes fishing on Sundays.

der **Fischer** NOUN (PL die **Fischer**)
fisherman

die **Fischerei** NOUN
fishing

der **Fischhändler** NOUN (PL die **Fischhändler**)
fishmonger

fit ADJECTIVE
fit ◊ *Ich halte mich mit Schwimmen fit.* I keep fit by swimming.

das **Fitnesszentrum** NOUN (PL die **Fitnesszentren**)
fitness centre

fix ADJECTIVE
♦ **fix und fertig (1)** finished ◊ *Alles war fix und fertig.* Everything was finished.
♦ **fix und fertig (2)** all in ◊ *Ich bin fix und fertig.* I'm all in.

der **Fixer** NOUN (PL die **Fixer**)
junkie

flach ADJECTIVE
[1] flat ◊ *Norddeutschland ist flach.* North Germany's flat.
[2] shallow ◊ *Ich brauche eine flache Schale.* I need a shallow bowl.

der **Flachbildschirm** NOUN (PL die **Flachbildschirme**)
flatscreen

die **Fläche** NOUN
area ◊ *eine Fläche von hundert Quadratkilometern* an area of a hundred square kilometres

das **Flachland** NOUN
lowland

flackern VERB
to flicker

die **Flagge** NOUN
flag

die **Flamme** NOUN
flame

die **Flasche** NOUN
bottle ◊ *eine Flasche Mineralwasser* a bottle of mineral water

der **Flaschenöffner** NOUN (PL die **Flaschenöffner**)
bottle-opener

flauschig ADJECTIVE
fluffy

der **Fleck** NOUN (PL die **Flecke**)
[1] stain ◊ *Der Wein hat einen Fleck auf dem Teppich gemacht.* The wine left a stain on the carpet.
[2] spot ◊ *Das ist ein hübscher Fleck.* This is a beautiful spot.

das **Fleckenmittel** NOUN (PL die **Fleckenmittel**)
stain remover

fleckig ADJECTIVE
[1] spotted ◊ *Ein Dalmatiner hat ein fleckiges Fell.* A Dalmatian has a spotted coat.
[2] stained ◊ *Die Tischdecke ist ganz fleckig.* The tablecloth's all stained.

die **Fledermaus** NOUN (PL die **Fledermäuse**)
bat

das **Fleisch** NOUN
meat ◊ *Ich esse kein Fleisch.* I don't eat meat.

die **Fleischbrühe** NOUN
meat stock

der **Fleischer** NOUN (PL die **Fleischer**)
butcher

die **Fleischerei** NOUN
butcher's

der **Fleiß** NOUN (GEN des **Fleißes**)
hard work ◊ *Mit etwas Fleiß könntest du deine Noten verbessern.* With a bit of hard work you could improve your marks.

fleißig ADJECTIVE
hard-working
♦ **Ich war heute schon fleißig.** I've already done quite a bit of work today.

flexibel ADJECTIVE
flexible

flicken VERB
to mend

die **Fliege** NOUN
[1] fly

F

[2] bow tie ◊ *Er trug eine Fliege.* He was wearing a bow tie.

fliegen VERB (IMPERFECT **flog**, PERFECT **ist geflogen**)
to fly

fliehen VERB (IMPERFECT **floh**, PERFECT **ist geflohen**)
to flee

die **Fliese** NOUN
tile

das **Fließband** NOUN (PL die **Fließbänder**)
assembly line

fließen VERB (IMPERFECT **floss**, PERFECT **ist geflossen**)
to flow

fließend ADJECTIVE, ADVERB
[1] running ◊ *fließendes Wasser* running water
[2] fluent ◊ *Sie spricht fließend Englisch.* She is fluent in English.

flink ADJECTIVE
nimble

die **Flitterwochen** FEM PL NOUN
honeymoon

flitzen VERB (PERFECT **ist geflitzt**)
to dash

die **Flocke** NOUN
flake ◊ *eine Schneeflocke* a snowflake

flog VERB *see* **fliegen**

der **Floh** NOUN (PL die **Flöhe**)
flea

der **Flohmarkt** NOUN (PL die **Flohmärkte**)
flea market

die **Floskel** NOUN
set phrase

floss VERB *see* **fließen**

die **Flosse** NOUN
[1] fin ◊ *die Flosse eines Hais* a shark's fin
[2] flipper ◊ *Er hat seine Flossen mit ins Schwimmbad genommen.* He took his flippers with him to the swimming baths.

die **Flöte** NOUN
[1] flute ◊ *Cordula spielt Flöte.* Cordula plays the flute.
[2] recorder ◊ *Phil spielt Flöte.* Phil plays the recorder.

fluchen VERB
to curse

flüchtig ADJECTIVE
at large ◊ *Der Einbrecher ist noch flüchtig.* The burglar's still at large.
♦ **jemanden nur flüchtig kennen** to know somebody only superficially

der **Flüchtling** NOUN (PL die **Flüchtlinge**)
refugee

der **Flug** NOUN (PL die **Flüge**)
flight ◊ *Der Flug nach Atlanta ist verspätet.* The flight to Atlanta's been delayed.

das **Flugblatt** NOUN (PL die **Flugblätter**)
leaflet

der **Flügel** NOUN (PL die **Flügel**)

[1] wing ◊ *die Flügel des Adlers* the eagle's wings
[2] grand piano

der **Fluggast** NOUN (PL die **Fluggäste**)
airline passenger

die **Fluggesellschaft** NOUN
airline

der **Flughafen** NOUN (PL die **Flughäfen**)
airport

der **Fluglotse** NOUN (GEN des **Fluglotsen**, PL die **Fluglotsen**)
air traffic controller

der **Flugplan** NOUN (PL die **Flugpläne**)
flight schedule

der **Flugplatz** NOUN (GEN des **Flugplatzes**, PL die **Flugplätze**)
[1] airport ◊ *Wir bringen dich zum Flugplatz.* We'll take you to the airport.
[2] airfield ◊ *Dieser Flugplatz ist nur für Privatflugzeuge.* This airfield is only for private planes.

der **Flugschein** NOUN (PL die **Flugscheine**)
plane ticket

das **Flugticket** NOUN (PL die **Flugtickets**)
plane ticket

das **Flugzeug** NOUN (PL die **Flugzeuge**)
aeroplane

die **Flugzeugentführung** NOUN
hijacking

das **Fluor** NOUN
fluorine

der **Flur** NOUN (PL die **Flure**)
corridor
Be careful! Flur does not mean floor.

der **Fluss** NOUN (GEN des **Flusses**, PL die **Flüsse**)
river

das **Flüsschen** NOUN (PL die **Flüsschen**)
little river

flüssig ADJECTIVE
liquid

die **Flüssigkeit** NOUN
liquid

das **Flussufer** NOUN (PL die **Flussufer**)
river bank ◊ *am Flussufer* on the river bank

flüstern VERB
to whisper

die **Flut** NOUN (PL die **Fluten**)
[1] flood ◊ *Wir haben eine Flut von Briefen bekommen.* We received a flood of letters.
[2] high tide ◊ *Das Schiff läuft bei Flut aus.* The ship sails at high tide.

das **Flutlicht** NOUN (PL die **Flutlichter**)
floodlight

der **Föhn** NOUN (PL die **Föhne**)
[1] foehn wind ◊ *Heute ist Föhn.* There's a foehn wind blowing today.

ⓘ *The foehn wind is a dry, warm wind usually found to the north of the Alps.*

2 hair dryer

föhnen VERB
to blow-dry

die **Folge** NOUN
1 result ◊ *Er starb an den Folgen des Unfalls.* He died as a result of the accident.
♦ **etwas zur Folge haben** to result in something ◊ *Deine Faulheit wird schlechte Noten zur Folge haben.* Your laziness will result in bad marks.
♦ **Folgen haben** to have consequences ◊ *Das wird schlimme Folgen haben.* That'll have serious consequences.
2 episode ◊ *Hast du die letzte Folge der "Lindenstraße" gesehen?* Did you see the latest episode of "Lindenstraße"?
♦ **ein Roman in Folgen** a serialized novel

folgen VERB (PERFECT **ist gefolgt**)
to follow ◊ *Uns ist ein grünes Auto gefolgt.* We were followed by a green car. ◊ *Folgen Sie dem Wagen da.* Follow that car.
♦ **Ich konnte ihm nicht folgen.** I couldn't follow what he was saying.
♦ **Meine Kinder folgen nicht immer.** My children don't always do what they're told.

folgend ADJECTIVE
following

die **Folgerung** NOUN
conclusion

folglich ADVERB
consequently

folgsam ADJECTIVE
obedient

die **Folie** NOUN
foil

foltern VERB
to torture

der **Fön** Ⓡ NOUN (PL die **Föne**)
hair dryer

fordern VERB
to demand

die **Forderung** NOUN
demand

die **Forelle** NOUN
trout ◊ *drei Forellen* three trout

die **Form** NOUN
1 shape ◊ *Das Auto hat eine elegante Form.* The car has an elegant shape.
2 mould ◊ *Das Metall wird in eine Form gegossen.* The metal is poured into a mould.
3 baking tin

das **Format** NOUN (PL die **Formate**)
format

formatieren VERB (PERFECT **hat formatiert**)
to format

die **Formel** NOUN
formula

formen VERB
to form

förmlich ADJECTIVE
formal

das **Formular** NOUN (PL die **Formulare**)
form ◊ *ein Formular ausfüllen* to fill in a form

formulieren VERB (PERFECT **hat formuliert**)
to formulate

der **Forscher** NOUN (PL die **Forscher**)
1 research scientist ◊ *Die Forscher haben noch keinen Impfstoff gegen Aids entwickelt.* Research scientists have still not developed an AIDS vaccine.
2 explorer ◊ *Ein Gruppe von Forschern ist im Amazonasgebiet verschollen.* A group of explorers is missing in the Amazon region.

die **Forschung** NOUN
research

fort ADVERB
gone ◊ *Mein Geldbeutel ist fort.* My purse is gone.
♦ **und so fort** and so on
♦ **in einem fort** on and on
♦ **Fort mit dir!** Away with you!

sich **fortbewegen** VERB (PERFECT **hat sich fortbewegt**)
to move

fortbleiben VERB (IMPERFECT **blieb fort,** PERFECT **ist fortgeblieben**)
to stay away

fortfahren VERB (PRESENT **fährt fort,** IMPERFECT **fuhr fort,** PERFECT **ist fortgefahren**)
1 to leave ◊ *Sie sind gestern fortgefahren.* They left yesterday.
2 to continue ◊ *Er fuhr in seiner Rede fort.* He continued with his speech.

fortgeschritten ADJECTIVE
advanced

der **Fortschritt** NOUN (PL die **Fortschritte**)
progress ◊ *Fortschritte machen* to make progress

fortschrittlich ADJECTIVE
progressive

fortsetzen VERB (PERFECT **hat fortgesetzt**)
to continue

die **Fortsetzung** NOUN
1 continuation ◊ *die Fortsetzung des Krieges* the continuation of the war
2 sequel ◊ *Hast du die Fortsetzung gelesen?* Have you read the sequel?
♦ **Morgen kommt die Fortsetzung des Krimis.** The detective story will be continued tomorrow.
♦ **Fortsetzung folgt** to be continued

das **Foto** NOUN (PL die **Fotos**)
photo

der **Fotoapparat** NOUN (PL die **Fotoapparate**)
camera

F

der **Fotograf** NOUN (GEN des **Fotografen**, PL die **Fotografen**)
photographer

> Be careful! **Fotograf** does not mean **photograph**.

die **Fotografie** NOUN

1 photography ◊ *Die Fotografie ist sein Hobby.* His hobby is photography.

2 photograph ◊ *Ich habe eine Fotografie davon gesehen.* I've seen a photograph of it.

fotografieren VERB (PERFECT **hat fotografiert**)

1 to take a photo of ◊ *Kannst du uns mal fotografieren?* Can you take a photo of us?

2 to take photographs ◊ *Ich fotografiere in den Ferien nie.* I never take photographs on holiday.

die **Fotokopie** NOUN

das **Fotohandy** NOUN (PL die **Fotohandys**)
camera phone

Fr. ABBREVIATION (= *Frau*)

1 Mrs

2 Ms

die **Fracht** NOUN
freight ◊ *Frachtkosten* freight charges

die **Frage** NOUN
question ◊ *Könntest du bitte meine Frage beantworten?* Could you please answer my question?

♦ **jemandem eine Frage stellen** to ask somebody a question

♦ **in Frage kommen/stellen** see **infrage**

der **Fragebogen** NOUN (PL die **Fragebogen**)
questionnaire

fragen VERB
to ask ◊ *Kann ich dich was fragen?* Can I ask you something?

das **Fragezeichen** NOUN (PL die **Fragezeichen**)
question mark

fraglich ADJECTIVE
doubtful ◊ *Es ist sehr fraglich, ob wir kommen können.* It's very doubtful whether we can come.

der **Franc** NOUN (GEN des **Franc**, PL die **Francs**)
franc ◊ *Er bezahlte 500 Franc.* He paid 500 francs.

der **Franken** NOUN (PL die **Franken**)
franc ◊ *Er bezahlte 50 Franken.* He paid 50 francs.

♦ **der Schweizer Franken** the Swiss franc

frankieren VERB (PERFECT **hat frankiert**)

♦ **einen Brief frankieren** to put a stamp on a letter

♦ **ein frankierter Briefumschlag** a stamped self-addressed envelope

Frankreich NEUT NOUN
France

♦ **aus Frankreich** from France

♦ **in Frankreich** in France

♦ **nach Frankreich** to France

der **Franzose** NOUN (GEN des **Franzosen**, PL die **Franzosen**)
Frenchman

♦ **Er ist Franzose.** He's French.

♦ **die Franzosen** the French

die **Französin** NOUN
Frenchwoman

♦ **Sie ist Französin.** She's French.

das **Französisch** NOUN (GEN des **Französischen**)

see also **französisch** ADJECTIVE

French ◊ *Er lernt Französisch in der Schule.* He's learning French at school.

französisch ADJECTIVE

see also **das Französisch** NOUN

French

fraß VERB see **fressen**

die **Frau** NOUN

1 woman ◊ *Sie ist eine nette Frau.* She's a nice woman.

2 wife ◊ *Herr Arnold ist mit seiner Frau gekommen.* Mr Arnold came with his wife.

♦ **Sehr geehrte Frau Braun (1)** Dear Mrs Braun

♦ **Sehr geehrte Frau Braun (2)** Dear Ms Braun

> 🛈 Generally **Frau** is used to address all women whether married or not.

♦ **Frau Doktor** Doctor

der **Frauenarzt** NOUN (GEN des **Frauenarztes**, PL die **Frauenärzte**)
gynaecologist

die **Frauenbewegung** NOUN
women's movement

das **Fräulein** NOUN (PL die **Fräulein**)

1 young lady

2 Miss ◊ *Liebes Fräulein Dümmler* Dear Miss Dümmler

> 🛈 **Fräulein** is hardly ever used nowadays and **Frau** is used instead to address all women whether married or not.

frech ADJECTIVE
cheeky

die **Frechheit** NOUN
cheek

frei ADJECTIVE
free

♦ **Ist der Platz hier frei?** Is this seat taken?

♦ **Soll ich einen Platz für dich frei halten?** Shall I keep a seat for you?

♦ **"Einfahrt frei halten"** "keep clear"

♦ **Wir haben im Momente keine freien Stellen.** We haven't got any vacancies at the moment.

♦ **ein freier Mitarbeiter** a freelancer
♦ **im Freien** in the open air

das **Freibad** NOUN (PL die **Freibäder**)
open-air swimming pool ◊ *Im Sommer gehe ich gern ins Freibad.* I like going to the open-air swimming pool in the summer.

freibekommen VERB (IMPERFECT **bekam frei,** PERFECT **hat freibekommen**)
♦ **jemanden freibekommen** to get somebody released
♦ **einen Tag freibekommen** to get a day off

freigebig ADJECTIVE
generous

freihalten VERB *see* **frei**

die **Freiheit** NOUN
1 freedom
2 liberty ◊ *sich Freiheiten herausnehmen* to take liberties

freilassen VERB (PRESENT **lässt frei,** IMPERFECT **ließ frei,** PERFECT **hat freigelassen**)
to free

freinehmen VERB (PRESENT **nimmt frei,** IMPERFECT **nahm frei,** PERFECT **hat freigenommen**)
♦ **sich einen Tag freinehmen** to take a day off ◊ *Ich werde mir morgen einen Tag freinehmen.* I'm taking the day off tomorrow.

der **Freitag** NOUN (PL die **Freitage**)
Friday ◊ *am Freitag* on Friday

freitags ADVERB
on Fridays

freiwillig ADJECTIVE
voluntary

die **Freizeit** NOUN
spare time ◊ *Was machst du in deiner Freizeit?* What do you do in your spare time?

die **Freizeitbeschäftigung** NOUN
leisure activity

der **Freizeitpark** NOUN (PL die **Freizeitparks**)
amusement park

das **Freizeitzentrum** NOUN (PL die **Freizeitzentren**)
leisure centre

fremd ADJECTIVE
1 strange ◊ *eine fremde Umgebung* strange surroundings
2 foreign ◊ *fremde Länder und Sprachen* foreign countries and languages
♦ **Ich bin in London fremd.** I'm a stranger to London.

der **Fremdenverkehr** NOUN
tourism

das **Fremdenzimmer** NOUN (PL die **Fremdenzimmer**)
guest room

die **Fremdsprache** NOUN
foreign language

das **Fremdwort** NOUN (PL die **Fremdwörter**)
foreign word

fressen VERB (PRESENT **frisst,** IMPERFECT **fraß,** PERFECT **hat gefressen**)
to eat
♦ **Er frisst wie ein Schwein.** He eats like a pig.

die **Freude** NOUN
1 joy ◊ *Welche Freude!* What joy!
2 delight ◊ *Zu meiner Freude hatten wir gestern keine Schule.* To my delight we didn't have any school yesterday.
♦ **Ich wollte dir eine Freude machen.** I wanted to make you happy.

freuen VERB
♦ **sich freuen** to be glad ◊ *Ich freue mich, dass du gekommen bist.* I'm glad you've come. ◊ *Freut mich!* Pleased to meet you.
♦ **Freust du dich denn gar nicht?** Aren't you pleased at all?
♦ **sich auf etwas freuen** to look forward to something ◊ *Wir freuen uns darauf, euch zu sehen.* We're looking forward to seeing you.
♦ **sich über etwas freuen** to be pleased with something ◊ *Sie hat sich sehr über das Geschenk gefreut.* She was very pleased with the present.
♦ **Dein Brief hat mich sehr gefreut.** Your letter made me very happy.

der **Freund** NOUN (PL die **Freunde**)
1 friend ◊ *Alle meine Freunde waren da.* All my friends were there.
2 boyfriend ◊ *Hast du einen Freund?* Have you got a boyfriend?

die **Freundin** NOUN
1 friend ◊ *Karla kommt mit ihrer Freundin.* Karla's coming with her friend.
2 girlfriend ◊ *Tobias hat keine Freundin.* Tobias hasn't got a girlfriend.

freundlich ADJECTIVE
1 friendly ◊ *ein freundliches Lächeln* a friendly smile
2 kind ◊ *Das ist sehr freundlich von Ihnen.* That's very kind of you.

freundlicherweise ADVERB
kindly ◊ *Er hat uns freundlicherweise geholfen.* He kindly helped us.

die **Freundlichkeit** NOUN
friendliness

die **Freundschaft** NOUN
friendship

der **Frieden** NOUN (PL die **Frieden**)
peace
♦ **im Frieden** in peacetime

der **Friedhof** NOUN (PL die **Friedhöfe**)
cemetery

friedlich ADJECTIVE
peaceful

frieren VERB (IMPERFECT **fror,** PERFECT **hat gefroren**)

☞

to freeze ◊ *Ich friere.* I'm freezing.
◆ **Letzte Nacht hat es gefroren.** It was frosty last night.
die **Frikadelle** NOUN
rissole
frisch ADJECTIVE
fresh ◊ *frische Milch* fresh milk ◊ *ein frischer Wind* a fresh wind
◆ **Frisch gestrichen!** Wet paint!
◆ **sich frisch machen** to freshen oneself up
der **Friseur** NOUN (PL die **Friseure**)
hairdresser
die **Friseuse** NOUN
hairdresser
frisieren VERB (PERFECT **hat frisiert**)
◆ **jemanden frisieren** to do somebody's hair
◆ **sich frisieren** to do one's hair
frisst VERB see **fressen**
die **Frist** NOUN
deadline ◊ *eine Frist einhalten* to meet a deadline
die **Frisur** NOUN
hairdo
Frl. ABBREVIATION (= *Fräulein*)
Miss
froh ADJECTIVE
happy ◊ *frohe Gesichter* happy faces
◆ **Ich bin froh, dass ...** I'm glad that ...
fröhlich ADJECTIVE
cheerful
die **Fröhlichkeit** NOUN
cheerfulness
fromm ADJECTIVE
devout
der **Fronleichnam** NOUN
Corpus Christi ◊ *an Fronleichnam* on Corpus Christi

> ❶ *Fronleichnam is the second Thursday after Whitsun and is a public holiday in predominantly Catholic areas.*

fror VERB see **frieren**
der **Frosch** NOUN (PL die **Frösche**)
frog
der **Frost** NOUN (PL die **Fröste**)
frost ◊ *ein strenger Frost* a hard frost
frösteln VERB
to shiver
das **Frottee** NOUN (GEN des **Frottees**)
towelling
das **Frottiertuch** NOUN (PL die **Frottiertücher**)
towel
die **Frucht** NOUN (PL die **Früchte**)
fruit
fruchtbar ADJECTIVE
[1] fruitful ◊ *ein fruchtbares Gespräch* a fruitful conversation
[2] fertile ◊ *fruchtbarer Boden* fertile soil
der **Fruchtsaft** NOUN (PL die **Fruchtsäfte**)

fruit juice
früh ADJECTIVE, ADVERB
early ◊ *Komm lieber etwas früher.* It's better if you come a bit earlier.
◆ **heute früh** this morning
früher ADJECTIVE, ADVERB
[1] former ◊ *eine frühere Schülerin unserer Schule* a former pupil of our school
[2] once ◊ *Hier stand früher ein Haus.* A house once stood here.
◆ **Früher war das anders.** That used to be different.
frühestens ADVERB
at the earliest
das **Frühjahr** NOUN (PL die **Frühjahre**)
spring ◊ *im Frühjahr* in spring
der **Frühling** NOUN (PL die **Frühlinge**)
spring ◊ *im Frühling* in spring
das **Frühstück** NOUN
breakfast
frühstücken VERB
to have breakfast
frustrieren VERB (PERFECT **hat frustriert**)
to frustrate
der **Fuchs** NOUN (GEN des **Fuchses,** PL die **Füchse**)
fox
fügen VERB
to join ◊ *Er fügte ein Teil an ein anderes.* He joined one piece to another.
◆ **sich fügen** to be obedient
fühlen VERB
to feel ◊ *Fühl mal, wie weich das ist.* Feel how soft it is. ◊ *Ich fühle mich wohl.* I feel fine. ◊ *Ich fühle mich krank.* I feel ill.
fuhr VERB see **fahren**
führen VERB
[1] to lead ◊ *Sie führte uns nach draußen.* She led us outside.
◆ **ein Geschäft führen** to run a business
[2] to be winning ◊ *Welche Mannschaft führt?* Which team's winning?
der **Führer** NOUN (PL die **Führer**)
[1] leader ◊ *der Parteiführer* the party leader
[2] guide ◊ *Unser Führer zeigte uns alle Sehenswürdigkeiten.* Our guide showed us all the sights.
[3] guidebook ◊ *Hast du einen Führer von Rom?* Have you got a guidebook of Rome?
der **Führerschein** NOUN (PL die **Führerscheine**)
driving licence
◆ **Wann hast du deinen Führerschein gemacht?** When did you sit your driving test?
die **Führung** NOUN
[1] lead ◊ *Unsere Mannschaft liegt in Führung.* Our team is in the lead.
[2] management ◊ *Das Geschäft hat unter neuer Führung wiedereröffnet.*

The business has reopened under new management.

3 guided tour ◊ *Führungen durchs Museum finden stündlich statt.* There are guided tours of the museum every hour.

füllen VERB

1 to fill ◊ *Sie füllte das Glas bis zum Rand.* She filled the glass to the brim.

2 to stuff ◊ *Heute gibt es gefüllte Paprika.* We're having stuffed peppers today.

der **Füller** NOUN (PL die **Füller**)

fountain pen

der **Füllfederhalter** NOUN (PL die **Füllfederhalter**)

fountain pen

die **Füllung** NOUN

filling

das **Fundament** NOUN (PL die **Fundamente**)

foundations

das **Fundbüro** NOUN (PL die **Fundbüros**)

lost property office

fundiert ADJECTIVE

sound ◊ *fundierte Englischkenntnisse* a sound knowledge of English

fünf NUMBER

see also **die Fünf** NOUN

five

die **Fünf** NOUN

see also **fünf** NUMBER

1 five

2 poor

ℹ *German marks range from one (sehr gut) to six (ungenügend).*

fünfhundert NUMBER

five hundred

fünfte ADJECTIVE

fifth ◊ *Ich erkläre dir das jetzt zum fünften Mal.* This is the fifth time I've explained this to you. ◊ *Er kam als Fünfter.* He was the fifth to arrive.

fünfzehn NUMBER

fifteen

fünfzig NUMBER

fifty

der **Funke** NOUN (GEN des **Funkens**, PL die **Funken**)

spark

funkeln VERB

to sparkle

das **Funkgerät** NOUN (PL die **Funkgeräte**)

radio set

die **Funktion** NOUN

function

funktionieren VERB (PERFECT **hat funktioniert**)

to work

die **Funktionstaste** NOUN

function key

für PREPOSITION

*The preposition **für** takes the accusative.*

for ◊ *Das ist für dich.* This is for you.

♦ **was für** what kind of ◊ *Was für ein Fahrrad hast du?* What kind of bike have you got?

♦ **das Für und Wider** the pros and cons

die **Furcht** NOUN

fear

furchtbar ADJECTIVE

terrible

sich **fürchten** VERB

to be afraid ◊ *Ich fürchte mich vor diesem Mann.* I'm afraid of that man.

fürchterlich ADJECTIVE

awful

füreinander ADVERB

for each other

fürs = **für das**

der **Fuß** NOUN (GEN des **Fußes**, PL die **Füße**)

1 foot ◊ *Mir tun die Füße weh.* My feet hurt.

2 leg ◊ *Der Tisch hat vier Füße.* The table's got four legs.

♦ **zu Fuß** on foot

der **Fußball** NOUN (PL die **Fußbälle**)

football

der **Fußballplatz** NOUN (GEN des **Fußballplatzes**, PL die **Fußballplätze**)

football pitch

das **Fußballspiel** NOUN (PL die **Fußballspiele**)

football match

der **Fußballspieler** NOUN (PL die **Fußballspieler**)

footballer

der **Fußboden** NOUN (PL die **Fußböden**)

floor

der **Fußgänger** NOUN (PL die **Fußgänger**)

pedestrian

die **Fußgängerzone** NOUN

pedestrian precinct

das **Fußgelenk** NOUN (PL die **Fußgelenke**)

ankle

der **Fußweg** NOUN (PL die **Fußwege**)

footpath

das **Futter** NOUN (PL die **Futter**)

1 feed ◊ *BSE entstand durch verseuchtes Futter.* BSE was the result of contaminated feed.

♦ **Hast du Futter für die Katze gekauft?** Have you bought cat food?

2 lining ◊ *Der Mantel hat ein Futter aus Pelz.* The coat has a fur lining.

füttern VERB

1 to feed ◊ *Kannst du bitte das Baby füttern?* Can you feed the baby, please?

2 to line ◊ *Der Mantel ist gefüttert.* The coat's lined.

das **Futur** NOUN (PL die **Future**)

future

F

G

g ABBREVIATION (= *Gramm*)
  g
gab VERB *see* **geben**
die **Gabel** NOUN
  fork
gähnen VERB
  to yawn
die **Galerie** NOUN
  gallery
die **Gameshow** NOUN
  gameshow
gammeln VERB
  to bum around
der **Gang** NOUN (PL die **Gänge**)
  1 corridor
  2 aisle ◇ *Ich hätte gern einen Platz am Gang.* I'd like an aisle seat.
  3 gear ◇ *Mein Fahrrad hat zehn Gänge.* My bike has ten gears.
  4 course ◇ *Das war erst der zweite Gang, und ich bin schon satt.* That was only that second course and I'm full already.
  ◆ **etwas in Gang bringen** to get something off the ground ◇ *Sie hat das Projekt in Gang gebracht.* She got the project off the ground.
die **Gans** NOUN (PL dle **Gänse**)
  goose
das **Gänseblümchen** NOUN (PL die **Gänseblümchen**)
  daisy
die **Gänsehaut** NOUN
  goose pimples
ganz ADJECTIVE, ADVERB
  1 whole ◇ *die ganze Welt* the whole world ◇ *ganz Europa* the whole of Europe
  ◆ **sein ganzes Geld** all his money
  2 quite ◇ *ganz gut* quite good
  ◆ **ganz und gar nicht** not at all
  ◆ **Es sieht ganz so aus.** It really looks like it.
ganztags ADVERB
  full time ◇ *ganztags arbeiten* to work full time
die **Ganztagsschule** NOUN
  all-day school
die **Ganztagsstelle** NOUN
  full-time job
gar ADJECTIVE, ADVERB
  done ◇ *Die Kartoffeln sind gar.* The potatoes are done.
  ◆ **gar nicht** not at all ◇ *Sie hat sich gar nicht gefreut.* She was not at all pleased. ◇ *gar nicht schlecht* not bad at all
  ◆ **gar nichts** nothing at all ◇ *Ich habe gar nichts zu tun.* I have nothing at all to do.

◆ **Ich habe gar nichts verstanden.** I didn't understand anything at all.
◆ **gar niemand** nobody at all
die **Garage** NOUN
  garage *(for parking)*
garantieren VERB (PERFECT **hat garantiert**)
  to guarantee
  ◆ **Er kommt garantiert.** He's sure to come.
die **Garderobe** NOUN
  cloakroom ◇ *Ich habe meinen Mantel an der Garderobe abgegeben.* I left my coat in the cloakroom.
die **Gardine** NOUN
  curtain ◇ *die Gardinen zuziehen* to shut the curtains
der **Garten** NOUN (PL die **Gärten**)
  garden
das **Gas** NOUN (GEN des **Gases**, PL die **Gase**)
  gas ◇ *Wir kochen mit Gas.* We cook with gas.
  ◆ **Gas geben** to accelerate
der **Gasherd** NOUN (PL die **Gasherde**)
  gas cooker
das **Gaspedal** NOUN (PL die **Gaspedale**)
  accelerator
die **Gasse** NOUN
  lane ◇ *die schmalen Gassen der Altstadt* the narrow lanes of the old town
der **Gast** NOUN (PL die **Gäste**)
  guest ◇ *Wir haben Gäste aus England.* We've got guests from England.
  ◆ **bei jemandem zu Gast sein** to be somebody's guest
das **Gästehaus** NOUN (GEN des **Gästehauses**, PL die **Gästehäuser**)
  guest house
gastfreundlich ADJECTIVE
  hospitable
die **Gastfreundschaft** NOUN
  hospitality
der **Gastgeber** NOUN (PL die **Gastgeber**)
  host
die **Gastgeberin** NOUN
  hostess
das **Gasthaus** NOUN (GEN des **Gasthauses**, PL die **Gasthäuser**)
  inn
der **Gasthof** NOUN (PL die **Gasthöfe**)
  inn
die **Gaststätte** NOUN
  pub

> *i* In Germany there's practically no difference between pubs and restaurants. You can eat or drink in a **Gaststätte**, families are welcome and the opening hours are flexible.

geb. ABBREVIATION (= *geboren*)
 1 born ◊ *Peter Schmitz, geb. 1965* Peter Schmitz, born 1965
 2 née ◊ *Frau Dümmler, geb. Schnorr* Mrs Dümmler, née Schnorr

das **Gebäck** NOUN (PL die **Gebäcke**)
 pastry ◊ *Kuchen und Gebäck* cakes and pastries

gebären VERB (PRESENT **gebiert**, IMPERFECT **gebar**, PERFECT **hat geboren**)
 to give birth to

das **Gebäude** NOUN (PL die **Gebäude**)
 building

geben VERB (PRESENT **gibt**, IMPERFECT **gab**, PERFECT **hat gegeben**)
 to give ◊ *Gib ihm bitte das Geld.* Please give him the money. ◊ *Kannst du dieses Buch bitte deiner Mutter geben.* Could you give this book to your mother, please.
 ♦ **Karten geben** to deal
 ♦ **es gibt** there is ◊ *Hier gibt es ein schönes Freibad.* There's a lovely open-air pool here. ◊ *In Stuttgart gibt es viele Parks.* There are many parks in Stuttgart. ◊ *Wenn wir zu spät kommen, gibt es Ärger.* There will be trouble if we arrive late.
 ♦ **Was gibt's?** What's up?
 ♦ **Was gibt es im Kino?** What's on at the cinema?
 ♦ **sich geschlagen geben** to admit defeat
 ♦ **Das wird sich schon geben.** That'll sort itself out.

das **Gebet** NOUN (PL die **Gebete**)
 prayer

gebeten VERB *see* **bitten**

das **Gebiet** NOUN (PL die **Gebiete**)
 1 area ◊ *ein bewaldetes Gebiet* a wooded area
 2 field ◊ *Er ist Experte auf diesem Gebiet.* He's an expert in this field.

gebildet ADJECTIVE
 cultured

das **Gebirge** NOUN (PL die **Gebirge**)
 mountain chain ◊ *Die Alpen sind ein großes Gebirge.* The Alps are a large mountain chain.
 ♦ **ins Gebirge fahren** to go to the mountains

das **Gebiss** NOUN (GEN des **Gebisses**, PL die **Gebisse**)
 1 teeth ◊ *Sie hat ein gesundes Gebiss.* She's got healthy teeth.
 2 dentures ◊ *Opas Gebiss lag auf dem Tisch.* Grandpa's dentures were lying on the table.

gebissen VERB *see* **beißen**

geblieben VERB *see* **bleiben**

geboren VERB *see* **gebären**

geboren ADJECTIVE
 1 born ◊ *Wann bist du geboren?* When were you born?
 2 née ◊ *Frau Dümmler, geborene Schnorr* Mrs Dümmler, née Schnorr

geborgen ADJECTIVE
 safe ◊ *Ich fühle mich bei dir geborgen.* I feel safe with you.

geboten VERB *see* **bieten**

gebracht VERB *see* **bringen**

gebraten ADJECTIVE
 fried

der **Gebrauch** NOUN (PL die **Gebräuche**)
 use ◊ *Der Gebrauch dieses Geräts ist sehr einfach.* This machine is very easy to use.
 ♦ **Sitten und Gebräuche** customs and traditions

gebrauchen VERB (PERFECT **hat gebraucht**)
 to use

die **Gebrauchsanweisung** NOUN
 directions for use ◊ *Wo ist die Gebrauchsanweisung?* Where are the directions for use?

gebraucht ADJECTIVE
 used

der **Gebrauchtwagen** NOUN (PL die **Gebrauchtwagen**)
 second-hand car

gebrochen VERB *see* **brechen**

die **Gebühr** NOUN
 fee

die **Gebühreneinheit** NOUN
 unit (*telephone*)

gebührenfrei ADJECTIVE
 free of charge
 ♦ **ein gebührenfreier Anruf** Freefone ® call

gebührenpflichtig ADJECTIVE
 subject to a charge
 ♦ **eine gebührenpflichtige Verwarnung** a fine

gebunden VERB *see* **binden**

die **Geburt** NOUN
 birth ◊ *bei der Geburt* at the birth

gebürtig ADJECTIVE
 native of ◊ *ein gebürtiger Schweizer* a native of Switzerland

das **Geburtsdatum** NOUN (PL die **Geburtsdaten**)
 date of birth

der **Geburtsort** NOUN (PL die **Geburtsorte**)
 birthplace

der **Geburtstag** NOUN (PL die **Geburtstage**)
 birthday ◊ *Herzlichen Glückwunsch zum Geburtstag!* Happy Birthday!

das **Gebüsch** NOUN (PL die **Gebüsche**)
 bushes

gedacht VERB *see* **denken**

das **Gedächtnis** NOUN (GEN des **Gedächtnisses**, PL die **Gedächtnisse**)
 memory ◊ *Ich habe ein schlechtes Gedächtnis.* I've got a bad memory.

G

der **Gedanke** NOUN (GEN des **Gedankens**, PL die **Gedanken**)
thought
♦ **sich über etwas Gedanken machen** to think about something ◊ *Ich habe mir Gedanken über das gemacht, was du gesagt hast.* I've thought about what you said.

der **Gedankenstrich** NOUN (PL die **Gedankenstriche**)
dash

das **Gedeck** NOUN (PL die **Gedecke**)
1 cover ◊ *ein Gedeck für drei Personen* covers for three people
2 set menu ◊ *Sie bestellte ein Gedeck.* She ordered the set menu.

gedeihen VERB (IMPERFECT **gedieh**, PERFECT **ist gediehen**)
to thrive

das **Gedenken** NOUN
♦ **zum Gedenken an jemanden** in memory of somebody

das **Gedicht** NOUN (PL die **Gedichte**)
poem

das **Gedränge** NOUN
crush ◊ *Vor der Kinokasse herrschte großes Gedränge.* There was a huge crush at the cinema box office.

die **Geduld** NOUN
patience

sich **gedulden** VERB (PERFECT **hat sich geduldet**)
to be patient

geduldig ADJECTIVE
patient

gedurft VERB see **dürfen**

geehrt ADJECTIVE
♦ **Sehr geehrter Herr Butterfeld** Dear Mr Butterfeld

geeignet ADJECTIVE
suitable

die **Gefahr** NOUN
danger ◊ *in Gefahr schweben* to be in danger
♦ **Gefahr laufen, etwas zu tun** to run the risk of doing something
♦ **auf eigene Gefahr** at one's own risk

gefährden VERB (PERFECT **hat gefährdet**)
to endanger

gefährlich ADJECTIVE
dangerous

das **Gefälle** NOUN (PL die **Gefälle**)
gradient

gefallen (1) VERB see **fallen**

gefallen (2) VERB (PRESENT **gefällt**, IMPERFECT **gefiel**, PERFECT **hat gefallen**)
see also **der Gefallen** NOUN
♦ **Es gefällt mir.** I like it.
♦ **Das Geschenk hat ihr gefallen.** She liked the present.
♦ **Er gefällt mir.** I like him.
♦ **Das gefällt mir an ihm.** That's one thing I like about him.

♦ **sich etwas gefallen lassen** to put up with something ◊ *Eine solche Frechheit lasse ich mir nicht gefallen.* I'm not putting up with cheek like that.

der **Gefallen** NOUN (PL die **Gefallen**)
see also **gefallen** VERB
favour ◊ *Könntest du mir einen Gefallen tun?* Could you do me a favour?

gefangen VERB see **fangen**
♦ **jemanden gefangen nehmen** to take somebody prisoner

der **Gefangene** NOUN (GEN des/der
die **Gefangenen**, PL die **Gefangenen**)
prisoner ◊ *Ein Gefangener ist geflohen.* A prisoner has escaped.

gefangennehmen VERB see **gefangen**

die **Gefangenschaft** NOUN
captivity

das **Gefängnis** NOUN (GEN des **Gefängnisses**, PL die **Gefängnisse**)
prison

die **Gefängnisstrafe** NOUN
prison sentence

das **Gefäß** NOUN (GEN des **Gefäßes**, PL die **Gefäße**)
container

gefasst ADJECTIVE
composed ◊ *Sie war sehr gefasst.* She was very composed.
♦ **auf etwas gefasst sein** to be prepared for something ◊ *Ich war schon aufs Schlimmste gefasst.* I was prepared for the worst.

geflogen VERB see **fliegen**

geflossen VERB see **fließen**

das **Geflügel** NOUN
poultry

gefragt ADJECTIVE
in demand ◊ *Er ist ein sehr gefragter Künstler.* He's an artist very much in demand. ◊ *Handwerker sind sehr gefragt.* Tradesmen are in great demand.

gefräßig ADJECTIVE
greedy

das **Gefrierfach** NOUN (PL die **Gefrierfächer**)
icebox

gefriergetrocknet ADJECTIVE
freeze-dried

die **Gefriertruhe** NOUN
deep-freeze

gefroren ADJECTIVE
frozen

das **Gefühl** NOUN (PL die **Gefühle**)
feeling ◊ *Sie hat ein Gefühl für Kunst.* She's got a feeling for art.
♦ **etwas im Gefühl haben** to have a feel for something

gefühlsmäßig ADJECTIVE
instinctive

gefüllt ADJECTIVE
stuffed ◊ *gefüllte Auberginen* stuffed aubergines

gefunden VERB *see* **finden**

gegangen VERB *see* **gehen**

gegeben VERB *see* **geben**

gegen PREPOSITION

> *The preposition **gegen** takes the accusative.*

[1] against ◊ *Ich bin gegen diese Idee.* I'm against this idea. ◊ *nichts gegen jemanden haben* to have nothing against somebody
♦ **ein Mittel gegen Schnupfen** something for colds
♦ **Maske gegen Botha** Maske versus Botha
[2] towards ◊ *gegen Osten* towards the east ◊ *gegen Abend* towards evening
♦ **gegen einen Baum fahren** to drive into a tree
[3] round about ◊ *gegen drei Uhr* round about three o'clock

die **Gegend** NOUN
area ◊ *die Gegend um Ulm* the area around Ulm

das **Gegenmittel** NOUN (PL die **Gegenmittel**)
antidote

der **Gegensatz** NOUN (GEN des **Gegensatzes,** PL die **Gegensätze**)
contrast
♦ **Im Gegensatz zu mir ist er gut in Mathe.** Unlike me, he's good at maths.

gegenseitig ADJECTIVE
mutual ◊ *gegenseitiges Vertrauen* mutual trust
♦ **sich gegenseitig helfen** to help each other

der **Gegenstand** NOUN (PL die **Gegenstände**)
object

das **Gegenteil** NOUN
opposite ◊ *Das ist das Gegenteil von schön.* That's the opposite of lovely.
♦ **im Gegenteil** on the contrary

gegenüber PREPOSITION, ADVERB

> *The preposition **gegenüber** takes the dative.*

[1] opposite ◊ *Die Apotheke ist gegenüber.* The chemist's is opposite. ◊ *Er saß mir gegenüber.* He sat opposite me.
[2] towards ◊ *Sie waren mir gegenüber sehr freundlich.* They were very friendly towards me.

der **Gegenverkehr** NOUN
oncoming traffic

die **Gegenwart** NOUN
present ◊ *in der Gegenwart leben* to live in the present

gegessen VERB *see* **essen**

der **Gegner** NOUN (PL die **Gegner**)
opponent

gegrillt ADJECTIVE
grilled

das **Gehackte** NOUN (GEN des **Gehackten**)
mince ◊ *Ein Kilo Gehacktes, bitte.* A kilo of mince, please.

das **Gehalt** NOUN (PL die **Gehälter**)
salary ◊ *Er verdient ein gutes Gehalt.* He earns a good salary.

gehässig ADJECTIVE
spiteful

geheim ADJECTIVE
secret
♦ **geheim halten** to keep secret

das **Geheimnis** NOUN (GEN des **Geheimnisses,** PL die **Geheimnisse**)
[1] secret ◊ *Kannst du ein Geheimnis behalten?* Can you keep a secret?
[2] mystery ◊ *die Geheimnisse der Erde* the Earth's mysteries

geheimnisvoll ADJECTIVE
mysterious

die **Geheimnummer** NOUN
ex-directory number
♦ **Wir haben eine Geheimnummer.** We're ex-directory.

gehemmt ADJECTIVE
inhibited

gehen VERB (IMPERFECT **ging,** PERFECT **ist gegangen**)
[1] to go ◊ *Wir gehen jetzt.* We're going now. ◊ *schwimmen gehen* to go swimming
[2] to walk ◊ *Sollen wir gehen oder den Bus nehmen?* Shall we walk or go by bus?
♦ **Wie geht es dir?** How are you?
♦ **Wie geht's?** How are things?
♦ **Mir geht's gut.** I'm fine.
♦ **Ihm geht's gut.** He's fine.
♦ **Es geht.** Not bad.
♦ **Geht das?** Is that possible?
♦ **Geht's noch?** Can you manage?
♦ **Das geht nicht.** That's not on.
♦ **um etwas gehen** to be about something ◊ *In dem Film geht es um einen Bankraub.* The film's about a bank robbery.
♦ **Hier geht es um sehr viel Geld.** There's a lot of money at stake here.

der **Gehilfe** NOUN (GEN des **Gehilfen,** PL die **Gehilfen**)
assistant

das **Gehirn** NOUN (PL die **Gehirne**)
brain

die **Gehirnerschütterung** NOUN
concussion

gehoben VERB *see* **heben**

geholfen VERB *see* **helfen**

gehorchen VERB (PERFECT **hat gehorcht**)
to obey ◊ *Du solltest deinem Vater gehorchen.* You should obey your father. ◊ *Ein Hund sollte lernen zu gehorchen.* A dog should learn to obey.

gehören VERB (PERFECT **hat gehört**)

G

☞

♦ **jemandem gehören** to belong to somebody ◊ *Dieses Buch gehört mir.* This book belongs to me.

♦ **Das gehört sich einfach nicht.** That just isn't done.

gehorsam ADJECTIVE
see also **der Gehorsam** NOUN
obedient

der **Gehorsam** NOUN
see also **gehorsam** ADJECTIVE
obedience

der **Gehsteig** NOUN (PL die **Gehsteige**)
pavement

der **Gehweg** NOUN (PL die **Gehwege**)
pavement

der **Geier** NOUN (PL die **Geier**)
vulture

die **Geige** NOUN
violin ◊ *Wiltrud spielt Geige.* Wiltrud plays the violin.

geil ADJECTIVE
[1] horny ◊ *Wenn er das sieht, wird er geil.* When he sees that, he'll get horny.
[2] cool ◊ *Das war eine geile Party.* That was a cool party. ◊ *ein geiler Song* a cool song

die **Geisel** NOUN
hostage

der **Geist** NOUN (PL die **Geister**)
[1] ghost
[2] mind ◊ *Er hat einen regen Geist.* He has a lively mind.
♦ **Seine Rede sprühte vor Geist.** His speech was very witty.

geistesabwesend ADJECTIVE
absent-minded

geisteskrank ADJECTIVE
mentally ill

die **Geisteskrankheit** NOUN
mental illness

geistig ADJECTIVE
intellectual ◊ *ihre geistigen Fähigkeiten* her intellectual capabilities
♦ **geistige Getränke** alcoholic drinks
♦ **geistig behindert** mentally handicapped

der **Geiz** NOUN (GEN des **Geizes**)
meanness

der **Geizhals** NOUN (GEN des **Geizhalses**, PL die **Geizhälse**)
miser

geizig ADJECTIVE
mean

gekannt VERB see **kennen**

geknickt ADJECTIVE
dejected ◊ *Er war total geknickt.* He was completely dejected.

gekonnt VERB see **können**

gekonnt ADJECTIVE
skilful

das **Gekritzel** NOUN
scrawl

das **Gel** NOUN (PL die **Gele**)

gel

das **Gelächter** NOUN
laughter

geladen VERB see **laden**

geladen ADJECTIVE
[1] loaded ◊ *eine geladene Waffe* a loaded weapon
♦ **geladene Gäste** invited guests
[2] live ◊ *Vorsicht, der Zaun ist geladen.* Careful, the fence is live.
♦ **geladen sein** to be furious ◊ *Meine Mutter war geladen.* My mother was furious.

gelähmt ADJECTIVE
paralysed

das **Gelände** NOUN (PL die **Gelände**)
[1] grounds ◊ *auf dem Gelände der Schule* on the school grounds
[2] terrain ◊ *unwegsames Gelände* difficult terrain
♦ **Wir sind mit dem Mountainbike durchs Gelände gefahren.** We cycled cross-country on our mountain bikes.
♦ **ein Baugelände** a building site

gelangweilt ADJECTIVE
bored

gelassen VERB see **lassen**

gelassen ADJECTIVE
calm ◊ *Sie blieb gelassen.* She remained calm.

geläufig ADJECTIVE
common ◊ *ein geläufiger Begriff* a common term
♦ **Das ist mir nicht geläufig.** I'm not familiar with that.

gelaunt ADJECTIVE
♦ **gut gelaunt** in a good mood
♦ **schlecht gelaunt** in a bad mood
♦ **Wie ist er gelaunt?** What sort of mood's he in?

gelb ADJECTIVE
[1] yellow
[2] amber ◊ *Die Ampel war gelb.* The traffic lights were at amber.

die **Gelbsucht** NOUN
jaundice

das **Geld** NOUN (PL die **Gelder**)
money
♦ **etwas zu Geld machen** to sell something off

der **Geldautomat** NOUN (GEN des **Geldautomaten**, PL die **Geldautomaten**)
cash dispenser

der **Geldbeutel** NOUN (PL die **Geldbeutel**)
purse

der **Geldschein** NOUN (PL die **Geldscheine**)
banknote

die **Geldstrafe** NOUN
fine

das **Geldstück** NOUN (PL die **Geldstücke**)
coin

die **Geldtasche** NOUN

wallet

der **Geldwechsel** NOUN
changing of money ◊ *Beim Geldwechsel muss man eine Gebühr bezahlen.* There is a charge for changing money.
♦ **"Geldwechsel"** "bureau de change"

gelegen VERB *see* **liegen**

die **Gelegenheit** NOUN
1 opportunity ◊ *Sobald ich eine Gelegenheit bekomme ...* As soon as I get an opportunity ... ◊ *bei jeder Gelegenheit* at every opportunity
2 occasion ◊ *Bei dieser Gelegenheit trug sie das blaue Kostüm.* On this occasion she wore her blue suit.

gelegentlich ADVERB
1 occasionally ◊ *Gelegentlich gehe ich ganz gern ins Kino.* I occasionally like going to the cinema.
2 some time or other ◊ *Ich werde mich gelegentlich darum kümmern.* I'll do it some time or other.

das **Gelenk** NOUN (PL die **Gelenke**)
joint (*in body*)

gelenkig ADJECTIVE
supple

gelernt ADJECTIVE
skilled

geliehen VERB *see* **leihen**

gelingen VERB (IMPERFECT **gelang**, PERFECT **ist gelungen**)
to succeed ◊ *Sein Plan ist ihm nicht gelungen.* His plan didn't succeed.
♦ **Es ist mir gelungen, ihn zu überzeugen.** I succeeded in convincing him.
♦ **Der Kuchen ist gelungen.** The cake turned out well.

gelten VERB (PRESENT **gilt**, IMPERFECT **galt**, PERFECT **hat gegolten**)
to be valid ◊ *Dein Ausweis gilt nicht mehr.* Your passport is no longer valid.
♦ **es gilt, etwas zu tun** it's necessary to do something ◊ *Es gilt, sich zu entscheiden.* It's necessary to make a decision.
♦ **jemandem gelten** to be aimed at somebody ◊ *Diese Bemerkung hat dir gegolten.* This comment was aimed at you.
♦ **etwas gelten lassen** to accept something
♦ **Was gilt die Wette?** What do you bet?

gelungen VERB *see* **gelingen**

gelungen ADJECTIVE
successful

das **Gemälde** NOUN (PL die **Gemälde**)
painting ◊ *ein Gemälde von Rembrandt* a painting by Rembrandt

gemein ADJECTIVE
mean ◊ *Das war gemein!* That was mean!
♦ **etwas gemein haben mit** to have something in common with ◊ *Mit solchen Leuten habe ich nichts gemein.* I don't have anything in common with people like that.

gemeinsam ADJECTIVE, ADVERB
1 joint ◊ *gemeinsame Anstrengungen* joint efforts
♦ **ein gemeinsames Abendessen** dinner together
2 together ◊ *Wir sind gemeinsam zum Lehrer gegangen.* We went together to the teacher.
♦ **etwas gemeinsam haben** to have something in common ◊ *Wir haben viel gemeinsam.* We've a lot in common.

gemischt ADJECTIVE
mixed

gemocht VERB *see* **mögen**

das **Gemüse** NOUN (PL die **Gemüse**)
vegetables ◊ *Gemüse ist gesund.* Vegetables are healthy.

gemusst VERB *see* **müssen**

gemustert ADJECTIVE
patterned

das **Gemüt** NOUN (PL die **Gemüter**)
nature ◊ *Sie hat ein fröhliches Gemüt.* She has a happy nature.
♦ **die Gemüter erregen** to arouse strong feelings

gemütlich ADJECTIVE
1 cosy ◊ *eine gemütliche Wohnung* a cosy flat
♦ **ein gemütlicher Abend** a pleasant evening
2 good-natured ◊ *Sie ist ein gemütlicher Mensch.* She's good-natured.

das **Gen** NOUN (PL die **Gene**)
gene

genannt VERB *see* **nennen**

genau ADJECTIVE, ADVERB
1 exact ◊ *Ich brauche genaue Zahlen.* I need exact figures.
♦ **Diese Übersetzung ist nicht sehr genau.** This translation isn't very accurate.
2 exactly ◊ *Genau das habe ich auch gesagt.* That's exactly what I said. ◊ *Sie hatte genau dasselbe Kleid an.* She was wearing exactly the same dress. ◊ *Das ist genau anders herum.* That's exactly the opposite.
♦ **etwas genau nehmen** to take something seriously
♦ **genau genommen** strictly speaking

die **Genauigkeit** NOUN
accuracy

genauso ADVERB
♦ **genauso gut** just as good

genehmigen VERB (PERFECT **hat genehmigt**)
to approve
♦ **sich etwas genehmigen** to treat oneself to something ◊ *Ich werde mir jetzt ein Eis genehmigen.* I'm going to treat myself to an ice cream.

G

die **Genehmigung** NOUN
  [1] permission ◊ *Für den Umbau brauchen wir eine Genehmigung.* We need permission for the conversion.
  [2] permit ◊ *Hier ist meine Genehmigung.* Here's my permit.

die **Generation** NOUN
  generation

Genf NEUT NOUN
  Geneva
  ◆ **der Genfer See** Lake Geneva

genial ADJECTIVE
  brilliant

das **Genick** NOUN (PL die **Genicke**)
  back of the neck
  ◆ **Ich hätte mir fast das Genick gebrochen.** I nearly broke my neck.

das **Genie** NOUN (PL die **Genies**)
  genius

genießbar ADJECTIVE
  [1] edible ◊ *Das Essen war nicht genießbar.* The meal wasn't edible.
  [2] drinkable ◊ *Probier mal, ob der Tee genießbar ist.* Try the tea and see if it's drinkable.

genießen VERB (IMPERFECT **genoss**, PERFECT **hat genossen**)
  to enjoy ◊ *Wir haben die Ferien genossen.* We enjoyed our holidays.

genmanipuliert ADJECTIVE
  genetically modified ◊ *genmanipulierte Lebensmittel* genetically modified food

genommen VERB *see* **nehmen**

die **Gentechnologie** NOUN
  genetic engineering

genug ADJECTIVE
  enough ◊ *Wir haben genug Geld.* We've got enough money. ◊ *gut genug* good enough

genügen VERB (PERFECT **hat genügt**)
  to be enough ◊ *Das genügt noch nicht.* That isn't enough.
  ◆ **jemandem genügen** to be enough for somebody ◊ *Genügt dir das eine Stück?* Is one piece enough for you?

genügend ADJECTIVE
  sufficient

der **Genuss** NOUN (GEN des **Genusses**, PL die **Genüsse**)
  [1] pleasure ◊ *Es war ein Genuss!* That was sheer pleasure!
  [2] consumption ◊ *der Genuss von Alkohol* the consumption of alcohol
  ◆ **in den Genuss von etwas kommen** to receive the benefit of something

genüsslich ADVERB
  with relish

geöffnet ADJECTIVE
  open

die **Geografie** NOUN
  geography

die **Geometrie** NOUN
  geometry

das **Gepäck** NOUN
  luggage

die **Gepäckannahme** NOUN
  luggage office

die **Gepäckaufbewahrungsstelle** NOUN
  left-luggage office

die **Gepäckausgabe** NOUN
  baggage reclaim

gepflegt ADJECTIVE
  [1] well-groomed ◊ *gepflegte Hände* well-groomed hands
  [2] well-kept ◊ *ein gepflegter Park* a well-kept park

gerade ADJECTIVE, ADVERB
  [1] straight ◊ *eine gerade Strecke* a straight stretch
  [2] upright ◊ *eine gerade Haltung* an upright posture
  ◆ **eine gerade Zahl** an even number
  [3] just ◊ *Du kommst gerade richtig.* You've come just at the right time. ◊ *Das ist es ja gerade!* That's just it! ◊ *Er wollte gerade aufstehen.* He was just about to get up.
  ◆ **gerade erst** only just ◊ *Ich bin gerade erst gekommen.* I've only just arrived.
  ◆ **gerade noch** only just ◊ *Das geht gerade noch.* That's only just OK.
  ◆ **gerade deshalb** that's exactly why
  ◆ **gerade du** you of all people ◊ *Warum gerade ich?* Why me of all people?
  ◆ **nicht gerade** not exactly ◊ *Das war nicht gerade nett.* That wasn't exactly nice.

geradeaus ADVERB
  straight ahead

gerannt VERB *see* **rennen**

das **Gerät** NOUN (PL die **Geräte**)
  [1] gadget ◊ *ein Gerät zum Papierschneiden* a gadget for cutting paper
  [2] appliance ◊ *ein Haushaltsgerät* a household appliance
  [3] tool ◊ *ein Gartengerät* a garden tool
  [4] apparatus ◊ *Wir haben heute an den Geräten geturnt.* We did gymnastics on the apparatus today.
  [5] equipment ◊ *Geräte zum Angeln* fishing equipment

geraten VERB (PRESENT **gerät**, IMPERFECT **geriet**, PERFECT **ist geraten**)
  [1] to thrive ◊ *Hier geraten die Pflanzen.* Plants thrive here.
  [2] to turn out ◊ *Ihre Kinder sind alle gut geraten.* All their children have turned out well. ◊ *Der Kuchen ist mir nicht geraten.* The cake hasn't turned out well.
  ◆ **in etwas geraten** to get into something ◊ *Wir sind in den Stau geraten.* We got into a traffic jam.
  ◆ **in Angst geraten** to get frightened
  ◆ **nach jemandem geraten** to take after somebody

geräuchert ADJECTIVE
smoked

das **Geräusch** NOUN (PL die **Geräusche**)
sound

gerecht ADJECTIVE
fair ◊ *Das ist nicht gerecht!* That's not fair!

die **Gerechtigkeit** NOUN
justice

das **Gerede** NOUN
gossip ◊ *Das ist alles nur Gerede.* That's all just gossip.

geregelt ADJECTIVE
1 steady ◊ *eine geregelte Arbeit* a steady job
2 regular ◊ *geregelte Mahlzeiten* regular meals

gereizt ADJECTIVE
irritable

das **Gericht** NOUN (PL die **Gerichte**)
1 court ◊ *Wir sehen uns vor Gericht.* I'll see you in court.
2 dish ◊ *ein leckeres Gericht* a tasty dish
♦ **das Jüngste Gericht** the Last Judgement

gerieben VERB *see* **reiben**

gering ADJECTIVE
1 small ◊ *eine geringe Menge* a small amount
2 low ◊ *geringe Beteiligung* low participation
♦ **eine geringe Zeit** a short time

geringschätzig ADJECTIVE
disparaging

geringste ADJECTIVE
least ◊ *Das ist meine geringste Sorge.* That's the least of my worries.

geritten VERB *see* **reiten**

gern ADVERB
gladly ◊ *Das habe ich gern getan.* I did it gladly.
♦ **gern mögen** to like ◊ *Ich mag diese Art von Musik gern.* I like this kind of music.
♦ **etwas gern tun** to like doing something ◊ *Ich schwimme gern.* I like swimming.
♦ **Ich hätte gern ...** I'd like ... ◊ *Ich hätte gern ein Zitroneneis.* I'd like a lemon ice cream.
♦ **Er möchte jetzt gern nach Hause.** He'd like to go home now.
♦ **Ja, gern!** Yes, please.
♦ **Gern geschehen!** It's a pleasure.

gernhaben VERB (PRESENT **hat gern,** IMPERFECT **hatte gern,** PERFECT **hat gerngehabt**)
to like ◊ *Ich habe sie sehr gern.* I like her a lot.

gerochen VERB *see* **riechen**

die **Gerste** NOUN
barley

der **Geruch** NOUN (PL die **Gerüche**)
smell

das **Gerücht** NOUN (PL die **Gerüchte**)
rumour

das **Gerümpel** NOUN
junk

gesalzen VERB *see* **salzen**

gesalzen ADJECTIVE
♦ **gesalzene Preise** hefty prices

gesamt ADJECTIVE
whole ◊ *die gesamte Klasse* the whole class
♦ **die gesamten Kosten** the total cost
♦ **gesamte Werke** complete works
♦ **im Gesamten** all in all

die **Gesamtschule** NOUN
comprehensive school

> ⓘ *Gesamtschulen* are the exception rather than the rule in Germany.

gesandt VERB *see* **senden**

das **Geschäft** NOUN (PL die **Geschäfte**)
1 shop ◊ *In welchem Geschäft hast du das gekauft?* Which shop did you buy that in?
2 business ◊ *Die Geschäfte gehen gut.* Business is good.
3 deal ◊ *Ich schlage dir ein Geschäft vor.* I'll make a deal with you.

die **Geschäftsfrau** NOUN
businesswoman

der **Geschäftsmann** NOUN (PL die **Geschäftsmänner**)
businessman

die **Geschäftszeiten** FEM PL NOUN
business hours

geschehen VERB (PRESENT **geschieht,** IMPERFECT **geschah,** PERFECT **ist geschehen**)
to happen ◊ *Was ist geschehen?* What's happened? ◊ *Was ist mit ihm geschehen?* What's happened to him?

gescheit ADJECTIVE
clever

das **Geschenk** NOUN (PL die **Geschenke**)
present

die **Geschichte** NOUN
1 story ◊ *eine lustige Geschichte* a funny story
2 history ◊ *die deutsche Geschichte* German history
3 business ◊ *die Geschichte mit dem verschwundenen Pass* the business of the missing passport

geschichtlich ADJECTIVE
historical

geschickt ADJECTIVE
skilful

geschieden VERB *see* **scheiden**

geschieden ADJECTIVE
divorced

geschienen VERB *see* **scheinen**

das **Geschirr** NOUN
crockery ◊ *In welchem Schrank steht das Geschirr?* What cupboard is the crockery kept in?

G

♦ **das Geschirr spülen** to do the dishes

die **Geschirrspülmaschine** NOUN
dishwasher

das **Geschirrtuch** NOUN (PL die **Geschirrtücher**)
dish cloth

das **Geschlecht** NOUN (PL die **Geschlechter**)
1 sex ◊ *ein Kind weiblichen Geschlechts* a child of the female sex
2 gender ◊ *Welches Geschlecht hat dieses Substantiv?* What gender is this noun?

die **Geschlechtskrankheit** NOUN
sexually transmitted disease

der **Geschlechtsverkehr** NOUN
sexual intercourse

geschlossen VERB *see* **schließen**

geschlossen ADJECTIVE
shut
♦ **"Geschlossen"** "Closed"

der **Geschmack** NOUN (PL die **Geschmäcke**)
taste ◊ *Das ist nicht nach meinem Geschmack.* This is not to my taste.
♦ **Geschmack an etwas finden** to come to like something ◊ *Sie hat inzwischen Geschmack an dieser Art von Sport gefunden.* In the meantime she's come to like this kind of sport.

geschmacklos ADJECTIVE
1 tasteless ◊ *Die Suppe war ziemlich geschmacklos.* The soup was pretty tasteless.
2 in bad taste ◊ *Das war ein geschmackloser Witz.* That joke was in bad taste.

geschmackvoll ADJECTIVE
tasteful

geschnitten VERB *see* **schneiden**

geschossen VERB *see* **schießen**

geschrieben VERB *see* **schreiben**

geschrien VERB *see* **schreien**

geschützt ADJECTIVE
protected

das **Geschwafel** NOUN
silly talk

das **Geschwätz** NOUN
chatter

geschwätzig ADJECTIVE
talkative

die **Geschwindigkeit** NOUN
speed

die **Geschwindigkeitsbeschränkung** NOUN
speed limit

die **Geschwindigkeitskontrolle** NOUN
speed check

die **Geschwister** PL NOUN
brothers and sisters

geschwommen VERB *see* **schwimmen**

das **Geschwür** NOUN (PL die **Geschwüre**)
ulcer

gesellig ADJECTIVE
sociable

die **Gesellschaft** NOUN
1 society ◊ *die Gesellschaft verändern* to change society
2 company
♦ **jemandem Gesellschaft leisten** to keep somebody company

gesessen VERB *see* **sitzen**

das **Gesetz** NOUN (GEN des **Gesetzes**, PL die **Gesetze**)
law

gesetzlich ADJECTIVE
legal
♦ **gesetzlicher Feiertag** public holiday

das **Gesicht** NOUN (PL die **Gesichter**)
face

der **Gesichtsausdruck** NOUN
expression

gespannt ADJECTIVE
1 strained ◊ *Die Lage in Nordirland ist gespannt.* The situation in Northern Ireland is strained.
2 eager ◊ *gespannte Zuhörer* eager listeners
♦ **Ich bin gespannt, ob ...** I wonder whether ...
♦ **auf etwas gespannt sein** to look forward to something ◊ *Ich bin auf das Fest gespannt.* I'm looking forward to the party.

das **Gespenst** NOUN (PL die **Gespenster**)
ghost

gesperrt ADJECTIVE
closed off

das **Gespräch** NOUN (PL die **Gespräche**)
1 conversation ◊ *ein langes Gespräch* a long conversation
2 call ◊ *Frau Morris, ein Gespräch für Sie.* Mrs Morris, there's a call for you.

gesprächig ADJECTIVE
talkative

gesprochen VERB *see* **sprechen**

gesprungen VERB *see* **springen**

die **Gestalt** NOUN
1 shape ◊ *die Gestalt der Skulptur* the shape of the sculpture
♦ **Gestalt annehmen** to take shape ◊ *Mein Referat nimmt langsam Gestalt an.* My assignment is slowly taking shape.
2 figure ◊ *Ich konnte eine dunkle Gestalt im Garten erkennen.* I could see a dark figure in the garden.
♦ **in Gestalt von** in the form of

gestalten VERB (PERFECT **hat gestaltet**)
to lay out ◊ *Wer hat euren Garten gestaltet?* Who laid out your garden?
♦ **Wie gestaltest du deine Freizeit?** How do you spend your spare time?

gestanden VERB *see* **stehen**

das **Geständnis** NOUN (GEN des **Geständnisses**, PL die **Geständnisse**)
confession

der **Gestank** NOUN
stench

gestatten VERB (PERFECT **hat/ist gestattet**)
to allow
♦ **Gestatten Sie?** May I?
gestattet ADJECTIVE
permitted ◊ *Das ist nicht gestattet.* That is not permitted.

die **Geste** NOUN
gesture

gestehen VERB (IMPERFECT **gestand,** PERFECT **hat gestanden**)
to confess

das **Gestein** NOUN (PL die **Gesteine**)
rock ◊ *vulkanisches Gestein* volcanic rock

das **Gestell** NOUN (PL die **Gestelle**)
[1] frame ◊ *ein Brillengestell* spectacle frames
[2] rack ◊ *ein Gestell für Weinflaschen* a wine rack

gestern ADVERB
yesterday
♦ **gestern Abend** yesterday evening
♦ **gestern Morgen** yesterday morning

gestohlen VERB see **stehlen**

gestorben VERB see **sterben**

gestört ADJECTIVE
disturbed

gestreift ADJECTIVE
striped

gesund ADJECTIVE
healthy
♦ **wieder gesund werden** to get better

die **Gesundheit** NOUN
health
♦ **Gesundheit!** Bless you!

gesundheitlich ADJECTIVE, ADVERB
health ◊ *gesundheitliche Probleme* health problems
♦ **Wie geht es Ihnen gesundheitlich?** How's your health?

gesungen VERB see **singen**

getan VERB see **tun**

das **Getränk** NOUN (PL die **Getränke**)
drink

die **Getränkekarte** NOUN
wine list

der **Getränkemarkt** NOUN (PL die **Getränkemärkte**)
drinks cash-and-carry

sich **getrauen** VERB (PERFECT **hat sich getraut**)
to dare ◊ *Sie hat sich nicht getraut hineinzugehen.* She didn't dare go in.

das **Getreide** NOUN (PL die **Getreide**)
cereals

getrennt ADJECTIVE
separate

das **Getriebe** NOUN (PL die **Getriebe**)
gearbox

getrieben VERB see **treiben**

getroffen VERB see **treffen**

getrunken VERB see **trinken**

geübt ADJECTIVE
experienced

gewachsen VERB see **wachsen**

gewachsen ADJECTIVE
♦ **jemandem gewachsen sein** to be a match for somebody ◊ *Er war seinem Gegner gewachsen.* He was a match for his opponent.
♦ **Sie ist den Kindern nicht gewachsen.** She can't cope with the children.
♦ **einer Sache gewachsen sein** to be up to something ◊ *Meinst du, du bist dieser Aufgabe gewachsen?* Do you think you're up to this job?

gewagt ADJECTIVE
risky

die **Gewalt** NOUN
[1] force ◊ *die Gewalt des Aufpralls* the force of the impact
[2] power ◊ *die staatliche Gewalt* the power of the state
[3] violence ◊ *Gewalt gegen Kinder* violence against children
♦ **mit aller Gewalt** with all one's might

gewaltig ADJECTIVE
tremendous ◊ *eine gewaltige Menge* a tremendous amount ◊ *Sie hat sich gewaltig angestrengt.* She tried tremendously hard.
♦ **ein gewaltiger Irrtum** a huge mistake

gewalttätig ADJECTIVE
violent

gewann VERB see **gewinnen**

das **Gewässer** NOUN (PL die **Gewässer**)
waters

das **Gewebe** NOUN (PL die **Gewebe**)
[1] fabric ◊ *ein feines Gewebe* a fine fabric
[2] tissue ◊ *Die Gewebeprobe hat ergeben, dass alles in Ordnung ist.* The tissue samples showed that there's nothing wrong.

das **Gewehr** NOUN (PL die **Gewehre**)
gun

die **Gewerkschaft** NOUN
trade union

> ⓘ Unions in Germany are mainly organized within the **Deutscher Gewerkschaftsbund (DGB)**.

gewesen VERB see **sein**

das **Gewicht** NOUN (PL die **Gewichte**)
weight ◊ *das Gewicht meines Koffers* the weight of my case

gewieft ADJECTIVE
shrewd

der **Gewinn** NOUN (PL die **Gewinne**)
profit ◊ *Wir haben dieses Jahr einen Gewinn gemacht.* We've made a profit this year. ◊ *etwas mit Gewinn verkaufen* to sell something at a profit

G

gewinnen VERB (IMPERFECT **gewann,** PERFECT **hat gewonnen**)
to win ◊ *Sie hat den ersten Preis gewonnen.* She won first prize. ◊ *Er hat im Lotto gewonnen.* He had a win on the lottery.
♦ **an etwas gewinnen** to gain in something ◊ *Durch das neue Kunstmuseum hat die Stadt an Beliebtheit gewonnen.* As a result of the new art gallery the town has gained in popularity.

der **Gewinner** NOUN (PL die **Gewinner**)
winner

gewiss ADJECTIVE, ADVERB
certain ◊ *Zwischen den beiden besteht eine gewisse Ähnlichkeit.* There's a certain similarity between them.
♦ **Eine gewisse Frau Böttcher hat angerufen.** A Mrs Böttcher called.
♦ **Das weiß ich ganz gewiss.** I'm certain about that.
♦ **Das hat sie gewiss vergessen.** She must have forgotten.

das **Gewissen** NOUN (PL die **Gewissen**)
conscience

gewissenhaft ADJECTIVE
conscientious

gewissermaßen ADVERB
more or less

die **Gewissheit** NOUN
certainty

das **Gewitter** NOUN (PL die **Gewitter**)
thunderstorm

gewöhnen VERB (PERFECT **hat gewöhnt**)
♦ **sich an etwas gewöhnen** to get used to something ◊ *Ich muss mich erst an die neue Rechtschreibung gewöhnen.* I have to get used to the new spelling rules.
♦ **jemanden an etwas gewöhnen** to teach somebody something ◊ *Der Klassenlehrer hat versucht, seine Klasse an Disziplin zu gewöhnen.* The form teacher tried to teach his class discipline.

die **Gewohnheit** NOUN
habit ◊ *Es ist so eine Gewohnheit von mir, morgens Kaffee zu trinken.* I drink coffee in the morning. It's a habit of mine.
♦ **aus Gewohnheit** from habit
♦ **zur Gewohnheit werden** to become a habit

gewöhnlich ADJECTIVE
1 usual ◊ *Ich bin heute früh zu der gewöhnlichen Zeit aufgestanden.* I got up at my usual time this morning. ◊ *Ich stehe gewöhnlich um sieben Uhr auf.* I usually get up at seven o'clock.
2 ordinary ◊ *Das sind ganz gewöhnliche Leute.* They're quite ordinary people.
♦ **wie gewöhnlich** as usual

gewohnt ADJECTIVE
usual ◊ *Mir fehlt die gewohnte Umgebung.* I miss my usual surroundings.
♦ **etwas gewohnt sein** to be used to something ◊ *Ich bin es nicht gewohnt, dass man mir widerspricht.* I'm not used to being contradicted.

gewonnen VERB see **gewinnen**

geworden VERB see **werden**

geworfen VERB see **werfen**

das **Gewürz** NOUN (GEN des **Gewürzes,** PL die **Gewürze**)
spice

gewusst VERB see **wissen**

die **Gezeiten** PL NOUN
tides

gezogen VERB see **ziehen**

gezwungen VERB see **zwingen**

gibt VERB see **geben**

die **Gier** NOUN
greed

gierig ADJECTIVE
greedy ◊ *gierig nach Geld* greedy for money

gießen VERB (IMPERFECT **goss,** PERFECT **hat gegossen**)
to pour ◊ *Sie goss mir Wein ins Glas.* She poured wine into my glass.
♦ **die Blumen gießen** to water the flowers
♦ **Es gießt in Strömen.** It's pouring.

die **Gießkanne** NOUN
watering can

das **Gift** NOUN (PL die **Gifte**)
poison
*Be careful! The German word **Gift** does not mean **gift**.*

giftig ADJECTIVE
poisonous ◊ *eine giftige Pflanze* a poisonous plant

der **Giftmüll** NOUN
toxic waste

ging VERB see **gehen**

der **Gipfel** NOUN (PL die **Gipfel**)
1 peak ◊ *die schneebedeckten Gipfel* the snow-covered peaks
2 height ◊ *Das ist der Gipfel der Unverschämtheit.* That's the height of impudence.

der **Gips** NOUN (GEN des **Gipses,** PL die **Gipse**)
plaster ◊ *Ich muss die Risse mit Gips zuschmieren.* I'll have to fill in the cracks with plaster. ◊ *Sie hatte den rechten Arm in Gips.* Her right arm was in plaster.

der **Gipsverband** NOUN (PL die **Gipsverbände**)
plaster cast

die **Giraffe** NOUN
giraffe

das **Girokonto** NOUN (PL die **Girokonten**)
current account

die **Gitarre** NOUN
guitar ◊ *Ich spiele Gitarre.* I play the guitar.

glänzen VERB
to shine ◊ *Ihr Gesicht glänzte vor Freude.* Her face shone with joy.
♦ **Du hast in der Mathearbeit nicht gerade geglänzt.** You didn't exactly do brilliantly in your maths test.

glänzend ADJECTIVE
[1] shining ◊ *ein glänzendes Metall* shining metal
[2] brilliant ◊ *Das war eine glänzende Leistung.* That was a brilliant achievement.

das **Glas** NOUN (GEN des **Glases**, PL die **Gläser**)
glass

die **Glasscheibe** NOUN
pane

glatt ADJECTIVE
[1] smooth ◊ *Der Tisch hat eine glatte Oberfläche.* The table has a smooth surface.
[2] slippery ◊ *Pass auf, die Straßen sind glatt.* Be careful, the streets are slippery.
♦ **eine glatte Absage** a flat refusal
♦ **eine glatte Lüge** a downright lie
♦ **Das habe ich glatt vergessen.** It completely slipped my mind.

das **Glatteis** NOUN (GEN des **Glatteises**)
black ice ◊ *Bei Glatteis sollte man vorsichtig fahren.* When there's black ice, you have to drive carefully.

die **Glatze** NOUN
♦ **Er hat eine Glatze.** He's bald.
♦ **eine Glatze bekommen** to go bald

glauben VERB
[1] to believe ◊ *Ich habe kein Wort geglaubt.* I didn't believe a word.
[2] to think ◊ *Ich glaube, wir sind hier nicht willkommen.* I don't think we're welcome here.
♦ **jemandem glauben** to believe somebody ◊ *Ich glaube dir.* I believe you.
♦ **an etwas glauben** to believe in something ◊ *Glaubst du an ein Leben nach dem Tod?* Do you believe in life after death?

glaubwürdig ADJECTIVE
[1] credible ◊ *Das ist keine besonders glaubwürdige Geschichte.* That story's not particularly credible.
[2] trustworthy ◊ *Er ist ein glaubwürdiger Mensch.* He's a trustworthy person.

gleich ADJECTIVE, ADVERB
[1] same ◊ *Wir haben das gleiche Problem.* We have the same problem.
[2] identical ◊ *Bei einem Würfel sind alle Seiten gleich.* All the sides of a cube are identical.
[3] the same ◊ *Ich behandle alle meine Kinder gleich.* I treat all my children the same. ◊ *Sie waren genau gleich angezogen.* They were dressed exactly the same.
♦ **gleich groß** the same size

[4] equal ◊ *Wir wollen für die gleiche Arbeit auch die gleiche Bezahlung.* We want equal pay for equal work.
[5] straight away ◊ *Ich werde ihn gleich anrufen.* I'll call him straight away.
♦ **Ich bin gleich fertig.** I'll be ready in a minute.
♦ **Es ist mir gleich.** It's all the same to me.
♦ **Zwei mal zwei gleich vier.** Two times two equals four.
♦ **gleich nach** right after ◊ *Wir sind gleich nach dem Mittagessen abgefahren.* We left right after lunch.
♦ **gleich neben** right next to ◊ *Wir wohnen gleich neben der Schule.* We live right next to the school.

gleichaltrig ADJECTIVE
of the same age ◊ *gleichaltrige Schüler* pupils of the same age ◊ *Sie sind gleichaltrig.* They're the same age.

gleichartig ADJECTIVE
similar

gleichbedeutend ADJECTIVE
synonymous

die **Gleichberechtigung** NOUN
equal rights ◊ *die Gleichberechtigung der Frau* equal rights for women

gleichen VERB (IMPERFECT **glich**, PERFECT **hat geglichen**)
♦ **jemandem gleichen** to be like somebody ◊ *Du gleichst deinem Vater.* You're like your father.
♦ **einer Sache gleichen** to be like something ◊ *Unser Haus gleicht eurem.* Our house is like yours.
♦ **sich gleichen** to be alike

gleichfalls ADVERB
♦ **Danke gleichfalls!** The same to you.

das **Gleichgewicht** NOUN
balance

gleichgültig ADJECTIVE
[1] indifferent ◊ *Er zeigte sich ihr gegenüber ziemlich gleichgültig.* He seemed to be quite indifferent to her.
[2] not important ◊ *Es ist doch gleichgültig, wie wir das machen.* It's not important how we do it.

die **Gleichung** NOUN
equation

gleichzeitig ADVERB
at the same time ◊ *Ich kann doch nicht drei Dinge gleichzeitig tun.* I can't do three things at the same time.

das **Gleis** NOUN (GEN des **Gleises**, PL die **Gleise**)
[1] line ◊ *die Straßenbahngleise* the tram lines
[2] platform ◊ *Achtung auf Gleis drei.* Attention on platform three.

der **Gletscher** NOUN (PL die **Gletscher**)
glacier

gliedern VERB

G

☞

to structure ◊ *Du musst deinen Aufsatz besser gliedern.* You must structure your essay better.

die **Gliederung** NOUN
structure ◊ *Die Gliederung meines Aufsatzes habe ich schon.* I've already worked out the structure of my essay.

glimpflich ADJECTIVE
♦ **glimpflich davonkommen** to get off lightly

glitzern VERB
1 to glitter ◊ *Das Wasser glitzerte in der Sonne.* The water glittered in the sun.
2 to twinkle ◊ *Die Sterne glitzerten.* The stars twinkled.

die **Globalisierung** NOUN
globalization

die **Glocke** NOUN
bell
♦ **etwas an die große Glocke hängen** to shout something from the rooftops

glotzen VERB
to gawp

das **Glück** NOUN
1 luck ◊ *Ein vierblättriges Kleeblatt bringt Glück.* A four-leaf clover brings good luck.
♦ **Glück haben** to be lucky. ◊ *Ich habe viel Glück gehabt.* I was very lucky.
♦ **Viel Glück!** Good luck!
♦ **zum Glück** fortunately
2 happiness ◊ *Sie strahlte vor Glück.* She was beaming with happiness.

glücklich ADJECTIVE
1 happy ◊ *Ich bin sehr glücklich mit ihm.* I'm very happy with him. ◊ *Das waren glückliche Tage.* Those were happy days.
2 lucky ◊ *Das war ein glücklicher Zufall.* That was a lucky coincidence.

glücklicherweise ADVERB
fortunately

der **Glückwunsch** NOUN (PL die **Glückwünsche**)
congratulations ◊ *Herzlichen Glückwunsch zur bestandenen Prüfung.* Congratulations on passing your exam.
♦ **Herzlichen Glückwunsch zum Geburtstag.** Happy Birthday.

die **Glühbirne** NOUN
light bulb

GmbH ABBREVIATION (= *Gesellschaft mit beschränkter Haftung*)
limited company

das **Gold** NOUN
gold

golden ADJECTIVE
golden

der **Goldfisch** NOUN (PL die **Goldfische**)
goldfish ◊ *Ich habe zwei Goldfische.* I've got two goldfish.

der **Golf** NOUN (PL die **Golfe**)

see also **das Golf** NOUN
gulf ◊ *der Persische Golf* the Persian Gulf

das **Golf** NOUN
see also **der Golf** NOUN
golf ◊ *Mein Vater spielt Golf.* My father plays golf.

der **Golfplatz** NOUN (GEN des **Golfplatzes,** PL die **Golfplätze**)
golf course

der **Golfschläger** NOUN (PL die **Golfschläger**)
golf club ◊ *ein Satz Golfschläger* a set of golf clubs

der **Golfstrom** NOUN
the Gulf Stream

gönnen VERB
♦ **Sie gönnt mir offensichtlich meinen Erfolg nicht.** She obviously begrudges me my success.
♦ **sich etwas gönnen** to treat oneself to something ◊ *Ich werde mir ein Stück Kuchen gönnen.* I'm going to treat myself to a piece of cake.

googeln VERB
to Google®

der **Gott** NOUN (PL die **Götter**)
god
♦ **Mein Gott!** For heaven's sake! ◊ *Mein Gott, wie kann man nur so dumm sein!* For heaven's sake, how can you be so stupid!
♦ **Um Gottes willen!** For heaven's sake!
♦ **Grüß Gott!** Hello!
♦ **Gott sei Dank!** Thank God!

die **Göttin** NOUN
goddess

göttlich ADJECTIVE
divine

das **Grab** NOUN (PL die **Gräber**)
grave

graben VERB (PRESENT **gräbt,** IMPERFECT **grub,** PERFECT **hat gegraben**)
see also **der Graben** NOUN
to dig

der **Graben** NOUN (PL die **Gräben**)
see also **graben** VERB
ditch

der **Grad** NOUN (PL die **Grad**)
degree ◊ *dreißig Grad im Schatten* thirty degrees in the shade

die **Grafikkarte** NOUN
graphics card

grafisch ADJEKTIV
graphic

das **Gramm** NOUN (PL die **Gramme** or **Gramm**)
gram ◊ *hundert Gramm Käse* a hundred grams of cheese

die **Grammatik** NOUN
grammar

graphisch ADJECTIVE see **grafisch**

das **Gras** NOUN (GEN des **Grases,** PL die **Gräser**)
grass

grässlich ADJECTIVE

horrible

die Gräte NOUN
bone ◊ *Dieser Fisch hat zu viele Gräten.*
This fish has too many bones in it.

gratis ADVERB
free of charge

gratulieren VERB (PERFECT **hat gratuliert**)
♦ **jemandem gratulieren** to congratulate
somebody ◊ *Wir gratulierten ihr zum
bestandenen Examen.* We congratulated
her on passing her exam.
♦ **Gratuliere!** Congratulations!

grau ADJECTIVE
grey

das Graubrot NOUN (PL die **Graubrote**)
brown bread

der Gräuel NOUN (PL die **Gräuel**)
horror ◊ *die Gräuel des Bürgerkriegs* the
horrors of civil war
♦ **Rote Bete sind mir ein Gräuel.** I loathe
beetroot.

grauen VERB
♦ **Mir graut vor dem Mathetest.** I'm
dreading the maths test.

grauenhaft ADJECTIVE
horrible

grauhaarig ADJECTIVE
grey-haired

grausam ADJECTIVE
cruel

die Grausamkeit NOUN
cruelty

greifen VERB (IMPERFECT **griff**, PERFECT **hat
gegriffen**)
♦ **nach etwas greifen** to reach for
something ◊ *Er griff nach meiner Hand.*
He reached for my hand.
♦ **um sich greifen** to spread ◊ *Das Feuer
griff schnell um sich.* The fire spread
quickly.

grell ADJECTIVE
harsh ◊ *eine grelle Farbe* a harsh colour
♦ **ein greller Schrei** a piercing scream

die Grenze NOUN
1 border ◊ *Wir sind an der Grenze nach
Frankreich kontrolliert worden.* Our
papers were checked at the French
border.
2 boundary ◊ *Der Zaun ist die Grenze
zum Grundstück des Nachbarn.* The
fence marks the boundary with our
neighbour's property.
3 limit ◊ *die Grenzen des guten
Geschmacks* the limits of good taste

grenzen VERB
♦ **an etwas grenzen** to border on
something ◊ *Unser Grundstück grenzt an
das von Schmidts.* Our property borders
on the Schmidt's.
♦ **Das grenzt an Wahnsinn.** It verges on
madness.

grenzenlos ADJECTIVE
boundless

der Greuel NOUN *see* **Gräuel**

der Grieche NOUN (GEN des **Griechen,** PL die
Griechen)
Greek

Griechenland NEUT NOUN
Greece
♦ **aus Griechenland** from Greece
♦ **nach Griechenland** to Greece

die Griechin NOUN
Greek

griechisch ADJECTIVE
Greek

griesgrämig ADJECTIVE
grumpy

der Grieß NOUN (GEN des **Grießes**)
semolina

der Griff NOUN (PL die **Griffe**)
1 handle ◊ *Halte dich da an dem Griff
fest.* Hold on to the handle.
2 hold ◊ *Ich habe Judogriffe geübt.* I've
been practising judo holds.

griffbereit ADJECTIVE
handy ◊ *etwas griffbereit halten* to keep
something handy

der Grill NOUN (PL die **Grills**)
grill

grillen VERB
1 to grill ◊ *gegrillter Fisch* grilled fish
2 to have a barbecue ◊ *Wir wollen am
Sonntag grillen.* We'd like to have a
barbecue on Sunday.

grinsen VERB
to grin

die Grippe NOUN
flu

grob ADJECTIVE
1 coarse ◊ *grober Sand* coarse sand
2 rough ◊ *Sei nicht so grob zu deiner
Schwester.* Don't be so rough with your
sister.
3 serious ◊ *ein grober Fehler* a serious
mistake

der Groschen NOUN (PL die **Groschen**)
10-pfennig piece

groß ADJECTIVE, ADVERB
1 big ◊ *Das war mein größter Fehler.*
That was my biggest mistake. ◊ *Sie
haben ein großes Haus.* They have a big
house.
2 tall ◊ *Mein Bruder ist viel größer als
ich.* My brother is much taller than me.
◊ *Wie groß bist du?* How tall are you?
3 great ◊ *Das war eine große Leistung.*
That was a great achievement. ◊ *Er war
ein großer Politiker.* He was a great
politician.
♦ **großen Hunger haben** to be very hungry
♦ **die großen Ferien** the summer holidays
♦ **Er hat sich nicht groß angestrengt.** He
didn't try very hard.

G

◆ **Was soll ich da groß sagen?** What is there to say?

◆ **im Großen und Ganzen** on the whole

großartig ADJECTIVE
splendid

Großbritannien NEUT NOUN
Great Britain

◆ **aus Großbritannien** from Great Britain

◆ **in Großbritannien** in Great Britain

◆ **nach Großbritannien** to Great Britain

die **Größe** NOUN
⒈ size ◊ *Welche Schuhgröße hast du?* What size shoes do you take?
⒉ height ◊ *Im Pass steht bei den Angaben zur Person auch die Größe.* Your height's also included in your passport under personal details.

die **Großeltern** PL NOUN
grandparents

großenteils ADVERB
mostly

die **Großmutter** NOUN (PL die **Großmütter**)
grandmother

großschreiben VERB (IMPERFECT **schrieb groß**, PERFECT **hat großgeschrieben**)
to write in capitals

die **Großstadt** NOUN (PL die **Großstädte**)
city

größtenteils ADVERB
for the most part

der **Großvater** NOUN (PL die **Großväter**)
grandfather

großzügig ADJECTIVE, ADVERB
generous ◊ *Meine Eltern sind sehr großzügig.* My parents are very generous. ◊ *Sie hat großzügig darauf verzichtet.* She generously did without.

das **Grübchen** NOUN (PL die **Grübchen**)
dimple

grün ADJECTIVE
green ◊ *Die Ampel ist grün.* The traffic lights are at green.

der **Grund** NOUN (PL die **Gründe**)
⒈ reason ◊ *Nenn mir einen Grund, warum wir das nicht so machen können.* Give me one reason why we can't do it like this.

◆ **Aus welchem Grund ist er so böse?** Why is he so angry?

⒉ ground ◊ *Das Haus ist auf felsigem Grund gebaut.* The house is built on rocky ground.

⒊ bottom ◊ *Das Schiff sank auf den Grund des Meeres.* The ship sank to the bottom of the sea.

◆ **im Grunde genommen** basically

◆ **auf Grund** see **aufgrund**

◆ **zu Grunde** see **zugrunde**

gründen VERB
to found ◊ *Wir haben einen Fanklub gegründet.* We've founded a fan club.

gründlich ADJECTIVE, ADVERB

thorough ◊ *eine gründliche Vorbereitung zur Prüfung* thorough preparation for the exam ◊ *Wir haben das Haus gründlich geputzt.* We cleaned the house thoroughly.

◆ **Ich habe mich gründlich geirrt.** I was completely wrong.

der **Grundsatz** NOUN (GEN des **Grundsatzes**, PL die **Grundsätze**)
principle

grundsätzlich ADJECTIVE, ADVERB
⒈ fundamental ◊ *Es bleibt die grundsätzliche Frage, ob das erlaubt werden soll.* The fundamental question remains: should it be allowed?
⒉ basically ◊ *Grundsätzlich bin ich ja dafür, aber ...* Basically I'm in favour, but ...
⒊ on principle ◊ *Ich bin grundsätzlich gegen die Prügelstrafe.* I'm against corporal punishment on principle.

die **Grundschule** NOUN
primary school

die **Grünen** PL NOUN
the Greens

der **Grünstreifen** NOUN (PL die **Grünstreifen**)
central reservation

grunzen VERB
to grunt

die **Gruppe** NOUN
group

der **Gruselfilm** NOUN (PL die **Gruselfilme**)
horror film

gruselig ADJECTIVE
creepy

der **Gruß** NOUN (GEN des **Grußes**, PL die **Grüße**)
greeting

◆ **viele Grüße** best wishes

◆ **mit freundlichen Grüßen** yours sincerely

◆ **Grüße an** regards to ◊ *Grüße an deine Eltern.* Regards to your parents.

grüßen VERB
to say hello ◊ *Sie hat mich nicht gegrüßt.* She didn't say hello to me.

◆ **Grüß Lorna von mir.** Give Lorna my regards.

◆ **Lorna lässt dich grüßen.** Lorna sends her regards.

gucken VERB
to look

der **Gulasch** NOUN (PL die **Gulaschs**)
goulash

die **Gulaschsuppe** NOUN
goulash soup

gültig ADJECTIVE
valid

das **Gummi** NOUN (PL die **Gummis**)
You can also say der Gummi.
rubber ◊ *Die Reifen sind aus Gummi.* The tyres are made of rubber.

das **Gummiband** NOUN (PL die **Gummibänder**)

elastic band ◊ *Sie machte ein Gummiband um das Geschenk.* She put an elastic band round the present.

das **Gummibärchen** NOUN (PL die **Gummibärchen**)
jelly bear

günstig ADJECTIVE
convenient ◊ *Morgen wäre günstig.* Tomorrow would be convenient.
♦ **eine günstige Gelegenheit** a favourable opportunity
♦ **Das habe ich günstig bekommen.** It was a bargain.

die **Gurgel** NOUN
throat

gurgeln VERB
to gargle ◊ *Ich habe Halsschmerzen und brauche etwas zum Gurgeln.* I've got a sore throat and need something to gargle with.

die **Gurke** NOUN
cucumber ◊ *Sie mag Gurkensalat nicht.* She doesn't like cucumber salad.
♦ **saure Gurke** gherkin

der **Gurt** NOUN (PL die **Gurte**)
belt

der **Gürtel** NOUN (PL die **Gürtel**)
belt

gut ADJECTIVE, ADVERB
[1] good ◊ *Ich habe gute Noten bekommen.* I got good marks. ◊ *Sie ist ein guter Mensch.* She's a good person. ◊ *Das ist ein guter Witz.* That's a good joke.
♦ **In Englisch habe ich "gut".** I got a B in English.

> ❶ German marks range from one (**sehr gut**) to six (**ungenügend**).

♦ **Alles Gute!** All the best.

♦ **also gut** all right then ◊ *Also gut, ich komme.* All right then, I'll come.
[2] well ◊ *Sie hat das gut gemacht.* She did it well. ◊ *Ich kenne ihn gut.* I know him well.
♦ **gut schmecken** to taste good
♦ **gut drei Stunden** a good three hours
♦ **das kann gut sein** that may well be
♦ **Gut, aber ...** OK, but ...
♦ **Lass es gut sein.** That'll do.
♦ **Es ist zum Glück gut gegangen.** Fortunately it came off.
♦ **Mir geht's gut.** I'm fine.
♦ **gut gemeint** well-meant ◊ *ein gut gemeinter Rat* a well-meant piece of advice
♦ **gut tun** *see* **guttun**

die **Güter** NEUT PL NOUN
goods

gutgehen VERB *see* **gut**

gutgemeint ADJECTIVE *see* **gut**

das **Guthaben** NOUN (PL die **Guthaben**)
credit

gütig ADJECTIVE
kind

gutmütig ADJECTIVE
good-natured

der **Gutschein** NOUN (PL die **Gutscheine**)
voucher

guttun VERB (IMPERFECT **tat gut**, PERFECT **hat gutgetan**)
♦ **jemandem guttun** to do somebody good ◊ *Die Pause hat mir gutgetan.* The break did me good.

das **Gymnasium** NOUN (PL die **Gymnasien**)
grammar school

die **Gymnastik** NOUN
keep-fit ◊ *Ich mache einmal in der Woche Gymnastik.* I do keep-fit once a week.

G

H

das **Haar** NOUN (PL die **Haare**)
hair ◊ *Sie hat dunkle Haare.* She's got dark hair.
♦ **um ein Haar** nearly

die **Haarbürste** NOUN
hairbrush

das **Haarwaschmittel** NOUN (PL die **Haarwaschmittel**)
shampoo

haben VERB (PRESENT **hat**, IMPERFECT **hatte**, PERFECT **hat gehabt**)
to have ◊ *Ich habe einen neuen Pulli.* I've got a new pullover. ◊ *Sie hat ihn nicht gesehen.* She hasn't seen him.
♦ **Marek hat heute Geburtstag.** It's Marek's birthday today.
♦ **Wir haben zur Zeit Ferien.** We're on holiday at the moment.
♦ **Welches Datum haben wir heute?** What's the date today?
♦ **Hunger haben** to be hungry
♦ **Angst haben** to be afraid
♦ **Woher hast du das?** Where did you get that from?
♦ **Was hast du denn?** What's the matter with you?
♦ **Ich hätte gern ...** I would like ...

das **Hackfleisch** NOUN
mince

der **Hafen** NOUN (PL die **Häfen**)
harbour

die **Hafenstadt** NOUN (PL die **Hafenstädte**)
port

der **Hafer** NOUN
oats

die **Haferflocken** FEM PL NOUN
porridge oats

haftbar ADJECTIVE
responsible ◊ *Eltern sind für ihre Kinder haftbar.* Parents are responsible for their children.

haften VERB
to stick ◊ *Der Klebstreifen haftet nicht.* The adhesive tape isn't sticking.
♦ **haften für** to be responsible for

die **Haftpflichtversicherung** NOUN
third party insurance

der **Hagel** NOUN
hail

hageln VERB
♦ **Es hagelt.** It's hailing.

der **Hahn** NOUN (PL die **Hähne**)
[1] cock ◊ *Der Hahn krähte.* The cock crowed.
[2] tap ◊ *Der Hahn tropft.* The tap's dripping.

das **Hähnchen** NOUN (PL die **Hähnchen**)

chicken ◊ *Heute gibt es Hähnchen.* We're having chicken today.

der **Hai** NOUN (PL die **Haie**)
shark

der **Haken** NOUN (PL die **Haken**)
[1] hook ◊ *Häng deinen Anorak an den Haken.* Hang your anorak up on the hook.
[2] catch ◊ *Die Sache hat einen Haken.* There's a catch.

halb ADJECTIVE
half ◊ *ein halber Kuchen* half a cake ◊ *eine halbe Stunde* half an hour
♦ **halb eins** half past twelve

halbieren VERB (PERFECT **hat halbiert**)
to halve

das **Halbjahr** NOUN (PL die **Halbjahre**)
six months

halbjährlich ADJECTIVE
half-yearly

die **Halbpension** NOUN
half board

halbtags ADVERB
♦ **halbtags arbeiten** to work part-time

die **Halbtagsarbeit** NOUN
part-time job

die **Halbtagsschule** NOUN
half-time school

half VERB *see* **helfen**

die **Hälfte** NOUN
half

die **Halle** NOUN
hall ◊ *eine Messehalle* an exhibition hall

das **Hallenbad** NOUN (PL die **Hallenbäder**)
indoor swimming pool

hallo EXCLAMATION
hello!

der **Hals** NOUN (GEN des **Halses**, PL die **Hälse**)
[1] neck ◊ *Ich habe einen steifen Hals.* I've got a stiff neck.
[2] throat ◊ *Mir tut der Hals weh.* My throat's sore.
♦ **Hals über Kopf** in a rush

die **Halskette** NOUN
necklace

die **Halsschmerzen** MASC PL NOUN
sore throat ◊ *Ich habe Halsschmerzen.* I've got a sore throat.

das **Halstuch** NOUN (PL die **Halstücher**)
scarf

halt EXCLAMATION
stop!

haltbar ADJECTIVE
durable ◊ *Das ist ein sehr haltbares Material.* That's a very durable material.
♦ **Butter ist nur begrenzt haltbar.** Butter only keeps for a limited time.

♦ **"Mindestens haltbar bis ..."** "Best before ..."

halten VERB (PRESENT **hält**, IMPERFECT **hielt**, PERFECT **hat gehalten**)

1 to hold ◊ *Er hielt sie an der Hand.* He held her by the hand. ◊ *Kannst du das mal halten?* Can you hold that for a moment?

2 to keep ◊ *Obst hält nicht lange.* Fruit doesn't keep long.

♦ **Ihre Freundschaft hat lange gehalten.** Their friendship has lasted a long time.

3 to stop ◊ *Der Bus hielt vor dem Rathaus.* The bus stopped in front of the town hall.

♦ **halten für** to regard as ◊ *Man hält ihn für den besten Chirurgen in Deutschland.* He's regarded as being the best surgeon in Germany.

♦ **Ich habe sie für deine Mutter gehalten.** I took her for your mother.

♦ **halten von** to think of ◊ *Sie hält viel von dir.* She thinks a lot of you. ◊ *Ich halte nichts von dieser Methode.* I don't think much of this method.

♦ **sich rechts halten** to keep to the right

die **Haltestelle** NOUN
stop ◊ *die Haltestelle der Straßenbahn* the tram stop

haltmachen VERB to stop

die **Haltung** NOUN

1 posture ◊ *Er hat eine aufrechte Haltung.* He has an upright posture.

2 attitude ◊ *Ich bewundere deine Haltung in dieser Frage.* I admire your attitude in this issue.

Hamburg NEUT NOUN
Hamburg

> 🛈 The "Free Hanseatic City of Hamburg" is one of the 16 **Länder**. It is a "city-state" like Bremen and Berlin, and is Germany's principal seaport.

der **Hammer** NOUN (PL die **Hämmer**)
hammer

der **Hamster** NOUN (PL die **Hamster**)
hamster

hamstern VERB
to hoard

die **Hand** NOUN (PL die **Hände**)
hand

die **Handarbeit** NOUN

1 manual work ◊ *Handarbeit macht ihm mehr Spaß als geistige Arbeit.* He enjoys manual work more than intellectual work.

2 needlework ◊ *In Handarbeit hat sie eine Zwei.* She got a B in needlework.

der **Handball** NOUN
handball

die **Handbremse** NOUN
handbrake

das **Handbuch** NOUN (PL die **Handbücher**)
manual

der **Händedruck** NOUN
handshake

der **Handel** NOUN

1 trade ◊ *der Handel mit Osteuropa* trade with Eastern Europe

♦ **Dieses Gerät ist überall im Handel erhältlich.** This appliance is available in all shops and retail outlets.

2 deal ◊ *Wir haben einen Handel abgeschlossen.* We have concluded a deal.

handeln VERB

1 to act ◊ *Wir müssen schnell handeln.* We'll have to act quickly.

2 to trade ◊ *Er handelt mit Gebrauchtwaren.* He trades in second-hand goods.

♦ **mit jemandem handeln** to bargain with somebody ◊ *Ich habe versucht, mit ihm zu handeln, aber er wollte es mir nicht billiger geben.* I tried to bargain with him but he didn't want to give it to me any cheaper.

♦ **es handelt sich um ...** it's about ... ◊ *Sie wollte mir nicht sagen, worum es sich handelt.* She didn't want to tell me what it was about.

♦ **Hier handelt es sich um einen besonders schweren Fall von Allergie.** This is a particularly bad case of allergy.

♦ **handeln von** to be about ◊ *Die Geschichte handelt von einer kranken Frau.* The story's about a sick woman.

die **Handelsschule** NOUN
business school

das **Handgepäck** NOUN
hand luggage

der **Händler** NOUN (PL die **Händler**)
dealer ◊ *Ich habe meinen Computerhändler danach gefragt.* I asked my computer dealer about it.

handlich ADJECTIVE
handy

die **Handlung** NOUN

1 act ◊ *Das war eine unüberlegte Handlung.* That was a rash act.

2 plot ◊ *Ich habe die Handlung des Buches nicht genau verstanden.* I didn't really understand the plot of the book.

3 shop ◊ *eine Eisenwarenhandlung* an ironmonger's shop

die **Handschrift** NOUN
handwriting

der **Handschuh** NOUN (PL die **Handschuhe**)
glove

die **Handtasche** NOUN
handbag

das **Handtuch** NOUN (PL die **Handtücher**)
towel

das **Handy** NOUN (PL die **Handys**)
mobile phone

H

der **Hang** NOUN (PL die **Hänge**)
slope

hängen (1) VERB (IMPERFECT **hängte**, PERFECT **hat gehängt**)
[1] to hang ◊ *Sie hat die Wäsche auf die Leine gehängt.* She hung her washing on the line.
[2] to hang ◊ *Sie hängten den Verbrecher.* They hanged the criminal.

hängen (2) VERB (IMPERFECT **hing**, PERFECT **hat gehangen**)
to hang ◊ *An der Wand hing ein Bild von Picasso.* A painting by Picasso was hanging on the wall.
♦ **hängen an** to be attached to ◊ *Sie hat sehr an ihrem Vater gehangen.* She was very attached to her father.

Hannover NEUT NOUN
Hanover

das **Hansaplast** ® NOUN
Elastoplast ®

hänseln VERB
to tease

die **Hansestadt** NOUN (PL die **Hansestädte**)
Hanseatic town

> ℹ The **Hanse** (Hanseatic League) was a powerful association of cities which dominated Baltic trade in the Middle Ages. Even today, Bremen, Hamburg, Lübeck, Rostock and Wismar still call themselves **Hansestädte**.

harmlos ADJECTIVE
harmless

harmonisch ADJECTIVE
harmonious

hart ADJECTIVE
hard ◊ *hart wie Stein* as hard as stone ◊ *Wir haben hart gearbeitet.* We worked hard. ◊ *Diese Kritik hat sie hart getroffen.* This criticism hit her hard.
♦ **harte Worte** harsh words
♦ **Das ist hart.** That's tough.
♦ **ein hart gekochtes Ei** a hard-boiled egg

hartnäckig ADJECTIVE
stubborn

das **Haschisch** NOUN (GEN des **Haschisch**)
hashish

der **Hase** NOUN (GEN des **Hasen**, PL die **Hasen**)
hare

die **Haselnuss** NOUN (PL die **Haselnüsse**)
hazelnut

der **Hass** NOUN (GEN des **Hasses**)
hatred

hassen VERB (PERFECT **hat gehasst**)
to hate

hässlich ADJECTIVE
[1] ugly ◊ *Sie ist das hässlichste Mädchen der Klasse.* She's the ugliest girl in the class.
[2] nasty ◊ *Es ist hässlich, so etwas zu sagen.* It's nasty to say things like that.

hast VERB *see* **haben**

hastig ADJECTIVE
hasty

hat, hatte VERB *see* **haben**

der **Haufen** NOUN (PL die **Haufen**)
heap ◊ *In ihrem Schlafzimmer lag ein Haufen schmutziger Wäsche.* There was a heap of dirty washing lying in her bedroom.
♦ **ein Haufen ...** heaps of ... ◊ *Ich habe einen Haufen Fehler gemacht.* I've made heaps of mistakes. ◊ *Er hat einen Haufen Geld dafür bezahlt.* He paid heaps of money for it. ◊ *ein Haufen Leute* heaps of people

häufen VERB
♦ **sich häufen** to accumulate ◊ *Der Müll häufte sich in den Straßen.* The rubbish accumulated in the streets.
♦ **Die Fälle von Asthma häufen sich.** Cases of asthma are on the increase.

haufenweise ADVERB
[1] heaps of ◊ *Dort gibt es haufenweise Ameisen.* There are heaps of ants there. ◊ *Wiltrud hat haufenweise CDs.* Wiltrud has heaps of CDs.
[2] in droves ◊ *Sie sind haufenweise angekommen.* They came in droves.

häufig ADJECTIVE, ADVERB
[1] frequent ◊ *sein häufiges Fehlen* his frequent absences
[2] frequently ◊ *Er fehlt häufig.* He is frequently absent.

der **Hauptbahnhof** NOUN (PL die **Hauptbahnhöfe**)
main station

hauptberuflich ADVERB
full-time ◊ *Er ist hauptberuflich als Gärtner tätig.* He's employed full-time as a gardener.

das **Hauptfach** NOUN (PL die **Hauptfächer**)
main subject

das **Hauptgericht** NOUN (PL die **Hauptgerichte**)
main course

die **Hauptsache** NOUN
main thing
♦ **Hauptsache, du bist gesund.** The main thing is that you're healthy.

die **Hauptsaison** NOUN (PL die **Hauptsaisons**)
high season

die **Hauptschule** NOUN
secondary school

die **Hauptstadt** NOUN (PL die **Hauptstädte**)
capital ◊ *Berlin ist die Hauptstadt von Deutschland.* Berlin's the capital of Germany.

die **Hauptstraße** NOUN
main street

die **Hauptverkehrszeit** NOUN
rush hour

das **Hauptwort** NOUN (PL die **Hauptwörter**)
noun

das **Haus** NOUN (GEN des **Hauses**, PL die **Häuser**)
house
♦ **nach Hause** home ◊ *Ich muss jetzt nach Hause.* I'll have to go home now.
♦ **zu Hause** at home

die **Hausarbeit** NOUN
[1] housework ◊ *Am Wochenende hilft mein Vater bei der Hausarbeit.* My father helps with the housework at the weekend.
[2] homework ◊ *Wir haben eine Hausarbeit zum Thema Umweltverschmutzung auf.* We've got homework on the subject of pollution.

der **Hausarzt** NOUN (GEN des **Hausarztes**, PL die **Hausärzte**)
family doctor

die **Hausaufgaben** FEM PL NOUN
homework ◊ *Heute waren die Hausaufgaben nicht schwierig.* Our homework wasn't difficult today.

die **Hausfrau** NOUN
housewife

der **Haushalt** NOUN (PL die **Haushalte**)
[1] household ◊ *den Haushalt führen* to run the household
[2] budget ◊ *der Haushalt für 2002* the 2002 budget

der **Hausmeister** NOUN (PL die **Hausmeister**)
caretaker

die **Hausnummer** NOUN
house number

der **Hausschlüssel** NOUN (PL die **Hausschlüssel**)
front-door key

der **Hausschuh** NOUN (PL die **Hausschuhe**)
slipper

das **Haustier** NOUN (PL die **Haustiere**)
pet

die **Haustür** NOUN
front door

die **Hauswirtschaft** NOUN
home economics

die **Hauswirtschaftslehre** NOUN
home economics

die **Haut** NOUN (PL die **Häute**)
skin

die **Hautcreme** NOUN (PL die **Hautcremes**)
skin cream

Hbf. ABBREVIATION (= *Hauptbahnhof*)
central station

der **Hebel** NOUN (PL die **Hebel**)
lever

heben VERB (IMPERFECT **hob**, PERFECT **hat gehoben**)
to lift

die **Hecke** NOUN
hedge

die **Hefe** NOUN
yeast

das **Heft** NOUN (PL die **Hefte**)
[1] exercise book ◊ *Schreibt die Verbesserung in euer Heft.* Write the correction in your exercise book.
[2] issue ◊ *Hast du noch das letzte Heft von "Geo"?* Have you got the latest issue of "Geo"?

die **Heftklammer** NOUN
paper clip

das **Heftpflaster** NOUN (PL die **Heftpflaster**)
sticking plaster

die **Heftzwecke** NOUN
drawing pin

die **Heide** NOUN
moor ◊ *Wir haben einen Spaziergang durch die Heide gemacht.* We went for a walk over the moor.
♦ **die Lüneburger Heide** Lüneburg Heath

das **Heidekraut** NOUN
heather

die **Heidelbeere** NOUN
blueberry

heilbar ADJECTIVE
curable

heilen VERB (PERFECT **hat/ist geheilt**)
*For the perfect tense use **haben** when the verb has an object and **sein** when there is no object.*
[1] to cure ◊ *Viele Arten von Krebs kann man heilen.* Many kinds of cancer can be cured.
[2] to heal ◊ *Die Wunde ist schnell geheilt.* The wound healed quickly.

heilig ADJECTIVE
holy

der **Heiligabend** NOUN (PL die **Heiligabende**)
Christmas Eve

der **Heilige** NOUN (GEN des/der **Heiligen**, PL die
die **Heiligen**)
saint ◊ *Er ist auch kein Heiliger.* He's no saint.

das **Heilmittel** NOUN (PL die **Heilmittel**)
remedy

das **Heim** NOUN (PL die **Heime**)
see also **heim** ADVERB
home ◊ *ein Heim für Kinder mit Lernschwierigkeiten* a home for children with learning difficulties

heim ADVERB
see also **das Heim** NOUN
home ◊ *Ich muss jetzt heim.* I'll have to go home now.

die **Heimat** NOUN
homeland ◊ *Deutschland ist meine Heimat.* Germany's my homeland.

heimatlos ADJECTIVE
homeless

die **Heimfahrt** NOUN
journey home

heimgehen VERB (IMPERFECT **ging heim**, PERFECT **ist heimgegangen**)
to go home

H

heimkehren VERB (PERFECT **ist heimgekehrt**)
to return home

heimlich ADJECTIVE
secret ◊ *Er hat das heimlich gemacht.* He did it secretly.

die **Heimreise** NOUN
journey home

das **Heimspiel** NOUN (PL die **Heimspiele**)
home game

der **Heimweg** NOUN (PL die **Heimwege**)
way home

das **Heimweh** NOUN
homesickness

heimzahlen VERB (PERFECT **hat heimgezahlt**)
♦ **jemandem etwas heimzahlen** to pay somebody back for something

die **Heirat** NOUN
marriage

heiraten VERB
to get married ◊ *Sie heiraten morgen.* They're getting married tomorrow.
♦ **jemanden heiraten** to marry somebody

heiser ADJECTIVE
hoarse

die **Heiserkeit** NOUN
hoarseness

heiß ADJECTIVE
hot ◊ *Mir ist heiß.* I'm hot. ◊ *heiße Schokolade* hot chocolate

heißen VERB (IMPERFECT **hieß**, PERFECT **hat geheißen**)
1 to be called ◊ *Er heißt Marek.* He's called Marek.
2 to mean ◊ *Das heißt, dass wir morgen früh aufstehen müssen.* That means that we'll have to get up early tomorrow.
♦ **es heißt ...** it is said ...
♦ **das heißt** that is to say

heiter ADJECTIVE
1 cheerful ◊ *Ich war in heiterer Laune.* I was in a cheerful mood.
2 bright ◊ *Das Wetter wird heiter bis bewölkt.* The weather will be cloudy with bright spells.

heizen VERB
to heat

der **Heizkörper** NOUN (PL die **Heizkörper**)
radiator

die **Heizung** NOUN
heating

hektisch ADJECTIVE
hectic

der **Held** NOUN (GEN **des Helden**, PL die **Helden**)
hero

die **Heldin** NOUN
heroine

helfen VERB (PRESENT **hilft**, IMPERFECT **half**, PERFECT **hat geholfen**)
to help ◊ *Kann ich dir helfen?* Can I help you? ◊ *Die Tablette hat geholfen.* The pill helped.
♦ **jemandem bei etwas helfen** to help somebody with something
♦ **sich zu helfen wissen** to be resourceful ◊ *Er weiß sich zu helfen.* He's very resourceful.
♦ **Es hilft nichts, du musst ...** It's no use, you'll have to ...

hell ADJECTIVE
bright ◊ *Hier ist es schön hell.* It's nice and bright here.
♦ **Sie hat einen hellen Teint.** She has a clear complexion.
♦ **eine helle Farbe** a light colour
♦ **ein Helles** a light beer

hellblau ADJECTIVE
light blue

hellblond ADJECTIVE
ash-blond

der **Helm** NOUN (PL die **Helme**)
helmet

das **Hemd** NOUN (PL die **Hemden**)
shirt
♦ **ein Unterhemd** a vest

die **Hemmung** NOUN
inhibition ◊ *Er hat furchtbare Hemmungen.* He has terrible inhibitions.

der **Henkel** NOUN (PL die **Henkel**)
handle ◊ *ein Eimer ohne Henkel* a bucket without a handle

die **Henne** NOUN
hen

her ADVERB
ago ◊ *Das ist fünf Jahre her.* That was five years ago.
♦ **von ... her** from ... ◊ *von England her* from England ◊ *von weit her* from a long way away
♦ **Wo bist du her?** Where do you come from?
♦ **Komm her zu mir.** Come here.
♦ **Her damit!** Hand it over!
♦ **Wo hat er das her?** Where did he get that from?

herab ADVERB
down

herabhängen VERB (IMPERFECT **hing herab**, PERFECT **hat herabgehangen**)
to hang down

herablassen VERB (PRESENT **lässt herab**, IMPERFECT **ließ herab**, PERFECT **hat herabgelassen**)
to lower ◊ *die Rollläden herablassen* to lower the blinds
♦ **sich herablassen, etwas zu tun** to condescend to do something

herablassend ADJECTIVE
condescending

heran ADVERB
♦ **Näher heran!** Come closer!

heranfahren VERB (PRESENT **fährt heran**, IMPERFECT **fuhr heran**, PERFECT **ist herangefahren**) to drive up ◊ *Kannst du noch etwas näher an die Garage heranfahren?* Can you drive closer up to the garage?

herauf ADVERB
up ◊ *Komm hier herauf.* Come up here.

heraus ADVERB
out

herausbekommen VERB (IMPERFECT **bekam heraus**, PERFECT **hat herausbekommen**)
1 to get out ◊ *Ich habe den Fleck nicht herausbekommen.* I didn't get the stain out.
2 to find out ◊ *Ich muss herausbekommen, warum er das gemacht hat.* I'll have to find out why he did it.

herausfordern VERB (PERFECT **hat herausgefordert**)
to challenge

herauskommen VERB (IMPERFECT **kam heraus**, PERFECT **ist herausgekommen**)
to come out ◊ *Die Maus ist aus ihrem Loch herausgekommen.* The mouse came out of its hole.
♦ *Dabei kommt nichts heraus.* Nothing will come of it.

herausnehmen VERB (PRESENT **nimmt heraus**, IMPERFECT **nahm heraus**, PERFECT **hat herausgenommen**)
to take out ◊ *Sie hat das Lesezeichen aus dem Buch herausgenommen.* She took the bookmark out of the book.
♦ **sich etwas herausnehmen** to take liberties ◊ *Du nimmst dir wirklich etwas zu viel heraus.* You really do take far too many liberties.

herausrücken VERB (PERFECT **hat/ist herausgerückt**)

*For the perfect tense use **haben** when the verb has an object and **sein** when there is no object.*

to fork out ◊ *Er wollte kein Geld herausrücken.* He didn't want to fork out any money.
♦ **mit etwas herausrücken** to come out with something ◊ *Endlich ist er mit der Wahrheit herausgerückt.* He finally came out with the truth.

sich **herausstellen** VERB (PERFECT **hat sich herausgestellt**)
to turn out ◊ *Es stellte sich heraus, dass ...* It turned out that ...

herausziehen VERB (IMPERFECT **zog heraus**, PERFECT **hat herausgezogen**)
to pull out

herb ADJECTIVE
bitter ◊ *eine herbe Enttäuschung* a bitter disappointment ◊ *ein herber Geschmack* a bitter taste

herbei ADVERB
over ◊ *Alle eilten herbei.* Everyone hurried over.

die **Herbergseltern** PL NOUN

wardens (*in youth hostel*)

die **Herbergsmutter** NOUN (PL die **Herbergsmütter**)
warden (*in youth hostel*)

der **Herbergsvater** NOUN (PL die **Herbergsväter**)
warden (*in youth hostel*)

herbringen VERB (IMPERFECT **brachte her**, PERFECT **hat hergebracht**)
to bring here

der **Herbst** NOUN (PL die **Herbste**)
autumn ◊ *im Herbst* in autumn

die **Herbstferien** PL NOUN
autumn holidays

herbstlich ADJECTIVE
autumnal

der **Herd** NOUN (PL die **Herde**)
cooker ◊ *ein Herd mit vier Platten* a cooker with four rings

die **Herde** NOUN
herd ◊ *eine Herde Kühe* a herd of cows
♦ **eine Schafherde** a flock of sheep

herein ADVERB
in ◊ *Noch mehr Menschen drängten herein.* Even more people pushed their way in. ◊ *Das Wasser strömte herein.* The water poured in.
♦ **Herein!** Come in!

hereinbitten VERB (IMPERFECT **bat herein**, PERFECT **hat hereingebeten**)
to ask in

hereinfallen VERB (PRESENT **fällt herein**, IMPERFECT **fiel herein**, PERFECT **ist hereingefallen**)
♦ **auf etwas hereinfallen** to fall for something ◊ *Auf einen solch plumpen Trick falle ich nicht herein.* I'm not falling for an obvious trick like that. ◊ *Sie ist auf einen Betrüger hereingefallen.* She fell for a swindler.

hereinkommen VERB (IMPERFECT **kam herein**, PERFECT **ist hereingekommen**)
to come in

hereinlassen VERB (PRESENT **lässt herein**, IMPERFECT **ließ herein**, PERFECT **hat hereingelassen**)
to let in

hereinlegen VERB (PERFECT **hat hereingelegt**)
♦ **jemanden hereinlegen** to take somebody for a ride ◊ *Er will dich bloß hereinlegen.* He's just trying to take you for a ride.

hergeben VERB (PRESENT **gibt her**, IMPERFECT **gab her**, PERFECT **hat hergegeben**)
to hand over ◊ *Gib das Buch her!* Hand over the book!
♦ **sich zu etwas hergeben** to lend one's name to something

hergehen VERB (IMPERFECT **ging her**, PERFECT **ist hergegangen**)
♦ **hinter jemandem hergehen** to follow somebody

H

☞

♦ **Es geht hoch her.** There are a lot of goings-on.

herhören VERB (PERFECT **hat hergehört**)
<u>to listen</u> ◊ *Alle mal herhören!* Listen everybody!

der **Hering** NOUN (PL die **Heringe**)
<u>herring</u>

herkommen VERB (IMPERFECT **kam her**, PERFECT **ist hergekommen**)
<u>to come</u> ◊ *Komm mal her!* Come here!

die **Herkunft** NOUN (PL die **Herkünfte**)
<u>origin</u>

das **Heroin** NOUN
<u>heroin</u>

der **Herr** NOUN (GEN des **Herrn**, PL die **Herren**)
1 <u>gentleman</u> ◊ *Er ist ein feiner Herr.* He's a fine gentleman.
2 <u>Lord</u> ◊ *Herr, gib uns Frieden!* Lord, give us peace.
♦ **Herr Mosbacher** Mr Mosbacher
♦ **Mein Herr!** Sir!
♦ **Meine Herren!** Gentlemen!

herrlich ADJECTIVE
<u>marvellous</u>

herrschen VERB
1 <u>to reign</u> ◊ *Wann hat Karl der Große geherrscht?* When did Charlemagne reign?
2 <u>to be</u> ◊ *Hier herrschen ja schöne Zustände.* This is a fine state of affairs. ◊ *Es herrscht noch Ungewissheit, wann das gemacht werden soll.* It's still uncertain when it's to be done.

herstellen VERB (PERFECT **hat hergestellt**)
<u>to manufacture</u>

der **Hersteller** NOUN (PL die **Hersteller**)
<u>manufacturer</u>

die **Herstellung** NOUN
<u>manufacture</u>

herüber ADVERB
1 <u>over here</u> ◊ *Er kam langsam zu uns herüber.* He came slowly over to us.
2 <u>across</u> ◊ *Sie versuchte, zu uns herüberzuschwimmen.* She tried to swim across to us.

herum ADVERB
<u>round</u> ◊ *Mach ein rotes Band herum.* Tie a red band round it.
♦ **um etwas herum** round something ◊ *Sie gingen ums Haus herum.* They went round the house.

herumführen VERB (PERFECT **hat herumgeführt**)
<u>to show around</u>

herumgehen VERB (IMPERFECT **ging herum**, PERFECT **ist herumgegangen**)
<u>to walk about</u> ◊ *Wir sind ein paar Stunden in der Stadt herumgegangen.* We walked about the town for a couple of hours.

♦ **um etwas herumgehen** to walk round something ◊ *Sie ging um den Tisch herum.* She walked round the table.

herumkommen VERB (IMPERFECT **kam herum**, PERFECT **ist herumgekommen**)
<u>to come round</u> ◊ *Ich sah sie um die Kurve herumkommen.* I saw her coming round the corner.
♦ **Sie ist schon viel herumgekommen.** She's seen a lot of the world.

sich **herumsprechen** VERB (PRESENT **spricht sich herum**, IMPERFECT **sprach sich herum**, PERFECT **hat sich herumgesprochen**)
<u>to get around</u>

herunter ADVERB
<u>down</u>

heruntergekommen ADJECTIVE
<u>run-down</u>

herunterkommen VERB (IMPERFECT **kam herunter**, PERFECT **ist heruntergekommen**)
1 <u>to come down</u> ◊ *Sie ist zu uns heruntergekommen.* She came down to us.
2 <u>to become run-down</u> ◊ *Das Haus ist in den letzten Jahren ziemlich heruntergekommen.* The house has become rather run-down in the past few years.

herunterladen VERB (PRESENT **lädt herunter**, IMPERFECT **lud herunter**, PERFECT **hat heruntergeladen**)
<u>to download</u> (*computer*) ◊ *eine Datei herunterladen* to download a file

hervorbringen VERB (IMPERFECT **brachte hervor**, PERFECT **hat hervorgebracht**)
<u>to produce</u>

hervorragend ADJECTIVE
<u>excellent</u>

hervorrufen VERB (IMPERFECT **rief hervor**, PERFECT **hat hervorgerufen**)
<u>to cause</u>

das **Herz** NOUN (GEN des **Herzens**, PL die **Herzen**)
1 <u>heart</u> ◊ *Es bricht mir fast das Herz.* It almost breaks my heart.
2 <u>hearts</u> ◊ *Herz ist Trumpf.* Hearts is trumps.

der **Herzinfarkt** NOUN (PL die **Herzinfarkte**)
<u>heart attack</u>

herzlich ADJECTIVE
<u>warm</u> ◊ *ein herzlicher Empfang* a warm welcome ◊ *Wir wurden herzlich begrüßt.* We were warmly welcomed.
♦ **Herzlich willkommen in Bamberg.** Welcome to Bamberg.
♦ **Herzlichen Glückwunsch!** Congratulations!
♦ **Herzliche Grüße.** Best wishes.

herzlos ADJECTIVE
<u>heartless</u>

der **Herzschlag** NOUN (PL die **Herzschläge**)
1 <u>heartbeat</u> ◊ *bei jedem Herzschlag* with every heartbeat

[2] heart attack ◊ *Er hat einen Herzschlag bekommen.* He had a heart attack.

Hessen NEUT NOUN
Hesse

> ❶ **Hessen** is one of the 16 **Länder**. Its capital is Wiesbaden, yet its biggest city is Frankfurt am Main, which is Germany's principal financial centre and home to the Bundesbank.

das **Heu** NOUN
hay
♦ **Geld wie Heu** stacks of money

heulen VERB
[1] to howl ◊ *Die Wölfe heulten.* The wolves were howling.
[2] to cry ◊ *Jetzt fang nicht gleich an zu heulen.* Now don't start crying.

der **Heuschnupfen** NOUN
hay fever ◊ *Sie leidet an Heuschnupfen.* She suffers from hay fever.

heute ADVERB
today
♦ **heute Abend** this evening
♦ **heute Morgen** this morning
♦ **heute früh** this morning

heutig ADJECTIVE
today's ◊ *die heutige Jugend* today's youth

heutzutage ADVERB
nowadays

die **Hexe** NOUN
witch

hexen VERB
♦ **Ich kann doch nicht hexen.** I can't work miracles.

der **Hexenschuss** NOUN (GEN des **Hexenschusses**)
lumbago

hielt VERB *see* **halten**

hier ADVERB
here ◊ *hier drinnen* in here
♦ **Hier spricht Lisa.** This is Lisa.
♦ **hier bleiben** to stay here

hierher ADVERB
here

hiesig ADJECTIVE
local ◊ *die hiesige Bevölkerung* the local population

hieß VERB *see* **heißen**

die **Hilfe** NOUN
help
♦ **Erste Hilfe** first aid
♦ **Hilfe!** Help!

das **Hilfemenü** NOUN (PL die **Hilfemenüs**)
help menu

hilflos ADJECTIVE
helpless

hilfreich ADJECTIVE
helpful

hilfsbereit ADJECTIVE
ready to help

hilft VERB *see* **helfen**

die **Himbeere** NOUN
raspberry

der **Himmel** NOUN (PL die **Himmel**)
[1] sky ◊ *ein wolkenloser Himmel* a cloudless sky
[2] heaven ◊ *in den Himmel kommen* to go to heaven

himmelblau ADJECTIVE
sky-blue

die **Himmelsrichtung** NOUN
♦ **die vier Himmelsrichtungen** the four points of the compass

himmlisch ADJECTIVE
heavenly

hin ADVERB
♦ **hin und zurück** there and back
♦ **hin und her** to and fro
♦ **Wo ist er hin?** Where has he gone?
♦ **Geld hin, Geld her** money or no money
♦ **auf meine Bitte hin** at my request

hinab ADVERB
down

hinauf ADVERB
up

hinaufsteigen VERB (IMPERFECT **stieg hinauf**, PERFECT **ist hinaufgestiegen**)
to climb ◊ *Wir sind auf den Berg hinaufgestiegen.* We climbed up the mountain.

hinaus ADVERB
out

hinausgehen VERB (IMPERFECT **ging hinaus**, PERFECT **ist hinausgegangen**)
to go out ◊ *Sie ist kurz hinausgegangen.* She's gone out for a minute.
♦ **über etwas hinausgehen** to exceed something ◊ *Das geht weit über meine Erwartungen hinaus.* That far exceeds my expectations.

hinausschieben VERB (IMPERFECT **schob hinaus**, PERFECT **hat hinausgeschoben**)
to put off ◊ *Sie haben die Entscheidung hinausgeschoben.* They put the decision off.

hinauswerfen VERB (PRESENT **wirft hinaus**, IMPERFECT **warf hinaus**, PERFECT **hat hinausgeworfen**)
to throw out

hindern VERB
♦ **jemanden an etwas hindern** to prevent somebody from doing something ◊ *Ich konnte ihn nicht am Weggehen hindern.* I couldn't prevent him from going.

das **Hindernis** NOUN (GEN des **Hindernisses**, PL die **Hindernisse**)
obstacle

hinein ADVERB
in ◊ *Hinein mit dir!* In you go!

hineingehen VERB (IMPERFECT **ging hinein**, PERFECT **ist hineingegangen**)

H

☞

to go in ◊ *Geh doch hinein.* Go in.

♦ **hineingehen in** to go into ◊ *Sie traute sich nicht, ins Zimmer hineinzugehen.* She didn't dare go into the room.

♦ **Meinst du, der Koffer geht noch in den Kofferraum hinein?** Do you think there's still room for the case in the boot?

hineinpassen VERB (PERFECT **hat hineingepasst**)

to fit ◊ *Der Schlüssel passt nicht hinein.* The key doesn't fit.

♦ **hineinpassen in** to fit into ◊ *Dein Koffer passt gerade noch in den Kofferraum hinein.* Your case just fits into the boot.

die **Hinfahrt** NOUN
outward journey

hinfallen VERB (PRESENT **fällt hin**, IMPERFECT **fiel hin**, PERFECT **ist hingefallen**)

to fall ◊ *Sie stolperte und fiel hin.* She stumbled and fell.

der **Hinflug** NOUN (PL die **Hinflüge**)
outward flight

hinhalten VERB (PRESENT **hält hin**, IMPERFECT **hielt hin**, PERFECT **hat hingehalten**)

to hold out ◊ *Sie hielt ihren Teller hin.* She held out her plate.

♦ **jemanden hinhalten** to put somebody off

hinken VERB
to limp

hinlegen VERB (PERFECT **hat hingelegt**)

to put down ◊ *Leg das Buch dort drüben hin.* Put the book down over there.

♦ **sich hinlegen** to lie down

hinnehmen VERB (PRESENT **nimmt hin**, IMPERFECT **nahm hin**, PERFECT **hat hingenommen**)

to put up with ◊ *Das kann ich nicht länger hinnehmen.* I can't put up with this any longer.

die **Hinreise** NOUN
outward journey

sich **hinsetzen** VERB (PERFECT **hat sich hingesetzt**)
to sit down

hinstellen VERB (PERFECT **hat hingestellt**)

to put ◊ *Wo soll ich die Vase hinstellen?* Where shall I put the vase?

♦ **Er stellte sich vor den Lehrer hin.** He went over and stood in front of the teacher.

hinten ADVERB

at the back ◊ *Er sitzt ganz hinten.* He sits at the very back.

hinter PREPOSITION

Use the accusative to express movement or a change of place. Use the dative when there is no change of place.

⬚1 behind ◊ *Stell dich hinter deine Schwester.* Stand behind your sister. ◊ *Ich saß hinter ihr.* I was sitting behind her.

⬚2 after ◊ *Wir hatten kurz hinter Köln eine Panne.* We broke down just after Cologne.

hintere ADJECTIVE

back ◊ *die hinteren Reihen* the back rows

♦ **der hintere Reifen** the rear tyre

hintereinander ADVERB
one after the other

♦ **dreimal hintereinander** three times in a row

der **Hintergrund** NOUN (PL die **Hintergründe**)
background

hinterher ADVERB
afterwards

der **Hintern** NOUN (GEN des **Hintern**, PL die **Hintern**)
bottom

das **Hinterrad** NOUN (PL die **Hinterräder**)
back wheel

hinüber ADVERB
over

hinübergehen VERB (IMPERFECT **ging hinüber**, PERFECT **ist hinübergegangen**)
to go over

hinunter ADVERB
down

hinunterschlucken VERB (PERFECT **hat hinuntergeschluckt**)
to swallow

der **Hinweg** NOUN (PL die **Hinwege**)
way there ◊ *auf dem Hinweg* on the way there

der **Hinweis** NOUN (GEN des **Hinweises**, PL die **Hinweise**)

⬚1 hint ◊ *Er hat mir nicht den kleinsten Hinweis gegeben, wie ich das machen soll.* He didn't give me the slightest hint as to how I was supposed to do it.

⬚2 instruction ◊ *Hinweise zur Bedienung* operating instructions

hinweisen VERB (IMPERFECT **wies hin**, PERFECT **hat hingewiesen**)

♦ **jemanden auf etwas hinweisen** to point something out to somebody

hinzufügen VERB (PERFECT **hat hinzugefügt**)
to add

das **Hirn** NOUN (PL die **Hirne**)
brain

der **Hirsch** NOUN (PL die **Hirsche**)
stag

historisch ADJECTIVE
historic

die **Hitparade** NOUN
charts

die **Hitze** NOUN
heat

hitzefrei ADJECTIVE

♦ **hitzefrei haben** to have time off school because of excessively hot weather

ⓘ *If the temperature reaches 28°C - 30°C at 10 a.m., then German children are sent home early and any afternoon lessons are cancelled.*

die **Hitzewelle** NOUN

heat wave

der **Hitzschlag** NOUN (PL die **Hitzschläge**)
heatstroke

das **Hobby** NOUN (PL die **Hobbys**)
hobby

das **Hoch** NOUN (PL die **Hochs**)

> see also **hoch** ADJECTIVE

1 cheer ◊ *Ein Hoch auf die Gastgeber!*
Three cheers for the hosts!

2 area of high pressure ◊ *ein Hoch
über dem Atlantik* an area of high
pressure over the Atlantic

hoch ADJECTIVE

> see also **das Hoch** NOUN

high ◊ *zehn Meter hoch* ten metres
high

> *Before a noun or after an article, use*
> **hohe**.

◊ *ein hoher Zaun* a high fence
♦ **Das ist mir zu hoch.** That's above my
head.

hochachtungsvoll ADVERB
yours faithfully

hochbegabt ADJECTIVE
extremely talented

das **Hochdeutsch** NOUN (GEN des
Hochdeutschen)
High German

der **Hochdruck** NOUN
high pressure

das **Hochgebirge** NOUN (PL die **Hochgebirge**)
high mountains

das **Hochhaus** NOUN (GEN des **Hochhauses**, PL
die **Hochhäuser**)
multistorey building

hochheben VERB (IMPERFECT **hob hoch**,
PERFECT **hat hochgehoben**)
to lift up

hochnäsig ADJECTIVE
stuck-up

die **Hochsaison** NOUN (PL die **Hochsaisons**)
high season

die **Hochschule** NOUN
1 college
2 university

die **Hochschulreife** NOUN
♦ **Sie hat die Hochschulreife.** She's got her
A-levels.

der **Hochsommer** NOUN (PL die **Hochsommer**)
high summer

der **Hochsprung** NOUN (PL die **Hochsprünge**)
high jump

höchst ADVERB
extremely

höchste ADJECTIVE
highest ◊ *Die Zugspitze ist der höchste
Berg Deutschlands.* The Zugspitze is the
highest mountain in Germany.

höchstens ADVERB
at most

die **Höchstgeschwindigkeit** NOUN
maximum speed

die **Höchsttemperatur** NOUN
maximum temperature

höchstwahrscheinlich ADVERB
most probably

die **Hochzeit** NOUN
wedding

der **Hochzeitstag** NOUN (PL die **Hochzeitstage**)
1 wedding day ◊ *An ihrem
Hochzeitstag trug sie ein wunderschönes
Kleid.* She wore a beautiful dress on her
wedding day.

2 wedding anniversary ◊ *Morgen ist
ihr zehnter Hochzeitstag.* It's their tenth
wedding anniversary tomorrow.

der **Hocker** NOUN (PL die **Hocker**)
stool

der **Hof** NOUN (PL die **Höfe**)
1 yard ◊ *Die Kinder spielen im Hof.* The
children are playing in the yard.

2 farm ◊ *Dieser Bauer hat den größten
Hof im Dorf.* This farmer has the largest
farm in the village.

hoffen VERB
to hope ◊ *Ich hoffe, er kommt noch.* I
hope he's coming.

♦ **auf etwas hoffen** to hope for something
◊ *Wir hoffen auf besseres Wetter.* We're
hoping for better weather.

hoffentlich ADVERB
hopefully ◊ *Hoffentlich kommt er bald.*
Hopefully he'll come soon. ◊ *Das passiert
hoffentlich nie wieder.* Hopefully that
won't happen again.

♦ **Hoffentlich nicht.** I hope not.

die **Hoffnung** NOUN
hope

hoffnungslos ADJECTIVE
hopeless

hoffnungsvoll ADJECTIVE
hopeful

höflich ADJECTIVE
polite

die **Höflichkeit** NOUN
politeness

hohe ADJECTIVE

> **hohe** is the form of **hoch** used before a
> noun.

high ◊ *ein hoher Zaun* a high fence

die **Höhe** NOUN
height

der **Höhepunkt** NOUN (PL die **Höhepunkte**)
climax ◊ *der Höhepunkt des Abends* the
climax of the evening

höher ADJECTIVE, ADVERB
higher

hohl ADJECTIVE
hollow

die **Höhle** NOUN
cave

holen VERB
to get ◊ *Ich hole ihn.* I'll get him.

H

♦ **jemanden holen lassen** to send for somebody

Holland NEUT NOUN
Holland
♦ **aus Holland** from Holland
♦ **in Holland** in Holland
♦ **nach Holland** to Holland

der **Holländer** NOUN (PL die **Holländer**)
Dutchman
♦ **Er ist Holländer.** He's Dutch.
♦ **die Holländer** the Dutch

die **Holländerin** NOUN
Dutchwoman
♦ **Sie ist Holländerin.** She's Dutch.

holländisch ADJECTIVE
Dutch

die **Hölle** NOUN
hell

das **Holz** NOUN (GEN des **Holzes**, PL die **Hölzer**)
wood

die **Holzkohle** NOUN
charcoal

die **Homepage** NOUN
home page

homosexuell ADJECTIVE
homosexual

der **Honig** NOUN (PL die **Honige**)
honey

die **Honigmelone** NOUN
honeydew melon

der **Hopfen** NOUN (PL die **Hopfen**)
hops

hörbar ADJECTIVE
audible

horchen VERB
[1] to listen ◊ *Er horchte auf das kleinste Geräusch.* He listened for the slightest noise.
[2] to eavesdrop ◊ *Du hast an der Tür gehorcht!* You've been eavesdropping at the door!

hören VERB
to hear ◊ *Ich höre dich nicht.* I can't hear you.
♦ **Musik hören** to listen to music
♦ **Radio hören** to listen to the radio

der **Hörer** NOUN (PL die **Hörer**)
receiver ◊ *Sie hat einfach den Hörer aufgelegt.* She simply put down the receiver.

der **Horizont** NOUN (PL die **Horizonte**)
horizon ◊ *am Horizont* on the horizon

horizontal ADJECTIVE
horizontal

das **Horn** NOUN (PL die **Hörner**)
horn

der **Horror** NOUN
horror

der **Horrorfilm** NOUN (PL die **Horrorfilme**)
horror film

der **Horrorroman** NOUN (PL die **Horrorromane**)
horror novel

die **Hose** NOUN
trousers ◊ *eine Hose* a pair of trousers
*Be careful! The German word **Hose** does not mean **hose**.*

der **Hosenanzug** NOUN (PL die **Hosenanzüge**)
trouser suit

die **Hosentasche** NOUN
trouser pocket

der **Hosenträger** NOUN (PL die **Hosenträger**)
braces

das **Hotel** NOUN (PL die **Hotels**)
hotel

Hr. ABBREVIATION (= *Herr*)
Mr

hübsch ADJECTIVE
pretty

der **Hubschrauber** NOUN (PL die **Hubschrauber**)
helicopter

das **Hufeisen** NOUN (PL die **Hufeisen**)
horseshoe

die **Hüfte** NOUN
hip

der **Hügel** NOUN (PL die **Hügel**)
hill

hügelig ADJECTIVE
hilly

das **Huhn** NOUN (PL die **Hühner**)
chicken ◊ *Huhn mit Reis* chicken with rice

die **Hummel** NOUN
bumblebee

der **Hummer** NOUN (PL die **Hummer**)
lobster

der **Humor** NOUN
humour
♦ **Humor haben** to have a sense of humour

humorvoll ADJECTIVE
humorous

der **Hund** NOUN (PL die **Hunde**)
dog

die **Hundehütte** NOUN
kennel

hundemüde ADJECTIVE
dog-tired

hundert NUMBER
a hundred

der **Hunger** NOUN
hunger
♦ **Hunger haben** to be hungry

hungrig ADJECTIVE
hungry

die **Hupe** NOUN
horn ◊ *auf die Hupe drücken* to sound the horn

hupen VERB
to sound the horn

hüpfen VERB (PERFECT **ist gehüpft**)
to hop

der **Hürdenlauf** NOUN (PL die **Hürdenläufe**)
hurdles

der **Husten** NOUN

> see also **husten** VERB

cough ◊ *Sie hat Husten.* She has a cough.

husten VERB

> see also **der Husten** NOUN

to cough

das **Hustenbonbon** NOUN (PL die **Hustenbonbons**)

cough drop

der **Hustensaft** NOUN (PL die **Hustensäfte**)

cough mixture

der **Hut** NOUN (PL die **Hüte**)

> see also **die Hut** NOUN

hat

die **Hut** NOUN

> see also **der Hut** NOUN

♦ **auf der Hut sein** to be on one's guard

hüten VERB

to look after ◊ *Silke hütet heute Abend unsere Kinder.* Silke's looking after our children this evening.

♦ **ein Geheimnis hüten** to keep a secret

♦ **sich hüten, etwas zu tun** to take care not to do something ◊ *Ich werde mich hüten, ihr das zu sagen.* I'll take care not to say that to her.

♦ **sich hüten vor** to be on one's guard against ◊ *Hüte dich vor ihm, er lügt.* Be on your guard against him, he's a liar.

die **Hütte** NOUN

hut

hygienisch ADJECTIVE

hygienic

hypnotisieren VERB (PERFECT **hat hypnotisiert**)

to hypnotize

hysterisch ADJECTIVE

hysterical ◊ *Sie wurde hysterisch.* She became hysterical.

H

I

IC ABBREVIATION (= *Intercityzug*)
  Intercity train
ICE ABBREVIATION (= *Intercityexpress*)
  Intercity Express train
ich PRONOUN
  I ◊ *Ich weiß nicht.* I don't know.
  ♦ **Ich bin's!** It's me!
das **Icon** NOUN (PL die **Icons**)
  icon (*computer*) ◊ *ein Icon anklicken* to
  click on an icon
das **Ideal** NOUN
  see also **ideal** ADJECTIVE
  ideal
ideal ADJECTIVE
  see also **das Ideal** NOUN
  ideal
die **Idee** NOUN
  idea
identifizieren VERB (PERFECT **hat
  identifiziert**)
  to identify
identisch ADJECTIVE
  identical
die **Ideologie** NOUN
  ideology
ideologisch ADJECTIVE
  ideological
der **Idiot** NOUN (GEN des **Idioten**, PL die **Idioten**)
  idiot
idiotisch ADJECTIVE
  idiotic
der **Igel** NOUN (PL die **Igel**)
  hedgehog
ihm PRONOUN
  ihm is the dative of **er** *and* **es**.
  1 him ◊ *Kannst du ihm sagen, wie spät
  es ist?* Can you tell him what the time is?
  2 to him ◊ *Gib es ihm!* Give it to him.
  3 it ◊ *Das Meerschweinchen hat Hunger,
  gib ihm was zu essen.* The guinea pig's
  hungry, give it something to eat.
ihn PRONOUN
  ihn is the accusative of **er**.
  him ◊ *Ich habe ihn gesehen.* I saw him.
ihnen PRONOUN
  see also **Ihnen** PRONOUN
  ihnen is the dative of **sie** *(plural)*.
  1 them ◊ *Ich sage es ihnen.* I'll tell them.
  2 to them ◊ *Gib es ihnen.* Give it to
  them.
Ihnen PRONOUN
  see also **ihnen** PRONOUN
  Ihnen is the dative of **Sie**.
  1 you ◊ *Darf ich Ihnen etwas zu trinken
  anbieten?* May I offer you something to
  drink?
  2 to you ◊ *Darf ich Ihnen das geben?*
  May I give this to you?

ihr PRONOUN
  see also **ihr** ADJECTIVE, **ihr** ADJECTIVE
  1 you ◊ *Habt ihr das gesehen?* Did you
  see that?

  ⓘ *The familiar form of address* **ihr** *is
  used when addressing family
  members, friends, children under 16
  and pets.*

  ◊ *Ihr seid es.* It's you.
  ihr is also the dative of **sie** *(singular)*.
  2 her ◊ *Kannst du ihr das bitte
  ausrichten?* Can you please tell her?
  ♦ **Er steht neben ihr.** He's standing beside
  her.
  3 to her ◊ *Gib es ihr.* Give it to her.
ihr ADJECTIVE
  see also **ihr** ADJECTIVE, **ihr** PRONOUN
  1 her ◊ *Ihr Vater ist nett.* Her father's
  nice. ◊ *Ihre Mutter hat mir das gesagt.*
  Her mother told me. ◊ *Das ist ihr
  Fahrrad.* That's her bike. ◊ *Ihre Eltern
  sind prima.* Her parents are great.
  2 hers ◊ *Das ist nicht ihr Füller, ihrer ist
  schwarz.* That's not her pen, hers is
  black. ◊ *Meine Mutter heißt Ulla, ihre
  auch.* My mother's called Ulla, so is hers.
  ◊ *Mein Fahrrad war kaputt, also habe ich
  ihres genommen.* My bike was broken,
  so I took hers. ◊ *Seine Noten sind
  schlecht, ihre sind viel besser.* His marks
  are bad, hers are much better.
  3 their ◊ *Das ist ihr Lehrer.* That's their
  teacher. ◊ *Ihre Englischlehrerin ist netter
  als unsere.* Their English teacher's nicer
  than ours. ◊ *Ihr Haus liegt gleich neben
  unserem.* Their house is right next door
  to ours. ◊ *die Bäume und ihre Blätter* the
  trees and their leaves
  4 theirs ◊ *Das ist nicht ihr Lehrer, ihrer
  heißt Herr Schulz.* That's not their
  teacher, theirs is called Mr Schulz.
  ◊ *Unsere Schule macht einen
  Wandertag, ihre nicht.* Our school is
  going rambling, theirs isn't. ◊ *Das ist
  nicht ihr Haus, ihres ist in der
  Hauptstraße.* That's not their house,
  theirs is on the main road. ◊ *Unsere
  Lehrer sind streng, ihre sind viel netter.*
  Our teachers are strict, theirs are much
  nicer.
Ihr ADJECTIVE
  see also **ihr** ADJECTIVE, **ihr** PRONOUN
  1 your ◊ *Ihr Vater ist nett.* Your father's
  nice. ◊ *Ihre Mutter hat mir das gesagt.*
  Your mother told me. ◊ *Ist das Ihr
  Fahrrad?* Is that your bike? ◊ *Leben Ihre
  Eltern noch?* Are your parents still alive?

2 yours ◊ *Das ist nicht Ihr Füller, Ihrer ist hier.* That's not your pen, yours is here. ◊ *Meine Mutter heißt Ulla, wie heißt Ihre?* My mother's called Ulla, what's yours called? ◊ *Mein Fahrrad ist kaputt, kann ich Ihres nehmen?* My bike's broken, can I take yours? ◊ *Unsere Kinder sind nicht so artig wie Ihre.* Our children aren't as well-behaved as yours.

ihretwegen ADVERB

see also **Ihretwegen**

ihretwegen refers to sie (singular or plural).

1 for her sake ◊ *Ich habe ihretwegen auf den Urlaub verzichtet.* I went without a holiday for her sake.

2 on her account ◊ *Er hat sich ihretwegen furchtbar aufgeregt.* He got terribly upset on her account.

3 as far as she's concerned ◊ *Sie sagt, dass du ihretwegen ruhig gehen kannst.* She says that as far as she's concerned you can go.

4 for their sake ◊ *Wir haben ihretwegen auf den Urlaub verzichtet.* We went without a holiday for their sake.

5 on their account ◊ *Er hat sich ihretwegen furchtbar aufgeregt.* He got terribly upset on their account.

6 as far as they're concerned ◊ *Sie sagen, dass du ihretwegen ruhig gehen kannst.* They say that as far as they're concerned you can go.

Ihretwegen ADVERB

see also **ihretwegen**

Ihretwegen refers to Sie.

1 for your sake ◊ *Ich habe Ihretwegen auf den Urlaub verzichtet.* I went without a holiday for your sake.

2 on your account ◊ *Er hat sich Ihretwegen furchtbar aufgeregt.* He got terribly upset on your account.

die **Illustrierte** NOUN (GEN der **Illustrierten**)
　magazine

im = in dem

der **Imbiss** NOUN (GEN des **Imbisses**, PL die **Imbisse**)
　snack

die **Imbisshalle** NOUN
　snack bar

der **Imbissstand** NOUN (PL die **Imbissstände**)
　hot-dog stand

die **Imbissstube** NOUN
　snack bar

immatrikulieren VERB (PERFECT **hat immatrikuliert**)
　to register (*at university*)

immer ADVERB
　always ◊ *Du kommst immer zu spät.* You're always late.

◆ **immer wieder** again and again
◆ **immer noch** still
◆ **immer noch nicht** still not

◆ **für immer** forever
◆ **immer wenn ich ...** every time I ...
◆ **immer schöner** more and more beautiful
◆ **immer trauriger** sadder and sadder
◆ **wer auch immer** whoever
◆ **was auch immer** whatever

immerhin ADVERB
　at least

das **Imperfekt** NOUN (PL die **Imperfekte**)
　imperfect

impfen VERB
　to vaccinate ◊ *jemanden gegen etwas impfen* to vaccinate somebody against something

der **Impfstoff** NOUN (PL die **Impfstoffe**)
　vaccine

die **Impfung** NOUN
　vaccination

imponieren VERB (PERFECT **hat imponiert**)
　to impress ◊ *jemandem imponieren* to impress somebody

der **Import** NOUN (PL die **Importe**)
　import

importieren VERB (PERFECT **hat importiert**)
　to import

improvisieren VERB (PERFECT **hat improvisiert**)
　to improvise

imstande ADJECTIVE
◆ **imstande sein, etwas zu tun** to be able to do something

in PREPOSITION

Use the accusative to express movement or a change of place. Use the dative when there is no change of place.

1 in ◊ *Es ist im Schrank.* It's in the cupboard. ◊ *Sie ist in der Stadt.* She's in town. ◊ *Sie wurde rot im Gesicht.* She went red in the face.

2 into ◊ *Lege es in diese Schublade.* Put it into this drawer. ◊ *Sie geht in die Stadt.* She's going into town.

◆ **in der Schule sein** to be at school
◆ **in die Schule gehen** to go to school
◆ **in diesem Jahr** this year
◆ **heute in zwei Wochen** two weeks today
◆ **bis ins zwanzigste Jahrhundert** into the twentieth century
◆ **in sein** to be in ◊ *Inline-Skates sind jetzt in.* In-line skates are in at the moment.

inbegriffen ADVERB
　included

der **Inder** NOUN (PL die **Inder**)
　Indian

die **Inderin** NOUN
　Indian

der **Indianer** NOUN (PL die **Indianer**)
　Native American

die **Indianerin** NOUN
　Native American

indianisch ADJECTIVE
　Native American

das **Indien** NOUN
India
♦ **aus Indien** from India
♦ **nach Indien** to India
indisch ADJECTIVE
Indian
indiskutabel ADJECTIVE
out of the question
die **Industrie** NOUN
industry
das **Industriegebiet** NOUN (PL die **Industriegebiete**)
industrial area
die **Industriestadt** NOUN (PL die **Industriestädte**)
industrial town
der **Infarkt** NOUN (PL die **Infarkte**)
coronary
die **Infektion** NOUN
infection
der **Infinitiv** NOUN (PL die **Infinitive**)
infinitive
infizieren VERB (PERFECT **hat infiziert**)
to infect
♦ **sich bei jemandem infizieren** to catch something from somebody
die **Inflation** NOUN
inflation
infolge PREPOSITION
*The preposition **infolge** takes the genitive.*
as a result of
infolgedessen ADVERB
consequently
die **Informatik** NOUN
computer science
der **Informatiker** NOUN (PL die **Informatiker**)
computer scientist
die **Information** NOUN
information ◊ *Weitere Informationen lassen wir Ihnen zukommen.* We will send you further information.
das **Informationsbüro** NOUN (PL die **Informationsbüros**)
information bureau
informieren VERB (PERFECT **hat informiert**)
to inform
♦ **sich über etwas informieren** to find out about something
♦ **sich über jemanden informieren** to make enquiries about somebody
infrage ADVERB
♦ **etwas infrage stellen** to question something
♦ **nicht infrage kommen** to be out of the question
der **Ingenieur** NOUN (PL die **Ingenieure**)
engineer
die **Ingenieurschule** NOUN
school of engineering
der **Ingwer** NOUN
ginger

der **Inhaber** NOUN (PL die **Inhaber**)
owner
♦ **der Inhaber einer Lizenz** the licence holder
der **Inhalt** NOUN (PL die **Inhalte**)
[1] contents ◊ *Der Inhalt der Flasche war grün.* The contents of the bottle were green.
[2] content ◊ *Fasse den Inhalt dieser Geschichte zusammen.* Summarize the content of this story.
[3] volume ◊ *Berechne den Inhalt des Würfels.* Calculate the volume of the cube.
die **Inhaltsangabe** NOUN
summary
das **Inhaltsverzeichnis** NOUN (GEN des **Inhaltsverzeichnisses,** PL die **Inhaltsverzeichnisse**)
table of contents
inkl. ABBREVIATION (= *inklusive*)
incl.
inklusive PREPOSITION, ADVERB
*The preposition **inklusive** takes the genitive.*
[1] inclusive of ◊ *ein Computer inklusive Bildschirm* a computer inclusive of monitor
[2] included ◊ *Die Bedienung ist inklusive.* Service is included.
das **Inland** NOUN
♦ **im In- und Ausland** at home and abroad
der **Inline-Skater** NOUN (PL die **Inline-Skater**)
rollerblader
die **Inline-Skaterin** NOUN
rollerblader
die **Inline-Skates** PL NOUN
in-line skates
innen ADVERB
inside
der **Innenminister** NOUN (PL die **Innenminister**)
Home Secretary
die **Innenpolitik** NOUN
domestic policy
innenpolitisch ADJECTIVE
internal
die **Innenstadt** NOUN (PL die **Innenstädte**)
town centre
innere ADJECTIVE
internal ◊ *die inneren Angelegenheiten des Landes* the internal matters of the country
die **Innereien** FEM PL NOUN
innards
innerhalb ADVERB, PREPOSITION
*The preposition **innerhalb** takes the genitive.*
[1] within ◊ *innerhalb von zwei Tagen* within two days
♦ **Ich schaffe das nicht innerhalb der gesetzten Frist.** I won't manage that by the deadline.
[2] during ◊ *Der Bus fährt nur innerhalb der Woche, nicht an Wochenenden.* The

bus only runs during the week, not at the
weekend.

inoffiziell ADJECTIVE
unofficial

ins = **in das**

insbesondere ADVERB
particularly

die **Inschrift** NOUN
inscription

das **Insekt** NOUN (PL die **Insekten**)
insect

der **Insektenstich** NOUN (PL die **Insektenstiche**)
insect bite

die **Insel** NOUN
island

insgesamt ADVERB
in all ◊ *Er hat insgesamt drei Fahrräder.*
He has three bikes in all. ◊ *Insgesamt
waren dreihundert Leute gekommen.* In
all, three hundred people came.

der **Instinkt** NOUN (PL die **Instinkte**)
instinct

instinktiv ADJECTIVE
instinctive

das **Instrument** NOUN (PL die **Instrumente**)
instrument

intellektuell ADJECTIVE
intellectual

intelligent ADJECTIVE
intelligent

die **Intelligenz** NOUN
intelligence

intensiv ADJECTIVE
intensive

der **Intercityexpress** NOUN (GEN des
Intercityexpresses, PL die
Intercityexpresse)
Intercity Express train

der **Intercityzug** NOUN (PL die **Intercityzüge**)
Intercity train

interessant ADJECTIVE
interesting

das **Interesse** NOUN (PL die **Interessen**)
interest
♦ **Interesse haben an** to be interested in
◊ *Hast du Interesse an einem
gebrauchten Notebook?* Are you
interested in a used notebook?
◊ *Manfred scheint Interesse an dir zu
haben.* Manfred seems to be interested
in you.

interessieren VERB (PERFECT **hat
interessiert**)
to interest ◊ *Es interessiert mich, was du
in den Ferien erlebt hast.* I'm interested
to know what you did in your holidays.
♦ **sich interessieren für** to be interested in
◊ *Ich interessiere mich für Kunst.* I'm
interested in art.

das **Internat** NOUN (PL die **Internate**)
boarding school

international ADJECTIVE

international

das **Internet** NOUN
Internet

der **Internet-Anbieter** NOUN (PL die **Internet-
Anbieter**)
Internet Service Provider

der **Internetbenutzer** NOUN (PL die
Internetbenutzer)
Internet user

das **Internet-Café** NOUN (PL die **Internet-Cafés**)
Internet café

interpretieren VERB (PERFECT **hat
interpretiert**)
to interpret

intransitiv ADJECTIVE
intransitive

inwiefern ADVERB
how far ◊ *Ich weiß nicht, inwiefern das
stimmt.* I don't know how far that's right.

inzwischen ADVERB
meanwhile

der **Irak** NOUN
Iraq
♦ **aus dem Irak** from Iraq
♦ **im Irak** in Iraq
♦ **in den Irak** to Iraq

irakisch ADJECTIVE
Iraqi

der **Iran** NOUN
Iran
♦ **aus dem Iran** from Iran
♦ **im Iran** in Iran
♦ **in den Iran** to Iran

iranisch ADJECTIVE
Iranian

der **Ire** NOUN (GEN des **Iren**, PL die **Iren**)
Irishman
♦ **die Iren** the Irish

irgend ADVERB
at all ◊ *Komm, wenn es irgend geht.*
Come if it's at all possible.

irgendein ADJECTIVE
[1] some ◊ *Irgendein Mann hat mir das
gesagt.* Some man told me. ◊ *Irgendeine
Ausrede wird dir schon einfallen.* You'll
think of some excuse.
♦ **Bring mir irgendein Getränk mit.** Bring
me something to drink.
♦ **Welchen Kuli willst du? – Irgendeinen.**
Which pen do you want? – Any one.
[2] any ◊ *Ich will nicht irgendeinen
Computer.* I don't just want any
computer. ◊ *Gibt es nicht irgendeine
Möglichkeit?* Isn't there any chance?

irgendetwas PRONOUN
[1] something ◊ *irgendetwas Schönes*
something nice
[2] anything ◊ *Hast du irgendetwas
gehört?* Did you hear anything?

irgendjemand PRONOUN

irgendwann ADVERB
sometime

irgendwas PRONOMEN
1 something ◊ *Er murmelte irgendwas.* He murmured something.
2 anything ◊ *Was soll ich anziehen? – Irgendwas.* What shall I wear? – Anything.

irgendwie ADVERB
somehow

irgendwo ADVERB
somewhere

irgendwohin ADVERB
somewhere ◊ *Ich habe das irgendwohin gelegt.* I've put it somewhere.
♦ **Stell es irgendwohin.** Put it anywhere.

die **Irin** NOUN
Irishwoman

irisch ADJECTIVE
Irish

Irland NEUT NOUN
Ireland
♦ **aus Irland** from Ireland
♦ **in Irland** in Ireland
♦ **nach Irland** to Ireland

die **Ironie** NOUN
irony

ironisch ADJECTIVE
ironic ◊ *Das war ironisch gemeint.* That was meant to be ironic.

irre ADJECTIVE, ADVERB
1 mad ◊ *Wer ist denn auf diese irre Idee gekommen?* Who thought up this mad idea?
2 fantastic ◊ *Das war ein irres Konzert.* That was a fantastic concert.
3 incredibly ◊ *Er ist irre schnell gefahren.* He drove incredibly fast. ◊ *Die Party war irre gut.* The party was incredibly good.

1 somebody ◊ *Das hat mir irgendjemand gesagt.* Somebody told me.
2 anybody ◊ *Hast du irgendjemanden gesehen?* Did you see anybody?

irreführen VERB (PERFECT **hat irregeführt**)
to mislead

irren VERB

*Use **haben** to form the perfect tense for **to be mistaken** but **sein** for **to wander about**.*

♦ **sich irren** to be mistaken ◊ *Du hast dich geirrt.* You were mistaken. to wander about ◊ *Sie ist durch die Straßen geirrt.* She wandered about the streets.

irrsinnig ADJECTIVE, ADVERB
1 crazy ◊ *Das ist doch eine irrsinnige Idee.* That's a crazy idea.
2 incredibly ◊ *Er ist irrsinnig schnell gefahren.* He drove incredibly fast.

der **Irrtum** NOUN (PL die **Irrtümer**)
mistake

der **Islam** NOUN
Islam

Island NEUT NOUN
Iceland
♦ **nach Island** to Iceland

Israel NEUT NOUN
Israel
♦ **aus Israel** from Israel
♦ **nach Israel** to Israel

der **Israeli** NOUN (PL die **Israelis**)
die Israeli ◊ *Sie ist mit einem Israeli verheiratet.* He is married to an Israeli.

israelisch ADJECTIVE
Israeli

isst VERB *see* **essen**

ist VERB *see* **sein**

Italien NEUT NOUN
Italy
♦ **aus Italien** from Italy
♦ **in Italien** in Italy
♦ **nach Italien** to Italy

der **Italiener** NOUN (PL die **Italiener**)
Italian

die **Italienerin** NOUN
Italian

italienisch ADJECTIVE
Italian

J

ja ADVERB
  1. yes ◇ *Hast du das gesehen? – Ja.* Did you see that? – Yes, I did.
  ◆ **Ich glaube ja.** I think so.
  2. really? ◇ *Ich habe mir ein neues Auto gekauft. – Ach ja?* I've bought a new car. – Really?
  ◆ **Ich habe gekündigt. – Ja?** I've quit. – Have you?
  ◆ **Du kommst, ja?** You're coming, aren't you?
  ◆ **Sei ja vorsichtig!** Do be careful.
  ◆ **Sie wissen ja, dass ...** As you know, ...
  ◆ **Tu das ja nicht!** Don't you dare do that!
  ◆ **Ich habe es ja gewusst.** I just knew it.
  ◆ **ja, also ...** well ... ◇ *Ja, also wenn ihr alle geht, dann gehe ich mit.* Well, if you're all going, then I'm going too.

die **Jacht** NOUN
  yacht

die **Jacke** NOUN
  1. jacket ◇ *Sie trug einen blauen Rock und eine schwarze Jacke.* She was wearing a blue skirt and a black jacket.
  2. cardigan ◇ *Wenn es dir kalt ist, solltest du eine Jacke anziehen.* If you're cold, you should put on a cardigan.

das **Jackett** NOUN (PL die **Jacketts**)
  jacket

die **Jagd** NOUN (PL die **Jagden**)
  1. hunt ◇ *Er fiel während der Jagd vom Pferd.* He fell off his horse during the hunt.
  2. hunting ◇ *Alan geht oft zur Jagd.* Alan often goes hunting.

jagen VERB
  *Use **haben** to form the perfect tense for **to hunt** or **to chase** but **sein** for **to race**.*
  1. to hunt ◇ *Sonntags geht er jagen.* He goes hunting on Sundays. ◇ *Er hat in Afrika Löwen gejagt.* He hunted lions in Africa. ◇ *Meine Katze jagt Mäuse.* My cat hunts mice.
  2. to chase ◇ *Die Polizei hat die Bankräuber gejagt, aber nicht eingeholt.* The police chased the bank robbers but didn't catch them.
  3. to race ◇ *Wir sind mit ihr ins Krankenhaus gejagt.* We raced with her to the hospital.
  ◆ **Damit kann man mich jagen.** I can't stand that.

das **Jahr** NOUN (PL die **Jahre**)
  year ◇ *Ich bin vierzehn Jahre alt.* I'm fourteen years old.
  ◆ **die Neunziger jahre** the nineties

jahrelang ADVERB
  for years

die **Jahreszeit** NOUN
  season
  ◆ **zu jeder Jahreszeit** throughout the year ◇ *Man bekommt inzwischen zu jeder Jahreszeit Erdbeeren.* You can now get strawberries throughout the year.

der **Jahrgang** NOUN (PL die **Jahrgänge**)
  ◆ **Sie ist mein Jahrgang.** She was born in the same year as me.
  ◆ **Welcher Jahrgang bist du?** In which year were you born?

das **Jahrhundert** NOUN (PL die **Jahrhunderte**)
  century

jährlich ADJECTIVE, ADVERB
  yearly

der **Jahrmarkt** NOUN (PL die **Jahrmärkte**)
  funfair

das **Jahrtausend** NOUN (PL die **Jahrtausende**)
  millennium

jähzornig ADJECTIVE
  hot-tempered

die **Jalousie** NOUN
  Venetian blind

der **Jammer** NOUN
  misery
  ◆ **Es ist ein Jammer, dass ...** It's a crying shame that ...

jämmerlich ADJECTIVE
  pitiful ◇ *ein jämmerliches Miauen* a pitiful miaowing
  ◆ **jämmerlich weinen** to cry bitterly

jammern VERB
  to whine ◇ *Hör auf zu jammern!* Stop whining.

der **Januar** NOUN (GEN des **Januar** or **Januars**, PL die **Januare**)
  January ◇ *im Januar* in January ◇ *am dritten Januar* on the third of January ◇ *Ulm, den 3. Januar 2005* Ulm, 3 January 2005 ◇ *Heute ist der dritte Januar.* Today is the third of January.

Japan NEUT NOUN
  Japan
  ◆ **aus Japan** from Japan
  ◆ **nach Japan** to Japan

der **Japaner** NOUN (PL die **Japaner**)
  Japanese

die **Japanerin** NOUN
  Japanese

japanisch ADJECTIVE
  Japanese

jaulen VERB
  to howl

jawohl ADVERB
  yes

je ADVERB, CONJUNCTION
  1. ever ◇ *Warst du je in Italien?* Have you ever been to Italy? ◇ *Hast du so was je*

☞

gesehen? Did you ever see anything like it?

2 **each** ◊ *Wir haben je zwei Stück bekommen.* We got two pieces each. ◊ *Sie zahlten je zehn Euro.* They paid ten euros each.

♦ **je nach** depending on ◊ *Je nach Größe sind sie verschieden teuer.* Prices vary depending on size.

♦ **je nachdem** it depends ◊ *Wir kommen vielleicht etwas später, je nachdem, wie lange wir unterwegs sind.* We'll perhaps be a little late, it depends how long we take to get there.

♦ **je nachdem, ob ...** depending on whether ... ◊ *Wir kommen vielleicht mit den Kindern, je nachdem ob sie Lust haben.* We'll come with the children depending on whether they feel like it or not.

♦ **je ... umso ...** the ... the ... ◊ *Je schneller er fuhr, umso mehr Angst hatte sie.* The faster he drove, the more frightened she was.

♦ **je eher, desto besser** the sooner the better

♦ **besser denn je** better than ever

♦ **Es geht mir besser denn je.** Things have never been better.

die **Jeans** NOUN (PL die **Jeans**)
jeans

♦ **eine Jeans** a pair of jeans ◊ *Ich habe mir eine neue Jeans gekauft.* I've bought myself a new pair of jeans.

jede ADJECTIVE, PRONOUN

1 **every** ◊ *Jeder Schüler bekommt ein Zeugnis.* Every pupil receives a report. ◊ *Ich besuche sie jede Woche.* I visit her every week. ◊ *Er gab jedem Mädchen ein Bonbon.* He gave every girl a sweet.

♦ **jeder** everybody ◊ *Jeder weiß, dass das nicht erlaubt ist.* Everybody knows that that's not allowed.

2 **each** ◊ *Jeder von euch bekommt ein Stück.* Each of you will get a piece. ◊ *Jede seiner Freundinnen war anders.* Each of his girlfriends was different.

♦ **Jedes der Kinder hat mir etwas geschenkt.** Each child gave me something.

jedenfalls ADVERB
in any case

jedermann PRONOUN
everyone

jederzeit ADVERB
at any time

jedesmal ADVERB
every time

jedoch ADVERB
however

jemals ADVERB
ever

jemand PRONOUN

1 **somebody** ◊ *Jemand hat mir gesagt, dass du krank bist.* Somebody told me that you were ill.

2 **anybody** ◊ *War jemand zu Hause?* Was anybody at home?

jene PRONOUN

1 **that** ◊ *in jener Zeit* at that time

2 **those** ◊ *in jenen Tagen* in those days

jetzt ADVERB
now ◊ *Sie ist jetzt in der Schweiz.* She's in Switzerland now.

jeweils ADVERB

♦ **jeweils zwei zusammen** two at a time

♦ **zu jeweils fünf Euro** at five euros each

der **Job** NOUN (PL die **Jobs**)
job

das **Jod** NOUN
iodine

jodeln VERB
to yodel

joggen VERB

Use **haben** for the perfect tense when you describe the activity and **sein** when you describe the motion.

to jog ◊ *Früher habe ich oft gejoggt.* I used to jog a lot. ◊ *Wir sind durch den Wald gejoggt.* We jogged through the woods.

das **Jogging** NOUN
jogging

der **Jogginganzug** NOUN (PL die **Jogginganzüge**)
tracksuit

der **Joghurt** NOUN (PL die **Joghurts**)
yogurt

der **Jogurt** NOUN (PL die **Jogurts**)
see **Joghurt**

die **Johannisbeere** NOUN
redcurrant ◊ *Johannisbeeren sind mir zu sauer.* Redcurrants are too sour for me.

♦ **Schwarze Johannisbeere** blackcurrant

der **Journalist** NOUN (GEN des **Journalisten**, PL die **Journalisten**)
journalist

jubeln VERB
to rejoice

das **Jubiläum** NOUN (PL die **Jubiläen**)
anniversary ◊ *Nächstes Jahr feiert unsere Schule ihr zwanzigjähriges Jubiläum.* Our school's celebrating its twentieth anniversary next year.

jucken VERB
to be itchy ◊ *Meine Nase juckt.* My nose is itchy.

♦ **Es juckt mich am Arm.** My arm's itchy.

♦ **Das juckt mich.** That's itchy.

der **Jude** NOUN (GEN des **Juden**, PL die **Juden**)
Jew

die **Jüdin** NOUN
Jew

jüdisch ADJECTIVE
Jewish

die **Jugend** NOUN
  youth ◊ *In meiner Jugend habe ich
  Fußball gespielt.* I used to play football in
  my youth. ◊ *die Jugend von heute* the
  youth of today

die **Jugendherberge** NOUN
  youth hostel

der **Jugendklub** NOUN (PL die **Jugendklubs**)
  youth club

jugendlich ADJECTIVE
  youthful ◊ *Er hat ein jugendliches
  Gesicht.* He has a youthful face. ◊ *Sie
  sieht sehr jugendlich aus.* She looks very
  youthful.

der **Jugendliche** NOUN (GEN des/der
die   **Jugendlichen**, PL die **Jugendlichen**)
  teenager ◊ *Ich habe einen Jugendlichen
  dabei beobachtet, wie er die Wand
  besprüht hat.* I watched a teenager spray
  the wall.

das **Jugendzentrum** NOUN (PL die
  Jugendzentren)
  youth centre

Jugoslawien NEUT NOUN
  Yugoslavia ◊ *das frühere Jugoslawien*
  the former Yugoslavia

jugoslawisch ADJECTIVE
  Yugoslavian

der **Juli** NOUN (GEN des **Juli** or **Julis**, PL die **Julis**)
  July ◊ *im Juli* in July ◊ *am dritten Juli* on
  the third of July ◊ *Ulm, den 3. Juli 2004*
  Ulm, 3 July 2004 ◊ *Heute ist der dritte
  Juli.* Today is the third of July.

jung ADJECTIVE
  young ◊ *Er ist drei Jahre jünger als ich.*
  He's three years younger than me.

der **Junge** NOUN (GEN des **Jungen**, PL die
  Jungen)
  | see also **das Junge** NOUN |
  boy ◊ *In unserer Klasse gibt es zehn
  Jungen und fünfzehn Mädchen.* There
  are ten boys and fifteen girls in our class.

das **Junge** NOUN (GEN des **Jungen**, PL die
  Jungen)
  | see also **der Junge** NOUN |
  young animal
  ♦ **eine Löwin mit ihren Jungen** a lioness
  with her young

die **Jungfrau** NOUN
  1 virgin
  2 Virgo ◊ *Veronika ist Jungfrau.*
  Veronika's Virgo.

jüngste ADJECTIVE
  1 youngest ◊ *Er ist der jüngste Schüler
  der Klasse.* He's the youngest pupil in the
  class.
  2 latest ◊ *die jüngsten Entwicklungen*
  the latest developments

der **Juni** NOUN (GEN des **Juni** or **Junis**, PL die
  Junis)
  June ◊ *im Juni* in June ◊ *am fünfzehnten
  Juni* on the fifteenth of June ◊ *Ulm, den
  3. Juni 2001* Ulm, 3 June 2001 ◊ *Heute ist
  der dritte Juni.* Today is the third of
  June.

der **Juwelier** NOUN (PL die **Juweliere**)
  jeweller

der **Jux** NOUN
  laugh ◊ *Das war ein Jux!* That was a
  laugh! ◊ *Wir haben das aus Jux
  gemacht.* We did it for a laugh.

J

K

das **Kabel** NOUN (PL die **Kabel**)
   1 wire ◊ *Das Kabel des Telefons ist zu kurz.* The telephone wire is too short.
   2 cable ◊ *Das Kabel der Seilbahn muss regelmäßig überprüft werden.* The cable on the cable car has to be checked regularly.

der **Kabelanschluss** NOUN (GEN des **Kabelanschlusses**, PL die **Kabelanschlüsse**)
   cable connection

das **Kabelfernsehen** NOUN
   cable television

die **Kabine** NOUN
   1 cabin ◊ *Wir hatten zu zweit eine Kabine auf dem Schiff.* The two of us shared a cabin on the ship.
   2 cubicle ◊ *Sie können das Kleid dort hinten in der Kabine anprobieren.* You can try the dress on in the cubicle over there.

der **Käfer** NOUN (PL die **Käfer**)
   beetle

der **Kaffee** NOUN (PL die **Kaffees** or **Kaffee**)
   coffee ◊ *Herr Ober, zwei Kaffee bitte.* Two coffees please, waiter.

die **Kaffeekanne** NOUN
   coffeepot

die **Kaffeepause** NOUN
   coffee break ◊ *Wir machten Kaffeepause.* We had a coffee break.

der **Käfig** NOUN (PL die **Käfige**)
   cage

kahl ADJECTIVE
   bald ◊ *sein kahler Kopf* his bald head
   ♦ **die kahlen Bäume im Winter** the bare trees in winter
   ♦ **kahl geschoren** shaven

der **Kai** NOUN (PL die **Kais**)
   quay

der **Kaiser** NOUN (PL die **Kaiser**)
   emperor

der **Kakao** NOUN (PL die **Kakaos** or **Kakao**)
   cocoa ◊ *Herr Ober, zwei Kakao bitte.* Two cups of cocoa please, waiter.

das **Kalb** NOUN (PL die **Kälber**)
   calf (*animal*)

das **Kalbfleisch** NOUN
   veal

der **Kalender** NOUN (PL die **Kalender**)
   1 calendar ◊ *An der Wand hing ein Kalender mit Bildern von Picasso.* A calendar with pictures by Picasso was hanging on the wall.
   2 diary ◊ *Sie holte ihren Kalender aus der Tasche.* She got her diary out of her bag.

der **Kalk** NOUN
   1 lime (*stone*)
   2 calcium ◊ *Ein Mangel an Kalk kann zu schlechten Zähnen führen.* A lack of calcium can lead to bad teeth.

die **Kalorie** NOUN
   calorie

kalorienarm ADJECTIVE
   low in calories

kalt ADJECTIVE
   cold ◊ *Heute ist es kälter als gestern.* It's colder today than yesterday.
   ♦ **Mir ist kalt.** I'm cold.
   ♦ **etwas kalt stellen** to chill something ◊ *Du solltest den Weißwein kalt stellen.* You should chill the white wine.

die **Kälte** NOUN
   1 cold ◊ *Bei dieser Kälte gehe ich nicht raus.* I'm not going out in this cold.
   2 coldness ◊ *Die Kälte des Wassers hat uns vom Baden abgehalten.* The coldness of the water stopped us from bathing.

kam VERB *see* **kommen**

das **Kamel** NOUN (PL die **Kamele**)
   camel

die **Kamera** NOUN (PL die **Kameras**)
   camera

der **Kamerad** NOUN (GEN des **Kameraden**, PL die **Kameraden**)
   friend

der **Kamillentee** NOUN (PL die **Kamillentees**)
   camomile tea

der **Kamin** NOUN (PL die **Kamine**)
   open fire
   ♦ **Wir saßen am Kamin.** We sat by the fire.

der **Kamm** NOUN (PL die **Kämme**)
   comb

kämmen VERB
   to comb ◊ *Sie kann es nicht leiden, wenn man sie kämmt.* She can't stand having her hair combed. ◊ *Ich muss meiner kleinen Schwester die Haare kämmen.* I have to comb my little sister's hair.
   ♦ **sich kämmen** to comb one's hair

der **Kampf** NOUN (PL die **Kämpfe**)
   1 fight ◊ *der Kampf zwischen Tyson und Bruno* the fight between Tyson and Bruno
   2 contest ◊ *Dieses Jahr findet der Kampf um den Pokal in Großbritannien statt.* The contest for the cup is taking place in Great Britain this year.
   3 struggle ◊ *Ich habe die Prüfung geschafft, aber es war ein Kampf.* I passed the exam but it was a struggle.

kämpfen VERB
   to fight

Kanada NEUT NOUN

Canada
- **aus Kanada** from Canada
- **in Kanada** in Canada
- **nach Kanada** to Canada

der **Kanadier** NOUN (PL die **Kanadier**)
Canadian

die **Kanadierin** NOUN
Canadian

kanadisch ADJECTIVE
Canadian

der **Kanal** NOUN (PL die **Kanäle**)
1 canal ◊ *Diese beiden Flüsse sind durch einen Kanal verbunden.* These two rivers are connected by a canal.
2 drain

die **Kanalinseln** FEM PL NOUN
Channel Islands

der **Kanaltunnel** NOUN (PL die **Kanaltunnel**)
Channel Tunnel

der **Kanarienvogel** NOUN (PL die **Kanarienvögel**)
canary

kanarisch ADJECTIVE
- **die Kanarischen Inseln** the Canaries

der **Kandidat** NOUN (GEN des **Kandidaten**, PL die **Kandidaten**)
candidate

das **Känguru** NOUN (PL die **Kängurus**)
kangaroo

das **Kaninchen** NOUN (PL die **Kaninchen**)
rabbit

der **Kanister** NOUN (PL die **Kanister**)
can ◊ *ein Benzinkanister* a petrol can

kann VERB *see* **können**

das **Kännchen** NOUN (PL die **Kännchen**)
pot ◊ *ein Kännchen Kaffee* a pot of coffee
- **ein Kännchen mit Milch** a jug of milk

die **Kanne** NOUN
1 pot (*for coffee*)
2 churn (*for milk*)
3 watering can

die **Kante** NOUN
edge

die **Kantine** NOUN
canteen ◊ *Mittags isst sie in der Kantine.* She eats in the canteen at lunchtime.

das **Kanu** NOUN (PL die **Kanus**)
canoe
- **Kanu fahren** to go canoeing

der **Kanzler** NOUN (PL die **Kanzler**)
chancellor

die **Kapelle** NOUN
1 chapel ◊ *Auf dem Berg stand eine Kapelle.* There was a chapel on the mountain.
2 band ◊ *Die Kapelle spielte einen Walzer.* The band was playing a waltz.

kapieren VERB (PERFECT **hat kapiert**)
to understand ◊ *Ich habe heute in Mathe nichts kapiert.* I didn't understand anything in maths today.

- **Sie hat den Witz nicht kapiert.** She didn't get the joke.

das **Kapital** NOUN
capital (*money*)

der **Kapitän** NOUN (PL die **Kapitäne**)
captain

das **Kapitel** NOUN (PL die **Kapitel**)
chapter

die **Kappe** NOUN
cap

kaputt ADJECTIVE
> *see also* **kaputtmachen** VERB

1 broken ◊ *Mein Computer ist kaputt.* My computer's broken.
- **Am Auto ist etwas kaputt.** There's something wrong with the car.
- **kaputt machen** to break ◊ *Mach mir bloß mein Fahrrad nicht kaputt!* Don't you dare break my bike! ◊ *Sie hat den Teller kaputt gemacht.* She's broken the plate.
2 knackered ◊ *Ich bin von der Wanderung total kaputt.* I'm completely knackered after the walk.

kaputtgehen VERB (IMPERFECT **ging kaputt**, PERFECT **ist kaputtgegangen**)
1 to break ◊ *Mein Computer ist gestern kaputtgegangen.* My computer broke yesterday.
2 (*material*)
to wear out
3 (*plant*)
to die
4 (*relationship*)
to break up

kaputtmachen VERB
> *see also* **kaputt** ADJECTIVE

to wear out ◊ *Die viele Arbeit macht mich noch kaputt.* All this work is wearing me out.
- **sich kaputtmachen** to wear oneself out ◊ *Du solltest mal Ferien machen, du machst dich ja kaputt.* You should take a holiday, you're wearing yourself out.

die **Kapuze** NOUN
hood ◊ *ein Anorak mit Kapuze* an anorak with a hood

der **Karfreitag** NOUN
Good Friday

die **Karibik** NOUN
the Caribbean ◊ *Wir fahren in die Karibik.* We're going to the Caribbean. ◊ *Wir machen in der Karibik Ferien.* We're spending our holidays in the Caribbean.

karibisch ADJECTIVE
- **die Karibischen Inseln** the Caribbean Islands

kariert ADJECTIVE
1 checked ◊ *Sie hatte ein kariertes Kleid an.* She was wearing a checked dress.
2 squared ◊ *Für Mathe brauchst du ein Heft mit kariertem Papier.* You need an

exercise book with squared paper for maths.

die **Karies** NOUN
tooth decay ◊ *Sie hat Karies.* She has tooth decay.

der **Karneval** NOUN (PL die **Karnevale** or **Karnevals**)
carnival

> ⓘ The German carnival season lasts from 11 November to Shrove Tuesday but most events, fancy-dress processions and parties take place in the week leading up to Ash Wednesday.

das **Karo** NOUN (PL die **Karos**)
1 square ◊ *Das Muster bestand aus kleinen Karos.* The pattern was made up of little squares.
2 diamonds ◊ *Karo ist Trumpf.* Diamonds is trumps.

die **Karotte** NOUN
carrot

die **Karriere** NOUN
career
◆ **Karriere machen** to get on ◊ *Es ist schwer für Frauen, in der Politik Karriere zu machen.* It's hard for women to get on in politics.

die **Karte** NOUN
1 card ◊ *Sie hat uns aus dem Urlaub eine Karte geschickt.* She sent us a card from her holiday. ◊ *Ich weiß nicht, welche Karte ich ausspielen soll.* I don't know which card I should play.
◆ **die Gelbe Karte** the yellow card
◆ **die Rote Karte** the red card
2 map ◊ *Sieh mal auf der Karte nach, wie weit wir noch fahren müssen.* Look on the map to see how far we still have to go.
3 menu ◊ *Der Ober brachte uns die Karte.* The waiter brought us the menu.
4 ticket ◊ *Kannst du Karten fürs Konzert besorgen?* Can you get us tickets for the concert? ◊ *Ich fahre morgen nach Bonn, die Karte habe ich schon gekauft.* I'm going to Bonn tomorrow, I've already bought my ticket.
◆ **alles auf eine Karte setzen** to put all one's eggs in one basket

das **Kartenspiel** NOUN (PL die **Kartenspiele**)
1 card game ◊ *Ich habe ein neues Kartenspiel gelernt.* I've learned a new card game.
2 pack of cards ◊ *Hast du ein Kartenspiel da?* Have you got a pack of cards?

die **Kartoffel** NOUN
potato

der **Kartoffelbrei** NOUN
mashed potatoes

der **Kartoffelsalat** NOUN (PL die **Kartoffelsalate**)
potato salad

der **Karton** NOUN (PL die **Kartons**)
1 cardboard ◊ *Wir haben das Bild auf Karton aufgezogen.* We mounted the picture on cardboard.
2 cardboard box ◊ *Sie packte die Bücher in einen Karton.* She packed the books in a cardboard box.

das **Karussell** NOUN (PL die **Karussells**)
roundabout ◊ *Ich möchte Karussell fahren.* I'd like to go on the roundabout.

der **Käse** NOUN (PL die **Käse**)
cheese

der **Käsekuchen** NOUN (PL die **Käsekuchen**)
cheesecake

die **Kaserne** NOUN
barracks ◊ *In unserer Nähe gibt es eine Kaserne.* There's a barracks near us.

die **Kasse** NOUN
1 till ◊ *Die meisten Geschäfte haben elektronische Kassen.* Most shops have an electronic till.
2 checkout ◊ *Es war nur eine von fünf Kassen besetzt.* Only one of the five checkouts was open.
◆ **an der Kasse** at the checkout
3 box office ◊ *Sie können Ihre Karten telefonisch vorbestellen und an der Kasse abholen.* You may order your tickets in advance and collect them from the box office.
4 ticket office ◊ *Karten fürs Fußballspiel bekommen Sie auch an der Kasse des Stadions.* You can also get tickets for the football match at the ticket office in the stadium.
5 cash box ◊ *Alle Barbeträge bewahren wir in dieser Kasse auf.* We keep all the cash in this cash box.
6 health insurance ◊ *Bei welcher Kasse sind Sie versichert?* What health insurance have you got?

> ⓘ In Germany one can choose between different health insurance schemes. There is no "National Health Service".

◆ **gut bei Kasse sein** to be in the money

der **Kassenzettel** NOUN (PL die **Kassenzettel**)
receipt

die **Kassette** NOUN
1 tape ◊ *Diesen Song habe ich auf Kassette.* I've got this song on tape. ◊ *eine Videokassette* a video tape
2 small box ◊ *Sie bewahrt ihren Schmuck in einer Kassette auf.* She keeps her jewellery in a small box.

der **Kassettenrekorder** NOUN (PL die **Kassettenrekorder**)
tape recorder

kassieren VERB (PERFECT **hat kassiert**)
to take ◊ *Die Polizei hat seinen Führerschein kassiert.* The police took his driving licence.
♦ **Der Parkwächter hat zehn Euro Parkgebühren kassiert.** The park attendant charged us ten euros to park the car.
♦ **Darf ich kassieren?** Would you like to pay now?

der **Kassierer** NOUN (PL die **Kassierer**)
cashier

die **Kastanie** NOUN
1 chestnut
2 chestnut tree

der **Kasten** NOUN (PL die **Kästen**)
1 box ◊ *Er warf den Brief in den Kasten.* He put the letter in the box.
2 case ◊ *Sie legte die Geige zurück in den Kasten.* She put the violin back in its case.
♦ **ein Kasten Bier** a crate of beer

der **Katalog** NOUN (PL die **Kataloge**)
catalogue

der **Katalysator** NOUN (PL die **Katalysatoren**)
catalytic converter ◊ *ein Auto mit Katalysator* a car with catalytic converter

katastrophal ADJECTIVE, ADVERB
catastrophic
♦ **katastrophal schlecht** appallingly bad

die **Katastrophe** NOUN
disaster

die **Kategorie** NOUN
category

der **Kater** NOUN (PL die **Kater**)
1 tomcat ◊ *Wir haben einen Kater und eine Katze.* We have a tomcat and a female cat.
2 hangover ◊ *Nach der Party hatte ich einen furchtbaren Kater.* I had a terrible hangover after the party.

die **Kathedrale** NOUN
cathedral

katholisch ADJECTIVE
Catholic

das **Kätzchen** NOUN (PL die **Kätzchen**)
kitten

die **Katze** NOUN
cat
♦ **für die Katz** for nothing

kauen VERB
to chew

der **Kauf** NOUN (PL die **Käufe**)
purchase ◊ *der Kauf eines Autos* the purchase of a car
♦ **ein guter Kauf** a bargain

kaufen VERB
to buy

der **Käufer** NOUN (PL die **Käufer**)
buyer

die **Kauffrau** NOUN
businesswoman

das **Kaufhaus** NOUN (GEN des **Kaufhauses,** PL die **Kaufhäuser**)
department store

der **Kaufmann** NOUN (PL die **Kaufleute**)
1 businessman ◊ *ein erfolgreicher Kaufmann* a successful businessman
2 grocer ◊ *zum Kaufmann gehen* to go to the grocer's

der **Kaugummi** NOUN (PL die **Kaugummis**)
chewing gum

kaum ADVERB
hardly ◊ *Ich habe kaum geschlafen.* I hardly slept.

der **Kegel** NOUN (PL die **Kegel**)
1 skittle
2 cone ◊ *die Form eines Kegels haben* to be shaped like a cone

die **Kegelbahn** NOUN
skittle alley

kegeln VERB
to play skittles

die **Kehle** NOUN
throat

der **Keil** NOUN (PL die **Keile**)
wedge

der **Keim** NOUN (PL die **Keime**)
1 shoot ◊ *Eine Woche nach der Aussaat zeigen sich die ersten Keime.* The first shoots appear a week after sowing.
2 germ ◊ *Das Mittel tötete die Keime ab.* The medicine killed the germs.
♦ **etwas im Keim ersticken** to nip something in the bud

kein ADJECTIVE, PRONOUN

> When combined with a noun, **kein** is used for masculine and neuter nouns, **keine** for feminine and plural nouns. On its own **keiner** is used for masculine, **keine** for feminine and plural, and **keines** or **keins** for neuter.

1 not ... any ◊ *Ich habe keine Geschwister.* I don't have any brothers or sisters. ◊ *Ich will keinen Streit.* I don't want any quarrelling. ◊ *Er zeigt kein Interesse an Computern.* He doesn't show any interest in computers. ◊ *Er behauptet, hier gäbe es Mäuse, ich habe aber noch keine gesehen.* He claims that there are mice here but I haven't seen any. ◊ *Von den Autos hat mir keines gefallen.* I din't like any of the cars.
2 no ◊ *Kein Tier könnte in diesem Klima überleben.* No animal could survive in this climate.
♦ **"Kein Zutritt"** "No entry"
♦ **Ich habe keine Lust.** I don't feel like it.
♦ **Ich habe keinen Hunger.** I'm not hungry.
3 nobody ◊ *Alle waren eingeladen, es ist aber keiner gekommen.* Everybody was invited but nobody came.
♦ **Ich kenne hier keinen.** I don't know anybody here.

K

♦ **Warum hat er eine Einladung bekommen und ich keine?** Why did he get an invitation and not me?

keinerlei ADJECTIVE
no ... whatsoever ◊ *Ich habe damit keinerlei Probleme.* I don't have any problems with it whatsoever.

keinesfalls ADVERB
on no account

keineswegs ADVERB
by no means

der **Keks** NOUN (PL die **Kekse**)
biscuit

der **Keller** NOUN (PL die **Keller**)
cellar

der **Kellner** NOUN (PL die **Kellner**)
waiter

die **Kellnerin** NOUN
waitress

kennen VERB (IMPERFECT **kannte,** PERFECT **hat gekannt**)
to know ◊ *Ich kenne ihn nicht.* I don't know him. ◊ *Ich kenne London gut.* I know London well.

kennenlernen VERB
[1] to meet ◊ *Sie hat ihren Freund bei einem Fußballspiel kennengelernt.* She met her boyfriend at a football match.
[2] to get to know ◊ *Ich würde ihn gern besser kennenlernen.* I'd like to get to know him better.
♦ **sich kennenlernen (1)** to meet ◊ *Wir haben uns auf einer Party kennengelernt.* We met at a party.
♦ **sich kennenlernen (2)** to get to know each other. ◊ *Wir haben uns im Laufe der Zeit immer besser kennengelernt.* We got to know each other better and better as time went on.

die **Kenntnis** NOUN (PL die **Kenntnisse**)
knowledge ◊ *Deutschkenntnisse wären von Vorteil.* Knowledge of German would be an advantage.
♦ **etwas zur Kenntnis nehmen** to note something
♦ **jemanden in Kenntnis setzen** to inform somebody

das **Kennzeichen** NOUN (PL die **Kennzeichen**)
mark ◊ *unveränderliche Kennzeichen* distinguishing marks
♦ **das Auto mit dem Kennzeichen S-MJ 2714** the car with the registration S-MJ 2714

der **Kerl** NOUN (PL die **Kerle**)
bloke
♦ **Sie ist ein netter Kerl.** She's a good sort.

der **Kern** NOUN (PL die **Kerne**)
[1] pip ◊ *Klementinen haben keine Kerne.* Clementines don't have any pips.
[2] stone ◊ *der Kern der Kirsche* the cherry stone
[3] kernel (*of nut*)
[4] nucleus

[5] core ◊ *der Reaktorkern* the reactor core
♦ **Wir sollten zum Kern des Problems kommen.** We should to get to the heart of the problem.

die **Kernenergie** NOUN
nuclear energy

kerngesund ADJECTIVE
fit as a fiddle

das **Kernkraftwerk** NOUN (PL die **Kernkraftwerke**)
nuclear power station

die **Kernwaffen** FEM PL NOUN
nuclear weapons

die **Kerze** NOUN
[1] candle ◊ *Sie zündete eine Kerze an.* She lit a candle.
[2] plug ◊ *Bei der Inspektion werden die Kerzen erneuert.* The plugs are changed while the car is being serviced.

die **Kette** NOUN
chain

keuchen VERB
to pant

der **Keuchhusten** NOUN
whooping cough ◊ *Meine Schwester hat Keuchhusten.* My sister has whooping cough.

die **Keule** NOUN
[1] club ◊ *Er schlug ihm mit einer Keule über den Kopf.* He hit him over the head with a club.
[2] leg ◊ *Beim Hähnchen mag ich am liebsten die Keule.* My favourite part of a chicken is the leg.

kg ABBREVIATION (= *Kilogramm*)
kg

kichern VERB
to giggle

der **Kiefer** NOUN (PL die **Kiefer**)
see also **die Kiefer** NOUN
jaw

die **Kiefer** NOUN
see also **der Kiefer** NOUN
pine tree

der **Kies** NOUN
gravel

das **Kilo** NOUN (PL die **Kilos** or **Kilo**)
kilo ◊ *Ich muss ein paar Kilos loswerden.* I need to lose a couple of kilos. ◊ *Ich hätte gern zwei Kilo Tomaten.* Can I have two kilos of tomatoes. ◊ *Ich wiege fünfzig Kilo.* I weigh eight stone.

das **Kilogramm** NOUN (PL die **Kilogramme** or **Kilogramm**)
kilogram ◊ *zwei Kilogramm Äpfel* two kilograms of apples

der **Kilometer** NOUN (PL die **Kilometer**)
kilometre ◊ *mit achtzig Kilometern pro Stunde* at fifty miles per hour

das **Kind** NOUN (PL die **Kinder**)
child

♦ **von Kind auf** from childhood

♦ **ein Kind bekommen** to have a baby

der **Kindergarten** NOUN (PL die **Kindergärten**)
kindergarten

die **Kindergärtnerin** NOUN
kindergarten teacher

das **Kindergeld** NOUN
child benefit

die **Kinderkrippe** NOUN
crèche

die **Kinderlähmung** NOUN
polio ◊ *Sie hatte als Kind
Kinderlähmung.* She had polio as a child.

kinderleicht ADJECTIVE
child's play ◊ *Es war kinderleicht.* It was
child's play.

das **Kindermädchen** NOUN (PL die
Kindermädchen)
nanny

der **Kinderpfleger** NOUN (PL die **Kinderpfleger**)
paediatric nurse

die **Kinderpflegerin** NOUN
paediatric nurse

die **Kindertagesstätte** NOUN
day nursery

der **Kinderwagen** NOUN (PL die **Kinderwagen**)
pram

die **Kindheit** NOUN
childhood

kindisch ADJECTIVE
childish
♦ **sich kindisch benehmen** to behave
childishly

kindlich ADJECTIVE
childlike

das **Kinn** NOUN (PL die **Kinne**)
chin

das **Kino** NOUN (PL die **Kinos**)
cinema ◊ *ins Kino gehen* to go to the
cinema

der **Kiosk** NOUN (PL die **Kioske**)
kiosk

die **Kirche** NOUN
church

die **Kirchweih** NOUN
funfair

die **Kirmes** NOUN (PL die **Kirmessen**)
funfair

die **Kirsche** NOUN
cherry

das **Kissen** NOUN (PL die **Kissen**)
[1] cushion ◊ *Auf dem Sofa lagen bunte
Kissen.* There were brightly-coloured
cushions on the sofa.
[2] pillow ◊ *Er schläft ohne Kissen.* He
sleeps without a pillow.

kitschig ADJECTIVE
kitschy

kitzeln VERB
to tickle

kitzlig ADJECTIVE

ticklish ◊ *Ich bin kitzlig an den Füßen.*
My feet are ticklish. ◊ *Das ist eine ganz
kitzlige Angelegenheit.* That's a very
ticklish matter.

die **Kiwi** NOUN (PL die **Kiwis**)
kiwi fruit

klagen VERB
[1] to wail ◊ *"Hätte ich doch nur auf dich
gehört", klagte er.* "If only I had listened
to you", he wailed.
♦ **über jemanden klagen** to complain about
somebody ◊ *Sie klagt dauernd über ihre
Kinder.* She's constantly complaining
about her children.
♦ **Sie klagt in letzter Zeit oft über
Kopfschmerzen.** She's been complaining
of headaches a lot recently.
[2] to sue ◊ *Wir werden gegen ihn
klagen.* We're going to sue him.
♦ **Sie hat mir ihr Leid geklagt.** She poured
out her sorrows to me.

die **Klammer** NOUN (PL die **Klammern**)
[1] bracket ◊ *Sie schrieb in Klammern
eine Erklärung dazu.* She wrote an
explanation in brackets.
[2] peg (clothes peg)
[3] brace (for teeth) ◊ *Viele Kinder müssen
eine Klammer tragen.* Many children
have to wear a brace.

die **Klamotten** PL NOUN
stuff ◊ *Pack deine Klamotten!* Get your
stuff!

der **Klang** NOUN (PL die **Klänge**)
sound

die **Klappe** NOUN
[1] flap ◊ *Über dem Briefkasten ist eine
Klappe.* There's a flap over the letterbox.
[2] valve ◊ *Die Klappe an seinem Herzen
hat ein Loch.* His heart valve has a hole
in it.
[3] trap ◊ *Er soll die Klappe halten.* He
should keep his trap shut.
♦ **Sie hat eine große Klappe.** She's got a
big mouth.

klappen VERB
to work ◊ *Das kann ja nicht klappen.*
That won't work. ◊ *Das Experiment hat
geklappt.* The experiment worked.
♦ **etwas klappen** to tip something ◊ *Sie
klappte den Sitz nach oben.* She tipped
up the seat. ◊ *Er klappte den Deckel der
Kiste nach hinten.* He tipped the lid of the
chest back.

klappern VERB
to rattle

der **Klappstuhl** NOUN (PL die **Klappstühle**)
folding chair

der **Klapptisch** NOUN (PL die **Klapptische**)
folding table

klar ADJECTIVE
clear ◊ *Das Wasser ist sehr klar.* The
water is very clear. ◊ *Ich brauche einen*

K

klaren Kopf. I need a clear head. ◊ *eine klare Antwort* a clear answer

♦ **Mir ist nicht klar, was er eigentlich will.** I'm not clear about what he really wants.

♦ **sich über etwas im Klaren sein** to be clear about something ◊ *Bist du dir über die Konsequenzen im Klaren?* Are you clear about the consequences?

♦ **Na klar!** Of course!

klären VERB

⟦1⟧ to clarify ◊ *Wir sollten diese Frage klären.* We should clarify this matter.

♦ **Ich muss zuerst mit meinen Eltern klären, ob das geht.** I'll have to ask my parents if it's OK.

♦ **Die Polizei hat diesen Fall nie geklärt.** The police have never solved this case.

⟦2⟧ to purify ◊ *In dieser Anlage wird das Abwasser geklärt.* The sewage is purified in this plant.

♦ **sich klären** to clear itself up ◊ *Dieses Problem hat sich inzwischen geklärt.* The problem has cleared itself up in the meantime.

die **Klarheit** NOUN

⟦1⟧ clarity

♦ **Wir brauchen in dieser Sache Klarheit.** This matter must be clarified.

⟦2⟧ clearness ◊ *die Klarheit des Wassers* the clearness of the water

die **Klarinette** NOUN

clarinet ◊ *Oliver spielt Klarinette.* Oliver plays the clarinet.

klarstellen VERB (PERFECT **hat klargestellt**)

to make clear ◊ *Ich möchte doch mal klarstellen, dass ich das nie gesagt habe.* I would like to make it quite clear that I never said that.

die **Klasse** NOUN

see also **klasse** ADJECTIVE

class ◊ *Wir sind in der ersten Klasse gefahren.* We travelled first class. ◊ *Unsere Klasse fährt nach England.* Our class is going to England.

♦ **große Klasse sein** to be great ◊ *Unser Sportlehrer ist große Klasse.* Our sports teacher's really great.

klasse ADJECTIVE

see also **die Klasse** NOUN

smashing ◊ *Er ist ein klasse Lehrer.* He's a smashing teacher.

die **Klassenarbeit** NOUN

test

🛈 The **Klassenarbeit** is the main form of assessment in German schools. Over the school year, German pupils write between 6 and 8 **Klassenarbeiten**, usually 45 minutes long, in their core subjects (generally maths, German and English).

◊ *Wir schreiben morgen in Englisch eine Klassenarbeit.* We've got a written English test tomorrow.

das **Klassenbuch** NOUN (PL die **Klassenbücher**)

class register

die **Klassenfahrt** NOUN (PL die **Klassenfahrten**)

class trip

der **Klassenkamerad** NOUN (GEN des **Klassenkameraden**, PL die **Klassenkameraden**)

classmate

die **Klassenkameradin** NOUN

classmate

der **Klassenlehrer** NOUN (PL die **Klassenlehrer**)

class teacher

die **Klassenlehrerin** NOUN

class teacher

der **Klassensprecher** NOUN (PL die **Klassensprecher**)

class representative

die **Klassensprecherin** NOUN

class representative

das **Klassenzimmer** NOUN (PL die **Klassenzimmer**)

classroom

klassisch ADJECTIVE

classical

der **Klatsch** NOUN (GEN des **Klatsches**)

gossip ◊ *Hast du schon den neuesten Klatsch gehört?* Have you heard the latest gossip?

klatschen VERB

⟦1⟧ to clap ◊ *Die Zuschauer klatschten.* The audience clapped.

⟦2⟧ to gossip ◊ *Über das Königshaus wird viel geklatscht.* There's a lot of gossip about the royal family.

⟦3⟧ to batter ◊ *Der Regen klatschte gegen die Scheiben.* The rain battered against the panes.

♦ **jemandem Beifall klatschen** to applaud somebody

klauen VERB (PERFECT **hat geklaut**)

to pinch

das **Klavier** NOUN

piano ◊ *Bettina spielt Klavier.* Bettina plays the piano.

kleben VERB

to stick ◊ *Ich habe die zerbrochene Vase wieder geklebt.* I've stuck the broken vase together again.

♦ **etwas an etwas kleben** to stick something on something ◊ *Sie hat das Bild der Gruppe an ihre Wand geklebt.* She stuck the picture of the band on her wall.

♦ **an etwas kleben** to stick to something ◊ *An der Windschutzscheibe klebten lauter tote Insekten.* There were lots of dead insects stuck to the windscreen.

♦ **Das klebt nicht.** It doesn't stick.

◆ **jemandem eine kleben** to thump
somebody

klebrig ADJECTIVE
sticky

der **Klebstoff** NOUN (PL die **Klebstoffe**)
glue

der **Klebstreifen** NOUN (PL die **Klebstreifen**)
adhesive tape

der **Klecks** NOUN (PL die **Kleckse**)
stain

der **Klee** NOUN
clover

das **Kleid** NOUN (PL die **Kleider**)
dress ◊ *Sie trug ein rotes Kleid.* She was
wearing a red dress.
◆ **Kleider** clothes ◊ *Er räumte seine Kleider
auf.* He put his clothes away.

der **Kleiderbügel** NOUN (PL die **Kleiderbügel**)
coat hanger

der **Kleiderschrank** NOUN (PL die
Kleiderschränke)
wardrobe

die **Kleidung** NOUN
clothing

das **Kleidungsstück** NOUN (PL die
Kleidungsstücke)
garment

klein ADJECTIVE
small ◊ *ein kleines Kind* a small child
◊ *ein kleiner Betrag* a small amount
◆ **als ich klein war** when I was little

das **Kleingeld** NOUN
small change

der **Klempner** NOUN (PL die **Klempner**)
plumber

klettern VERB (PERFECT **ist geklettert**)
to climb

klicken VERB
to click (*computer*) ◊ *mit der Maus klicken*
to click on the mouse

das **Klima** NOUN (PL die **Klimas**)
climate

die **Klimaanlage** NOUN
air conditioning

die **Klingel** NOUN
bell

klingeln VERB
to ring
◆ **Es klingelte.** The doorbell rang.

der **Klingelton** NOUN (PL die **Klingeltöne**)
ringtone

klingen VERB (IMPERFECT **klang**, PERFECT **hat
geklungen**)
to sound ◊ *Das Klavier klingt verstimmt.*
The piano sounds out of tune. ◊ *Du klingst
deprimiert.* You sound depressed.

die **Klinik** NOUN
clinic

die **Klinke** NOUN
handle (*of door*)

die **Klippe** NOUN
cliff

das **Klo** NOUN (PL die **Klos**)
loo

der **Klon** NOUN (PL die **Klone**)
clone

klonen VERB
to clone ◊ *ein geklontes Schaf* a cloned
sheep

klopfen VERB
[1] to knock ◊ *Sie klopfte an die Tür.* She
knocked on the door.
◆ **Es klopft.** There's somebody knocking on
the door.
[2] to pound ◊ *Mein Herz klopfte vor
Aufregung.* My heart was pounding with
excitement.
◆ **jemandem auf die Schulter klopfen** to
tap somebody on the shoulder

das **Kloster** NOUN (PL die **Klöster**)
[1] monastery
[2] convent

der **Klub** NOUN (PL die **Klubs**)
club (*association*)

klug ADJECTIVE
intelligent
◆ **Es wäre klüger gewesen, nichts zu
sagen.** It would have been more sensible
not to say anything.

die **Klugheit** NOUN
intelligence

km ABBREVIATION (= *Kilometer*)
km

knabbern VERB
to nibble ◊ *Sie knabberte an einem Keks.*
She nibbled a biscuit.

das **Knäckebrot** NOUN
crispbread

knacken VERB
to crack ◊ *Nüsse knacken* to crack nuts
◊ *einen Code knacken* to crack a code
◆ **ein Auto knacken** to break into a car

der **Knall** NOUN (PL die **Knalle**)
bang ◊ *Die Tür schlug mit einem Knall
zu.* The door closed with a bang.

knapp ADJECTIVE
[1] tight ◊ *Sie hatte einen sehr knappen
Pulli an.* She was wearing a very tight
pullover.
[2] scarce ◊ *Benzin ist knapp.* Petrol is
scarce.
◆ **knapp bei Kasse** short of money
◆ **Wenn das Taschengeld knapp wird, geht
sie zu ihren Großeltern.** When her
pocket money runs out she always goes
to her grandparents.
[3] just ◊ *Sie ist knapp fünfzehn Jahre alt.*
She has just turned fifteen.
◆ **eine knappe Stunde** just under an hour
◆ **knapp unter** just under ◊ *Das kostet
knapp unter tausend Euro.* That costs
just under a thousand euros.
◆ **Wir haben knapp verloren.** We only just
lost.

K

kneifen VERB (IMPERFECT **kniff**, PERFECT **hat gekniffen**)
> [1] to pinch ◊ *Er hat mich in den Arm geknifen.* He pinched my arm.
> [2] to back out ◊ *Als er springen sollte, hat er gekniffen.* When it was his turn to jump, he backed out.

die **Kneipe** NOUN
> pub

das **Knie** NOUN (PL die **Knie**)
> knee

der **Kniestrumpf** NOUN (PL die **Kniestrümpfe**)
> knee-length sock

knipsen VERB (PERFECT **hat geknipst**)
> [1] to take a snap ◊ *Die Touristen knipsten den Eiffelturm.* The tourists took snaps of the Eiffel Tower.
> [2] to punch ◊ *Der Schaffner knipste die Fahrkarten.* The ticket collector punched the tickets.

der **Knoblauch** NOUN
> garlic

die **Knoblauchzehe** NOUN
> clove of garlic

der **Knöchel** NOUN (PL die **Knöchel**)
> [1] knuckle ◊ *Ich habe mir die Knöchel an der rechten Hand geschürft.* I've scraped the knuckles of my right hand.
> [2] ankle ◊ *Bei dem Sprung habe ich mir den Knöchel verstaucht.* I sprained my ankle when I jumped.

der **Knochen** NOUN (PL die **Knochen**)
> bone

der **Knödel** NOUN (PL die **Knödel**)
> dumpling

der **Knopf** NOUN (PL die **Knöpfe**)
> button

der **Knoten** NOUN (PL die **Knoten**)
> [1] knot ◊ *Sie machte einen Knoten in die Schnur.* She tied a knot in the string.
> [2] bun ◊ *Sie trug das Haar in einem Knoten.* She wore her hair in a bun.
> [3] lump ◊ *Sie hat einen Knoten in der Brust entdeckt.* She noticed a lump in her breast.

der **Knüppel** NOUN (PL die **Knüppel**)
> [1] cudgel ◊ *Die Robbenbabys werden mit Knüppel erschlagen.* The baby seals are beaten with cudgels.
> [2] truncheon ◊ *Die Polizisten gingen mit Knüppeln gegen die Demonstranten vor.* The police used truncheons against the demonstrators.
> [3] joystick (*aeroplane*)

der **Koch** NOUN (PL die **Köche**)
> cook

kochen VERB
> [1] to cook ◊ *Was kochst du heute?* What are you cooking today?
> ◆ **Sie kann gut kochen.** She's a good cook.
> ◆ **Ich koche gern.** I like cooking.
> [2] to boil ◊ *Das Wasser kocht.* The water's boiling.

der **Kocher** NOUN (PL die **Kocher**)
> cooker

die **Köchin** NOUN
> cook

der **Kochtopf** NOUN (PL die **Kochtöpfe**)
> saucepan

der **Koffer** NOUN (PL die **Koffer**)
> suitcase

der **Kofferkuli** NOUN (PL die **Kofferkulis**)
> luggage trolley

der **Kofferraum** NOUN (PL die **Kofferräume**)
> boot (*of car*)

der **Kohl** NOUN
> cabbage

die **Kohle** NOUN
> [1] coal ◊ *Wir heizen mit Kohle.* We use coal for heating.
> [2] charcoal ◊ *Wir brauchen noch Kohle zum Grillen.* We need charcoal for the barbecue.
> [3] dough (*money*)
> ◆ **Ich habe keine Kohle.** I'm broke.

das **Kohlenfeuer** NOUN (PL die **Kohlenfeuer**)
> coal fire

der **Kohlenherd** NOUN (PL die **Kohlenherde**)
> coal-burning stove

das **Kohlenhydrat** NOUN (PL die **Kohlenhydrate**)
> carbohydrate

die **Kohlensäure** NOUN
> carbon dioxide
> ◆ **Mineralwasser mit Kohlensäure** sparkling mineral water

die **Kokosnuss** NOUN (PL die **Kokosnüsse**)
> coconut

der **Kollege** NOUN (GEN des **Kollegen**, PL die **Kollegen**)
> colleague

die **Kollegin** NOUN
> colleague

Köln NEUT NOUN
> Cologne
> ◆ **nach Köln** to Cologne

das **Kölnischwasser** NOUN
> eau de Cologne

der **Komfort** NOUN
> luxury ◊ *ein Auto mit allem Komfort* a luxury car

der **Komiker** NOUN (PL die **Komiker**)
> comedian

komisch ADJECTIVE
> funny ◊ *ein komischer Film* a funny film ◊ *ein komisches Gefühl* a funny feeling

das **Komma** NOUN (PL die **Kommas**)
> comma
> ◆ **zwei Komma drei (2,3)** two point three (2.3)

kommen VERB (IMPERFECT **kam**, PERFECT **ist gekommen**)
> [1] to come ◊ *Wann ist der Brief gekommen?* When did the letter come?

◇ *Kommst du auch zur Party?* Are you coming to the party too?

♦ **Komm gut nach Hause!** Safe journey home.

[2] to get ◇ *Wie komme ich zum Bahnhof?* How do I get to the station?

♦ **unter ein Auto kommen** to be run over by a car

[3] to appear ◇ *Es wird Frühling, die Schneeglöckchen kommen schon.* Spring is coming, the snowdrops are appearing.

♦ **Bei Felix kommen jetzt die zweiten Zähne.** Felix's second teeth are coming through.

[4] to go ◇ *Er ist gestern ins Krankenhaus gekommen.* He went into hospital yesterday. ◇ *Das kommt in den Schrank.* That goes in the cupboard.

♦ **Mit sechs kommt man in die Schule.** You start school at six.

♦ **Wer kommt zuerst?** Who's first?

♦ **Jetzt kommst du an die Reihe.** It's your turn now.

♦ **kommenden Sonntag** next Sunday

♦ **kommen lassen** to send for ◇ *Ich habe mir den Katalog kommen lassen.* I've sent for the catalogue. ◇ *Der Direktor hat ihn kommen lassen.* The headmaster sent for him.

♦ **auf etwas kommen** to think of something ◇ *Darauf bin ich nicht gekommen.* I didn't think of that.

♦ **Wie kommst du auf die Idee?** What gave you that idea?

♦ **Ich komme nicht auf seinen Namen.** His name escapes me.

♦ **Er kommt aus Bayern.** He comes from Bavaria. ◇ *Kiwis kommen aus Neuseeland.* Kiwi fruit come from New Zealand.

♦ **Sie ist durchs Abitur gekommen.** She got through her Abitur.

♦ **ums Leben kommen** to lose one's life ◇ *Sie ist bei einem Unfall ums Leben gekommen.* She lost her life in an accident.

♦ **Das kommt davon!** That's what you get!

♦ **zu sich kommen** to come round ◇ *Die Patientin ist noch nicht wieder zu sich gekommen.* The patient hasn't come round again yet.

♦ **zu etwas kommen (1)** to get something ◇ *Wie bist du zu dem Computer gekommen?* How did you get the computer?

♦ **zu etwas kommen (2)** to get round to something ◇ *Ich mache das, sobald ich dazu komme.* I'll do it as soon as I get round to it.

die **Kommode** NOUN
chest of drawers

der **Kommunismus** NOUN (GEN des **Kommunismus**)
communism

die **Komödie** NOUN
comedy

kompatibel ADJECTIVE
compatible

kompetent ADJECTIVE
competent

das **Kompliment** NOUN (PL die **Komplimente**)
compliment ◇ *Er hat ihr zu ihrem Kuchen ein Kompliment gemacht.* He complimented her on her cake.

kompliziert ADJECTIVE
complicated

der **Komponist** NOUN (GEN des **Komponisten**, PL die **Komponisten**)
composer

das **Kompott** NOUN (PL die **Kompotte**)
compote

der **Konditor** NOUN (PL die **Konditoren**)
pastry cook

die **Konditorei** NOUN
cake shop

das **Kondom** NOUN (PL die **Kondome**)
condom

die **Konfektion** NOUN
ready-to-wear clothing

der **Konflikt** NOUN (PL die **Konflikte**)
conflict

der **König** NOUN (PL die **Könige**)
king

die **Königin** NOUN
queen

königlich ADJECTIVE
royal

das **Königreich** NOUN (PL die **Königreiche**)
kingdom

♦ **das Vereinigte Königreich** the United Kingdom

die **Konjugation** NOUN
conjugation

konjugieren VERB (PERFECT **hat konjugiert**)
to conjugate

die **Konjunktion** NOUN
conjunction

der **Konjunktiv** NOUN (PL die **Konjunktive**)
subjunctive

die **Konkurrenz** NOUN

[1] competition ◇ *Auf diesem Sektor ist die Konkurrenz groß.* Competition is keen in this sector.

[2] competitors ◇ *Sie ist zur Konkurrenz gegangen.* She's gone over to our competitors.

können VERB (PRESENT **kann**, IMPERFECT **konnte**, PERFECT **hat gekonnt** or **können**)

see also **das Können** NOUN

*The past participle **können** is used when **können** is a modal auxiliary.*

[1] can ◇ *Kannst du schwimmen?* Can you swim? ◇ *Sie hat nicht früher kommen können.* She couldn't come earlier.

K

♦ **Morgen werde ich nicht kommen können.** I won't be able to come tomorrow.
♦ **Ich kann nicht ...** I can't ...
♦ **Ich kann nicht mehr. (1)** I can't go on.
◊ *Ich mache jetzt Schluss, ich kann nicht mehr.* I'll have to stop now, I can't go on.
♦ **Ich kann nicht mehr. (2)** I'm full up.
◊ *Willst du noch ein Stück Kuchen? – Nein danke, ich kann nicht mehr.* Would you like another piece of cake? – No thanks, I'm full up.
[2] may ◊ *Kann ich gehen?* May I go?
◊ *Sie könnten recht haben.* You may be right.
♦ **es kann sein, dass ...** it may be that ...
◊ *Es kann sein, dass ich etwas später komme.* It may be that I'll come a little later.
♦ **Kann ich mit?** Can I come with you?
♦ **Ich kann nichts dafür.** It's not my fault.
♦ **Das kann sein.** That's possible.
[3] to know ◊ *Er kann viele Geschichtszahlen.* He knows a lot of historical dates.
♦ **Können Sie Deutsch?** Can you speak German?
♦ **Sie kann keine Mathematik.** She can't do mathematics.

das **Können** NOUN
| see also **können** VERB |
ability ◊ *Sie hat ihr Können bewiesen.* She has proved her ability.

konnte VERB *see* **können**

konservativ ADJECTIVE
conservative

die **Konserve** NOUN
tinned food

die **Konservenbüchse** NOUN
tin

der **Konsonant** NOUN (GEN des **Konsonanten**, PL die **Konsonanten**)
consonant

der **Kontakt** NOUN (PL die **Kontakte**)
contact

die **Kontaktlinsen** FEM PL NOUN
contact lenses

der **Kontinent** NOUN (PL die **Kontinente**)
continent

das **Konto** NOUN (PL die **Konten**)
account ◊ *Geld auf ein Konto einzahlen* to pay money into an account

die **Kontrolle** NOUN
control ◊ *die Passkontrolle* passport control ◊ *Sie hat die Kontrolle über das Fahrzeug verloren.* She lost control of the vehicle. ◊ *etwas unter Kontrolle haben* to have something under control

der **Kontrolleur** NOUN (PL die **Kontrolleure**)
inspector

kontrollieren VERB (PERFECT **hat kontrolliert**)
to check ◊ *Kann ich bitte Ihre Fahrkarten*

kontrollieren? May I check your tickets please?

sich **konzentrieren** VERB (PERFECT **hat sich konzentriert**)
to concentrate ◊ *Ich kann mich nicht konzentrieren.* I can't concentrate.

das **Konzert** NOUN (PL die **Konzerte**)
[1] concert ◊ *Wir waren gestern Abend im Konzert.* We were at a concert yesterday evening.
[2] concerto ◊ *ein Konzert für Klavier und Violine* a concerto for piano and violin

der **Kopf** NOUN (PL die **Köpfe**)
head

der **Kopfhörer** NOUN (PL die **Kopfhörer**)
headphones

das **Kopfkissen** NOUN (PL die **Kopfkissen**)
pillow

der **Kopfsalat** NOUN (PL die **Kopfsalate**)
lettuce

die **Kopfschmerzen** MASC PL NOUN
headache ◊ *Ich habe Kopfschmerzen.* I've got a headache.

die **Kopie** NOUN
copy

kopieren VERB (PERFECT **hat kopiert**)
to copy
♦ **kopieren und einfügen** to copy and paste

das **Kopiergerät** NOUN (PL die **Kopiergeräte**)
photocopier

der **Korb** NOUN (PL die **Körbe**)
basket
♦ **jemandem einen Korb geben** to turn somebody down

der **Korken** NOUN (PL die **Korken**)
cork

der **Korkenzieher** NOUN (PL die **Korkenzieher**)
corkscrew

das **Korn** NOUN (PL die **Körner**)
corn

der **Körper** NOUN (PL die **Körper**)
body

körperbehindert ADJECTIVE
disabled

der **Körperteil** NOUN (PL die **Körperteile**)
part of the body

die **Korrektur** NOUN
correction ◊ *Wir müssen die Korrektur ins gleiche Heft wie die Arbeit schreiben.* We have to write the corrections in the same exercise book as the test. ◊ *Der Text war voller Korrekturen.* The text was full of corrections.
♦ **Die Mathelehrerin ist noch nicht fertig mit den Korrekturen.** The maths teacher hasn't finished her marking yet.

korrigieren VERB (PERFECT **hat korrigiert**)
to correct

die **Kosmetik** NOUN
cosmetics

kosmetisch ADJECTIVE
cosmetic

die **Kost** NOUN
[1] food ◊ *Sie ernährt sich von gesunder Kost.* She eats healthy food.
[2] board ◊ *Für Kost und Unterkunft ist gesorgt.* Board and lodging will be provided.

kostbar ADJECTIVE
precious ◊ *Du vergeudest meine kostbare Zeit.* You're wasting my precious time.

die **Kosten** PL NOUN
> see also **kosten** VERB

[1] costs ◊ *die Kosten tragen* to bear the costs
[2] expense ◊ *Bei vielen Kindern hat man auch viele Kosten.* Lots of children mean a lot of expense.
◆ **auf jemandes Kosten** at somebody's expense ◊ *Sie ist auf Kosten der Firma zu der Konferenz gefahren.* She went to the conference at the company's expense.

kosten VERB
> see also **die Kosten** NOUN

[1] to cost ◊ *Mein Fahrrad hat zweitausend Euro gekostet.* My bike cost two thousand euros.
◆ **Was kostet ...?** How much is ...?
[2] to taste ◊ *Willst du die Soße mal kosten?* Would you like to taste the sauce? ◊ *Koste mal, ob das schmeckt.* Taste it and see if it's good.

kostenlos ADJECTIVE
free of charge

köstlich ADJECTIVE
[1] hilarious ◊ *Das war ein köstlicher Film.* That was a hilarious film. ◊ *ein köstlicher Witz* a hilarious joke
[2] delicious (*food*)
◆ **sich köstlich amüsieren** to have a marvellous time

das **Kostüm** NOUN (PL die **Kostüme**)
costume
◆ **ein Damenkostüm** a ladies' suit

das **Kotelett** NOUN (PL die **Koteletts**)
chop

krabbeln VERB (PERFECT **ist gekrabbelt**)
to crawl

der **Krach** NOUN
[1] crash ◊ *Die Vase fiel mit einem lauten Krach zu Boden.* The vase fell on the ground with a loud crash.
[2] noise ◊ *Unsere Nachbarn machen viel Krach.* Our neighbours make a lot of noise.
[3] row ◊ *Sie hat Krach mit ihrem Freund.* She had a row with her boyfriend.

die **Kraft** NOUN (PL die **Kräfte**)
strength ◊ *Samson hat seine Kraft verloren.* Samson lost his strength.
◆ **Er hat viel Kraft.** He's very strong.
◆ **mit aller Kraft** with all one's might

◆ **Kinder kosten viel Kraft.** Children require a lot of energy.
◆ **Sie scheint magische Kräfte zu haben.** She seems to have magic powers.
◆ **Das Gesetz tritt am ersten August in Kraft.** The law comes into effect on the first of August.

das **Kraftfahrzeug** NOUN (PL die **Kraftfahrzeuge**)
motor vehicle

kräftig ADJECTIVE, ADVERB
[1] strong ◊ *Er ist ein kräftiger Junge.* He is a strong boy.
[2] hard ◊ *ein kräftiger Schlag* a hard blow ◊ *kräftig schütteln* to shake hard
◆ **kräftig üben** to practise a lot ◊ *Wenn du kräftig übst, dann schaffst du es.* If you practise a lot, you'll do it.

das **Kraftwerk** NOUN (PL die **Kraftwerke**)
power station

der **Kragen** NOUN (PL die **Kragen**)
collar

die **Kralle** NOUN
[1] claw ◊ *die Krallen der Katze* the cat's claws
[2] talon ◊ *die Krallen des Vogels* the bird's talons

der **Kram** NOUN
stuff ◊ *Ich habe den ganzen Kram weggeworfen.* I threw all the stuff away.
◆ **Mach doch deinen Kram allein!** Do it yourself!
◆ **Das passt mir nicht in den Kram.** It doesn't suit me.

krank ADJECTIVE
ill ◊ *Ich bin krank.* I'm ill. ◊ *Ich habe eine kranke Mutter.* My mother's ill.

das **Krankenhaus** NOUN (GEN des **Krankenhauses**, PL die **Krankenhäuser**)
hospital

die **Krankenkasse** NOUN
health insurance

> ⓘ *In Germany one can choose between different health insurance schemes. There is no "National Health Service".*

der **Krankenpfleger** NOUN (PL die **Krankenpfleger**)
male nurse

der **Krankenschein** NOUN (PL die **Krankenscheine**)
health insurance card

die **Krankenschwester** NOUN
nurse

die **Krankenversicherung** NOUN
health insurance

der **Krankenwagen** NOUN (PL die **Krankenwagen**)
ambulance

die **Krankheit** NOUN
illness

K

krankschreiben VERB (IMPERFECT **schrieb krank,** PERFECT **hat krankgeschrieben**)
♦ **jemanden krankschreiben** to give somebody a sick note ◊ *Der Arzt hat ihn für eine Woche krankgeschrieben.* The doctor gave him a sick note for a week.

kratzen VERB
to scratch
♦ **sich kratzen** to scratch oneself

kraus ADJECTIVE
frizzy ◊ *Sie hat krause Haare.* She has frizzy hair.

das **Kraut** NOUN (PL die **Kräuter**)
1 herb ◊ *eine Salatsoße mit frischen Kräutern* a salad dressing with fresh herbs
2 sauerkraut ◊ *Heute gibt es Würstchen mit Kraut.* We're having sausages and sauerkraut today.

die **Krawatte** NOUN
tie

kreativ ADJECTIVE
creative

der **Krebs** NOUN (GEN des **Krebses,** PL die **Krebse**)
1 crab ◊ *Krebse bewegen sich seitlich voran.* Crabs move sideways.
2 cancer ◊ *Sie ist an Krebs gestorben.* She died of cancer.
3 Cancer
♦ **Beate ist Krebs.** Beate's Cancer.

der **Kredit** NOUN (PL die **Kredite**)
credit ◊ *auf Kredit* on credit

die **Kreditkarte** NOUN
credit card

die **Kreide** NOUN
chalk

der **Kreis** NOUN (GEN des **Kreises,** PL die **Kreise**)
1 circle ◊ *Stellt euch im Kreis auf.* Form a circle. ◊ *mein Freundeskreis* my circle of friends
2 district ◊ *Blaubeuren liegt im Kreis Ulm.* Blaubeuren is in the district of Ulm.
♦ **im Kreis gehen** to go round in circles

kreischen VERB
to shriek ◊ *Sie kreischte laut.* She shrieked loudly.

der **Kreislauf** NOUN
circulation ◊ *Sie hat einen labilen Kreislauf.* She has bad circulation.

der **Kreisverkehr** NOUN (PL die **Kreisverkehre**)
roundabout

das **Kreuz** NOUN (GEN des **Kreuzes,** PL die **Kreuze**)
1 cross ◊ *Sie markierte die Stelle mit einem Kreuz.* She marked the place with a cross.
♦ **Mir tut das Kreuz weh.** My back's sore.
2 clubs ◊ *Kreuz ist Trumpf.* Clubs is trumps.

die **Kreuzung** NOUN
1 crossroads ◊ *An der Kreuzung fährst du links.* You go left at the crossroads.
2 cross ◊ *Das ist eine Kreuzung zwischen Pferd und Esel.* It's a cross between a horse and a donkey.

das **Kreuzworträtsel** NOUN (PL die **Kreuzworträtsel**)
crossword puzzle

kriechen VERB (IMPERFECT **kroch,** PERFECT **ist gekrochen**)
1 to crawl ◊ *Das Baby kroch zur Tür.* The baby crawled towards the door. ◊ *Der Verkehr kriecht.* The traffic is crawling.
2 to grovel ◊ *Er kriecht vor seinem Chef.* He's grovelling to his boss.

der **Krieg** NOUN (PL die **Kriege**)
war

kriegen VERB
to get ◊ *Ich kriege einen Schnupfen.* I'm getting a cold.
♦ **Sie kriegt ein Kind.** She's going to have a baby.

der **Krimi** NOUN (PL die **Krimis**)
thriller

der **Kriminalfilm** NOUN (PL die **Kriminalfilme**)
crime thriller

der **Kriminalroman** NOUN (PL die **Kriminalromane**)
detective story

kriminell ADJECTIVE
criminal

die **Krise** NOUN
crisis

kritisch ADJECTIVE
critical

kritisieren VERB (PERFECT **hat kritisiert**)
to criticize

Kroatien NEUT NOUN
Croatia
♦ **aus Kroatien** from Croatia
♦ **nach Kroatien** to Croatia

das **Krokodil** NOUN (PL die **Krokodile**)
crocodile

die **Krone** NOUN
crown

die **Kröte** NOUN
toad

der **Krug** NOUN (PL die **Krüge**)
1 jug ◊ *Sie stellte einen Krug Saft auf den Tisch.* She put a jug of juice on the table.
2 beer mug ◊ *Er trinkt sein Bier immer aus einem Krug.* He always drinks his beer out of a beer mug.

krumm ADJECTIVE
♦ **ein krummer Rücken** a humped back
♦ **Mach nicht so einen krummen Rücken.** Don't slouch.
♦ **Sitz nicht so krumm.** Sit up straight.

die **Küche** NOUN
1 kitchen
2 cooking ◊ *die französische Küche* French cooking

der **Kuchen** NOUN (PL die **Kuchen**)
1 cake ◊ *ein Marmorkuchen* a marble cake
2 flan ◊ *ein Obstkuchen* a fruit flan

der **Kuckuck** NOUN (PL die **Kuckucke**)
cuckoo

die **Kuckucksuhr** NOUN
cuckoo clock

die **Kugel** NOUN
1 bullet ◊ *Er wurde von einer Kugel getroffen.* He was hit by a bullet.
2 ball ◊ *Die Wahrsagerin hat eine Kugel aus Glas.* The fortune teller has a crystal ball.

der **Kugelschreiber** NOUN (PL die **Kugelschreiber**)
Biro ®

die **Kuh** NOUN (PL die **Kühe**)
cow

kühl ADJECTIVE
cool ◊ *Abends wurde es kühl.* In the evenings it got cool.

der **Kühler** NOUN (PL die **Kühler**)
radiator (*in car*)

der **Kühlschrank** NOUN (PL die **Kühlschränke**)
fridge

die **Kühltruhe** NOUN
freezer

kühn ADJECTIVE
bold

der **Kuli** NOUN (PL die **Kulis**)
Biro ®

die **Kultur** NOUN
1 culture
◆ **Kultur haben** to be cultured
2 civilization ◊ *die abendländische Kultur* Western civilization

der **Kulturbeutel** NOUN (PL die **Kulturbeutel**)
toilet bag

kulturell ADJECTIVE
cultural

der **Kümmel** NOUN (PL die **Kümmel**)
caraway seed

der **Kummer** NOUN
sorrow
◆ **Hast du Kummer?** Have you got problems?

kümmern VERB
to concern ◊ *Was kümmert mich seine Kritik?* Why should his criticism concern me?
◆ **Das kümmert mich nicht.** That doesn't worry me.
◆ **sich um jemanden kümmern** to look after somebody
◆ **sich um etwas kümmern** to see to something ◊ *Kannst du dich um meine Pflanzen kümmern?* Can you see to my plants? ◊ *Ich kümmere mich darum, dass das gemacht wird.* I'll see to it that it's done.

◆ **Sie kümmert sich nicht um das Gerede der Leute.** She doesn't care about what people say.

der **Kunde** NOUN (GEN des **Kunden,** PL die **Kunden**)
customer

kündigen VERB
1 to hand in one's notice ◊ *Die Arbeit gefällt mir nicht, ich werde kündigen.* I don't like the job, I'm going to hand in my notice.
◆ **die Stellung kündigen** to hand in one's notice
◆ **Der Chef hat ihr gekündigt.** The boss gave her her notice.
◆ **die Wohnung kündigen** to give notice on one's flat
2 to cancel ◊ *Ich habe mein Abonnement gekündigt.* I've cancelled my subscription.

die **Kündigung** NOUN
notice ◊ *Er reichte seine Kündigung ein.* He handed in his notice.

die **Kundin** NOUN
customer

die **Kundschaft** NOUN
customers

die **Kunst** NOUN (PL die **Künste**)
1 art ◊ *Sie interessiert sich für Kunst.* She's interested in art.
2 knack ◊ *Er beherrscht die Kunst, andere zu überzeugen.* He's got the knack of persuading others.
◆ **Das ist doch keine Kunst.** It's easy.

die **Kunstfaser** NOUN
man-made fibre

der **Künstler** NOUN (PL die **Künstler**)
artist

die **Künstlerin** NOUN
artist

künstlerisch ADJECTIVE
artistic ◊ *künstlerisch begabt sein* to have artistic talents

künstlich ADJECTIVE
artificial

der **Kunststoff** NOUN (PL die **Kunststoffe**)
synthetic material

das **Kunststück** NOUN (PL die **Kunststücke**)
trick

das **Kunstwerk** NOUN (PL die **Kunstwerke**)
work of art

das **Kupfer** NOUN
copper (*metal*)

die **Kupplung** NOUN
clutch ◊ *Bei Automatikwagen gibt es keine Kupplung.* Automatic cars don't have a clutch.

die **Kur** NOUN
health cure ◊ *eine Kur machen* to take a health cure

der **Kürbis** NOUN (GEN des **Kürbisses,** PL die **Kürbisse**)

K

☞

pumpkin

der **Kurort** NOUN (PL die **Kurorte**)
health resort

der **Kurs** NOUN (GEN des **Kurses**, PL die **Kurse**)
1 course ◊ *Ich mache einen Kurs, um Spanisch zu lernen.* I'm doing a course to learn Spanish.
2 rate ◊ *Wie ist der Kurs des Pfunds?* What's the rate for the pound?

die **Kurve** NOUN
1 bend ◊ *Ein Auto bog um die Kurve.* A car came round the bend.
2 curve ◊ *die Kurve eines Schaubilds* the curve on a graph

kurz ADJECTIVE
short ◊ *Sie hat kurze Haare.* She has short hair. ◊ *Wir fahren über Feuerbach, das ist kürzer.* We'll go via Feuerbach, it's shorter. ◊ *Sie hat eine kurze Rede gehalten.* She made a short speech.
♦ **kurz gesagt** in short
♦ **zu kurz kommen** to come off badly
♦ **den Kürzeren ziehen** to get the worst of it

die **Kurzarbeit** NOUN
short-time work

die **Kürze** NOUN

shortness

kürzen VERB
1 to shorten ◊ *Du solltest den Aufsatz etwas kürzen.* You should shorten your essay a little.
2 to cut ◊ *Mein Vater hat mir das Taschengeld gekürzt.* My father has cut my pocket money.

die **Kurzgeschichte** NOUN
short story

kürzlich ADVERB
recently

kurzsichtig ADJECTIVE
short-sighted

die **Kusine** NOUN
cousin

der **Kuss** NOUN (GEN des **Kusses**, PL die **Küsse**)
kiss

küssen VERB
to kiss ◊ *Sie hat mich geküsst.* She kissed me.
♦ **sich küssen** to kiss ◊ *Sie küssten sich.* They kissed.

die **Küste** NOUN
coast

L

l ABBREVIATION (= *Liter*)
l

das **Labor** NOUN (PL die **Labore** or **Labors**)
lab

lächeln VERB
see also **das Lächeln** NOUN
to smile

das **Lächeln** NOUN
see also **lächeln** VERB
smile

lachen VERB
to laugh

lächerlich ADJECTIVE
ridiculous

der **Lachs** NOUN (GEN des **Lachses**, PL die **Lachse**)
salmon ◊ *drei Lachse* three salmon

der **Lack** NOUN (PL die **Lacke**)
[1] varnish ◊ *Er hat das Holz mit Lack behandelt.* He treated the wood with varnish.
[2] paint ◊ *Der Lack an meinem Auto ist stumpf geworden.* The paint on my car has become dull.

lackieren VERB (PERFECT **hat lackiert**)
[1] to varnish ◊ *Ich lackiere mir die Nägel.* I'm varnishing my nails.
[2] to spray ◊ *Das Auto muss lackiert werden.* The car has to be sprayed.

der **Laden** NOUN (PL die **Läden**)
see also **laden** VERB
[1] shop ◊ *In welchem Laden hast du das gekauft?* Which shop did you buy it in?
[2] shutter ◊ *Im Sommer machen wir tagsüber die Läden zu.* In summer we close the shutters during the day.

laden VERB (PRESENT **lädt**, IMPERFECT **lud**, PERFECT **hat geladen**)
see also **der Laden** NOUN
[1] to load ◊ *Wir haben das Gepäck ins Auto geladen.* We loaded the luggage into the car. ◊ *Das Programm wird geladen.* The program is being loaded. ◊ *eine Waffe laden* to load a weapon
♦ **eine Batterie laden** to charge a battery
[2] to summon ◊ *Ich wurde als Zeugin geladen.* I was summoned as a witness.

die **Ladung** NOUN
[1] cargo ◊ *Das Flugzeug hatte zu viel Ladung an Bord.* The plane had too much cargo on board.
[2] loading ◊ *Ein Arbeiter ist bei der Ladung des Schiffes verunglückt.* A worker was injured while loading the ship.
[3] summons ◊ *Wenn Sie eine Ladung als Zeuge bekommen, müssen Sie erscheinen.* If you receive a summons to appear as a witness, you have to attend.
[4] charge ◊ *eine Ladung Dynamit* a charge of dynamite

die **Lage** NOUN
[1] situation ◊ *Die politische Lage auf dem Balkan ist brisant.* The political situation in the Balkans is explosive.
[2] layer ◊ *Die Torte bestand aus mehreren Lagen.* The gateau was made up of several layers.
♦ **in der Lage sein, etwas zu tun** to be in a position to do something

das **Lager** NOUN (PL die **Lager**)
[1] camp ◊ *Er fährt im Sommer in ein Lager der Pfadfinder.* He's going to a scout camp in the summer.
[2] warehouse ◊ *Die Fabrik hat ein eigenes Lager.* The factory has its own warehouse.
[3] stockroom ◊ *Die Verkäuferin hat im Lager nachgesehen.* The sales assistant looked in the stockroom.

lagern VERB
[1] to store ◊ *kühl lagern* to store in a cool place ◊ *trocken lagern* to store in a dry place
[2] to lay down ◊ *Der Verletzte sollte auf der Seite gelagert werden.* The injured person should be laid down on his side.
[3] to camp ◊ *Die Indianer lagerten am Fluss.* The Indians camped by the river.

lahm ADJECTIVE
[1] lame ◊ *Das Pferd ist lahm.* The horse is lame.
[2] slow ◊ *Er ist furchtbar lahm.* He is terribly slow.

lähmen VERB
to paralyse

die **Lähmung** NOUN
paralysis

der **Laib** NOUN (PL die **Laibe**)
loaf

der **Laie** NOUN (GEN des **Laien**, PL die **Laien**)
layman

das **Laken** NOUN (PL die **Laken**)
sheet (*on bed*)

die **Lakritze** NOUN
liquorice

das **Lamm** NOUN (PL die **Lämmer**)
lamb

das **Lammfleisch** NOUN
lamb (*meat*)

die **Lampe** NOUN
lamp

das **Lampenfieber** NOUN
stage fright

das **Land** NOUN (PL die **Länder**)
[1] country ◊ *Italien ist ein schönes Land.* Italy is a beautiful country. ◊ *Am*

☞

Wochenende fahren wir aufs Land. We're going to the country at the weekend.
- ◆ **auf dem Land** in the country
- ◆ **an Land** on land ◊ *Wenn wir wieder an Land sind …* When we're on land again …
- ② state ◊ *Die Bundesrepublik besteht aus sechzehn Ländern.* The Federal Republic consists of sixteen states.

der **Landarbeiter** NOUN (PL die **Landarbeiter**)
farm worker

die **Landarbeiterin** NOUN
farm worker

die **Landebahn** NOUN
runway

landen VERB (PERFECT **ist gelandet**)
to land

die **Landeskunde** NOUN
regional and cultural studies

die **Landkarte** NOUN
map

der **Landkreis** NOUN (GEN des **Landkreises**, PL die **Landkreise**)
administrative district

> ❶ *The German administrative hierarchy starts with the **Stadt/Gemeinde** (town/community), and continues via the **Landkreis** (administrative district) and **Land** (federal state) to the **Bund** (federation).*

ländlich ADJECTIVE
rural

die **Landschaft** NOUN
① countryside ◊ *Die toskanische Landschaft ist sehr schön.* The Tuscan countryside is very beautiful.
② landscape ◊ *Turner hat viele Landschaften gemalt.* Turner painted many landscapes.

die **Landstraße** NOUN
country road

die **Landung** NOUN
landing ◊ *Das Flugzeug verunglückte bei der Landung.* The plane crashed on landing.

der **Landwirt** NOUN (PL die **Landwirte**)
farmer

die **Landwirtschaft** NOUN
agriculture

lang ADJECTIVE
① long ◊ *Sie hat lange Haare.* She has long hair. ◊ *Das war eine lange Rede.* That was a long speech. ◊ *Sie war länger als erwartet weg.* She was away longer than expected. ◊ *Es wird nicht lang dauern.* It won't take long.
② tall ◊ *Mathis ist der Längste in unserer Klasse.* Mathis is the tallest in our class.

langatmig ADJECTIVE
long-winded

lange ADVERB

for a long time ◊ *Sie war lange krank.* She was ill for a long time.
- ◆ **lange dauern** to last a long time
- ◆ **lange brauchen** to take a long time

die **Länge** NOUN
length ◊ *Sie hat die Länge und Breite des Zimmers ausgemessen.* She measured the length and breadth of the room. ◊ *die Länge eines Films* the length of a film

langen VERB
to have enough ◊ *Meinst du das Geld langt?* Do you think we have enough money?
- ◆ **Das Fleisch hat nicht für alle gelangt.** There wasn't enough meat to go round.
- ◆ **Es langt mir.** I've had enough.
- ◆ **nach etwas langen** to reach for something ◊ *Er langte nach dem Apfel.* He reached for the apple.

die **Langeweile** NOUN
boredom

langfristig ADJECTIVE, ADVERB
long-term ◊ *eine langfristige Besserung* a long-term improvement ◊ *Wir müssen langfristig planen.* We have to plan long-term.

der **Langlauf** NOUN
cross-country skiing ◊ *Sie macht gern Langlauf.* She likes to go cross-country skiing.

länglich ADJECTIVE
longish

langsam ADJECTIVE, ADVERB
① slow
② slowly ◊ *langsam fahren* to drive slowly
- ◆ **Das wird langsam langweilig.** This is getting boring.

die **Langsamkeit** NOUN
slowness

der **Langschläfer** NOUN (PL die **Langschläfer**)
late riser

die **Langspielplatte** NOUN
LP

längst ADVERB
- ◆ **Das ist längst fertig.** That was finished a long time ago.
- ◆ **Das weiß ich längst.** I've known that for a long time.
- ◆ **Er ist längst nicht so gescheit wie seine Schwester.** He's far from being as bright as his sister.

längste ADJECTIVE
longest ◊ *der längste Tag des Jahres* the longest day of the year

langweilen VERB
to bore ◊ *Langweile ich dich?* Am I boring you?
- ◆ **sich langweilen** to be bored

langweilig ADJECTIVE
boring

langwierig ADJECTIVE
lengthy

der **Lappen** NOUN (PL die **Lappen**)
rag ◊ *mit einem feuchten Lappen* with a damp rag

der **Laptop** NOUN (PL die **Laptops**)
laptop

der **Lärm** NOUN
noise

der **Laser** NOUN (PL die **Laser**)
laser

lassen VERB (PRESENT **lässt**, IMPERFECT **ließ**, PERFECT **gelassen** or **lassen**)

*The past participle **lassen** is used when **lassen** is a modal auxiliary.*

[1] to stop ◊ *Du solltest das Rauchen lassen.* You should stop smoking. ◊ *Er kann das Trinken nicht lassen.* He can't stop drinking. ◊ *Sie kann's nicht lassen.* She won't stop doing it.

♦ **Lass das!** Stop that!

[2] to leave ◊ *Kann ich die Kinder hier lassen?* Can I leave the children here? ◊ *jemanden allein lassen* to leave somebody alone ◊ *Wir haben das Auto zu Hause gelassen.* We left the car at home. ◊ *etwas lassen, wie es ist* to leave something as it is

♦ **Lassen wir das!** Let's leave it.
♦ **Lass mal, ich mache das schon.** Leave it, I'll do it.
♦ **Lass mich!** Leave me alone.
♦ **jemanden irgendwohin lassen** to let somebody go somewhere ◊ *Sie lässt die Katze nicht ins Schlafzimmer.* She doesn't let the cat into the bedroom. ◊ *jemanden ins Haus lassen* to let somebody into the house
♦ **etwas machen lassen** to have something done ◊ *Ich habe mir den Katalog schicken lassen.* I had the catalogue sent to me. ◊ *Sie hat sich die Haare schneiden lassen.* She had her hair cut.
♦ **jemanden etwas tun lassen** to let somebody do something ◊ *Sie hat uns nicht ins Kino gehen lassen.* She didn't let us go to the cinema.
♦ **jemanden etwas wissen lassen** to let somebody know something
♦ **jemanden warten lassen** to keep somebody waiting
♦ **Das lässt sich machen.** That can be done.
♦ **Lass uns gehen.** Let's go.

lässig ADJECTIVE
casual

die **Last** NOUN
load ◊ *Er stöhnte unter der schweren Last.* He groaned under the heavy load.
♦ **jemandem zur Last fallen** to be a burden to somebody

lästern VERB

to make nasty remarks ◊ *Lästert ihr schon wieder über eure Lehrerin?* Are you making nasty remarks about your teacher again?

lästig ADJECTIVE
tiresome

der **Lastwagen** NOUN (PL die **Lastwagen**)
lorry

das **Latein** NOUN
Latin

Lateinamerika NEUT NOUN
Latin America

die **Laterne** NOUN
[1] lantern ◊ *Die Kinder trugen Laternen.* The children carried lanterns.
[2] streetlamp ◊ *Vor unserem Haus steht eine Laterne.* There's a streetlamp in front of our house.

der **Lauch** NOUN (PL die **Lauche**)
leek

der **Lauf** NOUN (PL die **Läufe**)
[1] run ◊ *Er machte einen Lauf durch den Wald.* He went for a run through the forest.
[2] race ◊ *Sie hat den Lauf über vierhundert Meter gewonnen.* She won the four-hundred-metre race.
[3] course ◊ *der Lauf des Flusses* the course of the river
[4] barrel ◊ *Er richtete den Lauf seiner Pistole auf mich.* He aimed the barrel of his pistol at me.
♦ **im Laufe der Woche** in the course of the week
♦ **einer Sache ihren Lauf lassen** to let something take its course

die **Laufbahn** NOUN
career

laufen VERB (PRESENT **läuft**, IMPERFECT **lief**, PERFECT **ist gelaufen**)
[1] to run ◊ *Sie liefen so schnell sie konnten.* They ran as fast as they could. ◊ *Er läuft Marathon.* He runs marathons.
[2] to walk ◊ *Wir mussten nach Hause laufen.* We had to walk home.

laufend ADJECTIVE, ADVERB
[1] running ◊ *bei laufendem Motor* with the engine running
[2] current ◊ *die laufenden Ausgaben* current expenses
♦ **auf dem Laufenden sein** to be up to date
♦ **auf dem Laufenden halten** to keep up to date
[3] always ◊ *Musst du mich laufend stören?* Do you always have to interrupt me?

der **Läufer** NOUN (PL die **Läufer**)
[1] runner ◊ *Die Läufer standen am Start.* The runners were at the start. ◊ *Im Flur liegt ein roter Läufer.* There's a red runner in the hall.
[2] bishop ◊ *Sie zog mit dem Läufer.* She moved her bishop.

L

die **Läuferin** NOUN
runner

die **Laufmasche** NOUN
ladder (*in tights*)

das **Laufwerk** NOUN (PL die **Laufwerke**)
disk drive ◊ *Die Diskette in Laufwerk A einlegen.* Put the diskette in disk drive A.

die **Laune** NOUN
mood ◊ *Was hat sie für eine Laune?* What kind of mood is she in? ◊ *Ich habe gute Laune.* I'm in a good mood.
♦ **Ich bin deine Launen leid.** I'm fed up with your bad moods.
♦ **Sie ist aus einer Laune heraus nach Italien gefahren.** She took it into her head to go off to Italy.

launisch ADJECTIVE
[1] temperamental ◊ *Sie ist ein sehr launischer Mensch.* She's very temperamental.
[2] bad-tempered ◊ *Er war heute schrecklich launisch.* He was terribly bad-tempered today.

die **Laus** NOUN (PL die **Läuse**)
louse

laut ADJECTIVE, ADVERB, PREPOSITION
see also der **Laut** NOUN
[1] loud ◊ *Ich mag laute Musik nicht.* I don't like loud music.
♦ **Hier ist es schrecklich laut.** It's terribly noisy here.
[2] loudly ◊ *Sie schrie so laut sie konnte.* She screamed as loudly as she could.
♦ **laut lesen** to read aloud
[3] according to ◊ *Laut unserem Vertrag ...* According to our contract ...

der **Laut** NOUN (PL die **Laute**)
see also **laut** ADJECTIVE
sound

lauten VERB
[1] to go ◊ *Wie lautet die zweite Strophe des Lieds?* How does the second verse of the song go?
[2] to be ◊ *Das Urteil lautete auf zehn Jahre Gefängnis.* The sentence was ten years' imprisonment.

läuten VERB
to ring ◊ *Die Glocken läuten.* The bells are ringing. ◊ *Ich habe geläutet, es hat aber niemand aufgemacht.* I rang but nobody answered.

lauter ADVERB
nothing but ◊ *Sie hat lauter Lügen erzählt.* She told nothing but lies.

die **Lautschrift** NOUN
phonetics

der **Lautsprecher** NOUN (PL die **Lautsprecher**)
loudspeaker

die **Lautstärke** NOUN
volume

lauwarm ADJECTIVE
lukewarm

die **Lawine** NOUN
avalanche

das **Leben** NOUN (PL die **Leben**)
see also **leben** VERB
life
♦ **ums Leben kommen** to lose one's life ◊ *Er ist bei einem Unfall ums Leben gekommen.* He lost his life in an accident.

leben VERB
see also **das Leben** NOUN
to live

lebend ADJECTIVE
living

lebendig ADJECTIVE
[1] alive ◊ *Er konnte lebendig aus den Trümmern geborgen werden.* He was rescued from the ruins alive.
[2] lively ◊ *Sie ist ein sehr lebendiges Kind.* She's a very lively child.

die **Lebensgefahr** NOUN
mortal danger ◊ *Die Geiseln waren in Lebensgefahr.* The hostages were in mortal danger.
♦ **"Lebensgefahr!"** "danger!"

lebensgefährlich ADJECTIVE
[1] dangerous ◊ *eine lebensgefährliche Kurve* a dangerous corner
[2] critical ◊ *eine lebensgefährliche Krankheit* a critical illness
♦ **lebensgefährlich verletzt** critically injured

die **Lebenshaltungskosten** PL NOUN
cost of living

lebenslänglich ADJECTIVE
for life
♦ **Er hat eine lebenslängliche Gefängnisstrafe bekommen.** He received a life sentence.

der **Lebenslauf** NOUN (PL die **Lebensläufe**)
CV (= curriculum vitae)

die **Lebensmittel** NEUT PL NOUN
food

das **Lebensmittelgeschäft** NOUN (PL die **Lebensmittelgeschäfte**)
grocer's shop

die **Lebensmittelvergiftung** NOUN
food poisoning

der **Lebensstandard** NOUN
standard of living

der **Lebensunterhalt** NOUN
livelihood

die **Lebensversicherung** NOUN
life insurance

die **Leber** NOUN
liver

der **Leberfleck** NOUN (PL die **Leberflecke**)
mole (*on skin*)

die **Leberwurst** NOUN (PL die **Leberwürste**)
liver sausage

das **Lebewesen** NOUN (PL die **Lebewesen**)
creature

lebhaft ADJECTIVE
lively

der **Lebkuchen** NOUN (PL die **Lebkuchen**)
gingerbread

lecken VERB
[1] to leak ◊ *Der Behälter leckt.* The container's leaking.
[2] to lick ◊ *Die Katze leckte sich das Fell.* The cat licked its fur. ◊ *Sie leckte am Eis.* She licked her ice.

lecker ADJECTIVE
delicious ◊ *lecker schmecken* to taste delicious

das **Leder** NOUN (PL die **Leder**)
leather

die **Lederhose** NOUN
leather trousers

> *ⓘ* **Lederhosen** *are the traditional dress in South Germany and Austria.*

ledig ADJECTIVE
single ◊ *"Familienstand: ledig"* "Marital status: single"

leer ADJECTIVE
empty ◊ *eine leere Flasche* an empty bottle ◊ *leere Drohungen* empty threats
♦ **ein leeres Blatt Papier** a blank sheet of paper
♦ **ein leerer Blick** a vacant expression
♦ **leer machen** to empty

die **Leere** NOUN
emptiness

leeren VERB
to empty

die **Leerung** NOUN
[1] emptying ◊ *Die Leerung der Mülltonnen erfolgt freitags.* The dustbins are emptied on Fridays.
[2] collection (*from postbox*) ◊ *"Nächste Leerung: 18 Uhr"* "Next collection: 6 p.m."

legal ADJECTIVE
legal

legen VERB
[1] to put ◊ *Sie legte das Kind ins Bett.* She put the child to bed. ◊ *Leg das Besteck in die Schublade.* Put the cutlery in the drawer. ◊ *Er legte das Buch aus der Hand.* He put the book down.
[2] to lay ◊ *Sie legten den Verletzten auf eine Decke.* They laid the injured man on a blanket. ◊ *Sie legte ihren Mantel über den Stuhl.* She laid her coat over the chair. ◊ *ein Ei legen* to lay an egg
♦ **sich legen (1)** to lie down ◊ *Sie legte sich auf das Sofa.* She lay down on the sofa. ◊ *Ich lege mich ins Bett.* I'm going to lie down. ◊ *Wir legten uns an den Strand.* We lay down on the beach.
♦ **sich legen (2)** to drop ◊ *Der Wind hat sich gelegt.* The wind has dropped.

♦ **Das wird sich legen.** That will sort itself out.

die **Lehne** NOUN
[1] arm ◊ *Sie saß auf der Lehne des Sofas.* She sat on the arm of the sofa.
[2] back ◊ *Der Sessel hat eine hohe Lehne.* The chair has a high back.

lehnen VERB
to lean

der **Lehnstuhl** NOUN (PL die **Lehnstühle**)
armchair

die **Lehre** NOUN
[1] apprenticeship ◊ *bei jemandem in die Lehre gehen* to serve one's apprenticeship with somebody
[2] lesson ◊ *Lass dir das eine Lehre sein!* Let that be a lesson to you!

lehren VERB (PERFECT **hat gelehrt**)
to teach

der **Lehrer** NOUN (PL die **Lehrer**)
teacher

die **Lehrerin** NOUN
teacher

das **Lehrerzimmer** NOUN (PL die **Lehrerzimmer**)
staff room

das **Lehrjahr** NOUN (PL die **Lehrjahre**)
year as an apprentice

der **Lehrling** NOUN (PL die **Lehrlinge**)
apprentice

der **Lehrplan** NOUN (PL die **Lehrpläne**)
syllabus

die **Lehrstelle** NOUN
apprenticeship

die **Leiche** NOUN
corpse

leicht ADJECTIVE
[1] light ◊ *leichtes Gepäck* light luggage
[2] easy ◊ *Die Klassenarbeit war leicht.* The class test was easy.
♦ **es sich leicht machen** to make things easy for oneself ◊ *Du machst es dir wirklich zu leicht.* You really make things too easy for yourself.

die **Leichtathletik** NOUN
athletics

leichtfallen VERB
♦ **jemandem leichtfallen** to be easy for somebody

leichtmachen VERB see **leicht**

der **Leichtsinn** NOUN
carelessness

leichtsinnig ADJECTIVE
careless

das **Leid** NOUN
> see also **leid** ADJECTIVE, **leidtun** VERB

sorrow
♦ **zu Leide** see **zuleide**

leid ADJECTIVE
> see also **das Leid** NOUN

♦ **etwas leid sein** to be tired of something ◊ *Ich bin deine ewigen Klagen leid.* I'm tired of your constant complaining.

L

☞

leiden VERB (IMPERFECT **litt**, PERFECT **hat gelitten**)
to suffer ◊ *Sie leidet an Asthma.* She suffers from asthma. ◊ *Wir leiden unter der Hitze.* We're suffering from the heat.
◆ **jemanden gut leiden können** to like somebody
◆ **Ich kann ihn nicht leiden.** I can't stand him.

leider ADVERB
unfortunately ◊ *Ich kann leider nicht kommen.* Unfortunately I can't come.
◆ **Ja, leider.** Yes, I'm afraid so.
◆ **Leider nicht.** I'm afraid not. ◊ *Er hat mir leider nicht geholfen.* I'm afraid he didn't help me.

leidtun VERB (IMPERFECT **tat leid**, PERFECT **hat leidgetan**)
◆ **Es tut mir leid.** I'm sorry.
◆ **Er tut mir leid.** I'm sorry for him.

leihen VERB (IMPERFECT **lieh**, PERFECT **hat geliehen**)
to lend ◊ *Kannst du mir fünfzig Euro leihen?* Can you lend me fifty euros?
◆ **sich etwas leihen** to borrow something ◊ *Das ist nicht mein Fahrrad, ich habe es mir von meiner Schwester geliehen.* That's not my bike, I've borrowed it from my sister.

der **Leim** NOUN (PL die **Leime**)
glue

die **Leine** NOUN
1 line ◊ *Sie hängte die Wäsche auf die Leine.* She hung the washing on the line.
2 lead ◊ *Hunde müssen an der Leine geführt werden.* Dogs must be kept on a lead.

das **Leinen** NOUN (PL die **Leinen**)
linen

leise ADJECTIVE, ADVERB
1 quiet ◊ *Seid bitte leise.* Please be quiet.
2 quietly ◊ *Sie sprach mit leiser Stimme.* She spoke quietly. ◊ *Sie kam ganz leise ins Zimmer.* She came into the room very quietly.

leisten VERB
1 to do ◊ *Du hast gute Arbeit geleistet.* You've done a good job.
2 to achieve ◊ *Sie hat viel geleistet im Leben.* She's achieved a lot in her life.
◆ **jemandem Gesellschaft leisten** to keep somebody company
◆ **sich etwas leisten** to treat oneself to something ◊ *Ich leiste mir heute einen freien Tag.* I'm going to treat myself to a day off today.
◆ **sich etwas leisten können** to be able to afford something ◊ *Ich kann mir keinen neuen Computer leisten.* I can't afford a new computer. ◊ *Ich kann es mir nicht leisten, schon wieder zu spät zu kommen.* I can't afford to be late again.

die **Leistung** NOUN

1 performance ◊ *Sie haben die Leistung des Motors verbessert.* They've improved the performance of the engine.
◆ **schulische Leistungen** school results
2 achievement ◊ *eine sportliche Leistung* a sporting achievement ◊ *Das war wirklich eine Leistung!* That really was an achievement.

leiten VERB
1 to direct ◊ *Das Wasser wird durch Rohre geleitet.* The water is directed through pipes.
2 to lead ◊ *eine Partei leiten* to lead a party
3 to run ◊ *Wer leitet diese Firma?* Who runs this company?
4 to chair ◊ *Wer hat die Versammlung geleitet?* Who chaired the meeting?
◆ **Metall leitet Strom besonders gut.** Metal is a good conductor of electricity.

der **Leiter** NOUN (PL die **Leiter**)
see also **die Leiter** NOUN
head ◊ *der Leiter des Museums* the head of the museum

die **Leiter** NOUN
see also **der Leiter** NOUN
ladder ◊ *eine Leiter hinaufklettern* to climb a ladder

die **Leitung** NOUN
1 management ◊ *Ihr wurde die Leitung der Abteilung übertragen.* She was entrusted with the management of the department.
◆ **Wer hatte bei der Diskussion die Leitung?** Who chaired the discussion?
2 direction ◊ *der Jugendchor unter Leitung von ...* the youth choir under the direction of ...
3 pipe ◊ *In unserer Straße werden neue Leitungen für Wasser und Gas verlegt.* They're laying new water and gas pipes in our road.
4 cable ◊ *Die Leitung steht unter Strom.* The cable is live.
5 line ◊ *Alle Leitungen waren besetzt.* All the lines were busy.
◆ **eine lange Leitung haben** to be slow on the uptake

die **Lektion** NOUN
lesson

die **Lektüre** NOUN
1 reading ◊ *Stör sie nicht bei der Lektüre.* Don't disturb her while she's reading.
2 reading matter ◊ *Das ist die richtige Lektüre für die Ferien.* That's the right reading matter for the holidays.
3 set text ◊ *Welche Lektüre habt ihr dieses Jahr in Englisch?* What are your set texts in English this year?
Be careful! **Lektüre** does not mean **lecture**.

lenken VERB

to steer ◊ *ein Fahrzeug lenken* to steer a car

♦ **Sie lenkte das Gespräch auf ein anderes Thema.** She led the conversation round to another subject.

das **Lenkrad** NOUN (PL die **Lenkräder**)
steering wheel

die **Lenkstange** NOUN
handlebars

lernen VERB
to learn

das **Lesebuch** NOUN (PL die **Lesebücher**)
reading book

lesen VERB (PRESENT **liest**, IMPERFECT **las**, PERFECT **hat gelesen**)
to read

leserlich ADJECTIVE
legible ◊ *eine leserliche Handschrift* legible handwriting ◊ *leserlich schreiben* to write legibly

das **Lesezeichen** NOUN (PL die **Lesezeichen**)
bookmark

letzte ADJECTIVE
1 last ◊ *In der letzten Arbeit habe ich eine Zwei geschrieben.* I got a "B" in the last test. ◊ *Ich habe noch einen letzten Wunsch.* I have one last wish. ◊ *letzte Woche* last week

♦ **als Letzter** last ◊ *Franz kam als Letzter.* Franz arrived last.

♦ **zum letzten Mal** for the last time
2 latest ◊ *Laut letzten Informationen kam es zu schweren Unruhen.* According to latest reports there were serious riots.

letztens ADVERB
lately

leuchten VERB
to shine ◊ *jemandem ins Gesicht leuchten* to shine a light in somebody's face

der **Leuchter** NOUN (PL die **Leuchter**)
candlestick

der **Leuchtstift** NOUN (PL die **Leuchtstifte**)
highlighter

der **Leuchtturm** NOUN (PL die **Leuchttürme**)
lighthouse

die **Leute** PL NOUN
people

das **Lexikon** NOUN (PL die **Lexika**)
encyclopedia

das **Licht** NOUN (PL die **Lichter**)
light

das **Lichtjahr** NOUN (PL die **Lichtjahre**)
light year

der **Lichtschalter** NOUN (PL die **Lichtschalter**)
light switch

das **Lid** NOUN (PL die **Lider**)
eyelid

der **Lidschatten** NOUN (PL die **Lidschatten**)
eyeshadow

lieb ADJECTIVE

dear ◊ *Liebe Bettina* Dear Bettina ◊ *Lieber Herr Schlüter* Dear Mr Schlüter

♦ **Das ist lieb von dir.** That's nice of you.

♦ **jemanden lieb haben** to be fond of somebody

die **Liebe** NOUN
love

lieben VERB
to love

liebenswürdig ADJECTIVE
kind

die **Liebenswürdigkeit** NOUN
kindness

lieber ADVERB
rather ◊ *Ich hätte jetzt lieber einen Kaffee.* I'd rather have a coffee just now. ◊ *Ich gehe lieber nicht.* I'd rather not go.

♦ **Lass das lieber!** I'd leave that if I were you.

♦ **Ich sage lieber nichts.** I'd better not say anything.

♦ **etwas lieber haben** to prefer something ◊ *Was hast du lieber, Mathe oder Chemie?* What do you prefer, maths or chemistry?

der **Liebesbrief** NOUN (PL die **Liebesbriefe**)
love letter

die **Liebesgeschichte** NOUN
love story

der **Liebeskummer** NOUN
♦ **Liebeskummer haben** to be lovesick

der **Liebesroman** NOUN (PL die **Liebesromane**)
romantic novel

liebevoll ADJECTIVE
loving

liebhaben VERB *see* **lieb**

der **Liebling** NOUN (PL die **Lieblinge**)
darling

Lieblings- PREFIX
favourite ◊ *Was ist dein Lieblingsfach?* What's your favourite subject?

liebste ADJECTIVE
favourite ◊ *Der Winter ist meine liebste Jahreszeit.* Winter is my favourite season.

♦ **am liebsten** best ◊ *Am liebsten lese ich Kriminalromane.* I like detective stories best.

das **Lied** NOUN (PL die **Lieder**)
song

lief VERB *see* **laufen**

liefern VERB
1 to deliver ◊ *Wir liefern die Möbel ins Haus.* We deliver the furniture to your door.
2 to supply ◊ *Das Kraftwerk liefert den Strom für die ganze Gegend.* The power station supplies electricity to the whole area.

♦ **den Beweis liefern** to produce proof

der **Lieferwagen** NOUN (PL die **Lieferwagen**)
van

L

liegen VERB (IMPERFECT **lag,** PERFECT **hat gelegen**)

1 to lie ◊ *Sie lag auf dem Bett.* She lay on the bed. ◊ *Wir haben den ganzen Tag am Strand gelegen.* We lay on the beach all day. ◊ *Auf meinem Schreibtisch liegt eine Menge Papier.* There's a lot of paper lying on my desk.

♦ **Es lag viel Schnee.** There was a lot of snow.

2 to be ◊ *Unser Haus liegt sehr zentral.* Our house is very central. ◊ *Ulm liegt an der Donau.* Ulm is on the Danube.

♦ **nach Süden liegen** to face south

♦ **Mir liegt viel daran.** It matters a lot to me.

♦ **Mir liegt nichts daran.** It doesn't matter to me.

♦ **Es liegt bei dir, ob ...** It's up to you whether ...

♦ **Sprachen liegen mir nicht.** Languages are not my thing.

♦ **Woran liegt es?** How come?

♦ **Das liegt am Wetter.** It's because of the weather.

♦ **liegen bleiben (1)** to lie in ◊ *Morgen ist Sonntag, da kann ich liegen bleiben.* It's Sunday tomorrow, so I can lie in.

♦ **liegen bleiben (2)** not to get up ◊ *Der verletzte Spieler blieb liegen.* The injured player didn't get up.

♦ **liegen bleiben (3)** to be left behind ◊ *Der Schirm ist liegen geblieben.* The umbrella's been left behind.

♦ **Unser Auto ist liegen geblieben.** Our car has broken down.

♦ **etwas liegen lassen** to leave something ◊ *Ich muss diese Arbeit liegen lassen.* I'll have to leave this job. ◊ *Ich habe meinen Schirm liegen lassen.* I've left my umbrella.

der **Liegestuhl** NOUN (PL die **Liegestühle**)
deck chair

der **Liegewagen** NOUN (PL die **Liegewagen**)
couchette

der **Lift** NOUN (PL die **Lifte** or **Lifts**)
lift (*elevator*)

die **Liga** NOUN (PL die **Ligen**)
league

lila ADJECTIVE
purple ◊ *Sie hatte einen lila Hut auf.* She was wearing a purple hat.

die **Limo** NOUN (PL die **Limos**)
lemonade

die **Limonade** NOUN
lemonade

die **Limone** NOUN
lime

das **Lineal** NOUN (PL die **Lineale**)
ruler ◊ *einen Strich mit dem Lineal ziehen* to draw a line with a ruler

die **Linie** NOUN
line

die **Linke** NOUN (GEN der **Linken**)

see also **linke** ADJECTIVE

1 left ◊ *Zu Ihrer Linken sehen Sie das Rathaus.* On your left you'll see the town hall.

2 left hand ◊ *Er schlug mit der Linken zu.* He hit out with his left hand.

linke ADJECTIVE

see also **die Linke** NOUN, **links** ADVERB

left ◊ *In Großbritannien fährt man auf der linken Seite.* In Great Britain they drive on the left. ◊ *Mein linkes Auge tut weh.* My left eye's hurting. ◊ *Er hat sich den linken Arm gebrochen.* He broke his left arm.

links ADVERB

see also **linke** ADJECTIVE

left ◊ *links abbiegen* to turn left

♦ **links fahren** to drive on the left

♦ **links überholen** to overtake on the left

♦ **Er schreibt mit links.** He writes with his left hand.

♦ **Links sehen Sie das Rathaus.** On the left you'll see the town hall.

♦ **links von der Kirche** to the left of the church

♦ **links von mir** on my left

♦ **links wählen** to vote for a left-wing party

♦ **etwas mit links machen** to do something easily

der **Linkshänder** NOUN (PL die **Linkshänder**)
♦ **Er ist Linkshänder.** He's left-handed.

die **Linkshänderin** NOUN
♦ **Sie ist Linkshänderin.** She's left-handed.

die **Linkskurve** NOUN
left-hand bend

der **Linksverkehr** NOUN
driving on the left
♦ **In Großbritannien ist Linksverkehr.** They drive on the left in Britain.

die **Linse** NOUN
1 lentil ◊ *Linsensuppe* lentil soup
2 lens ◊ *die Linse der Kamera* the camera lens

die **Lippe** NOUN
lip

der **Lippenstift** NOUN (PL die **Lippenstifte**)
lipstick

lispeln VERB
to lisp

die **Liste** NOUN
list

der **Liter** NOUN (PL die **Liter**)
You can also say **das Liter**.
litre

die **Literatur** NOUN
literature

live ADVERB
live

die **Lizenz** NOUN
licence

der **Lkw** NOUN (GEN des **Lkw** or **Lkws**, PL die **Lkws**) (= *Lastkraftwagen*)
  lorry

das **Lob** NOUN
  praise

loben VERB
  to praise

das **Loch** NOUN (PL die **Löcher**)
  hole

die **Locke** NOUN
  curl
  ◆ **Sie hat Locken.** She has curly hair.

der **Lockenwickler** NOUN (PL die **Lockenwickler**)
  curler

locker ADJECTIVE
  1 loose ◊ *ein lockerer Zahn* a loose tooth
  2 relaxed ◊ *eine lockere Atmosphäre* a relaxed atmosphere

lockerlassen VERB (PRESENT **lässt locker**, IMPERFECT **ließ locker**, PERFECT **hat lockergelassen**)
  ◆ **nicht lockerlassen** not to let up ◊ *Er ließ nicht locker mit seinen Fragen.* He didn't let up with his questions.

lockig ADJECTIVE
  curly

der **Löffel** NOUN (PL die **Löffel**)
  spoon
  ◆ **ein Löffel Zucker** a spoonful of sugar

die **Logik** NOUN
  logic

logisch ADJECTIVE
  logical

der **Lohn** NOUN (PL die **Löhne**)
  1 wages ◊ *Freitags wird der Lohn ausbezahlt.* The wages are paid on Fridays.
  2 reward ◊ *Das ist jetzt der Lohn für meine Mühe!* That's the reward for my efforts.

lohnen VERB
  ◆ **Das lohnt sich.** It's worth it.

lohnend ADJECTIVE
  worthwhile

die **Lohnsteuer** NOUN
  income tax

das **Lokal** NOUN (PL die **Lokale**)
  pub

die **Lokomotive** NOUN
  locomotive

das **Lorbeerblatt** NOUN (PL die **Lorbeerblätter**)
  bay leaf

das **Los** NOUN (GEN des **Loses**, PL die **Lose**)
  see also **los** ADJECTIVE
  lottery ticket ◊ *Mein Los hat gewonnen.* My lottery ticket has won.

los ADJECTIVE
  see also **das Los** NOUN
  loose ◊ *Die Schraube ist los.* The screw's loose.

◆ **Dort ist viel los.** There's a lot going on there.
◆ **Dort ist nichts los.** There's nothing going on there.
◆ **Was ist los?** What's the matter?
◆ **Den Schirm bist du los.** You've lost that umbrella for good.
◆ **Los!** Go on!

losbinden VERB (IMPERFECT **band los**, PERFECT **hat losgebunden**)
  to untie

löschen VERB
  to put out ◊ *ein Feuer löschen* to put out a fire ◊ *das Licht löschen* to put out the light
  ◆ **den Durst löschen** to quench one's thirst
  ◆ **eine Datei löschen** to delete a file
  ◆ **ein Tonband löschen** to erase a tape

die **Löschtaste** NOUN
  delete key

lose ADJECTIVE
  loose ◊ *lose Blätter* loose sheets ◊ *etwas lose verkaufen* to sell something loose
  ◆ **ein loses Mundwerk** a big mouth

lösen VERB
  1 to solve ◊ *ein Rätsel lösen* to solve a puzzle ◊ *ein Problem lösen* to solve a problem
  2 to loosen ◊ *Kannst du diesen Knoten lösen?* Can you loosen the knot?
  ◆ **etwas von etwas lösen** to remove something from something ◊ *Sie löste das Etikett vom Glas.* She removed the label from the jar.
  ◆ **sich lösen (1)** to come loose ◊ *Eine Schraube hatte sich gelöst.* A screw had come loose.
  ◆ **sich lösen (2)** to dissolve ◊ *Die Tablette löst sich in Wasser.* The pill dissolves in water.
  ◆ **sich lösen (3)** to resolve itself ◊ *Das Problem hat sich inzwischen gelöst.* The problem has resolved itself in the meantime.
  ◆ **eine Fahrkarte lösen** to buy a ticket

losfahren VERB (PRESENT **fährt los**, IMPERFECT **fuhr los**, PERFECT **ist losgefahren**)
  to leave

losgehen VERB (IMPERFECT **ging los**, PERFECT **ist losgegangen**)
  1 to set out ◊ *Wir sollten so langsam losgehen.* It's time we were setting out.
  2 to start ◊ *Wann geht der Film los?* When does the film start?
  ◆ **auf jemanden losgehen** to go for somebody ◊ *Er ging mit einem Messer auf sie los.* He went for her with a knife.

loslassen VERB (PRESENT **lässt los**, IMPERFECT **ließ los**, PERFECT **hat losgelassen**)
  to let go of

loslaufen VERB (PRESENT **läuft los**, IMPERFECT **lief los**, PERFECT **ist losgelaufen**)
  to run off

L

löslich ADJECTIVE
soluble

die **Lösung** NOUN
solution ◊ *Weißt du die Lösung des Rätsels?* Do you know the solution to the puzzle?

loswerden VERB (PRESENT **wird los**, IMPERFECT **wurde los**, PERFECT **ist losgeworden**)
to get rid of

das **Lotto** NOUN (PL die **Lottos**)
National Lottery

die **Lottozahlen** FEM PL NOUN
winning lottery numbers

der **Löwe** NOUN (GEN des **Löwen**, PL die **Löwen**)
1 lion
2 Leo ◊ *Manfred ist Löwe.* Manfred's Leo.

die **Lücke** NOUN
gap

die **Luft** NOUN (PL die **Lüfte**)
air ◊ *Ich brauche frische Luft.* I need some fresh air.
♦ **in der Luft liegen** to be in the air
♦ **jemanden wie Luft behandeln** to ignore somebody

der **Luftballon** NOUN (PL die **Luftballons** *or* **Luftballone**)
balloon

der **Luftdruck** NOUN
atmospheric pressure

das **Luftkissenboot** NOUN (PL die **Luftkissenboote**)
hovercraft

die **Luftlinie** NOUN
♦ **in der Luftlinie** as the crow flies

die **Luftmatratze** NOUN
air bed

die **Luftpost** NOUN
airmail ◊ *per Luftpost* by airmail

die **Luftverschmutzung** NOUN
air pollution

die **Lüge** NOUN
lie

lügen VERB (IMPERFECT **log**, PERFECT **hat gelogen**)
to lie ◊ *Ich müsste lügen, wenn ...* I would be lying if ...
♦ **Er lügt ständig.** He's always telling lies.

der **Lügner** NOUN (PL die **Lügner**)
liar

der **Lumpen** NOUN (PL die **Lumpen**)
rag ◊ *in Lumpen herumlaufen* to go around in rags

die **Lunge** NOUN
lung

die **Lungenentzündung** NOUN
pneumonia

die **Lupe** NOUN
magnifying glass
♦ **unter die Lupe nehmen** to scrutinize

die **Lust** NOUN
♦ **Lust haben, etwas zu tun** to feel like doing something ◊ *Hast du Lust, ins Kino zu gehen?* Do you feel like going to the cinema?
♦ **keine Lust haben, etwas zu tun** not to feel like doing something ◊ *Sie hatte keine Lust, mit auf die Party zu kommen.* She didn't feel like coming to the party.
♦ **Lust auf etwas haben** to feel like something ◊ *Ich habe Lust auf eine kalte Limonade.* I feel like some cold lemonade.

lustig ADJECTIVE
funny ◊ *eine lustige Geschichte* a funny story

lutschen VERB
to suck ◊ *am Daumen lutschen* to suck one's thumb

der **Lutscher** NOUN (PL die **Lutscher**)
lollipop

Luxemburg NEUT NOUN
Luxembourg
♦ **aus Luxemburg** from Luxembourg
♦ **nach Luxemburg** to Luxembourg

der **Luxus** NOUN (GEN des **Luxus**)
luxury

M

m ABBREVIATION (= *Meter*)
m

machbar ADJECTIVE
feasible

machen VERB

[1] to do ◊ *Hausaufgaben machen* to do one's homework ◊ *etwas sorgfältig machen* to do something carefully ◊ *Was machst du heute Nachmittag?* What are you doing this afternoon? ◊ *Lass mal, ich mach das schon.* Leave it, I'll do it.
♦ **eine Prüfung machen** to sit an exam
♦ **den Führerschein machen** to take driving lessons

[2] to make ◊ *aus Holz gemacht* made of wood ◊ *Kaffee machen* to make coffee ◊ *einen Fehler machen* to make a mistake ◊ *Krach machen* to make a noise ◊ *Das macht müde.* It makes you tired.
♦ **Schluss machen** to finish
♦ **ein Foto machen** to take a photo
♦ **das Radio leiser machen** to turn the radio down

[3] to cause ◊ *Das hat mir viel Mühe gemacht.* This caused me a lot of trouble. ◊ *Ich möchte Ihnen keine Schwierigkeiten machen.* I don't want to cause you any difficulties.
♦ **viel Arbeit machen** to cause a lot of work
♦ **Das macht die Kälte.** It's the cold that does that.

[4] to be ◊ *Drei und fünf macht acht.* Three and five is eight. ◊ *Was macht das?* How much is that? ◊ *Das macht acht Euro.* That's eight euros.
♦ **Was macht die Arbeit?** How's the work going?
♦ **Was macht dein Bruder?** How's your brother doing?
♦ **Das macht nichts.** That doesn't matter.
♦ **Die Kälte macht mir nichts.** I don't mind the cold.
♦ **sich machen** to come on ◊ *Eine Zwei in Physik, du machst dich!* A "B" in physics, you're coming on.
♦ **sich verständlich machen** to make oneself understood
♦ **sich nichts aus etwas machen** not to be very keen on something ◊ *Ich mache mir nichts aus Süßigkeiten.* I'm not very keen on sweets.
♦ **Mach's gut!** Take care!
♦ **Mach schon!** Come on!

die **Macht** NOUN (PL die **Mächte**)
power

das **Mädchen** NOUN (PL die **Mädchen**)
girl

der **Mädchenname** NOUN (GEN des **Mädchennamens**, PL die **Mädchennamen**)
maiden name

mag VERB *see* **mögen**

das **Magazin** NOUN
magazine ◊ *Ich habe das in einem Magazin gelesen.* I read it in a magazine.

der **Magen** NOUN (PL die **Magen** *or* **Mägen**)
stomach

die **Magenschmerzen** MASC PL NOUN
stomachache ◊ *Ich habe Magenschmerzen.* I've got a stomachache.

die **Magenverstimmung** NOUN
stomach upset

mager ADJECTIVE
[1] lean ◊ *mageres Fleisch* lean meat
[2] thin ◊ *Sie ist furchtbar mager.* She's terribly thin.

der **Magnet** NOUN (GEN des **Magnets** *or* **Magneten**, PL die **Magneten**)
magnet

magnetisch ADJECTIVE
magnetic

mähen VERB
to mow

mahlen VERB (PERFECT **hat gemahlen**)
to grind

die **Mahlzeit** NOUN
meal ◊ *Wir essen drei Mahlzeiten am Tag.* We eat three meals a day.

der **Mai** NOUN (GEN des **Mai** *or* **Mais**, PL die **Maie**)
May ◊ *im Mai* in May ◊ *am sechsten Mai* on 6 May ◊ *Ulm, den 6. Mai 2006* Ulm, 6 May 2006 ◊ *Heute ist der sechste Mai.* Today is the sixth of May.
♦ **der Erste Mai** May Day

das **Maiglöckchen** NOUN (PL die **Maiglöckchen**)
lily of the valley

der **Maikäfer** NOUN (PL die **Maikäfer**)
cockchafer

mailen VERB (PERFECT **hat gemailt**)
to e-mail ◊ *Hast du es gemailt?* Did you e-mail it?

die **Mailingliste** NOUN (PL die **Mailinglisten**)
mailing list

der **Mais** NOUN (GEN des **Maises**)
maize

die **Majonäse** NOUN
mayonnaise

der **Majoran** NOUN
marjoram

das **Mal** NOUN (PL die **Male**)
see also **mal** ADVERB
[1] time ◊ *das fünfte Mal* the fifth time ◊ *zum ersten Mal* for the first time ◊ *Wie viele Male hast du es versucht?* How many times have you tried?

☞

[2] mark ◊ *Sie hat ein rotes Mal im Gesicht.* She has a red mark on her face.

mal ADVERB

see also das Mal NOUN

times ◊ *zwei mal fünf* two times five ◊ *Wir haben sechsmal geklingelt.* We rang six times.

♦ **Warst du schon mal in Paris?** Have you ever been to Paris?

♦ **Wir möchten auch mal nach England fahren.** We'd like to go to England sometime.

malen VERB
to paint

der **Maler** NOUN (PL die **Maler**)
painter

malerisch ADJECTIVE
picturesque

das **Mallorca** NOUN
Majorca

♦ **nach Mallorca** to Majorca

malnehmen VERB (PRESENT **nimmt mal**, IMPERFECT **nahm mal**, PERFECT **hat malgenommen**)
to multiply

das **Malz** NOUN (GEN des **Malzes**)
malt

die **Mama** NOUN (PL die **Mamas**)
mum

die **Mami** NOUN (PL die **Mamis**)
mummy

man PRONOUN
you ◊ *Man kann nie wissen.* You never know. ◊ *Wie schreibt man das?* How do you spell that?

♦ **man sagt,** ... they say ...

♦ **Man hat mir gesagt** ... I was told that ...

der **Manager** NOUN (PL die **Manager**)
manager

manche PRONOUN
some ◊ *Manche Bücher sind langweilig.* Some books are boring. ◊ *Manche Schüler meinen wohl, man müsste keine Hausaufgaben machen.* Some pupils seem to think they don't have to do any homework.

manchmal ADVERB
sometimes

die **Mandarine** NOUN
mandarin orange

die **Mandel** NOUN
[1] almond ◊ *ein Kuchen mit Nüssen und Mandeln* a cake with nuts and almonds
[2] tonsil ◊ *Sie hat entzündete Mandeln.* Her tonsils are inflamed.

die **Mandelentzündung** NOUN
tonsillitis

der **Mangel** NOUN (PL die **Mängel**)
[1] lack ◊ *Schlafmangel* lack of sleep
[2] shortage ◊ *Der Mangel an Arbeitsplätzen führt zu immer größerer Arbeitslosigkeit.* The shortage of jobs is causing rising unemployment.
[3] fault ◊ *Das Gerät weist mehrere Mängel auf.* The appliance has several faults.

mangelhaft ADJECTIVE
[1] poor ◊ *Wegen seiner schlechten Grammatikkenntnisse hat er mangelhaft bekommen.* He got a poor mark because of his bad grammar.

ⓘ *German marks range from one (**sehr gut**) to six (**ungenügend**).*

[2] faulty ◊ *Mangelhafte Waren kann man zurückgehen lassen.* You can return faulty goods.

mangels PREPOSITION

*The preposition **mangels** takes the genitive.*

for lack of ◊ *Er wurde mangels Beweisen freigesprochen.* He was acquitted for lack of evidence.

die **Manieren** PL NOUN
manners ◊ *Sie hat keine Manieren.* She doesn't have any manners.

der **Mann** NOUN (PL die **Männer**)
[1] man ◊ *Es war ein Mann am Telefon.* There was a man on the phone.
[2] husband ◊ *Frau Maier kam mit ihrem Mann.* Mrs Maier came with her husband.

♦ **seinen Mann stehen** to hold one's own

♦ **Alle Mann an Deck!** All hands on deck!

männlich ADJECTIVE
[1] male ◊ *meine männlichen Kollegen* my male colleagues

♦ **Eine männliche Person wurde am Tatort gesehen.** A man was seen at the scene of the crime.
[2] masculine ◊ *ein männliches Substantiv* a masculine noun

die **Mannschaft** NOUN
[1] team ◊ *die deutsche Mannschaft* the German team
[2] crew ◊ *der Kapitän und seine Mannschaft* the captain and his crew

der **Mantel** NOUN (PL die **Mäntel**)
coat ◊ *Er hatte einen Mantel an.* He was wearing a coat.

die **Mappe** NOUN
[1] briefcase
[2] folder

*Be careful! **Mappe** does not mean **map**.*

das **Märchen** NOUN (PL die **Märchen**)
fairy tale

die **Margarine** NOUN
margarine

der **Marienkäfer** NOUN (PL die **Marienkäfer**)
ladybird

die **Marine** NOUN
navy ◊ *Er ist bei der Marine.* He's in the navy.

die **Marionette** NOUN
  puppet

die **Mark** NOUN (PL die **Mark**)
  mark ◊ *Das kostet fünf Mark.* It costs five
  marks.

die **Marke** NOUN
  ⓵ brand ◊ *Für diese Marke sieht man in
  letzter Zeit viel Werbung.* There's been a
  lot of advertising for this brand recently.
  ⓶ make ◊ *Welche Marke fährt dein
  Vater?* What make of car does your
  father drive?
  ⓷ voucher
  ♦ **eine Briefmarke** a postage stamp

die **Markenkleidung** NOUN
  brand-name clothing

die **Markenware** NOUN
  branded goods

markieren VERB (PERFECT **hat markiert**)
  to mark ◊ *Sie hat die Stelle mit
  Leuchtstift markiert.* She marked the
  place with a highlighter.

das **Markstück** NOUN (PL die **Markstücke**)
  one-mark piece

der **Markt** NOUN (PL die **Märkte**)
  market

der **Marktplatz** NOUN (GEN des **Marktplatzes**, PL
  die **Marktplätze**)
  market place

die **Marmelade** NOUN
  jam ◊*Erdbeermarmelade* strawberry jam
  ♦ **Orangenmarmelade** marmalade

der **Marmor** NOUN (PL die **Marmore**)
  marble

der **März** NOUN (GEN des **März** or **Märzes**, PL die
  Märze)
  March ◊ *im März* in March ◊ *am dritten
  März* on the third of March ◊ *Ulm, den 3.
  März 2001* Ulm, 3 March 2001 ◊ *Heute ist
  der dritte März.*Today is the third of March.

das **Marzipan** NOUN (PL die **Marzipane**)
  marzipan

die **Masche** NOUN
  ⓵ mesh ◊ *Das Netz hatte feine Maschen.*
  The net had a very fine mesh.
  ⓶ stitch
  ♦ **Das ist die neueste Masche.** That's the
  latest thing.

die **Maschine** NOUN
  ⓵ machine ◊ *Werkzeug wird heutzutage
  von Maschinen hergestellt.* Nowadays
  tools are manufactured by machines.
  ◊ *Kannst du die schmutzige Wäsche bitte
  in die Maschine tun?* Can you put the
  dirty washing in the machine?
  ⓶ engine ◊ *Dieses Motorrad hat eine
  starke Maschine.* This motorbike has a
  powerful engine.
  ⓷ typewriter
  ⓸ plane

das **Maschinengewehr** NOUN (PL die
  Maschinengewehre)
  machine gun

die **Masern** PL NOUN
  measles ◊ *Masern sind bei Erwachsenen
  ziemlich gefährlich.* Measles is quite
  dangerous for adults.

die **Maske** NOUN
  mask

sich **maskieren** VERB (PERFECT **hat sich maskiert**)
  ⓵ to disguise oneself ◊ *Die Täter hatten
  sich maskiert.* The culprits had disguised
  themselves.
  ⓶ to dress up ◊ *Als was wirst du dich
  maskieren?* What are you dressing up
  as?
  ♦ **Die Bankräuber waren maskiert.** The
  bank robbers were masked.

das **Maß** NOUN (GEN des **Maßes**, PL die **Maße**)
  ⟦ see also **die Maß** NOUN ⟧
  ⓵ measure ◊ *In Deutschland werden
  metrische Maße verwendet.* Metric
  measures are used in Germany.
  ♦ **Wie sind die Maße des Zimmers?** What
  are the measurements of the room?
  ⓶ extent ◊ *Sie war zu einem hohen Maß
  selbst schuld.* To a large extent she had
  only herself to blame.
  ♦ **Maß halten** *see* **maßhalten**

die **Maß** NOUN (PL die **Maß**)
  ⟦ see also **das Maß** NOUN ⟧
  litre of beer

die **Massage** NOUN
  massage

die **Masse** NOUN
  mass

massenhaft ADJECTIVE
  masses of ◊ *Du hast massenhaft Fehler
  gemacht.* You've made masses of
  mistakes.

die **Massenmedien** NEUT PL NOUN
  mass media

maßhalten VERB (PRESENT **hält maß**, IMPERFECT
  hielt maß, PERFECT **hat maßgehalten**)
  to show moderation

massieren VERB (PERFECT **hat massiert**)
  to massage ◊ *Kannst du mir bitte den
  Rücken massieren?* Can you massage my
  back, please?

mäßig ADJECTIVE
  moderate

der **Maßkrug** NOUN (PL die **Maßkrüge**)
  tankard

die **Maßnahme** NOUN
  step ◊ *Maßnahmen ergreifen* to take
  steps

der **Maßstab** NOUN (PL die **Maßstäbe**)
  ⓵ standard ◊ *Dieses Gerät setzt neue
  Maßstäbe.* This appliance sets new
  standards.
  ⓶ scale ◊ *In welchem Maßstab ist diese
  Karte?* What's the scale of this map?

der **Mast** NOUN (PL die **Maste** or **Masten**)

☞

1 mast ◊ *Am Mast hing die britische Fahne.* The Union Jack was hanging from the mast.

2 pylon ◊ *Neben unserem Garten steht ein Hochspannungsmast.* There's a high-tension pylon beside our garden.

das **Material** NOUN (PL die **Materialien**)
material ◊ *Aus welchem Material ist das gemacht?* What material is it made of? ◊ *Ich sammle Material für mein Referat.* I'm collecting material for my assignment.

materialistisch ADJECTIVE
materialistic
♦ **materialistisch eingestellt sein** to be materialistic

die **Mathe** NOUN
maths

die **Mathematik** NOUN
mathematics ◊ *Mathematik ist mein Lieblingsfach.* Mathematics is my favourite subject.

mathematisch ADJECTIVE
mathematical

der **Matjeshering** NOUN (PL die **Matjesheringe**)
young herring

die **Matratze** NOUN
mattress

der **Matrose** NOUN (GEN des **Matrosen,** PL die **Matrosen**)
sailor

der **Matsch** NOUN
1 mud ◊ *Deine Schuhe sind voller Matsch.* Your shoes are covered in mud.
2 slush

matschig ADJECTIVE
1 muddy ◊ *Nach dem Regen war der Weg sehr matschig.* The path was very muddy after the rain.
2 slushy ◊ *Bei matschigem Schnee macht das Skifahren keinen Spaß.* Skiing isn't fun when the snow is slushy.

matt ADJECTIVE
1 weak ◊ *Bei der Hitze fühle ich mich so matt.* I feel so weak in this heat.
2 dull ◊ *Ihre Augen waren ganz matt.* Her eyes were really dull.
3 matt ◊ *Möchten Sie die Abzüge Hochglanz oder matt?* Would you like the prints glossy or matt?
4 mate ◊ *Schach und matt* checkmate

die **Matte** NOUN
mat

die **Mauer** NOUN
wall

das **Maul** NOUN (PL die **Mäuler**)
mouth ◊ *Die Katze hatte einen Vogel im Maul.* The cat had a bird in its mouth.
♦ **Halt's Maul!** Shut your face!

der **Maulkorb** NOUN (PL die **Maulkörbe**)
muzzle

der **Maulwurf** NOUN (PL die **Maulwürfe**)
mole

der **Maurer** NOUN (PL die **Maurer**)
bricklayer

die **Maus** NOUN (PL die **Mäuse**)
mouse ◊ *Sie hat Angst vor Mäusen.* She's afraid of mice. ◊ *Du musst zweimal mit der Maus klicken.* You have to click the mouse twice.

die **Mausefalle** NOUN
mousetrap

der **Mausklick** NOUN (PL die **Mausklicks**)
mouse click
♦ **per Mausklick** by clicking the mouse

maximal ADJECTIVE, ADVERB
1 maximum ◊ *der maximale Betrag* the maximum amount
2 at most ◊ *Wir können maximal eine Woche wegfahren.* We can go away for a week at most.

die **Mayonnaise** NOUN
mayonnaise

der **Mechaniker** NOUN (PL die **Mechaniker**)
mechanic

mechanisch ADJECTIVE, ADVERB
mechanical ◊ *Das Gerät hat einen mechanischen Schaden.* The appliance has a mechanical fault.
♦ **etwas mechanisch tun** to do something mechanically

der **Mechanismus** NOUN (GEN des **Mechanismus,** PL die **Mechanismen**)
mechanism

meckern VERB
to moan ◊ *Müsst ihr über alles meckern?* Do you have to moan about everything?

das **Mecklenburg-Vorpommern** NOUN
Mecklenburg-Western Pomerania

> **ⓘ** *Mecklenburg-Vorpommern is one of the 16 Länder. Its capital is Schwerin. It is Germany's most rural and thinly populated Land, and is becoming increasingly popular with tourists.*

die **Medaille** NOUN
medal

die **Medien** PL NOUN
media

das **Medikament** NOUN (PL die **Medikamente**)
drug ◊ *verschreibungspflichtige Medikamente* prescribed drugs

die **Medizin** NOUN
medicine

medizinisch ADJECTIVE
medical

das **Meer** NOUN (PL die **Meere**)
sea ◊ *Wir wohnen am Meer.* We live by the sea.

der **Meeresspiegel** NOUN
sea level

der **Meerrettich** NOUN
horseradish

das **Meerschweinchen** NOUN (PL die **Meerschweinchen**)
guinea pig

das **Mehl** NOUN (PL die **Mehle**)
flour

mehr ADJECTIVE, ADVERB
more

mehrdeutig ADJECTIVE
ambiguous

mehrere ADJECTIVE
several

mehreres PRONOUN
several things

mehrfach ADJECTIVE, ADVERB
[1] many ◊ *Das Gerät hat mehrfache Verwendungsmöglichkeiten.* This gadget has many uses.
[2] repeated ◊ *Es ist mir erst nach mehrfachen Versuchen gelungen.* I only managed after repeated attempts. ◊ *Ich habe mehrfach versucht, dich zu erreichen.* I've tried repeatedly to get hold of you.

die **Mehrfahrtenkarte** NOUN
multi-journey ticket

die **Mehrheit** NOUN
majority

mehrmalig ADJECTIVE
repeated

mehrmals ADVERB
repeatedly

die **Mehrwertsteuer** NOUN
value added tax

die **Mehrzahl** NOUN
[1] majority ◊ *Die Mehrzahl der Schüler besitzt einen Computer.* The majority of pupils have a computer.
[2] plural ◊ *Wie heißt die Mehrzahl von "woman"?* What's the plural of "woman"?

meiden VERB (IMPERFECT **mied**, PERFECT **hat gemieden**)
to avoid

die **Meile** NOUN
mile

mein ADJECTIVE, PRONOUN
[1] my ◊ *Mein Englischlehrer ist nett.* My English teacher's nice. ◊ *Meine Mutter erlaubt es nicht.* My mother won't allow it. ◊ *Ich finde mein Buch nicht.* I can't find my book. ◊ *Meine Eltern sind klasse.* My parents are great.
[2] mine ◊ *Das ist nicht mein Füller, meiner ist blau.* That's not my pen, mine's blue. ◊ *Seine Mutter heißt Anne, meine auch.* His mother's called Anne, so's mine. ◊ *Wenn dein Fahrrad kaputt ist, kannst du meins nehmen.* If your bike's broken you can use mine. ◊ *Sie hat schlechte Noten, aber meine sind auch nicht besser.* Her marks are bad but mine aren't any better.

meinen VERB

[1] to think ◊ *Ich meine, wir sollten jetzt gehen.* I think we should go now. ◊ *Was meint deine Mutter zu deinem Freund?* What does your mother think about your boyfriend? ◊ *Sollen wir sie zur Party einladen, was meinst du?* Should we invite her to the party, what do you think?
[2] to say ◊ *Unser Lehrer meint, wir sollten am Wochenende keine Aufgaben machen.* Our teacher says that we shouldn't do any homework at the weekend.
[3] to mean ◊ *Was meint er mit diesem Wort?* What does he mean by this word? ◊ *Ich verstehe nicht, was du meinst.* I don't understand what you mean. ◊ *So habe ich das nicht gemeint.* I didn't mean it like that.
♦ **Das will ich meinen!** I should think so.

meinetwegen ADVERB
[1] for my sake ◊ *Ihr müsst meinetwegen nicht auf euren Urlaub verzichten.* You don't have to do without your holiday for my sake.
[2] on my account ◊ *Hat er sich meinetwegen so aufgeregt?* Did he get so upset on my account?
[3] as far as I'm concerned ◊ *Meinetwegen kannst du gehen.* As far as I'm concerned you can go.
♦ **Kann ich das machen? – Meinetwegen.** Can I do that? – I don't mind.

die **Meinung** NOUN
opinion ◊ *Er hat mich nach meiner Meinung zu diesem Punkt gefragt.* He asked for my opinion on this subject.
♦ **meiner Meinung nach** in my opinion ◊ *Meiner Meinung nach sollten Kinder nicht so viel fernsehen.* In my opinion children shouldn't watch so much television.
♦ **Ganz meine Meinung!** I quite agree.
♦ **jemandem die Meinung sagen** to give somebody a piece of one's mind
Be careful! **Meinung** does not mean **meaning**.

die **Meinungsumfrage** NOUN
opinion poll

meist ADVERB
usually ◊ *Samstags bin ich meist zu Hause.* I'm usually at home on Saturdays.

meiste ADJECTIVE
most ◊ *Die meisten Bücher habe ich schon gelesen.* I've already read most of the books. ◊ *Hast du die Bücher alle gelesen? – Ja, die meisten.* Have you read all the books? – Yes, most of them. ◊ *Die meisten meinen, das sei einfach.* Most people think it's easy. ◊ *Die meisten von euch kennen dieses Wort sicher.* Most of you must know this word.

M

♦ **am meisten (1)** most ◊ *Darüber hat sie sich am meisten aufgeregt.* This upset her most.

♦ **am meisten (2)** the most ◊ *Er hat am meisten gewonnen.* He won the most.

meistens ADVERB
usually ◊ *Samstags bin ich meistens zu Hause.* I'm usually at home on Saturdays.

der **Meister** NOUN (PL die **Meister**)
1 champion ◊ *Er ist deutscher Meister im Ringen.* He's the German wrestling champion.
2 master craftsman ◊ *Der Meister bildet Lehrlinge aus.* The master craftsman trains apprentices.

die **Meisterschaft** NOUN
championship ◊ *Wer hat die Meisterschaft gewonnen?* Who won the championship?

melden VERB (PERFECT **hat gemeldet**)
to report ◊ *Er meldete den Diebstahl bei der Polizei.* He reported the theft to the police.

♦ **sich melden (1)** to answer (*phone*) ◊ *Es meldet sich niemand.* There's no answer.

♦ **sich melden (2)** to put one's hand up (*in school*)

♦ **sich polizeilich melden** to register with the police

die **Melodie** NOUN
tune

die **Melone** NOUN
1 melon
2 bowler hat ◊ *Er trug eine Melone.* He was wearing a bowler hat.

die **Menge** NOUN
1 quantity ◊ *etwas in großen Mengen bestellen* to order a large quantity of something
2 crowd ◊ *Ich habe ihn in der Menge verloren.* I lost him in the crowd.

♦ **eine Menge** a lot of ◊ *Du hast eine Menge Fehler gemacht.* You've made a lot of mistakes. ◊ *Hast du CDs? – Ja, eine Menge.* Have you got any CDs? – Yes, lots.

der **Mensch** NOUN (GEN des **Menschen,** PL die **Menschen**)
human being ◊ *Es heißt, dass sich der Mensch durch die Sprache vom Tier unterscheidet.* It's said that what distinguishes human beings from animals is language.

♦ **Wie viele Menschen sind schon glücklich?** How many people are happy?

♦ **kein Mensch** nobody

der **Menschenverstand** NOUN
♦ **gesunder Menschenverstand** common sense

die **Menschheit** NOUN
mankind

menschlich ADJECTIVE
human

die **Mentalität** NOUN
mentality

das **Menü** NOUN (PL die **Menüs**)
set meal

merken VERB
to notice ◊ *Hat sie gemerkt, dass ich gefehlt habe?* Did she notice that I wasn't there? ◊ *Ich habe den Fehler nicht gemerkt.* I didn't notice the mistake.

♦ **sich etwas merken** to remember something ◊ *Dieses Wort kann ich mir nie merken.* I can never remember that word.

♦ **Das werd' ich mir merken!** I won't forget that in a hurry!

merkwürdig ADJECTIVE
odd

♦ **sich merkwürdig benehmen** to behave strangely

die **Messe** NOUN
1 fair ◊ *Auf der Messe wurden die neuesten Modelle gezeigt.* The latest models were shown at the fair.
2 mass ◊ *Sie geht jeden Sonntag zur Messe.* She goes to mass every Sunday.

messen VERB (PRESENT **misst,** IMPERFECT **maß,** PERFECT **hat gemessen**)
to measure ◊ *Hast du die Länge gemessen?* Have you measured the length?

♦ **bei jemandem Fieber messen** to take somebody's temperature

♦ **Mit ihm kannst du dich nicht messen.** You're no match for him.

das **Messer** NOUN (PL die **Messer**)
knife

das **Messgerät** NOUN (PL die **Messgeräte**)
gauge

das **Messing** NOUN
brass

das **Metall** NOUN (PL die **Metalle**)
metal

der **Meter** NOUN (PL die **Meter**)
metre

das **Metermaß** NOUN (GEN des **Metermaßes,** PL die **Metermaße**)
tape measure

die **Methode** NOUN
method

der **Metzger** NOUN (PL die **Metzger**)
butcher ◊ *Er ist Metzger.* He's a butcher. ◊ *beim Metzger* at the butcher's

die **Metzgerei** NOUN
butcher's

miauen VERB
to miaow

mich PRONOUN
mich is the accusative of ich.
1 me ◊ *Er hat mich zu seiner Party eingeladen.* He's invited me to his party.

2 myself ◊ *Ich sehe mich im Spiegel.* I can see myself in the mirror.

die **Miene** NOUN
look
♦ **eine finstere Miene machen** to look grim

mies ADJECTIVE
lousy ◊ *Mir geht's mies.* I feel lousy.

die **Miete** NOUN
rent
♦ **zur Miete wohnen** to live in rented accommodation

mieten VERB
1 to rent

ℹ It is far more usual to live in rented accommodation in Germany than it is in Britain. Flats are mainly rented unfurnished.

◊ *Wir haben eine Ferienwohnung gemietet.* We've rented a holiday flat.
2 to hire ◊ *Man kann am Flughafen ein Auto mieten.* You can hire a car at the airport.

das **Mietshaus** NOUN (GEN des **Mietshauses**, PL die **Mietshäuser**)
block of rented flats

der **Mietvertrag** NOUN (PL die **Mietverträge**)
lease

der **Mietwagen** NOUN (PL die **Mietwagen**)
rental car

das **Mikrofon** NOUN (PL die **Mikrofone**)
microphone

das **Mikroskop** NOUN (PL die **Mikroskope**)
microscope

die **Mikrowelle** NOUN
microwave

der **Mikrowellenherd** NOUN (PL die **Mikrowellenherde**)
microwave oven

die **Milch** NOUN
milk

mild ADJECTIVE
1 mild ◊ *eine milde Seife* a mild soap ◊ *mildes Wetter* mild weather
2 lenient ◊ *ein mildes Urteil* a lenient sentence ◊ *ein milder Richter* a lenient judge

das **Militär** NOUN
army ◊ *zum Militär gehen* to join the army

militärisch ADJECTIVE
military

die **Milliarde** NOUN
billion

der **Millimeter** NOUN (PL die **Millimeter**)
millimetre

die **Million** NOUN
million

der **Millionär** NOUN (PL die **Millionäre**)
millionaire ◊ *Er ist Millionär.* He's a millionaire.

die **Minderheit** NOUN
minority ◊ *in der Minderheit sein* to be in the minority

minderjährig ADJECTIVE
underage ◊ *Sie ist noch minderjährig.* She's still underage.

der **Minderjährige** NOUN (GEN des/der
die **Minderjährigen**, PL die **Minderjährigen**)
minor ◊ *Minderjährige dürfen keinen Alkohol kaufen.* Minors are not allowed to buy alcohol.

minderwertig ADJECTIVE
inferior

das **Mindestalter** NOUN
minimum age

mindeste ADJECTIVE
♦ **das Mindeste** the least ◊ *Das ist das Mindeste, was du tun kannst.* That's the least you can do.
♦ **nicht im Mindesten** not in the least ◊ *Sie war nicht im Mindesten überrascht.* She wasn't in the least surprised.
♦ **zum Mindesten** at least ◊ *Zum Mindesten hättest du ja anrufen können.* You could at least have phoned.

mindestens ADVERB
at least

das **Mineral** NOUN (PL die **Minerale** or **Mineralien**)
mineral

das **Mineralwasser** NOUN (PL die **Mineralwasser**)
mineral water

das **Minirock** NOUN (PL die **Miniröcke**)
miniskirt

der **Minister** NOUN (PL die **Minister**)
minister (*in government*)

das **Ministerium** NOUN (PL die **Ministerien**)
ministry

minus ADVERB
minus

die **Minute** NOUN
minute

mir PRONOUN
mir is the dative of ich.
1 me ◊ *Kannst du mir sagen, wie spät es ist?* Can you tell me the time?
2 to me ◊ *Gib es mir!* Give it to me.
♦ **mir nichts, dir nichts** just like that ◊ *Sie war mir nichts, dir nichts verschwunden.* She disappeared just like that.

mischen VERB
to mix

die **Mischung** NOUN
mixture

miserabel ADJECTIVE
dreadful ◊ *Mir geht's miserabel.* I feel dreadful.

missbilligen VERB (PERFECT **hat missbilligt**)
to disapprove of

der **Missbrauch** NOUN
abuse

M

der **Misserfolg** NOUN (PL die **Misserfolge**)
  failure
misshandeln VERB (PERFECT **hat misshandelt**)
  to ill-treat
missmutig ADJECTIVE
  sullen
misstrauen VERB (PERFECT **hat misstraut**)
  see also das Misstrauen NOUN
  ◆**jemandem misstrauen** to mistrust somebody
das **Misstrauen** NOUN
  see also misstrauen VERB
  suspicion
misstrauisch ADJECTIVE
  suspicious
das **Missverständnis** NOUN (GEN des **Missverständnisses**, PL die **Missverständnisse**)
  misunderstanding
missverstehen VERB (IMPERFECT **missverstand**, PERFECT **hat missverstanden**)
  to misunderstand
der **Mist** NOUN
  1 manure ◊ *Im Frühling werden die Felder mit Mist gedüngt.* The fields are fertilized with manure in the spring.
  2 rubbish ◊ *Warum isst du so einen Mist?* Why do you eat such rubbish? ◊ *Heute kommt wieder nur Mist im Fernsehen.* There's nothing but rubbish on TV again today. ◊ *Du redest Mist.* You're talking rubbish.
  ◆**Mist!** Blast!
  Be careful! The German word Mist does not mean mist.
die **Mistel** NOUN
  mistletoe
mit PREPOSITION, ADVERB
  The preposition mit takes the dative.
  1 with ◊ *Er ist mit seiner Freundin gekommen.* He came with his girlfriend. ◊ *mit Filzstift geschrieben* written with a felt-tip pen
  2 by ◊ *mit dem Auto* by car ◊ *mit der Bahn* by train ◊ *mit dem Bus* by bus
  ◆**mit zehn Jahren** at the age of ten
  ◆**Sie ist mit die Beste in ihrer Klasse.** She is one of the best in her class.
  ◆**Wollen Sie mit?** Do you want to come along?
der **Mitarbeiter** NOUN (PL die **Mitarbeiter**)
  1 colleague ◊ *meine Mitarbeiter und ich* my colleagues and I
  2 collaborator ◊ *die Mitarbeiter an diesem Projekt* the collaborators on this project
  3 employee ◊ *Die Firma hat 500 Mitarbeiter.* The company has 500 employees.
mitbringen VERB (IMPERFECT **brachte mit**, PERFECT **hat mitgebracht**)
  to bring along ◊ *Kann ich meine Freundin mitbringen?* Can I bring my girlfriend along?
  ◆**Wir haben Tante Anita ein Geschenk mitgebracht.** We took a present for Aunt Anita.
miteinander ADVERB
  with each another
der **Mitesser** NOUN (PL die **Mitesser**)
  blackhead
mitfahren VERB (PRESENT **fährt mit**, IMPERFECT **fuhr mit**, PERFECT **ist mitgefahren**)
  ◆**Wir fahren nach Berlin. Willst du mitfahren?** We're going to Berlin. Do you want to come too?
  ◆**Die Klasse fährt nach England, aber ich fahre nicht mit.** The class are going to England but I'm not going with them.
  ◆**Willst du mit uns im Auto mitfahren?** Do you want a lift in our car?
mitgeben VERB (PRESENT **gibt mit**, IMPERFECT **gab mit**, PERFECT **hat mitgegeben**)
  to give
das **Mitglied** NOUN (PL die **Mitglieder**)
  member
die **Mitgliedschaft** NOUN
  membership
mithelfen VERB (PRESENT **hilft mit**, IMPERFECT **half mit**, PERFECT **hat mitgeholfen**)
  to help
mitkommen VERB (IMPERFECT **kam mit**, PERFECT **ist mitgekommen**)
  1 to come along ◊ *Willst du nicht mitkommen?* Wouldn't you like to come along?
  2 to keep up ◊ *In Mathe komme ich nicht mit.* I can't keep up in maths.
das **Mitleid** NOUN
  1 sympathy
  ◆**Ich habe wirklich Mitleid mit dir.** I really sympathize with you.
  2 pity ◊ *Er kennt kein Mitleid.* He knows no pity.
mitmachen VERB (PERFECT **hat mitgemacht**)
  to join in
mitnehmen VERB (PRESENT **nimmt mit**, IMPERFECT **nahm mit**, PERFECT **hat mitgenommen**)
  1 to take ◊ *Kannst du den Brief zur Post mitnehmen?* Can you take the letter to the post office? ◊ *Ich habe meine Freundin zur Party mitgenommen.* I took my girlfriend to the party.
  ◆**Die Polizei ist gekommen und hat ihn mitgenommen.** The police came and took him away.
  ◆**zum Mitnehmen** to take away
  2 to affect ◊ *Die Scheidung ihrer Eltern hat sie sehr mitgenommen.* Her parents' divorce really affected her.
der **Mitschüler** NOUN (PL die **Mitschüler**)
  schoolmate
die **Mitschülerin** NOUN

schoolmate

mitspielen VERB
to join in ◊ *Willst du nicht mitspielen?*
Don't you want to join in?
♦ **Wer hat bei dem Match mitgespielt?**
Who played in the match?

der **Mittag** NOUN (PL die **Mittage**)
midday ◊ *gegen Mittag* around midday
♦ **zu Mittag essen** to have lunch
♦ **heute Mittag** at lunchtime
♦ **morgen Mittag** tomorrow lunchtime
♦ **gestern Mittag** yesterday lunchtime

das **Mittagessen** NOUN (PL die **Mittagessen**)
lunch

mittags ADVERB
at lunchtime

die **Mittagspause** NOUN
lunch break

die **Mitte** NOUN
middle

mitteilen VERB
♦ **jemandem etwas mitteilen** to inform
somebody of something

die **Mitteilung** NOUN
communication

das **Mittel** NOUN (PL die **Mittel**)
means ◊ *Wir werden jedes Mittel
einsetzen, um die Genehmigung zu
bekommen.* We will use every means to
gain approval. ◊ *ein Mittel zum Zweck* a
means to an end ◊ *Sie griff zu ziemlich
unfairen Mitteln.* She used rather unfair
means.
♦ **ein Mittel gegen Husten** something for a
cough
♦ **ein Mittel gegen Flecken** a stain remover
♦ **öffentliche Mittel** public funds

das **Mittelalter** NOUN
Middle Ages ◊ *im Mittelalter* in the
Middle Ages

Mitteleuropa NEUT NOUN
Central Europe

mittelgroß ADJECTIVE
[1] medium-sized ◊ *Bremen ist eine
mittelgroße Stadt.* Bremen is a medium-
sized city.
[2] of medium height ◊ *Christine ist
mittelgroß.* Christine is of medium
height.

mittelmäßig ADJECTIVE
mediocre

das **Mittelmeer** NOUN
the Mediterranean

der **Mittelpunkt** NOUN (PL die **Mittelpunkte**)
centre

der **Mittelstürmer** NOUN (PL die **Mittelstürmer**)
centre-forward

die **Mittelwelle** NOUN
medium wave

mitten ADVERB
in the middle ◊ *mitten auf der Straße* in
the middle of the street ◊ *mitten am Tag*
in the middle of the day ◊ *mitten in der
Nacht* in the middle of the night

die **Mitternacht** NOUN
midnight ◊ *um Mitternacht* at midnight

mittlere ADJECTIVE
[1] middle ◊ *Das mittlere von den
Fahrrädern ist meins.* The bike in the
middle is mine. ◊ *Der mittlere Teil des
Buches ist langweilig.* The middle section
of the book is boring.
[2] average ◊ *Die mittleren Temperaturen
liegen bei zwanzig Grad.* The average
temperature is twenty degrees.
♦ **mittleren Alters** middle-aged ◊ *eine Frau
mittleren Alters* a middle-aged woman
♦ **mittlere Reife** O-levels

mittlerweile ADVERB
meanwhile

der **Mittwoch** NOUN (PL die **Mittwoche**)
Wednesday ◊ *am Mittwoch* on
Wednesday

mittwochs ADVERB
on Wednesdays

der **Mixer** NOUN (PL die **Mixer**)
mixer (*kitchen appliance*)

das **Mobbing** NOUN
workplace bullying

die **Möbel** NEUT PL NOUN
furniture

das **Möbelstück** NOUN (PL die **Möbelstücke**)
piece of furniture

der **Möbelwagen** NOUN (PL die **Möbelwagen**)
removal van

das **Mobiltelefon** NOUN (PL die **Mobiltelefone**)
mobile phone

möblieren VERB (PERFECT **hat möbliert**)
to furnish ◊ *Sie hat ihre Wohnung sehr
geschmackvoll möbliert.* She has
furnished her flat very tastefully.
♦ **möbliert wohnen** to live in furnished
accommodation

möchte VERB see **mögen**

die **Mode** NOUN
fashion

das **Modell** NOUN (PL die **Modelle**)
model

modern ADJECTIVE
modern

modernisieren VERB (PERFECT **hat
modernisiert**)
to modernize

modisch ADJECTIVE
fashionable ◊ *Jane trägt sehr modische
Kleidung.* Jane wears very fashionable
clothes.

das **Mofa** NOUN (PL die **Mofas**)
small moped

mogeln VERB
to cheat

mögen VERB (PRESENT **mag**, IMPERFECT **mochte**,
PERFECT **hat gemocht** or **mögen**)

M

☞

The past participle mögen is used when mögen is a modal auxiliary.

to like ◊ *Ich mag Süßes.* I like sweet things. ◊ *Ich habe sie noch nie gemocht.* I've never liked her.

♦ **Ich möchte ...** I'd like ... ◊ *Ich möchte ein Erdbeereis.* I'd like a strawberry ice cream. ◊ *Er möchte in die Stadt.* He'd like to go into town. ◊ *Möchtest du ...?* Would you like ...?

♦ **Ich möchte nicht, dass du ...** I wouldn't like you to ... ◊ *Ich möchte nicht, dass du dich übergangen fühlst.* I wouldn't like you to feel you were being ignored.

♦ **Ich mag nicht mehr.** I've had enough.

♦ **etwas tun mögen** to like to do something ◊ *Magst du noch mit zu mir kommen?* Would you like to come back to my place? ◊ *Möchtest du etwas essen?* Would you like something to eat?

♦ **etwas nicht tun mögen** not to want to do something ◊ *Sie mag nicht bleiben.* She doesn't want to stay. ◊ *Ich möchte nicht, dass du so spät nach Hause kommst.* I don't want you coming home so late.

möglich ADJECTIVE
possible ◊ *Das ist gar nicht möglich!* That's not possible. ◊ *so viel wie möglich* as much as possible

möglicherweise ADVERB
possibly

die **Möglichkeit** NOUN
possibility
♦ **nach Möglichkeit** if possible

möglichst ADVERB
as ... as possible ◊ *Komm möglichst bald.* Come as soon as possible.

die **Möhre** NOUN
carrot

der **Moment** NOUN (PL die **Momente**)
moment ◊ *Wir müssen den richtigen Moment abwarten.* We have to wait for the right moment.
♦ **im Moment** at the moment
♦ **Moment mal!** Just a moment.

momentan ADJECTIVE, ADVERB
[1] momentary ◊ *Das ist nur eine momentane Schwäche.* It's only a momentary weakness.
[2] at the moment ◊ *Ich bin momentan sehr beschäftigt.* I'm very busy at the moment.

die **Monarchie** NOUN
monarchy

der **Monat** NOUN (PL die **Monate**)
month

monatelang ADVERB
for months

monatlich ADJECTIVE, ADVERB
monthly

die **Monatskarte** NOUN
monthly ticket

der **Mond** NOUN (PL die **Monde**)
moon

der **Monitor** NOUN (PL die **Monitore**)
monitor

der **Montag** NOUN (PL die **Montage**)
Monday ◊ *am Montag* on Monday

montags ADVERB
on Mondays

das **Moor** NOUN (PL die **Moore**)
moor

das **Moped** NOUN (PL die **Mopeds**)
moped

die **Moral** NOUN
[1] morals ◊ *Sie hat keine Moral.* She hasn't any morals.
[2] moral ◊ *Und die Moral der Geschichte ist: ...* And the moral of the story is: ...

moralisch ADJECTIVE
moral

der **Mord** NOUN (PL die **Morde**)
murder

der **Mörder** NOUN (PL die **Mörder**)
murderer
Be careful! Mörder does not mean murder.

die **Mörderin** NOUN
murderer

morgen ADVERB
see also **der Morgen** NOUN
tomorrow
♦ **morgen früh** tomorrow morning
♦ **Bis morgen!** See you tomorrow!

der **Morgen** NOUN (PL die **Morgen**)
see also **morgen** ADVERB
morning ◊ *Wir haben den ganzen Morgen Unterricht.* We've got lessons all morning.
♦ **Guten Morgen!** Good morning.

morgens ADVERB
in the morning ◊ *Morgens bin ich immer müde.* I'm always tired in the morning.
♦ **von morgens bis abends** from morning to night

morgig ADJECTIVE
tomorrow's ◊ *das morgige Fest* tomorrow's party
♦ **der morgige Tag** tomorrow

die **Mosel** NOUN
Moselle

das **Motiv** NOUN (PL die **Motive**)
motive ◊ *Was war sein Motiv?* What was his motive?

die **Motivation** NOUN
motivation

motivieren VERB (PERFECT **hat motiviert**)
to motivate

der **Motor** NOUN (PL die **Motoren**)
[1] engine ◊ *Das Auto hat einen starken Motor.* The car has a powerful engine.
[2] motor ◊ *ein Außenbordmotor* an outboard motor

das **Motorboot** NOUN (PL die **Motorboote**)

motorboat

das **Motorrad** NOUN (PL die **Motorräder**)
motorcycle

der **Motorroller** NOUN (PL die **Motorroller**)
scooter

die **Möwe** NOUN
seagull

die **Mücke** NOUN
midge

der **Mückenstich** NOUN (PL die **Mückenstiche**)
midge bite

müde ADJECTIVE
tired ◊ *Ich bin sehr müde.* I'm very tired.

die **Müdigkeit** NOUN
tiredness

die **Mühe** NOUN
trouble ◊ *Das macht gar keine Mühe.*
That's no trouble.
♦ **mit Müh und Not** with great difficulty
♦ **sich Mühe geben** to go to a lot of trouble
◊ *Die Gastgeberin hat sich viele Mühe gegeben.* The hostess went to a lot of trouble.
♦ **Du solltest dir in Englisch mehr Mühe geben.** You should try harder in English.

die **Mühle** NOUN
mill ◊ *In dieser Mühle wird Korn gemahlen.* Corn is ground in this mill.
◊ *Hast du eine Mühle, um den Kaffee zu mahlen?* Do you have a coffee mill?

der **Müll** NOUN
refuse

die **Müllabfuhr** NOUN
[1] disposal of rubbish ◊ *Die Gebühren für die Müllabfuhr sollen erhöht werden.*
The charges for the disposal of rubbish are to be increased.
[2] dustmen ◊ *Morgen kommt die Müllabfuhr.* The dustmen come tomorrow.

der **Mülleimer** NOUN (PL die **Mülleimer**)
rubbish bin

die **Mülltonne** NOUN
dustbin

die **Müllverbrennungsanlage** NOUN
waste incineration plant

multiplizieren VERB (PERFECT **hat multipliziert**)
to multiply

der **Mumps** NOUN (GEN des **Mumps**)
mumps ◊ *Mumps ist sehr unangenehm.*
Mumps is very unpleasant.

München NEUT NOUN
Munich
♦ **nach München** to Munich

der **Mund** NOUN (PL die **Münder**)
mouth
♦ **Halt den Mund!** Shut up!

der **Mundgeruch** NOUN
bad breath ◊ *Sie hat Mundgeruch.* She has bad breath.

die **Mundharmonika** NOUN
mouth organ

mündlich ADJECTIVE
oral ◊ *eine mündliche Prüfung* an oral exam

die **Munition** NOUN
ammunition

das **Münster** NOUN (PL die **Münster**)
cathedral

munter ADJECTIVE
lively

die **Münze** NOUN
coin

der **Münzfernsprecher** NOUN (PL die **Münzfernsprecher**)
payphone

murmeln VERB
to mumble ◊ *Er murmelte irgendwas vor sich hin.* He mumbled something.

mürrisch ADJECTIVE
sullen

die **Muschel** NOUN
[1] mussel ◊ *Ich esse gern Muscheln.* I like mussels.
[2] shell ◊ *Wir haben am Strand Muscheln gesammelt.* We collected shells on the beach.
[3] receiver ◊ *Du musst in die Muschel sprechen.* You have to speak into the receiver.

das **Museum** NOUN (PL die **Museen**)
museum

die **Musik** NOUN
music

musikalisch ADJECTIVE
musical ◊ *musikalisch begabt sein* to be musically gifted

die **Musikbox** NOUN
jukebox

der **Musiker** NOUN (PL die **Musiker**)
musician

das **Musikinstrument** NOUN (PL die **Musikinstrumente**)
musical instrument

musizieren VERB (PERFECT **hat musiziert**)
to make music

der **Muskat** NOUN (PL die **Muskate**)
nutmeg

der **Muskel** NOUN (PL die **Muskeln**)
muscle

das **Müsli** NOUN (PL die **Müsli**)
muesli

müssen VERB (PRESENT **muss**, IMPERFECT **musste**, PERFECT **hat gemusst** or **müssen**)
The past participle müssen is used when müssen is a modal auxiliary.
must ◊ *Ich muss es tun.* I must do it. ◊ *Er hat gehen müssen.* He had to go.
♦ **Ich musste es tun.** I had to do it.
♦ **Er muss es nicht tun.** He doesn't have to do it.
♦ **Muss ich?** Do I have to?
♦ **Muss das sein?** Is that really necessary?

M

- **Das hättest du nicht tun müssen.** You needn't have done that.
- **Es muss nicht wahr sein.** It needn't be true.
- **Sie hätten ihn fragen müssen.** You should have asked him.
- **Es muss geregnet haben.** It must have rained.
- **Ich muss mal.** I need the loo.

das **Muster** NOUN (PL die **Muster**)

1 pattern ◊ *ein Kleid mit einem geometrischen Muster* a dress with a geometric pattern

2 sample ◊ *Lass dir von dem Stoff doch ein Muster geben.* Ask them to give you a sample of the material.

der **Mut** NOUN

courage

- **Nur Mut!** Cheer up!
- **jemandem Mut machen** to encourage somebody

- **zu Mute** *see* **zumute**

mutig ADJECTIVE

courageous

die **Mutter (1)** NOUN (PL die **Mütter**)

mother ◊ *Meine Mutter erlaubt das nicht.* My mother doesn't allow that.

die **Mutter (2)** NOUN (PL die **Muttern**)

nut ◊ *Hast du die Mutter zu dieser Schraube gesehen?* Have you seen the nut for this bolt?

die **Muttersprache** NOUN

mother tongue

der **Muttertag** NOUN (PL die **Muttertage**)

Mother's Day

die **Mutti** NOUN (PL die **Muttis**)

mummy

die **Mütze** NOUN

cap

MwSt ABBREVIATION (= *Mehrwertsteuer*)

VAT (= value added tax)

N

na EXCLAMATION
well ◊ *Na, kommst du mit?* Well, are you coming?
♦ **Na gut.** Okay then.
♦ **Na ja, ...** Well, ...

der **Nabel** NOUN (PL die **Nabel**)
navel

nach PREPOSITION, ADVERB
The preposition **nach** *takes the dative.*
[1] to ◊ *nach Berlin* to Berlin ◊ *nach Italien* to Italy
♦ **nach Süden** south
♦ **nach links** left
♦ **nach rechts** right
♦ **nach oben** up
♦ **nach hinten** back
[2] after ◊ *Ich fange nach Weihnachten damit an.* I'll start on it after Christmas. ◊ *die nächste Straße nach der Kreuzung* the first street after the crossroads ◊ *einer nach dem anderen* one after the other ◊ *Nach Ihnen!* After you!
♦ **Ihm nach!** After him!
♦ **zehn nach drei** ten past three
[3] according to ◊ *Nach unserer Englischlehrerin wird das so geschrieben.* According to our English teacher, that's how it's spelt.
♦ **nach und nach** little by little
♦ **nach wie vor** still

nachahmen VERB (PERFECT **hat nachgeahmt**)
to imitate

der **Nachbar** NOUN (GEN des **Nachbarn**, PL die **Nachbarn**)
neighbour

die **Nachbarin** NOUN
neighbour

die **Nachbarschaft** NOUN
neighbourhood

nachdem CONJUNCTION
[1] after ◊ *Nachdem er gegangen war, haben wir Witze erzählt.* After he left we told jokes.
[2] since ◊ *Nachdem du sowieso zur Post gehst, könntest du mein Päckchen aufgeben?* Since you're going to the post office anyway, could you post my parcel?
♦ **je nachdem** it depends ◊ *Du kommst doch auch mit? – Je nachdem.* You're coming along too, aren't you? – It depends.
♦ **je nachdem, ob** depending on whether ◊ *Wir kommen mit dem Rad oder dem Auto, je nachdem, ob es regnet oder nicht.* We'll be coming by bike or by car, depending on whether it rains or not.

nachdenken VERB (IMPERFECT **dachte nach**, PERFECT **hat nachgedacht**)

♦ **nachdenken über** to think about ◊ *Ich habe über deine Frage nachgedacht.* I've been thinking about your question.

nachdenklich ADJECTIVE
pensive

nacheinander ADVERB
one after the other

nachgeben VERB (PRESENT **gibt nach**, IMPERFECT **gab nach**, PERFECT **hat nachgegeben**)
[1] to give way ◊ *Das Brett hat nachgegeben.* The plank gave way.
[2] to give in ◊ *Ich werde nicht nachgeben.* I won't give in.

nachgehen VERB (IMPERFECT **ging nach**, PERFECT **ist nachgegangen**)
♦ **jemandem nachgehen** to follow somebody
♦ **einer Sache nachgehen** to look into something ◊ *Wir werden Ihrer Beschwerde nachgehen.* We will look into your complaint.
♦ **Die Uhr geht nach.** The clock is slow.

nachgiebig ADJECTIVE
indulgent

nachher ADVERB
afterwards

die **Nachhilfestunde** NOUN
private lesson

der **Nachhilfeunterricht** NOUN
extra tuition

nachholen VERB (PERFECT **hat nachgeholt**)
[1] to catch up on ◊ *Weil er gefehlt hat, muss er jetzt viel nachholen.* As he was absent, he's got a lot to catch up on.
[2] to make up for ◊ *Wir konnten meinen Geburtstag nicht feiern, werden das aber nachholen.* We weren't able to celebrate my birthday, but we'll make up for it.
♦ **eine Prüfung nachholen** to do an exam at a later date

nachkommen VERB (IMPERFECT **kam nach**, PERFECT **ist nachgekommen**)
to come later ◊ *Wir gehen schon mal, du kannst ja später nachkommen.* We'll go on and you can come later.
♦ **einer Verpflichtung nachkommen** to fulfil an obligation

nachlassen VERB (PRESENT **lässt nach**, IMPERFECT **ließ nach**, PERFECT **hat nachgelassen**)
[1] to deteriorate ◊ *Seine Leistungen haben merklich nachgelassen.* His marks have deteriorated considerably.
♦ **Ihr Gedächtnis lässt nach.** Her memory is going.
♦ **Er hat nachgelassen.** He's got worse.

☞

2 to ease off ◊ *Die Schmerzen haben nachgelassen.* The pain has eased off.

3 to die down ◊ *sobald der Sturm nachlässt* as soon as the storm dies down

♦ **Der Händler hat mir zwanzig Euro nachgelassen.** The salesman gave me twenty euros off.

nachlässig ADJECTIVE
careless

♦ **etwas nachlässig machen** to do something carelessly ◊ *Sie macht ihre Hausaufgaben ziemlich nachlässig.* She does her homework pretty carelessly.

nachlaufen VERB (PRESENT **läuft nach**, IMPERFECT **lief nach**, PERFECT **ist nachgelaufen**)

♦ **jemandem nachlaufen** to run after somebody ◊ *Sie hat ihren Schirm vergessen, lauf ihr schnell nach.* She's forgotten her umbrella. Quick, run after her.

to chase ◊ *Er läuft allen Mädchen nach.* He chases all the girls.

nachmachen VERB (PERFECT **hat nachgemacht**)

1 to copy ◊ *Macht alle meine Bewegungen nach.* Copy all my movements.

2 to imitate ◊ *Sie kann unsere Mathelehrerin gut nachmachen.* She's good at imitating our maths teacher.

3 to forge ◊ *ein Gemälde nachmachen* to forge a painting

♦ **Das ist nicht echt, sondern nachgemacht.** This isn't genuine, it's a fake.

der **Nachmittag** NOUN (PL die **Nachmittage**)
afternoon ◊ *am Nachmittag* in the afternoon

♦ **heute Nachmittag** this afternoon

nachmittags ADVERB
in the afternoon

der **Nachname** NOUN (GEN des **Nachnamens**, PL die **Nachnamen**)
surname ◊ *Wie heißt du mit Nachnamen?* What's your surname?

nachprüfen VERB (PERFECT **hat nachgeprüft**)
to check ◊ *nachprüfen, ob* to check whether

die **Nachricht** NOUN

1 news ◊ *Wir haben noch keine Nachricht von ihr.* We still haven't had any news of her.

♦ **die Nachrichten** the news ◊ *Was kommt in den Nachrichten?* What's on the news?

2 message ◊ *Kannst du ihm eine Nachricht von mir übermitteln?* Can you give him a message from me?

nachschicken VERB (PERFECT **hat nachgeschickt**)
to forward

nachschlagen VERB (PRESENT **schlägt nach**, IMPERFECT **schlug nach**, PERFECT **hat nachgeschlagen**)

to look up (*in dictionary*)

nachsehen VERB (PRESENT **sieht nach**, IMPERFECT **sah nach**, PERFECT **hat nachgesehen**)

to check ◊ *Sieh mal nach, ob noch genügend Brot da ist.* Check whether we've still got enough bread. ◊ *Ich habe im Wörterbuch nachgesehen.* I've checked in the dictionary. ◊ *Mein Vater sieht immer meine Englischaufgaben nach.* My father always checks my English homework.

♦ **jemandem etwas nachsehen** to forgive somebody something ◊ *Den kleinen Fehler sollten wir ihm nachsehen.* We ought to forgive him this little mistake.

♦ **das Nachsehen haben** to come off worst

nachsenden VERB (IMPERFECT **sendete** or **sandte nach**, PERFECT **hat nachgesendet** or **nachgesandt**)

to send on ◊ *Ich habe ihr den Brief nachgesendet.* I've sent the letter on to her.

nachsichtig ADJECTIVE
lenient

nachsitzen VERB (IMPERFECT **saß nach**, PERFECT **hat nachgesessen**)

♦ **nachsitzen müssen** to be kept in ◊ *Er musste nachsitzen, weil er seine Hausaufgaben vergessen hatte.* He was kept in because he had forgotten to do his homework.

die **Nachspeise** NOUN
pudding ◊ *Was gibt's als Nachspeise?* What's for pudding?

nachsprechen VERB (PRESENT **spricht nach**, IMPERFECT **sprach nach**, PERFECT **hat nachgesprochen**)

♦ **jemandem nachsprechen** to repeat after somebody ◊ *Ich sage es vor, und ihr sprecht nach.* I'll say it, and you repeat after me. ◊ *Sie spricht ihrem Vater alles nach.* She repeats everything her father says.

nächste ADJECTIVE
see also **nahe**, **näher**

1 next ◊ *Wir nehmen den nächsten Zug.* We'll take the next train. ◊ *Beim nächsten Mal passt du besser auf.* Be more careful next time. ◊ *nächstes Jahr* next year

♦ **als Nächstes** next ◊ *Was machen wir als Nächstes?* What'll we do next?

♦ **Der Nächste bitte!** Next, please!

2 nearest ◊ *Wo ist hier die nächste Post?* Where's the nearest post office?

♦ **Das ist der nächste Weg.** That's the shortest way.

die **Nacht** NOUN (PL die **Nächte**)
night

♦ **Gute Nacht!** Good night.

der **Nachteil** NOUN (PL die **Nachteile**)
disadvantage

das **Nachthemd** NOUN (PL die **Nachthemden**)
nightshirt

die **Nachtigall** NOUN
nightingale

der **Nachtisch** NOUN
pudding ◊ *Was gibt's zum Nachtisch?*
What's for pudding?

der **Nachtklub** NOUN (PL die **Nachtklubs**)
night club

das **Nachtleben** NOUN
nightlife

nächtlich ADJECTIVE
nightly

nachträglich ADJECTIVE, ADVERB
[1] subsequent ◊ *eine nachträgliche
Korrektur* a subsequent correction
♦**nachträgliche Glückwünsche** belated
best wishes
[2] later ◊ *Nachträglich habe ich
eingesehen, dass das ein Fehler war.* I
later realized that it was a mistake.

die **Nachtruhe** NOUN
sleep ◊ *Ich brauche meine Nachtruhe.* I
need my sleep.

nachts ADVERB
at night

der **Nacken** NOUN (PL die **Nacken**)
nape of the neck

nackt ADJECTIVE
naked ◊ *Er war nackt.* He was naked.
♦**nackte Arme** bare arms
♦**nackte Tatsachen** plain facts

die **Nadel** NOUN
[1] needle ◊ *Ich brauche Nadel und
Faden.* I need a needle and thread.
[2] pin ◊ *Ich habe mich an der Nadel des
Ansteckers gestochen.* I've pricked
myself on the pin of my badge.

der **Nagel** NOUN (PL die **Nägel**)
nail

die **Nagelbürste** NOUN
nailbrush

die **Nagelfeile** NOUN
nailfile

der **Nagellack** NOUN (PL die **Nagellacke**)
nail varnish

nagelneu ADJECTIVE
brand-new

die **Nagelschere** NOUN
nail scissors ◊ *eine Nagelschere* a pair
of nail scissors

nagen VERB
to gnaw ◊ *an etwas nagen* to gnaw on
something

das **Nagetier** NOUN (PL die **Nagetiere**)
rodent

nahe ADJECTIVE, ADVERB, PREPOSITION
see also **näher**, **nächste**
[1] near ◊ *in der nahen Zukunft* in the
near future
♦**nahe bei** near ◊ *nahe bei der Kirche* near
the church

[2] close ◊ *Der Bahnhof ist ganz nah.* The
station's quite close. ◊ *nahe Verwandte*
close relatives ◊ *nahe Freunde* close
friends ◊ *Unser Haus ist nahe der
Universität.* Our house is close to the
university. ◊ *den Tränen nahe* close to tears.
♦**mit jemandem nah verwandt sein** to be
closely related to somebody
♦**der Nahe Osten** the Middle East
♦**Die Prüfungen rücken näher.** The exams
are getting closer.
♦**nahe daran sein, etwas zu tun** to be
close to doing something ◊ *Ich war nahe
daran aufzugeben.* I was close to giving
up.
♦**nahe liegend** see **naheliegend**

die **Nähe** NOUN
♦**in der Nähe** near ◊ *Unsere Schule liegt in
der Nähe des Bahnhofs.* Our school is
near the station. ◊ *Ich wohne in der Nähe
von Rostock.* I live near Rostock.
♦**aus der Nähe** close up ◊ *wenn man das
aus der Nähe betrachtet* if you look at it
close up

nahelegen VERB
♦**jemandem etwas nahelegen** to suggest
something to somebody

naheliegend ADJECTIVE
obvious

nähen VERB
to sew

näher ADJECTIVE, ADVERB
see also **nahe**, **nächste**
[1] nearer ◊ *Die Straßenbahnhaltestelle
ist näher als die Bushaltestelle.* The tram
stop is nearer than the bus stop.
[2] more detailed ◊ *Nähere Auskünfte
erteilt Ihnen unser Informationsdienst.*
Our information service will give you
more detailed information.
♦**Näheres** details ◊ *Ich wüsste gern
Näheres.* I'd like to have more details.
♦**näher kommen** to get closer

sich **nähern** VERB
to get closer ◊ *Wir näherten uns dem
Bahnhof.* We were approaching the
station.

nahezu ADVERB
nearly

nahm VERB see **nehmen**

die **Nähmaschine** NOUN
sewing machine

die **Nähnadel** NOUN
needle

nahrhaft ADJECTIVE
nourishing

die **Nahrung** NOUN
food ◊ *feste Nahrung* solid food

das **Nahrungsmittel** NOUN (PL die
Nahrungsmittel)
foodstuffs

die **Naht** NOUN (PL die **Nähte**)

N

seam ◊ *Die Hose ist an der Naht geplatzt.* The trousers have split along the seam.

der **Nahverkehr** NOUN
local traffic

der **Nahverkehrszug** NOUN (PL die **Nahverkehrszüge**)
local train

der **Name** NOUN (GEN des **Namens**, PL die **Namen**)
name ◊ *Mein Name ist ...* My name is ...
♦ **im Namen von** on behalf of

der **Namenstag** NOUN (PL die **Namenstage**)
name day

nämlich ADVERB
[1] you see ◊ *Sie ist nämlich meine beste Freundin.* You see, she's my best friend.
[2] that is to say ◊ *Nächstes Jahr, nämlich im März ...* Next year, that is to say in March ...
♦ **Ich kann nicht kommen, ich bin nämlich krank.** I can't come, I'm ill.

nannte VERB *see* **nennen**

nanu EXCLAMATION
well, well!

die **Narbe** NOUN
scar

die **Narkose** NOUN
anaesthetic

naschen VERB
♦ **Sie nascht gern.** She's got a sweet tooth.
♦ **Wer hat von der Torte genascht?** Who's been at the cake?

die **Nase** NOUN
nose ◊ *Meine Nase blutet.* My nose is bleeding.

das **Nasenbluten** NOUN
nosebleed ◊ *Ich hatte Nasenbluten.* I had a nosebleed.

nass ADJECTIVE
wet ◊ *Nach dem Regen war die Wäsche noch nässer.* After the rain, the washing was even wetter.

die **Nässe** NOUN
wetness

die **Nation** NOUN
nation

die **Nationalhymne** NOUN
national anthem

die **Nationalität** NOUN
nationality

die **Natur** NOUN
[1] country ◊ *Wir gehen gern in der Natur spazieren.* We like to go for a walk in the country.
[2] constitution ◊ *Sie hat eine robuste Natur.* She's got a strong constitution.

natürlich ADJECTIVE, ADVERB
[1] natural ◊ *Das ist ihre natürliche Haarfarbe.* That's her natural hair colour.
[2] of course ◊ *Wir kommen natürlich.* Of course we'll come. ◊ *Sie hat das*
natürlich wieder vergessen. She's forgotten it again, of course. ◊ *Ja, natürlich!* Yes, of course.

das **Naturschutzgebiet** NOUN (PL die **Naturschutzgebiete**)
nature reserve

der **Naturschutzpark** NOUN (PL die **Naturschutzparks**)
national park

die **Naturwissenschaft** NOUN
natural science

der **Naturwissenschaftler** NOUN (PL die **Naturwissenschaftler**)
scientist

der **Nazi** NOUN (PL die **Nazis**)
Nazi ◊ *Sie ist ein Nazi.* She's a Nazi.

der **Nebel** NOUN (PL die **Nebel**)
[1] mist
[2] fog

nebelig ADJECTIVE
[1] misty
[2] foggy

neben PREPOSITION

Use the accusative to express movement or a change of place. Use the dative when there is no change of place.

[1] next to ◊ *Dein Rad steht neben meinem.* Your bike's next to mine. ◊ *Stell dein Rad neben meines.* Put your bike next to mine.
[2] apart from

neben takes the dative in this sense.
◊ *Neben den Sehenswürdigkeiten haben wir uns auch ein Theaterstück angesehen.* Apart from the sights, we also saw a play.

nebenan ADVERB
next door

nebenbei ADVERB
[1] at the same time ◊ *Ich kann nicht Hausaufgaben machen und nebenbei fernsehen.* I can't do my homework and watch TV at the same time.
[2] on the side ◊ *Sie hat nebenbei noch einen anderen Job.* She has another job on the side.
♦ **Sie sagte ganz nebenbei, dass sie nicht mitkommen wollte.** She mentioned quite casually that she didn't want to come along.
♦ **Nebenbei bemerkt, ...** Incidentally, ...

nebenberuflich ADVERB
as a second job ◊ *Er ist nebenberuflich als Gärtner tätig.* He has a second job as a gardener.

nebeneinander ADVERB
side by side

das **Nebenfach** NOUN (PL die **Nebenfächer**)
subsidiary subject

der **Nebenfluss** NOUN (GEN des **Nebenflusses**, PL die **Nebenflüsse**)
tributary

nebenher ADVERB
1 on the side ◇ *Er verdient nebenher noch Geld durch Zeitungaustragen.* He also earns money on the side doing a paper round.
2 at the same time ◇ *Sie bügelt und sieht nebenher fern.* She does the ironing and watches TV at the same time.
3 alongside ◇ *Wir sind mit dem Rad gefahren, der Hund lief nebenher.* We rode our bikes and the dog ran alongside.

die **Nebenstraße** NOUN
side street

neblig ADJECTIVE
1 misty
2 foggy

nee ADVERB
no

der **Neffe** NOUN (GEN des **Neffen,** PL die **Neffen**)
nephew

negativ ADJECTIVE
see also **das Negativ** NOUN
negative ◇ *HIV-negativ* HIV-negative

das **Negativ** NOUN (PL die **Negative**)
see also **negativ** ADJECTIVE
negative ◇ *Kann ich von den Bildern das Negativ haben?* Can I have the negatives of these pictures?

nehmen VERB (PRESENT **nimmt,** IMPERFECT **nahm,** PERFECT **hat genommen**)
to take ◇ *Sie nahm fünf Euro aus dem Geldbeutel.* She took five euros out of her purse. ◇ *Wir nehmen besser den Bus in die Stadt.* We'd better take the bus into town. ◇ *Hast du deine Medizin genommen?* Have you taken your medicine? ◇ *Nimm ihn nicht ernst!* Don't take him seriously.
♦ **Ich nehme ein Erdbeereis.** I'll have a strawberry ice cream.
♦ **Nimm dir doch bitte!** Please help yourself.
♦ **Wir haben eine Kleinigkeit zu uns genommen.** We had a bite to eat.

der **Neid** NOUN
envy

neidisch ADJECTIVE
envious ◇ *Sie ist neidisch auf ihren Bruder.* She's envious of her brother.

nein ADVERB
no ◇ *Hast du das gesehen? – Nein.* Did you see that? – No, I didn't.
♦ **Ich glaube nein.** I don't think so.

die **Nektarine** NOUN
nectarine

die **Nelke** NOUN
1 carnation ◇ *Er brachte mir einen Strauß Nelken.* He brought me a bunch of carnations.
2 clove ◇ *Zum Glühwein braucht man Nelken.* You need cloves to make mulled wine.

nennen VERB (IMPERFECT **nannte,** PERFECT **hat genannt**)
1 to call ◇ *Sie haben ihren Sohn Manfred genannt.* They called their son Manfred. ◇ *Die Band nennt sich "Die Zerstörer".* The band call themselves "The Destroyers". ◇ *Wie nennt man ...?* What do you call ...?
2 to name ◇ *Kannst du mir einen Fluss in England nennen?* Can you name a river in England?

das **Neonlicht** NOUN
neon light

die **Neonröhre** NOUN
strip light

der **Nerv** NOUN (PL die **Nerven**)
nerve
♦ **jemandem auf die Nerven gehen** to get on somebody's nerves

die **Nervensäge** NOUN
pain in the neck

der **Nervenzusammenbruch** NOUN (PL die **Nervenzusammenbrüche**)
nervous breakdown

nervös ADJECTIVE
nervous

die **Nervosität** NOUN
nervousness

das **Nest** NOUN (PL die **Nester**)
1 nest ◇ *Der Vogel hat ein Nest gebaut.* The bird has built a nest.
2 dump ◇ *Wiblingen ist ein Nest.* Wiblingen is a dump.

nett ADJECTIVE
1 lovely ◇ *Vielen Dank für den netten Abend.* Thanks for a lovely evening.
2 nice ◇ *Wir haben uns nett unterhalten.* We had a nice talk.
3 kind ◇ *Wären Sie vielleicht so nett, mir zu helfen?* Would you be so kind as to help me? ◇ *Das war sehr nett von dir.* That was very kind of you.
♦ **Er war ganz nett frech.** He was pretty damn cheeky.

netto ADVERB
net ◇ *Sie verdient dreitausend Euro netto.* She earns three thousand euros net.

das **Netz** NOUN (GEN des **Netzes,** PL die **Netze**)
1 net ◇ *Die Fischer werfen ihre Netze aus.* The fishermen cast their nets. ◇ *Der Ball ging ins Netz.* The ball went into the net.
2 string bag ◇ *Sie packte die Einkäufe ins Netz.* She packed her shopping into a string bag.
3 network ◇ *ein weitverzweigtes Netz an Rohren* an extensive network of pipes ◇ *einen Computer ans Netz anschließen* to connect a computer to the network

neu ADJECTIVE

new ◊ *Ist der Pulli neu?* Is that pullover new? ◊ *Sie hat einen neuen Freund.* She's got a new boyfriend. ◊ *Ich bin neu hier.* I'm new here.

◆ **neue Sprachen** modern languages
◆ **neueste** latest ◊ *die neuesten Nachrichten* the latest news
◆ **seit Neuestem** recently
◆ **neu schreiben** to rewrite
◆ **Das ist mir neu!** That's news to me.

neuartig ADJECTIVE

new kind of ◊ *ein neuartiges Wörterbuch* a new kind of dictionary

die **Neugier** NOUN

curiosity

neugierig ADJECTIVE

curious

die **Neuheit** NOUN

1 new product ◊ *Auf der Messe werden alle Neuheiten vorgestellt.* All new products are presented at the trade fair.
2 newness ◊ *Ich muss mich erst auf die Neuheit dieser Situation einstellen.* I've still got to get used to the newness of the situation.

die **Neuigkeit** NOUN

news ◊ *Gibt es irgendwelche Neuigkeiten?* Is there any news?

das **Neujahr** NOUN

New Year

der **Neujahrstag** NOUN (PL die **Neujahrstage**)

New Year's Day

neulich ADVERB

the other day

neun NUMBER

nine

neunte ADJECTIVE

ninth ◊ *Heute ist der neunte Juni.* Today is the ninth of June.

neunzehn NUMBER

nineteen

neunzig NUMBER

ninety

neurotisch ADJECTIVE

neurotic

Neuseeland NEUT NOUN

New Zealand

◆ **aus Neuseeland** from New Zealand
◆ **nach Neuseeland** to New Zealand

der **Neuseeländer** NOUN (PL die **Neuseeländer**)

New Zealander

die **Neuseeländerin** NOUN

New Zealander

neutral ADJECTIVE

neutral

das **Neutrum** NOUN (PL die **Neutra** or **Neutren**)

neuter

nicht ADVERB

not ◊ *Ich bin nicht müde.* I'm not tired. ◊ *Er ist es nicht.* It's not him.
◆ **Er raucht nicht. (1)** He isn't smoking.

◆ **Er raucht nicht. (2)** He doesn't smoke.
◆ **Ich kann das nicht – Ich auch nicht.** I can't do it – Neither can I.
◆ **Es regnet nicht mehr.** It's not raining any more.
◆ **Nicht!** Don't!
◆ **Nicht berühren!** Do not touch!
◆ **Du bist müde, nicht wahr?** You're tired, aren't you?
◆ **Das ist schön, nicht wahr?** It's nice, isn't it?
◆ **Was du nicht sagst!** You don't say!

die **Nichte** NOUN

niece

der **Nichtraucher** NOUN (PL die **Nichtraucher**)

nonsmoker

nichts PRONOUN

nothing ◊ *nichts zu verzollen* nothing to declare ◊ *nichts Neues* nothing new
◆ **Ich habe nichts gesagt.** I didn't say anything.
◆ **Nichts ist so wie früher.** Things aren't what they used to be.
◆ **Das macht nichts.** It doesn't matter.
◆ **für nichts und wieder nichts** for nothing

der **Nichtschwimmer** NOUN (PL die **Nichtschwimmer**)

nonswimmer

nicken VERB

to nod

nie ADVERB

never ◊ *Das habe ich nie gesagt.* I never said that. ◊ *Das werde ich nie vergessen.* I'll never forget that. ◊ *Das habe ich noch nie gehört.* I've never heard that. ◊ *Ich war noch nie in Indien.* I've never been to India.
◆ **nie wieder** never again ◊ *Tu das nie wieder.* Don't ever do that again.
◆ **nie mehr** never again ◊ *Sie hat nie mehr geschrieben.* She never wrote to me again.
◆ **nie und nimmer** no way ◊ *Das kann nie und nimmer stimmen.* There's no way that can be right.

nieder ADJECTIVE, ADVERB

1 low ◊ *ein niederer Rang* a low rank
◆ **ein niederer Beamter** a low-ranking government officer
2 base ◊ *niedere Instinkte* base instincts
◆ **Nieder mit ...!** Down with ...! ◊ *Nieder mit dem Diktator!* Down with the dictator!

niedergeschlagen ADJECTIVE

dejected

die **Niederlage** NOUN

defeat

die **Niederlande** NEUT PL NOUN

the Netherlands
◆ **aus den Niederlanden** from the Netherlands
◆ **in den Niederlanden** in the Netherlands
◆ **in die Niederlande** to the Netherlands

der **Niederländer** NOUN (PL die **Niederländer**)
Dutchman
♦ **Er ist Niederländer.** He's Dutch.

die **Niederländerin** NOUN
Dutchwoman
♦ **Sie ist Niederländerin.** She's Dutch.

niederländisch ADJECTIVE
Dutch

Niedersachsen NEUT NOUN
Lower Saxony

> ⓘ *Niedersachsen is one of the 16 Länder. Its capital is Hannover. Its most important industries are mining and car manufacturing (Volkswagen). The Hannover Industrial Fair is the largest in the world.*

der **Niederschlag** NOUN (PL die **Niederschläge**)
precipitation
♦ **heftige Niederschläge** heavy rain
♦ **radioaktiver Niederschlag** radioactive fallout

niedlich ADJECTIVE
sweet ◊ *niedlich aussehen* to look sweet

niedrig ADJECTIVE
1 low ◊ *Die Decke ist sehr niedrig.* The ceiling is very low. ◊ *niedrige Temperaturen* low temperatures
2 shallow ◊ *Hier ist der Fluss niedriger.* The river is shallower here.
3 base ◊ *niedrige Motive* base motives

niemals ADVERB
never

niemand PRONOUN
1 nobody ◊ *Niemand hat mir Bescheid gesagt.* Nobody told me.
2 not ... anybody ◊ *Ich habe niemanden gesehen.* I haven't seen anybody. ◊ *Sie hat mit niemandem darüber gesprochen.* She hasn't mentioned it to anybody.

die **Niere** NOUN
kidney

nieseln VERB
to drizzle

niesen VERB
to sneeze

die **Niete** NOUN
1 stud ◊ *Jeans mit Nieten* jeans with studs
2 blank ◊ *Ich habe eine Niete gezogen.* I've drawn a blank.
♦ **In Mathe ist er eine Niete.** He's useless at maths.

das **Nikotin** NOUN
nicotine

nimmt VERB *see* **nehmen**

nirgends ADVERB
1 nowhere ◊ *Nirgends sonst gibt es so schöne Blumen.* Nowhere else will you find such beautiful flowers.
2 not ... anywhere ◊ *Hier gibt es nirgends ein Schwimmbad.* There isn't a swimming pool anywhere here. ◊ *Ich habe ihn nirgends gesehen.* I haven't seen him anywhere.

nirgendwo ADVERB *see* **nirgends**

das **Niveau** NOUN (PL die **Niveaus**)
level

noch ADVERB, CONJUNCTION
still ◊ *Ich habe noch Hunger.* I'm still hungry. ◊ *Das kann noch passieren.* That might still happen.
♦ **Bleib doch noch ein bisschen!** Stay a bit longer.
♦ **Das wirst du noch lernen.** You'll learn.
♦ **Er wird noch kommen.** He'll come.
♦ **heute noch** today
♦ **noch am selben Tag** the very same day
♦ **noch vor einer Woche** only a week ago
♦ **noch im neunzehnten Jahrhundert** as late as the nineteenth century
♦ **Wer noch?** Who else? ◊ *Wer war noch da?* Who else was there?
♦ **Was noch?** What else? ◊ *Was will er noch?* What else does he want?
♦ **noch nicht** not yet ◊ *Ich bin noch nicht fertig.* I haven't finished yet.
♦ **noch nie** never ◊ *Ich war noch nie in Leeds.* I've never been to Leeds.
♦ **immer noch** still ◊ *Du bist ja immer noch da!* How come you're still here? ◊ *Das Haus ist immer noch nicht fertig.* The house still isn't finished.
♦ **noch einmal** again
♦ **noch dreimal** three more times
♦ **noch einer** another one
♦ **noch größer** even bigger
♦ **Das ist noch besser.** That's better still.
♦ **Geld noch und noch** loads of money
♦ **weder ... noch ...** neither ... nor ...

nochmals ADVERB
again

der **Nominativ** NOUN (PL die **Nominative**)
nominative

Nordamerika NEUT NOUN
North America

der **Norden** NOUN
north

Nordirland NEUT NOUN
Northern Ireland
♦ **aus Nordirland** from Northern Ireland
♦ **in Nordirland** in Northern Ireland
♦ **nach Nordirland** to Northern Ireland

nördlich ADJECTIVE, PREPOSITION, ADVERB
northerly ◊ *Wir fuhren in nördlicher Richtung.* We drove in a northerly direction.
♦ **nördlich einer Sache** to the north of something ◊ *Das Kraftwerk liegt nördlich der Stadt.* The power station is to the north of the city.
♦ **nördlich von** north of ◊ *Düsseldorf liegt nördlich von Köln.* Düsseldorf is north of Cologne.

der **Nordosten** NOUN

northeast

der **Nordpol** NOUN
North Pole ◊ *am Nordpol* at the North Pole

Nordrhein-Westfalen NEUT NOUN
North Rhine-Westphalia

> **ⓘ** *Nordrhein-Westfalen is one of the 16 Länder. Its capital is Düsseldorf. It is Germany's most densely populated state, and includes the Ruhr district.*

die **Nordsee** NOUN
North Sea ◊ *Wir fahren an die Nordsee.* We're going to the North Sea. ◊ *Wir waren an der Nordsee.* We've been to the North Sea.

der **Nordwesten** NOUN
northwest

nörgeln VERB
to moan ◊ *Er hat immer etwas zu nörgeln.* He always finds something to moan about.

die **Norm** NOUN
standard ◊ *Für die meisten technischen Geräte gibt es Normen.* There are set standards for most technical equipment.

normal ADJECTIVE
normal

das **Normalbenzin** NOUN
regular petrol

> **ⓘ** *The type of petrol generally used in Germany is unleaded.*

normalerweise ADVERB
normally

Norwegen NEUT NOUN
Norway
♦ **aus Norwegen** from Norway
♦ **nach Norwegen** to Norway

der **Norweger** NOUN (PL die **Norweger**)
Norwegian

die **Norwegerin** NOUN
Norwegian

norwegisch ADJECTIVE
Norwegian

die **Not** NOUN
♦ **zur Not** if necessary ◊ *Zur Not kannst du ja später nachkommen.* You can join us later if necessary.

der **Notausgang** NOUN (PL die **Notausgänge**)
emergency exit

die **Notbremse** NOUN
emergency brake

der **Notdienst** NOUN (PL die **Notdienste**)
emergency service

notdürftig ADJECTIVE
makeshift ◊ *eine notdürftige Reparatur* a makeshift repair

die **Note** NOUN

1 mark ◊ *Max hat gute Noten.* Max has got good marks.
2 note ◊ *Welche Note hast du eben gespielt?* What note did you just play?

der **Notfall** NOUN (PL die **Notfälle**)
emergency

notfalls ADVERB
if need be

notieren VERB (PERFECT **hat notiert**)
to note down

nötig ADJECTIVE
necessary ◊ *wenn nötig* if necessary
♦ **etwas nötig haben** to need something

die **Notiz** NOUN
1 note ◊ *Sein Kalender ist voller Notizen.* His diary is full of notes.
2 item ◊ *Das stand heute in einer kleinen Notiz in der Zeitung.* There was a short item on it in the newspaper today.
♦ **Notiz nehmen von** to take notice of ◊ *Er hat von mir keine Notiz genommen.* He didn't take any notice of me.

der **Notizblock** NOUN (PL die **Notizblöcke**)
notepad

das **Notizbuch** NOUN (PL die **Notizbücher**)
notebook

notlanden VERB (PERFECT **ist notgelandet**)
to make an emergency landing

der **Notruf** NOUN (PL die **Notrufe**)
emergency call

die **Notrufsäule** NOUN
emergency telephone

notwendig ADJECTIVE
necessary

der **November** NOUN (GEN des **November** or **Novembers**, PL die **November**)
November ◊ *im November* in November ◊ *am neunten November* on the ninth of November ◊ *Freiburg, den 9. November 2000* Freiburg, 9 November 2000 ◊ *Heute ist der neunte November.* Today is the ninth of November.

Nr. ABBREVIATION (= *Nummer*)
No.

der **Nu** NOUN
♦ **im Nu** in an instant

nüchtern ADJECTIVE
1 sober ◊ *Nach drei Gläsern Wein bist du nicht mehr nüchtern.* After three glasses of wine you aren't sober any more. ◊ *nüchterne Tatsachen* sober facts
2 with an empty stomach ◊ *Kommen Sie nüchtern ins Krankenhaus.* Come to the hospital with an empty stomach.
♦ **auf nüchternen Magen** on an empty stomach
♦ **Wenn ich mir die Lage nüchtern betrachte ...** When I look at the situation in a matter-of-fact way ...

die **Nudel** NOUN
noodle ◊ *Es waren Nudeln in der Suppe.* There were noodles in the soup.

♦ **Nudeln** pasta ◊ *Nudeln sind meine Lieblingsspeise.* Pasta is my favourite food.

die **Null** NOUN

see also **null** NUMBER

① zero ◊ *Du musst zuerst eine Null wählen.* You have to dial zero first.

② nonentity ◊ *Er ist doch eine völlige Null.* He's a complete nonentity.

null NUMBER

see also **die Null** NOUN

① nil ◊ *Sie haben eins zu null gespielt.* They won one nil.

② no ◊ *Ich hatte null Fehler.* I had no mistakes.

♦ **null Uhr** midnight

♦ **null und nichtig** null and void

numerieren VERB see **nummerieren**

die **Nummer** NOUN

① number ◊ *Ich kann seine Nummer auswendig.* I know his number by heart.

② size ◊ *Die Schuhe sind eine Nummer zu groß.* These shoes are a size too big.

nummerieren VERB (PERFECT **hat nummeriert**)

to number

das **Nummernschild** NOUN (PL die **Nummernschilder**)

number plate

nun ADVERB, EXCLAMATION

① now ◊ *von nun an* from now on

② well ◊ *Nun, was gibt's Neues?* Well, what's new?

♦ **Das ist nun mal so.** That's the way it is.

nur ADVERB

only ◊ *Das hat nur zwanzig Euro*

gekostet. It only cost twenty euros. ◊ *Es sind nur fünf Leute da gewesen.* There were only five people there.

♦ **Wo bleibt er nur?** Where on earth can he be?

♦ **Was hat sie nur?** What on earth's wrong with her?

die **Nuss** NOUN (PL die **Nüsse**)

nut

der **Nutzen** NOUN

see also **nutzen** VERB

♦ **von Nutzen** useful ◊ *Sprachkenntnisse sind immer von Nutzen.* It's always useful to know a foreign language.

♦ **Das ist bestimmt zu deinem Nutzen.** It's for your own good.

nutzen VERB

see also **der Nutzen** NOUN

to help ◊ *Sprachkenntnisse können dir im Ausland viel nutzen.* Knowing a language can help you a lot abroad.

♦ **etwas nutzen** to make use of something ◊ *Du solltest die Zeit nutzen.* You ought to make use of the time.

♦ **Das nutzt ja doch nichts.** That's pointless.

♦ **Es nutzt alles nichts, wir müssen ...** There's no getting around it, we'll have to ...

nützen VERB see **nutzen**

nützlich ADJECTIVE

useful ◊ *sich nützlich machen* to make oneself useful

nutzlos ADJECTIVE

useless

N

O

o. Ä. ABBREVIATION (= *oder Ähnliche*)
or similar

die **Oase** NOUN
oasis

ob CONJUNCTION
[1] whether ◊ *Ich weiß nicht, ob ich kommen kann.* I don't know whether I can come.
[2] if ◊ *Sie fragt, ob du auch kommst.* She wants to know if you're coming too.
♦ **Ob das wohl wahr ist?** Can that be true?
♦ **Und ob!** You bet!

obdachlos ADJECTIVE
homeless

oben ADVERB
on top ◊ *oben auf dem Schrank* on top of the cupboard
♦ **oben auf dem Berg** up on the mountain
♦ **Die Schlafzimmer sind oben.** The bedrooms are upstairs.
♦ **nach oben** up ◊ *Der Fahrstuhl fährt nach oben.* The lift is going up. ◊ *Ich gehe nach oben in mein Zimmer.* I'm going up to my room.
♦ **von oben** down ◊ *Der Fahrstuhl kommt von oben.* The lift is going down. ◊ *Bringst du mir von oben die Bettwäsche mit?* Bring the bed clothes down with you.
♦ **oben ohne** topless
♦ **jemanden von oben bis unten ansehen** to look somebody up and down
♦ **Befehl von oben** orders from above

der **Ober** NOUN (PL die **Ober**)
waiter
♦ **Herr Ober!** Waiter!

obere ADJECTIVE
see also **oberste** ADJECTIVE
upper ◊ *die oberen Stockwerke* the upper floors
♦ **Nimm das obere Buch.** Take the book from the top of the pile.
♦ **die oberen Klassen** the senior classes

die **Oberfläche** NOUN
surface

oberflächlich ADJECTIVE
superficial ◊ *Er ist sehr oberflächlich in seiner Arbeit.* His work is very superficial.
♦ **jemanden nur oberflächlich kennen** to know somebody only slightly

das **Obergeschoss** NOUN (GEN des **Obergeschosses**, PL die **Obergeschosse**)
upper storey

das **Oberhaus** NOUN (GEN des **Oberhauses**)
upper chamber

der **Oberschenkel** NOUN (PL die **Oberschenkel**)
thigh

die **Oberschule** NOUN
grammar school

oberste ADJECTIVE
see also **obere** ADJECTIVE
topmost ◊ *Das Buch steht auf dem obersten Regalbrett.* The book is on the topmost shelf.
♦ **Sie ist in der obersten Klasse.** She's in the top class.

die **Oberstufe** NOUN
upper school

das **Oberteil** NOUN (PL die **Oberteile**)
upper part

die **Oberweite** NOUN
bust measurement

obgleich CONJUNCTION
although ◊ *Obgleich sie müde war, blieb sie lange auf.* Although she was tired, she stayed up late.

das **Objekt** NOUN (PL die **Objekte**)
object

das **Objektiv** NOUN (PL die **Objektive**)
see also **objektiv** ADJECTIVE
lens (*of camera*)

objektiv ADJECTIVE
see also **das Objektiv** NOUN
objective

das **Obst** NOUN
fruit

der **Obstbaum** NOUN (PL die **Obstbäume**)
fruit tree

der **Obstkuchen** NOUN (PL die **Obstkuchen**)
fruit tart

der **Obstsalat** NOUN (PL die **Obstsalate**)
fruit salad

obwohl CONJUNCTION
although ◊ *Obwohl sie müde war, blieb sie lange auf.* Although she was tired, she stayed up late.

der **Ochse** NOUN (GEN des **Ochsen**, PL die **Ochsen**)
ox

öde ADJECTIVE
dull ◊ *eine öde Landschaft* a dull landscape
♦ **Diese Arbeit ist echt öde.** This job's really the pits.

oder CONJUNCTION
or ◊ *entweder ich oder du* either me or you
♦ **Das stimmt, oder?** That's right, isn't it?

der **Ofen** NOUN (PL die **Öfen**)
[1] oven ◊ *Der Kuchen ist im Ofen.* The cake's in the oven.
[2] heater
♦ **Mach bitte den Ofen an, mir ist kalt.** Put the fire on, I'm cold.

offen ADJECTIVE

open ◊ *Das Fenster ist offen.* The window's open. ◊ *Die Banken sind bis sechzehn Uhr offen.* The banks are open until four o'clock. ◊ *Sie ist ein sehr offener Mensch.* She's a very open person.
* **offen gesagt** to be honest
* **Ich gebe dir eine offene Antwort.** I'll be frank with you.
* **eine offene Stelle** a vacancy

offenbleiben VERB (IMPERFECT **bleib offen,** PERFECT **ist offengeblieben**)
to remain open ◊ *Diese Möglichkeit bleibt uns noch offen.* This option remains open to us.

offensichtlich ADJECTIVE, ADVERB
[1] obvious ◊ *ein offensichtlicher Fehler* an obvious mistake
[2] obviously ◊ *Er ist offensichtlich nicht zufrieden.* He's obviously dissatisfied.

öffentlich ADJECTIVE
public
* **öffentliche Verkehrsmittel** public transport

die **Öffentlichkeit** NOUN
public ◊ *Die Öffentlichkeit wurde nicht informiert.* The public were not informed.
* **in aller Öffentlichkeit** in public

offiziell ADJECTIVE
official

der **Offizier** NOUN (PL die **Offiziere**)
officer

öffnen VERB
to open ◊ *jemandem die Tür öffnen* to open the door for somebody

der **Öffner** NOUN (PL die **Öffner**)
opener

die **Öffnung** NOUN
opening

die **Öffnungszeiten** FEM PL NOUN
opening times

oft ADVERB
see also **öfter** ADVERB
often ◊ *Wie oft warst du schon in London?* How often have you been to London?

öfter ADVERB
see also **oft** ADVERB
more often ◊ *Ich würde dich gern öfter besuchen.* I would like to visit you more often.
* **Sie war in letzter Zeit öfter krank.** She's been ill a lot recently.

öfters ADVERB
often

oh EXCLAMATION
oh ◊ *Oh, das wusste ich nicht.* Oh, I didn't know that.

ohne PREPOSITION, CONJUNCTION

*The preposition **ohne** takes the accusative.*

without ◊ *Ich fahre ohne meine Eltern in Ferien.* I'm going on holiday without my parents. ◊ *Ich habe das ohne Wörterbuch übersetzt.* I translated it without a dictionary.
* **Das ist nicht ohne.** It's not half bad.
* **ohne weiteres** easily ◊ *Das ist ohne weiteres in einer Woche zu schaffen.* That can easily be done in a week.
* **Du kannst doch nicht so ohne weiteres gehen.** You can't just leave.
* **ohne etwas zu tun** without doing something ◊ *Sie ist gegangen, ohne Bescheid zu sagen.* She left without telling anyone. ◊ *ohne zu fragen* without asking

die **Ohnmacht** NOUN
* **in Ohnmacht fallen** to faint

ohnmächtig ADJECTIVE
* **ohnmächtig werden** to faint
* **Sie ist ohnmächtig.** She's fainted.

das **Ohr** NOUN (PL die **Ohren**)
ear
* **Er hat sehr gute Ohren.** His hearing is very good.

die **Ohrenschmerzen** MASC PL NOUN
earache ◊ *Sie hat Ohrenschmerzen.* She's got earache.

die **Ohrfeige** NOUN
slap across the face

ohrfeigen VERB
* **jemanden ohrfeigen** to slap somebody across the face

der **Ohrring** NOUN (PL die **Ohrringe**)
earring

oje EXCLAMATION
oh dear!

ökologisch ADJECTIVE
ecological

der **Oktober** NOUN (GEN des **Oktober** or **Oktobers,** PL die **Oktober**)
October ◊ *im Oktober* in October ◊ *am dritten Oktober* on the third of October ◊ *Ulm, den 3. Oktober 2010* Ulm, 3 October 2010. ◊ *Heute ist der dritte Oktober.* Today is the third of October.

das **Oktoberfest** NOUN (PL die **Oktoberfeste**)
Munich beer festival

das **Öl** NOUN (PL die **Öle**)
oil

die **Ölfarbe** NOUN
oil paint

die **Ölheizung** NOUN
oil-fired central heating

ölig ADJECTIVE
oily

oliv ADJECTIVE
olive-green

die **Olive** NOUN
olive

der **Ölmessstab** NOUN (PL die **Ölmessstäbe**)
dipstick

O

die **Ölsardine** NOUN
sardine

der **Ölwechsel** NOUN (PL die **Ölwechsel**)
oil change

die **Olympiade** NOUN
Olympic Games

der **Olympiasieger** NOUN (PL die **Olympiasieger**)
Olympic champion

die **Olympiasiegerin** NOUN
Olympic champion

olympisch ADJECTIVE
Olympic

das **Ölzeug** NOUN
oilskins

die **Oma** NOUN (PL die **Omas**)
granny

das **Omelett** NOUN (PL die **Omeletts**)
omelette

die **Omi** NOUN (PL die **Omis**)
granny

der **Onkel** NOUN (PL die **Onkel**)
uncle

online ADVERB
on line

der **Opa** NOUN (PL die **Opas**)
grandpa

die **Oper** NOUN
1 opera ◊ *eine Oper von Verdi* an opera by Verdi
2 opera house ◊ *die Mailänder Oper* the Milan opera house

die **Operation** NOUN
operation

der **Operationssaal** NOUN (PL die **Operationssäle**)
operating theatre

die **Operette** NOUN
operetta

operieren VERB (PERFECT **hat operiert**)
to operate on ◊ *jemanden operieren* to operate on somebody
♦ **Sie muss operiert werden.** She has to have an operation.
♦ **Sie wurde am Auge operiert.** She had an eye operation.

das **Opfer** NOUN (PL die **Opfer**)
1 sacrifice ◊ *Das war ein großes Opfer für ihn.* It was a great sacrifice for him.
2 victim ◊ *Der Unfall hat viele Opfer gefordert.* The accident claimed a lot of victims.

der **Opi** NOUN (PL die **Opis**)
grandpa

die **Opposition** NOUN
opposition

die **Optik** NOUN
optics

der **Optiker** NOUN (PL die **Optiker**)
optician

optimal ADJECTIVE, ADVERB

optimum ◊ *Das ist die optimale Lösung.* That's the optimum solution.
♦ **Sie hat das optimal gelöst.** She solved it in the best possible way.
♦ **Wir haben den Platz optimal genutzt.** We made the best possible use of the space available.

der **Optimismus** NOUN (GEN des **Optimismus**)
optimism

der **Optimist** NOUN (GEN des **Optimisten**, PL die **Optimisten**)
optimist

optimistisch ADJECTIVE
optimistic

die **Orange** NOUN
see also **orange** ADJECTIVE
orange

orange ADJECTIVE
see also **die Orange** NOUN
orange

der **Orangensaft** NOUN (PL die **Orangensäfte**)
orange juice

das **Orchester** NOUN (PL die **Orchester**)
orchestra

ordentlich ADJECTIVE, ADVERB
1 tidy ◊ *Seine Wohnung ist sehr ordentlich.* His flat's very tidy. ◊ *Ich bin ein ordentlicher Mensch.* I'm a tidy person.
2 decent ◊ *Das sind ordentliche Leute.* They're decent people. ◊ *eine ordentliche Portion* a decent portion
♦ **Ich brauche jetzt etwas Ordentliches zu essen.** Now I need a decent meal.
3 respectable ◊ *Das ist eine ordentliche Leistung.* That's a respectable achievement.
4 neatly ◊ *Du solltest ordentlicher schreiben.* You should write more neatly.
5 properly ◊ *Kannst du dich nicht ordentlich benehmen?* Can't you behave properly?
♦ **Es hat ordentlich geschneit.** There's been a fair bit of snow.
♦ **Sie haben ihn ordentlich verprügelt.** They beat him up good and proper.

ordinär ADJECTIVE
vulgar
♦ **sich ordinär ausdrücken** to use vulgar expressions

ordnen VERB
to put in order

der **Ordner** NOUN (PL die **Ordner**)
file
♦ **Diese Unterlagen hefte ich in einem Ordner ab.** I'll file these documents away.

die **Ordnung** NOUN
order ◊ *Ruhe und Ordnung* law and order
♦ **Auf meinem Schreibtisch herrscht Ordnung.** On my desk, everything is in its place.
♦ **Sie liebt Ordnung.** She likes everything to be in its place.

◆ **Das hat schon alles seine Ordnung.**
Everything is as it should be.

◆ **Ordnung machen** to tidy up ◇ *Du solltest in deinem Zimmer Ordnung machen.*
You should tidy up your room.

◆ **Mit meinem Auto ist etwas nicht in Ordnung.** Something's wrong with my car.

◆ **etwas wieder in Ordnung bringen** to repair something ◇ *Er hat das defekte Gerät wieder in Ordnung gebracht.* He repaired the faulty appliance.

◆ **Ich muss meine Wohnung in Ordnung bringen.** I'll have to tidy up my flat.

◆ **Ist alles in Ordnung?** Is everything okay?

◆ **In Ordnung!** Okay!

das **Organ** NOUN (PL die **Organe**)
organ ◇ *die inneren Organe* internal organs

die **Organisation** NOUN
organization

organisch ADJECTIVE
organic

organisieren VERB (PERFECT **hat organisiert**)
to organize ◇ *Wer hat das Fest organisiert?* Who organized the party?

die **Orgel** NOUN
organ ◇ *Sie spielt Orgel.* She plays the organ.

der **Orient** NOUN
Orient

orientalisch ADJECTIVE
oriental

sich **orientieren** VERB (PERFECT **hat sich orientiert**)
[1] to find one's way around ◇ *Ich brauche einen Stadtplan, um mich besser orientieren zu können.* I need a city map to be able to find my way around better.
[2] to find out ◇ *Ich muss mich orientieren, wie das gehandhabt wird.* I'll have to find out what the procedure is.

die **Orientierung** NOUN
[1] bearings ◇ *Wir haben die Orientierung verloren.* We've lost our bearings.
[2] information ◇ *Diese Broschüre ist zu Ihrer Orientierung.* This brochure is for your information.

das **Original** NOUN (PL die **Originale**)
original

originell ADJECTIVE
original

der **Orkan** NOUN (PL die **Orkane**)
hurricane

der **Ort** NOUN (PL die **Orte**)
place
◆ **an Ort und Stelle** on the spot

die **Orthografie** NOUN
spelling

örtlich ADJECTIVE
local

das **Ortsgespräch** NOUN (PL die **Ortsgespräche**)
local phone call

der **Osten** NOUN
east

das **Osterei** NOUN (PL die **Ostereier**)
Easter egg

die **Osterferien** PL NOUN
Easter holidays

der **Osterhase** NOUN (GEN des **Osterhasen,** PL die **Osterhasen**)
Easter bunny

der **Ostermontag** NOUN (PL die **Ostermontage**)
Easter Monday

das **Ostern** NOUN (PL die **Ostern**)
Easter ◇ *an Ostern* at Easter

das **Österreich** NOUN
Austria

> **ⓘ** *Austria borders on Germany, the Czech Republic, Slovakia, Hungary, Slovenia, Italy and Switzerland. Its capital is Vienna and its currency the Schilling.*

◆ **aus Österreich** from Austria
◆ **in Österreich** in Austria
◆ **nach Österreich** to Austria

der **Österreicher** NOUN (PL die **Österreicher**)
Austrian

die **Österreicherin** NOUN
Austrian

österreichisch ADJECTIVE
Austrian

> **ⓘ** *People in Austria speak a dialect of German.*

östlich ADJECTIVE, PREPOSITION, ADVERB
easterly ◇ *in östlicher Richtung* in an easterly direction

◆ **östlich einer Sache** to the east of something ◇ *Das Kraftwerk liegt östlich der Stadt.* The power station is to the east of the city.

◆ **östlich von** east of ◇ *Jena liegt östlich von Erfurt.* Jena is east of Erfurt.

die **Ostsee** NOUN
Baltic ◇ *Wir fahren an die Ostsee.* We're going to the Baltic. ◇ *Wir waren an der Ostsee.* We've been to the Baltic.

oval ADJECTIVE
oval

der **Ozean** NOUN (PL die **Ozeane**)
ocean

das **Ozon** NOUN
ozone

das **Ozonloch** NOUN (PL die **Ozonlöcher**)
ozone hole

die **Ozonschicht** NOUN
ozone layer

O

P

das **Paar** NOUN (PL die **Paare**)
  1 pair ◊ *Ich habe ein Paar Schuhe gekauft.* I've bought a pair of shoes.
  2 couple ◊ *Sie sind ein sehr glückliches Paar.* They're a very happy couple.
  ♦ **ein paar** a few

paarmal ADVERB
  ♦ **ein paarmal** a few times

paarweise ADVERB
  in pairs ◊ *Sie hängt die Socken paarweise auf die Leine.* She's hanging out the socks in pairs. ◊ *Stellt euch bitte paarweise auf.* Line up in pairs, please.

das **Päckchen** NOUN (PL die **Päckchen**)
  1 small parcel ◊ *Wie viel kostet ein Päckchen ins Ausland?* How much does it cost to post a small parcel abroad?
  2 packet ◊ *Sie raucht ein Päckchen pro Tag.* She smokes a packet a day.

packen VERB
  1 to pack ◊ *Hast du deinen Koffer schon gepackt?* Have you already packed your suitcase?
  2 to grasp ◊ *Sie packte mich am Arm.* She grasped my arm.
  ♦ **Er hat die Prüfung nicht gepackt.** He didn't manage to get through the exam.

das **Packpapier** NOUN
  brown paper

die **Packung** NOUN
  packet ◊ *eine Packung Tee* a packet of tea ◊ *eine Packung Zigaretten* a packet of cigarettes
  ♦ **eine Packung Pralinen** a box of chocolates

pädagogisch ADJECTIVE
  educational

das **Paket** NOUN (PL die **Pakete**)
  1 packet ◊ *Ich habe ein Paket Waschpulver gekauft.* I bought a packet of washing powder.
  2 parcel ◊ *Die Gebühren für Pakete stehen in dieser Liste.* Parcel rates are in this list.

die **Paketannahme** NOUN
  parcels office

der **Palast** NOUN (PL die **Paläste**)
  palace

die **Palme** NOUN
  palm tree

die **Pampelmuse** NOUN
  grapefruit

die **Panik** NOUN
  panic

panisch ADJECTIVE
  ♦ **panische Angst vor etwas haben** to be terrified of something
  ♦ **panisch reagieren** to panic

die **Panne** NOUN
  1 breakdown ◊ *Wir hatten eine Panne auf der Autobahn.* We had a breakdown on the motorway.
  2 slip ◊ *Mir ist da eine kleine Panne passiert.* I made a slight slip.

der **Panzer** NOUN (PL die **Panzer**)
  1 tank ◊ *Die Armee setzte Panzer ein.* The army used tanks.
  2 shell ◊ *der Panzer einer Schildkröte* a tortoise's shell

der **Papa** NOUN (PL die **Papas**)
  daddy

der **Papagei** NOUN (PL die **Papageien**)
  parrot

das **Papier** NOUN (PL die **Papiere**)
  paper

der **Papierkorb** NOUN (PL die **Papierkörbe**)
  wastepaper basket

die **Papiertüte** NOUN
  paper bag

die **Pappe** NOUN
  cardboard

der **Paprika** NOUN (PL die **Paprikas**)
  1 paprika ◊ *Ich habe das Hähnchen mit Paprika gewürzt.* I've seasoned the chicken with paprika.
  2 pepper ◊ *Heute gibt es gefüllte Paprikas.* We're having stuffed peppers today.

der **Papst** NOUN (PL die **Päpste**)
  pope

die **Parabolantenne** NOUN
  satellite dish

das **Paradies** NOUN (GEN des **Paradieses,** PL die **Paradiese**)
  paradise

parallel ADJECTIVE
  parallel

die **Parallele** NOUN
  parallel

das **Pärchen** NOUN (PL die **Pärchen**)
  couple ◊ *Auf der Parkbank saß ein Pärchen.* There was a couple sitting on the bench in the park.

das **Parfüm** NOUN (PL die **Parfüms** or **Parfüme**)
  perfume

der **Pariser** NOUN (PL die **Pariser**)
  1 Parisian
  2 condom ◊ *Auf den meisten Toiletten gibt es Automaten mit Parisern.* Most toilets have condom machines.

die **Pariserin** NOUN
  Parisian

der **Park** NOUN (PL die **Parks**)
  park

die **Parkanlage** NOUN
  park

parken VERB
to park

das **Parkett** NOUN (PL die **Parkette** or **Parketts**)
stalls (theatre)

das **Parkhaus** NOUN (GEN des **Parkhauses**, PL die **Parkhäuser**)
multistorey car park

die **Parklücke** NOUN
parking space

der **Parkplatz** NOUN (GEN des **Parkplatzes**, PL die **Parkplätze**)
car park

die **Parkscheibe** NOUN
parking disc

der **Parkschein** NOUN
car-park ticket

die **Parkuhr** NOUN
parking meter

das **Parkverbot** NOUN (PL die **Parkverbote**)
◆ **Hier ist Parkverbot.** You're not allowed to park here.

das **Parlament** NOUN (PL die **Parlamente**)
parliament

die **Parole** NOUN
1 motto ◇ "Morgenstund hat Gold im Mund" ist seine Parole. His motto is: "The early bird catches the worm".
2 slogan ◇ ausländerfeindliche Parolen racist slogans

die **Partei** NOUN
party (political)
◆ **Partei für jemanden ergreifen** to take somebody's side

parteiisch ADJECTIVE
biased

das **Parterre** NOUN (PL die **Parterres**)
1 ground floor ◇ Wir wohnen im Parterre. We live on the ground floor.
2 stalls (theatre)

die **Partie** NOUN
1 area ◇ Die Creme auf die Augenpartie auftragen. Apply the cream to the area around the eyes.
2 game ◇ eine Partie Schach a game of chess
◆ **mit von der Partie sein** to join in

das **Partizip** NOUN (PL die **Partizipien**)
participle

der **Partner** NOUN (PL die **Partner**)
partner

die **Partnerin** NOUN
partner

die **Partnerstadt** NOUN (PL die **Partnerstädte**)
twin town

die **Party** NOUN (PL die **Partys**)
party ◇ eine Party veranstalten to have a party

der **Pass** NOUN (GEN des **Passes**, PL die **Pässe**)
1 passport ◇ Für Indien brauchst du einen Pass. You need a passport for India.
2 pass ◇ Im Winter ist der Pass gesperrt. The pass is closed in winter.

die **Passage** NOUN
passage
◆ **eine Einkaufspassage** a shopping arcade

der **Passagier** NOUN (PL die **Passagiere**)
passenger

passen VERB
1 to fit ◇ Die Hose passt nicht. The trousers don't fit. ◇ Es ist zu groß und passt nicht in meinen Koffer. It's too big and doesn't fit in my suitcase.
2 to suit ◇ Passt dir Dienstag? Does Tuesday suit you? ◇ Dieser Termin passt mir nicht. That date doesn't suit me.
◆ **Es passt mir nicht, dass du so frech bist.** I don't like you being so cheeky.
◆ **zu etwas passen** to go with something ◇ Der Rock passt nicht zu deiner Bluse. The skirt doesn't go with your blouse.
◆ **zu jemandem passen** to be right for somebody ◇ Er passt nicht zu dir. He's not right for you.
3 to pass ◇ Auf die Frage muss ich passen. I'll have to pass on that question.

passend ADJECTIVE
1 matching ◇ Ich muss jetzt dazu passende Schuhe kaufen. I now must buy some matching shoes.
◆ **Ich suche zu dem Rock noch eine passende Bluse.** I'm looking for a blouse to match this skirt.
2 appropriate ◇ Sie hat ein paar passende Worte gesprochen. She said a few appropriate words.
3 convenient ◇ Das ist nicht die passende Gelegenheit. This isn't a convenient time.

passieren VERB (PERFECT **ist passiert**)
to happen ◇ Was ist passiert? What happened? ◇ Mir ist etwas Lustiges passiert. Something funny happened to me.

das **Passiv** NOUN (PL die **Passive**)
see also **passiv** ADJECTIVE
passive

passiv ADJECTIVE, ADVERB
see also **das Passiv** NOUN
passive ◇ passives Rauchen passive smoking ◇ passiv zusehen to watch passively

das **Passivrauchen** NOUN
passive smoking

die **Passkontrolle** NOUN
passport control

das **Passwort** NOUN (PL die **Passwörter**)
password

die **Paste** NOUN
paste

die **Pastete** NOUN
pie (savoury)

der **Pate** NOUN (GEN des **Paten**, PL die **Paten**)
godfather

P

das Patenkind NOUN (PL die **Patenkinder**)
godchild

das Patent NOUN (PL die **Patente**)
patent

die Patentante NOUN
godmother

der Patient NOUN (GEN des **Patienten,** PL die **Patienten**)
patient

die Patientin NOUN
patient

die Patin NOUN
godmother

die Patrone NOUN
cartridge

patschnass ADJECTIVE
soaking wet

die Pauke NOUN
kettledrum ◇ *Er spielt Pauke.* He plays the kettledrum.
♦ **auf die Pauke hauen** to live it up

pauken VERB
[1] to swot ◇ *Vor der Arbeit habe ich ziemlich gepaukt.* I swotted quite a lot before the test.
[2] to swot up ◇ *Ich muss Vokabeln pauken.* I have to swot up my vocabulary.

die Pauschalreise NOUN
package tour

die Pause NOUN
[1] break ◇ *eine Pause machen* to have a break ◇ *die große Pause* the long break
[2] interval ◇ *In der Pause haben wir über das Stück gesprochen.* We talked about the play during the interval.

der Pazifik NOUN
Pacific

der PC NOUN (GEN des **PCs,** PL die **PCs**)
PC

das Pech NOUN
bad luck ◇ *Das war Pech!* That was bad luck.
♦ **Pech haben** to be unlucky
♦ **Pech!** Hard luck!

das Pedal NOUN (PL die **Pedale**)
pedal

der Pegel NOUN (PL die **Pegel**)
water level

peinlich ADJECTIVE
[1] embarrassing ◇ *eine peinliche Frage* an embarrassing question
[2] awkward ◇ *eine peinliche Angelegenheit* an awkward situation
♦ **Das ist mir aber peinlich.** I'm dreadfully sorry.
♦ **peinlich genau** painstakingly ◇ *Sie hat das peinlich genau überprüft.* She checked it painstakingly.

die Peitsche NOUN
whip

die Pelle NOUN
skin

die Pellkartoffeln FEM PL NOUN
potatoes boiled in their skins

der Pelz NOUN (GEN des **Pelzes,** PL die **Pelze**)
fur

das Pendel NOUN (PL die **Pendel**)
pendulum

pendeln VERB (PERFECT **ist gependelt**)
to commute ◇ *Er pendelt zwischen Tübingen und Stuttgart.* He commutes between Tübingen and Stuttgart.
♦ **Der Bus pendelt zwischen Bahnhof und Flughafen.** A shuttle bus runs between the station and the airport.

der Pendelverkehr NOUN
[1] shuttle service ◇ *Die Fluggesellschaft hat einen Pendelverkehr zwischen Köln und Berlin eingerichtet.* The airline set up a shuttle service between Cologne and Berlin.
[2] commuter traffic ◇ *Zwischen Tübingen und Stuttgart besteht ein reger Pendelverkehr.* There is heavy commuter traffic between Tübingen and Stuttgart.

der Pendler NOUN (PL die **Pendler**)
commuter

penetrant ADJECTIVE
[1] overpowering ◇ *ein penetranter Geruch* an overpowering smell
[2] pushy ◇ *ein penetranter Vertreter* a pushy salesman
♦ **penetrant werden** to get aggressive

der Penis NOUN (GEN des **Penis,** PL die **Penisse**)
penis

pennen VERB
to kip ◇ *Ich habe auf dem Fußboden gepennt.* I kipped on the floor.
♦ **Was macht er? – Er pennt.** What's he doing? – He's having a kip.

der Penner NOUN (PL die **Penner**)
dosser

die Pension NOUN
[1] pension ◇ *Er bezieht eine ordentliche Pension.* He gets a decent pension.
♦ **in Pension gehen** to retire
[2] guesthouse ◇ *Wir haben in einer Pension übernachtet.* We stayed overnight in a guesthouse.

pensioniert ADJECTIVE
retired

das Perfekt NOUN (PL die **Perfekte**)
see also **perfekt** ADJECTIVE
perfect

perfekt ADJECTIVE
see also **das Perfekt** NOUN
perfect ◇ *ein perfektes Alibi* a perfect alibi ◇ *perfekt passen* to fit perfectly

die Periode NOUN
period

die Perle NOUN
pearl

perplex ADJECTIVE

dumbfounded

die **Person** NOUN
person
♦ **ich für meine Person** ... personally I ...

das **Personal** NOUN
staff ◊ *das Hotelpersonal* the hotel staff

der **Personalausweis** NOUN (GEN des
Personalausweises, PL die
Personalausweise)
identity card

der **Personalchef** NOUN (PL die **Personalchefs**)
personnel manager

der **Personal Computer** NOUN (PL die
Personal Computer)
personal computer

die **Personalien** FEM PL NOUN
particulars

das **Personalpronomen** NOUN (PL die
Personalpronomen)
personal pronoun

der **Personenzug** NOUN (PL die **Personenzüge**)
passenger train

persönlich ADJECTIVE, ADVERB
[1] personal ◊ *das persönliche Fürwort*
the personal pronoun ◊ *eine persönliche
Beleidigung* a personal insult
◊ *persönlich werden* to get personal
[2] in person ◊ *persönlich erscheinen* to
appear in person
[3] personally ◊ *jemanden persönlich
kennen* to know somebody personally
◊ *Das war nicht persönlich gemeint.* It
wasn't meant personally.

die **Persönlichkeit** NOUN
personality

die **Perücke** NOUN
wig

der **Pessimismus** NOUN (GEN des **Pessimismus**)
pessimism

der **Pessimist** NOUN (GEN des **Pessimisten,** PL
die **Pessimisten**)
pessimist

pessimistisch ADJECTIVE
pessimistic

die **Pest** NOUN
plague
♦ **jemanden wie die Pest hassen** to loathe
somebody

die **Petersilie** NOUN
parsley

das **Petroleum** NOUN
paraffin

Pf ABBREVIATION (= *Pfennig*)
pfennig

der **Pfad** NOUN (PL die **Pfade**)
path

der **Pfadfinder** NOUN (PL die **Pfadfinder**)
boy scout

die **Pfadfinderin** NOUN
girl guide

das **Pfand** NOUN (PL die **Pfänder**)

[1] deposit ◊ *Auf der Flasche ist ein Pfand
von siebzig Cent.* There's a deposit of
seventy cents on the bottle.
[2] forfeit ◊ *Wer die Frage nicht
beantworten kann, muss ein Pfand
geben.* Anyone who cannot answer the
question must pay a forfeit.

die **Pfandflasche** NOUN
returnable bottle

die **Pfanne** NOUN
frying pan

der **Pfannkuchen** NOUN (PL die **Pfannkuchen**)
pancake

der **Pfarrer** NOUN (PL die **Pfarrer**)
parish priest

der **Pfau** NOUN (PL die **Pfauen**)
peacock

Pfd. ABBREVIATION (= *Pfund*)
pound (*weight*)

der **Pfeffer** NOUN (PL die **Pfeffer**)
pepper

das **Pfefferkorn** NOUN (PL die **Pfefferkörner**)
peppercorn

der **Pfefferkuchen** NOUN (PL die **Pfefferkuchen**)
gingerbread

das **Pfefferminzbonbon** NOUN (PL die
Pfefferminzbonbons)
peppermint

die **Pfefferminze** NOUN
mint

die **Pfeffermühle** NOUN
pepper mill

die **Pfeife** NOUN
[1] whistle
[2] pipe ◊ *Mein Bruder raucht Pfeife.* My
brother smokes a pipe.

pfeifen VERB (IMPERFECT **pfiff,** PERFECT **hat
gepfiffen**)
to whistle

der **Pfeil** NOUN (PL die **Pfeile**)
arrow

der **Pfennig** NOUN (PL die **Pfennige** or **Pfennig**)
pfennig
There were 100 Pfennige in a Mark.
◊ *Eine Kopie kostete dreißig Pfennig.*
One copy cost thirty pfennigs.

das **Pferd** NOUN (PL die **Pferde**)
horse

das **Pferderennen** NOUN (PL die **Pferderennen**)
[1] race meeting ◊ *Er geht regelmäßig zu
Pferderennen.* He regularly goes to race
meetings.
[2] horse-racing ◊ *Ich interessiere mich
nicht für Pferderennen.* I'm not interested
in horse-racing.

der **Pferdeschwanz** NOUN (GEN des
Pferdeschwanzes, PL die **Pferdeschwänze**)
ponytail

der **Pferdestall** NOUN (PL die **Pferdeställe**)
stable

das **Pfingsten** NOUN (GEN des **Pfingsten,** PL die
Pfingsten)

P

Whitsun ◊ *an Pfingsten* at Whitsun

der **Pfirsich** NOUN (PL die **Pfirsiche**)
peach

die **Pflanze** NOUN
plant

pflanzen VERB
to plant

das **Pflaster** NOUN (PL die **Pflaster**)
[1] plaster ◊ *Sie klebte ein Pflaster auf die Wunde.* She put a plaster on the cut.
[2] paving stones ◊ *Jemand hatte das Pflaster in der Fußgängerzone bemalt.* Somebody had been painting on the paving stones in the pedestrian precinct.

die **Pflaume** NOUN
plum

die **Pflege** NOUN
[1] care ◊ *Diese Pflanze braucht nicht viel Pflege.* This plant doesn't need much care. ◊ *ein Mittel zur Pflege von Leder* a leather-care product
[2] nursing ◊ *Ein krankes Baby braucht viel Pflege.* A sick baby needs a lot of nursing.
♦ **ein Kind in Pflege geben** to have a child fostered

die **Pflegeeltern** PL NOUN
foster parents

das **Pflegekind** NOUN (PL die **Pflegekinder**)
foster child

pflegeleicht ADJECTIVE
easy-care ◊ *ein pflegeleichter Stoff* an easy-care fabric
♦ **ein pflegeleichter Mensch** an uncomplicated person

pflegen VERB
[1] to nurse ◊ *Sie pflegt ihre kranke Mutter.* She's nursing her sick mother.
[2] to look after ◊ *Briten pflegen ihren Rasen.* The British look after their lawns.
♦ **Womit pflegst du dein Gesicht?** How do you care for your face?
♦ **gepflegte Hände** well-cared-for hands
♦ **gepflegt aussehen** to look well-groomed

der **Pfleger** NOUN (PL die **Pfleger**)
male nurse

die **Pflicht** NOUN
duty ◊ *Es ist deine Pflicht, dich darum zu kümmern.* It's your duty to take care of it.

pflichtbewusst ADJECTIVE
conscientious

das **Pflichtfach** NOUN (PL die **Pflichtfächer**)
compulsory subject

pflücken VERB
to pick ◊ *Wir haben Himbeeren gepflückt.* We picked raspberries. ◊ *einen Strauß pflücken* to pick a bunch of flowers

die **Pforte** NOUN
gate

der **Pförtner** NOUN (PL die **Pförtner**)
doorman

der **Pfosten** NOUN (PL die **Pfosten**)
post ◊ *Der Ball traf den Pfosten.* The ball hit the post.

die **Pfote** NOUN
paw ◊ *Der Hund hat schmutzige Pfoten.* The dog's paws are dirty.

pfui EXCLAMATION
ugh!

das **Pfund** NOUN (PL die **Pfunde** or **Pfund**)
pound ◊ *drei Pfund Äpfel* three pounds of apples ◊ *dreißig britische Pfund* thirty pounds sterling

pfuschen VERB
to be sloppy
♦ **Die Handwerker haben gepfuscht.** The craftsmen produced sloppy work.
♦ **jemandem ins Handwerk pfuschen** to stick one's nose into somebody's business

die **Pfütze** NOUN
puddle

die **Phantasie** NOUN *see* **Fantasie**

phantasieren VERB *see* **fantasieren**

phantastisch ADJECTIVE *see* **fantastisch**

die **Philosophie** NOUN
philosophy

philosophisch ADJECTIVE
philosophical

phlegmatisch ADJECTIVE
lethargic

die **Phonetik** NOUN
phonetics ◊ *Die Phonetik steht in eckigen Klammern.* Phonetics are given in square brackets.

phonetisch ADJECTIVE
phonetic

das **Photo** NOUN *see* **Foto**

die **Physik** NOUN
physics ◊ *Physik ist mein Lieblingsfach.* Physics is my favourite subject.

der **Physiker** NOUN (PL die **Physiker**)
physicist

physisch ADJECTIVE
physical

der **Pickel** NOUN (PL die **Pickel**)
[1] pimple ◊ *Du hast einen Pickel auf der Nase.* You've got a pimple on your nose.
[2] pickaxe ◊ *Die Arbeiter haben den Straßenbelag mit Pickeln aufgeschlagen.* The workers broke up the road surface with pickaxes.
[3] ice axe ◊ *Die Bergsteiger hatten Seile und Pickel dabei.* The mountaineers had ropes and ice axes with them.

pickelig ADJECTIVE
spotty

das **Picknick** NOUN (PL die **Picknicks**)
picnic ◊ *Picknick machen* to have a picnic

der **Piepser** NOUN (PL die **Piepser**)
bleeper

das **Piercing** NOUN (PL die **Piercings**)

1 body piercing

2 body jewellery

das **Pik** NOUN (PL die **Pik**)

spades ◊ *Pik ist Trumpf.* Spades is trumps.

pikant ADJECTIVE

spicy

die **Pille** NOUN

pill ◊ *Sie nimmt die Pille.* She's on the pill.

der **Pilot** NOUN (GEN des **Piloten**, PL die **Piloten**)

pilot

das **Pils** NOUN (GEN des **Pils**, PL die **Pils**)

Pilsner lager

der **Pilz** NOUN (GEN des **Pilzes**, PL die **Pilze**)

1 mushroom ◊ *eine Soße mit Pilzen* a mushroom sauce

2 toadstool ◊ *Der Fliegenpilz ist giftig.* The fly agaric is a toadstool.

pinkeln VERB

to pee

die **Pinnwand** NOUN (PL die **Pinnwände**)

noticeboard

der **Pinsel** NOUN (PL die **Pinsel**)

paintbrush

die **Pinzette** NOUN

tweezers ◊ *eine Pinzette* a pair of tweezers

der **Pirat** NOUN (GEN des **Piraten**, PL die **Piraten**)

pirate

die **Piste** NOUN

1 run ◊ *Wir sind die blaue Piste runtergefahren.* We skied down the blue run.

2 runway ◊ *Das Flugzeug stand auf der Piste und wartete auf die Starterlaubnis.* The plane stood on the runway waiting for clearance for takeoff.

die **Pistole** NOUN

pistol

die **Pizza** NOUN (PL die **Pizzas**)

pizza

der **Pkw** NOUN (GEN des **Pkw** or **Pkws**, PL die **Pkws**) (= *Personenkraftwagen*)

car

plagen VERB

to bother ◊ *Was plagt dich denn?* What's bothering you?

♦ **Mich plagen Zahnschmerzen.** I've got dreadful toothache.

♦ **Sie muss sich in der Schule ziemlich plagen.** She finds school hard going.

♦ **Mit diesem Problem plage ich mich schon seit einiger Zeit.** I've been wrestling with this problem for some time now.

das **Plakat** NOUN (PL die **Plakate**)

poster

der **Plan** NOUN (PL die **Pläne**)

1 plan ◊ *Unser Plan war, vor ihm da zu sein.* Our plan was to arrive before him.

2 map ◊ *Hast du einen Plan von München?* Have you got a map of Munich?

planen VERB

to plan ◊ *Wir planen unseren nächsten Urlaub.* We're planning our next holiday.

♦ **einen Mord planen** to plot a murder

der **Planet** NOUN (GEN des **Planeten**, PL die **Planeten**)

planet

planmäßig ADJECTIVE

1 according to plan ◊ *Alles verlief planmäßig.* Everything went according to plan.

2 scheduled ◊ *planmäßige Ankunft* scheduled arrival

♦ **Die Maschine ist planmäßig gelandet.** The plane landed on time.

das **Plastik** NOUN

see also **die Plastik** NOUN

plastic ◊ *Die meisten Spielzeuge sind heute aus Plastik.* Most toys these days are made of plastic.

die **Plastik** NOUN

see also **das Plastik** NOUN

sculpture

der **Plastikbeutel** NOUN (PL die **Plastikbeutel**)

plastic bag

die **Plastiktüte** NOUN

plastic bag

platt ADJECTIVE

flat ◊ *ein platter Reifen* a flat tyre ◊ *plattes Land* flat country

♦ **etwas platt drücken** to flatten something

♦ **Ich bin platt!** I'm flabbergasted!

plattdeutsch ADJECTIVE

low German

die **Platte** NOUN

1 plate ◊ *Sie stellte den Topf auf die Platte.* She put the saucepan on the plate.

♦ **eine Platte mit Käseaufschnitt** a platter of assorted cheeses

♦ **Die Platte des Tisches war zerkratzt.** The tabletop was scratched.

♦ **ein Loch mit einer Platte aus Holz abdecken** to cover a hole with a wooden board

2 record ◊ *Sie hat alle Platten der Beatles.* She's got all the Beatles' records.

der **Plattenspieler** NOUN (PL die **Plattenspieler**)

record player

der **Plattfuß** NOUN (GEN des **Plattfußes**, PL die **Plattfüße**)

flat foot

♦ **Sie hat Plattfüße.** She's flat-footed.

der **Platz** NOUN (GEN des **Platzes**, PL die **Plätze**)

1 place ◊ *Das ist ein schöner Platz zum Zelten.* That's a good place to pitch a tent. ◊ *Das Buch steht nicht an seinem Platz.* The book isn't in its place. ◊ *der erste Platz* the first place

P

☞

☐2 seat ◊ *Wir hatten Plätze in der ersten Reihe.* We had seats in the front row. ◊ *Ist hier noch ein Platz frei?* Are all these seats taken?

♦ **Platz nehmen** to take a seat

☐3 room ◊ *Das Sofa braucht zu viel Platz.* The sofa takes up too much room. ◊ *jemandem Platz machen* to make room for somebody

☐4 square ◊ *Auf dem Platz vor der Kirche ist zweimal die Woche Markt.* There's a market twice a week on the square in front of the church.

☐5 playing field

♦ **Der Schiedsrichter schickte ihn vom Platz.** The referee sent him off.

das **Plätzchen** NOUN (PL die **Plätzchen**)

☐1 spot ◊ *ein hübsches Plätzchen* a beautiful spot

☐2 biscuit ◊ *Zum Kaffee gab es Plätzchen.* There were biscuits with the coffee.

platzen VERB (PERFECT **ist geplatzt**)

☐1 to burst ◊ *Der Luftballon ist geplatzt.* The balloon has burst.

☐2 to explode ◊ *In der Innenstadt ist gestern eine Bombe geplatzt.* A bomb exploded in the town centre yesterday.

♦ **vor Wut platzen** to be livid

die **Platzkarte** NOUN
seat reservation

plaudern VERB
to chat

die **Pleite** NOUN

see also **pleite** ADJECTIVE

☐1 bankruptcy ◊ *die Pleite einer Firma* the bankruptcy of a company

♦ **Pleite machen** to go bust

☐2 flop ◊ *Die Veranstaltung war eine Pleite.* The event was a flop.

pleite ADJECTIVE

see also **die Pleite** NOUN

broke ◊ *Ich bin total pleite.* I'm stony-broke.

die **Plombe** NOUN
filling ◊ *Ich habe noch keine einzige Plombe.* I still haven't got a single filling.

plombieren VERB (PERFECT **hat plombiert**)
to fill ◊ *Ein Zahn muss plombiert werden.* One tooth will have to be filled.

plötzlich ADJECTIVE, ADVERB

☐1 sudden ◊ *ihr plötzliches Erscheinen* her sudden appearance

☐2 suddenly ◊ *Sie war plötzlich weg.* Suddenly she was gone.

plump ADJECTIVE
clumsy ◊ *plumpe Bewegungen* clumsy movements

♦ **ein plumper Körper** a shapeless body

♦ **eine plumpe Lüge** a blatant lie

der **Plural** NOUN (PL die **Plurale**)
plural

das **Plus** NOUN (GEN des **Plus**)

see also **plus** ADVERB

☐1 plus ◊ *Steht vor der Zahl ein Plus oder ein Minus?* Is there a plus or a minus in front of the figure?

☐2 profit ◊ *Die Firma hat dieses Jahr ein Plus gemacht.* The company has made a profit this year.

☐3 advantage ◊ *Sprachkenntnisse sind immer ein Plus.* Language skills are always an advantage.

plus ADVERB

see also **das Plus** NOUN

plus

das **Plutonium** NOUN
plutonium

PLZ ABBREVIATION (= *Postleitzahl*)
postcode

der **Po** NOUN (PL die **Pos**)
bum

der **Pokal** NOUN (PL die **Pokale**)

☐1 cup ◊ *Welche Mannschaft hat den Pokal gewonnen?* Which team won the cup?

☐2 goblet ◊ *Sie tranken Wein aus Pokalen.* They drank wine out of goblets.

das **Pokalspiel** NOUN (PL die **Pokalspiele**)
cup tie

der **Pol** NOUN (PL die **Pole**)
pole ◊ *am Pol* at the Pole

der **Pole** NOUN (GEN des **Polen**, PL die **Polen**)
Pole

♦ **Er ist Pole.** He's Polish.

Polen NEUT NOUN
Poland

♦ **aus Polen** from Poland

♦ **nach Polen** to Poland

die **Police** NOUN
insurance policy

polieren VERB (PERFECT **hat poliert**)
to polish

die **Polin** NOUN
Pole

♦ **Sie ist Polin.** She's Polish.

die **Politik** NOUN

☐1 politics ◊ *Politik interessiert mich nicht.* Politics doesn't interest me.

☐2 policy ◊ *die Politik Großbritanniens in Bezug auf BSE* Great Britain's policy on BSE

der **Politiker** NOUN (PL die **Politiker**)
politician

politisch ADJECTIVE
political

die **Polizei** NOUN
police

Note that Polizei is used with a singular verb and police with a plural verb.
◊ *Die Polizei ist noch nicht da.* The police haven't arrived yet.

der **Polizeibeamte** NOUN (GEN des **Polizeibeamten**, PL die **Polizeibeamten**) police officer ◇ *Wir wurden von einem Polizeibeamten angehalten.* We were stopped by a police officer.

die **Polizeibeamtin** NOUN
police officer ◇ *Sie ist Polizeibeamtin.* She's a police officer.

polizeilich ADJECTIVE
♦ **Er wird polizeilich gesucht.** The police are looking for him.

das **Polizeirevier** NOUN (PL die **Polizeireviere**)
police station

die **Polizeistunde** NOUN
closing time (*of bars*)

die **Polizeiwache** NOUN
police station

der **Polizist** NOUN (GEN des **Polizisten,** PL die **Polizisten**)
policeman ◇ *Dietmar ist Polizist.* Dietmar's a policeman.

die **Polizistin** NOUN
policewoman ◇ *Ursula ist Polizistin.* Ursula's a policewoman.

der **Pollen** NOUN (PL die **Pollen**)
pollen

polnisch ADJECTIVE
Polish

die **Polypen** PL NOUN
adenoids ◇ *Ihm wurden die Polypen entfernt.* He had his adenoids removed.

die **Pommes** PL NOUN
chips ◇ *Pommes mit Mayonnaise* chips with mayonnaise

die **Pommes frites** PL NOUN
chips ◇ *Würstchen mit Pommes frites* sausages and chips

pompös ADJECTIVE
ostentatious

das **Pony** NOUN (PL die **Ponys**)
see also **der Pony** NOUN
pony ◇ *Wir sind auf Ponys geritten.* We rode ponies.

der **Pony** NOUN (PL die **Ponys**)
see also **das Pony** NOUN
fringe ◇ *Sie trägt einen Pony.* She's got a fringe.

der **Pop** NOUN
pop

die **Popmusik** NOUN
pop music

poppig ADJECTIVE
bright ◇ *poppige Farben* bright colours

der **Popstar** NOUN (PL die **Popstars**)
pop star

die **Pore** NOUN
pore

die **Pornografie** NOUN
pornography

porös ADJECTIVE
porous

der **Porree** NOUN (PL die **Porrees**)
leek

das **Portemonnaie** NOUN (PL die **Portemonnaies**)
purse

der **Portier** NOUN (PL die **Portiers**)
porter

die **Portion** NOUN
portion ◇ *eine große Portion* a big portion ◇ *Zwei Portionen Pommes frites, bitte.* Two portions of chips, please.
♦ **Dazu gehört eine ordentliche Portion Mut.** You need quite a bit of courage for that.

das **Portmonee** NOUN (PL die **Portmonees**)
purse

das **Porto** NOUN (PL die **Portos**)
postage

Portugal NEUT NOUN
Portugal
♦ **aus Portugal** from Portugal
♦ **nach Portugal** to Portugal

der **Portugiese** NOUN (GEN des **Portugiesen,** PL die **Portugiesen**)
Portuguese

die **Portugiesin** NOUN
Portuguese

portugiesisch ADJECTIVE
Portuguese

das **Porzellan** NOUN
[1] porcelain ◇ *eine Figur aus Porzellan* a porcelain figurine
[2] china ◇ *Das Porzellan habe ich von meiner Oma geerbt.* I inherited the china from my grandma.

die **Posaune** NOUN
trombone ◇ *Franz spielt Posaune.* Franz plays the trombone.

positiv ADJECTIVE
positive ◇ *HIV-positiv* HIV-positive

das **Possessivpronomen** NOUN (PL die **Possessivpronomen**)
possessive pronoun

die **Post** NOUN
[1] post office ◇ *Bring bitte das Päckchen zur Post.* Please take the parcel to the post office.
[2] mail ◇ *Ist Post für mich gekommen?* Was there any mail for me?

das **Postamt** NOUN (PL die **Postämter**)
post office

die **Postanweisung** NOUN
postal order

der **Posten** NOUN (PL die **Posten**)
[1] post ◇ *Sie hat einen guten Posten als Chefsekretärin.* She's got a good post as a director's secretary.
[2] sentry ◇ *Die Armee hat vor dem Gebäude Posten aufgestellt.* The army posted sentries in front of the building.
[3] item ◇ *Dieser Posten ist nicht auf der Preisliste aufgeführt.* This item doesn't appear on the price list.

das **Poster** NOUN (PL die **Poster**)

P

poster

das **Postfach** NOUN (PL die **Postfächer**)
post office box

die **Postkarte** NOUN
postcard

postlagernd ADVERB
poste restante

die **Postleitzahl** NOUN
postcode

postwendend ADVERB
by return of post

das **Postwertzeichen** NOUN (PL die **Postwertzeichen**)
postage stamp

die **Pracht** NOUN
splendour

prächtig ADJECTIVE, ADVERB
1 magnificent ◊ *ein prächtiges Haus* a magnificent house
2 marvellous ◊ *Wir haben uns prächtig amüsiert.* We had a marvellous time.

prachtvoll ADJECTIVE
splendid

das **Prädikat** NOUN (PL die **Prädikate**)
predicate ◊ *Subjekt und Prädikat eines Satzes* subject and predicate of a sentence

prahlen VERB
to brag

der **Praktikant** NOUN (GEN des **Praktikanten**, PL die **Praktikanten**)
trainee

die **Praktikantin** NOUN
trainee

das **Praktikum** NOUN (GEN des **Praktikums**, PL die **Praktika**)
practical training ◊ *Sie absolviert ihr Praktikum.* She's doing her practical training.

praktisch ADJECTIVE
1 practical ◊ *ein praktischer Mensch* a practical person
2 handy ◊ *ein praktisches Gerät* a handy gadget
♦ **praktischer Arzt** general practitioner
♦ **praktisch begabt sein** to be good with one's hands

die **Praline** NOUN
chocolate

die **Präposition** NOUN
preposition

das **Präsens** NOUN (GEN des **Präsens**)
present tense

das **Präservativ** NOUN (PL die **Präservative**)
condom

der **Präsident** NOUN (GEN des **Präsidenten**, PL die **Präsidenten**)
president

die **Praxis** NOUN (PL die **Praxen**)
1 practical experience ◊ *Ihr fehlt die Praxis.* She lacks practical experience.

♦ **etwas in die Praxis umsetzen** to put something into practice
2 surgery ◊ *Kommen Sie zur Behandlung in die Praxis.* Come to the surgery for treatment.
3 practice ◊ *Mein Anwalt hat seine eigene Praxis aufgemacht.* My solicitor has opened his own practice.

die **Predigt** NOUN
sermon

der **Preis** NOUN (GEN des **Preises**, PL die **Preise**)
1 price ◊ *Die Preise für Computer sind gefallen.* Computer prices have fallen.
2 prize ◊ *Ihr Hund hat einen Preis gewonnen.* Her dog's won a prize.
♦ **um keinen Preis** not at any price

die **Preiselbeere** NOUN
cranberry

preisgünstig ADJECTIVE
inexpensive

die **Preislage** NOUN
price range

das **Preisschild** NOUN (PL die **Preisschilder**)
price tag

der **Preisträger** NOUN (PL die **Preisträger**)
prizewinner

preiswert ADJECTIVE
inexpensive

die **Prellung** NOUN
bruise

der **Premierminister** NOUN (PL die **Premierminister**)
prime minister

die **Presse** NOUN
press

pressen VERB
to press

der **Priester** NOUN (PL die **Priester**)
priest

prima ADJECTIVE
super ◊ *ein prima Hotel* a super hotel

der **Prinz** NOUN (GEN des **Prinzen**, PL die **Prinzen**)
prince

die **Prinzessin** NOUN
princess

das **Prinzip** NOUN (PL die **Prinzipien**)
principle
♦ **aus Prinzip** as a matter of principle

privat ADJECTIVE
private

der **Privatpatient** NOUN (GEN des **Privatpatienten**, PL die **Privatpatienten**)
private patient

die **Privatschule** NOUN
fee-paying school

das **Privileg** NOUN (PL die **Privilegien**)
privilege

pro PREPOSITION
*The preposition **pro** takes the accusative.*
per ◊ *zehn Euro pro Person* ten euros per person
♦ **einmal pro Woche** once a week

die **Probe** NOUN
　　[1] test ◊ *Wir müssen eine Probe machen, ob er geeignet ist.* We need to do a test to see if he's suitable.
　　[2] sample ◊ *Die Probe wird im Labor untersucht.* The sample's being examined in the laboratory.
　　[3] rehearsal ◊ *die letzte Probe vor der Aufführung* the final rehearsal before the performance
　　♦ **jemanden auf die Probe stellen** to test somebody

probieren VERB (PERFECT **hat probiert**)
　　to try ◊ *Probier mal eine andere Methode.* Try a different method. ◊ *Willst du mal von dem Käse probieren?* Would you like to try some of the cheese?

das **Problem** NOUN (PL die **Probleme**)
　　problem ◊ *Kein Problem!* No problem.

das **Produkt** NOUN (PL die **Produkte**)
　　product

die **Produktion** NOUN
　　[1] production ◊ *die Produktion von Luxusautos* the production of luxury cars
　　[2] output ◊ *Wir müssen unsere Produktion erhöhen.* We must increase our output.

produzieren VERB (PERFECT **hat produziert**)
　　to produce

der **Professor** NOUN (PL die **Professoren**)
　　professor

der **Profi** NOUN (PL die **Profis**)
　　pro ◊ *Er spielt wie ein Profi.* He plays like a pro.

der **Profit** NOUN (PL die **Profite**)
　　profit

profitieren VERB (PERFECT **hat profitiert**)
　　♦ **von etwas profitieren** to profit from something

das **Programm** NOUN (PL die **Programme**)
　　[1] programme ◊ *das Programm des heutigen Abends* this evening's programme
　　[2] program ◊ *Für die Kalkulation arbeite ich mit einem anderen Programm.* I've got a different program for spreadsheets.

programmieren VERB (PERFECT **hat programmiert**)
　　to program

der **Programmierer** NOUN (PL die **Programmierer**)
　　programmer

das **Projekt** NOUN (PL die **Projekte**)
　　project

das **Promille** NOUN (PL die **Promille**)
　　alcohol level ◊ *Er hatte drei Promille.* He had an alcohol level of three hundred milligrams in a hundred millilitres of blood.

das **Pronomen** NOUN (PL die **Pronomen**)
　　pronoun

der **Prophet** NOUN (GEN des **Propheten**, PL die **Propheten**)
　　prophet

die **Proportion** NOUN
　　proportion

die **Prosa** NOUN
　　prose

prosit EXCLAMATION
　　cheers!
　　♦ **Prosit Neujahr!** Happy New Year!

der **Prospekt** NOUN (PL die **Prospekte**)
　　brochure
　　*Be careful! **Prospekt** does not mean prospect.*

prost EXCLAMATION
　　cheers!

die **Prostituierte** NOUN (GEN der **Prostituierten**)
　　prostitute

die **Prostitution** NOUN
　　prostitution

das **Protein** NOUN (PL die **Proteine**)
　　protein

der **Protest** NOUN (PL die **Proteste**)
　　protest

protestantisch ADJECTIVE
　　Protestant

protestieren VERB (PERFECT **hat protestiert**)
　　to protest

das **Protokoll** NOUN (PL die **Protokolle**)
　　[1] minutes ◊ *Wer schreibt das Protokoll der heutigen Besprechung?* Who is taking the minutes of today's meeting?
　　[2] statement ◊ *Der Zeuge muss das polizeiliche Protokoll unterschreiben.* The witness must sign the statement he made to the police.

protzen VERB
　　to show off

protzig ADJECTIVE
　　showy ◊ *ein protziges Auto* a showy car

der **Proviant** NOUN (PL die **Proviante**)
　　provisions

provisorisch ADJECTIVE
　　provisional

provozieren VERB (PERFECT **hat provoziert**)
　　to provoke

das **Prozent** NOUN (PL die **Prozente**)
　　per cent ◊ *zehn Prozent* ten per cent

der **Prozess** NOUN (GEN des **Prozesses**, PL die **Prozesse**)
　　trial ◊ *der Prozess gegen die Terroristen* the trial of the terrorists
　　♦ **einen Prozess gewinnen** to win a case

prüde ADJECTIVE
　　prudish

prüfen VERB
　　[1] to test ◊ *Wir werden morgen in Chemie geprüft.* We're having a chemistry test tomorrow.
　　[2] to check ◊ *Vor der Reise sollte man den Ölstand prüfen.* You should check the oil before your journey.

P

der **Prüfer** NOUN (PL die **Prüfer**)
examiner

die **Prüfung** NOUN

[1] examination ◊ *Sie hat die Prüfung bestanden.* She's passed the examination.

[2] check ◊ *Bei der Prüfung der Bremsen haben wir einen Defekt festgestellt.* During a check on the brakes we found a fault.

der **Prügel** NOUN (PL die **Prügel**)
stick ◊ *Er schlug ihn mit einem Prügel.* He hit him with a stick.
♦ **Prügel bekommen** to get a hiding

die **Prügelei** NOUN
fight

prügeln VERB
to beat ◊ *Eltern sollten ihre Kinder nicht prügeln.* Parents shouldn't beat their children.
♦ **sich prügeln** to fight ◊ *Ich will mich nicht mit dir prügeln.* I don't want to fight you.

die **Prügelstrafe** NOUN
corporal punishment

psychisch ADJECTIVE
psychological

der **Psychologe** NOUN (GEN des **Psychologen,** PL die **Psychologen**)
psychologist ◊ *Ihr Vater ist Psychologe.* Her father is a psychologist.

die **Psychologie** NOUN
psychology

psychologisch ADJECTIVE
psychological

der **Psychotherapeut** NOUN (GEN des **Psychotherapeuten,** PL die **Psychotherapeuten**)
psychotherapist ◊ *Herr Müller ist Psychotherapeut.* Mr Müller is a psychotherapist.

die **Pubertät** NOUN
puberty ◊ *während der Pubertät* during puberty

das **Publikum** NOUN
audience

der **Pudding** NOUN (PL die **Puddinge** or **Puddings**)
blancmange

der **Puder** NOUN (PL die **Puder**)
powder

der **Puffer** NOUN (PL die **Puffer**)
buffer

der **Pulli** NOUN (PL die **Pullis**)
pullover

der **Pullover** NOUN (PL die **Pullover**)
pullover

der **Puls** NOUN (GEN des **Pulses,** PL die **Pulse**)
pulse
♦ **jemandem den Puls fühlen** to take somebody's pulse

das **Pult** NOUN (PL die **Pulte**)
desk

das **Pulver** NOUN (PL die **Pulver**)
powder

der **Pulverschnee** NOUN
powder snow

die **Pumpe** NOUN
pump

pumpen VERB

[1] to pump ◊ *Das Öl wird durch die Pipeline gepumpt.* The oil's pumped along the pipeline.

[2] to lend ◊ *Kannst du mir mal deinen Walkman pumpen?* Can you lend me your Walkman?

[3] to borrow ◊ *Ich habe mir das Rad meiner Schwester gepumpt.* I've borrowed my sister's bike.

der **Punkt** NOUN (PL die **Punkte**)

[1] full stop ◊ *Am Satzende steht ein Punkt.* A full stop goes at the end of a sentence.

[2] point ◊ *In diesem Punkt gebe ich dir recht.* On this point I agree with you.

[3] dot ◊ *Das Schiff war nur noch ein kleiner Punkt am Horizont.* The ship was only a small dot on the horizon.

pünktlich ADJECTIVE, ADVERB

[1] punctual ◊ *Sie ist nicht sehr pünktlich.* She's not very punctual.

[2] on time ◊ *Der Zug kam pünktlich an.* The train arrived on time.

die **Pünktlichkeit** NOUN
punctuality

die **Puppe** NOUN
doll

pur ADJECTIVE
pure ◊ *Das ist pures Gold.* That's pure gold. ◊ *Das ist doch der pure Wahnsinn.* But that's pure madness.
♦ **Whisky pur** neat whisky

die **Pute** NOUN
turkey

der **Puter** NOUN (PL die **Puter**)
turkey

putzen VERB

[1] to clean ◊ *Sie putzt jeden Samstag das Haus.* She cleans the house every Saturday.

[2] to wipe ◊ *Putz dir die Schuhe, bevor du reinkommst.* Wipe your shoes before you come in.
♦ **sich die Nase putzen** to blow one's nose
♦ **sich die Zähne putzen** to brush one's teeth

die **Putzfrau** NOUN
cleaner

der **Putzmann** NOUN (PL die **Putzmänner**)
cleaner

das **Puzzle** NOUN (PL die **Puzzles**)
jigsaw

der **Pyjama** NOUN (PL die **Pyjamas**)
pyjamas ◊ *ein Pyjama* a pair of pyjamas

die **Pyramide** NOUN
pyramid

Q

qm ABBREVIATION (= *Quadratmeter*)
m²

das **Quadrat** NOUN (PL die **Quadrate**)
square

quadratisch ADJECTIVE
square

der **Quadratmeter** NOUN (PL die **Quadratmeter**)
square metre ◇ *eine Wohnung von achtzig Quadratmetern* a flat of eighty square metres

quaken VERB
1 to croak (*frog*)
2 to quack (*duck*)

die **Qual** NOUN
1 agony ◇ *Treppensteigen ist für sie eine Qual.* Climbing the stairs is agony for her.
2 anguish ◇ *Die Qualen, die ich bei dieser Prüfung ausgestanden habe ...* The anguish I went through in that exam ...

quälen VERB
to treat cruelly ◇ *Tiere quälen* to treat animals cruelly
♦ **sich quälen (1)** to struggle ◇ *Sie quälte sich die Treppe hinauf.* She struggled up the steps.
♦ **sich quälen (2)** to torment oneself ◇ *Quäl dich nicht so!* Don't torment yourself like that.
♦ **Er muss sich in der Schule ziemlich quälen.** School's quite a trial for him.

die **Qualifikation** NOUN (PL die **Qualifikationen**)
qualification

sich **qualifizieren** VERB (PERFECT **hat sich qualifiziert**)
to qualify ◇ *Sie hat sich für die Weltmeisterschaft qualifiziert.* She qualified for the world championships.

qualifiziert ADJECTIVE
qualified

die **Qualität** NOUN
quality

die **Qualle** NOUN
jellyfish ◇ *zwei Quallen* two jellyfish

der **Qualm** NOUN
thick smoke

qualmen VERB
to smoke ◇ *Der Schornstein qualmt.* The chimney is smoking.

die **Quantität** NOUN
quantity

der **Quark** NOUN
quark

der **Quarz** NOUN (GEN des **Quarzes**)
quartz

quasseln VERB
to natter

der **Quatsch** NOUN
rubbish ◇ *Erzähl keinen Quatsch.* Don't talk rubbish.
♦ **Quatsch machen** to fool around
♦ **Mach keinen Quatsch!** Don't be foolish!

quatschen VERB
to natter

die **Quelle** NOUN
1 spring ◇ *heiße Quellen* hot springs
2 source ◇ *aus zuverlässiger Quelle* from a reliable source

quer ADVERB
1 diagonally ◇ *Die Streifen auf dem Stoff verlaufen quer.* The stripes run diagonally across the material.
♦ **quer auf dem Bett** across the bed
2 at right angles ◇ *Die Mannstraße verläuft quer zur Müllerstraße.* Mann Street runs at right angles to Müller Street.

die **Querflöte** NOUN
flute ◇ *Cordula spielt Querflöte.* Cordula plays the flute.

querschnittsgelähmt ADJECTIVE
paraplegic

die **Querstraße** NOUN
♦ **eine Straße mit vielen Querstraßen** a road with a lot of side streets off it
♦ **Biegen Sie an der zweiten Querstraße links ab.** Take the second street on the left.

quetschen VERB
1 to squash ◇ *Pass auf, dass die Tomaten nicht gequetscht werden.* Mind the tomatoes don't get squashed.
2 to cram ◇ *Sie quetschte das Kleid noch in ihren Koffer.* She crammed the dress into her case.
♦ **Ich habe mir den Finger in der Tür gequetscht.** I trapped my finger in the door.

die **Quetschung** NOUN
bruise

quietschen VERB
to squeak

quitt ADJECTIVE
quits ◇ *Jetzt sind wir quitt.* We're quits now.

die **Quittung** NOUN
receipt ◇ *Brauchen Sie eine Quittung?* Do you need a receipt?

R

der **Rabatt** NOUN (PL die **Rabatte**)
discount

die **Rache** NOUN
revenge

der **Rachen** NOUN (PL die **Rachen**)
throat

rächen VERB
- **etwas rächen** to avenge something
- **sich rächen** to take revenge
- **Das wird sich rächen.** You'll pay for that.

das **Rad** NOUN (PL die **Räder**)
1 wheel
2 bike ◊ *Wir sind mit dem Rad gekommen.* We came by bike.
- **Rad fahren** to cycle

der **Radar** NOUN (PL die **Radare**)
You can also say das Radar.
radar

die **Radarfalle** NOUN
speed trap

die **Radarkontrolle** NOUN
radar-controlled speed check

radebrechen VERB
- **Deutsch radebrechen** to speak broken German

radeln VERB (PERFECT **ist geradelt**)
to cycle ◊ *Wir sind an den Bodensee geradelt.* We cycled to Lake Constance.

radfahren VERB see **Rad**

der **Radfahrer** NOUN (PL die **Radfahrer**)
cyclist

der **Radfahrweg** NOUN (PL die **Radfahrwege**)
cycle track

der **Radiergummi** NOUN (PL die **Radiergummis**)
rubber

das **Radieschen** NOUN (PL die **Radieschen**)
radish

das **Radio** NOUN (PL die **Radios**)
radio

radioaktiv ADJECTIVE
radioactive

die **Radioaktivität** NOUN
radioactivity

das **Radrennen** NOUN (PL die **Radrennen**)
1 cycle race ◊ *Er hat an dem Radrennen teilgenommen.* He took part in the cycle race.
2 cycle racing ◊ *Sie begeistert sich für Radrennen.* She's a cycle racing fan.

der **Radsport** NOUN
cycling

der **Rahm** NOUN
cream

der **Rahmen** NOUN (PL die **Rahmen**)
frame ◊ *der Rahmen eines Bildes* the frame of a picture

- **im Rahmen des Möglichen** within the bounds of possibility

die **Rakete** NOUN
rocket

der **Rand** NOUN (PL die **Ränder**)
1 edge ◊ *Er stand am Rand des Schwimmbeckens.* He stood on the edge of the swimming pool.
2 rim ◊ *der Rand der Tasse* the rim of the cup
- **eine Brille mit Goldrand** a pair of gold-rimmed glasses
3 margin ◊ *Lass an der Seite des Blattes einen Rand.* Leave a margin at the edge of the page.
4 ring ◊ *In der Badewanne waren dunkle Ränder.* There were dark rings in the bath tub.
5 verge ◊ *Die Firma steht am Rand des Bankrotts.* The company's on the verge of bankruptcy.
- **außer Rand und Band** out of control

randalieren VERB (PERFECT **hat randaliert**)
to go on the rampage

der **Rang** NOUN (PL die **Ränge**)
1 rank (*military*) ◊ *Er steht im Rang eines Hauptmanns.* He has the rank of captain.
- **ein Mann ohne Rang und Namen** a man without any standing
2 circle (*theatre*) ◊ *erster Rang* dress circle ◊ *zweiter Rang* upper circle

ranzig ADJECTIVE
rancid

der **Rappen** NOUN (PL die **Rappen**)
rappen ◊ *Der Schweizer Franken hat hundert Rappen.* There're one hundred rappen in a Swiss franc.

ⓘ *In the French-speaking part of Switzerland you talk about **Centime** rather than **Rappen**.*

rasch ADJECTIVE, ADVERB
quick ◊ *Das war rasch gemacht.* That was quickly done.
- **Ich gehe noch rasch beim Bäcker vorbei.** I'll just pop round to the baker's.

der **Rasen** NOUN (PL die **Rasen**)
see also **rasen** VERB
lawn

rasen VERB (PERFECT **ist gerast**)
see also **der Rasen** NOUN
to race ◊ *Wir sind durch die engen Straßen gerast.* We raced along the narrow streets.

der **Rasenmäher** NOUN (PL die **Rasenmäher**)
lawnmower

der **Rasierapparat** NOUN (PL die **Rasierapparate**)
shaver

die **Rasiercreme** NOUN (PL die **Rasiercremes**)
shaving cream

rasieren VERB (PERFECT **hat rasiert**)
to shave
♦ **sich rasieren** to shave

die **Rasierklinge** NOUN
razor blade

das **Rasiermesser** NOUN (PL die **Rasiermesser**)
razor

das **Rasierwasser** NOUN (PL die **Rasierwasser**)
shaving lotion

die **Rasse** NOUN
1 race ◊ *Rassenunruhen* race riots
2 breed ◊ *Welche Rasse ist Ihr Hund?* What breed is your dog?

der **Rassenhass** NOUN (GEN des **Rassenhasses**)
racial hatred

die **Rassentrennung** NOUN
racial segregation

der **Rassismus** NOUN (GEN des **Rassismus**)
racism

die **Rast** NOUN
rest
♦ **Rast machen** to stop for a break

rasten VERB
to rest

das **Rasthaus** NOUN (PL die **Rasthäuser**)
services *(motorway)*

der **Rasthof** NOUN (PL die **Rasthöfe**)
services *(motorway)*

der **Rastplatz** NOUN (GEN des **Rastplatzes**, PL die **Rastplätze**)
lay-by

die **Raststätte** NOUN
service area

die **Rasur** NOUN
shaving

der **Rat** NOUN (PL die **Ratschläge**)
advice ◊ *Ich habe viele Ratschläge bekommen.* I've been given a lot of advice.
♦ **ein Rat** a piece of advice
♦ **Ich weiß keinen Rat.** I don't know what to do.
♦ **zu Rate** *see* **zurate**

die **Rate** NOUN
instalment

raten VERB (PRESENT **rät**, IMPERFECT **riet**, PERFECT **hat geraten**)
to guess ◊ *Rat mal, wie alt ich bin.* Guess how old I am.
♦ **jemandem raten** to advise somebody ◊ *Sie hat mir geraten, einen Arzt aufzusuchen.* She advised me to see a doctor.

das **Rathaus** NOUN (GEN des **Rathauses**, PL die **Rathäuser**)
town hall

die **Ration** NOUN
ration

rationalisieren VERB (PERFECT **hat rationalisiert**)
to rationalize

rationell ADJECTIVE
efficient

ratlos ADJECTIVE
at a loss ◊ *Ich bin ratlos, was ich tun soll.* I'm at a loss as to what to do.
♦ **Sie sah mich ratlos an.** She gave me a helpless look.

der **Ratschlag** NOUN (PL die **Ratschläge**)
piece of advice ◊ *Ich habe viele Ratschläge bekommen.* I've been given a lot of advice.

das **Rätsel** NOUN (PL die **Rätsel**)
1 puzzle ◊ *Sie löst gern Rätsel.* She likes solving puzzles.
2 mystery ◊ *Das ist mir ein Rätsel.* It's a mystery to me.

rätselhaft ADJECTIVE
mysterious
♦ **Es ist mir rätselhaft ...** It's a mystery to me ...

der **Ratskeller** NOUN (PL die **Ratskeller**)
town-hall restaurant

die **Ratte** NOUN
rat

rau ADJECTIVE
1 rough ◊ *raue Haut* rough skin
2 husky ◊ *eine raue Stimme* a husky voice
3 sore ◊ *ein rauer Hals* a sore throat
4 harsh ◊ *raues Wetter* harsh weather ◊ *ein rauer Wind* a harsh wind
♦ **Hier herrschen raue Sitten.** People here have rough-and-ready ways.

der **Raub** NOUN
robbery

das **Raubtier** NOUN (PL die **Raubtiere**)
predator

der **Rauch** NOUN
smoke

rauchen VERB
to smoke ◊ *Er raucht Pfeife.* He smokes a pipe.
♦ **"Rauchen verboten"** "No smoking"

der **Raucher** NOUN (PL die **Raucher**)
smoker

das **Raucherabteil** NOUN (PL die **Raucherabteile**)
smoking compartment

räuchern VERB
to smoke ◊ *Fisch räuchern* to smoke fish

das **Rauchfleisch** NOUN
smoked meat

rauh ADJECTIVE *see* **rau**

der **Raum** NOUN (PL die **Räume**)
1 space ◊ *Sie haben eine Rakete in den Raum geschossen.* They launched a

R

☞

rocket into space. ◊ *Raum und Zeit* space and time

2 room ◊ *Eine Wohnung mit vier Räumen ist nicht groß genug für uns.* A four-roomed flat isn't big enough for us. ◊ *Dieses Gerät braucht wenig Raum.* This appliance doesn't take up much room.

3 area ◊ *Im Raum Stuttgart kommt es morgen zu Gewittern.* There will be thunderstorms in the Stuttgart area tomorrow.

räumen VERB
1 to clear ◊ *Im Winter müssen die Bürgersteige von Schnee geräumt werden.* The pavements have to be cleared of snow in winter. ◊ *Die Polizei hat das besetzte Haus geräumt.* The police cleared the squat.

2 to move away from ◊ *Die Polizei forderte die Schaulustigen auf, die Unfallstelle zu räumen.* The police ordered the onlookers to move away from the scene of the accident.

3 to vacate ◊ *Bitte räumen Sie Ihr Zimmer bis spätestens zehn Uhr.* Please vacate your room by ten o'clock at the latest.

4 to clear away ◊ *Könnt ihr bitte das Geschirr vom Tisch räumen?* Could you clear away the dishes, please?

5 to put away ◊ *Räum bitte deine Spielsachen in den Schrank.* Please put your toys away in the cupboard.

die **Raumfähre** NOUN
space shuttle

die **Raumfahrt** NOUN
space travel

der **Rauminhalt** NOUN (PL die **Rauminhalte**)
volume

räumlich ADJECTIVE
spatial

die **Räumlichkeiten** FEM PL NOUN
premises

das **Raumschiff** NOUN (PL die **Raumschiffe**)
spaceship

der **Rausch** NOUN (PL die **Räusche**)
♦ einen Rausch haben to be drunk
♦ seinen Rausch ausschlafen to sleep it off

das **Rauschgift** NOUN (PL die **Rauschgifte**)
drug

der **Rauschgiftsüchtige** NOUN (GEN des/der
die **Rauschgiftsüchtigen**, PL die
Rauschgiftsüchtigen)
drug addict ◊ *Gestern wurde ein Rauschgiftsüchtiger tot aufgefunden.* A drug addict was found dead yesterday.

sich **räuspern** VERB
to clear one's throat

reagieren VERB (PERFECT **hat reagiert**)
1 to react ◊ *Wie hat sie auf diesen Vorwurf reagiert?* How did she react to the allegation?

2 to respond ◊ *Die Bremsen haben nicht reagiert.* The brakes didn't respond.

die **Reaktion** NOUN
reaction

reaktionär ADJECTIVE
reactionary

der **Reaktor** NOUN (PL die **Reaktoren**)
reactor

realisieren VERB (PERFECT **hat realisiert**)
1 to fulfil ◊ *Er hat seine Träume realisiert.* He's fulfilled his dreams.

2 carry out ◊ *Wir sollten diese Pläne realisieren.* We ought to carry out these plans.

3 realize ◊ *Sie hat gar nicht realisiert, dass er schon längst weg war.* She simply didn't realize that he had long since left.

realistisch ADJECTIVE
realistic

die **Realschule** NOUN
secondary school

> ❶ Pupils enter **Realschule** at the age of about ten, and leave after six years. It is not as academically oriented as the **Gymnasium**.

der **Rechen** NOUN (PL die **Rechen**)
rake

das **Rechnen** NOUN
> see also **rechnen** VERB

arithmetic ◊ *Bettina ist gut im Rechnen.* Bettina's good at arithmetic.

rechnen VERB
> see also **das Rechnen** NOUN

to work out ◊ *Lass mich rechnen, wie viel das wird.* Let me work out how much that's going to be.

♦ **Bettina kann gut rechnen.** Bettina's good at arithmetic.

♦ **Klinsmann wird zu den besten Fußballspielern gerechnet.** Klinsmann is regarded as one of the best footballers.

♦ **Man rechnet Mexico City zu den Megastädten.** Mexico City is classed as one of the metropolises.

♦ **rechnen mit (1)** to reckon with ◊ *Mit wie vielen Besuchern können wir rechnen?* How many visitors can we reckon with?

♦ **rechnen mit (2)** to reckon on ◊ *Mit dieser Reaktion hatte ich nicht gerechnet.* I hadn't reckoned on this reaction.

♦ **rechnen auf** to count on ◊ *Wir rechnen auf deine Unterstützung.* We're counting on your support.

der **Rechner** NOUN (PL die **Rechner**)
1 calculator ◊ *Ich habe das mit meinem Rechner nachgerechnet.* I've checked it with my calculator.

2 computer ◊ *Er hat sich für seinen Rechner einen neuen Prozessor gekauft.* He's bought a new CPU for his computer.

die **Rechnung** NOUN

1 calculations ◊ *Meine Rechnung ergibt, dass wir noch zweihundert Euro haben.* According to my calculations, we still have two hundred euros left.

2 invoice ◊ *Die Rechnung liegt der Sendung bei.* The invoice is enclosed.

das **Recht** NOUN (PL die **Rechte**)

see also **recht** ADJECTIVE, ADVERB

1 right ◊ *Es ist mein Recht, das zu erfahren.* It's my right to know that. ◊ *Ich habe ein Recht auf eine Erklärung.* I've got a right to an explanation.

♦ **im Recht sein** to be in the right ◊ *Obwohl er im Recht war, hat er nachgegeben.* Although he was in the right, he gave in.

♦ **etwas mit Recht tun** to be right to do something ◊ *Sie hat sich mit Recht beschwert.* She was right to complain.

2 law ◊ *Sie wurde nach deutschem Recht zu zehn Jahren Gefängnis verurteilt.* She was sentenced under German law to ten years' imprisonment.

♦ **Recht sprechen** to administer justice

recht ADJECTIVE, ADVERB

see also **das Recht** NOUN, **rechte** ADJECTIVE, **rechts** ADVERB

1 right ◊ *Es war nicht recht, dass du sie belogen hast.* It wasn't right of you to lie to her. ◊ *Dies ist nicht der rechte Moment, um darüber zu sprechen.* This isn't the right moment to talk about it.

♦ **Wenn ich dich recht verstehe ...** If I understand you correctly ...

♦ **Das geschieht dir recht!** Serves you right!

2 quite ◊ *Das scheint recht einfach.* It seems quite simple.

♦ **jemandem recht sein** to be all right with somebody ◊ *Wenn es deiner Mutter recht ist, übernachte ich gern bei euch.* If it's all right with your mother, I'd like to stay the night at your place.

♦ **Das ist mir recht.** That suits me.

♦ **es jemandem recht machen** to please somebody ◊ *Dir kann man es auch nie recht machen!* There's no pleasing you.

♦ **recht haben** to be right ◊ *Wer hat nun recht?* Who's right? ◊ *Sie will immer recht haben.* She always has to be right.

♦ **jemandem recht geben** to agree with somebody ◊ *Ich muss dir recht geben, das war nicht nett.* I have to agree with you – that wasn't nice.

♦ **Jetzt erst recht!** Now more than ever.

die **Rechte** NOUN (GEN der **Rechten**)

see also **rechte** ADJECTIVE, **das Rechte** NOUN

1 right ◊ *Zu Ihrer Rechten sehen Sie das Rathaus.* On your right you'll see the town hall.

2 right hand ◊ *Er schlug mit der Rechten zu.* He hit out with his right hand.

3 right-wing ◊ *eine Partei der Rechten* a right-wing party

rechte ADJECTIVE

see also **recht** ADJECTIVE, **die Rechte** NOUN, **das Rechte** NOUN, **rechts** ADVERB

right ◊ *In Deutschland fährt man auf der rechten Seite.* They drive on the right in Germany. ◊ *Mein rechtes Auge tut weh.* My right eye's hurting. ◊ *Er hat sich den rechten Arm gebrochen.* He broke his right arm.

das **Rechte** NOUN (GEN des **Rechten**)

see also **die Rechte** NOUN, **rechte** ADJECTIVE

right thing ◊ *Pass auf, dass du das Rechte sagst.* Make sure you say the right thing.

♦ **etwas Rechtes** something proper ◊ *Du solltest etwas Rechtes lernen.* You ought to learn something proper.

♦ **nichts Rechtes** nothing decent ◊ *Ich habe den ganzen Tag noch nichts Rechtes gegessen.* I haven't had anything decent to eat all day.

rechteckig ADJECTIVE
rectangular

rechtfertigen VERB
to justify ◊ *Wie kannst du dein Verhalten rechtfertigen?* How can you justify your behaviour?

♦ **sich rechtfertigen** to justify oneself

rechtmäßig ADJECTIVE
lawful

rechts ADVERB

see also **rechte** ADJECTIVE

right ◊ *rechts abbiegen* to turn right

♦ **rechts überholen** to overtake on the right

♦ **Er schreibt mit rechts.** He writes with his right hand.

♦ **Rechts sehen Sie das Rathaus.** On the right you'll see the town hall.

♦ **rechts von der Kirche** to the right of the church

♦ **rechts von mir** on my right

♦ **rechts wählen** to vote for a right-wing party

der **Rechtsanwalt** NOUN (PL die **Rechtsanwälte**)
lawyer

die **Rechtsanwältin** NOUN
lawyer

die **Rechtschreibung** NOUN
spelling

der **Rechtshänder** NOUN (PL die **Rechtshänder**)
♦ **Er ist Rechtshänder.** He's right-handed.

die **Rechtshänderin** NOUN
♦ **Sie ist Rechtshänderin.** She's right-handed.

die **Rechtskurve** NOUN
right-hand bend

der **Rechtsverkehr** NOUN
driving on the right
♦ **In Deutschland ist Rechtsverkehr.** They drive on the right in Germany.

R

rechtwinklig ADJECTIVE
right-angled

rechtzeitig ADJECTIVE, ADVERB
in time ◊ *Ich bitte um rechtzeitige Benachrichtigung.* Please let me know in time. ◊ *Wir sind rechtzeitig angekommen.* We arrived in time.

recyceln VERB (PERFECT **hat recycelt**)
to recycle

das **Recycling** NOUN
recycling

der **Redakteur** NOUN (PL die **Redakteure**)
editor

die **Redaktion** NOUN
[1] editing ◊ *die Redaktion eines Buches* the editing of a book
[2] editorial staff ◊ *Die Redaktion hat das Manuskript abgelehnt.* The editorial staff rejected the manuscript.
[3] editorial office ◊ *Er arbeitet in unserer Redaktion.* He works in our editorial office.

die **Rede** NOUN
speech ◊ *Er hat eine witzige Rede gehalten.* He made an amusing speech.
♦ **jemanden zur Rede stellen** to take somebody to task

reden VERB
[1] to talk ◊ *Wir haben über das Wetter geredet.* We talked about the weather. ◊ *Du redest Unsinn.* You're talking nonsense.
[2] to speak ◊ *Ich werde mit deiner Mutter reden.* I'll speak to your mother. ◊ *Ich rede nicht gern vor so vielen Menschen.* I don't like speaking in front of so many people. ◊ *Der Präsident redet zum Volk.* The President's speaking to the country.
[3] to say ◊ *Was reden die Leute über uns?* What are people saying about us?

die **Redewendung** NOUN
expression

der **Redner** NOUN (PL die **Redner**)
speaker

reduzieren VERB (PERFECT **hat reduziert**)
to reduce

das **Referat** NOUN (PL die **Referate**)
[1] assignment ◊ *Ich muss in Geografie ein Referat schreiben.* I have to write an assignment in geography.
[2] paper ◊ *Sie hat ein Referat über Shakespeare gehalten.* She gave a paper on Shakespeare.
[3] section ◊ *Er ist Leiter des Referats Umweltschutz.* He's head of the environmental protection section.

der **Reflex** NOUN (GEN des **Reflexes,** PL die **Reflexe**)
reflex

reflexiv ADJECTIVE
reflexive

die **Reform** NOUN
reform

das **Regal** NOUN (PL die **Regale**)
[1] bookcase ◊ *In ihrem Regal stehen viele Krimis.* There are a lot of detective stories in her bookcase.
[2] rack ◊ *ein Regal für Weinflaschen* a wine rack
[3] shelf ◊ *Auf dem Regal standen Kräuter.* There were herbs on the shelf.

die **Regel** NOUN
[1] rule ◊ *Keine Regel ohne Ausnahme.* The exception proves the rule.
[2] period ◊ *Meine Regel ist ausgeblieben.* I've missed a period.

regelmäßig ADJECTIVE, ADVERB
regular ◊ *in regelmäßigen Abständen* at regular intervals ◊ *Die Busse verkehren regelmäßig.* The buses run regularly.

die **Regelmäßigkeit** NOUN
regularity

regeln VERB
[1] to direct ◊ *Ein Polizist regelte den Verkehr.* A policeman was directing the traffic.
[2] to control ◊ *die Lautstärke regeln* to control the volume
[3] to settle ◊ *Ich habe da noch eine Sache mit ihm zu regeln.* I've still got something to settle with him.
[4] to arrange ◊ *Wir haben das so geregelt, dass er abwäscht und ich putze.* We've arranged things so that he washes the dishes and I do the cleaning.
♦ **sich von selbst regeln** to take care of itself

der **Regen** NOUN (PL die **Regen**)
rain

der **Regenbogen** NOUN (PL die **Regenbogen**)
rainbow

der **Regenmantel** NOUN (PL die **Regenmäntel**)
raincoat

der **Regenschauer** NOUN (PL die **Regenschauer**)
shower

der **Regenschirm** NOUN (PL die **Regenschirme**)
umbrella

der **Regenwurm** NOUN (PL die **Regenwürmer**)
earthworm

regieren VERB (PERFECT **hat regiert**)
[1] to govern ◊ *Wer regiert zur Zeit Russland?* Who governs Russia nowadays?
[2] to reign ◊ *Wann hat Elisabeth die Erste regiert?* When did Elizabeth the First reign?

die **Regierung** NOUN
[1] government ◊ *die deutsche Regierung* the German government
[2] reign ◊ *England unter der Regierung von Elisabeth der Zweiten* England during the reign of Elizabeth the Second

regnen VERB
to rain ◊ *Es regnet.* It's raining.

regnerisch ADJECTIVE
rainy

das **Reh** NOUN (PL die **Rehe**)
deer

reiben VERB (IMPERFECT **rieb**, PERFECT **hat gerieben**)
[1] to rub ◊ *Warum reibst du dir die Augen?* Why are you rubbing your eyes?
[2] to grate ◊ *Er rieb Käse über die Kartoffeln.* He grated cheese over the potatoes.

die **Reibung** NOUN
friction

das **Reich** NOUN (PL die **Reiche**)
see also **reich** ADJECTIVE
[1] empire ◊ *Das Reich Hadrians erstreckte sich bis Schottland.* Hadrian's empire reached as far as Scotland.
[2] kingdom ◊ *das Reich der Tiere* the animal kingdom
♦ **das Dritte Reich** the Third Reich

reich ADJECTIVE
see also **das Reich** NOUN
rich

reichen VERB
[1] to be enough ◊ *Der Kuchen wird nicht für alle reichen.* There won't be enough cake for everybody.
[2] to give ◊ *Sie reichte mir die Hand.* She gave me her hand.
♦ **jemandem etwas reichen** to pass somebody something ◊ *Kannst du mir bitte die Butter reichen?* Can you pass me the butter, please?
♦ **Nur ein Salat reicht ihm nicht.** A salad won't be enough for him.
♦ **Das Gehalt reicht ihr nicht, sie will mehr.** She can't get by on her salary, she wants more.
♦ **Mir reicht's!** I've had enough.
♦ **Unser Garten reicht bis zum Fluss.** Our garden goes right down to the river.

reif ADJECTIVE
[1] ripe ◊ *Die Äpfel sind noch nicht reif.* The apples aren't ripe yet.
[2] mature ◊ *Für sein Alter ist er schon sehr reif.* He's very mature for his age.

der **Reifen** NOUN (PL die **Reifen**)
[1] tyre ◊ *Mir ist ein Reifen geplatzt.* I've got a burst tyre.
[2] hoop ◊ *ein Hula-Hoop-Reifen* a hula hoop

der **Reifendruck** NOUN
tyre pressure

die **Reifenpanne** NOUN
puncture

die **Reihe** NOUN
row ◊ *Stellt euch in einer Reihe auf.* Stand in a row. ◊ *Wir saßen in der zweiten Reihe.* We sat in the second row.
♦ **Eine ganze Reihe von Menschen ist abergläubisch.** A whole lot of people are superstitious.

♦ **der Reihe nach** in turn
♦ **Er ist an der Reihe.** It's his turn.
♦ **an die Reihe kommen** to have one's turn

die **Reihenfolge** NOUN
order ◊ *alphabetische Reihenfolge* alphabetical order

das **Reihenhaus** NOUN (GEN des **Reihenhauses**, PL die **Reihenhäuser**)
terraced house

rein ADJECTIVE, ADVERB
[1] pure ◊ *Das ist reines Gold.* That's pure gold. ◊ *reine Seide* pure silk
[2] clean ◊ *Damit wird die Wäsche rein.* This will get the washing clean. ◊ *reine Luft* clean air ◊ *reine Haut* clear skin
[3] sheer ◊ *Das ist der reine Wahnsinn.* That's sheer madness. ◊ *Das ist das reinste Vergnügen.* It's sheer pleasure.
[4] purely ◊ *Rein technisch ist das machbar.* From a purely technical point of view it's feasible.
♦ **rein gar nichts** absolutely nothing
♦ **etwas ins Reine schreiben** to make a fair copy of something
♦ **etwas ins Reine bringen** to clear something up
[5] in ◊ *Deckel auf und rein mit dem Müll.* Off with the lid and in with the rubbish. ◊ *Los rein mit dir, Zeit fürs Bett!* Come on, in you come, it's time for bed.

der **Reinfall** NOUN (PL die **Reinfälle**)
let-down

die **Reinheit** NOUN
purity ◊ *die Reinheit des Biers* the purity of beer
♦ **Für die Reinheit Ihrer Wäsche ...** To get your washing really clean ...

reinigen VERB
to clean

die **Reinigung** NOUN
[1] cleaning ◊ *ein Mittel zur Reinigung der Polster* an cleaning agent for upholstery
[2] cleaner's ◊ *Bring bitte meine Hose in die Reinigung.* Please take my trousers to the cleaner's.
♦ **chemische Reinigung (1)** dry cleaning ◊ *Bei diesem Stoff empfehlen wir eine chemische Reinigung.* We recommend dry cleaning for this material.
♦ **chemische Reinigung (2)** dry cleaner's ◊ *Im Einkaufszentrum gibt es auch eine chemische Reinigung.* There's also a dry cleaner's in the shopping mall.

der **Reis** NOUN (GEN des **Reises**)
rice

die **Reise** NOUN
journey ◊ *Auf meiner letzten Reise durch Ägypten habe ich viel gesehen.* I saw a lot on my last journey through Egypt.
♦ **Reisen** travels ◊ *Auf seinen Reisen hat er viel erlebt.* He has experienced a lot on his travels.

R

♦ **Gute Reise!** Have a good journey.

das **Reiseandenken** NOUN (PL die **Reiseandenken**)
souvenir

das **Reisebüro** NOUN (PL die **Reisebüros**)
travel agency

der **Reisebus** NOUN (GEN des **Reisebusses**, PL die **Reisebusse**)
coach

der **Reiseführer** NOUN (PL die **Reiseführer**)
① guidebook ◊ Ich habe einen Reiseführer für Griechenland gekauft. I've bought a guidebook to Greece.
② travel guide ◊ Unser Reiseführer hat uns alles erklärt. Our travel guide explained everything to us.

der **Reiseleiter** NOUN (PL die **Reiseleiter**)
courier

reisen VERB (PERFECT **ist gereist**)
to travel ◊ Ich reise gern. I like travelling.
♦ **reisen nach** to go to ◊ In den Sommerferien wollen wir nach Griechenland reisen. We want to go to Greece in the summer holidays.

der **Reisende** NOUN (GEN des/der **Reisenden**, PL
die die **Reisenden**)
traveller ◊ Ein Reisender hatte sich verirrt. A traveller has got lost.

der **Reisepass** NOUN (GEN des **Reisepasses**, PL die **Reisepässe**)
passport

der **Reisescheck** NOUN (PL die **Reiseschecks**)
traveller's cheque

das **Reiseziel** NOUN (PL die **Reiseziele**)
destination

reißen VERB (IMPERFECT **riss**, PERFECT **hat/ist gerissen**)

> Use **haben** to form the perfect tense. Use **sein** to form the perfect tense for **to break**.

① to tear ◊ Er riss ihren Brief in tausend Stücke. He tore her letter into a thousand pieces. ◊ Sie riss sich die Kleider vom Leib. She tore her clothes off.
② to break ◊ Das Seil ist gerissen. The rope has broken.
③ to snatch ◊ Er hat mir den Geldbeutel aus der Hand gerissen. He snatched my purse from my hand.
④ to drag ◊ Sie hat ihn zu Boden gerissen. She dragged him to the floor.
⑤ to wrench ◊ Er riss das Steuer nach links. He wrenched the steering wheel to the left.
⑥ to tug ◊ Er riss an der Leine. He tugged at the rope.
♦ **Witze reißen** to crack jokes
♦ **etwas an sich reißen** to seize something ◊ Er hat versucht, die Macht an sich zu reißen. He tried to seize power.
♦ **Ich habe das Kind in letzter Minute an mich gerissen.** I pulled the child towards me in the nick of time.

♦ **sich um etwas reißen** to scramble for something ◊ Die Kinder haben sich um die Luftballons gerissen. The children scrambled for the balloons.

der **Reißnagel** NOUN (PL die **Reißnägel**)
drawing pin

der **Reißverschluss** NOUN (GEN des **Reißverschlusses**, PL die **Reißverschlüsse**)
zip

reiten VERB (IMPERFECT **ritt**, PERFECT **ist geritten**)
to ride

der **Reiter** NOUN (PL die **Reiter**)
rider

die **Reitschule** NOUN
riding school

der **Reiz** NOUN (GEN des **Reizes**, PL die **Reize**)
① charm ◊ der Reiz dieser Stadt the charm of this town ◊ Er war von ihren Reizen ganz begeistert. He was quite taken with her charms.
② appeal ◊ der Reiz der Großstadt the appeal of the big city

reizbar ADJECTIVE
irritable

reizen VERB
① to appeal to ◊ Diese Arbeit reizt mich sehr. The work greatly appeals to me. ◊ Es würde mich reizen, mal nach Kreta zu fahren. The idea of going to Crete appeals to me.
② to annoy ◊ Du musst den Hund nicht reizen. Don't annoy the dog.
③ to irritate ◊ Der Rauch reizt die Augen. Smoke irritates the eyes.

reizend ADJECTIVE
charming

reizvoll ADJECTIVE
attractive

die **Reklame** NOUN
① advertising ◊ Im Fernsehen gibt es viel zu viel Reklame. There's far too much advertising on television.
② advertisement ◊ zehn Seiten Reklame ten pages of advertisements

der **Rekord** NOUN (PL die **Rekorde**)
record ◊ Der Rekord liegt bei zehn Metern. The record is ten metres. ◊ einen neuen Rekord aufstellen to set a new record

der **Rektor** NOUN (PL die **Rektoren**)
① headteacher ◊ Der Rektor ist bei uns für die Stundenpläne zuständig. At our school, the headteacher's in charge of timetables.
② vice-chancellor ◊ Zu Semesterbeginn hält der Rektor eine Rede. At the beginning of term the vice-chancellor gives a speech.

das **Rektorat** NOUN (PL die **Rektorate**)
headteacher's office ◊ Franz, du sollst aufs Rektorat kommen. Franz, you're to go to the headteacher's office.

relativ ADVERB
relatively ◊ *Das ist relativ einfach.* That's
relatively easy.

relaxt ADJECTIVE
relaxed

die **Religion** NOUN
religion

die **Religionslehre** NOUN
religious education

religiös ADJECTIVE
religious

das **Rendezvous** NOUN (GEN des **Rendezvous**, PL
die **Rendezvous**)
date ◊ *Sie hatte gestern Abend ein
Rendezvous mit Michael.* She had a date
with Michael last night.

das **Rennen** NOUN (PL die **Rennen**)
| see also **rennen** VERB |
race ◊ *ein Pferderennen* a horse race
◊ *ein Autorennen* a motor race

rennen VERB (IMPERFECT **rannte**, PERFECT **ist
gerannt**)
| see also **das Rennen** NOUN |
to run

der **Rennfahrer** NOUN (PL die **Rennfahrer**)
racing driver

das **Rennpferd** NOUN (PL die **Rennpferde**)
racehorse

der **Rennwagen** NOUN (PL die **Rennwagen**)
racing car

renovieren VERB (PERFECT **hat renoviert**)
to renovate

rentabel ADJECTIVE
[1] lucrative ◊ *eine rentable Arbeit* a
lucrative job
[2] profitable ◊ *Das wäre nicht rentabel.*
That wouldn't be profitable.

die **Rentabilität** NOUN
profitability

die **Rente** NOUN
pension
♦ **in Rente gehen** to retire
Be careful! *Rente* does not mean *rent*.

sich **rentieren** VERB (PERFECT **hat sich rentiert**)
to be profitable ◊ *Das Geschäft rentiert
sich nicht mehr.* The business is no
longer profitable.
♦ **Das hat sich rentiert.** That was
worthwhile.

der **Rentner** NOUN (PL die **Rentner**)
pensioner

die **Reparatur** NOUN
repair

die **Reparaturwerkstatt** NOUN (PL die
Reparaturwerkstätten)
garage (*repair shop*)

reparieren VERB (PERFECT **hat repariert**)
to repair

die **Reportage** NOUN
[1] report ◊ *Ich habe eine Reportage über
die Zustände in Rumänien gelesen.* I read
a report about conditions in Romania.

[2] live commentary ◊ *Hast du im Radio
die Reportage des Europapokalspiels
gehört?* Did you hear the live
commentary on the European cup game
on the radio?

der **Reporter** NOUN (PL die **Reporter**)
reporter

das **Reptil** NOUN (PL die **Reptilien**)
reptile

die **Republik** NOUN
republic

republikanisch ADJECTIVE
republican

das **Reservat** NOUN (PL die **Reservate**)
reservation

die **Reserve** NOUN
reserve

das **Reserverad** NOUN (PL die **Reserveräder**)
spare wheel

reservieren VERB (PERFECT **hat reserviert**)
to reserve ◊ *Ich habe einen Tisch für
heute Abend reservieren lassen.* I've
reserved a table for this evening.

die **Reservierung** NOUN
reservation

der **Respekt** NOUN
respect

respektieren VERB (PERFECT **hat respektiert**)
to respect

respektlos ADJECTIVE
disrespectful

respektvoll ADJECTIVE
respectful

der **Rest** NOUN (PL die **Reste**)
[1] rest ◊ *Den Rest bezahle ich später.* I'll
pay the rest later. ◊ *Die meisten sind
früher gegangen, der Rest hat noch
lange gefeiert.* Most left early, but the
rest carried on celebrating for a long
time.
[2] left-over ◊ *Heute gab's die Reste von
gestern.* Today we had yesterday's left-
overs.
♦ **die Reste** the remains ◊ *Das sind die
Reste der alten Stadtmauer.* These are
the remains of the old town walls.

das **Restaurant** NOUN (PL die **Restaurants**)
restaurant

restaurieren VERB (PERFECT **hat restauriert**)
to restore

restlich ADJECTIVE
remaining

das **Resultat** NOUN (PL die **Resultate**)
result

retten VERB
to rescue

der **Rettich** NOUN (PL die **Rettiche**)
radish

die **Rettung** NOUN
[1] rescue ◊ *Alle zeigten bei der Rettung
großen Mut.* They all showed great
courage during the rescue.

R

☞

2 salvation ◊ *Das war meine Rettung.*
That was my salvation.

3 hope ◊ *seine letzte Rettung* his last
hope

das **Rettungsboot** NOUN (PL die
Rettungsboote)
lifeboat

der **Rettungsdienst** NOUN (PL die
Rettungsdienste)
rescue service

der **Rettungsring** NOUN (PL die **Rettungsringe**)
lifebelt

der **Rettungswagen** NOUN (PL die
Rettungswagen)
ambulance

die **Reue** NOUN
remorse ◊ *Der Täter zeigt keine Reue.*
The culprit doesn't show any remorse.

das **Revier** NOUN (PL die **Reviere**)
1 police station ◊ *Der Polizist nahm ihn
mit aufs Revier.* The policeman took him
to the police station.
2 territory ◊ *Das männliche Tier
verteidigt sein Revier.* The male animal
defends its territory.

die **Revolution** NOUN
revolution ◊ *die Revolution von 1789* the
revolution of 1789

der **Revolver** NOUN (PL die **Revolver**)
revolver

das **Rezept** NOUN (PL die **Rezepte**)
1 recipe ◊ *Kannst du mir mal das
Rezept von deinem Käsekuchen geben?*
Can you give me your cheesecake
recipe?
2 prescription ◊ *Dieses Medikament
bekommt man nur auf Rezept.* You
can only get this medicine on
prescription.

die **Rezeption** NOUN
reception

rezeptpflichtig ADJECTIVE
available only on prescription
♦ **rezeptpflichtige Medikamente**
prescribed drugs

das **R-Gespräch** NOUN (PL die **R-Gespräche**)
reverse charge call

der **Rhabarber** NOUN
rhubarb

der **Rhein** NOUN
Rhine

> ❶ The Rhine is 1320 km long and the
> entire 865 km which flows through
> Germany is navigable, making it an
> important inland waterway. It flows
> past such important cities as Karlsruhe,
> Mannheim, Ludwigshafen, Mainz,
> Cologne, Düsseldorf and Duisburg.

Rheinland-Pfalz NEUT NOUN
Rhineland-Palatinate

> ❶ *Rheinland-Pfalz is one of the 16
> Länder. Its capital is Mainz. It is home
> to the BASF chemicals giant and to
> Germany's biggest television network,
> ZDF (Channel 2).*

das **Rheuma** NOUN
rheumatism ◊ *Meine Oma hat Rheuma.*
My granny's got rheumatism.

der **Rhythmus** NOUN (GEN des **Rhythmus**, PL die
Rhythmen)
rhythm

richten VERB
1 to point ◊ *Er richtete das Fernrohr
zum Himmel.* He pointed the telescope at
the sky.
♦ **eine Waffe auf jemanden richten** to aim
a weapon at somebody
2 to prepare ◊ *Er hatte das Mittagessen
schon gerichtet.* He had already prepared
lunch.
♦ **etwas an jemanden richten** to address
something to somebody ◊ *Der Brief war
an meine Eltern gerichtet.* The letter was
addressed to my parents.
♦ **Ich richte mich ganz nach dir.** I'll do
whatever you want.
♦ **sich nach etwas richten (1)** to conform to
something ◊ *Auch du solltest dich
danach richten, wie wir das hier machen.*
You should conform to our way of doing
things.
♦ **sich nach etwas richten (2)** to be
determined by something ◊ *Das Angebot
richtet sich nach der Nachfrage.* Supply
is determined by demand.

der **Richter** NOUN (PL die **Richter**)
judge

richtig ADJECTIVE, ADVERB
1 right ◊ *Wir müssen den richtigen
Zeitpunkt abwarten.* We must wait for
the right moment. ◊ *Es war nicht richtig
von dir, ihn zu belügen.* It wasn't right of
you to lie to him.
♦ **Bin ich hier richtig?** Have I come to the
right place?
♦ **der Richtige** the right person
♦ **das Richtige** the right thing
2 correctly ◊ *Du hast das nicht richtig
geschrieben.* You haven't written that
correctly.
3 proper ◊ *Ich will ein richtiges
Motorrad und kein Moped.* I want a
proper motorbike, not a moped.
4 really ◊ *Wir waren richtig froh, als es
vorbei war.* We were really glad when it
was over.

die **Richtung** NOUN
direction ◊ *Wir gehen in die falsche
Richtung.* We are going in the wrong
direction. ◊ *in östlicher Richtung* in an
easterly direction

rieb VERB *see* **reiben**

riechen VERB (IMPERFECT **roch,** PERFECT **hat gerochen**)

to smell ◇ *Ich rieche Gas.* I can smell gas. ◇ *Das riecht gut.* That smells good. ◇ *Ich kann nichts riechen.* I can't smell anything.

◆**an etwas riechen** to smell something ◇ *Sie roch an der Rose.* She smelled the rose.

◆**nach etwas riechen** to smell of something ◇ *Hier riecht es nach Benzin.* It smells of petrol here.

◆**Ich kann ihn nicht riechen.** I can't stand him.

rief VERB *see* **rufen**

der **Riegel** NOUN (PL die **Riegel**)

[1] bolt ◇ *Sie schob den Riegel vor die Tür.* She bolted the door.

[2] bar ◇ *Für unterwegs haben wir einen Schokoriegel mitgenommen.* We've brought a bar of chocolate to eat on the way.

der **Riese** NOUN (GEN des **Riesen,** PL die **Riesen**)

giant

der **Riesenerfolg** NOUN (PL die **Riesenerfolge**)

enormous success

riesengroß ADJECTIVE

gigantic

das **Riesenrad** NOUN (PL die **Riesenräder**)

big wheel ◇ *mit dem Riesenrad fahren* to go on the big wheel

riesig ADJECTIVE

huge

riet VERB *see* **raten**

die **Rille** NOUN

groove

das **Rind** NOUN (PL die **Rinder**)

[1] (*male*)

ox

[2] (*female*)

cow

◆**Rinder** cattle ◇ *Seine Rinder sind im Sommer auf der Weide.* His cattle spend the summer on the meadow.

[3] beef ◇ *Wir essen kaum noch Rind.* We hardly eat beef any more.

die **Rinde** NOUN

[1] rind ◇ *Er schnitt die Rinde vom Käse ab.* He cut the rind off the cheese.

[2] crust ◇ *frisches Brot mit knuspriger Rinde* fresh crusty bread

[3] bark ◇ *Er ritzte ihren Namen in die Rinde einer Eiche.* He carved her name into the bark of an oak tree.

das **Rindfleisch** NOUN

beef

der **Ring** NOUN (PL die **Ringe**)

ring

das **Ringbuch** NOUN (PL die **Ringbücher**)

ring binder

das **Ringen** NOUN

wrestling ◇ *Ringen ist sein Hobby.* His hobby is wrestling.

der **Ringkampf** NOUN (PL die **Ringkämpfe**)

wrestling bout

der **Ringrichter** NOUN (PL die **Ringrichter**)

referee

ringsum ADVERB

all around ◇ *Wir sahen ringsum Menschen.* We saw people all around. ◇ *Er blickte ringsum.* He looked all around.

die **Rippe** NOUN

rib

das **Risiko** NOUN (PL die **Risiken**)

risk

riskant ADJECTIVE

risky

riskieren VERB (PERFECT **hat riskiert**)

to risk

der **Riss** NOUN (GEN des **Risses,** PL die **Risse**)

[1] crack ◇ *Die Maus verschwand durch einen Riss in der Mauer.* The mouse disappeared into a crack in the wall. ◇ *Der trockene Boden war voller Risse.* The dry soil was full of cracks.

[2] tear ◇ *Er hatte einen Riss in der Hose.* There was a tear in his trousers.

rissig ADJECTIVE

[1] cracked ◇ *Von der Trockenheit ist die Erde rissig geworden.* The soil is cracked as a result of the drought.

[2] chapped ◇ *Vom vielen Waschen hat sie ganz rissige Hände.* Her hands are all chapped from doing so much washing.

ritt VERB *see* **reiten**

der **Ritter** NOUN (PL die **Ritter**)

knight

der **Rivale** NOUN (GEN des **Rivalen,** PL die **Rivalen**)

rival

die **Robbe** NOUN

seal ◇ *ein Robbenbaby* a seal pup

der **Roboter** NOUN (PL die **Roboter**)

robot

roch VERB *see* **riechen**

der **Rock** NOUN (PL die **Röcke**)

skirt

der **Roggen** NOUN

rye

roh ADJECTIVE

[1] raw ◇ *rohes Fleisch* raw meat ◇ *Karotten esse ich am liebsten roh.* I like carrots best raw.

[2] callous ◇ *Sei nicht so roh.* Don't be so callous.

[3] rough ◇ *Er hat sie ziemlich roh mit sich gezogen.* He dragged her off pretty roughly.

das **Rohr** NOUN (PL die **Rohre**)

[1] pipe ◇ *Das Abwasser wird durch Rohre in die Kanalisation geleitet.* Sewage is fed into the sewer via pipes.

R

☞

2 cane ◇ *ein Stuhl aus Rohr* a cane chair

3 reeds ◇ *In dem Teich wuchs Rohr. Reeds were growing in the pond.*

der **Rohstoff** NOUN (PL die **Rohstoffe**)
raw material

der **Rolladen** NOUN *see* **Rollladen**

das **Rollbrett** NOUN (PL die **Rollbretter**)
skateboard

die **Rolle** NOUN

1 role ◇ *Der Schauspieler hat die Rolle des Königs gut gespielt.* The actor was good in the role of the king. ◇ *Die Rolle der Frau hat sich geändert.* The role of women has changed.

2 castor ◇ *ein Stuhl mit Rollen* a chair with castors

3 roll ◇ *eine Rolle Toilettenpapier* a roll of toilet paper

4 reel ◇ *Sie hat den Faden von der Rolle abgewickelt.* She unwound the thread from the reel.

♦ **keine Rolle spielen** not to matter ◇ *Das Wetter spielt keine Rolle.* The weather doesn't matter.

♦ **eine wichtige Rolle spielen bei** to play a major role in ◇ *Er hat bei der Planung des Abschlussfestes eine wichtige Rolle gespielt.* He played a major role in organizing the end-of-term party.

rollen VERB (PERFECT **hat/ist gerollt**)

*For the perfect tense use **haben** when the verb has an object and **sein** when there is no object.*

to roll ◇ *Sie haben den Stein den Berg hinuntergerollt.* They rolled the stone down the hill. ◇ *Der Ball ist direkt vor ein Auto gerollt.* The ball rolled right in front of a car.

der **Roller** NOUN (PL die **Roller**)
scooter

der **Rollkragen** NOUN (PL die **Rollkragen**)
polo neck

der **Rollladen** NOUN (PL die **Rollläden**)
shutter

der **Rollschuh** NOUN (PL die **Rollschuhe**)
roller skate

der **Rollstuhl** NOUN (PL die **Rollstühle**)
wheelchair

die **Rolltreppe** NOUN
escalator

Rom NEUT NOUN
Rome

♦ **nach Rom** to Rome

der **Roman** NOUN (PL die **Romane**)
novel

romantisch ADJECTIVE
romantic

römisch ADJECTIVE
Roman

röntgen VERB
to X-ray

rosa ADJECTIVE

pink ◇ *Sie hatte ein rosa Kleid an.* She was wearing a pink dress.

die **Rose** NOUN
rose

der **Rosenkohl** NOUN
Brussels sprouts ◇ *Rosenkohl ist mein Lieblingsgemüse.* Brussels sprouts are my favourite vegetable.

der **Rosenmontag** NOUN (PL die **Rosenmontage**)
Monday before Shrove Tuesday

> ℹ **Rosenmontag** is an important day in the carnival festivities. Cities such as Cologne, Düsseldorf and Mainz traditionally have long processions with carnival floats on **Rosenmontag**.

die **Rosine** NOUN
raisin

der **Rosmarin** NOUN
rosemary

die **Rosskastanie** NOUN
horse chestnut

der **Rost** NOUN (PL die **Roste**)
rust ◇ *An diesem Auto ist viel Rost.* This car has a lot of rust on it.

♦ **ein Bratrost** a grill

rosten VERB (PERFECT **ist gerostet**)
to rust

rösten VERB

1 to roast ◇ *geröstete Erdnüsse* roasted peanuts

2 to toast ◇ *Brot rösten* to toast bread

3 to grill ◇ *Würstchen auf dem Grill rösten* to grill sausages

rostig ADJECTIVE
rusty

rot ADJECTIVE
red ◇ *Sein Gesicht wurde immer röter.* His face got redder and redder.

♦ **in den roten Zahlen** in the red

♦ **das Rote Meer** the Red Sea

die **Röteln** PL NOUN
German measles ◇ *Röteln sind für schwangere Frauen gefährlich.* German measles is dangerous for pregnant women.

rothaarig ADJECTIVE
red-haired

der **Rotkohl** NOUN
red cabbage

der **Rotwein** NOUN (PL die **Rotweine**)
red wine

die **Roulade** NOUN
beef olive

die **Route** NOUN
route

der **Rowdy** NOUN (PL die **Rowdys**)
hooligan

die **Rübe** NOUN

beet ◊ *Der Bauer füttert die Kühe mit Rüben.* The farmer feeds his cows on beet.

◆**Gelbe Rübe** carrot

◆**Rote Rübe** beetroot

rüber ADVERB
over ◊ *Komm hier rüber, da siehst du besser.* Come over here, you'll get a better view.

der **Rücken** NOUN (PL die **Rücken**)

see also **rücken** VERB

back ◊ *Er schläft auf dem Rücken.* He sleeps on his back.

rücken VERB (PERFECT **ist/hat gerückt**)

see also **der Rücken** NOUN

For the perfect tense use **haben** *when the verb has an object and* **sein** *when there is no object.*

[1] to move over ◊ *Rück mal ein bisschen.* Move over a bit.

[2] to shift ◊ *Sie rückten den Tisch zur Seite.* They shifted the table to one side.

das **Rückenmark** NOUN
spinal cord

die **Rückenschmerzen** PL NOUN
backache ◊ *Sie hat Rückenschmerzen.* She has backache.

das **Rückenschwimmen** NOUN
backstroke

die **Rückfahrkarte** NOUN
return ticket

die **Rückfahrt** NOUN
return journey

der **Rückflug** NOUN (PL die **Rückflüge**)
return flight

die **Rückgabe** NOUN
return

rückgängig ADJECTIVE
◆**etwas rückgängig machen** to cancel something

das **Rückgrat** NOUN (PL die **Rückgrate**)
spine

die **Rückkehr** NOUN
return ◊ *bei unserer Rückkehr* on our return

das **Rücklicht** NOUN (PL die **Rücklichter**)
rear light

die **Rückreise** NOUN
return journey

der **Rucksack** NOUN (PL die **Rucksäcke**)
rucksack

die **Rücksicht** NOUN
consideration
◆**auf jemanden Rücksicht nehmen** to show consideration for somebody ◊ *Du solltest mehr Rücksicht auf deine Mitschüler nehmen.* You should show more consideration for your fellow pupils.

rücksichtslos ADJECTIVE
inconsiderate
◆**ein rücksichtsloser Fahrer** a reckless driver

rücksichtsvoll ADJECTIVE
considerate

der **Rücksitz** NOUN (PL die **Rücksitze**)
back seat ◊ *Dieser Sportwagen hat keine Rücksitze.* This sports car has no back seats.

◆**Kinder sollten auf dem Rücksitz mitfahren.** Children should travel in the back.

der **Rückspiegel** NOUN (PL die **Rückspiegel**)
rear-view mirror

das **Rückspiel** NOUN (PL die **Rückspiele**)
return match

der **Rücktritt** NOUN (PL die **Rücktritte**)
resignation

rückwärts ADVERB
backwards ◊ *rückwärts zählen* to count backwards

rückwärtsfahren VERB (PRESENT **fährt rückwärts,** IMPERFECT **fuhr rückwärts,** PERFECT **ist rückwärtsgefahren**)
to reverse ◊ *Er fuhr rückwärts in die Garage.* He reversed into the garage.

der **Rückwärtsgang** NOUN (PL die **Rückwärtsgänge**)
reverse gear

der **Rückweg** NOUN (PL die **Rückwege**)
way back

das **Ruder** NOUN (PL die **Ruder**)
[1] oar ◊ *ein Boot mit zwei Rudern* a boat with two oars
[2] rudder ◊ *Der Steuermann steht am Ruder.* The helmsman stands at the rudder.

das **Ruderboot** NOUN (PL die **Ruderboote**)
rowing boat

rudern VERB (PERFECT **hat/ist gerudert**)

Use **haben** *for the perfect tense when you describe the activity and* **sein** *when you describe the motion.*

to row ◊ *Zuerst hat er gerudert, dann sie.* First he rowed, then she did. ◊ *Wir sind über den See gerudert.* We rowed across the lake.

der **Ruf** NOUN (PL die **Rufe**)
[1] shout ◊ *Wir hörten seine Rufe.* We heard his shouts.
[2] reputation ◊ *Das schadet seinem Ruf.* This will damage his reputation.

rufen VERB (IMPERFECT **rief,** PERFECT **hat gerufen**)
[1] to call out ◊ *Ich habe gerufen, es hat mich aber niemand gehört.* I called out, but nobody heard me.
◆**Der Patient rief nach der Schwester.** The patient called for the nurse.
[2] to call ◊ *Wir sollten den Arzt rufen.* We ought to call the doctor. ◊ *Sie hat mir ein Taxi gerufen.* She called me a taxi.
[3] to shout ◊ *Sie rief um Hilfe.* She shouted for help.

die **Rufnummer** NOUN
telephone number

R

die **Ruhe** NOUN

   1 rest ◊ *Nach den anstrengenden Tagen brauche ich etwas Ruhe.* After the strain of the last few days I need a rest.

   2 peace ◊ *Jetzt kann ich in Ruhe arbeiten.* Now I can work in peace.

   3 peace and quiet ◊ *Die Kinder sind weg, ich genieße die Ruhe.* The children are out and I'm enjoying the peace and quiet.

   ♦ **in aller Ruhe** calmly

   ♦ **jemanden aus der Ruhe bringen** to unsettle somebody ◊ *Dieser Anruf hat mich aus der Ruhe gebracht.* The phone call unsettled me.

   4 silence ◊ *Ich bitte um etwas mehr Ruhe.* I would ask you for a bit more silence.

   ♦ **Ruhe!** Silence!

   ♦ **jemanden in Ruhe lassen** to leave somebody alone ◊ *Lass endlich deine Schwester in Ruhe.* Will you leave your sister alone!

   ♦ **sich zur Ruhe setzen** to retire

der **Ruhestand** NOUN

   retirement

   ♦ **Mein Vater ist im Ruhestand.** My father has retired.

die **Ruhestörung** NOUN

   breach of the peace

der **Ruhetag** NOUN

   day off ◊ *einen Ruhetag einlegen* to have a day off

   ♦ **"Mittwochs Ruhetag"** "closed on Wednesdays"

ruhig ADJECTIVE, ADVERB

   1 quiet ◊ *Im Haus war alles ruhig.* The house was completely quiet. ◊ *Die Kinder haben ruhig gespielt.* The children played quietly. ◊ *Seid endlich ruhig!* Will you be quiet!

   2 still ◊ *Bleib ruhig stehen, dann tut dir der Hund nichts.* If you keep still the dog won't hurt you.

   ♦ **eine ruhige Hand** a steady hand

   3 calm ◊ *Wie kannst du so ruhig bleiben?* How can you stay so calm? ◊ *Ich bin ganz ruhig in die Prüfung gegangen.* I went quite calmly into the exam.

   ♦ **ein ruhiges Gewissen** a clear conscience

   ♦ **Kommen Sie ruhig herein!** Come on in.

der **Ruhm** NOUN

   fame

das **Rührei** NOUN (PL die **Rühreier**)

   scrambled eggs

rühren VERB

   1 to stir ◊ *Sie rührte mit dem Löffel in der Soße.* She stirred the sauce with the spoon.

   2 to move ◊ *Ich kann meine Beine nicht rühren.* I can't move my legs.

   ♦ **sich rühren** to move ◊ *Sie hatte so Angst, dass sie sich nicht rührte.* She was so afraid that she didn't move.

   ♦ **jemanden rühren** to move somebody ◊ *Die Armut der Kinder hat uns gerührt.* The children's poverty moved us.

   ♦ **rühren an (1)** to touch ◊ *Rühr nicht an den Draht, da ist Strom drauf.* Don't touch the wire, it's live.

   ♦ **rühren an (2)** to bring up ◊ *An dieses Thema solltest du nicht rühren.* You shouldn't bring this subject up.

rührend ADJECTIVE

   touching ◊ *eine rührende Geschichte* a touching story ◊ *Er ist rührend naiv.* He's touchingly naive.

die **Ruine** NOUN

   ruin

ruinieren VERB (PERFECT **hat ruiniert**)

   to ruin

rülpsen VERB

   to belch

der **Rumäne** NOUN (GEN des **Rumänen,** PL die **Rumänen**)

   Romanian

Rumänien NEUT NOUN

   Romania

   ♦ **aus Rumänien** from Romania

   ♦ **nach Rumänien** to Romania

die **Rumänin** NOUN

   Romanian

rumänisch ADJECTIVE

   Romanian

der **Rummel** NOUN

   1 hullabaloo ◊ *Das war vielleicht ein Rummel in der Stadt.* There was quite a hullabaloo in town.

   2 fair ◊ *Wir sind auf dem Rummel Karussell gefahren.* We went on a roundabout at the fair.

der **Rummelplatz** NOUN (GEN des **Rummelplatzes,** PL die **Rummelplätze**)

   fairground

rund ADJECTIVE, ADVERB

   1 round ◊ *Sie hat ein rundes Gesicht.* She's got a round face.

   2 about ◊ *Das kostet rund hundert Euro.* It costs about a hundred euros.

   ♦ **rund um etwas** around something

die **Runde** NOUN

   1 lap ◊ *Das Auto fuhr ein paar Runden.* The car drove a few laps.

   2 round ◊ *Diese Runde zahle ich.* I'll get this round.

ⓘ *It isn't usual to buy rounds in Germany. Normally people just order what they want from the waiter, and pay when they leave. You can, however, buy a round* (**eine Runde schmeißen**) *if you're feeling generous.*

③ lap ◊ *Er liegt in der letzten Runde in Führung.* He's in the lead on the last lap.
④ party ◊ *Wir waren eine fröhliche Runde.* We were a merry party.

die **Rundfahrt** NOUN
round trip

der **Rundfunk** NOUN
broadcasting
♦ **im Rundfunk** on the radio

runter ADVERB
① off ◊ *Runter vom Tisch!* Get off the table!
② down ◊ *Dann ging's den Berg runter.* Then off we went down the mountain.

runterladen VERB (PRESENT **lädt runter,** IMPERFECT **lud runter,** PERFECT **hat runtergeladen**)
to download (*computer*) ◊ *eine Datei runterladen* to download a file

der **Ruß** NOUN (GEN des **Rußes**)
soot

der **Russe** NOUN (GEN des **Russen,** PL die **Russen**)
Russian

der **Rüssel** NOUN (PL die **Rüssel**)
① snout ◊ *der Rüssel eines Schweins* a pig's snout
② trunk ◊ *der Rüssel eines Elefanten* an elephant's trunk

rußig ADJECTIVE
sooty

die **Russin** NOUN
Russian

russisch ADJECTIVE
Russian

Russland NEUT NOUN
Russia
♦ **aus Russland** from Russia
♦ **nach Russland** to Russia

die **Rüstung** NOUN
① suit of armour ◊ *In der Burg standen ein paar rostige Rüstungen.* There were a couple of rusty suits of armour in the castle.
② armaments ◊ *Es wird viel Geld für Rüstung ausgegeben.* A lot of money is spent on armaments.

die **Rutschbahn** NOUN
slide

rutschen VERB (PERFECT **ist gerutscht**)
① to slip ◊ *Sie ist auf dem Eis gerutscht und hingefallen.* She slipped and fell on the ice. ◊ *Der Teller ist mir aus der Hand gerutscht.* The plate slipped out of my hand.
② to move over ◊ *Rutsch mal ein bisschen!* Move over a bit.

rutschig ADJECTIVE
slippery

R

S

der **Saal** NOUN (PL die **Säle**)
hall
das **Saarland** NOUN
Saarland

> ❶ The **Saarland** is one of the 16 **Länder**. Its capital is Saarbrücken. While its coal and steel industries have been in crisis, it still has flourishing ceramics and glass industries.

die **Sache** NOUN
[1] thing ◇ Räum bitte deine Sachen weg. Please put your things away. ◇ Pack warme Sachen ein. Pack warm things.
[2] matter ◇ Wir sollten diese Sache ausdiskutieren. We should discuss this matter fully. ◇ Die Polizei wird dieser Sache nachgehen. The police will investigate this affair.
[3] job ◇ Es ist deine Sache, dich darum zu kümmern. It's your job to see to it.
♦ **Mach keine Sachen!** Don't be silly!
♦ **Was machst du denn für Sachen?** The things you do!
♦ **zur Sache** to the point ◇ Komm endlich zur Sache! Get to the point!
sachlich ADJECTIVE
[1] objective ◇ ein sehr sachlicher Bericht a very objective report ◇ Du solltest sachlich bleiben. You should remain objective.
[2] factual ◇ Was er sagt, ist sachlich falsch. What he says is factually inaccurate.
sächlich ADJECTIVE
neuter
Sachsen NEUT NOUN
Saxony

> ❶ **Sachsen** is one of the 16 **Länder**. Its capital is Dresden. Its largest city, Leipzig, is famous for its industrial fair and was one of the main centres of the peaceful revolt against the DDR regime.

Sachsen-Anhalt NEUT NOUN
Saxony-Anhalt

> ❶ **Sachsen-Anhalt** is one of the 16 **Länder**. Its capital is Magdeburg. It has a rich cultural past: Martin Luther and Georg Friedrich Händel were born here, and the Bauhaus school of architecture was situated in Dessau.

sächsisch ADJECTIVE
Saxon

sachte ADVERB
softly
der **Sack** NOUN (PL die **Säcke**)
sack
die **Sackgasse** NOUN
cul-de-sac
der **Saft** NOUN (PL die **Säfte**)
juice
saftig ADJECTIVE
juicy
die **Säge** NOUN
saw
sagen VERB
[1] to say ◇ Ich kann noch nicht sagen, ob ich komme. I can't say yet if I'll come. ◇ Habe ich etwas Falsches gesagt? Have I said something wrong? ◇ Wie sagt man "danke" auf Japanisch? How do you say "thank you" in Japanese? ◇ Was sagst du zu meinem Vorschlag? What do you say to my suggestion? ◇ Sie sagt, sie habe das nicht gewusst. She says that she didn't know that.
♦ **Man sagt, dass ...** It's said that ...
[2] to tell ◇ Kannst du ihm bitte sagen, er soll seine Eltern anrufen. Can you tell him to call his parents. ◇ Ich werde es ihr sagen. I'll tell her. ◇ Sag ihm, er solle das nicht tun. Tell him he shouldn't do it. ◇ sagen Sie ihm, dass ... tell him that ...
♦ **etwas zu jemandem sagen** to call somebody something ◇ Die Kinder sagen Onja zu mir. The children call me Onja.
♦ **zu sagen haben** to have a say ◇ Du hast hier nichts zu sagen. You don't have a say in this matter.
♦ **Es hat nichts zu sagen, dass er sich noch nicht gemeldet hat.** The fact that he hasn't called doesn't mean anything.
sägen VERB
to saw
sagenhaft ADJECTIVE
[1] legendary ◇ der sagenhafte König Artus the legendary King Arthur
[2] terrific ◇ Das war ein sagenhaftes Glück. That was terrific luck.
sah VERB see **sehen**
die **Sahne** NOUN
cream
die **Saison** NOUN (PL die **Saisons**)
season
die **Saite** NOUN
string
das **Saiteninstrument** NOUN (PL die **Saiteninstrumente**)
stringed instrument
der **Sakko** NOUN (PL die **Sakkos**)
jacket

der **Salat** NOUN (PL die **Salate**)
  1 salad ◊ *Es gab verschiedene Salate.* There were various salads.
  2 lettuce ◊ *Am liebsten mag ich grünen Salat.* I like lettuce best.

die **Salatsoße** NOUN
  salad dressing

die **Salbe** NOUN
  ointment

der **Salbei** NOUN (GEN des **Salbeis**)
  sage

das **Salz** NOUN (GEN des **Salzes**)
  salt

  salzen VERB (PERFECT **hat gesalzen**)
  to salt

  salzig ADJECTIVE
  salty

die **Salzkartoffeln** FEM PL NOUN
  boiled potatoes

die **Salzstange** NOUN
  pretzel stick

das **Salzwasser** NOUN
  salt water

der **Samen** NOUN (PL die **Samen**)
  seed ◊ *Hast du die Blumensamen schon ausgesät?* Have you sown the flower seeds yet?

  sammeln VERB
  1 to collect ◊ *Er sammelt Briefmarken.* He collects stamps. ◊ *Altpapier wird gesammelt und wiedeverwertet.* Waste paper is collected and recycled.
  2 to gather ◊ *Wir haben Pilze gesammelt.* We gathered mushrooms.

die **Sammlung** NOUN
  collection

der **Samstag** NOUN (PL die **Samstage**)
  Saturday ◊ *am Samstag* on Saturday

  samstags ADVERB
  on Saturdays

der **Samt** NOUN (PL die **Samte**)
  | see also **samt** PREPOSITION |
  velvet

  samt PREPOSITION
  | see also **der Samt** NOUN |
  *The preposition **samt** takes the dative.*
  with ◊ *Sie kamen samt Kindern und Hund.* They came with their children and dog.

der **Sand** NOUN
  sand

die **Sandale** NOUN
  sandal

die **Sandburg** NOUN
  sand castle

  sandig ADJECTIVE
  sandy

der **Sandkasten** NOUN (PL die **Sandkästen**)
  sandpit

der **Sandstein** NOUN (PL die **Sandsteine**)
  sandstone

  sandstrahlen VERB

to sandblast ◊ *Die Gebäude wurden alle gesandstrahlt.* All the buildings were sandblasted.

der **Sandstrand** NOUN (PL die **Sandstrände**)
  sandy beach

  sandte VERB *see* **senden**

  sanft ADJECTIVE
  gentle ◊ *etwas sanft berühren* to touch something gently

  sang VERB *see* **singen**

der **Sänger** NOUN (PL die **Sänger**)
  singer

die **Sängerin** NOUN
  singer

die **Sardelle** NOUN
  anchovy

die **Sardine** NOUN
  sardine

der **Sarg** NOUN (PL die **Särge**)
  coffin

der **Sarkasmus** NOUN (GEN des **Sarkasmus,** PL die **Sarkasmen**)
  sarcasm

  saß VERB *see* **sitzen**

der **Satellit** NOUN (GEN des **Satelliten,** PL die **Satelliten**)
  satellite

das **Satellitenfernsehen** NOUN
  satellite television

  satt ADJECTIVE
  full ◊ *Ich bin satt.* I'm full.
  ◆ **Wir sind nicht satt geworden.** We didn't get enough to eat.
  ◆ **sich satt essen** to eat one's fill
  ◆ **satt machen** to be filling
  ◆ **satte Farben** rich colours ◊ *ein sattes Rot* a rich red
  ◆ **jemanden satt sein** to be fed up with somebody

der **Sattel** NOUN (PL die **Sättel**)
  saddle

  satthaben VERB (PRESENT **hat satt,** IMPERFECT **hatte satt,** PERFECT **hat sattgehabt**)
  ◆ **etwas satthaben** to be fed up with something

der **Satz** NOUN (GEN des **Satzes,** PL die **Sätze**)
  1 sentence ◊ *Bitte antworte mit einem ganzen Satz.* Please answer in a complete sentence.
  ◆ **ein Nebensatz** a subordinate clause
  ◆ **ein Adverbialsatz** an adverbial clause
  2 theorem ◊ *der Satz des Pythagoras* Pythagoras' theorem
  3 set ◊ *Becker hat den ersten Satz verloren.* Becker lost the first set. ◊ *ein Satz Schraubenschlüssel* a set of screwdrivers
  4 rate ◊ *Die Krankenversicherung hat ihre Sätze erhöht.* The health insurance has increased its rates.

das **Satzzeichen** NOUN (PL die **Satzzeichen**)
  punctuation mark

S

sauber ADJECTIVE
[1] clean ◊ *Die Wäsche ist nicht sauber geworden.* The washing hasn't come up clean.
[2] fine ◊ *Du bist mir ein sauberer Freund!* You're a fine friend!
♦ **sauber machen** to clean

die **Sauberkeit** NOUN
cleanness

die **Sauce** NOUN
sauce

sauer ADJECTIVE
[1] sour ◊ *Der Apfel ist sauer.* The apple is sour. ◊ *Die Milch ist sauer geworden.* The milk has turned sour.
[2] acid ◊ *saurer Regen* acid rain
[3] cross ◊ *Ich bin sauer auf meine Freundin.* I'm cross with my girlfriend.

der **Sauerbraten** NOUN (PL die **Sauerbraten**)
marinated beef

die **Sauerei** NOUN
[1] scandal ◊ *Es ist eine Sauerei, dass wir länger arbeiten müssen.* It's a scandal that we have to work longer hours.
[2] mess ◊ *Wer hat denn die Sauerei im Bad gemacht?* Who made the mess in the bathroom?
[3] obscenity ◊ *Über solche Sauereien kann ich nicht lachen.* I can't laugh at such obscenities.

das **Sauerkraut** NOUN
sauerkraut (*pickled cabbage*)

der **Sauerstoff** NOUN
oxygen

saufen VERB (PRESENT **säuft**, IMPERFECT **soff**, PERFECT **hat gesoffen**)
to booze

saugen VERB (IMPERFECT **saugte** *or* **sog**, PERFECT **hat gesaugt** *or* **gesogen**)
to suck

das **Säugetier** NOUN (PL die **Säugetiere**)
mammal

der **Säugling** NOUN (PL die **Säuglinge**)
infant

die **Säule** NOUN
column

die **Sauna** NOUN (PL die **Saunas**)
sauna

die **Säure** NOUN
acid ◊ *Die Säure hat den Stein zerfressen.* The acid has eaten away at the stone.

das **Saxofon** NOUN (PL die **Saxofone**)
saxophone ◊ *Er spielt Saxofon.* He plays the saxophone.

das **Saxophon** NOUN (PL die **Saxophone**)
see **Saxofon**

die **S-Bahn** NOUN
suburban railway

die **SB-Tankstelle** NOUN
self-service petrol station

das **Schach** NOUN
chess ◊ *Ich kann nicht Schach spielen.* I can't play chess.

das **Schachbrett** NOUN (PL die **Schachbretter**)
chessboard

die **Schachfigur** NOUN
chessman

die **Schachtel** NOUN
box

schade ADJECTIVE, EXCLAMATION
a pity ◊ *Es ist schade um das gute Essen.* It's a pity to waste good food. ◊ *Das ist aber schade.* That's a pity.
♦ **Wie schade!** What a pity! ◊ *Wie schade, dass du nicht mitkommen kannst.* What a pity you can't come.
♦ **für etwas zu schade sein** to be too good for something ◊ *Diese Decke ist doch zu schade für ein Picknick.* This blanket is too good for a picnic.
♦ **sich zu schade sein für etwas** to consider oneself too good for something ◊ *Du bist dir für so eine Arbeit wohl zu schade?* So you consider yourself too good for a job like that?

der **Schädel** NOUN (PL die **Schädel**)
skull

der **Schaden** NOUN (PL die **Schäden**)
see also **schaden** VERB
[1] damage ◊ *Der Schaden an seinem Auto war nicht so groß.* The damage to his car wasn't too bad.
[2] injury ◊ *Sie hat den Unfall ohne Schaden überstanden.* She came out of the accident without injury.
[3] disadvantage ◊ *Es soll dein Schaden nicht sein.* It won't be to your disadvantage.

schaden VERB
see also **der Schaden** NOUN
♦ **jemandem schaden** to harm somebody ◊ *Ich habe den Eindruck, dass sie mir schaden will.* I've got the feeling that she wants to harm me.
♦ **einer Sache schaden** to damage something ◊ *Das hat unserem Ruf geschadet.* That's damaged our reputation.
♦ **es kann nicht schaden ...** it can't do any harm ... ◊ *Es kann nicht schaden, wenn du die Vokabeln noch einmal wiederholst.* It can't do any harm for you to go over the vocabulary once more.

der **Schadenersatz** NOUN (GEN des **Schadenersatzes**)
compensation

schädigen VERB (PERFECT **hat geschädigt**)
to damage

schädlich ADJECTIVE
harmful ◊ *Rauchen ist schädlich.* Smoking is harmful. ◊ *Alkohol ist für die Leber schädlich.* Alcohol is harmful to your liver.

der **Schadstoff** NOUN (PL die **Schadstoffe**)
    harmful substance
das **Schaf** NOUN (PL die **Schafe**)
    sheep ◊ *zehn Schafe* ten sheep
der **Schäferhund** NOUN (PL die **Schäferhunde**)
    Alsatian
    schaffen (1) VERB (IMPERFECT **schuf**, PERFECT
    hat geschaffen)
    to create ◊ *Die Regierung will neue
    Arbeitsplätze schaffen.* The government
    wants to create new jobs.
    schaffen (2) VERB (IMPERFECT **schaffte**, PERFECT
    hat geschafft)
    to manage ◊ *Die Übersetzung schaffe
    ich heute noch.* I'll manage that
    translation today. ◊ *Er schafft das nicht
    allein.* He won't manage to do that on his
    own.
    ◆ **Wir haben den Zug gerade noch
    geschafft.** We just managed to catch the
    train.
    ◆ **eine Prüfung schaffen** to pass an exam
    ◆ **Ich bin geschafft!** I'm shattered!
der **Schal** NOUN (PL die **Schale** or **Schals**)
    scarf
die **Schale** NOUN
    [1] skin ◊ *eine Bananenschale* a banana
    skin
    [2] peel ◊ *die Kartoffelschalen* the potato
    peel ◊ *eine Zitronenschale* lemon peel
    [3] shell ◊ *Die Nussschalen nicht in den
    Kompost werfen.* Don't throw the
    nutshells onto the compost heap. ◊ *Diese
    Eier haben sehr dünne Schalen.* These
    eggs have very thin shells.
    [4] bowl ◊ *Auf dem Tisch stand eine
    Schale mit Obst.* There was a bowl of
    fruit on the table.
    schälen VERB
    [1] to peel ◊ *einen Apfel schälen* to peel
    an apple
    [2] to shell ◊ *Nüsse schälen* to shell nuts
    ◆ **sich schälen** to peel ◊ *Ich schäle mich auf
    der Nase.* My nose is peeling.
der **Schall** NOUN
    sound
der **Schalldämpfer** NOUN (PL die
    Schalldämpfer)
    silencer
die **Schallmauer** NOUN
    sound barrier
die **Schallplatte** NOUN
    record
    schalten VERB
    [1] to switch ◊ *den Herd auf "aus"
    schalten* to switch the oven to "off"
    [2] to change gear ◊ *Du solltest schalten.*
    You should change gear.
    ◆ **in den vierten Gang schalten** to change
    into fourth
    [3] to catch on ◊ *Ich habe zu spät
    geschaltet.* I caught on too late.
der **Schalter** NOUN (PL die **Schalter**)

[1] counter ◊ *Zahlen Sie bitte am Schalter
dort drüben.* Please pay at the counter
over there.
[2] switch ◊ *Wo ist der Lichtschalter?*
Where is the light switch?
das **Schaltjahr** NOUN (PL die **Schaltjahre**)
    leap year
sich **schämen** VERB
    to be ashamed ◊ *sich einer Sache
    schämen* to be ashamed of something
die **Schande** NOUN
    disgrace
    scharf ADJECTIVE
    [1] sharp ◊ *ein scharfes Messer* a sharp
    knife ◊ *eine scharfe Kurve* a sharp corner
    ◆ **ein scharfer Wind** a biting wind
    [2] hot ◊ *Indisches Essen ist schärfer als
    deutsches.* Indian food is hotter than
    German food.
    ◆ **scharfe Munition** live ammunition
    ◆ **scharf schießen** to shoot with live
    ammunition
    ◆ **scharf nachdenken** to think hard
    ◆ **auf etwas scharf sein** to be mad about
    something ◊ *Er ist ganz scharf auf
    Gummibärchen.* He is mad about jelly
    bears.
    ◆ **auf jemanden scharf sein** to fancy
    somebody ◊ *Ich glaube, Manfred ist
    scharf auf dich.* I think Manfred fancies
    you.
der **Schaschlik** NOUN (PL die **Schaschliks**)
    *You can also say **das Schaschlik**.*
    kebab
der **Schatten** NOUN (PL die **Schatten**)
    shadow
    ◆ **Wir saßen im Schatten.** We sat in the
    shade.
    schattig ADJECTIVE
    shady
der **Schatz** NOUN (GEN des **Schatzes**, PL die
    Schätze)
    [1] treasure ◊ *der Schatz der Piraten* the
    pirates' treasure
    [2] darling ◊ *Du bist ein Schatz!* You're a
    darling! ◊ *Mein Schatz.* My darling.
das **Schätzchen** NOUN (PL die **Schätzchen**)
    darling
    schätzen VERB
    [1] to guess ◊ *Schätz mal, wie viel das
    gekostet hat.* Guess how much that cost.
    ◆ **Man kann sein Alter schlecht schätzen.**
    It's difficult to tell how old he is.
    [2] to value ◊ *Ich werde die alte Uhr
    schätzen lassen.* I'm going to have the
    old clock valued.
    [3] to appreciate ◊ *Ich schätze deine Hilfe
    sehr.* I really appreciate your help.
das **Schaubild** NOUN (PL die **Schaubilder**)
    diagram
    schauen VERB
    to look ◊ *Schau mal an die Tafel.* Look at
    the board.

S

der Schauer NOUN (PL die **Schauer**)
1 shower ◊ *Für morgen sind Schauer angesagt.* Showers are forecast for tomorrow.
2 shudder ◊ *Ein Schauer überlief sie.* A shudder ran through her body.

die Schaufel NOUN
shovel

das Schaufenster NOUN (PL die **Schaufenster**)
shop window

der Schaufensterbummel NOUN (PL die **Schaufensterbummel**)
window shopping

die Schaukel NOUN
swing
schaukeln VERB
to swing

der Schaumgummi NOUN
foam rubber

das Schauspiel NOUN
play (*theatre*)

der Schauspieler NOUN (PL die **Schauspieler**)
actor

die Schauspielerin NOUN
actress

der Scheck NOUN (PL die **Schecks**)
cheque

das Scheckbuch NOUN (PL die **Scheckbücher**)
chequebook

das Scheckheft NOUN (PL die **Scheckhefte**)
cheque book

die Scheckkarte NOUN
cheque card

die Scheibe NOUN
slice ◊ *Sie belegte das Brot mit mehreren Scheiben Wurst.* She put several slices of cold meat on the bread.

der Scheibenwischer NOUN (PL die **Scheibenwischer**)
windscreen wiper

scheiden VERB (IMPERFECT **schied**, PERFECT **hat geschieden**)
♦ **sich scheiden lassen** to get a divorce
♦ **geschieden sein** to be divorced

die Scheidung NOUN
divorce

der Schein NOUN (PL die **Scheine**)
1 light ◊ *beim Schein einer Kerze* by the light of a candle
2 appearance ◊ *Der Schein trügt.* Appearances are deceptive.
3 note ◊ *Er hat in großen Scheinen bezahlt.* He paid in large notes.
4 certificate ◊ *Am Ende des Semesters bekommt man einen Schein.* You get a certificate at the end of the semester.
♦ **etwas zum Schein tun** to pretend to do something ◊ *Er ging zum Schein auf den Vorschlag ein.* He pretended to go along with the suggestion.

scheinbar ADVERB
apparently

scheinen VERB (IMPERFECT **schien**, PERFECT **hat geschienen**)
1 to shine ◊ *Die Sonne scheint.* The sun is shining.
2 to seem ◊ *Sie scheint glücklich zu sein.* She seems to be happy.

der Scheinwerfer NOUN (PL die **Scheinwerfer**)
1 headlamp ◊ *Die Scheinwerfer des entgegenkommenden Autos haben mich geblendet.* The headlamps of the approaching car blinded me.
2 floodlight ◊ *Die Scheinwerfer beleuchteten das Stadion.* The floodlights lit the stadium.
3 spotlight ◊ *Das Gemälde wird von einem Scheinwerfer angestrahlt.* The painting is lit up by a spotlight.

scheitern VERB (PERFECT **ist gescheitert**)
to fail

der Schenkel NOUN (PL die **Schenkel**)
thigh

schenken VERB
1 to give ◊ *Was haben dir deine Eltern zum Geburtstag geschenkt?* What did your parents give you for your birthday? ◊ *Das habe ich geschenkt bekommen.* I was given it as a present.
2 to pour ◊ *Sie schenkte ihm noch etwas Rotwein ins Glas.* She poured some more red wine into his glass.
♦ **sich etwas schenken** to skip something ◊ *Die Geigenstunde werde ich mir heute schenken.* I'm going to skip my violin lesson today.
♦ **Das ist geschenkt! (1)** That's a giveaway!
♦ **Das ist geschenkt! (2)** That's worthless!

die Scherbe NOUN
piece ◊ *eine Glasscherbe* a piece of glass

die Schere NOUN
1 scissors ◊ *eine Schere* a pair of scissors
2 shears ◊ *Wo ist die Schere, um die Hecke zu schneiden?* Where are the shears for cutting the hedge?

scheren (1) VERB (IMPERFECT **schor**, PERFECT **hat geschoren**)
♦ **Schafe scheren** to shear sheep

scheren (2) VERB (IMPERFECT **scherte**, PERFECT **hat geschert**)
to bother ◊ *Es schert mich wenig, was die Leute sagen.* It doesn't really bother me what people say.
♦ **sich um etwas scheren** to care about something ◊ *Sie schert sich nicht um die Spielregeln.* She doesn't care about the rules.
♦ **Scher dich um deine eigenen Angelegenheiten.** Mind your own business!
♦ **Scher dich zum Teufel!** Go to hell!

der **Scherz** NOUN (GEN des **Scherzes**, PL die **Scherze**)

> joke ◊ *Das war doch nur ein Scherz!* It was only a joke.
> ♦ **zum Scherz** for fun

scheußlich ADJECTIVE

> dreadful ◊ *Das Wetter war scheußlich.* The weather was dreadful.
> ♦ **Das tut scheußlich weh.** It hurts dreadfully.

der **Schi** NOUN (PL die **Schi** or **Schier**) *see* **Ski**

die **Schicht** NOUN

> [1] layer ◊ *Auf dem Weg lag eine Schicht Sand.* There was a layer of sand on the path.
> [2] class ◊ *soziale Schichten* social classes
> [3] shift ◊ *Mein Vater arbeitet Schicht.* My father works shifts.

schick ADJECTIVE

> stylish ◊ *ein schicker Hosenanzug* a stylish trouser suit
> ♦ **schick angezogen** stylishly dressed

schicken VERB

> to send ◊ *Ich habe ihr ein Päckchen geschickt.* I've sent her a parcel. ◊ *Sie hat ihren Sohn zum Bäcker geschickt.* She sent her son to the baker's.

das **Schicksal** NOUN

> fate

schieben VERB (IMPERFECT **schob**, PERFECT **hat geschoben**)

> to push ◊ *Wir mussten das Auto schieben.* We had to push the car. ◊ *Könnt ihr mal schieben?* Could you lot push?
> ♦ **die Schuld auf jemanden schieben** to put the blame on somebody

der **Schiedsrichter** NOUN (PL die **Schiedsrichter**)

> [1] referee ◊ *Der Schiedsrichter pfiff das Spiel an.* The referee blew the whistle to start the game.
> [2] umpire ◊ *Bei einem Tennisspiel sagt der Schiedsrichter den Spielstand an.* In a tennis match the umpire gives the score.

schief ADJECTIVE, ADVERB

> crooked ◊ *Die Wände des Hauses sind schief.* The walls of the house are crooked.
> ♦ **Das Bild hängt schief.** The picture isn't hanging straight.
> ♦ **der Schiefe Turm von Pisa** the Leaning Tower of Pisa
> ♦ **ein schiefer Blick** a funny look
> ♦ **Er hatte seinen Hut schief aufgesetzt.** He was wearing his hat at an angle.

schiefgehen VERB (IMPERFECT **ging schief**, PERFECT **ist schiefgegangen**)

> to go wrong

schielen VERB

> to squint

schien VERB *see* **scheinen**

die **Schiene** NOUN

> [1] rail ◊ *Die Schienen sind verrostet.* The rails have rusted.
> [2] splint ◊ *Sie hatte den Arm in einer Schiene.* She had her arm in a splint.

schießen VERB (IMPERFECT **schoss**, PERFECT **hat geschossen**)

> [1] to shoot ◊ *Nicht schießen!* Don't shoot! ◊ *Er hat ein Kaninchen geschossen.* He shot a rabbit. ◊ *Er hat auf einen Polizisten geschossen.* He shot at a policeman.
> [2] to kick ◊ *Sie schoss den Ball ins Tor.* She kicked the ball into the goal.

das **Schiff** NOUN (PL die **Schiffe**)

> ship

die **Schifffahrt** NOUN

> shipping

der **Schikoree** NOUN

> chicory

das **Schild** NOUN (PL die **Schilder**)

> sign ◊ *Das ist eine Einbahnstraße, hast du das Schild nicht gesehen?* This is a one-way street, didn't you see the sign?
> ♦ **ein Namensschild** a nameplate

die **Schildkröte** NOUN

> [1] tortoise
> [2] turtle

der **Schilling** NOUN (PL die **Schillinge** or **Schilling**)

> schilling ◊ *Das kostete hundert Schilling.* It cost a hundred schillings.

der **Schimmel** NOUN (PL die **Schimmel**)

> [1] mould ◊ *Auf dem Käse ist Schimmel.* There's mould on the cheese.
> [2] white horse ◊ *Sie ritt auf einem Schimmel.* She rode a white horse.

schimmelig ADJECTIVE

> mouldy

schimmeln VERB

> to go mouldy

der **Schimpanse** NOUN (GEN des **Schimpansen**, PL die **Schimpansen**)

> chimpanzee

schimpfen VERB

> to scold ◊ *Hat deine Mutter geschimpft?* Did your mother scold you?
> ♦ **auf jemanden schimpfen** to curse somebody ◊ *Schüler schimpfen gern auf ihre Lehrer.* Pupils like cursing their teachers.
> ♦ **über etwas schimpfen** to complain about something ◊ *Meine Kinder schimpfen über zu viel Hausaufgaben.* My children complain about having too much homework.

das **Schimpfwort** NOUN (PL die **Schimpfwörter**)

> term of abuse

der **Schinken** NOUN (PL die **Schinken**)

> ham

S

der Schirm NOUN (PL die **Schirme**)
umbrella ◊ *Nimm einen Schirm mit!*
Take an umbrella!
♦ **der Sonnenschirm** the sunshade
♦ **eine Mütze mit Schirm** a peaked cap

die Schlacht NOUN
battle

schlachten VERB
to slaughter

der Schlachter NOUN (PL die **Schlachter**)
butcher

das Schlachtfeld NOUN (PL die **Schlachtfelder**)
battlefield

der Schlachthof NOUN (PL die **Schlachthöfe**)
slaughterhouse

der Schlaf NOUN
sleep

der Schlafanzug NOUN (PL die **Schlafanzüge**)
pyjamas ◊ *ein Schlafanzug* a pair of
pyjamas

schlafen VERB (PRESENT **schläft**, IMPERFECT
schlief, PERFECT **hat geschlafen**)
to sleep ◊ *Hast du gut geschlafen?* Did
you sleep well? ◊ *Schlaf gut!* Sleep well.
♦ **schlafen gehen** to go to bed

schlaff ADJECTIVE
1 drained ◊ *Ich bin total schlaff.* I'm
drained.
♦ **Bei der Hitze bin ich so schlaff.** The heat
really takes it out of me.
2 exhausted ◊ *Nach der Gartenarbeit
war ich total schlaff.* I was completely
exhausted after working in the
garden.
3 slack ◊ *Das Seil ist zu schlaff.* The
rope is too slack.

schlaflos ADJECTIVE
sleepless

der Schlafraum NOUN (PL die **Schlafräume**)
dormitory

der Schlafsaal NOUN (PL die **Schlafsäle**)
dormitory

der Schlafsack NOUN (PL die **Schlafsäcke**)
sleeping bag

die Schlaftablette NOUN
sleeping pill

der Schlafwagen NOUN (PL die **Schlafwagen**)
sleeping car

das Schlafzimmer NOUN (PL die **Schlafzimmer**)
bedroom

der Schlag NOUN (PL die **Schläge**)
1 blow ◊ *ein Schlag auf den Kopf* a
blow to the head ◊ *Ich bin durchgefallen,
das ist ein Schlag.* I've failed, that's a
blow.
2 stroke ◊ *Mein Opa hat einen Schlag
gehabt und ist gelähmt.* My granddad's
had a stroke and he's now paralysed.
3 shock ◊ *Fass nicht an den Draht, sonst
bekommst du einen Schlag.* Don't touch
that wire, otherwise you'll get a shock.
♦ **Er hat von seinem Vater Schläge
bekommen.** His father gave him a hiding.

♦ **mit einem Schlag** all at once

schlagen VERB (PRESENT **schlägt**, IMPERFECT
schlug, PERFECT **hat geschlagen**)
1 to beat ◊ *Meine Eltern haben mich
noch nie geschlagen.* My parents have
never beaten me. ◊ *England hat Holland
vier zu eins geschlagen.* England beat
Holland four one. ◊ *Ihr Herz schlug
schneller.* Her heart beat faster.
♦ **Sahne schlagen** to whip cream
2 to hit ◊ *Er schlug mit dem Hammer
auf den Nagel.* He hit the nail with the
hammer. ◊ *Sie schlug mit der Faust auf
den Tisch.* She hit the table with her fist.
♦ **Er schlägt den Nagel in die Wand.** He
hammers the nail into the wall.
♦ **Die Uhr schlägt zehn.** The clock strikes
ten.
♦ **Es hat eben zehn geschlagen.** It's just
struck ten.
♦ **nach jemandem schlagen** to take after
somebody ◊ *Sie schlägt nach ihrer
Mutter.* She takes after her mother.
♦ **sich gut schlagen** to do well ◊ *Er hat sich
in der Prüfung gut geschlagen.* He did
well in the exam.

der Schlager NOUN (PL die **Schlager**)
hit

der Schläger NOUN (PL die **Schläger**)
1 thug ◊ *Franz ist ein Schläger.* Franz is
a thug.
2 bat ◊ *Baseball und Tischtennis spielt
man mit einem Schläger.* You play
baseball and table tennis with a bat.
3 racket ◊ *Für Tennis, Federball und
Squash braucht man einen Schläger.*
You need a racket for tennis, badminton
and squash.
♦ **ein Golfschläger** a golf club
♦ **ein Hockeyschläger** a hockey stick

die Schlägerei NOUN
fight

schlagfertig ADJECTIVE
quick-witted

die Schlagsahne NOUN
whipped cream

die Schlagzeile NOUN
headline

das Schlagzeug NOUN (PL die **Schlagzeuge**)
drums ◊ *Er spielt Schlagzeug.* He plays
the drums. ◊ *Am Schlagzeug: Freddy
Braun.* On drums: Freddy Braun.

der Schlagzeuger NOUN (PL die **Schlagzeuger**)
drummer

der Schlamm NOUN
mud

schlampen VERB
to be sloppy
♦ **Bei den Hausaufgaben hast du
geschlampt.** Your homework's sloppy.

die Schlamperei NOUN

[1] untidiness ◊ *Deine Schlamperei regt mich auf.* Your untidiness gets on my nerves.

[2] sloppy work ◊ *So eine Schlamperei kannst du doch nicht abgeben.* You can't possibly hand in such sloppy work.

schlampig ADJECTIVE
sloppy

die **Schlange** NOUN
[1] snake ◊ *eine giftige Schlange* a poisonous snake
[2] queue ◊ *Vor dem Kino stand eine lange Schlange.* There was a long queue outside the cinema.
♦ **Schlange stehen** to queue ◊ *Wir mussten für die Karten Schlange stehen.* We had to queue for the tickets.

schlank ADJECTIVE
slim ◊ *Sie ist sehr schlank.* She's very slim.

die **Schlankheitskur** NOUN
diet ◊ *eine Schlankheitskur machen* to be on a diet

schlapp ADJECTIVE
worn out ◊ *Ich fühle mich schlapp.* I feel worn out.

schlau ADJECTIVE
cunning

der **Schlauch** NOUN (PL die **Schläuche**)
[1] hose ◊ *Er hat den Garten mit dem Schlauch gespritzt.* He watered the garden with the hose.
[2] inner tube ◊ *Ich brauche einen neuen Schlauch für mein Fahrrad.* I need a new inner tube for my bike.

das **Schlauchboot** NOUN (PL die **Schlauchboote**)
rubber dinghy

schlecht ADJECTIVE, ADVERB
[1] bad ◊ *Er ist in Mathe schlecht.* He is bad at maths. ◊ *Meine Augen werden immer schlechter.* My eyes are getting worse.
♦ **ein schlechtes Gewissen** a guilty conscience
♦ **Die Milch ist schlecht geworden.** The milk's turned.
[2] badly ◊ *Ich habe schlecht geschlafen.* I slept badly.
♦ **schlecht gelaunt** in a bad mood
♦ **Mir ist schlecht.** I feel sick.
♦ **ein schlecht bezahlter Job** a poorly paid job
♦ **Ihm geht es schlecht.** He's in a bad way.

schlechtmachen VERB
♦ **jemanden schlechtmachen** to run somebody down ◊ *Du solltest ihn nicht dauernd schlechtmachen.* You shouldn't constantly run him down.

schleichen VERB (IMPERFECT **schlich**, PERFECT **ist geschlichen**)
to creep

die **Schleife** NOUN
[1] loop ◊ *Der Fluss macht eine Schleife.* The river makes a loop.
[2] bow ◊ *Sie hatte eine Schleife im Haar.* She had a bow in her hair.

Schleswig-Holstein NEUT NOUN
Schleswig-Holstein

> ⓘ **Schleswig-Holstein** is one of the 16 **Länder**. Its capital is Kiel. It is Germany's northernmost state, bordered by the North Sea and the Baltic, and by Denmark in the north.

die **Schleuder** NOUN
[1] catapult ◊ *Er hat mit seiner Schleuder ein Fenster getroffen.* He hit a window with his catapult.
[2] spin-dryer ◊ *Tu die nassen Sachen in die Schleuder.* Put your wet things in the spin-dryer.

schleudern VERB (PERFECT **hat/ist geschleudert**)
*For the perfect tense use **haben** when the verb has an object and **sein** when there is no object.*
[1] to hurl ◊ *Sie hat das Buch in die Ecke geschleudert.* She hurled the book into the corner.
[2] to spin ◊ *Du solltest die nasse Wäsche schleudern.* You should spin the wet washing.
[3] to skid ◊ *Das Auto ist geschleudert.* The car skidded.

schlief VERB see **schlafen**

schließen VERB (IMPERFECT **schloss**, PERFECT **hat geschlossen**)
to shut ◊ *Schließ bitte das Fenster.* Please shut the window. ◊ *Wann schließen die Geschäfte?* When do the shops shut? ◊ *Sie hatte die Augen geschlossen.* She had her eyes shut. ◊ *Der Betrieb wurde geschlossen.* The company was shut down.
♦ **mit jemandem Freundschaft schließen** to make friends with somebody
♦ **etwas aus etwas schließen** to gather something from something ◊ *Aus dem, was er sagte, schließe ich, dass er nicht mitkommen will.* I gather from what he said that he doesn't want to come.
♦ **Schließ bitte nicht von dir auf andere.** Don't judge others by your own standards.

schließlich ADVERB
finally
♦ **schließlich doch** after all

schlimm ADJECTIVE
bad

schlimmer ADJECTIVE
worse

schlimmste ADJECTIVE
underline{worst} ◊ *mein schlimmster Feind* my worst enemy

S

schlimmstenfalls ADVERB
at the worst

der **Schlips** NOUN
tie (necktie)

der **Schlitten** NOUN (PL die **Schlitten**)
sledge ◊ Im Winter sind wir viel Schlitten gefahren. We went sledging a lot in the winter.

das **Schlittenfahren** NOUN
sledging

der **Schlittschuh** NOUN (PL die **Schlittschuhe**)
skate
♦ **Schlittschuh laufen** to skate

der **Schlitz** NOUN (GEN des **Schlitzes**, PL die **Schlitze**)
1 slit ◊ Der Rock hat hinten einen Schlitz. The skirt has a slit at the back.
2 slot ◊ Du musst das Zwei-Euro-Stück in den Schlitz werfen. You have to put the two-euro coin in the slot.
3 flies ◊ Der Schlitz an deiner Hose ist auf. Your flies are open.

das **Schloss** NOUN (GEN des **Schlosses**, PL die **Schlösser**)
1 lock ◊ Sie steckte den Schlüssel ins Schloss. She put the key in the lock.
2 clasp ◊ Kannst du mir bitte das Schloss an meiner Kette aufmachen? Can you please open the clasp of my necklace?
3 chateau ◊ das Schloss in Versailles the chateau of Versailles

schloss VERB see **schließen**

schluchzen VERB
to sob

der **Schluckauf** NOUN
hiccups ◊ Er hatte einen Schluckauf. He had hiccups.

schlucken VERB
to swallow

schludern VERB
to do sloppy work

schlug VERB see **schlagen**

der **Schluss** NOUN (GEN des **Schlusses**, PL die **Schlüsse**)
1 end ◊ am Schluss des Jahres at the end of the year
♦ **Das Buch hat einen traurigen Schluss.** The book has a sad ending.
2 conclusion ◊ Ich habe meine Schlüsse gezogen. I've drawn my conclusions.
♦ **zum Schluss** finally ◊ Zum Schluss haben wir noch ein Lied gesungen. Finally we sang a song.
♦ **Schluss machen** to finish ◊ Wir sollten langsam Schluss machen. We should be finishing now.
♦ **mit jemandem Schluss machen** to finish with somebody ◊ Warum hast du mit Manfred Schluss gemacht? Why did you finish with Manfred?

der **Schlüssel** NOUN (PL die **Schlüssel**)
key ◊ Wo ist mein Fahrradschlüssel? Where's the key for my bike? ◊ der Schlüssel zum Erfolg the key to success

das **Schlüsselbein** NOUN (PL die **Schlüsselbeine**)
collar bone

der **Schlüsselbund** NOUN (PL die **Schlüsselbunde**)
bunch of keys

der **Schlüsselring** NOUN (PL die **Schlüsselringe**)
keyring

der **Schlussverkauf** NOUN
sales ◊ Dieses Kleid habe ich im Schlussverkauf bekommen. I got this dress in the sales.

schmal ADJECTIVE
narrow ◊ ein schmaler Durchgang a narrow passageway
♦ **Sie hat ein schmales Gesicht.** She has a thin face.
♦ **Du bist schmäler geworden.** You've lost weight.
Be careful! **schmal** does not mean **small**.

schmatzen VERB
to eat noisily

schmecken VERB
to taste ◊ Wie schmeckt eine Mango? What does a mango taste like? ◊ Das schmeckt gut. That tastes good.
♦ **Es schmeckt ihm.** He likes it.

schmeicheln VERB
♦ **jemandem schmeicheln** to flatter somebody

schmeißen VERB (IMPERFECT **schmiss**, PERFECT **hat geschmissen**)
to throw

schmelzen VERB (PRESENT **schmilzt**, IMPERFECT **schmolz**, PERFECT **hat/ist geschmolzen**)
For the perfect tense use **haben** when the verb has an object and **sein** when there is no object.
to melt ◊ Sie haben Schnee geschmolzen. They melted snow. ◊ Das Eis ist geschmolzen. The ice has melted.

der **Schmerz** NOUN (GEN des **Schmerzes**, PL die **Schmerzen**)
1 pain ◊ ein stechender Schmerz in der Seite a stabbing pain in the side
2 grief ◊ Sie verbarg ihren Schmerz über diesen Verlust. She hid her grief over her loss.

schmerzen VERB (PERFECT **hat geschmerzt**)
to hurt

das **Schmerzmittel** NOUN (PL die **Schmerzmittel**)
painkiller

die **Schmerztablette** NOUN
painkiller

der **Schmetterling** NOUN (PL die **Schmetterlinge**)
butterfly

die **Schminke** NOUN
   make-up

schminken VERB
   to make up ◊ *Hast du dir die Augen geschminkt?* Have you made up your eyes?
   ♦ **Ich schminke mich selten.** I seldom use make-up.

schmollen VERB
   to sulk

der **Schmuck** NOUN
   1 jewellery ◊ *Sie trägt selten Schmuck.* She seldom wears jewellery.
   2 decoration ◊ *bunte Kugeln als Schmuck für den Weihnachtsbaum* bright baubles as Christmas tree decorations

schmücken VERB
   to decorate

schmuggeln VERB
   to smuggle

schmusen VERB
   to cuddle ◊ *Sie hat mit Felix geschmust.* She cuddled Felix.

der **Schmutz** NOUN (GEN des **Schmutzes**)
   dirt

schmutzig ADJECTIVE
   dirty

der **Schnabel** NOUN (PL die **Schnäbel**)
   beak ◊ *Der Schnabel der Amsel ist gelb.* The blackbird's beak is yellow.

die **Schnalle** NOUN
   buckle

der **Schnaps** NOUN (GEN des **Schnapses**, PL die **Schnäpse**)
   schnapps

schnarchen VERB
   to snore

schnaufen VERB
   to puff

die **Schnauze** NOUN
   1 nose ◊ *Der Hund hat eine kalte Schnauze.* The dog has a cold nose.
   2 gob ◊ *Halt die Schnauze!* Shut your gob!
   ♦ **die Schnauze von etwas voll haben** to be fed up to the back teeth of something

sich **schnäuzen** VERB
   to blow one's nose

die **Schnecke** NOUN
   snail
   ♦ **eine Nacktschnecke** a slug

der **Schnee** NOUN
   snow ◊ *Heute Nacht ist viel Schnee gefallen.* A lot of snow fell last night.

der **Schneeball** NOUN (PL die **Schneebälle**)
   snowball

der **Schneemann** NOUN (PL die **Schneemänner**)
   snowman

der **Schneepflug** NOUN (PL die **Schneepflüge**)
   snowplough

schneiden VERB (IMPERFECT **schnitt,** PERFECT **hat geschnitten**)
   to cut ◊ *Kannst du bitte Brot schneiden?* Can you cut some bread, please? ◊ *jemandem die Haare schneiden* to cut somebody's hair ◊ *Du solltest dir die Haare schneiden lassen.* You should have your hair cut.
   ♦ **sich schneiden (1)** to cut oneself ◊ *Ich habe mich geschnitten.* I've cut myself. ◊ *Ich habe mir in den Finger geschnitten.* I've cut my finger.
   ♦ **sich schneiden (2)** to intersect ◊ *Die beiden Geraden schneiden sich.* The two straight lines intersect.

schneien VERB
   ♦ **Es schneit.** It's snowing.

schnell ADJECTIVE, ADVERB
   1 fast ◊ *Sie hat ein schnelles Auto.* She has a fast car. ◊ *Sie ist schnell gefahren.* She drove fast.
   2 quickly ◊ *Ich rief schnell einen Krankenwagen.* I quickly phoned for an ambulance.
   ♦ **Ich gehe noch schnell bei meiner Freundin vorbei.** I'm just popping in to my girlfriend's.

die **Schnelligkeit** NOUN
   speed

der **Schnellimbiss** NOUN (GEN des **Schnellimbisses,** PL die **Schnellimbisse**)
   snack bar

schnellstens ADVERB
   as quickly as possible

der **Schnellzug** NOUN (PL die **Schnellzüge**)
   express train

sich **schneuzen** VERB *see* **schnäuzen**

der **Schnitt** NOUN (PL die **Schnitte**)
   1 cut ◊ *Der Schnitt blutet.* The cut's bleeding. ◊ *Das Kleid hat einen eleganten Schnitt.* The dress has an elegant cut.
   2 average ◊ *Ich habe im Zeugnis einen Schnitt von drei.* I've got an average of C in my report.
   3 pattern ◊ *Hast du zu dem Rock einen Schnitt?* Have you got a pattern for this skirt?

schnitt VERB *see* **schneiden**

der **Schnittlauch** NOUN
   chive

die **Schnittstelle** NOUN
   interface

die **Schnittwunde** NOUN
   cut

das **Schnitzel** NOUN (PL die **Schnitzel**)
   escalope ◊ *Ich bestelle mir ein Schnitzel.* I'm going to order an escalope.

schnitzen VERB
   to carve

der **Schnorchel** NOUN (PL die **Schnorchel**)
   snorkel

S

schnüffeln VERB
to sniff

der **Schnuller** NOUN (PL die **Schnuller**)
dummy ◊ *Das Baby saugte am Schnuller.* The baby sucked the dummy.

der **Schnupfen** NOUN (PL die **Schnupfen**)
cold ◊ *Meine Schwester hat Schnupfen.* My sister has a cold.

die **Schnur** NOUN (PL die **Schnüre**)
[1] string ◊ *Du solltest eine Schnur um das Päckchen machen.* You should put string round the parcel.
[2] flex ◊ *Die Schnur von der Lampe ist zu kurz.* The flex of the lamp is too short.

der **Schnurrbart** NOUN (PL die **Schnurrbärte**)
moustache

schnurren VERB
to purr

der **Schnürsenkel** NOUN (PL die **Schnürsenkel**)
shoelace

der **Schock** NOUN (PL die **Schocks**)
shock

schockieren VERB (PERFECT **hat schockiert**)
to shock

die **Schokolade** NOUN
chocolate ◊ *eine heiße Schokolade* a hot chocolate

schon ADVERB
already ◊ *Ich bin schon fertig.* I've already finished.
♦ **Ist er schon da?** Is he there yet?
♦ **Warst du schon einmal da?** Have you ever been there?
♦ **Ich war schon einmal da.** I've been there before.
♦ **Das war schon immer so.** That's always been the case.
♦ **Hast du schon gehört?** Have you heard?
♦ **schon oft** often
♦ **schon der Gedanke** the very thought
♦ **Du wirst schon sehen.** You'll see.
♦ **Das wird schon noch gut.** That'll be OK.
♦ **ja schon, aber ...** yes, but ...
♦ **schon möglich** possible
♦ **Schon gut!** OK!
♦ **Du weißt schon.** You know.
♦ **Komm schon!** Come on!

schön ADJECTIVE
[1] beautiful ◊ *Sie haben ein schönes Haus.* They have a beautiful house.
[2] nice ◊ *Es waren schöne Ferien.* The holidays were nice. ◊ *Schönes Wochenende!* Have a nice weekend.
♦ **sich schön machen** to make oneself look nice
♦ **Schöne Grüße an deine Eltern!** Regards to your parents.
♦ **Sie ist ganz schön frech.** She's pretty damn cheeky.
♦ **na schön** very well ◊ *Na schön, dann geht halt spielen.* Very well then, go and play.

schonend ADJECTIVE, ADVERB
gentle ◊ *jemandem etwas schonend beibringen* to break something gently to somebody

die **Schönheit** NOUN
beauty

sich **schönmachen** VERB *see* **schön**

schöpfen VERB
to ladle ◊ *Sie schöpfte Suppe in die Teller.* She ladled soup into the plates.
♦ **Luft schöpfen** to get some air

die **Schöpfung** NOUN
creation

der **Schornstein** NOUN (PL die **Schornsteine**)
chimney

schoss VERB *see* **schießen**

der **Schotte** NOUN (GEN des **Schotten,** PL die **Schotten**)
Scot
♦ **Er ist Schotte.** He's Scottish.

die **Schottin** NOUN
Scot
♦ **Sie ist Schottin.** She's Scottish.

schottisch ADJECTIVE
Scottish

Schottland NEUT NOUN
Scotland
♦ **aus Schottland** from Scotland
♦ **in Schottland** in Scotland
♦ **nach Schottland** to Scotland

schräg ADJECTIVE
sloping ◊ *Das Haus hat ein schräges Dach.* The house has a sloping roof.
♦ **etwas schräg stellen** to put something at an angle
♦ **schräg gegenüber** diagonally opposite

der **Schrägstrich** NOUN (PL die **Schrägstriche**)
slash

der **Schrank** NOUN (PL die **Schränke**)
[1] cupboard ◊ *Der Besen ist im Schrank in der Küche.* The broom's in the cupboard in the kitchen.
[2] wardrobe ◊ *Ich räume meine Kleider in den Schrank.* I'll put my clothes away in the wardrobe.

die **Schranke** NOUN
barrier

die **Schrankwand** NOUN (PL die **Schrankwände**)
wall unit

die **Schraube** NOUN
[1] screw
[2] bolt

der **Schraubenschlüssel** NOUN (PL die **Schraubenschlüssel**)
spanner

der **Schraubenzieher** NOUN (PL die **Schraubenzieher**)
screwdriver

der **Schreck** NOUN

fright ◊ *Ich habe einen furchtbaren Schreck bekommen.* I got a terrible fright.

schreckhaft ADJECTIVE
jumpy

schrecklich ADJECTIVE, ADVERB
1 terrible ◊ *Das Wetter war schrecklich schlecht.* The weather was terrible.
2 terribly ◊ *Das tut schrecklich weh.* It hurts terribly. ◊ *Es tut mir schrecklich leid.* I'm terribly sorry.

der **Schrei** NOUN (PL die **Schreie**)
1 scream ◊ *Als sie die Spinne sah, stieß sie einen Schrei aus.* When she saw the spider she let out a scream.
2 shout ◊ *Wir hörten einen Schrei um Hilfe.* We heard a shout for help.

der **Schreibblock** NOUN (PL die **Schreibblöcke**)
writing pad

schreiben VERB (IMPERFECT **schrieb**, PERFECT **hat geschrieben**)
1 to write ◊ *Ich habe ihr einen Brief geschrieben.* I've written her a letter.
♦ **Wir schreiben morgen eine Arbeit in Englisch.** We've got a written English test tomorrow.
♦ **Wir sollten uns schreiben.** We should write to each other.
2 to spell ◊ *Wie schreibt man seinen Namen?* How do you spell his name?

die **Schreibmaschine** NOUN
typewriter

das **Schreibpapier** NOUN
notepaper

der **Schreibtisch** NOUN (PL die **Schreibtische**)
desk

die **Schreibwaren** FEM PL NOUN
stationery

das **Schreibwarengeschäft** NOUN (PL die **Schreibwarengeschäfte**)
stationery shop

das **Schreibzeug** NOUN
writing materials

schreien VERB (IMPERFECT **schrie**, PERFECT **hat geschrien**)
1 to scream ◊ *Sie schrie vor Schmerzen.* She screamed with pain.
2 to shout ◊ *Wir haben geschrien, du hast uns aber nicht gehört.* We shouted but you didn't hear us.

der **Schreiner** NOUN (PL die **Schreiner**)
joiner

schrieb VERB see **schreiben**

die **Schrift** NOUN
1 writing ◊ *Sie hat eine schöne Schrift.* She has lovely writing.
2 font ◊ *Welche Schrift soll ich für das Dokument nehmen?* Which font should I use for the document?

schriftlich ADJECTIVE, ADVERB
written ◊ *eine schriftliche Entschuldigung* a written apology

♦ **etwas schriftlich festhalten** to put something in writing

der **Schriftsteller** NOUN (PL die **Schriftsteller**)
writer

schrill ADJECTIVE
shrill

der **Schritt** NOUN (PL die **Schritte**)
1 step ◊ *Er machte einen vorsichtigen Schritt nach vorn.* He took a careful step forward.
2 walk ◊ *Ich habe dich an deinem Schritt erkannt.* I recognized you by your walk.
3 pace ◊ *Sie ging mit schnellen Schritten nach Hause.* She walked home at a brisk pace.
♦ **Schritt fahren** to drive at walking pace

der **Schrott** NOUN
scrap metal

schrumpfen VERB (PERFECT **ist geschrumpft**)
1 to shrink ◊ *Der Pulli ist in der Wäsche geschrumpft.* The pullover shrank in the wash.
2 to shrivel ◊ *Die Äpfel sind geschrumpft.* The apples have shrivelled.

die **Schublade** NOUN
drawer

schüchtern ADJECTIVE
shy

der **Schuh** NOUN (PL die **Schuhe**)
shoe

die **Schuhcreme** NOUN (PL die **Schuhcremes**)
shoe polish

die **Schuhgröße** NOUN
shoe size ◊ *Welche Schuhgröße hast du?* What shoe size are you?

die **Schularbeiten** FEM PL NOUN
homework ◊ *Hast du deine Schularbeiten schon gemacht?* Have you done your homework?

die **Schulaufgaben** FEM PL NOUN
homework ◊ *Heute haben wir keine Schulaufgaben bekommen.* We didn't get any homework today.

das **Schulbuch** NOUN (PL die **Schulbücher**)
school book

die **Schuld** NOUN
see also **schuld** ADJECTIVE
1 guilt ◊ *Seine Schuld konnte nicht bewiesen werden.* His guilt couldn't be proved.
2 fault ◊ *Es war deine Schuld, dass wir zu spät kamen.* It was your fault that we arrived late.
♦ **jemandem Schuld geben** to blame somebody

schuld ADJECTIVE
see also **die Schuld** NOUN
♦ **an etwas schuld sein** to be to blame for something ◊ *Du bist an der Verspätung schuld.* You are to blame for the delay.

S

☞

♦ **Sie ist schuld, dass wir eine Strafarbeit bekommen haben.** It's her fault that we got lines.

♦ **Er ist schuld.** It's his fault.

die **Schulden** PL NOUN

see also **schulden** VERB

debt ◊ *Ich muss noch meine Schulden bei dir bezahlen.* I still have to pay off my debts to you. ◊ *Staatsschulden* national debt

schulden VERB

see also **die Schulden** NOUN

to owe ◊ *Was schulde ich dir?* How much do I owe you?

schuldig ADJECTIVE

guilty ◊ *Meinst du, dass die Angeklagte schuldig ist?* Do you think that the accused is guilty?

♦ **jemandem etwas schuldig sein** to owe somebody something ◊ *Was bin ich dir schuldig?* How much do I owe you?

♦ **Er ist mir noch immer eine Antwort schuldig.** He still hasn't given me an answer.

der **Schuldirektor** NOUN (PL die **Schuldirektoren**)

headmaster

die **Schuldirektorin** NOUN

headmistress

die **Schule** NOUN

school ◊ *in der Schule* at school

der **Schüler** NOUN (PL die **Schüler**)

pupil

die **Schülerin** NOUN

pupil

die **Schülervertretung** NOUN

pupil representation

die **Schulferien** PL NOUN

school holidays

schulfrei ADJECTIVE

♦ **ein schulfreier Tag** a holiday

♦ **Sonntag ist schulfrei.** Sunday isn't a school day.

der **Schulhof** NOUN (PL die **Schulhöfe**)

playground

das **Schuljahr** NOUN (PL die **Schuljahre**)

school year

die **Schulmappe** NOUN

school bag

schulpflichtig ADJECTIVE

of school age

die **Schulstunde** NOUN

period

der **Schultag** NOUN (PL die **Schultage**)

♦ **mein erster Schultag** my first day at school

die **Schultasche** NOUN

school bag

die **Schulter** NOUN

shoulder

die **Schulverwaltung** NOUN

school administration

das **Schulzeugnis** NOUN (GEN des **Schulzeugnisses,** PL die **Schulzeugnisse**)

school report

schummeln VERB

to cheat ◊ *Du schummelst!* You're cheating!

die **Schuppe** NOUN

scale ◊ *Der Fisch hat glänzende Schuppen.* The fish has shiny scales.

♦ **Schuppen** dandruff ◊ *ein Haarwaschmittel gegen Schuppen* an anti-dandruff shampoo

die **Schürze** NOUN

apron

der **Schuss** NOUN (GEN des **Schusses,** PL die **Schüsse**)

shot ◊ *Wir hörten einen Schuss.* We heard a shot.

die **Schüssel** NOUN

bowl

die **Schusswaffe** NOUN

firearm

der **Schuster** NOUN (PL die **Schuster**)

cobbler

der **Schutt** NOUN

rubble ◊ *Der Schutt von der Baustelle wird morgen weggebracht.* The rubble from the building site will be removed tomorrow.

♦ **Schutt abladen verboten!** No dumping!

der **Schuttabladeplatz** NOUN (GEN des **Schuttabladeplatzes,** PL die **Schuttabladeplätze**)

refuse dump

schütteln VERB

to shake

♦ **sich schütteln** to shake oneself

schütten VERB

1 to pour ◊ *Soll ich dir Saft ins Glas schütten?* Shall I pour you some juice?

2 to spill ◊ *Pass auf, dass du den Kaffee nicht auf die Tischdecke schüttest.* Be careful that you don't spill coffee on the tablecloth.

♦ **Es schüttet.** It's pouring down.

der **Schutz** NOUN (GEN des **Schutzes**)

1 protection ◊ *Zum Schutz gegen die Sonne solltest du dich eincremen.* You should put some cream on to protect against the sun.

2 shelter ◊ *Sie suchten Schutz in der Berghütte.* They took shelter in a mountain hut.

♦ **jemanden in Schutz nehmen** to stand up for somebody

der **Schütze** NOUN (GEN des **Schützen,** PL die **Schützen**)

1 marksman ◊ *Er ist ein guter Schütze.* He's a good marksman.

2 Sagittarius ◊ *Martin ist Schütze.* Martin's Sagittarius.

schützen VERB

to protect ◊ *Diese Creme schützt die Haut gegen Sonnenbrand.* This cream protects the skin from sunburn.
- **sich gegen etwas schützen** to protect oneself from something ◊ *Schützen Sie sich gegen Sonnenbrand.* Protect yourself from sunburn.

schwach ADJECTIVE
weak ◊ *Ihre Stimme wurde immer schwächer.* Her voice became weaker and weaker.
- **Das war eine schwache Leistung!** That wasn't very good.

die **Schwäche** NOUN
weakness

der **Schwächling** NOUN (PL die **Schwächlinge**)
weakling

der **Schwachsinn** NOUN
balderdash

schwachsinnig ADJECTIVE
idiotic ◊ *So eine schwachsinnige Idee!* What an idiotic idea!

der **Schwager** NOUN (PL die **Schwäger**)
brother-in-law

die **Schwägerin** NOUN
sister-in-law

der **Schwamm** NOUN (PL die **Schwämme**)
sponge

schwamm VERB *see* **schwimmen**

schwanger ADJECTIVE
pregnant ◊ *Sie ist im dritten Monat schwanger.* She's three months pregnant.

schwanken VERB
[1] to sway ◊ *Das Schiff schwankte.* The ship swayed.
[2] to stagger ◊ *Er schwankte und fiel dann um.* He staggered and fell down.
[3] to fluctuate ◊ *Die Temperaturen schwanken.* Temperatures are fluctuating. ◊ *Der Kurs des Pfunds schwankt.* The exchange rate of the pound is fluctuating.

der **Schwanz** NOUN (GEN des **Schwanzes,** PL die **Schwänze**)
tail

schwänzen VERB
to skive off ◊ *Ich habe heute die Turnstunde geschwänzt.* I skived off PE today.

der **Schwarm** NOUN (PL die **Schwärme**)
swarm ◊ *ein Schwarm Fliegen* a swarm of flies
- **Er ist mein Schwarm.** I have a crush on him.

schwärmen VERB (PERFECT **hat/ist geschwärmt**)

Use **sein** *to form the perfect tense for to swarm.*

to swarm ◊ *Die Bienen sind aus dem Bienenstock geschwärmt.* The bees swarmed out of the hive.

- **schwärmen für** to have a crush on ◊ *Sie schwärmt für ihren Mathelehrer.* She has a crush on her maths teacher.
- **schwärmen von** to rave about ◊ *Er hat von dem Konzert geschwärmt.* He raved about the concert.

schwarz ADJECTIVE
black ◊ *Der Himmel wurde immer schwärzer.* The sky turned blacker and blacker.
- **Schwarzes Brett** notice board
- **ins Schwarze treffen** to hit the bull's eye

das **Schwarzbrot** NOUN (PL die **Schwarzbrote**)
brown rye bread

der **Schwarze** NOUN (GEN des/der **Schwarzen,** PL
die die **Schwarzen**)
black

schwarzfahren VERB (PRESENT **fährt schwarz,** IMPERFECT **fuhr schwarz,** PERFECT **ist schwarzgefahren**)
- **Sie fährt in der Straßenbahn immer schwarz.** She never pays her tram fare.

schwarzsehen VERB (PRESENT **sieht schwarz,** IMPERFECT **sah schwarz,** PERFECT **hat schwarzgesehen**)
to look on the black side of things ◊ *Sieh doch nicht immer so schwarz.* Don't always look on the black side of things.

der **Schwarzwald** NOUN
Black Forest

schwarz-weiß ADJECTIVE
black and white

schwätzen VERB
to chatter

der **Schwätzer** NOUN (PL die **Schwätzer**)
windbag

der **Schwede** NOUN (GEN des **Schweden,** PL die **Schweden**)
Swede
- **Er ist Schwede.** He's Swedish.

Schweden NEUT NOUN
Sweden
- **aus Schweden** from Sweden
- **nach Schweden** to Sweden

die **Schwedin** NOUN
Swede

schwedisch ADJECTIVE
Swedish

der **Schwefel** NOUN
sulphur

schweigen VERB (IMPERFECT **schwieg,** PERFECT **hat geschwiegen**)
[1] to be silent ◊ *Die Kinder finden es schwierig, mehr als fünf Minuten lang zu schweigen.* The children find it difficult to be silent for more than five minutes.
[2] to stop talking ◊ *Sag ihm, er soll schweigen.* Tell him to stop talking.

das **Schwein** NOUN (PL die **Schweine**)
pig

♦ **Schwein haben** to be really lucky ◊ *Da hatten wir ja noch mal Schwein.* We were really lucky there.

der **Schweinebraten** NOUN (PL die **Schweinebraten**)
roast pork

das **Schweinefleisch** NOUN
pork

die **Schweinerei** NOUN

1 scandal ◊ *Es ist eine Schweinerei, dass wir länger arbeiten müssen.* It's a scandal that we have to work longer hours.

2 mess ◊ *Wer hat denn die Schweinerei im Bad gemacht?* Who made the mess in the bathroom?

3 obscenity ◊ *Über solche Schweinereien kann ich nicht lachen.* I can't laugh at such obscenities.

der **Schweiß** NOUN (GEN des **Schweißes**)
sweat

die **Schweiz** NOUN
Switzerland

ⓘ *Switzerland is bordered by Germany, Austria, Liechtenstein, Italy and France. Its capital is Berne and its currency the Franken. Roughly 60% of the population (mainly in the North and East) speak a German dialect. French, Italian and Rhaeto-Romanic are also spoken.*

♦ **aus der Schweiz** from Switzerland
♦ **in der Schweiz** in Switzerland
♦ **in die Schweiz** to Switzerland

der **Schweizer** NOUN (PL die **Schweizer**)
Swiss ◊ *die Schweizer* the Swiss

die **Schweizerin** NOUN
Swiss

schweizerisch ADJECTIVE
Swiss

die **Schwellung** NOUN
swelling

schwer ADJECTIVE, ADVERB

1 heavy ◊ *Ich habe einen schweren Koffer.* I have a heavy suitcase. ◊ *Er hat eine schwere Erkältung.* He has a heavy cold.

♦ **Ich habe einen schweren Kopf.** I've got a headache.

2 difficult ◊ *Die Mathearbeit war schwer.* The maths test was difficult.

♦ **Sie ist schwer in Ordnung.** She's a great person.

♦ **Er ist schwer verletzt.** He's badly injured.

schwerfallen VERB (PRESENT **fällt schwer**, IMPERFECT **fiel schwer**, PERFECT **ist schwergefallen**)

♦ **jemandem schwerfallen** to be difficult for somebody ◊ *Das dürfte dir nicht schwerfallen.* That shouldn't be too difficult for you.

das **Schwert** NOUN (PL die **Schwerter**)
sword

die **Schwester** NOUN

1 sister ◊ *Meine Schwester ist jünger als ich.* My sister's younger than me.

2 nurse ◊ *Die Schwester hat mir eine Schmerztablette gegeben.* The nurse gave me a painkiller.

die **Schwiegereltern** PL NOUN
parents-in-law

die **Schwiegermutter** NOUN (PL die **Schwiegermütter**)
mother-in-law

der **Schwiegersohn** NOUN (PL die **Schwiegersöhne**)
son-in-law

die **Schwiegertochter** NOUN (PL die **Schwiegertöchter**)
daughter-in-law

der **Schwiegervater** NOUN (PL die **Schwiegerväter**)
father-in-law

schwierig ADJECTIVE
difficult

die **Schwierigkeit** NOUN
difficulty

das **Schwimmbad** NOUN (PL die **Schwimmbäder**)
swimming pool

das **Schwimmbecken** NOUN (PL die **Schwimmbecken**)
swimming pool

schwimmen VERB (IMPERFECT **schwamm**, PERFECT **ist geschwommen**)

1 to swim ◊ *Er kann nicht schwimmen.* He can't swim.

2 to float ◊ *Auf dem Fluss schwammen Äste.* Branches were floating on the river.

3 to flounder ◊ *Bei der Prüfung bin ich ganz schön geschwommen.* I really floundered in the exam.

die **Schwimmweste** NOUN
life jacket

der **Schwindel** NOUN

1 dizzy spell

2 fraud ◊ *Der Schwindel wurde entdeckt.* The fraud was discovered.

schwindelfrei ADJECTIVE

♦ **schwindelfrei sein** to have a good head for heights ◊ *Ich bin nicht schwindelfrei.* I don't have a good head for heights.

schwindeln VERB
to fib

schwindlig ADJECTIVE
dizzy

♦ **Mir ist schwindlig.** I feel dizzy.

der **Schwips** NOUN (GEN des **Schwipses**, PL die **Schwipse**)

♦ **einen Schwips haben** to be tipsy

schwitzen VERB
to sweat

schwören VERB (IMPERFECT **schwor**, PERFECT **hat geschworen**)
to swear

schwul ADJECTIVE
gay

schwül ADJECTIVE
close

der **Schwule** NOUN (GEN des/der **Schwulen**, PL die **Schwulen**)
gay ◊ *Ich habe nichts gegen Schwule.* I have nothing against gays.

der **Schwung** NOUN (PL die **Schwünge**)
swing ◊ *Sie setzte das Pendel in Schwung.* She started the pendulum swinging.
♦ **Der Party fehlte irgendwie der Schwung.** The party never really got going.
♦ **Ein heißes Bad wird mich wieder in Schwung bringen.** A hot bath will get me going again.

sechs NUMBER
see also **die Sechs** NOUN
six

die **Sechs** NOUN
see also **sechs** NUMBER
1 six
2 unsatisfactory

> ℹ️ *German marks range from one (**sehr gut**) to six (**ungenügend**).*

sechshundert NUMBER
six hundred

sechste ADJECTIVE
sixth ◊ *Er kam als Sechster.* He was the sixth to arrive.

das **Sechstel** NOUN (PL die **Sechstel**)
sixth

sechzehn NUMBER
sixteen

sechzig NUMBER
sixty

die **See** NOUN
see also **der See** NOUN
sea ◊ *auf See* at sea
♦ **Wir fahren im Sommer an die See.** We're going to the seaside in the summer.

der **See** NOUN (PL die **Seen**)
see also **die See** NOUN
lake ◊ *der Genfer See* Lake Geneva

der **Seehund** NOUN (PL die **Seehunde**)
seal

seekrank ADJECTIVE
seasick

der **Seelachs** NOUN (GEN des **Seelachses**, PL die **Seelachse**)
rock salmon

die **Seele** NOUN
soul

seelenruhig ADVERB
calmly

der **Seeräuber** NOUN (PL die **Seeräuber**)
pirate

das **Segel** NOUN (PL die **Segel**)
sail

das **Segelboot** NOUN (PL die **Segelboote**)
yacht

das **Segelfliegen** NOUN
gliding

das **Segelflugzeug** NOUN (PL die **Segelflugzeuge**)
glider

segeln VERB (PERFECT **ist gesegelt**)
to sail

das **Segelschiff** NOUN (PL die **Segelschiffe**)
sailing ship

der **Segen** NOUN (PL die **Segen**)
blessing

sehen VERB (PRESENT **sieht**, IMPERFECT **sah**, PERFECT **hat gesehen**)
1 to see ◊ *Hast du den Film schon gesehen?* Have you seen the film yet?
♦ **siehe Seite fünf** see page five
2 to look ◊ *Sieh mal an die Tafel.* Look at the board.
♦ **schlecht sehen** to have bad eyesight ◊ *Sie sieht schlecht.* She has bad eyesight.
♦ **mal sehen, ob ...** let's see if ... ◊ *Mal sehen, ob Post für mich gekommen ist.* Let's see if there's any post for me.
♦ **Kommst du mit? – Mal sehen.** Are you coming? – I'll see.

sehenswert ADJECTIVE
worth seeing

die **Sehenswürdigkeiten** FEM PL NOUN
sights

sich **sehnen** VERB
♦ **sich sehnen nach** to long for

die **Sehnsucht** NOUN (PL die **Sehnsüchte**)
longing

sehnsüchtig ADJECTIVE
longing

sehr ADVERB
1 very ◊ *Das ist sehr schön.* That's very nice.
♦ **sehr gut** very good

> ℹ️ *German marks range from one (**sehr gut**) to six (**ungenügend**).*

2 a lot ◊ *Sie hat sehr geweint.* She cried a lot.
♦ **zu sehr** too much
♦ **Sehr geehrter Herr Ahlers** Dear Mr Ahlers

die **Seide** NOUN
silk

die **Seife** NOUN
soap

die **Seifenoper** NOUN
soap opera

das **Seil** NOUN (PL die **Seile**)

S

1 rope ◇ *Sie hatten ihn mit einem Seil gefesselt.* They had tied him up with a rope.

2 cable ◇ *das Seil des Skilifts* the cable of the ski lift

die **Seilbahn** NOUN
cable car

sein VERB (PRESENT **ist**, IMPERFECT **war**, PERFECT **ist gewesen**)

see also **sein** ADJECTIVE

to be ◇ *Ich bin müde.* I'm tired. ◇ *Du bist doof.* You're stupid. ◇ *Er ist reich.* He's rich. ◇ *Sie ist Lehrerin.* She's a teacher. ◇ *Es ist kalt.* It's cold. ◇ *Wir sind Schüler am Gymnasium.* We're pupils at the grammar school. ◇ *Ihr seid spät dran.* You're late. ◇ *Sie sind vom Zirkus.* They're from the circus. ◇ *Wir waren dort.* We were there. ◇ *Wir sind im Schwimmbad gewesen.* We've been to the swimming pool. ◇ *Seien Sie nicht böse.* Don't be angry.

◆ **Das wäre gut.** That would be a good thing.

◆ **Wenn ich Sie wäre ...** If I were you ...

◆ **Das wär's.** That's it.

◆ **Morgen bin ich in Rom.** Tomorrow I'll be in Rome.

◆ **Waren Sie mal in Rom?** Have you ever been to Rome?

◆ **Mir ist kalt.** I'm cold.

◆ **Was ist?** What's the matter?

◆ **Ist was?** Is something the matter?

◆ **es sei denn, dass ...** unless ...

◆ **wie dem auch sei** be that as it may

◆ **Wie wäre es mit ...?** How about ...?

◆ **Lass das sein!** Stop that!

sein ADJECTIVE

see also **sein** VERB

1 his ◇ *Sein Deutschlehrer ist nett.* His German teacher's nice. ◇ *Seine Mutter erlaubt das nicht.* His mother doesn't allow it. ◇ *Das ist sein Buch.* That's his book. ◇ *Seine Eltern sind klasse.* His parents are great. ◇ *Das ist nicht mein Füller, das ist seiner.* That's not my pen, it's his. ◇ *Meine Mutter heißt Anne, seine auch.* My mother's called Anne, so is his. ◇ *Mein Fahrrad war kaputt, also habe ich seins genommen.* My bike was broken, so I took his. ◇ *Ich habe schlechte Noten, aber seine sind nicht besser.* My marks are bad, but his aren't much better.

2 its ◇ *Der Fuchs kam aus seiner Höhle.* The fox came out of its lair. ◇ *Jedes Buch hat seinen Platz.* Each book has its place.

seiner PRONOUN

seiner is the genitive of *er*.

of him ◇ *Wir gedenken seiner.* We're thinking of him.

seinetwegen ADVERB

1 for his sake ◇ *Ihr müsst seinetwegen nicht auf euren Urlaub verzichten.* You don't have to do without your holiday for his sake.

2 on his account ◇ *Hat sie sich seinetwegen so aufgeregt?* Did she get so upset on his account?

3 as far as he's concerned ◇ *Er sagt, dass du seinetwegen gehen kannst.* He says that as far as he's concerned you can go.

seit PREPOSITION, CONJUNCTION

The preposition **seit** *takes the dative.*

since ◇ *Seit er verheiratet ist, spielt er nicht mehr Fußball.* He's stopped playing football since he got married. ◇ *Seit letztem Jahr habe ich nichts mehr von ihm gehört.* I haven't heard anything from him since last year.

◆ **Er ist seit einer Woche hier.** He's been here for a week.

◆ **seit Langem** for a long time

seitdem ADVERB, CONJUNCTION

since ◇ *Seitdem sie im Gymnasium ist, hat sie kaum mehr Zeit.* Since she's been going to grammar school, she's hardly had any time.

◆ **Ich habe seitdem nichts mehr von ihr gehört.** I haven't heard from her since then.

die **Seite** NOUN

1 side ◇ *Die rechte Seite des Autos war beschädigt.* The right side of the car was damaged.

2 page ◇ *Das steht auf Seite fünfzig.* It's on page fifty.

das **Seitenstechen** NOUN
stitch ◇ *Ich habe Seitenstechen.* I've got a stitch.

der **Sekretär** NOUN
secretary

das **Sekretariat** NOUN (PL die **Sekretariate**)
secretary's office

die **Sekretärin** NOUN
secretary

der **Sekt** NOUN (PL die **Sekte**)
sparkling wine

die **Sekunde** NOUN
second ◇ *zehn Sekunden* ten seconds

selber PRONOUN = **selbst**

selbst PRONOUN, ADVERB

1 on one's own ◇ *Das Kind kann sich selbst anziehen.* The child can get dressed on her own. ◇ *Ich werde schon selbst eine Lösung finden.* I'll find a solution on my own.

◆ **ich selbst** I myself

◆ **er selbst** he himself

◆ **wir selbst** we ourselves

◆ **Sie ist die Liebenswürdigkeit selbst.** She's kindness itself.

◆ **Er braut sein Bier selbst.** He brews his own beer.

♦ **Wie geht's? – Gut, und selbst?** How are things? – Fine, and yourself?

♦ **von selbst** by itself ◊ *Die Bombe ist von selbst losgegangen.* The bomb went off by itself.

2 even ◊ *Selbst meine Mutter findet Oasis gut.* Even my mother likes Oasis.

♦ **selbst wenn** even if ◊ *Du musst das machen, selbst wenn du keine Lust hast.* You have to do it even if you don't feel like it.

selbständig ADJECTIVE *see* **selbstständig**

die **Selbstbedienung** NOUN
self-service

selbstbewusst ADJECTIVE
self-confident

der **Selbstmord** NOUN (PL die **Selbstmorde**)
suicide ◊ *Selbstmord begehen* to commit suicide

selbstsicher ADJECTIVE
self-assured

selbstständig ADJECTIVE
independent ◊ *Du solltest langsam selbstständiger werden.* It's about time you started to become more independent. ◊ *ein selbstständiger Staat* an independent country

♦ **Kannst du das nicht selbstständig entscheiden?** Can't you decide on your own?

♦ **sich selbstständig machen** to become self-employed

♦ **Sie hat sich als Übersetzerin selbstständig gemacht.** She set herself up as a self-employed translator.

selbstsüchtig ADJECTIVE
selfish

die **Selbstverpflegung** NOUN
self-catering

selbstverständlich ADJECTIVE, ADVERB
1 obvious ◊ *Das ist für mich durchaus nicht selbstverständlich.* It's not at all obvious to me.

♦ **Es ist doch selbstverständlich, dass man da hilft.** It goes without saying that you should help.

♦ **Ich halte das für selbstverständlich.** I take that for granted.

2 of course ◊ *Ich habe mich selbstverständlich sofort bedankt.* Of course I said thank you immediately. ◊ *Kommt er mit? – Selbstverständlich.* Is he coming? – Of course. ◊ *Ich habe selbstverständlich nicht unterschrieben.* Of course I didn't sign.

das **Selbstvertrauen** NOUN
self-confidence

selig ADJECTIVE
blissful ◊ *Er hatte ein seliges Lächeln auf dem Gesicht.* He had a blissful smile on his face.

♦ **Sie war selig, als sie ihn sah.** She was overjoyed to see him.

der **Sellerie** NOUN
celeriac

selten ADJECTIVE, ADVERB
1 rare ◊ *eine seltene Pflanze* a rare plant
2 rarely ◊ *Wir gehen selten ins Kino.* We rarely go to the cinema.

seltsam ADJECTIVE
curious

das **Semester** NOUN (PL die **Semester**)
semester

das **Semikolon** NOUN (PL die **Semikolons** *or* **Semikola**)
semicolon

das **Seminar** NOUN (PL die **Seminare**)
seminar ◊ *Ich mache dieses Semester ein Seminar über Steinbeck.* I'm doing a seminar on Steinbeck this semester.

die **Semmel** NOUN
roll

die **Sendefolge** NOUN
series

senden VERB (IMPERFECT **sendete** *or* **sandte**, PERFECT **hat gesendet** *or* **gesandt**)
1 to send ◊ *Bitte senden Sie mir Ihren neuesten Katalog.* Please send me your latest catalogue.
2 to broadcast ◊ *Der Spielfilm wird im dritten Programm gesendet.* The film will be broadcast on Channel three. ◊ *Wir senden bis Mitternacht.* We broadcast until midnight.

die **Sendereihe** NOUN
series

die **Sendung** NOUN
1 transmission ◊ *Während der Sendung darf das Studio nicht betreten werden.* Nobody's allowed to enter the studio during transmission.
2 programme ◊ *Kennst du die Sendung "Tiere im Zoo"?* Do you know the programme "Animals in the Zoo"?
3 consignment ◊ *Für Sie ist eine Sendung mit Mustern angekommen.* A consignment of samples has arrived for you.

der **Senf** NOUN (PL die **Senfe**)
mustard

der **Senior** NOUN (PL die **Senioren**)
senior citizen

die **Sensation** NOUN
sensation

sensibel ADJECTIVE
sensitive ◊ *Sie ist ein sehr sensibler Mensch.* She's a very sensitive person.
Be careful! **sensibel** does not mean **sensible**.

sentimental ADJECTIVE
sentimental ◊ *Nun werd nicht sentimental!* Now don't get sentimental.

der **September** NOUN
September ◊ *im September* in September ◊ *am elften September* on

S

☞

the eleventh of September ◊ *Ulm, den
11. September 2003* Ulm, 11 September
2003 ◊ *Heute ist der elfte September.*
Today is the eleventh of September.

die **Serie** NOUN
series

seriös ADJECTIVE
respectable
> Be careful! **seriös** does not mean
> **serious**.

der **Server** NOUN (PL die **Server**)
server

das **Service** NOUN (GEN des **Service** or **Services**,
PL die **Service**)
| see also **der Service** NOUN |
set ◊ *Sie hat ein hübsches Teeservice
aus Porzellan.* She has a lovely china tea
set.

der **Service** NOUN (GEN des **Service**, PL die
Services)
| see also **das Service** NOUN |
service ◊ *In dem Hotel ist der Service
ausgezeichnet.* The service in the hotel is
excellent.

die **Serviette** NOUN
serviette

servus EXCLAMATION
1 hello!
2 goodbye!

der **Sessel** NOUN (PL die **Sessel**)
armchair

der **Sessellift** NOUN (PL die **Sessellifte**)
chairlift

setzen VERB
to put ◊ *Sie setzte das Kind auf den
Stuhl.* She put the child on the chair. ◊ *Er
setzte das Glas an den Mund.* He put the
glass to his lips. ◊ *Hast du meinen
Namen auf die Liste gesetzt?* Have you
put my name on the list?
♦ **ein Komma setzen** to put a comma
♦ **jemandem eine Frist setzen** to set
somebody a deadline
♦ **sich setzen (1)** to settle ◊ *Der Kaffeesatz
hat sich gesetzt.* The coffee grounds have
settled.
♦ **sich setzen (2)** to sit down ◊ *Setz dich
doch!* Do sit down! ◊ *Er setzte sich aufs
Sofa.* He sat down on the sofa.
♦ **Sie setzte sich aufs Fahrrad.** She got on
her bike.
♦ **auf etwas setzen** to bet on something
◊ *Er hat hundert Euro auf die Nummer
zwei gesetzt.* He bet a hundred euros on
number two.

die **Seuche** NOUN
epidemic

seufzen VERB
to sigh

der **Sex** NOUN (GEN des **Sex** or **Sexes**)
sex

sexuell ADJECTIVE
sexual

das **Shampoo** NOUN (PL die **Shampoos**)
shampoo

das **Shoppingcenter** NOUN (PL die
Shoppingcenter)
shopping centre

Sibirien NEUT NOUN
Siberia

sich PRONOUN
1 himself ◊ *Er redet mit sich selbst.* He's
talking to himself.
herself
◊ *Sie spricht nicht gern über sich selbst.*
She doesn't like to talk about herself.
◊ *Sie hat sich einen Pullover gekauft.* She
bought herself a jumper.
itself
◊ *Das Boot hat sich wieder aufgerichtet.*
The boat righted itself.
2 themselves ◊ *Meine Eltern haben sich
ein neues Auto gekauft.* My parents have
bought themselves a new car. ◊ *Sie
bleiben gern unter sich.* They keep
themselves to themselves.
3 each other ◊ *Sie lieben sich.* They
love each other.
♦ **Sie wäscht sich.** She's washing herself.
♦ **Sie wäscht sich die Haare.** She's
washing her hair.
♦ **Er schneidet sich die Nägel.** He's cutting
his nails.
♦ **Man fragt sich, ob ...** One wonders
whether ...
♦ **Sie wiederholen sich.** You're repeating
yourself.
♦ **Haben Sie Ihren Ausweis bei sich?** Do
you have your pass on you?
♦ **Er hat nichts bei sich.** He's got nothing
on him.
♦ **Dieses Auto fährt sich gut.** This car
drives well.
♦ **Dieser Artikel verkauft sich gut.** This
article sells well.
♦ **Hier sitzt es sich gut.** This is a good
place to sit.

sicher ADJECTIVE, ADVERB
1 safe ◊ *Das ist ein sehr sicheres Auto.*
It's a very safe car.
2 certain ◊ *Der Termin ist noch nicht
sicher.* The date isn't certain yet.
♦ **Ich bin nicht sicher.** I'm not sure.
3 reliable ◊ *eine sichere Methode* a
reliable method
♦ **vor jemandem sicher sein** to be safe from
somebody ◊ *In einer Großstadt ist man
vor Taschendieben nicht sicher.* You're
never safe from pickpockets in a city.
♦ **vor etwas sicher sein** to be safe from
something ◊ *Bei ihr ist man vor
Überraschungen nie sicher.* With her
you're never safe from surprises.
4 definitely ◊ *Sie kommt sicher nicht
mehr.* She's definitely not coming
anymore.

- ◆ **Er weiß das sicher schon.** I'm sure he knows that already.
- ◆ **sicher nicht** surely not
- ◆ **Aber sicher!** Of course!

die **Sicherheit** NOUN
safety ◇ *Tragen Sie einen Helm zu Ihrer eigenen Sicherheit.* Wear a helmet for your own safety. ◇ *Diese Maßnahmen dienen der Sicherheit der Fluggäste.* These measures are for passenger safety.
- ◆ **Hier sind wir in Sicherheit.** We're safe here.
- ◆ **Ich kann nicht mit Sicherheit sagen, ob ich komme.** I can't say for sure if I'll come.

der **Sicherheitsgurt** NOUN (PL die **Sicherheitsgurte**)
seat belt

sicherlich ADVERB
certainly

sichern VERB
to secure ◇ *Maßnahmen, die Arbeitsplätze sichern* measures to secure jobs
- ◆ **Daten sichern** to back up data ◇ *Die Daten werden stündlich auf Band gesichert.* The data are backed up onto tape every hour.
- ◆ **jemandem etwas sichern** to secure something for somebody ◇ *Ich habe dir einen guten Platz gesichert.* I've secured a good place for you.

die **Sicherung** NOUN
1 securing ◇ *Maßnahmen zur Sicherung der Arbeitsplätze* measures for securing jobs
2 fuse ◇ *Die Sicherung ist durchgebrannt.* The fuse has blown.

die **Sicherungskopie** NOUN
backup copy

die **Sicht** NOUN
view ◇ *Wir hatten eine gute Sicht auf die Berge.* We had a good view of the mountains. ◇ *Du versperrst mir die Sicht.* You're blocking my view.
- ◆ **auf lange Sicht** on a long-term basis
- ◆ **aus jemandes Sicht** as somebody sees it ◇ *Aus meiner Sicht ist das zu schaffen.* As I see it, it can be done.

sichtbar ADJECTIVE
visible

Sie PRONOUN
see also **sie** PRONOUN
you

> **ℹ** *The formal form of address **Sie** (singular and plural) is used when addressing people you don't know or your superiors. Teachers say **Sie** to children over the age of 16.*

◇ *Möchten Sie mitkommen?* Would you like to come? ◇ *Ich kenne Sie.* I know you.

sie PRONOUN
see also **Sie** PRONOUN
1 she ◇ *Sie ist sehr hübsch.* She's very pretty.
2 it ◇ *Schöne Tasche, ist sie neu?* Lovely bag, is it new? ◇ *Kann ich deine Tasche haben, oder brauchst du sie noch?* Can I have your bag or do you need it?
3 her ◇ *Ich kenne sie nicht.* I don't know her.
4 they ◇ *Sie sind alle gekommen.* They all came.
5 them ◇ *Ich habe sie alle eingeladen.* I've invited all of them.

das **Sieb** NOUN (PL die **Siebe**)
1 sieve ◇ *Wir sollten da Mehl durch ein Sieb schütten.* We should rub the flour through a sieve.
2 strainer ◇ *Hast du ein Teesieb?* Have you got a tea strainer?

sieben NUMBER
seven

siebenhundert NUMBER
seven hundred

siebte ADJECTIVE
seventh ◇ *Er kam als Siebter.* He was the seventh to arrive.

siebzehn NUMBER
seventeen

siebzig NUMBER
seventy

die **Siedlung** NOUN
1 settlement ◇ *eine indianische Siedlung* an Indian settlement
2 estate ◇ *Sie wohnt in unserer Siedlung.* She lives on our estate.

der **Sieg** NOUN (PL die **Siege**)
victory

siegen VERB
to win ◇ *Welche Mannschaft hat gesiegt?* Which team won?

der **Sieger** NOUN (PL die **Sieger**)
winner ◇ *Brasilien war 1994 Sieger der Fußballweltmeisterschaft.* Brazil was the winner of the 1994 World Cup.

siehe VERB *see* **sehen**

siezen VERB
to address as "Sie"

> **ℹ** *The formal form of address **Sie** (singular and plural) is used when addressing people you don't know or your superiors. Teachers say **Sie** to children over the age of 16.*

die **Silbe** NOUN
syllable

das **Silber** NOUN
silver

S

das **Silvester** NOUN (PL die **Silvester**)
  New Year's Eve
  simsen VERB (IMPERFECT **simste,** PERFECT **hat gesimst**)
  to text
  singen VERB (IMPERFECT **sang,** PERFECT **hat gesungen**)
  to sing
der **Singular** NOUN (PL die **Singulare**)
  singular
  sinken VERB (IMPERFECT **sank,** PERFECT **ist gesunken**)
  [1] to sink ◊ *Das Schiff ist gesunken.* The ship has sunk.
  [2] to fall ◊ *Die Preise für Häuser sind gesunken.* House prices have fallen.
der **Sinn** NOUN (PL die **Sinne**)
  [1] sense ◊ *die fünf Sinne* the five senses
  [2] meaning ◊ *Ich verstehe den Sinn dieses Satzes nicht.* I don't understand the meaning of this sentence.
  ◆ **Sinn für etwas haben** to have a sense of something ◊ *Sie hat viel Sinn für Humor.* She has a great sense of humour.
  ◆ **jemandem in den Sinn kommen** to come to somebody ◊ *Die Idee kam mir plötzlich in den Sinn.* The idea suddenly came to me.
  ◆ **Es hat keinen Sinn.** There's no point.
  sinnlos ADJECTIVE
  [1] pointless ◊ *Es ist sinnlos, das zu tun.* It's pointless doing that.
  [2] meaningless ◊ *Er hat sinnloses Zeug geredet.* He talked meaningless rubbish.
  sinnvoll ADJECTIVE
  sensible
die **Situation** NOUN
  situation
der **Sitz** NOUN (GEN des **Sitzes,** PL die **Sitze**)
  seat
  sitzen VERB (IMPERFECT **saß,** PERFECT **hat gesessen**)
  to sit ◊ *Er saß auf dem Stuhl.* He was sitting on the chair.
  ◆ **sitzen bleiben (1)** to remain seated
  ◆ **sitzen bleiben (2)** to have to repeat a year

> ❶ In Germany, pupils do not automatically move up **(werden versetzt)** to the next class at the end of the school year. If their performance is not good enough, they have to repeat the year. This is known as **sitzen bleiben**.

◊ *Ich habe Angst, dass ich dieses Jahr sitzen bleibe.* I'm worried that I'll have to repeat this year.
  ◆ **Diese Hose sitzt.** These trousers fit well.
die **Sitzgelegenheit** NOUN
  place to sit down
der **Sitzplatz** NOUN (GEN des **Sitzplatzes,** PL die **Sitzplätze**)
  seat
die **Sitzung** NOUN
  meeting
der **Skandal** NOUN (PL die **Skandale**)
  scandal
  Skandinavien NEUT NOUN
  Scandinavia
  ◆ **aus Skandinavien** from Scandinavia
  ◆ **nach Skandinavien** to Scandinavia
  skandinavisch ADJECTIVE
  Scandinavian
das **Skelett** NOUN (PL die **Skelette**)
  skeleton
der **Ski** NOUN (PL die **Ski** or **Skier**)
  ski
  ◆ **Ski fahren** to ski
der **Skifahrer** NOUN (PL die **Skifahrer**)
  skier
das **Skilaufen** NOUN
  skiing
der **Skilehrer** NOUN (PL die **Skilehrer**)
  ski instructor
der **Skilift** NOUN (PL die **Skilifte** or **Skilifts**)
  ski lift
der **Skistock** NOUN (PL die **Skistöcke**)
  ski pole
der **Skorpion** NOUN (PL die **Skorpione**)
  [1] scorpion
  [2] Scorpio ◊ *Sie ist Skorpion.* She's Scorpio.
der **Slip** NOUN (PL die **Slips**)
  pants ◊ *ein Slip* a pair of pants
die **Slowakei** NOUN
  Slovakia
  ◆ **aus der Slowakei** from Slovakia
  ◆ **in die Slowakei** to Slovakia
der **Smoking** NOUN (PL die **Smokings**)
  dinner jacket
  SMS ABBREVIATION (= *Short Message Service*)
  text message ◊ *Ich schicke dir später eine SMS.* I'll text you later.
  SMV ABBREVIATION (= *Schülermitverwaltung*)
  school council
das **Snowboarding** NOUN
  snowboarding
  SO ADVERB, CONJUNCTION, EXCLAMATION
  [1] so ◊ *so schön* so nice ◊ *zwanzig oder so* twenty or so
  ◆ **so groß wie ...** as big as ...
  ◆ **das hat ihn so geärgert, dass ...** that annoyed him so much that ...
  ◆ **so einer wie ich** somebody like me
  [2] like that ◊ *Mach es nicht so.* Don't do it like that.
  ◆ **... oder so was ...** or something like that
  ◆ **Na so was!** Well, well!
  ◆ **und so weiter** and so on
  ◆ **Ich habe es so bekommen.** I got it for nothing.
  ◆ **so dass** so that

♦ **So?** Really?

♦ **So, das wär's.** So, that's it then.

sobald CONJUNCTION
as soon as

das **Söckchen** NOUN (PL die **Söckchen**)
ankle sock

die **Socke** NOUN
sock

sodass CONJUNCTION
so that

das **Sofa** NOUN (PL die **Sofas**)
sofa

sofort ADVERB
immediately

die **Software** NOUN
software

sogar ADVERB
even

sogleich ADVERB
straight away

die **Sohle** NOUN
sole

der **Sohn** NOUN (PL die **Söhne**)
son

solch PRONOUN
such ◊ *Sie ist solch eine nette Frau.*
She's such a nice lady.

♦ **ein solcher** a ... like that ◊ *Ein solcher Fehler sollte nicht passieren.* A mistake like that shouldn't happen. ◊ *Eine solche Wohnung würde mir auch gefallen.* I'd like a flat like that. ◊ *Ein solches Mountainbike hätte ich auch gern.* I'd also really like to have a mountain bike like that.

♦ **Solche Fehler solltest du nicht mehr machen.** You shouldn't be making mistakes like that any more.

♦ **eine solche Frechheit** such a cheek

der **Soldat** NOUN (GEN des **Soldaten**, PL die **Soldaten**)
soldier

solide ADJECTIVE
1 solid ◊ *Dieser Tisch ist aus solidem Holz.* This table is of solid wood.

♦ **Sie hat solide Grammatikkenntnisse.** Her grammar is sound.

2 respectable ◊ *Wir führen ein solides Leben.* We lead a respectable life. ◊ *Er ist solide geworden.* He's become respectable.

sollen VERB (IMPERFECT **sollte**, PERFECT **hat gesollt** or **sollen**)

*The past participle **sollen** is used when **sollen** is a modal auxiliary.*

1 to be supposed to ◊ *Ich soll um fünf Uhr dort sein.* I'm supposed to be there at five o'clock. ◊ *Was soll das heißen?* What's that supposed to mean? ◊ *Morgen soll es schön werden.* It's supposed to be nice tomorrow.

2 to have to ◊ *Du sollst sofort nach Hause.* You have to go home immediately. ◊ *Sie sagt, du sollst nach Hause kommen.* She says that you have to come home.

♦ **Sag ihm, er soll warten.** Tell him he's to wait.

3 should ◊ *Ich sollte meine Hausaufgaben machen.* I should do my homework. ◊ *Du hättest nicht gehen sollen.* You shouldn't have gone. ◊ *Was soll ich machen?* What should I do? ◊ *sollte das passieren, ...* if that should happen ...

♦ **Sie soll verheiratet sein.** She's said to be married.

♦ **man sollte glauben, dass ...** you would think that ...

♦ **Soll ich dir helfen?** Shall I help you?

♦ **Soll ich?** Shall I?

♦ **Ich hätte eigentlich nicht gesollt.** I really shouldn't have.

♦ **Was soll das?** What's all this?

♦ **Das sollst du nicht.** You shouldn't do that.

♦ **Was soll's?** What the hell!

der **Sommer** NOUN (PL die **Sommer**)
summer ◊ *im Sommer* in summer

die **Sommerferien** PL NOUN
summer holidays

sommerlich ADJECTIVE
1 summery ◊ *ein sommerliches Kleid* a summery dress
2 summer ◊ *sommerliche Kleidung* summer clothes ◊ *sommerliches Wetter* summer weather

der **Sommerschlussverkauf** NOUN (PL die **Sommerschlussverkäufe**)
summer sale

die **Sommersprossen** FEM PL NOUN
freckles

das **Sonderangebot** NOUN (PL die **Sonderangebote**)
special offer

sonderbar ADJECTIVE
strange

die **Sonderfahrt** NOUN
special trip

sondern CONJUNCTION
but

♦ **nicht nur ..., sondern auch** not only ..., but also

der **Sonderpreis** NOUN
special price

der **Sonnabend** NOUN (PL die **Sonnabende**)
Saturday ◊ *am Sonnabend* on Saturday

sonnabends ADVERB
on Saturdays

die **Sonne** NOUN
sun

sich **sonnen** VERB
to sun oneself

S

der **Sonnenbrand** NOUN (PL die **Sonnenbrände**)
sunburn

die **Sonnenbräune** NOUN
suntan

die **Sonnenbrille** NOUN
sunglasses ◊ *Sie trug eine Sonnenbrille.*
She was wearing sunglasses.

die **Sonnencreme** NOUN (PL die **Sonnencremes**)
suntan lotion

die **Sonnenenergie** NOUN
solar power

die **Sonnenmilch** NOUN
suntan lotion

das **Sonnenöl** NOUN (PL die **Sonnenöle**)
suntan oil

der **Sonnenschein** NOUN
sunshine

der **Sonnenschirm** NOUN (PL die **Sonnenschirme**)
sunshade

der **Sonnenstich** NOUN
sunstroke

sonnig ADJECTIVE
sunny

der **Sonntag** NOUN (PL die **Sonntage**)
Sunday ◊ *am Sonntag* on Sunday

sonntags ADVERB
on Sundays

sonst ADVERB, CONJUNCTION
[1] normally ◊ *Was ist mit dir? Du bist doch sonst nicht so still.* What's wrong with you? You're not normally so quiet. ◊ *Die Kinder sind sonst eigentlich artiger.* The children normally behave better.
[2] else ◊ *Wer sonst?* Who else? ◊ *Was sonst?* What else? ◊ *Sonst war niemand da.* Nobody else was there. ◊ *sonst nichts* nothing else
♦ **sonst noch** else ◊ *Was hast du sonst noch bekommen?* What else did you get?
♦ **Haben Sie sonst noch einen Wunsch?** Would you like anything else?
♦ **Sonst noch etwas?** Anything else?
♦ **sonst wo** somewhere else
[3] otherwise ◊ *Ich habe etwas Kopfschmerzen, aber sonst geht's mir gut.* I've got a headache, otherwise I feel fine. ◊ *Geh besser nach Hause, sonst macht sich deine Mutter Sorgen.* You'd better go home otherwise your mother will be worried.

sonstig ADJECTIVE
other

sooft CONJUNCTION
whenever

die **Sorge** NOUN
worry
♦ **Ich mache mir Sorgen.** I'm worried.

sorgen VERB

♦ **für jemanden sorgen** to look after somebody
♦ **für etwas sorgen** to see to something
♦ **sich um jemanden sorgen** to worry about somebody

sorgfältig ADJECTIVE
careful

die **Sorte** NOUN
[1] sort ◊ *Welche Sorte Äpfel ist das?* What sort of apple is that?
[2] brand ◊ *Welche Sorte Waschmittel verwenden Sie?* What brand of detergent do you use?

sortieren VERB (PERFECT **hat sortiert**)
to sort out

die **Soße** NOUN
[1] sauce ◊ *Eis mit Himbeersoße* ice cream with raspberry sauce
[2] gravy ◊ *Schweinebraten mit Soße* roast pork with gravy
[3] dressing ◊ *Salat mit einer Joghurtsoße* salad with a yoghurt dressing

das **Souvenir** NOUN (PL die **Souvenirs**)
souvenir

soviel ADVERB *see* **viel**

soviel CONJUNCTION
as far as
♦ **soviel ich weiß** as far as I know

soweit ADVERB *see* **weit**

soweit CONJUNCTION
as far as ◊ *Soweit ich weiß, kann er nicht kommen.* As far as I know, he can't come.

sowenig ADVERB *see* **wenig**

sowie CONJUNCTION
as soon as ◊ *Ich rufe an, sowie ich Bescheid weiß.* I'll phone as soon as I know.

sowieso ADVERB
anyway

sowohl CONJUNCTION
♦ **sowohl ... als auch** both ... and

sozial ADJECTIVE
social

der **Sozialdemokrat** NOUN (GEN des **Sozialdemokraten**, PL die **Sozialdemokraten**)
social democrat

die **Sozialhilfe** NOUN
social security ◊ *Sozialhilfe bekommen* to be on social security

die **Sozialkunde** NOUN
social studies

die **Sozialversicherung** NOUN
social security

die **Sozialwissenschaften** PL NOUN
social sciences

sozusagen ADVERB
so to speak

die **Spalte** NOUN

[1] crack ◇ *Durch die Trockenheit hatten sich tiefe Spalten gebildet.* Deep cracks had formed as a result of the dry spell.

[2] column ◇ *Der Text ist in zwei Spalten gedruckt.* The text is printed in two columns.

spalten VERB
to split

Spanien NEUT NOUN
Spain
 ◆ **aus Spanien** from Spain
 ◆ **in Spanien** in Spain
 ◆ **nach Spanien** to Spain

der **Spanier** NOUN (PL die **Spanier**)
Spaniard
 ◆ **Er ist Spanier.** He's Spanish.
 ◆ **die Spanier** the Spanish

die **Spanierin** NOUN
Spaniard
 ◆ **Sie ist Spanierin.** She's Spanish.

das **Spanisch** NOUN (GEN des **Spanischen**)
see also **spanisch** ADJECTIVE
Spanish ◇ *Er lernt Spanisch in der Schule.* He's learning Spanish at school.

spanisch ADJECTIVE
Spanish

spannend ADJECTIVE
exciting

die **Spannung** NOUN
[1] suspense ◇ *ein Film voller Spannung* a film full of suspense
 ◆ **Sie erwartet die Prüfungsergebnisse mit Spannung.** She can't wait for the exam results.
[2] tension ◇ *Das führte zu Spannungen zwischen den beiden Ländern.* That caused tension between the two countries.

das **Sparbuch** NOUN (PL die **Sparbücher**)
savings book

die **Sparbüchse** NOUN
money box

sparen VERB
to save ◇ *Wir müssen sparen.* We have to save. ◇ *Sie hat zweihundert Euro gespart.* She's saved two hundred euros. ◇ *Energie sparen* to save energy ◇ *Er spart für ein Mountainbike.* He's saving for a mountain bike.
 ◆ **sich etwas sparen (1)** not to bother with something ◇ *Den Film kannst du dir sparen.* Don't bother with that film.
 ◆ **sich etwas sparen (2)** to keep something to oneself ◇ *Spar dir deine Bemerkungen.* You can keep your remarks to yourself.
 ◆ **mit etwas sparen** to be sparing with something
 ◆ **an etwas sparen** to economize on something ◇ *Sie spart in letzter Zeit am Essen.* She's been economizing on food recently.

*Be careful! **sparen** does not mean **to spare.***

der **Spargel** NOUN
asparagus

die **Sparkasse** NOUN
savings bank

sparsam ADJECTIVE
[1] economical ◇ *ein sparsames Auto* an economical car ◇ *Wir sollten mit den Rohstoffen sparsam umgehen.* We should be economical with raw materials.
[2] thrifty ◇ *Sie ist sehr sparsam.* She's very thrifty.

das **Sparschwein** NOUN (PL die **Sparschweine**)
piggy bank

der **Spaß** NOUN (GEN des **Spaßes,** PL die **Späße**)
fun ◇ *Wir hatten in den Ferien viel Spaß.* We had great fun in the holidays.
 ◆ **Sie versteht keinen Spaß.** She has no sense of humour.
 ◆ **Skifahren macht mir Spaß.** I like skiing.
 ◆ **zum Spaß** for fun ◇ *Ich mache den Kurs nur zum Spaß.* I'm only doing the course for fun.
 ◆ **Ich habe das doch nur zum Spaß gesagt.** I only said it as a joke.
 ◆ **Viel Spaß!** Have fun!

spät ADJECTIVE, ADVERB
late ◇ *Es wird spät.* It's getting late.
 ◆ **Wir kamen zu spät.** We were late.
 ◆ **Wie spät ist es?** What's the time?

später ADJECTIVE, ADVERB
later
 ◆ **Bis später!** See you later!

spätestens ADVERB
at the latest

der **Spatz** NOUN (GEN des **Spatzen,** PL die **Spatzen**)
sparrow

spazieren VERB
 ◆ **spazieren fahren** to go for a drive
 ◆ **spazieren gehen** to go for a walk

der **Spaziergang** NOUN (PL die **Spaziergänge**)
walk ◇ *einen Spaziergang machen* to go for a walk

der **Speck** NOUN
bacon

das **Speerwerfen** NOUN
throwing the javelin

der **Speicher** NOUN (PL die **Speicher**)
[1] loft ◇ *Die alten Möbel sind auf dem Speicher.* The old furniture's in the loft.
[2] storehouse ◇ *Die alten Speicher am Hafen wurden zu Wohnungen umgebaut.* The old storehouses at the harbour were converted into flats.
[3] memory ◇ *Ich will den Speicher meines Computers erweitern.* I want to expand the memory of my computer.

speichern VERB (PERFECT **hat gespeichert**)
[1] to store ◇ *Energie speichern* to store energy

S

2 to save ◊ *eine Datei speichern* to save a file

das **Speiseeis** NOUN
ice cream

die **Speisekarte** NOUN
menu ◊ *Könnte ich bitte die Speisekarte haben?* Could I have the menu please?

der **Speisesaal** NOUN
dining room

der **Speisewagen** NOUN (PL die **Speisewagen**)
dining car

die **Spende** NOUN
donation

spenden VERB
to donate ◊ *Ich habe zwanzig Euro gespendet.* I've donated twenty euros.
♦ **Bitte spenden Sie für die Flüchtlinge.** Please give a donation for the refugees.
♦ **Blut spenden** to give blood
Be careful! **spenden** does not mean **to spend**.

der **Spender** NOUN (PL die **Spender**)
donor

spendieren VERB (PERFECT **hat spendiert**)
♦ **jemandem etwas spendieren** to stand somebody something ◊ *Mutti hat uns ein Eis spendiert.* Mum stood us an ice cream.

die **Sperre** NOUN
1 barrier ◊ *Vor dem Eingang befand sich eine Sperre.* There was a barrier in front of the entrance.
2 ban ◊ *Er erhielt eine Sperre von drei Monaten.* He got a three-month ban.

sperren VERB (PERFECT **hat gesperrt**)
1 to close ◊ *Die Polizei hat die Straße gesperrt.* The police closed the road.
2 to obstruct ◊ *Es ist verboten, gegnerische Spieler zu sperren.* Obstructing the opposition is not allowed.
3 to lock ◊ *Diese Dateien sind gesperrt.* These files are locked.

die **Spezialität** NOUN
speciality

der **Spiegel** NOUN (PL die **Spiegel**)
mirror ◊ *Er sah in den Spiegel.* He looked in the mirror.

das **Spiegelbild** NOUN (PL die **Spiegelbilder**)
reflection

das **Spiegelei** NOUN (PL die **Spiegeleier**)
fried egg

das **Spiel** NOUN (PL die **Spiele**)
1 game ◊ *Sollen wir ein Spiel spielen?* Shall we play a game? ◊ *Hast du das Spiel England gegen Deutschland gesehen?* Did you see the England-Germany game? ◊ *Sie hat das erste Spiel des zweiten Satzes verloren.* She lost the first game of the second set.
2 pack ◊ *Hast du ein Spiel Karten?* Do you have a pack of cards?
♦ **ein Theaterspiel** a play

spielen VERB

to play ◊ *Die Kinder spielen im Garten.* The children are playing in the garden.
◊ *Wollen wir Tennis spielen?* Shall we play tennis? ◊ *Wer spielt den Hamlet?* Who's playing Hamlet? ◊ *Wir haben um Geld gespielt.* We played for money.

spielend ADVERB
easily

der **Spieler** NOUN (PL die **Spieler**)
1 player ◊ *Wir brauchen noch einen dritten Spieler.* We still need a third player.
2 gambler ◊ *Er ist ein leidenschaftlicher Spieler.* He's a passionate gambler.

das **Spielfeld** NOUN (PL die **Spielfelder**)
pitch

der **Spielfilm** NOUN (PL die **Spielfilme**)
feature film

der **Spielplatz** NOUN (GEN des **Spielplatzes**, PL die **Spielplätze**)
playground

die **Spielregel** NOUN
rule ◊ *Ich erkläre euch die Spielregeln.* I'll explain the rules of the game to you.

die **Spielsachen** FEM PL NOUN
toys

der **Spielverderber** NOUN (PL die **Spielverderber**)
spoilsport

das **Spielzeug** NOUN (PL die **Spielzeuge**)
toy

das **Spielzimmer** NOUN (PL die **Spielzimmer**)
playroom

der **Spinat** NOUN
spinach

die **Spinne** NOUN
spider

spinnen VERB (IMPERFECT **spann**, PERFECT **hat gesponnen**)
1 to spin ◊ *Wolle spinnen* to spin wool
2 to be crazy ◊ *Du spinnst wohl!* You're crazy!

die **Spionage** NOUN
espionage

spionieren VERB (PERFECT **hat spioniert**)
to spy

spitz ADJECTIVE
pointed
♦ **ein spitzer Winkel** an acute angle
♦ **eine spitze Zunge** a sharp tongue
♦ **eine spitze Bemerkung** a caustic remark

spitze ADJECTIVE
great ◊ *Das war spitze!* That was great!

die **Spitze** NOUN
1 point ◊ *Die Spitze des Bleistifts ist abgebrochen.* The point of the pencil has broken off.
2 peak ◊ *Die Spitzen der Berge waren schneebedeckt.* The peaks of the mountains were covered with snow.
3 top ◊ *Welche Mannschaft liegt an der Spitze?* Which team is top?

4 lace ◊ *An ihrem Kleid war ein Kragen aus Spitze.* Her dress had a lace collar.

spitzen VERB
to sharpen

der **Spitzer** NOUN (PL die **Spitzer**)
pencil sharpener

der **Spitzname** NOUN (GEN des **Spitznamens**, PL die **Spitznamen**)
nickname

der **Splitter** NOUN (PL die **Splitter**)
splinter

sponsern VERB
to sponsor

der **Sport** NOUN
sport

die **Sportart** NOUN
sport ◊ *verschiedene Sportarten* various sports

der **Sportler** NOUN (PL die **Sportler**)
sportsman

die **Sportlerin** NOUN
sportswoman

sportlich ADJECTIVE
sporty ◊ *Bettina ist sehr sportlich.* Bettina is very sporty.

der **Sportplatz** NOUN (GEN des **Sportplatzes**, PL die **Sportplätze**)
sports field

der **Sportschuh** NOUN (PL die **Sportschuhe**)
trainer

der **Sportverein** NOUN (PL die **Sportvereine**)
sports club

das **Sportzentrum** NOUN (PL die **Sportzentren**)
sports centre

spotten VERB
♦**spotten über** to ridicule ◊ *Ich kann es nicht leiden, wenn man über mich spottet.* I can't stand being ridiculed.

sprach VERB *see* **sprechen**

die **Sprache** NOUN
language

der **Sprachführer** NOUN (PL die **Sprachführer**)
phrase book

das **Sprachlabor** NOUN (PL die **Sprachlabors** or **Sprachlabore**)
language laboratory

sprachlich ADJECTIVE
linguistic

sprachlos ADJECTIVE
speechless

sprang VERB *see* **springen**

sprechen VERB (PRESENT **spricht**, IMPERFECT **sprach**, PERFECT **hat gesprochen**)
1 to talk ◊ *Seid bitte ruhig, wenn ich spreche.* Please be quiet, I'm talking. ◊ *Du sprichst so leise.* You talk so quietly. ◊ *Wir haben von dir gesprochen.* We were talking about you.
2 to say ◊ *Sie hat kein Wort gesprochen.* She didn't say a word.

3 to speak ◊ *Ich spreche Italienisch ziemlich schlecht.* I speak Italian pretty badly.
♦**jemanden sprechen** to speak to somebody ◊ *Der Direktor will dich sprechen.* The headmaster wants to speak to you.
♦**mit jemandem über etwas sprechen** to speak to somebody about something
♦**Das spricht für ihn.** That's a point in his favour.

die **Sprechstunde** NOUN
surgery (*doctor's*)

spricht VERB *see* **sprechen**

das **Sprichwort** NOUN (PL die **Sprichwörter**)
proverb

springen VERB (IMPERFECT **sprang**, PERFECT **ist gesprungen**)
1 to jump ◊ *Er sprang über den Zaun.* He jumped over the fence.
2 to crack ◊ *Das Glas ist gesprungen.* The glass has cracked.

die **Spritze** NOUN
1 syringe ◊ *Die Spritze muss steril sein.* The syringe has to be sterile.
2 injection ◊ *Der Arzt hat mir eine Spritze gegeben.* The doctor gave me an injection.
3 nozzle ◊ *Die Spritze am Gartenschlauch ist nicht dicht.* The nozzle on the garden hose leaks.

spritzen VERB (PERFECT **hat/ist gespritzt**)
*Use **haben** to form the perfect tense. Use **sein** to form the perfect tense for to spurt out.*
1 to spray ◊ *Er hat sein Fahrrad grün gespritzt.* He's sprayed his bike green.
♦**den Garten spritzen** to water the garden
♦**jemanden nass spritzen** to splash somebody
♦**Als er durch die Pfütze fuhr, hat es gespritzt.** When he drove through the puddle, the water splashed up.
2 to spurt out ◊ *Das Wasser ist nach allen Seiten gespritzt.* The water spurted out all over the place. ◊ *Das Blut spritzte aus der Wunde.* The blood spurted out of the wound.

der **Sprudel** NOUN (PL die **Sprudel**)
mineral water
♦**süßer Sprudel** lemonade

sprühen VERB (PERFECT **hat/ist gesprüht**)
*For the perfect tense use **haben** when the verb has an object and **sein** when there is no object. Use **haben** to form the perfect tense for to sparkle.*
1 to spray ◊ *Sie hat Haarspray auf ihre Haare gesprüht.* She sprayed her hair with hairspray.
2 to fly ◊ *In alle Richtungen sind Funken gesprüht.* Sparks flew in all directions.

S

☞

3 to sparkle ◊ *Er hat gestern Abend vor Witz gesprüht.* He was sparkling with humour yesterday evening.

der **Sprung** NOUN (PL die **Sprünge**)
1 jump ◊ *Das war ein weiter Sprung.* That was a long jump.
2 crack ◊ *Die Tasse hat einen Sprung.* There is a crack in the cup.

das **Sprungbrett** NOUN (PL die **Sprungbretter**)
springboard

die **Spucke** NOUN
spit

spucken VERB
to spit

das **Spülbecken** NOUN (PL die **Spülbecken**)
kitchen sink

die **Spüle** NOUN
kitchen sink

spülen VERB
1 to rinse ◊ *Wollsachen muss man gut spülen.* Woollens have to be rinsed well.
2 to wash up ◊ *Wenn du spülst, dann trockne ich ab.* If you wash up I'll dry.

die **Spülmaschine** NOUN
dishwasher

das **Spülmittel** NOUN (PL die **Spülmittel**)
washing-up liquid

die **Spur** NOUN
1 track ◊ *Wir sahen Spuren im Sand.* We saw tracks in the sand. ◊ *Das Band hat eine Spur für Bilder und eine andere für den Ton.* The tape has one track for pictures and another for sound.
2 lane ◊ *Der Fahrer vor mir hat plötzlich die Spur gewechselt.* The driver in front of me suddenly changed lane.
3 trace ◊ *Auf ihrem Gesicht sah man die Spuren der Anstrengung.* You could see the traces of strain on her face.
4 trail ◊ *Die Polizei verfolgte seine Spur.* The police followed his trail.
♦ *Das Essen war eine Spur zu scharf.* The meal was a touch too spicy.

spüren VERB
to feel

der **Staat** NOUN (PL die **Staaten**)
state
♦ **die Vereinigten Staaten von Amerika** the United States of America

staatlich ADJECTIVE
1 state ◊ *staatliche Fördermittel* state subsidies ◊ *ein staatliche Schule* a state school
2 state-run ◊ *eine staatliche Einrichtung* a state-run organization

die **Staatsangehörigkeit** NOUN
nationality

stabil ADJECTIVE
1 stable ◊ *Die Lage ist stabil.* The situation is stable.
2 sturdy ◊ *stabile Möbel* sturdy furniture

der **Stachel** NOUN (PL die **Stacheln**)
1 spike ◊ *Ich habe mir die Hose an einem Stachel aufgerissen.* I've torn my trousers on a spike.
2 spine ◊ *Ein Igel hat Stacheln.* A hedgehog has spines. ◊ *Dieser Kaktus hat lange Stacheln.* This cactus has long spines.
3 sting ◊ *Ich habe versucht, den Stachel der Biene herauszuziehen.* I tried to take the bee sting out.

die **Stachelbeere** NOUN
gooseberry

der **Stacheldraht** NOUN (PL die **Stacheldrähte**)
barbed wire

das **Stadion** NOUN (PL die **Stadien**)
stadium

die **Stadt** NOUN (PL die **Städte**)
town

der **Stadtbummel** NOUN (PL die **Stadtbummel**)
stroll through the town

städtisch ADJECTIVE
municipal

der **Stadtkreis** NOUN (PL die **Stadtkreise**)
town borough

die **Stadtmitte** NOUN
town centre

der **Stadtplan** NOUN (PL die **Stadtpläne**)
street map

der **Stadtrand** NOUN (PL die **Stadtränder**)
outskirts

die **Stadtrundfahrt** NOUN
tour of the city

der **Stadtteil** NOUN (PL die **Stadtteile**)
part of town

das **Stadtwappen** NOUN (PL die **Stadtwappen**)
municipal coat of arms

das **Stadtzentrum** NOUN (PL die **Stadtzentren**)
city centre

der **Staffellauf** NOUN (PL die **Staffelläufe**)
relay race

der **Stahl** NOUN
steel

stahl VERB see **stehlen**

der **Stall** NOUN (PL die **Ställe**)
stable ◊ *Die Pferde sind im Stall.* The horses are in the stable.
♦ **ein Hühnerstall** a henhouse

der **Stamm** NOUN (PL die **Stämme**)
1 trunk ◊ *Der Baum hat einen dicken Stamm.* The tree has a thick trunk.
2 tribe ◊ *Er gehört zum Stamm der Bantus.* He belongs to the Bantu tribe.
3 stem ◊ *Die Endung wird an den Stamm des Verbs angehängt.* The ending's added to the stem of the verb.

stammen VERB
♦ **stammen aus** to come from

der **Stammgast** NOUN (PL die **Stammgäste**)
regular customer

der **Stammtisch** NOUN (PL die **Stammtische**)
table for the regulars

i In Germany it is usual for a group of friends to reserve a table in the same pub or restaurant for the same time each week.

der **Stand** NOUN (PL die **Stände**)
    ① state ◊ *Was ist der Stand der Dinge?* What's the state of affairs?
    ② score ◊ *Sie sind beim Stand von eins zu eins in die Pause.* The score was one all at half-time.
    ③ stand ◊ *An welchen Stand hast du den Luftballon gekauft?* Which stand did you buy the balloon at?
    ④ level ◊ *Prüf mal den Ölstand.* Check the oil level.
    ◆ **zu Stande** see **zustande**
stand VERB see **stehen**
ständig ADJECTIVE
    constant ◊ *Musst du ständig stören?* Do you constantly have to interrupt?
der **Standort** NOUN (PL die **Standorte**)
    location
der **Stapel** NOUN (PL die **Stapel**)
    pile
starb VERB see **sterben**
stark ADJECTIVE
    ① strong ◊ *Mein Bruder ist stärker als du.* My brother's stronger than you.
    ② heavy ◊ *starke Regenfälle* heavy rain
    ◆ **starke Kopfschmerzen** a splitting headache
    ③ great ◊ *Das war stark!* That was great!
der **Start** NOUN (PL die **Starts**)
    ① start ◊ *Es waren über hundert Läufer am Start.* There were over a hundred runners at the start.
    ② takeoff ◊ *Die Maschine war bereit zum Start.* The machine was ready for takeoff.
starten VERB
    ① to start ◊ *Wann startet das Rennen?* When does the race start?
    ② to take off ◊ *Das Flugzeug startet gleich.* The plane is about to take off.
die **Station** NOUN
    ① station ◊ *An welcher Station müssen wir aussteigen?* Which station do we have to get off at?
    ② hospital ward ◊ *Der Patient wurde auf eine andere Station verlegt.* The patient's been moved to another ward.
statt CONJUNCTION, PREPOSITION
    *The preposition **statt** takes the genitive or the dative.*
    instead of ◊ *Statt nach Hause zu gehen, sind wir noch in die Disco.* Instead of going home, we went to the disco. ◊ *Sie kam statt ihres Bruders.* She came instead of her brother.
stattfinden VERB (IMPERFECT **fand statt**, PERFECT **hat stattgefunden**)
    to take place

der **Stau** NOUN (PL die **Staus**)
    traffic jam ◊ *Wir sind im Stau stecken geblieben.* We were stuck in a traffic jam.
der **Staub** NOUN
    dust
    ◆ **Staub wischen** to dust
staubig ADJECTIVE
    dusty
staubsaugen VERB (PERFECT **hat staubgesaugt**)
    to hoover
der **Staubsauger** NOUN (PL die **Staubsauger**)
    vacuum cleaner
staunen VERB
    to be astonished
die **Stauung** NOUN
    congestion
Std. ABBREVIATION (= *Stunde*)
    hr.
das **Steak** NOUN (PL die **Steaks**)
    steak
stechen VERB (PRESENT **sticht**, IMPERFECT **stach**, PERFECT **hat gestochen**)
    ① to prick ◊ *Ich habe mich mit der Nadel gestochen.* I've pricked myself with the needle.
    ② to sting ◊ *Mich hat eine Biene gestochen.* A bee stung me.
    ③ to bite ◊ *Reibe dich ein, damit du nicht gestochen wirst.* Rub something on so that you won't be bitten.
    ④ to take ◊ *Sie hat meine Dame mit dem König gestochen.* She took my queen with her king.
die **Steckdose** NOUN
    socket
stecken VERB
    ① to put ◊ *Sie steckte ihren Geldbeutel in die Tasche.* She put her purse in her bag.
    ② to insert ◊ *Stecken Sie die Münze in den Schlitz.* Insert the coin into the slot.
    ③ to stick ◊ *Steck deinen Finger nicht in das Loch!* Don't stick your finger in the hole.
    ④ to pin ◊ *Ich steckte das Abzeichen an meine Jacke.* I pinned the badge onto my jacket.
    ⑤ to be stuck ◊ *Wir stecken im Stau.* We are stuck in a traffic jam.
    ◆ **Wo steckt sie nur?** Where on earth is she?
der **Stecker** NOUN (PL die **Stecker**)
    plug
die **Stecknadel** NOUN
    pin
stehen VERB (IMPERFECT **stand**, PERFECT **hat gestanden**)
    ① to stand ◊ *Es war so voll, dass wir stehen mussten.* It was so full that we had to stand.

S

2 to be ◊ *Vor unserem Haus steht eine Kastanie.* There's a chestnut tree in front of our house.

3 to say ◊ *In der Zeitung steht, dass das Wetter besser wird.* It says in the newspaper that the weather will improve.

♦ **zum Stehen kommen** to come to a halt ◊ *Der Verkehr kam zum Stehen.* The traffic came to a halt.

♦ **Es steht schlecht um ihn.** Things are bad for him.

♦ **jemandem stehen** to suit somebody ◊ *Blau steht dir gut.* Blue suits you.

♦ **Wie steht's? (1)** How are things?

♦ **Wie steht's? (2)** What's the score?

♦ **stehen bleiben** to stop ◊ *Meine Uhr ist stehen geblieben.* My watch has stopped.

die **Stehlampe** NOUN
standard lamp

stehlen VERB (PRESENT **stiehlt**, IMPERFECT **stahl**, PERFECT **hat gestohlen**)
to steal

steif ADJECTIVE
stiff

steigen VERB (IMPERFECT **stieg**, PERFECT **ist gestiegen**)

1 to rise ◊ *Der Ballon stieg zum Himmel.* The balloon rose into the sky.

2 to climb ◊ *Sie ist auf die Leiter gestiegen.* She climbed up the ladder.

♦ **in etwas steigen** to get into something ◊ *Er stieg ins Auto.* He got into the car.

♦ **Sie stieg in den Zug.** She got on the train.

♦ **auf etwas steigen** to get on something ◊ *Sie stieg aufs Fahrrad.* She got on her bike.

die **Steigung** NOUN
incline

steil ADJECTIVE
steep

der **Stein** NOUN (PL die **Steine**)
stone

der **Steinbock** NOUN (PL die **Steinböcke**)
Capricorn ◊ *Er ist Steinbock.* He's Capricorn.

steinig ADJECTIVE
stony

die **Stelle** NOUN

1 place ◊ *Ich habe mir die Stelle im Buch angestrichen.* I've marked the place in the book.

♦ **an dieser Stelle** here

2 job ◊ *Ich suche eine neue Stelle.* I'm looking for a new job.

3 office ◊ *Bei welcher Stelle kann man einen Pass bekommen?* In which office can you get a passport?

♦ **An deiner Stelle würde ich das nicht tun.** I wouldn't do it if I were you.

stellen VERB

1 to put ◊ *Ich habe die Vase auf den Tisch gestellt.* I put the vase on the table.

2 to set ◊ *Stell deine Uhr nach meiner.* Set your watch by mine.

3 to supply ◊ *Die Lehrbücher werden gestellt.* The course books will be supplied.

♦ **sich irgendwohin stellen** to stand somewhere ◊ *Stellt euch bitte an die Wand.* Please stand against the wall.

♦ **sich stellen** to give oneself up ◊ *Der Dieb hat sich gestellt.* The thief gave himself up.

♦ **sich dumm stellen** to pretend to be stupid

die **Stellenanzeige** NOUN
job advertisement

die **Stellung** NOUN
position ◊ *In welcher Stellung schläfst du?* Which position do you sleep in? ◊ *Er hat eine gute Stellung.* He has a good position.

♦ **zu etwas Stellung nehmen** to comment on something

der **Stellvertreter** NOUN (PL die **Stellvertreter**)
deputy

der **Stempel** NOUN (PL die **Stempel**)
stamp

stempeln VERB
to stamp

♦ **jemanden zum Sündenbock stempeln** to make somebody a scapegoat

die **Steppdecke** NOUN
quilt

die **Sterbehilfe** NOUN
euthanasia

sterben VERB (PRESENT **stirbt**, IMPERFECT **starb**, PERFECT **ist gestorben**)
to die

die **Stereoanlage** NOUN
stereo

der **Stern** NOUN (PL die **Sterne**)
star ◊ *die Sterne am Himmel* the stars in the sky

das **Sternzeichen** NOUN (PL die **Sternzeichen**)
star sign ◊ *Was ist dein Sternzeichen?* What star sign are you?

das **Steuer** NOUN (PL die **Steuer**)

see also **die Steuer** NOUN

wheel ◊ *Wer saß am Steuer?* Who was at the wheel?

die **Steuer** NOUN

see also **das Steuer** NOUN

tax ◊ *Wir müssen viel Steuern bezahlen.* We have to pay a lot of tax.

das **Steuerrad** NOUN (PL die **Steuerräder**)
steering wheel

der **Steward** NOUN (PL die **Stewards**)
steward

die **Stewardess** NOUN (PL die **Stewardessen**)
stewardess

der **Stich** NOUN (PL die **Stiche**)

☐1 bite ◊ *Das Mittel schützt vor Stichen.* This gives protection from bites. ◊ *ein Mückenstich* a midge bite

♦ **ein Bienenstich** a bee sting

☐2 stab ◊ *Er tötete sie mit zwölf Stichen.* He killed her by stabbing her twelve times.

☐3 stitch ◊ *Sie hat den Aufhänger mit ein paar Stichen angenäht.* She sewed on the loop with a couple of stitches. ◊ *Die Wunde wurde mit drei Stichen genäht.* Three stitches were put in the wound.

☐4 trick ◊ *Ich habe beim letzten Spiel keinen Stich gemacht.* I didn't win any tricks in the last game.

☐5 engraving ◊ *ein Kupferstich* a copper engraving

♦ **jemanden im Stich lassen** to leave somebody in the lurch

sticken VERB
to embroider

der **Stickstoff** NOUN
nitrogen

der **Stiefel** NOUN (PL die **Stiefel**)
boot

das **Stiefkind** NOUN (PL die **Stiefkinder**)
stepchild

die **Stiefmutter** NOUN (PL die **Stiefmütter**)
stepmother

der **Stiefvater** NOUN (PL die **Stiefväter**)
stepfather

stiehlt VERB see **stehlen**

der **Stiel** NOUN (PL die **Stiele**)
☐1 handle ◊ *der Stiel des Besens* the broom handle
☐2 stem ◊ *Er hat den Stiel der Tulpe abgeknickt.* He snapped the stem off the tulip.

der **Stier** NOUN (PL die **Stiere**)
☐1 bull ◊ *Der Stier wurde getötet.* The bull was killed.
☐2 Taurus ◊ *Brigitte ist Stier.* Brigitte's Taurus.

der **Stift** NOUN (PL die **Stifte**)
☐1 peg ◊ *Das Brett wird mit Stiften an der Wand befestigt.* The board is fixed to the wall with pegs.
☐2 crayon ◊ *Sebastian hat lauter bunte Stifte bekommen.* Sebastian got lots of coloured crayons.
☐3 pencil ◊ *Schreib lieber mit Kuli als mit einem Stift.* I'd rather you wrote with a Biro than a pencil.

stiften VERB
♦ **Sie hat eine Runde Eis gestiftet.** She bought us all an ice cream.
♦ **Unruhe stiften** to cause trouble

der **Stil** NOUN (PL die **Stile**)
style

still ADJECTIVE
quiet ◊ *Seid mal still.* Be quiet.
♦ **Sie stand ganz still.** She stood quite still.

die **Stille** NOUN

quietness
♦ **in aller Stille** quietly

stillhalten VERB (PRESENT **hält still,** IMPERFECT **hielt still,** PERFECT **hat stillgehalten**)
to keep still

stillschweigend ADVERB
tacitly

die **Stimme** NOUN
☐1 voice ◊ *Er hat eine laute Stimme.* He has a loud voice.
☐2 vote ◊ *Er bekam nur zwanzig Stimmen.* He only got twenty votes.
♦ **Wem hast du deine Stimme gegeben?** Who did you vote for?

stimmen VERB
to be right ◊ *Die Übersetzung stimmt nicht.* The translation isn't right. ◊ *Das stimmt nicht!* That's not right!
♦ **ein Instrument stimmen** to tune an instrument
♦ **stimmen für** to vote for
♦ **stimmen gegen** to vote against
♦ **Stimmt so!** Keep the change.

die **Stimmung** NOUN
mood

stinken VERB (IMPERFECT **stank,** PERFECT **hat gestunken**)
to stink

das **Stipendium** NOUN (PL die **Stipendien**)
grant

stirbt VERB see **sterben**

die **Stirn** NOUN
forehead

der **Stock (1)** NOUN (PL die **Stöcke**)
stick ◊ *Er hat ihn mit einem Stock geschlagen.* He hit him with a stick.

der **Stock (2)** NOUN (PL die **Stock** or **Stockwerke**)
floor ◊ *Wir wohnen im dritten Stock.* We live on the third floor.

der **Stoff** NOUN (PL die **Stoffe**)
☐1 fabric ◊ *Das ist ein hübscher Stoff.* That's a pretty fabric.
☐2 material ◊ *Ich sammle Stoff für mein Referat.* I'm collecting material for my assignment.

stöhnen VERB
to groan

stolpern VERB (PERFECT **ist gestolpert**)
☐1 to stumble ◊ *Er ist gestolpert und gefallen.* He stumbled and fell.
☐2 to trip ◊ *Er ist über einen Stein gestolpert.* He tripped over a stone.

stolz ADJECTIVE
proud ◊ *Ich bin stolz auf dich.* I'm proud of you.

der **Stöpsel** NOUN (PL die **Stöpsel**)
plug

stören VERB
to disturb ◊ *Störe ich?* Am I disturbing you? ◊ *Ich will nicht länger stören.* I won't disturb you any longer.

S

♦ **Stört es dich, wenn ich rauche?** Do you mind if I smoke?

♦ **Das stört meine Konzentration.** That's stopping me from concentrating.

♦ **Die Leitung war gestört.** It was a bad line.

♦ **sich an etwas stören** to worry about something ◊ *Stör dich nicht an der Schrift, der Inhalt ist wichtig.* Don't worry about the writing, it's the content that counts.

störend ADJECTIVE
disturbing

die **Störung** NOUN
1 interruption ◊ *Diese dauernden Störungen regen mich auf.* These constant interruptions are getting on my nerves.
2 interference ◊ *Es war eine Störung beim Bild.* There was interference to the picture.

stoßen VERB (PRESENT **stößt**, IMPERFECT **stieß**, PERFECT **hat gestoßen**)

♦ **den Kopf an etwas stoßen** to bump one's head on something ◊ *Ich habe mir an der niedrigen Decke den Kopf gestoßen.* I bumped my head on the low ceiling.

♦ **sich stoßen** to bump oneself ◊ *Sie hat einen blauen Fleck, wo sie sich gestoßen hat.* She has a bruise where she bumped herself.

♦ **sich an etwas stoßen** to take exception to something ◊ *Sie hat sich an seinem schlechten Benehmen gestoßen.* She took exception to his bad behaviour.

♦ **an etwas stoßen** to bump into something ◊ *Pass auf, dass du nicht an die Statue stößt.* Watch out that you don't bump into the statue.

♦ **auf etwas stoßen** to come across ◊ *Heute bin ich auf dem Flohmarkt auf ein tolles Buch gestoßen.* I came across a great book at the flea market today.

stottern VERB
to stutter

Str. ABBREVIATION (= *Straße*)
St

die **Strafarbeit** NOUN
lines ◊ *Ich habe eine Strafarbeit bekommen.* I got lines.

die **Strafe** NOUN
1 punishment ◊ *Zur Strafe müsst ihr länger bleiben.* You'll be kept in after school as a punishment.

♦ **eine Gefängnisstrafe** a prison sentence
2 fine ◊ *Er musste eine Strafe von fünfzig Euro bezahlen.* He had to pay a fifty euro fine.

der **Strahl** NOUN (PL die **Strahlen**)
1 ray ◊ *radioaktive Strahlen* radioactive rays ◊ *ein Sonnenstrahl* a ray of sunlight

♦ **ein Lichtstrahl** a beam of light

2 jet ◊ *ein Wasserstrahl* a jet of water

strahlen VERB
1 to shine ◊ *Die Sterne strahlten hell.* The stars shone brightly.
2 to beam ◊ *Sie strahlte, als sie das hörte.* She beamed when she heard that.

die **Strahlung** NOUN
radiation

der **Strand** NOUN (PL die **Strände**)
1 beach ◊ *Wir haben den ganzen Tag am Strand gelegen.* We lay on the beach all day.
2 shore ◊ *Das wurde an den Strand gespült.* That was washed up on the shore.

die **Strapaze** NOUN
strain

strapazieren VERB (PERFECT **hat strapaziert**)
1 to be hard on ◊ *Du hast heute deinen Computer ganz schön strapaziert.* You've been really hard on your computer today.
2 to wear out ◊ *Die Wanderung hat uns ziemlich strapaziert.* The walk has really worn us out.

die **Straße** NOUN
1 street ◊ *In welcher Straße wohnt Eva?* Which street does Eva live in?
2 road ◊ *Wir sind die Straße entlang der Küste gefahren.* We drove along the coast road.

die **Straßenbahn** NOUN
tram

der **Strauß** NOUN (GEN des **Straußes**, PL die **Sträuße**)
bunch of flowers ◊ *Wir haben unserer Gastgeberin einen Strauß mitgebracht.* We brought our hostess a bunch of flowers.

der **Streber** NOUN (PL die **Streber**)
swot

die **Strecke** NOUN
1 distance ◊ *Wir haben diese Strecke an einem Tag zurückgelegt.* We covered this distance in one day. ◊ *Bis zu ihm ist es noch eine ziemliche Strecke.* It's still quite a distance to his place.
2 line ◊ *Auf der Strecke zwischen Stuttgart und Ulm gab es ein Zugunglück.* There's been a train accident on the Stuttgart to Ulm line.

der **Streich** NOUN (PL die **Streiche**)
trick ◊ *Sie haben dem Lehrer einen Streich gespielt.* They played a trick on the teacher.

streicheln VERB
to stroke

streichen VERB (IMPERFECT **strich**, PERFECT **hat gestrichen**)
1 to stroke ◊ *Sie strich über seine Haare.* She stroked his hair.
2 to spread ◊ *Sie strich Honig aufs Brot.* She spread honey on the bread.

♦ **Butter aufs Brot streichen** to butter bread

3 to paint ◊ *Ich muss dringend mein Zimmer streichen.* I really must paint my room.

4 to delete ◊ *Den zweiten Satz kannst du streichen.* You can delete the second sentence.

5 to cancel ◊ *Der Direktor hat den Schulausflug gestrichen.* The headmaster has cancelled the school trip.

das **Streichholz** NOUN (GEN des **Streichholzes**, PL die **Streichhölzer**)
match

der **Streifen** NOUN (PL die **Streifen**)
strip

der **Streifenwagen** NOUN (PL die **Streifenwagen**)
patrol car

der **Streik** NOUN (PL die **Streiks**)
strike

streiken VERB
to go on strike
♦ **Sie streiken.** They're on strike.

der **Streit** NOUN (PL die **Streite**)
argument

sich **streiten** VERB (IMPERFECT **stritt**, PERFECT **hat gestritten**)
to argue ◊ *Sie streiten sich ständig.* They argue constantly.
♦ **Darüber lässt sich streiten.** That's debatable.

streng ADJECTIVE
1 strict ◊ *Meine Eltern sind furchtbar streng.* My parents are terribly strict.
2 severe ◊ *Es war ein strenger Winter.* It was a severe winter. ◊ *Das wird streng bestraft.* That will be severely punished.
3 sharp ◊ *Wo kommt der strenge Geruch her?* Where's that sharp smell coming from?

der **Stress** NOUN (GEN des **Stresses**)
stress
♦ **Ich bin im Stress!** I'm stressed out.

stressen VERB (PRESENT **stresst**, IMPERFECT **stresste**, PERFECT **hat gestresst**)
to put under stress

stressig ADJECTIVE
stressful

der **Strich** NOUN (PL die **Striche**)
1 line ◊ *Mach einen Strich unter die Spalte.* Draw a line under the column.
2 stroke ◊ *Mit ein paar Strichen zeichnete er ein Haus.* He drew a house with a couple of strokes.
♦ **auf den Strich gehen** to be on the game

der **Strichkode** NOUN (PL die **Strichkodes**)
bar code

der **Strichpunkt** NOUN (PL die **Strichpunkte**)
semicolon

der **Strick** NOUN (PL die **Stricke**)
rope

stricken VERB
to knit

das **Stroh** NOUN
straw

der **Strohhalm** NOUN (PL die **Strohhalme**)
drinking straw

der **Strom** NOUN (PL die **Ströme**)
current ◊ *der Wechselstrom* alternating current
♦ **Vorsicht, auf dem Draht ist Strom.** Be careful, the wire is live.
♦ **Sie haben den Strom abgeschaltet.** They've cut off the electricity.
♦ **Ein Strom von Zuschauern kam aus dem Stadion.** A stream of spectators was coming out of the stadium.

die **Strömung** NOUN
current

der **Strumpf** NOUN (PL die **Strümpfe**)
stocking

die **Strumpfhose** NOUN
tights ◊ *eine Strumpfhose* a pair of tights

das **Stück** NOUN (PL die **Stücke**)
1 piece ◊ *Sie schnitt ein Stück Käse ab.* She cut off a piece of cheese.
2 play ◊ *Wir haben ein Stück von Brecht angesehen.* We saw a play by Brecht.

das **Stückchen** NOUN (PL die **Stückchen**)
little piece

der **Student** NOUN (GEN des **Studenten**, PL die **Studenten**)
student

die **Studentin** NOUN
student

studieren VERB (PERFECT **hat studiert**)
to study ◊ *Mein Bruder studiert Physik.* My brother's studying physics.

das **Studium** NOUN (PL die **Studien**)
studies

die **Stufe** NOUN
1 step ◊ *Vorsicht, Stufe!* Mind the step!
2 stage ◊ *Er hat bereits eine fortgeschrittene Stufe erreicht.* He's already reached an advanced stage. ◊ *eine Entwicklungsstufe* a stage of development

der **Stuhl** NOUN (PL die **Stühle**)
chair

stumm ADJECTIVE
1 silent ◊ *Sie blieb stumm.* She remained silent.
2 dumb ◊ *Sie ist von Geburt an stumm.* She's been dumb from birth.

stumpf ADJECTIVE
blunt ◊ *Er wurde mit einem stumpfen Gegenstand am Kopf getroffen.* He was hit on the head with a blunt object.
♦ **ein stumpfer Winkel** an obtuse angle

stumpfsinnig ADJECTIVE
mindless

die **Stunde** NOUN

S

☞

1 hour ◊ *Ich komme in einer Stunde.* I'll come in an hour.

2 lesson ◊ *Was haben wir in der letzten Stunde behandelt?* What did we do in the last lesson?

der **Stundenplan** NOUN (PL die **Stundenpläne**)
   timetable

stündlich ADJECTIVE
   hourly ◊ *stündlich verkehren* to run hourly

stur ADJECTIVE
   obstinate

der **Sturm** NOUN (PL die **Stürme**)
   storm

stürmen VERB (PERFECT **ist/hat gestürmt**)
   *Use **sein** to form the perfect tense for **to storm (out)**. Use **haben** to form the perfect tense for all other meanings.*
   to storm ◊ *Er ist aus dem Zimmer gestürmt.* He stormed out of the room.
   ◊ *Die Polizei hat das Gebäude gestürmt.* The police stormed the building.
   ♦ **Es stürmt.** There's a gale blowing.

stürmisch ADJECTIVE
   stormy

der **Sturz** NOUN (GEN des **Sturzes**, PL die **Stürze**)
   1 fall ◊ *Bei dem Sturz hat sie sich das Bein gebrochen.* She broke her leg in the fall.
   2 overthrow ◊ *Alle freuten sich über den Sturz des Diktators.* Everybody was pleased about the overthrow of the dictator.

stürzen VERB (PERFECT **hat/ist gestürzt**)
   *Use **sein** to form the perfect tense. Use **haben** to form the perfect tense for **to overthrow** and for **sich stürzen**.*
   1 to fall ◊ *Sie ist vom Pferd gestürzt.* She fell off a horse.
   ♦ **Das Flugzeug ist ins Meer gestürzt.** The plane crashed into the sea.
   2 to rush ◊ *Er kam ins Zimmer gestürzt.* He rushed into the room.
   3 to overthrow ◊ *Die Regierung wurde gestürzt.* The government has been overthrown.
   ♦ **sich stürzen** to plunge ◊ *Sie stürzte sich ins Wasser.* She plunged into the water.
   ♦ **Er hat sich vom Fernsehturm gestürzt.** He threw himself off the television tower.

der **Sturzhelm** NOUN (PL die **Sturzhelme**)
   crash helmet

die **Stütze** NOUN
   support

das **Styropor** ® NOUN
   polystyrene

das **Subjekt** NOUN (PL die **Subjekte**)
   subject

das **Substantiv** NOUN (PL die **Substantive**)
   noun

subtrahieren VERB (PERFECT **hat subtrahiert**)
   to subtract

die **Subvention** NOUN
   subsidy

die **Suche** NOUN
   search

suchen VERB
   to look for ◊ *Ich suche meinen Radiergummi.* I'm looking for my rubber.
   ◊ *Wir haben gesucht, es aber nicht gefunden.* We looked for it but couldn't find it.
   ♦ **Er wird von der Polizei gesucht.** The police are looking for him.
   ♦ **nach etwas suchen** to look for something ◊ *Wonach suchst du?* What are you looking for?

die **Suchmaschine** NOUN
   search engine (*Internet*)

süchtig ADJECTIVE
   addicted ◊ *heroinsüchtig* addicted to heroin

der **Süchtige** NOUN (GEN des/der **Süchtigen**, PL
die   die **Süchtigen**)
   addict ◊ *Ein Süchtiger hat uns erzählt, wie er süchtig geworden ist.* An addict told us how he became addicted.

Südafrika NEUT NOUN
   South Africa
   ♦ **aus Südafrika** from South Africa
   ♦ **nach Südafrika** to South Africa

Südamerika NEUT NOUN
   South America
   ♦ **aus Südamerika** from South America
   ♦ **nach Südamerika** to South America

der **Süden** NOUN
   south

südlich ADJECTIVE, PREPOSITION, ADVERB
   southerly ◊ *in südlicher Richtung* in a southerly direction
   ♦ **südlich einer Sache** to the south of something ◊ *Das Kraftwerk liegt südlich der Stadt.* The power station's to south of the city.
   ♦ **südlich von** south of ◊ *Das liegt südlich von Rom.* It is south of Rome.

der **Südosten** NOUN
   southeast

der **Südpol** NOUN
   South Pole ◊ *am Südpol* at the South Pole

der **Südwesten** NOUN
   southwest

die **Summe** NOUN
   total

summen VERB
   1 to buzz ◊ *Die Bienen summten.* The bees were buzzing.
   2 to hum ◊ *Sie summte vor sich hin.* She was humming. ◊ *Er hat ein Lied gesummt.* He hummed a song.

der **Sumpf** NOUN (PL die **Sümpfe**)
   swamp

die **Sünde** NOUN

sin

das **Super** NOUN
  four star ◊ *Ich tanke Super.* My car takes
  four star.

das **Superbenzin** NOUN
  four-star petrol

der **Superlativ** NOUN (PL die **Superlative**)
  superlative

der **Supermarkt** NOUN (PL die **Supermärkte**)
  supermarket

die **Suppe** NOUN
  soup

das **Surfbrett** NOUN (PL die **Surfbretter**)
  surfboard

  surfen VERB (PERFECT **hat gesurft**)
  to surf
  ◆ **im Internet surfen** to surf the Net

  süß ADJECTIVE
  sweet

die **Süßigkeit** NOUN
  sweet ◊ *Sie isst gern Süßigkeiten.* She
  likes eating sweets.

der **Süßstoff** NOUN (PL die **Süßstoffe**)
  sweetener

die **Süßwaren** PL NOUN
  confectionery

der **Süßwarenladen** NOUN (PL die
  Süßwarenläden)
  sweetshop

das **Süßwasser** NOUN
  fresh water

das **Symbol** NOUN (PL die **Symbole**)
  symbol

  symmetrisch ADJECTIVE
  symmetrical

die **Sympathie** NOUN
  fondness ◊ *Ihre Sympathie für ihn ist
  offensichtlich.* Her fondness for him is
  obvious.

  sympathisch ADJECTIVE
  likeable ◊ *Er ist ein sympathischer
  Mensch.* He's a likeable person.
  ◆ **Er ist mir sympathisch.** I like him.
  Be careful! **sympathisch** *does not mean*
  sympathetic.

die **Synagoge** NOUN
  synagogue

  synchronisieren VERB (PERFECT **hat
  synchronisiert**)
  to dub ◊ *ein synchronisierter Film* a
  dubbed film

das **Synonym** NOUN (PL die **Synonyme**)
  synonym

  synthetisch ADJECTIVE
  synthetic

das **System** NOUN (PL die **Systeme**)
  system

  systematisch ADJECTIVE
  systematic

die **Szene** NOUN
  scene

S

T

der **Tabak** NOUN (PL die **Tabake**)
tobacco

die **Tabelle** NOUN
table

die **Tabellenkalkulation** NOUN
spreadsheet

das **Tablett** NOUN (PL die **Tablette**)
tray

die **Tablette** NOUN
tablet

der **Tachometer** NOUN (PL die **Tachometer**)
speedometer

tadellos ADJECTIVE
faultless

die **Tafel** NOUN
blackboard ◊ *Der Lehrer schrieb das Wort an die Tafel.* The teacher wrote the word on the blackboard.
♦ **eine Tafel Schokolade** a bar of chocolate

der **Tag** NOUN (PL die **Tage**)
1 day ◊ *Ich war den ganzen Tag weg.* I was away all day.
2 daylight ◊ *Wir möchten noch bei Tag ankommen.* We want to arrive in daylight.
♦ **an den Tag kommen** to come to light
♦ **Guten Tag!** Hello!

das **Tageblatt** NOUN (PL die **Tageblätter**)
daily newspaper

das **Tagebuch** NOUN (PL die **Tagebücher**)
diary ◊ *ein Tagebuch führen* to keep a diary

tagelang ADVERB
for days

der **Tagesanbruch** NOUN
dawn ◊ *bei Tagesanbruch* at dawn

das **Tagesgericht** NOUN (PL die **Tagesgerichte**)
dish of the day

die **Tageskarte** NOUN
1 menu of the day
2 day ticket

das **Tageslicht** NOUN
daylight

der **Tageslichtprojektor** NOUN (PL die **Tageslichtprojektoren**)
overhead projector

die **Tagesschau** NOUN
TV news

die **Tageszeit** NOUN
time of day

die **Tageszeitung** NOUN
daily paper

täglich ADJECTIVE, ADVERB
daily

tagsüber ADVERB
during the day

die **Taille** NOUN
waist

der **Takt** NOUN (PL die **Takte**)
tact ◊ *Sie behandelte die Sache mit viel Takt.* She showed great tact in dealing with the matter.
♦ **Er hat überhaupt keinen Takt.** He's completely tactless.
♦ **den Takt angeben** to keep time
♦ **im Stundentakt** at hourly intervals

die **Taktik** NOUN
tactics ◊ *Das ist die falsche Taktik.* Those are the wrong tactics.

taktisch ADJECTIVE
tactical ◊ *Das war taktisch unklug.* That was a tactical mistake.

taktlos ADJECTIVE
tactless

taktvoll ADJECTIVE
tactful

das **Tal** NOUN (PL die **Täler**)
valley

das **Talent** NOUN (PL die **Talente**)
talent

talentiert ADJECTIVE
talented

die **Talkshow** NOUN (PL die **Talkshows**)
chat show

der **Tampon** NOUN (PL die **Tampons**)
tampon

der **Tank** NOUN (PL die **Tanks**)
tank

tanken VERB
to get petrol ◊ *Wir müssen noch tanken.* We still have to get petrol.

die **Tankstelle** NOUN
petrol station

der **Tankwart** NOUN (PL die **Tankwarte**)
petrol pump attendant

die **Tanne** NOUN
fir

der **Tannenzapfen** NOUN (PL die **Tannenzapfen**)
fir cone

die **Tante** NOUN
aunt

der **Tanz** NOUN (GEN des **Tanzes,** PL die **Tänze**)
dance

tanzen VERB
to dance

die **Tanzschule** NOUN
dancing school

> ❢ It is very common for German boys and girls to go to a **Tanzschule** when they are about 14.

die **Tapete** NOUN
wallpaper

tapezieren VERB (PERFECT **hat tapeziert**)

to wallpaper
tapfer ADJECTIVE
brave
die **Tapferkeit** NOUN
bravery
die **Tasche** NOUN
[1] pocket ◇ *Er hatte die Hände in der Hosentasche.* He had his hands in his trouser pockets.
[2] bag ◇ *Sie kann ihre Tasche nicht finden.* She can't find her bag.
das **Taschenbuch** NOUN (PL die **Taschenbücher**)
paperback
der **Taschendieb** NOUN
pickpocket
das **Taschengeld** NOUN (PL die **Taschengelder**)
pocket money
die **Taschenlampe** NOUN
torch
das **Taschenmesser** NOUN (PL die **Taschenmesser**)
penknife
der **Taschenrechner** NOUN (PL die **Taschenrechner**)
pocket calculator
das **Taschentuch** NOUN (PL die **Taschentücher**)
handkerchief
die **Tasse** NOUN
cup ◇ *eine Tasse Tee* a cup of tea
die **Tastatur** NOUN
keyboard
die **Taste** NOUN
[1] button ◇ *Welche Taste muss ich drücken, um die Waschmaschine anzustellen?* What button do I have to press to start the washing machine?
[2] key ◇ *Bei der Schreibmaschine und der Computertastatur gibt es eine Hochstelltaste.* There's a shift key on the typewriter and the computer keyboard.
die **Tat** NOUN (PL die **Taten**)
deed ◇ *Das war eine tapfere Tat.* That was a brave deed. ◇ *eine gute Tat* a good deed
♦ *Der Beschuldigte hat die Tat gestanden.* The accused confessed to the crime.
♦ **in der Tat** indeed
tat VERB *see* **tun**
der **Täter** NOUN (PL die **Täter**)
culprit
tätig ADJECTIVE
♦ **tätig sein** to work ◇ *Er ist als Journalist tätig.* He works as a journalist.
die **Tätigkeit** NOUN
[1] activity ◇ *kriminelle Tätigkeiten* criminal activities
[2] occupation ◇ *Welche Tätigkeit übt dein Vater aus?* What's your father's occupation?
tätowieren VERB (PERFECT **hat tätowiert**)
to tattoo

die **Tatsache** NOUN
fact
tatsächlich ADJECTIVE, ADVERB
[1] actual ◇ *Der tatsächliche Grund war ein anderer als der, den sie angegeben hatte.* The actual reason was different from the one she gave.
[2] really ◇ *Das hat sie tatsächlich gesagt.* She really did say that. ◇ *Er ist tatsächlich rechtzeitig gekommen.* He really has come in time.
taub ADJECTIVE
deaf ◇ *Sie ist auf dem rechten Ohr taub.* She's deaf in her right ear.
die **Taube** NOUN
[1] pigeon ◇ *die Tauben auf dem Marktplatz* the pigeons in the market square
[2] dove ◇ *die Friedenstaube* the dove of peace
die **Taubheit** NOUN
deafness
taubstumm ADJECTIVE
deaf-mute
tauchen VERB (PERFECT **hat/ist getaucht**)
*Use **haben** for the perfect tense when you describe the activity and **sein** when you describe the motion.*
[1] to dip ◇ *Sie hat ihren Zeh ins Wasser getaucht.* She dipped her toe into the water.
[2] to dive ◇ *Als Kind habe ich viel getaucht.* I used to dive a lot as a child. ◇ *Er ist nach dem versunkenen Schatz getaucht.* He dived in search of the sunken treasure.
der **Taucheranzug** NOUN (PL die **Taucheranzüge**)
diving suit
tauen VERB
♦ **Es taut.** It's thawing.
die **Taufe** NOUN
christening
taufen VERB
to christen
taugen VERB
♦ **nichts taugen** to be no good ◇ *Das Programm taugt nichts.* The program's no good.
tauschen VERB
to exchange
täuschen VERB
[1] to deceive ◇ *Du hast mich bewusst getäuscht.* You deliberately deceived me.
[2] to be deceptive ◇ *Der äußere Anschein täuscht oft.* Appearances are often deceptive.
♦ **sich täuschen** to be wrong
die **Täuschung** NOUN
deception
♦ **eine optische Täuschung** an optical illusion

T

tausend NUMBER
thousand

das **Taxi** NOUN (GEN des **Taxis**, PL die **Taxis**)
taxi

der **Taxifahrer** NOUN (PL die **Taxifahrer**)
taxi driver

der **Taxistand** NOUN (PL die **Taxistände**)
taxi rank

die **Technik** NOUN
1 technology ◊ *hoch entwickelte Technik* advanced technology
♦ **die Gentechnik** genetic engineering
2 technique ◊ *Sie beherrscht diese Technik des Hochsprungs noch nicht.* She hasn't mastered this high-jump technique yet.

der **Techniker** NOUN (PL die **Techniker**)
technician

technisch ADJECTIVE
technical

die **Technologie** NOUN
technology

der **TEE** NOUN (= *Trans-Europ-Express*)
Trans-Europe Express

der **Tee** NOUN (PL die **Tees**)
tea ◊ *Tee mit Milch und Zucker* tea with milk and sugar ◊ *Tee mit Zitrone* lemon tea
♦ **der Kamillentee** camomile tea

der **Teebeutel** NOUN (PL die **Teebeutel**)
tea bag

die **Teekanne** NOUN
teapot

der **Teelöffel** NOUN (PL die **Teelöffel**)
teaspoon
♦ **ein Teelöffel Zucker** a teaspoonful of sugar

der **Teer** NOUN
tar

das **Teesieb** NOUN (PL die **Teesiebe**)
tea strainer

der **Teich** NOUN (PL die **Teiche**)
pond

der **Teig** NOUN (PL die **Teige**)
dough

die **Teigwaren** FEM PL NOUN
pasta

der **Teil** NOUN (PL die **Teile**)
You can also say das Teil.
1 part ◊ *der erste Teil des Buches* the first part of the book
♦ **das Ersatzteil** the spare part
2 share ◊ *Ich möchte meinen Teil am Gewinn.* I would like my share of the profit.
3 component part ◊ *Er hat das Fahrrad in seine Teile zerlegt.* He dismantled the bike into its component parts.
♦ **Sie waren zum Teil beschädigt.** Some of them were damaged.

teilen VERB
to divide

♦ **mit jemandem teilen** to share with somebody

teilnehmen VERB (PRESENT **nimmt teil**, IMPERFECT **nahm teil**, PERFECT **hat teilgenommen**)
♦ **an etwas teilnehmen** to take part in something ◊ *Du solltest am Wettbewerb teilnehmen!* You ought to take part in the competition.

der **Teilnehmer** NOUN (PL die **Teilnehmer**)
participant

teils ADVERB
partly

teilweise ADVERB
in parts ◊ *Das Buch war teilweise sehr spannend.* The book was thrilling in parts.
♦ **Sie waren teilweise beschädigt.** Some of them were damaged.

die **Teilzeitarbeit** NOUN
part-time work

der **Teilzeitjob** NOUN (PL die **Teilzeitjobs**)
part-time job

der **Teint** NOUN (PL die **Teints**)
complexion

die **Telearbeit** NOUN
teleworking

das **Telefax** NOUN (GEN des **Telefax**, PL die **Telefaxe**)
fax

das **Telefon** NOUN (PL die **Telefone**)
telephone

der **Telefonanruf** NOUN (PL die **Telefonanrufe**)
telephone call

das **Telefonat** NOUN (PL die **Telefonate**)
phone call

das **Telefonbuch** NOUN (PL die **Telefonbücher**)
phone book

das **Telefonhäuschen** NOUN (PL die **Telefonhäuschen**)
telephone box

der **Telefonhörer** NOUN (PL die **Telefonhörer**)
receiver ◊ *Er nahm den Telefonhörer ab.* He picked up the receiver.

telefonieren VERB (PERFECT **hat telefoniert**)
to telephone
♦ **Ich habe gestern mit ihr telefoniert.** I talked to her on the phone yesterday.

telefonisch ADJECTIVE
telephone ◊ *eine telefonische Nachricht* a telephone message
♦ **Sie können mich telefonisch erreichen.** You can contact me by phone.

die **Telefonkarte** NOUN
phonecard

die **Telefonnummer** NOUN
telephone number

die **Telefonzelle** NOUN
telephone box

das **Telegramm** NOUN (PL die **Telegramme**)
telegram

das **Teleobjektiv** NOUN (PL die **Teleobjektive**)
telephoto lens

das **Teleskop** NOUN (PL die **Teleskope**)
telescope

der **Teller** NOUN (PL die **Teller**)
plate

das **Temperament** NOUN (PL die **Temperamente**)
♦ **Sie hat das Stück mit Temperament gespielt.** She gave a lively rendition of the piece.
♦ **Sie hat ein ziemlich lebhaftes Temperament.** She's quite a vivacious person.

temperamentvoll ADJECTIVE
vivacious

die **Temperatur** NOUN
temperature

das **Tempo** NOUN (PL die **Tempos**)
1 speed ◊ *Er ist mit einem irren Tempo gefahren.* He drove at breakneck speed.
2 rate ◊ *Wir müssen unser Arbeitstempo steigern.* We must increase our work rate.

tendieren VERB (PERFECT **hat tendiert**)
♦ **zu etwas tendieren** to tend towards something

das **Tennis** NOUN (GEN des **Tennis**)
tennis

der **Tennisplatz** NOUN (GEN des **Tennisplatzes**, PL die **Tennisplätze**)
tennis court

der **Tennisschläger** NOUN (PL die **Tennisschläger**)
tennis racket

der **Tennisspieler** NOUN (PL die **Tennisspieler**)
tennis player

der **Teppich** NOUN (PL die **Teppiche**)
carpet

der **Teppichboden** NOUN (PL die **Teppichböden**)
wall-to-wall carpet

der **Termin** NOUN (PL die **Termine**)
1 date ◊ *Habt ihr einen Termin ausgemacht?* Have you arranged a date?
2 deadline ◊ *Ich muss den Aufsatz bis zu dem Termin fertig haben.* I must have the essay finished by that deadline.
3 appointment ◊ *Ich habe einen Termin beim Zahnarzt.* I've got an appointment with the dentist.

der **Terminkalender** NOUN (PL die **Terminkalender**)
appointments diary

die **Terrasse** NOUN
terrace

der **Terror** NOUN
terror

der **Terrorismus** NOUN (GEN des **Terrorismus**)
terrorism

der **Terrorist** NOUN (GEN des **Terroristen**, PL die **Terroristen**)
terrorist

der **Tesafilm** ® NOUN

Sellotape ®

der **Test** NOUN (PL die **Tests**)
test

das **Testament** NOUN (PL die **Testamente**)
will ◊ *sein Testament machen* to make one's will

testen VERB
to test

teuer ADJECTIVE
expensive

der **Teufel** NOUN (PL die **Teufel**)
devil

der **Text** NOUN (PL die **Texte**)
1 text ◊ *Lest den Text auf Seite zehn.* Read the text on page ten.
2 lyrics ◊ *Kannst du mir den Text von dem Song übersetzen?* Can you translate the lyrics of the song for me?

die **Textilien** FEM PL NOUN
textiles

die **Textverarbeitung** NOUN
word processing

das **Textverarbeitungssystem** NOUN (PL die **Textverarbeitungssysteme**)
word processor

das **Theater** NOUN (PL die **Theater**)
1 theatre ◊ *Wir gehen ins Theater.* We're going to the theatre.
♦ **Theater spielen** to act
2 fuss ◊ *Mach nicht so ein Theater!* Don't make such a fuss.

das **Theaterstück** NOUN (PL die **Theaterstücke**)
play

die **Theke** NOUN
1 bar ◊ *Er stand an der Theke und trank ein Bier.* He stood at the bar drinking a beer.
2 counter ◊ *Das bekommen Sie an der Käsetheke.* You'll get that at the cheese counter.

das **Thema** NOUN (PL die **Themen**)
subject

die **Themse** NOUN
Thames

theoretisch ADJECTIVE
theoretical ◊ *rein theoretisch betrachtet* from a purely theoretical point of view

die **Theorie** NOUN
theory

die **Therapie** NOUN
therapy

das **Thermometer** NOUN (PL die **Thermometer**)
thermometer

die **Thermosflasche** NOUN
Thermos ®

die **These** NOUN
thesis

der **Thriller** NOUN (PL die **Thriller**)
thriller

der **Thron** NOUN (PL die **Throne**)
throne

T

der **Thunfisch** NOUN (PL die **Thunfische**)
tuna

das **Thüringen** NOUN
Thuringia

> ℹ️ **Thüringen** is one of the 16 **Länder**.
> Its capital is Erfurt. With its extensive
> forests, it is sometimes called
> "Germany's green heartland". It is not
> only rural, however: the Zeiss precision
> engineering company is based in Jena.

der **Thymian** NOUN (PL die **Thymiane**)
thyme

ticken VERB
to tick ◊ *Die Uhr tickte.* The clock was
ticking.
♦ **Du tickst ja nicht richtig!** You're off your
rocker!

das **Tief** NOUN (PL die **Tiefs**)
see also **tief** ADJECTIVE
depression ◊ *ein Tief über
Norddeutschland* a depression over
North Germany

tief ADJECTIVE
see also **das Tief** NOUN
[1] deep ◊ *Wie tief ist das Wasser?* How
deep's the water?
[2] low (neckline, price, note) ◊ *ein tief
ausgeschnittenes Kleid* a low-cut dress

der **Tiefdruck** NOUN
low pressure

die **Tiefe** NOUN
depth

die **Tiefgarage** NOUN
underground garage

tiefgekühlt ADJECTIVE
frozen

die **Tiefkühlkost** NOUN
frozen food

die **Tiefkühltruhe** NOUN
freezer

die **Tiefsttemperatur** NOUN
minimum temperature

das **Tier** NOUN (PL die **Tiere**)
animal

der **Tierarzt** NOUN (GEN des **Tierarztes,** PL die
Tierärzte)
vet

der **Tiergarten** NOUN (PL die **Tiergärten**)
zoo

tierisch ADJECTIVE
animal ◊ *tierische Fette* animal fats
♦ **Du hast dich tierisch benommen.** You
behaved terribly.

der **Tierkreis** NOUN (GEN des **Tierkreises**)
zodiac

die **Tierquälerei** NOUN
cruelty to animals

der **Tiger** NOUN (PL die **Tiger**)
tiger

die **Tinte** NOUN
ink

der **Tintenfisch** NOUN (PL die **Tintenfische**)
squid

der **Tipp** NOUN (PL die **Tipps**)
tip

tippen VERB
[1] to tap ◊ *Sie tippte leicht an die Statue.*
She lightly tapped the statue.
[2] to type ◊ *Tippst du dein Referat?* Are
you typing your assignment?
♦ **Mein Freund tippt im Lotto.** My friend
plays the lottery.
♦ **Auf wen tippst du bei den Wahlen?**
Who're you tipping to win the elections?

der **Tippfehler** NOUN (PL die **Tippfehler**)
typing error

Tirol NEUT NOUN
Tyrol

der **Tiroler** NOUN (PL die **Tiroler**)
Tyrolean

die **Tirolerin** NOUN
Tyrolean

der **Tisch** NOUN (PL die **Tische**)
table ◊ *bei Tisch* at table

die **Tischdecke** NOUN
tablecloth

der **Tischler** NOUN (PL die **Tischler**)
joiner

das **Tischtennis** NOUN
table tennis

das **Tischtuch** NOUN (PL die **Tischtücher**)
tablecloth

der **Titel** NOUN (PL die **Titel**)
title

der **Toast** NOUN (PL die **Toasts**)
toast

das **Toastbrot** NOUN (PL die **Toastbrote**)
bread for toasting

der **Toaster** NOUN (PL die **Toaster**)
toaster

toben VERB
[1] to rage ◊ *Der Sturm tobte die ganze
Nacht.* The storm raged all night long.
♦ **Wenn er das erfährt, wird er toben.** If he
finds out he'll go mad.
[2] to romp about ◊ *Die Kinder toben im
Garten.* The children are romping about
in the garden.

die **Tochter** NOUN (PL die **Töchter**)
daughter

der **Tod** NOUN (PL die **Tode**)
death

todernst ADJECTIVE, ADVERB
grave ◊ *ein todernstes Gesicht* a grave
face
♦ **Er hat das todernst gesagt.** He said it in
deadly earnest.

die **Todesstrafe** NOUN
death penalty

todkrank ADJECTIVE
critically ill

tödlich ADJECTIVE

deadly ◊ *eine tödliche Waffe* a deadly weapon
♦ **ein tödlicher Unfall** a fatal accident
todmüde ADJECTIVE
exhausted
todschick ADJECTIVE
smart
die **Toilette** NOUN
toilet
das **Toilettenpapier** NOUN
toilet paper
tolerant ADJECTIVE
tolerant
toll ADJECTIVE
terrific
die **Tollwut** NOUN
rabies
die **Tomate** NOUN
tomato
das **Tomatenmark** NOUN
tomato purée
der **Ton** NOUN (PL die **Töne**)
1 sound ◊ *Es war kein Ton zu hören.* Not a sound could be heard.
2 note ◊ *Mit welchen Ton fängt das Lied an?* What note does the song start on?
3 tone of voice ◊ *Sein Ton gefiel mir nicht.* I didn't like his tone of voice.
4 shade ◊ *Pastelltöne sind in.* Pastel shades are in.
5 stress ◊ *Bei Substantiven liegt der Ton meist auf der ersten Silbe.* Nouns are usually stressed on the first syllable.
das **Tonband** NOUN (PL die **Tonbänder**)
tape
das **Tonbandgerät** NOUN (PL die **Tonbandgeräte**)
tape recorder
die **Tonne** NOUN
ton ◊ *Es wiegt drei Tonnen.* It weighs three tons.
der **Topf** NOUN (PL die **Töpfe**)
pot
das **Tor** NOUN (PL die **Tore**)
1 gate ◊ *Das Tor war offen.* The gate was open.
2 goal ◊ *Wer hat das zweite Tor geschossen?* Who scored the second goal?
der **Torf** NOUN
peat
die **Torte** NOUN
1 gateau
2 flan
der **Torwart** NOUN (PL die **Torwarte**)
goalkeeper
tot ADJECTIVE
dead
♦ **Er war sofort tot.** He was killed instantly.
total ADJECTIVE, ADVERB
1 complete ◊ *Das ist doch der totale Wahnsinn.* But that's complete madness.

2 completely ◊ *Das ist total verrückt.* That's completely mad.
totalitär ADJECTIVE
totalitarian
der **Totalschaden** NOUN (PL die **Totalschäden**)
complete write-off
der/die **Tote** NOUN (GEN des/der **Toten**, PL die **Toten**)
dead body ◊ *Auf der Straße lag ein Toter.* There was a dead body lying in the road.
♦ **die Toten begraben** to bury the dead
töten VERB
to kill
sich **totlachen** VERB (PERFECT **hat sich totgelacht**)
to laugh one's head off
die **Tour** NOUN (PL die **Touren**)
trip ◊ *auf Tour gehen* to go on a trip
♦ **auf vollen Touren** at full speed
der **Tourismus** NOUN (GEN des **Tourismus**)
tourism
der **Tourist** NOUN (GEN des **Touristen**, PL die **Touristen**)
tourist
die **Touristenklasse** NOUN
tourist class
die **Tournee** NOUN
tour ◊ *Bon Jovi auf Tournee* Bon Jovi on tour ◊ *auf Tournee gehen* to go on tour
die **Tracht** NOUN
traditional costume ◊ *Im Schwarzwald tragen die Frauen noch Tracht.* Women still wear traditional costume in the Black Forest.
♦ **eine Tracht Prügel** a sound beating
die **Tradition** NOUN
tradition
traditionell ADJECTIVE
traditional
traf VERB *see* **treffen**
tragbar ADJECTIVE
portable ◊ *ein tragbarer Fernseher* a portable TV
träge ADJECTIVE
sluggish
tragen VERB (PRESENT **trägt**, IMPERFECT **trug**, PERFECT **hat getragen**)
1 to carry ◊ *Kannst du meinen Koffer tragen?* Can you carry my case?
2 to bear ◊ *die Verantwortung tragen* to bear responsibility
3 (clothes, glasses)
to wear ◊ *Sie trug ein weißes Kleid und eine Sonnenbrille.* She was wearing a white dress and sunglasses.
♦ **Ich trag's mit Fassung.** I'll just have to grin and bear it.
die **Tragetasche** NOUN
carrier bag
die **Trägheit** NOUN
laziness
tragisch ADJECTIVE
tragic

T

die **Tragödie** NOUN
tragedy

der **Trainer** NOUN (PL die **Trainer**)
coach

trainieren VERB (PERFECT **hat trainiert**)
[1] to train ◊ *Sie trainiert täglich für den Wettkampf.* She trains for the competition every day.
[2] to coach ◊ *Wer trainiert diese Tennisspielerin?* Who coaches this tennis player?
[3] to practise ◊ *Diese Übung muss ich noch mehr trainieren.* I need to practise this exercise more.

das **Training** NOUN (PL die **Trainings**)
training

der **Trainingsanzug** NOUN (PL die **Trainingsanzüge**)
track suit

trampen VERB
to hitchhike

der **Tramper** NOUN (PL die **Tramper**)
hitchhiker

die **Tramperin** NOUN
hitchhiker

die **Träne** NOUN
tear ◊ *in Tränen ausbrechen* to burst into tears

das **Tränengas** NOUN (GEN des **Tränengases**)
tear gas

trank VERB *see* **trinken**

die **Transplantation** NOUN
transplant ◊ *eine Herztransplantation* a heart transplant
♦ *eine Hauttransplantation* a skin graft

der **Transport** NOUN (PL die **Transporte**)
transport

transportieren VERB (PERFECT **hat transportiert**)
to transport

das **Transportmittel** NOUN (PL die **Transportmittel**)
means of transport

die **Traube** NOUN
grape

der **Traubenzucker** NOUN (PL die **Traubenzucker**)
glucose

trauen VERB
♦ *jemandem trauen* to trust somebody
♦ *sich trauen* to dare ◊ *Ich wette, du traust dich nicht!* I bet you don't dare.

der **Traum** NOUN (PL die **Träume**)
dream

träumen VERB
to dream ◊ *Ich habe von dir geträumt.* I dreamt about you.

traumhaft ADJECTIVE
wonderful ◊ *Es waren traumhafte Ferien.* It was a wonderful holiday.

traurig ADJECTIVE
sad

die **Traurigkeit** NOUN
sadness

das **Treffen** NOUN (PL die **Treffen**)
| *see also* **treffen** VERB |
meeting

treffen VERB (PRESENT **trifft**, IMPERFECT **traf**, PERFECT **hat getroffen**)
| *see also* **das Treffen** NOUN |
[1] to hit ◊ *Er hat die Zielscheibe getroffen.* He hit the target. ◊ *Sie wurde am Kopf getroffen.* She was hit on the head.
♦ *Du hast nicht getroffen.* You missed.
[2] to meet ◊ *Ich habe ihn gestern im Supermarkt getroffen.* I met him yesterday in the supermarket. ◊ *Wir sind in London auf ihn getroffen.* We met him in London.
♦ *sich treffen* to meet ◊ *Wir treffen uns am Bahnhof.* We'll meet at the station. ◊ *Sie treffen sich einmal in der Woche.* They meet once a week.
[3] to affect ◊ *Die Bemerkung hat sie sehr getroffen.* The remark affected her deeply.
♦ *eine Entscheidung treffen* to make a decision
♦ *Maßnahmen treffen* to take steps
♦ *es traf sich, dass ...* it so happened that ...
♦ *Das trifft sich gut!* How very convenient!

treffend ADJECTIVE
pertinent

der **Treffer** NOUN (PL die **Treffer**)
[1] hit ◊ *Das Schiff musste einen Volltreffer hinnehmen.* The ship took a direct hit.
[2] goal ◊ *Klinsmann hat einen Treffer erzielt.* Klinsmann scored a goal. ◊ *Ich hatte vier Treffer im Lotto.* I got four numbers in the lottery.

der **Treffpunkt** NOUN (PL die **Treffpunkte**)
meeting place

treiben VERB (IMPERFECT **trieb**, PERFECT **hat/ist getrieben**)
*Use **haben** to form the perfect tense. Use sein to form the perfect tense for **to drift**.*
[1] to drive ◊ *Sie trieben die Kühe auf das Feld.* They drove the cows into the field.
♦ *Sport treiben* to do sport
♦ *Unsinn treiben* to fool around
♦ *jemanden zu etwas treiben* to drive somebody to something ◊ *Du treibst mich zur Verzweiflung.* You drive me to despair.
♦ *Sie hat uns zur Eile getrieben.* She made us hurry up.
[2] to drift ◊ *Das Schiff ist aufs Meer getrieben.* The ship drifted out to sea.

das **Treibhaus** NOUN (GEN des **Treibhauses**, PL die **Treibhäuser**)
greenhouse

der **Treibhauseffekt** NOUN

greenhouse effect

der **Treibstoff** NOUN (PL die **Treibstoffe**)
fuel

trennen VERB
[1] to separate ◊ *Er hat die beiden Raufbolde getrennt.* He separated the two ruffians.
[2] to make a distinction between ◊ *Diese beiden Begriffe muss man sauber trennen.* You have to make a clear distinction between these two concepts.
[3] to hyphenate ◊ *Wie wird dieses Wort getrennt?* Where do you hyphenate this word?
♦ **sich trennen** to separate ◊ *Die beiden haben sich getrennt.* The two of them have separated.
♦ **Du solltest dich von ihm trennen.** You ought to leave him.
♦ **sich von etwas trennen** to part with something ◊ *Ich trenne mich ungern von dem Buch.* I'm loath to part with this book.

die **Trennung** NOUN
separation

die **Treppe** NOUN
stairs

das **Treppenhaus** NOUN (GEN des **Treppenhauses**, PL die **Treppenhäuser**)
staircase

treten VERB (PRESENT **tritt**, IMPERFECT **trat**, PERFECT **hat/ist getreten**)

*For the perfect tense use **haben** when the verb has an object and **sein** when there is no object.*

[1] to step ◊ *Sie ist in die Pfütze getreten.* She stepped in the puddle. ◊ *Er trat auf die Bremse.* He stepped on the brakes. ◊ *Er trat ans Mikrofon.* He stepped up to the microphone.
♦ **mit jemandem in Verbindung treten** to get in touch with somebody
♦ **in Erscheinung treten** to appear
♦ **Mir sind die Tränen in die Augen getreten.** Tears came to my eyes.
[2] to kick ◊ *Sie hat mich getreten.* She kicked me.
[3] to tread ◊ *Er ist mir auf den Fuß getreten.* He trod on my foot.
♦ **Sie trat nach dem Hund.** She kicked the dog.

treu ADJECTIVE
faithful ◊ *Bist du mir auch treu gewesen?* Have you been faithful to me?

die **Treue** NOUN
faithfulness

die **Tribüne** NOUN
[1] grandstand ◊ *Die Fans auf der Tribüne pfiffen.* The fans on the grandstand whistled.

[2] platform ◊ *Der Redner stand auf einer Tribüne.* The speaker stood on a platform.

der **Trichter** NOUN (PL die **Trichter**)
[1] funnel ◊ *Sie hat das Öl mit einem Trichter in die Flasche gefüllt.* She used a funnel to fill the bottle with oil.
[2] crater ◊ *Das Gelände war von Bombentrichtern übersät.* The area was pitted with bomb craters.

der **Trick** NOUN (PL die **Tricks**)
trick ◊ *Das war ein fauler Trick.* That was a dirty trick.

der **Trickfilm** NOUN (PL die **Trickfilme**)
cartoon

trieb VERB *see* **treiben**

trifft VERB *see* **treffen**

das **Trimester** NOUN (PL die **Trimester**)
term (*university*)

der **Trimm-dich-Pfad** NOUN (PL die **Trimm-dich-Pfade**)
keep-fit trail

sich **trimmen** VERB (PERFECT **hat getrimmt**)
to keep fit

trinkbar ADJECTIVE
drinkable

trinken VERB (IMPERFECT **trank**, PERFECT **hat getrunken**)
to drink
♦ **Ich habe zu viel getrunken.** I've had too much to drink.

das **Trinkgeld** NOUN (PL die **Trinkgelder**)
tip ◊ *Er gab dem Taxifahrer ein großzügiges Trinkgeld.* He gave the taxi driver a generous tip.

die **Trinkhalle** NOUN
refreshment kiosk

das **Trinkwasser** NOUN (PL die **Trinkwässer**)
drinking water

trocken ADJECTIVE
dry

trocknen VERB
to dry

der **Trödel** NOUN
junk

der **Trödelmarkt** NOUN (PL die **Trödelmärkte**)
flea market

trödeln VERB
to dawdle

die **Trommel** NOUN
drum ◊ *Er spielt Trommel.* He plays the drums.

das **Trommelfell** NOUN (PL die **Trommelfelle**)
eardrum

trommeln VERB
to drum

die **Trompete** NOUN
trumpet ◊ *Sie spielt Trompete.* She plays the trumpet.

der **Trompeter** NOUN (PL die **Trompeter**)
trumpeter

die **Tropen** PL NOUN

T

tropics

der **Tropfen** NOUN (PL die **Tropfen**)
drop

tropisch ADJECTIVE
tropical

der **Trost** NOUN
consolation

trösten VERB
to console

trostlos ADJECTIVE
bleak ◊ *eine trostlose Landschaft* a bleak landscape

der **Trostpreis** NOUN (GEN des **Trostpreises**, PL die **Trostpreise**)
consolation prize

der **Trottel** NOUN (PL die **Trottel**)
prat

der **Trotz** NOUN (GEN des **Trotzes**)
see also **trotz** PREPOSITION
defiance ◊ *ihm zum Trotz* in defiance of him
♦ **etwas aus Trotz tun** to do something defiantly

trotz PREPOSITION
see also **der Trotz** NOUN
*The preposition **trotz** takes the dative or genitive.*
in spite of

trotzdem ADVERB
all the same ◊ *Ich gehe trotzdem.* I'm going all the same.

trotzig ADJECTIVE
defiant

trüb ADJECTIVE
[1] dull ◊ *Es war ein trüber Tag.* It was a dull day.
[2] cloudy ◊ *Das Wasser war trüb.* The water was cloudy.
[3] gloomy ◊ *Die Zukunftsaussichten sind ziemlich trüb.* Prospects for the future are pretty gloomy.

der **Trubel** NOUN
hurly-burly

der **Trübsinn** NOUN
gloom

trübsinnig ADJECTIVE
gloomy

trug VERB *see* **tragen**

trügen VERB (IMPERFECT **trog**, PERFECT **hat getrogen**)
to be deceptive ◊ *Der Schein trügt.* Appearances are deceptive.

der **Trugschluss** NOUN (GEN des **Trugschlusses**, PL die **Trugschlüsse**)
false conclusion

die **Trümmer** PL NOUN
[1] wreckage ◊ *die Trümmer des Flugzeugs* the wreckage of the aeroplane
[2] ruins ◊ *Nach dem Bombenangriff war die Stadt voller Trümmer.* After the air raid the town was in ruins.

der **Trumpf** NOUN (PL die **Trümpfe**)
trump ◊ *Herz ist Trumpf.* Hearts is trumps.

die **Trunkenheit** NOUN
drunkenness
♦ **Trunkenheit am Steuer** drink-driving

die **Truppen** FEM PL NOUN
troops

der **Truthahn** NOUN (PL die **Truthähne**)
turkey

der **Tscheche** NOUN (GEN des **Tschechen**, PL die **Tschechen**)
Czech

die **Tschechin** NOUN
Czech

tschechisch ADJECTIVE
Czech ◊ *die Tschechische Republik* the Czech Republic

tschüs EXCLAMATION
cheerio!

das **T-Shirt** NOUN (PL die **T-Shirts**)
T-shirt

die **Tube** NOUN
tube ◊ *eine Tube Zahnpasta* a tube of toothpaste

das **Tuch** NOUN (PL die **Tücher**)
[1] cloth ◊ *Mit welchem Tuch soll ich abstauben?* Which cloth should I use for dusting?
[2] towel ◊ *Nimm dir ein großes Tuch ins Schwimmbad mit.* Take a large towel with you to the swimming baths.
[3] scarf ◊ *Sie hatte ein seidenes Tuch um den Hals.* She wore a silk scarf around her neck.

tüchtig ADJECTIVE
competent ◊ *Er ist ein sehr tüchtiger Mensch.* He's a very competent person.
♦ **Er nahm einen tüchtigen Schluck aus der Flasche.** He took a hefty swig from the bottle.

die **Tugend** NOUN
virtue

die **Tulpe** NOUN
tulip

der **Tumor** NOUN (PL die **Tumore**)
tumour

tun VERB (IMPERFECT **tat**, PERFECT **hat getan**)
[1] to do ◊ *Was sollen wir jetzt tun?* What shall we do now? ◊ *Er hat den ganzen Tag nichts getan.* He hasn't done anything all day. ◊ *Kann ich etwas für dich tun?* Can I do anything for you? ◊ *Was kann ich für Sie tun?* What can I do for you?
[2] to put ◊ *Sie tat die Teller in den Schrank.* She put the plates in the cupboard.
[3] to act ◊ *Tu nicht so unschuldig!* Don't act so innocent.
[4] to pretend ◊ *Sie tat, als ob sie schliefe.* She pretended to be sleeping.

◊ *Er ist nicht krank, er tut nur so.* He isn't ill, he's only pretending.

♦ **Der Hund tut dir bestimmt nichts.** The dog won't hurt you.

♦ **Hoffentlich hast du dir bei dem Sturz nichts getan.** I hope you didn't hurt yourself when you fell.

♦ **Es tut sich viel.** A lot's happening.

♦ **Ein belegtes Brot tut es auch.** A sandwich will do.

♦ **mit etwas zu tun haben** to have something to do with something ◊ *Seine Laune hat etwas mit seiner Krankheit zu tun.* His mood has something to do with his illness.

♦ **Mit ihm will ich nichts zu tun haben.** I won't have anything to do with him.

♦ **Das tut nichts zur Sache.** That's neither here nor there.

der **Tunfisch** NOUN (PL die **Tunfische**)
  tuna

der **Tunnel** NOUN (PL die **Tunnel**)
  tunnel

der **Tupfen** NOUN (PL die **Tupfen**)
  dot

die **Tür** NOUN
  door

der **Türke** NOUN (GEN des **Türken**, PL die **Türken**)
  Turk

die **Türkei** NOUN
  Turkey
  ♦ **aus der Türkei** from Turkey
  ♦ **in der Türkei** in Turkey
  ♦ **in die Türkei** to Turkey

die **Türkin** NOUN
  Turk

  türkis ADJECTIVE
  turquoise

  türkisch ADJECTIVE
  Turkish

der **Turm** NOUN (PL die **Türme**)
  1 tower ◊ *die Türme der Burg* the castle towers
  2 steeple ◊ *Das Ulmer Münster hat den höchsten Kirchturm der Welt.* Ulm Cathedral has the world's highest steeple.

3 rook ◊ *Er machte einen Zug mit dem Turm.* He moved his rook.

das **Turnen** NOUN
  see also **turnen** VERB
  1 gymnastics ◊ *Die Russinnen sind im Turnen gut.* The Russian women are good at gymnastics.
  2 physical education ◊ *Wir haben in der vierten Stunde Turnen.* We have PE in the fourth period.

turnen VERB
  see also **das Turnen** NOUN
  1 to do gymnastics ◊ *Sie turnt nicht gern.* She doesn't like doing gymnastics.
  2 to perform ◊ *Sie hat die Kür hervorragend geturnt.* She performed the free programme brilliantly.

die **Turnhalle** NOUN
  gym

die **Turnhose** NOUN
  gym shorts ◊ *eine Turnhose* a pair of gym shorts

das **Turnier** NOUN (PL die **Turniere**)
  tournament

der **Turnschuh** NOUN (PL die **Turnschuhe**)
  trainer ◊ *ein Paar Turnschuhe* a pair of trainers

der **Turnverein** NOUN (PL die **Turnvereine**)
  sports club

das **Turnzeug** NOUN
  gym things ◊ *Wo ist mein Turnzeug?* Where are my gym things?

die **Tüte** NOUN
  bag

der **TÜV** NOUN (PL die **TÜVs**)
  (= *Technischer Überwachungsverein*)
  MOT ◊ *Mein Auto ist nicht durch den TÜV gekommen.* My car failed its MOT.

der **Typ** NOUN (PL die **Typen**)
  1 type ◊ *Er ist ein athletischer Typ.* He's an athletic type.
  2 bloke ◊ *der Typ da drüben* the bloke over there

typisch ADJECTIVE
  typical ◊ *typisch für* typical of

T

U

die **U-Bahn** NOUN
> underground ◊ *mit der U-Bahn fahren* to travel by underground

die **U-Bahn-Station** NOUN
> underground station

übel ADJECTIVE
> bad ◊ *ein übler Geruch* a bad smell ◊ *eine üble Lage* a bad situation ◊ *Nicht übel!* Not bad.
> ♦ **jemandem ist übel** somebody feels sick
> ♦ **Sie hat dir die Bemerkung übel genommen.** She was offended by your remark.

die **Übelkeit** NOUN
> nausea

übelnehmen VERB *see* **übel**

üben VERB
> to practise

über PREPOSITION, ADVERB

Use the accusative to express movement or a change of place. Use the dative when there is no change of place.

> **1** over ◊ *Über dem Tisch hängt eine Lampe.* There's a lamp hanging over the table. ◊ *Sie legten ein Brett über das Loch.* They put a board over the hole. ◊ *Flugzeuge dürfen nicht über dieses Gebiet fliegen.* Planes are not allowed to fly over this area. ◊ *Über Weihnachten bin ich zu Hause.* I'm at home over Christmas. ◊ *Wir fahren über die Feiertage zu meinen Eltern.* We're going to my parents over the holidays. ◊ *Kinder über zwölf Jahren* children over twelve years of age ◊ *Das hat über hundert Euro gekostet.* It cost over a hundred euros.
> ♦ **Das Flugzeug flog hoch über der Stadt.** The plane flew high above the town.
> ♦ **Ich bin den ganzen Tag über zu Hause.** I'm at home all day long.
> ♦ **zwei Grad über null** two degrees above zero
> ♦ **ein Scheck über zweihundert Euro** a cheque for two hundred euros
> **2** across ◊ *Er ging quer über das Feld.* He went across the field.
> **3** via ◊ *nach Köln über Aachen* to Cologne via Aachen ◊ *über Satellit* via satellite
> **4** about ◊ *Wir haben über das Wetter geredet.* We talked about the weather. ◊ *ein Buch über ...* a book about ...
> **5** through ◊ *Ich habe den Job über einen Freund bekommen.* I got the job through a friend.
> ♦ **über jemanden lachen** to laugh at somebody

> ♦ **Sie liebt ihn über alles.** She loves him more than anything.
> ♦ **über und über** over and over
> ♦ **über kurz oder lang** sooner or later
> ♦ **etwas über haben** to be fed up with something ◊ *Ich habe Kartoffeln langsam über.* I'm getting fed up with potatoes.

überall ADVERB
> everywhere

sich **überanstrengen** VERB (PERFECT **hat sich überanstrengt**)
> to overexert oneself

überaus ADVERB
> exceedingly

überbieten VERB (IMPERFECT **überbot,** PERFECT **hat überboten**)
> to outbid ◊ *Er bot zweitausend Euro, aber wir haben ihn überboten.* He bid two thousand euros but we outbid him.
> ♦ **einen Rekord überbieten** to break a record
> ♦ **sich überbieten** to excel oneself

der **Überblick** NOUN (PL die **Überblicke**)
> **1** view ◊ *Von hier aus hat man einen guten Überblick über das Gelände.* You can get a good view of the area from here.
> **2** overview ◊ *ein Überblick über die unregelmäßigen Verben* an overview of irregular verbs
> **3** overall impression ◊ *Ich muss mir erst mal einen Überblick verschaffen.* I have to get an overall impression first.
> ♦ **den Überblick verlieren** to lose track of things
> ♦ **Sie hat den Überblick über ihre Arbeit verloren.** She has no idea where she is with her work.

überdenken VERB (IMPERFECT **überdachte,** PERFECT **hat überdacht**)
> to think over

der **Überdruss** NOUN (GEN des **Überdrusses**)
> ♦ **bis zum Überdruss** ad nauseam

übereifrig ADJECTIVE
> overeager

übereinander ADVERB
> one on top of the other ◊ *Sie legte die Bücher übereinander.* She put one book on top of the other.
> ♦ **übereinander sprechen** to talk about each other

überempfindlich ADJECTIVE
> hypersensitive

überfahren VERB (PRESENT **überfährt,** IMPERFECT **überfuhr,** PERFECT **hat überfahren**)
> to run over ◊ *Die Katze wurde von einem Auto überfahren.* The cat was run over by a car.

die **Überfahrt** NOUN
crossing

der **Überfall** NOUN (PL die **Überfälle**)
[1] raid ◊ *ein Banküberfall* a bank raid
◊ *ein Überfall auf ein fremdes Land* a
raid on a foreign country
[2] assault ◊ *Er wurde das Opfer eines
Überfalls.* He was the victim of an
assault.

überfallen VERB (PRESENT **überfällt**, IMPERFECT
überfiel, PERFECT **hat überfallen**)
[1] to attack ◊ *Sie ist im Park überfallen
worden.* She was attacked in the park.
♦ **eine Bank überfallen** to raid a bank
[2] to descend on ◊ *Am Wochenende hat
mich meine Freundin mit ihren Eltern
überfallen.* My girlfriend and her parents
descended on me at the weekend.

überfällig ADJECTIVE
overdue

überfliegen VERB (IMPERFECT **überflog**, PERFECT
hat überflogen)
[1] to fly over ◊ *Flugzeuge dürfen
Wohngebiete nicht überfliegen.* Planes
are not allowed to fly over residential
areas.
[2] to skim through ◊ *Ich habe das Buch
nur überflogen.* I only skimmed through
the book.

überflüssig ADJECTIVE
superfluous

überfordern VERB (PERFECT **hat überfordert**)
to ask too much of ◊ *Unser Mathelehrer
überfordert uns.* Our maths teacher asks
too much of us.
♦ **Du solltest dich nicht überfordern.** You
shouldn't overtax yourself.

überfüllt ADJECTIVE
[1] overcrowded ◊ *Die Gefängnisse sind
völlig überfüllt.* The prisons are
completely overcrowded.
♦ **Die Straßen waren überfüllt.** The streets
were crowded with people.
[2] oversubscribed ◊ *Der Computerkurs
ist überfüllt.* The computer course is
oversubscribed.

der **Übergang** NOUN (PL die **Übergänge**)
[1] crossing ◊ *ein Fußgängerübergang* a
pedestrian crossing
[2] transition ◊ *der Übergang vom
Sommer zum Herbst* the transition from
summer to autumn

übergeben VERB (PRESENT **übergibt**, IMPERFECT
übergab, PERFECT **hat übergeben**)
to hand over ◊ *Sie hat uns die Schlüssel
übergeben.* She handed the keys over to
us.
♦ **sich übergeben** to be sick

überglücklich ADJECTIVE
overjoyed

überhaupt ADVERB
[1] at all ◊ *Kannst du überhaupt Auto
fahren?* Can you drive a car at all? ◊ *Hast*

du überhaupt zugehört? Have you been
listening at all? ◊ *Ich habe überhaupt
keine Lust.* I don't feel like it at all.
[2] in general ◊ *Die Engländer sind
überhaupt sehr höflich.* In general the
English are very polite.
♦ **überhaupt nicht** not at all ◊ *Der Film hat
mir überhaupt nicht gefallen.* I didn't like
the film at all.
♦ **überhaupt nichts** nothing at all ◊ *Was
hat er gesagt? – Überhaupt nichts.* What
did he say? – Nothing at all.
♦ **Er hat überhaupt nichts gesagt.** He
didn't say anything at all.

überheblich ADJECTIVE
arrogant

überholen VERB (PERFECT **hat überholt**)
[1] to overtake ◊ *Er hat rechts überholt.*
He overtook on the right.
[2] to check over ◊ *Ich muss mein
Fahrrad überholen.* I have to check my
bike over.

überholt ADJECTIVE
out-of-date

das **Überholverbot** NOUN (PL die
Überholverbote)
restriction on overtaking

überhören VERB (PERFECT **hat überhört**)
[1] not to hear ◊ *Sie hat das Klingeln
überhört.* She didn't hear the bell.
[2] to ignore ◊ *Deine Frechheit überhöre
ich.* I shall ignore your cheek.

überlassen VERB (PRESENT **überlässt**, IMPERFECT
überließ, PERFECT **hat überlassen**)
♦ **jemandem etwas überlassen** to leave
something up to somebody ◊ *Ich
überlasse es dir, wann du das machst.* I'll
leave it up to you when you do it.

überlasten VERB (PERFECT **hat überlastet**)
to overload ◊ *Der Aufzug war überlastet.*
The lift was overloaded.
♦ **Ich fühle mich überlastet.** I feel
overworked.

überleben VERB (PERFECT **hat überlebt**)
to survive

überlegen VERB (PERFECT **hat überlegt**)
see also **überlegen** ADJECTIVE
to think about ◊ *Ich muss mir deinen
Vorschlag überlegen.* I'll have to think
about your suggestion. ◊ *Überleg doch
mal.* Think about it.

überlegen ADJECTIVE
see also **überlegen** VERB
better ◊ *Er ist ihr in Englisch überlegen.*
He's better at English than she is.
♦ **Unsere Mannschaft hat überlegen
gewonnen.** Our team won convincingly.

die **Überlegung** NOUN
consideration

die **Überlieferung** NOUN
tradition

überlisten VERB (PERFECT **hat überlistet**)

U

to outwit

überm = über dem

übermäßig ADJECTIVE
excessive

übermorgen ADVERB
the day after tomorrow

übernächste ADJECTIVE
next but one
◆ **An der übernächsten Haltestelle muss ich aussteigen.** I need to get off at the next stop but one.

übernachten VERB (PERFECT **hat übernachtet**)
◆ **bei jemandem übernachten** to spend the night at somebody's house

die **Übernachtung** NOUN
overnight stay
◆ **Übernachtung mit Frühstück** bed and breakfast

übernehmen VERB (PRESENT **übernimmt**, IMPERFECT **übernahm**, PERFECT **hat übernommen**)
to take over ◊ *Er hat das Geschäft seines Vaters übernommen.* He's taken over his father's business. ◊ *Er hat das Amt des Klassensprechers übernommen.* He took over as class representative.
◆ **sich übernehmen** to take on too much

überprüfen VERB (PERFECT **hat überprüft**)
to check

überqueren VERB (PERFECT **hat überquert**)
to cross

überraschen VERB (PERFECT **hat überrascht**)
to surprise

überrascht ADJECTIVE
surprised

die **Überraschung** NOUN
surprise

überreden VERB (PERFECT **hat überredet**)
to persuade ◊ *Kannst du sie nicht überreden mitzukommen?* Can't you persuade her to come?

übers = über das

das **Überschallflugzeug** NOUN (PL die **Überschallflugzeuge**)
supersonic jet

überschätzen VERB (PERFECT **hat überschätzt**)
to overestimate

überschlagen VERB (PRESENT **überschlägt**, IMPERFECT **überschlug**, PERFECT **hat überschlagen**)
to estimate ◊ *Wir sollten die Kosten für das Fest überschlagen.* We should estimate how much the party will cost.
◆ **eine Seite überschlagen** to miss a page
◆ **Das Auto hat sich überschlagen.** The car rolled over.

überschnappen VERB (PERFECT **ist übergeschnappt**)
to flip one's lid ◊ *Du bist wohl übergeschnappt!* You've flipped your lid!

die **Überschrift** NOUN
heading

der **Überschuss** NOUN (GEN des **Überschusses**, PL die **Überschüsse**)
◆ **ein Überschuss an** a surplus of

überschüssig ADJECTIVE
surplus

überschütten VERB (PERFECT **hat überschüttet**)
◆ **jemanden mit etwas überschütten** to shower somebody with something ◊ *Sie haben uns mit Geschenken überschüttet.* They showered us with presents.

die **Überschwemmung** NOUN
flood

übersehen VERB (PRESENT **übersieht**, IMPERFECT **übersah**, PERFECT **hat übersehen**)
[1] to overlook ◊ *Sie hat ein paar Fehler übersehen.* She overlooked a couple of mistakes.
[2] to see ◊ *Wir können die Folgen noch nicht übersehen.* We can't see the consequences yet.

übersetzen VERB (PERFECT **hat übersetzt**)
to translate ◊ *Übersetzt den Text ins Englische.* Translate the text into English.

der **Übersetzer** NOUN (PL die **Übersetzer**)
translator

die **Übersetzerin** NOUN
translator

die **Übersetzung** NOUN
translation ◊ *Das war eine schwierige Übersetzung.* That was a difficult translation.

die **Übersicht** NOUN
[1] view ◊ *Von hier aus hat man eine gute Übersicht.* You get a good view from here.
[2] overview ◊ *eine Übersicht über die unregelmäßigen Verben* an overview of irregular verbs

übersichtlich ADJECTIVE
clear ◊ *Die Tabelle ist nicht besonders übersichtlich.* The table isn't particularly clear. ◊ *etwas übersichtlich gestalten* to arrange something clearly
◆ **ein übersichtliches Gelände** open country

überspringen VERB (IMPERFECT **übersprang**, PERFECT **hat übersprungen**)
[1] to jump over ◊ *Er hat die Hürde übersprungen.* He jumped over the hurdle.
[2] to skip ◊ *Das nächste Kapitel können wir überspringen.* We can skip the next chapter.

überstehen VERB (IMPERFECT **überstand**, PERFECT **hat überstanden**)
[1] to get over ◊ *Wir haben das Schlimmste überstanden.* We've got over the worst.

2 to survive ◊ *Die Pflanze hat den Winter nicht überstanden.* The plant didn't survive the winter.

übersteigen VERB (IMPERFECT **überstieg**, PERFECT **hat überstiegen**)
to exceed

überstimmen VERB (PERFECT **hat überstimmt**)
to outvote

die **Überstunden** FEM PL NOUN
overtime ◊ *Er macht viele Überstunden.* He does a lot of overtime.

überstürzen VERB (PERFECT **hat überstürzt**)
to rush ◊ *Du solltest nichts überstürzen.* You shouldn't rush into things.
♦ **sich überstürzen** to follow one another in rapid succession ◊ *Die Ereignisse überstürzten sich.* One event followed another in rapid succession.

überstürzt ADJECTIVE
rash ◊ *eine überstürzte Entscheidung* a rash decision
♦ **Sie sind überstürzt abgereist.** They left in a rush.

übertragen VERB (PRESENT **überträgt**, IMPERFECT **übertrug**, PERFECT **hat übertragen**)
see also **übertragen** ADJECTIVE
1 to broadcast ◊ *Wir übertragen das Spiel live.* We're broadcasting the game live.
2 to copy ◊ *Sie hat den Text in ihr Heft übertragen.* She copied the text into her exercise book.
♦ **eine Krankheit übertragen** to transmit an illness
♦ **Sie hat mir diese Aufgabe übertragen.** She has assigned this task to me.
♦ **sich übertragen auf** to spread to ◊ *Ihre Nervosität hat sich auf die Kinder übertragen.* Her nervousness spread to the children.

übertragen ADJECTIVE
see also **übertragen** VERB
figurative ◊ *die übertragene Bedeutung eines Wortes* the figurative meaning of a word

übertreffen VERB (PRESENT **übertrifft**, IMPERFECT **übertraf**, PERFECT **hat übertroffen**)
to surpass

übertreiben VERB (IMPERFECT **übertrieb**, PERFECT **hat übertrieben**)
to exaggerate

die **Übertreibung** NOUN
exaggeration

übertrieben ADJECTIVE
excessive

überwachen VERB (PERFECT **hat überwacht**)
1 to supervise ◊ *Wer soll die Kinder überwachen?* Who will supervise the children?
2 to keep under surveillance ◊ *Die Polizei überwacht ihn.* The police are keeping him under surveillance.

überwältigend ADJECTIVE
overwhelming

überweisen VERB (IMPERFECT **überwies**, PERFECT **hat überwiesen**)
to transfer

überwinden VERB (IMPERFECT **überwand**, PERFECT **hat überwunden**)
to overcome ◊ *Jetzt haben wir alle Schwierigkeiten überwunden.* Now we've overcome all difficulties.
♦ **sich überwinden** to force oneself ◊ *Ich musste mich überwinden, das zu essen.* I had to force myself to eat it.

überzeugen VERB (PERFECT **hat überzeugt**)
to convince

überzeugend ADJECTIVE
convincing

die **Überzeugung** NOUN
conviction ◊ *Er sagte es ohne große Überzeugung.* He said it without much conviction.

üblich ADJECTIVE
usual

das **U-Boot** NOUN (PL die **U-Boote**)
submarine

übrig ADJECTIVE
remaining ◊ *Die übrigen Gäste sind auch bald gegangen.* The remaining guests left soon afterwards.
♦ **Ist noch Kuchen übrig?** Is there any cake left?
♦ **die übrigen** the others
♦ **das Übrige** the rest
♦ **im Übrigen** besides
♦ **übrig bleiben** to be left
♦ **übrig lassen** to leave ◊ *Habt ihr uns etwas Kuchen übrig gelassen?* Have you left us any cake?

übrigens ADVERB
by the way ◊ *Übrigens, du schuldest mir noch zehn Euro.* By the way, you still owe me ten euros.

übrighaben VERB (PRESENT **hat übrig**, IMPERFECT **hatte übrig**, PERFECT **hat übriggehabt**)
♦ **für jemanden etwas übrighaben** to be fond of somebody

übriglassen VERB see **übrig**

die **Übung** NOUN
1 practice ◊ *Mir fehlt die Übung.* I need more practice.
♦ **Übung macht den Meister.** Practice makes perfect.
2 exercise ◊ *Bitte macht jetzt Übung dreizehn.* Please do exercise thirteen now. ◊ *eine Turnübung* a gym exercise

das **Ufer** NOUN (PL die **Ufer**)
1 bank ◊ *Wir saßen am Ufer des Rheins.* We sat on the bank of the Rhine.
2 shore ◊ *Treibholz, das ans Ufer gespült wurde* driftwood which was washed up onto the shore

U

die **Uhr** NOUN
1 clock ◊ *Die Uhr am Bahnhof sollte richtig gehen.* The station clock should be right.
2 watch ◊ *Er sah auf seine Uhr.* He looked at his watch.
♦ **Wie viel Uhr ist es?** What time is it?
♦ **ein Uhr** one o'clock
♦ **zwanzig Uhr** eight o'clock in the evening
♦ **um fünf Uhr** at five o'clock

der **Uhrzeiger** NOUN (PL die **Uhrzeiger**)
hand

der **Uhrzeigersinn** NOUN
♦ **im Uhrzeigersinn** clockwise
♦ **entgegen dem Uhrzeigersinn** anticlockwise

die **Uhrzeit** NOUN
time

ulkig ADJECTIVE
funny

der **Ultraschall** NOUN
ultrasound

um PREPOSITION, CONJUNCTION, ADVERB
see also **umso** CONJUNCTION

The preposition um takes the accusative.
1 round ◊ *Sie legte sich einen Schal um den Hals.* She wrapped a scarf round her neck. ◊ *Wir sind um die Stadt herumgefahren.* We drove round the town.
♦ **um Weihnachten** around Christmas
2 at ◊ *um acht Uhr* at eight o'clock
3 by ◊ *etwas um vier Zentimeter kürzen* to shorten something by four centimetres
♦ **um zehn Prozent teurer** ten per cent more expensive
♦ **um vieles besser** better by far
♦ **der Kampf um den Titel** the battle for the title
♦ **um Geld spielen** to play for money
♦ **um ... willen** for the sake of ...

um ... willen takes the genitive.
◊ *um deinetwillen* for your sake ◊ *um meiner Mutter willen* for my mother's sake
♦ **um ... zu** in order to ...

um ... zu is used with the infinitive.
◊ *Ich gehe in die Schule, um etwas zu lernen.* I go to school in order to learn something.
♦ **zu klug, um zu ...** too clever to ...
4 about ◊ *um die dreißig Leute* about thirty people
♦ **Die zwei Stunden sind um.** The two hours are up.

umarmen VERB (PERFECT **hat umarmt**)
to hug ◊ *Sie umarmten sich.* They hugged.

umblättern VERB (PERFECT **hat umgeblättert**)
to turn over

umbringen VERB (IMPERFECT **brachte um**, PERFECT **hat umgebracht**)
to kill

umdrehen VERB (PERFECT **hat umgedreht**)
to turn round ◊ *Dreh das Bild mal um.* Turn the picture round.
♦ **sich umdrehen** to turn round

umfallen VERB (PRESENT **fällt um**, IMPERFECT **fiel um**, PERFECT **ist umgefallen**)
to fall down

der **Umfang** NOUN
1 extent ◊ *Der Umfang der Arbeiten war am Anfang nicht absehbar.* The extent of the work couldn't be seen at the beginning.
2 circumference ◊ *Berechnet den Umfang des Kreises.* Calculate the circumference of the circle.

die **Umfrage** NOUN
poll

der **Umgang** NOUN
♦ **Solche Leute sind kein Umgang für dich.** You shouldn't go about with people like that.
♦ **Sie ist erfahren im Umgang mit Kindern.** She's very experienced in dealing with children.
♦ **Für Schüler ist der Umgang mit dem Computer selbstverständlich geworden.** It's become a matter of course for pupils to work with computers.

umgänglich ADJECTIVE
sociable

die **Umgangsformen** FEM PL NOUN
manners

die **Umgangssprache** NOUN
colloquial language

umgeben VERB (PRESENT **umgibt**, IMPERFECT **umgab**, PERFECT **hat umgeben**)
to surround

die **Umgebung** NOUN
1 surroundings ◊ *ein Haus in schöner Umgebung* a house in beautiful surroundings
2 environment ◊ *Diese Pflanze wächst am besten in sonniger Umgebung.* This plant grows best in a sunny environment.

umgehen (1) VERB (IMPERFECT **ging um**, PERFECT **ist umgegangen**)
Note that here the stress is on um.
♦ **mit jemandem grob umgehen** to treat somebody roughly
♦ **mit Geld sparsam umgehen** to be careful with one's money
♦ **Sie kann nicht gut mit Geld umgehen.** She's not very good with money.

umgehen (2) VERB (IMPERFECT **umging**, PERFECT **hat umgangen**)
Note that here the stress is on gehen.
to avoid ◊ *Dieses Problem sollten wir besser umgehen.* It would be better if we could avoid this problem.

umgehend ADJECTIVE
immediate

die **Umgehungsstraße** NOUN
bypass

umgekehrt ADJECTIVE, ADVERB

[1] reverse ◊ *in umgekehrter Reihenfolge* in reverse order

♦ **Es war nicht so, es war genau umgekehrt.** It wasn't like that, it was exactly the opposite.

[2] the other way around ◊ *Du musst das Bild umgekehrt hängen.* You'll have to hang the picture the other way round. ◊ *Mach das doch umgekehrt, und fang hiermit an.* Do it the other way round and start here.

♦ **... und umgekehrt** ... and vice versa

umhauen VERB (PERFECT **hat umgehauen**)

[1] to bowl over ◊ *Die Neuigkeit wird dich umhauen.* The news will bowl you over.

[2] to fell ◊ *Sie haben die alte Eiche umgehauen.* They've felled the old oak tree.

umherziehen VERB (IMPERFECT **zog umher**, PERFECT **ist umhergezogen**)
to wander from place to place

sich **umhören** VERB (PERFECT **hat sich umgehört**)
to ask around

umkehren VERB (PERFECT **hat/ist umgekehrt**)

*For the perfect tense use **haben** when the verb has an object and **sein** when there is no object.*

[1] to turn back ◊ *Wir sind auf halbem Weg umgekehrt.* We turned back halfway.

[2] to turn round ◊ *Warum hast du das Bild umgekehrt?* Why did you turn the picture round?

[3] to turn inside out ◊ *Sie hat ihre Tasche umgekehrt, den Schlüssel aber nicht gefunden.* She turned her bag inside out but couldn't find the key.

[4] to turn upside down ◊ *Kehr mal den Eimer um, dann kann ich mich draufstellen.* Turn the bucket upside down so that I can stand on it.

umkippen VERB (PERFECT **hat/ist umgekippt**)

*For the perfect tense use **haben** when the verb has an object and **sein** when there is no object.*

[1] to tip over ◊ *Der Stuhl ist umgekippt.* The chair tipped over.

[2] to overturn ◊ *Sie haben das Boot umgekippt.* They overturned the boat.

[3] to keel over ◊ *Wenn ich Blut sehe, kippe ich immer um.* I keel over whenever I see blood.

die **Umkleidekabine** NOUN
changing cubicle

der **Umkleideraum** NOUN (PL die **Umkleideräume**)
changing room

umkommen VERB (IMPERFECT **kam um**, PERFECT **ist umgekommen**)
to be killed ◊ *Alle Passagiere sind umgekommen.* All the passengers were killed.

der **Umkreis** NOUN (GEN des **Umkreises**, PL die **Umkreise**)
neighbourhood

♦ **im Umkreis von** within a radius of

die **Umlage** NOUN

♦ **Wir haben eine Umlage gemacht.** We shared the costs.

der **Umlaut** NOUN (PL die **Umlaute**)
umlaut

umlegen VERB (PERFECT **hat umgelegt**)

[1] to put on ◊ *Du solltest dir eine Jacke umlegen.* You should put on a jacket.

♦ **die Kosten für etwas umlegen** to divide the cost of something

[2] to bump off ◊ *Er ist von der Mafia umgelegt worden.* He was bumped off by the Mafia.

umleiten VERB (PERFECT **hat umgeleitet**)
to divert

die **Umleitung** NOUN
diversion

umrechnen VERB (PERFECT **hat umgerechnet**)
to convert

die **Umrechnung** NOUN
conversion

der **Umrechnungskurs** NOUN (GEN des **Umrechnungskurses**, PL die **Umrechnungskurse**)
rate of exchange

der **Umriss** NOUN (GEN des **Umrisses**, PL die **Umrisse**)
outline

umrühren VERB (PERFECT **hat umgerührt**)
to stir

ums = **um das**

der **Umsatz** NOUN (GEN des **Umsatzes**, PL die **Umsätze**)
turnover

umschalten VERB (PERFECT **hat umgeschaltet**)
to switch ◊ *Schalt bitte ins zweite Programm um.* Please switch over to Channel two.

♦ **Die Ampel hat auf Gelb umgeschaltet.** The traffic lights changed to amber.

♦ **Wir schalten um ins Studio.** We'll now go back to the studio.

sich **umschauen** VERB (PERFECT **hat sich umgeschaut**)
to look round

der **Umschlag** NOUN (PL die **Umschläge**)

[1] cover ◊ *Alle meine Mathehefte haben einen schwarzen Umschlag.* All my maths exercise books have a black cover.

[2] jacket ◊ *Ich habe den Umschlag von dem Wörterbuch abgemacht.* I took the jacket off the dictionary.

U

3 envelope ◊ *Sie steckte den Brief in den Umschlag.* She put the letter in the envelope.

4 compress ◊ *Bei Fieber helfen kalte Umschläge.* Cold compresses help if you have a temperature.

die **Umschweife** MASC PL NOUN
 ◆ **ohne Umschweife** without beating about the bush

sich **umsehen** VERB (PRESENT **sieht sich um,** IMPERFECT **sah sich um,** PERFECT **hat sich umgesehen)**
 to look around ◊ *Als sie Schritte hörte, sah sie sich um.* When she heard steps, she looked around.
 ◆ **sich nach etwas umsehen** to look for something ◊ *Ich sehe mich zurzeit nach einer neuen Wohnung um.* I'm looking for a new flat at the moment.

umso CONJUNCTION
 so much ◊ *umso besser* so much the better ◊ *umso schlimmer* so much the worse
 ◆ **Je mehr ich höre, umso weniger verstehe ich.** The more I hear the less I understand.

umsonst ADVERB
 1 in vain ◊ *Wir haben umsonst gewartet.* We waited in vain.
 2 for nothing ◊ *Wir sind umsonst ins Museum gekommen.* We got into the museum for nothing.
 ◆ **Diese Broschüre gibt es umsonst.** This brochure is free of charge.

der **Umstand** NOUN (PL die **Umstände)**
 circumstance ◊ *unter keinen Umständen* under no circumstances
 ◆ **Wenn es keine Umstände macht.** If it's no trouble.
 ◆ **unter Umständen** possibly
 ◆ **in anderen Umständen sein** to be pregnant

umständlich ADJECTIVE
 1 complicated ◊ *Das ist aber umständlich, wie du das machst.* The way you do it is complicated.
 2 long-winded ◊ *eine umständliche Erklärung* a long-winded explanation
 ◆ **Werner ist ziemlich umständlich.** Werner makes life difficult for himself.

umsteigen VERB (IMPERFECT **stieg um,** PERFECT **ist umgestiegen)**
 to change ◊ *Wir müssen in München umsteigen.* We have to change in Munich.

umstellen (1) VERB (PERFECT **hat umgestellt)**
 *Note that here the stress is on **um**.*
 to move ◊ *Ich werde meinen Schreibtisch umstellen.* I'm going to move my desk.
 ◆ **Wann wurde in Großbritannien auf metrische Maße umgestellt?** When did Great Britain go over to the metric system?

 ◆ **sich umstellen** to adapt ◊ *Jetzt, wo das Baby da ist, müssen wir uns umstellen.* Now that the baby's here we have to adapt.

umstellen (2) VERB (PERFECT **hat umstellt)**
 *Note that here the stress is on **stellen**.*
 to surround ◊ *Die Polizei hat das Haus umstellt.* The police have surrounded the house.

umstritten ADJECTIVE
 controversial ◊ *ein umstrittenes Thema* a controversial subject

der **Umtausch** NOUN
 exchange

umtauschen VERB (PERFECT **hat umgetauscht)**
 to exchange

der **Umweg** NOUN (PL die **Umwege)**
 detour ◊ *Wir haben einen Umweg gemacht.* We made a detour.

die **Umwelt** NOUN
 environment

umweltfeindlich ADJECTIVE
 ecologically harmful

umweltfreundlich ADJECTIVE
 environment-friendly

der **Umweltschützer** NOUN (PL die **Umweltschützer)**
 environmentalist

die **Umweltverschmutzung** NOUN
 environmental pollution

umwerfen VERB (PRESENT **wirft um,** IMPERFECT **warf um,** PERFECT **hat umgeworfen)**
 to knock over ◊ *Wer hat den Stuhl umgeworfen?* Who knocked the chair over?
 ◆ **Diese Nachricht hat mich umgeworfen.** The news really threw me.

umwerfend ADJECTIVE
 fantastic

umziehen VERB (IMPERFECT **zog um,** PERFECT **hat/ist umgezogen)**
 *Use **haben** to form the perfect tense. Use **sein** to form the perfect tense for **to move**.*
 1 to change ◊ *Ich habe Carolin heute schon zweimal umgezogen.* I've already changed Carolin's clothes twice today.
 ◆ **sich umziehen** to get changed ◊ *Wenn ich mich umgezogen habe, können wir gehen.* We can go when I've got changed.
 2 to move ◊ *Mein Freund ist nach Bremen umgezogen.* My friend's moved to Bremen.

der **Umzug** NOUN (PL die **Umzüge)**
 1 move ◊ *Alle meine Freunde haben beim Umzug geholfen.* All my friends helped with the move.
 2 procession ◊ *Zu Karneval finden überall Umzüge statt.* There are processions everywhere during the Carnival.

unabhängig ADJECTIVE
independent

die **Unabhängigkeit** NOUN
independence

unangebracht ADJECTIVE
uncalled-for

unangenehm ADJECTIVE
unpleasant

die **Unannehmlichkeiten** FEM PL NOUN
trouble ◇ *Das gibt Unannehmlichkeiten mit dem Klassenlehrer.* That'll cause trouble with the class teacher.

unanständig ADJECTIVE
improper

unartig ADJECTIVE
naughty

unaufmerksam ADJECTIVE
inattentive

unausgeglichen ADJECTIVE
moody

unausstehlich ADJECTIVE
intolerable

unbeabsichtigt ADJECTIVE
unintentional

unbedeutend ADJECTIVE
unimportant

unbedingt ADJECTIVE, ADVERB
1 unconditional ◇ *Ich verlange unbedingten Gehorsam.* I demand unconditional obedience.
2 really ◇ *Er wollte unbedingt nach Hause.* He really wanted to go home. ◇ *Den Film musst du dir unbedingt ansehen.* You really have to see that film.

unbefriedigend ADJECTIVE
unsatisfactory

unbefriedigt ADJECTIVE
unsatisfied

unbegreiflich ADJECTIVE
inconceivable

unbehaglich ADJECTIVE
uncomfortable ◇ *Mir war's unbehaglich.* I felt uncomfortable. ◇ *Der Stuhl ist unbehaglich.* The chair is uncomfortable.
♦ **ein unbehagliches Gefühl** an uneasy feeling

unbekannt ADJECTIVE
unknown

unbeliebt ADJECTIVE
unpopular

unbequem ADJECTIVE
uncomfortable ◇ *Das Bett ist unbequem.* The bed's uncomfortable.
♦ **Er ist ein sehr unbequemer Mensch.** He's a very awkward person.

unbesetzt ADJECTIVE
vacant

unbestimmt ADJECTIVE
1 indefinite ◇ *der unbestimmte Artikel* the indefinite article

2 uncertain ◇ *Es ist noch unbestimmt, wann wir Ferien machen.* It's still uncertain when we're going on holiday.

unbewusst ADJECTIVE
unconscious

und CONJUNCTION
and
♦ **und so weiter** and so on
♦ **Na und?** So what?

undankbar ADJECTIVE
ungrateful

undeutlich ADJECTIVE
indistinct

uneben ADJECTIVE
uneven

unehrlich ADJECTIVE
dishonest

unempfindlich ADJECTIVE
practical ◇ *Wir brauchen für das Sofa einen unempfindlichen Bezug.* We need a practical cover for the sofa.
♦ **Ich bin gegen Kälte unempfindlich.** I don't feel the cold.

unendlich ADJECTIVE
infinite

unentschieden ADJECTIVE
undecided
♦ **unentschieden enden** to end in a draw

unerfahren ADJECTIVE
inexperienced

unerfreulich ADJECTIVE
unpleasant

unerträglich ADJECTIVE
unbearable ◇ *Die Schmerzen sind unerträglich.* The pain's unbearable.

unerwünscht ADJECTIVE
undesirable

unfähig ADJECTIVE
incapable ◇ *zu etwas unfähig sein* to be incapable of something

unfair ADJECTIVE
unfair

der **Unfall** NOUN (PL die **Unfälle**)
accident

unfreundlich ADJECTIVE
unfriendly

die **Unfreundlichkeit** NOUN
unfriendliness

der **Unfug** NOUN
1 mischief ◇ *Die Kinder machen dauernd Unfug.* The children are always getting up to mischief.
2 nonsense ◇ *Red nicht so einen Unfug.* Don't talk such nonsense.

der **Ungar** NOUN (GEN des **Ungarn**, PL die **Ungarn**)
Hungarian

die **Ungarin** NOUN
Hungarian

ungarisch ADJECTIVE
Hungarian

Ungarn NEUT NOUN

U

☞

Hungary
♦ **aus Ungarn** from Hungary
♦ **nach Ungarn** to Hungary

ungebildet ADJECTIVE
uneducated

die **Ungeduld** NOUN
impatience

ungeduldig ADJECTIVE
impatient

ungeeignet ADJECTIVE
unsuitable

ungefähr ADJECTIVE
approximate ◊ *Kannst du mir eine ungefähre Zeit nennen?* Can you give me an approximate time? ◊ *um ungefähr zwei Uhr* at approximately two o'clock

ungefährlich ADJECTIVE
harmless

das **Ungeheuer** NOUN (PL die **Ungeheuer**)
see also **ungeheuer** ADJECTIVE, ADVERB
monster ◊ *das Ungeheuer von Loch Ness* the Loch Ness monster

ungeheuer ADJECTIVE, ADVERB
see also **das Ungeheuer** NOUN
1 huge ◊ *eine ungeheure Menge* a huge amount
2 extremely ◊ *Das war ungeheuer nett von dir.* That was extremely nice of you.

ungehörig ADJECTIVE
impertinent

der **Ungehorsam** NOUN
see also **ungehorsam** ADJECTIVE
disobedience

ungehorsam ADJECTIVE
see also **der Ungehorsam** NOUN
disobedient

ungeklärt ADJECTIVE
unsolved ◊ *ein ungeklärtes Rätsel* an unsolved puzzle

ungelegen ADJECTIVE
inconvenient ◊ *Ich hoffe, ich komme nicht ungelegen.* I hope I haven't come at an inconvenient time.

ungelernt ADJECTIVE
unskilled ◊ *ein ungelernter Arbeiter* an unskilled worker

ungemütlich ADJECTIVE
1 uncomfortable ◊ *ein ungemütlicher Stuhl* an uncomfortable chair
2 disagreeable ◊ *Jetzt wird er ungemütlich.* Now he's going to get disagreeable.

ungenau ADJECTIVE
inaccurate

ungenießbar ADJECTIVE
1 inedible ◊ *Das Essen war ungenießbar.* The food was inedible.
2 undrinkable ◊ *Diese Limonade ist ungenießbar.* This lemonade's undrinkable.

3 unbearable ◊ *Du bist heute aber ungenießbar.* You're really unbearable today.

ungenügend ADJECTIVE
1 insufficient ◊ *eine ungenügende Menge* an insufficient amount
2 unsatisfactory

🛈 German marks range from one (**sehr gut**) to six (**ungenügend**).

---

ungepflegt ADJECTIVE
♦ **ein ungepflegter Garten** a neglected garden
♦ **ungepflegte Hände** uncared-for hands

ungerade ADJECTIVE
♦ **eine ungerade Zahl** an odd number

ungerecht ADJECTIVE
unjust

die **Ungerechtigkeit** NOUN
injustice

ungern ADVERB
reluctantly

ungeschickt ADJECTIVE
clumsy

ungestört ADJECTIVE
undisturbed

ungesund ADJECTIVE
unhealthy

ungewiss ADJECTIVE
uncertain

die **Ungewissheit** NOUN
uncertainty

ungewöhnlich ADJECTIVE
unusual

ungewohnt ADJECTIVE
unaccustomed

das **Ungeziefer** NOUN
vermin

ungezogen ADJECTIVE
rude

ungezwungen ADJECTIVE
natural

unglaublich ADJECTIVE
incredible

das **Unglück** NOUN (PL die **Unglücke**)
1 accident ◊ *Er ist bei einem Unglück ums Leben gekommen.* He lost his life in an accident.
2 misfortune ◊ *Lass sie in ihrem Unglück nicht allein.* Don't leave her alone in her misfortune.
♦ **Eine schwarze Katze bringt Unglück.** A black cat means bad luck.

unglücklich ADJECTIVE
1 unhappy ◊ *Sie ist furchtbar unglücklich.* She's terribly unhappy.
2 unfortunate ◊ *ein unglücklicher Zufall* an unfortunate coincidence ◊ *eine unglückliche Formulierung* an unfortunate choice of words

♦ **Sie ist unglücklich gefallen.** She fell awkwardly.

unglücklicherweise ADVERB
unfortunately

ungültig ADJECTIVE
invalid

ungünstig ADJECTIVE
unfavourable

unheilbar ADJECTIVE
incurable

unheimlich ADJECTIVE, ADVERB
1 weird ◊ *Das war ein unheimliches Geräusch.* That was a weird noise.
♦ **Mir wird's etwas unheimlich.** I'm getting a bit scared.
2 incredibly ◊ *Das hat mich unheimlich gefreut.* I was incredibly pleased about it.

unhöflich ADJECTIVE
impolite

die **Uni** NOUN (PL die **Unis**)
uni

die **Uniform** NOUN
uniform

uninteressant ADJECTIVE
uninteresting

die **Universität** NOUN
university

die **Unkenntnis** NOUN
ignorance

unklar ADJECTIVE
unclear
♦ **über etwas im Unklaren sein** to be unclear about something ◊ *Ich bin mir über mein Berufsziel noch im Unklaren.* I'm still unclear about what I want to do.
♦ **jemanden über etwas im Unklaren lassen** to leave somebody in the dark about something

unklug ADJECTIVE
unwise

die **Unkosten** PL NOUN
expenses

unleserlich ADJECTIVE
illegible

unlogisch ADJECTIVE
illogical

unlösbar ADJECTIVE
insoluble ◊ *ein unlösbares Problem* an insoluble problem

unmissverständlich ADJECTIVE
unmistakeable

unmittelbar ADJECTIVE
immediate

unmöglich ADJECTIVE
impossible

die **Unmöglichkeit** NOUN
impossibility

unmoralisch ADJECTIVE
immoral

unnötig ADJECTIVE
unnecessary

unordentlich ADJECTIVE
untidy

die **Unordnung** NOUN
disorder

unparteiisch ADJECTIVE
impartial

unpassend ADJECTIVE
1 inappropriate ◊ *unpassende Kleidung* inappropriate clothes
2 inopportune ◊ *zu einer unpassenden Zeit* at an inopportune time

unpersönlich ADJECTIVE
impersonal ◊ *das unpersönliche Fürwort* the impersonal pronoun

unpraktisch ADJECTIVE
unpractical

unpünktlich ADJECTIVE
♦ **Sie ist immer unpünktlich.** She's always late.

das **Unrecht** NOUN
see also **unrecht** ADJECTIVE
wrong ◊ *ein großes Unrecht* a great wrong
♦ **zu Unrecht** wrongly

unrecht ADJECTIVE
see also **das Unrecht** NOUN
wrong ◊ *Du tust ihr unrecht.* You are wronging her.
♦ **unrecht haben** to be wrong

unregelmäßig ADJECTIVE
irregular ◊ *ein unregelmäßiges Verb* an irregular verb

unreif ADJECTIVE
1 not ripe ◊ *Der Apfel ist noch unreif.* The apple's not ripe yet.
2 immature ◊ *Elisabeth ist noch furchtbar unreif.* Elisabeth's still terribly immature.

unrichtig ADJECTIVE
incorrect

die **Unruhe** NOUN
unrest

der **Unruhestifter** NOUN (PL die **Unruhestifter**)
troublemaker

unruhig ADJECTIVE
restless

uns PRONOUN
uns is the accusative and dative of wir.
1 us ◊ *Sie haben uns eingeladen.* They've invited us.
2 to us ◊ *Sie haben es uns gegeben.* They gave it to us.
3 ourselves ◊ *Wir fragen uns, ob das sein muss.* We're asking ourselves whether that is necessary.
4 each other ◊ *Wir lieben uns.* We love each other.

unschlagbar ADJECTIVE
invincible

die **Unschuld** NOUN
innocence

unschuldig ADJECTIVE
innocent

U

unselbstständig ADJECTIVE
dependent

unser ADJECTIVE

1 our ◊ *Unser Deutschlehrer ist nett.* Our German teacher's nice. ◊ *Unsere Mathelehrerin ist streng.* Our maths teacher's strict. ◊ *Unser Haus ist ganz in der Nähe der Schule.* Our house is very near the school. ◊ *Unsere Lehrer sind prima.* Our teachers are great.

2 ours ◊ *Das ist nicht euer Lehrer, das ist unserer.* He's not your teacher, he's ours. ◊ *Seine Note war besser als unsere.* His mark was better than ours. ◊ *Wenn du kein Wörterbuch hast, kannst du unseres mitbenutzen.* If you don't have a dictionary, you can use ours. ◊ *Deine Eltern sind netter als unsere.* Your parents are nicer than ours.

unseretwegen ADVERB

1 for our sake ◊ *Ihr braucht unseretwegen nicht zu warten.* You needn't wait for our sake.

2 on our account ◊ *Hat sie sich unseretwegen so aufgeregt?* Did she get so upset on our account?

3 as far as we're concerned ◊ *Unseretwegen kann man das gern anders machen.* As far as we're concerned you're welcome to do it differently.

unsicher ADJECTIVE

1 uncertain ◊ *Es ist unsicher, ob wir kommen können.* It's uncertain whether we can come.

2 insecure ◊ *Elisabeth ist sehr unsicher.* Elisabeth's very insecure.

unsichtbar ADJECTIVE
invisible

der **Unsinn** NOUN
nonsense ◊ *Unsinn erzählen* to talk nonsense
♦ **Unsinn machen** to do silly things

unsportlich ADJECTIVE
not sporty ◊ *Tobias ist ziemlich unsportlich.* Tobias is not at all sporty.
♦ **unsportliches Verhalten** unsportsmanlike behaviour

unsre = **unsere**

unsympathisch ADJECTIVE
unpleasant ◊ *ein unsympathischer Mensch* an unpleasant person
♦ **Er ist mir unsympathisch.** I don't like him.

unten ADVERB

1 at the bottom ◊ *Das beste Buch lag unten auf dem Stapel.* The best book was at the bottom of the pile.

2 downstairs ◊ *Mutter ist unten in der Küche.* Mother's downstairs in the kitchen.

3 at the bottom ◊ *Er stand unten an der Treppe.* He was standing at the bottom of the stairs. ◊ *unten am Berg* at the bottom of the mountain
♦ **nach unten** down

unter PREPOSITION

1 under

Use the accusative to express movement or a change of place. Use the dative when there is no change of place.

◊ *Die Katze lag unter dem Tisch.* The cat lay under the table. ◊ *Der Ball rollte unter den Tisch.* The ball rolled under the table. ◊ *unter achtzehn Jahren* under eighteen years of age
♦ **Die Temperaturen sanken unter null.** The temperatures dropped below zero degrees.

2 among ◊ *Unter den Büchern war auch ein Atlas.* There was also an atlas among the books.
♦ **Sie waren unter sich.** They were by themselves.
♦ **einer unter ihnen** one of them
♦ **unter anderem** among other things

das **Unterbewusstsein** NOUN
subconscious

unterbrechen VERB (PRESENT **unterbricht**, IMPERFECT **unterbrach**, PERFECT **hat unterbrochen**)
to interrupt

die **Unterbrechung** NOUN
interruption

unterdrücken VERB (PERFECT **hat unterdrückt**)
to suppress ◊ *Sie unterdrückte ein Lächeln.* She suppressed a smile.
♦ **Menschen unterdrücken** to oppress people

untere ADJECTIVE
lower ◊ *die unteren Stockwerke* the lower floors

die **Unterführung** NOUN
underpass

untergehen VERB (IMPERFECT **ging unter**, PERFECT **ist untergegangen**)

1 to sink

2 to set ◊ *sobald die Sonne untergegangen ist ...* as soon as the sun has set ...
♦ **Die Welt geht unter.** The world's coming to an end.
♦ **Seine Rede ging im Lärm unter.** His speech was drowned out by the noise.

das **Untergeschoss** NOUN
basement

unterhalb PREPOSITION

*The preposition **unterhalb** takes the genitive.*

below ◊ *Ihr Haus befindet sich unterhalb der Kirche.* Her house is below the church.

unterhalten VERB (PRESENT **unterhält**, IMPERFECT **unterhielt**, PERFECT **hat unterhalten**)

1 to entertain ◊ *Sie hat uns den ganzen Abend mit lustigen Geschichten unterhalten.* She entertained us with funny stories all evening.

2 to run ◊ *Das Schwimmbad wird von der Stadt unterhalten.* The swimming pool is run by the town council.

♦ **sich unterhalten** to talk ◊ *Wir haben uns über dich unterhalten.* We talked about you.

unterhaltsam ADJECTIVE
entertaining

die **Unterhaltung** NOUN
1 talk ◊ *Es war eine sehr aufschlussreiche Unterhaltung.* It was a very informative talk.
2 entertainment ◊ *Zur Unterhaltung der Gäste spielt die örtliche Musikkapelle.* Entertainment will be provided by the local brass band.

das **Unterhemd** NOUN (PL die **Unterhemden**)
vest

die **Unterhose** NOUN
underpants ◊ *eine Unterhose* a pair of underpants

die **Unterkunft** NOUN (PL die **Unterkünfte**)
accommodation

der **Untermieter** NOUN (PL die **Untermieter**)
lodger

das **Unternehmen** NOUN (PL die **Unternehmen**)
see also **unternehmen** VERB
enterprise

unternehmen VERB (PRESENT **unternimmt**, IMPERFECT **unternahm**, PERFECT **hat unternommen**)
see also **das Unternehmen** NOUN
♦ **Was sollen wir heute unternehmen?** What shall we do today?

der **Unternehmer** NOUN (PL die **Unternehmer**)
entrepreneur

unternehmungslustig ADJECTIVE
enterprising

der **Unterricht** NOUN
lessons ◊ *Nachmittags haben wir selten Unterricht.* We seldom have lessons in the afternoon.

unterrichten VERB (PERFECT **hat unterrichtet**)
1 to teach ◊ *Sie unterrichtet Englisch.* She teaches English.
♦ **Wer unterrichtet euch in Sport?** Who do you have for sport?
2 to inform ◊ *Wir müssen deine Eltern davon unterrichten.* We'll have to inform your parents.

das **Unterrichtsfach** NOUN (PL die **Unterrichtsfächer**)
subject

der **Unterrock** NOUN (PL die **Unterröcke**)
underskirt

untersagt ADJECTIVE
forbidden

unterschätzen VERB (PERFECT **hat unterschätzt**)
to underestimate

unterscheiden VERB (IMPERFECT **unterschied**, PERFECT **hat unterschieden**)
to distinguish ◊ *Man muss zwischen Sachlichkeit und Unfreundlichkeit unterscheiden.* You have to distinguish between objectivity and unfriendliness.
♦ **sich unterscheiden** to differ

der **Unterschied** NOUN (PL die **Unterschiede**)
difference
♦ **im Unterschied zu** as distinct from

unterschiedlich ADJECTIVE
different ◊ *Sie haben sehr unterschiedliche Begabungen.* They have very different talents. ◊ *Sie sind unterschiedlich groß.* They're different sizes.
♦ **Das Wetter war sehr unterschiedlich.** The weather was mixed.

unterschreiben VERB (IMPERFECT **unterschrieb**, PERFECT **hat unterschrieben**)
to sign ◊ *Du musst das Zeugnis unterschreiben lassen.* You have to have the report signed.

die **Unterschrift** NOUN
signature

unterste ADJECTIVE
bottom ◊ *Es ist im untersten Fach.* It's on the bottom shelf.
♦ **Sie ist in der untersten Klasse.** She's in the first form.

sich **unterstellen (1)** VERB (PERFECT **hat sich untergestellt**)
*Note that here the stress is on **unter**.*
to take shelter ◊ *Es hat so stark geregnet, dass wir uns unterstellen mussten.* It was raining so heavily that we had to take shelter.

unterstellen (2) VERB (PERFECT **hat unterstellt**)
*Note that here the stress is on **stellen**.*
to imply ◊ *Willst du mir vielleicht unterstellen, dass ich das absichtlich getan habe?* Are you perhaps implying that I did it on purpose?

unterstreichen VERB (IMPERFECT **unterstrich**, PERFECT **hat unterstrichen**)
to underline

die **Unterstufe** NOUN
lower school

unterstützen VERB (PERFECT **hat unterstützt**)
to support

die **Unterstützung** NOUN
support

untersuchen VERB (PERFECT **hat untersucht**)
to examine

die **Untersuchung** NOUN
examination

die **Untertasse** NOUN
saucer ◊ *eine fliegende Untertasse* a flying saucer

U

das **Unterteil** NOUN (PL die **Unterteile**)
lower part

unterteilen VERB (PERFECT **hat unterteilt**)
to divide up

der **Untertitel** NOUN (PL die **Untertitel**)
subtitle

die **Unterwäsche** NOUN
underwear

unterwegs ADVERB
on the way

untreu ADJECTIVE
unfaithful

untrinkbar ADJECTIVE
undrinkable

untröstlich ADJECTIVE
inconsolable

unübersichtlich ADJECTIVE
unclear

ununterbrochen ADJECTIVE
uninterrupted

unveränderlich ADJECTIVE
unchangeable

unverantwortlich ADJECTIVE
irresponsible

unverbesserlich ADJECTIVE
incorrigible

unverbleit ADJECTIVE
unleaded ◊ *Ich fahre unverbleit.* I use
unleaded.

unvergesslich ADJECTIVE
unforgettable

unvermeidlich ADJECTIVE
unavoidable

unvernünftig ADJECTIVE
foolish

unverschämt ADJECTIVE
impudent

die **Unverschämtheit** NOUN
impudence

unverständlich ADJECTIVE
unintelligible
♦ **Es ist mir unverständlich, wie ...** I just
don't understand how ...

unverzeihlich ADJECTIVE
unpardonable

unvollkommen ADJECTIVE
imperfect

unvollständig ADJECTIVE
incomplete

unvorbereitet ADJECTIVE
unprepared

unvoreingenommen ADJECTIVE
unbiased

unvorsichtig ADJECTIVE
careless

unvorstellbar ADJECTIVE
inconceivable

unwahr ADJECTIVE
untrue

unwahrscheinlich ADJECTIVE, ADVERB
1 unlikely ◊ *eine unwahrscheinliche*
Geschichte an unlikely story
2 incredibly ◊ *Ich habe mich*
unwahrscheinlich gefreut. I was
incredibly pleased.

unwichtig ADJECTIVE
unimportant

unwirksam ADJECTIVE
ineffective

unzählig ADJECTIVE
countless

unzerbrechlich ADJECTIVE
unbreakable

unzertrennlich ADJECTIVE
inseparable

unzufrieden ADJECTIVE
dissatisfied

unzutreffend ADJECTIVE
incorrect

uralt ADJECTIVE
ancient

der **Ureinwohner** NOUN (PL die **Ureinwohner**)
original inhabitant

der **Urin** NOUN (PL die **Urine**)
urine

die **Urkunde** NOUN
certificate

der **Urlaub** NOUN (PL die **Urlaube**)
holiday ◊ *Wir fahren morgen in Urlaub.*
We're going on holiday tomorrow.

die **Ursache** NOUN
cause
♦ **Keine Ursache!** That's all right.

ursprünglich ADJECTIVE, ADVERB
1 original ◊ *Wir mussten unsere*
ursprünglichen Pläne aufgeben. We had
to abandon our original plans.
2 originally ◊ *Ursprünglich wollten wir*
nach Griechenland fahren. We originally
wanted to go to Greece.

das **Urteil** NOUN (PL die **Urteile**)
1 opinion ◊ *Wie lautet dein Urteil?*
What's your opinion?
2 sentence ◊ *Die Richter haben das*
Urteil noch nicht verkündet. The judges
haven't passed sentence yet.

urteilen VERB
to judge

der **Urwald** NOUN (PL die **Urwälder**)
jungle

die **Urzeit** NOUN
prehistoric times

die **USA** PL NOUN
USA
♦ **aus den USA** from the USA
♦ **in den USA** in the USA
♦ **nach den USA** to the USA

usw. ABBREVIATION (= *und so weiter*)
etc

utopisch ADJECTIVE
utopian

V

vage ADJECTIVE
vague

der **Vampir** NOUN (PL die **Vampire**)
vampire

die **Vanille** NOUN
vanilla

die **Vase** NOUN
vase

der **Vater** NOUN (PL die **Väter**)
father

väterlich ADJECTIVE
fatherly

das **Vaterunser** NOUN (PL die **Vaterunser**)
Lord's prayer

der **Vati** NOUN (PL die **Vatis**)
daddy

der **Vegetarier** NOUN (PL die **Vegetarier**)
vegetarian

die **Vegetarierin** NOUN
vegetarian

vegetarisch ADJECTIVE
vegetarian

das **Veilchen** NOUN (PL die **Veilchen**)
violet

die **Vene** NOUN
vein

das **Ventil** NOUN (PL die **Ventile**)
valve

der **Ventilator** NOUN (PL die **Ventilatoren**)
fan

verabreden VERB (PERFECT **hat verabredet**)
to arrange ◊ *Wir sollten Zeit und Ort des Treffens verabreden.* We ought to arrange when and where to meet.
♦ **sich mit jemandem verabreden** to arrange to meet somebody
♦ **mit jemandem verabredet sein** to have arranged to meet somebody ◊ *Ich bin mit meiner Mutter verabredet.* I've arranged to meet my mother.
♦ **Ich bin heute Abend mit meiner Freundin verabredet.** I'm seeing my girlfriend tonight.

die **Verabredung** NOUN
date
♦ **Ich habe um fünf eine Verabredung mit meiner Mutter.** I'm meeting my mother at five.

verabschieden VERB (PERFECT **hat verabschieden**)
to say goodbye to ◊ *Wir verabschiedeten unsere Gäste.* We said goodbye to our guests.
♦ **sich verabschieden** to take one's leave

verallgemeinern VERB (PERFECT **hat verallgemeinert**)
to generalize

veralten VERB (PERFECT **ist veraltet**)
to become obsolete

veränderlich ADJECTIVE
changeable

verändern VERB (PERFECT **hat verändert**)
to change
♦ **sich verändern** to change ◊ *Sie hat sich in den letzten beiden Monaten verändert.* She's changed in the last couple of months.

die **Veränderung** NOUN
change

die **Veranlagung** NOUN
disposition ◊ *eine nervöse Veranlagung* a nervous disposition

veranlassen VERB (PERFECT **hat veranlasst**)
♦ **etwas veranlassen** to have something done
♦ **Was hat dich veranlasst, so zu reagieren?** What made you react like that?
♦ **sich veranlasst sehen, etwas zu tun** to be prompted to do something

veranschaulichen VERB (PERFECT **hat veranschaulicht**)
to illustrate

veranstalten VERB (PERFECT **hat veranstaltet**)
to organize

der **Veranstalter** NOUN (PL die **Veranstalter**)
organizer

die **Veranstaltung** NOUN
event

verantworten VERB (PERFECT **hat verantwortet**)
to take responsibility for ◊ *Wenn das nicht klappt, hast du das zu verantworten.* If it doesn't work, you'll have to take responsibility for it.
♦ **Das kann ich nicht verantworten.** I couldn't possibly allow that.

verantwortlich ADJECTIVE
responsible

die **Verantwortung** NOUN
responsibility

verantwortungsbewusst ADJECTIVE
responsible

verantwortungslos ADJECTIVE
irresponsible

verarbeiten VERB (PERFECT **hat verarbeitet**)
1 to process ◊ *In diesem Werk wird Metall verarbeitet.* Metal is processed in this factory.
♦ **etwas zu etwas verarbeiten** to make something into something ◊ *Der Plastikmüll wird zu Parkbänken verarbeitet.* Plastic waste is made into park benches.

☞

②to digest ◊ *Ich muss die Reiseeindrücke erst noch verarbeiten.* I still have to digest my impressions from the journey.

verärgern VERB (PERFECT **hat verärgert**)
to annoy

das **Verb** NOUN (PL die **Verben**)
verb

der **Verband** NOUN (PL die **Verbände**)
①dressing
◆ *Die Schwester hat ihm einen Verband angelegt.* The nurse dressed his wound.
②association ◊ *Die Bauern haben sich zu einem Verband zusammengeschlossen.* The farmers have formed an association.

der **Verbandskasten** NOUN (PL die **Verbandskästen**)
first-aid box

das **Verbandszeug** NOUN
first-aid kit

verbergen VERB (PRESENT **verbirgt**, IMPERFECT **verbarg**, PERFECT **hat verborgen**)
to hide
◆ **sich vor jemandem verbergen** to hide from somebody

verbessern VERB (PERFECT **hat verbessert**)
①to improve ◊ *Ich konnte meine Noten verbessern.* I was able to improve my marks.
②to correct ◊ *Meine Mutter hat meine Hausaufgaben verbessert.* My mother corrected my homework.
◆ **sich verbessern** to improve ◊ *In Mathe habe ich mich verbessert.* I've improved in maths.

die **Verbesserung** NOUN
①improvement ◊ *eine Verbesserung seiner Leistungen* an improvement in his work
②correction ◊ *Schreibt bitte die Verbesserung ins Heft.* Please write the correction in your exercise book.

verbiegen VERB (IMPERFECT **verbog**, PERFECT **hat verbogen**)
to bend

verbieten VERB (IMPERFECT **verbot**, PERFECT **hat verboten**)
to forbid ◊ *Meine Mutter hat mir verboten, mit Frank auszugehen.* My mother forbade me to go out with Frank.

verbinden VERB (IMPERFECT **verband**, PERFECT **hat verbunden**)
①to combine ◊ *Ich habe das Nützliche mit dem Angenehmen verbunden.* I was able to combine business with pleasure.
②to bandage ◊ *Die Wunde muss verbunden werden.* The wound has to be bandaged.
◆ **jemandem die Augen verbinden** to blindfold somebody

③to connect ◊ *Ein Kanal verbindet die beiden Flüsse.* A canal connects the two rivers.
④to put through ◊ *Können Sie mich bitte mit Frau Karl verbinden?* Can you put me through to Mrs Karl, please? ◊ *Ich verbinde!* I'm putting you through.
◆ **Sie sind falsch verbunden.** You've got the wrong number.

verbindlich ADJECTIVE
①definite ◊ *Ich hätte gern eine verbindliche Antwort.* I'd like a definite answer.
②obliging ◊ *Die Verkäuferin war äußerst verbindlich.* The shop assistant was extremely obliging.

die **Verbindung** NOUN (PL die **Verbindungen**)
①connection ◊ *Es gibt eine direkte Verbindungen nach München.* There is a direct connection to Munich.
②communication ◊ *eine telefonische Verbindung* a telephone communication
◆ **eine chemische Verbindung** a compound

verbleit ADJECTIVE
leaded

verblüffen VERB (PERFECT **hat verblüfft**)
to amaze

die **Verblüffung** NOUN
amazement

verbluten VERB (PERFECT **ist verblutet**)
to bleed to death

verborgen ADJECTIVE
hidden

das **Verbot** NOUN (PL die **Verbote**)
ban ◊ *Die Regierung verhängte ein Verbot für Rindfleischimporte aus England.* The government imposed a ban on beef imports from England.

verboten ADJECTIVE
forbidden
◆ **Rauchen verboten!** No smoking

der **Verbrauch** NOUN
consumption

verbrauchen VERB (PERFECT **hat verbraucht**)
to use up ◊ *Das Gerät verbraucht viel Strom.* The machine uses up a lot of electricity.

der **Verbraucher** NOUN (PL die **Verbraucher**)
consumer

der **Verbrauchermarkt** NOUN (PL die **Verbrauchermärkte**)
hypermarket

das **Verbrechen** NOUN (PL die **Verbrechen**)
crime

der **Verbrecher** NOUN (PL die **Verbrecher**)
criminal

verbreiten VERB (PERFECT **hat verbreitet**)
①to spread ◊ *eine Krankheit verbreiten* to spread a disease
②to broadcast ◊ *eine Nachricht verbreiten* to broadcast a message

♦ **sich verbreiten** to spread ◊ *Die Seuche hat sich inzwischen im ganzen Land verbreitet.* The epidemic has since spread all over the country. ◊ *Die Nachricht von seinem Tod hat sich schnell verbreitet.* The news of his death spread quickly.

verbrennen VERB (IMPERFECT **verbrannte,** PERFECT **hat verbrannt**)
[1] to burn ◊ *In dieser Anlage wird Müll verbrannt.* Waste is burnt in this plant.
[2] to cremate ◊ *Sie möchte nach ihrem Tod verbrannt werden.* She'd like to be cremated when she dies.

verbringen VERB (IMPERFECT **verbrachte,** PERFECT **hat verbracht**)
to spend ◊ *Wir haben das Wochenende im Schwarzwald verbracht.* We spent the weekend in the Black Forest.

verbrühen VERB (PERFECT **hat verbrüht**)
to scald ◊ *Ich habe mir den Arm verbrüht.* I've scalded my arm.
♦ **sich verbrühen** to scald oneself ◊ *Pass auf, dass du dich nicht verbrühst.* Careful you don't scald yourself.

der **Verdacht** NOUN (PL die **Verdachte**)
suspicion

verdächtig ADJECTIVE
suspicious

verdächtigen VERB (PERFECT **hat verdächtigt**)
to suspect

verdammt ADJECTIVE, ADVERB
damned ◊ *Diese verdammten Fliegen!* These damned flies!
♦ **Verdammt noch mal!** Damn it all!
♦ **Verdammt!** Damn!

verdampfen VERB (PERFECT **ist verdampft**)
to evaporate

verdanken VERB (PERFECT **hat verdankt**)
♦ **jemandem sein Leben verdanken** to owe one's life to somebody ◊ *Sie verdankt ihm ihr Leben.* She owes her life to him.

verdauen VERB (PERFECT **hat verdaut**)
to digest

verdaulich ADJECTIVE
♦ **Das ist schwer verdaulich.** That's hard to digest.

die **Verdauung** NOUN
digestion

verderben VERB (PRESENT **verdirbt,** IMPERFECT **verdarb,** PERFECT **hat/ist verdorben**)
*Use **haben** to form the perfect tense. Use **sein** to form the perfect tense for **to go bad.***
[1] to ruin ◊ *Du verdirbst dir bei dem schlechten Licht die Augen.* You'll ruin your eyes in this bad light. ◊ *Er hat mir den Urlaub verdorben.* He ruined my holiday.
[2] to corrupt ◊ *Geld verdirbt den Menschen.* Money corrupts people.

♦ **es mit jemandem verderben** to get into somebody's bad books ◊ *Sie will es mit keinem verderben.* She doesn't want to get into anybody's bad books.
[3] to go bad ◊ *Die Wurst ist verdorben.* The sausage has gone bad.

verdienen VERB (PERFECT **hat verdient**)
[1] to earn ◊ *Wie viel verdient dein Vater?* How much does your father earn?
[2] to deserve ◊ *Du hast die Strafe verdient.* You deserved the punishment.

verdoppeln VERB (PERFECT **hat verdoppelt**)
to double

verdreifachen VERB (PERFECT **hat verdreifacht**)
to treble

verdünnen VERB (PERFECT **hat verdünnt**)
to dilute

verdunsten VERB (PERFECT **ist verdunstet**)
to evaporate

verdursten VERB (PERFECT **ist verdurstet**)
to die of thirst

verdutzt ADJECTIVE
nonplussed

der **Verein** NOUN (PL die **Vereine**)
club ◊ *ein Sportverein* a sports club

vereinbar ADJECTIVE
♦ **mit etwas vereinbar** compatible with something

vereinbaren VERB (PERFECT **hat vereinbart**)
to agree on

die **Vereinbarung** NOUN
agreement

vereinen VERB (PERFECT **hat vereint**)
[1] to unite ◊ *Das geteilte Land wurde wieder vereint.* The divided country was reunited.
[2] to reconcile ◊ *Ich kann das nicht mit meinem Gewissen vereinen.* I can't reconcile that with my conscience.
♦ **Mit vereinten Kräften schaffen wir das.** If we all pull together, we'll manage to do it.
♦ **die Vereinten Nationen** the United Nations

vereinfachen VERB (PERFECT **hat vereinfacht**)
to simplify

vereinigen VERB (PERFECT **hat vereinigt**)
to unite

vereinzelt ADJECTIVE
isolated ◊ *vereinzelte Schauer* isolated showers

vererben VERB (PERFECT **hat vererbt**)
to leave ◊ *Meine Oma hat mir all ihre Bücher vererbt.* My granny left me all her books.
♦ **sich vererben** to be hereditary ◊ *Krampfadern vererben sich.* Varicose veins are hereditary.

verfahren VERB (PRESENT **verfährt,** IMPERFECT **verfuhr,** PERFECT **hat/ist verfahren**)

V

1 to proceed ◊ *Wie sollen wir verfahren?* How shall we proceed?

2 to use up ◊ *Wir haben 50 Liter Benzin verfahren.* We have used up 50 litres of petrol.

♦ **Wir haben uns verfahren.** We have lost our way.

das **Verfahren** NOUN (PL die **Verfahren**)

1 process ◊ *Das ist ein neuartiges Verfahren zum Recyceln von Plastik.* This is a new recycling process for plastic.

2 proceedings ◊ *ein Verfahren gegen jemanden einleiten* to bring proceedings against somebody

die **Verfassung** NOUN

1 constitution ◊ *Die Opposition hat eine Änderung der Verfassung beantragt.* The opposition's called for an amendment to the constitution.

2 state ◊ *Ich bin nicht in der Verfassung, da mitzumachen.* I'm in no state to join in.

verfaulen VERB (PERFECT **ist verfault**)
to rot

verflixt ADJECTIVE
damn

verfolgen VERB (PERFECT **hat verfolgt**)

1 to pursue ◊ *Die Polizei verfolgte die Täter.* The police pursued the culprits.

♦ **Die Hunde verfolgten ihre Fährte.** The dogs tracked them.

2 to persecute ◊ *In vielen Ländern werden Minderheiten verfolgt.* Minorities are persecuted in many countries.

die **Verfolgung** NOUN

1 hunt ◊ *Die Verfolgung der Täter war erfolgreich.* The hunt for the culprits had a successful outcome.

2 persecution ◊ *die Verfolgung von Minderheiten* the persecution of minorities

verfügbar ADJECTIVE
available

die **Verfügung** NOUN

♦ **etwas zur Verfügung haben** to have something at one's disposal ◊ *Nicht alle Schüler haben einen Computer zur Verfügung.* Not all pupils have a computer at their disposal.

♦ **Die Bibliothek steht allen Schülern zur Verfügung.** The library's open to all pupils.

♦ **Sollten Sie meine Hilfe brauchen, stehe ich Ihnen zur Verfügung.** If you should need my help, I will be at your service.

verführen VERB (PERFECT **hat verführt**)

1 to tempt ◊ *Verführ mich nicht, ich habe schon zwei Stück Kuchen gegessen.* Don't tempt me, I've already had two pieces of cake.

2 to seduce ◊ *Er hat versucht, sie zu verführen.* He tried to seduce her.

vergammeln VERB (PERFECT **ist vergammelt**)

to go off ◊ *Pfui, das Fleisch ist ja total vergammelt.* Ugh, the meat's gone right off.

♦ **etwas vergammeln lassen** to let something go ◊ *Wir haben den Garten ziemlich vergammeln lassen.* We've rather let the garden go.

die **Vergangenheit** NOUN
past ◊ *in der Vergangenheit* in the past

vergasen VERB (PERFECT **hat vergast**)
to gas

der **Vergaser** NOUN (PL die **Vergaser**)
carburettor

vergaß VERB *see* **vergessen**

vergeben VERB (PRESENT **vergibt**, IMPERFECT **vergab**, PERFECT **hat vergeben**)

to forgive ◊ *Kannst du mir noch einmal vergeben?* Can you forgive me one more time? ◊ *Diese Lüge werde ich dir nie vergeben.* I'll never forgive you for that lie.

♦ **vergeben sein** to be taken ◊ *Tut mir leid, die Stelle ist schon vergeben.* Sorry, the job's already taken.

♦ **Er ist schon vergeben.** He's already spoken for.

vergeblich ADVERB, ADJECTIVE
in vain ◊ *Wir haben uns vergeblich bemüht.* We tried, but in vain. ◊ *All mein Reden war vergeblich.* All my words were in vain.

vergehen VERB (IMPERFECT **verging**, PERFECT **ist vergangen**)
to pass

♦ **Wie schnell die Zeit doch vergeht!** How time flies!

♦ **Mir ist der Appetit vergangen.** I've lost my appetite.

♦ **sich an jemandem vergehen** to indecently assault somebody ◊ *Er soll sich an kleinen Mädchen vergangen haben.* He's said to have indecently assaulted young girls.

vergessen VERB (PRESENT **vergisst**, IMPERFECT **vergaß**, PERFECT **hat vergessen**)
to forget ◊ *Ich habe seinen Namen vergessen.* I've forgotten his name.

♦ **Vergiss nicht, die Blumen zu gießen.** Remember to water the flowers.

vergesslich ADJECTIVE
forgetful

vergeuden VERB (PERFECT **hat vergeudet**)
to squander

vergewaltigen VERB (PERFECT **hat vergewaltigt**)
to rape ◊ *Er hat eine Frau vergewaltigt.* He raped a woman.

die **Vergewaltigung** NOUN
rape

sich **vergewissern** VERB (PERFECT **hat sich vergewissert**)
to make sure

vergiften VERB (PERFECT **hat vergiftet**)

to poison

die **Vergiftung** NOUN
poisoning

das **Vergissmeinnicht** NOUN (PL die **Vergissmeinnicht**)
forget-me-not

vergisst VERB *see* **vergessen**

der **Vergleich** NOUN (PL die **Vergleiche**)
comparison
♦ **im Vergleich zu** compared with

vergleichen VERB (IMPERFECT **verglich**, PERFECT **hat verglichen**)
to compare ◊ *Er hat mein Wörterbuch mit seinem verglichen.* He compared my dictionary with his. ◊ *Man kann doch Äpfel und Birnen nicht vergleichen.* You can't compare apples and pears.

das **Vergnügen** NOUN (PL die **Vergnügen**)
pleasure
♦ **Viel Vergnügen!** Have fun!

vergnügt ADJECTIVE
cheerful

vergraben VERB (PRESENT **vergräbt**, IMPERFECT **vergrub**, PERFECT **hat vergraben**)
to bury

vergrößern VERB (PERFECT **hat vergrößert**)
[1] to enlarge ◊ *Ich habe das Foto vergrößern lassen.* I had the photo enlarged.
[2] to extend ◊ *Wir wollen das Haus vergrößern.* We want to extend the house.
♦ **sich vergrößern** to grow larger ◊ *Die Klasse hat sich stark vergrößert.* The class has grown considerably larger.

die **Vergrößerung** NOUN
[1] enlargement ◊ *Kann man mit dem Kopierer auch Vergrößerungen machen?* Can you do enlargements with the copier as well?
[2] expansion ◊ *eine Vergrößerung der Firma* an expansion of the company

das **Vergrößerungsglas** NOUN (GEN des **Vergrößerungsglases**, PL die **Vergrößerungsgläser**)
magnifying glass

verhaften VERB (PERFECT **hat verhaftet**)
to arrest

das **Verhalten** NOUN
see also **verhalten** VERB
behaviour

sich **verhalten** VERB (PRESENT **verhält sich**, IMPERFECT **verhielt sich**, PERFECT **hat sich verhalten**)
see also **das Verhalten** NOUN
to behave ◊ *Er hat sich uns gegenüber sehr fair verhalten.* He behaved very fairly towards us.

das **Verhältnis** NOUN (GEN des **Verhältnisses**, PL die **Verhältnisse**)

Vergiftung → verhören

[1] affair ◊ *Er hat ein Verhältnis mit einer verheirateten Frau.* He's having an affair with a married woman.
[2] proportion ◊ *Unser Gehalt steht in keinem Verhältnis zu unserer Leistung.* Our salary is not in proportion to our efforts.
♦ **Verhältnisse (1)** conditions ◊ *Wenn die Verhältnisse anders wären, könnten wir die Arbeit schneller beenden.* If conditions were different we could get the work finished sooner.
♦ **Verhältnisse (2)** background ◊ *Er kommt aus bescheidenen Verhältnissen.* He comes from a modest background.
♦ **über seine Verhältnisse leben** to live beyond one's means

verhältnismäßig ADVERB
relatively

verhandeln VERB (PERFECT **hat verhandelt**)
to negotiate ◊ *Sie verhandeln einen Waffenstillstand.* They're negotiating a ceasefire.
♦ **Mein Fall wird nächste Woche vor dem Arbeitsgericht verhandelt.** My case is being heard by the industrial tribunal next week.

die **Verhandlung** NOUN
[1] negotiation ◊ *die Friedensverhandlungen* peace negotiations ◊ *Wir sind mit der Firma noch in Verhandlung.* We're still involved in negotiations with the company.
[2] trial ◊ *Die Verhandlung gegen Klitt ist morgen.* Klitt's trial is tomorrow.
[3] hearing ◊ *die Verhandlung vor dem Arbeitsgericht* the hearing before the industrial tribunal

verharmlosen VERB (PERFECT **hat verharmlost**)
to play down

verhauen VERB (PERFECT **hat verhauen**)
to beat up

verheerend ADJECTIVE
devastating

verheimlichen VERB (PERFECT **hat verheimlicht**)
♦ **jemandem etwas verheimlichen** to keep something secret from somebody

verheiratet ADJECTIVE
married

verhexen VERB (PERFECT **hat verhext**)
♦ **Es ist wie verhext.** It's jinxed.

verhindern VERB (PERFECT **hat verhindert**)
to prevent
♦ **verhindert sein** to be unable to make it ◊ *Ich bin leider verhindert.* I'm afraid I can't make it.

verhören VERB (PERFECT **hat verhört**)
[1] to interrogate ◊ *Die Polizei hat ihn verhört.* The police interrogated him.
[2] to examine ◊ *Der Zeuge wurde verhört.* The witness was examined.

V

♦ **sich verhören** to mishear ◊ *Ich muss mich wohl verhört haben.* I must have misheard.

verhungern VERB (PERFECT **ist verhungert**)
to starve to death

das **Verhütungsmittel** NOUN (PL die **Verhütungsmittel**)
contraceptive

sich **verirren** VERB (PERFECT **hat sich verirrt**)
to get lost ◊ *Wir hatten uns im Nebel verirrt.* We lost our way in the fog.

der **Verkauf** NOUN (PL die **Verkäufe**)
sale

verkaufen VERB (PERFECT **hat verkauft**)
to sell

der **Verkäufer** NOUN (PL die **Verkäufer**)
shop assistant ◊ *Der Verkäufer hat uns sehr gut beraten.* The shop assistant was extremely helpful.

die **Verkäuferin** NOUN
shop assistant ◊ *Sie ist Verkäuferin in einer Modeboutique.* She's a shop assistant in a fashion boutique.

der **Verkehr** NOUN
1 traffic ◊ *Heute war viel Verkehr auf den Straßen.* There was heavy traffic on the roads today.
2 intercourse ◊ *Haben Sie mit der Frau Verkehr gehabt?* Did you have intercourse with this woman?

die **Verkehrsampel** NOUN
traffic lights

das **Verkehrsamt** NOUN (PL die **Verkehrsämter**)
tourist office

die **Verkehrsmeldung** NOUN
traffic announcement

das **Verkehrsmittel** NOUN (PL die **Verkehrsmittel**)
means of transport

das **Verkehrsnetz** NOUN (GEN des **Verkehrsnetzes**, PL die **Verkehrsnetze**)
traffic network

das **Verkehrsschild** NOUN (PL die **Verkehrsschilder**)
road sign

der **Verkehrsunfall** NOUN (PL die **Verkehrsunfälle**)
traffic accident

das **Verkehrszeichen** NOUN (PL die **Verkehrszeichen**)
traffic sign

verkehrt ADJECTIVE
wrong ◊ *Das war die verkehrte Antwort.* That was the wrong answer.
♦ **verkehrt herum** back to front ◊ *Du hast deinen Pulli verkehrt herum an.* You've got your pullover on back to front.

sich **verkleiden** VERB (PERFECT **hat sich verkleidet**)
to dress up ◊ *Sie verkleidete sich als Hexe.* She dressed up as a witch.

verkleinern VERB (PERFECT **hat verkleinert**)
to reduce ◊ *Wir sollten den Zeilenabstand verkleinern.* We should reduce the line spacing.
♦ **sich verkleinern** to grow smaller ◊ *Die Klasse hat sich stark verkleinert.* The class has grown considerably smaller.

verklemmt ADJECTIVE
inhibited

der **Verlag** NOUN (PL die **Verlage**)
publisher

verlangen VERB (PERFECT **hat verlangt**)
to ask for ◊ *Ich verlange etwas mehr Verständnis.* I'm asking for a bit more understanding. ◊ *Wie viel hat er dafür verlangt?* How much did he ask for it?
♦ **Er hat zwanzig Euro dafür verlangt.** He charged twenty euros for it.
♦ **etwas von jemandem verlangen** to expect something of somebody ◊ *Unser Chemielehrer verlangt zu viel von uns.* Our chemistry teacher expects too much of us.

verlängern VERB (PERFECT **hat verlängert**)
1 to extend ◊ *Wir haben die Ferien um eine Woche verlängert.* We've extended our holiday by a week.
2 to lengthen ◊ *Wir müssen das Seil verlängern.* We'll have to lengthen the rope.

die **Verlängerungsschnur** NOUN (PL die **Verlängerungsschnüre**)
extension cable

verlassen VERB (PRESENT **verlässt**, IMPERFECT **verließ**, PERFECT **hat verlassen**)
see also **verlassen** ADJECTIVE
to leave ◊ *Er hat seine Frau und Kinder verlassen.* He's left his wife and children.
♦ **Verlassen Sie sofort das Gebäude!** Get out of the building immediately.
♦ **sich verlassen auf** to depend on ◊ *Ich kann mich doch auf dich verlassen.* I hope I can depend on you.

verlassen ADJECTIVE
see also **verlassen** VERB
1 deserted ◊ *eine verlassene Gegend* a deserted area ◊ *die verlassene Ehefrau* the deserted wife
2 empty ◊ *ein verlassenes Haus* an empty house
♦ **Sie fühlte sich allein und verlassen.** She felt all alone.

sich **verlaufen** VERB (PRESENT **verläuft sich**, IMPERFECT **verlief sich**, PERFECT **hat sich verlaufen**)
1 to get lost ◊ *Wir haben uns im Wald verlaufen.* We got lost in the forest.
2 to disperse ◊ *Nach Ende der Veranstaltung verlief sich die Menge.* After the event the crowd dispersed.

verlegen ADJECTIVE
embarrassed

♦ **nicht verlegen um** never at a loss for ◊ *Sie ist nie um eine Ausrede verlegen.* She's never at a loss for an excuse.

der **Verleih** NOUN (PL die **Verleihe**)
hire
♦ **ein Fahrradverleih** a bicycle hire shop

verleihen VERB (IMPERFECT **verlieh**, PERFECT **hat verliehen**)
1 to lend ◊ *Ich habe mein Wörterbuch an sie verliehen.* I've lent her my dictionary.
2 to hire out ◊ *Ich suche jemanden, der Fahrräder verleiht.* I'm looking for somebody who hires out bikes.
3 to award ◊ *Sie hat einen Preis verliehen bekommen.* She was awarded a prize.

verleiten VERB (PERFECT **hat verleitet**)
♦ **jemanden dazu verleiten, etwas zu tun** to tempt somebody into doing something

verlernen VERB (PERFECT **hat verlernt**)
to forget

verletzen VERB (PERFECT **hat verletzt**)
1 to hurt ◊ *Deine Bemerkung hat mich verletzt.* Your remark hurt me.
2 to injure ◊ *Sie ist schwer verletzt.* She's seriously injured.
♦ **ein Gesetz verletzen** to violate a law

der **Verletzte** NOUN (GEN des/der **Verletzten**, PL
die   die **Verletzten**)
injured person ◊ *Auf der Straße lag ein Verletzter.* An injured person was lying in the street.

die **Verletzung** NOUN
injury
♦ **Er hatte schwere Verletzungen.** He was seriously injured.
♦ **Das ist eine Verletzung der Spielregeln.** That's against the rules of the game.

sich **verlieben** VERB (PERFECT **hat sich verliebt**)
♦ **sich in jemanden verlieben** to fall in love with somebody

verliebt ADJECTIVE
in love ◊ *Ich bin in Anke verliebt.* I'm in love with Anke.

verlieren VERB (IMPERFECT **verlor**, PERFECT **hat verloren**)
to lose

der **Verlierer** NOUN (PL die **Verlierer**)
loser

sich **verloben** VERB (PERFECT **hat sich verlobt**)
♦ **sich mit jemandem verloben** to get engaged to somebody

der **Verlobte** NOUN (GEN des **Verlobten**, PL die **Verlobten**)
see also **die Verlobte** NOUN
fiancé ◊ *Mathias ist mein Verlobter.* Mathias is my fiancé.

die **Verlobte** NOUN (GEN der **Verlobten**, PL die **Verlobten**)
see also **der Verlobte** NOUN
fiancée ◊ *Ingrid ist seine Verlobte.* Ingrid's his fiancée.

die **Verlobung** NOUN
engagement

verlor, verloren VERB *see* **verlieren**

verloren ADJECTIVE
lost ◊ *die verlorene Zeit wieder einholen* to make up for lost time
♦ **verlorene Eier** poached eggs
♦ **verloren gehen** to get lost

die **Verlosung** NOUN
raffle

der **Verlust** NOUN (PL die **Verluste**)
loss

vermehren VERB (PERFECT **hat vermehrt**)
increase ◊ *Die Firma hat ihren Umsatz vermehrt.* The company has increased its turnover.
♦ **sich vermehren** to reproduce ◊ *Wie vermehren sich Regenwürmer?* How do earthworms reproduce?

vermeiden VERB (IMPERFECT **vermied**, PERFECT **hat vermieden**)
to avoid

vermieten VERB (PERFECT **hat vermietet**)
1 to let ◊ *"Zimmer zu vermieten"* "Rooms to let"
2 to rent ◊ *Sie vermietet Zimmer.* She rents rooms.
3 to hire out ◊ *Wir vermieten Boote und Fahrräder.* We hire out boats and bikes.

der **Vermieter** NOUN (PL die **Vermieter**)
landlord

die **Vermieterin** NOUN
landlady

vermissen VERB (PERFECT **hat vermisst**)
to miss ◊ *Ich habe dich vermisst.* I missed you.
♦ **Ich vermisse eines meiner Bücher.** One of my books is missing.

das **Vermögen** NOUN (PL die **Vermögen**)
wealth
♦ **ein Vermögen kosten** to cost a fortune

vermuten VERB (PERFECT **hat vermutet**)
1 to guess ◊ *Ich kann nur vermuten, was er damit gemeint hat.* I can only guess what he meant by that.
♦ **Man vermutet, dass er im Ausland ist.** He is thought to be abroad.
2 to suspect ◊ *Die Polizei vermutet, dass er der Täter ist.* The police suspect that he's the culprit.
3 to suppose ◊ *Ich vermute, dass er das noch nicht weiß.* I don't suppose that he knows that yet.

vermutlich ADJECTIVE, ADVERB
1 probable ◊ *die vermutliche Ursache* the probable cause
2 probably ◊ *Sie ist vermutlich schon gegangen.* She has probably already left.

die **Vermutung** NOUN

V

1 supposition ◊ *Das legt die Vermutung nahe, dass sie schon gegangen ist.* It seems a likely supposition that she's already gone.

2 suspicion ◊ *Die Polizei hat eine Vermutung, wer der Täter gewesen sein könnte.* The police have a suspicion as to who the culprit could have been.

vernachlässigen VERB (PERFECT **hat vernachlässigt**)
to neglect

vernichten VERB (PERFECT **hat vernichtet**)
to destroy
♦ **Insekten vernichten** to exterminate insects
♦ **Unkraut vernichten** to eradicate weeds

vernichtend ADJECTIVE
crushing ◊ *Unsere Mannschaft wurde vernichtend geschlagen.* Our team suffered a crushing defeat.
♦ **ein vernichtender Blick** a withering look
♦ **eine vernichtende Kritik** a scathing review

die **Vernunft** NOUN
reason

vernünftig ADJECTIVE
reasonable ◊ *Sei doch vernünftig!* Be reasonable! ◊ *ein vernünftiger Preis* a reasonable price
♦ **etwas Vernünftiges essen** to eat something decent

veröffentlichen VERB (PERFECT **hat veröffentlicht**)
to publish

die **Verpackung** NOUN
packing

das **Verpackungsmaterial** NOUN (PL die **Verpackungsmaterialien**)
packaging

verpassen VERB (PERFECT **hat verpasst**)
to miss
♦ **jemandem eine Ohrfeige verpassen** to give somebody a clip round the ear

verpflegen VERB (PERFECT **hat verpflegt**)
to cater for ◊ *Die Flüchtlinge wurden vom Roten Kreuz verpflegt.* The Red Cross catered for the refugees.

die **Verpflegung** NOUN
food ◊ *Für Ihre Verpflegung wird gesorgt.* Food will be laid on. ◊ *Die Verpflegung im Schullandheim war gut.* The food at the school camp was good.

verpflichten VERB (PERFECT **hat verpflichtet**)
to sign ◊ *Der VfB will Köpke verpflichten.* VfB want to sign Köpke.
♦ **sich verpflichten, etwas zu tun** to promise to do something ◊ *Du hast dich verpflichtet, für die Musik zu sorgen.* You promised to organize the music.
♦ **Sie haben sich verpflichtet, für Ersatz zu sorgen.** You undertook to find a replacement.

♦ **verpflichtet sein, etwas zu tun** to be obliged to do something
♦ **Er ist zum Stillschweigen verpflichtet.** He's sworn to silence.
♦ **Das verpflichtet Sie zu nichts.** This doesn't commit you to anything.
♦ **jemandem zu Dank verpflichtet sein** to be obliged to somebody

verprügeln VERB (PERFECT **hat verprügelt**)
to beat up

verraten VERB (PRESENT **verrät**, IMPERFECT **verriet**, PERFECT **hat verraten**)
1 to betray ◊ *Er hat seine Mittäter verraten.* He betrayed his accomplices.
2 to report ◊ *Fritz hat uns beim Lehrer verraten.* Fritz reported us to the teacher.
3 to tell ◊ *Verrate mir doch, wer es war.* Tell me who it was. ◊ *Ich habe dieses Geheimnis niemandem verraten.* I haven't told anyone the secret.
♦ **sich verraten** to give oneself away

verregnet ADJECTIVE
rainy

verreisen VERB (PERFECT **ist verreist**)
to go away ◊ *Ich möchte diesen Sommer verreisen.* I'd like to go away this summer.
♦ **Wir wollen nach Israel verreisen.** We intend to go to Israel.

verrenken VERB (PERFECT **hat verrenkt**)
to sprain ◊ *Er hat sich den Knöchel verrenkt.* He sprained his ankle.

verrosten VERB (PERFECT **ist verrostet**)
to rust

verrückt ADJECTIVE
crazy

der **Verrückte** NOUN (GEN des/der **Verrückten**, PL
die die **Verrückten**)
maniac ◊ *Er ist gefahren wie ein Verrückter.* He drove like a maniac.

die **Verrücktheit** NOUN
madness

verrufen ADJECTIVE
disreputable

der **Vers** NOUN (GEN des **Verses**, PL die **Verse**)
verse

der **Versager** NOUN (PL die **Versager**)
failure

versalzen VERB (PERFECT **hat versalzen**)
to put too much salt in ◊ *Sie hat die Suppe versalzen.* She put too much salt in the soup.
♦ **Die Suppe ist versalzen.** There's too much salt in the soup.

versammeln VERB (PERFECT **hat versammelt**)
to assemble

die **Versammlung** NOUN
meeting

das **Versandhaus** NOUN (GEN des **Versandhauses**, PL die **Versandhäuser**)
mail-order firm

versäumen VERB (PERFECT **hat versäumt**)
to miss ◊ *Ich habe wegen Krankheit drei Stunden versäumt.* I missed three lessons due to illness.
♦ **es versäumen, etwas zu tun** to fail to do something ◊ *Sie hat es versäumt, sich rechtzeitig anzumelden.* She failed to register in time.
♦ **Sie sollten nicht versäumen, sich die Kathedrale anzusehen.** Don't miss a visit to the cathedral.

sich **verschätzen** VERB (PERFECT **hat sich verschätzt**)
to misjudge

verschenken VERB (PERFECT **hat verschenkt**)
to give away

verschicken VERB (PERFECT **hat verschickt**)
to send away

verschieben VERB (IMPERFECT **verschob**, PERFECT **hat verschoben**)
to postpone ◊ *Wir müssen das Fest verschieben.* We'll have to postpone the party.

verschieden ADJECTIVE
different ◊ *Die zwei Brüder sind sehr verschieden.* The two brothers are very different.
♦ **verschiedene** various ◊ *Wir haben verschiedene Sehenswürdigkeiten besichtigt.* We've seen various sights.
♦ **Sie sind verschieden groß.** They are different sizes.

verschlafen VERB (PRESENT **verschläft**, IMPERFECT **verschlief**, PERFECT **hat verschlafen**)
see also **verschlafen** ADJECTIVE
1 to sleep in ◊ *Tut mir leid, ich habe verschlafen.* Sorry, I slept in.
2 to sleep through ◊ *Er hat den ganzen Vormittag verschlafen.* He slept through the whole morning.
3 to forget ◊ *Ich habe deinen Geburtstag total verschlafen.* I completely forgot your birthday.

verschlafen ADJECTIVE
see also **verschlafen** VERB
sleepy ◊ *Sie sah mich mit einem verschlafenen Blick an.* She gave me a sleepy look. ◊ *ein verschlafenes kleines Dorf* a sleepy little village

verschlechtern VERB (PERFECT **hat verschlechtert**)
to make worse ◊ *Das verschlechtert die Lage.* That makes the situation worse.
♦ **Sie hat ihre Noten gewaltig verschlechtert.** Her marks have got considerably worse.
♦ **sich verschlechtern** to get worse ◊ *Die Lage hat sich verschlechtert.* The situation's got worse. ◊ *In Englisch habe ich mich verschlechtert.* My marks in English have got worse.

♦ **Sein Gesundheitszustand hat sich noch weiter verschlechtert.** His condition has deteriorated even further.

verschleißen VERB (IMPERFECT **verschliss**, PERFECT **hat verschlissen**)
to wear out ◊ *eine verschlissene Jacke* a worn-out jacket

verschlimmern VERB (PERFECT **hat verschlimmert**)
to make worse ◊ *Du verschlimmerst alles, wenn du weiter lügst.* You'll make everything worse if you go on lying.
♦ **sich verschlimmern** to get worse ◊ *Die Lage hat sich verschlimmert.* The situation's got worse.

verschlucken VERB (PERFECT **hat verschluckt**)
to swallow ◊ *Ich habe eine Gräte verschluckt.* I've swallowed a fish bone.
♦ **sich verschlucken** to choke ◊ *Ich habe mich an einer Erdnuss verschluckt.* I choked on a peanut.

der **Verschluss** NOUN (GEN des **Verschlusses**, PL die **Verschlüsse**)
1 cap ◊ *Die Flasche hat einen kindersicheren Verschluss.* The bottle has a childproof cap.
2 fastening ◊ *Kannst du mir den Verschluss an meinem Kleid aufmachen?* Can you undo the fastening of my dress?
3 catch ◊ *der Verschluss der Tasche* the catch of the bag ◊ *der Verschluss an einer Halskette* the catch of a necklace

verschmutzen VERB (PERFECT **hat verschmutzt**)
to soil
♦ **Die Straße war stark verschmutzt.** The road was very dirty.
♦ **die Umwelt verschmutzen** to pollute the environment

verschneit ADJECTIVE
covered with snow
♦ **eine verschneite Straße** a snow-covered road

verschonen VERB (PERFECT **hat verschont**)
♦ **jemanden mit etwas verschonen** to spare somebody something ◊ *Sie verschonte mich mit den ganzen Einzelheiten.* She spared me all the details.

verschreiben VERB (IMPERFECT **verschrieb**, PERFECT **hat verschrieben**)
to prescribe ◊ *Der Arzt hat mir Antibiotika verschrieben.* The doctor prescribed me antibiotics.
♦ **sich verschreiben** to make a spelling mistake

verschreibungspflichtig ADJECTIVE
available on prescription only
♦ **verschreibungspflichtige Medikamente** prescribed drugs

verschütten VERB (PERFECT **hat verschüttet**)

V

☞

to spill ◊ *Sie hat den Kaffee verschüttet.* She spilt the coffee.

♦ **verschüttet werden** to be buried ◊ *Bei dem Erdbeben wurden zahlreiche Menschen verschüttet.* Many people were buried in the earthquake.

verschweigen VERB (IMPERFECT **verschwieg**, PERFECT **hat verschwiegen**)

♦ **jemandem etwas verschweigen** to keep something from somebody

verschwenden VERB (PERFECT **hat verschwendet**)

to waste ◊ *Zeit verschwenden* to waste time

die **Verschwendung** NOUN

waste

verschwinden VERB (IMPERFECT **verschwand**, PERFECT **ist verschwunden**)

to disappear

verschwitzt ADJECTIVE

sweaty

verschwommen ADJECTIVE

blurred

das **Versehen** NOUN (PL die **Versehen**)

oversight ◊ *Das war ein Versehen.* It was an oversight.

♦ **aus Versehen** by mistake

versehentlich ADVERB

by mistake

versenden VERB (IMPERFECT **versendete** or **versandte**, PERFECT **hat versendet** or **versandt**)

to dispatch

versessen ADJECTIVE

♦ **auf etwas versessen sein** to be mad about something ◊ *Sie ist ganz versessen auf ihn.* She's mad about him.

versetzen VERB (PERFECT **hat versetzt**)

to transfer ◊ *Mein Vater wird nach Berlin versetzt.* My father's being transferred to Berlin.

♦ **jemanden in die nächste Klasse versetzen** to move somebody up into the next class

> ⓘ In Germany, pupils do not automatically move up **(werden versetzt)** to the next class at the end of the school year. If their performance is not good enough, they have to repeat the school year. This is known as **sitzen bleiben**.

♦ **jemanden versetzen** to stand somebody up ◊ *Meine Freundin hat mich versetzt.* My girlfriend stood me up.

♦ **sich in jemandes Lage versetzen** to put oneself in somebody's shoes ◊ *Wenn du dich einmal in meine Lage versetzt ...* If you put yourself in my shoes ...

♦ **jemandem einen Schlag versetzen** to hit somebody

♦ **jemandem einen Tritt versetzen** to kick somebody

♦ **jemanden in gute Laune versetzen** to put somebody in a good mood

verseuchen VERB (PERFECT **hat verseucht**)

to contaminate

versichern VERB (PERFECT **hat versichert**)

[1] to assure ◊ *Er hat mir versichert, dass das stimmt.* He assured me that this is correct.

[2] to insure ◊ *Wir sind nicht gegen Diebstahl versichert.* We are not insured against theft.

die **Versicherung** NOUN

insurance

sich **versöhnen** VERB (PERFECT **hat sich versöhnt**)

to make up ◊ *Na, habt ihr euch wieder versöhnt?* Well, have you two made up again?

♦ **sich mit jemandem versöhnen** to make it up with somebody ◊ *Ich habe mich wieder mit ihm versöhnt.* I made it up with him again.

versorgen VERB (PERFECT **hat versorgt**)

to supply ◊ *Von hier aus wird die Stadt mit Elektrizität versorgt.* The town is supplied with electricity from here.

♦ **einen Kranken versorgen** to look after a patient

♦ **Wer versorgt die Blumen während der Ferien?** Who's watering the plants during the holidays?

♦ **eine Familie versorgen** to support a family

sich **verspäten** VERB (PERFECT **hat sich verspätet**)

to be late

verspätet ADJECTIVE

late ◊ *die verspätete Ankunft* the late arrival

♦ **der verspätete Flug** the delayed flight

♦ **verspätete Glückwünsche** belated best wishes

die **Verspätung** NOUN

delay

♦ **Verspätung haben** to be late

das **Versprechen** NOUN (PL die **Versprechen**)

> see also **versprechen** VERB

promise ◊ *Sie hat ihr Versprechen gehalten.* She kept her promise.

versprechen VERB (PRESENT **verspricht**, IMPERFECT **versprach**, PERFECT **hat versprochen**)

> see also **das Versprechen** NOUN

to promise ◊ *Du hast es versprochen.* You promised.

♦ **Ich habe mir von dem Kurs mehr versprochen.** I expected more from this course.

der **Verstand** NOUN

mind

♦ **den Verstand verlieren** to go out of one's mind

♦ **über jemandes Verstand gehen** to be beyond somebody

verständigen VERB (PERFECT **hat verständigt**)
to inform ◊ *Wir müssen ihre Eltern verständigen.* We must inform her parents.

♦ **sich verständigen** to communicate ◊ *Wir konnten uns auf Englisch verständigen.* We were able to communicate in English.

♦ **sich auf etwas verständigen** to agree on something ◊ *Wir haben uns auf folgendes Vorgehen verständigt.* We've agreed on the following plan of action.

verständlich ADJECTIVE
understandable

♦ **sich verständlich ausdrücken** to express oneself clearly

verständnisvoll ADJECTIVE
understanding ◊ *Meine Eltern sind sehr verständnisvoll.* My parents are very understanding.

verstärken VERB (PERFECT **hat verstärkt**)
to strengthen ◊ *Wir müssen den Karton verstärken.* We'll have to strengthen the box. ◊ *ein Team verstärken* to strengthen a team

♦ **den Ton verstärken** to amplify the sound

♦ **Das verstärkt die Schmerzen.** That makes the pain worse.

der **Verstärker** NOUN (PL die **Verstärker**)
amplifier

die **Verstärkung** NOUN
reinforcements ◊ *Wir brauchen Verstärkung.* We need reinforcements.

verstauchen VERB (PERFECT **hat verstaucht**)
to sprain ◊ *Ich habe mir den Knöchel verstaucht.* I've sprained my ankle.

das **Versteck** NOUN (PL die **Verstecke**)
hiding place

verstecken VERB (PERFECT **hat versteckt**)
to hide

verstehen VERB (IMPERFECT **verstand,** PERFECT **hat verstanden**)
to understand ◊ *Ich habe die Frage nicht verstanden.* I didn't understand the question. ◊ *Ich verstehe nicht.* I don't understand.

♦ **sich verstehen** to get on ◊ *Die beiden verstehen sich blendend.* The two of them get on marvellously.

♦ **Das versteht sich von selbst.** That goes without saying.

verstellbar ADJECTIVE
adjustable

verstellen VERB (PERFECT **hat verstellt**)
1 to adjust ◊ *Man kann die Höhe verstellen.* The height can be adjusted.
2 to reset ◊ *Wer hat die Uhr verstellt?* Who reset the clock?

3 to block ◊ *Der Ausgang war mit Kisten verstellt.* The exit was blocked by crates.
4 to disguise ◊ *Sie hat ihre Stimme verstellt.* She disguised her voice.

♦ **sich verstellen** to put on an act

verstimmt ADJECTIVE
1 out of tune ◊ *Meine Geige ist verstimmt.* My violin's out of tune.
2 cross ◊ *Worüber bist du denn so verstimmt?* What are you so cross about?

♦ **ein verstimmter Magen** an upset stomach

verstopft ADJECTIVE
1 blocked ◊ *ein verstopfter Abfluss* a blocked drain
2 constipated ◊ *Ich bin seit gestern verstopft.* I've been constipated since yesterday.

die **Verstopfung** NOUN
1 obstruction ◊ *eine Verstopfung im Rohr* an obstruction in the pipe
2 constipation ◊ *Ich habe Verstopfung.* I'm constipated.

verstreuen VERB (PERFECT **hat verstreut**)
to scatter

der **Versuch** NOUN (PL die **Versuche**)
1 attempt ◊ *Ich habe den Versuch gemacht, Spanisch zu lernen.* I made an attempt to learn Spanish. ◊ *Sie ist schon beim ersten Versuch gescheitert.* She failed at the very first attempt.
2 experiment ◊ *Versuche mit Tieren lehnen wir ab.* We disapprove of experiments with animals.

versuchen VERB (PERFECT **hat versucht**)
to try ◊ *Ich versuche zu kommen.* I'll try to come. ◊ *Willst du mal die Soße versuchen?* Would you like to try the sauce?

♦ **sich an etwas versuchen** to try one's hand at something ◊ *Ich habe mich am Töpfern versucht.* I tried my hand at pottery.

das **Versuchskaninchen** NOUN (PL die **Versuchskaninchen**)
guinea pig

vertagen VERB (PERFECT **hat vertagt**)
to adjourn

vertauschen VERB (PERFECT **hat vertauscht**)
1 to mix up ◊ *Die Babys wurden im Krankenhaus vertauscht.* They mixed the babies up at the hospital. ◊ *Er hat offensichtlich seinen Mantel mit meinem vertauscht.* He must have got his coat and mine mixed up.
2 to exchange ◊ *Er hat seinen Sportwagen mit einem Familienwagen vertauscht.* He exchanged his sports car for a family car.

verteidigen VERB (PERFECT **hat verteidigt**)
to defend

der **Verteidiger** NOUN (PL die **Verteidiger**)

[1] defender ◊ *Der Verteidiger wurde gefoult.* The defender was fouled.

[2] defence counsel ◊ *Wer ist der Verteidiger des Angeklagten?* Who's counsel for the defence?

verteilen VERB (PERFECT **hat verteilt**)

[1] to hand out ◊ *Sie verteilte die Hefte an die Schüler.* She handed the exercise books out to the pupils.

[2] to spread ◊ *Die Salbe sollte gleichmäßig auf der Haut verteilt werden.* The ointment should be spread evenly over the skin.

der **Vertrag** NOUN (PL die **Verträge**)

[1] contract ◊ *ein Arbeitsvertrag* a contract of employment

[2] treaty ◊ *ein Friedensvertrag* a peace treaty

vertragen VERB (PRESENT **verträgt**, IMPERFECT **vertrug**, PERFECT **hat vertragen**)

[1] to be able to stand ◊ *Ich vertrage die Hitze nicht.* I can't stand the heat.

[2] to tolerate ◊ *Ich kann eine solche Behandlung nicht vertragen.* I can't tolerate such treatment.

♦ **sich vertragen** to get along ◊ *Die beiden vertragen sich blendend.* The two of them get along marvellously.

♦ **sich wieder vertragen** to patch things up ◊ *Na, vertragt ihr euch wieder?* Well, have you patched things up again?

verträglich ADJECTIVE

[1] good-natured ◊ *ein verträglicher Mensch* a good-natured person

[2] easily digestible ◊ *Im Sommer sollte man nur leicht verträgliche Speisen zu sich nehmen.* In summer, you should only eat easily digestible food.

♦ **Das Medikament ist gut verträglich.** The drug has no side effects.

das **Vertrauen** NOUN

see also **vertrauen** VERB

trust ◊ *Vertrauen zu jemandem haben* to have trust in somebody

vertrauen VERB (PERFECT **hat vertraut**)

see also **das Vertrauen** NOUN

♦ **jemandem vertrauen** to trust somebody

♦ **vertrauen auf** to rely on ◊ *Ich vertraue auf dich.* I'm relying on you.

♦ **Ich vertraue auf mein Glück.** I'm trusting my luck.

vertraulich ADJECTIVE

[1] confidential ◊ *ein vertrauliches Gespräch* a confidential talk

[2] familiar ◊ *Ich verbiete mir diesen vertraulichen Ton.* I'll not have you talking to me in such familiar way.

vertraut ADJECTIVE

familiar ◊ *vertraute Gesichter* familiar faces

vertreiben VERB (IMPERFECT **vertrieb**, PERFECT **hat vertrieben**)

[1] to drive ◊ *Er hat uns von seinem Grundstück vertrieben.* He drove us off his land. ◊ *Während des Krieges wurden viele Menschen aus ihrer Heimat vertrieben.* Many people were driven from their homes during the war.

[2] to sell ◊ *Wir vertreiben Hardware und Software.* We sell hardware and software.

♦ **sich die Zeit vertreiben** to pass the time ◊ *Ich habe mir die Zeit mit Kreuzworträtseln vertrieben.* I passed the time doing crosswords.

vertreten VERB (PRESENT **vertritt**, IMPERFECT **vertrat**, PERFECT **hat vertreten**)

[1] to stand in for ◊ *Während ich in Urlaub bin, vertritt mich Frau Wengel.* While I'm on holiday, Mrs Wengel's standing in for me.

[2] to represent ◊ *Die Lobby vertritt die Interessen der Wirtschaft.* The lobby represents business interests.

♦ **eine Meinung vertreten** to hold an opinion

♦ **sich den Fuß vertreten** to twist one's ankle ◊ *Ich habe mir den Fuß vertreten.* I've twisted my ankle.

♦ **sich die Beine vertreten** to stretch one's legs ◊ *Ich will mir nur etwas die Beine vertreten.* I just want to stretch my legs a bit.

der **Vertreter** NOUN (PL die **Vertreter**)

sales representative ◊ *Er ist Vertreter für Collins.* He's a sales representative for Collins.

der **Vertrieb** NOUN (PL die **Vertriebe**)

[1] sale ◊ *Der Vertrieb von Raubkopien steht unter Strafe.* The sale of pirate copies is punishable by law.

[2] marketing department ◊ *Sie arbeitet im Vertrieb.* She works in the marketing department.

sich **vertun** VERB (IMPERFECT **vertat sich**, PERFECT **hat sich vertan**)

to make a mistake

verübeln VERB (PERFECT **hat verübelt**)

♦ **jemandem etwas verübeln** to be cross with somebody because of something

verüben VERB (PERFECT **hat verübt**)

to commit

verunglücken VERB (PERFECT **ist verunglückt**)

to have an accident ◊ *Sie sind mit dem Auto verunglückt.* They've had a car accident.

verursachen VERB (PERFECT **hat verursacht**)

to cause

verurteilen VERB (PERFECT **hat verurteilt**)

to condemn

vervielfältigen VERB (PERFECT **hat vervielfältigt**)

to copy

vervollständigen VERB (PERFECT **hat vervollständigt**)
to complete

sich **verwählen** VERB (PERFECT **hat sich verwählt**)
to dial the wrong number

die **Verwaltung** NOUN
administration ◊ *Er arbeitet in der Verwaltung.* He works in administration.

verwandt ADJECTIVE
♦ **mit jemandem verwandt sein** to be related to somebody

der **Verwandte** NOUN (GEN des/der
die Verwandten, PL die **Verwandten**)
relative ◊ *Ein Verwandter von mir ist gestern gestorben.* A relative of mine died yesterday.

die **Verwandtschaft** NOUN
relations ◊ *Die ganze Verwandtschaft war eingeladen.* All my relations were invited.

verwechseln VERB (PERFECT **hat verwechselt**)
[1] to confuse ◊ *Du darfst die beiden Begriffe nicht verwechseln.* You mustn't confuse the two ideas.
[2] to mix up ◊ *Sie haben offensichtlich die Mäntel verwechselt.* They must have got their coats mixed up.
♦ **verwechseln mit (1)** to confuse with ◊ *Ich verwechsle "akut" immer mit "aktuell".* I always confuse "akut" with "aktuell".
♦ **verwechseln mit (2)** to mistake for ◊ *Ich habe dich mit deiner Schwester verwechselt.* I mistook you for your sister.
♦ **Sie sind zum Verwechseln ähnlich.** They're the spitting image of each other.

die **Verwechslung** NOUN
mix-up

verweigern VERB (PERFECT **hat verweigert**)
♦ **jemandem etwas verweigern** to refuse somebody something ◊ *Sie verweigerte ihm das Besuchsrecht für die Kinder.* She refused him access to the children.
♦ **den Gehorsam verweigern** to refuse to obey
♦ **die Aussage verweigern** to refuse to testify

der **Verweis** NOUN (GEN des **Verweises**, PL die **Verweise**)
reprimand ◊ *Er hat für sein Zuspätkommen einen schweren Verweis bekommen.* He was given a severe reprimand for being late.

verwelken VERB (PERFECT **ist verwelkt**)
to fade

verwenden VERB (IMPERFECT **verwendete or verwandte**, PERFECT **hat verwendet or verwandt**)
[1] to use ◊ *Verwenden Sie einen Computer?* Do you use a computer?
[2] (*effort, time, work*)

to spend ◊ *Ich habe auf diesen Aufsatz viel Zeit verwendet.* I spent a lot of time on this essay.

verwerten VERB (PERFECT **hat verwertet**)
to utilize

verwesen VERB (PERFECT **ist verwest**)
to decay

verwickeln VERB (PERFECT **hat verwickelt**)
♦ **sich verwickeln** to get tangled ◊ *Die Schnur hat sich verwickelt.* The line's got tangled.
♦ **jemanden in etwas verwickeln** to involve somebody in something ◊ *Ich möchte in diese Angelegenheit nicht verwickelt werden.* I don't want to get involved in this business.

verwickelt ADJECTIVE
complicated ◊ *Das ist eine ziemlich verwickelte Angelegenheit.* This is a pretty complicated matter.

verwirren VERB (PERFECT **hat verwirrt**)
[1] to confuse ◊ *Jetzt hast du mich total verwirrt.* Now you've completely confused me.
[2] to tangle up (*thread*) ◊ *Die Katze hat die Wolle verwirrt.* The cat's tangled the wool up.

verwöhnen VERB (PERFECT **hat verwöhnt**)
to spoil

verwunden VERB (PERFECT **hat verwundet**)
to wound

der **Verwundete** NOUN (GEN des/der
die Verwundeten, PL die **Verwundeten**)
injured person ◊ *Der Arzt versorgt gerade einen Verwundeten.* The doctor is just attending to an injured person.

die **Verwundung** NOUN
injury

sich **verzählen** VERB (PERFECT **hat sich verzählt**)
to miscount

das **Verzeichnis** NOUN (GEN des **Verzeichnisses**, PL die **Verzeichnisse**)
list ◊ *Am Ende des Buches ist ein Verzeichnis aller Fachbegriffe.* At the end of the book there's a list of all the technical terms.
♦ **das Inhaltsverzeichnis** the table of contents
♦ **das Dateienverzeichnis** the file directory

verzeihen VERB (IMPERFECT **verzieh**, PERFECT **hat verziehen**)
to forgive ◊ *jemandem etwas verzeihen* to forgive somebody for something

die **Verzeihung** NOUN
forgiveness
♦ **Verzeihung, ich wollte Sie nicht treten.** Sorry, I didn't mean to kick you.
♦ **Verzeihung, aber können Sie mir sagen, wie spät es ist?** Excuse me, could you tell me what time it is?

verzichten VERB (PERFECT **hat verzichtet**)
♦ **auf etwas verzichten (1)** to do without something ◊ *Ich werde heute wohl auf*

meinen Mittagsschlaf verzichten müssen.
It looks like I'll have to do without my
afternoon nap today. ◊ *Ich verzichte auf
deine Hilfe.* I can do without your help.
- ◆ **auf etwas verzichten (2)** to forego
  something ◊ *Er hat auf eine Bezahlung
  verzichtet.* He forewent payment. ◊ *Ich
  verzichte nicht auf meine Rechte.* I won't
  forego my rights.

die **Verzierung** NOUN
decoration

verzögern VERB (PERFECT **hat verzögert**)
to delay

verzollen VERB (PERFECT **hat verzollt**)
to pay duty on ◊ *Den Whisky müssen
Sie verzollen.* You have to pay duty on
that whisky.
- ◆ **Haben Sie etwas zu verzollen?** Have you
  anything to declare?

die **Verzögerung** NOUN
delay

verzweifeln VERB (PERFECT **ist verzweifelt**)
to despair

verzweifelt ADJECTIVE
desperate

die **Verzweiflung** NOUN
despair

der **Vetter** NOUN (PL die **Vettern**)
cousin

das **Video** NOUN (PL die **Videos**)
video

das **Videogerät** NOUN (PL die **Videogeräte**)
video recorder

der **Videorekorder** NOUN (PL die
Videorekorder)
video recorder

das **Vieh** NOUN
cattle ◊ *Das Vieh ist auf der Weide.* The
cattle are out in the meadow.

viel ADJECTIVE, ADVERB
[1] a lot of ◊ *Sie haben viel Arbeit.*
They've got a lot of work.
[2] much ◊ *Wir haben nicht viel Geld.* We
haven't got much money. ◊ *Wir haben
nicht viel gelernt.* We didn't learn much.
- ◆ **Vielen Dank!** Thank you very much.
[3] a lot ◊ *Wir haben viel gesehen.* We
saw a lot.
- ◆ **viel zu wenig** far too little
- ◆ **Viel Glück!** Good luck.
- ◆ **so viel** so much ◊ *Sie hat so viel gelernt.*
  She's learned so much. ◊ *Rede nicht so
  viel.* Don't talk so much.
- ◆ **so viel wie** as much as ◊ *Sie hat so viel
  wie ich bekommen.* She got as much as I
  did. ◊ *so viel wie möglich* as much as
  possible
- ◆ **wie viel?** how much?
- ◆ **zu viel** too much
- ◆ **viel versprechend** promising

viele PL PRONOUN
[1] a lot of ◊ *Sie hat viele Bücher.* She's
got a lot of books.

[2] many ◊ *Er hat nicht viele Fehler
gemacht.* He didn't make many mistakes.
◊ *Viele Schüler mögen Chemie nicht.*
Many pupils don't like chemistry.
- ◆ **Viele wissen das nicht.** A lot of people
  don't know that.

vieles PRONOUN
many things ◊ *Vieles war neu für mich.*
Many things were new to me.

vielleicht ADVERB
perhaps

vielmals ADVERB
- ◆ **Danke vielmals!** Many thanks!

vielseitig ADJECTIVE
many-sided

vielversprechend ADJECTIVE *see* **viel**

vier NUMBER
see also **die Vier** NOUN
four

die **Vier** NOUN
see also **vier** NUMBER
[1] four
[2] adequate

> **ⓘ** German marks range from one (**sehr
> gut**) to six (**ungenügend**).

das **Viereck** NOUN (PL die **Vierecke**)
[1] rectangle
[2] square

viereckig ADJECTIVE
[1] rectangular
[2] square

vierte ADJECTIVE
fourth ◊ *Sie hat erst beim vierten
Klingeln abgenommen.* She didn't
answer until the fourth ring. ◊ *Er kam als
Vierter.* He was the fourth to arrive.

das **Viertel** NOUN (PL die **Viertel**)
quarter ◊ *Viertel vor zwei* quarter to two

das **Vierteljahr** NOUN (PL die **Vierteljahre**)
quarter

vierteljährlich ADJECTIVE
quarterly

vierteln VERB
[1] to divide by four ◊ *wenn man den
Betrag viertelt ...* if you divide the
amount by four ...
[2] to cut into quarters ◊ *Sie hat den
Kuchen geviertelt.* She cut the cake into
quarters.

die **Viertelnote** NOUN
crotchet

die **Viertelstunde** NOUN
quarter of an hour

vierzehn NUMBER
fourteen
- ◆ **in vierzehn Tagen** In a fortnight

vierzehntägig ADJECTIVE
fortnightly

vierzig NUMBER
forty

die **Villa** NOUN (PL die **Villen**)
villa
virtuell ADJECTIVE
virtual ◊ *die virtuelle Realität* virtual
reality
der **Virus** NOUN (GEN des **Virus,** PL die **Viren**)
virus ◊ *Er ist an einem Virus erkrankt.* He
caught a virus. ◊ *Im Computersystem ist
ein Virus.* There's a computer virus in the
system.
die **Visen** PL NOUN *see* **Visum**
die **Visitenkarte** NOUN
business card
das **Visum** NOUN (PL die **Visen**)
visa
das **Vitamin** NOUN (PL die **Vitamine**)
vitamin
der **Vogel** NOUN (PL die **Vögel**)
bird
 ◆ **einen Vogel haben** to have a screw loose
 ◆ **jemandem den Vogel zeigen** to make a
rude sign

> ℹ *In Germany you make a rude sign at
> somebody by tapping your forehead to
> show that you think they are stupid.*

die **Vokabel** NOUN
word
das **Vokabular** NOUN (PL die **Vokabulare**)
vocabulary
der **Vokal** NOUN (PL die **Vokale**)
vowel
das **Volk** NOUN (PL die **Völker**)
[1] people ◊ *das einfache Volk* the simple
people
[2] nation ◊ *das deutsche Volk* the
German nation
das **Volksfest** NOUN (PL die **Volksfeste**)
fair
die **Volkshochschule** NOUN
adult education classes
die **Volkswirtschaft** NOUN
economics
voll ADJECTIVE
full
 ◆ **voll und ganz** completely
 ◆ **jemanden für voll nehmen** to take
somebody seriously
vollends ADVERB
completely
völlig ADJECTIVE, ADVERB
[1] complete ◊ *bis zur völligen
Erschöpfung* to the point of complete
exhaustion
[2] completely ◊ *Das ist völlig
unmöglich.* That's completely
impossible. ◊ *Ich bin völlig deiner
Meinung.* I completely agree with you.
volljährig ADJECTIVE
of age ◊ *volljährig werden* to come of
age

vollkommen ADJECTIVE
perfect ◊ *vollkommen richtig* perfectly
right
 ◆ **vollkommen unmöglich** completely
impossible
das **Vollkornbrot** NOUN (PL die **Vollkornbrote**)
wholemeal bread
vollmachen VERB
to fill up
die **Vollmacht** NOUN
power of attorney
der **Vollmond** NOUN
full moon ◊ *bei Vollmond* at full moon
die **Vollpension** NOUN
full board
vollschlank ADJECTIVE
plump (*person*)
 ◆ **Mode für Vollschlanke** fashion for the
fuller figure
vollständig ADJECTIVE
complete
volltanken VERB
to fill up (*car*)
die **Vollwertkost** NOUN
wholefood
vom = **von dem**
von PREPOSITION
> *von takes the dative.*
[1] from ◊ *von Hamburg nach Kiel* from
Hamburg to Kiel
 ◆ **Wir sind um fünf von Hamburg
losgefahren.** We left Hamburg at five.
 ◆ **von ... bis** from ... to ◊ *von morgens bis
abends* from morning to night
 ◆ **von ... an** from ... ◊ *Von Mai an wohnen
wir in Regensburg.* We'll be living in
Regensburg from May.
 ◆ **von ... aus** from ... ◊ *Ich habe es vom
Fenster aus gesehen.* I saw it from my
window.
 ◆ **etwas von sich aus tun** to do something
of one's own accord ◊ *Du solltest das
von dir aus machen.* You should do it of
your own accord.
 ◆ **von mir aus** I don't mind ◊ *Von mir aus
können wir gehen.* I don't mind if we go.
 ◆ **Von wo bist du?** Where are you from?
 ◆ **Von wann ist der Brief?** When's the
letter from?
[2] by ◊ *Ich bin von einem Hund gebissen
worden.* I was bitten by a dog. ◊ *ein
Gedicht von Schiller* a poem by Schiller
 ◆ **von etwas kommen** to be caused by
something ◊ *Der Husten kommt vom
Rauchen.* The cough is caused by
smoking.
[3] of ◊ *ein Freund von mir* a friend of
mine ◊ *Wie nett von dir!* How nice of you!
 ◆ **jeweils zwei von zehn** two out of every ten
[4] about ◊ *Er erzählte vom Urlaub.* He
talked about his holiday.
 ◆ **Von wegen!** No way!
voneinander ADVERB

V

from each other

vor PREPOSITION, ADVERB

Use the accusative to express movement or a change of place. Use the dative when there is no change of place.

1 in front of ◊ *Er stand vor dem Spiegel.* He stood in front of the mirror. ◊ *Stell den Stuhl vor das Fenster.* Put the chair in front of the window.

2 before ◊ *Der Artikel steht vor dem Substantiv.* The article goes before the noun. ◊ *Bei Fragen stellt man das Verb vor das Substantiv.* In questions, put the verb before the noun. ◊ *Vor der Kirche links abbiegen.* Turn left just before you get to the church. ◊ *Du solltest vor der Prüfung mehr lernen.* You ought to study more before the exam. ◊ *Ich war vor ihm da.* I was there before him.

3 ago ◊ *vor zwei Tagen* two days ago ◊ *vor einem Jahr* a year ago

♦ **Es ist fünf vor vier.** It's five to four.

♦ **vor Kurzem** a little while ago

4 with ◊ *vor Wut* with rage ◊ *vor Liebe* with love

♦ **vor Hunger sterben** to die of hunger

♦ **vor lauter Arbeit** because of work

♦ **vor allem** above all

♦ **vor und zurück** backwards and forwards

vorankommen VERB (IMPERFECT **kam voran,** PERFECT **ist vorangekommen**)
to make progress

voraus ADVERB
ahead ◊ *Fahr du schon mal voraus.* You go on ahead. ◊ *Er war seiner Zeit voraus.* He was ahead of his time.

♦ **im Voraus** in advance

vorausgehen VERB (IMPERFECT **ging voraus,** PERFECT **ist vorausgegangen**)

1 to go on ahead ◊ *Geht ihr voraus, ich komme nach.* Go on ahead, I'll catch up with you.

2 to precede ◊ *Der Schlägerei ging ein Streit voraus.* The fight was preceded by an argument.

voraussetzen VERB (PERFECT **hat vorausgesetzt**)
to assume ◊ *Ich setze voraus, dass du auch kommst.* I assume that you're coming too.

♦ **Gute Englischkenntnisse werden vorausgesetzt.** A good command of English is essential.

♦ **vorausgesetzt, dass ...** provided that ...

die **Voraussetzung** NOUN
prerequisite

♦ **unter der Voraussetzung, dass ...** provided that ...

voraussichtlich ADVERB
probably

vorbei ADVERB
past ◊ *Fahren Sie am Rathaus vorbei.* Drive past the town hall.

♦ **Ich sehe noch kurz bei ihr vorbei.** I'll just pop round to her place.

♦ **vorbei sein** to be over ◊ *Damit ist es nun vorbei.* That's all over now.

vorbeigehen VERB (IMPERFECT **ging vorbei,** PERFECT **ist vorbeigegangen**)
to go past ◊ *Er ging vorbei, ohne zu grüßen.* He went past without saying hello.

♦ **an etwas vorbeigehen** to go past something ◊ *Sie ist am Schaufenster vorbeigegangen, ohne es zu beachten.* She went past the shop window without looking at it.

♦ **bei jemandem vorbeigehen** to call in at somebody's ◊ *Kannst du beim Bäcker vorbeigehen?* Can you call in at the baker's? ◊ *Ich gehe noch schnell bei meiner Freundin vorbei.* I'm just going to call in at my girlfriend's.

vorbeikommen VERB (IMPERFECT **kam vorbei,** PERFECT **ist vorbeigekommen**)

♦ **bei jemandem vorbeikommen** to drop in on somebody

vorbereiten VERB (PERFECT **hat vorbereitet**)
to prepare

die **Vorbereitung** NOUN
preparation

vorbeugen VERB (PERFECT **hat vorgebeugt**)

♦ **sich vorbeugen** to lean forward

♦ **einer Sache vorbeugen** to prevent something ◊ *um einer Erkältung vorzubeugen* to prevent a cold

vorbeugend ADJECTIVE
preventive

die **Vorbeugung** NOUN
prevention ◊ *zur Vorbeugung gegen* for the prevention of

das **Vorbild** NOUN (PL die **Vorbilder**)
role model ◊ *Er ist mein Vorbild.* He's my role model.

♦ **sich jemanden zum Vorbild nehmen** to follow somebody's example ◊ *Du solltest dir deinen Bruder zum Vorbild nehmen.* You ought to follow your brother's example.

vordere ADJECTIVE
front ◊ *Das Haus hat einen vorderen und einen hinteren Eingang.* The house has a front door and a back door.

die **Vorderseite** NOUN
front

vorderste ADJECTIVE
front ◊ *die vorderste Reihe* the front row

♦ **Gebt das bitte an den vordersten Schüler durch.** Please pass it to the pupil at the front.

voreilig ADJECTIVE
hasty ◊ *Du solltest nicht voreilig urteilen.* You shouldn't make hasty judgements.

voreingenommen ADJECTIVE
biased

vorenthalten VERB (PRESENT **enthält vor,** IMPERFECT **enthielt vor,** PERFECT **hat vorenthalten**)
- **jemandem etwas vorenthalten** to withhold something from somebody

vorerst ADVERB
for the moment

die **Vorfahrt** NOUN
right of way
- **Vorfahrt achten!** Give way!

der **Vorfall** NOUN (PL die **Vorfälle**)
incident

vorführen VERB (PERFECT **hat vorgeführt**)
to show

der **Vorgänger** NOUN (PL die **Vorgänger**)
predecessor

das **Vorgehen** NOUN
| see also **vorgehen** VERB |
action

vorgehen VERB (IMPERFECT **ging vor,** PERFECT **ist vorgegangen**)
| see also **das Vorgehen** NOUN |
[1] to go on ahead ◊ *Geht ihr vor, ich komme nach.* Go on ahead, I'll catch up.
[2] to go up to ◊ *Sie ging ans Rednerpult vor.* She went up to the lectern.
[3] to proceed ◊ *Ich weiß nicht, wie wir vorgehen sollen.* I don't know how we should proceed.
- **Die Uhr geht vor.** The clock is fast.
- **Was geht hier vor?** What's going on here?

der **Vorgeschmack** NOUN
foretaste

vorgestern ADVERB
the day before yesterday

vorhaben VERB (PRESENT **hat vor,** IMPERFECT **hatte vor,** PERFECT **hat vorgehabt**)
to intend ◊ *Wir haben vor, nach Italien zu fahren.* We intend to go to Italy. ◊ *Was hast du vor?* What do you intend to do?
- **Ich habe heute viel vor.** I've got a lot planned for today.
- **Was hast du heute Abend vor?** What are you doing this evening?

der **Vorhang** NOUN (PL die **Vorhänge**)
curtain

vorher ADVERB
beforehand

die **Vorhersage** NOUN
forecast

vorhersehbar ADJECTIVE
predictable

vorhersehen VERB (PRESENT **sieht vorher,** IMPERFECT **sah vorher,** PERFECT **hat vorhergesehen**)
to foresee

vorhin ADVERB
just now

vorig ADJECTIVE
previous

vorkommen VERB (IMPERFECT **kam vor,** PERFECT **ist vorgekommen**)
[1] to happen ◊ *So ein Fehler sollte nicht vorkommen.* A mistake like that shouldn't happen.
- **jemandem vorkommen** to seem to somebody ◊ *Das kommt mir komisch vor.* That seems funny to me.
- **sich dumm vorkommen** to feel stupid ◊ *Ich kam mir dumm vor.* I felt stupid.
[2] to come out ◊ *Komm endlich hinter dem Schrank vor.* Come out from behind that cupboard, will you?

vorläufig ADJECTIVE
provisional

vorlaut ADJECTIVE
impertinent

vorlesen VERB (PRESENT **liest vor,** IMPERFECT **las vor,** PERFECT **hat vorgelesen**)
to read out

vorletzte ADJECTIVE
last but one ◊ *Ich wohne im vorletzten Haus.* My house is the last but one.

die **Vorliebe** NOUN
partiality
- **Sie hat eine Vorliebe für Krimis.** She's partial to detective stories.

der **Vormittag** NOUN (PL die **Vormittage**)
morning ◊ *am Vormittag* in the morning

vormittags ADVERB
in the morning

vorn ADVERB
in front ◊ *Der deutsche Schwimmer liegt vorn.* The German swimmer is in front.
- **nach vorn** to the front
- **von vorn anfangen** to start at the beginning

der **Vorname** NOUN (GEN des **Vornamens,** PL die **Vornamen**)
first name

vornehm ADJECTIVE
[1] distinguished ◊ *eine vornehme Familie* a distinguished family
[2] refined ◊ *sich vornehm ausdrücken* to use refined language ◊ *vornehme Manieren* refined manners
[3] posh ◊ *ein vornehmes Hotel* a posh hotel
[4] elegant ◊ *eine vornehme Dame* an elegant lady
- **Tu nicht so vornehm!** Don't put on airs and graces.

vornehmen VERB (PRESENT **nimmt vor,** IMPERFECT **nahm vor,** PERFECT **hat vorgenommen**)
- **sich etwas vornehmen** to resolve to do something

vornherein ADVERB
- **von vornherein** from the start

der **Vorort** NOUN (PL die **Vororte**)
suburb

der **Vorrat** NOUN (PL die **Vorräte**)

V

stock ◊ *solange der Vorrat reicht* while stocks last

vorrätig ADJECTIVE
in stock

die **Vorrichtung** NOUN
device

der **Vorsatz** NOUN (GEN des **Vorsatzes**, PL die **Vorsätze**)
intention ◊ *Er hat lauter gute Vorsätze.* His intentions are all good.

der **Vorschlag** NOUN (PL die **Vorschläge**)
suggestion

vorschlagen VERB (PRESENT **schlägt vor**, IMPERFECT **schlug vor**, PERFECT **hat vorgeschlagen**)
to suggest

die **Vorschrift** NOUN
rule ◊ *Das ist gegen die Vorschriften.* It's against the rules.

die **Vorsicht** NOUN
caution
♦ **Vorsicht! (1)** Look out!
♦ **Vorsicht! (2)** Caution!
♦ **Vorsicht, Stufe!** Mind the step!

vorsichtig ADJECTIVE
careful

vorsichtshalber ADVERB
just in case

die **Vorsilbe** NOUN
prefix

die **Vorspeise** NOUN
starter

der **Vorsprung** NOUN (PL die **Vorsprünge**)
lead ◊ *Wir haben einen Vorsprung vor unseren Konkurrenten gewonnen.* We have gained a lead over our competitors.

die **Vorstadt** NOUN (PL die **Vorstädte**)
suburbs

vorstellbar ADJECTIVE
conceivable

vorstellen VERB (PERFECT **hat vorgestellt**)
♦ **sich etwas vorstellen** to imagine something ◊ *Stell dir mal vor, wir wären jetzt im Urlaub.* Imagine we were on holiday right now.
♦ **jemanden jemandem vorstellen** to introduce somebody to somebody ◊ *Darf ich Ihnen meinen Mann vorstellen?* May I introduce my husband to you?

die **Vorstellung** NOUN
1 performance ◊ *Die Vorstellung endet gegen zehn Uhr.* The performance ends at about ten.
2 idea ◊ *Hast du eine Vorstellung, wie wir das machen sollen?* Have you got any idea how we should do that?

das **Vorstellungsgespräch** NOUN (PL die **Vorstellungsgespräche**)
interview (*for job*)

vortäuschen VERB (PERFECT **hat vorgetäuscht**)
to feign

der **Vorteil** NOUN (PL die **Vorteile**)
advantage
♦ **im Vorteil sein** to have the advantage

der **Vortrag** NOUN (PL die **Vorträge**)
talk ◊ *einen Vortrag halten* to give a talk

vorüber ADVERB
over

vorübergehend ADJECTIVE
passing
♦ **Das Geschäft ist vorübergehend geschlossen.** The shop's temporarily closed.

das **Vorurteil** NOUN (PL die **Vorurteile**)
prejudice

der **Vorverkauf** NOUN (PL die **Vorverkäufe**)
advance booking

die **Vorwahl** NOUN
dialling code

die **Vorwahlnummer** NOUN
dialling code

der **Vorwand** NOUN (PL die **Vorwände**)
pretext

vorwärts ADVERB
forward

der **Vorwärtsgang** NOUN (PL die **Vorwärtsgänge**)
forward gear

vorwegnehmen VERB (PRESENT **nimmt vorweg**, IMPERFECT **nahm vorweg**, PERFECT **hat vorweggenommen**)
to anticipate

vorwerfen VERB (PRESENT **wirft vor**, IMPERFECT **warf vor**, PERFECT **hat vorgeworfen**)
♦ **jemandem etwas vorwerfen** to accuse somebody of something
♦ **sich nichts vorzuwerfen haben** to have nothing to reproach oneself for

vorwiegend ADVERB
predominantly

das **Vorwort** NOUN (PL die **Vorworte**)
preface

der **Vorwurf** NOUN (PL die **Vorwürfe**)
reproach
♦ **jemandem Vorwürfe machen** to reproach somebody
♦ **Ich mache mir solche Vorwürfe!** I blame myself.

vorzeigen VERB (PERFECT **hat vorgezeigt**)
to show

vorziehen VERB (IMPERFECT **zog vor**, PERFECT **hat vorgezogen**)
1 to prefer ◊ *Was ziehst du vor: Kaffee oder Tee?* Do you prefer coffee or tea?
2 to pull forward ◊ *Du solltest den Stuhl etwas vorziehen.* You should pull your chair forward a bit.

vulgär ADJECTIVE
vulgar ◊ *sich vulgär ausdrücken* to use vulgar language

der **Vulkan** NOUN (PL die **Vulkane**)
volcano

W

die **Waage** NOUN
 1 scales ◇ *Die Waage stimmt nicht genau.* The scales aren't accurate.
 2 Libra ◇ *Ulla ist Waage.* Ulla's Libra.
waagerecht ADJECTIVE
 horizontal
wach ADJECTIVE
 ♦ **wach sein** to be awake
die **Wache** NOUN
 guard ◇ *Wache stehen* to stand guard
das **Wachs** NOUN (GEN des **Wachses**, PL die **Wachse**)
 wax
wachsen VERB (PRESENT **wächst**, IMPERFECT **wuchs**, PERFECT **ist gewachsen**)
 to grow
das **Wachstum** NOUN
 growth
wackelig ADJECTIVE
 wobbly
die **Wade** NOUN
 calf ◇ *Ich habe mich an der Wade verletzt.* I've hurt my calf.
die **Waffe** NOUN
 weapon
die **Waffel** NOUN
 1 waffle ◇ *Heute gab's zum Mittagessen Waffeln.* We had waffles for lunch today.
 2 wafer ◇ *Willst du eine Waffel zu deinem Eis?* Would you like a wafer with your ice?
der **Wagen** NOUN (PL die **Wagen**)
 see also **wagen** VERB
 1 car ◇ *Seid ihr mit dem Wagen da?* Did you come by car?
 2 carriage ◇ *ein Eisenbahnwagen* a railway carriage
 ♦ **ein Pferdewagen** a cart
wagen VERB
 see also **der Wagen** NOUN
 ♦ **es wagen, etwas zu tun** to dare to do something
 ♦ **sich irgendwohin wagen** to dare to go somewhere
der **Wagenheber** NOUN (PL die **Wagenheber**)
 jack (*for car*)
waghalsig ADJECTIVE
 foolhardy
die **Wahl** NOUN (PL die **Wahlen**)
 1 choice ◇ *Du hast die Wahl.* It's your choice.
 2 election ◇ *Wann sind die nächsten Wahlen?* When are the next elections?
wählen VERB
 1 to choose ◇ *Du kannst wählen, entweder das rote oder das grüne.* You can choose, either the red one or the green one.

 2 to vote ◇ *Wer wurde zum Klassensprecher gewählt?* Who was voted class representative?
 ♦ **Wählt Kowalski!** Vote for Kowalski.
 ♦ **Nächsten Sonntag wird gewählt.** There are elections next Sunday.
 3 to dial ◇ *Sie wählte die Nummer ihrer Freundin.* She dialled her friend's number.
wählerisch ADJECTIVE
 particular
das **Wahlfach** NOUN (PL die **Wahlfächer**)
 optional subject
der **Wahnsinn** NOUN
 madness
wahnsinnig ADJECTIVE, ADVERB
 1 mad ◇ *Wer hatte denn diese wahnsinnige Idee?* Whose mad idea was it?
 2 incredibly ◇ *Das Kleid war wahnsinnig schön.* The dress was incredibly pretty. ◇ *Das tut wahnsinnig weh.* It's incredibly sore.
wahr ADJECTIVE
 true ◇ *eine wahre Geschichte* a true story
 ♦ **Sie ist verheiratet, nicht wahr?** She's married, isn't she?
während PREPOSITION, CONJUNCTION
 *The preposition **während** takes the genitive.*
 1 during ◇ *Was hast du während der Ferien gemacht?* What did you do during the holidays?
 2 while ◇ *Sie sah fern, während sie ihre Hausaufgaben machte.* She was watching TV while she was doing her homework.
 3 whereas ◇ *Er ist ganz nett, während seine Frau unhöflich ist.* He's quite nice, whereas his wife's impolite.
wahrhaben VERB
 ♦ **etwas nicht wahrhaben wollen** to refuse to admit something
die **Wahrheit** NOUN
 truth
wahrnehmen VERB (PRESENT **nimmt wahr**, IMPERFECT **nahm wahr**, PERFECT **hat wahrgenommen**)
 to perceive
der **Wahrsager** NOUN (PL die **Wahrsager**)
 fortune teller
die **Wahrsagerin** NOUN
 fortune teller
wahrscheinlich ADJECTIVE, ADVERB
 1 likely ◇ *Das ist nicht sehr wahrscheinlich.* That's not very likely.
 2 probably ◇ *Er kommt wahrscheinlich nicht.* He's probably not coming.

die **Wahrscheinlichkeit** NOUN
probability ◇ *aller Wahrscheinlichkeit
nach* in all probability

die **Währung** NOUN
currency

der **Wal** NOUN (PL die **Wale**)
whale

der **Wald** NOUN (PL die **Wälder**)
[1] wood ◇ *Hinter unserem Haus ist ein
Wald.* There's a wood behind our house.
[2] forest ◇ *die Wälder Kanadas* the
forests of Canada

Wales NEUT NOUN
Wales
♦ **aus Wales** from Wales
♦ **in Wales** in Wales
♦ **nach Wales** to Wales

der **Walfisch** NOUN (PL die **Walfische**)
whale

der **Waliser** NOUN (PL die **Waliser**)
Welshman
♦ **Er ist Waliser.** He's Welsh.
♦ **die Waliser** the Welsh

die **Waliserin** NOUN
Welshwoman
♦ **Sie ist Waliserin.** She's Welsh.

walisisch ADJECTIVE
Welsh

der **Walkman** ® NOUN (PL die **Walkmen** or
Walkmans)
Walkman ®

die **Walnuss** NOUN (PL die **Walnüsse**)
walnut

die **Wand** NOUN (PL die **Wände**)
wall

der **Wanderer** NOUN (PL die **Wanderer**)
rambler

die **Wanderin** NOUN
rambler

wandern VERB (PERFECT **ist gewandert**)
to hike ◇ *Wir sind am Wochenende
gewandert.* We went hiking at the
weekend.

die **Wanderung** NOUN
hike

der **Wandschrank** NOUN (PL die
Wandschränke)
wall cupboard

wann ADVERB
when

das **Wappen** NOUN (PL die **Wappen**)
coat of arms

war VERB see **sein**

die **Ware** NOUN
goods

das **Warenhaus** NOUN (GEN des **Warenhauses**,
PL die **Warenhäuser**)
department store

warf VERB see **werfen**

warm ADJECTIVE
warm ◇ *Heute ist es wärmer als gestern.*
It's warmer today than yesterday.

♦ **ein warmes Essen** a hot meal
♦ **Mir ist warm.** I'm warm.

die **Wärme** NOUN
warmth

die **Wärmflasche** NOUN
hot-water bottle

das **Warndreieck** NOUN (PL die **Warndreiecke**)
warning triangle

warnen VERB
to warn ◇ *jemanden vor etwas warnen*
to warn somebody of something

die **Warnung** NOUN
warning

warten VERB
to wait ◇ *Ich habe eine Stunde gewartet.*
I waited an hour.
♦ **warten auf** to wait for ◇ *Ich warte
draußen auf dich.* I'll wait outside for
you.
♦ **auf sich warten lassen** to take a long
time

der **Warteraum** NOUN (PL die **Warteräume**)
waiting room

der **Wartesaal** NOUN (PL die **Wartesäle**)
waiting room (*in station*)

das **Wartezimmer** NOUN (PL die **Wartezimmer**)
waiting room

warum ADVERB
why

was PRONOUN
[1] what ◇ *Was hast du gesagt?* What did
you say?
♦ **Was für ein ...** What kind of ... ◇ *Was für
ein Fahrrad hast du?* What kind of bike
do you have?
♦ **Was für eine Enttäuschung!** What a
disappointment!
[2] something ◇ *Heute gibt's was
Leckeres zum Mittagessen.* We're having
something delicious for lunch today.

waschbar ADJECTIVE
washable

das **Waschbecken** NOUN (PL die **Waschbecken**)
washbasin

die **Wäsche** NOUN
washing ◇ *Wäsche waschen* to do the
washing
♦ **Tu dein Hemd in die Wäsche.** Put your
shirt in the wash.
♦ **die Bettwäsche** bed linen
♦ **die Unterwäsche** underwear

die **Wäscheklammer** NOUN
clothes peg

die **Wäscheleine** NOUN
washing line

waschen VERB (PRESENT **wäscht**, IMPERFECT
wusch, PERFECT **hat gewaschen**)
to wash
♦ **sich waschen** to have a wash
♦ **sich die Hände waschen** to wash one's
hands ◇ *Ich muss mir die Hände
waschen.* I'll have to wash my hands.

der **Waschlappen** NOUN (PL die **Waschlappen**)
face cloth

die **Waschmaschine** NOUN
washing machine

das **Waschmittel** NOUN (PL die **Waschmittel**)
detergent

das **Waschpulver** NOUN (PL die **Waschpulver**)
washing powder

der **Waschraum** NOUN (PL die **Waschräume**)
washroom

der **Waschsalon** NOUN (PL die **Waschsalons**)
launderette

das **Wasser** NOUN (PL die **Wasser** or **Wässer**)
water

wasserdicht ADJECTIVE
waterproof

der **Wasserfall** NOUN (PL die **Wasserfälle**)
waterfall

die **Wasserfarbe** NOUN
watercolour

der **Wasserhahn** NOUN (PL die **Wasserhähne**)
tap

der **Wassermann** NOUN
Aquarius ◊ *Gerda ist Wassermann.*
Gerda's Aquarius.

die **Wassermelone** NOUN
water melon

der **Wasserstoff** NOUN
hydrogen

die **Watte** NOUN
cotton wool

das **WC** NOUN (PL die **WCs**)
WC

der **Webmaster** NOUN (PL die **Webmaster**)
webmaster

das **Web-Magazin** NOUN (PL die **Web-Magazine**)
webzine

die **Webseite** NOUN
web page

die **Website** NOUN (PL die **Websites**)
website

der **Wechsel** NOUN (PL die **Wechsel**)
change

der **Wechselkurs** NOUN (GEN des **Wechselkurses,** PL die **Wechselkurse**)
rate of exchange

wechseln VERB
1 to change ◊ *Wir mussten einen Reifen wechseln.* We had to change a tyre.
◊ *Wie viel Geld wechselst du?* How much money are you changing?
♦ **Blicke wechseln** to exchange glances
2 to have change ◊ *Können Sie wechseln?* Do you have any change?
◊ *Kannst du mir zwanzig Euro in Münzen wechseln?* Have you got change for twenty euros?

die **Wechselstube** NOUN
bureau de change

wecken VERB
to wake up

der **Wecker** NOUN (PL die **Wecker**)
alarm clock

weder CONJUNCTION
neither
♦ **weder ... noch ...** neither ... nor ...

der **Weg** NOUN (PL die **Wege**)
see also **weg** ADVERB
1 way ◊ *Es gibt sicher einen Weg, das zu reparieren.* There must be a way to repair it.
2 path ◊ *Ein Weg führte zur Kapelle hinauf.* A path led up to the chapel.
3 route ◊ *Welchen Weg habt ihr genommen?* Which route did you take?
♦ **sich auf den Weg machen** to be on one's way
♦ **jemandem aus dem Weg gehen** to keep out of somebody's way

weg ADVERB
see also **der Weg** NOUN
away ◊ *Geh weg!* Go away!
♦ **Weg da!** Out of the way!
♦ **Finger weg!** Hands off!
♦ **Er war schon weg.** He'd already left.

wegbleiben VERB (IMPERFECT **blieb weg,** PERFECT **ist weggeblieben**)
to stay away

wegen PREPOSITION
*The preposition **wegen** takes the dative or sometimes the genitive.*
because of ◊ *Wegen dir bin ich zu spät gekommen.* Because of you I arrived late.
◊ *Wegen des schlechten Wetters wurde die Veranstaltung abgesagt.* The event was cancelled because of the bad weather.

weggehen VERB (IMPERFECT **ging weg,** PERFECT **ist weggegangen**)
to go away

weglassen VERB (PRESENT **lässt weg,** IMPERFECT **ließ weg,** PERFECT **hat weggelassen**)
to leave out

weglaufen VERB (PRESENT **läuft weg,** IMPERFECT **lief weg,** PERFECT **ist weggelaufen**)
to run away

weglegen VERB (PERFECT **hat weggelegt**)
to put aside

wegmachen VERB (PERFECT **hat weggemacht**)
to get rid of ◊ *einen Fleck wegmachen* to get rid of a stain
♦ **die Satteltasche vom Fahrrad wegmachen** to take the saddlebag off the bike

wegmüssen VERB (PRESENT **muss weg,** IMPERFECT **musste weg,** PERFECT **hat weggemusst** or **wegmüssen**)
to have to go

wegnehmen VERB (PRESENT **nimmt weg,** IMPERFECT **nahm weg,** PERFECT **hat weggenommen**)
to take away

W

wegtun VERB (IMPERFECT **tat weg**, PERFECT **hat weggetan**)
to put away

der **Wegweiser** NOUN (PL die **Wegweiser**)
signpost

wegwerfen VERB (PRESENT **wirft weg**, IMPERFECT **warf weg**, PERFECT **hat weggeworfen**)
to throw away

das **Weh** NOUN (PL die **Wehe**)
ache

weh ADJECTIVE *see* **wehtun**

der **Wehrdienst** NOUN (PL die **Wehrdienste**)
military service

> *Young men are generally conscripted into the **Wehrdienst** when they leave school. The basic period of military service is 10 months.*

der **Wehrdienstverweigerer** NOUN (PL die **Wehrdienstverweigerer**)
conscientious objector

sich **wehren** VERB
to defend oneself

die **Wehrpflicht** NOUN
compulsory military service

wehtun VERB (IMPERFECT **tat weh**, PERFECT **hat wehgetan**)
[1] to hurt ◊ *Mein Bein tut weh.* My leg hurts.
[2] to be sore ◊ *Mein Hals tut weh.* My throat's sore.
♦ **sich wehtun** to hurt oneself ◊ *Hast du dir wehgetan?* Have you hurt yourself?
♦ **jemandem wehtun** to hurt somebody ◊ *Ich möchte dir nicht wehtun, aber das war nicht sehr intelligent.* I don't want to hurt you, but that really wasn't very clever.

das **Weibchen** NOUN (PL die **Weibchen**)
female

weiblich ADJECTIVE
feminine ◊ *ein weibliches Substantiv* a feminine noun

weich ADJECTIVE
soft ◊ *ein weiches Bett* a soft bed

sich **weigern** VERB
to refuse

das **Weihnachten** NOUN (GEN des **Weihnachten**)
Christmas ◊ *an Weihnachten* at Christmas
♦ **Frohe Weihnachten!** Merry Christmas.

die **Weihnachtsferien** PL NOUN
Christmas holidays

das **Weihnachtslied** NOUN (PL die **Weihnachtslieder**)
Christmas carol

der **Weihnachtsmann** NOUN (PL die **Weihnachtsmänner**)
Father Christmas

der **Weihnachtsmarkt** NOUN (PL die **Weihnachtsmärkte**)
Christmas fair

der **Weihnachtstag** NOUN (PL die **Weihnachtstage**)
♦ **der erste Weihnachtstag** Christmas Day
♦ **der zweite Weihnachtstag** Boxing Day

weil CONJUNCTION
because

die **Weile** NOUN
while ◊ *Es wird eine Weile dauern.* It'll take a while.

der **Wein** NOUN (PL die **Weine**)
wine

der **Weinberg** NOUN (PL die **Weinberge**)
vineyard

die **Weinbergschnecke** NOUN
snail

der **Weinbrand** NOUN (PL die **Weinbrände**)
brandy

weinen VERB
to cry
♦ **Das ist zum Weinen.** It's enough to make you cry.

das **Weinglas** NOUN (GEN des **Weinglases**, PL die **Weingläser**)
wine glass

die **Weinkarte** NOUN
wine list

der **Weinkeller** NOUN (PL die **Weinkeller**)
[1] wine cellar
[2] wine bar

die **Weinprobe** NOUN
wine tasting

die **Weinstube** NOUN
wine bar

die **Weintraube** NOUN
grape

die **Weise** NOUN
way ◊ *Die Art und Weise, wie er uns behandelt hat.* The way he treated us.
♦ **Es ist egal, auf welche Weise du das machst.** It doesn't matter how you do it.
♦ **auf diese Weise** in this way

die **Weisheit** NOUN
wisdom

der **Weisheitszahn** NOUN (PL die **Weisheitszähne**)
wisdom tooth

weiß VERB *see* **wissen**

weiß ADJECTIVE
white

das **Weißbrot** NOUN (PL die **Weißbrote**)
white bread

der **Weißwein** NOUN (PL die **Weißweine**)
white wine

weit ADJECTIVE, ADVERB
[1] long ◊ *Das ist eine weite Reise.* That's a long journey. ◊ *Das war sein weitester Wurf.* That was his longest throw.
[2] far ◊ *Wie weit ist es ...?* How far is it ...? ◊ *Nach Berlin ist es weiter als nach*

München. It's further to Berlin than to Munich.

③ baggy ◊ *Sie hatte einen weiten Pulli an.* She was wearing a baggy pullover.

◆ **ein weiter Begriff** a broad idea

◆ **in weiter Ferne** in the far distance

◆ **Das geht zu weit.** That's going too far.

◆ **so weit sein** to be ready ◊ *Ich bin so weit.* I'm ready.

◆ **so weit wie möglich** as far as possible

◆ **Ich bin so weit zufrieden.** By and large I'm quite satisfied.

weitaus ADVERB
by far

weiter ADJECTIVE, ADVERB
further ◊ *Wenn du noch weitere Fragen hast ...* If you have any further questions ... ◊ *Alles Weitere besprechen wir morgen.* We can discuss any further details tomorrow.

◆ **ohne weiteres** just like that ◊ *Ich kann doch nicht so ohne weiteres gehen.* I can't go just like that.

◆ **Ich könnte das ohne weiteres tun.** I could do that no problem.

◆ **weiter nichts** nothing else

◆ **weiter niemand** nobody else

weiterarbeiten VERB (PERFECT **hat weitergearbeitet**)
to go on working

sich **weiterbilden** VERB (PERFECT **hat sich weitergebildet**)
to continue one's education

die **Weiterbildung** NOUN
further education

die **Weiterfahrt** NOUN
continuation of the journey

weitergehen VERB (IMPERFECT **ging weiter**, PERFECT **ist weitergegangen**)
to go on

weiterhin ADVERB

◆ **etwas weiterhin tun** to go on doing something

weiterleiten VERB (PERFECT **hat weitergeleitet**)
to pass on

weitermachen VERB (PERFECT **hat weitergemacht**)
to continue

der **Weitsprung** NOUN
long jump

der **Weizen** NOUN
wheat

welche PRONOUN

① which ◊ *Welcher Mann?* Which man? ◊ *Welche Frau?* Which woman? ◊ *Welches Mädchen?* Which girl? ◊ *Welcher von beiden?* Which of the two? ◊ *Welchen hast du genommen?* Which one did you take?

◆ **Welch eine Überraschung!** What a surprise!

◆ **Welche Freude!** What joy!

② some ◊ *Ich habe Kirschen, willst du welche?* I have some cherries, would you like some? ◊ *Ich habe welche.* I have some. ◊ *Bei den Programmen gibt es welche, die echt schwierig sind.* There are some programs that are really difficult. ◊ *Ich habe kein Geld dabei, wenn du welches hast, musst du zahlen.* I don't have any money, if you have some then you'll have to pay.

③ any ◊ *Ich brauche Briefmarken, hast du welche?* I need stamps, have you got any? ◊ *Ich brauche Kleingeld, hast du welches?* I need change, have you got any?

die **Welle** NOUN
wave

die **Wellenlänge** NOUN
wavelength

die **Wellenlinie** NOUN
wavy line

der **Wellensittich** NOUN (PL die **Wellensittiche**)
budgie

die **Welt** NOUN
world

das **Weltall** NOUN
universe

weltberühmt ADJECTIVE
world-famous

der **Weltkrieg** NOUN (PL die **Weltkriege**)
world war

der **Weltmeister** NOUN (PL die **Weltmeister**)
world champion

der **Weltraum** NOUN
space

wem PRONOUN

wem is the dative of wer.

to whom

◆ **Wem hast du das Buch gegeben?** Who did you give the book to?

◆ **Mit wem bist du gekommen?** Who did you come with?

wen PRONOUN

wen is the accusative of wer.

whom

◆ **Wen hast du gesehen?** Who did you see?

wenig ADJECTIVE, ADVERB
little

◆ **so wenig wie** as little as ◊ *Er macht so wenig wie möglich.* He does as little as possible. ◊ *Ich habe so wenig Geld wie du.* I have as little money as you.

◆ **zu wenig** too little

wenige PL PRONOUN
few ◊ *Das wissen nur wenige.* Only a few people know that.

weniger ADJECTIVE, ADVERB

① less ◊ *Ich habe weniger Geld als du.* I have less money than you.

② fewer ◊ *Ich habe weniger Fehler gemacht.* I've made fewer mistakes.

W

3 minus ◊ *Zehn weniger drei ist sieben.* Ten minus three is seven.
- **Unser Geld wird immer weniger.** Our money's running out.

wenigste ADJECTIVE
least ◊ *Das ist das wenigste, was ich tun kann.* That's the least I can do.
- **am wenigsten** the least ◊ *Die Clowns haben mir am wenigsten gefallen.* I liked the clowns the least.

wenigstens ADVERB
at least

wenn CONJUNCTION
1 if ◊ *Wenn er anruft, sag mir Bescheid.* If he calls, tell me.
- **selbst wenn …** even if …
- **wenn ich doch …** if only I …
2 when ◊ *Wenn ich nach Hause komme, dusche ich erst mal.* When I get home, the first thing I'm going to do is have a shower.
- **immer wenn** whenever ◊ *Immer wenn ich frage, lacht er nur.* Whenever I ask, he just laughs.

wer PRONOUN
who
Be careful! wer does not mean where.

die **Werbeagentur** NOUN
advertising agency

das **Werbefernsehen** NOUN
commercial television

werben VERB (PRESENT **wirbt**, IMPERFECT **warb**, PERFECT **hat geworben**)
to advertise ◊ *Im Fernsehen wird zu viel geworben.* There's too much advertising on TV.
- **Mitglieder werben** to recruit members

der **Werbespot** NOUN (PL die **Werbespots**)
commercial

die **Werbung** NOUN
advert ◊ *Hast du die Werbung für den neuen Schokoriegel gesehen?* Have you seen the advert for the new chocolate bar? ◊ *Wenn Werbung kommt, schalte ich um.* I switch over when the adverts come on.
- **Er arbeitet in der Werbung.** He works in advertising.
- **für etwas Werbung machen** to advertise something

werden VERB (PRESENT **wird**, IMPERFECT **wurde**, PERFECT **ist geworden** or bei Passiv **worden**)
1 to become ◊ *Sie ist Lehrerin geworden.* She became a teacher. ◊ *Er ist reich geworden.* He became rich. ◊ *Was ist aus ihm geworden?* What became of him?
- **Erster werden** to come first
- **Was willst du einmal werden?** What do you want to be?
- **rot werden** to turn red
- **Es ist gut geworden.** It turned out well.
- **Die Fotos sind gut geworden.** The photos have come out well.
- **Es ist nichts geworden.** It came to nothing.
- **Es wird Tag.** It's getting light.
- **Es wird Nacht.** It's getting dark.
- **Mir wird kalt.** I'm getting cold.
- **Mir wird schlecht.** I feel sick.
- **Das muss anders werden.** That'll have to change.
2 will
werden is used to form the future tense.
◊ *Er wird es tun.* He'll do it.
- **Er wird das nicht tun.** He won't do it.
- **Es wird gleich regnen.** It's going to rain.
3 to be
werden is used to form the passive.
◊ *gebraucht werden* to be needed ◊ *Er ist erschossen worden.* He's been shot.
◊ *Mir wurde gesagt, dass …* I was told that …
werden is used to form the conditional tense.
- **Ich würde …** I would …
- **Er würde gern …** He'd like to …
- **Ich würde lieber …** I'd rather …
- **Sie wird in der Küche sein.** She'll be in the kitchen.

werfen VERB (PRESENT **wirft**, IMPERFECT **warf**, PERFECT **hat geworfen**)
to throw

das **Werken** NOUN
handicrafts

die **Werkstatt** NOUN (PL die **Werkstätten**)
1 workshop ◊ *eine Werkstatt für Behinderte* a workshop for the handicapped
2 garage ◊ *Das Auto ist in der Werkstatt.* The car's in the garage.

der **Werktag** NOUN (PL die **Werktage**)
working day

werktags ADVERB
on working days

das **Werkzeug** NOUN (PL die **Werkzeuge**)
tool

der **Wert** NOUN (PL die **Werte**)
see also **wert** ADJECTIVE
value
- **Wert legen auf** to attach importance to ◊ *Sie legt großen Wert auf rechtzeitiges Erscheinen.* She attaches great importance to punctuality.
- **Es hat doch keinen Wert.** There's no point.

wert ADJECTIVE
see also **der Wert** NOUN
worth ◊ *Wie viel ist das Bild wert?* How much is that picture worth? ◊ *Das ist nichts wert.* It's not worth anything.
◊ *Das ist viel wert.* It's worth a lot.

wertlos ADJECTIVE
worthless

wertvoll ADJECTIVE

valuable

das **Wesen** NOUN (PL die **Wesen**)
manner ◊ *Er hat ein freundliches Wesen.*
He has a friendly manner.

wesentlich ADJECTIVE
significant

weshalb ADVERB
why

die **Wespe** NOUN
wasp

der **Wespenstich** NOUN (PL die **Wespenstiche**)
wasp sting

wessen PRONOUN
wessen is the genitive of wer.
whose

die **Weste** NOUN
waistcoat

der **Westen** NOUN
west

der **Western** NOUN (PL die **Western**)
western

westlich ADJECTIVE, PREPOSITION, ADVERB
westerly ◊ *in westlicher Richtung* in a
westerly direction
◆ **westlich einer Sache** to the west of
something ◊ *Das Kraftwerk liegt westlich
der Stadt.* The power station's to the
west of the city.
◆ **westlich von** west of ◊ *Essen liegt
westlich von Bochum.* Essen's west of
Bochum.

weswegen ADVERB
why

der **Wettbewerb** NOUN (PL die **Wettbewerbe**)
competition

die **Wette** NOUN
bet

wetten VERB
to bet ◊ *Ich wette, du fällst durchs
Examen.* I bet you fail the exam.

das **Wetter** NOUN
weather

der **Wetterbericht** NOUN (PL die
Wetterberichte)
weather report

die **Wetterlage** NOUN (PL die **Wetterlagen**)
weather situation

die **Wettervorhersage** NOUN
weather forecast

der **Wettkampf** NOUN (PL die **Wettkämpfe**)
contest

der **Wettlauf** NOUN (PL die **Wettläufe**)
race

wichtig ADJECTIVE
important

der **Widder** NOUN (PL die **Widder**)
1 ram
2 Aries ◊ *Horst ist Widder.* Horst's Aries.

widerlich ADJECTIVE
disgusting

widerspenstig ADJECTIVE
wilful

widersprechen VERB (PRESENT **widerspricht,**
IMPERFECT **widersprach,** PERFECT **hat
widersprochen**)
◆ **jemandem widersprechen** to contradict
somebody

der **Widerspruch** NOUN (PL die **Widersprüche**)
contradiction

der **Widerstand** NOUN (PL die **Widerstände**)
resistance

widerwillig ADJECTIVE
unwilling

widmen VERB
1 to dedicate ◊ *Er hat das Buch seiner
Mutter gewidmet.* He dedicated the book
to his mother.
2 to devote ◊ *Sie widmet ihrer Familie
viel Zeit.* She devotes a lot of time to her
family.
◆ **sich einer Sache widmen** to devote
oneself to something ◊ *Jetzt kann ich
mich meinen Hobbys widmen.* Now I can
devote myself to my hobbies.

wie ADVERB
how ◊ *Wie groß?* How big? ◊ *Wie
schnell?* How fast? ◊ *Wie schön!* How
lovely! ◊ *Und wie!* And how!
◆ **Wie wär's?** How about it?
◆ **Wie geht's dir?** How are you?
◆ **Wie ist er?** What's he like?
◆ **Wie gut du das kannst!** You're very
good at it.
◆ **Wie bitte? (1)** Pardon? ◊ *Wie bitte, was
haben Sie gesagt?* Pardon, what did you say?
◆ **Wie bitte? (2)** What? ◊ *Wie bitte, du
willst zweitausend Euro von mir haben?*
What? You want me to give you two
thousand euros?
◆ **so schön wie ...** as beautiful as ...
◆ **wie ich schon sagte** as I said
◆ **wie du** like you
◆ **singen wie ein ...** to sing like a ...
◆ **wie zum Beispiel** such as

wieder ADVERB
again ◊ *wieder da sein* to be back again
◊ *Gehst du schon wieder?* Are you off
again?
◆ **wieder ein ...** another ... ◊ *wenn du
wieder einen Geldbeutel findest ...* if you
find another purse ...

wiederaufbereiten (PERFECT **hat
wiederaufbereitet**)
to recycle

wiederbekommen VERB (IMPERFECT **bekam
wieder,** PERFECT **hat wiederbekommen**)
to get back

wiedererkennen VERB (IMPERFECT **erkannte
wieder,** PERFECT **hat wiedererkannt**)
to recognize

wiederholen VERB (PERFECT **hat wiederholt**)
to repeat

die **Wiederholung** NOUN
1 repetition ◊ *Es darf keine
Wiederholung dieses Vorfalls geben.*

There must be no repetition of this incident.

2 repeat ◊ *Im Fernsehen kommen zu viele Wiederholungen.* There are too many repeats on TV.

das **Wiederhören** NOUN
◆ **Auf Wiederhören!** Goodbye! (*on telephone, radio*)

wiedersehen VERB (PRESENT **sieht wieder,** IMPERFECT **sah wieder,** PERFECT **hat wiedergesehen**)
to see again
◆ **Auf Wiedersehen!** Goodbye.

wiedervereinigen VERB (PERFECT **hat wiedervereinigt**)
to reunify ◊ *das wiedervereinigte Deutschland* reunified Germany

wiederverwerten VERB (PERFECT **hat wiederverwertet**)
to recycle

die **Wiederverwertung** NOUN
recycling

die **Wiege** NOUN
cradle

wiegen VERB (IMPERFECT **wog,** PERFECT **hat gewogen**)
to weigh ◊ *Ich habe mich gestern gewogen.* I weighed myself yesterday.

Wien NEUT NOUN
Vienna

die **Wiese** NOUN
meadow

wieso ADVERB
why

wie viel ADJECTIVE
how much ◊ *Wie viel hat das gekostet?* How much did it cost?
◆ **wie viel Menschen** how many people

wievielmal ADVERB
how often

wievielte ADJECTIVE
◆ **Zum wievielten Mal?** How many times?
◆ **Den Wievielten haben wir?** What's the date?
◆ **Der wievielte Besucher war er?** How many visitors were there before him?

wieweit CONJUNCTION
to what extent

wild ADJECTIVE
wild

wildfremd ADJECTIVE
◆ **ein wildfremder Mensch** a complete stranger

das **Wildleder** NOUN (PL die **Wildleder**)
suede

will VERB *see* **wollen**

der **Wille** NOUN (GEN des **Willens,** PL die **Willen**)
will ◊ *Ich habe es aus freiem Willen getan.* I did it of my own free will.

willkommen ADJECTIVE
welcome ◊ *Herzlich willkommen!* Welcome!

◆ **jemanden willkommen heißen** to welcome somebody

wimmeln VERB
◆ **Es wimmelt von ...** It's teeming with ...

die **Wimper** NOUN
eyelash

die **Wimperntusche** NOUN
mascara

der **Wind** NOUN (PL die **Winde**)
wind

die **Windel** NOUN
nappy ◊ *Kannst du dem Baby die Windeln wechseln?* Can you change the baby's nappy?

die **Windenergie** NOUN
wind energy

windig ADJECTIVE
windy ◊ *Es ist windig.* It's windy.

die **Windmühle** NOUN
windmill

die **Windpocken** PL NOUN
chickenpox ◊ *Windpocken sind ansteckend.* Chickenpox is catching.

die **Windschutzscheibe** NOUN
windscreen

das **Windsurfen** NOUN
windsurfing

der **Winkel** NOUN (PL die **Winkel**)
1 angle ◊ *ein spitzer Winkel* an acute angle
2 corner ◊ *Ich habe jeden Winkel des Zimmers durchsucht.* I've searched every corner of the room.

winken VERB
to wave ◊ *jemandem winken* to wave to somebody

der **Winter** NOUN (PL die **Winter**)
winter ◊ *im Winter* in winter

winzig ADJECTIVE
tiny

wir PRONOUN
we ◊ *Wir kommen.* We're coming.
◆ **wir alle** all of us
◆ **Wir sind's.** It's us.

der **Wirbel** NOUN (PL die **Wirbel**)
1 vertebra ◊ *Sie hat sich einen Wirbel gebrochen.* She's broken a vertebra.
2 hubbub ◊ *der Wirbel vor Weihnachten* the hubbub before Christmas
3 stir ◊ *Das hat für einigen Wirbel gesorgt.* That caused quite a stir.

die **Wirbelsäule** NOUN
spine

wird VERB *see* **werden**

wirft VERB *see* **werfen**

wirken VERB
1 to have an effect ◊ *Die Tablette wirkt schon.* The pill's already having an effect.
2 to seem ◊ *Er wirkte traurig.* He seemed sad.

wirklich ADJECTIVE, ADVERB

1 real ◊ *Er ist ein wirklicher Freund.* He's a real friend.
2 really ◊ *Das ist wirklich passiert.* That really happened. ◊ *Ich weiß es wirklich nicht.* I really don't know.

die **Wirklichkeit** NOUN
reality

wirksam ADJECTIVE
effective

die **Wirkung** NOUN
effect ◊ *Wirkung auf etwas haben* to have an effect on something

wirr ADJECTIVE
confused

der **Wirrwarr** NOUN
chaos

der **Wirsing** NOUN
savoy cabbage

wirst VERB *see* **werden**

der **Wirt** NOUN (PL die **Wirte**)
landlord

die **Wirtin** NOUN
landlady

die **Wirtschaft** NOUN
1 pub ◊ *Wir sind in einer Wirtschaft eingekehrt.* We stopped at a pub.
2 economy ◊ *Die Wirtschaft leidet unter der Rezession.* The economy's suffering because of the recession.

wirtschaftlich ADJECTIVE
1 economical ◊ *Die große Packung ist wirtschaftlicher.* The large packet's more economical.
2 economic ◊ *ein wirtschaftlicher Aufschwung* an economic upswing

die **Wirtschaftslehre** NOUN
economics

das **Wirtshaus** NOUN (GEN des **Wirtshauses**, PL die **Wirtshäuser**)
inn

wischen VERB
to wipe

der **Wischlappen** NOUN (PL die **Wischlappen**)
cloth (*for cleaning*)

das **Wissen** NOUN
see also **wissen** VERB
knowledge

wissen VERB (PRESENT **weiß**, IMPERFECT **wusste**, PERFECT **hat gewusst**)
see also **das Wissen** NOUN
to know ◊ *Sie weiß sehr viel.* She knows a lot. ◊ *Ich weiß es nicht.* I don't know.
♦ *Was weiß ich!* How should I know?

die **Wissenschaft** NOUN
science

der **Wissenschaftler** NOUN (PL die **Wissenschaftler**)
scientist

wissenschaftlich ADJECTIVE
scientific

die **Witwe** NOUN
widow ◊ *Sie ist Witwe.* She's a widow.

der **Witwer** NOUN (PL die **Witwer**)
widower ◊ *Er ist Witwer.* He's a widower.

der **Witz** NOUN (GEN des **Witzes**, PL die **Witze**)
joke ◊ *einen Witz erzählen* to tell a joke

der **Witzbold** NOUN (PL die **Witzbolde**)
joker

witzig ADJECTIVE
funny

wo ADVERB
where ◊ *Wo warst du?* Where were you?
Be careful! **wo** does not mean **who**.

woanders ADVERB
elsewhere

die **Woche** NOUN
week ◊ *nächste Woche* next week

das **Wochenende** NOUN (PL die **Wochenenden**)
weekend ◊ *am Wochenende* at the weekend

der **Wochenendtrip** NOUN (PL die **Wochenendtrips**)
weekend trip

wochenlang ADJECTIVE, ADVERB
for weeks

der **Wochentag** NOUN (PL die **Wochentage**)
weekday

wochentags ADVERB
on weekdays

wöchentlich ADJECTIVE, ADVERB
weekly

wofür ADVERB
what ... for ◊ *Wofür brauchst du das Geld?* What do you need the money for?

wog VERB *see* **wiegen**

woher ADVERB
where ... from ◊ *Woher sind Sie?* Where do you come from?

wohin ADVERB
1 where ... to ◊ *Wohin zieht ihr um?* Where are you moving to?
2 where ◊ *Wohin gehst du?* Where are you going?

das **Wohl** NOUN
see also **wohl** ADVERB
benefit ◊ *zu eurem Wohl* for your benefit
♦ *Zum Wohl!* Cheers!

wohl ADVERB
see also **das Wohl** NOUN
probably ◊ *Das hat er wohl vergessen.* He's probably forgotten.
♦ *Es ist wohl gestohlen worden.* It must have been stolen.
♦ *Das ist doch wohl nicht dein Ernst!* Surely you're not being serious!
♦ *Das mag wohl sein.* That may well be.
♦ *Ob das wohl stimmt?* I wonder if that's true.
♦ *Er weiß das sehr wohl.* He knows that perfectly well.
♦ *Ich muss wohl oder übel hingehen.* I have to go whether I like it or not.

sich **wohlfühlen** VERB
1 to be happy ◊ *Ich fühle mich in*

W

☞

diesem Haus sehr wohl. I'm very happy in this house.

[2] to feel well ◊ *Sie fühlte sich nicht wohl.* She didn't feel well.

die **Wohltätigkeitsorganisation** NOUN
charitable organization

wohlweislich ADVERB
prudently

der **Wohnblock** NOUN (PL die **Wohnblocks**)
block of flats

wohnen VERB
to live ◊ *Ich wohne in Bremen.* I live in Bremen.

die **Wohngemeinschaft** NOUN
♦*Ich wohne in einer Wohngemeinschaft.* I share a flat.

das **Wohnheim** NOUN (PL die **Wohnheime**)
[1] home ◊ *ein Wohnheim für ältere Menschen* a home for senior citizens
♦*ein Studentenwohnheim* a hall of residence
[2] hostel

der **Wohnort** NOUN (PL die **Wohnorte**)
place of residence

der **Wohnsitz** NOUN (GEN des **Wohnsitzes,** PL die **Wohnsitze**)
place of residence

die **Wohnung** NOUN
flat

der **Wohnwagen** NOUN (PL die **Wohnwagen**)
caravan

das **Wohnzimmer** NOUN (PL die **Wohnzimmer**)
living room

der **Wolf** NOUN (PL die **Wölfe**)
wolf

die **Wolke** NOUN
cloud

der **Wolkenkratzer** NOUN (PL die **Wolkenkratzer**)
skyscraper

wolkenlos ADJECTIVE
cloudless

wolkig ADJECTIVE
cloudy

die **Wolle** NOUN
wool

wollen VERB (PRESENT **will,** IMPERFECT **wollte,** PERFECT **hat gewollt** *or* **wollen**)
The past participle **wollen** *is used when* **wollen** *is a modal auxiliary.*
to want ◊ *Er hat nicht gewollt.* He didn't want to. ◊ *Er wollte das nicht.* He didn't want it. ◊ *Ich will nach Hause.* I want to go home.
♦**Wenn du willst.** If you like.
♦**etwas tun wollen** to want to do something ◊ *Er hat unbedingt gehen wollen.* He really wanted to go.
♦**Ich wollte, ich wäre ...** I wish I were ...

womit ADVERB
[1] with which ◊ *Das ist der Gegenstand,*

womit er erschlagen wurde. This is the instrument with which he was killed.
[2] what ... with ◊ *Womit hast du das repariert?* What did you repair it with?

womöglich ADVERB
probably

wonach ADVERB
[1] what ... for ◊ *Das war genau, wonach er gesucht hatte.* That was just what he had been looking for.
[2] what ... by ◊ *Wonach sollen wir die Uhr stellen?* What shall we set the clock by?

woran ADVERB
♦**das Paket, woran dieser Zettel hing** the parcel the note was attached to
♦**die Krankheit, woran sie gestorben ist** the illness she died of
♦**Woran war dieser Zettel befestigt?** What was this note attached to?
♦**Woran ist er gestorben?** What did he die of?

worauf ADVERB
what ... on ◊ *Worauf soll ich den Computer stellen?* What shall I put the computer on?
♦**der Tisch, worauf der Computer steht** the table the computer is on

woraus ADVERB
♦**das Material, woraus es hergestellt ist** the material it is made of
♦**das Leck, woraus Gas strömte** the hole gas was pouring out of
♦**Woraus ist diese Statue?** What's the statue made of?
♦**Woraus kamen die Schreie?** Where did the cries come from?

worin ADVERB
what ... in ◊ *Worin war das versteckt?* What was it hidden in?
♦**die Schublade, worin der Schlüssel ist** the drawer the key is in
♦**Worin besteht der Unterschied?** What's the difference?

das **Wort** NOUN (PL die **Wörter** *or* **Worte**)
word ◊ *Sie sprach ein paar bewegende Worte.* She said a few moving words. ◊ *Manche Wörter werden wie im Französischen ausgesprochen.* Some words are pronounced as in French.
♦**jemanden beim Wort nehmen** to take somebody at his word ◊ *Ich nahm sie beim Wort.* I took her at her word.
♦**mit anderen Worten** in other words

das **Wörterbuch** NOUN (PL die **Wörterbücher**)
dictionary

wörtlich ADJECTIVE
literal

der **Wortschatz** NOUN (GEN des **Wortschatzes**)
vocabulary

das **Wortspiel** NOUN (PL die **Wortspiele**)
pun

worüber ADVERB
- **das Thema, worüber wir reden** the subject we're talking about
- **der Tisch, worüber eine Lampe hing** the table a lamp was hanging over
- **Worüber habt ihr gesprochen?** What did you talk about?

worunter ADVERB
what ... under ◇ *Worunter hat sich die Katze verkrochen?* What did the cat crawl under?
- **der Tisch, worunter die Katze lag** the table the cat was lying under

wovon ADVERB
- **Das war es, wovon wir sprachen.** That was what we were talking about.
- **das Essen, wovon ihm schlecht wurde** the food which made him ill
- **Wovon habt ihr gesprochen?** What did you talk about?
- **Wovon ist ihm schlecht geworden?** What made him ill?

wovor ADVERB
- **das Haus, wovor du stehst** the house you're standing in front of
- **die Arbeit, wovor sie am meisten Angst hat** the test which she's most afraid of
- **Wovor hast du Angst?** What are you afraid of?

wozu ADVERB
1 why ◇ *Wozu willst du das wissen?* Why do you want to know that?
2 what ... for ◇ *Wozu dient dieser Schalter?* What's this switch for? ◇ *Wozu brauchst du einen Computer?* What do you need a computer for?

das **Wrack** NOUN (PL die **Wracks**)
wreck

der **Wucher** NOUN
- **Das ist Wucher!** That's daylight robbery!

wund ADJECTIVE
sore ◇ *Ich habe mir die Füße beim Einkaufen wund gelaufen.* My feet are sore from going round the shops.

die **Wunde** NOUN
wound

das **Wunder** NOUN (PL die **Wunder**)
miracle
- **es ist kein Wunder** it's no wonder

wunderbar ADJECTIVE
wonderful

wundern VERB
to surprise ◇ *Diese Frage hat mich sehr gewundert.* This question really surprised me.
- **sich wundern über** to be surprised at ◇ *Ich wundere mich immer wieder über ihr Wissen.* I'm always surprised at how much she knows. ◇ *Ich wundere mich, dass er noch nicht angerufen hat.* I'm surprised that he hasn't phoned yet.
- **Ich muss mich schon über dich wundern.** I must say you surprise me.

- **Es wundert mich, dass du das fragst.** I'm surprised you ask.
- **Er wird sich noch wundern!** He's in for a surprise!

wunderschön ADJECTIVE
beautiful

wundervoll ADJECTIVE
wonderful

der **Wunsch** NOUN (PL die **Wünsche**)
wish

wünschen VERB
to wish ◇ *Ich wünsche dir viel Erfolg!* I wish you every success.
- **sich etwas wünschen** to want something ◇ *Ich wünsche mir zum Geburtstag Inline-Skates.* I want in-line skates for my birthday.

wurde VERB *see* **werden**

der **Wurf** NOUN (PL die **Würfe**)
throw

der **Würfel** NOUN (PL die **Würfel**)
1 dice ◇ *zwei Würfel* two dice ◇ *Wir haben Würfel gespielt.* We played dice.
2 cube ◇ *Ein Würfel hat sechs gleich große Flächen.* A cube has six equal surfaces.

würfeln VERB
1 to throw a dice ◇ *Ich bin dran mit Würfeln.* It's my turn to throw the dice.
2 to dice ◇ *den Speck würfeln* to dice the bacon

der **Würfelzucker** NOUN
lump sugar

der **Wurm** NOUN (PL die **Würmer**)
worm

die **Wurst** NOUN (PL die **Würste**)
1 sausage ◇ *Leberwurst* liver sausage
2 cold meat
- **Das ist mir Wurst.** I don't give a toss.

das **Würstchen** NOUN (PL die **Würstchen**)
sausage

die **Würstchenbude** NOUN
hot dog stand

die **Würze** NOUN
seasoning

die **Wurzel** NOUN
root

wusch VERB *see* **waschen**

wusste VERB *see* **wissen**

die **Wüste** NOUN
desert

die **Wut** NOUN
rage
- **eine Wut haben** to be furious

der **Wutanfall** NOUN (PL die **Wutanfälle**)
fit of rage

wütend ADJECTIVE
furious ◇ *Ich bin wütend auf ihn.* I'm furious with him.

WWW ABBREVIATION (= World Wide Web)
WWW
- **eine WWW-Seite** a web page

W

X

x-beliebig ADJECTIVE
  any ... whatever ◊ *Wähle eine x-beliebige Zahl.* Choose any number whatever.
x-mal ADVERB
  any number of times ◊ *Ich habe es ihm x-mal gesagt.* I've told him any number of times.
das **Xylofon** NOUN (PL die **Xylofone**)
  xylophone
das **Xylophon** NOUN (PL die **Xylophone**)
  see **Xylofon**

Y

das **Yoga** NOUN (GEN des **Yoga** or **Yogas**)
  yoga
das **Ypsilon** NOUN (GEN des **Ypsilon** or **Ypsilons**, PL die **Ypsilons**)
  the letter Y

Z

die **Zacke** NOUN
> peak ◊ *die Zacke einer Fieberkurve* the peak of a temperature chart
> ♦ **eine Bergzacke** a jagged peak
> ♦ **die Zacken der Gabel** the prongs of the fork
> ♦ **die Zacken des Kamms** the teeth of the comb

zaghaft ADJECTIVE
> timid

zäh ADJECTIVE
> [1] tough ◊ *Das Steak ist zäh.* The steak's tough. ◊ *Ich bin zäh, ich halte es noch eine Weile aus.* I'm tough, I can stand it for a bit yet.
> [2] slow-moving ◊ *Der Verkehr war zäh.* Traffic was slow-moving.

die **Zahl** NOUN
> number

zahlen VERB
> to pay ◊ *Wie viel hast du dafür gezahlt?* How much did you pay for it?
> ♦ **Zahlen bitte!** The bill, please!

zählen VERB
> to count ◊ *Ich zähle bis drei.* I'll count to three. ◊ *Ich habe die Hefte gezählt.* I've counted the exercise books.
> ♦ **zählen auf** to count on ◊ *Wir zählen auf dich.* We're counting on you.
> ♦ **zählen zu** to be one of ◊ *Er zählt zu den besseren Schülern.* He's one of the better pupils.

zahlreich ADJECTIVE
> numerous

die **Zahlung** NOUN
> payment

das **Zahlwort** NOUN (PL die **Zahlwörter**)
> numeral

zahm ADJECTIVE
> tame

der **Zahn** NOUN (PL die **Zähne**)
> tooth

der **Zahnarzt** NOUN (GEN des **Zahnarztes**, PL die **Zahnärzte**)
> dentist

die **Zahnbürste** NOUN
> toothbrush

die **Zahncreme** NOUN (PL die **Zahncremes**)
> toothpaste

das **Zahnfleisch** NOUN
> gums ◊ *Mein Zahnfleisch blutet.* My gums are bleeding.

die **Zahnpasta** NOUN (PL die **Zahnpasten**)
> toothpaste

die **Zahnschmerzen** MASC PL NOUN
> toothache ◊ *Zahnschmerzen haben* to have toothache

der **Zahnstein** NOUN
> tartar

der **Zahnstocher** NOUN (PL die **Zahnstocher**)
> toothpick

die **Zange** NOUN
> [1] pliers ◊ *Ich brauche eine isolierte Zange.* I need a pair of insulated pliers.
> [2] pincers ◊ *die Zangen eines Hummers* a lobster's pincers

zappeln VERB
> [1] to wriggle ◊ *Der Fisch zappelt noch.* The fish is still wriggling.
> [2] to fidget ◊ *Hör auf zu zappeln.* Stop fidgeting.

zart ADJECTIVE
> [1] soft ◊ *zarte Haut* soft skin
> [2] gentle ◊ *eine zarte Berührung* a gentle touch
> [3] delicate ◊ *zarte Farben* delicate colours ◊ *Sie ist ein sehr zartes Kind.* She's a very delicate child.
> ♦ **zartes Fleisch** tender meat

zärtlich ADJECTIVE
> loving ◊ *Mein Freund ist sehr zärtlich.* My boyfriend's very loving. ◊ *ein zärtlicher Kuss* a loving kiss ◊ *eine zärtliche Berührung* a loving touch

die **Zauberei** NOUN
> magic

der **Zaun** NOUN (PL die **Zäune**)
> fence

z. B. ABBREVIATION (= *zum Beispiel*)
> e.g.

das **ZDF** ABBREVIATION (= *Zweites Deutsches Fernsehen*)
> German TV channel

der **Zebrastreifen** NOUN (PL die **Zebrastreifen**)
> zebra crossing

die **Zehe** NOUN
> toe ◊ *die große Zehe* the big toe
> ♦ **eine Knoblauchzehe** a clove of garlic

zehn NUMBER
> ten

zehnte ADJECTIVE
> tenth

das **Zeichen** NOUN (PL die **Zeichen**)
> sign

der **Zeichentrickfilm** NOUN (PL die **Zeichentrickfilme**)
> animated cartoon

zeichnen VERB
> to draw ◊ *Marek kann gut zeichnen.* Marek's good at drawing. ◊ *Sie hat eine Maus gezeichnet.* She's drawn a mouse.

die **Zeichnung** NOUN
> drawing

der **Zeigefinger** NOUN (PL die **Zeigefinger**)
> index finger

zeigen VERB

zeigen VERB

[1] to show ◊ *Sie hat mir ihre Fotos gezeigt.* She showed me her photos. ◊ *Zeig mal, was du da hast.* Show us what you've got there.

[2] to point ◊ *Sie zeigte an die Tafel.* She pointed to the blackboard.

♦ **zeigen auf** to point at ◊ *Man zeigt nicht mit dem Finger auf Menschen.* Don't point at people.

♦ **es wird sich zeigen** time will tell ◊ *Es wird sich zeigen, ob er das kann.* Time will tell whether he can do it.

♦ **Es zeigte sich, dass ...** It turned out that ... ◊ *Es zeigte sich, dass der Text zu schwierig war.* It turned out that the text was too difficult.

der **Zeiger** NOUN (PL die **Zeiger**)

[1] hand ◊ *der kleine Zeiger der Uhr* the little hand of the clock

[2] pointer ◊ *der Zeiger der Waage* the pointer of the scales

die **Zeile** NOUN

line ◊ *Ich schreibe ihr ein paar Zeilen.* I'm going to write her a few lines.

die **Zeit** NOUN

[1] time ◊ *Wir haben keine Zeit mehr.* We haven't got any more time. ◊ *Um welche Zeit seid ihr nach Hause gekommen?* What time did you get home?

[2] tense ◊ *die Zeiten der Vergangenheit* the past tenses

♦ **zur Zeit** at the moment

♦ **sich Zeit lassen** to take one's time ◊ *Da hast du dir aber viel Zeit gelassen.* You've been taking your time.

♦ **von Zeit zu Zeit** from time to time

♦ **Zeit raubend** see **zeitraubend**

zeitlich ADJECTIVE

chronological

die **Zeitlupe** NOUN

slow motion ◊ *in Zeitlupe* in slow motion

zeitraubend ADJECTIVE

time-consuming

der **Zeitraum** NOUN (PL die **Zeiträume**)

period ◊ *innerhalb dieses Zeitraums* within this period

die **Zeitschrift** NOUN

magazine

die **Zeitung** NOUN

newspaper

der **Zeitungskiosk** NOUN (PL die **Zeitungskioske**)

newspaper kiosk

der **Zeitungsstand** NOUN (PL die **Zeitungsstände**)

newspaper stand

die **Zeitverschwendung** NOUN

waste of time ◊ *Das ist doch Zeitverschwendung!* That's just a waste of time.

das **Zeitwort** NOUN (PL die **Zeitwörter**)

verb

die **Zelle** NOUN

[1] cell ◊ *Im Alter sterben die Zellen ab.* Cells die off in old age.

[2] call box ◊ *Ich rufe aus einer Zelle an.* I'm phoning from a call box.

das **Zelt** NOUN (PL die **Zelte**)

tent

zelten VERB

to camp

der **Zeltplatz** NOUN (GEN des **Zeltplatzes,** PL die **Zeltplätze**)

camp site

der **Zement** NOUN (PL die **Zemente**)

cement

zensieren VERB (PERFECT **hat zensiert**)

[1] to censor ◊ *Der Film wurde zensiert.* The film was censored.

[2] to give a mark ◊ *Wie hat deine Deutschlehrerin den Aufsatz zensiert?* What mark did your German teacher give you for your essay?

die **Zensur** NOUN

mark ◊ *Ich habe durchweg gute Zensuren.* I've got good marks in everything.

der **Zentimeter** NOUN (PL die **Zentimeter**)

centimetre

der **Zentner** NOUN (PL die **Zentner**)

hundredweight ◊ *drei Zentner* three hundredweight

zentral ADJECTIVE

central

die **Zentrale** NOUN

[1] head office ◊ *Das Gerät müssen wir in der Zentrale anfordern.* We'll have to order the appliance from the head office.

[2] switchboard ◊ *Du musst dich über die Zentrale verbinden lassen.* You have to go through the switchboard.

die **Zentralheizung** NOUN

central heating

das **Zentrum** NOUN (PL die **Zentren**)

centre

zerbrechen VERB (PRESENT **zerbricht,** IMPERFECT **zerbrach,** PERFECT **hat/ist zerbrochen**)

*For the perfect tense use **haben** when the verb has an object and **sein** when there is no object.*

to break ◊ *Sie hat den Teller zerbrochen.* She's broken the plate. ◊ *Der Teller ist zerbrochen.* The plate broke.

zerbrechlich ADJECTIVE

fragile

zerreißen VERB (IMPERFECT **zerriss,** PERFECT **hat/ist zerrissen**)

*For the perfect tense use **haben** when the verb has an object and **sein** when there is no object.*

[1] to tear to pieces ◊ *Sie hat seinen Brief zerrissen.* She tore his letter to pieces.

♦ **Sie hatte völlig zerrissene Kleider an.**
Her clothes were all tattered.
2 to tear ◊ *Der Umschlag ist unterwegs zerrissen.* The envelope got torn in the post.

zerren VERB
to drag ◊ *Er zerrte sie in die Büsche.* He dragged her into the bushes.
♦ **zerren an** to tug at ◊ *Der Hund zerrte an der Leine.* The dog tugged at its leash.

zerrissen VERB *see* **zerreißen**

zerschlagen VERB (PRESENT **zerschlägt**, IMPERFECT **zerschlug**, PERFECT **hat zerschlagen**)
to smash ◊ *Sie haben alles Porzellan zerschlagen.* They smashed all the china.
♦ **sich zerschlagen** to fall through ◊ *Unsere Ferienpläne haben sich zerschlagen.* Our holiday plans have fallen through.

zerschneiden VERB (IMPERFECT **zerschnitt**, PERFECT **hat zerschnitten**)
to cut up

der **Zerstäuber** NOUN (PL die **Zerstäuber**)
atomizer

zerstören VERB (PRESENT **hat zerstört**)
to destroy

die **Zerstörung** NOUN
destruction

zerstreuen VERB (PERFECT **hat zerstreut**)
1 to entertain ◊ *Er hat uns mit lustigen Geschichten zerstreut.* He entertained us with amusing stories.
2 to scatter ◊ *Warum hast du die Blätter im ganzen Zimmer zerstreut?* Why have you scattered the papers all over the room? ◊ *Unsere Familie ist über ganz Deutschland zerstreut.* Our family's scattered all over Germany.
♦ **jemandes Angst zerstreuen** to allay somebody's fears

zerstreut ADJECTIVE
1 absent-minded ◊ *Er ist furchtbar zerstreut.* He's terribly absent-minded.
2 scattered ◊ *Sie sammelte die zerstreuten Seiten auf.* She picked up the scattered pages.

der **Zettel** NOUN (PL die **Zettel**)
1 note ◊ *Auf dem Küchentisch liegt ein Zettel für dich.* There's a note on the kitchen table for you.
2 piece of paper ◊ *Sie schrieb seine Telefonnummer auf einen Zettel.* She wrote his telephone number on a piece of paper.
3 form ◊ *Wenn du dem Klub beitreten willst, musst du diesen Zettel ausfüllen.* If you want to join the club you'll have to fill in this form.

das **Zeug** NOUN
1 stuff ◊ *Was ist das für ein Zeug?* What's this stuff? ◊ *mein Sportzeug* my sports stuff
2 gear ◊ *mein Angelzeug* my fishing gear

♦ **dummes Zeug** nonsense ◊ *Das ist doch dummes Zeug.* That's just a lot of nonsense.
♦ **das Zeug haben zu** to have the makings of ◊ *Er hat das Zeug zum Lehrer.* He has the makings of a teacher.

der **Zeuge** NOUN (GEN des **Zeugen**, PL die **Zeugen**)
witness

die **Zeugin** NOUN
witness

das **Zeugnis** NOUN (GEN des **Zeugnisses**, PL die **Zeugnisse**)
report ◊ *Oliver hat ein sehr gutes Zeugnis.* Oliver's got a very good report.

die **Ziege** NOUN
goat

der **Ziegel** NOUN (PL die **Ziegel**)
1 brick ◊ *eine Mauer aus Ziegeln* a brick wall
2 tile ◊ *Deutsche Dächer sind meist mit roten Ziegeln gedeckt.* German roofs are usually covered with red tiles.

ziehen VERB (IMPERFECT **zog**, PERFECT **hat/ist gezogen**)

Use **sein** to form the perfect tense for **to move** (house) and **to roam**. Use **haben** for **to move** (in chess), **to draw** and **to pull**.

1 to draw ◊ *Er hat eine Niete gezogen.* He drew a blank.
2 to pull ◊ *Sie zog mich am Ärmel.* She pulled at my sleeve.
3 to move ◊ *Sie sind nach Wuppertal gezogen.* They've moved to Wuppertal. ◊ *Er zog mit seinem Turm.* He moved his rook.
4 to roam ◊ *Früher zogen die Zigeuner durchs Land.* In the old days, gypsies used to roam the countryside.
♦ **Es zieht.** There's a draught.
♦ **sich in die Länge ziehen** to be drawn out

das **Ziel** NOUN (PL die **Ziele**)
1 destination ◊ *Unser heutiges Ziel ist Bonn.* Our destination today is Bonn.
2 finishing line ◊ *Er ging als Erster durchs Ziel.* He was the first to cross the finishing line.
3 target ◊ *Ulm war das Ziel eines Bombenangriffs.* Ulm was the target of an air raid.
4 goal ◊ *Es ist nicht mein Ziel im Leben, reich zu werden.* Getting rich is not my goal in life.

zielen VERB
to aim ◊ *Er hat auf seine Beine gezielt.* He aimed at his legs.

die **Zielscheibe** NOUN
target ◊ *Er traf die Zielscheibe mit seinem ersten Schuss.* He hit the target with his first shot.

ziemlich ADJECTIVE, ADVERB

Z

☞

1 quite ◊ *Das war eine ziemliche Katastrophe.* That was quite a disaster.
2 fair ◊ *eine ziemliche Menge Fehler* a fair number of mistakes
3 rather ◊ *Er war ziemlich sauer.* He was rather cross.
♦ **ziemlich viel** quite a bit ◊ *Wir haben ziemlich viel erledigt.* We've got through quite a bit.

sich **zieren** VERB
to act coy

zierlich ADJECTIVE
dainty

die **Ziffer** NOUN
figure

zig ADJECTIVE
umpteen

die **Zigarette** NOUN
cigarette

der **Zigarettenautomat** NOUN (GEN des **Zigarettenautomaten**, PL die **Zigarettenautomaten**)
cigarette machine

die **Zigarettenschachtel** NOUN
cigarette packet

das **Zigarillo** NOUN (PL die **Zigarillos**)
You can also say der Zigarillo.
cigarillo

die **Zigarre** NOUN
cigar

der **Zigeuner** NOUN (PL die **Zigeuner**)
gipsy

die **Zigeunerin** NOUN
gipsy

das **Zimmer** NOUN (PL die **Zimmer**)
room
♦ **"Zimmer frei"** "Vacancies"

das **Zimmermädchen** NOUN (PL die **Zimmermädchen**)
chambermaid

der **Zimmernachweis** NOUN (GEN des **Zimmernachweises**, PL die **Zimmernachweise**)
accommodation office

der **Zimt** NOUN
cinnamon

das **Zinn** NOUN
1 tin ◊ *In Cornwall wurde früher Zinn abgebaut.* They used to mine tin in Cornwall.
2 pewter ◊ *Mein Bruder sammelt Zinn.* My brother collects pewter.

der **Zins** NOUN (GEN des **Zinses**, PL die **Zinsen**)
interest ◊ *acht Prozent Zinsen* eight per cent interest

das **Zip-Laufwerk** NOUN (PL die **Zip-Laufwerke**)
zip drive

zirka ADVERB
approximately

der **Zirkus** NOUN (GEN des **Zirkus**, PL die **Zirkusse**)
circus

zischen VERB
to hiss

das **Zitat** NOUN (PL die **Zitate**)
quotation

zitieren VERB (PERFECT **hat zitiert**)
to quote

die **Zitrone** NOUN
lemon

die **Zitronenlimonade** NOUN
lemonade

der **Zitronensaft** NOUN (PL die **Zitronensäfte**)
lemon juice

zittern VERB
to tremble ◊ *vor Angst zittern* to tremble with fear
♦ **Sie zitterte vor Kälte.** She was shivering.

der **Zivildienst** NOUN
community service

> ⓘ Instead of doing national service in the German armed forces, young men can opt to do community service as **Zivildienstleistende** or **Zivis**, for example with the Red Cross or in an old people's home.

die **Zivilisation** NOUN
civilization

zögern VERB
to hesitate

der **Zoll** NOUN (PL die **Zölle**)
1 customs ◊ *Wir mussten am Zoll lange warten.* We had to wait a long time at customs.
2 duty ◊ *Darauf musst du Zoll bezahlen.* You have to pay duty on that.

der **Zollbeamte** NOUN (GEN des **Zollbeamten**, PL die **Zollbeamten**)
customs official ◊ *Ein Zollbeamter hat unser Auto durchsucht.* A customs official searched our car.

zollfrei ADJECTIVE
duty-free

die **Zollkontrolle** NOUN
customs check

die **Zone** NOUN
zone

der **Zoo** NOUN (PL die **Zoos**)
zoo

zoologisch ADJECTIVE
zoological

der **Zopf** NOUN (PL die **Zöpfe**)
1 plait ◊ *Man stellt sich deutsche Mädchen immer mit zwei blonden Zöpfen vor.* You always imagine German girls as having two blonde plaits.
2 pigtail ◊ *Sie hatte ihre Haare zu einem Zopf zusammengebunden.* She had put her hair into a pigtail.

der **Zorn** NOUN
anger

zornig ADJECTIVE

angry

zu PREPOSITION, CONJUNCTION, ADVERB

The preposition zu takes the dative.

 1 to ◊ *zum Bahnhof gehen* to go to the station ◊ *zum Arzt gehen* to go to the doctor ◊ *zur Schule gehen* to go to school ◊ *zur Kirche gehen* to go to church ◊ *Genau das habe ich zu ihm gesagt.* That's exactly what I said to him. ◊ *Sollen wir zu euch gehen?* Shall we go to your place?

♦ **Sie sah zu ihm hin.** She looked towards him.

♦ **zum Fenster herein** through the window
♦ **zu meiner Linken** on my left

zu is used with the infinitive.

◊ *etwas zu essen* something to eat

♦ **um besser sehen zu können** in order to see better

♦ **ohne es zu wissen** without knowing it
 2 at ◊ *zu Ostern* at Easter

♦ **zu Hause** at home
♦ **bis zum ersten Mai (1)** until the first of May ◊ *Das Sonderangebot gilt bis zum ersten Mai.* The special offer is valid until the first of May.

♦ **bis zum ersten Mai (2)** by the first of May ◊ *Bis zum ersten Mai muss mein Referat fertig sein.* My assignment has to be finished by the first of May.

♦ **zu meinem Geburtstag** for my birthday
♦ **zu meiner Zeit** in my time
 3 with ◊ *Wein zum Essen trinken* to drink wine with one's meal

♦ **sich zu jemandem setzen** to sit down beside somebody

♦ **Setz dich doch zu uns.** Come and sit with us.

♦ **Anmerkungen zu etwas** notes on something
 4 for ◊ *Wasser zum Waschen* water for washing

♦ **Papier zum Schreiben** paper to write on
♦ **zu etwas werden** to develop into something ◊ *Sie ist zu einer hübschen jungen Dame geworden.* She's developed into an attractive young lady.

♦ **jemanden zu etwas machen** to make somebody something ◊ *Sie haben mich zur Klassensprecherin gemacht.* They made me class representative.

♦ **drei zu zwei** three two ◊ *Unsere Mannschaft hat drei zu zwei gewonnen.* Our team won three two.

♦ **das Stück zu drei Euro** at three euros each

♦ **zum ersten Mal** for the first time
♦ **zu meiner Freude** to my delight
♦ **zum Scherz** as a joke
♦ **zu Fuß** on foot
♦ **Es ist zum Weinen.** It's enough to make you cry.

 5 too ◊ *zu schnell* too fast ◊ *zu sehr* too much
 6 closed ◊ *Die Geschäfte haben zu.* The shops are closed.

♦ **zu sein** to be shut ◊ *Das Fenster war zu.* The window was shut.

zuallererst ADVERB
first of all

zuallerletzt ADVERB
last of all

das **Zubehör** NOUN (PL die **Zubehöre**)
accessories ◊ *Das Zubehör kostet extra.* You pay extra for the accessories.

zubereiten VERB (PERFECT **hat zubereitet**)
to prepare

zubinden VERB (IMPERFECT **band zu**, PERFECT **hat zugebunden**)
to tie up

zubringen VERB (IMPERFECT **brachte zu**, PERFECT **hat zugebracht**)
to spend ◊ *Ich habe viel Zeit bei ihnen zugebracht.* I spent a lot of time with them.

die **Zucchini** PL NOUN
courgette

züchten VERB
 1 to breed ◊ *Er züchtet Tauben.* He breeds pigeons.
 2 to grow ◊ *Mein Vater züchtet Rosen.* My father grows roses.

zucken VERB
 1 to twitch ◊ *Seine Mundwinkel zuckten.* The corners of his mouth twitched.
 2 to flash ◊ *Ein Blitz zuckte durch die Nacht.* Lightning flashed across the night sky.

♦ **mit den Schultern zucken** to shrug one's shoulders

der **Zucker** NOUN
 1 sugar ◊ *Ich nehme keinen Zucker in den Tee.* I don't take sugar in my tea.
 2 diabetes ◊ *Meine Tante hat Zucker.* My aunt's got diabetes.

der **Zuckerguss** NOUN (GEN des **Zuckergusses**, PL die **Zuckergüsse**)
icing

zuckerkrank ADJECTIVE
diabetic

die **Zuckerkrankheit** NOUN
diabetes

zudecken VERB (PERFECT **hat zugedeckt**)
 1 to cover up ◊ *Man sollte das Loch zudecken.* They ought to cover up the hole.
 2 to tuck up ◊ *Sie deckte die Kinder zu.* She tucked the children up.

zueinander ADVERB
 1 to one another ◊ *Seid nett zueinander.* Be nice to one another.

♦ **Wir haben viel Vertrauen zueinander.** We trust each other.

Z

☞

2 together ◊ *Wir halten zueinander, egal, was kommt.* Whatever happens, we'll stick together.

zuerst ADVERB

1 first ◊ *Was soll ich zuerst machen?* What shall I do first? ◊ *Er ist zuerst gekommen, dann kam seine Schwester.* He arrived first, then his sister.

2 at first ◊ *Zuerst war sie noch etwas schüchtern.* At first, she was still a bit shy.

♦ **zuerst einmal** first of all ◊ *Wir sollten zuerst einmal klären, was das kostet.* First of all we ought to check how much it costs.

die **Zufahrt** NOUN

approach road

♦ **"keine Zufahrt"** "no access"

der **Zufall** NOUN (PL die **Zufälle**)

1 chance ◊ *Wie es der Zufall so wollte ...* As chance would have it ...

♦ **durch Zufall** by chance ◊ *Ich habe es durch Zufall gefunden.* I found it by chance.

2 coincidence ◊ *Es war schon ein Zufall, dass ich ihm in London begegnet bin.* It was quite a coincidence that I met him in London. ◊ *Was für ein glücklicher Zufall!* What a happy coincidence! ◊ *So ein Zufall!* What a coincidence!

zufällig ADJECTIVE, ADVERB

1 chance ◊ *eine zufällige Begegnung* a chance meeting

2 by chance ◊ *Ich habe das Restaurant ganz zufällig gefunden.* I found the restaurant quite by chance.

♦ **Ich habe zufällig Zeit.** I happen to have time.

3 by any chance ◊ *Hast du zufällig mein Heft gesehen?* Have you seen my exercise book by any chance?

zufrieden ADJECTIVE

satisfied ◊ *Ich bin mit deinen Leistungen nicht zufrieden.* I'm not satisfied with your work. ◊ *Bist du jetzt zufrieden?* Are you satisfied now? ◊ *ein zufriedener Gesichtsausdruck* a satisfied expression

zufrieren VERB (IMPERFECT **fror zu,** PERFECT **ist zugefroren**)

to freeze over ◊ *Der See ist zugefroren.* The lake's frozen over.

der **Zug** NOUN (PL die **Züge**)

1 train ◊ *Wir sind mit dem Zug gefahren.* We went by train.

2 draught ◊ *Hier ist ein furchtbarer Zug.* There's a terrible draught in here.

3 move ◊ *Du bist am Zug.* It's your move.

4 gulp ◊ *Er trank das Glas auf einen Zug leer.* He emptied the glass in one gulp.

5 trait ◊ *Sein Geiz ist ein unangenehmer Zug an ihm.* His meanness is an unpleasant trait.

♦ **etwas in vollen Zügen genießen** to enjoy something to the full

die **Zugabe** NOUN

1 free gift ◊ *Beim Kauf von drei Packungen bekommen Sie einen Dosierlöffel als Zugabe.* Buy three packets and get a measuring spoon as a free gift.

2 encore ◊ *Die Zuhörer brüllten: "Zugabe, Zugabe".* The audience roared: "encore, encore".

zugeben VERB (PRESENT **gibt zu,** IMPERFECT **gab zu,** PERFECT **hat zugegeben**)

to admit ◊ *Gib doch zu, dass du dich getäuscht hast.* Admit you were wrong. ◊ *Sie wollte ihren Irrtum nicht zugeben.* She didn't want to admit her mistake.

zugehen VERB (IMPERFECT **ging zu,** PERFECT **ist zugegangen**)

to shut ◊ *Die Tür geht nicht zu.* The door won't shut.

♦ **auf jemanden zugehen** to walk up to somebody ◊ *Sie ging auf den Mann zu und fragte ihn nach dem Weg.* She walked up to the man and asked him the way.

♦ **auf etwas zugehen** to walk towards something ◊ *Sie ging auf den Eingang zu, kehrte dann aber wieder um.* She walked towards the entrance but then turned back again.

♦ **Es geht dort seltsam zu.** There are strange goings-on there.

♦ **dem Ende zugehen** to be nearing the end

der **Zugführer** NOUN (PL die **Zugführer**)

chief guard (*on train*)

zugig ADJECTIVE

draughty

zügig ADJECTIVE

swift ◊ *eine zügige Entscheidung* a swift decision

zugreifen VERB (IMPERFECT **griff zu,** PERFECT **hat zugegriffen**)

1 to help oneself ◊ *Greift ungeniert zu, es ist genügend Kuchen da!* Feel free to help yourselves, there's plenty of cake.

2 to seize ◊ *Er sah das Seil und griff zu.* He saw the rope and seized it.

3 to lend a hand ◊ *Du könntest ruhig ein bisschen zugreifen und mich nicht alles allein machen lassen.* You could at least lend a hand a bit instead of letting me do everything.

zugrunde ADVERB

♦ **elend zugrunde gehen** to come to a wretched end ◊ *Er fing an zu trinken und ging elend zugrunde.* He took to drink and came to a wretched end.

♦ **zugrunde richten** to destroy ◊ *Alkohol und Drogen haben sie zugrunde gerichtet.* Alcohol and drugs have destroyed her.

♦ **einer Sache etwas zugrunde legen** to base something on something ◊ *Diesem Film liegt ein Roman zugrunde.* This film is based on a novel.

zugunsten PREPOSITION

*The preposition **zugunsten** takes the dative or the genitive.*

in favour of ◊ *Das Gericht entschied zugunsten des Angeklagten.* The court decided in favour of the accused.

zugutekommen VERB

♦ **jemandem zugutekommen** to stand somebody in good stead ◊ *Meine Englischkenntnisse sind mir im Urlaub zugutegekommen.* My knowledge of English stood me in good stead on holiday.

das **Zuhause** NOUN (GEN des **Zuhause**)
home

zuhören VERB (PERFECT **hat zugehört**)
to listen ◊ *Du hörst mir ja gar nicht zu.* You're not listening to me at all.

der **Zuhörer** NOUN (PL die **Zuhörer**)
listener

zukommen VERB (IMPERFECT **kam zu,** PERFECT **ist zugekommen**)

♦ **auf jemanden zukommen** to come up to somebody ◊ *Er kam auf uns zu und fragte uns, wie spät es ist.* He came up to us and asked what time it was.

♦ **jemandem etwas zukommen lassen** to give somebody something ◊ *Mein Onkel hat mir etwas Geld zukommen lassen.* My uncle gave me some money.

♦ **etwas auf sich zukommen lassen** to take something as it comes ◊ *Warum lässt du diese Sache nicht einfach auf dich zukommen?* Why don't you just take things as they come?

die **Zukunft** NOUN
future ◊ *in Zukunft* in the future

die **Zukunftspläne** PL NOUN
plans for the future

zulassen VERB (PRESENT **lässt zu,** IMPERFECT **ließ zu,** PERFECT **hat zugelassen**)

[1] to allow ◊ *Ich kann es nicht zulassen, dass du so spät noch fernsiehst.* I can't allow you to watch TV so late.

[2] to register ◊ *Hast du dein Moped schon zugelassen?* Have you registered your moped yet?

[3] to leave closed ◊ *Bitte lass das Fenster zu.* Please leave the window closed.

♦ **Lass den Brief zu.** Don't open the letter.

zulässig ADJECTIVE
permissible

zuleide ADVERB

♦ **jemandem etwas zuleide tun** to hurt somebody ◊ *Bitte tu ihr nichts zuleide.* Please don't hurt her.

zuletzt ADVERB

[1] last ◊ *Wir sollten das zuletzt machen.* We should do that last.

[2] in the end ◊ *Zuletzt hat sie es dann doch verstanden.* In the end she understood.

zuliebe ADVERB

♦ **jemandem zuliebe** to please somebody ◊ *Er ist mir zuliebe zu Hause geblieben.* He stayed at home to please me.

zum = **zu dem**

zumachen VERB (PERFECT **hat zugemacht**)

[1] to shut ◊ *Mach bitte die Tür zu.* Please shut the door.

[2] to fasten ◊ *Kannst du mal bitte mein Kleid zumachen?* Can you fasten my dress, please?

zumindest ADVERB
at least

zumute ADVERB

♦ **Wie ist ihm zumute?** How does he feel?

zumuten VERB (PERFECT **hat zugemutet**)

♦ **jemandem etwas zumuten** to ask something of somebody ◊ *Das kann ich ihm nicht zumuten.* I can't ask that of him.

die **Zumutung** NOUN

♦ **Das ist eine Zumutung!** That's asking too much.

zunächst ADVERB
first of all ◊ *Wir sollten zunächst diese Frage klären.* We ought to clear this issue up first of all.

♦ **zunächst einmal** to start with

zunehmen VERB (PRESENT **nimmt zu,** IMPERFECT **nahm zu,** PERFECT **hat zugenommen**)

[1] to increase ◊ *Der Lärm nahm zu.* The noise increased.

[2] to put on weight ◊ *Ich habe schon wieder zugenommen.* I've put on weight yet again.

♦ **Er hat fünf Kilo zugenommen.** He's put on five kilos.

die **Zuneigung** NOUN
affection

♦ **Ich empfinde große Zuneigung für ihn.** I'm very fond of him.

die **Zunge** NOUN
tongue

zur = **zu der**

zurate ADVERB

♦ **jemanden zurate ziehen** to consult somebody

zurechnungsfähig ADJECTIVE
compos mentis

sich **zurechtfinden** VERB (IMPERFECT **fand sich zurecht,** PERFECT **hat sich zurechtgefunden**)
to find one's way

zurechtkommen VERB (IMPERFECT **kam zurecht,** PERFECT **ist zurechtgekommen**)
to manage

zurechtlegen VERB (PERFECT **hat zurechtgelegt**)

Z

☞

to sort out ◇ *Ich habe die Sachen für die Ferien schon zurechtgelegt.* I've already sorted out my things for my holiday.

♦ **sich eine Ausrede zurechtlegen** to think up an excuse ◇ *Na, welche Ausrede hast du dir denn diesmal zurechtgelegt?* Well, what excuse have you thought up this time?

zurück ADVERB
back

zurückbekommen VERB (IMPERFECT **bekam zurück,** PERFECT **hat zurückbekommen**)
to get back

zurückbringen VERB (IMPERFECT **brachte zurück,** PERFECT **hat zurückgebracht**)
to bring back

zurückerstatten VERB (PERFECT **hat zurückerstattet**)
to refund

zurückfahren VERB (PRESENT **fährt zurück,** IMPERFECT **fuhr zurück,** PERFECT **ist/hat zurückgefahren**)

*For the perfect tense use **haben** when the verb has an object and **sein** when there is no object.*

to return ◇ *Wann fahrt ihr zurück?* When do you return?

♦ **jemanden zurückfahren** to drive somebody back ◇ *Sie hat mich nach Hause zurückgefahren.* She drove me back home.

zurückgeben VERB (PRESENT **gibt zurück,** IMPERFECT **gab zurück,** PERFECT **hat zurückgegeben**)
to give back ◇ *Gib mir bitte mein Buch zurück.* Please give me my book back.

zurückgehen VERB (IMPERFECT **ging zurück,** PERFECT **ist zurückgegangen**)
1 to go back ◇ *Wir sollten zurückgehen, bevor es zu spät wird.* We should go back before it gets too late.
2 to recede ◇ *Das Hochwasser ist zurückgegangen.* The floodwater receded.
3 to fall ◇ *Die Nachfrage geht zurück.* Demand is falling.

♦ **zurückgehen auf** to date back to ◇ *Die Gründung der Stadt Aachen geht auf Karl den Großen zurück.* The founding of the city of Aachen dates back to Charlemagne.

zurückhaltend ADJECTIVE
reserved ◇ *Er ist sehr zurückhaltend.* He is very reserved.

zurückkehren VERB (PERFECT **ist zurückgekehrt**)
to return

zurückkommen VERB (IMPERFECT **kam zurück,** PERFECT **ist zurückgekommen**)
to come back ◇ *Er kam nach dem Film zurück.* He came back after the film.
◇ *Darf ich auf das zurückkommen, was*

Sie vorhin gesagt haben? May I come back to what you were saying earlier?

♦ **Komm nicht zu spät zurück.** Don't be too late back.

zurücklegen VERB (PERFECT **hat zurückgelegt**)
1 to put back ◇ *Leg das Buch bitte an seinen Platz zurück.* Please put the book back in its place.
2 to put by ◇ *Wir haben für die Ferien etwas Geld zurückgelegt.* We've put some money by for the holidays.
3 to put aside ◇ *Können Sie mir diesen Pulli bitte zurücklegen?* Could you put this pullover aside for me, please?
4 to cover ◇ *Wir haben heute zweihundert Kilometer zurückgelegt.* We've covered two hundred kilometres today.

zurücknehmen VERB (PRESENT **nimmt zurück,** IMPERFECT **nahm zurück,** PERFECT **hat zurückgenommen**)
to take back

zurückrufen VERB (PERFECT **hat zurückgerufen**)
to call back ◇ *Können Sie mich morgen zurückrufen?* Can you call me back tomorrow?

zurücktreten VERB (PRESENT **tritt zurück,** IMPERFECT **trat zurück,** PERFECT **ist zurückgetreten**)
1 to step back ◇ *Treten Sie etwas zurück bitte!* Step back a bit, please.
2 to resign ◇ *Warum ist er zurückgetreten?* Why did he resign?

zurückzahlen VERB (PERFECT **hat zurückgezahlt**)
to repay ◇ *Du solltest endlich das geliehene Geld zurückzahlen.* It's high time you repaid the money you borrowed.

zurückziehen VERB (IMPERFECT **zog zurück,** PERFECT **hat zurückgezogen**)
to pull back ◇ *Sie zog die Hand zurück.* She pulled her hand back.

♦ **ein Angebot zurückziehen** to withdraw an offer

♦ **sich zurückziehen** to retire ◇ *Sie hat sich in ihr Zimmer zurückgezogen.* She has retired to her room. ◇ *Er hat sich aus dem öffentlichen Leben zurückgezogen.* He has retired from public life.

zusagen VERB (PERFECT **hat zugesagt**)
1 to promise ◇ *Er hat mir seine Hilfe zugesagt.* He promised to help me.
2 to accept an invitation ◇ *Die meisten Gäste haben zugesagt.* Most of the guests have accepted the invitation.

♦ **jemandem zusagen** to appeal to somebody ◇ *Das Konzert hat mir nicht zugesagt.* The concert didn't appeal to me.

zusammen ADVERB

together

zusammenbleiben VERB (IMPERFECT **blieb zusammen**, PERFECT **sind zusammengeblieben**)

to stay together

zusammenbrechen VERB (PRESENT **bricht zusammen**, IMPERFECT **brach zusammen**, PERFECT **ist zusammengebrochen**)

1 to collapse ◊ *Das Gebäude ist zusammengebrochen.* The building collapsed.

2 to break down ◊ *Als sie von seinem Tod erfuhr, ist sie zusammengebrochen.* When she heard of his death she broke down.

zusammenfassen VERB (PERFECT **hat zusammengefasst**)

to summarize ◊ *Sie fasste das Gesagte noch einmal kurz zusammen.* She briefly summarized once again what had been said.

die **Zusammenfassung** NOUN

summary

der **Zusammenhang** NOUN (PL die **Zusammenhänge**)

connection ◊ *Gibt es einen Zusammenhang zwischen diesen Ereignissen?* Is there a connection between these events?

♦ **im Zusammenhang mit** in connection with ◊ *Zwei Männer wurden im Zusammenhang mit dem Mord verhört.* Two men were questioned in connection with the murder.

♦ **aus dem Zusammenhang** out of context ◊ *Du hast mich aus dem Zusammenhang zitiert.* You've quoted me out of context.

zusammenhängen VERB (IMPERFECT **hing zusammen**, PERFECT **hat zusammengehangen**)

to be connected ◊ *Die beiden Ereignisse hängen miteinander zusammen.* The two events are connected.

zusammenkommen VERB (IMPERFECT **kam zusammen**, PERFECT **ist zusammengekommen**)

1 to meet up ◊ *Früher sind wir öfter zusammengekommen.* We used to meet up more often.

2 to come together ◊ *Es ist alles zusammengekommen.* Everything came together.

zusammenlegen VERB (PERFECT **hat zusammengelegt**)

1 to fold ◊ *Sie legte die Wäsche zusammen.* She folded the washing.

2 to merge ◊ *Die beiden Klassen sollen zusammengelegt werden.* The two classes are to be merged.

3 to combine ◊ *Wir können unsere Geburtstagspartys doch zusammenlegen.* We can combine our birthday parties.

4 to club together ◊ *Wir haben zusammengelegt und ihr eine CD gekauft.* We clubbed together and bought her a CD.

zusammennehmen VERB (PRESENT **nimmt zusammen**, IMPERFECT **nahm zusammen**, PERFECT **hat zusammengenommen**)

to summon up ◊ *Ich musste meinen ganzen Mut zusammennehmen.* I had to summon up all my courage.

♦ **alles zusammengenommen** all in all

♦ **sich zusammennehmen** to pull oneself together

zusammenpassen VERB (PERFECT **hat zusammengepasst**)

1 to be well suited ◊ *Die beiden passen gut zusammen.* The two are well suited.

2 to go together ◊ *Der Pulli und die Hose passen nicht zusammen.* The pullover and the trousers don't go together.

zusammenschreiben VERB (IMPERFECT **schrieb zusammen**, PERFECT **hat zusammengeschrieben**)

♦ **Schreibt man dieses Wort zusammen oder auseinander?** Is this written as one word or two?

das **Zusammensein** NOUN

get-together ◊ *ein gemütliches Zusammensein* a cosy get-together

zusammenstellen VERB (PERFECT **hat zusammengestellt**)

1 to put together ◊ *Stellt alle Stühle zusammen.* Put all the chairs together.

2 to compile ◊ *Ich habe eine Wunschliste zusammengestellt.* I've compiled a list of presents I'd like.

der **Zusammenstoß** NOUN (GEN des **Zusammenstoßes**, PL die **Zusammenstöße**)

collision

zusammenstoßen VERB (PRESENT **stößt zusammen**, IMPERFECT **stieß zusammen**, PERFECT **sind zusammengestoßen**)

to collide

zusammenzählen VERB (PERFECT **hat zusammengezählt**)

to add up

zusätzlich ADJECTIVE, ADVERB

1 additional ◊ *Wir sollen eine zusätzliche Englischstunde bekommen.* We're to get an additional English lesson.

2 in addition ◊ *Zusätzlich zu den Matheaufgaben muss ich noch Physik machen.* I still have some physics to do in addition to my maths homework.

zuschauen VERB (PERFECT **hat zugeschaut**)

to watch ◊ *Habt ihr beim Match zugeschaut?* Did you watch the match?

die **Zuschauer** MASC PL NOUN

audience ◊ *Die Zuschauer haben geklatscht.* The audience clapped.

Z

zuschicken → zwar

zuschicken VERB (PERFECT **hat zugeschickt**)
♦ **jemandem etwas zuschicken** to send somebody something ◊ *Wir werden Ihnen unseren Katalog zuschicken.* We'll send you our catalogue.

der **Zuschlag** NOUN (PL die **Zuschläge**)
underline surcharge ◊ *Für den ICE brauchst du einen Zuschlag.* You have to pay a surcharge if you go by Intercity Express.

zuschlagpflichtig ADJECTIVE
subject to a surcharge ◊ *Der ICE ist zuschlagpflichtig.* The Intercity Express is subject to a surcharge.

zusehen VERB (PRESENT **sieht zu**, IMPERFECT **sah zu**, PERFECT **hat zugesehen**)
to watch ◊ *Wir haben beim Match zugesehen.* We watched the match. ◊ *Er stand nur dabei und sah zu.* He just stood there watching.
♦ **jemandem zusehen** to watch somebody ◊ *Ich habe ihr dabei zugesehen, wie sie ihr Zimmer aufräumte.* I watched her tidy up her room.
♦ **zusehen, dass etwas gemacht wird** to make sure something is done ◊ *Sieh zu, dass die Kinder früh ins Bett kommen.* Make sure that the children go to bed early.

zusenden VERB (IMPERFECT **sendete** *or* **sandte zu**, PERFECT **hat zugesendet** *or* **zugesandt**)
to send ◊ *Wir werden Ihnen unseren Prospekt zusenden.* We'll send you our brochure.

der **Zustand** NOUN (PL die **Zustände**)
1 state ◊ *Das Haus war in einem furchtbaren Zustand.* The house was in an awful state. ◊ *Das sind hier ja schreckliche Zustände.* This is a terrible state of affairs.
2 condition ◊ *Das Auto ist noch in gutem Zustand.* The car's still in good condition.

zustande ADVERB
♦ **zustande bringen** to bring about
♦ **zustande kommen** to come about

zuständig ADJECTIVE
♦ **Dafür bin ich nicht zuständig.** That's not my responsibility.
♦ **der zuständige Beamte** the official in charge

zustimmen VERB (PERFECT **hat zugestimmt**)
to agree ◊ *Ich stimme dir zu.* I agree with you.

die **Zustimmung** NOUN
1 consent ◊ *Du brauchst die Zustimmung deiner Eltern.* You need your parents' consent.
2 approval ◊ *wenn das deine Zustimmung findet* if that meets with your approval

zustoßen VERB (PRESENT **stößt zu**, IMPERFECT **stieß zu**, PERFECT **ist zugestoßen**)

to happen ◊ *Ihm ist doch hoffentlich nichts zugestoßen.* Let's hope nothing's happened to him.

die **Zutaten** FEM PL NOUN
ingredients

zutreffen VERB (PRESENT **trifft zu**, IMPERFECT **traf zu**, PERFECT **hat zugetroffen**)
1 to be true ◊ *Es trifft nicht zu, dass ich das Buch mitgenommen habe.* It's not true that I took the book with me.
2 to apply ◊ *Diese Beschreibung trifft nicht auf sie zu.* This description doesn't apply to her.

zutreffend ADJECTIVE
♦ **Zutreffendes bitte unterstreichen.** Please underline where applicable.

zuverlässig ADJECTIVE
reliable

zuversichtlich ADJECTIVE
confident

zuviel ADVERB *see* **viel**

zuvor ADVERB
before ◊ *der Tag zuvor* the day before

zuwenig ADVERB *see* **wenig**

zuwider ADVERB
♦ **Spinnen sind mir zuwider.** I detest spiders.

zuziehen VERB (IMPERFECT **zog zu**, PERFECT **hat zugezogen**)
1 to draw ◊ *Es wird dunkel, zieh bitte die Vorhänge zu.* It's getting dark, please draw the curtains.
2 to call in ◊ *Wir sollten einen Fachmann zuziehen.* We should call in an expert.
♦ **sich etwas zuziehen** to catch something ◊ *Ich habe mir eine Erkältung zugezogen.* I've caught a cold.

zuzüglich PREPOSITION
*The preposition **zuzüglich** takes the genitive.*
plus ◊ *zweihundert Euro zuzüglich der Spesen* two hundred euros plus expenses

der **Zwang** NOUN (PL die **Zwänge**)
compulsion

zwängen VERB
to squeeze

zwanglos ADJECTIVE
informal ◊ *ein zwangloses Gespräch* an informal talk

zwanzig NUMBER
twenty

zwar ADVERB
although ◊ *Ich habe das zwar gesagt, aber es war nicht so gemeint.* Although I said it, it wasn't meant like that.
♦ **das ist zwar ..., aber ...** that may be ... but ... ◊ *Das ist zwar viel, aber mir reicht es nicht.* That may be a lot, but it's not enough for me.

♦ **Sie ist zwar klug, aber diesmal hat sie unrecht.** She may be clever, but she's wrong this time.
♦ **und zwar am Sonntag** on Sunday to be precise
♦ **und zwar so schnell, dass ...** in fact, so quickly that ...

der **Zweck** NOUN (PL die **Zwecke**)
    1 purpose ◊ *Was ist der Zweck Ihres Besuchs?* What's the purpose of your visit?
    2 point ◊ *Was ist der Zweck dieser Übung?* What's the point of this exercise? ◊ *Es hat keinen Zweck.* There's no point.

zwecklos ADJECTIVE
    pointless

zwei NUMBER
    see also **die Zwei** NOUN
    two

die **Zwei** NOUN
    see also **zwei** NUMBER
    1 two
    2 good

    ⓘ *German marks range from one (**sehr gut**) to six (**ungenügend**).*

zweideutig ADJECTIVE
    1 ambiguous ◊ *Sie hat sich zweideutig ausgedrückt.* She expressed herself very ambiguously.
    2 suggestive ◊ *Er macht immer so zweideutige Witze.* He's always making such suggestive jokes.

zweierlei ADJECTIVE
♦ **zweierlei Stoff** two different kinds of material
♦ **Das sind doch zweierlei Dinge.** They're two different things.
♦ **zweierlei Meinung** of differing opinions

zweifach ADJECTIVE, ADVERB
    1 double ◊ *die zweifache Menge* double the quantity
    2 twice ◊ *Der Brief war zweifach gefaltet.* The letter had been folded twice.

der **Zweifel** NOUN (PL die **Zweifel**)
    doubt ◊ *ohne Zweifel* without doubt

zweifelhaft ADJECTIVE
    1 doubtful ◊ *Es ist noch zweifelhaft, ob wir kommen.* It's still doubtful whether we're coming.
    2 dubious ◊ *eine zweifelhafte Lösung* a dubious solution
♦ **ein zweifelhaftes Kompliment** a backhanded compliment

zweifellos ADVERB
    doubtless
♦ **Sie hat sich zweifellos bemüht.** There's no doubt that she tried.

zweifeln VERB

♦ **an etwas zweifeln** to doubt something ◊ *Ich zweifle an der Richtigkeit dieser Aussage.* I doubt the truth of this statement.
♦ **zweifeln, ob** to doubt whether ◊ *Ich zweifle, ob wir das schaffen.* I doubt whether we'll make it.

der **Zweig** NOUN (PL die **Zweige**)
    branch

die **Zweigstelle** NOUN
    branch ◊ *Die nächste Zweigstelle ist in Villach.* The nearest branch is in Villach.

zweihundert NUMBER
    two hundred

zweimal ADVERB
    twice

zweisprachig ADJECTIVE
    bilingual

zweispurig ADJECTIVE
    two-lane

zweit ADVERB
♦ **zu zweit (1)** together ◊ *Wir fahren zu zweit in die Ferien.* We're going on holiday together.
♦ **zu zweit (2)** in twos ◊ *Stellt euch zu zweit auf.* Line up in twos.

zweitbeste ADJECTIVE
    second best

zweite ADJECTIVE
    second ◊ *Er kam als Zweiter.* He was the second to arrive.

zweitens ADVERB
    secondly

zweitgrößte ADJECTIVE
    second largest

zweitklassig ADJECTIVE
    inferior

zweitletzte ADJECTIVE
    last but one ◊ *Er ging als Zweitletzter durchs Ziel.* He was last but one to cross the finishing line.

der **Zwerg** NOUN (PL die **Zwerge**)
    dwarf

die **Zwetschge** NOUN
    damson

der **Zwieback** NOUN (PL die **Zwiebacke**)
    rusk

die **Zwiebel** NOUN
    onion ◊ *Sebastian mag keine Zwiebeln.* Sebastian doesn't like onions.

der **Zwilling** NOUN (PL die **Zwillinge**)
    twin ◊ *Diese Zwillinge sehen sich zum Verwechseln ähnlich.* The twins are the spitting image of each other.
♦ **Zwillinge** Gemini ◊ *Michael ist Zwilling.* Michael's Gemini.

zwingen VERB (IMPERFECT **zwang**, PERFECT **hat gezwungen**)
    to force

zwinkern VERB

Z

to wink ◊ *Als sie das sagte, zwinkerte er wissend.* When she said that he winked knowingly.

zwischen PREPOSITION

Use the accusative to express movement or a change of place. Use the dative when there is no change of place.

between ◊ *Er stand zwischen den beiden Mädchen.* He was standing between the two girls. ◊ *Stell deinen Stuhl zwischen unsere.* Put your chair between ours.

das **Zwischending** NOUN
cross ◊ *Das ist ein Zwischending zwischen Schreibmaschine und Computer.* It's a cross between a typewriter and a computer.

zwischendurch ADVERB
in between ◊ *Wir haben zwischendurch eine Pause gemacht.* We had a break in between.

der **Zwischenfall** NOUN (PL die **Zwischenfälle**)
incident

die **Zwischenfrage** NOUN
question

die **Zwischenlandung** NOUN
stopover

zwischenmenschlich ADJECTIVE
interpersonal ◊ *zwischenmenschliche Beziehungen* interpersonal relationships

zwitschern VERB
to chirp

zwölf NUMBER
twelve

Zypern NEUT NOUN
Cyprus
♦ **aus Zypern** from Cyprus
♦ **nach Zypern** to Cyprus

GERMAN IN ACTION

PUZZLES AND WORDGAMES

The wordgames on the following pages have been designed to give you practice in using your dictionary. Make sure you read the "Dictionary Skills" section at the front of this book before you start. Don't worry, there are answers at the end of the wordgames in case you get really stuck!

WORDGAME 1

▶ CHOOSING THE RIGHT TRANSLATION ◀

Complete the crossword below by looking up the English words in the list and finding the correct German translations. There is a slight catch, however! All the English words have more than one German translation, but only one will fit correctly into the crossword. Beside each English word we have given you a clue, telling you whether the correct translation is a noun, adjective, adverb or verb.

1. HELP (NOUN)
2. CLOSE (ADVERB)
3. ALONE (ADVERB)
4. LIGHT (ADJECTIVE)
5. KICK (VERB)
6. ROLL (NOUN)

7. DARK (ADJECTIVE)
8. COLD (NOUN)
9. ALTERNATIVE (NOUN)
10. EMPTY (ADJECTIVE)
11. DELAY (VERB)
12. KIND (ADJECTIVE)

▶ NOUNS ◀

a. This list contains the singular form of some German nouns. Use your dictionary to find the plural form. Remember that the plural may appear separately, or it may be shown in the same entry as the singular form. Don't forget, if the plural form is regular, it won't be shown in the dictionary.

b. Use your dictionary to find the genitive of the following nouns. If it is irregular, the genitive form appears in brackets and in bold on the line below the singular form. Remember that if the genitive form is regular, it won't be shown in the dictionary.

SINGULAR	PLURAL
das Haus	
der Garten	
das Pferd	
die Freundin	
das Abendessen	
das Abonnement	
die Frau	
der Gast	
die Fahrt	
der Mann	

SINGULAR	GENITIVE
der Arzt	
der Bär	
die Hose	
das Kind	
der Laden	
der Herr	
die Maus	
der August	
die Bluse	
der Astronaut	

327

WORDGAME 3

▶ VERB TENSES ◀

Use the German verb tables on pages 344 to 356 to help you fill in the blanks in the table below.

INFINITIVE	PRESENT	IMPERFECT	PERFECT	FUTURE
machen				du
gehen		er		
	ihr habt			
lesen	du			
fahren			wir	
beginnen				ich
essen	er			
können			ich	
			sie hat geholfen	
schwimmen			er	
tun		es		
sprechen				er
nehmen		ich		
wollen	ich			
		wir standen		

► ANSWERS ◄

WORDGAME 1

1. Hilfe
2. knapp
3. allein
4. leicht
5. treten
6. Rolle
7. dunkel
8. Kälte
9. Alternative
10. leer
11. verschieben
12. nett

WORDGAME 2a

Plural forms
1. die Häuser
2. die Gärten
3. die Pferde
4. die Freundinnen
5. die Abendessen
6. die Abonnements
7. die Frauen
8. die Gäste
9. die Fahrten
10. die Männer

WORDGAME 2b

Genitive forms
1. des Arztes
2. des Bären
3. der Hose
4. des Kinds *or* des Kindes
5. des Ladens
6. des Herrn
7. der Maus
8. des August *or* des Augustes
9. der Bluse
10. des Astronauten

WORDGAME 3

1. du wirst machen
2. er ging
3. haben
4. du liest
5. wir sind gefahren
6. ich werde beginnen
7. er isst
8. ich habe gekonnt
9. helfen
10. er ist geschwommen
11. es tat
12. er wird sprechen
13. ich nahm
14. ich will
15. stehen

CORRESPONDENCE

▶ LETTER

München, 15 Mai 2008

Place & Date

Liebe Oma und Opa!

Vielen Dank für die CDs, die Ihr mir zum Geburtstag geschickt habt. Sie sind von zwei meiner Lieblingsgruppen, und ich höre sie mir sehr gerne an.

Ansonsten gibt es nicht viel Neues. Die meiste Zeit lerne ich für die Prüfungen, die in zwei Wochen beginnen. Ich hoffe, dass ich alle bestehe. Nur vor der Matheprüfung graut es mir, denn in Mathe bin ich gar nicht gut.

Mutti erzählte mir, dass Ihr nächste Woche nach England in den Urlaub fahrt. Ich wünsche Euch schöne und erholsame Tage dort.

Herzliche Grüße von Eurer

Franziska

Or:
Viele liebe Grüße von ...
Alles Liebe, Eure ...

STARTING A PERSONAL LETTER

Vielen Dank für Deinen Brief ...
Ich habe mich sehr gefreut, von Dir zu hören.
Es tut mir leid, dass ich nicht früher geschrieben habe.

Thanks for your letter ...
It is lovely to hear from you.
Sorry I haven't written sooner.

ENDING A PERSONAL LETTER

Bitte antworte bald!
Viele Grüße an ...
... lässt vielmals grüßen.

Write soon!
Give my love to ...
... sends his/her best wishes.

CORRESPONDENCE

▶ EMAIL

> To give your email address to someone in German, say:
> **"claudia at n t online Punkt d e"**

	Neue Nachricht
An:	claudia@nt-online.de
Von:	susan@comp.net
Betreff:	Konzert am 11.2.
cc:	gernhausen@intercom.de
bcc:	

Anhang	Senden

Hallo alle zusammen!

Ich habe gerade das neue Album von "Rockstar" gekauft. Es ist absolute Spitze. Ich habe noch zwei Karten extra bekommen, für das Konzert, das "Rockstar" nächste Woche in Hamburg gibt. Ich hoffe, Ihr kommt beide mit.

Bis bald! Susan

Neue Nachricht	New message
An	To
Von	From
Betreff	Subject
cc	cc
bcc	bcc
Anhang	Attachment
Senden	Send

TELEPHONE

▶ WHEN YOUR NUMBER ANSWERS

– **Guten Tag. Spreche ich mit Jenny?**
– Hello! Is that Jenny?

– **Könnte ich bitte mit Tom sprechen?**
– Could I speak to Tom, please?

– **Können Sie ihm bitte sagen, dass er mich anrufen soll.**
– Would you ask him to call me back?

▶ ANSWERING THE TELEPHONE

– **Guten Tag. Hier ist Susan.**   – Hello! It's Susan speaking.

– **Am Apparat.**   – Speaking.

– **Wer ist am Apparat, bitte?**   – Who's speaking?

▶ WHEN THE SWITCHBOARD ANSWERS

– **Wer is am Apparat, bitte?**   – Who shall I say is calling?

– **Ich verbinde Sie.**   – I'm putting you through.

– **Bitte bleiben Sie am Apparat.**   – Please hold.

– **Wollen Sie eine Nachricht hinterlassen?** – Would you like to leave a message?

▶ DIFFICULTIES

– **Ich komme nicht durch.**
– I can't get through.

– **Sie haben sich verwählt.**
– I'm afraid you have the wrong number.

– **Die Verbindung ist sehr schlecht.**
– This is a very bad line.

– **Ihr Telefon is kaputt.**
– Their phone is out of order.

NUMBERS

1	**eins**	11	**elf**	21	**einundzwanzig**
2	**zwei**	12	**zwölf**	30	**dreißig**
3	**drei**	13	**dreizehn**	40	**vierzig**
4	**vier**	14	**vierzehn**	50	**fünfzig**
5	**fünf**	15	**fünfzehn**	60	**sechzig**
6	**sechs**	16	**sechzehn**	70	**siebzig**
7	**sieben**	17	**siebzehn**	80	**achtzig**
8	**acht**	18	**achtzehn**	90	**neunzig**
9	**neun**	19	**neunzehn**	100	**hundert**
10	**zehn**	20	**zwanzig**		

101	**hundert(und)eins**
200	**zweihundert**
201	**zweihundert(und)eins**

1,000	**tausend**
1,001	**tausend(und)eins**
1,000,000	**eine Million**

▶ FRACTIONS etc

1/2	**ein Halb**
1/3	**ein Drittel**
1/4	**ein Viertel**
1/5	**ein Fünftel**
0.5	**null Komma fünf (0,5)**
3.4	**drei Komma vier (3,4)**
6.89	**sechs Komma acht neun (6,89)**
10%	**zehn Prozent**
100%	**hundert Prozent**

▶ EXAMPLES

auf Seite neunzehn	on page nineteen
im siebten Kapitel	in chapter seven
im Maßstab eins zu fünfundzwanzig	on the scale of one to twenty-five

NUMBERS

1st	**erste (1.)**	14th	**vierzehnte (14.)**
2nd	**zweite (2.)**	15th	**fünfzehnte (15.)**
3rd	**dritte (3.)**	16th	**sechzehnte (16.)**
4th	**vierte (4.)**	17th	**siebzehnte (17.)**
5th	**fünfte (5.)**	18th	**achtzehnte (18.)**
6th	**sechste (6.)**	19th	**neunzehnte (19.)**
7th	**siebte (7.)**	20th	**zwanzigste (20.)**
8th	**achte (8.)**	21st	**einundzwanzigste (21.)**
9th	**neunte (9.)**	30th	**dreißigste (30.)**
10th	**zehnte (10.)**	100th	**hundertste (100.)**
11th	**elfte (11.)**	101st	**hunderterste (101.)**
12th	**zwölfte (12.)**	1000th	**tausendste (1000.)**
13th	**dreizehnte (13.)**		

Horst war Erster

▶ EXAMPLES

er wohnt im fünften Stock	he lives on the fifth floor
er war Dritter	he came in third
ein Vlertel des Kuchens	a quarter of the cake

DATE

▶ WOCHENTAGE

Montag
Dienstag
Mittwoch
Donnerstag
Freitag
Samstag
Sonntag

Wann?

am Montag
montags
jeden Montag
letzten Dienstag
nächsten Freitag
Samstag in einer Woche
nächsten Samstag in zwei Wochen

▶ DAYS OF THE WEEK

Monday
Tuesday
Wednesday
Thursday
Friday
Saturday
Sunday

When?

on Monday
on Mondays
every Monday
last Tuesday
next Friday
a week on Saturday
two weeks on Saturday

▶ MONATE

Januar
Februar
März
April
Mai
Juni
Juli
August
September
Oktober
November
Dezember

Wann?

im Februar
am 1. *or* **ersten Dezember 2009**
zweitausendneun

Was haben wir heute?
Heute ist...
Montag, 26. Mai *or*
  Montag, der sechsundzwanzigste Mai

▶ MONTHS OF THE YEAR

January
February
March
April
May
June
July
August
September
October
November
December

When?

in February
on December 1st 2009
in two thousand and nine

What day is it?
It's...
Monday, the 26th May *or*
  Monday, the twenty-sixth of May

TIME

Wie spät ist es?	What time is it? What's the time?	**Um wie viel Uhr?**	At what time?
Es ist...	It's...		

ein Uhr

zehn nach eins

Viertel nach eins

halb zwei

zwanzig vor zwei

Viertel vor zwei

um Mitternacht

um Mittag

um ein Uhr (nachmittags)

um acht Uhr (abends)

In Germany times are often given in the twenty-four hour clock.

um 11.15
or
elf Uhr fünfzehn

um 20.45
or
zwanzig Uhr fünfundvierzig

FALSE FRIENDS

German ≠ English

aktuell ≠ actual

ein **aktuelles** Thema   →   a **topical** issue

The film is based on   →   Der Film basiert auf **wirklichen**
  actual events.   Begebenheiten.

also ≠ also

Was sollen wir **also** tun?   →   What shall we do, **then**?

My sister **also** came.   →   Meine Schwester ist **auch** gekommen.

Angel ≠ angel

Die **Angel** ist kaputt.   →   The **fishing rod** is broken.

She's an **angel**!   →   Sie ist ein **Engel**!

bekommen ≠ become

Was hast du zum Geburtstag   →   What did you **get** for your birthday?
  bekommen?

He wants to **become** a   →   Er will ein berühmter Schriftsteller
  famous writer.   **werden**.

brav ≠ brave

Die Kinder waren **brav**.   →   The children were **good**.

Be **brave**!   →   Sei **mutig**!

Chips ≠ chips

Möchtet ihr **Chips**?   →   Would you like some **crisps**?

We bought some **chips**.   →   Wir haben **Pommes frites** gekauft.

eventuell ≠ eventual

Eventuell komme ich später nach.   →   **Perhaps** I'll come later.

Eventually he passed his   →   Er bestand **schließlich** die
  driving test.   Fahrprüfung.

Fabrik ≠ fabric

Die **Fabrik** wird nächstes Jahr geschlossen.	→	The **factory** will be closed down next year.
400 metres of **fabric**	→	400 Meter **Stoff**

fast ≠ fast

Es ist **fast** Mitternacht.	→	It's **almost** midnight.
a **fast** car	→	ein **schnelles** Auto

Flur ≠ floor

Der **Flur** muss sauber gemacht werden.	→	The **corridor** must be cleaned.
She is sitting on the **floor**.	→	Sie sitzt auf dem **Fußboden**.

Fotograf ≠ photograph

Er ist **Fotograf**.	→	He is a **photographer**.
I took a **photograph**.	→	Ich habe ein **Foto** gemacht.

Gift ≠ gift

Dieses **Gift** wirkt schnell.	→	This **poison** acts fast.
The necklace is a **gift** from my father.	→	Die Halskette ist ein **Geschenk** von meinem Vater.

Hose ≠ hose

eine **Hose**	→	a pair of **trousers**
a garden **hose**	→	ein **Gartenschlauch**

Lektüre ≠ lecture

Stör sie nicht bei der **Lektüre**. → Don't disturb her while she is **reading**.

He is giving a **lecture** at the art gallery. → Er hält einen **Vortrag** in der Kunstgalerie.

Mappe ≠ map

Die Fotos sind in einer **Mappe**. → The photographs are in a **folder**.

a road **map** → eine Straßen**karte**

Meinung ≠ meaning

meiner **Meinung** nach → in my **opinion**

The **meaning** of this word is not clear. → Die **Bedeutung** dieses Wortes ist nicht klar.

Mist ≠ mist

Du redest **Mist**. → You're talking **rubbish**.

morning **mist** → Morgen**nebel**

Mörder ≠ murder

Er ist ein **Mörder**. → He's a **murderer**.

He has been charged with **murder**. → Er ist des **Mordes** angeklagt.

Prospekt ≠ prospect

ein **Prospekt** mit Urlaubsreisen → a holiday **brochure**

It will improve my career **prospects**. → Das wird meine **Berufsaussichten** verbessern.

Rente ≠ rent

Seine **Rente** reicht nicht aus. → His **pension** isn't enough.

I am behind with my **rent** this month. → Ich habe die **Miete** diesen Monat noch nicht bezahlt.

schmal ≠ small

ein **schmaler** Durchgang → a **narrow** passageway

I have a **small** car. → Ich habe ein **kleines** Auto.

sensibel ≠ sensible

Sie ist ein sehr **sensibler** Mensch. → She's a very **sensitive** person.

Be **sensible**! → Sie **vernünftig**!

seriös ≠ serious

Er ist ein **seriöser** Geschäftsmann. → He is a **respectable** businessman.

Are you **serious**? → Ist das dein **Ernst**?

sparen ≠ spare

Wir müssen **sparen**. → We must **save**.

There's no room to **spare**. → Es ist kein Platz **übrig**.

sympathisch ≠ sympathetic

Er ist ein **sympatischer** Mensch. → He is a **likeable** person.

She is a **sympathetic** listener. → Sie hört **verständnisvoll** zu.

wer ≠ where

Wer ist das? → **Who** is that?

Where do you live? → **Wo** wohnst du?

wo ≠ who

Wo warst du? → **Where** were you?

Who said that? → **Wer** hat das gesagt?

GERMAN VERB TABLES

▶ CONTENTS

GERMAN VERB TABLES

This section contains thirteen important German verbs that you need to learn. German verbs fall mainly into two categories – **regular** (weak) and **irregular** – and it is important to learn which verbs fall into which category.

At the top of each table you will find the infinitive, the imperative and the past participle, plus examples of how you might want to use the verb. The lower section of the tables shows you how to form six tenses of the verb:

PRESENT	e.g. ich sage = **I say** *or* **I am saying**
IMPERFECT	e.g. ich sagte = **I was saying** *or* **I said**
PERFECT	e.g. ich habe gesagt = **I said** *or* **I have said**
FUTURE	e.g. ich werde sagen = **I will say**
CONDITIONAL	e.g. ich würde sagen = **I would say**
PRESENT SUBJUNCTIVE	e.g. ich sage = **I say**

▶ REGULAR (WEAK) VERBS

German regular verbs follow a set pattern. Once you have learnt this pattern, you will be able to form *any* regular verb.

HOW TO FORM A REGULAR VERB

i. a) To form the present and imperfect tense, take the infinitive minus the last two letters.
    This is called the **stem** e.g. *machen* → **mach**

ii. Next add the appropriate **ending**. You need to ask yourself two questions:
    a) **Who** is doing the verb (ich, du, er *etc*)?
    b) **When** are they doing it (in the present, the past or the future)?

Look at the verb tables for **machen**. The endings can be tagged onto the stem of *any* regular verb.

▶ HABEN, SEIN AND WERDEN

Haben (to have) and **sein** (to be) are very important verbs which **must** be learnt. You use them to say "I have" *etc* or "I am" *etc*. The present tense of **haben** and **sein** are also used to form the **perfect tense**. In most cases, **haben** is used to form the perfect tense, but verbs of movement like **gehen** (to go) and **fahren** (to drive) use **sein** e.g. the German for "he has gone" is **er *ist* gegangen**, not **er *hat* gegangen**. You will have to learn which verbs use **sein**.

HOW TO FORM THE PERFECT TENSE

a) Take the infinitive of a German verb e.g. **lachen**
b) Does it use **haben** or **sein** to form the perfect tense? **Lachen** uses **haben**
c) Take the present tense form of **haben** or **sein** that goes with the person who **did** the action e.g. **he** laughed – the German for "he" is **er**, so to form the perfect tense of **lachen** we use **er hat**

d) Add the **past participle** – this is shown near the top of each verb table. If you want to form the past participle of *any* regular verb, simply take the infinitive of the verb, add **ge** to it, knock off the last two letters and add **t** e.g. **ge**lieb**t**, **ge**setz**t**. For a regular separable verb, add **ge** between the prefix and the stem, knock off the last two letters and add **t** e.g. ab**ge**hol**t**. In our example, **lachen** is a regular verb, so the past participle is ge + lach + t → **gelacht**.
e) The German for "he laughed" is "**er hat gelacht**"

Werden (to become) is also used to form the **future tense**, and the conditional tense of **werden** is used in forming the **conditional tense** of *any* verb.

HOW TO FORM THE FUTURE AND CONDITIONAL TENSES

a) To form the future tense, take the present tense form of **werden** that goes with the person who **will do** the action e.g. **he** will speak – the German for "he" is **er**, so to form the future tense of **sprechen** we use **er wird**. To form the conditional tense – he would speak – take the conditional tense of **werden** for **er** – **er würde**
b) Add the infinitive of the German verb e.g. **sprechen**
c) The German for "he will speak" is "**er wird sprechen**", and for "he would speak" is "**er würde sprechen**"

▶IRREGULAR VERBS

Many German verbs are irregular and this means that you have to learn them individually. One type of irregular verb in German is the strong verb, which changes the vowel in the past tense and does not add **t** in the past participle e.g. **gehen - ging - gegangen**. There are tables showing different types of irregular verbs in this section, including several of the most important ones. When you are translating from German and meet an unfamiliar verb form, you may be able to guess from the context that it comes from one of these verbs, and you can use the verb table to check. The most common irregular verb parts are listed on the German side of the dictionary, so you could also look there.

HOW TO USE THE VERB TABLES

You will find some useful example phrases at the top of each verb table, but if you can't find what you need to say or write in German there, use the verb table itself to help you. Imagine that you want to find the German for "he is going". Here's how to do it:

a) Look up **go** on the English-German side of the dictionary to find the German translation **gehen**
b) Turn to the verb table section of your dictionary and find **gehen**
c) When is he going? He is going **now**, so look for the heading *PRESENT*
d) Who is going? **He** is. The German for "he" is **er** so look for **er** under the *PRESENT* heading
e) The German for "he is going" is "**er geht**"

GERMAN VERB TABLES

▶ machen

to do *or* to make

IMPERATIVE

mach
macht
machen Sie

PAST PARTICIPLE

gemacht

EXAMPLE PHRASES

Was **machst** *du?* What are you doing?
Ich **habe** *die Betten* **gemacht**.
I made the beds.
Ich **werde** *es morgen* **machen**.
I'll do it tomorrow.

PRESENT		*IMPERFECT*	
ich	mache	ich	machte
du	machst	du	machtest
er	macht	er	machte
wir	machen	wir	machten
ihr	macht	ihr	machtet
sie	machen	sie	machten

PERFECT		*CONDITIONAL*	
ich	habe gemacht	ich	würde machen
du	hast gemacht	du	würdest machen
er	hat gemacht	er	würde machen
wir	haben gemacht	wir	würden machen
ihr	habt gemacht	ihr	würdet machen
sie	haben gemacht	sie	würden machen

FUTURE		*PRESENT SUBJUNCTIVE*	
ich	werde machen	ich	mache
du	wirst machen	du	machest
er	wird machen	er	mache
wir	werden machen	wir	machen
ihr	werdet machen	ihr	machet
sie	werden machen	sie	machen

GERMAN VERB TABLES

▶ wissen

to know

EXAMPLE PHRASES

*Ich **weiß** nicht.* I don't know.
*Er **hat** nichts davon **gewusst**.*
  He didn't know anything about it.
*Sie **wussten**, wo das Kino war.*
  They knew where the cinema was.

IMPERATIVE

wisse
wisset
wissen Sie

PAST PARTICIPLE

gewusst

PRESENT

ich	weiß
du	weißt
er	weiß
wir	wissen
ihr	wisst
sie	wissen

PERFECT

ich	habe gewusst
du	hast gewusst
er	hat gewusst
wir	haben gewusst
ihr	habt gewusst
sie	haben gewusst

FUTURE

ich	werde wissen
du	wirst wissen
er	wird wissen
wir	werden wissen
ihr	werdet wissen
sie	werden wissen

IMPERFECT

ich	wusste
du	wusstest
er	wusste
wir	wussten
ihr	wusstet
sie	wussten

CONDITIONAL

ich	würde wissen
du	würdest wissen
er	würde wissen
wir	würden wissen
ihr	würdet wissen
sie	würden wissen

PRESENT SUBJUNCTIVE

ich	wisse
du	wissest
er	wisse
wir	wissen
ihr	wisset
sie	wissen

GERMAN VERB TABLES

▶ sich waschen

to wash (oneself)

IMPERATIVE

wasch dich
wascht euch
waschen Sie sich

EXAMPLE PHRASES

*Ich **habe mir** die Hände **gewaschen**.*
I washed my hands.
*Er **wäscht sich** jeden Tag.*
He washes every day.
*Die Katze **wusch sich** in der Sonne.*
The cat was washing itself in the sunshine.

PAST PARTICIPLE

gewaschen

PRESENT

ich wasche mich
du wäschst dich
er wäscht sich
wir waschen uns
ihr wascht euch
sie waschen sich

PERFECT

ich habe mich gewaschen
du hast dich gewaschen
er hat sich gewaschen
wir haben uns gewaschen
ihr habt euch gewaschen
sie haben sich gewaschen

FUTURE

ich werde mich waschen
du wirst dich waschen
er wird sich waschen
wir werden uns waschen
ihr werdet euch waschen
sie werden sich waschen

IMPERFECT

ich wusch mich
du wuschest dich
er wusch sich
wir wuschen uns
ihr wuscht euch
sie wuschen sich

CONDITIONAL

ich würde mich waschen
du würdest dich waschen
er würde sich waschen
wir würden uns waschen
ihr würdet euch waschen
sie würden sich waschen

PRESENT SUBJUNCTIVE

ich wasche mich
du waschest dich
er wasche sich
wir waschen uns
ihr waschet euch
sie waschen sich

GERMAN VERB TABLES

▶ aufstehen

to get up or to stand up

EXAMPLE PHRASES

Ich muss früh **aufstehen**.
 I have to get up early.
Als er hereinkam, **stand** *ich* **auf**.
 I stood up when he entered.
Die ganze Klasse **ist aufgestanden**.
 The whole class stood up.

PAST PARTICIPLE

aufgestanden

IMPERATIVE

steh auf
steht auf
stehen Sie auf

PRESENT

ich stehe auf
du stehst auf
er steht auf
wir stehen auf
ihr steht auf
sie stehen auf

PERFECT

ich bin aufgestanden
du bist aufgestanden
er ist aufgestanden
wir sind aufgestanden
ihr seid aufgestanden
sie sind aufgestanden

FUTURE

ich werde aufstehen
du wirst aufstehen
er wird aufstehen
wir werden aufstehen
ihr werdet aufstehen
sie werden aufstehen

IMPERFECT

ich stand auf
du standst auf
er stand auf
wir standen auf
ihr standet auf
sie standen auf

CONDITIONAL

ich würde aufstehen
du würdest aufstehen
er würde aufstehen
wir würden aufstehen
ihr würdet aufstehen
sie würden aufstehen

PRESENT SUBJUNCTIVE

ich stehe auf
du stehest auf
er stehe auf
wir stehen auf
ihr stehet auf
sie stehen auf

GERMAN VERB TABLES

▶ können

can *or* to be able to

EXAMPLE PHRASES

Er **kann** *gut schwimmen.* He can swim well.
Sie **konnte** *kein Wort Deutsch.* She couldn't speak a word of German.
Kann *ich gehen?* Can I go?

PAST PARTICIPLE

gekonnt *or* können

PRESENT		IMPERFECT	
ich	kann	ich	konnte
du	kannst	du	konntest
er	kann	er	konnte
wir	können	wir	konnten
ihr	könnt	ihr	konntet
sie	können	sie	konnten

PERFECT		CONDITIONAL	
ich	habe gekonnt	ich	könnte
du	hast gekonnt	du	könntest
er	hat gekonnt	er	könnte
wir	haben gekonnt	wir	könnten
ihr	habt gekonnt	ihr	könntet
sie	haben gekonnt	sie	könnten

FUTURE		PRESENT SUBJUNCTIVE	
ich	werde können	ich	könne
du	wirst können	du	könnest
er	wird können	er	könne
wir	werden können	wir	können
ihr	werdet können	ihr	könnet
sie	werden können	sie	können

GERMAN VERB TABLES

▶ müssen

must *or* to have to

EXAMPLE PHRASES

Ich **muss** *aufs Klo.* I must go to the loo.
Wir **müssen** *jeden Abend unsere Hausaufgaben machen.*
  We have to do our homework every night.
Sie **hat** *abwaschen* **müssen**. She had to wash up.

PAST PARTICIPLE

gemusst *or* müssen

PRESENT	IMPERFECT
ich muss	ich musste
du musst	du musstest
er muss	er musste
wir müssen	wir mussten
ihr müsst	ihr musstet
sie müssen	sie mussten

PERFECT	CONDITIONAL
ich habe gemusst	ich müsste
du hast gemusst	du müsstest
er hat gemusst	er müsste
wir haben gemusst	wir müssten
ihr habt gemusst	ihr müsstet
sie haben gemusst	sie müssten

FUTURE	PRESENT SUBJUNCTIVE
ich werde müssen	ich müsse
du wirst müssen	du müssest
er wird müssen	er müsse
wir werden müssen	wir müssen
ihr werdet müssen	ihr müsset
sie werden müssen	sie müssen

GERMAN VERB TABLES

▶ fahren

to drive *or* to go

IMPERATIVE

fahr
fahrt
fahren Sie

EXAMPLE PHRASES

Sie **fahren** *mit dem Bus in die Schule.*
They go to school by bus.
Rechts **fahren!** Drive on the right!
Ich **bin** *mit der Familie nach Spanien*
gefahren. I went to Spain with
my family.

PAST PARTICIPLE

gefahren

PRESENT		*IMPERFECT*	
ich	fahre	ich	fuhr
du	fährst	du	fuhrst
er	fährt	er	fuhr
wir	fahren	wir	fuhren
ihr	fahrt	ihr	fuhrt
sie	fahren	sie	fuhren

PERFECT		*CONDITIONAL*	
ich	bin gefahren	ich	würde fahren
du	bist gefahren	du	würdest fahren
er	ist gefahren	er	würde fahren
wir	sind gefahren	wir	würden fahren
ihr	seid gefahren	ihr	würdet fahren
sie	sind gefahren	sie	würden fahren

FUTURE		*PRESENT SUBJUNCTIVE*	
ich	werde fahren	ich	fahre
du	wirst fahren	du	fahrest
er	wird fahren	er	fahre
wir	werden fahren	wir	fahren
ihr	werdet fahren	ihr	fahret
sie	werden fahren	sie	fahren

GERMAN VERB TABLES

▶ gehen

to go

EXAMPLE PHRASES

Die Kinder **gingen** *ins Haus.*
  The children went into the house.
Wie **geht** *es dir?* How are you?
Wir **sind** *gestern schwimmen* **gegangen**.
  We went swimming yesterday.

IMPERATIVE

geh
geht
gehen Sie

PAST PARTICIPLE

gegangen

PRESENT		*IMPERFECT*	
ich	gehe	ich	ging
du	gehst	du	gingst
er	geht	er	ging
wir	gehen	wir	gingen
ihr	geht	ihr	gingt
sie	gehen	sie	gingen

PERFECT		*CONDITIONAL*	
ich	bin gegangen	ich	würde gehen
du	bist gegangen	du	würdest gehen
er	ist gegangen	er	würde gehen
wir	sind gegangen	wir	würden gehen
ihr	seid gegangen	ihr	würdet gehen
sie	sind gegangen	sie	würden gehen

FUTURE		*PRESENT SUBJUNCTIVE*	
ich	werde gehen	ich	gehe
du	wirst gehen	du	gehest
er	wird gehen	er	gehe
wir	werden gehen	wir	gehen
ihr	werdet gehen	ihr	gehet
sie	werden gehen	sie	gehen

GERMAN VERB TABLES

▶ kommen

to come

IMPERATIVE

komm
kommt
kommen Sie

EXAMPLE PHRASES

Er **kam** *die Straße entlang.*
  He was coming along the street.
Ich **komme** *zu deiner Party.*
  I'm coming to your party.
Woher **kommst** *du?*
  Where do you come from?

PAST PARTICIPLE

gekommen

PRESENT

ich komme
du kommst
er kommt
wir kommen
ihr kommt
sie kommen

IMPERFECT

ich kam
du kamst
er kam
wir kamen
ihr kamt
sie kamen

PERFECT

ich bin gekommen
du bist gekommen
er ist gekommen
wir sind gekommen
ihr seid gekommen
sie sind gekommen

CONDITIONAL

ich würde kommen
du würdest kommen
er würde kommen
wir würden kommen
ihr würdet kommen
sie würden kommen

FUTURE

ich werde kommen
du wirst kommen
er wird kommen
wir werden kommen
ihr werdet kommen
sie werden kommen

PRESENT SUBJUNCTIVE

ich komme
du kommest
er komme
wir kommen
ihr kommet
sie kommen

GERMAN VERB TABLES

▶ essen

to eat

EXAMPLE PHRASES

Ich **esse** *kein Fleisch.* I don't eat meat.
Wir **haben** *nichts* **gegessen**.
  We haven't had anything to eat.
Ich möchte was **essen**.
  I'd like something to eat.

IMPERATIVE

iss
esst
essen Sie

PAST PARTICIPLE

gegessen

PRESENT		IMPERFECT	
ich	esse	ich	aß
du	isst	du	aßest
er	isst	er	aß
wir	essen	wir	aßen
ihr	esst	ihr	aßt
sie	essen	sie	aßen

PERFECT		CONDITIONAL	
ich	habe gegessen	ich	würde essen
du	hast gegessen	du	würdest essen
er	hat gegessen	er	würde essen
wir	haben gegessen	wir	würden essen
ihr	habt gegessen	ihr	würdet essen
sie	haben gegessen	sie	würden essen

FUTURE		PRESENT SUBJUNCTIVE	
ich	werde essen	ich	esse
du	wirst essen	du	essest
er	wird essen	er	esse
wir	werden essen	wir	essen
ihr	werdet essen	ihr	esset
sie	werden essen	sie	essen

GERMAN VERB TABLES

► haben

to have

IMPERATIVE

hab
habt
haben Sie

EXAMPLE PHRASES

Hast *du eine Schwester?*
 Have you got a sister?
Er **hatte** *Hunger.* He was hungry.
Ich **hätte** *gern ein Eis.*
 I'd like an ice cream.
Sie **hat** *heute Geburtstag.*
 It's her birthday today.

PAST PARTICIPLE

gehabt

PRESENT

ich habe
du hast
er hat
wir haben
ihr habt
sie haben

PERFECT

ich habe gehabt
du hast gehabt
er hat gehabt
wir haben gehabt
ihr habt gehabt
sie haben gehabt

FUTURE

ich werde haben
du wirst haben
er wird haben
wir werden haben
ihr werdet haben
sie werden haben

IMPERFECT

ich hatte
du hattest
er hatte
wir hatten
ihr hattet
sie hatten

CONDITIONAL

ich hätte
du hättest
er hätte
wir hätten
ihr hättet
sie hätten

PRESENT SUBJUNCTIVE

ich habe
du habest
er habe
wir haben
ihr habet
sie haben

GERMAN VERB TABLES

▶ sein

to be

EXAMPLE PHRASES

*Er **ist** zehn Jahre alt.* He is ten years old.
*Mir **ist** kalt.* I'm cold.
*Wir **waren** gestern im Theater.*
   We were at the theatre yesterday.
Seid *ruhig!* Be quiet!

IMPERATIVE

sei
seid
seien Sie

PAST PARTICIPLE

gewesen

PRESENT		*IMPERFECT*	
ich	bin	ich	war
du	bist	du	warst
er	ist	er	war
wir	sind	wir	waren
ihr	seid	ihr	wart
sie	sind	sie	waren

PERFECT		*CONDITIONAL*	
ich	bin gewesen	ich	wäre
du	bist gewesen	du	wärst
er	ist gewesen	er	wäre
wir	sind gewesen	wir	wären
ihr	seid gewesen	ihr	wärt
sie	sind gewesen	sie	wären

FUTURE		*PRESENT SUBJUNCTIVE*	
ich	werde sein	ich	sei
du	wirst sein	du	seiest
er	wird sein	er	sei
wir	werden sein	wir	seien
ihr	werdet sein	ihr	seiet
sie	werden sein	sie	seien

GERMAN VERB TABLES

▶ werden

to become

IMPERATIVE

werde
werdet
werden Sie

EXAMPLE PHRASES

Mir **wird** *schlecht*. I feel ill.
Ich will Lehrerin **werden**.
 I want to be a teacher.
Der Kuchen **ist** *gut* **geworden**.
 The cake turned out well.

PAST PARTICIPLE

geworden

PRESENT

ich	werde
du	wirst
er	wird
wir	werden
ihr	werdet
sie	werden

IMPERFECT

ich	wurde
du	wurdest
er	wurde
wir	wurden
ihr	wurdet
sie	wurden

PERFECT

ich	bin geworden
du	bist geworden
er	ist geworden
wir	sind geworden
ihr	seid geworden
sie	sind geworden

CONDITIONAL

ich	würde werden
du	würdest werden
er	würde werden
wir	würden werden
ihr	würdet werden
sie	würden werden

FUTURE

ich	werde werden
du	wirst werden
er	wird werden
wir	werden werden
ihr	werdet werden
sie	werden werden

PRESENT SUBJUNCTIVE

ich	werde
du	werdest
er	werde
wir	werden
ihr	werdet
sie	werden

GERMAN IRREGULAR VERB FORMS

* verbs which use 'sein'

INFINITIVE	PRESENT INDICATIVE 2nd pers sing	◆ 3rd pers sing	IMPERFECT INDICATIVE	PAST PARTICIPLE
backen	bäckst	◆ bäckt	backte or buk	gebacken
befehlen	befiehlst	◆ befiehlt	befahl	befohlen
beginnen	beginnst	◆ beginnt	begann	begonnen
beißen	beißt	◆ beißt	biss	gebissen
bewegen	bewegst	◆ bewegt	bewog	bewogen
biegen	biegst	◆ biegt	bog	gebogen
bieten	bietest	◆ bietet	bot	geboten
binden	bindest	◆ bindet	band	gebunden
bitten	bittest	◆ bittet	bat	gebeten
blasen	bläst	◆ bläst	blies	geblasen
bleiben*	bleibst	◆ bleibt	blieb	geblieben
braten	brätst	◆ brät	briet	gebraten
brechen*	brichst	◆ bricht	brach	gebrochen
brennen	brennst	◆ brennt	brannte	gebrannt
bringen	bringst	◆ bringt	brachte	gebracht
denken	denkst	◆ denkt	dachte	gedacht
dringen*	dringst	◆ dringt	drang	gedrungen
dürfen	darfst	◆ darf	durfte	gedurft
empfangen	empfängst	◆ empfängt	empfing	empfangen
empfehlen	empfiehlst	◆ empfiehlt	empfahl	empfohlen
erschrecken*	erschrickst	◆ erschrickt	erschrak	erschrocken
essen	isst	◆ isst	aß	gegessen
fahren*	fährst	◆ fährt	fuhr	gefahren
fallen*	fällst	◆ fällt	fiel	gefallen
fangen	fängst	◆ fängt	fing	gefangen
fechten	fichtst	◆ ficht	focht	gefochten
finden	findest	◆ findet	fand	gefunden
flechten	flichtst	◆ flicht	flocht	geflochten
fliegen*	fliegst	◆ fliegt	flog	geflogen
fliehen*	fliehst	◆ flieht	floh	geflohen
fließen*	fließt	◆ fließt	floss	geflossen
fressen	frisst	◆ frisst	fraß	gefressen
frieren	frierst	◆ friert	fror	gefroren
gebären	gebierst	◆ gebiert	gebar	geboren
geben	gibst	◆ gibt	gab	gegeben
gedeihen*	gedeihst	◆ gedeiht	gedieh	gediehen
gehen*	gehst	◆ geht	ging	gegangen
gelingen*	-	◆ gelingt	gelang	gelungen
gelten	giltst	◆ gilt	galt	gegolten

INFINITIVE	PRESENT INDICATIVE 2nd pers sing	◆ 3rd pers sing	IMPERFECT INDICATIVE	PAST PARTICIPLE
genießen	genießt	◆ genießt	genoss	genossen
geraten*	gerätst	◆ gerät	geriet	geraten
geschehen*	-	◆ geschieht	geschah	geschehen
gewinnen	gewinnst	◆ gewinnt	gewann	gewonnen
gießen	gießt	◆ gießt	goss	gegossen
gleichen	gleichst	◆ gleicht	glich	geglichen
gleiten*	gleitest	◆ gleitet	glitt	geglitten
graben	gräbst	◆ gräbt	grub	gegraben
greifen	greifst	◆ greift	griff	gegriffen
haben	hast	◆ hat	hatte	gehabt
halten	hältst	◆ hält	hielt	gehalten
hängen	hängst	◆ hängt	hing	gehangen
hauen	haust	◆ haut	hieb	gehauen
heben	hebst	◆ hebt	hob	gehoben
heißen	heißt	◆ heißt	hieß	geheißen
helfen	hilfst	◆ hilft	half	geholfen
kennen	kennst	◆ kennt	kannte	gekannt
klingen	klingst	◆ klingt	klang	geklungen
kneifen	kneifst	◆ kneift	kniff	gekniffen
kommen*	kommst	◆ kommt	kam	gekommen
können	kannst	◆ kann	konnte	gekonnt
kriechen*	kriechst	◆ kriecht	kroch	gekrochen
laden	lädst	◆ lädt	lud	geladen
lassen	lässt	◆ lässt	ließ	gelassen
laufen*	läufst	◆ läuft	lief	gelaufen
leiden	leidest	◆ leidet	litt	gelitten
leihen	leihst	◆ leiht	lieh	geliehen
lesen	liest	◆ liest	las	gelesen
liegen*	liegst	◆ liegt	lag	gelegen
lügen	lügst	◆ lügt	log	gelogen
mahlen	mahlst	◆ mahlt	mahlte	gemahlen
meiden	meidest	◆ meidet	mied	gemieden
messen	misst	◆ misst	maß	gemessen
misslingen*	-	◆ misslingt	misslang	misslungen
mögen	magst	◆ mag	mochte	gemocht
müssen	musst	◆ muss	musste	gemusst
nehmen	nimmst	◆ nimmt	nahm	genommen
nennen	nennst	◆ nennt	nannte	genannt
pfeifen	pfeifst	◆ pfeift	pfiff	gepfiffen
raten	rätst	◆ rät	riet	geraten
reiben	reibst	◆ reibt	rieb	gerieben
reißen*	reißt	◆ reißt	riss	gerissen

INFINITIVE	PRESENT INDICATIVE 2nd pers sing	♦ 3rd pers sing	IMPERFECT INDICATIVE	PAST PARTICIPLE
reiten*	reitest	♦ reitet	ritt	geritten
rennen*	rennst	♦ rennt	rannte	gerannt
riechen	riechst	♦ riecht	roch	gerochen
ringen	ringst	♦ ringt	rang	gerungen
rufen	rufst	♦ ruft	rief	gerufen
salzen	salzt	♦ salzt	salzte	gesalzen
saufen	säufst	♦ säuft	soff	gesoffen
saugen	saugst	♦ saugt	sog	gesogen or gesaugt
schaffen	schaffst	♦ schafft	schuf	geschaffen
scheiden*	scheidest	♦ scheidet	schied	geschieden
scheinen	scheinst	♦ scheint	schien	geschienen
scheißen	scheißt	♦ scheißt	schiss	geschissen
scheren	scherst	♦ schert	schor	geschoren
schieben	schiebst	♦ schiebt	schob	geschoben
schießen	schießt	♦ schießt	schoss	geschossen
schlafen	schläfst	♦ schläft	schlief	geschlafen
schlagen	schlägst	♦ schlägt	schlug	geschlagen
schleichen*	schleichst	♦ scheicht	schlich	geschlichen
schließen	schließt	♦ schließt	schloss	geschlossen
schmeißen	schmeißt	♦ schmeißt	schmiss	geschmissen
schmelzen*	schmilzt	♦ schmilzt	schmolz	geschmolzen
schneiden	schneidest	♦ schneidet	schnitt	geschnitten
schreiben	schreibst	♦ schreibt	schrieb	geschrieben
schreien	schreist	♦ schreit	schrie	geschrien
schweigen	schweigst	♦ schweigt	schwieg	geschwiegen
schwimmen*	schwimmst	♦ schwimmt	schwamm	geschwommen
schwingen	schwingst	♦ schwingt	schwang	geschwungen
schwören	schwörst	♦ schwört	schwor	geschworen
sehen	siehst	♦ sieht	sah	gesehen
sein*	bist	♦ ist	war	gewesen
senden	sendest	♦ sendet	sandte	gesandt
singen	singst	♦ singt	sang	gesungen
sinken*	sinkst	♦ sinkt	sank	gesunken
sitzen*	sitzt	♦ sitzt	saß	gesessen
sollen	sollst	♦ soll	sollte	gesollt
speien	speist	♦ speit	spie	gespie(e)n
spinnen	spinnst	♦ spinnt	spann	gesponnen
sprechen	sprichst	♦ spricht	sprach	gesprochen
springen*	springst	♦ springt	sprang	gesprungen
stechen	stichst	♦ sticht	stach	gestochen
stecken	steckst	♦ steckt	steckte or stak	gesteckt
stehen	stehst	♦ steht	stand	gestanden

INFINITIVE	PRESENT INDICATIVE 2nd pers sing	3rd pers sing	IMPERFECT INDICATIVE	PAST PARTICIPLE
stehlen	stiehlst	♦ stiehlt	stahl	gestohlen
steigen*	steigst	♦ steigt	stieg	gestiegen
sterben*	stirbst	♦ stirbt	starb	gestorben
stinken	stinkst	♦ stinkt	stank	gestunken
stoßen	stößt	♦ stößt	stieß	gestoßen
streichen	streichst	♦ streicht	strich	gestrichen
streiten	streitest	♦ streitet	stritt	gestritten
tragen	trägst	♦ trägt	trug	getragen
treffen	triffst	♦ trifft	traf	getroffen
treiben*	treibst	♦ treibt	trieb	getrieben
treten*	trittst	♦ tritt	trat	getreten
trinken	trinkst	♦ trinkt	trank	getrunken
trügen	trügst	♦ trügt	trog	getrogen
tun	tust	♦ tut	tat	getan
verderben	verdirbst	♦ verdirbt	verdarb	verdorben
vergessen	vergisst	♦ vergisst	vergaß	vergessen
verlieren	verlierst	♦ verliert	verlor	verloren
verschwinden	verschwindest	♦ verschwindet	verschwand	verschwunden
verzeihen	verzeihst	♦ verzeiht	verzieh	verziehen
wachsen*	wächst	♦ wächst	wuchs	gewachsen
waschen	wäschst	♦ wäscht	wusch	gewaschen
weisen	weist	♦ weist	wies	gewiesen
werben	wirbst	♦ wirbt	warb	geworben
werden*	wirst	♦ wird	wurde	geworden
werfen	wirfst	♦ wirft	warf	geworfen
wiegen	wiegst	♦ wiegt	wog	gewogen
winden	windest	♦ windet	wand	gewunden
wissen	weißt	♦ weiß	wusste	gewusst
wollen	willst	♦ will	wollte	gewollt
ziehen*	ziehst	♦ zieht	zog	gezogen
zwingen	zwingst	♦ zwingt	zwang	gezwungen

ENGLISH ~ GERMAN

A

A NOUN
die Eins (*school mark*) (PL die Einsen) ◊ *I got an A for my essay.* Ich habe für meinen Aufsatz eine Eins bekommen.

a ARTICLE

> In the nominative use **ein** for masculine and neuter nouns, **eine** for feminine nouns.

〔1〕 ein ◊ *a man* ein Mann ◊ *I saw a man.* Ich habe einen Mann gesehen. ◊ *a child* ein Kind ◊ *an apple* ein Apfel
〔2〕 eine ◊ *a woman* eine Frau ◊ *He gave it to a woman.* Er hat es einer Frau gegeben.

> You do not translate **a** when you want to describe what somebody does for a living.

◊ *He's a butcher.* Er ist Metzger. ◊ *She's a doctor.* Sie ist Ärztin.
♦ **once a week** einmal pro Woche
♦ **thirty kilometres an hour** dreißig Kilometer in der Stunde
♦ **thirty pence a kilo** dreißig Pence das Kilo
♦ **a hundred pounds** einhundert Pfund

AA NOUN (= *Automobile Association*)
der ADAC

to **abandon** VERB
〔1〕 (*place*)
verlassen (PRESENT verlässt, IMPERFECT verließ, PERFECT hat verlassen)
〔2〕 (*plan, idea*)
aufgeben (PRESENT gibt auf, IMPERFECT gab auf, PERFECT hat aufgegeben)

abbey NOUN
das Kloster (PL die Klöster)

abbreviation NOUN
die Abkürzung

ability NOUN
die Fähigkeit
♦ **to have the ability to do something** fähig sein, etwas zu tun

able ADJECTIVE
♦ **to be able to do something** etwas tun können

to **abolish** VERB
abschaffen (PERFECT hat abgeschafft)

abortion NOUN
die Abtreibung
♦ **She had an abortion.** Sie hat abgetrieben.

about PREPOSITION, ADVERB
〔1〕 wegen (*concerning*) ◊ *I'm phoning about tomorrow's meeting.* Ich rufe wegen des morgigen Treffens an.
〔2〕 etwa (*approximately*) ◊ *It takes about ten hours.* Es dauert etwa zehn Stunden. ◊ *about a hundred pounds* etwa hundert Pfund ◊ *at about eleven o'clock* um etwa elf Uhr
〔3〕 in ... herum (*around*) ◊ *to walk about the town* in der Stadt herumlaufen
〔4〕 über ◊ *a book about the London Underground* ein Buch über die Londoner U-Bahn
♦ **to be about to do something** gerade etwas tun wollen ◊ *I was about to go out.* Ich wollte gerade gehen.
♦ **to talk about something** über etwas reden ◊ *We talked about the weather.* Wir haben über das Wetter geredet.
♦ **What's the film about?** Wovon handelt der Film?
♦ **How about going to the cinema?** Wie wär's, wenn wir ins Kino gingen?

above PREPOSITION, ADVERB
über ◊ *above forty degrees* über vierzig Grad

> Use the accusative to express movement or a change of place. Use the dative when there is no change of place.

◊ *He put his hands above his head.* Er hielt die Hände über den Kopf. ◊ *The lamp is hanging above the table.* Die Lampe hängt über dem Tisch.
♦ **the flat above** die Wohnung darüber
♦ **mentioned above** oben erwähnt
♦ **above all** vor allem

abroad ADVERB
〔1〕 im Ausland ◊ *She lives abroad.* Sie lebt im Ausland.
〔2〕 ins Ausland ◊ *to go abroad* ins Ausland gehen

abrupt ADJECTIVE
brüsk ◊ *He was a bit abrupt with me.* Er war etwas brüsk zu mir.

abruptly ADVERB
plötzlich ◊ *He got up abruptly.* Er stand plötzlich auf.

absence NOUN
die Abwesenheit

absent ADJECTIVE
abwesend

absent-minded ADJECTIVE
zerstreut ◊ *She's a bit absent-minded.* Sie ist etwas zerstreut.

absolutely ADVERB
〔1〕 völlig (*completely*) ◊ *Beate's absolutely right.* Beate hat völlig recht.
〔2〕 ganz sicher ◊ *Do you think it's a good idea? – Absolutely!* Meinst du, das ist eine gute Idee? – Ganz sicher!

absurd ADJECTIVE
absurd ◊ *That's absurd!* Das ist absurd!

abuse NOUN
| see also **abuse** VERB |

der Missbrauch (*of power, drugs*)
- **child abuse** die Kindesmisshandlung
- **to shout abuse at somebody** jemanden beschimpfen

to **abuse** VERB

see also **abuse** NOUN

missbrauchen (PERFECT hat missbraucht)
◊ *to abuse drugs* Drogen missbrauchen
- **abused children** misshandelte Kinder

abusive ADJECTIVE
beleidigend ◊ *He became abusive.* Er wurde beleidigend.

academic ADJECTIVE
- **the academic year** das Studienjahr

academy NOUN
die Akademie ◊ *a military academy* eine Militärakademie

to **accelerate** VERB
beschleunigen (PERFECT hat beschleunigt)

accelerator NOUN
das Gaspedal (PL die Gaspedale)

accent NOUN
der Akzent (PL die Akzente) ◊ *He's got a German accent.* Er hat einen deutschen Akzent.

to **accept** VERB
annehmen (PRESENT nimmt an, IMPERFECT nahm an, PERFECT hat angenommen)

acceptable ADJECTIVE
annehmbar

access NOUN
[1] der Zugang ◊ *He has access to confidential information.* Er hat Zugang zu vertraulichen Informationen.
[2] das Besuchsrecht ◊ *Her ex-husband has access to the children.* Ihr geschiedener Mann hat ein Besuchsrecht.

accessible ADJECTIVE
erreichbar ◊ *It's only accessible via a secret entrance.* Es ist nur durch einen Geheimeingang erreichbar.

accessory NOUN
- **fashion accessories** die Modeartikel PL

accident NOUN
der Unfall (PL die Unfälle) ◊ *to have an accident* einen Unfall haben
- **by accident (1)** (*by mistake*) versehentlich ◊ *The burglar killed him by accident.* Der Einbrecher hat ihn versehentlich getötet.
- **by accident (2)** (*by chance*) zufällig ◊ *She met him by accident.* Sie ist ihm zufällig begegnet.

accidental ADJECTIVE
zufällig

to **accommodate** VERB
unterbringen (IMPERFECT brachte unter, PERFECT hat untergebracht)
- **The hotel can accommodate fifty people.** Das Hotel hat Platz für fünfzig Gäste.

accommodation NOUN
die Unterkunft (PL die Unterkünfte)

to **accompany** VERB

begleiten (PERFECT hat begleitet)

accord NOUN
- **of his own accord** aus eigenem Antrieb
◊ *He left of his own accord.* Er ist aus eigenem Antrieb gegangen.

accordingly ADVERB
entsprechend

according to PREPOSITION
laut ◊ *According to him, everyone had gone.* Laut ihm waren alle weggegangen.

accordion NOUN
das Akkordeon (PL die Akkordeons)

account NOUN
[1] das Konto (PL die Konten) ◊ *a bank account* ein Bankkonto
- **to do the accounts** die Buchführung machen
[2] (*report*)
der Bericht (PL die Berichte)
- **He gave a detailed account of what happened.** Er berichtete genau, was passiert war.
- **to take something into account** etwas berücksichtigen
- **on account of** wegen ◊ *We couldn't go out on account of the bad weather.* Wir konnten wegen des schlechten Wetters nicht raus.
- **to account for** erklären ◊ *If she was ill, that would account for her poor results.* Wenn sie krank war, dann würde das ihre schlechten Resultate erklären.

accountable ADJECTIVE
- **to be accountable to someone** jemandem gegenüber verantwortlich sein

accountancy NOUN
die Buchführung

accountant NOUN
[1] (*bookkeeper*)
der Buchhalter (PL die Buchhalter)
die Buchhalterin
◊ *She's an accountant.* Sie ist Buchhalterin.
[2] (*tax consultant*)
der Steuerberater (PL die Steuerberater)
die Steuerberaterin

accuracy NOUN
die Genauigkeit

accurate ADJECTIVE
genau ◊ *accurate information* genaue Information

accurately ADVERB
genau

accusation NOUN
der Vorwurf (PL die Vorwürfe)

to **accuse** VERB
- **to accuse somebody of something (1)** jemanden einer Sache beschuldigen
◊ *She accused her husband of lying.* Sie beschuldigte ihren Mann, er würde lügen.

A

♦ **to accuse somebody of something (2)**
(*police*) jemanden einer Sache anklagen
◊ *The police are accusing her of murder.*
Die Polizei klagt sie wegen Mordes an.

ace NOUN
das Ass (GEN des Asses, PL die Asse) ◊ *the ace of hearts* das Herzass

ache NOUN
see also **ache** VERB
der Schmerz (GEN des Schmerzes, PL die Schmerzen) ◊ *I have an ache in my side.*
Ich habe Schmerzen in der Seite.

to **ache** VERB
see also **ache** NOUN
wehtun (IMPERFECT tat weh, PERFECT hat wehgetan) ◊ *My leg's aching.* Mein Bein tut weh.

to **achieve** VERB
1 (*an aim*)
erreichen (PERFECT hat erreicht)
2 (*victory*)
erringen (IMPERFECT errang, PERFECT hat errungen)

achievement NOUN
die Leistung ◊ *That was quite an achievement.* Das war eine Leistung.

acid NOUN
die Säure

acid rain NOUN
der saure Regen

acne NOUN
die Akne ◊ *She's got acne.* Sie hat Akne.

to **acquit** VERB
♦ **to be acquitted** freigesprochen werden
◊ *He was acquitted of murder.* Er wurde von der Mordanklage freigesprochen.

acre NOUN
der Morgen (PL die Morgen)

acrobat NOUN
der Akrobat (GEN des Akrobaten, PL die Akrobaten)
die Akrobatin
◊ *He's an acrobat.* Er ist Akrobat.

across PREPOSITION, ADVERB
über
Use the accusative to express movement or a change of place. Use the dative when there is no change of place.
◊ *the shop across the road* der Laden über der Straße ◊ *to walk across the road* über die Straße gehen
♦ **across from** (*opposite*) gegenüber +DAT
◊ *He sat down across from her.* Er setzte sich ihr gegenüber.

to **act** VERB
see also **act** NOUN
1 spielen (*in play, film*) ◊ *He acts really well.* Er spielt wirklich gut. ◊ *She's acting the part of Juliet.* Sie spielt die Rolle der Julia.
2 handeln (*take action*) ◊ *The police acted quickly.* Die Polizei hat schnell gehandelt.

♦ **She acts as his interpreter.** Sie übersetzt für ihn.

act NOUN
see also **act** VERB
der Akt (*in play*) (PL die Akte) ◊ *in the first act* im ersten Akt

action NOUN
die Handlung
♦ **The film was full of action.** In dem Film gab es viel Action.
♦ **to take firm action against somebody** hart gegen jemanden vorgehen

active ADJECTIVE
aktiv ◊ *He's a very active person.* Er ist ein sehr aktiver Mensch. ◊ *an active volcano* ein aktiver Vulkan

activity NOUN
die Tätigkeit
♦ **outdoor activities** die Betätigung im Freien SING

actor NOUN
der Schauspieler (PL die Schauspieler)
◊ *Brad Pitt is a well-known actor.* Brad Pitt ist ein bekannter Schauspieler.

actress NOUN
die Schauspielerin ◊ *Julia Roberts is a well-known actress.* Julia Roberts ist eine bekannte Schauspielerin.

actual ADJECTIVE
wirklich ◊ *The film is based on actual events.* Der Film basiert auf wirklichen Begebenheiten.
*Be careful not to translate **actual** by aktuell.*

actually ADVERB
1 wirklich (*really*) ◊ *Did it actually happen?* Ist das wirklich passiert?
2 eigentlich (*in fact*) ◊ *Actually, I don't know him at all.* Eigentlich kenne ich ihn überhaupt nicht.

acupuncture NOUN
die Akupunktur

ad NOUN
1 die Anzeige (*in paper*)
2 die Werbung (*on TV, radio*)

AD ABBREVIATION
n. Chr. (= nach Christus) ◊ *in 800 AD* im Jahre 800 n. Chr.

to **adapt** VERB
bearbeiten (PERFECT hat bearbeitet) ◊ *His novel was adapted for television.*
Sein Roman wurde fürs Fernsehen bearbeitet.
♦ **to adapt to something** (*get used to*) sich in etwas eingewöhnen ◊ *He adapted to his new school very quickly.* Er hat sich in der neuen Schule sehr schnell eingewöhnt.

adaptor NOUN
der Adapter (PL die Adapter)

to **add** VERB

hinzufügen (PERFECT hat hinzugefügt)
◊ *Add two eggs to the mixture.* Fügen Sie dem Teig zwei Eier hinzu.

♦ **to add up** zusammenzählen ◊ *Add the figures up.* Zähle die Zahlen zusammen.

addict NOUN
(*drug addict*)
der Süchtige (GEN des Süchtigen, PL die Süchtigen)
die Süchtige (GEN der Süchtigen) ◊ *an addict (man)* ein Süchtiger

♦ **Martin's a football addict.** Martin ist ein Fußballnarr.

addicted ADJECTIVE
süchtig ◊ *She's addicted to heroin.* Sie ist heroinsüchtig. ◊ *She's addicted to soap operas.* Sie ist süchtig nach Seifenopern.

addition NOUN

♦ **in addition** außerdem ◊ *He's broken his leg and, in addition, he's caught a cold.* Er hat sich das Bein gebrochen, und außerdem hat er einen Schnupfen bekommen.

♦ **in addition to** zusätzlich zu ◊ *In addition to the price of the cassette, there's a charge for postage.* Zusätzlich zum Preis der Kassette wird eine Versandgebühr berechnet.

address NOUN

see also **address** VERB

die Adresse ◊ *What's your address?* Wie ist Ihre Adresse?

to **address** VERB

see also **address** NOUN

1 (*envelope, letter*)
adressieren (PERFECT hat adressiert)
2 (*speak to*)
sprechen zu (PRESENT spricht, IMPERFECT sprach, PERFECT hat gesprochen) ◊ *She addressed the audience.* Sie sprach zum Publikum.

adjective NOUN
das Adjektiv (PL die Adjektive)

to **adjust** VERB
einstellen (PERFECT hat eingestellt) ◊ *He adjusted the seat to the right height.* Er stellte den Stuhl auf die richtige Höhe ein.

♦ **to adjust to something** (*get used to*) sich in etwas eingewöhnen ◊ *He adjusted to his new school very quickly.* Er hat sich in der neuen Schule schnell eingewöhnt.

adjustable ADJECTIVE
verstellbar

administration NOUN
die Verwaltung

admiral NOUN
der Admiral (PL die Admirale)

to **admire** VERB
bewundern (PERFECT hat bewundert)

admission NOUN

der Eintritt ◊ *"admission free"* "Eintritt frei"

to **admit** VERB
zugeben (PRESENT gibt zu, IMPERFECT gab zu, PERFECT hat zugegeben) ◊ *I must admit that ...* Ich muss zugeben, dass ... ◊ *He admitted that he'd done it.* Er gab zu, dass er es getan hat.

adolescence NOUN
die Pubertät

adolescent NOUN
der Jugendliche (GEN des Jugendlichen, PL die Jugendlichen)
die Jugendliche (GEN der Jugendlichen) ◊ *an adolescent (male)* ein Jugendlicher

to **adopt** VERB
1 (*child*)
adoptieren (PERFECT hat adoptiert) ◊ *Phil was adopted.* Phil wurde adoptiert.
2 (*idea*)
übernehmen (PRESENT übernimmt, IMPERFECT übernahm, PERFECT hat übernommen) ◊ *The system of multiple choice questions has been adopted for many exams.* Das Multiple-Choice-System ist für viele Prüfungen übernommen worden.

adopted ADJECTIVE
adoptiert

♦ **an adopted son** ein Adoptivsohn

adoption NOUN
die Adoption

to **adore** VERB
bewundern (PERFECT hat bewundert)

Adriatic Sea NOUN
die Adria

adult NOUN
der Erwachsene (GEN des Erwachsenen, PL die Erwachsenen)
die Erwachsene (GEN der Erwachsenen) ◊ *an adult (man)* ein Erwachsener

♦ **adult education** die Erwachsenenbildung

to **advance** VERB

see also **advance** NOUN

1 (*move forward*)
vorrücken (PERFECT ist vorgerückt) ◊ *The troops are advancing.* Die Truppen rücken vor.
2 (*progress*)
Fortschritte machen ◊ *Technology has advanced a lot.* Die Technik hat große Fortschritte gemacht.

advance NOUN

see also **advance** VERB

♦ **in advance** vorher ◊ *They bought the tickets in advance.* Sie haben die Karten vorher gekauft.

advance booking NOUN
die Vorbestellung ◊ *Reductions are offered for advance booking.* Bei Vorbestellung gibt es Rabatt.

♦ **Advance booking is essential.** Es ist wichtig vorzubestellen.

A

advanced ADJECTIVE
fortgeschritten

advantage NOUN
der Vorteil (PL die Vorteile) ◊ *Going to university has many advantages.* Das Studium hat viele Vorteile.

♦ **to take advantage of something** etwas ausnützen ◊ *He took advantage of the good weather to go for a walk.* Er hat das schöne Wetter ausgenützt und einen Spaziergang gemacht.

♦ **to take advantage of somebody** jemanden ausnützen ◊ *The company was taking advantage of its employees.* Die Firma nützte ihre Angestellten aus.

adventure NOUN
das Abenteuer (PL die Abenteuer)

adverb NOUN
das Adverb (PL die Adverbien)

advert NOUN *see* **advertisement**

to **advertise** VERB
annoncieren (PERFECT hat annonciert) ◊ *Jobs are advertised in the paper.* Stellenangebote werden in der Zeitung annonciert.

advertisement NOUN
1 die Anzeige (*in paper*)
2 die Werbung (*on TV, radio*)

advertising NOUN
die Werbung ◊ *She works in advertising.* Sie ist in der Werbung tätig. ◊ *They've increased spending on advertising.* Sie geben mehr Geld für Werbung aus.

advice NOUN
der Rat ◊ *to give somebody advice* jemandem einen Rat geben

♦ **a piece of advice** ein Rat ◊ *He gave me a good piece of advice.* Er gab mir einen guten Rat.

to **advise** VERB
raten (PRESENT rät, IMPERFECT riet, PERFECT hat geraten) ◊ *He advised me to wait.* Er riet mir zu warten. ◊ *He advised me not to go there.* Er hat mir geraten, nicht dorthin zu gehen.

aerial NOUN
die Antenne

aerobics PL NOUN
das Aerobic ◊ *I'm going to aerobics tonight.* Ich mache heute Abend Aerobic.

aeroplane NOUN
das Flugzeug (PL die Flugzeuge)

aerosol NOUN
der Spray (PL die Sprays)

affair NOUN
1 (*romantic*)
das Verhältnis (GEN des Verhältnisses, PL die Verhältnisse) ◊ *to have an affair with somebody* mit jemandem ein Verhältnis haben
2 (*event*)

die Angelegenheit

to **affect** VERB
1 (*influence*)
beeinflussen (PERFECT hat beeinflusst) ◊ *Does violence on television affect children's behaviour?* Beeinflusst Gewalt im Fernsehen das Verhalten von Kindern?
2 (*have effect on*)
beeinträchtigen (PERFECT hat beeinträchtigt) ◊ *The bad weather has affected sales.* Das schlechte Wetter hat den Absatz beeinträchtigt.

♦ **It affects me deeply.** Es geht mir sehr nahe.

affectionate ADJECTIVE
liebevoll

to **afford** VERB
sich leisten ◊ *I can't afford a new pair of jeans.* Ich kann mir keine neue Jeans leisten. ◊ *We can't afford to go on holiday.* Wir können es uns nicht leisten, in Urlaub zu fahren.

afraid ADJECTIVE
♦ **to be afraid of something** vor etwas Angst haben ◊ *I'm afraid of spiders.* Ich habe Angst vor Spinnen.

♦ **I'm afraid I can't come.** ich kann leider nicht kommen.

♦ **I'm afraid so.** Ja, leider.

♦ **I'm afraid not.** Leider nicht.

Africa NOUN
Afrika NEUT

♦ **from Africa** aus Afrika

♦ **to Africa** nach Afrika

African ADJECTIVE
see also **African** NOUN
afrikanisch

African NOUN
see also **African** ADJECTIVE
der Afrikaner (PL die Afrikaner)
die Afrikanerin

after PREPOSITION, ADVERB, CONJUNCTION
nach +DAT ◊ *after dinner* nach dem Abendessen ◊ *He ran after me.* Er rannte mir nach.

♦ **soon after** kurz danach

♦ **after I'd had a rest** nachdem ich mich ausgeruht hatte

♦ **After having eaten I left.** Nachdem ich gegessen hatte, ging ich.

♦ **after all** schließlich

afternoon NOUN
der Nachmittag (PL die Nachmittage)

♦ **three o'clock in the afternoon** drei Uhr nachmittags

♦ **this afternoon** heute Nachmittag

♦ **on Saturday afternoon** Samstag Nachmittag

afters SING *or* PL NOUN
der Nachtisch SING (PL die Nachtische)

aftershave NOUN
das After-shave (PL die After-shaves)

afterwards ADVERB
danach ◊ *She left not long afterwards.*
Sie ging kurz danach.

again ADVERB
1 wieder (*once more*) ◊ *They're friends
again.* Sie sind wieder Freunde.
2 noch einmal (*one more time*) ◊ *Can
you tell me again?* Kannst du mir das
noch einmal sagen?
♦ **not ... again** nie mehr ◊ *I won't go there
again.* Dort gehe ich nie mehr hin.
♦ **Do it again!** Mach's noch mal!
♦ **Not again!** Nicht schon wieder!
♦ **again and again** immer wieder

against PREPOSITION
gegen ◊ *He leant against the wall.* Er
lehnte gegen die Wand. ◊ *I'm against
nuclear testing.* Ich bin gegen Atomtests.

age NOUN
das Alter (PL die Alter) ◊ *an age limit* eine
Altersgrenze
♦ **at the age of sixteen** mit sechzehn
♦ **I haven't been to the cinema for ages.**
Ich war schon ewig nicht mehr im Kino.

aged ADJECTIVE
♦ **aged ten** zehn Jahre alt

agenda NOUN
die Tagesordnung

agent NOUN
der Agent (GEN des Agenten, PL die
Agenten)
die Agentin
♦ **an estate agent** ein Immobilienmakler
♦ **a travel agent** ein Reisebüro

aggressive ADJECTIVE
aggressiv

ago ADVERB
♦ **two days ago** vor zwei Tagen
♦ **two years ago** vor zwei Jahren
♦ **not long ago** vor Kurzem
♦ **How long ago did it happen?** Wie lange
ist das her?

agony NOUN
♦ **He was in agony.** Er hatte furchtbare
Schmerzen.

to **agree** VERB
♦ **to agree with somebody** jemandem
zustimmen ◊ *I agree with your sister.* Ich
stimme deiner Schwester zu.
♦ **to agree to do something** bereit sein,
etwas zu tun ◊ *He agreed to go and pick
her up.* Er war bereit, sie abzuholen.
♦ **to agree that ...** (*admit*) zugeben, dass ...
◊ *I agree that it's difficult.* Ich gebe zu,
dass das schwierig ist.
♦ **Garlic doesn't agree with me.** Ich
vertrage Knoblauch nicht.

agreed ADJECTIVE
ausgemacht ◊ *at the agreed time* zur
ausgemachten Zeit

agreement NOUN
die Abmachung
♦ **to be in agreement** übereinstimmen
◊ *Everybody was in agreement with Ray.*
Alle stimmten mit Ray überein.

agricultural ADJECTIVE
landwirtschaftlich

agriculture NOUN
die Landwirtschaft

ahead ADVERB
voraus ◊ *We sent him on ahead.* Wir
schickten ihn voraus.
♦ **The Germans are five points ahead.** Die
Deutschen führen mit fünf Punkten.
♦ **She looked straight ahead.** Sie sah
geradeaus.
♦ **ahead of time** vorzeitig
♦ **to plan ahead** vorausplanen
♦ **Go ahead!** Ja bitte!

aid NOUN
♦ **in aid of charity** für wohltätige Zwecke

AIDS NOUN
das Aids (GEN des Aids) ◊ *He died of
AIDS.* Er starb an Aids.

to **aim** VERB
see also **aim** NOUN
♦ **to aim at** zielen auf +ACC ◊ *He aimed a gun
at me.* Er zielte mit der Pistole auf mich.
♦ **The film is aimed at children.** Der Film ist
für Kinder gedacht.
♦ **to aim to do something** beabsichtigen,
etwas zu tun ◊ *Janice aimed to leave at
five o'clock.* Janice beabsichtigte, um
fünf Uhr zu gehen.

aim NOUN
see also **aim** VERB
das Ziel (PL die Ziele) ◊ *The aim of the
festival is to raise money.* Ziel des
Festivals ist, Geld aufzutreiben.

air NOUN
die Luft (PL die Lüfte)
♦ **to get some fresh air** frische Luft
schnappen
♦ **by air** mit dem Flugzeug ◊ *I prefer to
travel by air.* Ich reise lieber mit dem
Flugzeug.

air-conditioned ADJECTIVE
mit Klimaanlage

air conditioning NOUN
die Klimaanlage

Air Force NOUN
die Luftwaffe

air hostess NOUN
die Stewardess (PL die Stewardessen)
◊ *She's an air hostess.* Sie ist
Stewardess.

airline NOUN
die Fluggesellschaft

airmail NOUN
♦ **by airmail** mit Luftpost

airplane NOUN US
das Flugzeug (PL die Flugzeuge)

airport NOUN
der Flughafen (PL die Flughäfen)

aisle NOUN
> **1** (*in church*)
> der <u>Mittelgang</u> (PL die Mittelgänge)
> **2** (*in plane*)
> der <u>Gang</u> (PL die Gänge) ◊ *an aisle seat*
> ein Platz am Gang

alarm NOUN
> der <u>Alarm</u> (*warning*) (PL die Alarme)
> ♦ **a fire alarm** ein Feueralarm

alarm clock NOUN
> der <u>Wecker</u> (PL die Wecker)

album NOUN
> das <u>Album</u> (PL die Alben)

alcohol NOUN
> der <u>Alkohol</u>

alcoholic NOUN
> | see also **alcoholic** ADJECTIVE |
> der <u>Alkoholiker</u> (PL die Alkoholiker)
> die <u>Akoholikerin</u>
> ◊ *He's an alcoholic.* Er ist Alkoholiker.

alcoholic ADJECTIVE
> | see also **alcoholic** NOUN |
> <u>alkoholisch</u> ◊ *alcoholic drinks*
> alkoholische Getränke

alert ADJECTIVE
> **1** <u>aufgeweckt</u> (*bright*) ◊ *He's a very alert
> baby.* Er ist ein sehr aufgewecktes Baby.
> **2** <u>wachsam</u> (*paying attention*) ◊ *We must
> stay alert.* Wir müssen wachsam bleiben.

A levels PL NOUN
> das <u>Abitur</u> SING

> ❶ Germans take their **Abitur** at the age
> of 19. The students sit examinations in
> a variety of subjects to attain an overall
> grade. If you pass, you have the right
> to a place at university.

alike ADVERB
> ♦ **to look alike** sich ähnlich sehen ◊ *The
> two sisters look alike.* Die beiden
> Schwestern sehen sich ähnlich.

alive ADJECTIVE
> <u>am Leben</u>

all ADJECTIVE, PRONOUN, ADVERB
> **1** <u>alle</u> ◊ *all the books* alle Bücher
> ♦ **all the time** die ganze Zeit
> ♦ **all day** den ganzen Tag
> **2** <u>alles</u> ◊ *He ate it all.* Er hat alles
> gegessen. ◊ *I ate all of it.* Ich habe alles
> gegessen.
> ♦ **All of us went.** Wir sind alle
> hingegangen.
> ♦ **after all** schließlich ◊ *After all, nobody
> can make us go.* Schließlich kann uns
> niemand zwingen hinzugehen.
> ♦ **all alone** ganz allein ◊ *She's all alone.* Sie
> ist ganz allein.
> ♦ **not at all** überhaupt nicht ◊ *I'm not tired
> at all.* Ich bin überhaupt nicht müde.
> ♦ **The score is five all.** Es steht fünf zu
> fünf.

allergic ADJECTIVE
> <u>allergisch</u>
> ♦ **to be allergic to something** allergisch
> gegen etwas sein ◊ *I'm allergic to cats.*
> Ich bin allergisch gegen Katzen.

allergy NOUN
> die <u>Allergie</u> (PL die Allergien)

alley NOUN
> die <u>Gasse</u>

to **allow** VERB
> ♦ **to be allowed to do something** etwas
> tun dürfen ◊ *He's not allowed to go out
> at night.* Er darf abends nicht ausgehen.
> ♦ **to allow somebody to do something**
> jemandem erlauben, etwas zu tun ◊ *His
> mum allowed him to go out.* Seine
> Mama hat ihm erlaubt auszugehen.

all right ADVERB
> **1** <u>gut</u> (*okay*) ◊ *Everything turned out all
> right.* Alles ist gut gegangen.
> ♦ **Are you all right?** Bist du in Ordnung?
> **2** <u>okay</u> (*not bad*) ◊ *The film was all right.*
> Der Film war okay.
> **3** <u>einverstanden</u> (*when agreeing*) ◊ *We'll
> talk about it later. – All right.* Wir reden
> später darüber. – Einverstanden.
> ♦ **Is that all right with you?** Ist das okay?

almond NOUN
> die <u>Mandel</u> (PL die Mandeln)

almost ADVERB
> <u>fast</u> ◊ *I've almost finished.* Ich bin fast
> fertig.

alone ADJECTIVE, ADVERB
> <u>allein</u> ◊ *She lives alone.* Sie lebt allein.
> ♦ **to leave somebody alone** jemanden in
> Ruhe lassen ◊ *Leave her alone!* Lass sie
> in Ruhe!
> ♦ **to leave something alone** etwas nicht
> anfassen ◊ *Leave my things alone!* Fass
> meine Sachen nicht an!

along PREPOSITION, ADVERB
> <u>entlang</u> ◊ *Chris was walking along the
> beach.* Chris ging am Strand entlang.
> ♦ **all along** die ganze Zeit ◊ *He was lying to
> me all along.* Er hat mich die ganze Zeit
> belogen.

aloud ADVERB
> <u>laut</u> ◊ *He read the poem aloud.* Er las das
> Gedicht vor.

alphabet NOUN
> das <u>Alphabet</u> (PL die Alphabete)

Alps PL NOUN
> die <u>Alpen</u> FEM PL

already ADVERB
> <u>schon</u> ◊ *Liz had already gone.* Liz war
> schon weg.

also ADVERB
> <u>auch</u>
> *Be careful not to translate **also** by the
> German word **also**.*

altar NOUN
> der <u>Altar</u> (PL die Altare)

to **alter** VERB
> <u>verändern</u> (PERFECT hat verändert)

alternate ADJECTIVE
♦ **on alternate days** abwechselnd jeden zweiten Tag

alternative NOUN
see also **alternative** ADJECTIVE
die Alternative ◊ *Fruit is a healthy alternative to chocolate.* Obst ist eine gesunde Alternative zu Schokolade.
♦ **You have no alternative.** Du hast keine andere Wahl.
♦ **There are several alternatives.** Es gibt mehrere Möglichkeiten.

alternative ADJECTIVE
see also **alternative** NOUN
andere ◊ *an alternative solution* eine andere Lösung ◊ *an alternative suggestion* ein anderer Vorschlag
♦ **alternative medicine** die alternative Medizin

alternatively ADVERB
♦ **Alternatively, we could just stay at home.** Wir könnten auch zu Hause bleiben.

although CONJUNCTION
obwohl ◊ *Although she was tired, she stayed up late.* Obwohl sie müde war, blieb sie lange auf.

altogether ADVERB
[1] insgesamt (*in total*) ◊ *You owe me twenty pounds altogether.* Du schuldest mir insgesamt zwanzig Pfund.
[2] ganz (*completely*) ◊ *I'm not altogether happy with your work.* Ich bin mit Ihrer Arbeit nicht ganz zufrieden.

aluminium NOUN (US **aluminum**)
das Aluminium

always ADVERB
immer ◊ *He's always moaning.* Er beklagt sich immer.

am VERB *see* **be**

a.m. ABBREVIATION
morgens ◊ *at four a.m.* um vier Uhr morgens

amateur NOUN
der Amateur (PL die Amateure)
die Amateurin
◊ *He's an amateur.* Er ist Amateur.

to **amaze** VERB
♦ **to be amazed** erstaunt sein ◊ *I was amazed that I managed to do it.* Ich war erstaunt, dass ich es geschafft habe.

amazing ADJECTIVE
[1] erstaunlich (*surprising*) ◊ *That's amazing news!* Das sind erstaunliche Neuigkeiten!
[2] ausgezeichnet (*excellent*) ◊ *Vivian's an amazing cook.* Vivian ist eine ausgezeichnete Köchin.

ambassador NOUN
der Botschafter (PL die Botschafter)
die Botschafterin

amber ADJECTIVE
♦ **an amber light** eine gelbe Ampel

ambition NOUN
der Ehrgeiz (GEN des Ehrgeizes)

ambitious ADJECTIVE
ehrgeizig ◊ *She's very ambitious.* Sie ist sehr ehrgeizig.

ambulance NOUN
der Krankenwagen (PL die Krankenwagen)

amenities PL NOUN
♦ **The hotel has very good amenities.** Das Hotel hat viel zu bieten.

America NOUN
Amerika NEUT
♦ **from America** aus Amerika
♦ **in America** in Amerika
♦ **to America** nach Amerika

American ADJECTIVE
see also **American** NOUN
amerikanisch ◊ *He's American.* Er ist Amerikaner. ◊ *She's American.* Sie ist Amerikanerin.

American NOUN
see also **American** ADJECTIVE
der Amerikaner (PL die Amerikaner)
die Amerikanerin
♦ **the Americans** die Amerikaner

among PREPOSITION
unter +DAT ◊ *I was among friends.* Ich war unter Freunden.
♦ **among other things** unter anderem

amount NOUN
[1] der Betrag (PL die Beträge) ◊ *a large amount of money* ein großer Geldbetrag
[2] die Menge ◊ *a huge amount of rice* eine enorme Menge Reis

amp NOUN
[1] (*of electricity*)
das Ampère (GEN des Ampère, PL die Ampère)
[2] (*for hi-fi*)
der Verstärker (PL die Verstärker)

amplifier NOUN
der Verstärker (*for hi-fi*) (PL die Verstärker)

to **amuse** VERB
belustigen (PERFECT hat belustigt)
♦ **He was most amused by the story.** Er fand die Geschichte sehr lustig.

amusement NOUN
das Vergnügen (*enjoyment*) (PL die Vergnügen)
♦ **amusement arcade** die Spielhalle

amusement arcade NOUN
die Spielhalle

an ARTICLE *see* **a**

to **analyse** VERB
analysieren (PERFECT hat analysiert)

analysis NOUN
die Analyse

to **analyze** VERB US
analysieren (PERFECT hat analysiert)

ancestor NOUN
der Vorfahr (GEN des Vorfahren, PL die Vorfahren)
die Vorfahrin

anchor NOUN
der Anker (PL die Anker)

ancient ADJECTIVE
alt ◇ *This is an ancient custom.* Das ist ein alter Brauch.
♦ **ancient Greece** das antike Griechenland
♦ **an ancient monument** ein historisches Denkmal

and CONJUNCTION
und ◇ *you and me* du und ich ◇ *Two and two are four.* Zwei und zwei gibt vier.
◇ *He talked and talked.* Er redete und redete.
♦ **Please try and come!** Versuche bitte zu kommen!
♦ **better and better** immer besser

angel NOUN
der Engel (PL die Engel)
*Be careful not to translate **angel** by the German word **Angel**.*

anger NOUN
die Wut

angle NOUN
der Winkel (PL die Winkel)

angler NOUN
der Angler (PL die Angler)
die Anglerin

angling NOUN
das Angeln ◇ *His favourite hobby is angling.* Angeln ist sein Lieblingshobby.

angry ADJECTIVE
böse ◇ *Dad looks very angry.* Papa sieht sehr böse aus.
♦ **to be angry with somebody** mit jemandem böse sein ◇ *Mum's really angry with you.* Mama ist sehr böse mit dir.
♦ **to get angry** wütend werden

animal NOUN
das Tier (PL die Tiere)

ankle NOUN
der Fußknöchel (PL die Fußknöchel)

anniversary NOUN
der Jahrestag (PL die Jahrestage)
♦ **wedding anniversary** der Hochzeitstag

to **announce** VERB
ankündigen (PERFECT hat angekündigt)

announcement NOUN
die Ankündigung

to **annoy** VERB
ärgern ◇ *He's really annoying me.* Er ärgert mich echt.
♦ **to get annoyed** wütend werden ◇ *I saw that he was getting annoyed.* Ich sah, dass er wütend wurde.

annoying ADJECTIVE
ärgerlich ◇ *It's really annoying.* Es ist wirklich ärgerlich.

annual ADJECTIVE

jährlich ◇ *an annual meeting* ein jährliches Treffen

anonymous ADJECTIVE
anonym

anorak NOUN
der Anorak (PL die Anoraks)

another ADJECTIVE
*Use **noch ein** for masculine and neuter nouns, **noch eine** for feminine nouns.*
[1] noch ein ◇ *I bought another hat.* Ich habe noch einen Hut gekauft. ◇ *Would you like another piece of cake?* Möchtest du noch ein Stück Kuchen?
noch eine ◇ *Would you like another cup of tea?* Möchten Sie noch eine Tasse Tee?
*Use **ein anderer** for masculine, **eine andere** for feminine and **ein anderes** for neuter nouns.*
[2] (*different*)
ein anderer ◇ *Could you show me another hat?* Könnten Sie mir einen anderen Hut zeigen?
eine andere ◇ *My girlfriend goes to another school.* Meine Freundin besucht eine andere Schule.
ein anderes ◇ *Have you got another shirt?* Haben Sie noch ein anderes Hemd?
♦ **another time** ein andermal

to **answer** VERB
see also **answer** NOUN
beantworten (PERFECT hat beantwortet)
◇ *Can you answer my question?* Kannst du meine Frage beantworten?
♦ **to answer the phone** ans Telefon gehen
♦ **to answer the door** aufmachen ◇ *Can you answer the door, please?* Kannst du bitte aufmachen?

answer NOUN
see also **answer** VERB
[1] die Antwort (*to question*)
[2] die Lösung (*to problem*)

answering machine NOUN
der Anrufbeantworter (PL die Anrufbeantworter)

ant NOUN
die Ameise

to **antagonize** VERB
verärgern (PERFECT hat verärgert) ◇ *He didn't want to antagonize her.* Er wollte sie nicht verärgern.

Antarctic NOUN
die Antarktis

anthem NOUN
♦ **the national anthem** die Nationalhymne

antibiotic NOUN
das Antibiotikum (PL die Antibiotika)

antidepressant NOUN
das Antidepressivum (PL die Antidepressiva)

antique NOUN

☞

die Antiquität (*furniture*)

antique shop NOUN
der Antiquitätenladen (PL die Antiquitätenläden)

antiseptic NOUN
das Antiseptikum (PL die Antiseptika)

any ADJECTIVE, PRONOUN, ADVERB
In most cases any is not translated.
◇ *Would you like any bread?* Möchten Sie Brot? ◇ *Have you got any mineral water?* Haben Sie Mineralwasser?
Use kein for not any.
◇ *We haven't got any milk left.* Wir haben keine Milch mehr. ◇ *I haven't got any money.* Ich habe kein Geld. ◇ *I haven't got any books.* Ich habe keine Bücher.
◇ *Sorry, we haven't got any.* Tut mir leid, wir haben keine.
♦ **any more (1)** (*additional*) noch etwas
◇ *Would you like any more coffee?* Möchten Sie noch etwas Kaffee?
♦ **any more (2)** (*no longer*) nicht mehr ◇ *I don't love him any more.* Ich liebe ihn nicht mehr.

anybody PRONOUN
1 jemand (*in question*) ◇ *Has anybody got a pen?* Hat jemand etwas zum Schreiben?
2 jeder (*no matter who*) ◇ *Anybody can learn to swim.* Jeder kann schwimmen lernen.
Use niemand for not ... anybody.
◇ *I can't see anybody.* Ich kann niemanden sehen.

anyhow ADVERB
sowieso ◇ *He doesn't want to go out and anyhow he's not allowed.* Er will nicht ausgehen, und er darf es sowieso auch nicht.

anyone PRONOUN
1 jemand (*in question*) ◇ *Has anyone got a pen?* Hat jemand etwas zum Schreiben?
2 jeder (*no matter who*) ◇ *Anyone can learn to swim.* Jeder kann schwimmen lernen.
Use niemand for not ... anyone.
◇ *I can't see anyone.* Ich kann niemanden sehen.

anything PRONOUN
1 etwas (*in question*) ◇ *Would you like anything to eat?* Möchtest du etwas zu essen?
2 alles (*no matter what*) ◇ *Anything could happen.* Alles könnte passieren.
Use nichts for not ... anything.
◇ *I can't hear anything.* Ich kann nichts hören.

anyway ADVERB
sowieso ◇ *He doesn't want to go out and anyway he's not allowed.* Er will nicht ausgehen, und er darf es sowieso auch nicht.

anywhere ADVERB
1 irgendwo (*in question*) ◇ *Have you seen my coat anywhere?* Hast du irgendwo meinen Mantel gesehen?
2 überall ◇ *You can buy stamps almost anywhere.* Man kann fast überall Briefmarken kaufen.
Use nirgends for not ... anywhere.
3 nirgends ◇ *I can't find it anywhere.* Ich kann es nirgends finden.

apart ADVERB
♦ **The two towns are ten kilometres apart.** Die zwei Städte liegen zehn Kilometer voneinander entfernt.
♦ **apart from** abgesehen von ◇ *Apart from that, everything's fine.* Davon abgesehen ist alles in Ordnung.

apartment NOUN
die Wohnung

to **apologize** VERB
sich entschuldigen (PERFECT hat sich entschuldigt) ◇ *He apologized for being late.* Er entschuldigte sich für sein Zuspätkommen.
♦ **I apologize!** Ich bitte um Entschuldigung!

apology NOUN
die Entschuldigung

apostrophe NOUN
der Apostroph (PL die Apostrophe)

apparatus NOUN
der Apparat (PL die Apparate)

apparent ADJECTIVE
offensichtlich

apparently ADVERB
offensichtlich

to **appeal** VERB
see also **appeal** NOUN
bitten (IMPERFECT bat, PERFECT hat gebeten) ◇ *They appealed for help.* Sie baten um Hilfe.
♦ **to appeal to somebody** (*attract*) jemanden reizen ◇ *Does that appeal to you?* Reizt dich das?

appeal NOUN
see also **appeal** VERB
der Aufruf (PL die Aufrufe)

to **appear** VERB
1 (*come into view*)
kommen (IMPERFECT kam, PERFECT ist gekommen) ◇ *The bus appeared around the corner.* Der Bus kam um die Ecke.
♦ **to appear on TV** im Fernsehen auftreten
2 (*seem*)
scheinen (IMPERFECT schien, PERFECT hat geschienen) ◇ *She appeared to be asleep.* Sie schien zu schlafen.

appearance NOUN
das Äußere (*looks*) (GEN des Äußeren)
◇ *She takes great care over her appearance.* Sie achtet sehr auf ihr Äußeres.

appendicitis NOUN
die Blinddarmentzündung

appetite NOUN
der Appetit

to **applaud** VERB
klatschen

applause NOUN
der Beifall

apple NOUN
der Apfel (PL die Äpfel)
♦ **an apple tree** ein Apfelbaum MASC

applicant NOUN
der Bewerber (PL die Bewerber)
die Bewerberin
◊ There were a hundred applicants for
the job. Es gab hundert Bewerber für die
Stelle.

application NOUN
♦ **a job application** eine Bewerbung

application form NOUN
[1] (for job)
das Bewerbungsformular (PL die
Bewerbungsformulare)
[2] (for university)
das Anmeldeformular (PL die
Anmeldeformulare)

to **apply** VERB
♦ **to apply for a job** sich für eine Stelle
bewerben ◊ She applied for the job as a
secretary. Sie bewarb sich für die
Sekretärinnenstelle.
♦ **to apply to** (be relevant) zutreffen auf
◊ This rule doesn't apply to me. Diese
Regel trifft auf mich nicht zu.

appointment NOUN
der Termin (PL die Termine) ◊ I've got a
dental appointment. Ich habe einen
Zahnarzttermin.

to **appreciate** VERB
zu schätzen wissen (PRESENT weiß zu
schätzen, IMPERFECT wusste zu schätzen,
PERFECT hat zu schätzen gewusst) ◊ I really
appreciate your help. Ich weiß deine
Hilfe wirklich zu schätzen.

apprentice NOUN
der Lehrling (PL die Lehrlinge)
der Lehrling is also used for women.
◊ She is an apprentice. Sie ist Lehrling.

to **approach** VERB
[1] (get nearer to)
sich nähern ◊ He approached the house.
Er näherte sich dem Haus.
[2] (tackle)
angehen (IMPERFECT ging an, PERFECT hat
angegangen) ◊ to approach a problem
ein Problem angehen

appropriate ADJECTIVE
passend ◊ That dress isn't very
appropriate for an interview. Dieses Kleid
ist für ein Vorstellungsgespräch nicht
sehr passend.

approval NOUN
die Zustimmung

to **approve** VERB

♦ **to approve of** gutheißen ◊ I don't
approve of his choice. Ich heiße seine
Wahl nicht gut.
♦ **They didn't approve of his girlfriend.** Sie
hatten etwas gegen seine Freundin.

approximate ADJECTIVE
ungefähr

apricot NOUN
die Aprikose

April NOUN
der April ◊ in April im April
♦ **April Fool's Day** der erste April
♦ **April Fool!** April, April!

apron NOUN
die Schürze

Aquarius NOUN
der Wassermann ◊ I'm Aquarius. Ich bin
Wassermann.

Arab ADJECTIVE
see also **Arab** NOUN
arabisch ◊ the Arab countries die
arabischen Länder

Arab NOUN
see also **Arab** ADJECTIVE
der Araber (PL die Araber)
die Araberin

Arabic ADJECTIVE
arabisch

arch NOUN
der Bogen (PL die Bögen)

archaeologist NOUN (US **archeologist**)
der Archäologe (GEN des Archäologen, PL
die Archäologen)
die Archäologin
◊ She's an archaeologist. Sie ist
Archäologin.

archaeology NOUN
die Archäologie

archbishop NOUN
der Erzbischof (PL die Erzbischöfe)

archeologist NOUN US
der Archäologe (GEN des Archäologen, PL
die Archäologen)
die Archäologin
◊ She's an archaeologist. Sie ist
Archäologin.

archeology NOUN US
die Archäologie

architect NOUN
der Architekt (GEN des Architekten, PL die
Architekten)
die Architektin
◊ She's an architect. Sie ist Architektin.

architecture NOUN
die Architektur

Arctic NOUN
die Arktis

are VERB see **be**

area NOUN
[1] die Gegend ◊ She lives in the London
area. Sie lebt in der Gegend von London.

2 das Viertel (PL die Viertel) ◊ *My favourite area of London is Soho.* Soho ist mein Lieblingsviertel von London.
3 die Fläche ◊ *The field has an area of one thousand square metres.* Das Feld hat eine Fläche von eintausend Quadratmetern.

Argentina NOUN
Argentinien NEUT
♦ **from Argentina** aus Argentinien
♦ **to Argentina** nach Argentinien

Argentinian ADJECTIVE
argentinisch

to **argue** VERB
streiten (IMPERFECT stritt, PERFECT hat gestritten) ◊ *They never stop arguing.* Sie streiten dauernd.

argument NOUN
der Streit (PL die Streite)
♦ **to have an argument** Streit haben ◊ *They had an argument.* Sie hatten Streit.

Aries NOUN
der Widder ◊ *I'm Aries.* Ich bin Widder.

arm NOUN
der Arm (PL die Arme)

armchair NOUN
der Sessel (PL die Sessel)

armour NOUN (US **armor**)
die Rüstung
♦ **a suit of armour** eine Rüstung

army NOUN
die Armee (PL die Armeen)

around PREPOSITION, ADVERB
1 um ◊ *She wore a scarf around her neck.* Sie trug einen Schal um den Hals.
2 etwa (*approximately*) ◊ *It costs around a hundred pounds.* Es kostet etwa einhundert Pfund.
3 gegen (*date, time*) ◊ *Let's meet at around eight p.m.* Treffen wir uns gegen acht Uhr abends.
♦ **around here (1)** (*nearby*) hier in der Nähe ◊ *Is there a chemist's around here?* Gibt es hier in der Nähe eine Apotheke?
♦ **around here (2)** (*in this area*) hier in der Gegend ◊ *He lives around here.* Er wohnt hier in der Gegend.

to **arrange** VERB
♦ **to arrange to do something** verabreden, etwas zu tun ◊ *They arranged to go out together on Friday.* Sie haben verabredet, am Freitag zusammen auszugehen.
♦ **to arrange a meeting** ein Treffen ausmachen ◊ *Can we arrange a meeting?* Können wir ein Treffen ausmachen?
♦ **to arrange a party** eine Party vorbereiten

arrangement NOUN
der Plan (*plan*) (PL die Pläne)
♦ **They made arrangements to go out on Friday night.** Sie haben verabredet, am Freitagabend auszugehen.

to **arrest** VERB
see also **arrest** NOUN
verhaften (PERFECT hat verhaftet) ◊ *The police have arrested five people.* Die Polizei hat fünf Leute verhaftet.

arrest NOUN
see also **arrest** VERB
die Verhaftung
♦ **You're under arrest!** Sie sind verhaftet!

arrival NOUN
die Ankunft (PL die Ankünfte)

to **arrive** VERB
ankommen (IMPERFECT kam an, PERFECT ist angekommen) ◊ *I arrived at five o'clock.* Ich bin um fünf Uhr angekommen.

arrogant ADJECTIVE
arrogant

arrow NOUN
der Pfeil (PL die Pfeile)

art NOUN
die Kunst (PL die Künste)

artery NOUN
die Arterie

art gallery NOUN
die Kunstgalerie

article NOUN
der Artikel (PL die Artikel) ◊ *a newspaper article* ein Zeitungsartikel

artificial ADJECTIVE
künstlich

artist NOUN
der Künstler (PL die Künstler)
die Künstlerin
◊ *She's an artist.* Sie ist Künstlerin.

artistic ADJECTIVE
künstlerisch

as CONJUNCTION, ADVERB
1 als (*while*) ◊ *He came in as I was leaving.* Er kam herein, als ich gehen wollte.
♦ **He works as a waiter in the holidays.** In den Ferien jobbt er als Kellner.
2 da (*since*) ◊ *As it's Sunday, you can have a lie-in.* Da es Sonntag ist, kannst du ausschlafen.
♦ **as ... as** so ... wie ◊ *Peter's as tall as Michael.* Peter ist so groß wie Michael. ◊ *Her coat cost twice as much as mine.* Ihr Mantel hat doppelt so viel wie meiner gekostet.
♦ **as much ... as** so viel ... wie ◊ *I haven't got as much money as you.* Ich habe nicht so viel Geld wie du.
♦ **as soon as possible** sobald wie möglich ◊ *I'll do it as soon as possible.* Ich tue es sobald wie möglich.
♦ **as from tomorrow** ab morgen ◊ *As from tomorrow, the shops will stay open until ten p.m.* Ab morgen haben die Geschäfte bis zehn Uhr abends auf.
♦ **as if** als ob
♦ **as though** als ob

Note that **als ob** is followed by the subjunctive.
◊ *She acted as though she hadn't seen me.* Sie tat so, als ob sie mich nicht sähe.

asap ABBREVIATION (= *as soon as possible*)
sobald wie möglich

ash NOUN
die Asche

ashamed ADJECTIVE
♦**to be ashamed** sich schämen ◊ *You should be ashamed of yourself!* Du solltest dich schämen!

ashtray NOUN
der Aschenbecher (PL die Aschenbecher)

Asia NOUN
Asien NEUT
♦**from Asia** aus Asien
♦**to Asia** nach Asien

Asian ADJECTIVE
see also **Asian** NOUN
asiatisch ◊ *He's Asian.* Er ist Asiate.
◊ *She's Asian.* Sie ist Asiatin.

Asian NOUN
see also **Asian** ADJECTIVE
der Asiate (GEN des Asiaten, PL die Asiaten)
die Asiatin

to **ask** VERB
[1] (*inquire, request*)
fragen ◊ *"Have you finished?" she asked.* "Bist du fertig?" fragte sie.
♦**to ask somebody something** jemanden etwas fragen ◊ *He asked her how old she was.* Er fragte sie, wie alt sie ist.
♦**to ask for something** um etwas bitten ◊ *He asked for a cup of tea.* Er bat um eine Tasse Tee.
♦**to ask somebody to do something** jemanden bitten, etwas zu tun ◊ *She asked him to do the shopping.* Sie bat ihn einzukaufen.
♦**to ask about something** sich nach etwas erkundigen ◊ *I asked about train times to Leeds.* Ich habe mich nach Zugverbindungen nach Leeds erkundigt.
♦**to ask somebody a question** jemanden etwas fragen
[2] (*invite*)
einladen (PRESENT lädt ein, IMPERFECT lud ein, PERFECT hat eingeladen) ◊ *Have you asked Matthew to the party?* Hast du Matthew zur Party eingeladen?
♦**He asked her out.** (*on a date*) Er hat sie um ein Rendezvous gebeten.

asleep ADJECTIVE
♦**to be asleep** schlafen ◊ *He's asleep.* Er schläft.
♦**to fall asleep** einschlafen ◊ *I fell asleep in front of the TV.* Ich bin beim Fernsehen eingeschlafen.

asparagus NOUN
der Spargel (PL die Spargel)

aspect NOUN

der Aspekt (PL die Aspekte)

aspirin NOUN
die Schmerztablette

asset NOUN
der Vorteil (PL die Vorteile) ◊ *Her experience will be an asset to the firm.* Ihre Erfahrung wird für die Firma von Vorteil sein.

assignment NOUN
das Referat (*in school*) (PL die Referate)

assistance NOUN
die Hilfe

assistant NOUN
[1] (*in shop*)
der Verkäufer (PL die Verkäufer)
die Verkäuferin
[2] (*helper*)
der Assistent (GEN des Assistenten, PL die Assistenten)
die Assistentin

association NOUN
der Verband (PL die Verbände)

assortment NOUN
[1] die Auswahl (*choice*) ◊ *a large assortment of cheeses* eine große Auswahl an Käse
[2] die Mischung (*mixture*) ◊ *an assortment of biscuits* eine Keksmischung

to **assume** VERB
annehmen (PRESENT nimmt an, IMPERFECT nahm an, PERFECT hat angenommen) ◊ *I assume she won't be coming.* Ich nehme an, dass sie nicht kommt.

to **assure** VERB
versichern (PERFECT hat versichert) ◊ *He assured me he was coming.* Er versicherte mir, dass er kommt.

asthma NOUN
das Asthma ◊ *I've got asthma.* Ich habe Asthma.

to **astonish** VERB
erstaunen (PERFECT hat erstaunt) ◊ *She was astonished.* Sie war erstaunt.

astonishing ADJECTIVE
erstaunlich

astrology NOUN
die Astrologie

astronaut NOUN
der Astronaut (GEN des Astronauten, PL die Astronauten)
die Astronautin

astronomy NOUN
die Astronomie

asylum NOUN
das Asyl ◊ *to ask for asylum* um Asyl bitten

asylum-seeker NOUN
der Asylbewerber (PL die Asylbewerber)
die Asylbewerberin

at PREPOSITION

1 um ◊ *at four o'clock* um vier Uhr
2 an ◊ *at Christmas* an Weihnachten
◊ *What are you doing at the weekend?*
Was machst du am Wochenende?
♦ **at night** nachts
3 mit ◊ *at fifty kilometres per hour* mit
fünfzig Stundenkilometern
4 in ◊ *at school* in der Schule
♦ **at home** zu Hause
♦ **two at a time** jeweils zwei
♦ **at the races** beim Pferderennen
5 at (*@ symbol*)

ate VERB *see* **eat**

Athens NOUN
Athen NEUT
♦ **from Athens** aus Athen

athlete NOUN
der Athlet (GEN des Athleten, PL die
Athleten)
die Athletin

athletic ADJECTIVE
athletisch

athletics NOUN
die Leichtathletik ◊ *I like watching the
athletics on TV.* Ich sehe mir im
Fernsehen gern Leichtathletik an.

Atlantic NOUN
der Atlantik

atlas NOUN
der Atlas (GEN des Atlasses, PL die
Atlanten)

atmosphere NOUN
die Atmosphäre

atom NOUN
das Atom (PL die Atome)

atomic ADJECTIVE
♦ **an atomic bomb** eine Atombombe

to **attach** VERB
festbinden (IMPERFECT band fest, PERFECT hat
festgebunden) ◊ *They attached a rope to
the car.* Sie banden ein Seil am Auto fest.
♦ **Please find attached ...** Anbei erhalten
Sie ...

attached ADJECTIVE
♦ **to be attached to somebody** an jemandem hängen ◊ *He's very attached to his
family.* Er hängt sehr an seiner Familie.

attachment NOUN
der Anhang (*to e-mail*) (PL die Anhänge)

to **attack** VERB
see also **attack** NOUN
angreifen (IMPERFECT griff an, PERFECT hat
angegriffen) ◊ *The dog attacked me.* Der
Hund hat mich angegriffen.

attack NOUN
see also **attack** VERB
der Angriff (PL die Angriffe)

attempt NOUN
see also **attempt** VERB
der Versuch (PL die Versuche) ◊ *She
gave up after several attempts.* Sie gab
nach mehreren Versuchen auf.

to **attempt** VERB
see also **attempt** NOUN
versuchen (PERFECT hat versucht)
♦ **to attempt to do something** versuchen,
etwas zu tun ◊ *I attempted to write a
song.* Ich habe versucht, ein Lied zu
schreiben.

to **attend** VERB
teilnehmen (PRESENT nimmt teil, IMPERFECT
nahm teil, PERFECT hat teilgenommen) ◊ *to
attend a meeting* an einem Treffen
teilnehmen

attention NOUN
die Aufmerksamkeit
♦ **to pay attention to something** auf etwas
achten ◊ *He didn't pay attention to what I
was saying.* Er hat nicht darauf geachtet,
was ich sagte.

attic NOUN
der Speicher (PL die Speicher)

attitude NOUN
die Einstellung

attorney NOUN US
der Rechtsanwalt (PL die Rechtsanwälte)
die Rechtsanwältin
◊ *My mother's an attorney.* Meine Mutter
ist Rechtsanwältin.

to **attract** VERB
anziehen (IMPERFECT zog an, PERFECT hat
angezogen) ◊ *The Lake District attracts
lots of tourists.* Der Lake District zieht
viele Touristen an.

attraction NOUN
die Attraktion ◊ *a tourist attraction* eine
Touristenattraktion

attractive ADJECTIVE
attraktiv ◊ *She's very attractive.* Sie ist
sehr attraktiv.

aubergine NOUN
die Aubergine

auction NOUN
die Auktion

audience NOUN
die Zuschauer MASC PL (*in theatre*) ◊ *The
audience laughed loudly.* Die Zuschauer
lachten laut.

audition NOUN
1 (*of actor*)
die Vorsprechprobe
2 (*of musician*)
das Vorspiel (PL die Vorspiele)

August NOUN
der August ◊ *in August* im August

aunt NOUN
die Tante ◊ *my aunt* meine Tante

aunty NOUN
die Tante ◊ *my aunty* meine Tante

au pair NOUN
das Au-pair-Mädchen (PL die Au-pair-
Mädchen) ◊ *She's an au pair.* Sie ist Au-
pair-Mädchen.

Australia NOUN
Australien NEUT
♦**from Australia** aus Australien
♦**in Australia** in Australien
♦**to Australia** nach Australien

Australian ADJECTIVE
see also **Australian** NOUN
australisch ◊ *He's Australian.* Er ist
Australier. ◊ *She's Australian.* Sie ist
Australierin.

Australian NOUN
see also **Australian** ADJECTIVE
der Australier (PL die Australier)
die Australierin
♦**the Australians** die Australier

Austria NOUN
Österreich NEUT
♦**from Austria** aus Österreich
♦**in Austria** in Österreich
♦**to Austria** nach Österreich

Austrian ADJECTIVE
see also **Austrian** NOUN
österreichisch ◊ *He's Austrian.* Er ist
Österreicher. ◊ *She's Austrian.* Sie ist
Österreicherin.

Austrian NOUN
see also **Austrian** ADJECTIVE
der Österreicher (PL die Österreicher)
die Österreicherin
♦**the Austrians** die Österreicher

author NOUN
der Autor (PL die Autoren)
die Autorin
◊ *She's a famous author.* Sie ist eine
berühmte Autorin.

autobiography NOUN
die Autobiografie

autograph NOUN
das Autogramm (PL die Autogramme)
◊ *May I have your autograph?* Kann ich
Ihr Autogramm haben?

automatic ADJECTIVE
automatisch ◊ *an automatic door* eine
automatische Tür

automatically ADVERB
automatisch

autumn NOUN
der Herbst (PL die Herbste) ◊ *in autumn*
im Herbst

availability NOUN
die Erhältlichkeit (*of goods*)
♦**subject to availability** falls vorrätig

available ADJECTIVE
erhältlich ◊ *Free brochures are available
on request.* Auf Anfrage sind kostenlose
Prospekte erhältlich.
♦**Is Mr Cooke available today?** Ist Herr
Cooke heute zu sprechen?

avalanche NOUN
die Lawine

avenue NOUN
die Allee

average NOUN
see also **average** ADJECTIVE
der Durchschnitt (PL die Durchschnitte)
◊ *on average* im Durchschnitt

average ADJECTIVE
see also **average** NOUN
durchschnittlich ◊ *the average price* der
durchschnittliche Preis

avocado NOUN
die Avocado (PL die Avocados)

to **avoid** VERB
[1] meiden (IMPERFECT mied, PERFECT hat
gemieden) ◊ *He avoids her when she's in
a bad mood.* Er meidet sie, wenn sie
schlechte Laune hat.
[2] vermeiden ◊ *You should avoid going
out on your own at night.* Du solltest
vermeiden, nachts allein auszugehen.

awake ADJECTIVE
♦**to be awake** wach sein ◊ *Is she awake?*
Ist sie wach? ◊ *He was still awake.* Er war
noch wach.

award NOUN
der Preis (PL die Preise) ◊ *He's won an
award.* Er hat einen Preis bekommen.

aware ADJECTIVE
♦**to be aware that...** sich bewusst sein,
dass...
♦**to be aware of something** etw merken
◊ *We are aware of what is happening.*
Wir merken, was geschieht.
♦**not that I am aware of** nicht dass ich
wüsste

away ADJECTIVE, ADVERB
weg (*not here*) ◊ *Felix is away today.* Felix
ist heute weg. ◊ *He's away for a week.* Er
ist eine Woche lang weg.
♦**The town's two kilometres away.** Die
Stadt ist zwei Kilometer entfernt.
♦**The coast is two hours away by car.** Zur
Küste sind es mit dem Auto zwei Stunden.
♦**Go away!** Geh weg!

away match NOUN
das Auswärtsspiel (PL die
Auswärtsspiele) ◊ *Our team has an away
match this week.* Unsere Mannschaft hat
diese Woche ein Auswärtsspiel.

awful ADJECTIVE
schrecklich ◊ *That's awful!* Das ist
schrecklich!
♦**an awful lot of ...** furchtbar viel ... ◊ *an
awful lot of work* furchtbar viel Arbeit

awfully ADVERB
furchtbar ◊ *I'm awfully sorry.* Es tut mir
furchtbar leid.

awkward ADJECTIVE
[1] schwierig (*difficult*) ◊ *an awkward
situation* eine schwierige Situation
[2] unangenehm (*embarrassing*) ◊ *an
awkward question* eine unangenehme
Frage

axe NOUN
die Axt (PL die Äxte)

B

BA ABBREVIATION (= *Bachelor of Arts*)
der Magister (PL die Magister)
◆ **She's got a BA in History.** Sie hat einen Magistertitel in Geschichte.

baby NOUN
das Baby (PL die Babys)

baby carriage NOUN US
der Buggy (PL die Buggys)

to **babysit** VERB
babysitten ◊ *Veronika is babysitting for her friend.* Veronika babysittet bei ihrer Freundin.

babysitter NOUN
der Babysitter (PL die Babysitter)
die Babysitterin

babysitting NOUN
das Babysitten

bachelor NOUN
der Junggeselle (GEN des Junggesellen, PL die Junggesellen) ◊ *He's a bachelor.* Er ist Junggeselle.

back NOUN
see also **back** ADJECTIVE, VERB

1 (*of person, horse, book*)
der Rücken (PL die Rücken)
2 (*of page, house*)
die Rückseite ◊ *Write your name on the back.* Schreiben Sie Ihren Namen auf die Rückseite.
◆ **in the back of the car** hinten im Auto
◆ **at the back** hinten ◊ *He's sitting at the back.* Er sitzt hinten.

back ADJECTIVE, ADVERB
see also **back** NOUN, VERB

hintere ◊ *the back wheel of my bike* das hintere Rad meines Fahrrads
◆ **the back seat** der Rücksitz
◆ **the back door** die Hintertür
◆ **to get back** zurückkommen ◊ *What time did you get back?* Wann bist du zurückgekommen?
◆ **We went there by bus and walked back.** Wir sind mit dem Bus hingefahren und zu Fuß zurückgegangen.
◆ **He's not back yet.** Er ist noch nicht zurück.
◆ **to call somebody back** jemanden zurückrufen ◊ *I'll call back later.* Ich rufe später zurück.

to **back** VERB
see also **back** NOUN, ADJECTIVE

◆ **to back somebody** für jemanden sein ◊ *I'm backing the Labour Party.* Ich bin für die Labour-Party.
◆ **to back a horse** auf ein Pferd setzen ◊ *He backed the wrong horse.* Er hat auf das falsche Pferd gesetzt.

◆ **to back out** einen Rückzieher machen ◊ *They promised to help and then backed out.* Sie haben versprochen zu helfen, haben dann aber einen Rückzieher gemacht.
◆ **to back somebody up** jemanden unterstützen

backache NOUN
die Rückenschmerzen MASC PL ◊ *to have backache* Rückenschmerzen haben

backbone NOUN
das Rückgrat (PL die Rückgrate)

to **backfire** VERB
schiefgehen (*go wrong*) (IMPERFECT ging schief, PERFECT ist schiefgegangen)

background NOUN
der Hintergrund (PL die Hintergründe)
◊ *a house in the background* ein Haus im Hintergrund ◊ *his family background* sein familiärer Hintergrund
◆ **background noise** die Hintergrundgeräusche NEUT PL

backhand NOUN
die Rückhand (PL die Rückhände)

backing NOUN
die Unterstützung (*support*)

backpack NOUN
der Rucksack (PL die Rucksäcke)

backpacker NOUN
der Wanderer (PL die Wanderer)
die Wanderin

back pain NOUN
die Rückenschmerzen MASC PL ◊ *to have back pain* Rückenschmerzen haben

backside NOUN
der Hintern (GEN des Hintern, PL die Hintern)

backstroke NOUN
das Rückenschwimmen

backup NOUN
die Unterstützung (*support*)
◆ **a backup file** eine Sicherungsdatei

backwards ADVERB
zurück ◊ *to take a step backwards* einen Schritt zurück machen
◆ **to fall backwards** nach hinten fallen

back yard NOUN
der Hinterhof (PL die Hinterhöfe)

bacon NOUN
der Speck ◊ *bacon and eggs* Eier mit Speck

bad ADJECTIVE
1 schlecht ◊ *a bad film* ein schlechter Film ◊ *the bad weather* das schlechte Wetter ◊ *to be in a bad mood* schlechte Laune haben ◊ *not bad* nicht schlecht ◊ *That's not bad at all.* Das ist gar nicht schlecht.

B

♦ **to be bad at something** in etwas schlecht sein ◊ *I'm really bad at maths.* In Mathe bin ich wirklich schlecht.

2 <u>schlimm</u> (*serious*) ◊ *a bad accident* ein schlimmer Unfall

3 <u>böse</u> (*naughty*) ◊ *You bad boy!* Du böser Junge!

♦ **to go bad** (*food*) schlecht werden

♦ **I feel bad about it.** Das tut mir echt leid.

badge NOUN
1 (*metal*)
der <u>Button</u> (PL die Buttons)
2 (*sticker*)
der <u>Aufkleber</u> (PL die Aufkleber)

badly ADVERB
<u>schlecht</u> ◊ *badly paid* schlecht bezahlt
♦ **badly wounded** schwer verletzt
♦ **He's badly in need of some money.** Er braucht dringend Geld.

badminton NOUN
das <u>Badminton</u> ◊ *to play badminton* Badminton spielen

bad-tempered ADJECTIVE
♦ **to be bad-tempered (1)** (*by nature*) griesgrämig sein ◊ *He's a really bad-tempered person.* Er ist wirklich ein griesgrämiger Mensch.
♦ **to be bad-tempered (2)** (*temporarily*) schlechte Laune haben ◊ *He was really bad-tempered yesterday.* Er hatte gestern wirklich schlechte Laune.

to **baffle** VERB
<u>verblüffen</u> (PERFECT hat verblüfft) ◊ *She was baffled.* Sie war verblüfft.

bag NOUN
die <u>Tasche</u>
♦ **an old bag** (*person*) eine alte Schachtel

baggage NOUN
das <u>Gepäck</u>

baggage reclaim NOUN
die <u>Gepäckausgabe</u>

baggy ADJECTIVE
<u>weit</u> (*clothes*)

bagpipes PL NOUN
der <u>Dudelsack</u> (PL die Dudelsäcke) ◊ *Ed plays the bagpipes.* Ed spielt Dudelsack.

to **bake** VERB
<u>backen</u> (PRESENT bäckt, IMPERFECT backte, PERFECT hat gebacken) ◊ *to bake a cake* einen Kuchen backen

baked beans PL NOUN
die <u>gebackenen Bohnen</u> PL

baker NOUN
der <u>Bäcker</u> (PL die Bäcker)
die <u>Bäckerin</u>
◊ *He's a baker.* Er ist Bäcker.

bakery NOUN
die <u>Bäckerei</u>

baking ADJECTIVE
♦ **It's baking in here!** Hier ist es furchtbar heiß!

balance NOUN
see also **balance** VERB
das <u>Gleichgewicht</u> ◊ *to lose one's balance* das Gleichgewicht verlieren

to **balance** VERB
see also **balance** NOUN
<u>balancieren</u> (PERFECT ist balanciert) ◊ *I balanced on the window ledge.* Ich balancierte auf dem Fensterbrett.
♦ **The boxes were carefully balanced.** Die Kartons befanden sich genau im Gleichgewicht.

balanced ADJECTIVE
<u>ausgewogen</u> ◊ *a balanced diet* eine ausgewogene Ernährung

balcony NOUN
der <u>Balkon</u> (PL die Balkone)

bald ADJECTIVE
<u>glatzköpfig</u>
♦ **to be bald** eine Glatze haben

ball NOUN
der <u>Ball</u> (PL die Bälle)

ballet NOUN
das <u>Ballett</u> (PL die Ballette)
Note that you pronounce the "tt" in German.
◊ *We went to a ballet.* Wir sind ins Ballett gegangen. ◊ *ballet lessons* Ballettstunden

ballet dancer NOUN
der <u>Balletttänzer</u> (PL die Balletttänzer)
die <u>Balletttänzerin</u>

ballet shoes PL NOUN
die <u>Ballettschuhe</u> MASC PL

balloon NOUN
der <u>Luftballon</u> (*at parties*) (PL die Luftballone)
♦ **a hot-air balloon** ein Heißluftballon

ballpoint pen NOUN
der <u>Kugelschreiber</u> (PL die Kugelschreiber)

ban NOUN
see also **ban** VERB
das <u>Verbot</u> (PL die Verbote)

to **ban** VERB
see also **ban** NOUN
<u>verbieten</u> (IMPERFECT verbot, PERFECT hat verboten) ◊ *to ban somebody from doing something* jemandem verbieten, etwas zu tun
♦ **She was banned from driving.** Sie bekam Fahrverbot.

banana NOUN
die <u>Banane</u> ◊ *a banana skin* eine Bananenschale

band NOUN
1 (*rock band*)
die <u>Band</u> (PL die Bands)
2 (*brass band*)
die <u>Kapelle</u>

bandage NOUN
see also **bandage** VERB
der <u>Verband</u> (PL die Verbände)

to **bandage** VERB

> see also **bandage** NOUN

verbinden (IMPERFECT verband, PERFECT hat verbunden) ◊ *The nurse bandaged his arm.* Die Schwester verband ihm den Arm.

Band-Aid ® NOUN US

das Heftpflaster (PL die Heftpflaster)

bandit NOUN

der Bandit (GEN des Banditen, PL die Banditen)

bang NOUN

> see also **bang** VERB

1 der Knall (PL die Knalle) ◊ *I heard a loud bang.* Ich habe einen lauten Knall gehört.

2 der Schlag (PL die Schläge) ◊ *a bang on the head* ein Schlag auf den Kopf

♦ **Bang!** Peng!

to **bang** VERB

> see also **bang** NOUN

anschlagen (*part of body*) (PRESENT schlägt an, IMPERFECT schlug an, PERFECT hat angeschlagen) ◊ *I banged my head.* Ich habe mir den Kopf angeschlagen.

♦ **to bang the door** die Tür zuknallen

♦ **to bang on the door** gegen die Tür hämmern

banger NOUN

die Bratwurst (PL die Bratwürste) ◊ *bangers and mash* Bratwürste mit Kartoffelbrei

bank NOUN

1 (*financial*)

die Bank (PL die Banken)

2 (*of river, lake*)

das Ufer (PL die Ufer)

to **bank on** VERB

sich verlassen auf (PRESENT verlässt, IMPERFECT verließ, PERFECT hat verlassen) ◊ *I was banking on your coming today.* Ich hatte mich darauf verlassen, dass du heute kommst. ◊ *I wouldn't bank on it.* Ich würde mich nicht darauf verlassen.

bank account NOUN

das Bankkonto (PL die Bankkonten)

banker NOUN

der Banker (PL die Banker)

die Bankerin

bank holiday NOUN

der Feiertag (PL die Feiertage)

banknote NOUN

die Banknote

bankrupt ADJECTIVE

bankrott

banned ADJECTIVE

verboten

bar NOUN

1 (*pub*)

die Bar (PL die Bars)

2 (*counter*)

die Theke

♦ **a bar of chocolate** eine Tafel Schokolade

♦ **a bar of soap** ein Stück Seife

barbaric ADJECTIVE

barbarisch

barbecue NOUN

das Barbecue (PL die Barbecues)

♦ **We could have a barbecue this evening.** Wir könnten heute Abend grillen.

barber NOUN

der Herrenfriseur (PL die Herrenfriseure)

bare ADJECTIVE

nackt

barefoot ADJECTIVE, ADVERB

barfuß ◊ *The children go around barefoot.* Die Kinder laufen barfuß herum. ◊ *She was barefoot.* Sie war barfuß.

barely ADVERB

kaum ◊ *I could barely hear what she was saying.* Ich konnte kaum hören, was sie sagte.

bargain NOUN

das Schnäppchen (PL die Schnäppchen) ◊ *It was a bargain!* Das war ein Schnäppchen!

barge NOUN

der Kahn (PL die Kähne)

to **bark** VERB

bellen

barmaid NOUN

die Bardame ◊ *She's a barmaid.* Sie ist Bardame.

barman NOUN

der Barkeeper (PL die Barkeeper) ◊ *He's a barman.* Er ist Barkeeper.

barn NOUN

die Scheune

barrel NOUN

das Fass (GEN des Fasses, PL die Fässer)

barrier NOUN

die Schranke

bartender NOUN US

der Barkeeper (PL die Barkeeper)

base NOUN

1 (*basis*)

die Basis (PL die Basen) ◊ *a good base for a successful career* eine gute Basis für eine erfolgreiche Karriere

2 (*of lamp, mountain*)

der Fuß (GEN des Fußes, PL die Füße)

3 (*of container*)

der Boden (PL die Böden)

4 (*for paint, make-up*)

die Grundlage

5 (*military*)

der Stützpunkt (PL die Stützpunkte)

baseball NOUN

der Baseball ◊ *a baseball cap* eine Baseballmütze

based ADJECTIVE

♦ **based on** basierend auf +DAT

basement NOUN

das Untergeschoss (GEN des Untergeschosses, PL die Untergeschosse)

B

to **bash** VERB

see also **bash** NOUN

♦**to bash something** auf etwas einschlagen ◊ *They tried to bash the door in.* Sie versuchten, die Tür einzuschlagen.

bash NOUN

see also **bash** VERB

♦**I'll have a bash.** Ich versuch's mal.

basic ADJECTIVE

1 elementar (*knowledge, education*)

♦**basic vocabulary** der Grundwortschatz

♦**It's a basic model.** Es ist ein Grundmodell.

2 einfach ◊ *The accommodation is pretty basic.* Die Unterkunft ist sehr einfach.

basically ADVERB

eigentlich ◊ *Basically, I just don't like him.* Eigentlich mag ich ihn nicht.

basics PL NOUN

die Grundlagen FEM PL

basil NOUN

das Basilikum

basin NOUN

(*washbasin*)

das Waschbecken (PL die Waschbecken)

basis NOUN

♦**on a daily basis** täglich

♦**on a regular basis** regelmäßig

basket NOUN

der Korb (PL die Körbe)

basketball NOUN

der Basketball

bass NOUN

der Bass (GEN des Basses, PL die Bässe) ◊ *He plays bass.* Er spielt Bass. ◊ *He's a bass.* Er singt Bass.

♦**a bass drum** eine Basstrommel

♦**a bass guitar** eine Bassgitarre

bassoon NOUN

das Fagott (PL die Fagotte) ◊ *I play the bassoon.* Ich spiele Fagott.

bat NOUN

1 (*for cricket, rounders, table tennis*)

der Schläger (PL die Schläger)

2 (*animal*)

die Fledermaus (PL die Fledermäuse)

bath NOUN

1 das Bad (PL die Bäder) ◊ *a hot bath* ein heißes Bad

♦**to have a bath** baden

2 (*bathtub*)

die Badewanne ◊ *There's a spider in the bath.* In der Badewanne ist eine Spinne.

to **bathe** VERB

baden

bathing suit NOUN US

der Badeanzug (PL die Badeanzüge)

bathroom NOUN

das Badezimmer (PL die Badezimmer)

baths PL NOUN

das Schwimmbad (PL die Schwimmbäder)

bath towel NOUN

das Badetuch (PL die Badetücher)

batter NOUN

der Pfannkuchenteig

battery NOUN

die Batterie

battle NOUN

die Schlacht ◊ *the Battle of Hastings* die Schlacht von Hastings

♦**It was a battle, but we managed in the end.** Es war ein Kampf, aber wir haben es schließlich geschafft.

battleship NOUN

das Schlachtschiff (PL die Schlachtschiffe)

bay NOUN

die Bucht

BC ABBREVIATION (= *before Christ*) v. Chr. (= vor Christus) ◊ *in 200 BC* im Jahre 200 v. Chr.

to **be** VERB

sein (PRESENT ist, IMPERFECT war, PERFECT ist gewesen) ◊ *I'm tired.* Ich bin müde. ◊ *You're late.* Du bist spät dran. ◊ *She's English.* Sie ist Engländerin. ◊ *It's cold.* Es ist kalt. ◊ *It's a nice day.* Es ist ein schöner Tag. ◊ *It's four o'clock.* Es ist vier Uhr. ◊ *I'm fourteen.* Ich bin vierzehn. ◊ *We are all happy.* Wir sind alle glücklich. ◊ *I've been ill.* Ich war krank. ◊ *I've never been to Dresden.* Ich war noch nie in Dresden.

♦**to be beaten** geschlagen werden

Questions like "isn't it?" don't exist in German.

◊ *She's pretty, isn't she?* Sie ist hübsch, nicht wahr? ◊ *The film was good, wasn't it?* Der Film war gut, nicht wahr?

You do not translate a when you want to describe somebody's occupation.

◊ *She's a doctor.* Sie ist Ärztin. ◊ *He's a student.* Er ist Student. ◊ *He's a bachelor.* Er ist Junggeselle.

♦**I'm cold.** Mir ist kalt.

♦**I'm hungry.** Ich habe Hunger.

beach NOUN

der Strand (PL die Strände)

bead NOUN

die Perle

beak NOUN

der Schnabel (PL die Schnäbel)

beam NOUN

der Strahl (PL die Strahlen)

beans PL NOUN

1 die Bohnen FEM PL

2 die gebackenen Bohnen FEM PL (*baked beans*)

☞

> ℹ️ *Few Germans eat baked beans and not many shops sell them.*

◊ *beans on toast* gebackene Bohnen in Tomatensoße auf Toast
♦ **broad beans** dicke Bohnen
♦ **green beans** grüne Bohnen
♦ **kidney beans** Kidneybohnen

bean sprouts PL NOUN
die Sojasprossen PL

bear NOUN

see also **bear** VERB

der Bär (GEN des Bären, PL die Bären)
to **bear** VERB

see also **bear** NOUN

ertragen (*endure*) (PRESENT erträgt, IMPERFECT ertrug, PERFECT hat ertragen) ◊ *I can't bear it.* Ich kann es nicht ertragen.
♦ **to bear up** sich halten
♦ **Bear up!** Kopf hoch!
♦ **If you would bear with me for a moment** ... Wenn Sie sich bitte einen Moment gedulden könnten ...

beard NOUN
der Bart (PL die Bärte) ◊ *He's got a beard.* Er hat einen Bart.
♦ **a man with a beard** ein bärtiger Mann

bearded ADJECTIVE
bärtig

beat NOUN

see also **beat** VERB

der Rhythmus (GEN des Rhythmus, PL die Rhythmen)
to **beat** VERB

see also **beat** NOUN

schlagen (PRESENT schlägt, IMPERFECT schlug, PERFECT hat geschlagen) ◊ *We beat them three nil.* Wir haben sie drei zu null geschlagen.
♦ **Beat it!** Hau ab! (*informal*)
♦ **to beat somebody up** (*informal*) jemanden zusammenschlagen

beautiful ADJECTIVE
schön

beautifully ADVERB
schön

beauty NOUN
die Schönheit

beauty spot NOUN
das schöne Fleckchen (PL die schönen Fleckchen)

became VERB *see* **become**

because CONJUNCTION
weil ◊ *I did it because ...* Ich habe es getan, weil ...
♦ **because of** wegen ◊ *because of the weather* wegen des Wetters
to **become** VERB
werden (PRESENT wird, IMPERFECT wurde, PERFECT ist geworden) ◊ *He became a*

famous writer. Er wurde ein berühmter Schriftsteller.

> *Be careful not to translate* **to become** *by* **bekommen.**

bed NOUN
das Bett (PL die Betten) ◊ *in bed* im Bett
♦ **to go to bed** ins Bett gehen ◊ *to go to bed with somebody* mit jemandem ins Bett gehen

bed and breakfast NOUN
das Zimmer mit Frühstück (PL die Zimmer mit Frühstück) ◊ *How much is it for bed and breakfast?* Wie viel kostet das Zimmer mit Frühstück?
♦ **We stayed in a bed and breakfast.** Wir waren in einer Frühstückspension.

bedclothes PL NOUN
die Bettwäsche SING

bedding NOUN
das Bettzeug

bedroom NOUN
das Schlafzimmer (PL die Schlafzimmer)

bedsit NOUN
das möblierte Zimmer (GEN des möblierten Zimmers, PL die möblierten Zimmer)

bedspread NOUN
die Tagesdecke

bedtime NOUN
♦ **Ten o'clock is my usual bedtime.** Ich gehe normalerweise um zehn Uhr ins Bett.
♦ **Bedtime!** Ab ins Bett!

bee NOUN
die Biene

beef NOUN
das Rindfleisch
♦ **roast beef** das Roastbeef

beefburger NOUN
die Frikadelle

been VERB *see* **be**

beer NOUN
das Bier (PL die Biere *or* Bier)

> *When ordering more than one beer use the plural form* **Bier.**

◊ *Two beers, please!* Zwei Bier bitte!

beetle NOUN
der Käfer (PL die Käfer)

beetroot NOUN
die Rote Bete

before PREPOSITION, CONJUNCTION, ADVERB
1 vor ◊ *before Tuesday* vor Dienstag
2 bevor ◊ *Before opening the packet, read the instructions.* Lesen Sie die Bedienungsanleitung, bevor Sie die Packung aufmachen. ◊ *I'll phone before I leave.* Ich rufe an, bevor ich gehe.
3 schon (*already*) ◊ *I've seen this film before.* Ich habe diesen Film schon gesehen. ◊ *Have you been to Scotland before?* Warst du schon einmal in Schottland?
♦ **the day before** am Tag davor

B

♦ **the week before** die Woche davor

beforehand ADVERB
vorher

to **beg** VERB
1 (*for money*)
betteln
2 anflehen (PERFECT hat angefleht) ◊ *He begged me to stop.* Er flehte mich an aufzuhören.

began VERB *see* **begin**

beggar NOUN
der Bettler (PL die Bettler)
die Bettlerin

to **begin** VERB
anfangen (PRESENT fängt an, IMPERFECT fing an, PERFECT hat angefangen)
♦ **to begin doing something** anfangen, etwas zu tun

beginner NOUN
der Anfänger (PL die Anfänger)
die Anfängerin
◊ *I'm just a beginner.* Ich bin noch Anfänger.

beginning NOUN
der Anfang (PL die Anfänge) ◊ *in the beginning* am Anfang

begun VERB *see* **begin**

behalf NOUN
♦ **on behalf of somebody** für jemanden ◊ *on her behalf* für sie

to **behave** VERB
sich benehmen (PRESENT benimmt sich, IMPERFECT benahm sich, PERFECT hat sich benommen) ◊ *He behaved like an idiot.* Er hat sich wie ein Idiot benommen. ◊ *She behaved very badly.* Sie hat sich sehr schlecht benommen.
♦ **to behave oneself** sich anständig benehmen ◊ *Did the children behave themselves?* Haben sich die Kinder anständig benommen?
♦ **Behave!** Sei brav!

behaviour NOUN (US **behavior**)
das Benehmen

behind PREPOSITION, ADVERB
see also **behind** NOUN
hinter
Use the accusative to express movement or a change of place. Use the dative when there is no change of place.
◊ *the wall behind the television* die Wand hinter dem Fernseher ◊ *The book fell behind the television.* Das Buch fiel hinter den Fernseher.
♦ **to be behind** (*late*) im Rückstand sein ◊ *I'm behind with my revision.* Ich bin mit dem Pauken im Rückstand.

behind NOUN
see also **behind** PREPOSITION, ADVERB
der Hintern (GEN des Hinterns, PL die Hintern)

beige ADJECTIVE

beige

Belgian ADJECTIVE
see also **Belgian** NOUN
belgisch
♦ **He's Belgian.** Er ist Belgier.
♦ **She's Belgian.** Sie ist Belgierin.

Belgian NOUN
see also **Belgian** ADJECTIVE
der Belgier (PL die Belgier)
die Belgierin
♦ **the Belgians** die Belgier

Belgium NOUN
Belgien NEUT
♦ **from Belgium** aus Belgien
♦ **in Belgium** in Belgien
♦ **to Belgium** nach Belgien

to **believe** VERB
glauben ◊ *I don't believe you.* Ich glaube dir nicht.
♦ **to believe in something** an etwas glauben ◊ *Do you believe in ghosts?* Glaubst du an Gespenster? ◊ *to believe in God* an Gott glauben

bell NOUN
1 (*doorbell, in school*)
die Klingel
♦ **to ring the bell** klingeln
♦ **When the bell rings the children go out into the playground.** Wenn es klingelt, gehen die Kinder auf den Schulhof.
2 (*in church*)
die Glocke
3 das Glöckchen (PL die Glöckchen)
◊ *Our cat has a bell on its neck.* Unsere Katze hat ein Glöckchen um den Hals.

belly NOUN
der Bauch (PL die Bäuche)

to **belong** VERB
gehören (PERFECT hat gehört)
♦ **to belong to somebody** jemandem gehören ◊ *Who does it belong to?* Wem gehört das? ◊ *That belongs to me.* Das gehört mir.
♦ **Do you belong to any clubs?** Bist du Mitglied in irgendeinem Klub?
♦ **Where does this belong?** Wo gehört das hin?

belongings PL NOUN
die Sachen FEM PL

below PREPOSITION, ADVERB
1 unterhalb ◊ *below the castle* unterhalb der Burg
2 unter
Use the accusative to express movement or a change of place. Use the dative when there is no change of place.
◊ *The bucket is below the sink.* Der Eimer ist unter der Spüle. ◊ *Put the cloth below the sink.* Leg das Tuch unter die Spüle.
3 darunter ◊ *on the floor below* im Stock darunter
♦ **ten degrees below freezing** zehn Grad unter null

belt NOUN
der Gürtel (PL die Gürtel)
beltway NOUN US
die Umgehungsstraße
bench NOUN
1 (*seat*)
die Bank (PL die Bänke)
2 (*for woodwork*)
die Werkbank (PL die Werkbänke)
bend NOUN
> *see also* **bend** VERB
1 die Kurve (*in road*)
2 die Biegung (*in river*)
to **bend** VERB
> *see also* **bend** NOUN
1 (*leg, arm*)
beugen ◇ *I can't bend my arm.* Ich kann
den Arm nicht beugen.
♦ **to bend down** sich bücken
♦ **to bend over** sich nach vorne beugen
2 (*object*)
verbiegen (IMPERFECT verbog, PERFECT hat
verbogen) ◇ *You've bent it.* Du hast es
verbogen.
♦ **It bends easily.** Das lässt sich leicht
biegen.
♦ **"do not bend"** "nicht knicken"
beneath PREPOSITION

> Use the accusative to express movement
> or a change of place. Use the dative
> when there is no change of place.

unter ◇ *He placed his football boots
beneath the chair.* Er stellte seine
Fußballschuhe unter den Stuhl. ◇ *She
found his jumper beneath the bed.* Sie
fand seinen Pullover unter dem Bett.
benefit NOUN
> *see also* **benefit** VERB
der Vorteil (*advantage*) (PL die
Vorteile)
♦ **unemployment benefit** die
Arbeitslosenunterstützung
to **benefit** VERB
> *see also* **benefit** NOUN
profitieren ◇ *You'll benefit from that
experience.* Du wirst von dieser
Erfahrung profitieren.
♦ **He benefited from the change.** Die
Veränderung hat ihm gutgetan.
bent VERB *see* **bend**
bent ADJECTIVE
verbogen ◇ *a bent fork* eine verbogene
Gabel
berserk ADJECTIVE
♦ **to go berserk** durchdrehen ◇ *She went
berserk.* Sie hat durchgedreht.
berth NOUN
1 (*on ship*)
die Koje
2 (*on train*)
der Schlafwagenplatz (PL die
Schlafwagenplätze)
beside PREPOSITION

neben

> Use the accusative to express movement
> or a change of place. Use the dative
> when there is no change of place.

◇ *the lamp beside the television* die
Lampe neben dem Fernseher ◇ *Put that
chair beside the television.* Stell den
Stuhl neben den Fernseher.
♦ **I was beside myself.** Ich war außer mir.
♦ **That's beside the point.** Das tut hier
nichts zur Sache.
besides ADVERB
außerdem ◇ *Besides, it's too expensive.*
Und außerdem ist es zu teuer.
best ADJECTIVE, ADVERB
1 beste ◇ *He's the best player in the
team.* Er ist der beste Spieler der
Mannschaft. ◇ *Janet's the best at maths.*
Janet ist in Mathe die Beste.
2 am besten ◇ *Emma sings best.* Emma
singt am besten.
♦ **to do one's best** sein Bestes tun ◇ *It's not
perfect, but I did my best.* Es ist nicht
vollkommen, aber ich habe mein Bestes
getan.
♦ **to make the best of it** das Beste daraus
machen ◇ *We'll have to make the best of
it.* Wir müssen das Beste daraus machen.
best man NOUN
der Trauzeuge (GEN des Trauzeugen, PL
die Trauzeugen)

> ⓘ There is no real equivalent in
> Germany to **best man**. A **Trauzeuge** is
> merely an official witness to the
> wedding ceremony.

bet NOUN
> *see also* **bet** VERB
die Wette ◇ *to make a bet* eine Wette
machen
to **bet** VERB
> *see also* **bet** NOUN
wetten
♦ **I bet you he won't come.** Wetten, dass er
nicht kommt.
♦ **I bet he forgot.** Wetten, dass er es
vergessen hat.
to **betray** VERB
verraten (PRESENT verrät, IMPERFECT verriet,
PERFECT hat verraten)
better ADJECTIVE, ADVERB
besser ◇ *This one's better than that one.*
Dieses hier ist besser als das da. ◇ *a
better way to do it* eine bessere Methode
◇ *You'd better do it straight away.* Das
machst du besser sofort. ◇ *I'd better go
home.* Ich gehe besser nach Hause.
◇ *That's better!* Das ist schon besser!
♦ **better still** noch besser ◇ *Go and see her
tomorrow, or better still, go today.* Geh
morgen zu ihr, oder noch besser, geh
heute.

B

♦ **to get better (1)** (*improve*) besser werden ◊ *I hope the weather gets better soon.* Ich hoffe, das Wetter wird bald besser. ◊ *My German is getting better.* Mein Deutsch wird besser.

♦ **to get better (2)** (*from illness*) sich erholen

♦ **I hope you get better soon.** Gute Besserung!

♦ **to feel better** sich besser fühlen ◊ *Are you feeling better now?* Fühlst du dich jetzt besser?

betting shop NOUN
das Wettbüro (PL die Wettbüros)

> *ⓘ There are very few betting shops in Germany and betting is far less popular than in the UK.*

between PREPOSITION

> *Use the accusative to express movement or a change of place. Use the dative when there is no change of place.*

zwischen ◊ *The cathedral is between the town hall and the river.* Der Dom liegt zwischen dem Rathaus und dem Fluss. ◊ *He sat down between the two girls.* Er setzte sich zwischen die beiden Mädchen. ◊ *between fifteen and twenty minutes* zwischen fünfzehn und zwanzig Minuten

to **beware** VERB
♦ **"Beware of the dog!"** "Vorsicht bissiger Hund!"

to **bewilder** VERB
verwirren ◊ *She was bewildered.* Sie war verwirrt.

beyond PREPOSITION
hinter ◊ *There was a lake beyond the mountain.* Hinter dem Berg war ein See.
♦ **beyond belief** nicht zu glauben
♦ **beyond repair** nicht mehr zu reparieren

biased ADJECTIVE
voreingenommen

Bible NOUN
die Bibel

bicycle NOUN
das Fahrrad (PL die Fahrräder)

bifocals PL NOUN
die Bifokalbrille ◊ *a pair of bifocals* eine Bifokalbrille

big ADJECTIVE
groß ◊ *a big house* ein großes Haus ◊ *a bigger house* ein größeres Haus ◊ *my big brother* mein großer Bruder ◊ *her big sister* ihre große Schwester
♦ **He's a big guy.** Er ist kräftig gebaut.

bigheaded ADJECTIVE
eingebildet

bike NOUN
das Fahrrad (PL die Fahrräder) ◊ *by bike* mit dem Fahrrad

bikini NOUN

der Bikini (PL die Bikinis)

bilingual ADJECTIVE
zweisprachig

bill NOUN
1 die Rechnung ◊ *the gas bill* die Gasrechnung
♦ **Can we have the bill, please?** Können wir bitte zahlen?
2 (*banknote*)
der Geldschein (PL die Geldscheine) ◊ *a dollar bill* ein Dollarschein

billiards SING NOUN
das Billard ◊ *to play billiards* Billard spielen

billion NOUN
die Milliarde

bin NOUN
1 (*indoors*)
der Abfalleimer (PL die Abfalleimer)
2 (*outside*)
der Mülleimer (PL die Mülleimer)

bingo NOUN
das Bingo

binoculars PL NOUN
das Fernglas (PL die Ferngläser) ◊ *a pair of binoculars* ein Fernglas

biochemistry NOUN
die Biochemie

biography NOUN
die Biografie

biology NOUN
die Biologie

bird NOUN
der Vogel (PL die Vögel)

bird-watching NOUN
♦ **My hobby's bird-watching.** Mein Hobby ist das Beobachten von Vögeln.

Biro ® NOUN
der Kuli (PL die Kulis)

birth NOUN
die Geburt ◊ *date of birth* das Geburtsdatum

birth certificate NOUN
die Geburtsurkunde

birth control NOUN
die Empfängnisverhütung ◊ *Before we go on holiday, we'd better talk about birth control.* Bevor wir in Urlaub fahren, sollten wir uns über Empfängnisverhütung unterhalten.

birthday NOUN
der Geburtstag (PL die Geburtstage) ◊ *When's your birthday?* Wann hast du Geburtstag? ◊ *a birthday cake* ein Geburtstagskuchen ◊ *a birthday card* eine Geburtstagskarte ◊ *I'm going to have a birthday party.* Ich gebe eine Geburtstagsparty.

biscuit NOUN
der Keks (PL die Kekse)

bishop NOUN
der Bischof (PL die Bischöfe)

bit VERB see **bite**

bit NOUN

das Stück (*piece*) (PL die Stücke) ◊ *Would you like another bit?* Möchtest du noch ein Stück? ◊ *a bit of cake* ein Stück Kuchen

♦ **a bit (1)** etwas ◊ *He's a bit mad.* Er ist etwas böse. ◊ *a bit too hot* etwas zu heiß

♦ **a bit (2)** ein bisschen ◊ *Wait a bit!* Warte ein bisschen! ◊ *Do you play football? – A bit.* Spielst du Fußball? – Ein bisschen.

♦ **a bit of** (*a little*) etwas ◊ *a bit of music* etwas Musik ◊ *It's a bit of a nuisance.* Das ist schon etwas ärgerlich.

♦ **to fall to bits** kaputtgehen

♦ **to take something to bits** etwas auseinandernehmen

♦ **bit by bit** nach und nach

bitch NOUN

1 (*female dog*)

die Hündin

to **bite** VERB

see also **bite** NOUN

1 (*person, dog*)

beißen (IMPERFECT biss, PERFECT hat gebissen)

2 (*insect*)

stechen (PRESENT sticht, IMPERFECT stach, PERFECT hat gestochen) ◊ *I got bitten by mosquitoes.* Ich bin von Mücken gestochen worden.

♦ **to bite one's nails** an den Nägeln kauen

bite NOUN

see also **bite** VERB

1 (*insect bite*)

der Stich (PL die Stiche)

2 (*animal bite*)

der Biss (GEN des Bisses, PL die Bisse)

♦ **to have a bite to eat** eine Kleinigkeit essen

bitter ADJECTIVE

see also **bitter** NOUN

1 bitter

2 bitterkalt (*weather, wind*) ◊ *It's bitter today.* Heute ist es bitterkalt.

bitter NOUN

see also **bitter** ADJECTIVE

das dunkle Bier (PL die dunklen Biere)

*ⓘ German beers are completely different from British ones. There is no real equivalent to **bitter**.*

black ADJECTIVE

schwarz ◊ *a black jacket* eine schwarze Jacke

♦ **She's black.** Sie ist eine Schwarze.

blackberry NOUN

die Brombeere

blackbird NOUN

die Amsel

blackboard NOUN

die Tafel

black coffee NOUN

der schwarze Kaffee (PL die schwarzen Kaffees)

blackcurrant NOUN

die Schwarze Johannisbeere

blackmail NOUN

see also **blackmail** VERB

die Erpressung ◊ *That's blackmail!* Das ist Erpressung!

to **blackmail** VERB

see also **blackmail** NOUN

erpressen (PERFECT hat erpresst) ◊ *He blackmailed her.* Er erpresste sie.

blackout NOUN

der Stromausfall (*power cut*) (PL die Stromausfälle)

♦ **to have a blackout** (*faint*) ohnmächtig werden

black pudding NOUN

die Blutwurst (PL die Blutwürste)

blacksmith NOUN

der Schmied ◊ *He's a blacksmith.* Er ist Schmied.

blade NOUN

die Klinge

to **blame** VERB

♦ **Don't blame me!** Ich bin nicht schuld!

♦ **I blame him.** Ich gebe ihm die Schuld.

♦ **He blamed it on my sister.** Er gab meiner Schwester die Schuld.

blank ADJECTIVE

see also **blank** NOUN

1 leer (*paper, page*)

2 unbespielt (*cassette, video*)

♦ **My mind went blank.** Ich hatte ein Brett vor dem Kopf.

blank NOUN

see also **blank** ADJECTIVE

die Lücke ◊ *Fill in the blanks.* Füllt die Lücken aus.

blank cheque NOUN

der Blankoscheck (PL die Blankoschecks)

blanket NOUN

die Decke

blast NOUN

♦ **a bomb blast** eine Bombenexplosion

blatant ADJECTIVE

unverschämt ◊ *a blatant liar* ein unverschämter Lügner

blaze NOUN

das Feuer (PL die Feuer)

blazer NOUN

der Blazer (PL die Blazer)

bleach NOUN

das Bleichmittel (PL die Bleichmittel)

bleached ADJECTIVE

gebleicht ◊ *bleached hair* gebleichtes Haar

bleak ADJECTIVE

trostlos ◊ *The future looks bleak.* Die Zukunft sieht trostlos aus.

to **bleed** VERB
    bluten ◊ *My nose is bleeding.* Ich blute
    aus der Nase.

bleeper NOUN
    der Piepser (PL die Piepser)

blender NOUN
    der Mixer (PL die Mixer)

to **bless** VERB
    segnen (*religiously*)
    ♦ **Bless you!** (*after sneezing*) Gesundheit!

blew VERB *see* **blow**

blind ADJECTIVE
    see also **blind** NOUN
    blind

blind NOUN
    see also **blind** ADJECTIVE
    das Rollo (*fabric*) (PL die Rollos)

blindfold NOUN
    see also **blindfold** VERB
    die Augenbinde

to **blindfold** VERB
    see also **blindfold** NOUN
    ♦ **to blindfold somebody** jemandem die
    Augen verbinden

to **blink** VERB
    zwinkern

bliss NOUN
    ♦ **It was bliss!** Es war eine Wonne!

blister NOUN
    die Blase

blizzard NOUN
    der Schneesturm (PL die
    Schneestürme)

blob NOUN
    der Tropfen (PL die Tropfen) ◊ *a blob of
    glue* ein Tropfen Klebstoff

block NOUN
    see also **block** VERB
    der Block (PL die Blöcke). ◊ *He lives in our
    block.* Er lebt in unserem Block.
    ♦ **a block of flats** ein Wohnblock MASC

to **block** VERB
    see also **block** NOUN
    blockieren (PERFECT hat blockiert)

blockage NOUN
    die Verstopfung (*in pipe or tube*) ◊ *The
    tea leaves created a blockage in the pipe.*
    Die Teeblätter haben eine Verstopfung
    im Rohr verursacht.

bloke NOUN
    der Typ (*informal*) (PL die Typen)

blonde ADJECTIVE
    blond ◊ *She's got blonde hair.* Sie hat
    blondes Haar.

blood NOUN
    das Blut

blood pressure NOUN
    der Blutdruck
    ♦ **to have high blood pressure** zu hohen
    Blutdruck haben

blood sports PL NOUN
    der Blutsport

blood test NOUN
    die Blutuntersuchung

bloody ADJECTIVE
    ♦ **bloody difficult** verdammt schwer
    (*informal*)
    ♦ **that bloody television** der
    Scheißfernseher (*informal*)
    ♦ **Bloody hell!** Scheiße! (*informal*)

blouse NOUN
    die Bluse

blow NOUN
    see also **blow** VERB
    der Schlag (PL die Schläge)

to **blow** VERB
    see also **blow** NOUN
    1 (*person*)
    blasen (PRESENT bläst, IMPERFECT blies, PERFECT
    hat geblasen)
    2 (*wind*)
    wehen
    ♦ **to blow one's nose** sich die Nase
    putzen ◊ *Blow your nose!* Putz dir die
    Nase!
    ♦ **to blow a whistle** pfeifen
    ♦ **to blow out a candle** eine Kerze
    ausblasen
    ♦ **to blow up (1)** in die Luft jagen ◊ *The
    terrorists blew up a police station.* Die
    Terroristen haben ein Polizeirevier in die
    Luft gejagt.
    ♦ **to blow up (2)** aufblasen ◊ *to blow
    up a balloon* einen Luftballon
    aufblasen
    ♦ **The house blew up.** Das Haus flog in die
    Luft.

blow-dry NOUN
    das Föhnen
    ♦ **A cut and blow-dry, please.** Schneiden
    und Föhnen bitte.

blown VERB *see* **blow**

blue ADJECTIVE
    blau ◊ *a blue dress* ein blaues
    Kleid
    ♦ **a blue film** ein Pornofilm MASC
    ♦ **It came out of the blue.** Das kam aus
    heiterem Himmel.

blues PL NOUN
    der Blues (*music*) SING (GEN des Blues)

to **bluff** VERB
    see also **bluff** NOUN
    bluffen

bluff NOUN
    see also **bluff** VERB
    der Bluff (PL die Bluffs) ◊ *It's just a bluff.*
    Das ist ein Bluff.

blunder NOUN
    der Schnitzer (PL die Schnitzer)

blunt ADJECTIVE
    1 unverblümt (*person*)
    2 stumpf (*knife*)

to **blush** VERB
    rot werden (PRESENT wird rot, IMPERFECT
    wurde rot, PERFECT ist rot geworden)

board NOUN
1 das Brett (PL die Bretter)
2 (*blackboard*)
die Tafel ◊ *Write it on the board.* Schreib es an die Tafel.
3 (*noticeboard*)
das Schwarze Brett (PL die Schwarzen Bretter)
♦ **on board** an Bord
♦ **full board** die Vollpension

boarder NOUN
der Internatsschüler (PL die Internatsschüler)
die Internatsschülerin

board game NOUN
das Brettspiel (PL die Brettspiele)

boarding card NOUN
die Bordkarte

boarding school NOUN
das Internat (PL die Internate) ◊ *I go to boarding school.* Ich gehe in ein Internat.

to **boast** VERB
prahlen ◊ *to boast about something* mit etwas prahlen

boat NOUN
das Boot (PL die Boote)

body NOUN
der Körper (PL die Körper)

bodybuilding NOUN
das Bodybuilding ◊ *He does bodybuilding.* Er macht Bodybuilding.

bodyguard NOUN
der Leibwächter (PL die Leibwächter)

bog NOUN
das Moor (*marsh*) (PL die Moore)

boil NOUN
see also **boil** VERB
der Furunkel (PL die Furunkel)

to **boil** VERB
see also **boil** NOUN
kochen ◊ *to boil some water* Wasser kochen ◊ *to boil an egg* ein Ei kochen ◊ *The water's boiling.* Das Wasser kocht.
♦ **to boil over** überkochen ◊ *The milk boiled over.* Die Milch ist übergekocht.

boiled ADJECTIVE
♦ **a soft-boiled egg** ein weich gekochtes Ei NEUT
♦ **boiled potatoes** Salzkartoffeln FEM PL

boiling ADJECTIVE
♦ **It's boiling in here!** Hier ist eine Bruthitze!
♦ **boiling hot** brütend heiß ◊ *a boiling hot day* ein brütend heißer Tag

bolt NOUN
1 (*on door*)
der Riegel (PL die Riegel)
2 (*with nut*)
der Bolzen (PL die Bolzen)

bomb NOUN
see also **bomb** VERB
die Bombe

Note that you pronounce the second "b" in German.

to **bomb** VERB
see also **bomb** NOUN
bombardieren (PERFECT hat bombardiert)

bomber NOUN
der Bomber (PL die Bomber)
Note that you pronounce the second "b" in German.

bombing NOUN
der Bombenangriff (PL die Bombenangriffe)

bond NOUN
die Bindung (*between people*) ◊ *There is a strong bond between the two brothers.* Zwischen den beiden Brüdern besteht eine enge Bindung.

bone NOUN
1 (*of human, animal*)
der Knochen (PL die Knochen)
2 (*of fish*)
die Gräte

bone dry ADJECTIVE
knochentrocken

bonfire NOUN
das Feuer (PL die Feuer)

bonnet NOUN
die Motorhaube (*of car*)

bonus NOUN
1 (*extra payment*)
der Bonus (PL die Bonusse)
2 (*added advantage*)
der Vorteil

book NOUN
see also **book** VERB
das Buch (PL die Bücher)

to **book** VERB
see also **book** NOUN
buchen ◊ *We haven't booked.* Wir haben nicht gebucht.

bookcase NOUN
1 (*open*)
das Bücherregal (PL die Bücherregale)
2 (*with doors*)
der Bücherschrank (PL die Bücherschränke)

booklet NOUN
die Broschüre

bookmark NOUN
das Lesezeichen (PL die Lesezeichen)

bookshelf NOUN
das Bücherbrett (PL die Bücherbretter)
♦ **bookshelves** das Bücherregal SING

bookshop NOUN
die Buchhandlung

to **boost** VERB
Auftrieb geben (PRESENT gibt, IMPERFECT gab, PERFECT hat gegeben) ◊ *The win boosted the team's morale.* Der Sieg gab der Mannschaft moralischen Auftrieb.

boot NOUN
1 (*of car*)
der Kofferraum (PL die Kofferräume)

B

2 (*footwear*)
der Stiefel (PL die Stiefel)
♦ **football boots** die Fußballschuhe MASC PL
booze NOUN
der Alkohol
border NOUN
die Grenze
bore VERB *see* **bear**
bored ADJECTIVE
♦ **to be bored** sich langweilen
♦ **I'm bored.** Ich langweile mich.
♦ **She gets bored easily.** Ihr wird schnell langweilig.
boredom NOUN
die Langeweile (GEN der Langenweile)
boring ADJECTIVE
langweilig
born ADJECTIVE
♦ **to be born** geboren werden ◊ *I was born in 1982.* Ich bin 1982 geboren.
borne VERB *see* **bear**
to **borrow** VERB
ausleihen (IMPERFECT lieh aus, PERFECT hat ausgeliehen) ◊ *Can I borrow your pen?* Kann ich deinen Schreiber ausleihen?
♦ **to borrow something from somebody** sich etwas von jemandem leihen ◊ *I borrowed some money from a friend.* Ich habe mir von einem Freund Geld geliehen.
Bosnia NOUN
Bosnien NEUT
♦ **from Bosnia** aus Bosnien
♦ **to Bosnia** nach Bosnien
Bosnian ADJECTIVE
bosnisch
boss NOUN
der Chef (PL die Chefs)
die Chefin
to **boss around** VERB
♦ **to boss somebody around** jemanden herumkommandieren
bossy ADJECTIVE
herrisch
both ADJECTIVE, PRONOUN
beide ◊ *We both went.* Wir sind beide gegangen. ◊ *Emma and Jane both went.* Emma und Jane sind beide gegangen. ◊ *Both of your answers are wrong.* Beide Antworten sind falsch. ◊ *Both of them have left.* Beide sind gegangen. ◊ *Both of us went.* Wir sind beide gegangen.
♦ **both ... and** sowohl ... als auch ◊ *He speaks both French and Italian.* Er spricht sowohl Französisch als auch Italienisch.
bother NOUN
see also **bother** VERB
der Ärger ◊ *We had a spot of bother with the car.* Wir hatten Ärger mit dem Auto.
♦ **No bother!** Kein Problem!
to **bother** VERB

see also **bother** NOUN
1 (*worry*)
beunruhigen (PERFECT hat beunruhigt) ◊ *Is something bothering you?* Beunruhigt dich etwas?
2 (*disturb*)
stören ◊ *I'm sorry to bother you.* Es tut mir leid, dass ich dich störe.
♦ **no bother** kein Problem
♦ **Don't bother!** Nicht nötig!
♦ **to bother to do something** es für nötig finden, etwas zu tun ◊ *He didn't bother to tell me about it.* Er hat es nicht für nötig gefunden, es mir zu sagen.
bottle NOUN
die Flasche
bottle bank NOUN
der Altglascontainer (PL die Altglascontainer)
bottle-opener NOUN
der Flaschenöffner (PL die Flaschenöffner)
bottom NOUN
see also **bottom** ADJECTIVE
1 (*of container, bag, sea*)
der Boden (PL die Böden)
2 (*buttocks*)
der Hintern (GEN des Hintern, PL die Hintern)
3 (*of list*)
das Ende (PL die Enden)
♦ **at the bottom of page two** unten auf Seite zwei
bottom ADJECTIVE
see also **bottom** NOUN
unterste ◊ *the bottom shelf* das unterste Regalbrett
♦ **the bottom sheet** das Bettlaken
bought VERB *see* **buy**
to **bounce** VERB
hüpfen (PERFECT ist gehüpft)
bouncer NOUN
der Rausschmeißer (PL die Rausschmeißer)
bound ADJECTIVE
♦ **He's bound to say that.** Er muss das ja sagen.
♦ **She's bound to come.** Sie kommt sicher.
boundary NOUN
die Grenze
bow NOUN
see also **bow** VERB
1 die Schleife (*knot*) ◊ *to tie a bow* eine Schleife machen
2 der Bogen (PL die Bogen) ◊ *a bow and arrow* ein Pfeil und Bogen
to **bow** VERB
see also **bow** NOUN
sich verneigen (PERFECT hat sich verneigt)
bowels PL NOUN
die Eingeweide NEUT PL
bowl NOUN

☞

see also **bowl** VERB
die Schale (*for soup, cereal*)

to **bowl** VERB

see also **bowl** NOUN
werfen (*in cricket*) (PRESENT wirft, IMPERFECT warf, PERFECT hat geworfen)

bowler NOUN
(*in cricket*)
der Werfer (PL die Werfer)
die Werferin

bowling NOUN
das Bowling
♦ **to go bowling** Bowling spielen
♦ **a bowling alley** eine Bowlingbahn

bowls SING NOUN
das Boccia (GEN des Boccia)
The "cc" in **Boccia** is pronounced like "ch" in church.
◊ *to play bowls* Boccia spielen

bow tie NOUN
die Fliege

box NOUN
die Schachtel ◊ *a box of matches* eine Schachtel Streichhölzer
♦ **a cardboard box** ein Karton MASC

boxer NOUN
der Boxer (PL die Boxer)

boxer shorts PL NOUN
die Boxershorts PL ◊ *He was wearing a pair of boxer shorts.* Er hatte Boxershorts an.

boxing NOUN
das Boxen

Boxing Day NOUN
der zweite Weihnachtsfeiertag

boy NOUN
der Junge (GEN des Jungen, PL die Jungen)

boyfriend NOUN
der Freund (PL die Freunde) ◊ *Have you got a boyfriend?* Hast du einen Freund?

bra NOUN
der BH (PL die BHs)

brace NOUN
die Zahnspange (*on teeth*) ◊ *She wears a brace.* Sie hat eine Zahnspange.

bracelet NOUN
das Armband (PL die Armbänder)

brackets PL NOUN
die Klammern FEM PL ◊ *in brackets* in Klammern

brain NOUN
das Gehirn (PL die Gehirne)

brainy ADJECTIVE
gescheit

brake NOUN

see also **brake** VERB
die Bremse

to **brake** VERB

see also **brake** NOUN
bremsen

branch NOUN
1 (*of tree*)
der Zweig (PL die Zweige)
2 (*of bank*)
die Filiale

brand NOUN
die Marke ◊ *a well-known brand of coffee* eine bekannte Kaffeemarke

brand name NOUN
der Markenname (GEN des Markennamens, PL die Markennamen)

brand-new ADJECTIVE
brandneu

brandy NOUN
der Weinbrand (PL die Weinbrände)

brass NOUN
das Messing (*metal*)
♦ **the brass section** die Blechbläser MASC PL

brass band NOUN
die Blaskapelle

brat NOUN
♦ **He's a spoiled brat.** Er ist ein verwöhnter Balg.

brave ADJECTIVE
mutig
Be careful not to translate **brave** by **brav**.

Brazil NOUN
Brasilien NEUT
♦ **from Brazil** aus Brasilien
♦ **to Brazil** nach Brasilien

bread NOUN
das Brot (PL die Brote) ◊ *bread and butter* Brot mit Butter
♦ **brown bread** das Graubrot
♦ **white bread** das Weißbrot

> ⓘ There is a huge variety of types of bread in Germany which can't simply be divided into brown and white.

break NOUN

see also **break** VERB
die Pause (*rest*) ◊ *to take a break* eine Pause machen ◊ *during morning break* während der Vormittagspause
♦ **the Christmas break** die Weihnachtsfeiertage MASC PL
♦ **Give me a break!** Mach mal halblang!

to **break** VERB

see also **break** NOUN
1 kaputt machen (PERFECT hat kaputt gemacht) ◊ *Careful, you'll break something!* Vorsicht, du machst sonst was kaputt!
2 (*record, law*)
brechen (PRESENT bricht, IMPERFECT brach, PERFECT hat gebrochen) ◊ *to break a promise* sein Versprechen brechen
♦ **to break one's leg** sich das Bein brechen ◊ *I broke my leg.* Ich habe mir das Bein gebrochen.
♦ **He broke his arm.** Er hat sich den Arm gebrochen.

B

3 (get broken)
brechen ◇ Careful, it'll break! Vorsicht,
es bricht!

to **break down** VERB
eine Panne haben (PRESENT hat eine
Panne, IMPERFECT hatte eine Panne, PERFECT
hat eine Panne gehabt) ◇ The car broke
down. Das Auto hatte eine Panne.

to **break in** VERB
einbrechen (PRESENT bricht ein, IMPERFECT
brach ein, PERFECT hat eingebrochen)

to **break into** VERB
einbrechen in (PRESENT bricht ein, IMPERFECT
brach ein, PERFECT ist eingebrochen)
◇ Thieves broke into the house. Diebe
brachen in das Haus ein.

to **break off** VERB
abbrechen (PRESENT bricht ab, IMPERFECT
brach ab, PERFECT hat abgebrochen) ◇ I
broke off a small piece. Ich habe ein
kleines Stück abgebrochen.

to **break open** VERB
aufbrechen (door, cupboard) (PRESENT
bricht auf, IMPERFECT brach auf, PERFECT hat
aufgebrochen)

to **break out** VERB
ausbrechen (PRESENT bricht aus, IMPERFECT
brach aus, PERFECT ist ausgebrochen)
◆ **to break out in a rash** einen Ausschlag
bekommen

to **break up** VERB
1 (crowd)
sich auflösen (PERFECT hat sich aufgelöst)
2 (meeting, party)
zu Ende gehen (IMPERFECT ging zu Ende,
PERFECT ist zu Ende gegangen)
3 (couple)
sich trennen
◆ **to break up a fight** eine Schlägerei
beenden
◆ **We break up next Wednesday.** Nächsten
Mittwoch ist der letzte Schultag.

breakdown NOUN
1 (in vehicle)
die Panne ◇ to have a breakdown eine
Panne haben
2 (mental)
der Nervenzusammenbruch (PL die
Nervenzusammenbrüche) ◇ to have a
breakdown einen
Nervenzusammenbruch haben

breakdown van NOUN
das Pannenfahrzeug (PL die
Pannenfahrzeuge)

breakfast NOUN
das Frühstück (PL die Frühstücke) ◇ What
would you like for breakfast? Was
möchtest du zum Frühstück?
◆ **to have breakfast** frühstücken

break-in NOUN
der Einbruch (PL die Einbrüche)

breast 'NOUN
die Brust (PL die Brüste)

◆ **chicken breast** die Hähnchenbrust

to **breast-feed** VERB
stillen

breaststroke NOUN
das Brustschwimmen

breath NOUN
der Atem
◆ **to have bad breath** Mundgeruch haben
◆ **to be out of breath** außer Atem sein
◆ **to get one's breath back** verschnaufen

to **breathe** VERB
atmen
◆ **to breathe in** einatmen
◆ **to breathe out** ausatmen

to **breed** VERB
see also **breed** NOUN
züchten ◇ to breed dogs Hunde züchten

breed NOUN
see also **breed** VERB
die Rasse

breeze NOUN
die Brise

brewery NOUN
die Brauerei

bribe NOUN
see also **bribe** VERB
die Bestechung

to **bribe** VERB
see also **bribe** NOUN
bestechen (PRESENT besticht, IMPERFECT
bestach, PERFECT hat bestochen)

brick NOUN
der Backstein (PL die Backsteine) ◇ a
brick wall eine Backsteinmauer

bricklayer NOUN
der Maurer (PL die Maurer)
die Maurerin

bride NOUN
die Braut (PL die Bräute)

bridegroom NOUN
der Bräutigam (PL die Bräutigame)

bridesmaid NOUN
die Brautjungfer

bridge NOUN
1 die Brücke ◇ a suspension bridge eine
Hängebrücke
2 das Bridge (GEN des Bridge) ◇ to play
bridge Bridge spielen

brief ADJECTIVE
kurz

briefcase NOUN
die Aktentasche

briefly ADVERB
kurz

briefs PL NOUN
die Unterhose ◇ a pair of briefs eine
Unterhose

bright ADJECTIVE
1 hell (light)
2 leuchtend (colour) ◇ a brighter colour
eine leuchtendere Farbe
◆ **bright blue** hellblau

3 intelligent ◊ *He's not very bright.* Er ist nicht besonders intelligent.

brilliant ADJECTIVE

1 prima (*wonderful*) ◊ *Brilliant!* Prima!

2 glänzend (*clever*) ◊ *a brilliant scientist* ein glänzender Wissenschaftler

to **bring** VERB

1 bringen (IMPERFECT brachte, PERFECT hat gebracht) ◊ *Could you bring me my trainers?* Könntest du mir meine Sportschuhe bringen?

2 (*bring along*) mitbringen ◊ *Bring warm clothes.* Bringt warme Kleidung mit! ◊ *Can I bring a friend?* Darf ich einen Freund mitbringen?

◆ **to bring about** herbeiführen

◆ **to bring back** zurückbringen

◆ **to bring forward** vorverlegen ◊ *The meeting was brought forward.* Die Sitzung wurde vorverlegt.

◆ **to bring up** aufziehen ◊ *She brought up five children on her own.* Sie hat fünf Kinder alleine aufgezogen.

Britain NOUN

Großbritannien NEUT

◆ **from Britain** aus Großbritannien

◆ **in Britain** in Großbritannien

◆ **to Britain** nach Großbritannien

◆ **Great Britain** Großbritannien

British ADJECTIVE

britisch

◆ **He's British.** Er ist Brite.

◆ **She's British.** Sie ist Britin.

◆ **the British** die Briten MASC PL

◆ **the British Isles** die Britischen Inseln

Brittany NOUN

die Bretagne

◆ **in Brittany** in der Bretagne

broad ADJECTIVE

breit (*wide*)

◆ **in broad daylight** am helllichten Tag

broadband NOUN

das Breitband

broadcast NOUN

see also **broadcast** VERB

die Sendung

to **broadcast** VERB

see also **broadcast** NOUN

senden ◊ *The interview was broadcast all over the world.* Das Interview wurde in der ganzen Welt gesendet.

broad-minded ADJECTIVE

tolerant

broccoli SING NOUN

die Brokkoli MASC PL

brochure NOUN

die Broschüre

to **broil** VERB US

grillen

broke VERB see **break**

broke ADJECTIVE

◆ **to be broke** (*without money*) pleite sein

broken VERB see **break**

broken ADJECTIVE

1 kaputt ◊ *It's broken.* Es ist kaputt.

2 gebrochen (*limb*) ◊ *He's got a broken arm.* Er hat einen gebrochenen Arm.

bronchitis NOUN

die Bronchitis

bronze NOUN

die Bronze ◊ *the bronze medal* die Bronzemedaille

brooch NOUN

die Brosche

broom NOUN

der Besen (PL die Besen)

brother NOUN

der Bruder (PL die Brüder) ◊ *my brother* mein Bruder ◊ *my big brother* mein großer Bruder

brother-in-law NOUN

der Schwager (PL die Schwäger)

brought VERB see **bring**

brown ADJECTIVE

braun

◆ **brown bread** das Graubrot

Brownie NOUN

der Wichtel (*Girl Guide*) (PL die Wichtel)

to **browse** VERB

browsen (*computer*) (PERFECT hat gebrowst)

◆ **to browse through a book** in einem Buch schmökern

browser NOUN

der Browser (*Internet*) (PL die Browser)

bruise NOUN

der blaue Fleck (PL die blauen Flecke)

brush NOUN

see also **brush** VERB

1 die Bürste

2 (*paintbrush*) der Pinsel (PL die Pinsel)

to **brush** VERB

see also **brush** NOUN

bürsten

◆ **to brush one's hair** sich die Haare bürsten ◊ *I brushed my hair.* Ich habe mir die Haare gebürstet.

◆ **to brush one's teeth** die Zähne putzen ◊ *I brush my teeth every night.* Ich putze jeden Abend die Zähne.

Brussels NOUN

Brüssel NEUT ◊ *to Brussels* nach Brüssel

Brussels sprouts PL NOUN

der Rosenkohl SING ◊ *The Brussel sprouts were salty.* Der Rosenkohl war versalzen.

brutal ADJECTIVE

brutal

BSc ABBREVIATION (= *Bachelor of Science*)

der Magister (PL die Magister)

◆ **She's got a BSc in Chemistry.** Sie hat einen Magistertitel in Chemie.

BSE NOUN (= *bovine spongiform encephalopathy*)
das BSE
bubble NOUN
die Blase
bubble bath NOUN
das Schaumbad (PL die Schaumbäder)
bubble gum NOUN
der Bubblegum (PL die Bubblegums)
bucket NOUN
der Eimer (PL die Eimer)
buckle NOUN
die Schnalle (*on belt, watch, shoe*)
Buddhism NOUN
der Buddhismus (GEN des Buddhismus)
◊ *Buddhism is the main religion of Sri Lanka.* Der Buddhismus ist die Hauptreligion in Sri Lanka.
Buddhist ADJECTIVE
buddhistisch
buddy NOUN US
der Kumpel (PL die Kumpel)
budget NOUN
see also **budget** VERB
das Budget (PL die Budgets)
to **budget** VERB
see also **budget** NOUN
einplanen (PERFECT hat eingeplant) ◊ *They budgeted $10 million for advertising.* Sie planten 10 Millionen Dollar für Werbung ein.
budgie NOUN
der Wellensittich (PL die Wellensittiche)
buffet NOUN
das Büfett (PL die Büfetts)
buffet car NOUN
der Speisewagen (PL die Speisewagen)
bug NOUN
1 (*insect*)
die Wanze
◆ **There are many bugs there.** Dort gibt es viel Ungeziefer.
◆ **a stomach bug** eine Magen-Darm-Infektion
◆ **There's a bug going round.** Da geht etwas herum.
2 (*in computer*)
der Programmfehler (PL die Programmfehler)
bugged ADJECTIVE
verwanzt ◊ *The room was bugged.* Das Zimmer war verwanzt.
to **build** VERB
bauen ◊ *They're going to build houses here.* Hier werden Häuser gebaut.
◆ **to build up** (*increase*) zunehmen
builder NOUN
1 (*owner of firm*)
der Bauunternehmer (PL die Bauunternehmer)
die Bauunternehmerin
2 (*worker*)
der Bauarbeiter (PL die Bauarbeiter)

die Bauarbeiterin
building NOUN
das Gebäude (PL die Gebäude)
built VERB see **build**
bulb NOUN
die Glühbirne (*electric*)
Bulgaria NOUN
Bulgarien NEUT
◆ **from Bulgaria** aus Bulgarien
◆ **to Bulgaria** nach Bulgarien
bull NOUN
der Stier (PL die Stiere)
bullet NOUN
die Kugel
bulletin board NOUN
das Schwarze Brett (*computer*) (PL die Schwarzen Bretter)
bullfighting NOUN
der Stierkampf (PL die Stierkämpfe)
bully NOUN
see also **bully** VERB
◆ **He's a big bully.** Er tyrannisiert andere gern.
to **bully** VERB
see also **bully** NOUN
tyrannisieren (PERFECT hat tyrannisiert)
bum NOUN
der Po (*informal: bottom*) (PL die Pos)
bum bag NOUN
die Gürteltasche
bump NOUN
see also **bump** VERB
1 (*lump*)
die Beule
2 (*minor accident*)
der Zusammenstoß (GEN des Zusammenstoßes, PL die Zusammenstöße)
◆ **We had a bump.** Es hat gebumst.
to **bump** VERB
see also **bump** NOUN
◆ **to bump into something** gegen etwas laufen ◊ *She bumped into the wall.* Sie ist gegen die Wand gelaufen.
◆ **We bumped into his car.** Wir sind in sein Auto gefahren.
◆ **I bumped into the headteacher.** Ich bin zufällig dem Rektor begegnet.
bumper NOUN
die Stoßstange
bumpy ADJECTIVE
holperig
bun NOUN
das Brötchen (PL die Brötchen)
bunch NOUN
◆ **a bunch of flowers** ein Blumenstrauß MASC
◆ **a bunch of grapes** eine Traube
◆ **a bunch of keys** ein Schlüsselbund MASC
bunches PL NOUN
die Rattenschwänze MASC PL ◊ *She has her hair in bunches.* Sie hat Rattenschwänze.

bungalow NOUN
der <u>Bungalow</u> (PL die Bungalows)
bunk NOUN
1 das <u>Bett</u> (PL die Betten)
2 (*on ship*)
die <u>Koje</u>
burger NOUN
der <u>Hamburger</u> (PL die Hamburger)
burglar NOUN
der <u>Einbrecher</u> (PL die Einbrecher)
die <u>Einbrecherin</u>
to **burglarize** VERB US
<u>einbrechen</u> in +ACC (PRESENT bricht ein,
IMPERFECT brach ein, PERFECT ist
eingebrochen)
♦ **Her house was burglarized.** Bei ihr
wurde eingebrochen.
burglary NOUN
der <u>Einbruch</u> (PL die Einbrüche)
to **burgle** VERB
<u>einbrechen</u> in +ACC (PRESENT bricht ein,
IMPERFECT brach ein, PERFECT ist
eingebrochen)
♦ **Her house was burgled.** Bei ihr wurde
eingebrochen.
burn NOUN
| *see also* **burn** VERB |
die <u>Verbrennung</u>
to **burn** VERB
| *see also* **burn** NOUN |
1 (*rubbish, documents*)
<u>verbrennen</u> (IMPERFECT verbrannte, PERFECT
hat verbrannt)
2 (*food*)
<u>anbrennen lassen</u> (PRESENT lässt
anbrennen, IMPERFECT ließ anbrennen,
PERFECT hat anbrennen lassen) ♦ *I burned
the cake.* Ich habe den Kuchen
anbrennen lassen.
3 (*CD, DVD*)
<u>brennen</u> (IMPERFECT brannte, PERFECT
hat gebrannt)
♦ **to burn oneself** sich verbrennen ♦ *I
burned myself on the oven door.* Ich
habe mich an der Ofentür verbrannt.
♦ **I've burned my hand.** Ich habe mir die
Hand verbrannt.
♦ **to burn down** abbrennen ♦ *The factory
burned down.* Die Fabrik ist abgebrannt.
to **burst** VERB
<u>platzen</u> (PERFECT ist geplatzt) ♦ *The balloon
burst.* Der Luftballon ist geplatzt.
♦ **to burst a balloon** einen Luftballon
platzen lassen
♦ **to burst out laughing** laut loslachen
♦ **to burst into flames** in Flammen
aufgehen
♦ **to burst into tears** in Tränen ausbrechen
to **bury** VERB
1 (*dead people, animals*)
<u>begraben</u> (PRESENT begräbt, IMPERFECT
begrub, PERFECT hat begraben) ♦ *We buried
my hamster in the garden.* Wir haben

meinen Hamster im Garten begraben.
2 (*things*)
<u>vergraben</u> ♦ *My dog buried a bone in
the flowerbed.* Mein Hund hat im
Blumenbeet einen Knochen vergraben.
bus NOUN
der <u>Bus</u> (GEN des Busses, PL die Busse)
♦ *the bus driver* der Busfahrer ♦ *a bus
stop* eine Bushaltestelle ♦ *the school bus*
der Schulbus
♦ **a bus pass** (*monthly*) eine Monatskarte
für den Bus

> ℹ *Almost all German cities operate an
> integrated public transport system; you
> can buy a weekly (**Wochenkarte**),
> monthly (**Monatskarte**) or yearly
> (**Jahreskarte**) pass which are valid for
> that period on all buses, trams and
> so on in a particular zone.*

♦ **a bus station** eine Bushaltestelle
♦ **a bus ticket** eine Busfahrkarte
bush NOUN
der <u>Busch</u> (PL die Büsche)
business NOUN
1 (*firm*)
die <u>Firma</u> (PL die Firmen) ♦ *He's got his
own business.* Er hat seine eigene
Firma.
2 (*commerce*)
das <u>Geschäft</u> (PL die Geschäfte) ♦ *a
business trip* eine Geschäftsreise
♦ **He's away on business.** Er ist
geschäftlich unterwegs.
♦ **It's none of my business.** Das geht mich
nichts an.
businessman NOUN
der <u>Geschäftsmann</u> (PL die
Geschäftsleute)
businesswoman NOUN
die <u>Geschäftsfrau</u>
busker NOUN
der <u>Straßenmusikant</u> (GEN des
Straßenmusikanten, PL die
Straßenmusikanten)
die <u>Straßenmusikantin</u>
bus stop NOUN
die <u>Bushaltestelle</u>
bust NOUN
der <u>Busen</u> (*chest*) (PL die Busen)
busy ADJECTIVE
1 <u>beschäftigt</u> (*person*)
2 <u>belebt</u> (*shop, street*)
3 <u>besetzt</u> (*phone line*)
♦ **It's been a busy day.** Es war viel los
heute.
busy signal NOUN US
das <u>Besetztzeichen</u> (PL die
Besetztzeichen)
but CONJUNCTION

aber ◊ *I'd like to come, but I'm busy.* Ich würde gerne kommen, aber ich habe zu tun.

butcher NOUN
der Metzger (PL die Metzger)
die Metzgerin
◊ *He's a butcher.* Er ist Metzger.

butcher's NOUN
die Metzgerei

butter NOUN
die Butter

butterfly NOUN
der Schmetterling (PL die Schmetterlinge)

buttocks PL NOUN
der Hintern SING (GEN des Hintern, PL die Hintern)

button NOUN
der Knopf (PL die Knöpfe)

to **buy** VERB
see also **buy** NOUN
kaufen ◊ *He bought me an ice cream.* Er hat mir ein Eis gekauft.
♦ **to buy something from somebody** etwas von jemandem kaufen ◊ *I bought a watch from him.* Ich habe von ihm eine Uhr gekauft.

buy NOUN
see also **buy** VERB
der Kauf (PL die Käufe) ◊ *It was a good buy.* Es war ein guter Kauf.

by PREPOSITION
1 von ◊ *The thieves were caught by the police.* Die Diebe wurden von der Polizei erwischt. ◊ *a painting by Picasso* ein Gemälde von Picasso
2 mit ◊ *by car* mit dem Auto ◊ *by train* mit dem Zug ◊ *by bus* mit dem Bus
3 bei (*close to*) ◊ *Where's the bank? – It's by the post office.* Wo ist die Bank? – Sie ist bei der Post.
♦ **by day** bei Tag
♦ **by night** bei Nacht
4 bis (*not later than*) ◊ *We have to be there by four o'clock.* Wir müssen bis vier Uhr dort sein.
♦ **by the time ...** bis ... ◊ *By the time I got there it was too late.* Bis ich dort war, war es zu spät.
♦ **That's fine by me.** Ist in Ordnung!
♦ **all by himself** ganz allein
♦ **all by herself** ganz allein
♦ **I did it all by myself.** Ich habe es ganz allein gemacht.
♦ **by the way** übrigens

bye EXCLAMATION
tschüs!

bypass NOUN
die Umgehungsstraße (*road*)

B

C

cab NOUN
das Taxi (PL die Taxis)

cabbage NOUN
der Kohl

cabin NOUN
die Kabine (on ship)

cabinet NOUN
◆**a bathroom cabinet** ein
Badezimmerschränkchen NEUT
◆**a drinks cabinet** eine Bar

cable NOUN
das Kabel (PL die Kabel)

cable car NOUN
die Drahtseilbahn

cable television NOUN
das Kabelfernsehen

cactus NOUN
der Kaktus (GEN des Kaktus, PL die
Kakteen)

cadet NOUN
◆**a police cadet** ein Polizeischüler MASC
◆**a cadet officer** ein Offiziersanwärter MASC

café NOUN
die Imbissstube

cage NOUN
der Käfig (PL die Käfige)

cagoule NOUN
die Windjacke

cake NOUN
der Kuchen (PL die Kuchen)

to **calculate** VERB
rechnen

calculation NOUN
die Rechnung

calculator NOUN
der Taschenrechner (PL die
Taschenrechner)

calendar NOUN
der Kalender (PL die Kalender)

calf NOUN
[1] (of cow)
das Kalb (PL die Kälber)
[2] (of leg)
die Wade

call NOUN
see also **call** VERB
der Anruf (by phone) (PL die Anrufe)
◊ *Thanks for your call.* Danke für Ihren
Anruf.
◆**a phone call** ein Telefongespräch NEUT
◆**to be on call** (doctor) Bereitschaftsdienst
haben ◊ *He's on call this evening.* Er hat
heute Abend Bereitschaftsdienst.

to **call** VERB
see also **call** NOUN
[1] (by phone)
anrufen (IMPERFECT rief an, PERFECT hat
angerufen) ◊ *I'll tell him you called.* Ich

sage ihm, dass du angerufen hast. ◊ *This
is the number to call.* Das ist die
Nummer, die du anrufen musst.
◆**to call back** (phone again) zurückrufen
◊ *I'll call back at six o'clock.* Ich rufe um
sechs Uhr zurück.
[2] (fetch)
rufen ◊ *We called the police.* Wir haben
die Polizei gerufen.
[3] (by name)
nennen (IMPERFECT nannte, PERFECT hat
genannt) ◊ *Everyone calls him Jimmy.*
Alle nennen ihn Jimmy.
◆**to be called** heißen ◊ *He's called Fluffy.*
Er heißt Fluffy. ◊ *What's she called?* Wie
heißt sie?
◆**to call somebody names** jemanden
beschimpfen
◆**to call for** abholen ◊ *I'll call for you at
half past two.* Ich hole dich um halb drei
ab.
◆**to call off** absagen ◊ *The match was
called off.* Das Spiel wurde abgesagt.

call box NOUN
die Telefonzelle

call centre NOUN
das Callcenter (PL die Callcenters)

calm ADJECTIVE
ruhig

to **calm down** VERB
sich beruhigen (PERFECT hat sich beruhigt)
◊ *Calm down!* Beruhige dich!

Calor gas ® NOUN
das Butangas

calorie NOUN
die Kalorie

calves PL NOUN see **calf**

camcorder NOUN
der Camcorder (PL die Camcorder)

came VERB see **come**

camel NOUN
das Kamel (PL die Kamele)

camera NOUN
[1] (for photos)
der Fotoapparat (PL die Fotoapparate)
[2] (for filming, TV)
die Kamera (PL die Kameras)

cameraman NOUN
der Kameramann (PL die
Kameramänner)

camera phone NOUN
das Fotohandy (PL die Fotohandys)

to **camp** VERB
see also **camp** NOUN
zelten

camp NOUN
see also **camp** VERB
das Lager (PL die Lager)

◆**a camp bed** eine Campingliege

campaign NOUN
> see also **campaign** VERB

die Kampagne

to **campaign** VERB
> see also **campaign** NOUN

sich einsetzen (PERFECT hat sich
eingesetzt) ◊ *They are campaigning for a*
change in the law. Sie setzen sich für
eine Gesetzesänderung ein.

camper NOUN
1 (*person*)
der Camper (PL die Camper)
die Camperin
2 (*van*)
das Wohnmobil (PL die Wohnmobile)

camping NOUN
das Camping
◆**to go camping** zelten ◊ *We went*
camping in Cornwall. Wir waren in
Cornwall zelten.

camping gas ® NOUN
das Campinggas

campsite NOUN
der Zeltplatz (PL die Zeltplätze)

campus NOUN
das Universitätsgelände (PL die
Universitätsgelände)

can NOUN
> see also **can** VERB

1 (*tin*)
die Dose ◊ *a can of sweetcorn* eine Dose
Mais ◊ *a can of beer* eine Dose Bier
2 (*jerry can*)
der Kanister (PL die Kanister) ◊ *a can of*
petrol ein Benzinkanister

can VERB
> see also **can** NOUN

können (PRESENT kann, IMPERFECT konnte,
PERFECT hat können) ◊ *I can't come.* Ich
kann nicht kommen. ◊ *Can I help you?*
Kann ich dir helfen? ◊ *You could hire a*
bike. Du könntest dir ein Fahrrad mieten.
◊ *I couldn't sleep because of the noise.*
Ich konnte wegen des Lärms nicht
schlafen. ◊ *I can swim.* Ich kann
schwimmen. ◊ *He can't drive.* Er kann
nicht Auto fahren. ◊ *Can you speak*
German? Können Sie Deutsch?
◆**That can't be true!** Das darf nicht wahr
sein!
◆**You could be right.** Da könntest du recht
haben.

Canada NOUN
Kanada NEUT
◆**from Canada** aus Kanada
◆**in Canada** in Kanada
◆**to Canada** nach Kanada

Canadian ADJECTIVE
> see also **Canadian** NOUN

kanadisch ◊ *He's Canadian.* Er ist
Kanadier. ◊ *She's Canadian.* Sie ist
Kanadierin.

Canadian NOUN
> see also **Canadian** ADJECTIVE

der Kanadier (PL die Kanadier)
die Kanadierin

canal NOUN
der Kanal (PL die Kanäle)

Canaries NOUN
◆**the Canaries** die Kanarischen Inseln PL

canary NOUN
der Kanarienvogel (PL die
Kanarienvögel)

to **cancel** VERB
1 absagen (PERFECT hat abgesagt) ◊ *The*
match was cancelled. Das Spiel wurde
abgesagt.
2 (*booking*)
stornieren (PERFECT hat storniert) ◊ *He*
cancelled his hotel booking. Er hat seine
Hotelreservierung storniert.

cancellation NOUN
die Absage

cancer NOUN
der Krebs (GEN des Krebses) ◊ *He's got*
cancer. Er hat Krebs.
◆**I'm Cancer.** Ich bin Krebs.

candidate NOUN
der Kandidat (GEN des Kandidaten, PL die
Kandidaten)
die Kandidatin

candle NOUN
die Kerze

candy NOUN US
1 (*sweet*)
das Bonbon (PL die Bonbons)
2 (*sweets*)
die Süßigkeit .

candyfloss NOUN
die Zuckerwatte

cannabis NOUN
das Cannabis (GEN des Cannabis)

canned ADJECTIVE
in Dosen (*food*) ◊ *canned beer* Bier in
Dosen

cannot VERB see **can**

canoe NOUN
das Kanu (PL die Kanus)

canoeing NOUN
◆**to go canoeing** Kanu fahren ◊ *We went*
canoeing. Wir gingen Kanu fahren.

can-opener NOUN
der Dosenöffner (PL die Dosenöffner)

can't VERB see **can**

canteen NOUN
die Kantine

canvas NOUN
die Leinwand (PL die Leinwände)

cap NOUN
1 (*hat*)
die Mütze
2 (*of bottle, tube*)
der Verschluss (GEN des Verschlusses, PL
die Verschlüsse)

C

capable ADJECTIVE
fähig

♦ **to be capable of doing something** etwas tun können ◊ *She is capable of looking after herself.* Sie kann auf sich selbst aufpassen.

capacity NOUN

[1] die Fähigkeit ◊ *He has the capacity to score a goal from almost any position.* Er hat die Fähigkeit, aus fast jeder Position ein Tor zu schießen.

[2] das Fassungsvermögen (*quantity*) ◊ *This tank has a capacity of fifty litres.* Der Tank hat ein Fassungsvermögen von fünfzig Litern.

cape NOUN
das Kap (PL die Kaps) ◊ *Cape Horn* Kap Hoorn

capital NOUN

[1] die Hauptstadt (PL die Hauptstädte) ◊ *Cardiff is the capital of Wales.* Cardiff ist die Hauptstadt von Wales.

[2] (*letter*)
der Großbuchstabe (GEN des Großbuchstaben, PL die Großbuchstaben) ◊ *Write your address in capitals.* Schreib deine Adresse in Großbuchstaben.

capitalism NOUN
der Kapitalismus (GEN des Kapitalismus)

capital punishment NOUN
die Todesstrafe

Capricorn NOUN
der Steinbock ◊ *I'm Capricorn.* Ich bin Steinbock.

to **capsize** VERB
kentern (PERFECT ist gekentert)

captain NOUN
der Kapitän (PL die Kapitäne)
die Kapitänin
◊ *She's captain of the hockey team.* Sie ist die Kapitänin der Hockeymannschaft.

caption NOUN
die Bildunterschrift

to **capture** VERB

[1] (*person*)
gefangen nehmen (PRESENT nimmt gefangen, IMPERFECT nahm gefangen, PERFECT hat gefangen genommen) ◊ *He was captured by the enemy.* Er wurde vom Feind gefangen genommen.

[2] (*animal*)
fangen (PRESENT fängt, IMPERFECT fing, PERFECT hat gefangen) ◊ *They managed to capture the lion.* Sie konnten den Löwen fangen.

car NOUN
das Auto (PL die Autos)

♦ **to go by car** mit dem Auto fahren ◊ *We went by car.* Wir sind mit dem Auto gefahren.

♦ **a car crash** ein Autounfall MASC

caramel NOUN

das Karamellbonbon (*sweet*) (PL die Karamellbonbons)

caravan NOUN
der Wohnwagen (PL die Wohnwagen) ◊ *a caravan site* ein Campingplatz für Wohnwagen

card NOUN
die Karte

♦ **a card game** ein Kartenspiel NEUT

cardboard NOUN
der Karton (PL die Kartons)

cardigan NOUN
die Strickjacke

card phone NOUN
das Kartentelefon (PL die Kartentelefone)

care NOUN

see also **care** VERB

die Vorsicht

♦ **with care** vorsichtig

♦ **to take care of** aufpassen auf +ACC ◊ *I take care of the children on Saturdays.* Ich passe samstags auf die Kinder auf.

♦ **Take care! (1)** (*Be careful!*) Sei vorsichtig!

♦ **Take care! (2)** (*Look after yourself!*) Pass auf dich auf!

to **care** VERB

see also **care** NOUN

♦ **to care about** achten auf +ACC ◊ *They care about their image.* Sie achten auf ihr Image.

♦ **I don't care!** Das ist mir egal! ◊ *She doesn't care.* Das ist ihr egal.

♦ **to care for somebody** (*patients, old people*) jemanden pflegen

career NOUN
die Karriere

careful ADJECTIVE
vorsichtig ◊ *Be careful!* Sei vorsichtig!

carefully ADVERB

[1] sorgsam ◊ *She carefully avoided the subject.* Sie vermied das Thema sorgsam.

[2] vorsichtig (*safely*) ◊ *Drive carefully!* Fahr vorsichtig!

♦ **Think carefully!** Denk gut nach!

careless ADJECTIVE

[1] schluderig (*work*)

♦ **a careless mistake** ein Flüchtigkeitsfehler MASC

[2] nachlässig (*person*) ◊ *She's very careless.* Sie ist sehr nachlässig.

[3] unvorsichtig ◊ *a careless driver* ein unvorsichtiger Fahrer

caretaker NOUN
der Hausmeister (PL die Hausmeister)
die Hausmeisterin

car ferry NOUN
die Autofähre

cargo NOUN
die Fracht

car hire NOUN
der Autoverleih (PL die Autoverleihe)

Caribbean ADJECTIVE

see also **Caribbean** NOUN

karibisch

Caribbean NOUN

see also **Caribbean** ADJECTIVE

⊡ die Karibik (*islands*) ◊ *We're going to the Caribbean.* Wir fahren in die Karibik. ◊ *He's from the Caribbean.* Er kommt aus der Karibik.

⊡ das Karibische Meer (*sea*)

caring ADJECTIVE

liebevoll

♦ **the caring professions** die Pflegeberufe

carnation NOUN

die Nelke

carnival NOUN

der Karneval (PL die Karnevale)

carol NOUN

♦ **a Christmas carol** ein Weihnachtslied NEUT

car park NOUN

der Parkplatz (PL die Parkplätze)

carpenter NOUN

der Schreiner (PL die Schreiner)
die Schreinerin
◊ *He's a carpenter.* Er ist Schreiner.

carpentry NOUN

die Schreinerei

carpet NOUN

der Teppich (PL die Teppiche) ◊ *a Persian carpet* ein Perserteppich

car phone NOUN

das Autotelefon (PL die Autotelefone)

carriage NOUN

der Eisenbahnwagen (PL die Eisenbahnwagen)

carrier bag NOUN

die Tragetasche

carrot NOUN

die Karotte

to **carry** VERB

tragen (PRESENT trägt, IMPERFECT trug, PERFECT hat getragen) ◊ *He carried her bag.* Er trug ihre Tasche.

♦ **a plane carrying a hundred passengers** ein Flugzeug mit hundert Passagieren an Bord

♦ **to carry on** weitermachen ◊ *She carried on talking.* Sie redete weiter. ◊ *Carry on!* Mach weiter!

♦ **to carry out** (*orders*) ausführen

carrycot NOUN

die Babytragetasche

cart NOUN

der Karren (PL die Karren)

carton NOUN

die Tüte (*of milk, juice*)

cartoon NOUN

⊡ (*film*)
der Zeichentrickfilm (PL die Zeichentrickfilme)

⊡ (*in newspaper*)
der Cartoon (PL die Cartoons)

♦ **a strip cartoon** ein Comic MASC

cartridge NOUN

die Patrone

to **carve** VERB

aufschneiden (*meat*) (IMPERFECT schnitt auf, PERFECT hat aufgeschnitten)

case NOUN

⊡ der Koffer (PL die Koffer) ◊ *I've packed my case.* Ich habe meinen Koffer gepackt.

⊡ der Fall (PL die Fälle) ◊ *in some cases* in manchen Fällen ◊ *Which case does "außer" take?* Welcher Fall steht nach "außer"?

♦ **in that case** in dem Fall ◊ *I don't want it. – In that case, I'll take it.* Ich will es nicht. – In dem Fall nehme ich es.

♦ **in case** für den Fall ◊ *in case it rains* für den Fall, dass es regnet

♦ **just in case** für alle Fälle ◊ *Take some money, just in case.* Nimm für alle Fälle Geld mit.

cash NOUN

das Bargeld ◊ *I desperately need some cash.* Ich brauche dringend Bargeld.

♦ **in cash** in bar ◊ *two thousand pounds in cash* zweitausend Pfund in bar

♦ **to pay cash** bar bezahlen

♦ **I'm a bit short of cash.** Ich bin etwas knapp bei Kasse.

♦ **a cash card** eine Geldautomatenkarte

♦ **the cash desk** die Kasse

♦ **a cash dispenser** ein Geldautomat MASC

♦ **a cash register** eine Registrierkasse

cashew nut NOUN

die Cashewnuss (PL die Cashewnüsse)

cashier NOUN

der Kassierer (PL die Kassierer)
die Kassiererin

cashmere NOUN

der Kaschmir ◊ *a cashmere sweater* ein Kaschmirpullover

casino NOUN

das Kasino (PL die Kasinos)

casserole NOUN

der Schmortopf (PL die Schmortöpfe)

♦ **a casserole dish** eine Kasserolle

cassette NOUN

die Kassette

♦ **cassette recorder** der Kassettenrekorder

♦ **cassette player** der Kassettenspieler

cast NOUN

die Besetzung ◊ *After the play, we met the cast.* Nach dem Stück haben wir die Besetzung kennengelernt.

castle NOUN

die Burg

casual ADJECTIVE

⊡ leger ◊ *I prefer casual clothes.* Ich trage lieber legere Kleidung.

⊡ lässig ◊ *a casual attitude* eine lässige Haltung

⊡ beiläufig ◊ *It was just a casual remark.* Es war nur eine beiläufige Bemerkung.

casually ADVERB
♦**to dress casually** sich leger kleiden
casualty NOUN
die Unfallstation (*hospital department*)
cat NOUN
die Katze
catalogue NOUN
der Katalog (PL die Kataloge)
catalytic converter NOUN
der Katalysator (PL die Katalysatoren)
catarrh NOUN
der Katarrh (PL die Katarrhe)
catastrophe NOUN
die Katastrophe
to catch VERB
1 fangen (PRESENT fängt, IMPERFECT fing,
PERFECT hat gefangen) ◊ *My cat catches
birds.* Meine Katze fängt Vögel.
♦**to catch a thief** einen Dieb fassen
♦**to catch somebody doing something**
jemanden dabei erwischen, wie er etwas
tut ◊ *If they catch you smoking ...* Wenn
sie dich beim Rauchen erwischen ...
2 (*bus, train*)
nehmen (PRESENT nimmt, IMPERFECT nahm,
PERFECT hat genommen) ◊ *We caught the
last bus.* Wir haben den letzten Bus
genommen.
3 (*hear*)
mitbekommen (IMPERFECT bekam mit,
PERFECT hat mitbekommen) ◊ *I didn't catch
his name.* Ich habe seinen Namen nicht
mitbekommen.
♦**to catch up** aufholen ◊ *I've got a lot to
catch up on.* Ich habe viel aufzuholen.
♦**to catch a cold** einen Schnupfen
bekommen
catching ADJECTIVE
ansteckend ◊ *It's not catching.* Das ist
nicht ansteckend.
catering NOUN
♦**Who did the catering?** Wer hat das Essen
und die Getränke geliefert?
cathedral NOUN
die Kathedrale
Catholic ADJECTIVE
see also **Catholic** NOUN
katholisch
Catholic NOUN
see also **Catholic** ADJECTIVE
der Katholik (GEN des Katholiken, PL die
Katholiken)
die Katholikin
♦**I'm a Catholic.** Ich bin katholisch.
cattle PL NOUN
das Vieh SING
caught VERB see **catch**
cauliflower NOUN
der Blumenkohl (PL die Blumenkohle)
cause NOUN
see also **cause** VERB
die Ursache ◊ *The cause of the fire was*

a short-circuit. Ein Kurzschluss war die
Ursache für das Feuer.
to cause VERB
see also **cause** NOUN
verursachen (PERFECT hat verursacht) ◊ *to
cause an accident* einen Unfall verursachen
cautious ADJECTIVE
vorsichtig
cautiously ADVERB
vorsichtig
cave NOUN
die Höhle
caviar NOUN
der Kaviar
CCTV ABBREVIATION (= *closed-circuit
television*)
die Videoüberwachung
CD NOUN
die CD (PL die CDs)
CD player NOUN
der CD-Spieler (PL die CD-Spieler)
CD-ROM NOUN
die CD-ROM (PL die CD-ROMs)
ceasefire NOUN
der Waffenstillstand (PL die
Waffenstillstände)
ceiling NOUN
die Decke
to celebrate VERB
feiern (*birthday*)
celebration NOUN
die Feier
celebrity NOUN
die Berühmtheit
celery NOUN
der Stangensellerie (GEN des
Stangensellerie, PL die Stangenselleries)
cell NOUN
die Zelle
cellar NOUN
der Keller (PL die Keller) ◊ *a wine cellar*
ein Weinkeller
cello NOUN
das Cello (PL die Celli) ◊ *I play the cello.*
Ich spiele Cello.
cell phone NOUN US
das Handy (PL die Handys)
cement NOUN
der Zement
cemetery NOUN
der Friedhof (PL die Friedhöfe)
cent NOUN
der Cent (PL die Cents or Cent)
*When talking about amounts of money
use the plural form **Cent**.*
◊ *twenty cents* zwanzig Cent
centenary NOUN
das hundertjährige Jubiläum (PL die
hundertjährigen Jubiläen)
center NOUN US
das Zentrum (PL die Zentren) ◊ *a sports
centre* ein Sportzentrum

centigrade ADJECTIVE
♦ **twenty degrees centigrade** zwanzig Grad Celsius
centimetre NOUN (US **centimeter**)
der Zentimeter (PL die Zentimeter)
◊ *twenty centimetres* zwanzig Zentimeter
central ADJECTIVE
zentral
central heating NOUN
die Zentralheizung
centre NOUN
das Zentrum (PL die Zentren) ◊ *a sports centre* ein Sportzentrum
century NOUN
das Jahrhundert (PL die Jahrhunderte)
◊ *the twentieth century* das zwanzigste Jahrhundert ◊ *the twenty-first century* das einundzwanzigste Jahrhundert
cereal NOUN
die Getreideflocken FEM PL ◊ *I have cereal for breakfast.* Zum Frühstück esse ich Getreideflocken.
ceremony NOUN
die Zeremonie
certain ADJECTIVE
1 sicher ◊ *I'm absolutely certain it was him.* Ich bin ganz sicher, dass er es war.
♦ **I don't know for certain.** Ich bin mir nicht sicher.
♦ **to make certain** sich vergewissern ◊ *I made certain the door was locked.* Ich habe mich vergewissert, dass die Tür abgeschlossen war.
2 bestimmt ◊ *a certain person* eine bestimmte Person
certainly ADVERB
natürlich ◊ *I certainly expected something better.* Ich habe natürlich etwas Besseres erwartet.
♦ **Certainly not!** Sicher nicht!
♦ **Was it a surprise? – It certainly was!** War's eine Überraschung? – Und ob!
certificate NOUN
die Urkunde
CFC NOUN (= *chlorofluorocarbon*)
der FCKW (= Fluorchlorkohlenwasserstoff)
chain NOUN
die Kette
chair NOUN
1 der Stuhl (PL die Stühle) ◊ *a table and four chairs* ein Tisch und vier Stühle
2 (*armchair*)
der Sessel (PL die Sessel)
chairlift NOUN
der Sessellift (PL die Sessellifte)
chairman NOUN
der Vorsitzende (GEN des Vorsitzenden, PL die Vorsitzenden) ◊ *a chairman* ein Vorsitzender
chalet NOUN
das Ferienhaus (PL die Ferienhäuser)
chalk NOUN

die Kreide
challenge NOUN
see also **challenge** VERB
die Herausforderung
to **challenge** VERB
see also **challenge** NOUN
♦ **She challenged me to a race.** Sie wollte mit mir um die Wette laufen.
challenging ADJECTIVE
anspruchsvoll ◊ *a challenging job* eine anspruchsvolle Arbeit
chambermaid NOUN
das Zimmermädchen (PL die Zimmermädchen)
champagne NOUN
der Champagner (PL die Champagner)
champion NOUN
der Meister (PL die Meister)
die Meisterin
championship NOUN
die Meisterschaft
chance NOUN
1 die Chance ◊ *Do you think I've got any chance?* Meinst du, ich habe eine Chance? ◊ *Their chances of winning are very good.* Ihre Gewinnchancen sind sehr gut.
2 die Möglichkeit ◊ *I'd like to have a chance to travel.* Ich hätte gern die Möglichkeit zu reisen.
♦ **I'll write when I get the chance.** Ich schreibe, sobald ich dazu komme.
♦ **by chance** zufällig ◊ *We met by chance.* Wir haben uns zufällig kennengelernt.
♦ **to take a chance** ein Risiko eingehen ◊ *I'm taking no chances!* Ich gehe kein Risiko ein!
♦ **No chance!** Denkste!
Chancellor of the Exchequer NOUN
der Schatzkanzler (PL die Schatzkanzler)
chandelier NOUN
der Kronleuchter (PL die Kronleuchter)
to **change** VERB
see also **change** NOUN
1 sich verändern (PERFECT hat sich verändert) ◊ *The town has changed a lot.* Die Stadt hat sich sehr verändert.
2 (*money, job*)
wechseln ◊ *I'd like to change fifty pounds.* Ich würde gern fünfzig Pfund wechseln. ◊ *He wants to change his job.* Er möchte den Job wechseln.
♦ **You have to change trains in Stuttgart.** Sie müssen in Stuttgart umsteigen.
♦ **I'm going to change my shoes.** Ich ziehe andere Schuhe an.
♦ **to change one's mind** es sich anders überlegen ◊ *I've changed my mind.* Ich habe es mir anders überlegt.
♦ **to change gear** schalten
3 sich umziehen (IMPERFECT zog sich um, PERFECT hat sich umgezogen) ◊ *She's*

C

changing to go out. Sie zieht sich zum Ausgehen um.
♦ **to get changed** sich umziehen ◊ *I'm going to get changed.* Ich ziehe mich um.
4 (*swap*)
umtauschen (PERFECT hat umgetauscht)
◊ *Can I change this sweater? It's too small.* Kann ich diesen Pullover umtauschen? Er ist zu klein.

change NOUN
see also **change** VERB
1 die Änderung
♦ **There's been a change of plan.** Die Pläne haben sich geändert.
♦ **a change of clothes** Kleidung zum Wechseln
♦ **for a change** zur Abwechslung ◊ *Let's play tennis for a change.* Lass uns zur Abwechslung Tennis spielen.
2 das Kleingeld (*money*) ◊ *I haven't got any change.* Ich habe kein Kleingeld.

changeable ADJECTIVE
wechselhaft

changing room NOUN
der Umkleideraum (PL die Umkleideräume)

channel NOUN
das Programm (*TV*) (PL die Programme)
◊ *There's football on the other channel.* Im anderen Programm gibt es Fußball.
♦ **the English Channel** der Ärmelkanal
♦ **the Channel Islands** die Kanalinseln
♦ **the Channel Tunnel** der Kanaltunnel

chaos NOUN
das Chaos (GEN des Chaos)

chap NOUN
der Kerl (PL die Kerle) ◊ *He's a nice chap.* Er ist ein netter Kerl.

chapel NOUN
die Kapelle (*part of church*)

chapter NOUN
das Kapitel (PL die Kapitel)

character NOUN
1 der Charakter (PL die Charaktere)
◊ *Give me some idea of his character.* Beschreiben Sie mir seinen Charakter.
♦ **She's quite a character.** Sie ist ein Unikum.
2 (*in play, film*)
die Figur ◊ *the character played by Tom Cruise* die Figur, die Tom Cruise spielt

characteristic NOUN
das Merkmal (PL die Merkmale)

charcoal NOUN
die Holzkohle

charge NOUN
see also **charge** VERB
die Gebühr ◊ *Is there a charge for delivery?* Wird für die Zustellung eine Gebühr erhoben? ◊ *an extra charge* eine Extragebühr
♦ **free of charge** kostenlos

♦ **to reverse the charges** ein R-Gespräch führen ◊ *I'd like to reverse the charges.* Ich möchte gern ein R-Gespräch führen.
♦ **to be on a charge** angeklagt sein ◊ *He's on a charge of murder.* Er ist des Mordes angeklagt.
♦ **to be in charge** die Verantwortung haben ◊ *Mrs Munday was in charge of the group.* Mrs Munday hatte die Verantwortung für die Gruppe.

to **charge** VERB
see also **charge** NOUN
1 (*money*)
verlangen (PERFECT hat verlangt) ◊ *How much did he charge you?* Wie viel hat er verlangt? ◊ *They charge ten pounds an hour.* Sie verlangen zehn Pfund die Stunde.
2 (*with crime*)
anklagen (PERFECT hat angeklagt) ◊ *The police have charged him with murder.* Die Polizei hat ihn des Mordes angeklagt.

charity NOUN
die Wohlfahrt ◊ *She does a lot of work for charity.* Sie arbeitet viel für die Wohlfahrt.
♦ **He gave the money to charity.** Er hat das Geld für wohltätige Zwecke gespendet.

charm NOUN
der Charme
Note that the "e" in **Charme** *is silent.*
◊ *He's got a lot of charm.* Er hat viel Charme.

charming ADJECTIVE
bezaubernd

chart NOUN
die Grafik ◊ *The chart shows the rise of unemployment.* Die Grafik stellt den Anstieg der Arbeitslosigkeit dar.
♦ **the charts** die Hitparade SING ◊ *This album is number one in the charts.* Dieses Album ist auf Platz eins der Hitparade.

charter flight NOUN
der Charterflug (PL die Charterflüge)

to **chase** VERB
see also **chase** NOUN
verfolgen (PERFECT hat verfolgt)

chase NOUN
see also **chase** VERB
die Verfolgung
♦ **a car chase** eine Verfolgungsjagd im Auto

chat NOUN
das Schwätzchen (PL die Schwätzchen)
◊ *to have a chat* ein Schwätzchen halten

chat room NOUN
der Chatroom (PL die Chatrooms)

chat show NOUN
die Talkshow (PL die Talkshows)

chauvinist NOUN
♦ **male chauvinist** der Chauvi

cheap ADJECTIVE

billig ◊ *a cheap T-shirt* ein billiges T-Shirt ◊ *It's cheaper by bus.* Mit dem Bus ist es billiger.

to **cheat** VERB

see also **cheat** NOUN

betrügen (IMPERFECT betrog, PERFECT hat betrogen) ◊ *He cheated me.* Er hat mich betrogen.

♦ **You're cheating!** (*in games, at school*) Du schummelst!

cheat NOUN

see also **cheat** VERB

der Betrüger (PL die Betrüger)
die Betrügerin

check NOUN

see also **check** VERB

[1] die Kontrolle ◊ *a security check* eine Sicherheitskontrolle

[2] US (*bill*)
die Rechnung
◊ *The waiter brought us the check.* Der Kellner brachte uns die Rechnung.

[3] US
der Scheck (PL die Schecks)
◊ *to write a check* einen Scheck ausstellen

to **check** VERB

see also **check** NOUN

nachsehen (PRESENT sieht nach, IMPERFECT sah nach, PERFECT hat nachgesehen) ◊ *I'll check the time of the train.* Ich sehe die Abfahrtszeiten des Zuges nach. ◊ *Could you check the oil, please?* Könnten Sie bitte das Öl nachsehen?

♦ **to check in** einchecken ◊ *What time do I have to check in?* Wann muss ich einchecken?

♦ **to check out** (*from hotel*) sich auschecken

checked ADJECTIVE

kariert ◊ *a checked shirt* ein kariertes Hemd

checkers SING NOUN US

Dame FEM ◊ *Checkers is her favourite game.* Dame ist ihr Lieblingsspiel.

check-in NOUN

der Check-in (PL die Check-ins)

checking account NOUN US

das Girokonto (PL die Girokonten)

checkout NOUN

die Kasse

check-up NOUN

der Check-up (PL die Check-ups)

cheddar NOUN

der Cheddar (PL die Cheddars)

cheek NOUN

[1] die Wange ◊ *He kissed her on the cheek.* Er küsste sie auf die Wange.

[2] die Frechheit ◊ *What a cheek!* So eine Frechheit!

cheeky ADJECTIVE

frech ◊ *Don't be cheeky!* Sei nicht so frech! ◊ *a cheeky smile* ein freches Lächeln

cheer NOUN

see also **cheer** VERB

der Hurraruf (PL die Hurrarufe)

♦ **to give a cheer** Hurra rufen

♦ **Cheers! (1)** (*good health*) Prost!

♦ **Cheers! (2)** (*thanks*) Danke schön!

to **cheer** VERB

see also **cheer** NOUN

[1] (*team*)
anfeuern (PERFECT hat angefeuert)

[2] (*speaker*)
zujubeln (PERFECT hat zugejubelt) ◊ *The speaker was cheered.* Dem Redner wurde zugejubelt.

♦ **to cheer somebody up** jemanden aufheitern ◊ *I was trying to cheer him up.* Ich habe versucht, ihn aufzuheitern.

♦ **Cheer up!** Kopf hoch!

cheerful ADJECTIVE

fröhlich

cheerio EXCLAMATION

tschüs

cheese NOUN

der Käse (PL die Käse)

chef NOUN

der Küchenchef (PL die Küchenchefs)

chemical NOUN

die Chemikalie

chemist NOUN

[1] (*pharmacist*)
der Apotheker (PL die Apotheker)
die Apothekerin

[2] (*pharmacy*)
die Apotheke ◊ *You get it from the chemist.* Du bekommst das in der Apotheke.

[3] (*shop selling toiletries*)
die Drogerie

[4] (*scientist*)
der Chemiker (PL die Chemiker)
die Chemikerin

chemistry NOUN

die Chemie ◊ *the chemistry lab* das Chemielabor

cheque NOUN

der Scheck (PL die Schecks) ◊ *to write a cheque* einen Scheck ausstellen ◊ *to pay by cheque* mit Scheck bezahlen

chequebook NOUN

das Scheckheft (PL die Scheckhefte)

> ⓘ *German banks provide customers with cheques in an envelope or wallet, usually ten at a time, rather than chequebooks.*

cherry NOUN

die Kirsche

chess NOUN

das Schach ◊ *to play chess* Schach spielen

chessboard NOUN

das Schachbrett (PL die Schachbretter)

chest NOUN
die Brust (*of person*) (PL die Brüste)
♦ **his chest measurement** seine Oberweite
♦ **a chest of drawers** eine Kommode

chestnut NOUN
die Kastanie

to **chew** VERB
kauen

chewing gum NOUN
der Kaugummi (PL die Kaugummis)

chick NOUN
das Küken (PL die Küken) ◊ *a hen and her chicks* eine Henne mit ihren Küken

chicken NOUN
1 (*food*)
das Hähnchen (PL die Hähnchen) ◊ *I bought a chicken in the supermarket.* Ich habe im Supermarkt ein Hähnchen gekauft.
2 (*live*)
das Huhn (PL die Hühner) ◊ *My mother used to keep chickens.* Meine Mutter hat früher Hühner gehalten.

chickenpox SING NOUN
die Windpocken PL ◊ *My sister has chickenpox.* Meine Schwester hat Windpocken.

chickpeas PL NOUN
die Kichererbsen PL

chief NOUN
see also **chief** ADJECTIVE
der Chef (PL die Chefs) ◊ *the chief of security* der Sicherheitschef

chief ADJECTIVE
see also **chief** NOUN
hauptsächlich ◊ *His chief reason for resigning was the low pay.* Der hauptsächliche Grund für seine Kündigung war die geringe Bezahlung.

child NOUN
das Kind (PL die Kinder) ◊ *all the children* alle Kinder

childish ADJECTIVE
kindisch

child minder NOUN
die Tagesmutter (PL die Tagesmütter)

children PL NOUN see **child**

Chile NOUN
Chile NEUT
♦ **from Chile** aus Chile
♦ **to Chile** nach Chile

to **chill** VERB
kalt stellen ◊ *Put the wine in the fridge to chill.* Stell den Wein kalt.

chilli NOUN
der Chili (PL die Chilis)
♦ **chilli peppers** die Peperoni PL

chilly ADJECTIVE
kühl

chimney NOUN
der Schornstein (PL die Schornsteine)

chin NOUN
das Kinn (PL die Kinne)

china NOUN
das Porzellan ◊ *a china plate* ein Porzellanteller MASC

China NOUN
China NEUT
♦ **from China** aus China
♦ **to China** nach China

Chinese ADJECTIVE
see also **Chinese** NOUN
chinesisch ◊ *a Chinese restaurant* ein chinesisches Restaurant
♦ **a Chinese man** ein Chinese
♦ **a Chinese woman** eine Chinesin

Chinese NOUN
see also **Chinese** ADJECTIVE
das Chinesisch (*language*) (GEN des Chinesischen)
♦ **the Chinese** (*people*) die Chinesen

chip NOUN
der Chip (*in computer*) (PL die Chips)

chips PL NOUN
1 die Pommes frites FEM PL (*fried potatoes*) ◊ *We bought some chips.* Wir haben Pommes frites gekauft.
2 die Kartoffelchips MASC PL (*crisps*)
Be caerful not to translate **chips** by the German word **Chips**.

chiropodist NOUN
der Fußpfleger (PL die Fußpfleger)
die Fußpflegerin
◊ *He's a chiropodist.* Er ist Fußpfleger.

chives PL NOUN
der Schnittlauch

chocolate NOUN
die Schokolade ◊ *a chocolate cake* ein Schokoladenkuchen ◊ *hot chocolate* heiße Schokolade

choice NOUN
die Wahl ◊ *I had no choice.* Ich hatte keine andere Wahl.

choir NOUN
der Chor (PL die Chöre) ◊ *I sing in the school choir.* Ich singe im Schulchor.

to **choke** VERB
ersticken (PERFECT ist erstickt) ◊ *Help him, he's choking!* Helft ihm, er erstickt!

to **choose** VERB
auswählen (PERFECT hat ausgewählt)
◊ *She chose the red shirt.* Sie hat das rote Hemd ausgewählt.

to **chop** VERB
see also **chop** NOUN
klein hacken (PERFECT hat klein gehackt)
◊ *She chopped the onions.* Sie hackte die Zwiebeln klein.

chop NOUN
see also **chop** VERB
das Kotelett (PL die Koteletts) ◊ *a pork chop* ein Schweinekotelett

chopsticks PL NOUN

die <u>Stäbchen</u> NEUT PL

chose VERB *see* **choose**

chosen VERB *see* **choose**

Christ NOUN
<u>Christus</u> (GEN Christi) ◊ *the birth of Christ*
die Geburt Christi

christening NOUN
die <u>Taufe</u>

Christian NOUN
| *see also* **Christian** ADJECTIVE |
der <u>Christ</u> (GEN des Christen, PL die
Christen)
die <u>Christin</u>

Christian ADJECTIVE
| *see also* **Christian** NOUN |
<u>christlich</u>

Christian name NOUN
der <u>Vorname</u> (GEN des Vornamens, PL die
Vornamen)

Christmas NOUN
<u>Weihnachten</u> NEUT ◊ *Happy Christmas!*
Fröhliche Weihnachten!
♦ **Christmas Day** der erste
Weihnachtsfeiertag
♦ **Christmas Eve** Heiligabend

> *ℹ️ Traditionally, in Germany gifts are
> exchanged on Christmas Eve.*

◊ *on Christmas Eve* an Heiligabend
♦ **a Christmas tree** ein Weihnachtsbaum
MASC
♦ **a Christmas card** eine Weihnachtskarte

> *ℹ️ Most Germans send very few
> Christmas cards.*

♦ **Christmas dinner** das Weihnachtsessen

> *ℹ️ Germans traditionally eat goose at
> Christmas rather than turkey.*

♦ **Christmas pudding**

> *ℹ️ Germans don't have any traditional
> dessert at Christmas. Most know what
> **Christmas pudding** is, but almost
> always refer to it as **Plumpudding**.*

to **chuck out** VERB
<u>rauswerfen</u> (PRESENT wirft raus, IMPERFECT
warf raus, PERFECT hat rausgeworfen)
◊ *You'll need to chuck out some of these
books.* Du musst ein paar von diesen
Büchern rauswerfen.

chunk NOUN
das <u>Stück</u> (PL die Stücke) ◊ *Cut the meat
into chunks.* Schneiden Sie das Fleisch in
Stücke.

church NOUN
die <u>Kirche</u> ◊ *I don't go to church every
Sunday.* Ich gehe nicht jeden Sonntag in
die Kirche.

♦ **the Church of England** die anglikanische
Kirche

cider NOUN
der <u>Apfelwein</u>

cigar NOUN
die <u>Zigarre</u>

cigarette NOUN
die <u>Zigarette</u>

cigarette lighter NOUN
der <u>Zigarettenanzünder</u> (PL die
Zigarettenanzünder)

cinema NOUN
das <u>Kino</u> (PL die Kinos) ◊ *I'm going to the
cinema this evening.* Ich gehe heute
Abend ins Kino.

cinnamon NOUN
der <u>Zimt</u>

circle NOUN
der <u>Kreis</u> (PL die Kreise)

circular ADJECTIVE
<u>rund</u>

circulation NOUN
1 der <u>Kreislauf</u> (*of blood*)
2 die <u>Auflage</u> (*of newspaper*)

circumstances PL NOUN
die <u>Umstände</u> MASC PL

circus NOUN
der <u>Zirkus</u> (GEN des Zirkus, PL die
Zirkusse)

citizen NOUN
der <u>Bürger</u> (PL die Bürger)
die <u>Bürgerin</u>
♦ **a German citizen** ein deutscher
Staatsbürger

city NOUN
die <u>Stadt</u> (PL die Städte)
♦ **the city centre** die Innenstadt ◊ *It's in the
city centre.* Es liegt in der Innenstadt.
♦ **the City** die Londoner City

city technology college NOUN
die <u>technische Fachschule</u>

civilization NOUN
die <u>Zivilisation</u>

civil servant NOUN
der <u>Beamte</u> (GEN des Beamten, PL die
Beamten)
die <u>Beamtin</u>

> *ℹ️ In Germany most teachers are
> **Beamte**.*

◊ *He's a civil servant.* Er ist Beamter.

civil war NOUN
der <u>Bürgerkrieg</u> (PL die Bürgerkriege)

to **claim** VERB
| *see also* **claim** NOUN |
1 <u>behaupten</u> (PERFECT hat behauptet)
◊ *He claims to have found the money.* Er
behauptet, er habe das Geld gefunden.
Note the use of the subjunctive.
2 (*receive*)

C

bekommen (IMPERFECT bekam, PERFECT hat bekommen) ◊ *She's claiming unemployment benefit.* Sie bekommt Arbeitslosenunterstützung.

♦ **to claim on one's insurance** seine Versicherung in Anspruch nehmen ◊ *We claimed on our insurance.* Wir haben unsere Versicherung in Anspruch genommen.

claim NOUN

see also **claim** VERB

der Anspruch (on insurance policy) (PL die Ansprüche)

♦ **to make a claim for damages** Schadenersatz beanspruchen

to **clap** VERB

klatschen (applaud) ◊ *The audience clapped.* Das Publikum klatschte.

♦ **to clap one's hands** klatschen

clarinet NOUN

die Klarinette ◊ *I play the clarinet.* Ich spiele Klarinette.

to **clash** VERB

1 (colours)

sich beißen (IMPERFECT bissen sich, PERFECT haben sich gebissen) ◊ *These two colours clash.* Diese beiden Farben beißen sich.

2 (events)

sich überschneiden (IMPERFECT überschnitt sich, PERFECT hat sich überschnitten) ◊ *The concert clashes with Ann's party.* Das Konzert überschneidet sich mit Anns Party.

clasp NOUN

der Verschluss (of necklace) (GEN des Verschlusses, PL die Verschlüsse)

class NOUN

1 die Klasse (group) ◊ *We're in the same class.* Wir sind in derselben Klasse.

2 die Stunde (lesson) ◊ *I go to dancing classes.* Ich nehme Tanzstunden.

classic ADJECTIVE

see also **classic** NOUN

klassisch ◊ *a classic example* ein klassisches Beispiel

classic NOUN

see also **classic** ADJECTIVE

der Klassiker (book, film) (PL die Klassiker)

classical ADJECTIVE

klassisch ◊ *I like classical music.* Ich mag klassische Musik.

classmate NOUN

der Klassenkamerad (GEN des Klassenkameraden, PL die Klassenkameraden)

die Klassenkameradin

classroom NOUN

das Klassenzimmer (PL die Klassenzimmer)

clause NOUN

1 (in legal document)

die Klausel

2 (in grammar)

der Satz (GEN des Satzes, PL die Sätze)

claw NOUN

1 die Kralle (of cat, dog)

2 die Klaue (of bird)

3 die Schere (of crab, lobster)

clean ADJECTIVE

see also **clean** VERB

sauber ◊ *a clean shirt* ein sauberes Hemd

to **clean** VERB

see also **clean** ADJECTIVE

sauber machen (PERFECT hat sauber gemacht)

cleaner NOUN

der Putzmann (PL die Putzmänner)

die Putzfrau

◊ *She's a cleaner.* Sie ist Putzfrau.

cleaner's NOUN

die Reinigung

cleaning lady NOUN

die Putzfrau

cleansing lotion NOUN

die Reinigungslotion

clear ADJECTIVE

see also **clear** VERB

1 klar ◊ *It's clear you don't believe me.* Es ist klar, dass du mir nicht glaubst.

2 frei (road, way) ◊ *The road's clear now.* Die Straße ist jetzt frei.

to **clear** VERB

see also **clear** ADJECTIVE

1 räumen ◊ *The police are clearing the road after the accident.* Die Polizei räumt die Straße nach dem Unfall.

2 (fog, mist)

sich auflösen (PERFECT hat sich aufgelöst) ◊ *The mist soon cleared.* Der Nebel löste sich bald auf.

♦ **to be cleared of a crime** von einem Verbrechen freigesprochen werden ◊ *She was cleared of murder.* Sie wurde von der Mordanklage freigesprochen.

♦ **to clear the table** den Tisch abräumen ◊ *I'll clear the table.* Ich räume den Tisch ab.

♦ **to clear up** aufräumen ◊ *Who's going to clear all this up?* Wer räumt das alles auf?

♦ **I think it's going to clear up.** (weather) Ich glaube, es hellt sich auf.

clearly ADVERB

klar ◊ *She explained it very clearly.* Sie hat es sehr klar erklärt. ◊ *The English coast was clearly visible.* Die englische Küste war klar zu sehen.

♦ **to speak clearly** deutlich sprechen

clementine NOUN

die Klementine

to **clench** VERB

♦ **She clenched her fists.** Sie ballte die Fäuste.

clerk NOUN
der Büroangestellte (GEN des Büroangestellten, PL die Büroangestellten)
die Büroangestellte (GEN der Büroangestellten) ◊ *She's a clerk.* Sie ist Büroangestellte.

clever ADJECTIVE
1 klug ◊ *She's very clever.* Sie ist sehr klug.
2 genial (*ingenious*) ◊ *a clever system* ein geniales System ◊ *What a clever idea!* Das ist eine geniale Idee!

to **click on** VERB
anklicken (*computer*) (PERFECT hat angeklickt) ◊ *to click on an icon* ein Icon anklicken
♦ **to click on the mouse** mit der Maus klicken

client NOUN
der Klient (GEN des Klienten, PL die Klienten)
die Klientin

cliff NOUN
die Klippe

climate NOUN
das Klima (PL die Klimas)

to **climb** VERB
1 steigen auf +ACC (IMPERFECT stieg, PERFECT ist gestiegen) ◊ *We're going to climb Snowdon.* Wir steigen auf den Snowdon.
2 (*stairs*)
hinaufgehen (IMPERFECT ging hinauf, PERFECT ist hinaufgegangen) ◊ *I watched him climb the stairs.* Ich sah ihn die Treppe hinaufgehen.
♦ **She finds it difficult to climb the stairs.** Das Treppensteigen fällt ihr schwer.

climber NOUN
der Kletterer (PL die Kletterer)
die Kletterin

climbing NOUN
das Klettern
♦ **to go climbing** klettern gehen ◊ *We're going climbing in Scotland.* Wir gehen in Schottland klettern.

clingfilm NOUN
die Frischhaltefolie

clinic NOUN
die Klinik

cloakroom NOUN
1 die Garderobe (*for coats*)
2 die Toilette (*toilet*)

clock NOUN
die Uhr
♦ **a grandfather clock** eine Standuhr
♦ **an alarm clock** ein Wecker MASC
♦ **a clock radio** ein Radiowecker MASC

clockwork NOUN
das Uhrwerk
♦ **to go like clockwork** wie am Schnürchen gehen (*informal*)

clog NOUN
1 (*modern*)
der Clog (PL die Clogs)
2 (*traditional, made of wood*)
der Holzschuh (PL die Holzschuhe)

clone NOUN
see also **clone** VERB
der Klon (PL die Klone)

to **clone** VERB
see also **clone** NOUN
klonen ◊ *a cloned sheep* ein geklontes Schaf

close ADJECTIVE, ADVERB
see also **close** VERB
1 nahe (*near*) ◊ *close relations* nahe Verwandte ◊ *I'm very close to my sister.* Ich stehe meiner Schwester sehr nahe.
♦ **The shops are very close.** Die Geschäfte sind ganz in der Nähe.
♦ **She's a close friend of mine.** Sie ist eine gute Freundin von mir.
♦ **Come closer!** Komm näher!
♦ **close to** in der Nähe +GEN ◊ *The youth hostel is close to the station.* Die Jugendherberge ist in der Nähe des Bahnhofs.
2 knapp (*contest*) ◊ *It's going to be very close.* Das wird sehr knapp.
3 schwül (*weather*) ◊ *It's close this afternoon.* Heute Nachmittag ist es schwül.

to **close** VERB
see also **close** ADJECTIVE
schließen (IMPERFECT schloss, PERFECT hat geschlossen) ◊ *What time does the pool close?* Wann schließt das Schwimmbad? ◊ *The doors close automatically.* Die Türen schließen automatisch.
♦ **Please close the door.** Bitte mach die Tür zu.

closed ADJECTIVE
geschlossen ◊ *The bank's closed.* Die Bank ist geschlossen.

closely ADVERB
genau (*look, examine*)

cloth NOUN
der Stoff (*material*) (PL die Stoffe)
♦ **a cloth** ein Lappen MASC ◊ *Wipe it with a damp cloth.* Wischen Sie es mit einem feuchten Lappen ab.

clothes PL NOUN
die Kleider NEUT PL ◊ *new clothes* neue Kleider
♦ **a clothes line** eine Wäscheleine
♦ **a clothes peg** eine Wäscheklammer

cloud NOUN
die Wolke

cloudy ADJECTIVE
bewölkt

clove NOUN
♦ **a clove of garlic** eine Knoblauchzehe

clown NOUN
der Clown (PL die Clowns)

C

club NOUN

der <u>Klub</u> (PL die Klubs) ◊ *a tennis club* ein Tennisklub ◊ *the youth club* der Jugendklub

♦ **clubs** (*in cards*) Kreuz NEUT ◊ *the ace of clubs* das Kreuzass

to **club together** VERB

<u>zusammenlegen</u> (PERFECT hat zusammengelegt) ◊ *We clubbed together to buy her a present.* Wir haben zusammengelegt, um ein Geschenk für sie zu kaufen.

clubbing NOUN

♦ **to go clubbing** in Klubs gehen

clue NOUN

der <u>Hinweis</u> (PL die Hinweise) ◊ *an important clue* ein wichtiger Hinweis

♦ **I haven't a clue.** Ich habe keine Ahnung.

clumsy ADJECTIVE

<u>tollpatschig</u> ◊ *Toby is even clumsier than his sister.* Toby ist noch tollpatschiger als seine Schwester.

clutch NOUN

see also **clutch** VERB

die <u>Kupplung</u> (*of car*)

to **clutch** VERB

see also **clutch** NOUN

<u>umklammern</u> (PERFECT hat umklammert) ◊ *She clutched my arm and begged me not to go.* Sie umklammerte meinen Arm und flehte mich an, nicht zu gehen.

clutter NOUN

der <u>Kram</u> ◊ *There's so much clutter in here.* Hier liegt so viel Kram herum.

coach NOUN

[1] der <u>Reisebus</u> (GEN des Reisebusses, PL die Reisebusse) ◊ *We went there by coach.* Wir sind mit dem Bus dorthin gefahren. ◊ *the coach station* der Busbahnhof ◊ *a coach trip* eine Busreise

[2] (*trainer*)

der <u>Trainer</u> (PL die Trainer)

die <u>Trainerin</u>

◊ *the German coach* der deutsche Trainer

coal NOUN

die <u>Kohle</u>

♦ **a coal mine** eine Kohlezeche

♦ **a coal miner** ein Bergarbeiter MASC

coarse ADJECTIVE

[1] <u>grob</u> ◊ *The bag was made of coarse black cloth.* Die Tasche war aus grobem schwarzem Stoff gemacht.

[2] <u>grobkörnig</u> ◊ *The sand is very coarse on that beach.* Der Sand an diesem Strand ist sehr grobkörnig.

coast NOUN

die <u>Küste</u> ◊ *It's on the west coast of Scotland.* Es liegt an der Westküste Schottlands.

coastguard NOUN

die <u>Küstenwache</u>

coat NOUN

der <u>Mantel</u> (PL die Mäntel) ◊ *a warm coat* ein warmer Mantel

♦ **a coat of paint** ein Anstrich MASC

coat hanger NOUN

der <u>Kleiderbügel</u> (PL die Kleiderbügel)

cobweb NOUN

das <u>Spinnennetz</u>

cocaine NOUN

das <u>Kokain</u>

cock NOUN

der <u>Hahn</u> (*bird*) (PL die Hähne)

cockerel NOUN

der <u>Hahn</u> (PL die Hähne)

cockney NOUN

der <u>Cockney</u> (PL die Cockneys) ◊ *I'm a cockney.* Ich bin Cockney.

cocoa NOUN

der <u>Kakao</u> (PL die Kakaos *or* Kakao) ◊ *a cup of cocoa* eine Tasse Kakao

*When ordering more than one cup of cocoa use the plural form **Kakao**.*

◊ *Two cocoas, please.* Zwei Kakao bitte.

coconut NOUN

die <u>Kokosnuss</u> (PL die Kokosnüsse)

cod NOUN

der <u>Kabeljau</u> (PL die Kabeljaue)

code NOUN

der <u>Code</u> (PL die Codes)

coffee NOUN

der <u>Kaffee</u> (PL die Kaffees *or* Kaffee) ◊ *A cup of coffee, please.* Eine Tasse Kaffee, bitte.

*When ordering more than one coffee use the plural form **Kaffee**.*

◊ *Two coffees, please.* Zwei Kaffee bitte.

coffeepot NOUN

die <u>Kaffeekanne</u>

coffee table NOUN

der <u>Couchtisch</u> (PL die Couchtische)

coffin NOUN

der <u>Sarg</u> (PL die Särge)

coin NOUN

die <u>Münze</u>

♦ **a five-mark coin** ein Fünfmarkstück NEUT

coincidence NOUN

der <u>Zufall</u> (PL die Zufälle)

coin phone NOUN

das <u>Münztelefon</u>

Coke ® NOUN

die <u>Cola</u> (PL die Colas) ◊ *a can of Coke* ® eine Dose Cola

colander NOUN

der <u>Seiher</u> (PL die Seiher)

cold ADJECTIVE

see also **cold** NOUN

<u>kalt</u> ◊ *The water's cold.* Das Wasser ist kalt. ◊ *It's cold today.* Heute ist es kalt.

*When you talk about a person being **cold**, you use the impersonal construction.*

◊ *I'm cold.* Mir ist kalt. ◊ *Are you cold?* Ist dir kalt?

cold NOUN

see also **cold** ADJECTIVE

[1] die Kälte ◊ *I can't stand the cold.* Ich kann Kälte nicht ausstehen.

[2] der Schnupfen (PL die Schnupfen) ◊ *to catch a cold* einen Schnupfen bekommen ◊ *to have a cold* einen Schnupfen haben ◊ *I've got a bad cold.* Ich habe einen üblen Schnupfen.

♦ **a cold sore** ein Fieberbläschen NEUT

coleslaw NOUN

der Krautsalat (PL die Krautsalate)

to **collapse** VERB

zusammenbrechen (PRESENT bricht zusammen, IMPERFECT brach zusammen, PERFECT ist zusammengebrochen) ◊ *He collapsed.* Er brach zusammen.

collar NOUN

[1] (*of coat, shirt*)

der Kragen (PL die Kragen)

[2] (*for animal*)

das Halsband (PL die Halsbänder)

collarbone NOUN

das Schlüsselbein (PL die Schlüsselbeine) ◊ *I broke my collarbone.* Ich habe mir das Schlüsselbein gebrochen.

colleague NOUN

der Kollege (GEN des Kollegen, PL die Kollegen)

die Kollegin

to **collect** VERB

[1] einsammeln (PERFECT hat eingesammelt) ◊ *The teacher collected the exercise books.* Der Lehrer hat die Hefte eingesammelt.

[2] sammeln ◊ *I collect stamps.* Ich sammle Briefmarken. ◊ *They're collecting for charity.* Sie sammeln für wohltätige Zwecke.

[3] (*come to fetch*)

abholen (PERFECT hat abgeholt) ◊ *Their mother collects them from school.* Ihre Mutter holt sie von der Schule ab.

collect call NOUN US

das R-Gespräch (PL die R-Gespräche)

collection NOUN

die Sammlung ◊ *my CD collection* meine CD-Sammlung ◊ *a collection for charity* eine Spendensammlung

collector NOUN

der Sammler (PL die Sammler)

die Sammlerin

college NOUN

die Fachhochschule

> ⓘ A *Fachhochschule* is an institute of higher education for pupils aged over 18, which combines academic studies with work experience. It is oriented towards the needs of industry and commerce.

to **collide** VERB

zusammenstoßen (PRESENT stößt zusammen, IMPERFECT stieß zusammen, PERFECT ist zusammengestoßen)

collie NOUN

der Collie (PL die Collies)

colliery NOUN

die Zeche

collision NOUN

der Zusammenstoß (GEN des Zusammenstoßes, PL die Zusammenstöße)

colon NOUN

der Doppelpunkt (*punctuation mark*)

colonel NOUN

der Oberst (GEN des Obersten, PL die Obersten)

colour NOUN (US **color**)

die Farbe ◊ *What colour is it?* Welche Farbe hat es?

♦ **a colour film** (*for camera*) ein Farbfilm MASC

colourful ADJECTIVE (US **colorful**)

farbig

colouring NOUN (US **coloring**)

der Farbstoff (*for food*) (PL die Farbstoffe)

comb NOUN

see also **comb** VERB

der Kamm (PL die Kämme)

to **comb** VERB

see also **comb** NOUN

♦ **to comb one's hair** sich kämmen ◊ *You haven't combed your hair.* Du hast dich nicht gekämmt.

combination NOUN

die Kombination

to **combine** VERB

vereinen (PERFECT hat vereint) ◊ *The film combines humour with suspense.* Der Film vereint Humor und Spannung.

to **come** VERB

kommen (IMPERFECT kam, PERFECT ist gekommen) ◊ *I'm coming!* Ich komme! ◊ *The letter came this morning.* Der Brief kam heute früh. ◊ *Can I come too?* Kann ich mitkommen? ◊ *Some friends came to see us.* Einige Freunde sind zu Besuch gekommen. ◊ *I'll come with you.* Ich komme mit dir.

♦ **to come across** zufällig finden ◊ *I came across a dress that I hadn't worn for years.* Ich fand zufällig ein Kleid, das ich schon Jahre nicht mehr an hatte.

♦ **She comes across as a nice girl.** Sie scheint ein nettes Mädchen zu sein.

♦ **to come back** zurückkommen ◊ *Come back!* Komm zurück!

♦ **to come down (1)** (*person, lift*) herunterkommen

♦ **to come down (2)** (*prices*) fallen

C

- ◆ **to come from** kommen aus ◇ *I come from Germany.* Ich komme aus Deutschland. ◇ *Where do you come from?* Woher kommen Sie?
- ◆ **to come in** hereinkommen ◇ *Come in!* Herein!
- ◆ **Come on!** Na komm!
- ◆ **to come out** herauskommen ◇ *when we came out of the cinema* als wir aus dem Kino kamen ◇ *It's just come out on video.* Es ist gerade als Video herausgekommen.
- ◆ **None of my photos came out.** Meine Fotos sind alle nichts geworden.
- ◆ **to come round** (*after faint, operation*) wieder zu sich kommen
- ◆ **to come up** heraufkommen ◇ *Come up here!* Komm hier herauf!
- ◆ **to come up to somebody** auf jemanden zukommen ◇ *She came up to me and kissed me.* Sie kam auf mich zu und küsste mich.

comedian NOUN
der Komiker (PL die Komiker)
die Komikerin

comedy NOUN
die Komödie

comfortable ADJECTIVE
bequem
- ◆ **I'm very comfortable, thanks.** Danke, ich fühle mich sehr wohl.

comic NOUN
das Comicheft (*magazine*) (PL die Comichefte)

comic strip NOUN
der Comicstrip (PL die Comicstrips)

coming ADJECTIVE
kommend ◇ *in the coming months* in den kommenden Monaten

comma NOUN
das Komma (PL die Kommas)

command NOUN
der Befehl (PL die Befehle)

comment NOUN

see also **comment** VERB

der Kommentar (PL die Kommentare) ◇ *He made no comment.* Er gab keinen Kommentar ab. ◇ *No comment!* Kein Kommentar!

to **comment** VERB

see also **comment** NOUN

- ◆ **to comment on something** eine Bemerkung zu etwas machen

commentary NOUN
der Kommentar (*on TV, radio*) (PL die Kommentare)

commentator NOUN
(*sports*)
der Sportreporter (PL die Sportreporter)
die Sportreporterin

commercial NOUN
der Werbespot (PL die Werbespots)

commission NOUN

die Provision

- ◆ **Salesmen work on commission.** Verkäufer arbeiten auf Provisionsbasis.

to **commit** VERB
- ◆ **to commit a crime** ein Verbrechen begehen
- ◆ **to commit oneself** sich festlegen ◇ *I don't want to commit myself.* Ich will mich nicht festlegen.
- ◆ **to commit suicide** Selbstmord begehen ◇ *He committed suicide.* Er beging Selbstmord.

committee NOUN
der Ausschuss (GEN des Ausschusses, PL die Ausschüsse)

common ADJECTIVE

see also **common** NOUN

gebräuchlich ◇ *"Smith" is a very common surname.* "Smith" ist ein sehr gebräuchlicher Nachname.
- ◆ **in common** gemein ◇ *We've got a lot in common.* Wir haben viel gemein.

common NOUN

see also **common** ADJECTIVE

die Gemeindewiese ◇ *We went for a walk on the common.* Wir sind auf der Gemeindewiese spazieren gegangen.

Commons PL NOUN
- ◆ **the House of Commons** das britische Unterhaus

common sense NOUN
der gesunde Menschenverstand ◇ *Use your common sense!* Benutze deinen gesunden Menschenverstand!

to **communicate** VERB
kommunizieren (PERFECT hat kommuniziert)

communication NOUN
die Kommunikation

communion NOUN
die Kommunion ◇ *my First Communion* meine Erstkommunion

communism NOUN
der Kommunismus (GEN des Kommunismus)

communist NOUN

see also **communist** ADJECTIVE

der Kommunist (GEN des Kommunisten, PL die Kommunisten)
die Kommunistin

communist ADJECTIVE

see also **communist** NOUN

kommunistisch
- ◆ **the Communist Party** die Kommunistische Partei

community NOUN
die Gemeinschaft
- ◆ **the local community** die Gemeinde

to **commute** VERB
pendeln (PERFECT ist gependelt) ◇ *She commutes between Liss and London.* Sie pendelt zwischen Liss und London.

compact disc NOUN
die Compact Disc (PL die Compact Discs)
♦ **compact disc player** der CD-Spieler

companion NOUN
der Gefährte (GEN des Gefährten, PL die
Gefährten)
die Gefährtin

company NOUN
⟦1⟧ das Unternehmen (PL die
Unternehmen) ◊ *He works for a big
company.* Er arbeitet für ein großes
Unternehmen.
⟦2⟧ die Gesellschaft ◊ *an insurance
company* eine Versicherungsgesellschaft
♦ **a theatre company** ein Theaterensemble
NEUT
♦ **to keep somebody company** jemandem
Gesellschaft leisten ◊ *I'll keep you
company.* Ich leiste dir Gesellschaft.

comparatively ADVERB
relativ

to **compare** VERB
vergleichen (IMPERFECT verglich, PERFECT hat
verglichen) ◊ *People always compare
him with his brother.* Die Leute
vergleichen ihn immer mit seinem
Bruder.
♦ **compared with** im Vergleich zu ◊ *Oxford
is small compared with London.* Im
Vergleich zu London ist Oxford klein.

comparison NOUN
der Vergleich (PL die Vergleiche)

compartment NOUN
das Abteil (PL die Abteile)

compass NOUN
der Kompass (GEN des Kompasses, PL die
Kompasse)

compensation NOUN
der Schadenersatz ◊ *They got two
thousand pounds compensation.* Sie
bekamen zweitausend Pfund
Schadenersatz.

compere NOUN
der Conférencier (PL die Conférenciers)

to **compete** VERB
teilnehmen (PRESENT nimmt teil, IMPERFECT
nahm teil, PERFECT hat teilgenommen)
◊ *I'm competing in the marathon.* Ich
nehme am Marathon teil.
♦ **to compete for something** um etwas
kämpfen ◊ *They are competing for a
place in the UEFA cup.* Sie kämpfen um
einen Platz im UEFA-Pokal.
♦ **There are fifty students competing for
six places.** Fünfzig Studenten bewerben
sich auf sechs Studienplätze.

competent ADJECTIVE
kompetent

competition NOUN
(*organized event*)
der Wettbewerb (PL die Wettbewerbe)
◊ *a singing competition* ein
Gesangswettbewerb

competitive ADJECTIVE
♦ **I'm a very competitive person.** Ich bin
ein sehr ehrgeiziger Mensch.

competitor NOUN
(*participant*)
der Teilnehmer (PL die Teilnehmer)
die Teilnehmerin

to **complain** VERB
sich beschweren (PERFECT hat sich
beschwert) ◊ *I'm going to complain to
the manager.* Ich werde mich beim
Geschäftsführer beschweren. ◊ *We
complained about the noise.* Wir haben
uns über den Lärm beschwert.

complaint NOUN
die Beschwerde ◊ *There were lots of
complaints about the food.* Es gab viele
Beschwerden über das Essen.

complete ADJECTIVE
vollständig

completely ADVERB
völlig

complexion NOUN
der Teint (PL die Teints)

complicated ADJECTIVE
kompliziert

compliment NOUN
| see also **compliment** VERB |
das Kompliment (PL die Komplimente)

to **compliment** VERB
| see also **compliment** NOUN |
♦ **They complimented me on my German.**
Sie haben mir Komplimente zu meinem
Deutsch gemacht.

complimentary ADJECTIVE
♦ **complimentary ticket** der Freifahrschein

to **compose** VERB
komponieren (*music*) (PERFECT hat
komponiert)
♦ **to be composed of something** aus etwas
bestehen ◊ *The team is composed of two
boys and three girls.* Die Mannschaft
besteht aus zwei Jungen und drei
Mädchen.

composer NOUN
der Komponist (GEN des Komponisten, PL
die Komponisten)
die Komponistin

comprehension NOUN
das Verständnis (*school exercise*)

comprehensive ADJECTIVE
umfassend ◊ *a comprehensive guide to
Greece* ein umfassender Reiseführer für
Griechenland

comprehensive school NOUN
die Gesamtschule

> ⓘ *Gesamtschulen* are the exception
> rather than the rule in Germany.

compromise NOUN
| see also **compromise** VERB |

der Kompromiss (GEN des Kompromisses, PL die Kompromisse)
◊ We reached a compromise. Wir haben einen Kompromiss gefunden.

to **compromise** VERB

see also **compromise** NOUN

einen Kompromiss schließen (IMPERFECT schloss, PERFECT hat geschlossen)

compulsory ADJECTIVE
obligatorisch

computer NOUN
der Computer (PL die Computer)

computer game NOUN
das Computerspiel (PL die Computerspiele)

computer programmer NOUN
der Programmierer (PL die Programmierer)
die Programmiererin
◊ She's a computer programmer. Sie ist Programmiererin.

computer science NOUN
die Informatik

computing NOUN
die Informatik

to **concentrate** VERB
sich konzentrieren (PERFECT hat sich konzentriert) ◊ I couldn't concentrate. Ich konnte mich nicht konzentrieren.

concentration NOUN
die Konzentration

concern NOUN

see also **concern** VERB

die Sorge ◊ to express concern about something Sorge über etwas ausdrücken

to **concern** VERB

see also **concern** NOUN

betreffen (PRESENT betrifft, IMPERFECT betraf, PERFECT hat betroffen) ◊ It concerns all of us. Es betrifft uns alle.

concerned ADJECTIVE
♦ **to be concerned** sich Sorgen machen ◊ I am concerned about him. Ich mache mir Sorgen um ihn.
♦ **as far as I'm concerned** was mich betrifft

concerning NOUN
bezüglich ◊ For further information concerning the job, contact Mr Ross. Für weitere Informationen bezüglich der Stelle wenden Sie sich an Herrn Ross.

concert NOUN
das Konzert (PL die Konzerte)

concrete NOUN
der Beton (PL die Betons)

to **condemn** VERB
verurteilen (PERFECT hat verurteilt)

condition NOUN
1 die Bedingung ◊ I'll do it, on one condition ... Ich mache es unter einer Bedingung ...
2 der Zustand (PL die Zustände) ◊ in good condition in gutem Zustand

conditional NOUN
der Konditional

conditioner NOUN
die Spülung (for hair)

condom NOUN
das Kondom (PL die Kondome)

to **conduct** VERB
dirigieren (orchestra) (PERFECT hat dirigiert)

conductor NOUN
der Dirigent (GEN des Dirigenten, PL die Dirigenten)
die Dirigentin

cone NOUN
1 die Eistüte ◊ an ice-cream cone eine Eistüte
2 (geometric shape)
der Kegel (PL die Kegel)
♦ **a traffic cone** ein Pylon MASC

conference NOUN
die Konferenz

to **confess** VERB
gestehen (IMPERFECT gestand, PERFECT hat gestanden) ◊ He finally confessed. Er hat schließlich gestanden. ◊ He confessed to the murder. Er hat den Mord gestanden.

confession NOUN
1 das Geständnis (GEN des Geständnisses, PL die Geständnisse)
◊ Her confession was made under duress. Ihr Geständnis war erzwungen.
2 (in church)
die Beichte ◊ My sister doesn't like going to confession. Meine Schwester geht ungern zur Beichte.

confetti NOUN
das Konfetti

confidence NOUN
1 das Vertrauen ◊ I've got confidence in you. Ich habe Vertrauen in dich.
2 das Selbstvertrauen ◊ She lacks confidence. Sie hat zu wenig Selbstvertrauen.

confident ADJECTIVE
1 zuversichtlich (sure of something) ◊ I'm confident everything will be okay. Ich bin zuversichtlich, dass alles gut gehen wird.
2 selbstbewusst (self-assured) ◊ She's seems a confident person. Sie scheint eine selbstbewusste Frau zu sein.

confidential ADJECTIVE
vertraulich

to **confirm** VERB
bestätigen (booking) (PERFECT hat bestätigt)

confirmation NOUN
die Bestätigung

conflict NOUN
der Konflikt (PL die Konflikte)

to **confuse** VERB
durcheinanderbringen (IMPERFECT brachte durcheinander, PERFECT hat durcheinandergebracht) ◊ Don't confuse me! Bring mich nicht durcheinander!

confused ADJECTIVE

durcheinander

confusing ADJECTIVE
verwirrend

confusion NOUN
das Durcheinander

to **congratulate** VERB
beglückwünschen (PERFECT hat beglückwünscht) ◊ *My friends congratulated me on passing the test.* Meine Freunde haben mich zur bestandenen Prüfung beglückwünscht.

congratulations PL NOUN
der Glückwunsch (PL die Glückwünsche) ◊ *Congratulations on your new job!* Herzlichen Glückwunsch zum neuen Job!

conjunction NOUN
die Konjunktion

conjurer NOUN
der Zauberkünstler (PL die Zauberkünstler)
die Zauberkünstlerin

connection NOUN
[1] der Zusammenhang (PL die Zusammenhänge) ◊ *There's no connection between the two events.* Es besteht kein Zusammenhang zwischen den beiden Ereignissen.
[2] (*electrical*)
der Kontakt (PL die Kontakte) ◊ *There's a loose connection.* Da ist ein Wackelkontakt.
[3] (*of trains, planes*)
der Anschluss (GEN des Anschlusses, PL die Anschlüsse) ◊ *We missed our connection.* Wir haben unseren Anschluss verpasst.

to **conquer** VERB
erobern (PERFECT hat erobert)

conscience NOUN
das Gewissen ◊ *I have a guilty conscience.* Ich habe ein schlechtes Gewissen.

conscious ADJECTIVE
bewusst ◊ *politically conscious* politisch bewusst ◊ *a conscious effort* eine bewusste Anstrengung
♦ **to be conscious of something (1)** (*know*) sich einer Sache bewusst sein ◊ *I was conscious of his disapproval.* Ich war mir seiner Missbilligung bewusst.
♦ **to be conscious of something (2)** (*notice*) etwas bemerken ◊ *She was conscious of Max looking at her.* Sie hatte bemerkt, dass Max sie ansah.

consciousness NOUN
das Bewusstsein
♦ **to lose consciousness** bewusstlos werden ◊ *I lost consciousness.* Ich wurde bewusstlos.

consequence NOUN
die Folge

consequently ADVERB
folglich

conservation NOUN
der Schutz ◊ *nature conservation* der Naturschutz

conservative ADJECTIVE
see also **conservative** NOUN
konservativ
♦ **the Conservative Party** die Konservative Partei

Conservative NOUN
see also **conservative** ADJECTIVE
der Konservative (GEN des Konservativen, PL die Konservativen)
die Konservative
◊ *a Conservative* (*man*) ein Konservativer
♦ **to vote Conservative** die Konservativen wählen
♦ **the Conservatives** die Konservativen

conservatory NOUN
der Wintergarten (PL die Wintergärten)

to **consider** VERB
in Erwägung ziehen (IMPERFECT zog in Erwägung, PERFECT hat in Erwägung gezogen) ◊ *We considered cancelling our holiday.* Wir zogen in Erwägung, den Urlaub abzusagen.
♦ **I'm considering the idea.** Ich denke darüber nach.
♦ **He considered it a waste of time.** Er hielt es für Zeitverschwendung.

considerate ADJECTIVE
aufmerksam ◊ *That was very considerate of you.* Das war sehr aufmerksam von dir.
♦ **not very considerate** nicht sehr rücksichtsvoll

considering PREPOSITION
[1] dafür, dass ◊ *Considering we were there for a month ...* Dafür, dass wir einen Monat da waren ...
[2] unter den Umständen ◊ *I got a good mark, considering.* Unter den Umständen bekam ich eine gute Note.

to **consist** VERB
♦ **to consist of** bestehen aus ◊ *The band consists of three guitarists and a drummer.* Die Band besteht aus drei Gitarristen und einem Schlagzeuger.

consistent ADJECTIVE
beständig ◊ *He's the team's most consistent player.* Er ist der beständigste Spieler der Mannschaft.

consonant NOUN
der Konsonant (GEN des Konsonanten, PL die Konsonanten)

constant ADJECTIVE
beständig

constantly ADVERB
dauernd

constipated ADJECTIVE
verstopft

to **construct** VERB
bauen

construction NOUN
der Bau

to **consult** VERB

[1] (*solicitor, doctor*)
um Rat fragen
[2] (*book*)
nachsehen in +DAT
(PRESENT sieht nach, IMPERFECT sah nach,
PERFECT hat nachgesehen) ◊ *You should
consult the dictionary.* Du solltest im
Wörterbuch nachsehen.

consumer NOUN
der Verbraucher (PL die Verbraucher)
die Verbraucherin

contact NOUN
see also **contact** VERB
der Kontakt (PL die Kontakte) ◊ *I'm in
contact with her.* Ich bin in Kontakt mit
ihr.

to **contact** VERB
see also **contact** NOUN
sich in Verbindung setzen mit ◊ *You
should contact us immediately.* Sie
sollten sich sofort mit uns in Verbindung
setzen.
♦ **Where can we contact you?** Wo können
wir Sie erreichen?

contact lenses PL NOUN
die Kontaktlinsen FEM PL

to **contain** VERB
enthalten (PRESENT enthält, IMPERFECT
enthielt, PERFECT hat enthalten)

container NOUN
der Behälter (PL die Behälter)

contempt NOUN
die Verachtung

contents PL NOUN
der Inhalt
♦ **table of contents** das Inhaltsverzeichnis

contest NOUN
der Wettbewerb (PL die Wettbewerbe)

contestant NOUN
der Teilnehmer (PL die Teilnehmer)
die Teilnehmerin

context NOUN
der Zusammenhang (PL die
Zusammenhänge)

continent NOUN
der Kontinent (PL die Kontinente) ◊ *How
many continents are there?* Wie viele
Kontinente gibt es?
♦ **the Continent** Kontinentaleuropa NEUT
◊ *on the Continent* in Kontinentaleuropa
♦ **I've never been to the Continent.** Ich war
noch nie auf dem Kontinent.

continental breakfast NOUN
das kleine Frühstück

continental quilt NOUN
die Steppdecke

to **continue** VERB
weitermachen (PERFECT hat
weitergemacht) ◊ *We will continue after
the break.* Wir machen nach der Pause
weiter.
♦ **Please continue!** Bitte fahren Sie fort!

♦ **She continued talking to her friend.** Sie
redete weiter mit ihrer Freundin.

continuous ADJECTIVE
laufend
♦ **continuous assessment** laufende
Leistungskontrolle

contraceptive NOUN
das Verhütungsmittel (PL die
Verhütungsmittel)

contract NOUN
der Vertrag (PL die Verträge)

to **contradict** VERB
widersprechen (PRESENT widerspricht,
IMPERFECT widersprach, PERFECT hat
widersprochen) ◊ *Don't contradict me!*
Widersprich mir nicht!

contrary NOUN
das Gegenteil
♦ **on the contrary** im Gegenteil

contrast NOUN
der Kontrast (PL die Kontraste)

to **contribute** VERB
[1] beitragen (PRESENT trägt bei, IMPERFECT
trug bei, PERFECT hat beigetragen) ◊ *The
treaty will contribute to world peace.* Der
Vertrag wird zum Weltfrieden beitragen.
[2] (*donate*)
spenden ◊ *She contributed ten pounds.*
Sie hat zehn Pfund gespendet.

contribution NOUN
der Beitrag (PL die Beiträge)

control NOUN
see also **control** VERB

die Kontrolle
♦ **to lose control** (*of vehicle*) die Kontrolle
verlieren ◊ *He lost control of the car.* Er
hat die Kontrolle über das Auto verloren.
♦ **the controls** (*of machine*) die
Bedienelemente NEUT PL
♦ **to be in control** das Sagen haben
♦ **to keep control** (*of people*) Disziplin
halten ◊ *He can't keep control of the
class.* Er kann in der Klasse keine
Disziplin halten.
♦ **out of control** (*child, class*) außer Rand
und Band

to **control** VERB
see also **control** NOUN

[1] (*country, organization*)
unter Kontrolle haben (PRESENT hat unter
Kontrolle, IMPERFECT hatte unter Kontrolle,
PERFECT hat unter Kontrolle gehabt)
[2] Disziplin halten in +DAT
(PRESENT hält Disziplin in, IMPERFECT hielt
Disziplin in, PERFECT hat Disziplin gehalten
in) ◊ *He can't control the class.* Er kann in
der Klasse keine Disziplin halten.
[3] unter Kontrolle halten ◊ *I couldn't
control the horse.* Ich konnte das Pferd
nicht mehr unter Kontrolle halten.
[4] (*regulate*)

regeln ◊ *You can control the volume using this knob.* Sie können mit diesem Knopf die Lautstärke regeln.
♦ **to control oneself** sich beherrschen

controversial ADJECTIVE
umstritten ◊ *a controversial book* ein umstrittenes Buch

convenient ADJECTIVE
günstig (*place*) ◊ *The hotel's convenient for the airport.* Das Hotel ist in günstiger Lage zum Flughafen. ◊ *It's not convenient for me right now.* Es ist gerade ungünstig.
♦ **Would Monday be convenient for you?** Würde dir Montag passen?

conventional ADJECTIVE
konventionell

convent school NOUN
die Klosterschule

conversation NOUN
die Unterhaltung
♦ **a German conversation class** deutsche Konversation

to **convert** VERB
umbauen (PERFECT hat umgebaut) ◊ *We've converted the loft into a spare room.* Wir haben den Speicher zu einem Gästezimmer umgebaut.

convict NOUN
see also **convict** VERB
der Häftling ◊ *an escaped convict* ein entflohener Häftling

to **convict** VERB
see also **convict** NOUN
überführen (PERFECT hat überführt) ◊ *He was convicted of the murder.* Er wurde des Mordes überführt.

conviction NOUN
die Überzeugung ◊ *She spoke with great conviction.* Sie sprach mit großer Überzeugung.
♦ **He has three previous convictions for robbery.** Er ist bereits dreimal wegen Raubes vorbestraft.

to **convince** VERB
überzeugen (PERFECT hat überzeugt) ◊ *I'm not convinced.* Ich bin nicht überzeugt.

to **cook** VERB
see also **cook** NOUN
kochen ◊ *I can't cook.* Ich kann nicht kochen. ◊ *She's cooking lunch.* Sie kocht das Mittagessen.
♦ **to be cooked** fertig sein ◊ *When the potatoes are cooked ...* Wenn die Kartoffeln fertig sind ...

cook NOUN
see also **cook** VERB
der Koch (PL die Köche)
die Köchin
◊ *Werner's an excellent cook.* Werner ist ein ausgezeichneter Koch.

cookbook NOUN

das Kochbuch (PL die Kochbücher)

cooker NOUN
der Herd (PL die Herde) ◊ *a gas cooker* ein Gasherd

cookery NOUN
das Kochen
♦ **a cookery class** ein Kochkurs MASC

cookie NOUN US
der Keks (GEN des Kekses, PL die Kekse)

cooking NOUN
das Kochen
♦ **I like cooking.** Ich koche gern.

cool ADJECTIVE
see also **cool** VERB
kühl ◊ *a cooler place* ein kühlerer Ort
♦ **to stay cool** (*keep calm*) ruhig bleiben ◊ *He stayed cool.* Er blieb ruhig.

to **cool** VERB
see also **cool** ADJECTIVE
kühlen
♦ **Just cool it!** Immer mit der Ruhe! (*informal*)

cooperation NOUN
die Zusammenarbeit

cop NOUN
der Polizist (GEN des Polizisten, PL die Polizisten)
die Polizistin

to **cope** VERB
es schaffen ◊ *It was hard, but we coped.* Es war schwer, aber wir haben es geschafft.
♦ **to cope with** bewältigen ◊ *She's got a lot of problems to cope with.* Sie hat eine Menge Probleme zu bewältigen.

copper NOUN
[1] das Kupfer ◊ *a copper bracelet* ein Kupferarmband
[2] (*police officer*)
der Polizist (GEN des Polizisten, PL die Polizisten)
die Polizistin

copy NOUN
see also **copy** VERB
[1] (*of letter, document*)
die Kopie
[2] (*of book*)
das Exemplar (PL die Exemplare)

to **copy** VERB
see also **copy** NOUN
[1] (*write down*)
abschreiben (IMPERFECT schrieb ab, PERFECT hat abgeschrieben) ◊ *She copied the sentence into her exercise book.* Sie schrieb den Satz in ihr Heft ab. ◊ *The teacher accused him of copying.* Der Lehrer warf ihm vor, abgeschrieben zu haben.
[2] (*person*)
nachmachen (PERFECT hat nachgemacht) ◊ *She always copies her sister.* Sie macht ihrer Schwester alles nach.

C

core → **council**

3 (computer)
kopieren (PERFECT hat kopiert) ◊ to copy and paste kopieren und einfügen
core NOUN
der Stein (of fruit)
cork NOUN
1 (of bottle)
der Korken (PL die Korken)
2 (material)
der Kork ◊ a cork table mat ein Korkuntersetzer MASC
corkscrew NOUN
der Korkenzieher (PL die Korkenzieher)
corn NOUN
1 (wheat)
das Getreide (PL die Getreide)
2 (sweetcorn)
der Mais
♦ corn on the cob der Maiskolben
corner NOUN
1 die Ecke ◊ in a corner of the room in einer Ecke des Zimmers ◊ the shop on the corner das Geschäft an der Ecke ◊ He lives just round the corner. Er wohnt gleich um die Ecke.
2 (in football)
der Eckball (PL die Eckbälle)
cornet NOUN
1 das Kornett (PL die Kornette) ◊ He plays the cornet. Er spielt Kornett.
2 (ice cream)
die Eistüte
cornflakes PL NOUN
die Cornflakes PL
cornstarch NOUN US
das Maismehl
Cornwall NOUN
Cornwall NEUT
♦ in Cornwall in Cornwall
corporal NOUN
der Stabsunteroffizier (PL die Stabsunteroffiziere)
corporal punishment NOUN
die Prügelstrafe
corpse NOUN
die Leiche
correct ADJECTIVE
see also **correct** VERB
richtig ◊ That's correct. Das ist richtig. ◊ the correct answer die richtige Antwort
to **correct** VERB
see also **correct** ADJECTIVE
korrigieren (PERFECT hat korrigiert)
correction NOUN
die Verbesserung
correctly ADVERB
richtig
correspondent NOUN
der Korrespondent (GEN des Korrespondenten, PL die Korrespondenten)
die Korrespondentin

corridor NOUN
der Korridor (PL die Korridore)
corruption NOUN
die Korruption
Corsica NOUN
Korsika NEUT
♦ from Corsica aus Korsika
♦ to Corsica nach Korsika
cosmetics PL NOUN
die Kosmetika NEUT PL
cosmetic surgery NOUN
die Schönheitschirurgie
to **cost** VERB
see also **cost** NOUN
kosten ◊ The meal cost fifty euros. Das Essen hat fünfzig Euro gekostet. ◊ How much does it cost? Wie viel kostet das? ◊ It costs too much. Das kostet zu viel.
cost NOUN
see also **cost** VERB
die Kosten PL ◊ the cost of living die Lebenshaltungskosten
♦ at all costs um jeden Preis
costume NOUN
das Kostüm (PL die Kostüme)
cosy ADJECTIVE
gemütlich
cot NOUN
1 (for children)
das Kinderbett (PL die Kinderbetten)
2 (camp bed)
die Campingliege
cottage NOUN
das kleine Haus (GEN des kleinen Hauses, PL die kleinen Häuser)
♦ a thatched cottage ein Haus mit Strohdach
cottage cheese NOUN
der Hüttenkäse
cotton NOUN
die Baumwolle ◊ a cotton shirt ein Baumwollhemd NEUT
♦ cotton candy die Zuckerwatte
♦ cotton wool die Watte
couch NOUN
die Couch (PL die Couches)
couchette NOUN
der Platz im Liegewagen (PL die Plätze im Liegewagen)
to **cough** VERB
see also **cough** NOUN
husten
cough NOUN
see also **cough** VERB
der Husten ◊ a bad cough ein schlimmer Husten ◊ I've got a cough. Ich habe Husten.
could VERB see **can**
council NOUN
der Gemeinderat (PL die Gemeinderäte) ◊ He's on the council. Er ist im Gemeinderat.

♦ **a council estate** eine Siedlung des sozialen Wohnungsbaus
♦ **a council house** eine Sozialwohnung

> *ℹ In Germany the council provides flats rather than houses.*

councillor NOUN
der Gemeinderat (PL die Gemeinderäte)
die Gemeinderätin
◊ *She's a local councillor.* Sie ist Gemeinderätin.

to **count** VERB
zählen
♦ **to count on** zählen auf +ACC ◊ *You can count on me.* Du kannst auf mich zählen.

counter NOUN
☐1 (*in shop*)
der Ladentisch (PL die Ladentische)
☐2 (*in post office, bank*)
der Schalter (PL die Schalter)
☐3 (*in game*)
die Spielmarke

country NOUN
das Land (PL die Länder) ◊ *the border between the two countries* die Grenze zwischen den beiden Ländern
♦ **in the country** auf dem Land ◊ *I live in the country.* Ich wohne auf dem Land.
♦ **country dancing** der Volkstanz

countryside NOUN
die Landschaft

county NOUN
die Grafschaft

> *ℹ The nearest German equivalent of a county would be a **Bundesland**.*

♦ **the county council** der Grafschaftsrat

> *ℹ The nearest German equivalent of a county council would be the **Landtag**.*

couple NOUN
das Paar (PL die Paare) ◊ *the couple who live next door* das Paar von nebenan
♦ **a couple** ein paar
> Note that in this sense **paar** is spelt with a small "p".
◊ *a couple of hours* ein paar Stunden
◊ *Could you wait a couple of minutes?* Könntest du ein paar Minuten warten?

courage NOUN
der Mut

courgette NOUN
die Zucchini (PL die Zucchini)

courier NOUN
☐1 (*for tourists*)
der Reiseleiter (PL die Reiseleiter)
die Reiseleiterin
☐2 (*delivery service*)

der Kurier (PL die Kuriere) ◊ *They sent it by courier.* Sie haben es mit Kurier geschickt.

course NOUN
☐1 der Kurs (PL die Kurse) ◊ *a German course* ein Deutschkurs ◊ *to go on a course* einen Kurs machen
☐2 der Gang (PL die Gänge) ◊ *the first course* der erste Gang
♦ **the main course** das Hauptgericht
☐3 der Platz (PL die Plätze) ◊ *a golf course* ein Golfplatz
♦ **of course** natürlich ◊ *Do you love me? – Of course I do!* Liebst du mich? – Aber natürlich!

court NOUN
☐1 (*of law*)
das Gericht (PL die Gerichte) ◊ *He was in court last week.* Er war letzte Woche vor Gericht.
☐2 (*tennis*)
der Platz (PL die Plätze) ◊ *There are tennis and squash courts.* Es gibt Tennis- und Squashplätze.

courtyard NOUN
der Hof (PL die Höfe)

cousin NOUN
☐1 (*man*)
der Vetter (PL die Vettern)
☐2 (*woman*)
die Cousine

cover NOUN
> see also **cover** VERB
☐1 (*of book*)
der Umschlag (PL die Umschläge)
☐2 (*of duvet*)
der Bezug (PL die Bezüge)

to **cover** VERB
> see also **cover** NOUN
☐1 bedecken (PERFECT hat bedeckt) ◊ *He covers his computer with a plastic hood.* Er bedeckt seinen Computer mit einer Plastikhülle.
♦ **My face was covered with mosquito bites.** Mein Gesicht war voller Mückenstiche.
☐2 decken ◊ *Our insurance didn't cover it.* Unsere Versicherung hat das nicht gedeckt.
♦ **to cover up a scandal** einen Skandal vertuschen

cow NOUN
die Kuh (PL die Kühe)

coward NOUN
der Feigling (PL die Feiglinge)
> *der Feigling is also used for women.*
◊ *She's a coward.* Sie ist ein Feigling.

cowardly ADJECTIVE
feige

cowboy NOUN
der Cowboy (PL die Cowboys)

crab NOUN
die Krabbe

crack NOUN

see also **crack** VERB

1 (_in wall_)
der Riss (GEN des Risses, PL die Risse)
2 (_in cup, window_)
der Sprung (PL die Sprünge)
3 (_drug_)
das Crack
♦ **I'll have a crack at it.** Ich werd's mal versuchen.

to **crack** VERB

see also **crack** NOUN

1 (_nut_)
knacken
2 (_egg_)
aufschlagen (PRESENT schlägt auf, IMPERFECT schlug auf, PERFECT hat aufgeschlagen)
♦ **to crack a joke** einen Witz reißen
♦ **to crack down on** hart durchgreifen ◊ _The police are cracking down on motorists who drive too fast._ Die Polizei greift hart gegen Fahrer durch, die zu schnell fahren.

cracked ADJECTIVE
kaputt (_cup, window_)

cracker NOUN
1 (_biscuit_)
der Cracker (PL die Cracker)
2 (_Christmas cracker_)
das Knallbonbon (PL die Knallbonbons)

cradle NOUN
die Wiege

craft NOUN
das Werken ◊ _We do craft at school._ Wir haben Werken in der Schule.
♦ **a craft centre** ein Kunstgewerbezentrum NEUT

craftsman NOUN
der Kunsthandwerker (PL die Kunsthandwerker)

to **cram** VERB
1 stopfen ◊ _We crammed our stuff into the boot._ Wir haben unsere Sachen in den Kofferraum gestopft.
2 pauken (_for exams_)

crane NOUN
der Kran (_machine_)

to **crash** VERB

see also **crash** NOUN

kaputt fahren (PRESENT fährt kaputt, IMPERFECT fuhr kaputt, PERFECT hat kaputt gefahren) ◊ _He's crashed his car._ Er hat sein Auto kaputt gefahren.
♦ **The plane crashed.** Das Flugzeug stürzte ab.
♦ **to crash into something** auf etwas fahren ◊ _My brother crashed into the back of a lorry._ Mein Bruder ist hinten auf einen Lastwagen gefahren.

crash NOUN

see also **crash** VERB

1 (_of car_)
der Unfall (PL die Unfälle)
2 (_of plane_)
das Unglück (PL die Unglücke)
♦ **a crash helmet** ein Sturzhelm MASC
♦ **a crash course** ein Crashkurs MASC

to **crawl** VERB

see also **crawl** NOUN

krabbeln (_baby_) (PERFECT ist gekrabbelt)

crawl NOUN

see also **crawl** VERB

das Kraulen
♦ **to do the crawl** kraulen

crazy ADJECTIVE
verrückt

cream ADJECTIVE

see also **cream** NOUN

cremefarben (_colour_)

cream NOUN

see also **cream** ADJECTIVE

die Sahne ◊ _strawberries and cream_ Erdbeeren mit Sahne ◊ _a cream cake_ eine Sahnetorte
♦ **cream cheese** der Frischkäse
♦ **sun cream** die Sonnencreme

crease NOUN
die Falte

creased ADJECTIVE
zerknittert

to **create** VERB
schaffen (IMPERFECT schuf, PERFECT hat geschaffen)

creation NOUN
die Schöpfung

creative ADJECTIVE
kreativ

creature NOUN
das Lebewesen (PL die Lebewesen)

crèche NOUN
die Kinderkrippe

credit NOUN
der Kredit (PL die Kredite) ◊ _on credit_ auf Kredit

credit card NOUN
die Kreditkarte

creep NOUN

see also **creep** VERB

♦ **It gives me the creeps.** Es ist mir nicht geheuer.

to **creep** VERB

see also **creep** NOUN

kriechen (IMPERFECT kroch, PERFECT ist gekrochen)

cress NOUN
die Kresse

crew NOUN
die Mannschaft

crew cut NOUN
der Bürstenhaarschnitt (PL die Bürstenhaarschnitte)

cricket NOUN
1 das Cricket

C

> ⓘ *Cricket is practically never played in Germany.*

◊ *I play cricket.* Ich spiele Cricket.
♦ **a cricket bat** ein Cricketschläger MASC
2 die <u>Grille</u> (*insect*)
crime NOUN
1 das <u>Verbrechen</u> (PL die Verbrechen)
◊ *Murder is a crime.* Mord ist ein Verbrechen.
2 (*lawlessness*)
die <u>Kriminalität</u> ◊ *Crime is rising.* Die Kriminalität nimmt zu.
criminal NOUN
see also **criminal** ADJECTIVE
der <u>Verbrecher</u> (PL die Verbrecher)
die <u>Verbrecherin</u>
criminal ADJECTIVE
see also **criminal** NOUN
kriminell ◊ *It's criminal!* Das ist kriminell!
♦ **It's a criminal offence.** Das ist eine strafbare Handlung.
♦ **to have a criminal record** vorbestraft sein
crippled ADJECTIVE
gelähmt ◊ *He was crippled in an accident.* Er ist seit einem Unfall gelähmt.
crisis NOUN
die <u>Krise</u>
crisp ADJECTIVE
knusprig (*food*)
crisps PL NOUN
die <u>Chips</u> MASC PL ◊ *a bag of crisps* eine Tüte Chips
criterion NOUN
das <u>Kriterium</u> (PL die Kriterien)
critic NOUN
der <u>Kritiker</u> (PL die Kritiker)
die <u>Kritikerin</u>
critical ADJECTIVE
kritisch
criticism NOUN
die <u>Kritik</u>
to **criticize** VERB
kritisieren (PERFECT hat kritisiert)
Croatia NOUN
<u>Kroatien</u> NEUT
♦ **from Croatia** aus Kroatien
♦ **to Croatia** nach Kroatien
to **crochet** VERB
<u>häkeln</u>
crocodile NOUN
das <u>Krokodil</u> (PL die Krokodile)
crook NOUN
der <u>Verbrecher</u> (*criminal*) (PL die Verbrecher)
crop NOUN
die <u>Ernte</u> ◊ *a good crop of apples* eine gute Apfelernte

cross NOUN
see also **cross** ADJECTIVE, VERB
das <u>Kreuz</u> (PL die Kreuze)
cross ADJECTIVE
see also **cross** NOUN, VERB
böse ◊ *to be cross about something* wegen etwas böse sein
to **cross** VERB
see also **cross** ADJECTIVE, NOUN
überqueren (*street, bridge*) (PERFECT hat überquert)
♦ **to cross out** durchstreichen
♦ **to cross over** hinübergehen
cross-country NOUN
das <u>Querfeldeinrennen</u> (*race*) (PL die Querfeldeinrennen)
♦ **cross-country skiing** der Langlauf
crossing NOUN
1 (*by boat*)
die <u>Überfahrt</u> ◊ *the crossing from Dover to Calais* die Überfahrt von Dover nach Calais
2 (*for pedestrians*)
der <u>Fußgängerüberweg</u> (PL die Fußgängerüberwege)
crossroads SING NOUN
die <u>Kreuzung</u>
crossword NOUN
das <u>Kreuzworträtsel</u> (PL die Kreuzworträtsel) ◊ *I like doing crosswords.* Ich mache gern Kreuzworträtsel.
to **crouch down** VERB
sich <u>niederkauern</u> (PERFECT hat sich niedergekauert)
crow NOUN
die <u>Krähe</u>
crowd NOUN
see also **crowd** VERB
die <u>Menge</u>
♦ **the crowd** (*at sports match*) die Zuschauer MASC PL
to **crowd** VERB
see also **crowd** NOUN
sich <u>drängen</u> ◊ *The children crowded round the model.* Die Kinder drängten sich um das Modell.
crowded ADJECTIVE
voll
crown NOUN
die <u>Krone</u>
crucifix NOUN
das <u>Kruzifix</u> (PL die Kruzifixe)
crude ADJECTIVE
ordinär (*vulgar*)
cruel ADJECTIVE
grausam
cruise NOUN
die <u>Kreuzfahrt</u> ◊ *to go on a Caribbean cruise* eine Karibikkreuzfahrt machen
crumb NOUN
der <u>Krümel</u> (PL die Krümel)

to **crush** VERB

> see also **crush** NOUN

[1] zerquetschen (PERFECT hat zerquetscht) ◊ *The tomatoes got crushed.* Die Tomaten wurden zerquetscht.

[2] (*finger*)

quetschen ◊ *I crushed my finger in the car door.* Ich habe mir den Finger in der Autotür gequetscht.

crush NOUN

> see also **crush** VERB

♦ **to have a crush on somebody** für jemanden schwärmen

crutch NOUN
die Krücke

cry NOUN

> see also **cry** VERB

der Schrei ◊ *With a cry, she rushed forward.* Mit einem Schrei rannte sie vorwärts.

♦ **to have a good cry** sich ausweinen

to **cry** VERB

> see also **cry** NOUN

weinen ◊ *The baby cried all night.* Das Baby hat die ganze Nacht geweint.

crystal NOUN
der Kristall (PL die Kristalle)

CTC NOUN (= *city technology college*)
die technische Fachschule

cub NOUN

[1] (*animal*)

das Junge (GEN des Jungen, PL die Jungen) ◊ *the lioness and her cub* die Löwin und ihr Junges

[2] (*scout*)

der Wölfling (PL die Wölflinge)

cube NOUN
der Würfel (PL die Würfel)

cubic ADJECTIVE

♦ **a cubic metre** ein Kubikmeter MASC

cucumber NOUN
die Gurke

cuddle NOUN

> see also **cuddle** VERB

♦ **Come and give me a cuddle.** Komm und nimm mich in den Arm.

to **cuddle** VERB

> see also **cuddle** NOUN

♦ **to cuddle somebody** jemanden in den Arm nehmen

cue NOUN
das Queue (*for snooker, pool*) (PL die Queues)

> *Queue is pronounced as if spelt "Kö".*

culottes PL NOUN
der Hosenrock (PL die Hosenröcke) ◊ *a pair of culottes* ein Hosenrock

culture NOUN
die Kultur

cunning ADJECTIVE
schlau

cup NOUN

[1] die Tasse ◊ *a china cup* eine Porzellantasse ◊ *a cup of coffee* eine Tasse Kaffee

[2] (*trophy*)

der Pokal (PL die Pokale)

cupboard NOUN
der Schrank (PL die Schränke)

to **cure** VERB

> see also **cure** NOUN

heilen

cure NOUN

> see also **cure** VERB

das Mittel (PL die Mittel) ◊ *There is no simple cure for the common cold.* Es gibt kein einfaches Mittel gegen Schnupfen.

curious ADJECTIVE
neugierig

curl NOUN

> see also **curl** VERB

die Locke

to **curl** VERB

> see also **curl** NOUN

in Locken legen (*hair*)

curly ADJECTIVE
lockig ◊ *When I was younger my hair was curlier.* Als ich jünger war, waren meine Haare lockiger.

currant NOUN
die Korinthe (*dried fruit*)

currency NOUN
die Währung ◊ *foreign currency* ausländische Währung

current NOUN

> see also **current** ADJECTIVE

die Strömung ◊ *The current is very strong.* Die Strömung ist sehr stark.

current ADJECTIVE

> see also **current** NOUN

aktuell ◊ *the current situation* die aktuelle Lage

current account NOUN
das Girokonto (PL die Girokonten)

current affairs PL NOUN
die Tagespolitik SING

curriculum NOUN
der Lehrplan (PL die Lehrpläne)

curriculum vitae NOUN
der Lebenslauf (PL die Lebensläufe)

curry NOUN
das Curry (PL die Currys)

curse NOUN
der Fluch (*spell*) (PL die Flüche)

curtain NOUN
der Vorhang (PL die Vorhänge)

cushion NOUN
das Kissen (PL die Kissen)

custard NOUN
die Vanillesoße (*for pouring*)

custody NOUN
das Sorgerecht (*of child*) ◊ *He got custody of his son.* Er bekam das Sorgerecht für seinen Sohn.

C

♦ **to be remanded in custody** inhaftiert werden

custom NOUN
der Brauch (PL die Bräuche) ◊ *It's an old custom.* Es ist ein alter Brauch.

customer NOUN
der Kunde (GEN des Kunden, PL die Kunden)
die Kundin

customs PL NOUN
der Zoll (PL die Zölle)

customs officer NOUN
der Zollbeamte (GEN des Zollbeamten, PL die Zollbeamten)
die Zollbeamtin
◊ *a customs officer (man)* ein Zollbeamter

cut NOUN
see also **cut** VERB
1 die Schnittwunde ◊ *He's got a cut on his forehead.* Er hat eine Schnittwunde an der Stirn.
2 die Senkung (in price)
3 die Kürzung (in spending)
♦ **a cut and blow-dry** Schneiden und Föhnen

to **cut** VERB
see also **cut** NOUN
1 schneiden (IMPERFECT schnitt, PERFECT hat geschnitten) ◊ *I'll cut some bread.* Ich schneide Brot.
♦ **I cut my foot on a piece of glass.** Ich habe mir den Fuß an einer Glasscherbe verletzt.
♦ **to cut oneself** sich schneiden ◊ *Watch you don't cut yourself!* Pass auf, dass du dich nicht schneidest!
2 (price)
senken
3 (spending)
kürzen
♦ **to cut down (1)** (tree) fällen
♦ **to cut down (2)** einschränken ◊ *I'm trying to cut down on coffee and cigarettes.* Ich versuche, meinen Kaffee- und Zigarettenkonsum einzuschränken.
♦ **The electricity was cut off.** Der Strom wurde abgestellt.
♦ **to cut up** (vegetables, meat) klein schneiden

cutback NOUN
die Kürzung ◊ *Over the past year there have been severe cutbacks in public services.* In den letzten Jahren gab es starke Kürzungen bei den öffentlichen Ausgaben.

cute ADJECTIVE
niedlich

cutlery NOUN
das Besteck (PL die Bestecke)

CV NOUN
der Lebenslauf (PL die Lebensläufe)

cybercafé NOUN
das Internet-Café (PL die Internet-Cafés)

to **cycle** VERB
see also **cycle** NOUN
Rad fahren (PRESENT fährt Rad, IMPERFECT fuhr Rad, PERFECT ist Rad gefahren) ◊ *I like cycling.* Ich fahre gern Rad.
♦ **I cycle to school.** Ich fahre mit dem Rad zur Schule.

cycle NOUN
see also **cycle** VERB
das Fahrrad (PL die Fahrräder) ◊ *a cycle ride* eine Fahrradfahrt

cycling NOUN
das Radfahren ◊ *My hobby is cycling.* Radfahren ist mein Hobby.

cyclist NOUN
der Radfahrer (PL die Radfahrer)
die Radfahrerin

cylinder NOUN
der Zylinder (PL die Zylinder)

Cyprus NOUN
Zypern NEUT
♦ **from Cyprus** aus Zypern
♦ **in Cyprus** auf Zypern
♦ **to Cyprus** nach Zypern

Czech ADJECTIVE
see also **Czech** NOUN
tschechisch
♦ **the Czech Republic** die Tschechische Republik

Czech NOUN
see also **Czech** ADJECTIVE
1 (person)
der Tscheche (GEN des Tschechen, PL die Tschechen)
die Tschechin
2 (language)
das Tschechisch (GEN des Tschechischen)

D

dad NOUN
der <u>Papa</u> (PL die Papas) ◊ *his dad* sein
Papa ◊ *I'll ask Dad.* Ich werde Papa
fragen.

daddy NOUN
der <u>Papa</u> (PL die Papas) ◊ *my daddy* mein
Papa

daffodil NOUN
die <u>Osterglocke</u>

daft ADJECTIVE
<u>verrückt</u>

daily ADJECTIVE, ADVERB
<u>täglich</u> ◊ *It's part of my daily routine.* Es
gehört zu meiner täglichen Routine.
◊ *The pool is open daily from nine a.m.
to six p.m.* Das Schwimmbad ist täglich
von neun bis achtzehn Uhr geöffnet.

dairy NOUN
die <u>Molkerei</u> (*company*)

dairy products PL NOUN
die <u>Milchprodukte</u> NEUT PL

daisy NOUN
das <u>Gänseblümchen</u> (PL die
Gänseblümchen)

dam NOUN
der <u>Damm</u> (PL die Dämme)

damage NOUN
> see also **damage** VERB

der <u>Schaden</u> (PL die Schäden) ◊ *The
storm did a lot of damage.* Der Sturm hat
viel Schaden angerichtet.

to **damage** VERB
> see also **damage** NOUN

<u>beschädigen</u> (PERFECT hat beschädigt)

damn NOUN
> see also **damn** ADJECTIVE

♦ **I don't give a damn!** Das ist mir
scheißegal! (*informal*)
♦ **Damn!** Verdammt! (*informal*)

damn ADJECTIVE, ADVERB
> see also **damn** NOUN

♦ **It's a damn nuisance!** Es ist verdammt
ärgerlich! (*informal*)

damp ADJECTIVE
<u>feucht</u>

dance NOUN
> see also **dance** VERB

der <u>Tanz</u> (PL die Tänze) ◊ *The last dance
was a waltz.* Der letzte Tanz war ein
Walzer. ◊ *Are you going to the dance
tonight?* Gehst du heute Abend zum
Tanz?

to **dance** VERB
> see also **dance** NOUN

<u>tanzen</u>

dancer NOUN
der <u>Tänzer</u> (PL die Tänzer)
die <u>Tänzerin</u>

dancing NOUN
das <u>Tanzen</u>
♦ **to go dancing** tanzen gehen ◊ *Let's go
dancing!* Lass uns tanzen gehen!

dandruff NOUN
die <u>Schuppen</u> FEM PL

Dane NOUN
der <u>Däne</u> (GEN des Dänen, PL die Dänen)
die <u>Dänin</u>

danger NOUN
die <u>Gefahr</u>
♦ **in danger** in Gefahr ◊ *His life is in
danger.* Sein Leben ist in Gefahr.
♦ **I'm in danger of failing maths.** Es könnte
durchaus sein, dass ich in Mathe
durchfalle.

dangerous ADJECTIVE
<u>gefährlich</u>

Danish ADJECTIVE
> see also **Danish** NOUN

<u>dänisch</u>

Danish NOUN
> see also **Danish** ADJECTIVE

das <u>Dänisch</u> (*language*) (GEN des
Dänischen)

Danube NOUN
die <u>Donau</u>

to **dare** VERB
<u>sich trauen</u>
♦ **to dare to do something** sich trauen,
etwas zu tun ◊ *I didn't dare to tell my
parents.* Ich habe mich nicht getraut, es
meinen Eltern zu sagen.
♦ **I dare say it'll be okay.** Ich denke, dass
das in Ordnung ist.

daring ADJECTIVE
<u>mutig</u>

dark ADJECTIVE
> see also **dark** NOUN

<u>dunkel</u> ◊ *It's dark.* Es ist dunkel. ◊ *It's
getting dark.* Es wird dunkel. ◊ *She's got
dark hair.* Sie hat dunkle Haare. ◊ *a dark
green sweater* ein dunkelgrüner Pullover

dark NOUN
> see also **dark** ADJECTIVE

die <u>Dunkelheit</u> ◊ *after dark* nach
Einbruch der Dunkelheit
♦ **in the dark** im Dunkeln
♦ **I'm afraid of the dark.** Ich habe Angst im
Dunkeln.

darkness NOUN
die <u>Dunkelheit</u>
♦ **The room was in darkness.** Das Zimmer
war dunkel.

darling NOUN
der <u>Liebling</u> (PL die Lieblinge)
> *der Liebling* is also used for women.

◊ *Thank you, darling!* Danke, Liebling!

dart NOUN
der Pfeil (PL die Pfeile)
♦ **to play darts** Darts spielen

dash NOUN

> see also **dash** VERB

der Bindestrich (*punctuation mark*)

to **dash** VERB

> see also **dash** NOUN

[1] rennen (IMPERFECT rannte, PERFECT ist gerannt) ◊ *Everyone dashed to the window.* Alle rannten zum Fenster.
[2] sich beeilen (PERFECT hat sich beeilt) ◊ *I've got to dash!* Ich muss mich beeilen!

dashboard NOUN
das Armaturenbrett (PL die Armaturenbretter)

data PL NOUN
die Daten PL

database NOUN
die Datenbank (*on computer*) (PL die Datenbanken)

date NOUN
[1] das Datum (PL die Daten) ◊ *my date of birth* mein Geburtsdatum
♦ **What's the date today?** der Wievielte ist heute?
♦ **to have a date with somebody** mit jemandem eine Verabredung haben ◊ *She's got a date with Ian tonight.* Sie hat heute Abend eine Verabredung mit Ian.
♦ **out of date (1)** (*passport*) abgelaufen
♦ **out of date (2)** (*technology*) veraltet
♦ **out of date (3)** (*clothes*) altmodisch
[2] (*fruit*)
die Dattel .

daughter NOUN
die Tochter (PL die Töchter)

daughter-in-law NOUN
die Schwiegertochter (PL die Schwiegertöchter)

dawn NOUN
das Morgengrauen ◊ *at dawn* im Morgengrauen

day NOUN
der Tag (PL die Tage) ◊ *We stayed in Vienna for three days.* Wir sind drei Tage in Wien geblieben. ◊ *I stayed at home all day.* Ich war den ganzen Tag zu Hause.
♦ **every day** jeden Tag
♦ **during the day** tagsüber
♦ **the day before** der Tag davor ◊ *the day before my birthday* der Tag vor meinem Geburtstag
♦ **the day after** der Tag danach ◊ *the day after my birthday* der Tag nach meinem Geburtstag
♦ **the day before yesterday** vorgestern ◊ *He arrived the day before yesterday.* Er ist vorgestern angekommen.

♦ **the day after tomorrow** übermorgen ◊ *We're leaving the day after tomorrow.* Wir fahren übermorgen ab.

dead ADJECTIVE, ADVERB
[1] tot ◊ *He was already dead when the doctor came.* Er war schon tot, als der Arzt kam.
♦ **He was shot dead.** Er wurde erschossen.
[2] völlig (*totally*) ◊ *You're dead right!* Du hast völlig recht!
♦ **dead on time** ganz pünktlich ◊ *The train arrived dead on time.* Der Zug kam ganz pünktlich an.

dead end NOUN
die Sackgasse

deadline NOUN
der Termin (PL die Termine) ◊ *We'll never meet the deadline.* Den Termin schaffen wir nie.

deaf ADJECTIVE
taub

deafening ADJECTIVE
ohrenbetäubend

deal NOUN

> see also **deal** VERB

das Geschäft (PL die Geschäfte)
♦ **It's a deal!** Abgemacht!
♦ **a great deal** viel ◊ *a great deal of money* viel Geld

to **deal** VERB

> see also **deal** NOUN

geben (*cards*) (PRESENT gibt, IMPERFECT gab, PERFECT hat gegeben) ◊ *It's your turn to deal.* Du gibst!
♦ **to deal with something** sich um etwas kümmern ◊ *He promised to deal with it immediately.* Er versprach, sich sofort darum zu kümmern.

dealer NOUN
der Händler (PL die Händler)
die Händlerin
◊ *a drug dealer* ein Drogenhändler ◊ *an antique dealer* ein Antiquitätenhändler

dear ADJECTIVE
[1] lieb
♦ **Dear Mrs Sinclair (1)** Liebe Frau Sinclair
♦ **Dear Mrs Sinclair (2)** (*more formal*) Sehr geehrte Frau Sinclair
♦ **Dear Sir/Madam** (*in a circular*) Sehr geehrte Damen und Herren
[2] teuer (*expensive*)

death NOUN
der Tod (PL die Tode) ◊ *after her death* nach ihrem Tod ◊ *I was bored to death.* Ich habe mich zu Tode gelangweilt.

debate NOUN

> see also **debate** VERB

die Debatte

to **debate** VERB

> see also **debate** NOUN

debattieren (PERFECT hat debattiert) ◊ *We debated the issue of capital punishment.*

D

☞

Wir haben die Frage der Todesstrafe
debattiert.

debt NOUN
die <u>Schulden</u> FEM PL ◊ *He's got a lot of
debts.* Er hat viel Schulden.
♦**to be in debt** verschuldet sein

decade NOUN
das <u>Jahrzehnt</u> (PL die Jahrzehnte)

decaffeinated ADJECTIVE
<u>entkoffeiniert</u>

decay NOUN
♦**tooth decay** die Karies

to **deceive** VERB
<u>täuschen</u>

December NOUN
der <u>Dezember</u> ◊ *in December* im
Dezember

decent ADJECTIVE
<u>ordentlich</u> ◊ *a decent education* eine
ordentliche Ausbildung

to **decide** VERB
[1] <u>beschließen</u> (IMPERFECT beschloss,
PERFECT hat beschlossen) ◊ *I decided to
write to her.* Ich habe beschlossen, ihr zu
schreiben. ◊ *I decided not to go.* Ich habe
beschlossen, nicht hinzugehen.
[2] <u>sich entscheiden</u> (IMPERFECT entschied
sich, PERFECT hat sich entschieden) ◊ *I can't
decide.* Ich kann mich nicht entscheiden.
◊ *Haven't you decided yet?* Hast du dich
noch nicht entschieden?
♦**to decide on something** über etwas
entscheiden ◊ *We haven't decided on the
name yet.* Wir haben noch nicht über den
Namen entschieden.

decimal ADJECTIVE
<u>dezimal</u> ◊ *the decimal system* das
Dezimalsystem

decision NOUN
die <u>Entscheidung</u> ◊ *to make a decision*
eine Entscheidung treffen

decisive ADJECTIVE
<u>entschlossen</u> (*person*)

deck NOUN
[1] (*of ship*)
das <u>Deck</u> (PL die Decks) ◊ *on deck* an
Deck
[2] (*of cards*)
das <u>Spiel</u> (PL die Spiele)

deckchair NOUN
der <u>Liegestuhl</u> (PL die Liegestühle)

to **declare** VERB
<u>erklären</u> (PERFECT hat erklärt)

to **decline** VERB
[1] <u>ablehnen</u> (PERFECT hat abgelehnt) ◊ *He
declined to comment.* Er lehnte einen
Kommentar ab.
[2] <u>zurückgehen</u> (IMPERFECT ging zurück,
PERFECT ist zurückgegangen) ◊ *The birth
rate has declined by five per cent.* Die
Geburtenrate ist um fünf Prozent
zurückgegangen.

to **decorate** VERB

[1] <u>dekorieren</u> (PERFECT hat dekoriert) ◊ *I
decorated the cake with glacé cherries.*
Ich habe den Kuchen mit glasierten
Kirschen dekoriert.
[2] (*paint*)
<u>streichen</u> (IMPERFECT strich, PERFECT hat
gestrichen)
[3] (*wallpaper*)
<u>tapezieren</u> (PERFECT hat tapeziert)

decorations PLURAL NOUN
der <u>Schmuck</u> ◊ *Christmas decorations*
der Weihnachtsschmuck

decrease NOUN
see also **decrease** VERB
die <u>Abnahme</u> ◊ *a decrease in the
number of unemployed people* eine
Abnahme der Arbeitslosenzahl

to **decrease** VERB
see also **decrease** NOUN
<u>abnehmen</u> (PRESENT nimmt ab, IMPERFECT
nahm ab, PERFECT hat abgenommen)

dedicated ADJECTIVE
<u>engagiert</u> ◊ *a very dedicated teacher* ein
sehr engagierter Lehrer

to **deduct** VERB
<u>abziehen</u> (IMPERFECT zog ab, PERFECT hat
abgezogen)

deep ADJECTIVE
<u>tief</u> (*water, hole, cut*) ◊ *How deep is the
lake?* Wie tief ist der See? ◊ *a hole four
metres deep* ein vier Meter tiefes Loch
◊ *He's got a deep voice.* Er hat eine tiefe
Stimme.
♦**to take a deep breath** tief einatmen
♦**The snow was really deep.** Es lag sehr
viel Schnee.

deeply ADVERB
<u>zutiefst</u> (*depressed*)

deer NOUN
das <u>Reh</u> (PL die Rehe)

defeat NOUN
see also **defeat** VERB
die <u>Niederlage</u>

to **defeat** VERB
see also **defeat** NOUN
<u>besiegen</u> (PERFECT hat besiegt)

defect NOUN
der <u>Defekt</u> (PL die Defekte)

defence NOUN
die <u>Verteidigung</u>

to **defend** VERB
<u>verteidigen</u> (PERFECT hat verteidigt)

defender NOUN
der <u>Verteidiger</u> (PL die Verteidiger)
die <u>Verteidigerin</u>

defense NOUN US
die <u>Verteidigung</u>

to **define** VERB
<u>definieren</u> (PERFECT hat definiert)

definite ADJECTIVE
[1] <u>genau</u> ◊ *I haven't got any definite
plans.* Ich habe noch keine genauen
Pläne.

②eindeutig ◊ *It's a definite improvement.* Es ist eine eindeutige Verbesserung.

③sicher ◊ *Perhaps we'll go to Spain, but it's not definite.* Vielleicht fahren wir nach Spanien, aber es ist noch nicht sicher.

♦ **He was definite about it.** Er war sich sehr sicher.

definitely ADVERB
eindeutig ◊ *He's definitely the best player.* Er ist eindeutig der beste Spieler.

♦ **He's the best player. – Definitely!** Er ist der beste Spieler. – Absolut!

♦ **I definitely think he'll come.** Ich bin sicher, dass er kommt.

definition NOUN
die Definition

degree NOUN
①der Grad (PL die Grade) ◊ *a temperature of thirty degrees* eine Temperatur von dreißig Grad
②der Universitätsabschluss (GEN des Universitätsabschlusses, PL die Universitätsabschlüsse) ◊ *a degree in English* ein Universitätsabschluss in Englisch

to **delay** VERB
see also **delay** NOUN
verschieben (IMPERFECT verschob, PERFECT hat verschoben) ◊ *We decided to delay our departure.* Wir haben beschlossen, unsere Abreise zu verschieben.

♦ **to be delayed** Verspätung haben ◊ *Our flight was delayed.* Unser Flug hatte Verspätung.

delay NOUN
see also **delay** VERB
die Verzögerung

♦ **without delay** unverzüglich

to **delete** VERB
löschen (*on computer, tape*)

deliberate ADJECTIVE
absichtlich

deliberately ADVERB
absichtlich ◊ *She did it deliberately.* Sie hat es absichtlich getan.

delicate ADJECTIVE
①zierlich ◊ *She has very delicate hands.* Sie hat sehr zierliche Hände.
②zerbrechlich (*object*) ◊ *That vase is very delicate.* Die Vase ist sehr zerbrechlich.
③anfällig (*often ill*) ◊ *She's a very delicate child.* Sie ist ein sehr anfälliges Kind.
④heikel (*situation*) ◊ *The situation is rather delicate.* Die Lage ist ziemlich heikel.

delicatessen SING NOUN
das Feinkostgeschäft (PL die Feinkostgeschäfte)

delicious ADJECTIVE
köstlich

delight NOUN
die Freude

delighted ADJECTIVE
hocherfreut ◊ *He'll be delighted to see you.* Er wird hocherfreut sein, dich zu sehen.

delightful ADJECTIVE
wunderbar (*meal, evening*)

to **deliver** VERB
①austragen (PRESENT trägt aus, IMPERFECT trug aus, PERFECT hat ausgetraten) ◊ *I deliver newspapers.* Ich trage Zeitungen aus.
②(*mail*)
ausliefern (PERFECT hat ausgeliefert)

delivery NOUN
die Lieferung

to **demand** VERB
see also **demand** NOUN
fordern

demand NOUN
see also **demand** VERB
die Nachfrage (*for product*)

demanding ADJECTIVE
anspruchsvoll ◊ *It's a very demanding job.* Es ist eine sehr anspruchsvolle Arbeit.

demo NOUN
die Demo (*protest*) (PL die Demos)

democracy NOUN
die Demokratie

democratic ADJECTIVE
demokratisch

to **demolish** VERB
abreißen (*building*) (IMPERFECT riss ab, PERFECT hat abgerissen)

to **demonstrate** VERB
①(*show*)
vorführen (PERFECT hat vorgeführt) ◊ *She demonstrated the technique.* Sie hat die Methode vorgeführt.
②(*protest*)
demonstrieren (PERFECT hat demonstriert) ◊ *to demonstrate against something* gegen etwas demonstrieren

demonstration NOUN
①die Vorführung (*of method, technique*)
②die Demonstration (*protest*)

demonstrator NOUN
(*protester*)
der Demonstrant (GEN des Demonstranten, PL die Demonstranten)
die Demonstrantin

denim NOUN
der Jeansstoff

♦ **a denim jacket** eine Jeansjacke

denims PL NOUN
die Jeans FEM PL (*jeans*) ◊ *a pair of denims* eine Jeans

D

Denmark NOUN
Dänemark NEUT
♦ **from Denmark** aus Dänemark
♦ **to Denmark** nach Dänemark

dense ADJECTIVE
1 dicht (*crowd, fog*)
2 dick (*smoke*)
♦ **He's so dense!** Er ist furchtbar blöd!
(*informal*)

dent NOUN
see also **dent** VERB
die Delle

to **dent** VERB
see also **dent** NOUN
eindellen (PERFECT hat eingedellt)

dental ADJECTIVE
♦ **dental treatment** die Zahnbehandlung
♦ **dental floss** die Zahnseide
♦ **dental surgeon** der Zahnarzt

dentist NOUN
der Zahnarzt (PL die Zahnärzte)
die Zahnärztin
◊ *Catherine is a dentist.* Catherine ist
Zahnärztin.

to **deny** VERB
leugnen ◊ *She denied everything.* Sie
hat alles geleugnet.

deodorant NOUN
das Deo (PL die Deos)

to **depart** VERB
1 (*person*)
abreisen (PERFECT ist abgereist)
2 (*train*)
abfahren (PRESENT fährt ab, IMPERFECT fuhr
ab, PERFECT ist abgefahren)

department NOUN
1 (*in shop*)
die Abteilung ◊ *the shoe department* die
Schuhabteilung
2 (*university, school*)
der Fachbereich (PL die Fachbereiche)
◊ *the English department* der
Fachbereich Englisch

department store NOUN
das Kaufhaus (GEN des Kaufhauses, PL die
Kaufhäuser)

departure NOUN
die Abfahrt

departure lounge NOUN
die Abflughalle

to **depend** VERB
♦ **to depend on** abhängen von ◊ *The price
depends on the quality.* Der Preis hängt
von der Qualität ab.
♦ **depending on the weather** je nach
Wetterlage
♦ **It depends.** Das kommt drauf an.

to **deport** VERB
abschieben (IMPERFECT schob ab, PERFECT hat
abgeschoben)

deposit NOUN
1 (*part payment*)

die Anzahlung ◊ *You have to pay a
deposit when you book.* Sie müssen eine
Anzahlung leisten, wenn Sie buchen.
2 (*when hiring something*)
die Kaution ◊ *You get the deposit back
when you return the bike.* Sie bekommen
die Kaution zurück, wenn Sie das Fahrrad
zurückbringen.
3 (*on bottle*)
das Pfand (PL die Pfänder)

depressed ADJECTIVE
deprimiert ◊ *I'm feeling depressed.* Ich
bin deprimiert.

depressing ADJECTIVE
deprimierend

depth NOUN
die Tiefe

deputy head NOUN
der Konrektor (PL die Konrektoren)
die Konrektorin

to **descend** VERB
hinuntersteigen (IMPERFECT stieg hinunter,
PERFECT ist hinuntergestiegen)

to **describe** VERB
beschreiben (IMPERFECT beschrieb, PERFECT
hat beschrieben)

description NOUN
die Beschreibung

desert NOUN
die Wüste

desert island NOUN
die einsame Insel

to **deserve** VERB
verdienen (PERFECT hat verdient) ◊ *He
deserves a holiday.* Er hat einen Urlaub
verdient.
♦ **She deserves to be punished.** Sie gehört
bestraft.

design NOUN
see also **design** VERB
1 das Design (PL die Designs) ◊ *fashion
design* das Modedesign
♦ **It's a completely new design.** Es ist eine
völlig neue Konstruktion.
2 (*pattern*)
das Muster (PL die Muster) ◊ *a geometric
design* ein geometrisches Muster

to **design** VERB
see also **design** NOUN
entwerfen (*clothes, furniture*) (PRESENT
entwirft, IMPERFECT entwarf, PERFECT hat
entworfen)

designer NOUN
(*of clothes*)
der Modeschöpfer (PL die
Modeschöpfer)
die Modeschöpferin
♦ **designer clothes** die Designerkleidung
SING

desire NOUN
see also **desire** VERB
das Verlangen (PL die Verlangen)

to **desire** VERB

> see also **desire** NOUN

wünschen ◊ *if desired* falls gewünscht

desk NOUN

[1] (*in office*)
der Schreibtisch (PL die Schreibtische)
[2] (*in school*)
die Bank (PL die Bänke)
[3] (*in hotel*)
die Rezeption
[4] (*at airport*)
der Schalter (PL die Schalter)

despair NOUN

die Verzweiflung
♦ **I was in despair.** Ich war verzweifelt.

desperate ADJECTIVE

verzweifelt ◊ *a desperate situation* eine
verzweifelte Lage
♦ **to get desperate** fast verzweifeln ◊ *I was
getting desperate.* Ich bin fast
verzweifelt.
♦ **I'm desperate for a drink.** Ich brauche
dringend etwas zu trinken.

desperately ADVERB

[1] äußerst ◊ *We're desperately worried.*
Wir sind äußerst besorgt.
[2] verzweifelt ◊ *He was desperately
trying to persuade her.* Er versuchte
verzweifelt, sie zu überzeugen.

to **despise** VERB

verachten (PERFECT hat verachtet)

despite PREPOSITION

trotz ◊ *despite the bad weather* trotz des
schlechten Wetters

dessert NOUN

der Nachtisch ◊ *for dessert* zum
Nachtisch

destination NOUN

das Ziel (PL die Ziele)

to **destroy** VERB

zerstören (PERFECT hat zerstört)

destruction NOUN

die Zerstörung

detached house NOUN

das Einzelhaus (GEN des Einzelhauses, PL
die Einzelhäuser)

detail NOUN

das Detail (PL die Details)
♦ **in detail** ganz genau

detailed ADJECTIVE

ausführlich

detective NOUN

der Detektiv (PL die Detektive)
die Detektivin
♦ **a private detective** ein Privatdetektiv
♦ **a detective story** eine Detektivgeschichte

detention NOUN

♦ **to get a detention** nachsitzen müssen
◊ *He got a detention for smoking.* Er
musste nachsitzen, weil er geraucht
hatte.

detergent NOUN

das Waschmittel (PL die Waschmittel)

determined ADJECTIVE

entschlossen
♦ **to be determined to do something**
entschlossen sein, etwas zu tun ◊ *She's
determined to marry him.* Sie ist
entschlossen, ihn zu heiraten.

detour NOUN

der Umweg (PL die Umwege)

devaluation NOUN

die Abwertung

devastated ADJECTIVE

am Boden zerstört ◊ *I was devastated.*
Ich war am Boden zerstört.

devastating ADJECTIVE

[1] erschütternd (*upsetting*)
[2] verheerend (*flood, storm*)

to **develop** VERB

[1] entwickeln (PERFECT hat entwickelt) ◊ *to
get a film developed* einen Film
entwickeln lassen
[2] sich entwickeln (PERFECT hat sich
entwickelt) ◊ *Girls develop faster than
boys.* Mädchen entwickeln sich schneller
als Jungen. ◊ *The argument developed
into a fight.* Der Streit entwickelte sich zu
einer Schlägerei.
♦ **developing country** das
Entwicklungsland

development NOUN

die Entwicklung ◊ *the latest
developments* die neuesten
Entwicklungen

device NOUN

das Gerät

devil NOUN

der Teufel (PL die Teufel) ◊ *Poor devil!*
Armer Teufel!

to **devise** VERB

sich ausdenken (IMPERFECT dachte sich
aus, PERFECT hat sich ausgedacht) ◊ *We have
devised a way to help him.* Wir haben uns
etwas ausgedacht, um ihm zu helfen.

devoted ADJECTIVE

♦ **He's completely devoted to her.** Er liebt
sie über alles.

diabetes NOUN

der Zucker ◊ *She's got diabetes.* Sie hat
Zucker.

diabetic NOUN

der Zuckerkranke (GEN des
Zuckerkranken, PL die Zuckerkranken)
die Zuckerkranke (GEN der
Zuckerkranken)
♦ **I'm a diabetic.** Ich habe Zucker.

diagonal ADJECTIVE

diagonal

diagram NOUN

das Diagramm (PL die Diagramme)

to **dial** VERB

wählen (*number*)
♦ **He dialled the wrong number.** Er hat sich
verwählt.

dialling tone NOUN

D

☞

das Amtszeichen (PL die Amtszeichen)

dialogue NOUN
der Dialog (PL die Dialoge)

diamond NOUN
der Diamant (GEN des Diamanten, PL die Diamanten) ◊ *a diamond ring* ein Diamantring MASC
◆**diamonds** (*in cards*) das Karo ◊ *the ace of diamonds* das Karoass

diaper NOUN US
die Windel

diarrhoea NOUN
der Durchfall (PL die Durchfälle) ◊ *I've got diarrhoea.* Ich habe Durchfall.

diary NOUN
1 der Kalender (PL die Kalender) ◊ *I've got her phone number in my diary.* Ich habe ihre Telefonnummer in meinem Kalender.
2 das Tagebuch (PL die Tagebücher) ◊ *I keep a diary.* Ich führe ein Tagebuch.

dice NOUN
der Würfel (PL die Würfel)

dictation NOUN
das Diktat (PL die Diktate)

dictator NOUN
der Diktator (PL die Diktatoren)

dictionary NOUN
das Wörterbuch (PL die Wörterbücher)

did VERB *see* **do**

to **die** VERB
sterben (PRESENT stirbt, IMPERFECT starb, PERFECT ist gestorben) ◊ *She's dying.* Sie stirbt. ◊ *He died last year.* Er ist letztes Jahr gestorben.
◆**to be dying to do something** es kaum erwarten können, etwas zu tun ◊ *I'm dying to see you.* Ich kann es kaum erwarten, dich zu sehen.

to **die down** VERB
nachlassen (PRESENT lässt nach, IMPERFECT ließ nach, PERFECT hat nachgelassen) ◊ *The wind is dying down.* Der Wind lässt nach.

diesel NOUN
1 (*fuel*)
der Diesel ◊ *Thirty litres of diesel, please.* Dreißig Liter Diesel, bitte.
2 (*car*)
der Diesel (PL die Diesel) ◊ *Our car's a diesel.* Unser Auto ist ein Diesel.

diet NOUN
see also **diet** VERB
1 die Nahrung ◊ *a healthy diet* gesunde Nahrung
2 die Diät (*for slimming*)
◆**I'm on a diet.** Ich mache eine Diät.

to **diet** VERB
see also **diet** NOUN
eine Diät machen ◊ *I've been dieting for two months.* Ich mache seit zwei Monaten eine Diät.

difference NOUN

der Unterschied (PL die Unterschiede)
◊ *There's not much difference in age between us.* Es besteht kein großer Altersunterschied zwischen uns.
◆**It makes no difference.** Das ist egal.

different ADJECTIVE
verschieden ◊ *We are very different.* Wir sind sehr verschieden.
◆**Berlin is different from London.** Berlin ist anders als London.

difficult ADJECTIVE
schwierig ◊ *It's difficult to choose.* Es ist schwierig, sich zu entscheiden.

difficulty NOUN
die Schwierigkeit ◊ *to have difficulty doing something* Schwierigkeiten haben, etwas zu tun
◆**without difficulty** problemlos

to **dig** VERB
1 (*hole*)
graben (PRESENT gräbt, IMPERFECT grub, PERFECT hat gegraben)
2 (*garden*)
umgraben (PERFECT hat umgegraben)
◆**to dig something up** etwas ausgraben

digestion NOUN
die Verdauung

digger NOUN
der Bagger (PL die Bagger)

digital ADJECTIVE
digital ◊ *the digital revolution* die digitale Revolution
◆**a digital camera** eine Digitalkamera
◆**a digital watch** eine Digitaluhr
◆**digital TV** das Digitalfernsehen

dim ADJECTIVE
1 schwach (*light*)
2 beschränkt (*stupid*)

dimension NOUN
das Maß (*measurement*) (GEN des Maßes, PL die Maße)

to **diminish** VERB
abnehmen (PRESENT nimmt ab, IMPERFECT nahm ab, PERFECT hat abgenommen)

din NOUN
der Krach (PL die Kräche)

diner NOUN US
die Gaststätte

dinghy NOUN
◆**a rubber dinghy** ein Gummiboot NEUT
◆**a sailing dinghy** ein Segelboot NEUT

dining car NOUN
der Speisewagen (PL die Speisewagen)

dining room NOUN
das Esszimmer (PL die Esszimmer)

dinner NOUN
1 (*at midday*)
das Mittagessen (PL die Mittagessen)
2 (*in the evening*)
das Abendessen (PL die Abendessen)

dinner jacket NOUN
die Smokingjacke

dinner party NOUN

die Abendgesellschaft
♦ **We're having a dinner party on Saturday.** Wir haben am Samstag Leute zum Essen eingeladen.

dinner time NOUN
die Essenszeit

dinosaur NOUN
der Dinosaurier (PL die Dinosaurier)

dip NOUN
see also **dip** VERB
der Dip (PL die Dips) ◊ *a spicy dip* ein pikanter Dip
♦ **to go for a dip** kurz mal ins Wasser gehen

to **dip** VERB
see also **dip** NOUN
1 tauchen ◊ *She dipped her hand in the water.* Sie tauchte ihre Hand ins Wasser.
2 tunken ◊ *He dipped a biscuit into his tea.* Er tunkte einen Keks in seinen Tee.

diploma NOUN
das Diplom (PL die Diplome)
♦ **She has a diploma in social work.** Sie hat Sozialarbeiterin gelernt.

diplomat NOUN
der Diplomat (GEN des Diplomaten, PL die Diplomaten)
die Diplomatin

diplomatic ADJECTIVE
diplomatisch

direct ADJECTIVE, ADVERB
see also **direct** VERB
direkt ◊ *the most direct route* der direkteste Weg ◊ *You can't fly to Stuttgart direct from Glasgow.* Sie können von Glasgow nicht direkt nach Stuttgart fliegen.

to **direct** VERB
see also **direct** ADJECTIVE
Regie führen bei (*film, play*) ◊ *Who directed the film?* Wer hat bei dem Film Regie geführt?

direction NOUN
die Richtung ◊ *We're going in the wrong direction.* Wir fahren in die falsche Richtung.
♦ **to ask somebody for directions** jemanden nach dem Weg fragen

director NOUN
1 (*of company*)
der Direktor (PL die Direktoren)
die Direktorin
2 (*of play, film*)
der Regisseur (PL die Regisseure)
die Regisseurin
3 (*of programme*)
der Leiter (PL die Leiter)
die Leiterin

directory NOUN
1 das Verzeichnis (GEN des Verzeichnisses, PL die Verzeichnisse) ◊ *file directory* das Dateiverzeichnis

2 (*telephone book*)
das Telefonbuch (PL die Telefonbücher)

dirt NOUN
der Schmutz

dirty ADJECTIVE
schmutzig ◊ *to get dirty* sich schmutzig machen ◊ *to get something dirty* etwas schmutzig machen ◊ *a dirty joke* ein schmutziger Witz

disabled ADJECTIVE
behindert
♦ **the disabled** die Behinderten MASC PL

disadvantage NOUN
der Nachteil (PL die Nachteile)

to **disagree** VERB
♦ **We always disagree.** Wir sind nie einer Meinung.
♦ **I disagree!** Ich bin anderer Meinung.
♦ **He disagreed with me.** Er war anderer Meinung als ich.

disagreement NOUN
die Meinungsverschiedenheit

to **disappear** VERB
verschwinden (IMPERFECT verschwand, PERFECT ist verschwunden)

disappearance NOUN
das Verschwinden

disappointed ADJECTIVE
enttäuscht

disappointing ADJECTIVE
enttäuschend

disappointment NOUN
die Enttäuschung

disaster NOUN
die Katastrophe

disastrous ADJECTIVE
katastrophal

disc NOUN
die Platte

discipline NOUN
die Disziplin

disc jockey NOUN
der Diskjockey (PL die Diskjockeys)

disco NOUN
die Disco (PL die Discos) ◊ *There's a disco at the school tonight.* Heute Abend gibt es in der Schule eine Disco.

to **disconnect** VERB
1 (*electrical equipment*)
ausstecken (PERFECT hat ausgesteckt)
2 (*telephone, water supply*)
abstellen (PERFECT hat abgestellt)

discount NOUN
der Rabatt (PL die Rabatte) ◊ *a discount of twenty per cent* zwanzig Prozent Rabatt
♦ **a discount for students** eine Studentenermäßigung

to **discourage** VERB
entmutigen (PERFECT hat entmutigt)
♦ **to get discouraged** sich entmutigen lassen ◊ *Don't get discouraged!* Lass dich nicht entmutigen!

D

to **discover** VERB
entdecken (PERFECT hat entdeckt)
discovery NOUN
die Entdeckung
discrimination NOUN
die Diskriminierung ◊ *racial
discrimination* die
Rassendiskriminierung
to **discuss** VERB
[1] besprechen (PRESENT bespricht, IMPERFECT
besprach, PERFECT hat besprochen) ◊ *I'll
discuss it with my parents.* Ich werde es
mit meinen Eltern besprechen.
[2] (*topic*)
diskutieren über +ACC (PERFECT hat
diskutiert) ◊ *We discussed the problem
of pollution.* Wir haben über das Problem
der Umweltverschmutzung diskutiert.
discussion NOUN
die Diskussion
disease NOUN
die Krankheit
disgraceful ADJECTIVE
schändlich
to **disguise** VERB
verkleiden (PERFECT hat verkleidet) ◊ *He
was disguised as a policeman.* Er war als
Polizist verkleidet.
disgusted ADJECTIVE
angewidert ◊ *I was absolutely
disgusted.* Ich war total angewidert.
disgusting ADJECTIVE
[1] widerlich (*food, smell*) ◊ *It looks
disgusting.* Es sieht widerlich aus.
[2] abscheulich (*disgraceful*) ◊ *That's
disgusting!* Das ist abscheulich!
dish NOUN
[1] die Schüssel ◊ *a china dish* eine
Porzellanschüssel
♦ **the dishes** das Geschirr SING
♦ **to do the dishes** abwaschen ◊ *He never
does the dishes.* Er wäscht nie ab.
[2] (*food*)
das Gericht (PL die Gerichte) ◊ *a
vegetarian dish* ein vegetarisches
Gericht
dishonest ADJECTIVE
unehrlich
dish soap NOUN US
das Spülmittel (PL die Spülmittel)
dish towel NOUN US
das Geschirrtuch (PL die Geschirrtücher)
dishwasher NOUN
die Geschirrspülmaschine
disinfectant NOUN
das Desinfektionsmittel (PL die
Desinfektionsmittel)
disk NOUN
die Platte
♦ **the hard disk** die Festplatte
♦ **a floppy disk** eine Diskette
diskette NOUN
die Diskette

to **dislike** VERB
see also **dislike** NOUN
nicht mögen (PRESENT mag nicht, IMPERFECT
mochte nicht, PERFECT hat nicht gemocht)
◊ *I've always disliked cabbage.* Kohl
habe ich noch nie gemocht.
dislike NOUN
see also **dislike** VERB
♦ **my likes and dislikes** was ich mag und
nicht mag
dismal ADJECTIVE
kläglich ◊ *a dismal failure* ein kläglicher
Fehlschlag
to **dismiss** VERB
entlassen (*employee*) (PRESENT entlässt,
IMPERFECT entließ, PERFECT hat
entlassen)
disobedient ADJECTIVE
ungehorsam
display NOUN
see also **display** VERB
die Auslage (*of goods*)
♦ **to be on display** ausgestellt sein ◊ *Her
best paintings were on display.* Ihre
besten Bilder waren ausgestellt.
♦ **a firework display** ein Feuerwerk NEUT
to **display** VERB
see also **display** NOUN
[1] zeigen ◊ *She proudly displayed her
medal.* Sie zeigte stolz ihre Medaille.
[2] (*in shop window*)
ausstellen (PERFECT hat ausgestellt) ◊ *The
fruit displayed in the shop window ...* Das
Obst, das im Schaufenster ausgestellt
war ...
disposable ADJECTIVE
zum Wegwerfen
♦ **disposable nappies** die Wegwerfwindeln
FEM PL
to **disqualify** VERB
disqualifizieren (PERFECT hat
disqualifiziert)
♦ **to be disqualified** disqualifiziert werden
◊ *He was disqualified.* Er wurde
disqualifiziert.
to **disrupt** VERB
[1] stören ◊ *Protesters disrupted the
meeting.* Protestierende haben die
Versammlung gestört.
[2] (*service*)
unterbrechen (PRESENT unterbricht,
IMPERFECT unterbrach, PERFECT hat
unterbrochen) ◊ *Train services are being
disrupted by the strike.* Der Zugverkehr
wird vom Streik unterbrochen.
dissatisfied ADJECTIVE
unzufrieden ◊ *We were dissatisfied with
the service.* Wir waren mit dem Service
unzufrieden.
to **dissolve** VERB
[1] auflösen (PERFECT hat aufgelöst) ◊ *We
dissolved the crystals in an acid solution.*

Wir lösten die Kristalle in einer
Säurelösung auf.
[2] sich auflösen ◊ *Sugar dissolves
quickly in hot tea.* Zucker löst sich in
heißem Tee schnell auf.

distance NOUN
die Entfernung ◊ *a distance of forty
kilometres* eine Entfernung von vierzig
Kilometern
♦ **It's within walking distance.** Man kann
zu Fuß hingehen.
♦ **in the distance** in der Ferne

distant ADJECTIVE
weit ◊ *in the distant future* in weiter
Zukunft

distillery NOUN
die Brennerei ◊ *a whisky distillery* eine
Whiskybrennerei

distinction NOUN
[1] die Unterscheidung ◊ *to make a
distinction between ...* unterscheiden
zwischen ...
[2] die Auszeichnung ◊ *I got a distinction
in my piano exam.* Ich habe meine
Klavierprüfung mit Auszeichnung
bestanden.

distinctive ADJECTIVE
auffällig

to **distract** VERB
ablenken (PERFECT hat abgelenkt)

to **distribute** VERB
verteilen (PERFECT hat verteilt)

district NOUN
[1] (*of town*)
das Viertel (PL die Viertel)
[2] (*of country*)
die Gegend

to **disturb** VERB
stören
♦ **I'm sorry to disturb you.** Verzeihen Sie
die Störung.

ditch NOUN
see also **ditch** VERB
der Graben (PL die Gräben)

to **ditch** VERB
see also **ditch** NOUN
Schluss machen mit (*informal*) ◊ *She's
just ditched her boyfriend.* Sie hat gerade
mit ihrem Freund Schluss gemacht.

dive NOUN
see also **dive** VERB
der Kopfsprung (PL die Kopfsprünge)

to **dive** VERB
see also **dive** NOUN
[1] tauchen (*under water*) ◊ *They are
diving for pearls.* Sie tauchen nach
Perlen.
[2] einen Kopfsprung machen (*into
water*) ◊ *She dived into the water.* Sie
machte einen Kopfsprung ins Wasser.

diver NOUN
(*with breathing apparatus*)
der Taucher (PL die Taucher)

die Taucherin

diversion NOUN
die Umleitung (*for traffic*)

to **divide** VERB
[1] teilen ◊ *Divide the pastry in half.*
Teilen Sie den Teig in zwei Teile.
◊ *Twelve divided by three is four.* Zwölf
geteilt durch drei macht vier.
[2] sich aufteilen (PERFECT hat sich
aufgeteilt) ◊ *We divided into two groups.*
Wir haben uns in zwei Gruppen
aufgeteilt.

diving NOUN
[1] das Tauchen (*under water*)
[2] das Springen (*into water*)
♦ **diving board** das Sprungbrett

division NOUN
[1] das Teilen ◊ *I'm not very good at
division.* Im Teilen bin ich nicht sehr gut.
♦ **the division of labour** die Arbeitsteilung
[2] (*in football*)
die Liga (PL die Ligen)

divorce NOUN
die Scheidung

divorced ADJECTIVE
geschieden ◊ *My parents are divorced.*
Meine Eltern sind geschieden.

DIY NOUN (= *do-it-yourself*)
das Heimwerken
♦ **to do DIY** Heimwerker sein
♦ **a DIY shop** ein Geschäft für Heimwerker
♦ **DIY superstore** der Baumarkt

dizzy ADJECTIVE
♦ **I feel dizzy.** Mir ist schwindlig.

DJ NOUN (= *disc jockey*)
der Diskjockey (PL die Diskjockeys)

to **do** VERB
[1] machen ◊ *What are you doing this
evening?* Was macht ihr heute Abend?
◊ *I haven't done my homework.* Ich habe
meine Hausaufgaben noch nicht
gemacht. ◊ *She did it by herself.* Sie hat
es allein gemacht.
[2] tun (IMPERFECT tat, PERFECT hat getan)
◊ *What shall I do?* Was soll ich tun? ◊ *I'll
do my best.* Ich werde mein Bestes tun.
◊ *I'll tell you what to do.* Ich sage dir, was
du tun sollst.
*In combination with certain nouns and
verbs do is not translated.*
◊ *I do a lot of cycling.* Ich fahre viel Rad.
◊ *She was doing her knitting.* Sie strickte.
◊ *to do the ironing* bügeln
♦ **to do well** erfolgreich sein ◊ *The firm is
doing well.* Die Firma ist sehr erfolgreich.
♦ **She's doing well at school.** Sie ist gut in
der Schule.
[3] (*be enough*)
reichen ◊ *It's not very good, but it'll do.*
Es ist nicht besonders gut, aber es wird
reichen. ◊ *That'll do, thanks.* Danke, das
reicht.

D

☞

In English do is used to make questions. In German, questions are expressed by reversing the order of verb and subject.

◊ *Do you like German food?* Magst du deutsches Essen? ◊ *Where does he live?* Wo wohnt er? ◊ *Do you speak English?* Sprechen Sie Englisch? ◊ *What do you do in your free time?* Was machen Sie in Ihrer Freizeit? ◊ *Where did you go for your holidays?* Wohin seid ihr in den Ferien gefahren?

Use nicht in negative sentences for don't.

◊ *I don't understand.* Ich verstehe nicht. ◊ *Why didn't you come?* Warum bist du nicht gekommen?

do is not translated when it is used in place of another verb.

◊ *I hate maths. – So do I.* Ich hasse Mathe. – Ich auch. ◊ *I didn't like the film. – Neither did I.* Ich mochte den Film nicht. – Ich auch nicht. ◊ *Do you like horses? – No, I don't.* Magst du Pferde? – Nein.

Questions like "doesn't it?" don't exist in German.

◊ *The bus stops at the youth hostel, doesn't it?* Der Bus hält an der Jugendherberge, nicht wahr? ◊ *You go swimming on Fridays, don't you?* Du gehst freitags schwimmen, nicht wahr?

♦ **How do you do?** Guten Tag!

♦ **to do up (1)** (*shoes, shirt, cardigan*) zumachen ◊ *Do up your shoes!* Mach deine Schuhe zu!

♦ **to do up (2)** (*renovate*) renovieren ◊ *They're doing up an old cottage.* Sie renovieren ein altes Haus.

♦ **I could do with a holiday.** Ich könnte einen Urlaub gebrauchen.

♦ **to do without** ohne etwas auskommen ◊ *I couldn't do without my computer.* Ich käme nicht ohne meinen Computer aus.

dock NOUN
das <u>Dock</u> (*for ships*) (PL die Docks)

doctor NOUN
der <u>Arzt</u> (PL die Ärzte)
die <u>Ärztin</u>
◊ *She's a doctor.* Sie ist Ärztin. ◊ *She'd like to be a doctor.* Sie möchte gerne Ärztin werden.

document NOUN
das <u>Dokument</u> (PL die Dokumente)

documentary NOUN
der <u>Dokumentarfilm</u> (PL die Dokumentarfilme)

to **dodge** VERB
ausweichen (*attacker*) (IMPERFECT wich aus, PERFECT ist ausgewichen) ◊ *to dodge something* einer Sache ausweichen

Dodgems Ⓡ PL NOUN

der <u>Autoskooter</u> SING (PL die Autoskooter)
◊ *to go on the Dodgems* Autoskooter fahren

does VERB *see* do

doesn't = does not

dog NOUN
der <u>Hund</u> (PL die Hunde) ◊ *Have you got a dog?* Hast du einen Hund?

do-it-yourself NOUN
das <u>Heimwerken</u>

dole NOUN
die <u>Arbeitslosenunterstützung</u>
♦ **to be on the dole** stempeln gehen ◊ *A lot of people are on the dole.* Viele Menschen gehen stempeln.
♦ **to go on the dole** sich arbeitslos melden

doll NOUN
die <u>Puppe</u>

dollar NOUN
der <u>Dollar</u> (PL die Dollars *or* Dollar)
When talking about amounts of money use the plural form Dollar.
◊ *That costs fifty dollars.* Das kostet fünfzig Dollar.

dolphin NOUN
der <u>Delfin</u> (PL die Delfine)

domestic ADJECTIVE
♦ **a domestic flight** ein Inlandsflug MASC

dominoes SING NOUN
♦ **to have a game of dominoes** Domino spielen

to **donate** VERB
spenden

done VERB *see* do

donkey NOUN
der <u>Esel</u> (PL die Esel)

donor NOUN
der <u>Spender</u> (PL die Spender)
die <u>Spenderin</u>

don't = do not

door NOUN
die <u>Tür</u>

doorbell NOUN
die <u>Klingel</u>
♦ **to ring the doorbell** klingeln
♦ **Suddenly the doorbell rang.** Es klingelte plötzlich.

doorman NOUN
der <u>Portier</u> (PL die Portiers)

doorstep NOUN
die <u>Eingangsstufe</u>

dormitory NOUN
der <u>Schlafsaal</u> (PL die Schlafsäle)

dose NOUN
die <u>Dosis</u> (PL die Dosen)

dosh NOUN
die <u>Kohle</u> (*informal: money*)

dot NOUN
(*on letter "i", in E-mail address*)
der <u>Punkt</u> (PL die Punkte)

♦ on the dot genau ◊ *He arrived at nine o'clock on the dot.* Er kam genau um neun Uhr.

to **double** VERB
see also **double** ADJECTIVE
sich verdoppeln (PERFECT hat sich verdoppelt) ◊ *The number of attacks has doubled.* Die Zahl der Überfälle hat sich verdoppelt.

double ADJECTIVE, ADVERB
see also **double** VERB
doppelt ◊ *a double helping* eine doppelte Portion
♦ to cost double doppelt so viel kosten ◊ *First-class tickets cost double.* Fahrscheine erster Klasse kosten doppelt so viel.
♦ a double bed ein Doppelbett NEUT
♦ a double room ein Doppelzimmer NEUT
♦ a double-decker bus ein Doppeldeckerbus MASC

double bass NOUN
der Kontrabass (GEN des Kontrabasses, PL die Kontrabässe) ◊ *I play the double bass.* Ich spiele Kontrabass.

to **double-click** VERB
doppelklicken (*computer*) (PERFECT hat doppelgeklickt)

double glazing NOUN
das Doppelfenster (PL die Doppelfenster)

doubles PL NOUN
das Doppel (*in tennis*) (PL die Doppel) ◊ *to play mixed doubles* gemischtes Doppel spielen

doubt NOUN
see also **doubt** VERB
der Zweifel (PL die Zweifel) ◊ *I have my doubts.* Ich habe meine Zweifel.

to **doubt** VERB
see also **doubt** NOUN
bezweifeln (PERFECT hat bezweifelt) ◊ *I doubt it.* Das bezweifle ich.
♦ to doubt that bezweifeln, dass ◊ *I doubt he'll agree.* Ich bezweifle, dass er zustimmt.

doubtful ADJECTIVE
♦ to be doubtful about doing something nicht wissen, ob man etwas tun soll ◊ *I'm doubtful about going by myself.* Ich weiß nicht, ob ich allein gehen soll.
♦ It's doubtful. Es ist fraglich.
♦ You sound doubtful. Du scheinst nicht sicher zu sein.

dough NOUN
der Teig (PL die Teige)

doughnut NOUN
der Berliner (PL die Berliner) ◊ *a jam doughnut* ein gefüllter Berliner

Dover NOUN
Dover NEUT ◊ *We went from Dover to Boulogne.* Wir sind von Dover nach Boulogne gefahren.

down ADVERB, ADJECTIVE, PREPOSITION

[1] unten (*below*) ◊ *His office is down on the first floor.* Sein Büro ist unten im ersten Stock. ◊ *It's down there.* Es ist da unten.
[2] auf den Boden (*to the ground*) ◊ *He threw down his racket.* Er warf seinen Schläger auf den Boden.
♦ They live just down the road. Sie wohnen etwas weiter unten.
♦ to come down herunterkommen ◊ *Come down here!* Komm herunter!
♦ to go down hinuntergehen ◊ *They went down into the cellar.* Sie gingen in den Keller hinunter.
♦ to sit down sich hinsetzen ◊ *Sit down!* Setz dich hin!
♦ to feel down niedergeschlagen sein ◊ *I'm feeling a bit down.* Ich bin etwas niedergeschlagen.
♦ The computer's down. Der Computer ist abgestürzt.

to **download** VERB
runterladen (*computer*) (PRESENT lädt runter, IMPERFECT lud runter, PERFECT hat runtergeladen) ◊ *to download a file* eine Datei runterladen

downpour NOUN
der Regenguss (GEN des Regengusses, PL die Regengüsse) ◊ *a sudden downpour* ein plötzlicher Regenguss

downstairs ADVERB, ADJECTIVE
[1] unten ◊ *The bathroom's downstairs.* Das Badezimmer ist unten.
♦ the people downstairs die Leute von unten
♦ to go downstairs nach unten gehen
[2] untere ◊ *the downstairs bathroom* das untere Badezimmer

downtown ADVERB US
im Stadtzentrum

to **doze** VERB
dösen
♦ to doze off einnicken

dozen NOUN
das Dutzend (PL die Dutzende *or* Dutzend)

When talking about more than one dozen use the plural form **Dutzend**.

◊ *two dozen* zwei Dutzend ◊ *a dozen eggs* ein Dutzend Eier
♦ I've told you that dozens of times. Ich habe dir das schon x-mal gesagt.

drab ADJECTIVE
trist (*clothes*)

draft NOUN US
der Luftzug (PL die Luftzüge)
♦ There's a draft! Es zieht!

to **drag** VERB
see also **drag** NOUN
schleppen (*thing, person*)

drag NOUN
see also **drag** VERB

♦ **It's a real drag!** Das ist echt öde!
(*informal*)
♦ **in drag** in Frauenkleidern ◊ *He was in drag.* Er hatte Frauenkleider an.

dragon NOUN
der Drache (GEN des Drachen, PL die Drachen)

drain NOUN
see also **drain** VERB
der Abfluss (GEN des Abflusses, PL die Abflüsse) ◊ *The drains are blocked.* Der Abfluss ist verstopft.

to **drain** VERB
see also **drain** NOUN
abtropfen lassen (*vegetables, pasta*)
(PRESENT lässt abtropfen, IMPERFECT ließ abtropfen, PERFECT hat abtropfen lassen)

draining board NOUN
das Ablaufbrett (PL die Ablaufbretter)

drainpipe NOUN
das Regenrohr (PL die Regenrohre)

drama NOUN
das Drama (PL die Dramen) ◊ *Drama is my favourite subject.* Drama ist mein Lieblingsfach.
♦ **drama school** die Schauspielschule ◊ *I'd like to go to drama school.* Ich würde gerne auf die Schauspielschule gehen.

dramatic ADJECTIVE
dramatisch ◊ *It was really dramatic!* Es war wirklich dramatisch! ◊ *a dramatic improvement* eine dramatische Besserung

drank VERB *see* **drink**

drapes PL NOUN US
die Vorhänge MASC PL

drastic ADJECTIVE
drastisch (*change*) ◊ *to take drastic action* drastische Maßnahmen ergreifen

draught NOUN
der Luftzug
♦ **There's a draught!** Es zieht!

draughts SING NOUN
Dame FEM ◊ *to play draughts* Dame spielen

draw NOUN
see also **draw** VERB
1 (*sport*)
das Unentschieden (PL die Unentschieden) ◊ *The game ended in a draw.* Das Spiel endete mit einem Unentschieden.
2 (*in lottery*)
die Ziehung ◊ *The draw takes place on Saturday.* Die Ziehung findet am Samstag statt.

to **draw** VERB
see also **draw** NOUN
1 malen ◊ *He's good at drawing.* Er kann gut malen. ◊ *to draw a picture* ein Bild malen
♦ **to draw a line** einen Strich machen

2 unentschieden spielen (*sport*) ◊ *We drew two all.* Wir haben zwei zu zwei gespielt.
♦ **to draw the curtains** die Vorhänge zuziehen
♦ **to draw lots** losen

to **draw on** VERB
zurückgreifen auf (IMPERFECT griff zurück, PERFECT hat zurückgegriffen) ◊ *He drew on his own experience to write the book.* Er griff beim Schreiben des Buches auf seine eigenen Erfahrungen zurück.

to **draw up** VERB
halten (PRESENT hält, IMPERFECT hielt, PERFECT hat gehalten) ◊ *The car drew up in front of the house.* Das Auto hielt vor dem Haus.

drawback NOUN
der Nachteil (PL die Nachteile)

drawer NOUN
die Schublade

drawing NOUN
die Zeichnung

drawing pin NOUN
die Reißzwecke

drawn VERB *see* **draw**

dreadful ADJECTIVE
1 furchtbar ◊ *a dreadful mistake* ein furchtbarer Fehler ◊ *You look dreadful.* (*ill*) Du siehst furchtbar aus. ◊ *I feel dreadful.* Ich fühle mich furchtbar.
2 schrecklich ◊ *The weather was dreadful.* Das Wetter war schrecklich.

to **dream** VERB
see also **dream** NOUN
träumen ◊ *I dreamt I was in Belgium.* Ich habe geträumt, ich sei in Belgien.
Note the use of the subjunctive.

dream NOUN
see also **dream** VERB
der Traum (PL die Träume) ◊ *It was just a dream.* Es war nur ein Traum. ◊ *a bad dream* ein böser Traum

to **drench** VERB
♦ **to get drenched** klatschnass werden ◊ *We got drenched.* Wir wurden klatschnass.

dress NOUN
see also **dress** VERB
das Kleid (PL die Kleider)

to **dress** VERB
see also **dress** NOUN
sich anziehen (IMPERFECT zog sich an, PERFECT hat sich angezogen) ◊ *I got up, dressed, and went downstairs.* Ich stand auf, zog mich an und ging hinunter.
♦ **to dress somebody** jemanden anziehen ◊ *She dressed the children.* Sie zog die Kinder an.
♦ **to get dressed** sich anziehen ◊ *I got dressed quickly.* Ich habe mich schnell angezogen.

D

◆ **to dress up** sich verkleiden ◊ *I dressed up as a ghost.* Ich habe mich als Gespenst verkleidet.

dressed ADJECTIVE
angezogen ◊ *I'm not dressed yet.* Ich bin noch nicht angezogen. ◊ *How was she dressed?* Wie war sie angezogen?

◆ **She was dressed in a green sweater and jeans.** Sie hatte einen grünen Pullover und Jeans an.

dresser NOUN
die Kommode (*furniture*)

dressing NOUN
das Dressing (*for salad*) (PL die Dressings)

dressing gown NOUN
der Morgenmantel (PL die Morgenmäntel)

dressing table NOUN
der Frisiertisch (PL die Frisiertische)

drew VERB *see* **draw**

drier NOUN
1 (*for washing*)
der Wäschetrockner (PL die Wäschetrockner)
2 (*for hair*)
der Haartrockner (PL die Haartrockner)

drift NOUN
see also **drift** VERB
◆ **a snow drift** eine Schneeverwehung

to **drift** VERB
see also **drift** NOUN
treiben (*boat, snow*) (IMPERFECT trieb, PERFECT ist getrieben)

drill NOUN
see also **drill** VERB
der Bohrer (PL die Bohrer)

to **drill** VERB
see also **drill** NOUN
bohren

to **drink** VERB
see also **drink** NOUN
trinken (IMPERFECT trank, PERFECT hat getrunken) ◊ *What would you like to drink?* Was möchtest du trinken? ◊ *She drank three cups of tea.* Sie trank drei Tassen Tee. ◊ *He'd been drinking.* Er hatte getrunken. ◊ *I don't drink.* Ich trinke nicht.

drink NOUN
see also **drink** VERB
1 das Getränk (PL die Getränke) ◊ *a cold drink* ein kaltes Getränk ◊ *a hot drink* ein heißes Getränk
2 (*alcoholic*)
der Drink (PL die Drinks)
◆ **They've gone out for a drink.** Sie sind etwas trinken gegangen.
◆ **to have a drink** etwas trinken

drinking water NOUN
das Trinkwasser

drive NOUN

see also **drive** VERB
1 die Fahrt ◊ *We've got a long drive tomorrow.* Wir haben morgen eine lange Fahrt.
◆ **to go for a drive** fahren ◊ *We went for a drive in the country.* Wir sind aufs Land gefahren.
2 die Auffahrt (*of house*) ◊ *He parked his car in the drive.* Er parkte sein Auto in der Auffahrt.

to **drive** VERB
see also **drive** NOUN
1 fahren (PRESENT fährt, IMPERFECT fuhr, PERFECT ist/hat gefahren) ◊ *My mother drives me to school.* Meine Mutter fährt mich in die Schule. ◊ *I drove down to London.* Ich bin nach London gefahren.
*When **fahren** is used with an object it takes **haben** not **sein**.*
◊ *He drove me home.* Er hat mich nach Hause gefahren.
2 (*operate a car*)
Auto fahren (PRESENT fährt Auto, IMPERFECT fuhr Auto, PERFECT ist Auto gefahren) ◊ *Can you drive?* Kannst du Auto fahren?
◆ **She's learning to drive.** Sie macht den Führerschein.
3 (*go by car*)
mit dem Auto fahren ◊ *Did you go by train? – No, we drove.* Seid ihr mit dem Zug gefahren? – Nein, wir sind mit dem Auto gefahren.
◆ **to drive somebody mad** jemanden wahnsinnig machen ◊ *He drives her mad.* Er macht sie wahnsinnig.

driver NOUN
der Fahrer (PL die Fahrer)
die Fahrerin
◊ *She's an excellent driver.* Sie ist eine ausgezeichnete Fahrerin. ◊ *He's a bus driver.* Er ist Busfahrer.

driver's license NOUN US
der Führerschein (PL die Führerscheine)

driving instructor NOUN
der Fahrlehrer (PL die Fahrlehrer)
die Fahrlehrerin
◊ *He's a driving instructor.* Er ist Fahrlehrer.

driving lesson NOUN
die Fahrstunde

driving licence NOUN
der Führerschein (PL die Führerscheine)

driving test NOUN
die Fahrprüfung
◆ **to take one's driving test** die Fahrprüfung machen ◊ *He's taking his driving test tomorrow.* Er macht morgen die Fahrprüfung.
◆ **She's just passed her driving test.** Sie hat gerade ihren Führerschein gemacht.

drizzle NOUN
see also **drizzle** VERB
der Nieselregen

to **drizzle** VERB

> see also **drizzle** NOUN

nieseln

drop NOUN

> see also **drop** VERB

der Tropfen (PL die Tropfen) ◊ *a drop of water* ein Wassertropfen

to **drop** VERB

> see also **drop** NOUN

1 fallen lassen (PRESENT lässt fallen, IMPERFECT ließ fallen, PERFECT hat fallen lassen) ◊ *I dropped the glass and it broke.* Ich habe das Glas fallen lassen, und es ist kaputtgegangen.

2 (*abandon*) aufgeben (PRESENT gibt auf, IMPERFECT gab auf, PERFECT hat aufgegeben) ◊ *I'm going to drop chemistry.* Ich gebe Chemie auf.

3 absetzen (PERFECT hat abgesetzt) ◊ *Could you drop me at the station?* Könntest du mich am Bahnhof absetzen?

drought NOUN die Dürre

drove VERB *see* **drive**

to **drown** VERB

ertrinken (IMPERFECT ertrank, PERFECT ist ertrunken) ◊ *A young boy drowned here yesterday.* Hier ist gestern ein kleiner Junge ertrunken.

drug NOUN

1 (*medicine*) das Medikament (PL die Medikamente) ◊ *They need food and drugs.* Sie brauchen Nahrung und Medikamente.

2 (*illegal*) die Droge ◊ *hard drugs* harte Drogen ◊ *soft drugs* weiche Drogen ◊ *to take drugs* Drogen nehmen

♦ **a drug addict** (*man*) ein Drogensüchtiger

♦ **She's a drug addict.** Sie ist drogensüchtig.

♦ **a drug pusher** ein Dealer MASC

♦ **a drug smuggler** ein Drogenschmuggler MASC

♦ **the drugs squad** das Rauschgiftdezernat

drugstore NOUN US der Drugstore (PL die Drugstores)

drum NOUN

die Trommel ◊ *an African drum* eine afrikanische Trommel

♦ **a drum kit** ein Schlagzeug NEUT

♦ **drums** das Schlagzeug SING ◊ *I play drums.* Ich spiele Schlagzeug.

drummer NOUN

(*in rock group*) der Schlagzeuger (PL die Schlagzeuger) die Schlagzeugerin

drunk VERB *see* **drink**

drunk ADJECTIVE

> see also **drunk** NOUN

betrunken ◊ *He was drunk.* Er war betrunken.

drunk NOUN

> see also **drunk** ADJECTIVE

der Betrunkene (GEN des Betrunkenen, PL die Betrunkenen) die Betrunkene (GEN der Betrunkenen) ◊ *a drunk* (*man*) ein Betrunkener ◊ *The streets were full of drunks.* Die Straßen waren voll von Betrunkenen.

dry ADJECTIVE

> see also **dry** VERB

trocken ◊ *The paint isn't dry yet.* Die Farbe ist noch nicht trocken.

♦ **a long dry period** eine lange Trockenzeit

to **dry** VERB

> see also **dry** ADJECTIVE

1 trocknen ◊ *The washing will dry quickly in the sun.* Die Wäsche wird in der Sonne schnell trocknen. ◊ *some dried flowers* getrocknete Blumen

♦ **to dry one's hair** sich die Haare föhnen ◊ *I haven't dried my hair yet.* Ich habe mir noch nicht die Haare geföhnt.

2 (*clothes*) trocknen lassen (PRESENT lässt trocknen, IMPERFECT ließ trocknen, PERFECT hat trocknen lassen) ◊ *There's nowhere to dry clothes here.* Hier kann man nirgends Kleider trocknen lassen.

♦ **to dry the dishes** das Geschirr abtrocknen

dry-cleaner's NOUN die Reinigung

dryer NOUN

der Wäschetrockner (*for clothes*) (PL die Wäschetrockner)

♦ **a tumble dryer** ein Wäschetrockner

♦ **a hair dryer** ein Föhn MASC

DTP ABBREVIATION (= *Desktop Publishing*) DTP

dubbed ADJECTIVE

synchronisiert ◊ *The film was dubbed into German.* Der Film war deutsch synchronisiert.

dubious ADJECTIVE

♦ **My parents were a bit dubious about it.** Meine Eltern hatten ihre Zweifel.

duck NOUN die Ente

due ADJECTIVE, ADVERB

♦ **to be due to do something** etwas tun sollen ◊ *He's due to arrive tomorrow.* Er soll morgen ankommen.

♦ **The plane's due in half an hour.** Das Flugzeug sollte in einer halben Stunde ankommen.

♦ **When's the baby due?** Wann kommt das Baby?

♦ **due to** wegen ◊ *The trip was cancelled due to bad weather.* Der Ausflug wurde wegen des schlechten Wetters abgesagt.

dug VERB *see* **dig**

dull ADJECTIVE

D

1 langweilig ◊ *He's nice, but a bit dull.* Er ist nett, aber ein bisschen langweilig.
2 trüb (*weather, day*)

dumb ADJECTIVE
1 taub
♦ **She's deaf and dumb.** Sie ist taubstumm.
2 blöd (*stupid*) ◊ *That was a really dumb thing I did!* Da habe ich etwas echt Blödes gemacht!

dummy NOUN
der Schnuller (*for baby*) (PL die Schnuller)

dump NOUN
see also **dump** VERB
♦ **It's a real dump!** Das ist ein Dreckloch! (*informal*)
♦ **a rubbish dump** eine Müllkippe

to **dump** VERB
see also **dump** NOUN
1 (*waste*)
abladen (PRESENT lädt ab, IMPERFECT lud ab, PERFECT hat abgeladen)
♦ **"no dumping"** "Schutt abladen verboten"
2 (*informal: get rid of*)
Schluss machen mit ◊ *He's just dumped his girlfriend.* Er hat gerade mit seiner Freundin Schluss gemacht.

dungarees PL NOUN
die Latzhose ◊ *a pair of dungarees* eine Latzhose

dungeon NOUN
das Verlies (PL die Verliese)

duration NOUN
die Dauer

during PREPOSITION
während ◊ *during the holidays* während der Ferien
♦ **during the day** tagsüber

dusk NOUN
die Dämmerung ◊ *at dusk* bei Dämmerung

dust NOUN
see also **dust** VERB
der Staub

to **dust** VERB
see also **dust** NOUN
abstauben (PERFECT hat abgestaubt) ◊ *I dusted the shelves.* Ich habe das Regal abgestaubt.
♦ **I hate dusting!** Ich hasse Staubwischen!

dustbin NOUN
der Mülleimer (PL die Mülleimer)

dustman NOUN
der Müllmann (PL die Müllmänner)
♦ **He's a dustman.** Er arbeitet bei der Müllabfuhr.

dusty ADJECTIVE
staubig

Dutch ADJECTIVE
see also **Dutch** NOUN
holländisch ◊ *She's Dutch.* Sie ist Holländerin.

Dutch NOUN
see also **Dutch** ADJECTIVE
das Holländisch (*language*) (GEN des Holländischen)
♦ **the Dutch** die Holländer MASC PL

Dutchman NOUN
der Holländer (PL die Holländer)

Dutchwoman NOUN
die Holländerin

duty NOUN
die Pflicht ◊ *It was his duty to tell the police.* Es war seine Pflicht, die Polizei zu informieren.
♦ **to be on duty** Dienst haben

duty-free ADJECTIVE
zollfrei
♦ **the duty-free shop** der Duty-free-Laden

duvet NOUN
das Deckbett (PL die Deckbetten)

DVD NOUN (= *digital video disc*)
die DVD (PL die DVDs)

dwarf NOUN
der Zwerg (PL die Zwerge)
die Zwergin

dye NOUN
see also **dye** VERB
der Farbstoff
♦ **hair dye** das Haarfärbemittel

to **dye** VERB
see also **dye** NOUN
färben ◊ *to dye sth red* etw rot färben ◊ *She has dyed her hair blonde.* Sie hat blond gefärbte Haare.

dynamic ADJECTIVE
dynamisch

dyslexia NOUN
die Legasthenie
♦ **She has dyslexia.** Sie ist Legasthenikerin.

E

each ADJECTIVE, PRONOUN
jeder ◊ *Each pupil has his own desk.*
Jeder Schüler hat seinen eigenen
Schreibtisch. ◊ *They have ten points
each.* Jeder hat zehn Punkte. ◊ *He gave
each of us ten pounds.* Er gab jedem von
uns zehn Pfund. ◊ *each day* jeder Tag
jede ◊ *Each dancer wore a different
costume.* Jede Tänzerin trug ein anderes
Kostüm. ◊ *He gave each of the dancers a
red rose.* Er gab jeder Tänzerin eine rote
Rose.
jedes ◊ *Each house in our street has its
own garden.* Jedes Haus in unserer
Straße hat einen eigenen Garten. ◊ *The
girls each have their own bedroom.*
Jedes der Mädchen hat sein eigenes
Zimmer.
◆**each other** einander ◊ *They hate each
other.* Sie hassen einander. ◊ *We wrote
to each other.* Wir haben einander
geschrieben.
◆**They don't know each other.** Sie kennen
sich nicht.

eager ADJECTIVE
◆**He was eager to tell us about his
experiences.** Er wollte uns unbedingt von
seinen Erfahrungen erzählen.

eagle NOUN
der Adler (PL die Adler)

ear NOUN
das Ohr (PL die Ohren)

earache NOUN
die Ohrenschmerzen MASC PL ◊ *to have
earache* Ohrenschmerzen haben

earlier ADVERB
1 vorher ◊ *I saw him earlier.* Ich habe
ihn vorher gesehen.
2 früher (*in the morning*) ◊ *I ought to get
up earlier.* Ich sollte früher aufstehen.

early ADVERB, ADJECTIVE
früh ◊ *I have to get up early.* Ich muss
früh aufstehen. ◊ *I came early to get a
good seat.* Ich bin früh gekommen, um
einen guten Platz zu bekommen.
◆**to have an early night** früh ins Bett
gehen

to **earn** VERB
verdienen (PERFECT hat verdient) ◊ *She
earns five pounds an hour.* Sie verdient
fünf Pfund in der Stunde.

earnings PL NOUN
der Verdienst (PL die Verdienste)

earring NOUN
der Ohrring (PL die Ohrringe)

earth NOUN
die Erde

earthquake NOUN
das Erdbeben (PL die Erdbeben)

easily ADVERB
leicht

east ADJECTIVE, ADVERB
see also **east** NOUN
◆**the east coast** die Ostküste
◆**an east wind** ein Ostwind MASC
nach Osten ◊ *We were travelling east.*
Wir sind nach Osten gefahren.
◆**east of** östlich von ◊ *It's east of London.*
Es liegt östlich von London.

east NOUN
see also **east** ADJECTIVE
der Osten ◊ *in the east* im Osten

Easter NOUN
Ostern NEUT ◊ *at Easter* an Ostern ◊ *We
went to my grandparents' for Easter.* Wir
sind über Ostern zu meinen Großeltern
gefahren.

Easter egg NOUN
das Osterei (PL die Ostereier)

eastern ADJECTIVE
östlich ◊ *the eastern part of the island*
der östliche Teil der Insel
◆**Eastern Europe** Osteuropa NEUT

easy ADJECTIVE
einfach

easy chair NOUN
der Sessel (PL die Sessel)

easy-going ADJECTIVE
locker ◊ *She's very easy-going.* Sie ist
echt locker.

to **eat** VERB
essen (PRESENT isst, IMPERFECT aß, PERFECT hat
gegessen) ◊ *Would you like something
to eat?* Möchtest du etwas essen?

EC NOUN (= *European Community*)
die EG (= *Europäische Gemeinschaft*)

eccentric ADJECTIVE
exzentrisch

echo NOUN
das Echo (PL die Echos)

ecology NOUN
die Ökologie

e-commerce NOUN
der E-Commerce (GEN des E-Commerce)

economic ADJECTIVE
rentabel (*profitable*)

economical ADJECTIVE
sparsam

economics SING NOUN
die Volkswirtschaft ◊ *He's studying
economics.* Er studiert Volkswirtschaft.

to **economize** VERB
sparen ◊ *to economize on something* mit
etwas sparen

economy NOUN
die Wirtschaft ◊ *the German economy*
die deutsche Wirtschaft

ecstasy NOUN
 das Ecstasy (*drug*) (GEN des Ecstasy)
♦ **to be in ecstasy** entzückt sein

ecu NOUN (= *European Currency Unit*)
 der Ecu (GEN des Ecu, PL die Ecu)

eczema NOUN
 der Hautausschlag (PL die
 Hautausschläge)

edge NOUN
 [1] der Rand (PL die Ränder) ◊ *They live
 on the edge of the moors.* Sie leben am
 Rand des Moors. ◊ *The country was on
 the edge of war.* Das Land stand am
 Rand eines Krieges.
 [2] (*of table*)
 die Kante
 [3] (*of lake*)
 das Ufer (PL die Ufer)

edgy ADJECTIVE
 nervös

Edinburgh NOUN
 Edinburgh NEUT

editor NOUN
 (*of newspaper*)
 der Redakteur (PL die Redakteure)
 die Redakteurin

educated ADJECTIVE
 gebildet

education NOUN
 [1] das Bildungswesen ◊ *There should
 be more investment in education.* Es
 sollte mehr Geld ins Bildungswesen
 investiert werden.
 [2] das Lehramt (*teaching*) ◊ *She works in
 education.* Sie ist im Lehramt tätig.

educational ADJECTIVE
 lehrreich (*experience*) ◊ *It was very
 educational.* Das war sehr lehrreich.

effect NOUN
 der Effekt (PL die Effekte) ◊ *special effects*
 Spezialeffekte

effective ADJECTIVE
 effektiv

efficient ADJECTIVE
 effizient

effort NOUN
 die Bemühung
♦ **to make an effort to do something** sich
 bemühen, etwas zu tun

e.g. ABBREVIATION
 z. B. (= zum Beispiel)

egg NOUN
 das Ei (PL die Eier) ◊ *a hard-boiled egg*
 ein hart gekochtes Ei ◊ *a soft-boiled egg*
 ein weich gekochtes Ei
♦ **a fried egg** ein Spiegelei
♦ **scrambled eggs** die Rühreier NEUT PL

egg cup NOUN
 der Eierbecher (PL die Eierbecher)

eggplant NOUN US
 die Aubergine

Egypt NOUN
 Ägypten NEUT ◊ *to Egypt* nach Ägypten

eight NUMBER
 acht ◊ *She's eight.* Sie ist acht.

eighteen NUMBER
 achtzehn ◊ *She's eighteen.* Sie ist
 achtzehn.

eighteenth ADJECTIVE
 achtzehnte
♦ **the eighteenth of August** der achtzehnte
 August

eighth ADJECTIVE
 achte ◊ *the eighth floor* der achte
 Stock
♦ **the eighth of August** der achte August

eighty NUMBER
 achtzig ◊ *She's eighty.* Sie ist achtzig.

Eire NOUN
 Irland NEUT
♦ **from Eire** aus Irland
♦ **in Eire** in Irland
♦ **to Eire** nach Irland

either ADVERB, CONJUNCTION, PRONOUN
 [1] auch kein ◊ *I don't like milk, and I
 don't like eggs either.* Ich mag keine
 Milch und ich mag auch keine Eier.
 [2] auch nicht ◊ *I've never been to Spain.
 – I haven't either.* Ich war noch nie in
 Spanien. – Ich auch nicht.
♦ **either ... or ...** entweder ... oder ... ◊ *You
 can have either ice cream or yoghurt.* Du
 kannst entweder Eis oder Joghurt haben.
♦ **either of them** einer von beiden ◊ *Take
 either of them.* Nimm einen von beiden.
♦ **I don't like either of them.** Ich mag
 keinen von beiden.

elastic NOUN
 das Gummiband (PL die Gummibänder)

elastic band NOUN
 das Gummiband (PL die Gummibänder)

elbow NOUN
 der Ellbogen (PL die Ellbogen)

elder ADJECTIVE
 älter ◊ *my elder sister* meine ältere
 Schwester

elderly ADJECTIVE
 älter ◊ *an elderly gentleman* ein älterer
 Herr
♦ **the elderly** ältere Leute PL

eldest ADJECTIVE
 älteste ◊ *my eldest brother* mein ältester
 Bruder ◊ *my eldest sister* meine älteste
 Schwester ◊ *He's the eldest.* Er ist der
 Älteste.

to **elect** VERB
 wählen

election NOUN
 die Wahl

electric ADJECTIVE
 elektrisch ◊ *an electric fire* ein
 elektrischer Ofen ◊ *an electric guitar* eine
 elektrische Gitarre
♦ **an electric blanket** eine Heizdecke

electrical ADJECTIVE
 elektrisch

E

♦ **an electrical engineer** ein Elektrotechniker

electrician NOUN
der Elektriker (PL die Elektriker)
die Elektrikerin
◊ *He's an electrician.* Er ist Elektriker.

electricity NOUN
der Strom ◊ *They cut off our electricity.* Sie haben den Strom abgestellt.

electronic ADJECTIVE
elektronisch

electronics SING NOUN
die Elektronik ◊ *My hobby is electronics.* Elektronik ist mein Hobby.

elegant ADJECTIVE
elegant

elementary school NOUN US
die Grundschule

elephant NOUN
der Elefant (GEN des Elefanten, PL die Elefanten)

elevator NOUN US
der Aufzug (PL die Aufzüge)

eleven NUMBER
elf ◊ *She's eleven.* Sie ist elf.

eleventh ADJECTIVE
elfte ◊ *the eleventh floor* der elfte Stock
♦ **the eleventh of August** der elfte August

else ADVERB
1 anders ◊ *somebody else* jemand anders ◊ *nobody else* niemand anders
◊ *somewhere else* irgendwo anders
◊ *anywhere else* irgendwo anders
2 anderes ◊ *nothing else* nichts anderes
◊ *something else* etwas anderes
◊ *anything else* etwas anderes
♦ **Would you like anything else?** Möchtest du noch etwas?
♦ **I don't want anything else.** Ich will nichts anderes.
♦ **Give me the money, or else!** Gib mir das Geld, sonst gibt's was!

email NOUN
see also **email** VERB
die E-Mail (PL die E-Mails) ◊ *My email address is ...* Meine E-Mail-Adresse ist ...

to **email** VERB
see also **email** NOUN
mailen (PERFECT hat gemailt) ◊ *Did you email it?* Hast du es gemailt?
♦ **to email somebody** jemandem eine E-Mail senden

embankment NOUN
die Böschung

embarrassed ADJECTIVE
verlegen ◊ *He seemed to be pretty embarrassed.* Er schien sehr verlegen.
♦ **I was really embarrassed.** Es war mir wirklich peinlich.

embarrassing ADJECTIVE
peinlich ◊ *It was so embarrassing.* Es war so peinlich.

embassy NOUN
die Botschaft

to **embroider** VERB
besticken (PERFECT hat bestickt)

embroidery NOUN
die Stickerei
♦ **I do embroidery.** Ich sticke.

emergency NOUN
der Notfall (PL die Notfälle) ◊ *This is an emergency!* Dies ist ein Notfall! ◊ *in an emergency* in einem Notfall
♦ **an emergency exit** ein Notausgang MASC
♦ **an emergency landing** eine Notlandung
♦ **the emergency services** die Rettungsdienste MASC PL

to **emigrate** VERB
auswandern (PERFECT ist ausgewandert)

emotion NOUN
das Gefühl (PL die Gefühle)

emotional ADJECTIVE
emotional (*person*)

emperor NOUN
der Kaiser (PL die Kaiser)

to **emphasize** VERB
betonen (PERFECT hat betont)

empire NOUN
das Reich (PL die Reiche)

to **employ** VERB
beschäftigen (PERFECT hat beschäftigt)
◊ *The factory employs six hundred people.* Die Fabrik beschäftigt sechshundert Leute.

employee NOUN
der Angestellte (GEN des Angestellten, PL die Angestellten)
die Angestellte (GEN der Angestellten)
◊ *He's an employee.* Er ist Angestellter.

employer NOUN
der Arbeitgeber (PL die Arbeitgeber)
die Arbeitgeberin

employment NOUN
die Beschäftigung

empty ADJECTIVE
see also **empty** VERB
leer

to **empty** VERB
see also **empty** ADJECTIVE
leeren
♦ **to empty something out** etwas ausleeren

to **encourage** VERB
ermutigen (PERFECT hat ermutigt)
♦ **to encourage somebody to do something** jemanden ermutigen, etwas zu tun

encouragement NOUN
die Ermutigung

encyclopedia NOUN
das Lexikon (PL die Lexika)

end NOUN
see also **end** VERB

das <u>Ende</u> (PL die Enden) ◊ *the end of the holidays* das Ende der Ferien ◊ *at the end of the street* am Ende der Straße ◊ *at the other end of the table* am anderen Ende des Tisches
- **the end of the film** der Schluss des Films
- **in the end** schließlich ◊ *In the end I decided to stay at home.* Schließlich habe ich beschlossen, zu Hause zu bleiben. ◊ *It turned out all right in the end.* Schließlich ging alles gut.
- **for hours on end** stundenlang

to **end** VERB
see also **end** NOUN
zu Ende sein (PRESENT ist zu Ende, IMPERFECT war zu Ende, PERFECT ist zu Ende gewesen) ◊ *What time does the film end?* Wann ist der Film zu Ende?
- **to end up doing something** schließlich etwas tun ◊ *I ended up walking home.* Ich bin schließlich zu Fuß nach Hause gegangen.

ending NOUN
der <u>Schluss</u> (GEN des Schlusses, PL die Schlüsse) ◊ *It was an exciting film, especially the ending.* Es war ein spannender Film, besonders am Schluss.

endless ADJECTIVE
endlos ◊ *The journey seemed endless.* Die Reise erschien endlos.

enemy NOUN
der <u>Feind</u> (PL die Feinde)
die <u>Feindin</u>

energetic ADJECTIVE
voller Energie (*person*)

energy NOUN
die <u>Energie</u>

engaged ADJECTIVE
1 <u>besetzt</u> (*busy, in use*) ◊ *I phoned, but it was engaged.* Ich habe angerufen, aber es war besetzt.
2 <u>verlobt</u> (*to be married*) ◊ *She's engaged to Brian.* Sie ist mit Brian verlobt.
- **to get engaged** sich verloben

engagement NOUN
die <u>Verlobung</u> ◊ *an engagement ring* ein Verlobungsring MASC

engine NOUN
der <u>Motor</u> (PL die Motoren)

engineer NOUN
1 der <u>Ingenieur</u> (PL die Ingenieure)
die <u>Ingenieurin</u>
◊ *He's an engineer.* Er ist Ingenieur.
2 (*train driver*)
der <u>Lokomotivführer</u> (PL die Lokomotivführer)

engineering NOUN
die <u>Technik</u> ◊ *genetic engineering* die Gentechnik
- **mechanical engineering** der Maschinenbau

England NOUN

England NEUT
- **from England** aus England
- **in England** in England
- **to England** nach England

*ⓘ Germans frequently use **England** to mean Great Britain or the United Kingdom.*

English ADJECTIVE
see also **English** NOUN
englisch
- **He's English.** Er ist Engländer.
- **She's English.** Sie ist Engländerin.
- **English people** die Engländer MASC PL

English NOUN
see also **English** ADJECTIVE
das <u>Englisch</u> (*language*) (GEN des Englischen) ◊ *Do you speak English?* Sprechen Sie Englisch?
- **the English** (*people*) die Engländer MASC PL

Englishman NOUN
der <u>Engländer</u> (PL die Engländer)

Englishwoman NOUN
die <u>Engländerin</u>

to **enjoy** VERB
<u>genießen</u> (IMPERFECT genoss, PERFECT hat genossen) ◊ *I really enjoyed my holidays.* Ich habe meine Ferien wirklich genossen.
- **Did you enjoy the film?** Hat dir der Film gefallen?
- **Did you enjoy your meal?** Hat es Ihnen geschmeckt?
- **to enjoy oneself** sich amüsieren ◊ *I really enjoyed myself.* Ich habe mich richtig amüsiert. ◊ *Did you enjoy yourselves at the party?* Habt ihr euch auf der Party amüsiert?

enjoyable ADJECTIVE
nett

enlargement NOUN
die <u>Vergrößerung</u> (*of photo*)

enormous ADJECTIVE
riesig

enough PRONOUN, ADJECTIVE
<u>genug</u> ◊ *enough time* genug Zeit ◊ *I didn't have enough money.* Ich hatte nicht genug Geld. ◊ *big enough* groß genug ◊ *warm enough* warm genug
- **Have you got enough?** Reicht dir das?
- **I've had enough!** Mir reicht's!
- **That's enough.** Das reicht.

to **enquire** VERB
sich <u>erkundigen</u> (PERFECT hat sich erkundigt)
- **to enquire about something** sich nach etwas erkundigen ◊ *I'm going to enquire about train times.* Ich werde mich nach den Abfahrtszeiten der Züge erkundigen.

enquiry NOUN

☞

die Untersuchung (*official investigation*)
♦ **to make an enquiry** sich erkundigen
◊ *I'd like to make an enquiry about hotels.* Ich möchte mich über Hotels erkundigen.

to **enter** VERB
betreten (*room*) (PRESENT betritt, IMPERFECT betrat, PERFECT hat betreten)
♦ **to enter a competition** an einem Wettbewerb teilnehmen

to **entertain** VERB
unterhalten (*guests*) (PRESENT unterhält, IMPERFECT unterhielt, PERFECT hat unterhalten)

entertainer NOUN
der Entertainer (PL die Entertainer)
die Entertainerin

entertaining ADJECTIVE
unterhaltsam

enthusiasm NOUN
die Begeisterung

enthusiast NOUN
♦ **a railway enthusiast** ein Eisenbahnfan MASC
♦ **She's a DIY enthusiast.** Sie ist begeisterte Heimwerkerin.

enthusiastic ADJECTIVE
begeistert

entire ADJECTIVE
ganz ◊ *the entire world* die ganze Welt

entirely ADVERB
ganz

entrance NOUN
der Eingang (PL die Eingänge)
♦ **an entrance exam** eine Aufnahmeprüfung
♦ **entrance fee** der Eintritt

entry NOUN
der Eingang (*way in*) (PL die Eingänge)
♦ **"no entry" (1)** (*on door*) "kein Zutritt"
♦ **"no entry" (2)** (*on road sign*) "Einfahrt verboten"
♦ **an entry form** ein Teilnahmeformular NEUT

entry phone NOUN
die Gegensprechanlage

envelope NOUN
der Umschlag (PL die Umschläge)

envious ADJECTIVE
neidisch

environment NOUN
die Umwelt

environmental ADJECTIVE
♦ **environmental pollution** die Umweltverschmutzung
♦ **environmental protection** der Umweltschutz

environment-friendly ADJECTIVE
umweltfreundlich

envy NOUN

see also **envy** VERB
der Neid

to **envy** VERB

see also **envy** NOUN
beneiden (PERFECT hat beneidet) ◊ *I don't envy you!* Ich beneide dich nicht!

epileptic NOUN
der Epileptiker (PL die Epileptiker)
die Epileptikerin

episode NOUN
die Folge (*of TV programme, story*)

equal ADJECTIVE

see also **equal** VERB
gleich

to **equal** VERB

see also **equal** ADJECTIVE
♦ **Ten times two equals twenty.** Zehn mal zwei ist gleich zwanzig.

equality NOUN
die Gleichheit

to **equalize** VERB
ausgleichen (*in sport*) (IMPERFECT glich aus, PERFECT hat ausgeglichen)

equator NOUN
der Äquator

equipment NOUN
die Ausrüstung ◊ *fishing equipment* die Anglerausrüstung ◊ *skiing equipment* die Skiausrüstung

equipped ADJECTIVE
♦ **equipped with** ausgerüstet mit
♦ **to be well equipped** gut ausgestattet sein

equivalent NOUN
das Äquivalent (PL die Äquivalente)
♦ **to be equivalent to something** einer Sache entsprechen ◊ *Twenty-five per cent is equivalent to a quarter.* Fünfundzwanzig Prozent entspricht einem Viertel.

error NOUN
der Fehler (PL die Fehler)

escalator NOUN
die Rolltreppe

escape NOUN

see also **escape** VERB
der Ausbruch (*from prison*) (PL die Ausbrüche)

to **escape** VERB

see also **escape** NOUN
ausbrechen (PRESENT bricht aus, IMPERFECT brach aus, PERFECT ist ausgebrochen) ◊ *A lion has escaped.* Ein Löwe ist ausgebrochen. ◊ *to escape from prison* aus dem Gefängnis ausbrechen

escort NOUN
die Eskorte ◊ *a police escort* eine Polizeieskorte

Eskimo NOUN
der Eskimo (PL die Eskimos)
die Eskimofrau

especially ADVERB

besonders ◊ *It's very hot there, especially in the summer.* Dort ist es sehr heiß, besonders im Sommer.

essay NOUN
der Aufsatz (PL die Aufsätze) ◊ *a history essay* ein Aufsatz in Geschichte

essential ADJECTIVE
wichtig ◊ *It's essential to bring warm clothes.* Es ist ganz wichtig, warme Kleidung mitzubringen.

estate NOUN
die Siedlung (*housing estate*) ◊ *I live on an estate.* Ich wohne in einer Siedlung.

estate agent NOUN
der Immobilienmakler (PL die Immobilienmakler)
die Immobilienmaklerin

estate car NOUN
der Kombiwagen (PL die Kombiwagen)

to **estimate** VERB
schätzen ◊ *They estimated it would take three weeks.* Sie schätzten, dass es drei Wochen dauern würde.

etc ABBREVIATION (= *et cetera*)
usw. (= und so weiter)

Ethiopia NOUN
Äthiopien NEUT ◊ *in Ethiopia* in Äthiopien

ethnic ADJECTIVE
[1] ethnisch (*racial*) ◊ *an ethnic minority* eine ethnische Minderheit
[2] folkloristisch (*clothes, music*)

e-ticket NOUN
das E-Ticket (PL die E-Tickets)

EU NOUN (= *European Union*)
die EU (= Europäische Union)

euro NOUN
der Euro (PL die Euros)

Eurocheque NOUN
der Eurocheque (PL die Eurocheques)

Europe NOUN
Europa NEUT
♦ **from Europe** aus Europa
♦ **in Europe** in Europa
♦ **to Europe** nach Europa

European ADJECTIVE
see also **European** NOUN
europäisch
♦ **He's European.** Er ist Europäer.

European NOUN
see also **European** ADJECTIVE
(*person*)
der Europäer (PL die Europäer)
die Europäerin

to **evacuate** VERB
evakuieren (PERFECT hat evakuiert)

eve NOUN
♦ **Christmas Eve** der Heilige Abend
♦ **New Year's Eve** Silvester NEUT

even ADVERB
see also **even** ADJECTIVE

sogar ◊ *I like all animals, even snakes.* Ich mag alle Tiere, sogar Schlangen.
♦ **even if** selbst wenn ◊ *I'd never do that, even if you asked me.* Ich würde das nie tun, selbst wenn du mich darum bitten würdest.
♦ **not even** nicht einmal ◊ *He never stops working, not even at the weekend.* Er hört nie auf zu arbeiten, nicht einmal am Wochenende.
♦ **even though** obwohl ◊ *He's never got any money, even though his parents are quite rich.* Er hat nie Geld, obwohl seine Eltern ziemlich reich sind.
♦ **I liked Hamburg even more than Munich.** Hamburg hat mir noch besser gefallen als München.

even ADJECTIVE
see also **even** ADVERB
gleichmäßig ◊ *an even layer of snow* eine gleichmäßige Schneeschicht
♦ **an even number** eine gerade Zahl
♦ **to get even with somebody** es jemandem heimzahlen

evening NOUN
der Abend (PL die Abende) ◊ *in the evening* am Abend ◊ *all evening* den ganzen Abend ◊ *yesterday evening* gestern Abend ◊ *tomorrow evening* morgen Abend
♦ **Good evening!** Guten Abend!

evening class NOUN
der Abendkurs (PL die Abendkurse)

event NOUN
das Ereignis (GEN des Ereignisses, PL die Ereignisse)
♦ **a sporting event** eine Sportveranstaltung

eventful ADJECTIVE
ereignisreich

eventual ADJECTIVE
schließlich
♦ **the eventual outcome** das Endergebnis
Be careful not to translate eventual by eventuell.

eventually ADVERB
schließlich

ever ADVERB
[1] schon einmal ◊ *Have you ever been to America?* Warst du schon einmal in Amerika? ◊ *Have you ever seen her?* Hast du sie schon einmal gesehen?
[2] je ◊ *the best I've ever seen* das Beste, was ich je gesehen habe
♦ **for the first time ever** das allererste Mal
♦ **ever since** seit ◊ *ever since I met him* seit ich ihn kenne
♦ **ever since then** seither

every ADJECTIVE
jeder ◊ *every pupil* jeder Schüler ◊ *every day* jeden Tag
jede ◊ *every mother* jede Mutter ◊ *every week* jede Woche

jedes ◊ *every child* jedes Kind ◊ *every year* jedes Jahr
♦ **every time** jedes Mal ◊ *Every time I see him, he's depressed.* Jedes Mal, wenn ich ihn sehe, ist er deprimiert.
♦ **every now and then** ab und zu

everybody PRONOUN
[1] alle ◊ *Everybody had a good time.* Alle hatten ihren Spaß.
[2] jeder ◊ *Everybody makes mistakes.* Jeder macht mal Fehler.

everyone PRONOUN
[1] alle ◊ *Everyone opened their presents.* Alle machten ihre Geschenke auf.
[2] jeder ◊ *Everyone should have a hobby.* Jeder sollte ein Hobby haben.

everything PRONOUN
alles ◊ *You've thought of everything!* Du hast an alles gedacht! ◊ *Money isn't everything.* Geld ist nicht alles.

everywhere ADVERB
überall ◊ *I looked everywhere, but I couldn't find it.* Ich habe überall nachgesehen, habe es aber nirgends gefunden. ◊ *There were policemen everywhere.* Überall waren Polizisten.

evil ADJECTIVE
böse

ex- PREFIX
Ex- ◊ *his ex-wife* seine Ex-Frau

exact ADJECTIVE
genau

exactly ADVERB
genau ◊ *exactly the same* genau das gleiche ◊ *It's exactly ten o'clock.* Es ist genau zehn Uhr.

to **exaggerate** VERB
übertreiben (IMPERFECT übertrieb, PERFECT hat übertrieben)

exaggeration NOUN
die Übertreibung

exam NOUN
die Prüfung ◊ *a German exam* eine Deutschprüfung ◊ *the exam results* die Prüfungsergebnisse

examination NOUN
die Prüfung
♦ **a medical examination** eine ärztliche Untersuchung

to **examine** VERB
untersuchen (PERFECT hat untersucht)
◊ *The doctor examined him.* Der Arzt untersuchte ihn.
♦ **He examined her passport.** Er prüfte ihren Pass.

examiner NOUN
der Prüfer (PL die Prüfer)
die Prüferin

example NOUN
das Beispiel (PL die Beispiele)
♦ **for example** zum Beispiel

excellent ADJECTIVE

ausgezeichnet ◊ *Her results were excellent.* Ihre Noten waren ausgezeichnet.

except PREPOSITION
außer ◊ *everyone except me* alle außer mir
♦ **except for** abgesehen von ◊ *It was super except for the weather.* Abgesehen vom Wetter war es super.
♦ **except that** außer, dass ◊ *The weather was great, except that it was a bit cold.* Das Wetter war toll, außer dass es etwas kalt war.

exception NOUN
die Ausnahme ◊ *to make an exception* eine Ausnahme machen

exceptional ADJECTIVE
außergewöhnlich

excess baggage NOUN
das Übergewicht (PL die Übergewichte)

to **exchange** VERB
tauschen ◊ *I exchanged the book for a video.* Ich habe das Buch gegen ein Video getauscht.

exchange rate NOUN
der Wechselkurs (PL die Wechselkurse)

excited ADJECTIVE
aufgeregt

exciting ADJECTIVE
aufregend

exclamation mark NOUN
das Ausrufezeichen (PL die Ausrufezeichen)

excuse NOUN
| see also **excuse** VERB |
die Entschuldigung

to **excuse** VERB
| see also **excuse** NOUN |
♦ **Excuse me!** Entschuldigung!

ex-directory ADJECTIVE
♦ **She's ex-directory.** Ihre Nummer steht nicht im Telefonbuch.

to **execute** VERB
[1] (*kill*)
hinrichten (PERFECT hat hingerichtet)
[2] (*plan*)
ausführen (PERFECT hat ausgeführt)

execution NOUN
die Hinrichtung (*punishment*) ◊ *His execution took place yesterday.* Seine Hinrichtung fand gestern statt.

executive NOUN
(*in business*)
der leitende Angestellte (GEN des leitenden Angestellten, PL die leitenden Angestellten)
die leitende Angestellte (GEN der leitenden Angestellten) ◊ *He's an executive.* Er ist leitender Angestellter.

exercise NOUN
[1] die Übung ◊ *an exercise book* ein Übungsheft

2 die Bewegung ◊ *You need more exercise.* Sie brauchen mehr Bewegung.
♦ **an exercise bike** ein Heimtrainer MASC
♦ **She does her exercises every morning.** Sie macht jeden Morgen ihre Gymnastik.

exhaust NOUN
der Auspuff
♦ **exhaust fumes** die Abgase PL

exhausted ADJECTIVE
erschöpft

exhaust pipe NOUN
das Auspuffrohr (PL die Auspuffrohre)

exhibition NOUN
die Ausstellung

to **exist** VERB
existieren (PERFECT hat existiert)
♦ **It doesn't exist.** Das gibt es nicht.

exit NOUN
der Ausgang (*way out*) (PL die Ausgänge)

exotic ADJECTIVE
exotisch

to **expect** VERB
1 erwarten (PERFECT hat erwartet) ◊ *I'm expecting him for dinner.* Ich erwarte ihn zum Abendessen. ◊ *She's expecting a baby.* Sie erwartet ein Kind. ◊ *I didn't expect that from him.* Das habe ich von ihm nicht erwartet.
2 annehmen (PRESENT nimmt an, IMPERFECT nahm an, PERFECT hat angenommen) ◊ *I expect he'll be late.* Ich nehme an, dass er sich verspäten wird. ◊ *I expect so.* Das nehme ich mal an.

expedition NOUN
die Expedition

to **expel** VERB
♦ **to get expelled** (*from school*) von der Schule verwiesen werden

expenses PL NOUN
die Kosten PL

expensive ADJECTIVE
teuer

experience NOUN
see also **experience** VERB
die Erfahrung

to **experience** VERB
see also **experience** NOUN
1 haben (PRESENT hat, IMPERFECT hatte, PERFECT hat gehabt) ◊ *They're experiencing some problems.* Sie haben einige Probleme.
2 (*feel*)
empfinden (IMPERFECT empfand, PERFECT hat empfunden) ◊ *He experienced fear and excitement.* Er empfand Angst und Aufregung.

experienced ADJECTIVE
erfahren

experiment NOUN
das Experiment (PL die Experimente)

expert NOUN

der Fachmann (PL die Fachleute)
die Fachfrau
◊ *He's a computer expert.* Er ist ein Computerfachmann.
♦ **He's an expert cook.** Er kocht ausgezeichnet.

to **expire** VERB
ablaufen (*passport*) (PRESENT läuft ab, IMPERFECT lief ab, PERFECT ist abgelaufen)

to **explain** VERB
erklären (PERFECT hat erklärt)

explanation NOUN
die Erklärung

to **explode** VERB
explodieren (PERFECT ist explodiert)

to **exploit** VERB
ausbeuten (PERFECT hat ausgebeutet)

exploitation NOUN
die Ausbeutung

to **explore** VERB
erkunden (*place*) (PERFECT hat erkundet)

explorer NOUN
der Forscher (PL die Forscher)
die Forscherin

explosion NOUN
die Explosion

explosive ADJECTIVE
see also **explosive** NOUN
explosiv

explosive NOUN
see also **explosive** ADJECTIVE
der Sprengstoff (PL die Sprengstoffe)

to **export** VERB
exportieren (PERFECT hat exportiert)

to **express** VERB
ausdrücken (PERFECT hat ausgedrückt)
♦ **to express oneself** sich ausdrücken ◊ *It's not easy to express oneself in a foreign language.* Es ist nicht einfach, sich in einer fremden Sprache auszudrücken.

expression NOUN
der Ausdruck (PL die Ausdrücke)
♦ **It's an English expression.** Das ist eine englische Redewendung.

expressway NOUN US
die Schnellstraße

extension NOUN
1 (*of building*)
der Anbau (PL die Anbauten)
2 (*telephone*)
der Apparat (PL die Apparate)
♦ **Extension 3137, please.** Apparat 3137, bitte.

extensive ADJECTIVE
1 ausgedehnt ◊ *The hotel is situated in extensive grounds.* Das Hotel liegt auf einem ausgedehnten Gelände.
2 umfangreich ◊ *My brother has an extensive knowledge of this subject.* Mein Bruder verfügt auf diesem Gebiet über ein umfangreiches Wissen.
♦ **extensive damage** schwere Schäden PL

E

extensively ADVERB
viel ◊ *He has travelled extensively.* Er ist viel gereist.

extent NOUN
♦**to some extent** in gewisser Weise

exterior ADJECTIVE
äußere ◊ *the exterior walls* die äußeren Wände

extinct ADJECTIVE
♦**to become extinct** aussterben
♦**to be extinct** ausgestorben sein ◊ *The species is almost extinct.* Diese Art ist fast ausgestorben.

extinguisher NOUN
der Feuerlöscher (*fire extinguisher*) (PL die Feuerlöscher)

extortionate ADJECTIVE
überzogen

extra ADJECTIVE, ADVERB
zusätzlich ◊ *an extra blanket* eine zusätzliche Decke
♦**to pay extra** extra bezahlen
♦**Breakfast is extra.** Frühstück wird extra berechnet.
♦**It costs extra.** Das kostet extra.

extraordinary ADJECTIVE
außergewöhnlich

extravagant ADJECTIVE
verschwenderisch (*person*)

extreme ADJECTIVE
extrem

extremely ADVERB
äußerst

extremist NOUN
der Extremist (GEN des Extremisten, PL die Extremisten)
die Extremistin

eye NOUN
das Auge (PL die Augen) ◊ *I've got green eyes.* Ich habe grüne Augen.
♦**to keep an eye on something** auf etwas aufpassen

eyebrow NOUN
die Augenbraue

eyelash NOUN
die Wimper

eyelid NOUN
das Augenlid (PL die Augenlider)

eyeliner NOUN
der Eyeliner (PL die Eyeliner)

eye shadow NOUN
der Lidschatten (PL die Lidschatten)

eyesight NOUN
das Sehvermögen ◊ *Her eyesight is deteriorating.* Ihr Sehvermögen lässt nach.
♦**to have good eyesight** gute Augen haben

F

fabric NOUN
der <u>Stoff</u> (PL die Stoffe)

fabulous ADJECTIVE
<u>traumhaft</u> ◇ *The show was fabulous.* Die Show war traumhaft.

face NOUN
see also **face** VERB
[1] (*of person*)
das <u>Gesicht</u> (PL die Gesichter)
[2] (*of clock*)
das <u>Zifferblatt</u> (PL die Zifferblätter)
[3] (*of cliff*)
die <u>Wand</u> (PL die Wände)
♦ **on the face of it** auf den ersten Blick
♦ **in the face of these difficulties** angesichts dieser Schwierigkeiten
♦ **face to face** Auge in Auge
♦ **a face cloth** ein Waschlappen MASC

to **face** VERB
see also **face** NOUN
<u>konfrontiert sein mit</u> (*place, problem*) (PRESENT ist konfrontiert mit, IMPERFECT war konfrontiert mit, PERFECT ist konfrontiert gewesen mit)
♦ **to face up to something** sich einer Sache stellen ◇ *You must face up to your responsibilities.* Sie müssen sich Ihrer Verantwortung stellen.

facilities PL NOUN
die <u>Einrichtungen</u> FEM PL
♦ **This school has excellent facilities.** Diese Schule ist ausgezeichnet ausgestattet.
♦ **toilet facilities** Toiletten FEM PL
♦ **cooking facilities** die Kochgelegenheit SING

fact NOUN
die <u>Tatsache</u>
♦ **in fact** tatsächlich

factory NOUN
die <u>Fabrik</u>

to **fade** VERB
[1] (*colour*)
<u>verblassen</u> (PERFECT ist verblasst) ◇ *The colour has faded in the sun.* Die Farbe ist in der Sonne verblasst.
♦ **My jeans have faded.** Meine Jeans sind verbleicht.
[2] <u>schwächer werden</u> (PRESENT wird schwächer, IMPERFECT wurde schwächer, PERFECT ist schwächer geworden) ◇ *The light was fading fast.* Das Licht wurde schnell schwächer.
[3] <u>abnehmen</u> (PRESENT nimmt ab, IMPERFECT nahm ab, PERFECT hat abgenommen) ◇ *The noise gradually faded.* Der Lärm nahm allmählich ab.

fag NOUN
die <u>Kippe</u> (*informal: cigarette*)

to **fail** VERB
see also **fail** NOUN
[1] <u>durchfallen in</u> +DAT (PRESENT fällt durch, IMPERFECT fiel durch, PERFECT ist durchgefallen) ◇ *I failed the history exam.* Ich bin in der Geschichtsprüfung durchgefallen.
[2] <u>durchfallen</u> ◇ *In our class, no one failed.* In unserer Klasse ist niemand durchgefallen.
[3] <u>versagen</u> (PERFECT hat versagt) ◇ *My brakes failed.* Meine Bremsen haben versagt.
♦ **to fail to do something** etwas nicht tun ◇ *She failed to return her library books.* Sie hat die Bücher aus der Bücherei nicht zurückgebracht.

fail NOUN
see also **fail** VERB
♦ **without fail** ganz bestimmt

failure NOUN
[1] das <u>Versagen</u> ◇ *a mechanical failure* ein mechanisches Versagen
♦ **feelings of failure** das Gefühl zu versagen
[2] der <u>Versager</u> (PL die Versager)
die <u>Versagerin</u>
◇ *He's a failure.* Er ist ein Versager.

faint ADJECTIVE
see also **faint** VERB
<u>schwach</u> ◇ *His voice was very faint.* Seine Stimme war sehr schwach.
♦ **I feel faint.** Mir ist schwindlig.

to **faint** VERB
see also **faint** ADJECTIVE
<u>ohnmächtig werden</u> (PRESENT wird ohnmächtig, IMPERFECT wurde ohnmächtig, PERFECT ist ohnmächtig geworden) ◇ *All of a sudden she fainted.* Plötzlich wurde sie ohnmächtig.

fair ADJECTIVE
see also **fair** NOUN
[1] <u>fair</u> ◇ *That's not fair.* Das ist nicht fair.
[2] <u>blond</u> (*hair*) ◇ *He's got fair hair.* Er hat blonde Haare.
[3] <u>hell</u> (*skin*) ◇ *people with fair skin* Menschen mit heller Haut
[4] <u>schön</u> (*weather*) ◇ *The weather was fair.* Das Wetter war schön.
[5] <u>gut</u> (*good enough*) ◇ *I have a fair chance of winning.* Ich habe gute Gewinnchancen.
[6] <u>ordentlich</u> (*sizeable*) ◇ *That's a fair distance.* Das ist eine ordentliche Entfernung.

fair NOUN
see also **fair** ADJECTIVE

das Volksfest (PL die Volksfeste) ◊ *They went to the fair.* Sie sind aufs Volksfest gegangen.
♦ **a trade fair** eine Handelsmesse

fairground NOUN
der Rummelplatz (PL die Rummelplätze)

fair-haired ADJECTIVE
blond

fairly ADVERB
① gerecht ◊ *The cake was divided fairly.* Der Kuchen wurde gerecht verteilt.
② ziemlich (*quite*) ◊ *That's fairly good.* Das ist ziemlich gut.

fairness NOUN
die Fairness

fairy NOUN
die Fee

fairy tale NOUN
das Märchen (PL die Märchen)

faith NOUN
① der Glaube (GEN des Glaubens) ◊ *the Catholic faith* der katholische Glaube
② das Vertrauen ◊ *People have lost faith in the government.* Die Menschen haben das Vertrauen in die Regierung verloren.

faithful ADJECTIVE
treu

faithfully ADVERB
♦ **Yours faithfully ...** (*in letter*) Hochachtungsvoll ...

fake NOUN
| see also **fake** ADJECTIVE |
die Fälschung ◊ *The painting was a fake.* Das Gemälde war eine Fälschung.

fake ADJECTIVE
| see also **fake** NOUN |
gefälscht ◊ *a fake certificate* eine gefälschte Urkunde
♦ **She wore fake fur.** Sie trug eine Pelzimitation.

fall NOUN
| see also **fall** VERB |
① der Sturz (GEN des Sturzes, PL die Stürze)
♦ **She had a nasty fall.** Sie ist übel gestürzt.
♦ **a fall of snow** ein Schneefall MASC
♦ **the Niagara Falls** die Niagarafälle
② US (*autumn*)
der Herbst (PL die Herbste)
◊ *in fall* im Herbst

to **fall** VERB
| see also **fall** NOUN |
① hinfallen (PRESENT fällt hin, IMPERFECT fiel hin, PERFECT ist hingefallen) ◊ *He tripped and fell.* Er ist gestolpert und hingefallen.
② fallen ◊ *Prices are falling.* Die Preise fallen.
♦ **to fall apart** auseinanderfallen ◊ *The book fell apart when he opened it.* Das Buch fiel auseinander, als er es öffnete.

♦ **to fall down (1)** (*person*) hinfallen ◊ *She's fallen down.* Sie ist hingefallen.
♦ **to fall down (2)** (*building*) einfallen ◊ *The wall fell down.* Die Mauer ist eingefallen.
♦ **to fall for (1)** hereinfallen auf +ACC ◊ *They fell for it.* Sie sind darauf hereingefallen.
♦ **to fall for (2)** sich verlieben in +ACC ◊ *She's falling for him.* Sie ist dabei, sich in ihn zu verlieben.
♦ **to fall off** herunterfallen von ◊ *The book fell off the shelf.* Das Buch ist vom Regal heruntergefallen.
♦ **to fall out** sich zerstreiten ◊ *Sarah's fallen out with her boyfriend.* Sarah hat sich mit ihrem Freund zerstritten.
♦ **to fall through** ins Wasser fallen ◊ *Our plans have fallen through.* Unsere Pläne sind ins Wasser gefallen.

false ADJECTIVE
falsch
♦ **a false alarm** falscher Alarm
♦ **false teeth** das Gebiss

fame NOUN
der Ruhm

familiar ADJECTIVE
vertraut ◊ *a familiar face* ein vertrautes Gesicht
♦ **to be familiar with something** mit etwas vertraut sein ◊ *I'm familiar with his work.* Ich bin mit seiner Arbeit vertraut.

family NOUN
die Familie
♦ **the Airlie family** die Familie Airlie

famine NOUN
die Hungersnot (PL die Hungersnöte)

famous ADJECTIVE
berühmt

fan NOUN
① (*hand-held*)
der Fächer (PL die Fächer)
② (*electric*)
der Ventilator (PL die Ventilatoren)
③ (*of person, band, sport*)
der Fan (PL die Fans)
der Fan is also used for women.
◊ *I'm a fan of Oasis.* Ich bin ein Fan von Oasis. ◊ *football fans* Fußballfans

fanatic NOUN
der Fanatiker (PL die Fanatiker)
die Fanatikerin

to **fancy** VERB
♦ **to fancy something** Lust auf etwas haben ◊ *I fancy an ice cream.* Ich habe Lust auf ein Eis.
♦ **to fancy doing something** Lust haben, etwas zu tun
♦ **He fancies her.** Er steht auf sie.

fancy dress NOUN
das Kostüm (PL die Kostüme)
♦ **He was wearing fancy dress.** Er war kostümiert.
♦ **a fancy-dress ball** ein Kostümball MASC

fantastic ADJECTIVE

fantastisch

far ADJECTIVE, ADVERB
weit ◊ *Is it far?* Ist es weit? ◊ *How far is it?* Wie weit ist es? ◊ *How far is it to Geneva?* Wie weit ist es nach Genf?
♦ **far from (1)** weit entfernt von ◊ *It's not far from London.* Es ist nicht weit von London entfernt.
♦ **far from (2)** überhaupt nicht ◊ *It's far from easy.* Es ist überhaupt nicht einfach.
♦ **How far have you got?** (*with a task*) Wie weit bist du gekommen?
♦ **at the far end** am anderen Ende ◊ *at the far end of the room* am anderen Ende des Zimmers
♦ **far better** viel besser
♦ **as far as I know** soviel ich weiß

fare NOUN
der Fahrpreis (PL die Fahrpreise)
♦ **half fare** halber Preis
♦ **full fare** voller Preis

Far East NOUN
der Ferne Osten ◊ *in the Far East* im Fernen Osten

farm NOUN
der Bauernhof (PL die Bauernhöfe)

farmer NOUN
der Bauer (GEN des Bauern, PL die Bauern)
die Bäuerin ◊ *He's a farmer.* Er ist Bauer.
♦ **a farmers' market** ein Bauernmarkt MASC

farmhouse NOUN
das Bauernhaus (GEN des Bauernhauses, PL die Bauernhäuser)

farming NOUN
die Landwirtschaft
♦ **dairy farming** die Milchwirtschaft

fascinating ADJECTIVE
faszinierend

fashion NOUN
die Mode
♦ **in fashion** in Mode

fashionable ADJECTIVE
modisch ◊ *Jane wears very fashionable clothes.* Jane trägt sehr modische Kleidung.
♦ **a fashionable restaurant** ein Restaurant, das in Mode ist

fast ADJECTIVE, ADVERB
schnell ◊ *He can run fast.* Er kann schnell laufen. ◊ *a fast car* ein schnelles Auto
♦ **That clock's fast.** Die Uhr geht vor.
♦ **He's fast asleep.** Er schläft fest.

*Be careful not to translate **fast** by the German word **fast**.*

fat ADJECTIVE
see also **fat** NOUN
dick (*person*)

fat NOUN
see also **fat** ADJECTIVE
das Fett (PL die Fette)
♦ **It's very high in fat.** Es ist sehr fett.

fatal ADJECTIVE
1 tödlich (*causing death*) ◊ *a fatal accident* ein tödlicher Unfall
2 fatal (*disastrous*) ◊ *He made a fatal mistake.* Er machte einen fatalen Fehler.

father NOUN
der Vater (PL die Väter) ◊ *my father* mein Vater
♦ **Father Christmas** der Weihnachtsmann

father-in-law NOUN
der Schwiegervater (PL die Schwiegerväter)

faucet NOUN US
der Wasserhahn (PL die Wasserhähne)

fault NOUN
1 (*mistake*)
die Schuld ◊ *It's my fault.* Es ist meine Schuld.
2 (*defect*)
der Fehler (PL die Fehler) ◊ *a mechanical fault* ein mechanischer Fehler

faulty ADJECTIVE
defekt ◊ *This machine is faulty.* Die Maschine ist defekt.

favour NOUN (US **favor**)
der Gefallen (PL die Gefallen)
♦ **to do somebody a favour** jemandem einen Gefallen tun ◊ *Could you do me a favour?* Könntest du mir einen Gefallen tun?
♦ **to be in favour of something** für etwas sein ◊ *I'm in favour of nuclear disarmament.* Ich bin für nukleare Abrüstung.

favourite ADJECTIVE (US **favorite**)
see also **favourite** NOUN
♦ **Blue's my favourite colour.** Blau ist meine Lieblingsfarbe.

favourite NOUN (US **favorite**)
see also **favourite** ADJECTIVE
1 der Liebling (PL die Lieblinge)
der Liebling is also used for women.
◊ *She's his favourite.* Sie ist sein Liebling.
2 der Favorit (PL die Favoriten)
die Favoritin
◊ *Liverpool are favourites to win the Cup.* Der FC Liverpool ist Favorit für den Pokal.

fax NOUN
see also **fax** VERB
das Fax (GEN des Fax, PL die Faxe)

to **fax** VERB
see also **fax** NOUN
faxen

fear NOUN
see also **fear** VERB
die Furcht

to **fear** VERB
see also **fear** NOUN
befürchten (PERFECT hat befürchtet) ◊ *You have nothing to fear.* Sie haben nichts zu befürchten.

feather NOUN

F

die <u>Feder</u>

feature NOUN
die <u>Eigenschaft</u> (*of person, object*) ◇ *an important feature* eine wichtige Eigenschaft

February NOUN
der <u>Februar</u> ◇ *in February* im Februar

fed VERB *see* **feed**

fed up ADJECTIVE
♦ **to be fed up with something** etwas satthaben ◇ *I'm fed up with him.* Ich habe ihn satt.

to **feed** VERB
<u>füttern</u> ◇ *Have you fed the cat?* Hast du die Katze gefüttert?
♦ **He worked hard to feed his family.** Er arbeitete hart, um seine Familie zu ernähren.

to **feel** VERB
① <u>sich fühlen</u> ◇ *I don't feel well.* Ich fühle mich nicht wohl. ◇ *I feel a bit lonely.* Ich fühle mich etwas einsam.
② <u>spüren</u> ◇ *I didn't feel much pain.* Ich habe keine großen Schmerzen gespürt.
③ <u>befühlen</u> (PERFECT hat befühlt) ◇ *The doctor felt his forehead.* Der Arzt hat ihm die Stirn befühlt.
♦ **I was feeling hungry.** Ich hatte Hunger.
♦ **I was feeling cold, so I went inside.** Mir war kalt, also bin ich ins Haus gegangen.
♦ **I feel like ...** (*want*) Ich habe Lust auf ... ◇ *Do you feel like an ice cream?* Hast du Lust auf ein Eis?

feeling NOUN
das <u>Gefühl</u> (PL die Gefühle) ◇ *a feeling of satisfaction* ein Gefühl der Befriedigung
♦ **an itchy feeling** ein Jucken NEUT

feet PL NOUN *see* **foot**

fell VERB *see* **fall**

felt VERB *see* **feel**

felt-tip pen NOUN
der <u>Filzschreiber</u> (PL die Filzschreiber)

female ADJECTIVE
> see also **female** NOUN

<u>weiblich</u> ◇ *a female animal* ein weibliches Tier ◇ *the female sex* das weibliche Geschlecht

> *In many cases, the ending indicates clearly whether the noun refers to a man or a woman and there is therefore no need for the word* **female**.

◇ *male and female students* Studenten und Studentinnen

female NOUN
> see also **female** ADJECTIVE

das <u>Weibchen</u> (*animal*) (PL die Weibchen)

feminine ADJECTIVE
<u>feminin</u>

feminist NOUN
der <u>Feminist</u> (GEN des Feministen, PL die Feministen)
die <u>Feministin</u>

fence NOUN
der <u>Zaun</u> (PL die Zäune)

fern NOUN
der <u>Farn</u> (PL die Farne)

ferocious ADJECTIVE
<u>wild</u>

ferry NOUN
die <u>Fähre</u>

fertile ADJECTIVE
<u>fruchtbar</u>

fertilizer NOUN
das <u>Düngemittel</u> (PL die Düngemittel)

festival NOUN
das <u>Festival</u> (PL die Festivals) ◇ *a jazz festival* ein Jazzfestival

to **fetch** VERB
① <u>holen</u> ◇ *Fetch the bucket.* Hol den Eimer.
② (*sell for*)
<u>einbringen</u> (IMPERFECT brachte ein, PERFECT hat eingebracht) ◇ *His painting fetched five thousand pounds.* Sein Bild hat fünftausend Pfund eingebracht.

fever NOUN
das <u>Fieber</u> (*temperature*)

few ADJECTIVE, PRONOUN
<u>wenige</u> (*not many*) ◇ *few books* wenige Bücher
♦ **a few** ein paar ◇ *a few hours* ein paar Stunden ◇ *How many apples do you want? – A few.* Wie viele Äpfel willst du? – Ein paar.
♦ **quite a few people** einige Leute

fewer ADJECTIVE
<u>weniger</u> ◇ *There are fewer people than there were yesterday.* Es sind weniger Leute da als gestern. ◇ *There are fewer pupils in this class.* In dieser Klasse sind weniger Schüler.

fiancé NOUN
der <u>Verlobte</u> (GEN des Verlobten, PL die Verlobten) ◇ *He's my fiancé.* Er ist mein Verlobter.

fiancée NOUN
die <u>Verlobte</u> (GEN der Verlobten, PL die Verlobten) ◇ *She's my fiancée.* Sie ist meine Verlobte.

fiction NOUN
die <u>Romane</u> MASC PL (*novels*)

field NOUN
① (*in countryside*)
das <u>Feld</u> (PL die Felder) ◇ *a field of wheat* ein Weizenfeld
② (*for sport*)
der <u>Platz</u> (GEN des Platzes, PL die Plätze) ◇ *a football field* ein Fußballplatz
③ (*subject*)
das <u>Gebiet</u> (PL die Gebiete) ◇ *He's an expert in his field.* Er ist Fachmann auf seinem Gebiet.

fierce ADJECTIVE
① <u>gefährlich</u> ◇ *The dog looked very fierce.* Der Hund sah sehr gefährlich aus.

2 heftig ◊ *a fierce attack* ein heftiger
Angriff
♦ **The wind was very fierce.** Es wehte ein
sehr scharfer Wind.
fifteen NUMBER
fünfzehn ◊ *I'm fifteen.* Ich bin fünfzehn.
fifteenth ADJECTIVE
fünfzehnte
♦ **the fifteenth of August** der fünfzehnte
August
fifth ADJECTIVE
fünfte ◊ *the fifth floor* der fünfte Stock
♦ **the fifth of August** der fünfte August
fifty NUMBER
fünfzig ◊ *He's fifty.* Er ist fünfzig.
fifty-fifty ADJECTIVE, ADVERB
halbe-halbe ◊ *They split the prize money
fifty-fifty.* Sie teilten das Preisgeld halbe-
halbe.
♦ **a fifty-fifty chance** eine fifty-fifty Chance
fight NOUN

see also **fight** VERB

1 die Schlägerei ◊ *There was a fight in
the pub.* In der Kneipe gab es eine
Schlägerei.
2 der Kampf (PL die Kämpfe) ◊ *the fight
against cancer* der Kampf gegen Krebs
to **fight** VERB

see also **fight** NOUN

1 (*physically*)
sich prügeln ◊ *They were fighting.* Sie
haben sich geprügelt.
2 (*quarrel*)
streiten (IMPERFECT stritt, PERFECT hat
gestritten) ◊ *He's always fighting with his
wife.* Er streitet dauernd mit seiner Frau.
3 (*combat*)
bekämpfen (PERFECT hat bekämpft) ◊ *The
doctors tried to fight the disease.* Die
Ärzte versuchten, die Krankheit zu
bekämpfen.
to **fight back** VERB
sich wehren
fighting NOUN
die Schlägerei ◊ *Fighting broke out
outside the pub.* Vor der Kneipe kam es
zu einer Schlägerei.
figure NOUN
1 die Zahl (*number*) ◊ *Can you give me
the exact figures?* Können Sie mir
genaue Zahlen nennen?
2 die Gestalt (*outline of person*) ◊ *Mary
saw the figure of a man on the bridge.*
Mary sah die Gestalt eines Mannes auf
der Brücke.
3 die Figur (*shape*) ◊ *She's got a good
figure.* Sie hat eine gute Figur. ◊ *I have to
watch my figure.* Ich muss auf meine
Figur achten.
4 die Persönlichkeit (*personality*) ◊ *She's
an important political figure.* Sie ist eine
wichtige politische Persönlichkeit.

to **figure out** VERB
1 ausrechnen (PERFECT hat ausgerechnet)
◊ *I'll try to figure out how much it'll cost.*
Ich versuche auszurechnen, wie viel das
kostet.
2 herausfinden (IMPERFECT fand heraus,
PERFECT hat herausgefunden) ◊ *I couldn't
figure out what it meant.* Ich konnte nicht
herausfinden, was das bedeutet.
3 schlau werden aus (PRESENT wird
schlau, IMPERFECT wurde schlau, PERFECT ist
schlau geworden) ◊ *I can't figure him out
at all.* Ich werde aus ihm überhaupt nicht
schlau.
file NOUN

see also **file** VERB

1 (*document*)
die Akte ◊ *Have we got a file on the
suspect?* Haben wir über den
Verdächtigen eine Akte?
2 (*folder*)
die Aktenmappe ◊ *She keeps all her
letters in a cardboard file.* Sie bewahrt all
ihre Briefe in einer Aktenmappe auf.
3 (*ring binder*)
der Aktenordner (PL die Aktenordner)
4 (*on computer*)
die Datei
5 (*for nails, metal*)
die Feile
to **file** VERB

see also **file** NOUN

1 (*papers*)
abheften (PERFECT hat abgeheftet)
2 (*nails, metal*)
feilen ◊ *I'll have to file my nails.* Ich
muss mir die Nägel feilen.
to **fill** VERB
füllen ◊ *She filled the glass with water.*
Sie füllte das Glas mit Wasser.
♦ **to fill in (1)** ausfüllen ◊ *Can you fill this
form in, please?* Können Sie bitte dieses
Formular ausfüllen?
♦ **to fill in (2)** auffüllen ◊ *He filled the hole
in with soil.* Er füllte das Loch mit Erde
auf.
♦ **to fill up** vollmachen ◊ *He filled the cup
up to the brim.* Er machte die Tasse bis
zum Rand voll.
♦ **Fill it up, please.** (*at petrol station*)
Volltanken, bitte.
film NOUN
der Film (PL die Filme)
film star NOUN
der Filmstar (PL die Filmstars)
der Filmstar is also used for women.
◊ *She's a film star.* Sie ist ein Filmstar.
filthy ADJECTIVE
schmutzig
final ADJECTIVE

see also **final** NOUN

1 letzte (*last*) ◊ *our final match of the
season* unser letztes Spiel der Saison

F

2 endgültig (*definite*) ◊ *a final decision* eine endgültige Entscheidung
♦ **I'm not going and that's final.** Ich gehe nicht, und damit basta.

final NOUN
see also **final** ADJECTIVE

das Finale (PL die Finale) ◊ *Boris Becker is in the final.* Boris Becker ist im Finale.

finally ADVERB
1 schließlich (*lastly*) ◊ *Finally, I would like to say …* Und schließlich möchte ich sagen …
2 letztendlich (*eventually*) ◊ *They finally decided to leave on Saturday instead of Friday.* Sie haben letztendlich beschlossen, am Samstag statt am Freitag zu fahren.

financial ADJECTIVE
finanziell

to **find** VERB
finden (IMPERFECT fand, PERFECT hat gefunden) ◊ *I can't find the exit.* Ich kann den Ausgang nicht finden. ◊ *Did you find your pen?* Hast du deinen Schreiber gefunden?
♦ **to find something out** etwas herausfinden ◊ *I'm determined to find out the truth.* Ich bin entschlossen, die Wahrheit herauszufinden.
♦ **to find out about (1)** (*make enquiries*) sich erkundigen nach ◊ *Try to find out about the cost of a hotel.* Versuche, dich nach dem Preis für ein Hotel zu erkundigen.
♦ **to find out about (2)** (*by chance*) erfahren ◊ *I found out about their affair.* Ich habe von ihrem Verhältnis erfahren.

fine ADJECTIVE, ADVERB
see also **fine** NOUN

1 ausgezeichnet (*very good*) ◊ *He's a fine musician.* Er ist ein ausgezeichneter Musiker.
♦ **How are you? – I'm fine.** Wie geht's? – Gut!
♦ **I feel fine.** Mir geht's gut.
♦ **The weather is fine today.** Das Wetter ist heute schön.
2 fein (*not coarse*) ◊ *She's got very fine hair.* Sie hat sehr feine Haare.

fine NOUN
see also **fine** ADJECTIVE

1 die Geldbuße ◊ *She got a fifty-pound fine.* Sie hat eine Geldbuße von fünfzig Pfund bekommen.
2 (*for traffic offence*)
der Strafzettel (PL die Strafzettel) ◊ *I got a fine for driving through a red light.* Ich habe einen Strafzettel bekommen, weil ich bei Rot über die Ampel gefahren bin.

finger NOUN
der Finger (PL die Finger)
♦ **my little finger** mein kleiner Finger

fingernail NOUN
der Fingernagel (PL die Fingernägel)

finish NOUN
see also **finish** VERB

das Finish (*of race*) (PL die Finishs) ◊ *We saw the finish of the London Marathon.* Wir sahen das Finish des Londoner Marathonlaufs.

to **finish** VERB
see also **finish** NOUN

1 fertig sein (PRESENT ist fertig, IMPERFECT war fertig, PERFECT ist fertig gewesen) ◊ *I've finished!* Ich bin fertig!
2 zu Ende sein (PRESENT ist zu Ende, IMPERFECT war zu Ende, PERFECT ist zu Ende gewesen) ◊ *The film has finished.* Der Film ist zu Ende.
♦ **I've finished the book.** Ich habe das Buch zu Ende gelesen.
♦ **to finish doing something** etwas zu Ende machen ◊ *Let me finish writing this letter.* Lass mich den Brief zu Ende schreiben.

Finland NOUN
Finnland NEUT
♦ **from Finland** aus Finnland
♦ **to Finland** nach Finnland

Finn NOUN
der Finne (GEN des Finnen, PL die Finnen)
die Finnin

Finnish ADJECTIVE
see also **Finnish** NOUN

finnisch
♦ **She's Finnish.** Sie ist Finnin.

Finnish NOUN
see also **Finnish** ADJECTIVE

(*language*)
das Finnisch (GEN des Finnischen)

fir NOUN
die Tanne
♦ **fir cone** der Tannenzapfen
♦ **fir tree** der Tannenbaum

fire NOUN
see also **fire** VERB

1 das Feuer (PL die Feuer) ◊ *He made a fire to warm himself up.* Er machte ein Feuer, um sich aufzuwärmen.
♦ **to be on fire** brennen
2 (*accidental*)
der Brand (PL die Brände)
♦ **The house was destroyed by fire.** Das Haus ist abgebrannt.
3 (*heater*)
die Heizung ◊ *Turn the fire on.* Mach die Heizung an.
♦ **the fire brigade** die Feuerwehr
♦ **a fire alarm** ein Feueralarm MASC
♦ **a fire engine** ein Feuerwehrauto NEUT
♦ **a fire escape** (*stairs*) eine Feuertreppe
♦ **a fire extinguisher** ein Feuerlöscher MASC
♦ **a fire station** eine Feuerwehrstation

to **fire** VERB
see also **fire** NOUN

schießen (*shoot*) (IMPERFECT schoss, PERFECT
hat geschossen) ◊ *She fired twice.* Sie
hat zweimal geschossen.
♦ **to fire at somebody** auf jemanden
schießen ◊ *The terrorist fired at the
crowd.* Der Terrorist hat in die Menge
geschossen.
♦ **to fire a gun** einen Schuss abgeben
♦ **to fire somebody** jemanden feuern ◊ *He
was fired from his job.* Er wurde aus
seinem Job gefeuert.

fireman NOUN
der Feuerwehrmann (PL die
Feuerwehrleute) ◊ *He's a fireman.* Er ist
Feuerwehrmann.

fireplace NOUN
der offene Kamin (PL die offenen
Kamine)

fireworks PL NOUN
das Feuerwerk (PL die Feuerwerke)
◊ *Are you going to see the
fireworks?* Seht ihr euch das Feuerwerk
an?

firm ADJECTIVE
see also **firm** NOUN
streng ◊ *to be firm with somebody*
streng mit jemandem sein

firm NOUN
see also **firm** ADJECTIVE
die Firma (PL die Firmen) ◊ *He works for
a large firm in London.* Er arbeitet für
eine große Firma in London.

first ADJECTIVE, ADVERB
see also **first** NOUN
[1] erste ◊ *my first boyfriend* mein
erster Freund ◊ *the first time* das erste
Mal
♦ **Rachel came first.** (*in exam, race*) Rachel
war Erste.
♦ **John came first.** (*in exam, race*) John war
Erster. ◊ *the first of August* der erste
August
[2] zuerst ◊ *I want to get a job, but first I
have to pass my exams.* Ich will mir
einen Job suchen, aber zuerst muss ich
meine Prüfung bestehen.
♦ **first of all** zuallererst

first NOUN
see also **first** ADJECTIVE
der Erste (GEN des Ersten, PL die Ersten)
die Erste (GEN der Ersten) ◊ *She was the
first to arrive.* Sie ist als Erste
angekommen.
♦ **at first** zuerst

first aid NOUN
die Erste Hilfe
♦ **a first aid kit** ein Verbandszeug NEUT

first-class ADJECTIVE
[1] erster Klasse ◊ *She has booked a
first-class ticket.* Sie hat ein Ticket erster
Klasse gebucht.
[2] erstklassig ◊ *a first-class meal* ein
erstklassiges Essen

ⓘ *In Germany there is no first-class or
second-class post. However, letters
cost more to send than postcards, so
you have to remember to say what you
are sending when buying stamps.
There is also an express service.*

firstly ADVERB
[1] zuerst ◊ *Firstly, let's see what the
book is about.* Wir wollen erst mal sehen,
wovon das Buch handelt.
[2] erstens ◊ *firstly ... secondly ...* erstens
... zweitens ...

fish NOUN
see also **fish** VERB
der Fisch (PL die Fische) ◊ *I caught three
fish.* Ich habe drei Fische gefangen.

to **fish** VERB
see also **fish** NOUN
fischen
♦ **to go fishing** fischen gehen ◊ *We went
fishing in the River Dee.* Wir haben im
River Dee gefischt.

fisherman NOUN
der Fischer (PL die Fischer) ◊ *He's a
fisherman.* Er ist Fischer.

fish finger NOUN
das Fischstäbchen (PL die Fischstäbchen)

fishing NOUN
das Angeln ◊ *My hobby is fishing.*
Angeln ist mein Hobby.

fishing boat NOUN
das Fischerboot (PL die Fischerboote)

fishing rod NOUN
die Angel

fishing tackle NOUN
das Angelzeug

fishmonger's NOUN
der Fischladen (PL die Fischläden)

fish sticks PL NOUN US
die Fischstäbchen

fist NOUN
die Faust (PL die Fäuste)

to **fit** VERB
see also **fit** ADJECTIVE, NOUN
[1] (*be the right size*)
passen (PERFECT hat gepasst) ◊ *Does it fit?*
Passt es?
[2] (*fix up*)
einbauen (PERFECT hat eingebaut) ◊ *He
fitted an alarm in his car.* Er hat eine
Alarmanlage in sein Auto eingebaut.
[3] (*attach*)
anbringen (IMPERFECT brachte an, PERFECT
hat angebracht) ◊ *She fitted a plug to the
hair dryer.* Sie brachte am Föhn einen
Stecker an.
♦ **to fit in (1)** (*match up*) passen zu ◊ *That
story doesn't fit in with what he told us.*
Diese Geschichte passt nicht zu dem,
was er uns gesagt hat.

☞

◆**to fit in (2)** (*person*) sich einpassen ◊ *She fitted in well at her new school.* Sie hat sich in ihrer neuen Schule gut eingepasst.

fit ADJECTIVE

see also **fit** VERB, NOUN

fit (*healthy*) ◊ *He felt relaxed and fit after his holiday.* Nach seinem Urlaub fühlte er sich entspannt und fit.

fit NOUN

see also **fit** ADJECTIVE, VERB

◆**to have a fit (1)** (*epileptic*) einen Anfall haben

◆**to have a fit (2)** (*be angry*) Zustände bekommen ◊ *My Mum will have a fit when she sees the carpet!* Meine Mutter bekommt Zustände, wenn sie den Teppich sieht!

fitted carpet NOUN

der Teppichboden (PL die Teppichböden)

fitted kitchen NOUN

die Einbauküche

fitting room NOUN

die Umkleidekabine

five NUMBER

fünf ◊ *He's five.* Er ist fünf.

to **fix** VERB

⓵ (*mend*)

reparieren (PERFECT hat repariert) ◊ *Can you fix my bike?* Kannst du mein Fahrrad reparieren?

⓶ (*decide*)

festlegen (PERFECT hat festgelegt) ◊ *Let's fix a date for the party.* Lass uns einen Tag für die Party festlegen. ◊ *They fixed a price for the car.* Sie haben einen Preis für das Auto festgelegt.

⓷ machen ◊ *Jan fixed some food for us.* Jan hat uns etwas zum Essen gemacht.

fixed ADJECTIVE

festgesetzt ◊ *at a fixed price* zu einem festgesetzten Preis

◆**at a fixed time** zu einer bestimmten Zeit

◆**My parents have very fixed ideas.** Meine Eltern haben ziemlich festgelegte Ansichten.

fizzy ADJECTIVE

mit Kohlensäure ◊ *I don't like fizzy drinks.* Ich mag keine Getränke mit Kohlensäure.

flabby ADJECTIVE

wabbelig

flag NOUN

die Fahne

flame NOUN

die Flamme

flamingo NOUN

der Flamingo (PL die Flamingos)

flan NOUN

⓵ (*sweet*)

der Kuchen (PL die Kuchen) ◊ *a raspberry flan* ein Himbeerkuchen

⓶ (*savoury*)

die Quiche (PL die Quiches) ◊ *a cheese*

and onion flan eine Käse-Zwiebel-Quiche

flannel NOUN

der Waschlappen (PL die Waschlappen)

to **flap** VERB

flattern mit ◊ *The bird flapped its wings.* Der Vogel flatterte mit den Flügeln.

flash NOUN

see also **flash** VERB

das Blitzlicht (PL die Blitzlichter) ◊ *Has your camera got a flash?* Hat dein Fotoapparat ein Blitzlicht?

◆**a flash of lightning** ein Blitz MASC

◆**in a flash** blitzschnell

to **flash** VERB

see also **flash** NOUN

⓵ blinken ◊ *The police car's blue light was flashing.* Das Blaulicht des Polizeiautos blinkte.

⓶ leuchten mit ◊ *They flashed a torch in his face.* Sie leuchteten ihm mit einer Taschenlampe ins Gesicht.

◆**She flashed her headlights.** Sie betätigte die Lichthupe.

flask NOUN

die Thermosflasche ®

flat ADJECTIVE

see also **flat** NOUN

⓵ flach ◊ *flat shoes* flache Schuhe

◆**a flat roof** ein Flachdach NEUT

⓶ platt (*tyre*) ◊ *I've got a flat tyre.* Ich habe einen platten Reifen.

flat NOUN

see also **flat** ADJECTIVE

die Wohnung ◊ *She lives in a flat.* Sie wohnt in einer Wohnung.

flatscreen ADJECTIVE

◆**a flatscreen TV** ein Flachbildschirm-Fernseher MASC

to **flatter** VERB

schmeicheln ◊ *Are you trying to flatter me?* Willst du mir schmeicheln? ◊ *I feel flattered.* Ich fühle mich geschmeichelt.

flavour NOUN

der Geschmack (PL die Geschmäcke) ◊ *This cheese has a very strong flavour.* Dieser Käse hat einen sehr pikanten Geschmack.

◆**Which flavour of ice cream would you like?** Was für ein Eis möchtest du?

flavouring NOUN

das Aroma (PL die Aromen)

flea NOUN

der Floh (PL die Flöhe)

flew VERB see **fly**

flexible ADJECTIVE

flexibel

◆**flexible working hours** gleitende Arbeitszeit

to **flick** VERB

schnipsen ◊ *She flicked the ash off her jumper.* Sie schnipste die Asche von ihrem Pullover.

◆ **to flick through a book** ein Buch durchblättern

to **flicker** VERB
  flackern ◊ *The light flickered.* Das Licht flackerte.

flight NOUN
  der Flug (PL die Flüge) ◊ *What time is the flight to Munich?* Um wie viel Uhr geht der Flug nach München?
◆ **a flight of stairs** eine Treppe

flight attendant NOUN
  der Flugbegleiter (PL die Flugbegleiter)
  die Flugbegleiterin

to **fling** VERB
  schmeißen (IMPERFECT schmiss, PERFECT hat geschmissen) ◊ *He flung the dictionary onto the floor.* Er schmiss das Wörterbuch auf den Boden.

to **float** VERB
  schwimmen (IMPERFECT schwamm, PERFECT ist geschwommen) ◊ *A leaf was floating on the water.* Auf dem Wasser schwamm ein Blatt.

flock NOUN
◆ **a flock of sheep** eine Schafherde
◆ **a flock of birds** ein Vogelschwarm NEUT

flood NOUN
  │ see also **flood** VERB │
  [1] die Überschwemmung ◊ *The rain has caused many floods.* Der Regen hat zu vielen Überschwemmungen geführt.
  [2] die Flut ◊ *He received a flood of letters.* Er erhielt eine Flut von Briefen.

to **flood** VERB
  │ see also **flood** NOUN │
  überschwemmen (PERFECT hat überschwemmt) ◊ *The river has flooded the village.* Der Fluss hat das Dorf überschwemmt.

flooding NOUN
  die Überschwemmung

floor NOUN
  [1] der Fußboden (PL die Fußböden)
◆ **a tiled floor** ein Fliesenboden
◆ **on the floor** auf dem Boden
  [2] (*storey*)
  der Stock (PL die Stock)
◆ **the first floor** der erste Stock ◊ *on the first floor* im ersten Stock
◆ **the ground floor** das Erdgeschoss
  Be careful not to translate **floor** *by* **Flur.**

flop NOUN
  der Flop (PL die Flops) ◊ *The film was a flop.* Der Film war ein Flop.

floppy disk NOUN
  die Diskette

florist NOUN
  der Florist (GEN des Floristen, PL die Floristen)
  die Floristin

flour NOUN
  das Mehl (PL die Mehle)

to **flow** VERB
  fließen (IMPERFECT floss, PERFECT ist geflossen) ◊ *Water was flowing from the pipe.* Aus dem Rohr floss Wasser.

flower NOUN
  │ see also **flower** VERB │
  die Blume

to **flower** VERB
  │ see also **flower** NOUN │
  blühen

flown VERB see **fly**

flu NOUN
  die Grippe ◊ *She's got flu.* Sie hat Grippe.

fluent ADJECTIVE
◆ **He speaks fluent German.** Er spricht fließend Deutsch.

flung VERB see **fling**

flush NOUN
  │ see also **flush** VERB │
  die Spülung (*of toilet*)

to **flush** VERB
  │ see also **flush** NOUN │
◆ **to flush the toilet** spülen

flute NOUN
  die Querflöte ◊ *I play the flute.* Ich spiele Querflöte.

fly NOUN
  │ see also **fly** VERB │
  die Fliege (*insect*)

to **fly** VERB
  │ see also **fly** NOUN │
  fliegen (IMPERFECT flog, PERFECT ist geflogen) ◊ *He flew from Berlin to New York.* Er flog von Berlin nach New York.
◆ **to fly away** wegfliegen ◊ *The bird flew away.* Der Vogel flog weg.

foal NOUN
  das Fohlen (PL die Fohlen)

focus NOUN
  │ see also **focus** VERB │
◆ **to be out of focus** unscharf sein ◊ *The house is out of focus in this photo.* Das Haus ist auf diesem Foto unscharf.

to **focus** VERB
  │ see also **focus** NOUN │
  scharf einstellen (PERFECT hat scharf eingestellt) ◊ *Try to focus the binoculars.* Versuch, das Fernglas scharf einzustellen.
◆ **to focus on something (1)** (*with camera, telescope*) etwas auf etwas einstellen ◊ *The cameraman focused on the bird.* Der Kameramann stellte die Kamera auf den Vogel ein.
◆ **to focus on something (2)** (*concentrate*) sich auf etwas konzentrieren ◊ *Let's focus on the plot of the play.* Wir wollen uns auf die Handlung des Stücks konzentrieren.

fog NOUN
  der Nebel (PL die Nebel)

foggy ADJECTIVE

F

neblig ◊ *a foggy day* ein nebliger Tag

foil NOUN
die <u>Alufolie</u> (*kitchen foil*) ◊ *She wrapped the meat in foil.* Sie wickelte das Fleisch in Alufolie.

fold NOUN
> see also **fold** VERB

die <u>Falte</u>

to **fold** VERB
> see also **fold** NOUN

<u>falten</u> ◊ *He folded the newspaper in half.* Er faltete die Zeitung in der Mitte zusammen.
- ◆ **to fold up (1)** zusammenfalten (*paper*)
- ◆ **to fold up (2)** zusammenklappen (*chair*)
- ◆ **to fold one's arms** die Arme verschränken ◊ *She folded her arms.* Sie verschränkte die Arme.

folder NOUN
1 die <u>Mappe</u> ◊ *She kept all her letters in a folder.* Sie bewahrte all ihre Briefe in einer Mappe auf.
2 (*ring binder*)
der <u>Ordner</u> (PL die Ordner)

folding ADJECTIVE
- ◆ **a folding chair** ein Klappstuhl MASC
- ◆ **a folding bed** ein Klappbett NEUT

to **follow** VERB
<u>folgen</u> (PERFECT ist gefolgt) ◊ *She followed him.* Sie folgte ihm.
- ◆ **You go first and I'll follow.** Geh du vor, ich komme nach.

following ADJECTIVE
<u>folgend</u> ◊ *the following day* am folgenden Tag

fond ADJECTIVE
- ◆ **to be fond of somebody** jemanden gernhaben ◊ *I'm very fond of her.* Ich habe sie sehr gern.

food NOUN
die <u>Nahrung</u>
- ◆ **We need to buy some food.** Wir müssen etwas zum Essen kaufen.
- ◆ **cat food** das Katzenfutter
- ◆ **dog food** das Hundefutter

food processor NOUN
die <u>Küchenmaschine</u>

fool NOUN
der <u>Idiot</u> (GEN des Idioten, PL die Idioten)
die <u>Idiotin</u>

foot NOUN
1 (*of person*)
der <u>Fuß</u> (GEN des Fußes, PL die Füße) ◊ *My feet are aching.* Mir tun die Füße weh.
- ◆ **on foot** zu Fuß
2 (*12 inches*)
der <u>Fuß</u> (PL die Fuß)

> 🛈 In Germany measurements are in metres and centimetres rather than feet and inches. A foot is about 30 centimetres.

◊ *Dave is six foot tall.* Dave ist ein Meter achtzig groß. ◊ *That mountain is five thousand feet high.* Dieser Berg ist eintausendsechshundert Meter hoch.

football NOUN
der <u>Fußball</u> (PL die Fußbälle) ◊ *I like playing football.* Ich spiele gern Fußball. ◊ *Paul threw the football over the fence.* Paul warf den Fußball über den Zaun.

footballer NOUN
der <u>Fußballer</u> (PL die Fußballer)
die <u>Fußballerin</u>

football player NOUN
der <u>Fußballspieler</u> (PL die Fußballspieler)
die <u>Fußballspielerin</u>
◊ *He's a famous football player.* Er ist ein bekannter Fußballspieler.

footpath NOUN
der <u>Fußweg</u> (PL die Fußwege) ◊ *Jane followed the footpath through the forest.* Jane ging den Fußweg durch den Wald entlang.

footprint NOUN
der <u>Fußabdruck</u> (PL die Fußabdrücke)
◊ *He saw some footprints in the sand.* Er sah Fußabdrücke im Sand.

footstep NOUN
der <u>Schritt</u> (PL die Schritte) ◊ *I can hear footsteps on the stairs.* Ich höre Schritte auf der Treppe.

for PREPOSITION
> *There are several ways of translating* **for**. *Scan the examples to find one that is similar to what you want to say.*

1 <u>für</u> ◊ *a present for me* ein Geschenk für mich ◊ *He works for the government.* Er arbeitet für die Regierung. ◊ *I'll do it for you.* Ich mache es für dich. ◊ *Are you for or against the idea?* Bist du für oder gegen die Idee? ◊ *Oxford is famous for its university.* Oxford ist für seine Universität berühmt. ◊ *I sold it for five pounds.* Ich habe es für fünf Pfund verkauft.
- ◆ **What for?** Wofür? ◊ *Give me some money! – What for?* Gib mir Geld! – Wofür? ◊ *What's it for?* Wofür ist das?

> *When referring to periods of time, use* **lang** *for the future and completed action in the past, and* **seit** *(with the German verb in the present tense) for something that started in the past and is still going on.*

2 <u>lang</u> ◊ *He worked in Germany for two years.* Er hat zwei Jahre lang in Deutschland gearbeitet. ◊ *She will be away for a month.* Sie wird einen Monat lang weg sein.
- ◆ **There are road works for three kilometres.** Es gibt dort über drei Kilometer Bauarbeiten.

3 <u>seit</u> ◊ *He's been learning German for two years.* Er lernt seit zwei Jahren

Deutsch. ◊ *She's been away for a month.* Sie ist seit einem Monat weg.
- ◆**What's the German for "lion"?** Wie sagt man "lion" auf Deutsch?
- ◆**It's time for lunch.** Es ist Zeit zum Mittagessen.
- ◆**the train for London** der Zug nach London
- ◆**for sale** zu verkaufen ◊ *The factory's for sale.* Die Fabrik ist zu verkaufen.

to **forbid** VERB
verbieten (IMPERFECT verbot, PERFECT hat verboten)
- ◆**to forbid somebody to do something** jemandem verbieten, etwas zu tun ◊ *I forbid you to go out tonight!* Ich verbiete dir, heute Abend auszugehen!

forbidden ADJECTIVE
verboten ◊ *Smoking is strictly forbidden.* Rauchen ist streng verboten.

force NOUN
see also **force** VERB
die Gewalt ◊ *the forces of nature* die Naturgewalten
- ◆**The force of the explosion blew out all the windows.** Die Explosion war so stark, dass alle Fenster kaputtgingen.
- ◆**in force** in Kraft ◊ *The new law has been in force since May.* Das neue Gesetz ist seit Mai in Kraft.

to **force** VERB
see also **force** NOUN
zwingen (IMPERFECT zwang, PERFECT hat gezwungen) ◊ *They forced him to open the safe.* Sie zwangen ihn, den Safe aufzumachen.

forecast NOUN
- ◆**the weather forecast** die Wettervorhersage

foreground NOUN
der Vordergrund ◊ *in the foreground* im Vordergrund

forehead NOUN
die Stirn

foreign ADJECTIVE
ausländisch

foreigner NOUN
der Ausländer (PL die Ausländer)
die Ausländerin

to **foresee** VERB
vorhersehen (PRESENT sieht vorher, IMPERFECT sah vorher, PERFECT hat vorhergesehen) ◊ *He had foreseen the problem.* Er hatte das Problem vorhergesehen.

forest NOUN
der Wald (PL die Wälder)

forever ADVERB
1 für immer ◊ *He's gone forever.* Er ist für immer weg.
2 dauernd (*always*) ◊ *She's forever complaining.* Sie beklagt sich dauernd.

forgave VERB see **forgive**

to **forge** VERB
fälschen ◊ *She tried to forge his signature.* Sie versuchte, seine Unterschrift zu fälschen.

forged ADJECTIVE
gefälscht ◊ *forged banknotes* gefälschte Banknoten

to **forget** VERB
vergessen (PRESENT vergisst, IMPERFECT vergaß, PERFECT hat vergessen) ◊ *I've forgotten his name.* Ich habe seinen Namen vergessen. ◊ *I'm sorry, I completely forgot!* Tut mir leid, das habe ich total vergessen!

forgetful ADJECTIVE
vergesslich

to **forgive** VERB
- ◆**to forgive somebody** jemandem verzeihen ◊ *I forgive you.* Ich verzeihe dir.
- ◆**to forgive somebody for doing something** jemandem verzeihen, etwas getan zu haben ◊ *She forgave him for forgetting her birthday.* Sie verzieh ihm, dass er ihren Geburtstag vergessen hat.

forgot, forgotten VERB see **forget**

fork NOUN
1 die Gabel (*for eating, gardening*) ◊ *He ate his chips with a fork.* Er aß seine Pommes frites mit einer Gabel.
2 die Gabelung (*in road*)
- ◆**There was a fork in the road.** Die Straße gabelte sich.

form NOUN
1 (*paper*)
das Formular (PL die Formulare) ◊ *to fill in a form* ein Formular ausfüllen
2 (*type*)
die Form ◊ *I'm against hunting in any form.* Ich bin gegen die Jagd in jeglicher Form.
- ◆**in top form** in Topform
- ◆**She's in the fourth form.** Sie ist in der zehnten Klasse.

formal ADJECTIVE
1 formell (*occasion*) ◊ *a formal dinner* ein formelles Abendessen
2 förmlich (*person*)
3 gehoben (*language*) ◊ *In English, "residence" is a formal term.* Auf Englisch ist "residence" ein gehobener Ausdruck.
- ◆**formal clothes** die Gesellschaftskleidung SING
- ◆**He's got no formal qualifications.** Er hat keinen offiziellen Abschluss.

former ADJECTIVE
früher ◊ *a former pupil* ein früherer Schüler ◊ *the former Prime Minister* der frühere Premierminister

formerly ADVERB
früher

fort NOUN

F

das <u>Fort</u> (PL die Forts)
forth ADVERB
- **to go back and forth** hin- und hergehen
- **and so forth** und so weiter

forthcoming ADJECTIVE
<u>kommend</u> ◊ *It will be discussed at the forthcoming meeting.* Darüber wird auf der kommenden Besprechung diskutiert werden.

fortnight NOUN
- **a fortnight** vierzehn Tage ◊ *I'm going on holiday for a fortnight.* Ich verreise für vierzehn Tage.

fortunate ADJECTIVE
- **to be fortunate** Glück haben ◊ *He was extremely fortunate to survive.* Es war Glück, dass er überlebt hat.
- **It's fortunate that I remembered the map.** Zum Glück habe ich an die Landkarte gedacht.

fortunately ADVERB
<u>zum Glück</u> ◊ *Fortunately, it didn't rain.* Zum Glück hat es nicht geregnet.

fortune NOUN
das <u>Vermögen</u> (PL die Vermögen) ◊ *Kate earns a fortune!* Kate verdient ein Vermögen!
- **to tell somebody's fortune** jemandem wahrsagen

forty NUMBER
<u>vierzig</u> ◊ *He's forty.* Er ist vierzig.

forward ADVERB
> see also **forward** VERB
- **to move forward** sich vorwärtsbewegen

to **forward** VERB
> see also **forward** ADVERB
<u>nachsenden</u> (IMPERFECT sandte nach, PERFECT hat nachgesandt) ◊ *He forwarded all her letters.* Er sandte alle ihre Briefe nach.

to **foster** VERB
in Pflege nehmen (PRESENT nimmt, IMPERFECT nahm, PERFECT hat genommen) ◊ *She has fostered more than fifteen children.* Sie hat mehr als fünfzehn Kinder in Pflege genommen.

foster child NOUN
das <u>Pflegekind</u> (PL die Pflegekinder) ◊ *She's their foster child.* Sie ist ihr Pflegekind.

fought VERB *see* **fight**

foul ADJECTIVE
> see also **foul** NOUN
<u>furchtbar</u> ◊ *The weather was foul.* Das Wetter war furchtbar. ◊ *What a foul smell!* Was für ein furchtbarer Gestank!

foul NOUN
> see also **foul** ADJECTIVE
das <u>Foul</u> (PL die Fouls) ◊ *Ferguson committed a foul.* Ferguson hat ein Foul begangen.

found VERB *see* **find**

to **found** VERB

<u>gründen</u> ◊ *Baden-Powell founded the Scout Movement.* Baden-Powell hat die Pfadfinderbewegung gegründet.

foundations PL NOUN
das <u>Fundament</u> (PL die Fundamente)

fountain NOUN
der <u>Brunnen</u> (PL die Brunnen)

fountain pen NOUN
der <u>Füllfederhalter</u> (PL die Füllfederhalter)

four NUMBER
<u>vier</u> ◊ *She's four.* Sie ist vier.

fourteen NUMBER
<u>vierzehn</u> ◊ *I'm fourteen.* Ich bin vierzehn.

fourteenth ADJECTIVE
<u>vierzehnte</u>
- **the fourteenth of August** der vierzehnte August

fourth ADJECTIVE
<u>vierte</u> ◊ *the fourth floor* der vierte Stock
- **the fourth of August** der vierte August

fox NOUN
der <u>Fuchs</u> (GEN des Fuchses, PL die Füchse)

fragile ADJECTIVE
<u>zerbrechlich</u>

frame NOUN
(*for picture*)
der <u>Rahmen</u> (PL die Rahmen)

France NOUN
<u>Frankreich</u> NEUT
- **from France** aus Frankreich
- **in France** in Frankreich
- **to France** nach Frankreich

frantic ADJECTIVE
- **I was going frantic.** Ich bin fast durchgedreht.
- **I was frantic with worry.** Ich habe mir furchtbare Sorgen gemacht.

fraud NOUN
$\boxed{1}$ (*crime*)
der <u>Betrug</u> ◊ *He was jailed for fraud.* Er kam wegen Betrugs ins Gefängnis.
$\boxed{2}$ (*person*)
der <u>Betrüger</u> (PL die Betrüger)
die <u>Betrügerin</u>
◊ *He's not a real doctor, he's a fraud.* Er ist kein echter Arzt, er ist ein Betrüger.

freckles PL NOUN
die <u>Sommersprossen</u> PL

free ADJECTIVE
> see also **free** VERB
$\boxed{1}$ <u>kostenlos</u> (*free of charge*) ◊ *a free brochure* eine kostenlose Broschüre
$\boxed{2}$ <u>frei</u> (*not busy, not taken*) ◊ *Is this seat free?* Ist dieser Platz frei?
- **"admission free"** "Eintritt frei"
- **Are you free after school?** Hast du nach der Schule Zeit?

to **free** VERB
> see also **free** ADJECTIVE
<u>befreien</u> (PERFECT hat befreit)

freedom NOUN

die <u>Freiheit</u>
freeway NOUN ⃞US⃞
  die <u>Autobahn</u>
to **freeze** VERB
  ⃞1⃞ <u>gefrieren</u> (IMPERFECT gefror, PERFECT ist
  gefroren) ◊ *The water had frozen.* Das
  Wasser war gefroren.
  ⃞2⃞ (*food*)
  <u>einfrieren</u> ◊ *She froze the rest of the
  raspberries.* Sie hat die restlichen
  Himbeeren eingefroren.
freezer NOUN
  der <u>Gefrierschrank</u> (PL die
  Gefrierschränke)
freezing ADJECTIVE
  ◆ **It's freezing!** Es ist eiskalt! (*informal*)
  ◆ **I'm freezing!** Mir ist eiskalt! (*informal*)
  ◆ **three degrees below freezing** drei Grad
  minus
freight NOUN
  die <u>Fracht</u> (*goods*)
  ◆ **a freight train** ein Güterzug MASC
French ADJECTIVE
  ⃞ *see also* **French** NOUN ⃞
  <u>französisch</u> ◊ *He's French.* Er ist
  Franzose. ◊ *She's French.* Sie ist
  Französin.
French NOUN
  ⃞ *see also* **French** ADJECTIVE ⃞
  das <u>Französisch</u> (*language*) (GEN des
  Französischen) ◊ *Do you speak French?*
  Sprechen Sie Französisch?
  ◆ **the French** (*people*) die Franzosen MASC
  PL
French beans PL NOUN
  die <u>grünen Bohnen</u> FEM PL ◊ *She's very
  fond of French beans.* Sie mag grüne
  Bohnen besonders gern.
French fries PL NOUN
  die <u>Pommes frites</u> PL
French horn NOUN
  das <u>Waldhorn</u> (PL die Waldhörner) ◊ *I
  play the French horn.* Ich spiele
  Waldhorn.
French kiss NOUN
  der <u>Zungenkuss</u> (GEN des Zungenkusses,
  PL die Zungenküsse)
French loaf NOUN
  das <u>Stangenbrot</u> (PL die Stangenbrote)
Frenchman NOUN
  der <u>Franzose</u> (GEN des Franzosen, PL die
  Franzosen)
French windows PL NOUN
  die <u>Verandatür</u>
Frenchwoman NOUN
  die <u>Französin</u>
frequent ADJECTIVE
  <u>häufig</u> ◊ *frequent showers* häufige
  Niederschläge
  ◆ **There are frequent buses to the town
  centre.** Es gehen häufig Busse ins
  Stadtzentrum.

fresh ADJECTIVE
  <u>frisch</u> ◊ *I need some fresh air.* Ich
  brauche frische Luft.
to **freshen up** VERB
  <u>sich frisch machen</u> ◊ *I'd like to go and
  freshen up.* Ich würde mich gerne frisch
  machen.
to **fret** VERB
  <u>sich verrückt machen</u> ◊ *Don't fret about
  your exams.* Mach dich wegen der
  Prüfung nicht verrückt.
Friday NOUN
  der <u>Freitag</u> (PL die Freitage) ◊ *on Friday*
  am Freitag ◊ *every Friday* jeden Freitag
  ◊ *last Friday* letzten Freitag ◊ *next Friday*
  nächsten Freitag
  ◆ **on Fridays** freitags
fridge NOUN
  der <u>Kühlschrank</u> (PL die Kühlschränke)
fried ADJECTIVE
  <u>gebraten</u> ◊ *fried onions* gebratene
  Zwiebeln
  ◆ **a fried egg** ein Spiegelei NEUT
friend NOUN
  der <u>Freund</u> (PL die Freunde)
  die <u>Freundin</u>
friendly ADJECTIVE
  <u>freundlich</u> ◊ *She's really friendly.* Sie ist
  wirklich freundlich. ◊ *Liverpool is a very
  friendly city.* Liverpool ist eine sehr
  freundliche Stadt.
friendship NOUN
  die <u>Freundschaft</u>
fright NOUN
  der <u>Schrecken</u> (PL die Schrecken) ◊ *I got
  a terrible fright!* Ich habe einen
  furchtbaren Schrecken bekommen!
to **frighten** VERB
  <u>Angst machen</u> ◊ *Horror films frighten
  him.* Horrorfilme machen ihm Angst.
frightened ADJECTIVE
  ◆ **to be frightened** Angst haben ◊ *I'm
  frightened!* Ich habe Angst!
  ◆ **to be frightened of something** vor
  etwas Angst haben ◊ *Anna's frightened
  of spiders.* Anna hat Angst vor
  Spinnen.
frightening ADJECTIVE
  <u>beängstigend</u>
fringe NOUN
  der <u>Pony</u> (*of hair*) (PL die Ponys) ◊ *She's
  got a fringe.* Sie hat einen Pony.
Frisbee ® NOUN
  das <u>Frisbee</u> ®
  (PL die Frisbees) ◊ *to play Frisbee* Frisbee
  spielen
fro ADVERB
  ◆ **to and fro** hin und her
frog NOUN
  der <u>Frosch</u> (PL die Frösche)
from PREPOSITION

F

☞

1 aus (*from country, town*) ◊ *I'm from Yorkshire.* Ich bin aus Yorkshire. ◊ *I come from Perth.* Ich bin aus Perth.

♦ **Where do you come from?** Woher sind Sie?

2 von (*from person*) ◊ *a letter from my sister* ein Brief von meiner Schwester

♦ **The hotel is one kilometre from the beach.** Das Hotel ist einen Kilometer vom Strand entfernt.

3 ab (*number*) ◊ *from ten pounds* ab zehn Pfund ◊ *from the age of fourteen* ab vierzehn

♦ **from ... to ... (1)** (*distance*) von ... nach ... ◊ *He flew from London to Paris.* Er flog von London nach Paris.

♦ **from ... to ... (2)** (*time*) von ... bis ... ◊ *from one o'clock to two* von eins bis zwei

♦ **The price was reduced from ten pounds to five.** Der Preis war von zehn auf fünf Pfund herabgesetzt.

♦ **from ... onwards** ab ... ◊ *We'll be at home from seven o'clock onwards.* Wir werden ab sieben Uhr zu Hause sein.

front NOUN

see also **front** ADJECTIVE

die Vorderseite ◊ *the front of the house* die Vorderseite des Hauses

♦ **in front** davor ◊ *a house with a car in front* ein Haus mit einem Auto davor

♦ **in front of** vor

Use the accusative to express movement or a change of place. Use the dative when there is no change of place.

◊ *He stood in front of the house.* Er stand vor dem Haus. ◊ *He ran in front of a bus.* Er lief vor einen Bus. ◊ *the car in front of us* das Auto vor uns

♦ **in the front** (*of car*) vorn ◊ *I was sitting in the front.* Ich saß vorn.

♦ **at the front of the train** vorn im Zug

front ADJECTIVE

see also **front** NOUN

vordere ◊ *the front row* die vordere Reihe ◊ *the front seats of the car* die vorderen Sitze des Autos

♦ **the front door** die Haustür

frontier NOUN

die Grenze

frost NOUN

der Frost (PL die Fröste)

frosting NOUN US

der Zuckerguss (GEN des Zuckergusses)

frosty ADJECTIVE

frostig ◊ *It's frosty today.* Heute ist es frostig.

to **frown** VERB

die Stirn runzeln ◊ *He frowned.* Er runzelte die Stirn.

froze, frozen VERB *see* **freeze**

frozen ADJECTIVE

see also **freeze**

tiefgefroren (*food*) ◊ *frozen chips* tiefgefrorene Pommes frites

fruit NOUN

1 die Frucht (PL die Früchte) ◊ *an exotic fruit* eine exotische Frucht

2 das Obst ◊ *Fruit is very healthy.* Obst ist sehr gesund.

♦ **fruit juice** der Fruchtsaft

♦ **a fruit salad** ein Obstsalat MASC

fruit machine NOUN

der Spielautomat (GEN des Spielautomaten, PL die Spielautomaten)

frustrated ADJECTIVE

frustriert

to **fry** VERB

braten (PRESENT brät, IMPERFECT briet, PERFECT hat gebraten) ◊ *Fry the onions for five minutes.* Braten Sie die Zwiebeln fünf Minuten lang.

frying pan NOUN

die Bratpfanne

fuel NOUN

das Benzin (for car, aeroplane) (PL die Benzine) ◊ *to run out of fuel* kein Benzin mehr haben

to **fulfil** VERB

erfüllen (PERFECT hat erfüllt) ◊ *Robert fulfilled his dream of becoming a pilot.* Robert hat sich seinen Traum erfüllt und ist Pilot geworden.

full ADJECTIVE, ADVERB

1 voll ◊ *The tank's full.* Der Tank ist voll.

2 ausführlich ◊ *He asked for full information on the job.* Er bat um ausführliche Informationen über die Stelle.

♦ **your full name** Name und Vornamen

♦ **My full name is Ian John Marr.** Ich heiße Ian John Marr.

♦ **I'm full.** (*after meal*) Ich bin satt.

♦ **at full speed** mit Höchstgeschwindigkeit ◊ *He drove at full speed.* Er fuhr Höchstgeschwindigkeit.

♦ **There was a full moon.** Es war Vollmond.

full stop NOUN

der Punkt (PL die Punkte)

full-time ADJECTIVE, ADVERB

ganztags ◊ *She works full-time.* Sie arbeitet ganztags.

♦ **She's got a full-time job.** Sie hat einen Ganztagsjob.

fully ADVERB

ganz ◊ *He hasn't fully recovered from his illness.* Er hat sich noch nicht ganz von seiner Krankheit erholt.

fumes PL NOUN

die Abgase NEUT PL ◊ *The factory gave out dangerous fumes.* Die Fabrik stieß gefährliche Abgase aus.

♦ **exhaust fumes** Autoabgase

fun ADJECTIVE

see also **fun** NOUN

lustig ◊ *She's a fun person.* Sie ist ein lustiger Mensch.

fun NOUN

see also **fun** ADJECTIVE

◆**to have fun** Spaß haben ◊ *We had great fun playing in the snow.* Wir hatten beim Spielen im Schnee unseren Spaß.

◆**for fun** zum Spaß ◊ *He entered the competition just for fun.* Er hat am Wettbewerb nur zum Spaß mitgemacht.

◆**to make fun of somebody** sich über jemanden lustig machen ◊ *They made fun of him.* Sie machten sich über ihn lustig.

◆**It's fun!** Das macht Spaß!

◆**Have fun!** Viel Spaß!

funds PL NOUN

◆**to raise funds** Spenden sammeln

funeral NOUN
die Beerdigung

funfair NOUN
das Volksfest (PL die Volksfeste)

funny ADJECTIVE

[1] lustig (*amusing*) ◊ *It was really funny.* Es war wirklich lustig.

[2] komisch (*strange*) ◊ *There's something funny about him.* Er hat etwas Komisches an sich.

fur NOUN

[1] der Pelz (GEN des Pelzes, PL die Pelze) ◊ *a fur coat* ein Pelzmantel MASC

[2] das Fell (PL die Felle) ◊ *the dog's fur* das Fell des Hundes

furious ADJECTIVE
wütend ◊ *Dad was furious with me.*

Papa war wütend auf mich.

furniture NOUN
die Möbel NEUT PL ◊ *a piece of furniture* ein Möbelstück NEUT

further ADVERB, ADJECTIVE
weiter entfernt ◊ *London is further from Manchester than Leeds is.* London ist weiter von Manchester entfernt als Leeds.

◆**How much further is it?** Wie weit ist es noch?

further education NOUN
die Weiterbildung

fuse NOUN
die Sicherung ◊ *The fuse has blown.* Die Sicherung ist durchgebrannt.

fuss NOUN
die Aufregung ◊ *What's all the fuss about?* Was soll die ganze Aufregung?

◆**to make a fuss** Theater machen ◊ *He's always making a fuss about nothing.* Er macht immer Theater wegen nichts.

fussy ADJECTIVE
pingelig ◊ *She is very fussy about her food.* Sie ist mit dem Essen sehr pingelig.

future NOUN

[1] die Zukunft

◆**in future** in Zukunft ◊ *Be more careful in future.* Sei in Zukunft vorsichtiger.

◆**What are your plans for the future?** Was für Zukunftspläne haben Sie?

[2] das Futur (*in grammar*) ◊ *Put this sentence into the future.* Setzt diesen Satz ins Futur.

F

G

to **gain** VERB
  ◆ **to gain weight** zunehmen
  ◆ **to gain speed** schneller werden
  gallery NOUN
  die <u>Galerie</u> ◇ *an art gallery* eine
  Kunstgalerie
to **gamble** VERB
  <u>spielen</u>
  gambler NOUN
  der <u>Spieler</u> (PL die Spieler)
  die <u>Spielerin</u>
  gambling NOUN
  das <u>Glücksspiel</u> (PL die Glücksspiele)
  ◆ **He likes gambling.** Er spielt gern.
  game NOUN
  das <u>Spiel</u> (PL die Spiele) ◇ *The children
  were playing a game.* Die Kinder spielten
  ein Spiel. ◇ *a game of football* ein
  Fußballspiel ◇ *a game of cards* ein
  Kartenspiel
  gang NOUN
  die <u>Gang</u> (PL die Gangs)
  gangster NOUN
  der <u>Gangster</u> (PL die Gangster)
  gap NOUN
  1 die <u>Lücke</u> ◇ *There's a gap in the
  hedge.* In der Hecke ist eine Lücke.
  2 die <u>Pause</u> ◇ *a gap of four years* eine
  Pause von vier Jahren
  garage NOUN
  1 (*for parking cars*)
  die <u>Garage</u>
  2 (*for repairs*)
  die <u>Werkstatt</u> (PL die Werkstätten)
  garbage NOUN
  der <u>Müll</u> ◇ *the garbage can* die
  Mülltonne
  ◆ **That's garbage!** Das ist Blödsinn!
  garden NOUN
  der <u>Garten</u> (PL die Gärten)
  gardener NOUN
  der <u>Gärtner</u> (PL die Gärtner)
  die <u>Gärtnerin</u>
  ◇ *He's a gardener.* Er ist Gärtner.
  gardening NOUN
  die <u>Gartenarbeit</u> ◇ *Margaret loves
  gardening.* Margaret liebt
  Gartenarbeit.
  gardens PL NOUN
  der <u>Park</u> SING (PL die Parks)
  garlic NOUN
  der <u>Knoblauch</u>
  garment NOUN
  das <u>Kleidungsstück</u> (PL die
  Kleidungsstücke)
  gas NOUN
  1 das <u>Gas</u> (PL die Gase)
  ◆ **a gas cooker** ein Gasherd MASC

◆ **a gas cylinder** eine Gasflasche
  ◆ **a gas fire** ein Gasofen MASC
  ◆ **a gas leak** eine undichte Stelle in der
  Gasleitung
  2 das <u>Benzin</u> US
  ◆ **a gas station** eine Tankstelle
  gasoline NOUN US
  das <u>Benzin</u>
  gate NOUN
  1 (*of garden*)
  das <u>Tor</u> (PL die Tore)
  2 (*of field*)
  das <u>Gatter</u> (PL die Gatter)
  3 (*at airport*)
  der <u>Flugsteig</u> (PL die Flugsteige)
  gateau NOUN
  die <u>Torte</u>
to **gather** VERB
  <u>sich versammeln</u> (*assemble*) (PERFECT
  haben sich versammelt) ◇ *People
  gathered in front of Buckingham Palace.*
  Menschen versammelten sich vor dem
  Buckingham-Palast.
  ◆ **to gather speed** schneller werden ◇ *The
  train gathered speed.* Der Zug wurde
  schneller.
  gave VERB *see* **give**
  gay ADJECTIVE
  <u>schwul</u> (*homosexual*)
to **gaze** VERB
  ◆ **to gaze at something** etwas anstarren
  ◇ *He gazed at her.* Er starrte sie an.
  GCSE NOUN (= *General Certificate of
  Secondary Education*)
  die <u>mittlere Reife</u>
  gear NOUN
  1 (*in car*)
  der <u>Gang</u> (PL die Gänge) ◇ *in first gear* im
  ersten Gang
  ◆ **to change gear** schalten
  2 die <u>Ausrüstung</u> ◇ *camping gear* die
  Campingausrüstung
  ◆ **your sports gear** (*clothes*) dein Sportzeug
  NEUT
  gear lever NOUN
  der <u>Schalthebel</u> (PL die Schalthebel)
  gearshift NOUN US
  der <u>Schaltknüppel</u> (PL die Schaltknüppel)
  geese PL NOUN *see* **goose**
  gel NOUN
  das <u>Gel</u> (PL die Gele)
  Note that in German the "g" in **Gel** *is
  pronounced like the "g" in girl.*
  ◇ *hair gel* das Haargel
  gem NOUN
  der <u>Edelstein</u> (PL die Edelsteine)
  Gemini SING NOUN

die <u>Zwillinge</u> MASC PL ◊ *I'm Gemini.* Ich bin Zwilling.

gender NOUN
das <u>Geschlecht</u> (PL die Geschlechter)

general NOUN
see also **general** ADJECTIVE
der <u>General</u> (PL die Generäle)

general ADJECTIVE
see also **general** NOUN
<u>allgemein</u>
♦ **in general** im Allgemeinen

general election NOUN
die <u>allgemeinen Wahlen</u> FEM PL

general knowledge NOUN
die <u>Allgemeinbildung</u>

generally ADVERB
<u>normalerweise</u> ◊ *I generally go shopping on Saturday.* Ich gehe normalerweise samstags einkaufen.

generation NOUN
die <u>Generation</u> ◊ *the younger generation* die jüngere Generation

generator NOUN
der <u>Generator</u> (PL die Generatoren)

generous ADJECTIVE
<u>großzügig</u> ◊ *That's very generous of you.* Das ist sehr großzügig von Ihnen.

genetic ADJECTIVE
<u>genetisch</u>

genetically ADVERB
<u>genetisch</u>
♦ **genetically modified** genmanipuliert

Geneva NOUN
<u>Genf</u> NEUT ◊ *to Geneva* nach Genf
♦ **Lake Geneva** der Genfer See

genius NOUN
das <u>Genie</u> (PL die Genies) ◊ *She's a genius!* Sie ist ein Genie!

gentle ADJECTIVE
<u>sanft</u>

gentleman NOUN
der <u>Gentleman</u> (PL die Gentlemen)
♦ **Good morning, gentlemen.** Guten Morgen, meine Herren.

gently ADVERB
<u>sanft</u>

gents SING NOUN
die <u>Herrentoilette</u>
♦ **"gents"** (*on sign*) "Herren"

genuine ADJECTIVE
[1] <u>echt</u> (*real*) ◊ *These are genuine diamonds.* Das sind echte Diamanten.
[2] <u>geradlinig</u> (*sincere*) ◊ *She's a very genuine person.* Sie ist ein sehr geradliniger Mensch.

geography NOUN
die <u>Geografie</u>

gerbil NOUN
die <u>Wüstenrennmaus</u> (PL die Wüstenrennmäuse)

germ NOUN
die <u>Bazille</u>

German ADJECTIVE
see also **German** NOUN
<u>deutsch</u> ◊ *He is German.* Er ist Deutscher. ◊ *She is German.* Sie ist Deutsche.
♦ **German shepherd** der Schäferhund

German NOUN
see also **German** ADJECTIVE
[1] (*person*)
der <u>Deutsche</u> (GEN des Deutschen, PL die Deutschen)
die <u>Deutsche</u> (GEN der Deutschen) ◊ *a German (man)* ein Deutscher
♦ **the Germans** die Deutschen
[2] (*language*)
das <u>Deutsch</u> (GEN des Deutschen) ◊ *Do you speak German?* Sprechen sie Deutsch?

German measles NOUN
die <u>Röteln</u> PL ◊ *to have German measles* die Röteln haben

Germany NOUN
<u>Deutschland</u> NEUT
♦ **from Germany** aus Deutschland
♦ **in Germany** in Deutschland
♦ **to Germany** nach Deutschland

gesture NOUN
die <u>Geste</u>

to **get** VERB
[1] (*receive*)
<u>bekommen</u> (IMPERFECT bekam, PERFECT hat bekommen) ◊ *I got lots of presents.* Ich habe viele Geschenke bekommen. ◊ *He got first prize.* Er hat den ersten Preis bekommen. ◊ *Jackie got good exam results.* Jackie hat gute Noten bekommen.
♦ **have got** haben ◊ *How many have you got?* Wie viele hast du?
[2] (*fetch*)
<u>holen</u> ◊ *Get help!* Hol Hilfe!
[3] (*catch*)
<u>fassen</u> ◊ *They've got the thief.* Sie haben den Dieb gefasst.
[4] (*train, bus*)
<u>nehmen</u> (PRESENT nimmt, IMPERFECT nahm, PERFECT hat genommen) ◊ *I'm getting the bus into town.* Ich nehme den Bus in die Stadt.
[5] (*understand*)
<u>verstehen</u> (IMPERFECT verstand, PERFECT hat verstanden) ◊ *I don't get the joke.* Ich verstehe den Witz nicht.
[6] (*go*)
<u>kommen</u> (IMPERFECT kam, PERFECT ist gekommen) ◊ *How do you get to the castle?* Wie kommt man zur Burg?
[7] (*become*)
<u>werden</u> (PRESENT wird, IMPERFECT wurde, PERFECT ist geworden) ◊ *to get old* alt werden
♦ **to get something done** etwas machen lassen ◊ *to get something repaired* etwas

G

reparieren lassen ◊ *to get one's hair cut* sich die Haare schneiden lassen

♦ **to get something for somebody** etwas für jemanden holen ◊ *The librarian got the book for me.* Die Bibliothekarin holte mir das Buch.

♦ **to have got to do something** etwas tun müssen ◊ *I've got to tell him.* Ich muss es ihm sagen.

♦ **to get away** entkommen ◊ *One of the burglars got away.* Einer der Einbrecher ist entkommen.

♦ **You'll never get away with it.** Das wird man dir niemals durchgehen lassen.

♦ **to get back (1)** zurückkommen ◊ *What time did you get back?* Wann seid ihr zurückgekommen?

♦ **to get back (2)** zurückbekommen ◊ *He got his money back.* Er hat sein Geld zurückbekommen.

♦ **to get down** herunterkommen ◊ *Get down from there!* Komm da runter!

♦ **to get in** heimkommen ◊ *What time did you get in last night?* Wann bist du heute Nacht nach Hause gekommen?

♦ **to get into** einsteigen in +ACC ◊ *Sharon got into the car.* Sharon stieg ins Auto ein.

♦ **to get off (1)** (*vehicle*) aussteigen aus ◊ *Isobel got off the train.* Isobel stieg aus dem Zug aus.

♦ **to get off (2)** (*bike*) absteigen von ◊ *He got off his bike.* Er stieg vom Fahrrad ab.

♦ **to get on (1)** (*vehicle*) einsteigen in +ACC ◊ *Phyllis got on the bus.* Phyllis stieg in den Bus ein.

♦ **to get on (2)** (*bike*) steigen auf +ACC ◊ *Carol got on her bike.* Carol stieg auf ihr Fahrrad.

♦ **to get on with somebody** sich mit jemandem verstehen ◊ *He doesn't get on with his parents.* Er versteht sich nicht mit seinen Eltern. ◊ *We got on really well.* Wir haben uns wirklich gut verstanden.

♦ **to get out** aussteigen aus ◊ *Jason got out of the car.* Jason stieg aus dem Auto aus.

♦ **Get out!** Raus!

♦ **to get something out** etwas hervorholen ◊ *She got the map out.* Sie holte die Karte hervor.

♦ **to get over something (1)** sich von etwas erholen ◊ *It took her a long time to get over the illness.* Sie brauchte lange Zeit, um sich von der Krankheit zu erholen.

♦ **to get over something (2)** etwas überwinden ◊ *He managed to get over the problem.* Er konnte das Problem überwinden.

♦ **to get round to something** zu etwas kommen ◊ *I'll get round to it eventually.* Ich werde schon noch dazu kommen.

♦ **to get together** sich treffen ◊ *Could we get together this evening?* Könnten wir uns heute abend treffen?

♦ **to get up** aufstehen ◊ *What time do you get up?* Wann stehst du auf?

ghetto blaster NOUN
das tragbare Kofferradio (PL die tragbaren Kofferradios)

ghost NOUN
das Gespenst (PL die Gespenster)

giant ADJECTIVE
> see also **giant** NOUN

riesig ◊ *They ate a giant meal.* Sie haben ein riesiges Essen vertilgt.

giant NOUN
> see also **giant** ADJECTIVE

der Riese (GEN des Riesen, PL die Riesen)
die Riesin

gift NOUN
1 (*present*)
das Geschenk (PL die Geschenke)
2 (*talent*)
die Begabung

♦ **to have a gift for something** für etwas begabt sein ◊ *Dave has a gift for painting.* Dave ist künstlerisch begabt.

*Be careful not to translate **gift** by the German word **Gift**.*

gifted ADJECTIVE
begabt ◊ *Janice is a gifted pianist.* Janice ist eine begabte Pianistin.

gift shop NOUN
der Geschenkladen (PL die Geschenkläden)

gigantic ADJECTIVE
riesengroß

to **giggle** VERB
kichern

gin NOUN
der Gin (PL die Gins *or* Gin)

*When ordering more than one gin use the plural form **Gin**.*

◊ *Three gins, please.* Drei Gin bitte.

♦ **a gin and tonic** ein Gin Tonic

ginger NOUN
> see also **ginger** ADJECTIVE

der Ingwer ◊ *Add a teaspoon of ginger.* Fügen Sie einen Teelöffel Ingwer zu.

ginger ADJECTIVE
> see also **ginger** NOUN

rot ◊ *David has ginger hair.* David hat rote Haare.

gipsy NOUN
der Zigeuner (PL die Zigeuner)
die Zigeunerin

giraffe NOUN
die Giraffe

girl NOUN
das Mädchen (PL die Mädchen)
◊ *They've got a girl and two boys.* Sie haben ein Mädchen und zwei Jungen.

◊ *a five-year-old girl* ein fünfjähriges Mädchen

♦ **an English girl** eine junge Engländerin

girlfriend NOUN
die <u>Freundin</u> ◊ *Damon's girlfriend is called Justine.* Damons Freundin heißt Justine. ◊ *She often went out with her girlfriends.* Sie ging oft mit ihren Freundinnen aus.

to **give** VERB
<u>geben</u> (PRESENT **gibt**, IMPERFECT **gab**, PERFECT **hat gegeben**)

♦ **to give something to somebody** jemandem etwas geben ◊ *He gave me ten pounds.* Er gab mir zehn Pfund.

♦ **to give something back to somebody** jemandem etwas zurückgeben ◊ *I gave the book back to him.* Ich habe ihm das Buch zurückgegeben.

♦ **to give in** nachgeben ◊ *His mum gave in and let him watch TV.* Seine Mama hat nachgegeben und ihn fernsehen lassen.

♦ **to give out** austeilen ◊ *The teacher gave out the books.* Der Lehrer hat die Bücher ausgeteilt.

♦ **to give up** aufgeben ◊ *I couldn't do it, so I gave up.* Ich habe es nicht gekonnt, also habe ich aufgegeben.

♦ **to give up doing something** etwas aufgeben ◊ *He gave up smoking.* Er hat das Rauchen aufgegeben.

♦ **to give oneself up** sich ergeben ◊ *The thief gave himself up.* Der Dieb hat sich ergeben.

♦ **to give way** (*in traffic*) die Vorfahrt achten

glad ADJECTIVE
<u>froh</u> ◊ *She's glad she's done it.* Sie ist froh, dass sie es getan hat.

glamorous ADJECTIVE
<u>glamourös</u> (*person*)

to **glance** VERB
> see also **glance** NOUN

♦ **to glance at something** einen Blick auf etwas werfen ◊ *Peter glanced at his watch.* Peter warf einen Blick auf seine Uhr.

glance NOUN
> see also **glance** VERB

der <u>Blick</u> (PL die Blicke) ◊ *at first glance* auf den ersten Blick

to **glare** VERB
♦ **to glare at somebody** jemanden wütend ansehen ◊ *He glared at me.* Er sah mich wütend an.

glaring ADJECTIVE
♦ **a glaring mistake** ein eklatanter Fehler

glass NOUN
das <u>Glas</u> (GEN des Glases, PL die Gläser) ◊ *a glass of milk* ein Glas Milch

glasses PL NOUN
die <u>Brille</u> ◊ *Veronika wears glasses.* Veronika trägt eine Brille.

to **gleam** VERB
funkeln ◊ *Her eyes gleamed with excitement.* Ihre Augen funkelten vor Aufregung.

glider NOUN
das <u>Segelflugzeug</u> (PL die Segelflugzeuge)

gliding NOUN
das <u>Segelfliegen</u> ◊ *My hobby is gliding.* Segelfliegen ist mein Hobby.

glimpse NOUN
♦ **to catch a glimpse of somebody** jemanden kurz zu sehen bekommen

to **glitter** VERB
glitzern

global ADJECTIVE
<u>weltweit</u>

♦ **on a global scale** weltweit

global warming NOUN
die <u>Erwärmung der Erdatmosphäre</u>

globe NOUN
der <u>Globus</u> (GEN des Globus, PL die Globen)

gloomy ADJECTIVE
1 <u>düster</u> ◊ *He lives in a small gloomy flat.* Er wohnt in einer kleinen, düsteren Wohnung.

2 <u>niedergeschlagen</u> ◊ *She's been feeling very gloomy recently.* Sie fühlt sich in letzter Zeit sehr niedergeschlagen.

glorious ADJECTIVE
<u>herrlich</u>

glove NOUN
der <u>Handschuh</u> (PL die Handschuhe)

glove compartment NOUN
das <u>Handschuhfach</u> (PL die Handschuhfächer)

to **glow** VERB
<u>leuchten</u> ◊ *He bought a watch which glows in the dark.* Er kaufte eine Uhr, die im Dunkeln leuchtet.

glue NOUN
> see also **glue** VERB

der <u>Klebstoff</u> (PL die Klebstoffe)

to **glue** VERB
> see also **glue** NOUN

<u>kleben</u> ◊ *to glue something together* etwas zusammenkleben

GM ABBREVIATION (= *genetically modified*)
<u>genmanipuliert</u> ◊ *GM food* genmanipulierte Lebensmittel PL

GMO NOUN (= *genetically modified organism*)
der <u>genmanipulierte Organismus</u> (GEN des genmanipulierten Organismus, PL die genmanipulierten Organismen)

go NOUN
> see also **go** VERB

♦ **to have a go at doing something** etwas versuchen ◊ *He had a go at making a cake.* Er hat versucht, einen Kuchen zu backen.

♦ **Whose go is it?** Wer ist dran?

G

to go VERB

see also **go** NOUN

1 gehen (IMPERFECT ging, PERFECT ist gegangen) ◊ *I'm going to the cinema tonight.* Ich gehe heute Abend ins Kino. ◊ *I'm going now.* Ich gehe jetzt.

2 (*leave*)

weggehen ◊ *Where's Thomas? – He's gone.* Wo ist Thomas? – Er ist weggegangen.

3 (*vehicle*)

fahren (PRESENT fährt, IMPERFECT fuhr, PERFECT ist gefahren) ◊ *My car won't go.* Mein Auto fährt nicht.

♦ **to go home** nach Hause gehen ◊ *I go home at about four o'clock.* Ich gehe um etwa vier Uhr nach Hause.

♦ **to go for a walk** einen Spaziergang machen ◊ *Shall we go for a walk?* Sollen wir einen Spaziergang machen?

♦ **How did it go?** Wie ist es gelaufen?

♦ **I'm going to do it tomorrow.** Ich werde es morgen tun.

♦ **It's going to be difficult.** Es wird schwierig werden.

to go after VERB

nachgehen (*follow*)

+DAT (IMPERFECT ging nach, PERFECT ist nachgegangen) ◊ *I went after him.* Ich ging ihm nach.

♦ **Quick, go after them!** Schnell, ihnen nach!

to go ahead VERB

vorangehen (IMPERFECT ging voran, PERFECT ist vorangegangen)

♦ **to go ahead with something** etwas durchführen

to go around VERB

herumgehen (IMPERFECT ging herum, PERFECT ist herumgegangen) ◊ *There's a rumour going around that they're getting married.* Es geht das Gerücht um, sie würden heiraten.

to go away VERB

weggehen (IMPERFECT ging weg, PERFECT ist weggegangen) ◊ *Go away!* Geh weg!

to go back VERB

zurückgehen (IMPERFECT ging zurück, PERFECT ist zurückgegangen) ◊ *We went back to the same place.* Wir sind an denselben Ort zurückgegangen.

♦ **Is he still here? – No, he's gone back home.** Ist er noch hier? – Nein, er ist nach Hause gegangen.

to go by VERB

vorbeigehen (IMPERFECT ging vorbei, PERFECT ist vorbeigegangen) ◊ *Two policemen went by.* Zwei Polizisten gingen vorbei.

to go down VERB

1 (*person*)

hinuntergehen (IMPERFECT ging hinunter, PERFECT ist hinuntergegangen) ◊ *to go down the stairs* die Treppe hinuntergehen

2 (*decrease*)

sinken (IMPERFECT sank, PERFECT ist gesunken) ◊ *The price of computers has gone down.* Die Preise für Computer sind gesunken.

3 (*deflate*)

Luft verlieren (IMPERFECT verlor Luft, PERFECT hat Luft verloren) ◊ *My airbed kept going down.* Meine Luftmatratze verlor dauernd Luft.

♦ **My brother's gone down with flu.** Mein Bruder hat die Grippe bekommen.

to go for VERB

angreifen (*attack*) (IMPERFECT griff an, PERFECT hat angegriffen) ◊ *Suddenly the dog went for me.* Der Hund griff mich plötzlich an.

♦ **Go for it!** (*go on*) Na los!

to go in VERB

hineingehen (IMPERFECT ging hinein, PERFECT ist hineingegangen) ◊ *He knocked on the door and went in.* Er klopfte und ging hinein.

to go off VERB

1 losgehen (IMPERFECT ging los, PERFECT ist losgegangen) ◊ *The bomb went off.* Die Bombe ging los. ◊ *The fire alarm went off.* Der Feueralarm ging los.

2 klingeln ◊ *My alarm clock goes off at seven every morning.* Mein Wecker klingelt jeden Morgen um sieben Uhr.

3 schlecht werden (PRESENT wird schlecht, IMPERFECT wurde schlecht, PERFECT ist schlecht geworden)

♦ **The milk's gone off.** Die Milch ist sauer geworden.

4 (*go away*)

weggehen ◊ *He went off in a huff.* Er ist beleidigt weggegangen.

to go on VERB

1 (*happen*)

los sein (PRESENT ist los, IMPERFECT war los, PERFECT ist los gewesen) ◊ *What's going on?* Was ist los?

2 (*carry on*)

dauern ◊ *The concert went on until eleven o'clock at night.* Das Konzert hat bis nach elf Uhr nachts gedauert.

♦ **to go on doing something** etwas weiter tun ◊ *He went on reading.* Er las weiter.

♦ **to go on at somebody** an jemandem herumkritisieren ◊ *My parents always go on at me.* Meine Eltern kritisieren dauernd an mir herum.

♦ **Go on!** Na los! ◊ *Go on, tell me what the problem is!* Na los, sag mir, wo das Problem ist!

to go out VERB

ausgehen (IMPERFECT ging aus, PERFECT ist ausgegangen) ◊ *Are you going out*

tonight? Gehst du heute Abend aus?
◊ *Suddenly the lights went out.* Plötzlich ging das Licht aus.
♦ **to go out with somebody** mit jemandem ausgehen ◊ *Are you going out with him?* Gehst du mit ihm aus?

to **go past** VERB
♦ **to go past something** an etwas vorbeigehen ◊ *He went past the shop.* Er ging an dem Geschäft vorbei.

to **go round** VERB
♦ **to go round a corner** um die Ecke biegen
♦ **to go round to somebody's house** jemanden besuchen
♦ **to go round a museum** sich ein Museum ansehen
♦ **to go round the shops** einen Einkaufsbummel machen

to **go through** VERB
<u>fahren durch</u> (*by car*) (PRESENT fährt, IMPERFECT fuhr, PERFECT ist gefahren)
♦ **We went through London to get to Birmingham.** Wir sind über London nach Birmingham gefahren.

to **go up** VERB
1 (*person*)
<u>hinaufgehen</u> (IMPERFECT ging hinauf, PERFECT ist hinaufgegangen) ◊ *to go up the stairs* die Treppe hinaufgehen
2 (*increase*)
<u>steigen</u> (IMPERFECT stieg, PERFECT ist gestiegen) ◊ *The price has gone up.* Der Preis ist gestiegen.
♦ **to go up in flames** in Flammen aufgehen ◊ *The whole factory went up in flames.* Die ganze Fabrik ist in Flammen aufgegangen.

to **go with** VERB
<u>passen zu</u> ◊ *Does this blouse go with that skirt?* Passt diese Bluse zu dem Rock?

goal NOUN
1 (*sport*)
das <u>Tor</u> (PL die Tore) ◊ *to score a goal* ein Tor schießen
2 (*aim*)
das <u>Ziel</u> (PL die Ziele) ◊ *His goal is to become the world champion.* Sein Ziel ist es, Weltmeister zu werden.

goalkeeper NOUN
der <u>Torwart</u> (PL die Torwarte)

goat NOUN
die <u>Ziege</u>
♦ **goat's cheese** der Ziegenkäse

god NOUN
der <u>Gott</u> (PL die Götter) ◊ *I believe in God.* Ich glaube an Gott.

goddaughter NOUN
die <u>Patentochter</u> (PL die Patentöchter)

godfather NOUN
der <u>Patenonkel</u> (PL die Patenonkel)

godmother NOUN
die <u>Patentante</u>

godson NOUN
der <u>Patensohn</u> (PL die Patensöhne)

goes VERB *see* **go**

goggles PL NOUN
die <u>Schutzbrille</u>

gold NOUN
das <u>Gold</u> ◊ *They found some gold.* Sie haben Gold gefunden.
♦ **a gold necklace** eine goldene Halskette

goldfish NOUN
der <u>Goldfisch</u> (PL die Goldfische) ◊ *I've got five goldfish.* Ich habe fünf Goldfische.

gold-plated ADJECTIVE
<u>vergoldet</u>

golf NOUN
das <u>Golf</u> ◊ *My dad plays golf.* Mein Papa spielt Golf.
♦ **a golf club (1)** (*stick*) ein Golfschläger MASC
♦ **a golf club (2)** (*place*) ein Golfklub MASC

golf course NOUN
der <u>Golfplatz</u> (GEN des Golfplatzes, PL die Golfplätze)

gone VERB *see* **go**

good ADJECTIVE
1 <u>gut</u> ◊ *It's a very good film.* Das ist ein sehr guter Film.
♦ **Vegetables are good for you.** Gemüse ist gesund.
♦ **to be good at something** gut in etwas sein ◊ *Maree's very good at maths.* Maree ist sehr gut in Mathe.
2 <u>freundlich</u> (*kind*) ◊ *They were very good to me.* Sie waren sehr freundlich zu mir. ◊ *That's very good of you.* Das ist sehr freundlich von Ihnen.
3 <u>artig</u> (*not naughty*) ◊ *Be good!* Sei artig!
♦ **for good** für immer ◊ *One day he left for good.* Eines Tages ist er für immer weggegangen.
♦ **Good morning!** Guten Morgen!
♦ **Good afternoon!** Guten Tag!
♦ **Good evening!** Guten Abend!
♦ **Good night!** Gute Nacht!
♦ **It's no good complaining.** Es hat keinen Wert, sich zu beklagen.

goodbye EXCLAMATION
<u>auf Wiedersehen</u>

Good Friday NOUN
der <u>Karfreitag</u> (PL die Karfreitage)

good-looking ADJECTIVE
<u>gut aussehend</u>
♦ **Andrew's very good-looking.** Andrew sieht sehr gut aus.

good-natured ADJECTIVE
<u>gutmütig</u>

goods PL NOUN
die <u>Ware</u> (*in shop*)
♦ **a goods train** ein Güterzug MASC

to **Google**® VERB
<u>googeln</u>

goose NOUN

G

die <u>Gans</u> (PL die Gänse)
gooseberry NOUN
die <u>Stachelbeere</u>

gorgeous ADJECTIVE
[1] <u>hinreißend</u> ◊ *She's gorgeous!* Sie sieht hinreißend aus!
[2] <u>herrlich</u> ◊ *The weather was gorgeous.* Das Wetter war herrlich.

gorilla NOUN
der <u>Gorilla</u> (PL die Gorillas)

gospel NOUN
das <u>Evangelium</u> (PL die Evangelien)

gossip NOUN
see also **gossip** VERB
[1] (*rumours*)
der <u>Tratsch</u> ◊ *Tell me the gossip!* Erzähl mir den neuesten Tratsch!
[2] (*woman*)
die <u>Klatschtante</u> ◊ *She's such a gossip!* Sie ist eine furchtbare Klatschtante!
[3] (*man*)
das <u>Klatschweib</u> (PL die Klatschweiber) ◊ *What a gossip!* So ein Klatschweib!

to **gossip** VERB
see also **gossip** NOUN
[1] <u>schwatzen</u> (*chat*) ◊ *They were always gossiping.* Sie haben dauernd geschwatzt.
[2] <u>tratschen</u> (*about somebody*) ◊ *They gossiped about her.* Sie haben über sie getratscht.

got VERB *see* **get**

gotten VERB *see* **get**

government NOUN
die <u>Regierung</u>

GP NOUN (= *General Practitioner*)
der <u>praktische Arzt</u> (PL die praktischen Ärzte)
die <u>praktische Ärztin</u>

GPS NOUN (= *global positioning system*)
das <u>GPS</u> (PL die GPS)

to **grab** VERB
<u>packen</u> ◊ *She grabbed her umbrella and ran out of the door.* Sie packte ihren Schirm und lief zur Tür hinaus.

graceful ADJECTIVE
<u>anmutig</u>

grade NOUN
[1] die <u>Note</u> (*mark*) ◊ *He got good grades in his exams.* Er hat in der Prüfung gute Noten bekommen.
[2] die <u>Klasse</u> (*class*) ◊ *Which grade are you in?* In welcher Klasse bist du?

grade school NOUN US
die <u>Grundschule</u>

gradual ADJECTIVE
<u>allmählich</u>

gradually ADVERB
<u>allmählich</u> ◊ *We got used to it.* Wir haben uns daran gewöhnt.

graduate NOUN
see also **graduate** VERB
der <u>Hochschulabsolvent</u> (GEN des Hochschulabsolventen, PL die Hochschulabsolventen)
die <u>Hochschulabsolventin</u>

to **graduate** VERB
see also **graduate** NOUN
das <u>Examen machen</u>

graffiti PL NOUN
die <u>Graffiti</u> PL

grain NOUN
das <u>Korn</u> (PL die Körner)

gram NOUN
das <u>Gramm</u> (PL die Gramme *or* Gramm)
When specifying a quantity of something use the plural form **Gramm**.
◊ *five hundred grams of cheese* fünfhundert Gramm Käse

grammar NOUN
die <u>Grammatik</u>

grammar school NOUN
das <u>Gymnasium</u> (PL die Gymnasien)

> ⓘ **Gymnasium** education begins after year 4 of the **Grundschule** and lasts until year 13.

grammatical ADJECTIVE
<u>grammatisch</u>

gramme NOUN
das <u>Gramm</u> (PL die Gramme *or* Gramm)
When specifying a quantity of something use the plural form **Gramm**.
◊ *five hundred grammes of cheese* fünfhundert Gramm Käse

grand ADJECTIVE
<u>prachtvoll</u> ◊ *Samantha lives in a very grand house.* Samantha wohnt in einem prachtvollen Haus.

grandchild NOUN
der <u>Enkel</u> (PL die Enkel)

granddad NOUN
der <u>Opa</u> (PL die Opas) ◊ *my granddad* mein Opa

granddaughter NOUN
die <u>Enkelin</u>

grandfather NOUN
der <u>Großvater</u> (PL die Großväter) ◊ *my grandfather* mein Großvater

grandma NOUN
die <u>Oma</u> (PL die Omas) ◊ *my grandma* meine Oma

grandmother NOUN
die <u>Großmutter</u> (PL die Großmütter) ◊ *my grandmother* meine Großmutter

grandpa NOUN
der <u>Opa</u> (PL die Opas) ◊ *my grandpa* mein Opa

grandparents PL NOUN
die <u>Großeltern</u> PL ◊ *my grandparents* meine Großeltern

grandson NOUN
der Enkel (PL die Enkel)

granny NOUN
die Oma (PL die Omas) ◇ *my granny*
meine Oma

grant NOUN
1 (*for study*)
das Stipendium (PL die Stipendien)
2 (*for industry, organization*)
die Unterstützung

grape NOUN
die Traube

grapefruit NOUN
die Grapefruit (PL die Grapefruits)

graph NOUN
die grafische Darstellung

graphics PL NOUN
die Grafik SING

to **grasp** VERB
1 (*with hand*)
packen
2 verstehen (IMPERFECT verstand, PERFECT
hat verstanden) ◇ *I couldn't grasp the
difference.* Ich habe den Unterschied
nicht verstanden.

grass NOUN
das Gras (GEN des Grases) ◇ *The grass is
long.* Das Gras ist hoch.
♦ **to cut the grass** den Rasen mähen

grasshopper NOUN
die Heuschrecke

to **grate** VERB
reiben (IMPERFECT rieb, PERFECT hat gerieben)
◇ *to grate some cheese* Käse reiben

grateful ADJECTIVE
dankbar

grave NOUN
das Grab (PL die Gräber)

gravel NOUN
der Kies

graveyard NOUN
der Friedhof (PL die Friedhöfe)

gravy NOUN
die Bratensoße

grease NOUN
das Fett (PL die Fette)

greasy ADJECTIVE
fettig ◇ *He has greasy hair.* Er hat fettige
Haare.
♦ **The food was very greasy**. Das Essen
war sehr fett.

great ADJECTIVE
1 toll ◇ *That's great!* Das ist toll!
2 groß (*big*) ◇ *a great mansion* eine
große Villa

Great Britain NOUN
Großbritannien NEUT
♦ **from Great Britain** aus Großbritannien
♦ **in Great Britain** in Großbritannien
♦ **to Great Britain** nach Großbritannien

great-grandfather NOUN
der Urgroßvater (PL die Urgroßväter)

great-grandmother NOUN
die Urgroßmutter (PL die Urgroßmütter)

Greece NOUN
Griechenland NEUT
♦ **from Greece** aus Griechenland
♦ **to Greece** nach Griechenland

greedy ADJECTIVE
gierig ◇ *I want some more cake. – Don't
be so greedy!* Ich möchte noch etwas
Kuchen. – Sei nicht so gierig!

Greek ADJECTIVE
see also **Greek** NOUN
griechisch ◇ *I love Greek food.* Ich mag
griechisches Essen sehr gern. ◇ *Dionysis
is Greek.* Dionysis ist Grieche. ◇ *She's
Greek.* Sie ist Griechin.

Greek NOUN
see also **Greek** ADJECTIVE
1 (*person*)
der Grieche (GEN des Griechen, PL die
Griechen)
die Griechin
2 (*language*)
das Griechisch (GEN des Griechischen)

green ADJECTIVE
see also **green** NOUN
grün ◇ *a green car* ein grünes Auto ◇ *a
green salad* ein grüner Salat
♦ **the Green Party** die Grünen MASC PL

green NOUN
see also **green** ADJECTIVE
das Grün ◇ *a dark green* ein dunkles
Grün
♦ **greens** (*vegetables*) das Grüngemüse SING
♦ **the Greens** (*party*) die Grünen

greengrocer's NOUN
der Gemüsehändler (PL die
Gemüsehändler)

greenhouse NOUN
das Treibhaus (GEN des Treibhauses, PL
die Treibhäuser)
♦ **the greenhouse effect** der
Treibhauseffekt

Greenland NOUN
Grönland NEUT

to **greet** VERB
begrüßen (PERFECT hat begrüßt) ◇ *He
greeted me with a kiss.* Er begrüßte mich
mit einem Kuss.

greeting NOUN
♦ **Greetings from Bangor!** Grüße aus
Bangor!

greetings card NOUN
die Grußkarte

grew VERB *see* **grow**

grey ADJECTIVE
grau ◇ *She's got grey hair.* Sie hat graue
Haare. ◇ *He's going grey.* Er wird grau.

grey-haired ADJECTIVE
grauhaarig

grid NOUN
1 (*on map*)

G

das <u>Gitter</u> (PL die Gitter)
[2] (of electricity)
das <u>Netz</u> (GEN des Netzes, PL die Netze)

grief NOUN
der <u>Kummer</u>

grill NOUN
see also **grill** VERB
der <u>Grill</u> (of cooker) (PL die Grills)
♦ **a mixed grill** ein Grillteller MASC

to **grill** VERB
see also **grill** NOUN
<u>grillen</u>

grim ADJECTIVE
<u>schlimm</u> ◊ Things look grim. Es sieht schlimm aus.

to **grin** VERB
see also **grin** NOUN
<u>grinsen</u> ◊ Dave grinned at me. Dave grinste mich an.

grin NOUN
see also **grin** VERB
das <u>Grinsen</u>

to **grind** VERB
[1] (coffee, pepper)
<u>mahlen</u> (PERFECT hat gemahlen)
[2] (meat)
<u>hacken</u>

to **grip** VERB
<u>packen</u> ◊ I gripped his shirt and pulled him to the ground. Ich packte ihn am Hemd und zog ihn zu Boden.

gripping ADJECTIVE
<u>spannend</u> (exciting)

grit NOUN
der <u>Splitt</u> (PL die Splitte)

to **groan** VERB
see also **groan** NOUN
<u>stöhnen</u> ◊ He groaned with pain. Er stöhnte vor Schmerzen.

groan NOUN
see also **groan** VERB
das <u>Stöhnen</u> (of pain)

grocer NOUN
der <u>Lebensmittelhändler</u> (PL die Lebensmittelhändler)
die <u>Lebensmittelhändlerin</u>
◊ He's a grocer. Er ist Lebensmittelhändler.

groceries PL NOUN
die <u>Einkäufe</u> MASC PL

grocer's (shop) NOUN
das <u>Lebensmittelgeschäft</u> (PL die Lebensmittelgeschäfte)

grocery store NOUN US
das <u>Lebensmittelgeschäft</u> (PL die Lebensmittelgeschäfte)

groom NOUN
der <u>Bräutigam</u> (bridegroom) (PL die Bräutigame) ◊ the groom and his best man der Bräutigam und sein Trauzeuge

to **grope** VERB

♦ **to grope for something** nach etwas tasten ◊ He groped for the light switch. Er tastete nach dem Lichtschalter.

gross ADJECTIVE
<u>abscheulich</u> (revolting) ◊ It was really gross! Es war wirklich abscheulich!

grossly ADVERB
<u>total</u> ◊ We're grossly underpaid. Wir sind total unterbezahlt.

ground NOUN
see also **ground** VERB
[1] (earth)
der <u>Boden</u> (PL die Böden) ◊ The ground's wet. Der Boden ist nass.
[2] (for sport)
der <u>Platz</u> (GEN des Platzes, PL die Plätze)
◊ a football ground ein Fußballplatz
[3] (reason)
der <u>Grund</u> (PL die Gründe) ◊ We've got grounds for complaint. Wir haben Grund zur Klage.
♦ **on the ground** auf dem Boden ◊ We sat on the ground. Wir saßen auf dem Boden.

ground VERB see **grind**
see also **ground** NOUN
♦ **ground coffee** gemahlener Kaffee

group NOUN
die <u>Gruppe</u>

to **grow** VERB
[1] (plant, person, animal)
<u>wachsen</u> (PRESENT wächst, IMPERFECT wuchs, PERFECT ist gewachsen) ◊ Grass grows quickly. Gras wächst schnell. ◊ Haven't you grown! Bist du aber gewachsen!
♦ **to grow a beard** sich einen Bart wachsen lassen ◊ You should grow a beard. Du solltest dir einen Bart wachsen lassen.
♦ **He's grown out of his jacket.** Er ist aus der Jacke herausgewachsen.
[2] (increase)
<u>zunehmen</u> (PRESENT nimmt zu, IMPERFECT nahm zu, PERFECT hat zugenommen) ◊ The number of unemployed people has grown. Die Zahl der Arbeitslosen hat zugenommen.
[3] (cultivate)
<u>anbauen</u> (PERFECT hat angebaut) ◊ My Dad grows potatoes. Mein Papa baut Kartoffeln an.
♦ **to grow up** erwachsen werden ◊ Oh, grow up! Werd endlich erwachsen!

to **growl** VERB
<u>knurren</u>

grown VERB see **grow**

growth NOUN
das <u>Wachstum</u> ◊ economic growth das Wirtschaftswachstum

grub NOUN
die <u>Fressalien</u> FEM PL (informal)

grudge NOUN
♦ **to bear a grudge against somebody** einen Groll gegen jemanden haben

◇ He's always borne a grudge against me. Er hat schon immer einen Groll gegen mich gehabt.

gruesome ADJECTIVE
furchtbar

guarantee NOUN

see also **guarantee** VERB

die Garantie ◇ a five-year guarantee eine Garantie von fünf Jahren

to **guarantee** VERB

see also **guarantee** NOUN

garantieren (PERFECT hat garantiert) ◇ I can't guarantee he'll come. Ich kann nicht garantieren, dass er kommt.

to **guard** VERB

see also **guard** NOUN

bewachen (PERFECT hat bewacht) ◇ They guarded the palace. Sie bewachten den Palast.

♦ **to guard against something** gegen etwas Vorsichtsmaßnahmen ergreifen

guard NOUN

see also **guard** VERB

(of train)
der Zugbegleiter (PL die Zugbegleiter)
die Zugbegleiterin

♦ **a security guard** ein Wachtmann MASC
♦ **a guard dog** ein Wachhund MASC

to **guess** VERB

see also **guess** NOUN

raten (PRESENT rät, IMPERFECT riet, PERFECT hat geraten) ◇ Can you guess what it is? Rate mal, was das ist. ◇ to guess wrong falsch raten

guess NOUN

see also **guess** VERB

die Vermutung ◇ It's just a guess. Es ist nur eine Vermutung.

♦ **Have a guess!** Rate mal!

guest NOUN
der Gast (PL die Gäste)

der Gast is also used for women.

◇ She is our guest. Sie ist unser Gast.
◇ We have guests staying with us. Wir haben Gäste.

guesthouse NOUN
die Pension ◇ We stayed overnight in a guesthouse. Wir haben in einer Pension übernachtet.

guide NOUN

[1] (book)
der Führer (PL die Führer) ◇ We bought a guide to Cologne. Wir haben einen Führer von Köln gekauft.

[2] (person)
der Führer (PL die Führer)

die Führerin
◇ The guide showed us round the castle. Unser Führer hat uns die Burg gezeigt.

[3] (Girl Guide)
die Pfadfinderin

♦ **the Guides** die Pfadfinderinnen

guidebook NOUN
der Führer (PL die Führer)

guide dog NOUN
der Blindenhund (PL die Blindenhunde)

guilty ADJECTIVE
schuldig ◇ to feel guilty sich schuldig fühlen ◇ She was found guilty. Sie wurde schuldig gesprochen.

guinea pig NOUN
das Meerschweinchen (PL die Meerschweinchen)

guitar NOUN
die Gitarre ◇ I play the guitar. Ich spiele Gitarre.

gum NOUN
der Kaugummi (chewing gum) (PL die Kaugummis)

♦ **gums** (in mouth) das Zahnfleisch SING

gun NOUN
[1] (small)
die Pistole
[2] (rifle)
das Gewehr (PL die Gewehre)

gunpoint NOUN
♦ **at gunpoint** mit Waffengewalt

gust NOUN
♦ **a gust of wind** ein Windstoß MASC

guts PL NOUN
der Mumm (informal: courage) ◇ He's certainly got guts. Er hat wirklich Mumm.

♦ **I hate his guts.** Ich kann ihn nicht ausstehen.

guy NOUN
der Typ (PL die Typen) ◇ Who's that guy? Wer ist der Typ?

♦ **He's a nice guy.** Er ist ein netter Kerl.

gym NOUN
die Turnhalle
♦ **gym classes** die Turnstunden

gymnast NOUN
der Turner (PL die Turner)
die Turnerin
◇ She's a gymnast. Sie ist Turnerin.

gymnastics NOUN
das Turnen
♦ **to do gymnastics** turnen

gypsy NOUN
der Zigeuner (PL die Zigeuner)
die Zigeunerin

G

H

habit NOUN
die <u>Angewohnheit</u> ◊ *a bad habit* eine schlechte Angewohnheit

hacker NOUN
der <u>Hacker</u> (PL die Hacker)
die <u>Hackerin</u>

had VERB *see* **have**

haddock NOUN
der <u>Schellfisch</u>

hadn't = **had not**

hail NOUN
see also **hail** VERB
der <u>Hagel</u>

to **hail** VERB
see also **hail** NOUN
<u>hageln</u> ◊ *It's hailing.* Es hagelt.

hair NOUN
die <u>Haare</u> NEUT PL ◊ *She's got long hair.* Sie hat lange Haare. ◊ *He's got black hair.* Er hat schwarze Haare. ◊ *He's losing his hair.* Ihm gehen die Haare aus.
♦ **to brush one's hair** sich die Haare bürsten ◊ *I brush my hair every morning.* Ich bürste mir jeden Morgen die Haare.
♦ **to wash one's hair** sich die Haare waschen ◊ *I need to wash my hair.* Ich muss mir die Haare waschen.
♦ **to have one's hair cut** sich die Haare schneiden lassen ◊ *I've just had my hair cut.* Ich habe mir gerade die Haare schneiden lassen.
♦ **a hair** ein Haar NEUT

hairbrush NOUN
die <u>Haarbürste</u>

hair clip NOUN
die <u>Haarspange</u>

haircut NOUN
der <u>Haarschnitt</u> (PL die Haarschnitte)
♦ **to have a haircut** sich die Haare schneiden lassen ◊ *I've just had a haircut.* Ich habe mir gerade die Haare schneiden lassen.

hairdresser NOUN
der <u>Friseur</u> (PL die Friseure)
die <u>Friseuse</u>
◊ *He's a hairdresser.* Er ist Friseur.

hairdresser's NOUN
der <u>Friseur</u> (PL die Friseure) ◊ *at the hairdresser's* beim Friseur

hair dryer NOUN
der <u>Haartrockner</u> (PL die Haartrockner)

hair gel NOUN
das <u>Haargel</u> (PL die Haargele)

*In German the "g" in **Haargel** is pronounced like the "g" in girl.*

hairgrip NOUN
die <u>Haarklemme</u>

hair spray NOUN
der <u>Haarspray</u> (PL die Haarsprays)

hairstyle NOUN
die <u>Frisur</u>

hairy ADJECTIVE
<u>haarig</u> ◊ *He's got hairy legs.* Er hat die haarige Beine.

half NOUN
see also **half** ADJECTIVE
1 die <u>Hälfte</u> ◊ *half of the cake* die Hälfte des Kuchens
2 die <u>Kinderfahrkarte</u> (*ticket*) ◊ *A half to York, please.* Ein Kinderfahrkarte nach York bitte.
♦ **two and a half** zweieinhalb
♦ **half an hour** eine halbe Stunde
♦ **half past ten** halb elf
♦ **half a kilo** ein halbes Kilo
♦ **to cut something in half** etwas in zwei Teile schneiden

half ADJECTIVE, ADVERB
see also **half** NOUN
1 <u>halb</u> ◊ *a half chicken* ein halbes Hähnchen
2 <u>fast</u> ◊ *He was half asleep.* Er schlief fast.

half-hour NOUN
die <u>halbe Stunde</u>

half-price ADJECTIVE, ADVERB
♦ **at half-price** zum halben Preis

half-term NOUN
die <u>kleinen Ferien</u> PL

half-time NOUN
die <u>Halbzeit</u>

halfway ADVERB
1 <u>auf halber Strecke</u> ◊ *halfway between Oxford and London* auf halber Strecke zwischen Oxford und London
2 <u>in der Mitte</u> ◊ *halfway through the chapter* in der Mitte des Kapitels

hall NOUN
1 (*in house*)
der <u>Flur</u> (PL die Flure)
2 der <u>Saal</u> (PL die Säle) ◊ *the village hall* der Gemeindesaal
♦ **hall of residence** das Wohnheim

Hallowe'en NOUN
der <u>Abend vor Allerheiligen</u>

hallway NOUN
der <u>Flur</u> (PL die Flure)

halt NOUN
♦ **to come to a halt** zum Stehen kommen

ham NOUN
der <u>Schinken</u> (PL die Schinken) ◊ *a ham sandwich* ein Schinkensandwich NEUT

hamburger NOUN
der <u>Hamburger</u> (PL die Hamburger)

hammer NOUN
der <u>Hammer</u> (PL die Hämmer)

hamster NOUN
der Hamster (PL die Hamster)

hand NOUN

see also **hand** VERB

1 (*of person*)
die Hand (PL die Hände)
♦ **to give somebody a hand** jemandem helfen ◊ *Can you give me a hand?* Kannst du mir mal helfen?
♦ **on the one hand ..., on the other hand ...** einerseits ..., anderseits ...
2 (*of clock*)
der Zeiger (PL die Zeiger)

to **hand** VERB

see also **hand** NOUN

reichen ◊ *He handed me the book.* Er reichte mir das Buch.
♦ **to hand something in** etwas abgeben ◊ *Martin handed his exam paper in.* Martin gab seine Prüfungsarbeit ab.
♦ **to hand something out** etwas austeilen ◊ *The teacher handed out the books.* Der Lehrer teilte die Bücher aus.
♦ **to hand something over** etwas übergeben ◊ *She handed the keys over to me.* Sie übergab mir die Schlüssel.

handbag NOUN
die Handtasche

handball NOUN
1 der Handball (*sport*)
2 das Handspiel (*foul*)

handbook NOUN
das Handbuch (PL die Handbücher)

handcuffs PL NOUN
die Handschellen FEM PL

handkerchief NOUN
das Taschentuch (PL die Taschentücher)

handle NOUN

see also **handle** VERB

1 (*of door*)
die Klinke
2 (*of cup*)
der Henkel (PL die Henkel)
3 (*of knife*)
der Griff (PL die Griffe)
4 (*of saucepan*)
der Stiel (PL die Stiele)

to **handle** VERB

see also **handle** NOUN

♦ **He handled it well.** Er hat das gut gemacht.
♦ **Kath handled the travel arrangements.** Kath hat sich um die Reisevorbereitungen gekümmert.
♦ **She's good at handling children.** Sie kann gut mit Kindern umgehen.

handlebars PL NOUN
die Lenkstange SING

handmade ADJECTIVE
handgemacht

handsome ADJECTIVE
gut aussehend ◊ *a handsome man* ein gut aussehender Mann

♦ **He's very handsome.** Er sieht sehr gut aus.

handwriting NOUN
die Handschrift

handy ADJECTIVE
1 praktisch ◊ *This knife's very handy.* Dieses Messer ist sehr praktisch.
2 zur Hand ◊ *Have you got a pen handy?* Hast du einen Schreiber zur Hand?

to **hang** VERB
1 aufhängen (PERFECT hat aufgehängt) ◊ *Mike hung the painting on the wall.* Mike hängte das Bild an der Wand auf.
2 hängen ◊ *They hanged the criminal.* Sie hängten den Verbrecher.
♦ **to hang around** rumhängen ◊ *On Saturdays we hang around in the park.* Samstags hängen wir im Park rum.
♦ **to hang on** warten ◊ *Hang on a minute, please.* Bitte warte einen Moment.
♦ **to hang up (1)** (*clothes*) aufhängen ◊ *Hang your jacket up on the hook.* Häng deine Jacke am Haken auf.
♦ **to hang up (2)** (*phone*) auflegen ◊ *I tried to phone him but he hung up on me.* Ich habe versucht, mit ihm zu telefonieren, aber er hat einfach aufgelegt.

hanger NOUN
der Bügel (*for clothes*) (PL die Bügel)

hang-gliding NOUN
das Drachenfliegen
♦ **to go hang-gliding** Drachen fliegen gehen

hangover NOUN
der Kater (PL die Kater) ◊ *to have a hangover* einen Kater haben

to **happen** VERB
passieren (PERFECT ist passiert) ◊ *What's happened?* Was ist passiert?
♦ **as it happens** zufälligerweise ◊ *As it happens I saw him yesterday.* Zufälligerweise habe ich ihn gestern gesehen.

happily ADVERB
1 fröhlich ◊ *"Don't worry!" he said happily.* "Mach dir keine Sorgen!" sagte er fröhlich.
2 zum Glück (*fortunately*) ◊ *Happily, everything went well.* Zum Glück ging alles gut.

happiness NOUN
das Glück

happy ADJECTIVE
glücklich ◊ *Janet looks happy.* Janet sieht glücklich aus.
♦ **I'm very happy with your work.** Ich bin sehr zufrieden mit Ihrer Arbeit.
♦ **Happy birthday!** Herzlichen Glückwunsch zum Geburtstag!

harbour NOUN
der Hafen (PL die Häfen)

H

hard ADJECTIVE, ADVERB

[1] hart ◇ *This cheese is very hard.* Dieser Käse ist sehr hart. ◇ *He's worked very hard.* Er hat sehr hart gearbeitet.

[2] schwierig ◇ *This question's too hard for me.* Diese Frage ist für mich zu schwierig.

hard disk NOUN

die Festplatte (*of computer*)

hardly ADVERB

kaum ◇ *I've hardly got any money.* Ich habe kaum Geld. ◇ *I hardly know you.* Ich kenne Sie kaum.

♦ **hardly ever** fast nie

hard up ADJECTIVE

pleite

hardware NOUN

die Hardware

hare NOUN

der Feldhase (GEN des Feldhasen, PL die Feldhasen)

to **harm** VERB

♦ **to harm somebody** jemandem wehtun ◇ *I didn't mean to harm you.* Ich wollte Ihnen nicht wehtun.

♦ **to harm something** einer Sache schaden ◇ *Chemicals harm the environment.* Chemikalien schaden der Umwelt.

harmful ADJECTIVE

schädlich ◇ *harmful chemicals* schädliche Chemikalien

harmless ADJECTIVE

harmlos ◇ *Most spiders are harmless.* Die meisten Spinnen sind harmlos.

harsh ADJECTIVE

[1] hart ◇ *He deserves a harsh punishment for what he did.* Er verdient es, hart bestraft zu werden für das, was er getan hat.

[2] rau ◇ *She's got a very harsh voice.* Sie hat eine sehr raue Stimme.

harvest NOUN

die Ernte

has VERB *see* **have**

hasn't = **has not**

hat NOUN

der Hut (PL die Hüte)

to **hate** VERB

hassen ◇ *I hate maths.* Ich hasse Mathe.

hatred NOUN

der Hass (GEN des Hasses)

haunted ADJECTIVE

verwunschen ◇ *a haunted house* ein verwunschenes Haus

to **have** VERB

[1] haben (PRESENT hat, IMPERFECT hatte, PERFECT hat gehabt) ◇ *Have you got a sister?* Hast du eine Schwester? ◇ *He's got blue eyes.* Er hat blaue Augen. ◇ *I've got a cold.* Ich habe eine Erkältung.

The perfect tense of most verbs is formed with **haben**.

◇ *They have eaten.* Sie haben gegessen. ◇ *Have you done your homework?* Hast du deine Hausaufgaben gemacht?

Questions like "hasn't he?" don't exist in German.

◇ *He's done it, hasn't he?* Er hat es getan, nicht wahr?

have *is not translated when it is used in place of another verb.*

◇ *Have you got any money? – No, I haven't.* Hast du Geld? – Nein. ◇ *Does she have any pets? – Yes, she has.* Hat sie Haustiere? – Ja. ◇ *He hasn't done his homework. – Yes, he has.* Er hat seine Hausaufgaben nicht gemacht. – Doch.

[2] sein (PRESENT ist, IMPERFECT war, PERFECT ist gewesen)

The perfect tense of some verbs is formed with **sein**.

◇ *They have arrived.* Sie sind angekommen. ◇ *Has he gone?* Ist er gegangen?

have *plus noun is sometimes translated by a German verb.*

◇ *He had his breakfast.* Er hat gefrühstückt. ◇ *to have a shower* duschen ◇ *to have a bath* baden

♦ **to have got to do something** etwas tun müssen ◇ *She's got to do it.* Sie muss es tun.

♦ **to have a party** eine Party machen

♦ **I had my hair cut yesterday.** Ich habe mir gestern die Haare schneiden lassen.

haven't = **have not**

hay NOUN

das Heu

hay fever NOUN

der Heuschnupfen ◇ *Do you get hay fever?* Hast du manchmal Heuschnupfen?

hazelnut NOUN

die Haselnuss (PL die Haselnüsse)

he PRONOUN

er ◇ *He loves dogs.* Er liebt Hunde.

head NOUN

see also **head** VERB

[1] (*of person*)

der Kopf (PL die Köpfe) ◇ *The wine went to my head.* Der Wein ist mir in den Kopf gestiegen.

[2] (*of private or primary school*)

der Rektor (PL die Rektoren)

die Rektorin

[3] (*of state secondary school*)

der Direktor (PL die Direktoren)

die Direktorin

[4] (*leader*)

das Oberhaupt (PL die Oberhäupter) ◇ *a head of state* ein Staatsoberhaupt

♦ **to have a head for figures** gut mit Zahlen umgehen können

♦ **Heads or tails? – Heads.** Kopf oder Wappen? – Kopf.

to **head** VERB
> see also **head** NOUN

♦**to head for something** auf etwas
zugehen ◊ *He headed straight for the
bar.* Er ging direkt auf die Theke zu.

headache NOUN
die Kopfschmerzen MASC PL ◊ *I've got a
headache.* Ich habe Kopfschmerzen.

headlight NOUN
der Scheinwerfer (PL die Scheinwerfer)

headline NOUN
die Schlagzeile

headmaster NOUN
[1] (*of private or primary school*)
der Rektor (PL die Rektoren)
[2] (*of state secondary school*)
der Direktor (PL die Direktoren)

headmistress NOUN
[1] (*of private or primary school*)
die Rektorin
[2] (*of state secondary school*)
die Direktorin

headphones PL NOUN
der Kopfhörer (PL die Kopfhörer) ◊ *a set
of headphones* ein Kopfhörer

headquarters PL NOUN
das Hauptquartier ◊ *The bank's
headquarters are in London.* Das
Hauptquartier der Bank ist in London.

headteacher NOUN
[1] (*of private or primary school*)
der Rektor (PL die Rektoren)
die Rektorin
[2] (*of state secondary school*)
der Direktor (PL die Direktoren)
die Direktorin

to **heal** VERB
heilen

health NOUN
die Gesundheit

healthy ADJECTIVE
gesund ◊ *Lesley's a healthy person.*
Lesley ist gesund. ◊ *a healthy diet* eine
gesunde Ernährung

heap NOUN
der Haufen (PL die Haufen) ◊ *a rubbish
heap* ein Müllhaufen

to **hear** VERB
hören ◊ *He heard the dog bark.* Er hörte
den Hund bellen. ◊ *She can't hear very
well.* Sie hört nicht gut. ◊ *I heard that she
was ill.* Ich habe gehört, dass sie krank
war. ◊ *Did you hear the good news?* Hast
du die gute Nachricht gehört?

♦**to hear about something** von etwas
hören

♦**to hear from somebody** von jemandem
hören ◊ *I haven't heard from him
recently.* Ich habe in letzter Zeit nichts
von ihm gehört.

heart NOUN
das Herz (GEN des Herzens, PL die Herzen)

♦**to learn something by heart** etwas
auswendig lernen

♦**the ace of hearts** das Herzass

heart attack NOUN
der Herzinfarkt (PL die Herzinfarkte)

heartbroken ADJECTIVE
zutiefst betrübt

heat NOUN
> see also **heat** VERB
die Hitze

to **heat** VERB
> see also **heat** NOUN
erhitzen (PERFECT hat erhitzt) ◊ *Heat gently
for five minutes.* Erhitzen Sie es bei
schwacher Hitze fünf Minuten lang.

♦**to heat up (1)** (*cooked food*) aufwärmen
◊ *He heated the soup up.* Er hat die
Suppe aufgewärmt.

♦**to heat up (2)** (*water, oven*) heiß werden
◊ *The water is heating up.* Das Wasser
wird heiß.

heater NOUN
der Heizofen (PL die Heizöfen) ◊ *an
electric heater* ein elektrischer Heizofen

heather NOUN
das Heidekraut (PL die Heidekräuter)

heating NOUN
die Heizung

heaven NOUN
der Himmel (PL die Himmel)

heavily ADVERB
schwer ◊ *The car was heavily loaded.*
Das Auto war schwer beladen.

♦**He drinks heavily.** Er trinkt viel.

♦**It was raining heavily.** Es regnete stark.

heavy ADJECTIVE
[1] schwer ◊ *This bag's very heavy.* Diese
Tasche ist sehr schwer.

♦**heavy rain** starker Regen
[2] anstrengend (*busy*) ◊ *I've got a very
heavy week ahead.* Ich habe eine
anstrengende Woche vor mir.

♦**to be a heavy drinker** viel trinken

he'd = he would, = he had

hedge NOUN
die Hecke

hedgehog NOUN
der Igel (PL die Igel)

heel NOUN
der Absatz (GEN des Absatzes, PL die
Absätze)

height NOUN
[1] die Größe (*of person*)
[2] die Höhe (*of object, mountain*)

heir NOUN
der Erbe (GEN des Erben, PL die Erben)

heiress NOUN
die Erbin

held VERB *see* **hold**

helicopter NOUN
der Hubschrauber (PL die Hubschrauber)

hell NOUN

H

☞

die <u>Hölle</u>
♦ **Hell!** Mist! (*informal*)
he'll = **he will**, = **he shall**
hello EXCLAMATION
<u>hallo</u>
helmet NOUN
der <u>Helm</u> (PL die Helme)
to **help** VERB

see also **help** NOUN

<u>helfen</u> (PRESENT hilft, IMPERFECT half, PERFECT hat geholfen)
♦ **to help somebody** jemandem helfen
◇ *Can you help me?* Kannst du mir helfen?
♦ **Help!** Hilfe!
♦ **Help yourself!** Bedienen Sie sich!
♦ **He can't help it.** Er kann nichts dafür.
help NOUN

see also **help** VERB

die <u>Hilfe</u> ◇ *Do you need any help?* Brauchst du Hilfe?
helpful ADJECTIVE
<u>hilfreich</u> ◇ *a helpful suggestion* ein hilfreicher Vorschlag
♦ **He was very helpful.** Er war eine große Hilfe.
help menu NOUN
das <u>Hilfemenü</u> (PL die Hilfemenüs)
hen NOUN
die <u>Henne</u>
her ADJECTIVE

see also **her** PRONOUN

<u>ihr</u> ◇ *her father* ihr Vater ◇ *her mother* ihre Mutter ◇ *her child* ihr Kind ◇ *her parents* ihre Eltern

*Do not use **ihr** with parts of the body.*

◇ *She's going to wash her hair.* Sie wäscht sich die Haare. ◇ *She's cleaning her teeth.* Sie putzt sich die Zähne. ◇ *She's hurt her foot.* Sie hat sich am Fuß verletzt.
her PRONOUN

see also **her** ADJECTIVE

[1] <u>sie</u> ◇ *I can see her.* Ich kann sie sehen. ◇ *Look at her!* Sieh sie an! ◇ *Who is it? – It's her again.* Wer ist da? – Sie ist es schon wieder. ◇ *I'm older than her.* Ich bin älter als sie.

*Use **sie** after prepositions which take the accusative.*

◇ *I was thinking of her.* Ich habe an sie gedacht.
[2] <u>ihr</u>

*Use **ihr** after prepositions which take the dative.*

◇ *I'm going with her.* Ich gehe mit ihr mit. ◇ *He sat next to her.* Er saß neben ihr.

*Use **ihr** when **her** means **to her**.*

◇ *I gave her a book.* Ich gab ihr ein Buch. ◇ *I told her the truth.* Ich habe ihr die Wahrheit gesagt.
herb NOUN

das <u>Kraut</u> (PL die Kräuter)
here ADVERB
<u>hier</u> ◇ *I live here.* Ich wohne hier.
◇ *Here's Helen.* Hier ist Helen. ◇ *Here are the books.* Hier sind die Bücher. ◇ *Here he is!* Da ist er ja!
hero NOUN
der <u>Held</u> (GEN des Helden, PL die Helden)
◇ *He's a real hero!* Er ist ein echter Held!
heroin NOUN
das <u>Heroin</u> ◇ *Heroin is a hard drug.* Heroin ist eine harte Droge.
♦ **a heroin addict** (*man*) ein Heroinsüchtiger
♦ **She's a heroin addict.** Sie ist heroinsüchtig.
heroine NOUN
die <u>Heldin</u> ◇ *the heroine of the novel* die Heldin des Romans
hers PRONOUN
[1] <u>ihrer</u> ◇ *Is this her coat? – No, hers is black.* Ist das ihr Mantel? – Nein, ihrer ist schwarz.
<u>ihre</u> ◇ *Is this her cup? – No, hers is red.* Ist das ihre Tasse? – Nein, ihre ist rot.
<u>ihres</u> ◇ *Is this her car? – No, hers is white.* Ist das ihr Auto? – Nein, ihres ist weiß.
[2] <u>ihre</u> ◇ *my parents and hers* meine Eltern und ihre ◇ *I have my reasons and she has hers.* Ich habe meine Gründe und sie hat ihre.
♦ **Is this hers?** Gehört das ihr? ◇ *This book is hers.* Dieses Buch gehört ihr. ◇ *Whose is this? – It's hers.* Wem gehört das? – Es gehört ihr.
herself PRONOUN
[1] <u>sich</u> ◇ *She's hurt herself.* Sie hat sich verletzt. ◇ *She talked mainly about herself.* Sie redete hauptsächlich über sich selbst.
[2] <u>selbst</u> ◇ *She did it herself.* Sie hat es selbst gemacht.
♦ **by herself** allein ◇ *She doesn't like travelling by herself.* Sie verreist nicht gern allein.
he's = **he is**, = **he has**
to **hesitate** VERB
<u>zögern</u>
heterosexual ADJECTIVE
<u>heterosexuell</u>
hi EXCLAMATION
<u>hallo</u>
hiccups PL NOUN
der <u>Schluckauf</u> SING ◇ *He had the hiccups.* Er hatte einen Schluckauf.
to **hide** VERB
<u>sich verstecken</u> (PERFECT hat sich versteckt) ◇ *He hid behind a bush.* Er versteckte sich hinter einem Busch.
♦ **to hide something** etwas verstecken
◇ *Paula hid the present.* Paula hat das Geschenk versteckt.
hide-and-seek NOUN

♦ **to play hide-and-seek** Verstecken spielen

hideous ADJECTIVE
scheußlich

hi-fi NOUN
die Hi-Fi-Anlage

high ADJECTIVE, ADVERB
hoch ◊ *It's too high.* Es ist zu hoch.
◊ *How high is the wall?* Wie hoch ist die
Mauer? ◊ *The wall's two metres high.*
Die Mauer ist zwei Meter hoch.
Before a noun or after an article, use
hohe.
◊ *She's got a very high voice.* Sie hat
eine sehr hohe Stimme. ◊ *a high price*
ein hoher Preis ◊ *a high temperature*
eine hohe Temperatur ◊ *at high speed*
mit hoher Geschwindigkeit
♦ **It's very high in fat.** Es ist sehr fetthaltig.
♦ **to be high** (*on drugs*) high sein (*informal*)
♦ **to get high** (*on drugs*) high werden
(*informal*) ◊ *to get high on crack* von
Crack high werden

higher education NOUN
die Hochschulbildung

high-heeled ADJECTIVE
♦ **high-heeled shoes** hochhackige Schuhe

high jump NOUN
der Hochsprung (*sport*) (PL die
Hochsprünge)

highlight NOUN
see also **highlight** VERB
der Höhepunkt (PL die Höhepunkte) ◊ *the*
highlight of the evening der Höhepunkt
des Abends

to **highlight** VERB
see also **highlight** NOUN
markieren (PERFECT hat markiert) ◊ *She*
highlighted the word in yellow. Sie
markierte das Wort in Gelb.

highlighter NOUN
der Textmarker (PL die Textmarker)

high-rise NOUN
das Hochhaus (GEN des Hochhauses, PL
die Hochhäuser) ◊ *I live in a high-rise.* Ich
wohne in einem Hochhaus.

high school NOUN
das Gymnasium (PL die Gymnasien)

to **hijack** VERB
entführen (PERFECT hat entführt)

hijacker NOUN
der Entführer (PL die Entführer)
die Entführerin

hike NOUN
die Wanderung

hiking NOUN
♦ **to go hiking** wandern gehen

hilarious ADJECTIVE
urkomisch ◊ *It was hilarious!* Es war
urkomisch!

hill NOUN
der Hügel (PL die Hügel) ◊ *She walked up*
the hill. Sie ging den Hügel hinauf.

hill-walking NOUN
das Bergwandern
♦ **to go hill-walking** Bergwanderungen
machen

him PRONOUN
1 ihn ◊ *I can see him.* Ich kann ihn
sehen. ◊ *Look at him!* Sieh ihn an!
Use **ihn** *after prepositions which take the*
accusative.
◊ *I did it for him.* Ich habe es für ihn getan.
2 ihm
Use **ihm** *after prepositions which take*
the dative.
◊ *I travelled with him.* Ich bin mit ihm
gereist. ◊ *I haven't heard from him.* Ich
habe nichts von ihm gehört.
Use **ihm** *when* **him** *means to him.*
◊ *I gave him a book.* Ich gab ihm ein
Buch. ◊ *I told him the truth.* Ich habe ihm
die Wahrheit gesagt.
3 er ◊ *It's him again.* Er ist es schon
wieder. ◊ *I'm older than him.* Ich bin älter
als er.

himself PRONOUN
1 sich ◊ *He's hurt himself.* Er hat sich
verletzt. ◊ *He talked mainly about*
himself. Er redete hauptsächlich über
sich selbst.
2 selbst ◊ *He did it himself.* Er hat es
selbst gemacht.
♦ **by himself** allein ◊ *He was travelling by*
himself. Er reiste allein.

Hindu ADJECTIVE
hinduistisch
♦ **a Hindu temple** ein Hindutempel MASC

hint NOUN
see also **hint** VERB
die Andeutung ◊ *to drop a hint* eine
Andeutung machen
♦ **I can take a hint.** Ich verstehe schon.

to **hint** VERB
see also **hint** NOUN
andeuten (PERFECT hat angedeutet) ◊ *He*
hinted that I had a good chance of
getting the job. Er deutete an, dass ich
gute Chancen habe, die Stelle zu
bekommen.

hip NOUN
die Hüfte

hippie NOUN
der Hippie (PL die Hippies)
der Hippie is also used for women.
◊ *She was a hippie.* Sie war ein Hippie.

hippo NOUN
das Nilpferd (PL die Nilpferde)

to **hire** VERB
see also **hire** NOUN
1 mieten ◊ *to hire a car* ein Auto mieten
2 (*person*)
anstellen (PERFECT hat angestellt) ◊ *They*
hired a cleaner. Sie haben eine Putzfrau
angestellt.

hire NOUN

H

☞

see also **hire** VERB

der Verleih (PL die Verleihe)
- **car hire** der Autoverleih
- **for hire** zu vermieten

hire car NOUN
der Mietwagen (PL die Mietwagen)

his ADJECTIVE

see also **his** PRONOUN

sein ◊ *his father* sein Vater ◊ *his mother* seine Mutter ◊ *his child* sein Kind ◊ *his parents* seine Eltern

*Do not use **sein** with parts of the body.*
◊ *He's going to wash his hair.* Er wäscht sich die Haare. ◊ *He's cleaning his teeth.* Er putzt sich die Zähne. ◊ *He's hurt his foot.* Er hat sich am Fuß verletzt.

his PRONOUN

see also **his** ADJECTIVE

[1] seiner ◊ *Is this his coat? – No, his is black.* Ist das sein Mantel? – Nein, seiner ist schwarz.
seine ◊ *Is this his cup? – No, his is red.* Ist das seine Tasse? – Nein, seine ist rot.
seines ◊ *Is this his car? – No, his is white.* Ist das sein Auto? – Nein, seines ist weiß.
[2] seine ◊ *my parents and his* meine Eltern und seine ◊ *I have my reasons and he has his.* Ich habe meine Gründe und er hat seine.
- **Is this his?** Gehört das ihm? ◊ *This book is his.* Dieses Buch gehört ihm. ◊ *Whose is this? – It's his.* Wem gehört das? – Das gehört ihm.

history NOUN
die Geschichte

to **hit** VERB

see also **hit** NOUN

[1] schlagen (PRESENT schlägt, IMPERFECT schlug, PERFECT hat geschlagen) ◊ *Andrew hit him.* Andrew hat ihn geschlagen.
[2] anfahren (PRESENT fährt an, IMPERFECT fuhr an, PERFECT hat angefahren) ◊ *He was hit by a car.* Er wurde von einem Auto angefahren.
[3] treffen (PRESENT trifft, IMPERFECT traf, PERFECT hat getroffen) ◊ *The arrow hit the target.* Der Pfeil traf sein Ziel.
- **to hit it off with somebody** sich gut mit jemandem verstehen ◊ *She hit it off with his parents.* Sie hat sich mit seinen Eltern gut verstanden.

hit NOUN

see also **hit** VERB

[1] (*song*)
der Hit (PL die Hits) ◊ *Blur's latest hit* Blurs neuester Hit
[2] (*success*)
der Erfolg (PL die Erfolge) ◊ *The film was a massive hit.* Der Film war ein enormer Erfolg.

hitch NOUN

das Problem (PL die Probleme) ◊ *There's been a slight hitch.* Es gab ein kleineres Problem.

to **hitchhike** VERB
per Anhalter fahren (PRESENT fährt, IMPERFECT fuhr, PERFECT ist gefahren)

hitchhiker NOUN
der Anhalter (PL die Anhalter)
die Anhalterin

hitchhiking NOUN
das Trampen ◊ *Hitchhiking can be dangerous.* Trampen kann gefährlich sein.

hit man NOUN
der Killer (PL die Killer)

HIV-negative ADJECTIVE
HIV-negativ

HIV-positive ADJECTIVE
HIV-positiv

hobby NOUN
das Hobby (PL die Hobbys) ◊ *What are your hobbies?* Welche Hobbys haben Sie?

hockey NOUN
das Hockey ◊ *I play hockey.* Ich spiele Hockey.

to **hold** VERB
[1] (*hold on to*)
halten (PRESENT hält, IMPERFECT hielt, PERFECT hat gehalten) ◊ *Hold this end of the rope, please.* Halt bitte dieses Ende des Seils.
- **She held a bottle in her hand.** Sie hatte eine Flasche in der Hand.
[2] (*contain*)
fassen ◊ *This bottle holds two litres.* Diese Flasche fasst zwei Liter.
- **to hold a meeting** eine Versammlung abhalten
- **Hold the line!** (*on telephone*) Bleiben Sie am Apparat!
- **Hold it!** (*wait*) Sekunde!
- **to get hold of something** (*obtain*) etwas bekommen ◊ *I couldn't get hold of it.* Ich habe es nicht bekommen.

to **hold on** VERB
[1] (*keep hold*)
sich festhalten (PRESENT hält sich fest, IMPERFECT hielt sich fest, PERFECT hat sich festgehalten) ◊ *The cliff was slippery, but he managed to hold on.* Die Klippe war sehr rutschig, aber er konnte sich festhalten.
- **to hold on to something (1)** sich an etwas klammern ◊ *He held on to the railing.* Er klammerte sich an das Geländer.
- **to hold on to something (2)** etwas behalten ◊ *He held on to the book, just in case.* Er hat das Buch vorsichtshalber behalten.
[2] (*wait*)
warten ◊ *Hold on, I'm coming!* Warte, ich komme!

♦**Hold on!** (*on telephone*) Bleiben Sie am Apparat!

to **hold up** VERB
♦**to hold up one's hand** die Hand heben ◊ *Peter held up his hand.* Peter hob die Hand.
♦**to hold somebody up** (*delay*) jemanden aufhalten ◊ *I was held up at the office.* Ich wurde im Büro aufgehalten.
♦**to hold up a bank** (*rob*) eine Bank überfallen

hold-up NOUN
1 (*at bank*)
der Überfall (PL die Überfälle)
2 (*delay*)
die Verzögerung
3 (*traffic jam*)
der Stau (PL die Staus)

hole NOUN
das Loch (PL die Löcher)

holiday NOUN
1 (*from school*)
die Ferien PL ◊ *Did you have a good holiday?* Hattet ihr schöne Ferien?
♦**on holiday** in den Ferien ◊ *to go on holiday* in die Ferien fahren ◊ *We are on holiday.* Wir haben Ferien.
♦**the school holidays** die Schulferien
2 (*from work*)
der Urlaub (PL die Urlaube) ◊ *Did you have a good holiday?* Hattet ihr einen schönen Urlaub?
♦**on holiday** im Urlaub ◊ *to go on holiday* in Urlaub fahren ◊ *We are on holiday.* Wir sind im Urlaub.
3 (*public holiday*)
der Feiertag (PL die Feiertage) ◊ *Next Wednesday is a holiday.* Nächsten Mittwoch ist ein Feiertag.
4 (*day off*)
der freie Tag (PL die freien Tage)
♦**He took a day's holiday.** Er nahm einen Tag frei.
♦**a holiday camp** ein Ferienlager NEUT

Holland NOUN
Holland NEUT
♦**from Holland** aus Holland
♦**in Holland** in Holland
♦**to Holland** nach Holland

hollow ADJECTIVE
hohl

holly NOUN
die Stechpalme

holy ADJECTIVE
heilig

home NOUN
see also **home** ADVERB
das Zuhause (GEN des Zuhause)
♦**at home** zu Hause
♦**Make yourself at home.** Machen Sie es sich bequem.

home ADVERB
see also **home** NOUN

1 zu Hause ◊ *to be at home* zu Hause sein
2 nach Hause ◊ *to go home* nach Hause gehen
♦**to get home** nach Hause kommen ◊ *What time did he get home?* Wann ist er nach Hause gekommen?

home address NOUN
die Adresse ◊ *What's your home address?* Wie ist Ihre Adresse?

homeland NOUN
das Heimatland (PL die Heimatländer)

homeless ADJECTIVE
obdachlos
♦**the homeless** die Obdachlosen MASC PL

home match NOUN
das Heimspiel (PL die Heimspiele)

homeopathy NOUN
die Homöopathie

home page NOUN
die Homepage (*Internet*) (PL die Homepages)

homesick ADJECTIVE
♦**to be homesick** Heimweh haben

homework NOUN
die Hausaufgaben FEM PL ◊ *Have you done your homework?* Hast du deine Hausaufgaben gemacht? ◊ *my geography homework* meine Erdkundeaufgaben

homosexual ADJECTIVE
see also **homosexual** NOUN
homosexuell

homosexual NOUN
see also **homosexual** ADJECTIVE
der Homosexuelle (GEN des Homosexuellen, PL die Homosexuellen) ◊ *a homosexual* (*man*) ein Homosexueller

honest ADJECTIVE
ehrlich ◊ *She's an honest person.* Sie ist ein ehrlicher Mensch. ◊ *He was very honest with her.* Er war sehr ehrlich zu ihr.

honestly ADVERB
ehrlich ◊ *I honestly don't know.* Ich weiß es ehrlich nicht.

honesty NOUN
die Ehrlichkeit

honey NOUN
der Honig

honeymoon NOUN
die Flitterwochen FEM PL

honour NOUN
die Ehre

hood NOUN
1 die Kapuze ◊ *a coat with a hood* ein Mantel mit Kapuze
2 die Motorhaube (*of car*)

hook NOUN
der Haken (PL die Haken) ◊ *He hung the painting on the hook.* Er hängte das Bild an den Haken.

H

+ **to take the phone off the hook** das Telefon aushängen
+ **a fish-hook** ein Angelhaken

hooligan NOUN
der <u>Rowdy</u> (PL die Rowdys)

hooray EXCLAMATION
<u>hurra</u>

Hoover ® NOUN
der <u>Staubsauger</u> (PL die Staubsauger)

to **hoover** VERB
<u>staubsaugen</u> ◊ *She hoovered the lounge.* Sie hat im Wohnzimmer gestaubsaugt.

to **hop** VERB
<u>hüpfen</u> (PERFECT ist gehüpft)

to **hope** VERB

see also **hope** NOUN

<u>hoffen</u> ◊ *I hope he comes.* Ich hoffe, er kommt. ◊ *I'm hoping for good results.* Ich hoffe, dass ich gute Noten bekomme.
+ **I hope so.** Hoffentlich.
+ **I hope not.** Hoffentlich nicht.

hope NOUN

see also **hope** VERB

die <u>Hoffnung</u>
+ **to give up hope** die Hoffnung aufgeben ◊ *Don't give up hope!* Gib die Hoffnung nicht auf!

hopeful ADJECTIVE
1 <u>zuversichtlich</u> ◊ *I'm hopeful.* Ich bin zuversichtlich.
+ **He's hopeful of winning.** Er rechnet sich Gewinnchancen aus.
2 <u>aussichtsreich</u> (*situation*)
+ **The prospects look hopeful.** Die Aussichten sind gut.

hopefully ADVERB
<u>hoffentlich</u> ◊ *Hopefully he'll make it in time.* Hoffentlich schafft er es noch.

hopeless ADJECTIVE
<u>hoffnungslos</u> ◊ *I'm hopeless at maths.* In Mathe bin ich ein hoffnungsloser Fall.

horizon NOUN
der <u>Horizont</u> (PL die Horizonte)

horizontal ADJECTIVE
<u>horizontal</u>

horn NOUN
1 (*of car*)
die <u>Hupe</u>
+ **He sounded his horn.** Er hat gehupt.
2 das <u>Horn</u> (PL die Hörner) ◊ *I play the horn.* Ich spiele Horn.

horoscope NOUN
das <u>Horoskop</u> (PL die Horoskope)

horrible ADJECTIVE
<u>furchtbar</u> ◊ *What a horrible dress!* Was für ein furchtbares Kleid!

to **horrify** VERB
<u>entsetzen</u> ◊ *I was horrified by the news.* Ich war über die Neuigkeiten entsetzt.

horrifying ADJECTIVE

<u>schrecklich</u> ◊ *a horrifying accident* ein schrecklicher Unfall

horror NOUN
der <u>Horror</u>

horror film NOUN
der <u>Horrorfilm</u> (PL die Horrorfilme)

horse NOUN
das <u>Pferd</u> (PL die Pferde)

horse-racing NOUN
das <u>Pferderennen</u> (PL die Pferderennen)

horseshoe NOUN
das <u>Hufeisen</u> (PL die Hufeisen)

hose NOUN
der <u>Schlauch</u> (PL die Schläuche) ◊ *a garden hose* ein Gartenschlauch
Be careful not to translate **hose** *by the German word* **Hose**.

hosepipe NOUN
der <u>Schlauch</u> (PL die Schläuche)

hospital NOUN
das <u>Krankenhaus</u> (GEN des Krankenhauses, PL die Krankenhäuser) ◊ *Take me to the hospital!* Bringen Sie mich ins Krankenhaus! ◊ *in hospital* im Krankenhaus

hospitality NOUN
die <u>Gastfreundschaft</u>

host NOUN
1 der <u>Gastgeber</u> (PL die Gastgeber)
die <u>Gastgeberin</u>
2 (*television*)
der <u>Moderator</u> (PL die Moderatoren)
die <u>Moderatorin</u>

hostage NOUN
die <u>Geisel</u> ◊ *to take somebody hostage* jemanden als Geisel nehmen

hostel NOUN
die <u>Herberge</u>

hostile ADJECTIVE
<u>feindlich</u>

hot ADJECTIVE
1 <u>heiß</u> (*warm*) ◊ *a hot bath* ein heißes Bad ◊ *a hot country* ein heißes Land ◊ *It's hot.* Es ist heiß. ◊ *It's very hot today.* Heute ist es sehr heiß.
When you talk about a person being **hot**, *you use the impersonal construction.*
◊ *I'm hot.* Mir ist heiß. ◊ *I'm too hot.* Mir ist es zu heiß.
2 <u>scharf</u> (*spicy*) ◊ *a very hot curry* ein sehr scharfes Curry

hot dog NOUN
der <u>Hotdog</u> (PL die Hotdogs)

hotel NOUN
das <u>Hotel</u> (PL die Hotels) ◊ *We stayed in a hotel.* Wir haben in einem Hotel übernachtet.

hour NOUN
die <u>Stunde</u> ◊ *She always takes hours to get ready.* Sie braucht immer Stunden, bis sie fertig ist.
+ **a quarter of an hour** eine Viertelstunde
+ **half an hour** eine halbe Stunde

♦**two and a half hours** zweieinhalb Stunden

hourly ADJECTIVE, ADVERB
stündlich ◊ *There are hourly buses.* Der Bus verkehrt stündlich.
♦**to be paid hourly** stundenweise bezahlt werden

house NOUN
das Haus (GEN des Hauses, PL die Häuser)
♦**at his house** bei ihm zu Hause
♦**We stayed at their house.** Wir haben bei ihnen übernachtet.

housewife NOUN
die Hausfrau ◊ *She's a housewife.* Sie ist Hausfrau.

housework NOUN
die Hausarbeit ◊ *to do the housework* die Hausarbeit machen

hovercraft NOUN
das Luftkissenfahrzeug (PL die Luftkissenfahrzeuge)

how ADVERB
wie ◊ *How old are you?* Wie alt bist du? ◊ *How far is it to Edinburgh?* Wie weit ist es nach Edinburgh? ◊ *How long have you been here?* Wie lange sind Sie schon hier? ◊ *How are you?* Wie geht's?
♦**How much?** Wie viel? ◊ *How much sugar do you want?* Wie viel Zucker willst du?
♦**How many?** Wie viele? ◊ *How many pupils are there in the class?* Wie viele Schüler sind in der Klasse?

however CONJUNCTION
aber ◊ *This, however, isn't true.* Das ist aber nicht wahr.

to **howl** VERB
heulen

HTML ABBREVIATION (= *hypertext markup language*)
HTML

to **hug** VERB
see also **hug** NOUN
umarmen (PERFECT hat umarmt) ◊ *He hugged her.* Er umarmte sie.

hug NOUN
see also **hug** VERB
♦**to give somebody a hug** jemanden umarmen ◊ *She gave them a hug.* Sie umarmte sie.

huge ADJECTIVE
riesig

to **hum** VERB
summen ◊ *She hummed to herself.* Sie summte vor sich hin.

human ADJECTIVE
menschlich ◊ *the human body* der menschliche Körper

human being NOUN
der Mensch (GEN des Menschen, PL die Menschen)

humble ADJECTIVE
bescheiden

humour NOUN
der Humor
♦**to have a sense of humour** Humor haben

hundred NUMBER
♦**a hundred** einhundert ◊ *a hundred euros* einhundert Euro
♦**five hundred** fünfhundert
♦**five hundred and one** fünfhundertundeins
♦**hundreds of people** Hunderte von Menschen

hung VERB *see* **hang**

Hungarian ADJECTIVE
ungarisch

Hungary NOUN
Ungarn NEUT
♦**from Hungary** aus Ungarn
♦**to Hungary** nach Ungarn

hunger NOUN
der Hunger

hungry ADJECTIVE
♦**to be hungry** Hunger haben

to **hunt** VERB
jagen ◊ *People used to hunt wild boar.* Menschen haben früher Wildschweine gejagt.
♦**to go hunting** auf die Jagd gehen
♦**The police are hunting the killer.** Die Polizei sucht den Mörder.
♦**to hunt for something** (*search*) nach etwas suchen ◊ *I hunted everywhere for that book.* Ich habe überall nach diesem Buch gesucht.

hunting NOUN
das Jagen ◊ *I'm against hunting.* Ich bin gegen Jagen.
♦**fox-hunting** die Fuchsjagd

hurdle NOUN
die Hürde ◊ *the 100 metres hurdles* die 100 Meter Hürden

hurricane NOUN
der Orkan (PL die Orkane)

to **hurry** VERB
see also **hurry** NOUN
eilen (PERFECT ist geeilt) ◊ *Sharon hurried back home.* Sharon eilte nach Hause.
♦**Hurry up!** Beeil dich!

hurry NOUN
see also **hurry** VERB
♦**to be in a hurry** in Eile sein
♦**to do something in a hurry** etwas auf die Schnelle machen
♦**There's no hurry.** Das eilt nicht.

to **hurt** VERB
see also **hurt** ADJECTIVE
wehtun (IMPERFECT tat weh, PERFECT hat wehgetan) ◊ *That hurts.* Das tut weh. ◊ *My leg hurts.* Mein Bein tut weh. ◊ *It hurts to have a tooth out.* Es tut weh, wenn einem ein Zahn gezogen wird.
♦**to hurt somebody (1)** jemandem wehtun ◊ *You're hurting me!* Du tust mir weh!

H

☞

♦ **to hurt somebody (2)** (*offend*) jemanden verletzen ◊ *His remarks hurt me.* Seine Bemerkungen haben mich verletzt.

♦ **to hurt oneself** sich wehtun ◊ *I fell over and hurt myself.* Ich bin hingefallen und habe mir wehgetan.

hurt ADJECTIVE

see also **hurt** VERB

verletzt ◊ *Is he badly hurt?* Ist er schlimm verletzt? ◊ *He was hurt in the leg.* Er hatte ein verletztes Bein. ◊ *Luckily, nobody got hurt.* Zum Glück wurde niemand verletzt. ◊ *I was hurt by what he said.* Was er sagte hat mich verletzt.

husband NOUN
der Ehemann (PL die Ehemänner)

hut NOUN
die Hütte

hymn NOUN
das Kirchenlied (PL die Kirchenlieder)

hypermarket NOUN
der Verbrauchermarkt (PL die Verbrauchermärkte)

hyphen NOUN
der Bindestrich (PL die Bindestriche)

I

I PRONOUN
ich ◇ *I speak German.* Ich spreche
Deutsch. ◇ *Ann and I* Ann und ich

ice NOUN
1 das <u>Eis</u>
• **There was ice on the lake.** Der See war
gefroren.
2 das <u>Glatteis</u> (*on road*)

iceberg NOUN
der <u>Eisberg</u> (PL die Eisberge)

icebox NOUN US
der <u>Kühlschrank</u> (PL die
Kühlschränke)

ice cream NOUN
das <u>Eis</u> (PL die Eis) ◇ *vanilla ice cream*
das Vanilleeis

ice cube NOUN
der <u>Eiswürfel</u> (PL die Eiswürfel)

ice hockey NOUN
das <u>Eishockey</u> ◇ *I like ice hockey.* Ich
mag Eishockey.

Iceland NOUN
<u>Island</u> NEUT
• **from Iceland** aus Island
• **to Iceland** nach Island

ice lolly NOUN
das <u>Eis am Stiel</u>

ice rink NOUN
die <u>Eisbahn</u>

ice-skating NOUN
das <u>Schlittschuhlaufen</u>
• **I like ice-skating.** Ich laufe gern
Schlittschuh.
• **to go ice-skating** Schlittschuh laufen
gehen

icing NOUN
der <u>Zuckerguss</u> (*on cake*) (GEN des
Zuckergusses)
• **icing sugar** der Puderzucker

icon NOUN
das <u>Icon</u> (*computer*) (PL die Icons) ◇ *to
click on an icon* ein Icon anklicken

icy ADJECTIVE
eiskalt ◇ *There was an icy wind.* Es
wehte ein eiskalter Wind.
• **The roads are icy.** Die Straßen sind
vereist.

I'd = I had, = I would

idea NOUN
die <u>Idee</u> ◇ *Good idea!* Gute Idee!

ideal ADJECTIVE
ideal

identical ADJECTIVE
identisch ◇ *identical to* identisch mit

identification NOUN
die <u>Identifikation</u>
• **Have you got any identification?** Können
Sie sich ausweisen?

to **identify** VERB
identifizieren (PERFECT hat identifiziert)

identity card NOUN
der <u>Personalausweis</u> (PL die
Personalausweise)

idiom NOUN
die <u>Redewendung</u>

idiot NOUN
der <u>Idiot</u> (GEN des Idioten, PL die Idioten)
die <u>Idiotin</u>

idiotic ADJECTIVE
idiotisch

idle ADJECTIVE
faul (*lazy*) ◇ *to be idle* faul sein
• **It's just idle gossip.** Das ist nur sinnloses
Geschwätz.
• **I asked out of idle curiosity.** Ich habe aus
reiner Neugier gefragt.

i.e. ABBREVIATION
d. h. (= das heißt)

if CONJUNCTION
1 <u>wenn</u> ◇ *You can have it if you like.*
Wenn du willst, kannst du es haben.
2 <u>ob</u> (*whether*) ◇ *Do you know if he's
there?* Weißt du, ob er da ist?
• **if only** wenn doch nur ◇ *If only I had
more money!* Wenn ich doch nur mehr
Geld hätte!
• **if not** falls nicht ◇ *Are you coming? If
not, I'll go with Mark.* Kommst du? Falls
nicht, gehe ich mit Mark.

ignorant ADJECTIVE
unwissend

to **ignore** VERB
1 <u>nicht beachten</u> (PERFECT hat nicht
beachtet) ◇ *She ignored my advice.* Sie
hat meinen Rat nicht beachtet.
2 <u>ignorieren</u> (PERFECT hat ignoriert) ◇ *She
saw me, but she ignored me.* Sie sah
mich, hat mich aber ignoriert.
• **Just ignore him!** Beachte ihn einfach
nicht!

ill ADJECTIVE
krank (*sick*)
• **to be taken ill** krank werden ◇ *She was
taken ill while on holiday.* Sie wurde im
Urlaub krank.

I'll = I will

illegal ADJECTIVE
illegal

illegible ADJECTIVE
unleserlich

illness NOUN
die <u>Krankheit</u>

to **ill-treat** VERB
misshandeln (PERFECT hat misshandelt)

illusion NOUN
die <u>Illusion</u>

illustration NOUN
die Illustration

I'm = I am

image NOUN
das Image (*public image*) (GEN des Image,
PL die Images) ◊ *The company has
changed its image.* Die Firma hat sich ein
anderes Image zugelegt.

imagination NOUN
die Fantasie ◊ *You need a lot of
imagination to be a writer.* Als
Schriftsteller braucht man viel Fantasie.
♦ **It's just your imagination!** Das bildest du
dir nur ein!

to **imagine** VERB
sich vorstellen (PERFECT hat sich
vorgestellt) ◊ *You can imagine how I felt!*
Du kannst dir vorstellen, wie mir zumute
war!
♦ **Is he angry? – I imagine so.** Ist er böse? –
Ich denke schon.

to **imitate** VERB
nachmachen (PERFECT hat nachgemacht)

imitation NOUN
die Imitation

immediate ADJECTIVE
sofortig ◊ *We need an immediate
answer.* Wir brauchen eine sofortige
Antwort.
♦ **in the immediate future** in unmittelbarer
Zukunft

immediately ADVERB
sofort ◊ *I'll do it immediately.* Ich mache
es sofort.

immigrant NOUN
der Einwanderer (PL die Einwanderer)
die Einwanderin

immigration NOUN
die Einwanderung

immoral ADJECTIVE
unmoralisch

immune ADJECTIVE
♦ **to be immune to something** gegen
etwas immun sein ◊ *She is immune to
measles.* Sie ist gegen Masern
immun.

impartial ADJECTIVE
unparteiisch

impatience NOUN
die Ungeduld

impatient ADJECTIVE
ungeduldig ◊ *People are getting
impatient.* Die Leute werden ungeduldig.

impersonal ADJECTIVE
unpersönlich

to **implement** VERB
ausführen (PERFECT hat ausgeführt) ◊ *It'll
take a few months to implement the
plan.* Es wird ein paar Monate dauern,
bis der Plan ausgeführt ist.

to **imply** VERB

1 andeuten (PERFECT hat angedeutet)
◊ *Are you implying I did it on purpose?*
Wollen Sie damit andeuten, ich hätte das
absichtlich getan?

2 bedeuten (PERFECT hat bedeutet) ◊ *It
implies a lot of work.* Das bedeutet viel
Arbeit.

to **import** VERB
importieren (PERFECT hat importiert)

importance NOUN
die Wichtigkeit ◊ *the importance of a
good knowledge of German* die
Wichtigkeit guter Deutschkenntnisse

important ADJECTIVE
wichtig

to **impose** VERB
auferlegen (PERFECT hat auferlegt) ◊ *to
impose a penalty* eine Strafe auferlegen

impossible ADJECTIVE
unmöglich

to **impress** VERB
beeindrucken (PERFECT hat beeindruckt)
◊ *She's trying to impress you.* Sie will
dich beeindrucken.

impressed ADJECTIVE
beeindruckt ◊ *I'm very impressed!* Ich
bin sehr beeindruckt!

impression NOUN
der Eindruck (PL die Eindrücke) ◊ *I was
under the impression that ...* Ich hatte
den Eindruck, dass ...

impressive ADJECTIVE
beeindruckend

to **improve** VERB

1 (*make better*)
verbessern (PERFECT hat verbessert) ◊ *The
hotel has improved its service.* Das Hotel
hat den Service verbessert.

2 (*get better*)
besser werden (PRESENT wird besser,
IMPERFECT wurde besser, PERFECT ist besser
geworden) ◊ *The weather is improving.*
Das Wetter wird besser. ◊ *My German
has improved.* Mein Deutsch ist besser
geworden.

improvement NOUN

1 (*of condition*)
die Verbesserung ◊ *It's a great
improvement.* Das ist eine gewaltige
Verbesserung.

2 (*of learner*)
der Fortschritt (PL die Fortschritte)
◊ *There's been an improvement in his
German.* Er hat in Deutsch Fortschritte
gemacht.

in PREPOSITION, ADVERB
*Use the accusative to express movement
or a change of place. Use the dative
when there is no change of place.*

1 in ◊ *It's in my bag.* Es ist in meiner
Tasche. ◊ *Put it in my bag.* Tu es in
meine Tasche. ◊ *I read it in this book.* Ich
habe es in diesem Buch gelesen. ◊ *Write*

it in your address book. Schreib es in dein Adressbuch. ◊ *in hospital* im Krankenhaus ◊ *in school* in der Schule ◊ *in London* in London ◊ *in Germany* in Deutschland ◊ *in Switzerland* in der Schweiz ◊ *in May* im Mai ◊ *in spring* im Frühling ◊ *in the rain* im Regen ◊ *I'll see you in three weeks.* Ich sehe dich in drei Wochen.

Sometimes in is not translated.

◊ *It happened in 1996.* Es geschah 1996. ◊ *in the morning* morgens ◊ *in the afternoon* nachmittags ◊ *at six in the evening* um sechs Uhr abends

[2] mit ◊ *the boy in the blue shirt* der Junge mit dem blauen Hemd ◊ *It was written in pencil.* Es war mit Bleistift geschrieben. ◊ *in a loud voice* mit lauter Stimme ◊ *She paid in dollars.* Sie hat mit Dollar bezahlt.

[3] auf ◊ *in German* auf Deutsch ◊ *in English* auf Englisch

in is sometimes translated using the genitive.

◊ *the best pupil in the class* der beste Schüler der Klasse ◊ *the tallest person in the family* der Größte der Familie

♦ **in the beginning** am Anfang
♦ **in the country** auf dem Land
♦ **in time** rechtzeitig ◊ *We arrived in time for dinner.* Wir kamen rechtzeitig zum Abendessen.
♦ **in here** hier drin ◊ *It's hot in here.* Hier drin ist es heiß.
♦ **one person in ten** einer von zehn
♦ **to be in** (*at home, work*) da sein ◊ *He wasn't in.* Er war nicht da.
♦ **to ask somebody in** jemanden hereinbitten

inaccurate ADJECTIVE
[1] ungenau (*not precise*) ◊ *an inaccurate translation* eine ungenaue Übersetzung
[2] unrichtig (*not correct*) ◊ *What he said was inaccurate.* Was er sagte war unrichtig.

inadequate ADJECTIVE
unzulänglich

incentive NOUN
die Motivation ◊ *There is no incentive to work.* Es gibt keine Motivation zu arbeiten.

inch NOUN
der Zoll (PL die Zoll)

ⓘ In Germany measurements are given in metres and centimetres rather than feet and inches. An inch is about 2.5 centimetres.

♦ **six inches** fünfzehn Zentimeter
incident NOUN
der Vorfall (PL die Vorfälle)
inclined ADJECTIVE

♦ **to be inclined to do something** dazu tendieren, etwas zu tun ◊ *He's inclined to arrive late.* Er tendiert dazu, zu spät zu kommen.

to **include** VERB
einschließen (IMPERFECT schloss ein, PERFECT hat eingeschlossen) ◊ *Service is not included.* Bedienung ist nicht eingeschlossen.

including PREPOSITION
inklusive ◊ *That will be two hundred marks, including VAT.* Das macht zweihundert Mark, inklusive Mehrwertsteuer.

inclusive ADJECTIVE
♦ **The inclusive price is two hundred marks.** Das kostet alles in allem zweihundert Mark.
♦ **inclusive of VAT** inklusive Mehrwertsteuer

income NOUN
das Einkommen (PL die Einkommen)
income tax NOUN
die Einkommensteuer
incompetent ADJECTIVE
inkompetent
incomplete ADJECTIVE
unvollständig
inconsistent ADJECTIVE
[1] widersprüchlich
♦ **to be inconsistent with** ... im Widerspruch stehen zu ...
[2] unbeständig ◊ *Your work this year has been very inconsistent.* Die Qualität deiner Arbeit war dieses Jahr sehr unbeständig.

inconvenience NOUN
♦ **I don't want to cause any inconvenience.** Ich möchte keine Umstände machen.

inconvenient ADJECTIVE
♦ **That's very inconvenient for me.** Das passt mir gar nicht.

incorrect ADJECTIVE
unrichtig

increase NOUN
see also **increase** VERB
die Zunahme ◊ *an increase in road accidents* eine Zunahme an Verkehrsunfällen

to **increase** VERB
see also **increase** NOUN
[1] (*traffic, number*)
zunehmen (PRESENT nimmt zu, IMPERFECT nahm zu, PERFECT hat zugenommen)
◊ *Traffic on motorways has increased.* Der Verkehr auf den Autobahnen hat zugenommen.
[2] (*price, demand*)
steigen (IMPERFECT stieg, PERFECT ist gestiegen) ◊ *with increasing demand* bei steigender Nachfrage
[3] (*pain, wind*)

stärker werden (PRESENT wird stärker, IMPERFECT wurde stärker, PERFECT ist stärker geworden) ◊ *The wind has increased.* Der Wind ist stärker geworden.
♦ **to increase in size** größer werden
♦ **to increase something** etwas erhöhen ◊ *They have increased the price.* Sie haben den Preis erhöht.
♦ **increased cost of living** höhere Lebenshaltungskosten
incredible ADJECTIVE
unglaublich
indecisive ADJECTIVE
unentschlossen (*person*)
indeed ADVERB
wirklich ◊ *It's very hard indeed.* Es ist wirklich schwer.
♦ **Know what I mean? – Indeed I do.** Weißt du, was ich meine? – Ja, ganz genau.
♦ **Thank you very much indeed!** Ganz herzlichen Dank!
independence NOUN
die Unabhängigkeit
independent ADJECTIVE
unabhängig
♦ **an independent school** eine Privatschule
index NOUN
das Verzeichnis (*in book*) (GEN des Verzeichnisses, PL die Verzeichnisse)
India NOUN
Indien NEUT
♦ **from India** aus Indien
♦ **to India** nach Indien
Indian ADJECTIVE
| see also **Indian** NOUN |
1 indisch
2 indianisch (*American Indian*)
Indian NOUN
| see also **Indian** ADJECTIVE |
(*person*)
der Inder (PL die Inder)
die Inderin
♦ **an American Indian** ein Indianer MASC
to **indicate** VERB
1 zeigen ◊ *His reaction indicates how he feels about it.* Seine Reaktion zeigt, was er davon hält.
2 (*make known*)
andeuten (PERFECT hat angedeutet) ◊ *He indicated that he may resign.* Er hat angedeutet, dass er vielleicht zurücktritt.
3 (*technical device*)
anzeigen (PERFECT hat angezeigt) ◊ *The gauge indicated a very high temperature.* Das Messgerät zeigte eine sehr hohe Temperatur an.
♦ **to indicate left** links blinken
indicator NOUN
der Blinker (*in car*) (PL die Blinker)
indigestion NOUN
die Magenverstimmung
♦ **I've got indigestion.** Ich habe eine Magenverstimmung.

individual NOUN
| see also **individual** ADJECTIVE |
das Individuum (PL die Individuen)
individual ADJECTIVE
| see also **individual** NOUN |
individuell
indoor ADJECTIVE
♦ **an indoor swimming pool** ein Hallenbad
indoors ADVERB
im Haus ◊ *They're indoors.* Sie sind im Haus.
♦ **to go indoors** hineingehen ◊ *We'd better go indoors.* Wir gehen besser hinein.
industrial ADJECTIVE
industriell
industrial estate NOUN
das Industriegebiet (PL die Industriegebiete)
industry NOUN
die Industrie ◊ *the tourist industry* die Tourismusindustrie ◊ *the oil industry* die Erdölindustrie
♦ **I'd like to work in industry.** Ich würde gern in der freien Wirtschaft arbeiten.
inefficient ADJECTIVE
ineffizient
inevitable ADJECTIVE
unvermeidlich
inexpensive ADJECTIVE
preiswert ◊ *an inexpensive hotel* ein preiswertes Hotel
♦ **inexpensive holidays** günstige Ferien
inexperienced ADJECTIVE
unerfahren
infant school NOUN
die Grundschule

> ❶ The Grundschule is a primary school which children attend from the age of 6 to 10. Many children attend **Kindergarten** before going to the **Grundschule**.

infection NOUN
die Entzündung ◊ *an ear infection* eine Ohrenentzündung ◊ *a throat infection* eine Halsentzündung
infectious ADJECTIVE
ansteckend ◊ *It's not infectious.* Es ist nicht ansteckend.
infinitive NOUN
der Infinitiv (PL die Infinitive)
infirmary NOUN
das Krankenhaus (GEN des Krankenhauses, PL die Krankenhäuser)
inflatable ADJECTIVE
♦ **an inflatable mattress** eine Luftmatratze
♦ **an inflatable dinghy** ein Gummiboot NEUT
inflation NOUN
die Inflation
influence NOUN

see also **influence** VERB
der Einfluss (GEN des Einflusses, PL die Einflüsse) ◇ *He's a bad influence on her.* Er hat einen schlechten Einfluss auf sie.
to **influence** VERB
see also **influence** NOUN
beeinflussen (PERFECT hat beeinflusst)
influenza NOUN
die Grippe
to **inform** VERB
informieren (PERFECT hat informiert)
♦ **to inform somebody of something** jemanden über etwas informieren ◇ *Nobody informed me of the new plan.* Niemand hat mich über den neuen Plan informiert.
informal ADJECTIVE
1 locker (*person*)
2 zwanglos (*party*) ◇ *"informal dress"* "zwanglose Kleidung"
3 umgangssprachlich (*colloquial*)
♦ **informal language** die Umgangssprache
♦ **an informal visit** ein inoffizieller Besuch
information NOUN
die Information ◇ *important information* wichtige Informationen
♦ **a piece of information** eine Information
♦ **Could you give me some information about trains to Berlin?** Können Sie mir Auskunft über Zugverbindungen nach Berlin geben?
information office NOUN
die Auskunft (PL die Auskünfte)
information technology NOUN
die Informationstechnik
infuriating ADJECTIVE
äußerst ärgerlich
ingenious ADJECTIVE
genial
ingredient NOUN
die Zutat
inhabitant NOUN
(*of country, town*)
der Einwohner (PL die Einwohner)
die Einwohnerin
to **inherit** VERB
erben ◇ *She inherited her father's house.* Sie erbte das Haus ihres Vaters.
initials PL NOUN
die Initialen FEM PL ◇ *Her initials are CDT.* Ihre Initialen sind CDT.
initiative NOUN
die Initiative
to **inject** VERB
spritzen (*drug*) ◇ *He injected himself with heroin.* Er hat sich Heroin gespritzt.
injection NOUN
die Spritze
to **injure** VERB
verletzen (PERFECT hat verletzt)
injured ADJECTIVE
verletzt

injury NOUN
die Verletzung
injury time NOUN
♦ **to play injury time** nachspielen
injustice NOUN
die Ungerechtigkeit
ink NOUN
die Tinte
in-laws PL NOUN
die Schwiegereltern PL
inn NOUN
das Gasthaus (GEN des Gasthauses, PL die Gasthäuser)
inner ADJECTIVE
♦ **the inner city** die Innenstadt
inner tube NOUN
der Schlauch (PL die Schläuche)
innocent ADJECTIVE
unschuldig
inquest NOUN
die gerichtliche Untersuchung
to **inquire** VERB
♦ **to inquire about something** sich nach etwas erkundigen
inquiries office NOUN
die Auskunft (PL die Auskünfte)
inquiry NOUN
die Untersuchung (*official investigation*)
inquisitive ADJECTIVE
neugierig
insane ADJECTIVE
wahnsinnig
inscription NOUN
die Inschrift
insect NOUN
das Insekt (PL die Insekten)
insect repellent NOUN
das Insektenschutzmittel (PL die Insektenschutzmittel)
insensitive ADJECTIVE
gefühllos
to **insert** VERB
einwerfen (PRESENT wirft ein, IMPERFECT warf ein, PERFECT hat eingeworfen) ◇ *I inserted a coin.* Ich warf eine Münze ein.
inside NOUN
see also **inside** ADVERB
das Innere (GEN des Inneren)
inside ADVERB, PREPOSITION
see also **inside** NOUN
innen ◇ *inside and outside* innen und außen
♦ **They're inside.** Sie sind drinnen.
♦ **to go inside** hineingehen
♦ **Come inside!** Kommt herein!
Use the accusative to express movement or a change of place. Use the dative when there is no change of place.
♦ **inside the house (1)** im Haus ◇ *She was inside the house.* Sie war im Haus.
♦ **inside the house (2)** ins Haus ◇ *She went inside the house.* Sie ging ins Haus.

I

insincere ADJECTIVE
unaufrichtig

to **insist** VERB
darauf bestehen (IMPERFECT bestand darauf, PERFECT hat darauf bestanden) ◊ *I didn't want to, but he insisted.* Ich wollte nicht, aber er hat darauf bestanden.
♦ **to insist on doing something** darauf bestehen, etwas zu tun ◊ *She insisted on paying.* Sie hat darauf bestanden zu bezahlen.
♦ **He insisted he was innocent.** Er beteuerte seine Unschuld.

to **inspect** VERB
kontrollieren (PERFECT hat kontrolliert)

inspector NOUN
(*police*)
der Kommissar (PL die Kommissare)
die Kommissarin
◊ *Inspector Jill Brown* Kommissarin Jill Brown

to **install** VERB
installieren (PERFECT hat installiert)

instalment NOUN (US **installment**)
[1] die Rate ◊ *to pay in instalments* in Raten zahlen
[2] die Folge (*of TV, radio serial*)
[3] der Teil (*of publication*)

instance NOUN
♦ **for instance** zum Beispiel

instant ADJECTIVE
sofortig ◊ *It was an instant success.* Es war ein sofortiger Erfolg.
♦ **instant coffee** der Pulverkaffee

instantly ADVERB
sofort

instead ADVERB
♦ **instead of (1)** (*followed by noun*) anstelle von ◊ *Use honey instead of sugar.* Nehmen Sie Honig anstelle von Zucker.
♦ **instead of (2)** (*followed by verb*) statt ◊ *We played tennis instead of going swimming.* Wir spielten Tennis statt schwimmen zu gehen.
♦ **The pool was closed, so we played tennis instead.** Das Schwimmbad war zu, also spielten wir stattdessen Tennis.

instinct NOUN
der Instinkt (PL die Instinkte)

institute NOUN
das Institut

institution NOUN
die Institution

to **instruct** VERB
anweisen (IMPERFECT wies an, PERFECT hat angewiesen)
♦ **to instruct somebody to do something** jemanden anweisen, etwas zu tun ◊ *She instructed us to wait outside.* Sie wies uns an, draußen zu warten.

instructions PL NOUN

[1] die Anweisungen FEM PL ◊ *Follow the instructions carefully.* Befolgen Sie die Anweisungen genau.
[2] die Gebrauchsanweisung (*manual*)
◊ *Where are the instructions?* Wo ist die Gebrauchsanweisung?

instructor NOUN
der Lehrer (PL die Lehrer)
die Lehrerin
◊ *a skiing instructor* ein Skilehrer ◊ *a driving instructor* ein Fahrlehrer

instrument NOUN
das Instrument (PL die Instrumente) ◊ *Do you play an instrument?* Spielst du ein Instrument?

insufficient ADJECTIVE
unzureichend

insulin NOUN
das Insulin

insult NOUN
see also **insult** VERB
die Beleidigung

to **insult** VERB
see also **insult** NOUN
beleidigen (PERFECT hat beleidigt)

insurance NOUN
die Versicherung ◊ *his car insurance* seine Kraftfahrzeugversicherung
♦ **an insurance policy** eine Versicherungspolice

intelligent ADJECTIVE
intelligent

to **intend** VERB
♦ **to intend to do something** beabsichtigen, etwas zu tun ◊ *I intend to do German at university.* Ich beabsichtige, Deutsch zu studieren.

intense ADJECTIVE
stark

intensive ADJECTIVE
intensiv

intention NOUN
die Absicht

intercom NOUN
die Sprechanlage

interest NOUN
see also **interest** VERB
das Interesse (PL die Interessen) ◊ *to show an interest in something* Interesse an etwas zeigen ◊ *What interests do you have?* Welche Interessen hast du?
♦ **My main interest is music.** Ich interessiere mich hauptsächlich für Musik.

to **interest** VERB
see also **interest** NOUN
interessieren (PERFECT hat interessiert) ◊ *It doesn't interest me.* Das interessiert mich nicht.
♦ **to be interested in something** sich für etwas interessieren ◊ *I'm not interested*

in politics. Ich interessiere mich nicht für Politik.

interesting ADJECTIVE
<u>interessant</u>

interior NOUN
das <u>Innere</u> (GEN des Inneren)

interior designer NOUN
der <u>Innenarchitekt</u> (GEN des Innenarchitekten, PL die Innenarchitekten)
die <u>Innenarchitektin</u>

intermediate ADJECTIVE
♦ **an intermediate course** ein Kurs für fortgeschrittene Anfänger

internal ADJECTIVE
<u>innere</u> ◊ *the internal organs* die inneren Organe

international ADJECTIVE
<u>international</u>

Internet NOUN
das <u>Internet</u> ◊ *on the Internet* im Internet

Internet café NOUN
das <u>Internet-Café</u> (PL die Internet-Cafés)

Internet user NOUN
der <u>Internetbenutzer</u> (PL die Internetbenutzer)
die <u>Internetbenutzerin</u>

to **interpret** VERB
<u>übersetzen</u> (PERFECT hat übersetzt) ◊ *Steve couldn't speak German, so his friend interpreted.* Steve konnte kein Deutsch, also übersetzte sein Freund.

interpreter NOUN
der <u>Dolmetscher</u> (PL die Dolmetscher)
die <u>Dolmetscherin</u>

to **interrupt** VERB
<u>unterbrechen</u> (PRESENT unterbricht, IMPERFECT unterbrach, PERFECT hat unterbrochen)

interruption NOUN
die <u>Unterbrechung</u>

interval NOUN
die <u>Pause</u> (*in play, concert*)

interview NOUN
| see also **interview** VERB |
[1] das <u>Interview</u> (*on TV, radio*) (PL die Interviews)
[2] (*for job*)
das <u>Vorstellungsgespräch</u> (PL die Vorstellungsgespräche)

to **interview** VERB
| see also **interview** NOUN |
<u>interviewen</u> (*on TV, radio*) (PERFECT hat interviewt) ◊ *I was interviewed on the radio.* Ich wurde im Radio interviewt.

interviewer NOUN
(*on TV, radio*)
der <u>Moderator</u> (PL die Moderatoren)
die <u>Moderatorin</u>

intimate ADJECTIVE
<u>eng</u> ◊ *an intimate friendship* eine enge Freundschaft

♦ **my intimate feelings** meine innersten Gefühle

into PREPOSITION
<u>in</u>
> In this sense **in** is followed by the accusative.

◊ *He got into the car.* Er stieg ins Auto.
◊ *I'm going into town.* Ich gehe in die Stadt. ◊ *Translate it into German.* Übersetze das ins Deutsche. ◊ *Divide into two groups.* Teilt euch in zwei Gruppen.

intranet NOUN
das <u>Intranet</u> (PL die Intranets)

to **introduce** VERB
<u>vorstellen</u> (PERFECT hat vorgestellt) ◊ *He introduced me to his parents.* Er stellte mich seinen Eltern vor.

introduction NOUN
die <u>Einleitung</u> (*in book*)

intruder NOUN
der <u>Eindringling</u> (PL die Eindringlinge)
der Eindringling is also used for women.

intuition NOUN
die <u>Intuition</u>

to **invade** VERB
<u>eindringen in</u> +ACC (IMPERFECT drang ein, PERFECT ist eingedrungen) ◊ *to invade a country* in ein Land eindringen

invalid NOUN
der <u>Kranke</u> (GEN des Kranken, PL die Kranken)
die <u>Kranke</u> (GEN der Kranken) ◊ *an invalid (man)* ein Kranker

to **invent** VERB
<u>erfinden</u> (IMPERFECT erfand, PERFECT hat erfunden)

invention NOUN
die <u>Erfindung</u>

inventor NOUN
der <u>Erfinder</u> (PL die Erfinder)
die <u>Erfinderin</u>

to **invest** VERB
<u>investieren</u> (PERFECT hat investiert)

investigation NOUN
die <u>Untersuchung</u> (*police*)

investment NOUN
die <u>Investition</u>

invigilator NOUN
die <u>Aufsicht</u>
die Aufsicht is also used for men.
◊ *You have to ask the invigilator.* Du musst die Aufsicht fragen.

invisible ADJECTIVE
<u>unsichtbar</u>

invitation NOUN
die <u>Einladung</u>

to **invite** VERB
<u>einladen</u> (PRESENT lädt ein, IMPERFECT lud ein, PERFECT hat eingeladen) ◊ *He's not invited.* Er ist nicht eingeladen. ◊ *to invite somebody to a party* jemanden zu einer Party einladen

I

to **involve** VERB

mit sich bringen (IMPERFECT brachte mit sich, PERFECT hat mit sich gebracht) ◊ *This will involve a lot of work.* Das wird viel Arbeit mit sich bringen.

♦ **His job involves a lot of travelling.** Er muss in seinem Job viel reisen.

♦ **to be involved in something** (*crime, drugs*) in etwas verwickelt sein ◊ *He was involved in the murder.* Er war in den Mord verwickelt.

♦ **to be involved with somebody** (*in relationship*) mit jemandem eine Beziehung haben

♦ **I don't want to get involved.** Ich will damit nichts zu tun haben.

iPod® NOUN

der iPod® (PL die iPods)

IQ NOUN (= *intelligence quotient*)

der IQ (GEN des IQ, PL die IQ) (= Intelligenzquotient)

Iran NOUN

der Iran

Note that the definite article is used in German for countries which are masculine.

♦ **from Iran** aus dem Iran

♦ **in Iran** im Iran

♦ **to Iran** in den Iran

Iraq NOUN

der Irak

Note that the definite article is used in German for countries which are masculine.

♦ **from Iraq** aus dem Irak

♦ **in Iraq** im Irak

♦ **to Iraq** in den Irak

Iraqi NOUN

see also **Iraqi** ADJECTIVE

der Iraker (PL die Iraker)

die Irakerin

Iraqi ADJECTIVE

see also **Iraqi** NOUN

irakisch

Ireland NOUN

Irland NEUT

♦ **from Ireland** aus Irland

♦ **in Ireland** in Irland

♦ **to Ireland** nach Irland

Irish ADJECTIVE

see also **Irish** NOUN

irisch ◊ *Irish music* irische Musik

♦ **He's Irish.** Er ist Ire.

♦ **She's Irish.** Sie ist Irin.

Irish NOUN

see also **Irish** ADJECTIVE

das Irisch (*language*) (GEN des Irischen)

♦ **the Irish** (*people*) die Iren MASC PL

Irishman NOUN

der Ire (GEN des Iren, PL die Iren)

Irishwoman NOUN

die Irin

iron NOUN

see also **iron** VERB

1 (*metal*)

das Eisen

2 (*for clothes*)

das Bügeleisen (PL die Bügeleisen)

to **iron** VERB

see also **iron** NOUN

bügeln

ironic ADJECTIVE

ironisch

ironing NOUN

das Bügeln

♦ **to do the ironing** bügeln

ironing board NOUN

das Bügelbrett

ironmonger's (shop) NOUN

die Eisenwarenhandlung

irrelevant ADJECTIVE

irrelevant

irresponsible ADJECTIVE

verantwortungslos (*person*)

♦ **That was irresponsible of him.** Das war unverantwortlich von ihm.

irritating ADJECTIVE

nervend

is VERB *see* **be**

Islam NOUN

Note that the definite article is used in German.

der Islam

Islamic ADJECTIVE

islamisch ◊ *Islamic fundamentalists* islamische Fundamentalisten

♦ **Islamic law** das Recht des Islams

island NOUN

die Insel

isle NOUN

♦ **the Isle of Man** die Insel Man

♦ **the Isle of Wight** die Insel Wight

isolated ADJECTIVE

abgelegen (*place*)

♦ **She feels very isolated.** Sie fühlt sich sehr isoliert.

ISP ABBREVIATION (= *Internet Service Provider*)

der Internet-Anbieter (PL die Internet-Anbieter)

Israel NOUN

Israel NEUT

♦ **from Israel** aus Israel

♦ **to Israel** nach Israel

Israeli NOUN

see also **Israeli** ADJECTIVE

der Israeli (GEN des Israeli, PL die Israeli)

die Israeli (GEN der Israeli)

Israeli ADJECTIVE

see also **Israeli** NOUN

israelisch

♦ **He's Israeli.** Er ist Israeli.

issue NOUN

see also **issue** VERB

1 die <u>Frage</u> (*matter*) ◊ *a controversial issue* eine umstrittene Frage
2 die <u>Ausgabe</u> (*of magazine*)

to **issue** VERB

> *see also* **issue** NOUN

<u>ausgeben</u> (*equipment, supplies*) (PRESENT gibt aus, IMPERFECT gab aus, PERFECT hat ausgegeben)

it PRONOUN

Remember to check if **it** *stands for a masculine, feminine or neuter noun, and use the appropriate gender and case.*

1 <u>er</u> ◊ *Where's my hat? – It's on the table.* Wo ist mein Hut? – Er ist auf dem Tisch.

<u>sie</u>
◊ *What happened to your watch? – It broke.* Was ist mit deiner Uhr passiert? – Sie ist kaputtgegangen.

<u>es</u>
◊ *Have you seen her new dress, it's very pretty.* Hast du ihr neues Kleid gesehen, es ist sehr hübsch.

2 <u>ihn</u> ◊ *Where's my hat? – I haven't seen it.* Wo ist mein Hut? – Ich habe ihn nicht gesehen.

<u>sie</u>
◊ *Where's your jacket? – I've lost it.* Wo ist deine Jacke? – Ich habe sie verloren.

<u>es</u>
◊ *You can have my ruler, I don't need it anymore.* Du kannst mein Lineal haben, ich brauche es nicht mehr.

♦ **It's raining.** Es regnet.
♦ **It's six o'clock.** Es ist sechs Uhr.
♦ **It's Friday tomorrow.** Morgen ist Freitag.
♦ **Who is it? – It's me.** Wer ist's? – Ich bin's.
♦ **It's expensive.** Das ist teuer.

Italian ADJECTIVE

> *see also* **Italian** NOUN

<u>italienisch</u>
♦ **She's Italian.** Sie ist Italienerin.

Italian NOUN

> *see also* **Italian** ADJECTIVE

1 (*person*)
der <u>Italiener</u> (PL die Italiener)
die <u>Italienerin</u>
2 (*language*)
das <u>Italienisch</u> (GEN des Italienischen)

italics PL NOUN
die <u>Kursivschrift</u>
♦ **in italics** kursiv

Italy NOUN
<u>Italien</u> NEUT
♦ **from Italy** aus Italien
♦ **in Italy** in Italien
♦ **to Italy** nach Italien

to **itch** VERB
<u>jucken</u> ◊ *It itches.* Es juckt. ◊ *My head's itching.* Mein Kopf juckt.

itchy ADJECTIVE
♦ **My arm is itchy.** Mein Arm juckt.

it'd = **it had,** = **it would**

item NOUN
der <u>Artikel</u> (*object*) (PL die Artikel)

itinerary NOUN
die <u>Reiseroute</u>

it'll = **it will**

its ADJECTIVE

Remember to check if **its** *refers back to a masculine, feminine or neuter noun, and use the appropriate gender and case.*

<u>sein</u> ◊ *The dog is in its kennel.* Der Hund ist in seiner Hütte.
<u>ihr</u> ◊ *The cup is in its usual place.* Die Tasse ist an ihrem üblichen Platz.
<u>sein</u> ◊ *The baby is in its cot.* Das Baby ist in seinem Bett.

it's = **it is,** = **it has**

itself PRONOUN
1 <u>sich</u> ◊ *The dog scratched itself.* Der Hund kratzte sich.
2 <u>selbst</u> ◊ *The heating switches itself off.* Die Heizung schaltet von selbst aus.

I've = **I have**

I

J

jab NOUN
die Spritze (*injection*)

jack NOUN
[1] (*for car*)
der Wagenheber (PL die Wagenheber)
[2] (*playing card*)
der Bube (GEN des Buben, PL die Buben)

jacket NOUN
die Jacke
♦ **jacket potatoes** gebackene Kartoffeln

jackpot NOUN
der Jackpot (PL die Jackpots) ◊ *to win the jackpot* den Jackpot gewinnen

jail NOUN
see also **jail** VERB
das Gefängnis (GEN des Gefängnisses, PL die Gefängnisse)
♦ **She was sent to jail.** Sie musste ins Gefängnis.

to **jail** VERB
see also **jail** NOUN
einsperren (PERFECT hat eingesperrt)
♦ **He was jailed for ten years.** Er hat zehn Jahre Gefängnis bekommen.

jam NOUN
die Marmelade ◊ *strawberry jam* Erdbeermarmelade
♦ **a traffic jam** ein Verkehrsstau MASC

jam jar NOUN
das Marmeladenglas (GEN des Marmeladenglases, PL die Marmeladengläser)

jammed ADJECTIVE
♦ **The window's jammed.** Das Fenster klemmt.

jam-packed ADJECTIVE
brechend voll ◊ *The room was jam-packed.* Der Raum war brechend voll.

janitor NOUN
der Hausmeister (PL die Hausmeister)
die Hausmeisterin
◊ *He's a janitor.* Er ist Hausmeister.

January NOUN
der Januar ◊ *in January* im Januar

Japan NOUN
Japan NEUT
♦ **from Japan** aus Japan
♦ **to Japan** nach Japan

Japanese ADJECTIVE
see also **Japanese** NOUN
japanisch

Japanese NOUN
see also **Japanese** ADJECTIVE
[1] (*person*)
der Japaner (PL die Japaner)
die Japanerin
♦ **the Japanese** die Japaner MASC PL
[2] (*language*)

das Japanisch (GEN des Japanischen)

jar NOUN
das Glas (GEN des Glases, PL die Gläser)
◊ *an empty jar* ein leeres Glas ◊ *a jar of honey* ein Glas Honig

jaundice NOUN
die Gelbsucht ◊ *She's suffering from jaundice.* Sie hat Gelbsucht.

javelin NOUN
der Speer (PL die Speere)

jaw NOUN
der Kiefer (PL die Kiefer)

jazz NOUN
der Jazz (GEN des Jazz)

jealous ADJECTIVE
eifersüchtig

jeans PL NOUN
die Jeans FEM PL ◊ *a pair of jeans* eine Jeans

Jehovah's Witness NOUN
der Zeuge Jehovas (GEN des Zeugen Jehovas, PL die Zeugen Jehovas)
die Zeugin Jehovas
◊ *She's a Jehovah's Witness.* Sie ist Zeugin Jehovas.

Jello ® NOUN US
der Wackelpudding

jelly NOUN
[1] der Wackelpudding (*dessert*)
[2] die Marmelade (*jam*)

jellyfish NOUN
die Qualle

jersey NOUN
der Pullover (PL die Pullover)

Jesus NOUN
Jesus MASC (GEN des Jesus)

jet NOUN
das Düsenflugzeug (*plane*) (PL die Düsenflugzeuge)

jetlag NOUN
♦ **to be suffering from jetlag** unter der Zeitverschiebung leiden

jetty NOUN
die Mole

Jew NOUN
der Jude (GEN des Juden, PL die Juden)
die Jüdin

jewel NOUN
der Edelstein (*stone*) (PL die Edelsteine)

jeweller NOUN
der Juwelier (PL die Juweliere)
die Juwelierin
◊ *He's a jeweller.* Er ist Juwelier.

jeweller's shop NOUN

das Juweliergeschäft (PL die Juweliergeschäfte)

jewellery NOUN
der Schmuck

Jewish ADJECTIVE
jüdisch

jigsaw NOUN
das Puzzle (PL die Puzzles)

job NOUN
1 der Job (PL die Jobs) ◊ *He's lost his job.* Er hat seinen Job verloren. ◊ *I've got a Saturday job.* Ich habe einen Samstagsjob.
2 (*chore, task*)
die Arbeit ◊ *That was a difficult job.* Das war eine schwierige Arbeit.

job centre NOUN
das Arbeitsamt (PL die Arbeitsämter)

jobless ADJECTIVE
arbeitslos

jockey NOUN
der Jockey (PL die Jockeys)

to **jog** VERB
joggen

jogging NOUN
das Jogging ◊ *I like jogging.* Ich mag Jogging.
◆ **to go jogging** joggen

john NOUN US
das Klo (*informal*) (PL die Klos)

to **join** VERB
1 (*become member of*)
beitreten (PRESENT tritt bei, IMPERFECT trat bei, PERFECT ist beigetreten) ◊ *I'm going to join the tennis club.* Ich trete dem Tennisklub bei.
2 (*accompany*)
sich anschließen (IMPERFECT schloss sich an, PERFECT hat sich angeschlossen) ◊ *Do you mind if I join you?* Macht es dir etwas aus, wenn ich mich dir anschließe?

to **join in** VERB
1 mitmachen (PERFECT hat mitgemacht) ◊ *He doesn't join in with what we do.* Er macht nicht mit bei den Dingen, die wir tun.
2 einstimmen (PERFECT hat eingestimmt) ◊ *She started singing, and the audience joined in.* Sie begann zu singen, und das Publikum stimmte mit ein.

joiner NOUN
der Schreiner (PL die Schreiner)
die Schreinerin
◊ *She's a joiner.* Sie ist Schreinerin.

joint NOUN
1 (*in body*)
das Gelenk (PL die Gelenke)
2 (*of meat*)
der Braten (PL die Braten)
3 (*drugs*)
der Joint (PL die Joints)

joke NOUN

see also **joke** VERB
der Witz (GEN des Witzes, PL die Witze)
◊ *to tell a joke* einen Witz erzählen

to **joke** VERB
see also **joke** NOUN
Spaß machen ◊ *I'm only joking.* Ich mache nur Spaß.

jolly ADJECTIVE
fröhlich

Jordan NOUN
Jordanien NEUT (*country*)
◆ **from Jordan** aus Jordanien
◆ **to Jordan** nach Jordanien

to **jot down** VERB
notieren (PERFECT hat notiert)

jotter NOUN
der Notizblock (*pad*) (PL die Notizblöcke)

journalism NOUN
der Journalismus (GEN des Journalismus)

journalist NOUN
der Journalist (GEN des Journalisten, PL die Journalisten)
die Journalistin
◊ *She's a journalist.* Sie ist Journalistin.

journey NOUN
1 die Reise ◊ *I don't like long journeys.* Ich mag lange Reisen nicht.
◆ **to go on a journey** eine Reise machen
2 die Fahrt (*to school, work*) ◊ *The journey to school takes about half an hour.* Die Fahrt zur Schule dauert etwa eine halbe Stunde.
◆ **a bus journey** eine Busfahrt

joy NOUN
die Freude

joystick NOUN
der Joystick (*for computer game*) (PL die Joysticks)

judge NOUN
see also **judge** VERB
der Richter (PL die Richter)
die Richterin
◊ *She's a judge.* Sie ist Richterin.

to **judge** VERB
see also **judge** NOUN
beurteilen (*assess*) (PERFECT hat beurteilt)
◊ *You can judge for yourself which is better.* Du kannst das selbst beurteilen, welches besser ist.

judo NOUN
das Judo (GEN des Judo) ◊ *My hobby is judo.* Judo ist mein Hobby.

jug NOUN
der Krug (PL die Krüge)

juggler NOUN
der Jongleur
die Jongleurin

juice NOUN
der Saft (PL die Säfte) ◊ *orange juice* der Orangensaft

J

July NOUN
  der <u>Juli</u> ◊ *in July* im Juli
jumble sale NOUN
  der <u>Flohmarkt</u> (PL die Flohmärkte)
to **jump** VERB
  <u>springen</u> (IMPERFECT sprang, PERFECT ist
  gesprungen) ◊ *to jump out of the*
  window aus dem Fenster springen ◊ *to*
  jump off the roof vom Dach
  springen
  ♦ **to jump over something** über etwas
  springen ◊ *He jumped over the fence.* Er
  sprang über den Zaun.
jumper NOUN
  1 der <u>Pullover</u> (PL die Pullover)
  2 (*dress*)
  das <u>Trägerkleid</u> (PL die
  Trägerkleider)
junction NOUN
  1 (*of roads*)
  die <u>Kreuzung</u>
  2 (*motorway exit*)
  die <u>Ausfahrt</u>
June NOUN
  der <u>Juni</u> ◊ *in June* im Juni
jungle NOUN
  der <u>Dschungel</u> (PL die Dschungel)
junior NOUN
  ♦ **the juniors** die Grundschüler MASC PL
junior school NOUN
  die <u>Grundschule</u>

ⓘ The **Grundschule** is a primary
school which children attend from the
age of 6 to 10.

---

junk NOUN
  der <u>Krempel</u> (*old things*) ◊ *The attic's full*
  of junk. Der Speicher ist voller Krempel.
  ♦ **to eat junk food** Junkfood essen
  ♦ **a junk shop** ein Trödelladen MASC
jury NOUN
  die <u>Geschworenen</u> MASC PL (*in court*)
just ADVERB
  1 <u>gerade</u> (*barely*) ◊ *We had just enough*
  money. Wir hatten gerade genug Geld.
  ◊ *just in time* gerade noch rechtzeitig
  2 <u>kurz</u> (*shortly*) ◊ *just after Christmas*
  kurz nach Weihnachten
  3 <u>genau</u> (*exactly*) ◊ *just here* genau hier
  4 <u>eben</u> (*this minute*) ◊ *I did it just now.*
  Ich habe es eben gemacht. ◊ *He's just*
  arrived. Er ist eben angekommen.
  ♦ **I'm rather busy just now.** Ich bin gerade
  ziemlich beschäftigt.
  ♦ **I'm just coming!** Ich komme schon!
  5 <u>nur</u> (*only*) ◊ *It's just a suggestion.* Es
  ist nur ein Vorschlag.
justice NOUN
  die <u>Gerechtigkeit</u>
to **justify** VERB
  <u>rechtfertigen</u>

K

kangaroo NOUN
das Känguru (PL die Kängurus)

karate NOUN
das Karate (GEN des Karate) ◊ *I like karate.* Ich mag Karate.

kebab NOUN
der Kebab (PL die Kebabs)

keen ADJECTIVE
⓵ begeistert (*enthusiastic*) ◊ *He doesn't seem very keen.* Er scheint nicht gerade begeistert.
⓶ eifrig (*hardworking*) ◊ *She's a keen student.* Sie ist eine eifrige Studentin.
♦ **to be keen on something** etwas mögen ◊ *I'm keen on maths.* Ich mag Mathe. ◊ *I'm not very keen on maths.* Ich mag Mathe nicht besonders.
♦ **to be keen on somebody** (*fancy them*) auf jemanden stehen ◊ *He's keen on her.* Er steht auf sie.
♦ **to be keen on doing something** Lust haben, etwas zu tun ◊ *I'm not very keen on going.* Ich habe keine große Lust zu gehen.

to **keep** VERB
⓵ (*retain*)
behalten (PRESENT behält, IMPERFECT behielt, PERFECT hat behalten) ◊ *You can keep it.* Das kannst du behalten.
⓶ (*remain*)
sein (PRESENT ist, IMPERFECT war, PERFECT ist gewesen) ◊ *Keep quiet!* Sei still!
♦ **Keep still!** Halt still!
♦ **I keep forgetting my keys.** Ich vergesse dauernd meine Schlüssel.
♦ **to keep on doing something (1)** (*continue*) etwas weiter tun ◊ *He kept on reading.* Er las weiter.
♦ **to keep on doing something (2)** (*repeatedly*) etwas dauernd tun ◊ *The car keeps on breaking down.* Das Auto ist dauernd kaputt.
♦ **"keep out"** "Kein Zutritt"
♦ **to keep up** mithalten ◊ *Matthew walks so fast I can't keep up.* Matthew geht so schnell, da kann ich nicht mithalten.

keep-fit NOUN
die Gymnastik ◊ *I like keep-fit.* Ich mache gern Gymnastik.
♦ **I go to keep-fit classes.** Ich gehe zur Gymnastik.

kennel NOUN
die Hundehütte

kept VERB *see* **keep**

kerosene NOUN US
das Petroleum

kettle NOUN
der
Wasserkessel (PL die Wasserkessel)

key NOUN
der Schlüssel (PL die Schlüssel)

keyboard NOUN
⓵ (*of piano, computer*)
die Tastatur
⓶ (*of electric organ*)
das Keyboard (PL die Keyboards)
◊ *... with Mike Moran on keyboards* ... mit Mike Moran am Keyboard

keyring NOUN
der Schlüsselring (PL die Schlüsselringe)

kick NOUN
| see also **kick** VERB |
der Tritt (PL die Tritte)

to **kick** VERB
| see also **kick** NOUN |
treten (PRESENT tritt, IMPERFECT trat, PERFECT hat getreten) ◊ *He kicked me.* Er hat mich getreten. ◊ *He kicked the ball hard.* Er trat kräftig gegen den Ball.
♦ **to kick off** (*in football*) anfangen

kick-off NOUN
der Anstoß (GEN des Anstoßes, PL die Anstöße) ◊ *Kick-off is at ten o'clock.* Um zehn Uhr ist Anstoß.

kid NOUN
| see also **kid** VERB |
das Kind (*child*) (PL die Kinder)

to **kid** VERB
| see also **kid** NOUN |
Spaß machen ◊ *I'm just kidding.* Ich mache nur Spaß.

to **kidnap** VERB
entführen (PERFECT hat entführt)

kidney NOUN
die Niere ◊ *He's got kidney trouble.* Er hat Nierenprobleme. ◊ *I don't like kidneys.* Ich mag Nieren nicht.

to **kill** VERB
töten
♦ **to be killed** umkommen ◊ *He was killed in a car accident.* Er kam bei einem Unfall um. ◊ *Luckily, nobody was killed.* Zum Glück ist niemand dabei umgekommen.
♦ **to kill oneself** sich umbringen ◊ *He killed himself.* Er hat sich umgebracht.

killer NOUN
⓵ (*murderer*)
der Mörder (PL die Mörder)
die Mörderin
◊ *The police are searching for the killer.* Die Polizei sucht nach dem Mörder.
⓶ (*hitman*)
der Killer (PL die Killer) ◊ *a hired killer* ein Auftragskiller
♦ **Meningitis can be a killer.** Hirnhautentzündung kann tödlich sein.

kilo NOUN

das <u>Kilo</u> (PL die Kilos or Kilo)
*When specifying a quantity of something use the plural form **Kilo**.*
◊ *ten marks a kilo* zehn Mark das Kilo ◊ *three kilos of tomatoes* drei Kilo Tomaten

kilometre NOUN
der <u>Kilometer</u> (PL die Kilometer) ◊ *a hundred kilometres* hundert Kilometer

kilt NOUN
der <u>Kilt</u> (PL die Kilts)

kind ADJECTIVE
see also **kind** NOUN

<u>nett</u>
♦ **to be kind to somebody** zu jemandem nett sein
♦ **Thank you for being so kind.** Vielen Dank, dass Sie so nett waren.

kind NOUN
see also **kind** ADJECTIVE

die <u>Art</u> ◊ *It's a kind of sausage.* Es ist eine Art Wurst.
♦ **a new kind of dictionary** ein neuartiges Wörterbuch

kindergarten NOUN
der <u>Kindergarten</u> (PL die Kindergärten)

ⓘ *Many German children go to **Kindergarten** from the age of 3 to 6.*

kindly ADVERB
<u>freundlicherweise</u>

kindness NOUN
die <u>Freundlichkeit</u>

king NOUN
der <u>König</u> (PL die Könige)

kingdom NOUN
das <u>Königreich</u> (PL die Königreiche)

kiosk NOUN
1 (*phone box*)
die <u>Telefonzelle</u>
2 der <u>Kiosk</u> (PL die Kioske) ◊ *a newspaper kiosk* ein Zeitungskiosk

kipper NOUN
der <u>Räucherhering</u> (PL die Räucherheringe)

kiss NOUN
see also **kiss** VERB

der <u>Kuss</u> (GEN des Kusses, PL die Küsse)
◊ *a passionate kiss* ein leidenschaftlicher Kuss

to **kiss** VERB
see also **kiss** NOUN

1 <u>küssen</u> ◊ *He kissed her passionately.* Er küsste sie leidenschaftlich.
2 <u>sich küssen</u> ◊ *They kissed.* Sie küssten sich.

kit NOUN
1 (*clothes for sport*)
das <u>Zeug</u> ◊ *I've forgotten my gym kit.* Ich habe mein Sportzeug vergessen.

2 der <u>Kasten</u> (PL die Kästen) ◊ *a tool kit* ein Werkzeugkasten ◊ *a first-aid kit* ein Erste-Hilfe-Kasten
♦ **puncture repair kit** das Flickzeug
♦ **sewing kit** das Nähzeug

kitchen NOUN
die <u>Küche</u> ◊ *a fitted kitchen* eine Einbauküche
♦ **the kitchen units** die Küchenschränke
♦ **a kitchen knife** ein Küchenmesser NEUT

kite NOUN
der <u>Drachen</u> (PL die Drachen)

kitten NOUN
das <u>Kätzchen</u> (PL die Kätzchen)

knee NOUN
das <u>Knie</u> (PL die Knie) ◊ *He was on his knees.* Er lag auf den Knien.

to **kneel (down)** VERB
<u>sich hinknien</u> (PERFECT hat sich hingekniet)

knew VERB *see* **know**

knickers PL NOUN
die <u>Unterhose</u> ◊ *a pair of knickers* eine Unterhose

knife NOUN
das <u>Messer</u> (PL die Messer)
♦ **a sheath knife** ein Fahrtenmesser
♦ **a penknife** ein Taschenmesser

to **knit** VERB
<u>stricken</u>

knitting NOUN
das <u>Stricken</u>
♦ **I like knitting.** Ich stricke gern.

knives PL NOUN *see* **knife**

knob NOUN
1 (*on door*)
der <u>Griff</u>
2 (*on radio, TV*)
der <u>Knopf</u> (PL die Knöpfe)

to **knock** VERB
see also **knock** NOUN

<u>klopfen</u> ◊ *to knock on the door* an die Tür klopfen
♦ **Someone's knocking at the door.** Es klopft.
♦ **She was knocked down by a car.** Ein Auto hat sie umgefahren.
♦ **to knock somebody out (1)** (*stun*) jemanden bewusstlos schlagen ◊ *They knocked out the watchman.* Sie haben den Wächter bewusstlos geschlagen.
♦ **to knock somebody out (2)** (*defeat*) jemanden schlagen ◊ *Liverpool knocked Aston Villa out of the cup.* Der FC Liverpool hat Aston Villa im Pokalspiel geschlagen.
♦ **They were knocked out early in the tournament.** Sie schieden beim Turnier früh aus.
♦ **to knock something over** etwas umstoßen ◊ *I accidentally knocked the milk over.* Ich habe aus Versehen die Milch umgestoßen.

knock NOUN

see also **knock** VERB

♦**There was a knock on the door.** Es hat geklopft.

knot NOUN

der Knoten (PL die Knoten)

to **know** VERB

*Use **wissen** for knowing facts, **kennen** for knowing people and places.*

[1] wissen (PRESENT weiß, IMPERFECT wusste, PERFECT hat gewusst) ◊ *It's a long way. – Yes, I know.* Es ist weit. – Ja, ich weiß. ◊ *I don't know.* Ich weiß nicht. ◊ *I don't know what to do.* Ich weiß nicht, was ich tun soll. ◊ *I don't know how to do it.* Ich weiß nicht, wie ich es machen soll.

[2] kennen (IMPERFECT kannte, PERFECT hat gekannt) ◊ *I know her.* Ich kenne sie. ◊ *I know Berlin well.* Ich kenne Berlin gut.

♦**I don't know any French.** Ich kann kein Französisch.

♦**to know that ...** wissen, dass ... ◊ *I know that you like chocolate.* Ich weiß, dass du Schokolade magst. ◊ *I didn't know that your dad was a policeman.* Ich wusste nicht, dass dein Vater Polizist ist.

♦**to know about something (1)** (*be aware of*) von etwas wissen ◊ *Do you know about the meeting this afternoon?* Weißt du von dem Treffen heute Nachmittag?

♦**to know about something (2)** (*be knowledgeable about*) sich mit etwas auskennen ◊ *He knows a lot about cars.* Er kennt sich mit Autos aus. ◊ *I don't know much about computers.* Mit Computern kenne ich mich nicht besonders aus.

♦**to get to know somebody** jemanden kennenlernen

♦**How should I know?** (*I don't know!*) Wie soll ich das wissen?

♦**You never know!** Man kann nie wissen!

know-all NOUN

der Besserwisser (PL die Besserwisser) die Besserwisserin ◊ *He's such a know-all!* So ein Besserwisser!

know-how NOUN

das Know-how (GEN des Know-how)

knowledge NOUN

[1] das Wissen (*general knowledge*) ◊ *Our knowledge of the universe is limited.* Unser Wissen über das Universum ist begrenzt.

[2] die Kenntnisse FEM PL (*things learnt*) ◊ *my knowledge of German* meine Deutschkenntnisse

knowledgeable ADJECTIVE

♦**to be knowledgeable about something** viel über etwas wissen ◊ *She is very knowledgeable about physics.* Sie weiß viel über Physik.

♦**She's very knowledgeable about computers.** Sie kennt sich mit Computern gut aus.

known VERB *see* **know**

Koran NOUN

der Koran

Korea NOUN

Korea NEUT

♦**from Korea** aus Korea

♦**to Korea** nach Korea

kosher ADJECTIVE

koscher

K

L

lab NOUN (= *laboratory*)
das <u>Labor</u> (PL die Labors)
♦ **a lab technician** ein Laborant MASC

label NOUN
1 (*sticker*)
der <u>Aufkleber</u> (PL die Aufkleber)
2 (*on clothes*)
das <u>Etikett</u> (PL die Etiketts)
3 (*for luggage*)
der <u>Anhänger</u> (PL die
Anhänger)

laboratory NOUN
das <u>Labor</u> (PL die Labors)

labor union NOUN US
die <u>Gewerkschaft</u>

Labour NOUN
die <u>Labour-Party</u> ◊ *My parents vote
Labour.* Meine Eltern wählen die
Labour-Party.
♦ **the Labour Party** die Labour-Party

labourer NOUN
der <u>Arbeiter</u> (PL die Arbeiter)
die <u>Arbeiterin</u>
♦ **a farm labourer** ein Landarbeiter

lace NOUN
1 (*of shoe*)
der <u>Schnürsenkel</u> (PL die
Schnürsenkel)
2 die <u>Spitze</u> ◊ *a lace collar* ein
Spitzenkragen

lack NOUN
der <u>Mangel</u> (PL die Mängel) ◊ *He got the
job, despite his lack of experience.* Er
bekam die Stelle trotz seines Mangels an
Erfahrung.

lacquer NOUN
der <u>Lack</u> (PL die Lacke)

lad NOUN
der <u>Junge</u> (GEN des Jungen, PL die
Jungen)

ladder NOUN
1 die <u>Leiter</u>
2 die <u>Laufmasche</u> (*in tights*)

lady NOUN
die <u>Dame</u> ◊ *a young lady* eine junge
Dame
♦ **Ladies and gentlemen ...** Meine Damen
und Herren ...
♦ **the ladies'** die Damentoilette

ladybird NOUN
der <u>Marienkäfer</u> (PL die
Marienkäfer)

to **lag behind** VERB
<u>hinterherhinken</u> (PERFECT ist
hinterhergehinkt)

lager NOUN
das <u>helle Bier</u> (PL die hellen Biere)

ⓘ *German beers are completely
different from British ones. There is no
real equivalent to **lager**.*

laid VERB *see* **lay**

laid-back ADJECTIVE
<u>locker</u>

lain VERB *see* **lie**

lake NOUN
der <u>See</u> (PL die Seen)
♦ **Lake Geneva** der Genfer See
♦ **Lake Constance** der Bodensee

lamb NOUN
das <u>Lamm</u> (PL die Lämmer)
♦ **a lamb chop** ein Lammkotelett NEUT

lame ADJECTIVE
<u>lahm</u>
♦ **My pony is lame.** Mein Pony lahmt.

lamp NOUN
dle <u>Lampe</u>

lamppost NOUN
der <u>Laternenpfahl</u> (PL die
Laternenpfähle)

lampshade NOUN
der <u>Lampenschirm</u>

land NOUN
see also **land** VERB
das <u>Land</u> (PL die Länder) ◊ *a piece of land*
ein Stück Land

to **land** VERB
see also **land** NOUN
(*plane, passenger*)
<u>landen</u> (PERFECT ist gelandet)

landing NOUN
1 (*of plane*)
die <u>Landung</u>
2 (*of staircase*)
der <u>Treppenabsatz</u> (GEN des
Treppenabsatzes, PL die Treppenabsätze)

landlady NOUN
die <u>Vermieterin</u>

landlord NOUN
der <u>Vermieter</u> (PL die Vermieter)

landmark NOUN
das <u>Wahrzeichen</u> (PL die Wahrzeichen)
◊ *Big Ben is one of London's landmarks.*
Big Ben ist eines der Wahrzeichen
Londons.

landowner NOUN
der <u>Grundbesitzer</u> (PL die Grundbesitzer)
die <u>Grundbesitzerin</u>

landscape NOUN
die <u>Landschaft</u>

lane NOUN
1 (*in country*)
das <u>Sträßchen</u> (PL die Sträßchen)
2 (*on motorway*)

die <u>Spur</u>

language NOUN
die <u>Sprache</u> ◊ *Greek is a difficult language.* Griechisch ist eine schwierige Sprache.
♦ **to use bad language** Kraftausdrücke benutzen

language laboratory NOUN
das <u>Sprachlabor</u> (PL die Sprachlabors)

lap NOUN
die <u>Runde</u> (*sport*) ◊ *I ran ten laps.* Ich bin zehn Runden gelaufen.
♦ **on my lap** auf meinem Schoß

laptop NOUN
der <u>Laptop</u> (*computer*) (PL die Laptops)

larder NOUN
die <u>Speisekammer</u>

large ADJECTIVE
<u>groß</u> ◊ *a large house* ein großes Haus ◊ *a large dog* ein großer Hund

largely ADVERB
<u>größtenteils</u>

laser NOUN
der <u>Laser</u> (PL die Laser)

lass NOUN
das <u>Mädchen</u> (PL die Mädchen)

last ADJECTIVE, ADVERB
| *see also* **last** VERB |

1 <u>letzte</u> ◊ *one last time* ein letztes Mal ◊ *the last question* die letzte Frage ◊ *last Friday* letzten Freitag ◊ *last week* letzte Woche
2 <u>als Letzte</u> ◊ *He arrived last.* Er kam als Letzter an.
3 <u>zuletzt</u> ◊ *I've lost my bag. – When did you see it last?* Ich habe meine Tasche verloren. – Wann hast du sie zuletzt gesehen?
♦ **When I last saw him, he was wearing a blue shirt.** Als ich ihn das letzte Mal sah, trug er ein blaues Hemd.
♦ **the last time** das letzte Mal ◊ *the last time I saw her* als ich sie das letzte Mal sah ◊ *That's the last time I take your advice!* Das ist das letzte Mal, dass ich auf deinen Rat höre!
♦ **last night (1)** (*evening*) gestern Abend ◊ *I got home at midnight last night.* Ich bin gestern Abend um Mitternacht nach Hause gekommen.
♦ **last night (2)** (*sleeping hours*) heute Nacht ◊ *I couldn't sleep last night.* Ich konnte heute Nacht nicht schlafen.
♦ **at last** endlich

to **last** VERB
| *see also* **last** ADJECTIVE |

<u>dauern</u> ◊ *The concert lasts two hours.* Das Konzert dauert zwei Stunden.

lastly ADVERB
<u>schließlich</u> ◊ *Lastly I'd like to mention that ...* Und schließlich möchte ich erwähnen, dass ...

late ADJECTIVE, ADVERB

1 <u>zu spät</u> ◊ *Hurry up or you'll be late!* Beeil dich, du kommst sonst zu spät! ◊ *I'm often late for school.* Ich komme oft zu spät zur Schule.
♦ **to arrive late** zu spät kommen ◊ *She arrived late.* Sie kam zu spät.
2 <u>spät</u> ◊ *I went to bed late.* Ich bin spät ins Bett gegangen. ◊ *in the late afternoon* am späten Nachmittag
♦ **in late May** Ende Mai

lately ADVERB
<u>in letzter Zeit</u> ◊ *I haven't seen him lately.* Ich habe ihn in letzter Zeit nicht gesehen.

later ADVERB
<u>später</u> ◊ *I'll do it later.* Ich mache es später.
♦ **See you later!** Bis später!

latest ADJECTIVE
<u>neueste</u> ◊ *the latest news* die neuesten Nachrichten ◊ *their latest album* ihr neuestes Album
♦ **at the latest** spätestens ◊ *by ten o'clock at the latest* bis spätestens zehn Uhr

Latin NOUN
das <u>Latein</u> ◊ *I do Latin.* Ich lerne Latein.

Latin America NOUN
<u>Lateinamerika</u> NEUT
♦ **from Latin America** aus Lateinamerika
♦ **to Latin America** nach Lateinamerika

Latin American ADJECTIVE
<u>lateinamerikanisch</u>

laugh NOUN
| *see also* **laugh** VERB |

das <u>Lachen</u>
♦ **It was a good laugh.** (*it was fun*) Es war lustig.

to **laugh** VERB
| *see also* **laugh** NOUN |

<u>lachen</u>
♦ **to laugh at something** über etwas lachen ◊ *She didn't laugh at my joke.* Sie hat über meinen Witz nicht gelacht.
♦ **to laugh at somebody** jemanden auslachen ◊ *They laughed at her.* Sie lachten sie aus.

to **launch** VERB
1 <u>auf den Markt bringen</u> (*product*) (IMPERFECT brachte, PERFECT hat gebracht)
2 <u>abschießen</u> (*rocket*) (IMPERFECT schoss ab, PERFECT hat abgeschossen)

Launderette ® NOUN
der <u>Waschsalon</u> (PL die Waschsalons)

Laundromat ® NOUN US
der <u>Waschsalon</u> (PL die Waschsalons)

laundry NOUN
die <u>Wäsche</u> (*clothes*)

lavatory NOUN
die <u>Toilette</u>

lavender NOUN
der <u>Lavendel</u>

law NOUN

L

1 das Gesetz (GEN des Gesetzes, PL die Gesetze) ◊ *It's against the law.* Das ist gegen das Gesetz.

2 (*subject*)

Jura ◊ *My sister's studying law.* Meine Schwester studiert Jura.

lawn NOUN

der Rasen (PL die Rasen)

lawnmower NOUN

der Rasenmäher (PL die Rasenmäher)

law school NOUN US

die juristische Fakultät

lawyer NOUN

der Rechtsanwalt (PL die Rechtsanwälte)

die Rechtsanwältin

◊ *My mother's a lawyer.* Meine Mutter ist Rechtsanwältin.

to **lay** VERB

lay is also a form of lie (2) VERB.

legen ◊ *She laid the baby in her cot.* Sie legte das Baby ins Bettchen.

♦ **to lay the table** den Tisch decken

♦ **to lay something on (1)** (*provide*) etwas bereitstellen ◊ *They laid on extra buses.* Sie stellten zusätzliche Busse bereit.

♦ **to lay something on (2)** (*prepare*) etwas vorbereiten ◊ *They had laid on a meal.* Sie hatten ein Essen vorbereitet.

♦ **to lay off** entlassen ◊ *My father's been laid off.* Mein Vater ist entlassen worden.

lay-by NOUN

der Rastplatz (GEN des Rastplatzes, PL die Rastplätze)

layer NOUN

die Schicht

layout NOUN

das Design (*of house, garden*) (PL die Designs)

lazy ADJECTIVE

faul

lb. ABBREVIATION (= *pound*)

Pfund

to **lead** VERB

see also lead (1) NOUN AND lead (2) NOUN

führen ◊ *the street that leads to the station* die Straße, die zum Bahnhof führt

♦ **to lead the way** vorangehen ◊ *She led the way.* Sie ist vorangegangen.

♦ **to lead somebody away** jemanden abführen ◊ *The police led the man away.* Die Polizei führte den Mann ab.

lead (1) NOUN

see also lead VERB AND lead (2) NOUN

1 (*cable*)

das Kabel (PL die Kabel)

2 (*for dog*)

die Hundeleine

♦ **to be in the lead** in Führung sein ◊ *Our team is in the lead.* Unsere Mannschaft ist in Führung.

lead (2) NOUN

see also lead VERB AND lead (1) NOUN

das Blei (*metal*)

leaded petrol NOUN

das verbleite Benzin

leader NOUN

1 (*of expedition, gang*)

der Führer (PL die Führer)

die Führerin

2 (*of political party*)

der Anführer (PL die Anführer)

die Anführerin

lead-free ADJECTIVE

♦ **lead-free petrol** das bleifreie Benzin

lead singer NOUN

der Leadsinger (PL die Leadsinger)

die Leadsingerin

leaf NOUN

das Blatt (PL die Blätter)

leaflet NOUN

der Prospekt (*advertising*) (PL die Prospekte) ◊ *They sent me a leaflet describing their products.* Sie haben mir einen Prospekt über ihre Produkte geschickt.

league NOUN

die Liga (GEN der Liga, PL die Ligen) ◊ *the Premier League* die erste Liga

> ⓘ The **Premier League** is similar to the German **Bundesliga**.

♦ **They are at the top of the league.** Sie sind Tabellenführer.

leak NOUN

see also leak VERB

die undichte Stelle ◊ *a gas leak* eine undichte Stelle in der Gasleitung

to **leak** VERB

see also leak NOUN

1 (*pipe*)

undicht sein (PRESENT ist undicht, IMPERFECT war undicht, PERFECT ist undicht gewesen)

2 (*water*)

auslaufen (PRESENT läuft aus, IMPERFECT lief aus, PERFECT ist ausgelaufen)

3 (*gas*)

austreten (PRESENT tritt aus, IMPERFECT trat aus, PERFECT ist ausgetreten)

to **lean** VERB

sich lehnen ◊ *Don't lean over too far.* Lehn dich nicht zu weit vor. ◊ *She leant out of the window.* Sie lehnte sich zum Fenster hinaus.

♦ **to lean forward** sich nach vorn beugen

♦ **to lean on something** sich auf etwas stützen ◊ *He leant on the wall.* Er stützte sich auf die Mauer.

♦ **to be leaning against something** gegen etwas gelehnt sein ◊ *The ladder was leaning against the wall.* Die Leiter war gegen die Wand gelehnt.

♦ **to lean something against a wall** etwas an einer Mauer anlehnen ◊ *He leant his bike against the wall.* Er lehnte sein Fahrrad an der Mauer an.

to **leap** VERB
springen (IMPERFECT sprang, PERFECT ist gesprungen) ◊ *He leapt out of his chair when his team scored.* Er sprang vom Stuhl auf, als seine Mannschaft ein Tor schoss.

leap year NOUN
das Schaltjahr (PL die Schaltjahre)

to **learn** VERB
lernen ◊ *I'm learning to ski.* Ich lerne Ski fahren.

learner NOUN
♦ **She's a quick learner.** Sie lernt schnell.
♦ **German learners** (*people learning German*) Deutschschüler MASC PL

learner driver NOUN
der Fahrschüler (PL die Fahrschüler)
die Fahrschülerin

learnt VERB *see* **learn**

least ADVERB, ADJECTIVE, PRONOUN
♦ **the least (1)** (*followed by noun*) wenigste ◊ *It takes the least time to do.* Das braucht die wenigste Zeit. ◊ *She has the least money.* Sie hat das wenigste Geld.
♦ **the least (2)** (*followed by adjective*) am wenigsten ... ◊ *the least intelligent pupil* der am wenigsten intelligente Schüler ◊ *the least attractive woman* die am wenigsten attraktive Frau ◊ *the least interesting book* das am wenigsten interessante Buch
♦ **the least (3)** (*after a verb*) am wenigsten ◊ *Maths is the subject I like the least.* Mathe ist das Fach, das ich am wenigsten mag.
♦ **It's the least I can do.** Das ist das wenigste, was ich tun kann.
♦ **at least (1)** mindestens ◊ *It'll cost at least two hundred pounds.* Das kostet mindestens zweihundert Pfund.
♦ **at least (2)** wenigstens ◊ *... but at least nobody was hurt.* ... aber wenigstens wurde niemand verletzt.
♦ **It's totally unfair – at least, that's my opinion.** Das ist total ungerecht – zumindest meiner Meinung nach.

leather NOUN
das Leder (PL die Leder) ◊ *a black leather jacket* eine schwarze Lederjacke

to **leave** VERB
see also **leave** NOUN
1 (*deliberately*)
lassen (PRESENT lässt, IMPERFECT ließ, PERFECT hat gelassen) ◊ *He always leaves his camera in the car.* Er lässt immer seinen Fotoapparat im Auto.
2 (*by mistake*)
vergessen (PRESENT vergisst, IMPERFECT vergaß, PERFECT hat vergessen) ◊ *I've left my book at home.* Ich habe mein Buch zu Hause vergessen.

♦ **Make sure you don't leave anything behind.** Passen Sie auf, dass Sie nichts liegen lassen.
3 (*bus, train*)
abfahren (PRESENT fährt ab, IMPERFECT fuhr ab, PERFECT ist abgefahren) ◊ *The bus leaves at eight.* Der Bus fährt um acht ab.
4 (*plane*)
abfliegen (IMPERFECT flog ab, PERFECT ist abgeflogen) ◊ *The plane leaves at six.* Das Flugzeug fliegt um sechs ab.
5 (*person*)
weggehen (IMPERFECT ging weg, PERFECT ist weggegangen) ◊ *She's just left.* Sie ist eben weggegangen.
♦ **My sister left home last year.** Meine Schwester ist letztes Jahr von zu Hause weggezogen.
6 (*abandon*)
verlassen (PRESENT verlässt, IMPERFECT verließ, PERFECT hat verlassen) ◊ *She left her husband.* Sie hat ihren Mann verlassen.
♦ **to leave somebody alone** jemanden in Ruhe lassen ◊ *Leave me alone!* Lass mich in Ruhe!
♦ **to leave out** auslassen ◊ *You've left out a comma.* Du hast ein Komma ausgelassen.
♦ **I felt really left out.** Ich fühlte mich richtig ausgeschlossen.

leave NOUN
see also **leave** VERB
der Urlaub (*from job, army*) (PL die Urlaube) ◊ *My brother is on leave for a week.* Mein Bruder hat eine Woche Urlaub.

leaves PL NOUN *see* **leaf**

Lebanon NOUN
der Libanon
Note that the definite article is used in German for countries which are masculine.
♦ **from Lebanon** aus dem Libanon
♦ **in Lebanon** im Libanon
♦ **to Lebanon** in den Libanon

lecture NOUN
see also **lecture** VERB
1 (*public*)
der Vortrag (PL die Vorträge)
2 (*at university*)
die Vorlesung
Be careful not to translate lecture by Lektüre.

to **lecture** VERB
see also **lecture** NOUN
1 unterrichten (PERFECT hat unterrichtet) ◊ *She lectures at the technical college.* Sie unterrichtet an der Fachschule.
2 (*tell off*)
belehren (PERFECT hat belehrt) ◊ *He's always lecturing us.* Er belehrt uns andauernd.

L

lecturer NOUN
der Dozent (GEN des Dozenten, PL die Dozenten)
die Dozentin
◊ *She's a lecturer.* Sie ist Dozentin.

led VERB *see* **lead**

leek NOUN
der Lauch (PL die Lauche)

left VERB *see* **leave**

left ADJECTIVE, ADVERB
see also **left** NOUN
1 linke ◊ *the left foot* der linke Fuß ◊ *my left arm* mein linker Arm ◊ *your left hand* deine linke Hand ◊ *her left eye* ihr linkes Auge
2 links ◊ *Turn left at the traffic lights.* Biegen Sie an der Ampel links ab.
♦ **Look left!** Sehen Sie nach links!
♦ **I haven't got any money left.** Ich habe kein Geld mehr.

left NOUN
see also **left** ADJECTIVE
die linke Seite
♦ **on the left** links ◊ *Remember to drive on the left.* Vergiss nicht, links zu fahren.

left-hand ADJECTIVE
♦ **the left-hand side** die linke Seite
♦ **It's on the left-hand side.** Es liegt links.

left-handed ADJECTIVE
linkshändig

left-luggage office NOUN
die Gepäckaufbewahrung

leg NOUN
das Bein (PL die Beine) ◊ *I've broken my leg.* Ich habe mir das Bein gebrochen.
♦ **a chicken leg** eine Hähnchenkeule
♦ **a leg of lamb** eine Lammkeule

legal ADJECTIVE
legal

leggings PL NOUN
die Leggings PL

leisure NOUN
die Freizeit ◊ *What do you do in your leisure time?* Was machen Sie in Ihrer Freizeit?

leisure centre NOUN
das Freizeitzentrum (PL die Freizeitzentren)

lemon NOUN
die Zitrone

lemonade NOUN
die Limonade

to **lend** VERB
leihen (IMPERFECT lieh, PERFECT hat geliehen) ◊ *I can lend you some money.* Ich kann dir Geld leihen.

length NOUN
die Länge
♦ **It's about a metre in length.** Es ist etwa einen Meter lang.

lens NOUN
1 (*contact lens*)
die Kontaktlinse
2 (*of spectacles*)
das Glas (GEN des Glases, PL die Gläser)
3 (*of camera*)
das Objektiv (PL die Objektive)

Lent NOUN
die Fastenzeit ◊ *during Lent* während der Fastenzeit

lent VERB *see* **lend**

lentil NOUN
die Linse

Leo NOUN
der Löwe (GEN des Löwen) ◊ *I'm Leo.* Ich bin Löwe.

leotard NOUN
der Gymnastikanzug (PL die Gymnastikanzüge)

lesbian NOUN
die Lesbierin
♦ **She's a lesbian.** Sie ist lesbisch.

less PRONOUN, ADVERB, ADJECTIVE
weniger ◊ *A bit less, please.* Etwas weniger, bitte. ◊ *I've got less time for hobbies now.* Ich habe jetzt weniger Zeit für Hobbys.
♦ **He's less intelligent than his brother.** Er ist nicht so intelligent wie sein Bruder.
♦ **less than** weniger als ◊ *It costs less than a hundred euros.* Es kostet weniger als hundert Euro. ◊ *less than half* weniger als die Hälfte ◊ *He spent less than me.* Er hat weniger als ich ausgegeben. ◊ *I've got less than you.* Ich habe weniger als du.

lesson NOUN
1 die Lektion ◊ *"Lesson Sixteen"* (*in textbook*) "Lektion sechzehn"
2 die Stunde (*class*) ◊ *The lessons last forty minutes each.* Eine Stunde dauert je vierzig Minuten.

to **let** VERB
1 (*allow*)
lassen (PRESENT lässt, IMPERFECT ließ, PERFECT hat gelassen)
♦ **to let somebody do something** jemanden etwas tun lassen ◊ *Let me have a look.* Lass mich mal sehen. ◊ *My mother won't let me go out tonight.* Meine Mutter lässt mich heute Abend nicht ausgehen.
♦ **to let somebody down** jemanden enttäuschen ◊ *I won't let you down.* Ich werde dich nicht enttäuschen.
♦ **to let somebody know** jemandem Bescheid sagen ◊ *I'll let you know as soon as possible.* Ich sage Ihnen sobald wie möglich Bescheid.
♦ **to let go** (*release*) loslassen ◊ *Let me go!* Lass mich los!
♦ **to let in** hineinlassen ◊ *They wouldn't let me in because I was under eighteen.* Sie wollten mich nicht hineinlassen, weil ich noch nicht achtzehn bin.

♦**Let's go to the cinema!** Lass uns ins Kino gehen!
♦**Let's go!** Gehen wir!
②(*hire out*)
vermieten (PERFECT hat vermietet)
♦**"to let"** "zu vermieten"

letter NOUN
①der Brief (PL die Briefe) ◊ *She wrote me a long letter.* Sie hat mir einen langen Brief geschrieben.
②(*of alphabet*)
der Buchstabe (GEN des Buchstaben, PL die Buchstaben) ◊ *A is the first letter of the alphabet.* A ist der erste Buchstabe des Alphabets.

letterbox NOUN
der Briefkasten (PL die Briefkästen)

lettuce NOUN
der Kopfsalat (PL die Kopfsalate)

leukaemia NOUN
die Leukämie ◊ *He suffers from leukaemia.* Er leidet an Leukämie.

level ADJECTIVE
see also **level** NOUN
eben ◊ *A snooker table must be perfectly level.* Ein Snookertisch muss ganz eben sein.

level NOUN
see also **level** ADJECTIVE
①(*of river, lake*)
der Wasserstand (PL die Wasserstände) ◊ *The level of the river is rising.* Der Wasserstand des Flusses steigt.
②(*height*)
die Höhe ◊ *at eye level* in Augenhöhe
♦**A levels** das Abitur

ℹ *Germans take their **Abitur** at the age of 19. The students sit examinations in a variety of subjects to attain an overall grade. If you pass, you have the right to a place at university.*

level crossing NOUN
der Bahnübergang (PL die Bahnübergänge)

lever NOUN
der Hebel (PL die Hebel)

liable ADJECTIVE
♦**He's liable to lose his temper.** Er wird leicht wütend.

liar NOUN
der Lügner (PL die Lügner)
die Lügnerin

liberal ADJECTIVE
liberal (*opinions*)
♦**the Liberal Democrats** die Liberaldemokraten

liberation NOUN
die Befreiung

Libra NOUN
die Waage ◊ *I'm Libra.* Ich bin Waage.

librarian NOUN

der Bibliothekar (PL die Bibliothekare)
die Bibliothekarin
◊ *She's a librarian.* Sie ist Bibliothekarin.

library NOUN
①die Bücherei (*public lending library*)
②die Bibliothek (*of school, university*)

Libya NOUN
Libyen NEUT
♦**from Libya** aus Libyen
♦**to Libya** nach Libyen

licence NOUN
der Schein (PL die Scheine)
♦**a driving licence** ein Führerschein

to **lick** VERB
lecken

lid NOUN
der Deckel (PL die Deckel)

lie NOUN
see also **lie (1)** VERB AND **lie (2)** VERB
die Lüge ◊ *That's a lie!* Das ist eine Lüge!
♦**to tell a lie** lügen

to **lie (1)** VERB
see also **lie** NOUN AND **lie (2)** VERB
lügen (*not tell the truth*) (IMPERFECT log, PERFECT hat gelogen) ◊ *I know she's lying.* Ich weiß, dass sie lügt.

to **lie (2)** VERB
see also **lie** NOUN AND **lie (1)** VERB
liegen (IMPERFECT lag, PERFECT hat gelegen) ◊ *He was lying on the sofa.* Er lag auf dem Sofa. ◊ *When I'm on holiday I lie on the beach all day.* In den Ferien liege ich den ganzen Tag am Strand.
♦**to lie down** sich hinlegen
♦**to be lying down** liegen

lie-in NOUN
♦**to have a lie-in** ausschlafen ◊ *She has a lie-in on Sundays.* Sonntags schläft sie aus.

lieutenant NOUN
der Leutnant (PL die Leutnants)

life NOUN
das Leben (PL die Leben)

lifebelt NOUN
der Rettungsring (PL die Rettungsringe)

lifeboat NOUN
das Rettungsboot (PL die Rettungsboote)

lifeguard NOUN
①(*at beach*)
der Rettungsschwimmer (PL die Rettungsschwimmer)
die Rettungsschwimmerin
②(*at swimming pool*)
der Bademeister (PL die Bademeister)
die Bademeisterin

life jacket NOUN
die Schwimmweste

life-saving NOUN
das Rettungsschwimmen ◊ *I've done a course in life-saving.* Ich habe einen Kurs im Rettungsschwimmen gemacht.

L

lifestyle NOUN
der Lebensstil (PL die Lebensstile)

to **lift** VERB
| see also **lift** NOUN |

hochheben (IMPERFECT hob hoch, PERFECT hat hochgehoben) ◊ *It's too heavy, I can't lift it.* Es ist zu schwer, ich kann es nicht hochheben.

lift NOUN
| see also **lift** VERB |

der Aufzug (PL die Aufzüge) ◊ *The lift isn't working.* Der Aufzug geht nicht.
♦ **He gave me a lift to the cinema.** Er hat mich zum Kino gefahren.
♦ **Would you like a lift?** Wollen Sie mitfahren?

light ADJECTIVE
| see also **light** NOUN, VERB |

[1] leicht (*not heavy*) ◊ *a light jacket* eine leichte Jacke ◊ *a light meal* ein leichtes Essen
[2] hell (*colour*) ◊ *a light blue sweater* ein hellblauer Pullover

light NOUN
| see also **light** ADJECTIVE, VERB |

[1] das Licht (PL die Lichter) ◊ *to switch on the light* das Licht anmachen ◊ *to switch off the light* das Licht ausmachen
[2] die Lampe ◊ *There's a light by my bed.* Ich habe am Bett eine Lampe.
♦ **the traffic lights** die Ampel SING
♦ **Have you got a light?** (*for cigarette*) Haben Sie Feuer?

to **light** VERB
| see also **light** ADJECTIVE, NOUN |

anzünden (*candle, cigarette, fire*) (PERFECT hat angezündet)

light bulb NOUN
die Glühbirne

lighter NOUN
das Feuerzeug (*for cigarettes*) (PL die Feuerzeuge)

lighthouse NOUN
der Leuchtturm (PL die Leuchttürme)

lightning NOUN
der Blitz (GEN des Blitzes, PL die Blitze)
♦ **a flash of lightning** ein Blitz
♦ **There was a flash of lightning.** Es hat geblitzt.

to **like** VERB
| see also **like** PREPOSITION |

mögen (PRESENT mag, IMPERFECT mochte, PERFECT hat gemocht) ◊ *I don't like mustard.* Ich mag Senf nicht. ◊ *I like Paul, but I don't want to go out with him.* Ich mag Paul, aber ich will nicht mit ihm ausgehen.
♦ **I like riding.** Ich reite gern.
♦ **Would you like ...?** Möchtest du ...? ◊ *Would you like some coffee?* Möchtest du Kaffee? ◊ *Would you like to go for a*

walk? Möchtest du einen Spaziergang machen?
♦ **I'd like ...** Ich hätte gern ... ◊ *I'd like an orange juice, please.* Ich hätte gern einen Orangensaft, bitte.
♦ **I'd like to ...** Ich würde gern ... ◊ *I'd like to go to Russia one day.* Eines Tages würde ich gern nach Russland fahren. ◊ *I'd like to wash my hands.* Ich würde mir gern die Hände waschen.
♦ **... if you like** ... wenn du möchtest

like PREPOSITION
| see also **like** VERB |

[1] so (*this way*) ◊ *It's fine like that.* So ist es gut. ◊ *Do it like this.* Mach das so.
[2] wie (*similar to*) ◊ *a city like Munich* eine Stadt wie München ◊ *It's a bit like salmon.* Es ist ein bisschen wie Lachs.
♦ **What's the weather like?** Wie ist das Wetter?
♦ **to look like somebody** jemandem ähnlich sehen ◊ *You look like my brother.* Du siehst meinem Bruder ähnlich.

likely ADJECTIVE
wahrscheinlich ◊ *That's not very likely.* Das ist nicht sehr wahrscheinlich.
♦ **She's likely to come.** Sie kommt wahrscheinlich.
♦ **She's not likely to come.** Sie kommt wahrscheinlich nicht.

Lilo ® NOUN
die Luftmatratze

lime NOUN
die Limone (*fruit*)

limit NOUN
die Grenze
♦ **the speed limit** die Geschwindigkeitsbegrenzung

limousine NOUN
die Limousine

to **limp** VERB
hinken

line NOUN
[1] die Linie ◊ *a straight line* eine gerade Linie
[2] (*to divide, cancel*)
der Strich (PL die Striche) ◊ *Draw a line under each answer.* Machen Sie unter jede Antwort einen Strich.
[3] (*railway track*)
das Gleis (GEN des Gleises, PL die Gleise)
[4] die Schlange ◊ *to stand in line* Schlange stehen
♦ **Hold the line, please.** (*on telephone*) Bleiben Sie bitte am Apparat.
♦ **It's a very bad line.** (*on telephone*) Die Verbindung ist sehr schlecht.

linen NOUN
das Leinen ◊ *a linen jacket* eine Leinenjacke

liner NOUN

der Überseedampfer (*ship*) (PL die Überseedampfer)

linguist NOUN
♦**to be a good linguist** sprachbegabt sein ◊ *She's a good linguist.* Sie ist sehr sprachbegabt.

lining NOUN
das Futter (*of clothes*) (PL die Futter)

link NOUN
see also **link** VERB
1 der Zusammenhang (PL die Zusammenhänge) ◊ *the link between smoking and cancer* der Zusammenhang zwischen Rauchen und Krebs
2 (*computer*)
der Link (PL die Links)

to **link** VERB
see also **link** NOUN
verbinden (IMPERFECT verband, PERFECT hat verbunden)

lino NOUN
das Linoleum

lion NOUN
der Löwe (GEN des Löwen, PL die Löwen)

lioness NOUN
die Löwin

lip NOUN
die Lippe

to **lip-read** VERB
von den Lippen ablesen (PRESENT liest von den Lippen ab, IMPERFECT las von den Lippen ab, PERFECT hat von den Lippen abgelesen)
♦**I'm learning how to lip-read.** Ich lerne gerade Lippenlesen.

lip salve NOUN
der Lippenpflegestift (PL die Lippenpflegestifte)

lipstick NOUN
der Lippenstift (PL die Lippenstifte)

liqueur NOUN
der Likör (PL die Liköre)

liquid NOUN
die Flüssigkeit

liquidizer NOUN
der Mixer (PL die Mixer)

list NOUN
see also **list** VERB
die Liste

to **list** VERB
see also **list** NOUN
aufzählen (PERFECT hat aufgezählt) ◊ *List your hobbies.* Zählen Sie Ihre Hobbys auf.

to **listen** VERB
zuhören (PERFECT hat zugehört) ◊ *Listen to me!* Hör mir zu!
♦**Listen to this!** Hör dir das an!

listener NOUN
der Zuhörer (PL die Zuhörer)
die Zuhörerin

lit VERB see **light**

liter NOUN [US]
der Liter (PL die Liter)

literally ADVERB
buchstäblich (*completely*) ◊ *It was literally impossible to find a seat.* Es war buchstäblich unmöglich, einen Platz zu finden.
♦**to translate literally** wörtlich übersetzen

literature NOUN
die Literatur ◊ *I'm studying English Literature.* Ich studiere englische Literatur.

litre NOUN
der Liter (PL die Liter) ◊ *three litres* drei Liter

litter NOUN
der Abfall (PL die Abfälle)

litter bin NOUN
der Abfallkorb (PL die Abfallkörbe)

little ADJECTIVE
klein ◊ *a little girl* ein kleines Mädchen
♦**a little** ein bisschen ◊ *How much would you like? – Just a little.* Wie viel möchtest du? – Nur ein bisschen.
♦**very little** sehr wenig ◊ *We've got very little time.* Wir haben sehr wenig Zeit.
♦**little by little** nach und nach

live ADJECTIVE
see also **live** VERB
1 lebendig (*animal*)
2 live (*broadcast*)
♦**There's live music on Fridays.** Freitags gibt es Livemusik.

to **live** VERB
see also **live** ADJECTIVE
1 leben ◊ *I live with my grandmother.* Ich lebe bei meiner Großmutter.
◊ *They're not married, they're living together.* Sie sind nicht verheiratet, sie leben zusammen.
♦**to live on something** von etwas leben ◊ *He had to live on bread and water.* Er musste von Brot und Wasser leben. ◊ *He lives on benefit.* Er lebt von der Unterstützung.
2 wohnen (*in house, town*) ◊ *Where do you live?* Wo wohnst du? ◊ *I live in Edinburgh.* Ich wohne in Edinburgh.

lively ADJECTIVE
lebhaft ◊ *She's got a lively personality.* Sie ist ein lebhafter Typ.

liver NOUN
die Leber
♦**liver sausage** die Leberwurst

lives PL NOUN see **life**

living NOUN
♦**to make a living** sich seinen Lebensunterhalt verdienen ◊ *How do you make your living?* Wie verdienst du dir deinen Lebensunterhalt?
♦**What does she do for a living?** Was macht sie beruflich?

living room NOUN

L

☞

das Wohnzimmer (PL die Wohnzimmer)

lizard NOUN
die Echse

load NOUN

> see also **load** VERB

◆ **loads of** eine Menge ◊ *loads of people* eine Menge Leute ◊ *loads of money* eine Menge Geld

◆ **You're talking a load of rubbish!** Du redest vielleicht einen Unsinn!

to **load** VERB

> see also **load** NOUN

beladen (PRESENT belädt, IMPERFECT belud, PERFECT hat beladen) ◊ *He's loading the van right now.* Er belädt gerade den Lieferwagen.

loaf NOUN
der Laib (PL die Laibe)

◆ **a loaf of bread** ein Brot NEUT

loan NOUN

> see also **loan** VERB

das Darlehen (*money*) (PL die Darlehen)

to **loan** VERB

> see also **loan** NOUN

ausleihen (IMPERFECT lieh aus, PERFECT hat ausgeliehen)

to **loathe** VERB
verabscheuen (PERFECT hat verabscheut)
◊ *I loathe her.* Ich verabscheue sie.

loaves PL NOUN see **loaf**

lobster NOUN
der Hummer (PL die Hummer)

local ADJECTIVE
örtlich ◊ *the local police* die örtliche Polizei

◆ **the local paper** das Lokalblatt

◆ **a local call** ein Ortsgespräch NEUT

loch NOUN
der See (PL die Seen)

lock NOUN

> see also **lock** VERB

das Schloss (GEN des Schlosses, PL die Schlösser) ◊ *The lock is broken.* Das Schloss ist kaputt.

to **lock** VERB

> see also **lock** NOUN

abschließen (IMPERFECT schloss ab, PERFECT hat abgeschlossen) ◊ *Make sure you lock your door.* Schließen Sie die Tür ab.

◆ **to lock somebody out** jemanden aussperren ◊ *The door slammed and I was locked out.* Die Tür schlug zu und ich war ausgesperrt.

locker NOUN
das Schließfach (PL die Schließfächer)

◆ **the locker room** der Umkleideraum

◆ **the left-luggage lockers** die Gepäckschließfächer

locket NOUN
das Medaillon (PL die Medaillons)

lodger NOUN
der Untermieter (PL die Untermieter)

die Untermieterin

loft NOUN
der Speicher (PL die Speicher)

log NOUN
das Scheit (*of wood*) (PL die Scheite)

logical ADJECTIVE
logisch

to **log in** VERB
einloggen (*computer*) (PERFECT hat eingeloggt)

to **log off** VERB
ausloggen (*computer*) (PERFECT hat ausgeloggt)

to **log on** VERB
einloggen (*computer*) (PERFECT hat eingeloggt)

to **log out** VERB
ausloggen (*computer*) (PERFECT hat ausgeloggt)

lollipop NOUN
der Lutscher (PL die Lutscher)

lolly NOUN
das Eis am Stiel (*ice lolly*)

London NOUN
London NEUT

◆ **from London** aus London

◆ **to London** nach London

Londoner NOUN
der Londoner (PL die Londoner)
die Londonerin

loneliness NOUN
die Einsamkeit

lonely ADJECTIVE
einsam

◆ **to feel lonely** sich einsam fühlen ◊ *She feels a bit lonely.* Sie fühlt sich ein bisschen einsam.

long ADJECTIVE, ADVERB

> see also **long** VERB

lang ◊ *She's got long hair.* Sie hat lange Haare. ◊ *The room is six metres long.* Das Zimmer ist sechs Meter lang.

◆ **how long?** (*time*) wie lange? ◊ *How long did you stay there?* Wie lange bist du dortgeblieben? ◊ *How long is the flight?* Wie lange dauert der Flug?

> When you want to say how long you **have been** doing something, use the present tense in German.

◊ *How long have you been here?* Wie lange bist du schon da? ◊ *I've been waiting a long time.* Ich warte schon lange.

◆ **It takes a long time.** Das dauert lange.

◆ **as long as** solange ◊ *I'll come as long as it's not too expensive.* Ich komme mit, solange es nicht zu teuer ist.

to **long** VERB

> see also **long** ADJECTIVE

◆ **to long to do something** es kaum erwarten können, etwas zu tun ◊ *I'm* *longing to see my boyfriend again.* Ich kann es kaum erwarten, bis ich meinen Freund wiedersehe.

long-distance ADJECTIVE
♦ **a long-distance call** ein Ferngespräch NEUT

longer ADVERB
> see also **long** ADJECTIVE

♦ **They're no longer going out together.** Sie gehen nicht mehr miteinander.
♦ **I can't stand it any longer.** Ich halte das nicht länger aus.

long jump NOUN
der <u>Weitsprung</u> (PL die Weitsprünge)

loo NOUN
das <u>Klo</u> (*informal*) (PL die Klos) ◊ *Where's the loo?* Wo ist das Klo?
♦ **I need the loo.** (*informal*) Ich muss mal.

look NOUN
> see also **look** VERB

♦ **to have a look** ansehen ◊ *Have a look at this!* Sieh dir das mal an!
♦ **I don't like the look of it.** Das gefällt mir nicht.

to **look** VERB
> see also **look** NOUN

1 <u>sehen</u> (PRESENT sieht, IMPERFECT sah, PERFECT hat gesehen)
♦ **Look!** Sieh mal!
♦ **to look at something** etwas ansehen ◊ *Look at the picture.* Sieh dir das Bild an.
2 (*seem*)
<u>aussehen</u> (PERFECT hat ausgesehen) ◊ *She looks surprised.* Sie sieht überrascht aus. ◊ *That cake looks nice.* Der Kuchen sieht gut aus. ◊ *It looks fine.* Es sieht gut aus.
♦ **to look like somebody** jemandem ähnlich sehen ◊ *He looks like his brother.* Er sieht seinem Bruder ähnlich.
♦ **What does she look like?** Wie sieht sie aus?
♦ **Look out!** Pass auf!
♦ **to look after** sich kümmern um ◊ *I look after my little sister.* Ich kümmere mich um meine kleine Schwester.
♦ **to look for** suchen ◊ *I'm looking for my passport.* Ich suche meinen Pass.
♦ **to look forward to something** sich auf etwas freuen ◊ *I'm looking forward to the holidays.* Ich freue mich auf die Ferien.
♦ **Looking forward to hearing from you ...** In der Hoffnung, bald etwas von dir zu hören, ...
♦ **to look round** sich umsehen ◊ *I shouted and he looked round.* Ich habe gerufen, und er sah sich um. ◊ *I'm just looking round.* Ich sehe mich nur um. ◊ *I like looking round the shops.* Ich sehe mich gern in den Geschäften um.
♦ **to look round a museum** ein Museum ansehen

♦ **to look up** (*word, name*) nachschlagen ◊ *If you don't know a word, look it up in the dictionary.* Wenn du ein Wort nicht weißt, schlage es im Wörterbuch nach.

loose ADJECTIVE
<u>weit</u> (*clothes*)
♦ **loose change** das Kleingeld

lord NOUN
der <u>Lord</u> (*feudal*) (PL die Lords)
♦ **the House of Lords** das Oberhaus
♦ **the Lord** (*god*) Gott
♦ **Good Lord!** Großer Gott!

lorry NOUN
der <u>Lastwagen</u> (PL die Lastwagen)

lorry driver NOUN
der <u>Lastwagenfahrer</u> (PL die Lastwagenfahrer)
die <u>Lastwagenfahrerin</u>
◊ *He's a lorry driver.* Er ist Lastwagenfahrer.

to **lose** VERB
<u>verlieren</u> (IMPERFECT verlor, PERFECT hat verloren) ◊ *I've lost my purse.* Ich habe meinen Geldbeutel verloren.
♦ **to get lost** sich verlaufen ◊ *I was afraid of getting lost.* Ich hatte Angst, mich zu verlaufen.

loss NOUN
der <u>Verlust</u> (PL die Verluste)

lost VERB see **lose**

lost ADJECTIVE
<u>verloren</u>

lost-and-found NOUN US
das <u>Fundbüro</u> (PL die Fundbüros)

lost property office NOUN
das <u>Fundbüro</u> (PL die Fundbüros)

lot NOUN
♦ **a lot** viel
♦ **a lot of (1)** viel ◊ *He earns a lot of money.* Er verdient viel Geld.
♦ **a lot of (2)** viele ◊ *We saw a lot of interesting things.* Wir haben viele interessante Dinge gesehen.
♦ **lots of** eine Menge ◊ *She's got lots of money.* Sie hat eine Menge Geld. ◊ *He's got lots of friends.* Er hat eine Menge Freunde.
♦ **What did you do at the weekend? – Not a lot.** Was hast du am Wochenende gemacht? – Nicht viel.
♦ **Do you like football? – Not a lot.** Magst du Fußball? – Nicht besonders.
♦ **That's the lot.** Das ist alles.

lottery NOUN
das <u>Lotto</u>
♦ **to win the lottery** im Lotto gewinnen

loud ADJECTIVE
<u>laut</u> ◊ *The television is too loud.* Der Fernseher ist zu laut.

loudly ADVERB
<u>laut</u>

loudspeaker NOUN
der <u>Lautsprecher</u> (PL die Lautsprecher)

L

lounge NOUN
das Wohnzimmer (PL die Wohnzimmer)
lousy ADJECTIVE
lausig schlecht (*informal*) ◊ *The food in the canteen is lousy.* Das Essen in der Kantine ist lausig schlecht.
♦ **I feel lousy.** Mir geht's lausig schlecht.
love NOUN

see also **love** VERB

die Liebe
♦ **to be in love** verliebt sein ◊ *She's in love with Paul.* Sie ist in Paul verliebt.
♦ **to make love** sich lieben
♦ **Give Heike my love.** Grüß Heike von mir.
♦ **Love, Rosemary.** Alles Liebe, Rosemary.
to **love** VERB

see also **love** NOUN

1 (*person, thing*)
lieben ◊ *I love you.* Ich liebe dich. ◊ *I love chocolate.* Ich liebe Schokolade.
2 (*like a lot*)
mögen (PRESENT mag, IMPERFECT mochte, PERFECT hat gemocht) ◊ *Everybody loves her.* Alle mögen sie.
♦ **I'd love to come.** Ich würde liebend gern kommen.
♦ **I love skiing.** Ich fahre unheimlich gern Ski.
lovely ADJECTIVE
1 wunderbar ◊ *What a lovely surprise!* Was für eine wunderbare Überraschung!
2 schön (*pretty*) ◊ *They've got a lovely house.* Sie haben ein schönes Haus.
♦ **It's a lovely day.** Es ist ein herrlicher Tag.
♦ **She's a lovely person.** Sie ist ein sehr netter Mensch.
♦ **Is your meal OK? – Yes, it's lovely.** Schmeckt dein Essen? – Ja, prima.
♦ **Have a lovely time!** Viel Spaß!
lover NOUN
der Liebhaber (PL die Liebhaber)
die Liebhaberin
low ADJECTIVE, ADVERB
niedrig ◊ *low prices* niedrige Preise
♦ **That plane is flying very low.** Das Flugzeug fliegt sehr tief.
♦ **the low season** die Nebensaison ◊ *in the low season* in der Nebensaison
lower sixth NOUN
die zwölfte Klasse ◊ *He's in the lower sixth.* Er ist in der zwölften Klasse.
low-fat ADJECTIVE
mager
♦ **a low-fat yoghurt** ein Magerjoghurt MASC
loyalty NOUN
die Treue
loyalty card NOUN
die Kundenkarte
L-plates PL NOUN
das L-Schild (PL die L-Schilder)
luck NOUN
das Glück ◊ *She hasn't had much luck.* Sie hat nicht viel Glück gehabt.

♦ **Good luck!** Viel Glück!
♦ **Bad luck!** So ein Pech!
luckily ADVERB
zum Glück
lucky ADJECTIVE
♦ **to be lucky (1)** (*be fortunate*) Glück haben ◊ *He's lucky, he's got a job.* Er hat Glück, er hat Arbeit.
♦ **He wasn't hurt. – That was lucky!** Er wurde nicht verletzt. – Das war Glück!
♦ **to be lucky (2)** (*bring luck*) Glück bringen ◊ *Black cats are lucky in Britain.* In Großbritannien bringen schwarze Katzen Glück.
♦ **a lucky horseshoe** ein Glückshufeisen NEUT
luggage NOUN
das Gepäck
lukewarm ADJECTIVE
lauwarm
lump NOUN
1 das Stück (PL die Stücke) ◊ *a lump of coal* ein Stück Kohle
2 (*swelling*)
die Beule ◊ *He's got a lump on his forehead.* Er hat eine Beule an der Stirn.
lunatic NOUN
der Verrückte (GEN des Verrückten, PL die Verrückten)
die Verrückte (GEN der Verrückten) ◊ *a lunatic* (*man*) ein Verrückter
♦ **He's an absolute lunatic.** Er ist total verrückt.
lunch NOUN
das Mittagessen (PL die Mittagessen)
♦ **to have lunch** zu Mittag essen ◊ *We have lunch at twelve o'clock.* Wir essen um zwölf Uhr zu Mittag.
luncheon voucher NOUN
die Essensmarke
lung NOUN
die Lunge ◊ *lung cancer* der Lungenkrebs
luscious ADJECTIVE
köstlich
lush ADJECTIVE
üppig
lust NOUN
das Verlangen
Luxembourg NOUN
Luxemburg NEUT (*country, city*)
♦ **from Luxembourg** aus Luxemburg
♦ **to Luxembourg** nach Luxemburg
luxurious ADJECTIVE
luxuriös
luxury NOUN
der Luxus (GEN des Luxus) ◊ *It was luxury!* Das war wirklich ein Luxus!
♦ **a luxury hotel** ein Luxushotel NEUT
lying VERB *see* lie
lyrics PL NOUN
der Text SING (*of song*) (PL die Texte)

M

mac NOUN
der Regenmantel (PL die Regenmäntel)
macaroni SING NOUN
die Makkaroni PL
machine NOUN
die Maschine
machine gun NOUN
das Maschinengewehr
machinery NOUN
die Maschinen FEM PL
mackerel NOUN
die Makrele
mad ADJECTIVE
1 verrückt (*insane*) ◊ *You're mad!* Du
bist verrückt!
♦ **to be mad about** verrückt sein nach
◊ *Ann is mad about John.* Ann ist
verrückt nach John. ◊ *He's mad about
football.* Er ist verrückt nach Fußball.
2 wütend (*angry*) ◊ *She'll be mad when
she finds out.* Wenn sie das erfährt, wird
sie wütend sein.
♦ **to be mad at somebody** wütend auf
jemanden sein ◊ *She was mad at me.* Sie
war wütend auf mich.
madam NOUN
> *In German no form of address is
> normally used apart from* **Sie.**
◊ *Would you like to order, Madam?*
Möchten Sie bestellen?
made VERB *see* **make**
madly ADVERB
♦ **They're madly in love.** Sie sind
wahnsinnig verliebt.
madman NOUN
der Verrückte (GEN des Verrückten, PL die
Verrückten) ◊ *a madman* ein Verrückter
madness NOUN
der Wahnsinn ◊ *It's absolute madness.*
Das ist totaler Wahnsinn.
magazine NOUN
die Zeitschrift
maggot NOUN
die Made
magic ADJECTIVE
> *see also* **magic** NOUN
1 magisch (*magical*) ◊ *magic powers*
magische Kräfte
♦ **a magic trick** ein Zaubertrick MASC
♦ **a magic wand** ein Zauberstab MASC
2 echt toll (*brilliant*) ◊ *It was magic!* Es
war echt toll!
magic NOUN
> *see also* **magic** ADJECTIVE
das Zaubern ◊ *My hobby is magic.*
Zaubern ist mein Hobby.
magician NOUN
(*conjurer*)

der Zauberkünstler (PL die
Zauberkünstler)
die Zauberkünstlerin
magnet NOUN
der Magnet
magnificent ADJECTIVE
1 wundervoll (*beautiful*) ◊ *a magnificent
view* eine wundervolle Aussicht
2 ausgezeichnet (*outstanding*) ◊ *It was a
magnificent film.* Es war ein
ausgezeichneter Film.
magnifying glass NOUN
die Lupe
maid NOUN
die Hausangestellte (*servant*) (GEN der
Hausangestellten)
♦ **an old maid** (*spinster*) eine alte Jungfer
maiden name NOUN
der Mädchenname (GEN des
Mädchennamens, PL die
Mädchennamen)
mail NOUN
die Post ◊ *Here's your mail.* Hier ist
deine Post.
♦ **by mail** per Post
♦ **e-mail** (*electronic mail*) die E-Mail
mailbox NOUN US
der Briefkasten (PL die Briefkästen)
mailing list NOUN
die Mailingliste
mailman NOUN US
der Briefträger (PL die Briefträger)
main ADJECTIVE
♦ **the main problem** das Hauptproblem
♦ **the main thing** die Hauptsache
mainly ADVERB
hauptsächlich
main road NOUN
die Hauptstraße ◊ *I don't like cycling on
main roads.* Ich fahre nicht gern auf
Hauptstraßen Rad.
to **maintain** VERB
instand halten (*machine, building*) (PRESENT
hält instand, IMPERFECT hielt instand, PERFECT
hat instand gehalten)
maintenance NOUN
die Instandhaltung (*of machine,
building*)
maize NOUN
der Mais
majesty NOUN
die Majestät
♦ **Your Majesty** Eure Majestät
major ADJECTIVE
groß ◊ *a major problem* ein großes
Problem
♦ **in C major** in C-Dur
Majorca NOUN

☞

Mallorca NEUT ◊ *to Majorca* nach Mallorca

majority NOUN
die Mehrheit

make NOUN
see also **make** VERB
die Marke ◊ *What make is that car?*
Welche Marke ist das Auto?

to **make** VERB
see also **make** NOUN
[1] machen ◊ *He made it himself.* Er hat
es selbst gemacht. ◊ *I make my bed
every morning.* Ich mache jeden Morgen
mein Bett. ◊ *Two and two make four.*
Zwei und zwei macht vier.
♦ **to make lunch** das Mittagessen machen
◊ *She's making lunch.* Sie macht das
Mittagessen.
♦ **I'm going to make a cake.** Ich werde
einen Kuchen backen.
[2] (*manufacture*)
herstellen (PERFECT hat hergestellt) ◊ *made
in Germany* in Deutschland hergestellt
[3] (*earn*)
verdienen (PERFECT hat verdient) ◊ *He
makes a lot of money.* Er verdient viel
Geld.
♦ **to make somebody do something**
jemanden zwingen, etwas zu tun ◊ *My
mother makes me do my homework.*
Meine Mutter zwingt mich, meine
Hausaufgaben zu machen.
♦ **to make a phone call** telefonieren ◊ *I'd
like to make a phone call.* Ich würde gern
telefonieren.
♦ **to make fun of somebody** sich über
jemanden lustig machen ◊ *They made
fun of him.* Sie haben sich über ihn lustig
gemacht.
♦ **What time do you make it?** Wie viel Uhr
hast du?

to **make out** VERB
[1] entziffern (PERFECT hat entziffert) ◊ *I
can't make out the address on the label.*
Ich kann die Anschrift auf dem Anhänger
nicht entziffern.
[2] verstehen (IMPERFECT verstand, PERFECT
hat verstanden) ◊ *I can't make her out at
all.* Ich kann sie überhaupt nicht
verstehen.
[3] behaupten (PERFECT hat behauptet)
◊ *They're making out it was my fault.* Sie
behaupten, es wäre meine Schuld
gewesen.
♦ **to make a cheque out to somebody**
jemandem einen Scheck ausstellen

to **make up** VERB
[1] (*invent*)
erfinden (IMPERFECT erfand, PERFECT hat
erfunden) ◊ *He made up the whole story.*
Er hat die ganze Geschichte erfunden.
[2] (*after argument*)
sich versöhnen (PERFECT haben sich
versöhnt) ◊ *They had a quarrel, but soon*

made up. Sie haben sich gestritten, sich
aber bald wieder versöhnt.
♦ **to make oneself up** sich schminken
◊ *She spends hours making herself up.*
Sie schminkt sich immer stundenlang.

maker NOUN
der Hersteller (PL die Hersteller)
◊ *Germany's biggest car maker*
Deutschlands größter Autohersteller

make-up NOUN
das Make-up (PL die Make-ups)

Malaysia NOUN
Malaysia NEUT ◊ *to Malaysia* nach
Malaysia

male ADJECTIVE
männlich ◊ *a male kitten* ein männliches
Katzenjunges ◊ *Sex: male.* Geschlecht:
männlich

*In many cases, the ending in German
indicates clearly whether the noun refers
to a man or a woman and there is
therefore no need for the word* **male.**
◊ *male and female students* Studenten
und Studentinnen
♦ **a male chauvinist** ein Macho MASC
♦ **a male nurse** ein Krankenpfleger MASC

mall NOUN
das Einkaufszentrum (PL die
Einkaufszentren)

Malta NOUN
Malta NEUT
♦ **from Malta** aus Malta
♦ **to Malta** nach Malta

mammoth ADJECTIVE
monumental ◊ *a mammoth task* eine
monumentale Aufgabe

man NOUN
der Mann (PL die Männer) ◊ *an old man*
ein alter Mann

to **manage** VERB
[1] (*be in charge of*)
leiten ◊ *She manages a big store.* Sie
leitet ein großes Geschäft.
[2] (*band, football team*)
managen ◊ *He manages our band.* Er
managt unsere Band.
[3] (*get by*)
klarkommen (IMPERFECT kam klar, PERFECT
ist klargekommen) ◊ *We haven't got
much money, but we manage.* Wir haben
nicht viel Geld, aber wir kommen klar.
◊ *It's okay, I can manage.* Das ist okay,
ich komme klar.
[4] schaffen ◊ *Can you manage okay?*
Schaffst du es? ◊ *I can't manage all that.*
(*food*) Das schaffe ich nicht alles.
♦ **to manage to do something** es schaffen,
etwas zu tun
♦ **Luckily I managed to pass the exam.**
Zum Glück habe ich die Prüfung
geschafft.

manageable ADJECTIVE
machbar (*task*)

management NOUN
die <u>Leitung</u> (*organization*) ◊ *He's responsible for the management of the company.* Er ist für die Leitung des Unternehmens verantwortlich. ◊ *"under new management"* "unter neuer Leitung"

manager NOUN
1 (*of company, shop, restaurant*)
der <u>Geschäftsführer</u> (PL die Geschäftsführer)
die <u>Geschäftsführerin</u>
2 (*of performer, football team*)
der <u>Manager</u> (PL die Manager)
die <u>Managerin</u>

manageress NOUN
die <u>Geschäftsführerin</u>

mandarin NOUN
die <u>Mandarine</u> (*fruit*)

mango NOUN
die <u>Mango</u> (PL die Mangos)

mania NOUN
die <u>Manie</u>

maniac NOUN
der <u>Verrückte</u> (GEN des Verrückten, PL die Verrückten)
die <u>Verrückte</u> (GEN der Verrückten) ◊ *He drives like a maniac.* Er fährt wie ein Verrückter.

to **manipulate** VERB
<u>manipulieren</u> (PERFECT hat manipuliert)

mankind NOUN
die <u>Menschheit</u> ◊ *Is there any hope for mankind?* Gibt es noch Hoffnung für die Menschheit?

man-made ADJECTIVE
<u>synthetisch</u> (*fibre*)

manner NOUN
die <u>Art und Weise</u> ◊ *in this manner* auf diese Art und Weise
♦ **She behaves in an odd manner.** Sie benimmt sich eigenartig.
♦ **He has a confident manner.** Er wirkt selbstsicher.

manners PL NOUN
das <u>Benehmen</u> SING ◊ *good manners* gutes Benehmen
♦ **Her manners are appalling.** Sie benimmt sich schrecklich.
♦ **It's bad manners to speak with your mouth full.** Es gehört sich nicht, mit vollem Mund zu sprechen.

manpower NOUN
die <u>Arbeitskräfte</u> FEM PL

mansion NOUN
die <u>Villa</u> (PL die Villen)

mantelpiece NOUN
der <u>Kaminsims</u> (GEN des Kaminsimses, PL die Kaminsimse)

manual NOUN
das <u>Handbuch</u> (PL die Handbücher)

to **manufacture** VERB
<u>herstellen</u> (PERFECT hat hergestellt)

manufacturer NOUN
der <u>Hersteller</u> (PL die Hersteller)

manure NOUN
der <u>Mist</u>

manuscript NOUN
das <u>Manuskript</u> (PL die Manuskripte)

many ADJECTIVE, PRONOUN
<u>viele</u> ◊ *The film has many special effects.* In dem Film gibt es viele Spezialeffekte. ◊ *He hasn't got many friends.* Er hat nicht viele Freunde. ◊ *Were there many people at the concert?* Waren viele Leute in dem Konzert?
♦ **very many** sehr viele ◊ *I haven't got very many CDs.* Ich habe nicht sehr viele CDs.
♦ **Not many.** Nicht viele.
♦ **How many?** Wie viele? ◊ *How many do you want?* Wie viele möchten Sie?
♦ **How many euros do you get for one pound?** Wie viel Euro bekommt man für ein Pfund?
♦ **too many** zu viele ◊ *That's too many.* Das sind zu viele. ◊ *She makes too many mistakes.* Sie macht zu viele Fehler.
♦ **so many** so viele ◊ *I didn't know that so many would come.* Ich wusste nicht, dass so viele kommen würden. ◊ *I've never seen so many policemen.* Ich habe noch nie so viele Polizisten gesehen.

map NOUN
1 (*of country, area*)
die <u>Landkarte</u>
2 (*of town*)
der <u>Stadtplan</u> (PL die Stadtpläne)
*Be careful not to translate **map** by **Mappe**.*

marathon NOUN
der <u>Marathonlauf</u> (PL die Marathonläufe) ◊ *the London marathon* der Londoner Marathonlauf

marble NOUN
der <u>Marmor</u> ◊ *a marble statue* eine Marmorstatue
♦ **to play marbles** Murmeln spielen

March NOUN
der <u>März</u> ◊ *in March* im März

march NOUN
see also **march** VERB
der <u>Protestmarsch</u> (*demonstration*) (GEN des Protestmarsches, PL die Protestmärsche)

to **march** VERB
see also **march** NOUN
1 (*soldiers*)
<u>marschieren</u> (PERFECT ist marschiert)
2 (*protesters*)
<u>aufmarschieren</u> (PERFECT ist aufmarschiert)

mare NOUN
die <u>Stute</u>

margarine NOUN
die <u>Margarine</u>

margin NOUN

M

☞

der <u>Rand</u> (PL die Ränder) ◊ *I wrote notes in the margin.* Ich schrieb Notizen an den Rand.

marijuana NOUN
das <u>Marihuana</u>

marital status NOUN
der <u>Familienstand</u>

mark NOUN
see also **mark** VERB
1 (*in school*)
die <u>Note</u> ◊ *I get good marks for German.* Ich habe in Deutsch gute Noten.
2 (*stain*)
der <u>Fleck</u> (PL die Flecken) ◊ *You've got a mark on your shirt.* Du hast einen Fleck auf dem Hemd.
3 (*old German currency*)
die <u>Mark</u> (PL die Mark)

to **mark** VERB
see also **mark** NOUN
<u>korrigieren</u> (PERFECT hat korrigiert) ◊ *The teacher hasn't marked my homework yet.* Der Lehrer hat meine Hausarbeit noch nicht korrigiert.

market NOUN
der <u>Markt</u> (PL die Märkte)

marketing NOUN
das <u>Marketing</u> (GEN des Marketing)

marketplace NOUN
der <u>Marktplatz</u> (GEN des Marktplatzes, PL die Marktplätze)

marmalade NOUN
die <u>Orangenmarmelade</u>

maroon ADJECTIVE
<u>burgunderrot</u> (*colour*)

marriage NOUN
die <u>Ehe</u>

married ADJECTIVE
<u>verheiratet</u> ◊ *They are not married.* Sie sind nicht verheiratet. ◊ *They have been married for fifteen years.* Sie sind seit fünfzehn Jahren verheiratet.
♦ **a married couple** ein Ehepaar NEUT

marrow NOUN
der <u>Kürbis</u> (*vegetable*) (GEN des Kürbisses, PL die Kürbisse)

to **marry** VERB
<u>heiraten</u> ◊ *He wants to marry her.* Er will sie heiraten.
♦ **to get married** heiraten ◊ *My sister's getting married in June.* Meine Schwester heiratet im Juni.

marvellous ADJECTIVE
<u>wunderbar</u> ◊ *She's a marvellous cook.* Sie ist eine wunderbare Köchin. ◊ *The weather was marvellous.* Das Wetter war wunderbar.

marzipan NOUN
der <u>Marzipan</u> (PL die Marzipane)

mascara NOUN
die <u>Wimperntusche</u>

masculine ADJECTIVE
<u>männlich</u>

mashed potatoes PL NOUN
der <u>Kartoffelbrei</u> ◊ *sausages and mashed potatoes* Würstchen mit Kartoffelbrei

mask NOUN
die <u>Maske</u>

masked ADJECTIVE
<u>maskiert</u> ◊ *a masked man* ein maskierter Mann

mass NOUN
1 der <u>Haufen</u> (PL die Haufen) ◊ *a mass of books and papers* ein Haufen Bücher und Papiere
2 (*in church*)
die <u>Messe</u> ◊ *We go to mass on Sunday.* Wir gehen am Sonntag zur Messe.
♦ **the mass media** die Massenmedien

massage NOUN
die <u>Massage</u>

massive ADJECTIVE
<u>enorm</u>

to **master** VERB
<u>beherrschen</u> (PERFECT hat beherrscht) ◊ *to master a language* eine Sprache beherrschen

masterpiece NOUN
das <u>Meisterstück</u> (PL die Meisterstücke)

mat NOUN
der <u>Vorleger</u> (*doormat*) (PL die Vorleger)
♦ **a table mat** ein Untersetzer MASC
♦ **a place mat** ein Set NEUT

match NOUN
see also **match** VERB
1 das <u>Streichholz</u> (GEN des Streichholzes, PL die Streichhölzer) ◊ *a box of matches* eine Schachtel Streichhölzer
2 (*sport*)
das <u>Spiel</u> (PL die Spiele) ◊ *a football match* ein Fußballspiel

to **match** VERB
see also **match** NOUN
<u>passen zu</u> ◊ *The jacket matches the trousers.* Die Jacke passt zu der Hose. ◊ *These colours don't match.* Diese Farben passen nicht zueinander.

matching ADJECTIVE
<u>farblich aufeinander abgestimmt</u> ◊ *My bedroom has matching wallpaper and curtains.* Mein Schlafzimmer hat farblich aufeinander abgestimmte Tapeten und Vorhänge.

mate NOUN
der <u>Kumpel</u> (*informal*) (PL die Kumpel)
der Kumpel is also used for women.
◊ *On Friday night I go out with my mates.* Freitag Abend gehe ich mit meinen Kumpels aus.

material NOUN

1 (*cloth*)
der Stoff (PL die Stoffe)
2 (*information, data*)
das Material (PL die Materialien) ◊ *I'm
collecting material for my project.* Ich
sammle Material für mein Referat.
♦ **raw materials** die Rohstoffe

mathematics SING NOUN
die Mathematik

maths SING NOUN
die Mathe

matron NOUN
die Oberschwester (*in hospital*)

matter NOUN
see also **matter** VERB
die Angelegenheit ◊ *It's a serious
matter.* Das ist eine ernste
Angelegenheit.
♦ **It's a matter of life and death.** Es geht
um Leben und Tod.
♦ **What's the matter?** Was ist los?
♦ **as a matter of fact** tatsächlich

to **matter** VERB
see also **matter** NOUN
♦ **it doesn't matter (1)** (*I don't mind*) das
macht nichts ◊ *I can't give you the
money today. – It doesn't matter.* Ich
kann dir das Geld heute nicht geben. –
Das macht nichts.
♦ **it doesn't matter (2)** (*makes no difference*)
das ist egal ◊ *Shall I phone today or
tomorrow? – Whenever, it doesn't
matter.* Soll ich heute oder morgen
anrufen? – Wann du willst, das ist egal.
♦ **It matters a lot to me.** Das ist mir sehr
wichtig.

mattress NOUN
die Matratze

mature ADJECTIVE
reif ◊ *She's very mature for her age.* Sie
ist sehr reif für ihr Alter.

maximum NOUN
see also **maximum** ADJECTIVE
das Maximum (PL die Maxima)

maximum ADJECTIVE
see also **maximum** NOUN
♦ **The maximum speed is a hundred
kilometres per hour.** Die
Höchstgeschwindigkeit beträgt hundert
Stundenkilometer.
♦ **the maximum amount** der Höchstbetrag

May NOUN
der Mai ◊ *in May* im Mai
♦ **May Day** der Erste Mai

may VERB
♦ **He may come.** Er kommt vielleicht. ◊ *It
may rain.* Es regnet vielleicht.
♦ **Are you going to the party? – I don't
know, I may.** Gehst du zur Party? – Ich
weiß nicht, vielleicht.
♦ **May I smoke?** Darf ich rauchen?

maybe ADVERB

vielleicht ◊ *maybe not* vielleicht nicht ◊ *a
bit boring, maybe* vielleicht etwas
langweilig ◊ *Maybe she's at home.*
Vielleicht ist sie zu Hause. ◊ *Maybe he'll
change his mind.* Vielleicht überlegt er es
sich anders.

mayonnaise NOUN
die Mayonnaise

mayor NOUN
der Bürgermeister (PL die Bürgermeister)
die Bürgermeisterin

maze NOUN
der Irrgarten (PL die Irrgärten)

me PRONOUN
1 mich ◊ *Can you hear me?* Kannst du
mich hören? ◊ *Look at me!* Sieh mich an!
*Use **mich** after prepositions which take
the accusative.*
◊ *Is this present for me?* Ist das
Geschenk für mich? ◊ *Wait for me!* Warte
auf mich!
2 mir
*Use **mir** after prepositions which take
the dative.*
◊ *Will you come with me?* Kommst du
mit mir mit? ◊ *He sat next to me.* Er saß
neben mir.
*Use **mir** when **me** means **to me**.*
◊ *Give me the book, please!* Gib mir bitte
das Buch! ◊ *She told me the truth.* Sie
hat mir die Wahrheit erzählt.
3 ich ◊ *It's me!* Ich bin's! ◊ *Me too!* Ich
auch! ◊ *She's older than me.* Sie ist älter
als ich.

meal NOUN
das Essen (PL die Essen)

mealtime NOUN
♦ **at mealtimes** zur Essenszeit

to **mean** VERB
see also **mean** ADJECTIVE AND **means** NOUN
1 (*signify*)
bedeuten (PERFECT hat bedeutet) ◊ *What
does "besetzt" mean?* Was bedeutet
"besetzt"? ◊ *I don't know what it means.*
Ich weiß nicht, was es bedeutet.
2 (*mean to say*)
meinen ◊ *What do you mean?* Was
meinst du damit? ◊ *That's not what I
meant.* Das habe ich nicht gemeint.
◊ *Which one do you mean?* Welchen
meinst du? ◊ *Do you really mean it?*
Meinst du das wirklich?
♦ **to mean to do something** etwas tun
wollen ◊ *I didn't mean to offend you.* Ich
wollte dich nicht kränken.

mean ADJECTIVE
see also **mean** VERB AND **means** NOUN
1 geizig (*with money*) ◊ *He's too mean to
buy Christmas presents.* Er ist zu geizig,
um Weihnachtsgeschenke zu kaufen.
2 gemein (*unkind*) ◊ *You're being mean
to me.* Du bist gemein zu mir. ◊ *That's a*

M

really mean thing to say! Das ist gemein,
so etwas zu sagen!

meaning NOUN
die Bedeutung
> *Be careful not to translate* **meaning** *by* **Meinung.**

means NOUN
see also **mean** VERB AND ADJECTIVE
1 die Möglichkeit ◊ *a means of storing power* eine Möglichkeit, Energie zu speichern ◊ *We have the means to do that.* Wir haben die Möglichkeit, das zu tun.
2 das Mittel (PL die Mittel) ◊ *We have the means to renovate the house.* Wir haben die Mittel, um das Haus zu renovieren. ◊ *a means of transport* ein Transportmittel NEUT
♦ *He'll do it by any possible means.* Er wird es tun, egal wie.
♦ **by means of** mit ◊ *He got in by means of a stolen key.* Er kam mit einem gestohlenen Schlüssel hinein.
♦ **by all means** selbstverständlich ◊ *Can I come? – By all means!* Kann ich kommen? – Selbstverständlich!
♦ **by no means** keineswegs ◊ *That was by no means the end of the matter.* Damit war die Sache keineswegs erledigt.

meant VERB *see* **mean**

meanwhile ADVERB
inzwischen

measles SING NOUN
die Masern PL ◊ *She's got measles.* Sie hat Masern.

to **measure** VERB
1 ausmessen (PRESENT misst aus, IMPERFECT maß aus, PERFECT hat ausgemessen) ◊ *I measured the page.* Ich habe die Seite ausgemessen.
2 messen ◊ *The room measures three metres by four.* Das Zimmer misst drei auf vier Meter.

measurement NOUN
das Maß (*of object*) (PL die Maße) ◊ *What are the measurements of the room?* Wie sind die Maße des Zimmers? ◊ *What are your measurements?* Was sind Ihre Maße?
♦ **my waist measurement** meine Taillenweite
♦ **What's your neck measurement?** Welche Kragenweite haben Sie?

meat NOUN
das Fleisch ◊ *I don't eat meat.* Ich esse kein Fleisch.

Mecca NOUN
Mekka NEUT

mechanic NOUN
der Mechaniker (PL die Mechaniker)
die Mechanikerin
◊ *He's a mechanic.* Er ist Mechaniker.

mechanical ADJECTIVE

mechanisch

medal NOUN
die Medaille
♦ **the gold medal** die Goldmedaille

media PL NOUN
die Medien NEUT PL

median strip NOUN US
der Mittelstreifen (PL die Mittelstreifen)

medical ADJECTIVE
see also **medical** NOUN
medizinisch ◊ *medical treatment* die medizinische Behandlung
♦ **medical insurance** die Krankenversicherung
♦ **to have medical problems** gesundheitliche Probleme haben
♦ **She's a medical student.** Sie ist Medizinstudentin.

medical NOUN
see also **medical** ADJECTIVE
♦ **to have a medical** sich ärztlich untersuchen lassen

medicine NOUN
die Medizin ◊ *I want to study medicine.* Ich möchte Medizin studieren.
◊ *alternative medicine* die alternative Medizin ◊ *I need some medicine.* Ich brauche Medizin.

Mediterranean ADJECTIVE
südländisch (*person, character, scenery*)
♦ **the Mediterranean** das Mittelmeer

medium ADJECTIVE
mittlere ◊ *a man of medium height* ein Mann von mittlerer Größe

medium-sized ADJECTIVE
mittelgroß ◊ *a medium-sized town* eine mittelgroße Stadt

to **meet** VERB
1 (*by chance*)
treffen (PRESENT trifft, IMPERFECT traf, PERFECT hat getroffen) ◊ *I met Paul when I was walking the dog.* Ich habe Paul getroffen, als ich mit dem Hund spazieren war.
2 (*by arrangement*)
sich treffen ◊ *Let's meet in front of the tourist office.* Treffen wir uns doch vor dem Verkehrsbüro. ◊ *I'm going to meet my friends.* Ich treffe mich mit meinen Freunden.
3 (*get to know*)
kennenlernen (PERFECT hat kennengelernt)
◊ *I like meeting new people.* Ich lerne gerne neue Leute kennen.
♦ **Have you met him before?** Kennen Sie ihn?
4 (*pick up*)
abholen (PERFECT hat abgeholt) ◊ *I'll meet you at the station.* Ich hole dich am Bahnhof ab.

meeting NOUN
1 (*for work*)
die Besprechung ◊ *a business meeting* eine geschäftliche Besprechung

2 (*socially*)
das <u>Treffen</u> (PL die Treffen) ◊ *their first meeting* ihr erstes Treffen

mega ADJECTIVE
♦**He's mega rich.** Er ist superreich.
(*informal*)

melody NOUN
die <u>Melodie</u>

melon NOUN
die <u>Melone</u>

to **melt** VERB
<u>schmelzen</u> (PRESENT schmilzt, IMPERFECT schmolz, PERFECT ist geschmolzen) ◊ *The snow is melting.* Der Schnee schmilzt.

member NOUN
das <u>Mitglied</u> (PL die Mitglieder)
♦**a Member of Parliament (1)** (*man*) ein Abgeordneter
♦**a Member of Parliament (2)** (*woman*) eine Abgeordnete

membership NOUN
die <u>Mitgliedschaft</u> (*of party, union*) ◊ *I'm going to apply for membership.* Ich werde mich um Mitgliedschaft bewerben.

membership card NOUN
der <u>Mitgliedsausweis</u> (PL die Mitgliedsausweise)

memento NOUN
das <u>Andenken</u> (PL die Andenken)

memorial NOUN
das <u>Denkmal</u> (PL die Denkmäler) ◊ *a war memorial* ein Kriegerdenkmal

to **memorize** VERB
<u>auswendig lernen</u>

memory NOUN
1 das <u>Gedächtnis</u> (GEN des Gedächtnisses) ◊ *I haven't got a good memory.* Ich habe kein gutes Gedächtnis.
2 (*recollection*)
die <u>Erinnerung</u> ◊ *to bring back memories* Erinnerungen wachrufen
3 (*computer*)
der <u>Speicher</u> (GEN die Speicher)

men PL NOUN *see* **man**

to **mend** VERB
<u>flicken</u>

meningitis NOUN
die <u>Hirnhautentzündung</u>

mental ADJECTIVE
1 <u>geistig</u>
♦**a mental illness** eine Geisteskrankheit
2 <u>wahnsinnig</u> (*mad*) ◊ *You're mental!* Du bist wahnsinnig!
♦**a mental hospital** eine psychiatrische Klinik

to **mention** VERB
<u>erwähnen</u> (PERFECT hat erwähnt)
♦**Thank you! – Don't mention it!** Danke! – Bitte!

menu NOUN

1 die <u>Speisekarte</u> ◊ *Could I have the menu please?* Könnte ich bitte die Speisekarte haben?
2 (*on computer*)
das <u>Menü</u> (PL die Menüs)

merchant NOUN
der <u>Händler</u> (PL die Händler)
die <u>Händlerin</u>
◊ *a wine merchant* ein Weinhändler

mercy NOUN
die <u>Gnade</u>

mere ADJECTIVE
<u>bloß</u> ◊ *It's a mere formality.* Das ist eine bloße Formalität.
♦**a mere five percent** ganze fünf Prozent

meringue NOUN
die <u>Meringe</u>

merry ADJECTIVE
♦**Merry Christmas!** Fröhliche Weihnachten!

merry-go-round NOUN
das <u>Karussell</u> (PL die Karussells)

mess NOUN
die <u>Unordnung</u> ◊ *His bedroom's always in a mess.* In seinem Schlafzimmer herrscht ständig Unordnung.

to **mess about** VERB
♦**to mess about with something** (*interfere with*) an etwas herumfummeln ◊ *Stop messing about with my computer!* Hör auf, an meinem Computer herumzufummeln!
♦**Don't mess about with my things!** Lass meine Sachen in Ruhe!

to **mess up** VERB
♦**to mess something up** etwas durcheinanderbringen ◊ *My little brother has messed up my cassettes.* Mein kleiner Bruder hat meine Kassetten durcheinandergebracht.

message NOUN
die <u>Nachricht</u>

messenger NOUN
der <u>Bote</u> (GEN des Boten, PL die Boten)
die <u>Botin</u>

messy ADJECTIVE
1 <u>schmutzig</u> (*dirty*) ◊ *a messy job* eine schmutzige Arbeit
2 <u>unordentlich</u> (*untidy*) ◊ *Your room's really messy.* Dein Zimmer ist wirklich unordentlich. ◊ *She's so messy!* Sie ist so unordentlich!
♦**My writing is terribly messy.** Ich habe eine schreckliche Schrift.

met VERB *see* **meet**

metal NOUN
das <u>Metall</u> (PL die Metalle)

meter NOUN
1 (*for gas, electricity, taxi*)
der <u>Zähler</u> (PL die Zähler)
2 (*parking meter*)
die <u>Parkuhr</u>

method NOUN

M

☞

die <u>Methode</u>
Methodist NOUN
  der <u>Methodist</u> (GEN des Methodisten, PL
  die Methodisten)
  die <u>Methodistin</u>
  ◊ *She's a Methodist.* Sie ist Methodistin.
metre NOUN
  der <u>Meter</u> (PL die Meter)
metric ADJECTIVE
  <u>metrisch</u>
Mexico NOUN
  <u>Mexiko</u> NEUT
  ♦**from Mexico** aus Mexiko
  ♦**to Mexico** nach Mexiko
to **miaow** VERB
  <u>miauen</u> (PERFECT hat miaut)
mice PL NOUN *see* **mouse**
microchip NOUN
  der <u>Mikrochip</u> (PL die Mikrochips)
microphone NOUN
  das <u>Mikrofon</u> (PL die Mikrofone)
microscope NOUN
  das <u>Mikroskop</u> (PL die Mikroskope)
microwave NOUN
  die <u>Mikrowelle</u>
microwave oven NOUN
  der <u>Mikrowellenherd</u> (PL die
  Mikrowellenherde)
mid ADJECTIVE
  ♦**in mid May** Mitte Mai
midday NOUN
  der <u>Mittag</u> (PL die Mittage)
  ♦**at midday** um zwölf Uhr mittags
middle NOUN
  die <u>Mitte</u>
  ♦**in the middle of the road** mitten auf der
  Straße
  ♦**in the middle of the night** mitten in der
  Nacht
  ♦**the middle seat** der mittlere Sitz
middle-aged ADJECTIVE
  <u>mittleren Alters</u> ◊ *a middle-aged man*
  ein Mann mittleren Alters ◊ *She's*
  middle-aged. Sie ist mittleren Alters.
Middle Ages PL NOUN
  ♦**the Middle Ages** das Mittelalter
middle-class ADJECTIVE
  ♦**a middle-class family** eine Familie der
  Mittelschicht
Middle East NOUN
  der <u>Nahe Osten</u> ◊ *in the Middle East* im
  Nahen Osten
middle name NOUN
  der <u>zweite Vorname</u> (GEN des zweiten
  Vornamens, PL die zweiten Vornamen)
midge NOUN
  die <u>Mücke</u>
midnight NOUN
  die <u>Mitternacht</u>
  ♦**at midnight** um Mitternacht
midwife NOUN

die <u>Hebamme</u> ◊ *She's a midwife.* Sie ist
Hebamme.
might VERB
  Use **vielleicht** to express possibility.
  ◊ *He might come later.* Er kommt
  vielleicht später. ◊ *We might go to Spain*
  next year. Wir fahren nächstes Jahr
  vielleicht nach Spanien. ◊ *She might not*
  have understood. Sie hat es vielleicht
  nicht verstanden.
migraine NOUN
  die <u>Migräne</u> ◊ *I've got a migraine.* Ich
  habe Migräne.
mike NOUN
  das <u>Mikro</u> (PL die Mikros)
mild ADJECTIVE
  <u>mild</u> ◊ *The winters are quite mild.* Die
  Winter sind ziemlich mild.
mile NOUN
  die <u>Meile</u>

> ⓘ *In Germany distances and speeds*
> *are expressed in kilometres. A mile is*
> *about 1.6 kilometres.*

  ◊ *It's five miles from here.* Es ist acht
  Kilometer von hier. ◊ *at fifty miles per*
  hour mit achtzig Kilometern pro Stunde
  ♦**We walked miles!** Wir sind meilenweit
  gegangen!
military ADJECTIVE
  <u>militärisch</u>
milk NOUN
  see also **milk** VERB
  die <u>Milch</u> ◊ *tea with milk* der Tee mit
  Milch
to **milk** VERB
  see also **milk** NOUN
  <u>melken</u> (PERFECT hat gemolken)
milk chocolate NOUN
  die <u>Milchschokolade</u>
milkman NOUN
  der <u>Milchmann</u> (PL die Milchmänner)
  ◊ *He's a milkman.* Er ist Milchmann.
milk shake NOUN
  der <u>Milchshake</u> (PL die Milchshakes)
mill NOUN
  die <u>Mühle</u> (*for grain*)
millennium NOUN
  das <u>Jahrtausend</u>
millimetre NOUN
  der <u>Millimeter</u> (PL die Millimeter)
million NOUN
  die <u>Million</u>
millionaire NOUN
  der <u>Millionär</u> (PL die Millionäre)
  die <u>Millionärin</u>
to **mimic** VERB
  <u>nachmachen</u> (PERFECT hat nachgemacht)
mince NOUN
  das <u>Hackfleisch</u>
to **mind** VERB

see also **mind** NOUN

aufpassen auf +ACC (PERFECT hat
aufgepasst) ◊ *Could you mind the baby
this afternoon?* Kannst du heute
Nachmittag auf das Baby aufpassen?
◊ *Could you mind my bags for a few
minutes?* Können Sie für ein paar
Minuten auf mein Gepäck aufpassen?
♦ **Do you mind if I open the window?**
Macht es Ihnen etwas aus, wenn ich das
Fenster aufmache?
♦ **I don't mind.** Es macht mir nichts aus. ◊ *I
don't mind the noise.* Der Lärm macht
mir nichts aus.
♦ **Never mind!** Macht nichts!
♦ **Mind that bike!** Pass auf das Fahrrad
auf!
♦ **Mind the step!** Vorsicht Stufe!

mind NOUN

see also **mind** VERB

♦ **to make up one's mind** sich entscheiden
◊ *I haven't made up my mind yet.* Ich
habe mich noch nicht entschieden.
♦ **to change one's mind** es sich anders
überlegen ◊ *I've changed my mind.* Ich
habe es mir anders überlegt.
♦ **Are you out of your mind?** Bist du
wahnsinnig?

mine PRONOUN

see also **mine** NOUN

1 meiner ◊ *Is this your coat? – No,
mine's black.* Ist das dein Mantel? – Nein,
meiner ist schwarz.
meine ◊ *Is this your cup? – No, mine's
red.* Ist das deine Tasse? – Nein, meine
ist rot.
meines ◊ *Is this your car? – No, mine's
green.* Ist das dein Auto? – Nein, meines
ist grün.
2 meine ◊ *her parents and mine* ihre
Eltern und meine ◊ *Your hands are dirty,
mine are clean.* Deine Hände sind
schmutzig, meine sind sauber.
♦ **It's mine.** Das gehört mir. ◊ *This book is
mine.* Dieses Buch gehört mir. ◊ *Whose
is this? – It's mine.* Wem gehört das? – Es
gehört mir.

mine NOUN

see also **mine** PRONOUN

die Mine ◊ *a land mine* eine Landmine
♦ **a coal mine** ein Kohlebergwerk NEUT

miner NOUN
der Bergarbeiter (PL die Bergarbeiter)

mineral water NOUN
das Mineralwasser (PL die
Mineralwasser)

miniature NOUN
die Miniatur

minibus NOUN
der Minibus (GEN des Minibusses, PL die
Minibusse)

minicab NOUN
das Kleintaxi (PL die Kleintaxis)

Minidisc ® NOUN
die Minidisc ® (PL die Minidiscs)

minimum NOUN

see also **minimum** ADJECTIVE

das Minimum (PL die Minima)

minimum ADJECTIVE

see also **minimum** NOUN

♦ **minimum age** das Mindestalter
♦ **minimum amount** der Mindestbetrag
♦ **minimum wage** der Mindestlohn

miniskirt NOUN
der Minirock (PL die Miniröcke)

minister NOUN
1 (*in government*)
der Minister (PL die Minister)
die Ministerin
2 (*of church*)
der Pfarrer (PL die Pfarrer)
die Pfarrerin

ministry NOUN
das Ministerium (*in politics*) (PL die
Ministerien)

mink NOUN
der Nerz ◊ *a mink coat* ein Nerzmantel
MASC

minor ADJECTIVE
kleiner ◊ *a minor problem* ein kleineres
Problem ◊ *a minor operation* eine
kleinere Operation
♦ **in D minor** in d-Moll

minority NOUN
die Minderheit

mint NOUN
1 (*plant*)
die Pfefferminze ◊ *mint sauce* die
Pfefferminzsoße
2 (*sweet*)
das Pfefferminzbonbon (PL die
Pfefferminzbonbons)

minus PREPOSITION
minus ◊ *Sixteen minus three is thirteen.*
Sechzehn minus drei ist dreizehn. ◊ *It's
minus two degrees outside.* Draußen
hat es zwei Grad minus. ◊ *I got a B
minus.* Ich habe eine Zwei minus
bekommen.

ⓘ *In Germany, grades are given from
1 to 6, with 1 being the best.*

minute NOUN

see also **minute** ADJECTIVE

die Minute
♦ **Wait a minute!** Einen Augenblick!

minute ADJECTIVE

see also **minute** NOUN

winzig ◊ *Her flat is minute.* Ihre
Wohnung ist winzig.

miracle NOUN
das Wunder (PL die Wunder)

mirror NOUN
der Spiegel (PL die Spiegel)

to **misbehave** VERB

M

☞

sich schlecht benehmen (PRESENT benimmt sich schlecht, IMPERFECT benahm sich schlecht, PERFECT hat sich schlecht benommen)

miscellaneous ADJECTIVE

verschieden ◊ *miscellaneous items* verschiedene Artikel

mischief NOUN

die Dummheiten FEM PL ◊ *My little sister's always up to mischief.* Meine kleine Schwester macht dauernd Dummheiten.

mischievous ADJECTIVE

verschmitzt

miser NOUN

der Geizhals (GEN des Geizhalses, PL die Geizhälse)

miserable ADJECTIVE

① unglücklich (*person*) ◊ *You're looking miserable.* Du siehst richtig unglücklich aus.

② schrecklich (*weather*) ◊ *The weather was miserable.* Das Wetter war schrecklich.

♦ **to feel miserable** sich miserabel fühlen ◊ *I'm feeling miserable.* Ich fühle mich miserabel.

misery NOUN

① das Elend ◊ *All that money brought nothing but misery.* All das Geld hat nichts als Elend gebracht.

② der Miesepeter (*informal*) (PL die Miesepeter) ◊ *She's a real misery.* Sie ist ein richtiger Miesepeter.

misfortune NOUN

das Unglück (PL die Unglücke)

mishap NOUN

das Missgeschick (PL die Missgeschicke)

to **misjudge** VERB

falsch einschätzen (*person*) (PERFECT hat falsch eingeschätzt) ◊ *I've misjudged her.* Ich habe sie falsch eingeschätzt.

♦ **He misjudged the bend.** Er hat sich in der Kurve verschätzt.

to **mislay** VERB

verlegen (PERFECT hat verlegt) ◊ *I've mislaid my passport.* Ich habe meinen Pass verlegt.

to **mislead** VERB

irreführen (PERFECT hat irregeführt)

misleading ADJECTIVE

irreführend

misprint NOUN

der Druckfehler (PL die Druckfehler)

Miss NOUN

das Fräulein

> ⓘ *Nowadays it is regarded as old-fashioned to call somebody **Fräulein** and **Frau** is used instead.*

◊ *Miss Jones* Frau Jones

to **miss** VERB

verpassen (PERFECT hat verpasst) ◊ *Hurry or you'll miss the bus.* Beeil dich, sonst verpasst du den Bus! ◊ *to miss an opportunity* eine Gelegenheit verpassen

♦ **I miss you.** Du fehlst mir. ◊ *I'm missing my family.* Meine Familie fehlt mir.

♦ **He missed the target.** Er hat nicht getroffen.

missing ADJECTIVE

fehlend ◊ *the missing part* das fehlende Teil

♦ **to be missing** fehlen ◊ *My rucksack is missing.* Mein Rucksack fehlt. ◊ *Two members of the group are missing.* Zwei Mitglieder der Gruppe fehlen.

missionary NOUN

der Missionar (PL die Missionare) die Missionarin

mist NOUN

der Nebel (PL die Nebel)

*Be careful not to translate **mist** by the German word **Mist**.*

mistake NOUN

see also **mistake** VERB

der Fehler (PL die Fehler) ◊ *It was a mistake to buy those yellow shoes.* Es war ein Fehler, diese gelben Schuhe zu kaufen. ◊ *a spelling mistake* ein Rechtschreibfehler

♦ **to make a mistake (1)** (*in writing, speaking*) einen Fehler machen

♦ **to make a mistake (2)** (*get mixed up*) sich vertun ◊ *I'm sorry, I made a mistake.* Tut mir leid, ich habe mich vertan.

♦ **by mistake** aus Versehen ◊ *I took his bag by mistake.* Ich habe aus Versehen seine Tasche genommen.

to **mistake** VERB

see also **mistake** NOUN

♦ **He mistook me for my sister.** Er hat mich mit meiner Schwester verwechselt.

mistaken ADJECTIVE

♦ **to be mistaken** sich irren ◊ *If you think I'm going to get up at six o'clock, you're mistaken.* Wenn du meinst, ich würde um sechs Uhr aufstehen, dann irrst du dich.

mistakenly ADVERB

irrtümlicherweise

mistletoe NOUN

die Mistel

mistook VERB *see* **mistake**

mistress NOUN

① (*teacher*) die Lehrerin ◊ *our German mistress* unsere Deutschlehrerin

② (*lover*) die Geliebte (GEN der Geliebten) ◊ *He's got a mistress.* Er hat eine Geliebte.

to **mistrust** VERB

misstrauen (PERFECT hat misstraut) ◊ *I mistrust her.* Ich misstraue ihr.

misty ADJECTIVE

neblig ◊ *a misty morning* ein nebliger Morgen

to **misunderstand** VERB
missverstehen (IMPERFECT missverstand, PERFECT hat missverstanden) ◊ *Sorry, I misunderstood you.* Entschuldigung, ich habe Sie missverstanden.

misunderstanding NOUN
das Missverständnis (GEN des Missverständnisses, PL die Missverständnisse)

misunderstood VERB *see* **misunderstand**

mix NOUN
see also **mix** VERB
die Mischung ◊ *It's a mix of science fiction and comedy.* Es ist eine Mischung aus Science-Fiction und Komödie.
♦ **a cake mix** eine Backmischung

to **mix** VERB
see also **mix** NOUN
1 vermischen (PERFECT hat vermischt) ◊ *Mix the flour with the sugar.* Vermischen Sie das Mehl mit dem Zucker.
2 verbinden (IMPERFECT verband, PERFECT hat verbunden) ◊ *He's mixing business with pleasure.* Er verbindet das Geschäftliche mit dem Vergnügen.
♦ **to mix with somebody** (*associate*) mit jemandem verkehren
♦ **He doesn't mix much.** Er geht nicht viel unter Menschen.
♦ **to mix up** verwechseln ◊ *He always mixes me up with my sister.* Er verwechselt mich immer mit meiner Schwester. ◊ *The travel agent mixed up the bookings.* Das Reisebüro hat die Buchungen verwechselt.
♦ **I'm getting mixed up.** Ich werde ganz konfus.

mixed ADJECTIVE
gemischt ◊ *a mixed salad* ein gemischter Salat ◊ *a mixed school* eine gemischte Schule
♦ **a mixed grill** ein Grillteller MASC

mixer NOUN
der Mixer (*for food*) (PL die Mixer)

mixture NOUN
die Mischung ◊ *a mixture of spices* eine Gewürzmischung
♦ **cough mixture** der Hustensaft

mix-up NOUN
die Verwechslung

to **moan** VERB
sich beklagen (PERFECT hat sich beklagt) ◊ *She's always moaning.* Sie beklagt sich dauernd.

mobile NOUN
(*phone*)
das Handy (PL die Handys)

mobile home NOUN
das Wohnmobil (PL die Wohnmobile)

to **mock** VERB

see also **mock** ADJECTIVE
sich lustig machen über +ACC ◊ *Stop mocking him!* Mach dich nicht über ihn lustig!

mock ADJECTIVE
see also **mock** VERB
♦ **a mock exam** eine Übungsprüfung

mod cons PL NOUN
♦ **with all mod cons** mit allem Komfort

model NOUN
see also **model** ADJECTIVE, VERB
1 das Modell (PL die Modelle) ◊ *His car is the latest model.* Sein Auto ist das neueste Modell. ◊ *a model of the castle* ein Modell der Burg
2 (*fashion*)
das Mannequin (PL die Mannequins) ◊ *She's a famous model.* Sie ist ein berühmtes Mannequin.

model ADJECTIVE
see also **model** NOUN, VERB
♦ **a model plane** ein Modellflugzeug NEUT
♦ **a model railway** eine Modelleisenbahn
♦ **He's a model pupil.** Er ist ein vorbildlicher Schüler.

to **model** VERB
see also **model** NOUN, ADJECTIVE
als Model arbeiten ◊ *She was modelling in New York.* Sie arbeitete in New York als Model.
♦ **She was modelling a Paul Costello outfit.** Sie führte ein Outfit von Paul Costello vor.

modem NOUN
das Modem (PL die Modems)

moderate ADJECTIVE
gemäßigt ◊ *His views are quite moderate.* Er hat sehr gemäßigte Ansichten.
♦ **a moderate amount of alcohol** wenig Alkohol
♦ **a moderate price** ein annehmbarer Preis

modern ADJECTIVE
modern

to **modernize** VERB
modernisieren (PERFECT hat modernisiert)

modest ADJECTIVE
bescheiden

to **modify** VERB
ändern

moist ADJECTIVE
feucht ◊ *This cake is very moist.* Dieser Kuchen ist sehr feucht. ◊ *Sow the seeds in moist compost.* Säen Sie den Samen in feuchten Kompost.

moisture NOUN
die Feuchtigkeit

moisturizer NOUN
1 (*cream*)
die Feuchtigkeitscreme (PL die Feuchtigkeitscremes)
2 (*lotion*)

M

die <u>Feuchtigkeitslotion</u>
moldy ADJECTIVE US
<u>schimmlig</u>
mole NOUN
[1] (*animal*)
der <u>Maulwurf</u> (PL die Maulwürfe)
[2] (*on skin*)
der <u>Leberfleck</u> (PL die Leberflecke)
moment NOUN
der <u>Augenblick</u> (PL die Augenblicke)
◊ *Could you wait a moment?* Können Sie einen Augenblick warten? ◊ *in a moment* in einem Augenblick ◊ *Just a moment!* Einen Augenblick!
♦ **at the moment** momentan
♦ **any moment now** jeden Moment
◊ *They'll be arriving any moment now.* Sie können jeden Moment kommen.
momentous ADJECTIVE
<u>bedeutsam</u>
monarch NOUN
der <u>Monarch</u> (GEN des Monarchen, PL die Monarchen)
die <u>Monarchin</u>
monarchy NOUN
die <u>Monarchie</u>
monastery NOUN
das <u>Kloster</u> (PL die Klöster)
Monday NOUN
der <u>Montag</u> (PL die Montage) ◊ *on Monday* am Montag ◊ *every Monday* jeden Montag ◊ *last Monday* letzten Montag ◊ *next Monday* nächsten Montag
♦ **on Mondays** montags
money NOUN
das <u>Geld</u> (PL die Gelder) ◊ *I need to change some money.* Ich muss Geld wechseln.
♦ **to make money** Geld verdienen
mongrel NOUN
die <u>Promenadenmischung</u> ◊ *My dog's a mongrel.* Mein Hund ist eine Promenadenmischung.
monitor NOUN
der <u>Monitor</u> (*of computer*) (PL die Monitore)
monk NOUN
der <u>Mönch</u> (PL die Mönche)
monkey NOUN
der <u>Affe</u> (GEN des Affen, PL die Affen)
monopoly NOUN
das <u>Monopol</u>
♦ **to play Monopoly** ® Monopoly spielen
monotonous ADJECTIVE
<u>monoton</u>
monster NOUN
das <u>Monster</u> (PL die Monster)
month NOUN
der <u>Monat</u> (PL die Monate) ◊ *this month* diesen Monat ◊ *next month* nächsten Monat ◊ *last month* letzten Monat ◊ *every month* jeden Monat ◊ *at the end of the month* Ende des Monats

monthly ADJECTIVE
<u>monatlich</u>
monument NOUN
das <u>Denkmal</u> (PL die Denkmäler)
mood NOUN
die <u>Laune</u>
♦ **to be in a bad mood** schlechte Laune haben
♦ **to be in a good mood** gute Laune haben
moody ADJECTIVE
[1] <u>launisch</u> (*temperamental*)
[2] <u>schlecht gelaunt</u> (*in a bad mood*)
moon NOUN
der <u>Mond</u> (PL die Monde)
♦ **There's a full moon tonight.** Heute ist Vollmond.
♦ **to be over the moon** (*happy*) überglücklich sein
moor NOUN
┌─────────────────────┐
│ *see also* **moor** VERB │
└─────────────────────┘
das <u>Moor</u> (PL die Moore)
to **moor** VERB
┌─────────────────────┐
│ *see also* **moor** NOUN │
└─────────────────────┘
<u>festmachen</u> (*boat*) (PERFECT hat festgemacht)
mop NOUN
der <u>Mopp</u> (PL die Mopps) (*for floor*)
moped NOUN
das <u>Moped</u> (PL die Mopeds)
moral ADJECTIVE
┌─────────────────────┐
│ *see also* **moral** NOUN │
└─────────────────────┘
<u>moralisch</u>
moral NOUN
┌──────────────────────────┐
│ *see also* **moral** ADJECTIVE │
└──────────────────────────┘
die <u>Moral</u> ◊ *the moral of the story* die Moral der Geschichte
♦ **morals** die Moral SING
morale NOUN
die <u>Stimmung</u> ◊ *Their morale is very low.* Ihre Stimmung ist sehr schlecht.
more ADJECTIVE, PRONOUN, ADVERB
<u>mehr</u> ◊ *a bit more* etwas mehr ◊ *There are more girls in the class.* In der Klasse sind mehr Mädchen.
♦ **more than** mehr als ◊ *She practises more than I do.* Sie übt mehr als ich. ◊ *I spent more than two hundred euros.* Ich habe mehr als zweihundert Euro ausgegeben. ◊ *More girls than boys do German.* Mehr Mädchen als Jungen lernen Deutsch.

In comparisons you usually add **-er** *to the adjective.*

◊ *Could you speak more slowly?* Könnten Sie langsamer sprechen? ◊ *He's more intelligent than me.* Er ist intelligenter als ich. ◊ *Beer is more expensive in Britain.* Bier ist in Großbritannien teurer.

When referring to an additional amount, over and above what there already is, you usually use **noch**.

◊ *Is there any more?* Gibt es noch mehr?
◊ *Would you like some more?* Möchten
Sie noch etwas? ◊ *It'll take a few more
days.* Es braucht noch ein paar Tage.
◊ *Could I have some more chips?* Kann
ich noch Pommes frites haben? ◊ *Do you
want some more tea?* Möchten sie noch
Tee?
♦ **There isn't any more.** Es ist nichts mehr
da.
♦ **more or less** mehr oder weniger
♦ **more than ever** mehr denn je
moreover ADVERB
<u>außerdem</u>
morning NOUN
der <u>Morgen</u> (PL die Morgen) ◊ *every
morning* jeden Morgen
♦ **this morning** heute Morgen
♦ **tomorrow morning** morgen früh ◊ *I have
to get up at six tomorrow morning.* Ich
muss morgen früh um sechs aufstehen.
♦ **in the morning** morgens ◊ *at seven
o'clock in the morning* um sieben Uhr
morgens
♦ **a morning paper** eine Morgenzeitung
Morocco NOUN
<u>Marokko</u> NEUT
♦ **from Morocco** auf Marokko
♦ **to Morocco** nach Marokko
mortgage NOUN
die <u>Hypothek</u> (PL die Hypotheken)
Moscow NOUN
<u>Moskau</u> NEUT
♦ **to Moscow** nach Moskau
Moslem NOUN
der <u>Moslem</u> (PL die Moslems)
die <u>Moslime</u>
◊ *He's a Moslem.* Er ist Moslem.
mosque NOUN
die <u>Moschee</u>
mosquito NOUN
die <u>Stechmücke</u>
♦ **a mosquito bite** ein Mückenstich MASC
most ADVERB, ADJECTIVE, PRONOUN
  1 die <u>meisten</u> ◊ *most of my friends* die
meisten meiner Freunde ◊ *most of them*
die meisten von ihnen ◊ *most people* die
meisten Menschen ◊ *Most cats are
affectionate.* Die meisten Katzen sind
anhänglich.
  2 am <u>meisten</u> ◊ *what I hate most* was
ich am meisten hasse
♦ **most of the time** meist
♦ **most of the evening** fast den ganzen
Abend
♦ **most of the money** fast das ganze Geld
♦ **the most** am meisten ◊ *He's the one who
talks the most.* Er ist derjenige, der am
meisten redet.
♦ **to make the most of something** das
Beste aus etwas machen
♦ **at the most** höchstens ◊ *Two hours at
the most.* Höchstens zwei Stunden.

For the superlative you usually add **-ste**
to the adjective.
◊ *the most expensive seat* der teuerste
Platz ◊ *the most boring work* die
langweiligste Arbeit ◊ *the most
expensive restaurant* das teuerste
Restaurant
mostly ADVERB
♦ **The teachers are mostly quite nice.** Die
meisten unserer Lehrer sind ganz nett.
MOT NOUN
der <u>TÜV</u> (= Technischer
Überwachungsverein) ◊ *My car failed its
MOT.* Mein Auto ist nicht durch den TÜV
gekommen.
motel NOUN
das <u>Motel</u> (PL die Motels)
moth NOUN
die <u>Motte</u>
mother NOUN
die <u>Mutter</u> (PL die Mütter) ◊ *my mother*
meine Mutter
♦ **mother tongue** die Muttersprache
mother-in-law NOUN
die <u>Schwiegermutter</u> (PL die
Schwiegermütter)
Mother's Day NOUN
der <u>Muttertag</u> (PL die Muttertage)

ⓘ *In Germany* **Muttertag** *is on the
second Sunday in May.*

M

motionless ADJECTIVE
<u>bewegungslos</u>
motivated ADJECTIVE
<u>motiviert</u> ◊ *He is highly motivated.* Er ist
höchst motiviert.
motivation NOUN
die <u>Motivation</u>
motive NOUN
das <u>Motiv</u> (PL die Motive) ◊ *the motive
for the killing* das Motiv für den Mord
motor NOUN
der <u>Motor</u> (PL die Motoren) ◊ *The boat
has a motor.* Das Boot hat einen Motor.
motorbike NOUN
das <u>Motorrad</u> (PL die Motorräder)
motorboat NOUN
das <u>Motorboot</u> (PL die Motorboote)
motorcycle NOUN
das <u>Motorrad</u> (PL die Motorräder)
motorcyclist NOUN
der <u>Motorradfahrer</u> (PL die
Motorradfahrer)
die <u>Motorradfahrerin</u>
motorist NOUN
der <u>Autofahrer</u> (PL die Autofahrer)
die <u>Autofahrerin</u>
motor mechanic NOUN
der <u>Automechaniker</u> (PL die
Automechaniker)
die <u>Automechanikerin</u>
motor racing NOUN

das Autorennen (PL die Autorennen)
motorway NOUN
die Autobahn
mouldy ADJECTIVE
schimmlig
mountain NOUN
der Berg (PL die Berge)
♦ **a mountain bike** ein Mountainbike
NEUT
mountaineer NOUN
der Bergsteiger (PL die Bergsteiger)
die Bergsteigerin
mountaineering NOUN
das Bergsteigen
♦ **I go mountaineering.** Ich gehe
bergsteigen.
mountainous ADJECTIVE
bergig
mouse NOUN
die Maus (also for computer) (PL die
Mäuse) ◊ white mice weiße Mäuse
mouse mat NOUN
das Mousepad (computer) (PL die
Mousepads)
mousse NOUN
1 (food)
die Creme (PL die Cremes) ◊ chocolate
mousse die Schokoladencreme
2 (for hair)
der Schaumfestiger
moustache NOUN
der Schnurrbart (PL die Schnurrbärte)
◊ He's got a moustache. Er hat einen
Schnurrbart.
mouth NOUN
der Mund (PL die Münder)
mouthful NOUN
der Bissen (PL die Bissen)
mouth organ NOUN
die Mundharmonika (PL die
Mundharmonikas) ◊ I play the mouth
organ. Ich spiele Mundharmonika.
mouthwash NOUN
das Mundwasser (PL die Mundwasser)
move NOUN
see also **move** VERB
1 der Zug (PL die Züge) ◊ That was a
good move. Das war ein guter Zug.
♦ **It's your move.** Du bist dran.
2 der Umzug (PL die Umzüge) ◊ our
move from Oxford to Luton unser
Umzug von Oxford nach Luton
♦ **to get a move on** schneller machen
♦ **Get a move on!** Nun mach schon!
to **move** VERB
see also **move** NOUN
1 bewegen (PERFECT hat bewegt) ◊ I can't
move my arm. Ich kann den Arm nicht
bewegen. ◊ I was very moved by the
film. Der Film hat mich sehr bewegt.
♦ **Could you move your stuff?** Könntest du
dein Zeug wegtun?

♦ **Could you move your car?** Könnten Sie
Ihr Auto wegfahren?
2 sich bewegen ◊ Try not to move.
Versuche, dich nicht zu bewegen.
♦ **Don't move!** Keine Bewegung!
3 (vehicle)
fahren (PRESENT fährt, IMPERFECT fuhr, PERFECT
ist gefahren) ◊ The car was moving very
slowly. Das Auto fuhr sehr langsam.
♦ **to move house** umziehen ◊ She's
moving in July. Sie zieht im Juli um.
♦ **to move forward** sich vorwärtsbewegen
♦ **to move in** einziehen ◊ They're moving
in tomorrow. Sie ziehen morgen ein.
♦ **to move over** rücken ◊ Could you move
over a bit? Könnten Sie ein Stückchen
rücken?
movement NOUN
die Bewegung
movie NOUN
der Film (PL die Filme)
♦ **the movies** das Kino SING ◊ Let's go to the
movies! Lass uns ins Kino gehen!
moving ADJECTIVE
1 fahrend (not stationary) ◊ a moving bus
ein fahrender Bus
2 ergreifend (touching) ◊ a moving story
eine ergreifende Geschichte
to **mow** VERB
mähen ◊ to mow the lawn den Rasen
mähen
mower NOUN
der Rasenmäher (PL die Rasenmäher)
mown VERB see **mow**
MP NOUN (= Member of Parliament)
der Abgeordnete (GEN des
Abgeordneten, PL die Abgeordneten)
die Abgeordnete (GEN der Abgeordneten)
◊ an MP (man) ein Abgeordneter ◊ She's
an MP. Sie ist Abgeordnete.
mph ABBREVIATION (= miles per hour)
Meilen pro Stunde
MP3 player NOUN
der MP3-Spieler (PL die MP3-Spieler)
Mr NOUN (= Mister)
Herr
Mrs NOUN
Frau
MS NOUN (= multiple sclerosis)
MS ◊ She's got MS. Sie hat MS.
Ms NOUN
Frau

> ❶ Generally **Frau** is used to address all
> women whether married or not.

much ADJECTIVE, ADVERB, PRONOUN
1 viel ◊ I haven't got much money. Ich
habe nicht viel Geld. ◊ I haven't got very
much money. Ich habe nicht sehr viel
Geld. ◊ This is much better. Das ist viel
besser. ◊ I feel much better now. Ich
fühle mich jetzt viel besser.

2 **sehr**
*Use **sehr** with most verbs.*
◊ *I didn't like it much.* Es hat mir nicht sehr gefallen. ◊ *I enjoyed the film very much.* Der Film hat mir sehr gefallen.

3 **viel**
*Use **viel** with verbs implying physical activity.*
◊ *She doesn't travel much.* Sie reist nicht viel. ◊ *We didn't laugh much.* Wir haben nicht viel gelacht.

♦ **Do you go out much?** Gehst du oft aus?
♦ **Thank you very much.** Vielen Dank!
♦ **Not much.** Nicht viel. ◊ *What's on TV? – Not much.* Was kommt im Fernsehen? – Nicht viel. ◊ *What do you think of it? – Not much.* Was hältst du davon? – Nicht viel.

♦ **How much?** Wie viel? ◊ *How much do you want?* Wie viel möchtest du? ◊ *How much time have you got?* Wie viel Zeit hast du? ◊ *How much is it?* (*cost*) Wie viel kostet das?

♦ **too much** zu viel ◊ *That's too much!* Das ist zu viel! ◊ *It costs too much.* Das kostet zu viel. ◊ *They gave us too much homework.* Sie haben uns zu viele Hausaufgaben aufgegeben.

♦ **so much** so viel ◊ *I didn't think it would cost so much.* Ich hatte nicht gedacht, dass es so viel kosten würde. ◊ *I've never seen so much traffic.* Ich habe noch nie so viel Verkehr erlebt.

mud NOUN
der Schlamm

muddle NOUN
das Durcheinander
♦ **to be in a muddle** durcheinander sein ◊ *The photos are in a muddle.* Die Fotos sind durcheinander.

to **muddle up** VERB
verwechseln (*people*) (PERFECT hat verwechselt) ◊ *He muddles me up with my sister.* Er verwechselt mich mit meiner Schwester.
♦ **to get muddled up** durcheinanderkommen ◊ *I'm getting muddled up.* Ich komme durcheinander.

muddy ADJECTIVE
schlammig

muesli NOUN
das Müsli (PL die Müsli)

muffler NOUN US
der Schalldämpfer (PL die Schalldämpfer)

mug NOUN
see also **mug** VERB
der Becher (PL die Becher) ◊ *Do you want a cup or a mug?* Möchtest du eine Tasse oder einen Becher?
♦ **a beer mug** ein Bierkrug MASC

to **mug** VERB
see also **mug** NOUN

überfallen (PRESENT überfällt, IMPERFECT überfiel, PERFECT hat überfallen) ◊ *He was mugged in the city centre.* Er wurde in der Innenstadt überfallen.

mugger NOUN
der Straßenräuber (PL die Straßenräuber)
die Straßenräuberin

mugging NOUN
der Überfall (PL die Überfälle) ◊ *Mugging has increased in recent years.* Die Zahl der Überfälle hat in den letzten Jahren zugenommen.

muggy ADJECTIVE
schwül ◊ *It's muggy today.* Es ist schwül heute.

multiple choice test NOUN
der Multiple-Choice-Test (PL die Multiple-Choice-Tests)

multiple sclerosis NOUN
die multiple Sklerose ◊ *She's got multiple sclerosis.* Sie hat multiple Sklerose.

multiplication NOUN
die Multiplikation

to **multiply** VERB
multiplizieren (PERFECT hat multipliziert) ◊ *to multiply six by three* sechs mit drei multiplizieren

multi-storey car park NOUN
das Parkhaus (GEN des Parkhauses, PL die Parkhäuser)

mum NOUN
die Mama (PL die Mamas) ◊ *my mum* meine Mama ◊ *I'll ask Mum.* Ich frage Mama.

mummy NOUN
1 (*mum*)
die Mutti (PL die Muttis) ◊ *Mummy says I can go.* Mutti sagt, ich kann gehen.
2 (*Egyptian*)
die Mumie

mumps SING NOUN
der Mumps ◊ *My brother's got mumps.* Mein Bruder hat Mumps.

Munich NOUN
München NEUT
♦ **to Munich** nach München

murder NOUN
see also **murder** VERB
der Mord (PL die Morde)
*Be careful not to translate **murder** by **Mörder**.*

to **murder** VERB
see also **murder** NOUN
ermorden (PERFECT hat ermordet) ◊ *He was murdered.* Er wurde ermordet.

murderer NOUN
der Mörder (PL die Mörder)
die Mörderin

muscle NOUN
der Muskel (PL die Muskeln)

muscular ADJECTIVE
  muskulös
museum NOUN
  das Museum (PL die Museen)
mushroom NOUN
  1 der Pilz (PL die Pilze)
  2 (*button mushroom*)
  der Champignon (PL die Champignons)
  ◇ *mushroom omelette* das
  Champignonomelett
music NOUN
  die Musik
musical ADJECTIVE
  ┌─ see also **musical** NOUN ─┐
  musikalisch ◇ *I'm not musical.* Ich bin
  nicht musikalisch.
◆ **a musical instrument** ein
  Musikinstrument NEUT
musical NOUN
  ┌─ see also **musical** ADJECTIVE ─┐
  das Musical (PL die Musicals)
music centre NOUN
  die Stereoanlage
musician NOUN
  der Musiker (PL die Musiker)
  die Musikerin
Muslim NOUN
  der Moslem (PL die Moslems)
  die Moslime
  ◇ *He's a Muslim.* Er ist Moslem.
mussel NOUN
  die Miesmuschel
must VERB
  1 müssen (PRESENT muss, IMPERFECT
  musste, PERFECT hat gemusst) ◇ *I must buy
  some presents.* Ich muss Geschenke
  kaufen. ◇ *I really must go now.* Ich muss
  jetzt wirklich gehen. ◇ *You must be tired.*
  Du musst müde sein. ◇ *They must have
  plenty of money.* Sie müssen viel Geld
  haben. ◇ *You must come and see us.* Sie
  müssen uns besuchen.
  2 dürfen (PRESENT darf, IMPERFECT durfte,
  PERFECT hat gedurft)
  *Use **dürfen** in negative sentences.*
  ◇ *You mustn't say things like that.* So
  was darfst du nicht sagen.
◆ **You mustn't forget to send her a card.**
  Vergiss nicht, ihr eine Karte zu schicken.
mustard NOUN

  der Senf (PL die Senfe)
to **mutter** VERB
  murmeln
mutton NOUN
  das Hammelfleisch
mutual ADJECTIVE
  gegenseitig ◇ *The feeling was mutual.*
  Das Gefühl war gegenseitig.
◆ **a mutual friend** ein gemeinsamer Freund
my ADJECTIVE
  mein ◇ *my father* mein Vater ◇ *my aunt*
  meine Tante ◇ *my car* mein Auto ◇ *my
  parents* meine Eltern
◆ **my friend (1)** (*male*) mein Freund
◆ **my friend (2)** (*female*) meine Freundin
  *Do not use **mein** with parts of the body.*
  ◇ *I want to wash my hair.* Ich will mir die
  Haare waschen. ◇ *I'm going to clean my
  teeth.* Ich putze mir die Zähne. ◇ *I've hurt
  my foot.* Ich habe mich am Fuß verletzt.
myself PRONOUN
  1 mich ◇ *I've hurt myself.* Ich habe mich
  verletzt. ◇ *When I look at myself in the
  mirror ...* Wenn ich mich im Spiegel
  ansehe ... ◇ *I don't like talking about
  myself.* Ich rede nicht gern über mich
  selbst.
  2 mir ◇ *I said to myself ...* Ich sagte mir
  ... ◇ *I am not very pleased with myself.*
  Ich bin mit mir selbst nicht sehr
  zufrieden.
  3 selbst ◇ *I made it myself.* Ich habe es
  selbst gemacht.
◆ **by myself** allein ◇ *I don't like travelling
  by myself.* Ich verreise nicht gern allein.
mysterious ADJECTIVE
  rätselhaft
mystery NOUN
  das Rätsel (PL die Rätsel)
◆ **a murder mystery** (*novel*) ein Krimi MASC
myth NOUN
  1 (*legend*)
  der Mythos (GEN des Mythos, PL die
  Mythen) ◇ *a Greek myth* ein griechischer
  Mythos
  2 (*untrue idea*)
  das Märchen (PL die Märchen) ◇ *That's a
  myth.* Das ist ein Märchen.
mythology NOUN
  die Mythologie

N

to **nag** VERB
herumnörgeln an (*scold*) (PERFECT hat
herumgenörgelt) ◊ *She's always nagging
me.* Sie nörgelt dauernd an mir herum.

nail NOUN
der Nagel (PL die Nägel) ◊ *Don't bite your
nails!* Kau nicht an den Nägeln!

nailbrush NOUN
die Nagelbürste

nailfile NOUN
die Nagelfeile

nail scissors PL NOUN
die Nagelschere ◊ *a pair of nail scissors*
eine Nagelschere

nail varnish NOUN
der Nagellack (PL die Nagellacke)
♦ **nail varnish remover** der
Nagellackentferner

naked ADJECTIVE
nackt

name NOUN
der Name (GEN des Namens, PL die
Namen)
♦ **What's your name?** Wie heißt du?

nanny NOUN
das Kindermädchen (PL die
Kindermädchen) ◊ *She's a nanny.* Sie ist
Kindermädchen.

nap NOUN
das Nickerchen (PL die Nickerchen)
♦ **to have a nap** ein Nickerchen machen

napkin NOUN
die Serviette

nappy NOUN
die Windel

narrow ADJECTIVE
eng

narrow-minded ADJECTIVE
engstirnig

nasty ADJECTIVE
[1] übel (*bad*) ◊ *a nasty cold* eine üble
Erkältung ◊ *a nasty smell* ein übler
Geruch
[2] böse (*unfriendly*) ◊ *He gave me a nasty
look.* Er warf mir einen bösen Blick zu.

nation NOUN
die Nation

national ADJECTIVE
national
♦ **a national newspaper** eine überregionale
Zeitung
♦ **the national elections** die
Parlamentswahlen

> **ⓘ** In Germany the national elections
> are called **Bundestagswahlen**.

national anthem NOUN

die Nationalhymne

National Health Service NOUN
der staatliche Gesundheitsdienst

> **ⓘ** In Germany there are a large
> number of health schemes, not just a
> single service.

nationalism NOUN
der Nationalismus (GEN des
Nationalismus) ◊ *Scottish Nationalism*
der schottische Nationalismus

nationalist NOUN
der Nationalist (GEN des Nationalisten, PL
die Nationalisten)

nationality NOUN
die Staatsangehörigkeit

National Lottery NOUN
das Lotto

national park NOUN
der Nationalpark (PL die Nationalparks)

native ADJECTIVE
♦ **my native country** mein Heimatland
NEUT
♦ **native language** die Muttersprache
◊ *English is not their native language.*
Englisch ist nicht ihre Muttersprache.
♦ **a Native American** ein Indianer MASC

natural ADJECTIVE
natürlich

naturalist NOUN
der Naturforscher (PL die Naturforscher)
die Naturforscherin

naturally ADVERB
natürlich ◊ *Naturally, we were very
disappointed.* Natürlich waren wir sehr
enttäuscht.

nature NOUN
die Natur

naughty ADJECTIVE
böse ◊ *Naughty girl!* Böses Mädchen!
♦ **Don't be so naughty!** Sei nicht so
ungezogen!

navy NOUN
die Marine ◊ *He's in the navy.* Er ist bei
der Marine.

navy-blue ADJECTIVE
marineblau ◊ *a navy-blue shirt* ein
marineblaues Hemd

Nazi NOUN
der Nazi (PL die Nazis) ◊ *the Nazis* die
Nazis
der Nazi is also used for women.
◊ *She was a Nazi.* Sie war ein Nazi.

near ADJECTIVE
see also **near** PREPOSITION

nah ◊ *It's fairly near.* Es ist ziemlich nah.
◊ *It's near enough to walk.* Es ist nah
genug, um zu Fuß zu gehen.
♦ **nearest** nächste ◊ *Where's the nearest
service station?* Wo ist die nächste
Tankstelle? ◊ *The nearest shops were
three kilometres away.* Die nächsten
Geschäfte waren drei Kilometer weg.

near PREPOSITION, ADVERB
see also **near** ADJECTIVE
in der Nähe von ◊ *I live near Liverpool.*
Ich wohne in der Nähe von Liverpool.
◊ *near my house* in der Nähe meines
Hauses
♦ **near here** hier in der Nähe ◊ *Is there a
bank near here?* Ist hier in der Nähe eine
Bank?
♦ **near to** in der Nähe +GEN ◊ *It's very near to
the school.* Es ist ganz in der Nähe der
Schule.

nearby ADVERB, ADJECTIVE
1 in der Nähe ◊ *There's a supermarket
nearby.* Es gibt einen Supermarkt in der
Nähe.
2 nahe gelegen (*close*) ◊ *a nearby
garage* eine nahe gelegene Tankstelle

nearly ADVERB
fast ◊ *Dinner's nearly ready.* Das Essen
ist fast fertig. ◊ *I'm nearly fifteen.* Ich bin
fast fünfzehn. ◊ *I nearly missed the train.*
Ich habe fast meinen Zug verpasst.

neat ADJECTIVE
ordentlich ◊ *She has very neat writing.*
Sie hat eine sehr ordentliche Schrift.
♦ **a neat whisky** ein Whisky pur

neatly ADVERB
ordentlich ◊ *neatly folded* ordentlich
gefaltet ◊ *neatly dressed* ordentlich
gekleidet

necessarily ADVERB
♦ **not necessarily** nicht unbedingt

necessary ADJECTIVE
nötig

necessity NOUN
die Notwendigkeit ◊ *A car is a necessity,
not a luxury.* Ein Auto ist eine
Notwendigkeit und kein Luxus.

neck NOUN
1 (*of body*)
der Hals (GEN des Halses, PL die Hälse)
2 (*of garment*)
der Ausschnitt (PL die Ausschnitte) ◊ *a
V-neck sweater* ein Pullover mit
V-Ausschnitt

necklace NOUN
die Halskette

to **need** VERB
see also **need** NOUN
brauchen ◊ *I need a bigger size.* Ich
brauche eine größere Größe.
♦ **to need to do something** etwas tun
müssen ◊ *I need to change some money.*
Ich muss Geld wechseln.

need NOUN
see also **need** VERB
♦ **There's no need to book.** Man braucht
nicht zu buchen.

needle NOUN
die Nadel

needlework NOUN
die Handarbeit ◊ *We have needlework
lessons at school.* Wir haben
Handarbeitsunterricht an der Schule.

negative NOUN
see also **negative** ADJECTIVE
das Negativ (*photo*) (PL die Negative)

negative ADJECTIVE
see also **negative** NOUN
negativ ◊ *He's got a very negative
attitude.* Er hat eine sehr negative
Einstellung.

neglected ADJECTIVE
ungepflegt (*untidy*) ◊ *The garden is
neglected.* Der Garten ist ungepflegt.

negligee NOUN
das Negligé (PL die Negligés)

to **negotiate** VERB
verhandeln

negotiations PL NOUN
die Verhandlungen PL

neighbour NOUN
der Nachbar (GEN des Nachbarn, PL die
Nachbarn)
die Nachbarin
◊ *the neighbours' garden* der Garten der
Nachbarn

neighbourhood NOUN
die Nachbarschaft

neither PRONOUN, CONJUNCTION, ADVERB
weder noch ◊ *Carrots or peas? –
Neither, thanks.* Karotten oder Erbsen? –
Weder noch, danke.
♦ **Neither of them is coming.** Keiner von
beiden kommt.
♦ **neither ... nor ...** weder ... noch ...
◊ *Neither Sarah nor Tamsin is coming to
the party.* Weder Sarah noch Tamsin
kommen zur Party.
♦ **Neither do I.** Ich auch nicht. ◊ *I don't like
him. – Neither do I!* Ich mag ihn nicht. –
Ich auch nicht!
♦ **Neither have I.** Ich auch nicht. ◊ *I've
never been to Spain. – Neither have I.*
Ich war noch nie in Spanien. – Ich auch
nicht.

neon NOUN
das Neon ◊ *a neon light* eine
Neonlampe

nephew NOUN
der Neffe (GEN des Neffen, PL die Neffen)
◊ *my nephew* mein Neffe

nerve NOUN
der Nerv (PL die Nerven) ◊ *She
sometimes gets on my nerves.* Sie geht
mir manchmal auf die Nerven.

♦ **He's got a nerve!** Der hat vielleicht Nerven!

nerve-racking ADJECTIVE
nervenaufreibend

nervous ADJECTIVE
nervös (*tense*) ◇ *I bite my nails when I'm nervous.* Wenn ich nervös bin, kaue ich an den Nägeln.

♦ **to be nervous about something** vor etwas Angst haben ◇ *I'm a bit nervous about flying to Paris by myself.* Ich habe etwas Angst, allein nach Paris zu fliegen.

nest NOUN
das Nest (PL die Nester)

net NOUN
das Netz (GEN des Netzes, PL die Netze) ◇ *a fishing net* ein Fischnetz

Net NOUN
♦ **the Net** das Internet

netball NOUN
der Netzball

Netherlands PL NOUN
die Niederlande PL

Note that the definite article is used in German for countries which are plural.

♦ **from the Netherlands** aus den Niederlanden
♦ **in the Netherlands** in den Niederlanden
♦ **to the Netherlands** in die Niederlande

network NOUN
1 das Netz (GEN des Netzes, PL die Netze)
2 (*for computers*)
das Netzwerk (PL die Netzwerke)

neurotic ADJECTIVE
neurotisch

never ADVERB
nie ◇ *Have you ever been to Germany? – No, never.* Waren Sie schon mal in Deutschland? – Nein, nie. ◇ *I never write letters.* Ich schreibe nie Briefe. ◇ *Never again!* Nie wieder!

♦ **Never mind.** Macht nichts!

new ADJECTIVE
neu ◇ *her new boyfriend* ihr neuer Freund ◇ *I need a new dress.* Ich brauche ein neues Kleid.

newborn ADJECTIVE
♦ **a newborn baby** ein neugeborenes Kind

newcomer NOUN
der Neuling (PL die Neulinge)
der Neuling is also used for women.

news SING NOUN

Nachricht is a piece of news; Nachrichten is the news, for example on TV.

1 die Nachrichten FEM PL ◇ *good news* gute Nachrichten ◇ *I've had some bad news.* Ich habe schlechte Nachrichten bekommen. ◇ *I watch the news every evening.* Ich sehe mir jeden Abend die Nachrichten an. ◇ *I listen to the news every morning.* Ich höre jeden Morgen die Nachrichten.

2 die Nachricht ◇ *That's wonderful news!* Das ist eine wunderbare Nachricht!

newsagent NOUN
der Zeitungshändler (PL die Zeitungshändler)
die Zeitungshändlerin

news dealer NOUN US
der Zeitungshändler (PL die Zeitungshändler)
die Zeitungshändlerin

newspaper NOUN
die Zeitung ◇ *I deliver newspapers.* Ich trage Zeitungen aus.

newsreader NOUN
der Nachrichtensprecher (PL die Nachrichtensprecher)
die Nachrichtensprecherin

New Year NOUN
das Neujahr ◇ *to celebrate New Year* Neujahr feiern

♦ **Happy New Year!** Ein gutes neues Jahr!
♦ **New Year's Day** der Neujahrstag
♦ **New Year's Eve** das Silvester ◇ *a New Year's Eve party* eine Silvesterparty

New Zealand NOUN
Neuseeland NEUT
♦ **from New Zealand** aus Neuseeland
♦ **in New Zealand** in Neuseeland
♦ **to New Zealand** nach Neuseeland

New Zealander NOUN
der Neuseeländer (PL die Neuseeländer)
die Neuseeländerin

next ADJECTIVE, ADVERB, PREPOSITION
1 nächsten ◇ *next Saturday* nächsten Samstag ◇ *next week* nächste Woche ◇ *next year* nächstes Jahr ◇ *the next train* der nächste Zug

♦ **Next please!** Der Nächste, bitte!
2 danach (*afterwards*) ◇ *What happened next?* Was ist danach passiert?

♦ **What shall I do next?** Was soll ich als Nächstes machen?
♦ **next to** neben

Use the accusative to express movement or a change of place. Use the dative when there is no change of place.

◇ *I sat down next to my sister.* Ich setzte mich neben meine Schwester. ◇ *The post office is next to the bank.* Die Post ist neben der Bank.

♦ **the next day** am nächsten Tag ◇ *The next day we visited Heidelberg.* Am nächsten Tag haben wir Heidelberg besucht.
♦ **the next time** das nächste Mal ◇ *the next time you see her* wenn du sie das nächste Mal siehst
♦ **next door** nebenan ◇ *They live next door.* Sie wohnen nebenan. ◇ *the people next door* die Leute von nebenan
♦ **the next room** das Nebenzimmer

N

NHS NOUN (= *National Health Service*)
der staatliche Gesundheitsdienst

> 🛈 *In Germany there are a large number of health schemes, not just a single service.*

nice ADJECTIVE

1. nett (*kind*) ◊ *Your parents are nice.* Deine Eltern sind nett. ◊ *It was nice of you to remember my birthday.* Es war nett, dass du an meinen Geburtstag gedacht hast. ◊ *to be nice to somebody* nett zu jemandem sein

2. hübsch (*pretty*) ◊ *That's a nice dress!* Das ist ein hübsches Kleid! ◊ *Ulm is a nice town.* Ulm ist eine hübsche Stadt.

3. schön ◊ *nice weather* schönes Wetter ◊ *It's a nice day.* Es ist ein schöner Tag.

4. lecker (*food*) ◊ *This pizza's very nice.* Diese Pizza ist sehr lecker.

- **Have a nice time!** Viel Spaß!

nickname NOUN
der Spitzname (GEN des Spitznamens, PL die Spitznamen)

niece NOUN
die Nichte ◊ *my niece* meine Nichte

Nigeria NOUN
Nigeria NEUT ◊ *in Nigeria* in Nigeria

night NOUN

1. die Nacht (PL die Nächte) ◊ *I want a single room for two nights.* Ich möchte ein Einzelzimmer für zwei Nächte.

- **at night** nachts
- **Good night!** Gute Nacht!
- **a night club** ein Nachtklub MASC

2. (*evening*)
der Abend (PL die Abende) ◊ *last night* gestern Abend

nightdress NOUN
das Nachthemd (PL die Nachthemden)

nightie NOUN
das Nachthemd (PL die Nachthemden)

nightlife NOUN
das Nachtleben ◊ *There's plenty of nightlife.* Dort gibt es ein reges Nachtleben.

nightmare NOUN
der Albtraum (PL die Albträume) ◊ *I had a nightmare.* Ich hatte einen Albtraum. ◊ *It was a real nightmare!* Es war ein Albtraum!

nightshirt NOUN
das Nachthemd (PL die Nachthemden)

nil NOUN
null ◊ *We won one nil.* Wir haben eins zu null gewonnen.

nine NUMBER
neun ◊ *She's nine.* Sie ist neun.

nineteen NUMBER
neunzehn ◊ *She's nineteen.* Sie ist neunzehn.

nineteenth ADJECTIVE

neunzehnte
- **the nineteenth of August** der neunzehnte August

ninety NUMBER
neunzig ◊ *She's ninety.* Sie ist neunzig.

ninth ADJECTIVE
neunte ◊ *the ninth floor* der neunte Stock
- **the ninth of August** der neunte August

no ADVERB, ADJECTIVE

1. nein ◊ *Are you coming? – No.* Kommst du? – Nein. ◊ *Would you like some more? – No thank you.* Möchten Sie noch etwas? – Nein danke.

2. kein (*not any*) ◊ *There's no hot water.* Es gibt kein heißes Wasser. ◊ *There are no trains on Sundays.* Sonntags verkehren keine Züge. ◊ *No problem.* Kein Problem. ◊ *I've got no idea.* Ich habe keine Ahnung.

- **No way!** Auf keinen Fall!
- **"no smoking"** "Rauchen verboten"

nobody PRONOUN
niemand ◊ *Who's going with you? – Nobody.* Wer geht mit dir mit? – Niemand. ◊ *There was nobody in the office.* Es war niemand im Büro.

to **nod** VERB
nicken

noise NOUN
der Lärm ◊ *Please make less noise.* Macht bitte weniger Lärm.

noisy ADJECTIVE
laut ◊ *It's too noisy here.* Hier ist es zu laut.

to **nominate** VERB
nominieren (PERFECT hat nominiert) ◊ *She was nominated for the post.* Sie wurde für den Posten nominiert. ◊ *He was nominated for an Oscar.* Er war für einen Oskar nominiert.

none PRONOUN
keiner ◊ *None of my friends wanted to come.* Keiner meiner Freunde wollte kommen. ◊ *How many brothers have you got? – None.* Wie viele Brüder hast du? – Keinen.
keine ◊ *Where is the milk? – There's none left.* Wo ist die Milch? – Es ist keine mehr da.
keines ◊ *Which of the books have you read? – None.* Welches der Bücher hast du gelesen? – Keines.
- **There are none left.** Es sind keine mehr da.

nonsense NOUN
der Unsinn ◊ *She talks a lot of nonsense.* Sie redet viel Unsinn. ◊ *Nonsense!* Unsinn!

nonsmoker NOUN
der Nichtraucher (PL die Nichtraucher) die Nichtraucherin

◊ *She's a nonsmoker.* Sie ist
Nichtraucherin.
nonsmoking ADJECTIVE
♦ **a nonsmoking carriage** ein
Nichtraucherabteil NEUT
nonstop ADJECTIVE, ADVERB
1 nonstop ◊ *We flew nonstop.* Wir sind
nonstop geflogen.
♦ **a nonstop flight** ein Nonstop-Flug MASC
2 ununterbrochen ◊ *Liz talks nonstop.*
Liz redet ununterbrochen.
noodles PL NOUN
die Nudeln FEM PL
noon NOUN
der Mittag (PL die Mittage)
♦ **at noon** um zwölf Uhr mittags
no one PRONOUN
niemand ◊ *Who's going with you? – No
one.* Wer geht mit dir mit? – Niemand.
◊ *There was no one in the office.* Es war
niemand im Büro.
nor CONJUNCTION
♦ **neither ... nor** weder ... noch ◊ *neither
the cinema nor the swimming pool*
weder das Kino noch das Schwimmbad
♦ **Nor do I.** Ich auch nicht. ◊ *I didn't like the
film. – Nor did I.* Der Film hat mir nicht
gefallen. – Mir auch nicht.
♦ **Nor have I.** Ich auch nicht. ◊ *I haven't
seen him. – Nor have I.* Ich habe ihn nicht
gesehen. – Ich auch nicht.
normal ADJECTIVE
normal ◊ *at the normal time* zur
normalen Zeit ◊ *a normal car* ein
normales Auto
normally ADVERB
1 normalerweise (*usually*) ◊ *I normally
arrive at nine o'clock.* Normalerweise
komme ich um neun Uhr.
2 normal (*as normal*) ◊ *In spite of the
strike, the airports are working normally.*
Trotz des Streiks arbeiten die Flughäfen
normal.
Normandy NOUN
die Normandie
♦ **in Normandy** in der Normandie
north ADJECTIVE, ADVERB
see also **north** NOUN
♦ **the north coast** die Nordküste
♦ **a north wind** ein Nordwind MASC
nach Norden ◊ *We were travelling
north.* Wir sind nach Norden gefahren.
♦ **north of** nördlich von ◊ *It's north of
London.* Es liegt nördlich von London.
north NOUN
see also **north** ADJECTIVE
der Norden ◊ *in the north* im Norden
North America NOUN
Nordamerika NEUT
♦ **from North America** aus Nordamerika
♦ **to North America** nach Nordamerika
northbound ADJECTIVE

in Richtung Norden ◊ *Northbound
traffic is moving very slowly.* Der Verkehr
in Richtung Norden kommt nur sehr
langsam voran.
northeast NOUN
der Nordosten ◊ *in the northeast* im
Nordosten
northern ADJECTIVE
nördlich ◊ *the northern part of the island*
der nördliche Teil der Insel
♦ **Northern Europe** Nordeuropa NEUT
Northern Ireland NOUN
Nordirland NEUT
♦ **from Northern Ireland** aus Nordirland
♦ **in Northern Ireland** in Nordirland
♦ **to Northern Ireland** nach Nordirland
North Pole NOUN
der Nordpol
North Sea NOUN
die Nordsee
northwest NOUN
der Nordwesten ◊ *in the northwest* im
Nordwesten
Norway NOUN
Norwegen NEUT
♦ **from Norway** aus Norwegen
♦ **to Norway** nach Norwegen
Norwegian ADJECTIVE
see also **Norwegian** NOUN
norwegisch
♦ **He's Norwegian.** Er ist Norweger.
Norwegian NOUN
see also **Norwegian** ADJECTIVE
1 (*person*)
der Norweger (PL die Norweger)
die Norwegerin
2 (*language*)
das Norwegisch (GEN des Norwegischen)
nose NOUN
die Nase
nosebleed NOUN
das Nasenbluten ◊ *I often get
nosebleeds.* Ich habe oft Nasenbluten.
nosey ADJECTIVE
neugierig ◊ *She's very nosey.* Sie ist
sehr neugierig.
not ADVERB
1 nicht ◊ *Are you coming or not?*
Kommst du oder nicht? ◊ *I'm not sure.*
Ich bin nicht sicher. ◊ *It's not raining.* Es
regnet nicht.
♦ **not really** eigentlich nicht
♦ **not at all** überhaupt nicht
♦ **not yet** noch nicht ◊ *Have you finished?
– Not yet.* Bist du fertig? – Noch nicht.
◊ *They haven't arrived yet.* Sie sind noch
nicht angekommen.
2 nein ◊ *Can you lend me ten pounds? –
I'm afraid not.* Können Sie mir zehn
Pfund leihen? – Leider nein.
note NOUN
1 die Notiz

N

☞

♦ **to take notes** sich Notizen machen ◇ *You should take notes.* Du solltest dir Notizen machen.

2 (*letter*)
der Brief (PL die Briefe)

♦ **I'll write her a note.** Ich werde ihr schreiben.

3 (*banknote*)
der Schein (PL die Scheine) ◇ *a five-pound note* ein Fünfpfundschein

to **note down** VERB
aufschreiben (IMPERFECT schrieb auf, PERFECT hat aufgeschrieben)

notebook NOUN
1 das Notizbuch (PL die Notizbücher)
2 (*computer*)
der Notebookcomputer (PL die Notebookcomputer)

notepad NOUN
der Notizblock (PL die Notizblöcke)

notepaper NOUN
das Briefpapier

nothing NOUN
nichts ◇ *What's wrong? – Nothing.* Was ist los? – Nichts. ◇ *nothing special* nichts Besonderes ◇ *He does nothing.* Er tut nichts. ◇ *He ate nothing for breakfast.* Er hat nichts zum Frühstück gegessen.

notice NOUN
see also **notice** VERB
die Notiz (*sign*) ◇ *to put up a notice* eine Notiz aushängen ◇ *Don't take any notice of him!* Nimm keine Notiz von ihm!

♦ **a warning notice** ein Warnschild NEUT

to **notice** VERB
see also **notice** NOUN
bemerken (PERFECT hat bemerkt)

notice board NOUN
das Anschlagbrett (PL die Anschlagbretter)

nought NOUN
die Null

noun NOUN
das Substantiv (PL die Substantive)

novel NOUN
der Roman (PL die Romane)

novelist NOUN
der Romanautor (PL die Romanautoren)
die Romanautorin

November NOUN
der November ◇ *in November* im November

now ADVERB, CONJUNCTION
jetzt ◇ *What are you doing now?* Was tust du jetzt?

♦ **just now** gerade ◇ *I'm rather busy just now.* Ich bin gerade ziemlich beschäftigt. ◇ *I did it just now.* Ich habe es gerade getan.

♦ **by now** inzwischen ◇ *He should be there by now.* Er müsste inzwischen dort sein. ◇ *It should be ready by now.* Es müsste inzwischen fertig sein.

♦ **now and then** ab und zu

nowhere ADVERB
nirgends ◇ *nowhere else* sonst nirgends

nuclear ADJECTIVE
nuklear

♦ **nuclear power** die Kernkraft ◇ *a nuclear power station* ein Kernkraftwerk NEUT

nude ADJECTIVE
see also **nude** NOUN
nackt ◇ *to sunbathe nude* nackt sonnenbaden

nude NOUN
see also **nude** ADJECTIVE

♦ **in the nude** nackt

nudist NOUN
der Nudist (GEN des Nudisten, PL die Nudisten)
die Nudistin

nuisance NOUN
♦ **It's a nuisance.** Es ist sehr lästig.
♦ **Sorry to be a nuisance.** Tut mir leid, dass ich schon wieder ankomme.

numb ADJECTIVE
taub ◇ *numb with cold* taub vor Kälte

number NOUN
1 die Anzahl (*total amount*) ◇ *a large number of people* eine große Anzahl von Menschen
2 die Nummer (*of house, telephone, bank account*) ◇ *They live at number five.* Sie wohnen in der Nummer fünf. ◇ *What's your phone number?* Wie ist Ihre Telefonnummer?

♦ **You've got the wrong number.** Sie sind falsch verbunden.
3 die Zahl (*figure, digit*) ◇ *I can't read the second number.* Ich kann die zweite Zahl nicht lesen.

number plate NOUN
das Nummernschild (PL die Nummernschilder)

ⓘ The first letters of a German number plate allow you to tell where the car's owner lives. Thus L stands for Leipzig, LB for Ludwigsburg, LU for Ludwigshafen, etc.

nun NOUN
die Nonne ◇ *She's a nun.* Sie ist Nonne.

nurse NOUN
die Krankenschwester ◇ *She's a nurse.* Sie ist Krankenschwester.
der Krankenpfleger
◇ *He's a nurse.* Er ist Krankenpfleger.

nursery NOUN
1 (*for children*)
die Kindergarten (PL die Kindergärten)
2 (*for plants*)
die Baumschule

nursery school NOUN
der Kindergarten (PL die Kindergärten)

> *ⓘ German children go to **Kindergarten** from the age of 3 to 6.*

nursery slope NOUN
der <u>Idiotenhügel</u> (PL die Idiotenhügel)
nut NOUN
[1] die <u>Nuss</u> (PL die Nüsse)
[2] (*made of metal*)
die <u>Mutter</u>
nutmeg NOUN

der <u>Muskat</u>
nutritious ADJECTIVE
<u>nahrhaft</u>
nuts ADJECTIVE
♦**He's nuts.** Er spinnt. (*informal*)
nutter NOUN
♦**He's a nutter.** Er ist völlig durchgeknallt. (*informal*)
nylon NOUN
das <u>Nylon</u>

N

O

oak NOUN
die Eiche ◊ *an oak table* ein Eichentisch
MASC

oar NOUN
das Ruder (PL die Ruder)

oats PL NOUN
der Hafer

obedient ADJECTIVE
gehorsam

to **obey** VERB
gehorchen (PERFECT hat gehorcht) ◊ *She
didn't obey her mother.* Sie hat ihrer
Mutter nicht gehorcht.
♦ **to obey the rules** die Regeln befolgen

object NOUN
der Gegenstand (PL die Gegenstände)
◊ *a familiar object* ein vertrauter
Gegenstand

objection NOUN
der Einspruch (PL die Einsprüche)

objective NOUN
das Ziel (PL die Ziele)

oblong ADJECTIVE
länglich

oboe NOUN
die Oboe ◊ *I play the oboe.* Ich spiele
Oboe.

obscene ADJECTIVE
obszön

observant ADJECTIVE
aufmerksam

to **observe** VERB
beobachten (PERFECT hat beobachtet)

obsessed ADJECTIVE
besessen ◊ *He's completely obsessed
with trains.* Er ist von Zügen ganz
besessen.

obsession NOUN
die Leidenschaft ◊ *Football's an
obsession of mine.* Fußball ist meine
Leidenschaft.

obsolete ADJECTIVE
veraltet

obstacle NOUN
das Hindernis (GEN des Hindernisses, PL
die Hindernisse)

obstinate ADJECTIVE
stur

to **obstruct** VERB
behindern (PERFECT hat behindert) ◊ *A
lorry was obstructing the traffic.* Ein
Lastwagen hat den Verkehr
behindert.

to **obtain** VERB
erhalten (IMPERFECT erhielt, PERFECT hat
erhalten)

obvious ADJECTIVE
offensichtlich

obviously ADVERB
1 natürlich (*of course*) ◊ *Do you want to
pass the exam? – Obviously!* Willst du
die Prüfung bestehen? – Natürlich!
◊ *Obviously not!* Natürlich nicht!
2 offensichtlich (*visibly*) ◊ *She was
obviously exhausted.* Sie war
offensichtlich erschöpft.

occasion NOUN
die Gelegenheit ◊ *a special occasion*
eine besondere Gelegenheit
♦ **on several occasions** mehrmals

occasionally ADVERB
ab und zu

occupation NOUN
die Beschäftigung

to **occupy** VERB
besetzen (PERFECT hat besetzt) ◊ *That seat
is occupied.* Der Platz ist besetzt.

to **occur** VERB
passieren (*happen*) (PERFECT ist passiert)
◊ *The accident occurred yesterday.* Der
Unfall ist gestern passiert.
♦ **It suddenly occurred to me that ...**
Plötzlich ist mir eingefallen, dass ...

ocean NOUN
der Ozean (PL die Ozeane)

o'clock ADVERB
♦ **at four o'clock** um vier Uhr
♦ **It's five o'clock.** Es ist fünf Uhr.

October NOUN
der Oktober ◊ *in October* im Oktober

octopus NOUN
der Tintenfisch (PL die Tintenfische)

odd ADJECTIVE
1 eigenartig ◊ *That's odd!* Das ist
eigenartig!
2 ungerade ◊ *an odd number* eine
ungerade Zahl

of PREPOSITION
von ◊ *some photos of my holiday* Fotos
von meinen Ferien ◊ *three of us* drei von
uns ◊ *a friend of mine* ein Freund von
mir ◊ *That's very kind of you.* Das ist
sehr nett von Ihnen. ◊ *Can I have half of
that?* Kann ich die Hälfte davon haben?
*of is not translated when specifying a
quantity of something.*
◊ *a kilo of oranges* ein Kilo Orangen
*of is often expressed by using the
genitive.*
◊ *the end of the film* das Ende des Films
◊ *the top of the stairs* das obere Ende der
Treppe ◊ *the front of the house* die
Vorderseite des Hauses
♦ **a boy of ten** ein zehnjähriger Junge
♦ **the fourteenth of September** der
vierzehnte September

♦ **It's made of wood.** Es ist aus Holz.

off ADVERB, PREPOSITION, ADJECTIVE

> *For other expressions with* **off**, *see the*
> *verbs* **get, take, turn** *etc.*

[1] aus (*heater, light, TV*) ◊ *All the lights are*
off. Alle Lichter sind aus.

[2] zu (*tap, gas*) ◊ *Are you sure the tap is*
off? Bist du sicher, dass der Hahn zu ist?

[3] abgesagt (*cancelled*) ◊ *The match is*
off. Das Spiel wurde abgesagt.

♦ **to be off sick** krank sein

♦ **a day off** ein freier Tag

♦ **to take a day off work** sich einen Tag
freinehmen ◊ *I'm taking a day off work*
tomorrow. Ich werde mir morgen einen
Tag freinehmen.

♦ **She's off school today.** Sie ist heute
nicht in der Schule.

♦ **I must be off now.** Ich muss jetzt gehen.

♦ **I'm off.** Ich gehe jetzt.

offence NOUN
das Vergehen (*crime*) (PL die Vergehen)

offensive ADJECTIVE
anstößig

offer NOUN
see also **offer** VERB
das Angebot (PL die Angebote) ◊ *a good*
offer ein günstiges Angebot

♦ **"on special offer"** "im Sonderangebot"

to **offer** VERB
see also **offer** NOUN
anbieten (IMPERFECT bot an, PERFECT hat
angeboten) ◊ *He offered to help me.* Er
bot mir seine Hilfe an. ◊ *I offered to go*
with them. Ich habe ihnen angeboten
mitzugehen.

office NOUN
das Büro (PL die Büros) ◊ *She works in*
an office. Sie arbeitet in einem Büro.

♦ **doctor's office** die Arztpraxis

officer NOUN
der Offizier (*in army*) (PL die Offiziere)

♦ **a police officer** (*man*) ein Polizeibeamter

official ADJECTIVE
offiziell

off-licence NOUN
die Wein- und Spirituosenhandlung

off-peak ADJECTIVE
außerhalb der Stoßzeiten ◊ *It's cheaper*
to travel off-peak. Es ist billiger,
außerhalb der Stoßzeiten zu fahren.

♦ **off-peak calls** Gespräche zum
Billigtarif

offside ADJECTIVE
im Abseits (*in football*)

often ADVERB
oft ◊ *It often rains.* Es regnet oft. ◊ *How*
often do you go to church? Wie oft gehst
du in die Kirche? ◊ *I'd like to go skiing*
more often. Ich würde gern öfter Ski
fahren.

oil NOUN
see also **oil** VERB

[1] (*for lubrication, cooking*)
das Öl (PL die Öle)

♦ **an oil painting** ein Ölgemälde NEUT

[2] (*petroleum*)
das Erdöl ◊ *North Sea oil* Erdöl aus der
Nordsee

to **oil** VERB
see also **oil** NOUN
ölen

oil rig NOUN
die Bohrinsel ◊ *He works on an oil rig.*
Er arbeitet auf einer Bohrinsel.

oil slick NOUN
der Ölteppich (PL die Ölteppiche)

oil well NOUN
die Ölquelle

ointment NOUN
die Salbe

okay EXCLAMATION, ADJECTIVE
okay ◊ *Could you call back later? – Okay!*
Kannst du später anrufen? – Okay! ◊ *I'll*
meet you at six o'clock, okay? Ich treffe
dich um sechs Uhr, okay? ◊ *Is that okay?*
Ist das okay? ◊ *How was your holiday? –*
It was okay. Wie waren die Ferien? –
Okay.

♦ **I'll do it tomorrow, if that's okay with**
you. Ich mache das morgen, wenn du
einverstanden bist.

♦ **Are you okay?** Bist du in Ordnung?

old ADJECTIVE
alt ◊ *an old dog* ein alter Hund ◊ *old*
people alte Menschen ◊ *my old English*
teacher mein alter Englischlehrer ◊ *How*
old are you? Wie alt bist du? ◊ *He's ten*
years old. Er ist zehn Jahre alt. ◊ *my*
older brother mein älterer Bruder ◊ *my*
older sister meine ältere Schwester
◊ *She's two years older than me.* Sie ist
zwei Jahre älter als ich. ◊ *He's the oldest*
in the family. Er ist der Älteste der
Familie.

old age pensioner NOUN
der Rentner (PL die Rentner)
die Rentnerin
◊ *She's an old age pensioner.* Sie ist
Rentnerin.

old-fashioned ADJECTIVE
altmodisch ◊ *She wears old-fashioned*
clothes. Sie trägt altmodische Kleidung.
◊ *My parents are rather old-fashioned.*
Meine Eltern sind ziemlich
altmodisch.

olive NOUN
die Olive

olive oil NOUN
das Olivenöl (PL die Olivenöle)

Olympic ADJECTIVE
olympisch

♦ **the Olympics** die Olympischen Spiele

omelette NOUN
das Omelett (PL die Omeletts)

on PREPOSITION, ADVERB

O

see also **on** ADJECTIVE

There are several ways of translating **on**. Scan the examples to find one that is similar to what you want to say. For other expressions with **on** see the verbs **go**, **put**, **turn** etc.

1 auf

Use the accusative to express movement or a change of place. Use the dative when there is no change of place.

◇ *It's on the table.* Es ist auf dem Tisch. ◇ *Please, put it on the table.* Stell es bitte auf den Tisch. ◇ *on an island* auf einer Insel ◇ *on the left* auf der linken Seite

2 an ◇ *on Friday* am Freitag ◇ *on Christmas Day* am ersten Weihnachtsfeiertag ◇ *on the twentieth of June* am zwanzigsten Juni ◇ *on my birthday* an meinem Geburtstag

♦ **on Fridays** freitags

Use the accusative to express movement or a change of place. Use the dative when there is no change of place.

◇ *There was not a single picture on the wall.* An der Wand hing kein einziges Bild. ◇ *She hung a picture up on the wall.* Sie hängte ein Bild an die Wand.

3 in ◇ *on the second floor* im zweiten Stock ◇ *on TV* im Fernsehen ◇ *What's on TV?* Was kommt im Fernsehen? ◇ *I heard it on the radio.* Ich habe es im Radio gehört.

♦ **on the bus (1)** (*by bus*) mit dem Bus ◇ *I go into town on the bus.* Ich fahre mit dem Bus in die Stadt.

♦ **on the bus (2)** (*inside*) im Bus ◇ *There were no empty seats on the bus.* Es gab keinen freien Platz im Bus.

♦ **I go to school on my bike.** Ich fahre mit dem Fahrrad zur Schule.

♦ **on holiday** in den Ferien ◇ *They're on holiday.* Sie sind in den Ferien.

♦ **They are on strike.** Sie streiken.

on ADJECTIVE

see also **on** PREPOSITION

1 an (*heater, light, TV*) ◇ *I think I left the light on.* Ich glaube, ich habe das Licht angelassen. ◇ *Is the dishwasher on?* Ist die Spülmaschine an?

2 auf (*tap, gas*) ◇ *Leave the tap on.* Lass den Hahn auf.

♦ **What's on at the cinema?** Was gibt's im Kino?

once ADVERB

einmal ◇ *once a week* einmal pro Woche ◇ *once more* noch einmal ◇ *I've been to Germany once before.* Ich war schon einmal in Deutschland.

♦ **Once upon a time ...** Es war einmal ...

♦ **at once** sofort

♦ **once in a while** ab und zu

one NUMBER, PRONOUN

Use **ein** for masculine and neuter nouns, **eine** for feminine nouns.

1 ein ◇ *one man* ein Mann ◇ *one child* ein Kind ◇ *We stayed there for one day.* Wir sind einen Tag dortgeblieben.

2 eine ◇ *one minute* eine Minute ◇ *Do you need a stamp? – No thanks, I've got one.* Brauchst du eine Briefmarke? – Nein danke, ich habe eine. ◇ *I've got one brother and one sister.* Ich habe einen Bruder und eine Schwester.

3 eins

Use **eins** when counting.

◇ *one, two, three* eins, zwei, drei

4 man (*impersonal*) ◇ *One never knows.* Man kann nie wissen.

♦ **this one (1)** (*masculine*) dieser ◇ *Which foot hurts? – This one.* Welcher Fuß tut weh? – Dieser.

♦ **this one (2)** (*feminine*) diese ◇ *Which is your cup? – This one.* Welche ist deine Tasse? – Diese.

♦ **this one (3)** (*neuter*) dieses ◇ *Which is the best photo? – This one.* Welches ist das beste Foto? – Dieses.

♦ **that one (1)** (*masculine*) der da ◇ *Which pen did you use? – That one.* Welchen Schreiber hast du benützt? – Den da.

♦ **that one (2)** (*feminine*) die da ◇ *Which bag is yours? – That one.* Welche ist deine Tasche? – Die da.

♦ **that one (3)** (*neuter*) das da ◇ *Which is your car? – That one.* Welches ist Ihr Auto? – Das da.

oneself PRONOUN

1 sich ◇ *to hurt oneself* sich wehtun

2 selbst ◇ *It's quicker to do it oneself.* Es geht schneller, wenn man es selbst macht.

one-way ADJECTIVE

♦ **a one-way street** eine Einbahnstraße

onion NOUN

die Zwiebel ◇ *onion soup* die Zwiebelsuppe

on-line ADJECTIVE

online

only ADVERB, ADJECTIVE, CONJUNCTION

1 einzig ◇ *Monday is the only day I'm free.* Montag ist mein einziger Tag frei. ◇ *German is the only subject I like.* Deutsch ist das einzige Fach, das ich mag.

2 nur ◇ *How much was it? – Only twenty euros.* Wie viel hat es gekostet? – Nur zwanzig Euro. ◇ *We only want to stay for one night.* Wir wollen nur eine Nacht bleiben. ◇ *I'd like the same sweater, only in black.* Ich möchte den gleichen Pullover, nur in Schwarz.

♦ **an only child** ein Einzelkind NEUT

onwards ADVERB

ab ◇ *from July onwards* ab Juli

open ADJECTIVE

see also **open** VERB

offen ◊ *The window was open.* Das Fenster war offen.

♦ **The baker's is open on Sunday morning.** Die Bäckerei hat am Sonntagmorgen auf.

♦ **in the open air** im Freien

to **open** VERB

see also **open** ADJECTIVE

1 aufmachen (PERFECT hat aufgemacht) ◊ *Can I open the window?* Kann ich das Fenster aufmachen? ◊ *What time do the shops open?* Um wie viel Uhr machen die Geschäfte auf?

2 aufgehen (IMPERFECT ging auf, PERFECT ist aufgegangen) ◊ *The door opens automatically.* Die Tür geht automatisch auf. ◊ *The door opened and in came the teacher.* Die Tür ging auf, und der Lehrer kam herein.

opening hours PL NOUN
die Öffnungszeiten FEM PL

opera NOUN
die Oper

to **operate** VERB
bedienen (*machine*) (PERFECT hat bedient)

♦ **to operate on someone** jemanden operieren

operation NOUN
die Operation ◊ *a major operation* eine größere Operation

♦ **to have an operation** operiert werden ◊ *I have never had an operation.* Ich bin noch nie operiert worden.

operator NOUN
(*on telephone*)
der Telefonist (GEN des Telefonisten, PL die Telefonisten)
die Telefonistin

opinion NOUN
die Meinung ◊ *He asked me my opinion.* Er fragte mich nach meiner Meinung. ◊ *What's your opinion?* Was ist deine Meinung?

♦ **in my opinion** meiner Meinung nach

opinion poll NOUN
die Meinungsumfrage

opponent NOUN
der Gegner (PL die Gegner)
die Gegnerin

opportunity NOUN
die Gelegenheit

♦ **to have the opportunity to do something** die Gelegenheit haben, etwas zu tun ◊ *I've never had the opportunity to go to Germany.* Ich hatte noch nie die Gelegenheit, nach Deutschland zu fahren.

opposed ADJECTIVE

♦ **to be opposed to something** gegen etwas sein ◊ *I've always been opposed to violence.* Ich bin immer gegen Gewalt gewesen.

opposing ADJECTIVE
gegnerisch (*team*)

opposite ADJECTIVE, ADVERB, PREPOSITION
1 entgegengesetzt ◊ *It's in the opposite direction.* Es ist in der entgegengesetzten Richtung.

2 gegenüber ◊ *They live opposite.* Sie wohnen gegenüber. ◊ *the girl who was sitting opposite me* das Mädchen, das mir gegenüber saß

♦ **the opposite sex** das andere Geschlecht

opposition NOUN
die Opposition

optician NOUN
der Optiker (PL die Optiker)
die Optikerin
◊ *She's an optician.* Sie ist Optikerin.

optimist NOUN
der Optimist (GEN des Optimisten, PL die Optimisten)
die Optimistin
◊ *She's an optimist.* Sie ist Optimistin.

optimistic ADJECTIVE
optimistisch

option NOUN
1 (*choice*)
die Wahl ◊ *I've got no option.* Ich habe keine andere Wahl.

2 (*optional subject*)
das Wahlfach (PL die Wahlfächer) ◊ *I'm doing geology as my option.* Ich habe Geologie als Wahlfach.

optional ADJECTIVE
fakultativ

or CONJUNCTION
1 oder ◊ *Would you like tea or coffee?* Möchten Sie Tee oder Kaffee?

*Use **weder ... noch** in negative sentences.*

◊ *I don't eat meat or fish.* Ich esse weder Fleisch noch Fisch.

2 sonst (*otherwise*) ◊ *Hurry up or you'll miss the bus.* Beeil dich, sonst verpasst du den Bus.

♦ **Give me the money, or else!** Gib mir das Geld, sonst gibt's was!

oral ADJECTIVE

see also **oral** NOUN

mündlich ◊ *an oral exam* eine mündliche Prüfung

oral NOUN

see also **oral** ADJECTIVE

die mündliche Prüfung ◊ *I've got my German oral soon.* Ich habe bald meine mündliche Prüfung in Deutsch.

orange NOUN

see also **orange** ADJECTIVE

die Orange

♦ **an orange juice** ein Orangensaft MASC

orange ADJECTIVE

see also **orange** NOUN

orangerot (*colour*)

orchard NOUN
der Obstgarten (PL die Obstgärten)

orchestra NOUN
1 das Orchester (PL die Orchester) ◊ *I play in the school orchestra.* Ich spiele im Schulorchester.
2 (*stalls*)
das Parkett ◊ *We sat in the orchestra.* Wir saßen im Parkett.

order NOUN
see also **order** VERB
1 (*sequence*)
die Reihenfolge ◊ *in alphabetical order* in alphabetischer Reihenfolge
2 (*at restaurant, in shop*)
die Bestellung ◊ *The waiter took our order.* Der Ober nahm unsere Bestellung auf.
3 (*instruction*)
der Befehl (PL die Befehle) ◊ *That's an order.* Das ist ein Befehl.
♦ **in order to** um zu ◊ *He does it in order to earn money.* Er tut es, um Geld zu verdienen.
♦ **"out of order"** "außer Betrieb"

to **order** VERB
see also **order** NOUN
bestellen (PERFECT hat bestellt) ◊ *We ordered steak and chips.* Wir haben Steak mit Pommes frites bestellt. ◊ *Are you ready to order?* Möchten Sie bestellen?

to **order about** VERB
herumkommandieren (PERFECT hat herumkommandiert) ◊ *She was fed up with being ordered about.* Sie hatte es satt, herumkommandiert zu werden.

ordinary ADJECTIVE
1 gewöhnlich ◊ *an ordinary day* ein gewöhnlicher Tag
2 normal (*people*) ◊ *an ordinary family* eine normale Familie ◊ *He's just an ordinary guy.* Er ist ein ganz normaler Mensch.

organ NOUN
die Orgel (*instrument*) ◊ *I play the organ.* Ich spiele Orgel.

organic ADJECTIVE
biodynamisch (*fruit*)
♦ **organic vegetables** das Biogemüse SING

organization NOUN
die Organisation

to **organize** VERB
organisieren (PERFECT hat organisiert)

origin NOUN
der Ursprung (PL die Ursprünge)

original ADJECTIVE
originell ◊ *It's a very original idea.* Das ist eine sehr originelle Idee.
♦ **Our original plan was to go camping.** Ursprünglich wollten wir zelten.

originally ADVERB
ursprünglich

Orkney NOUN
die Orkneyinseln FEM PL
♦ **in Orkney** auf den Orkneyinseln

ornament NOUN
die Verzierung

orphan NOUN
das Waisenkind (PL die Waisenkinder) ◊ *She's an orphan.* Sie ist ein Waisenkind.

ostrich NOUN
der Strauß (GEN des Straußes, PL die Strauße)

other ADJECTIVE, PRONOUN
andere ◊ *Have you got these jeans in other colours?* Haben Sie diese Jeans in anderen Farben? ◊ *on the other side of the street* auf der anderen Straßenseite
♦ **the other day** neulich
♦ **the other one (1)** (*masculine*) der andere ◊ *This hat? – No, the other one.* Dieser Hut? – Nein, der andere.
♦ **the other one (2)** (*feminine*) die andere ◊ *This cup? – No, the other one.* Diese Tasse? – Nein, die andere.
♦ **the other one (3)** (*neuter*) das andere ◊ *This photo? – No, the other one.* Dieses Foto? – Nein, das andere.
♦ **the others** die anderen ◊ *The others are going but I'm not.* Die anderen gehen, ich nicht.

otherwise ADVERB, CONJUNCTION
sonst ◊ *Note down the number, otherwise you'll forget it.* Schreib dir die Nummer auf, sonst vergisst du sie. ◊ *Put some sunscreen on, you'll get burned otherwise.* Creme dich ein, sonst bekommst du einen Sonnenbrand. ◊ *I'm tired, but otherwise I'm fine.* Ich bin müde, aber sonst geht's mir gut.

ought VERB
*If you want to say that you feel obliged to do something, use the conditional tense of **sollen**.*
◊ *I ought to phone my parents.* Ich sollte meine Eltern anrufen. ◊ *You ought not to do that.* Du solltest das nicht tun.
*If you want to say that something is likely, use the conditional tense of **müssen**.*
◊ *He ought to win.* Er müsste gewinnen.

ounce NOUN
die Unze

our ADJECTIVE
unser ◊ *Our boss is quite nice.* Unser Chef ist ganz nett. ◊ *Our company is going to expand.* Unsere Firma wird expandieren. ◊ *Our house is quite big.* Unser Haus ist ziemlich groß. ◊ *Our neighbours are very nice.* Unsere Nachbarn sind sehr nett.
*Do not use **unser** with parts of the body.*
◊ *We had to shut our eyes.* Wir mussten die Augen zumachen.

ours PRONOUN

[1] unserer ◊ *Your garden is very big, ours is much smaller.* Euer Garten ist sehr groß, unserer ist viel kleiner.
unsere ◊ *Your school is very different from ours.* Eure Schule ist ganz anderes als unsere.
unseres ◊ *Your house is bigger than ours.* Euer Haus ist größer als unseres.
[2] unsere ◊ *Our teachers are strict. – Ours are too.* Unsere Lehrer sind streng. – Unsere auch.
♦ **Is this ours?** Gehört das uns? ◊ *This car is ours.* Das Auto gehört uns. ◊ *Whose is this? – It's ours.* Wem gehört das? – Uns.

ourselves PRONOUN

[1] uns ◊ *We really enjoyed ourselves.* Wir haben uns wirklich amüsiert.
[2] selbst ◊ *We built our garage ourselves.* Wir haben die Garage selbst gebaut.

out ADVERB

> There are several ways of translating *out*. Scan the examples to find one that is similar to what you want to say. For other expressions with *out*, see the verbs *go, put, turn* etc.

[1] draußen (*outside*) ◊ *It's cold out.* Es ist kalt draußen.
[2] aus (*light, fire*) ◊ *All the lights are out.* Alle Lichter sind aus.
♦ **She's out.** Sie ist weg. ◊ *She's out for the afternoon.* Sie ist den ganzen Nachmittag weg.
♦ **She's out shopping.** Sie ist zum Einkaufen.
♦ **out there** da draußen ◊ *It's cold out there.* Es ist kalt da draußen.
♦ **to go out** ausgehen ◊ *I'm going out tonight.* Ich gehe heute Abend aus.
♦ **to go out with somebody** mit jemandem gehen ◊ *I've been going out with him for two months.* Ich gehe seit zwei Monaten mit ihm.
♦ **out of (1)** aus ◊ *to drink out of a glass* aus einem Glas trinken
♦ **out of (2)** von ◊ *in nine cases out of ten* in neun von zehn Fällen
♦ **out of (3)** außerhalb ◊ *He lives out of town.* Er wohnt außerhalb der Stadt. ◊ *three kilometres out of town* drei Kilometer außerhalb der Stadt
♦ **out of curiosity** aus Neugier
♦ **out of work** arbeitslos
♦ **That is out of the question.** Das kommt nicht infrage.
♦ **You're out!** (*in game*) Du bist draußen!
♦ **"way out"** "Ausgang"

outbreak NOUN

der Ausbruch (PL die Ausbrüche) ◊ *a salmonella outbreak* ein Ausbruch von Salmonellenvergiftung ◊ *the outbreak of war* der Kriegsausbruch

outcome NOUN

das Ergebnis (PL die Ergebnisse)

outdoor ADJECTIVE

im Freien ◊ *outdoor activities* Aktivitäten im Freien
♦ **an outdoor swimming pool** ein Freibad NEUT

outdoors ADVERB

im Freien

outfit NOUN

das Outfit (PL die Outfits) ◊ *a cowboy outfit* ein Cowboyoutfit

outgoing ADJECTIVE

aufgeschlossen ◊ *She's very outgoing.* Sie ist sehr aufgeschlossen.

outing NOUN

der Ausflug (PL die Ausflüge) ◊ *to go on an outing* einen Ausflug machen

outline NOUN

[1] (*summary*)
der Grundriss (GEN des Grundrisses, PL die Grundrisse)
♦ **This is an outline of the plan.** Das ist der Grundriss des Plans.
[2] (*shape*)
der Umriss (GEN des Umrisses, PL die Umrisse) ◊ *We could see the outline of the mountain in the mist.* Wir konnten im Nebel den Umriss des Berges erkennen.

outlook NOUN

[1] die Einstellung (*attitude*) ◊ *my outlook on life* meine Einstellung zum Leben
[2] die Aussichten PL (*prospects*)

outrageous ADJECTIVE

[1] unerhört (*behaviour*)
[2] unverschämt (*price*)

outset NOUN

der Anfang (PL die Anfänge) ◊ *at the outset* am Anfang

outside NOUN

> see also **outside** ADJECTIVE

die Außenseite

outside ADJECTIVE, ADVERB, PREPOSITION

> see also **outside** NOUN

[1] äußere ◊ *the outside walls* die äußeren Mauern
[2] draußen ◊ *It's very cold outside.* Draußen ist es sehr kalt.
[3] außerhalb ◊ *outside the school* außerhalb der Schule ◊ *outside school hours* außerhalb der Schulzeit

outsize ADJECTIVE

übergroß

outskirts PL NOUN

der Stadtrand SING ◊ *on the outskirts of the town* am Stadtrand

outstanding ADJECTIVE

bemerkenswert

oval ADJECTIVE

oval

oven NOUN

der Backofen (PL die Backöfen)

O

over PREPOSITION, ADVERB, ADJECTIVE

1 über

Use the accusative to express movement or a change of place. Use the dative when there is no change of place.

◊ *The ball went over the wall.* Der Ball flog über die Mauer. ◊ *There's a mirror over the washbasin.* Über dem Becken ist ein Spiegel.

2 über +ACC (*more than*) ◊ *It's over ten kilos.* Es ist über zehn Kilo schwer. ◊ *The temperature was over thirty degrees.* Die Temperatur lag über dreißig Grad.

3 vorbei (*finished*) ◊ *I'll be happy when the exams are over.* Ich bin froh, wenn die Prüfungen vorbei sind.

♦ **over the holidays** die Ferien über
♦ **over Christmas** über Weihnachten
♦ **over here** hier
♦ **over there** dort
♦ **all over Scotland** in ganz Schottland

overall ADVERB

insgesamt (*generally*) ◊ *My results were quite good overall.* Insgesamt hatte ich ganz gute Noten.

overalls PL NOUN

der Overall SING (PL die Overalls)

overcast ADJECTIVE

bedeckt ◊ *The sky was overcast.* Der Himmel war bedeckt.

to **overcharge** VERB

zu viel berechnen (PERFECT hat zu viel berechnet) ◊ *He overcharged me.* Er hat mir zu viel berechnet. ◊ *They overcharged us for the meal.* Sie haben uns für das Essen zu viel berechnet.

overcoat NOUN

der Mantel (PL die Mäntel)

overdone ADJECTIVE

verkocht (*food*)

overdose NOUN

die Überdosis (*of drugs*) (PL die Überdosen) ◊ *to take an overdose* eine Überdosis nehmen

overdraft NOUN

der Überziehungskredit

to **overestimate** VERB

überschätzen (PERFECT hat überschätzt)

overhead projector NOUN

der Tageslichtprojektor (PL die Tageslichtprojektoren)

to **overlook** VERB

1 (*have view of*)

einen Blick haben auf +ACC (PRESENT hat einen Blick auf, IMPERFECT hatte einen Blick auf, PERFECT hat einen Blick auf gehabt) ◊ *The hotel overlooked the beach.* Vom Hotel hat man einen Blick auf den Strand.

2 (*forget about*)

übersehen (PRESENT übersieht, IMPERFECT übersah, PERFECT hat übersehen) ◊ *He had overlooked one important problem.* Er hatte ein wichtiges Problem übersehen.

overseas ADVERB

1 im Ausland ◊ *I'd like to work overseas.* Ich würde gern im Ausland arbeiten.

2 ins Ausland ◊ *His company has sent him overseas.* Seine Firma hat ihn ins Ausland geschickt.

oversight NOUN

das Versehen (PL die Versehen)

to **oversleep** VERB

verschlafen (PRESENT verschläft, IMPERFECT verschlief, PERFECT hat verschlafen) ◊ *I overslept this morning.* Ich habe heute morgen verschlafen.

to **overtake** VERB

überholen (PERFECT hat überholt) ◊ *He overtook me.* Er hat mich überholt.

overtime NOUN

die Überstunden FEM PL ◊ *to work overtime* Überstunden machen

overtook VERB *see* **overtake**

overweight ADJECTIVE

♦ **to be overweight** Übergewicht haben

to **owe** VERB

schulden

♦ **to owe somebody something** jemandem etwas schulden ◊ *You owe me five pounds.* Du schuldest mir fünf Pfund.

owing to PREPOSITION

wegen ◊ *owing to bad weather* wegen des schlechten Wetters

owl NOUN

die Eule

own ADJECTIVE

see also **own** VERB

eigen ◊ *I've got my own bathroom.* Ich habe mein eigenes Badezimmer.

♦ **I'd like a room of my own.** Ich hätte gern ein eigenes Zimmer.

♦ **on one's own** allein ◊ *on her own* allein ◊ *on our own* allein

to **own** VERB

see also **own** ADJECTIVE

besitzen (IMPERFECT besaß, PERFECT hat besessen) ◊ *My father owns a small business.* Mein Vater besitzt ein kleines Geschäft.

to **own up** VERB

zugeben (PRESENT gibt zu, IMPERFECT gab zu, PERFECT hat zugegeben) ◊ *to own up to something* etwas zugeben

owner NOUN

der Besitzer (PL die Besitzer)
die Besitzerin

oxygen NOUN

der Sauerstoff

oyster NOUN

die Auster

ozone layer NOUN

die Ozonschicht

P

PA NOUN (= personal assistant)
der <u>Chefsekretär</u> (PL die Chefsekretäre)
die <u>Chefsekretärin</u>
◇ *She's a PA.* Sie ist Chefsekretärin.
♦ **the PA system** (*public address*) die
Lautsprecheranlage

pace NOUN
das <u>Tempo</u> (*speed*) ◇ *Technology is
developing at a rapid pace.* Die
Technologie entwickelt sich in schnellem
Tempo.
♦ **He was walking at a brisk pace.** Er ging
mit schnellen Schritten.

Pacific NOUN
der <u>Pazifik</u>

pacifier NOUN US
der <u>Schnuller</u> (PL die Schnuller)

to **pack** VERB
  see also **pack** NOUN
<u>packen</u> ◇ *I'll help you pack.* Ich helfe
dir packen. ◇ *I've already packed my
case.* Ich habe meinen Koffer schon
gepackt.
♦ **Pack it in!** (*stop it*) Lass es!

pack NOUN
  see also **pack** VERB
1 (*packet*)
die <u>Packung</u> ◇ *a pack of cigarettes* eine
Packung Zigaretten
2 (*of yoghurts, cans*)
der <u>Pack</u> (PL die Packs) ◇ *a six-pack* ein
Sechserpack
♦ **a pack of cards** ein Spiel Karten NEUT

package NOUN
das <u>Paket</u> (PL die Pakete)
♦ **a package holiday** eine Pauschalreise

packed ADJECTIVE
<u>gerammelt voll</u> ◇ *The cinema was
packed.* Das Kino war gerammelt voll.

packed lunch NOUN
das <u>Lunchpaket</u> (PL die Lunchpakete)
♦ **I take a packed lunch to school.** Ich
nehme für mittags etwas zum Essen in
die Schule mit.

packet NOUN
die <u>Packung</u> ◇ *a packet of cigarettes* eine
Packung Zigaretten

pad NOUN
der <u>Notizblock</u> (*notepad*) (PL die
Notizblöcke)

to **paddle** VERB
  see also **paddle** NOUN
1 <u>paddeln</u> (*canoe*)
2 <u>planschen</u> (*in water*)

paddle NOUN
  see also **paddle** VERB
das <u>Paddel</u> (*for canoe*) (PL die Paddel)
♦ **to go for a paddle** planschen gehen

padlock NOUN
das <u>Vorhängeschloss</u> (GEN des
Vorhängeschlosses, PL die
Vorhängeschlösser)

page NOUN
  see also **page** VERB
die <u>Seite</u> (*of book*)

to **page** VERB
  see also **page** NOUN
♦ **to page somebody** jemanden per Pager
benachrichtigen

pager NOUN
der <u>Pager</u> (PL die Pager)

paid VERB *see* pay

paid ADJECTIVE
<u>bezahlt</u> ◇ *three weeks' paid holiday* drei
Wochen bezahlter Urlaub

pail NOUN
der <u>Eimer</u> (PL die Eimer)

pain NOUN
der <u>Schmerz</u> (GEN des Schmerzes, PL die
Schmerzen) ◇ *a terrible pain* ein
furchtbarer Schmerz
♦ **I've got pains in my stomach.** Ich habe
Bauchschmerzen.
♦ **to be in pain** Schmerzen haben ◇ *She's
in a lot of pain.* Sie hat starke Schmerzen.
♦ **He's a real pain.** Er geht einem echt auf
die Nerven. (*informal*)

painful ADJECTIVE
<u>schmerzhaft</u>
♦ **to suffer from painful periods** starke
Periodenschmerzen haben
♦ **to be painful** wehtun ◇ *Is it painful?* Tut
es weh?

painkiller NOUN
das <u>Schmerzmittel</u> (PL die
Schmerzmittel)

paint NOUN
  see also **paint** VERB
die <u>Farbe</u>

to **paint** VERB
  see also **paint** NOUN
1 <u>streichen</u> (IMPERFECT strich, PERFECT hat
gestrichen) ◇ *to paint something green*
etwas grün streichen
2 (*pictures*)
<u>malen</u> ◇ *She painted a picture of the
house.* Sie hat von dem Haus ein Bild
gemalt.

paintbrush NOUN
der <u>Pinsel</u> (PL die Pinsel)

painter NOUN
der <u>Maler</u> (PL die Maler)
die <u>Malerin</u>
♦ **a painter and decorator** ein Anstreicher

painting NOUN

☞

1 das <u>Malen</u> ◊ *My hobby is painting.*
Malen ist mein Hobby.

2 (*picture*)
das <u>Bild</u> (PL die Bilder) ◊ *a painting by
Picasso* ein Bild von Picasso

pair NOUN
das <u>Paar</u> (PL die Paare) ◊ *a pair of shoes*
ein Paar Schuhe

♦ **a pair of scissors** eine Schere
♦ **a pair of trousers** eine Hose
♦ **a pair of jeans** eine Jeans
♦ **in pairs** paarweise ◊ *We work in pairs.*
Wir arbeiten paarweise.

pajamas PL NOUN US
der <u>Schlafanzug</u> (PL die Schlafanzüge)
◊ *my pajamas* mein Schlafanzug

♦ **a pair of pajamas** ein Schlafanzug

Pakistan NOUN
<u>Pakistan</u> NEUT

♦ **from Pakistan** aus Pakistan
♦ **to Pakistan** nach Pakistan

Pakistani NOUN
see also **Pakistani** ADJECTIVE
der <u>Pakistani</u> (PL die Pakistani)
die <u>Pakistani</u>

Pakistani ADJECTIVE
see also **Pakistani** NOUN
pakistanisch

♦ **He's Pakistani.** Er ist Pakistani.

pal NOUN
der <u>Kumpel</u> (*informal*) (PL die
Kumpel)
der Kumpel is also used for women.

palace NOUN
der <u>Palast</u> (PL die Paläste)

pale ADJECTIVE
<u>blass</u> ◊ *You're very pale.* Du bist sehr
blass.

♦ **a pale blue shirt** ein hellblaues Hemd

Palestine NOUN
<u>Palästina</u> NEUT

♦ **from Palestine** aus Palästina
♦ **to Palestine** nach Palästina

Palestinian ADJECTIVE
see also **Palestinian** NOUN
palästinensisch

♦ **He's Palestinian.** Er ist Palästinenser.

Palestinian NOUN
see also **Palestinian** ADJECTIVE
der <u>Palästinenser</u> (PL die Palästinenser)
die <u>Palästinenserin</u>

palm NOUN
der <u>Handteller</u> (*of hand*) (PL die
Handteller)

♦ **a palm tree** eine Palme

pamphlet NOUN
die <u>Broschüre</u>

pan NOUN
1 (*saucepan*)
der <u>Topf</u> (PL die Töpfe)
2 (*frying pan*)
die <u>Pfanne</u>

pancake NOUN
der <u>Pfannkuchen</u> (PL die Pfannkuchen)

panic NOUN
see also **panic** VERB
die <u>Panik</u>

to **panic** VERB
see also **panic** NOUN
in Panik geraten (PRESENT gerät in Panik,
IMPERFECT geriet in Panik, PERFECT ist in Panik
geraten) ◊ *She panicked.* Sie geriet in
Panik.

♦ **Don't panic!** Nur keine Panik!

panther NOUN
der <u>Panther</u> (PL die Panther)

panties PL NOUN
der <u>Slip</u> (PL die Slips) ◊ *a pair of panties*
ein Slip

pantomime NOUN
das <u>Weihnachtsmärchen</u> (PL die
Weihnachtsmärchen)

pants PL NOUN
1 die <u>Unterhose</u> (*underwear*) ◊ *a pair of
pants* eine Unterhose
2 die <u>Hose</u> (*trousers*) ◊ *a pair of pants*
eine Hose

pantyhose PL NOUN US
die <u>Strumpfhose</u>

paper NOUN
1 das <u>Papier</u> (PL die Papiere) ◊ *a piece of
paper* ein Stück Papier ◊ *a paper towel*
ein Papierhandtuch
2 (*newspaper*)
die <u>Zeitung</u> ◊ *I saw an advert in the
paper.* Ich habe eine Anzeige in der
Zeitung gesehen.

♦ **an exam paper** eine Klausur

paperback NOUN
das <u>Taschenbuch</u> (PL die
Taschenbücher)

paper boy NOUN
der <u>Zeitungsjunge</u> (GEN des
Zeitungsjungen, PL die Zeitungsjungen)

paper clip NOUN
die <u>Büroklammer</u>

paper girl NOUN
das <u>Zeitungsmädchen</u> (PL die
Zeitungsmädchen)

paper round NOUN

♦ **to do a paper round** Zeitungen austragen

paperweight NOUN
der <u>Briefbeschwerer</u> (PL die
Briefbeschwerer)

paperwork NOUN
die <u>Schreibarbeit</u> ◊ *I've got a lot of
paperwork to do.* Ich habe eine Menge
Schreibarbeit zu erledigen.

parachute NOUN
der <u>Fallschirm</u> (PL die Fallschirme)

parade NOUN
die <u>Parade</u>

paradise NOUN
das <u>Paradies</u> (GEN des Paradieses, PL die
Paradiese)

paraffin NOUN
das Petroleum ◊ *a paraffin lamp* eine
Petroleumlampe

paragraph NOUN
der Paragraf (GEN des Paragrafen, PL die
Paragrafen)

parallel ADJECTIVE
parallel

paralyzed ADJECTIVE
gelähmt

paramedic NOUN
der Sanitäter (PL die Sanitäter)
die Sanitäterin

parcel NOUN
das Paket (PL die Pakete)

pardon NOUN
♦**Pardon?** Wie bitte?

parent NOUN
[1] der Vater (*father*)
[2] die Mutter (*mother*)
♦ **my parents** meine Eltern

Paris NOUN
Paris NEUT

park NOUN
see also **park** VERB
der Park (PL die Parks) ◊ *a national park*
ein Nationalpark ◊ *a theme park* ein
Themenpark
♦ **a car park** ein Parkplatz MASC

to **park** VERB
see also **park** NOUN
parken ◊ *Where can I park my car?* Wo
kann ich mein Auto parken?
♦ **We couldn't find anywhere to park.** Wir
haben nirgends einen Parkplatz
gefunden.

parking NOUN
das Parken ◊ *"no parking"* "Parken
verboten"

parking lot NOUN US
der Parkplatz (GEN des Parkplatzes, PL die
Parkplätze)

parking meter NOUN
die Parkuhr

parking ticket NOUN
der Strafzettel (PL die Strafzettel)

parliament NOUN
das Parlament (PL die Parlamente)

parole NOUN
♦ **on parole** auf Bewährung

parrot NOUN
der Papagei (PL die Papageien)

parsley NOUN
die Petersilie

part NOUN
[1] (*section*)
der Teil (PL die Teile) ◊ *The first part of
the film was boring.* Der erste Teil des
Films war langweilig.
[2] (*component*)
das Teil (PL die Teile) ◊ *spare parts*
Ersatzteile

[3] (*in play, film*)
die Rolle
♦ **to take part in something** an etwas
teilnehmen ◊ *A lot of people took part in
the demonstration.* An der
Demonstration haben viele Menschen
teilgenommen.

particular ADJECTIVE
bestimmt ◊ *I am looking for a particular
book.* Ich suche ein bestimmtes Buch.
♦ **Are you looking for anything particular?**
Suchen Sie nach etwas Bestimmtem?
♦ **nothing in particular** nichts Bestimmtes

particularly ADVERB
besonders

parting NOUN
der Scheitel (*in hair*) (PL die Scheitel)

partly ADVERB
zum Teil

partner NOUN
der Partner (PL die Partner)
die Partnerin

part-time ADJECTIVE, ADVERB
Teilzeit ◊ *a part-time job* eine
Teilzeitarbeit ◊ *She works part-time.* Sie
arbeitet Teilzeit.

party NOUN
[1] die Party (PL die Partys) ◊ *a birthday
party* eine Geburtstagsparty ◊ *a
Christmas party* eine Weihnachtsparty
◊ *a New Year party* eine Silvesterparty
[2] (*political*)
die Partei ◊ *the Conservative Party* die
Konservative Partei
[3] (*group*)
die Gruppe ◊ *a party of tourists* eine
Gruppe Touristen

pass NOUN
see also **pass** VERB
der Pass (GEN des Passes, PL die Pässe)
◊ *The pass was blocked with snow.* Der
Pass war zugeschneit. ◊ *That was a good
pass by Ferguson.* Das war ein guter
Pass von Ferguson.
♦ **to get a pass** (*in exam*) bestehen ◊ *She
got a pass in her piano exam.* Sie hat
ihre Klavierprüfung bestanden. ◊ *I got six
passes.* Ich habe in sechs Fächern
bestanden.
♦ **a bus pass (1)** (*monthly*) eine Monatskarte
für den Bus
♦ **a bus pass (2)** (*for old-age pensioners*) eine
Seniorenkarte für den Bus

> ⓘ *Almost all German cities operate an
> integrated public transport system; you
> can buy a weekly (**Wochenkarte**),
> monthly (**Monatskarte**) or yearly
> (**Jahreskarte**) pass which are valid for
> that period on all buses, trams and
> light railway vehicles in a particular
> zone.*

P

to **pass** VERB

> *see also* **pass** NOUN

1 (*give*)
geben (PRESENT gibt, IMPERFECT gab, PERFECT hat gegeben) ◊ *Could you pass me the salt, please?* Könntest du mir bitte das Salz geben?

2 (*go by*)
vergehen (IMPERFECT verging, PERFECT ist vergangen) ◊ *The time has passed quickly.* Die Zeit ist schnell vergangen.

3 (*on foot*)
vorbeigehen an +DAT (IMPERFECT ging vorbei, PERFECT ist vorbeigegangen) ◊ *I pass his house on my way to school.* Auf dem Weg zur Schule gehe ich an seinem Haus vorbei.

4 (*in vehicle*)
vorbeifahren an +DAT (PRESENT fährt vorbei, IMPERFECT fuhr vorbei, PERFECT ist vorbeigefahren) ◊ *We passed the post office.* Wir sind an der Post vorbeigefahren.

5 (*exam*)
bestehen (IMPERFECT bestand, PERFECT hat bestanden) ◊ *Did you pass?* Hast du bestanden?

♦ **to pass an exam** eine Prüfung bestehen ◊ *I hope I'll pass the exam.* Ich hoffe, dass ich die Prüfung bestehe.

to **pass out** VERB
ohnmächtig werden (*faint*) (PRESENT wird ohnmächtig, IMPERFECT wurde ohnmächtig, PERFECT ist ohnmächtig geworden)

passage NOUN
1 (*piece of writing*)
der Abschnitt (PL die Abschnitte) ◊ *Read the passage carefully.* Lest den Abschnitt sorgfältig durch.
2 (*corridor*)
der Gang (PL die Gänge)

passenger NOUN
der Passagier (PL die Passagiere)
die Passagierin

passion NOUN
die Leidenschaft

passive ADJECTIVE
passiv
♦ **passive smoking** das Passivrauchen

Passover NOUN
das Passahfest

passport NOUN
der Pass (GEN des Passes, PL die Pässe)
◊ *passport control* die Passkontrolle

password NOUN
das Passwort (PL die Passwörter)

past ADVERB, PREPOSITION

> *see also* **past** NOUN

nach (*beyond*) ◊ *It's on the right, just past the station.* Es ist auf der rechten Seite, gleich nach dem Bahnhof. ◊ *It's quarter past nine.* Es ist Viertel nach neun.

♦ **It's past midnight.** Es ist schon nach Mitternacht.
♦ **It's half past ten.** Es ist halb elf.
♦ **to go past (1)** (*vehicle*) vorbeifahren ◊ *The bus went past without stopping.* Der Bus ist vorbeigefahren, ohne anzuhalten. ◊ *The bus goes past our house.* Der Bus fährt an unserem Haus vorbei.
♦ **to go past (2)** (*on foot*) vorbeigehen ◊ *He went past without saying hello.* Er ging vorbei, ohne Hallo zu sagen. ◊ *I went past your house yesterday.* Ich bin gestern an eurem Haus vorbeigegangen.

past NOUN

> *see also* **past** ADVERB

die Vergangenheit ◊ *She lives in the past.* Sie lebt in der Vergangenheit.
♦ **in the past** (*previously*) früher ◊ *That was common in the past.* Das war früher üblich.

pasta NOUN
die Teigwaren FEM PL ◊ *Pasta is easy to cook.* Teigwaren sind leicht zu kochen.

paste NOUN
der Leim (*glue*) (PL die Leime)

pasteurized ADJECTIVE
pasteurisiert

pastime NOUN
der Zeitvertreib (PL die Zeitvertreibe) ◊ *Crossword puzzles are a popular pastime.* Kreuzworträtsel sind ein beliebter Zeitvertreib.
♦ **Her favourite pastime is knitting.** Stricken ist ihre Lieblingsbeschäftigung.

pastry NOUN
der Teig
♦ **pastries** (*cakes*) das Gebäck SING

to **pat** VERB
streicheln (*dog, cat*) (PERFECT hat gestreichelt)

patch NOUN
1 das Stück (PL die Stücke) ◊ *a patch of material* ein Stück Stoff
2 (*for flat tyre*)
der Flicken (PL die Flicken)
♦ **He's got a bald patch.** Er hat eine kahle Stelle.

patched ADJECTIVE
geflickt ◊ *a pair of patched jeans* eine geflickte Jeans

pâté NOUN
die Fleischpastete
♦ **liver pâté** die Leberwurst

path NOUN
der Weg (PL die Wege)

pathetic ADJECTIVE
schrecklich schlecht ◊ *Our team was pathetic.* Unsere Mannschaft war schrecklich schlecht.

patience NOUN

[1] die <u>Geduld</u> ◊ *He hasn't got much patience.* Er hat nicht viel Geduld.
[2] die <u>Patience</u> (*card game*) ◊ *to play patience* Patience spielen

patient NOUN

see also **patient** ADJECTIVE

der <u>Patient</u> (GEN des Patienten, PL die Patienten)
die <u>Patientin</u>

patient ADJECTIVE

see also **patient** NOUN

<u>geduldig</u>

patio NOUN
die <u>Terrasse</u>

patriotic ADJECTIVE
<u>patriotisch</u>

patrol NOUN
[1] die <u>Patrouille</u> (*military*)
[2] die <u>Streife</u> (*of police*)

patrol car NOUN
der <u>Streifenwagen</u> (PL die Streifenwagen)

pattern NOUN
das <u>Muster</u> (PL die Muster) ◊ *a geometric pattern* ein geometrisches Muster ◊ *a sewing pattern* ein Nähmuster

pause NOUN
die <u>Pause</u>

pavement NOUN
der <u>Bürgersteig</u> (PL die Bürgersteige)

pavilion NOUN
der <u>Pavillon</u> (PL die Pavillons)

paw NOUN
die <u>Pfote</u>

pay NOUN

see also **pay** VERB

die <u>Bezahlung</u>

to **pay** VERB

see also **pay** NOUN

<u>bezahlen</u> (PERFECT hat bezahlt) ◊ *They pay me more on Sundays.* Sie bezahlen mir sonntags mehr. ◊ *to pay by cheque* mit Scheck bezahlen ◊ *to pay by credit card* mit Kreditkarte bezahlen

♦ **to pay for something** für etwas bezahlen ◊ *I paid fifty euros for it.* Ich habe fünfzig Euro dafür bezahlt. ◊ *I paid for my ticket.* Ich habe meine Fahrkarte bezahlt.

♦ **to pay extra for something** für etwas extra bezahlen ◊ *You have to pay extra for parking.* Fürs Parken müssen Sie extra bezahlen.

♦ **to pay attention** aufpassen ◊ *You should pay more attention.* Du solltest besser aufpassen.

♦ **Don't pay any attention to him.** Beachte ihn einfach nicht.

♦ **to pay somebody a visit** jemanden besuchen ◊ *Paul paid us a visit last night.* Paul hat uns gestern Abend besucht.

♦ **to pay somebody back** (*money*) es jemandem zurückzahlen ◊ *I'll pay you*

patient → pedestrian crossing

back tomorrow. Ich zahle es dir morgen zurück.

payment NOUN
die <u>Bezahlung</u>

payphone NOUN
der <u>Münzfernsprecher</u> (PL die Münzfernsprecher)

PC NOUN (= *personal computer*)
der <u>PC</u> (PL die PCs) ◊ *She typed the report on her PC.* Sie hat den Bericht am PC erfasst.

PE NOUN (= *physical education*)
der <u>Sportunterricht</u>

pea NOUN
die <u>Erbse</u>

peace NOUN
[1] der <u>Frieden</u> (*after war*)
[2] die <u>Stille</u> (*quietness*)

peaceful ADJECTIVE
[1] <u>ruhig</u> (*calm*) ◊ *a peaceful afternoon* ein ruhiger Nachmittag
[2] <u>friedlich</u> (*not violent*) ◊ *a peaceful protest* ein friedlicher Protest

peach NOUN
der <u>Pfirsich</u> (PL die Pfirsiche)

peacock NOUN
der <u>Pfau</u> (PL die Pfauen)

peak NOUN
der <u>Gipfel</u> (*of mountain*) (PL die Gipfel)

♦ **the peak rate** der Spitzentarif ◊ *You pay the peak rate for calls at this time of day.* Um diese Tageszeit zahlt man fürs Telefonieren den Spitzentarif.

♦ **in peak season** in der Hochsaison

peanut NOUN
die <u>Erdnuss</u> (PL die Erdnüsse) ◊ *a packet of peanuts* eine Packung Erdnüsse

peanut butter NOUN
die <u>Erdnussbutter</u> ◊ *a peanut butter sandwich* ein Brot mit Erdnussbutter

pear NOUN
die <u>Birne</u>

pearl NOUN
die <u>Perle</u>

pebble NOUN
der <u>Kieselstein</u> (PL die Kieselsteine)

♦ **a pebble beach** ein Kieselstrand MASC

peckish ADJECTIVE
♦ **to feel a bit peckish** ein bisschen Hunger haben

peculiar ADJECTIVE
<u>eigenartig</u> ◊ *He's a peculiar person.* Er ist ein eigenartiger Mensch. ◊ *It tastes peculiar.* Es schmeckt eigenartig.

pedal NOUN
das <u>Pedal</u> (PL die Pedale)

pedestrian NOUN
der <u>Fußgänger</u> (PL die Fußgänger)
die <u>Fußgängerin</u>

pedestrian crossing NOUN
der <u>Fußgängerüberweg</u> (PL die Fußgängerüberwege)

P

pedestrianized ADJECTIVE
♦**a pedestrianized street** eine Fußgängerzone
pedigree ADJECTIVE
reinrassig (*animal*) ◊ *a pedigree labrador* ein reinrassiger Labrador
pee NOUN
♦**to have a pee** pinkeln (*informal*)
peek NOUN
♦**to have a peek at something** einen kurzen Blick auf etwas werfen ◊ *I had a peek at your new dress.* Ich habe einen kurzen Blick auf dein neues Kleid geworfen.
peel NOUN
  see also **peel** VERB
die Schale (*of orange*)
to **peel** VERB
  see also **peel** NOUN
  [1] schälen ◊ *Shall I peel the potatoes?* Soll ich die Kartoffeln schälen?
  [2] sich schälen ◊ *My nose is peeling.* Meine Nase schält sich.
peg NOUN
  [1] (*for coats*)
  der Haken (PL die Haken)
  [2] (*clothes peg*)
  die Wäscheklammer
  [3] (*tent peg*)
  der Hering (PL die Heringe)
Pekinese NOUN
der Pekinese (GEN des Pekinesen, PL die Pekinesen)
pelican crossing NOUN
die Fußgängerampel
pellet NOUN
die Schrotkugel (*for gun*)
pelvis NOUN
das Becken (PL die Becken)
pen NOUN
der Schreiber (PL die Schreiber)
to **penalize** VERB
bestrafen (PERFECT hat bestraft)
penalty NOUN
  [1] (*punishment*)
  die Strafe ◊ *the death penalty* die Todesstrafe
  [2] (*in football*)
  der Elfmeter (PL die Elfmeter)
  [3] (*in rugby*)
  der Strafstoß (GEN des Strafstoßes, PL die Strafstöße)
♦**a penalty shoot-out** ein Elfmeterschießen NEUT
pence PL NOUN
die Pence MASC PL
pencil NOUN
der Bleistift (PL die Bleistifte)
♦**in pencil** mit Bleistift
pencil case NOUN
das Federmäppchen (PL die Federmäppchen)
pencil sharpener NOUN

der Bleistiftspitzer (PL die Bleistiftspitzer)
pendant NOUN
der Anhänger (PL die Anhänger)
pen friend NOUN
der Brieffreund (PL die Brieffreunde)
die Brieffreundin
penguin NOUN
der Pinguin (PL die Pinguine)
penicillin NOUN
das Penizillin
penis NOUN
der Penis (GEN des Penis, PL die Penisse)
penitentiary NOUN US
das Gefängnis (GEN des Gefängnisses, PL die Gefängnisse)
penknife NOUN
das Taschenmesser (PL die Taschenmesser)
penny NOUN
der Penny (PL die Pennys *or* Pence)
pension NOUN
die Rente
pensioner NOUN
der Rentner (PL die Rentner)
die Rentnerin
pentathlon NOUN
der Fünfkampf (PL die Fünfkämpfe)
people PL NOUN
  [1] die Leute PL ◊ *The people were nice.* Die Leute waren nett. ◊ *a lot of people* viele Leute
  [2] die Menschen MASC PL (*individuals*) ◊ *six people* sechs Menschen ◊ *several people* mehrere Menschen
♦**German people** die Deutschen
♦**black people** die Schwarzen
♦**People say that ...** Man sagt, dass ...
pepper NOUN
  [1] der Pfeffer (*spice*) ◊ *Pass the pepper, please.* Gib mir mal bitte den Pfeffer.
  [2] die Paprikaschote (*vegetable*) ◊ *a green pepper* eine grüne Paprikaschote
peppermill NOUN
die Pfeffermühle
peppermint NOUN
das Pfefferminzbonbon (*sweet*) (PL die Pfefferminzbonbons)
♦**peppermint chewing gum** der Kaugummi mit Pfefferminzgeschmack
per PREPOSITION
pro ◊ *per day* pro Tag ◊ *per week* pro Woche
♦**thirty miles per hour** dreißig Meilen in der Stunde
per cent ADVERB
das Prozent ◊ *fifty per cent* fünfzig Prozent
percentage NOUN
der Prozentsatz (GEN des Prozentsatzes, PL die Prozentsätze)
percolator NOUN
die Kaffeemaschine

percussion NOUN
das <u>Schlagzeug</u> (PL die Schlagzeuge)
◊ *I play percussion.* Ich spiele
Schlagzeug.

perfect ADJECTIVE
<u>perfekt</u> ◊ *Manfred speaks perfect
English.* Manfred spricht perfekt
Englisch.

perfectly ADVERB
1 <u>ganz</u> ◊ *You know perfectly well what
happened.* Du weißt ganz genau, was
passiert ist.
2 <u>perfekt</u> (*very well*) ◊ *The system
worked perfectly.* Das System hat perfekt
funktioniert.

to **perform** VERB
<u>spielen</u> (*act, play*)

performance NOUN
1 die <u>Vorstellung</u> (*show*) ◊ *The
performance lasts two hours.* Die
Vorstellung dauert zwei Stunden.
2 die <u>Darstellung</u> (*acting*) ◊ *his
performance as Hamlet* seine Darstellung
des Hamlet
3 die <u>Leistung</u> (*results*) ◊ *the team's
poor performance* die schwache Leistung
der Mannschaft

perfume NOUN
das <u>Parfüm</u> (PL die Parfüme)

perhaps ADVERB
<u>vielleicht</u> ◊ *a bit boring, perhaps* etwas
langweilig vielleicht ◊ *Perhaps he's ill.*
Vielleicht ist er krank. ◊ *perhaps not*
vielleicht nicht

period NOUN
1 die <u>Zeit</u> ◊ *for a limited period* für eine
begrenzte Zeit
2 die <u>Epoche</u> (*in history*) ◊ *the Victorian
period* die viktorianische Epoche
3 die <u>Periode</u> (*menstruation*) ◊ *I'm
having my period.* Ich habe meine
Periode.
4 die <u>Stunde</u> (*lesson time*) ◊ *Each period
lasts forty minutes.* Jede Stunde dauert
vierzig Minuten.

perm NOUN
die <u>Dauerwelle</u> ◊ *She's got a perm.* Sie
hat eine Dauerwelle.
♦ **to have a perm** sich eine Dauerwelle
machen lassen ◊ *I'm going to have a
perm.* Ich lasse mir eine Dauerwelle
machen.

permanent ADJECTIVE
1 <u>dauerhaft</u> (*damage, solution,
relationship*) ◊ *We need a permanent
solution.* Wir brauchen eine dauerhafte
Lösung.
2 <u>dauernd</u> (*difficulties, tension*) ◊ *a
permanent headache* dauernde
Kopfschmerzen
3 <u>fest</u> (*job, address*) ◊ *I'm hoping to get a
permanent job.* Ich hoffe, ich finde eine
feste Arbeit.

permission NOUN
die <u>Erlaubnis</u> (PL die Erlaubnisse) ◊ *to
ask somebody's permission* jemanden
um Erlaubnis bitten
♦ **Could I have permission to leave early?**
Darf ich früher gehen?

permit NOUN
der <u>Schein</u> (PL die Scheine) ◊ *a fishing
permit* ein Angelschein

to **persecute** VERB
<u>verfolgen</u> (PERFECT hat verfolgt)

Persian ADJECTIVE
♦ **a Persian cat** eine Perserkatze

persistent ADJECTIVE
<u>hartnäckig</u> (*person*)

person NOUN
1 der <u>Mensch</u> (GEN des Menschen, PL die
Menschen) ◊ *She's a very nice person.*
Sie ist ein netter Mensch.
2 (*in grammar*)
die <u>Person</u> ◊ *first person singular* erste
Person Singular
♦ **in person** persönlich

personal ADJECTIVE
<u>persönlich</u>

personality NOUN
die <u>Persönlichkeit</u>

personally ADVERB
<u>persönlich</u> ◊ *I don't know him
personally.* Ich kenne ihn nicht
persönlich. ◊ *Personally I don't agree.* Ich
persönlich bin nicht einverstanden.

personal stereo NOUN
der <u>Walkman</u> ® (PL die Walkmans)

personnel NOUN
das <u>Personal</u>

perspiration NOUN
der <u>Schweiß</u>

to **persuade** VERB
<u>überreden</u> (PERFECT hat überredet)
♦ **to persuade somebody to do something**
jemanden überreden, etwas zu tun ◊ *She
persuaded me to go with her.* Sie hat
mich überredet mitzukommen.

Peru NOUN
<u>Peru</u> NEUT

Peruvian ADJECTIVE
<u>peruanisch</u>

pessimist NOUN
der <u>Pessimist</u> (GEN des Pessimisten, PL die
Pessimisten)
die <u>Pessimistin</u>
◊ *I'm a pessimist.* Ich bin Pessimist.

pessimistic ADJECTIVE
<u>pessimistisch</u>

pest NOUN
die <u>Nervensäge</u> (*person*) ◊ *He's a real
pest!* Er ist eine echte Nervensäge!

to **pester** VERB
<u>belästigen</u> (PERFECT hat belästigt) ◊ *I wish
she would stop pestering me.* Ich

P

wünschte, sie würde aufhören, mich zu
belästigen.
◆ **The children pestered her to take them
to the zoo.** Die Kinder ließen ihr keine
Ruhe, mit ihnen in den Zoo zu gehen.

pesticide NOUN
das Pestizid

pet NOUN
das Haustier (PL die Haustiere) ◊ *Have
you got a pet?* Hast du ein Haustier?
◆ **She's the teacher's pet.** Sie ist das
Schätzchen der Lehrerin.

petition NOUN
die Petition ◊ *a petition for the abolition
of school uniform* eine Petition für die
Abschaffung der Schuluniform

petrified ADJECTIVE
◆ **to be petrified of something** panische
Angst vor etwas haben ◊ *She's petrified
of spiders.* Sie hat panische Angst vor
Spinnen.

petrol NOUN
das Benzin (PL die Benzine)
◆ **unleaded petrol** bleifreies Benzin
◆ **leaded petrol** verbleites Benzin
◆ **Four-star petrol, please.** Super, bitte.

petrol station NOUN
die Tankstelle

petrol tank NOUN
der Benzintank (PL die Benzintanks)

phantom NOUN
der Geist (PL die Geister)

pharmacy NOUN
die Apotheke

pheasant NOUN
der Fasan (PL die Fasane)

philosophy NOUN
die Philosophie

phobia NOUN
die Phobie

phone NOUN
see also **phone** VERB
das Telefon (PL die Telefone) ◊ *Where's
the phone?* Wo ist das Telefon? ◊ *Is there
a phone here?* Gibt es hier ein Telefon?
◆ **by phone** telefonisch
◆ **to be on the phone (1)** (*speaking*)
telefonieren ◊ *She's on the phone at the
moment.* Sie telefoniert gerade.
◆ **to be on the phone (2)** (*connected*)
Telefonanschluss haben ◊ *They're not on
the phone.* Sie haben keinen
Telefonanschluss.
◆ **Can I use the phone, please?** Kann ich
mal bitte telefonieren?

to **phone** VERB
see also **phone** NOUN
anrufen (IMPERFECT rief an, PERFECT hat
angerufen) ◊ *I tried to phone you
yesterday.* Ich habe gestern versucht,
dich anzurufen.

phone bill NOUN
die Telefonrechnung

phone book NOUN
das Telefonbuch (PL die Telefonbücher)

phone box NOUN
die Telefonzelle

phone call NOUN
der Anruf (PL die Anrufe) ◊ *There's a
phone call for you.* Da ist ein Anruf für
Sie.
◆ **to make a phone call** telefonieren ◊ *Can I
make a phone call?* Kann ich
telefonieren?

phonecard NOUN
die Telefonkarte

phone number NOUN
die Telefonnummer

photo NOUN
das Foto (PL die Fotos) ◊ *to take a photo*
ein Foto machen ◊ *to take a photo of
somebody* ein Foto von jemandem
machen

photocopier NOUN
der Fotokopierer (PL die Fotokopierer)

photocopy NOUN
see also **photocopy** VERB
die Fotokopie

to **photocopy** VERB
see also **photocopy** NOUN
fotokopieren (PERFECT hat fotokopiert)

photograph NOUN
see also **photograph** VERB
das Foto (PL die Fotos) ◊ *to take a
photograph* ein Foto machen ◊ *to take a
photograph of somebody* ein Foto von
jemandem machen
*Be careful not to translate **photograph**
by Fotograf.*

to **photograph** VERB
see also **photograph** NOUN
fotografieren (PERFECT hat fotografiert)

photographer NOUN
der Fotograf (GEN des Fotografen, PL die
Fotografen)
die Fotografin
◊ *She's a photographer.* Sie ist
Fotografin.

photography NOUN
die Fotografie ◊ *My hobby is
photography.* Mein Hobby ist die
Fotografie.

phrase NOUN
die Wendung

phrase book NOUN
der Sprachführer (PL die Sprachführer)

physical ADJECTIVE
see also **physical** NOUN
körperlich (*of the body*) ◊ *physical
exercise* körperliche Bewegung
◆ **physical education** der Sportunterricht
◆ **physical therapist** (*man*) der
Krankengymnast

physical NOUN US
see also **physical** ADJECTIVE

die ärztliche Untersuchung

physicist NOUN
der Physiker (PL die Physiker)
die Physikerin
◊ *He's a physicist.* Er ist Physiker.

physics NOUN
die Physik ◊ *She teaches physics.* Sie
unterrichtet Physik.

physiotherapist NOUN
der Krankengymnast (GEN des
Krankengymnasten, PL die
Krankengymnasten)
die Krankengymnastin

physiotherapy NOUN
die Krankengymnastik

pianist NOUN
der Pianist (GEN des Pianisten, PL die
Pianisten)
die Pianistin

piano NOUN
das Klavier (PL die Klaviere) ◊ *I play the
piano.* Ich spiele Klavier. ◊ *I have piano
lessons.* Ich nehme Klavierstunden.

pick NOUN
| see also **pick** VERB |

♦**Take your pick!** Du hast die Wahl!

to **pick** VERB
| see also **pick** NOUN |

1 (*choose*)
auswählen (PERFECT hat ausgewählt) ◊ *I
picked the biggest piece.* Ich habe das
größte Stück ausgewählt.
2 (*fruit, flowers*)
pflücken

♦**to pick on somebody** auf jemandem
herumhacken ◊ *She's always picking on
me.* Sie hackt dauernd auf mir herum.

♦**to pick out** auswählen ◊ *I like them all –
it's difficult to pick one out.* Sie gefallen
mir alle – es ist schwierig, eins
auszuwählen.

♦**to pick up (1)** (*collect*) abholen ◊ *We'll
come to the airport to pick you up.* Wir
holen dich am Flughafen ab.

♦**to pick up (2)** (*from floor*) aufheben
◊ *Could you help me pick up the toys?*
Kannst du mir helfen, die Spielsachen
aufzuheben?

♦**to pick up (3)** (*learn*) aufschnappen
(*informal*) ◊ *I picked up some Spanish
during my holiday.* Ich habe während der
Ferien etwas Spanisch aufgeschnappt.

pickpocket NOUN
der Taschendieb (PL die Taschendiebe)
die Taschendiebin

picnic NOUN
das Picknick (PL die Picknicke)

♦**to have a picnic** picknicken ◊ *We had a
picnic on the beach.* Wir haben am
Strand gepicknickt.

picture NOUN

1 das Bild (PL die Bilder) ◊ *Children's
books have lots of pictures.*
Kinderbücher sind voller Bilder.

♦**to draw a picture of something** etwas
zeichnen

2 das Foto (PL die Fotos) ◊ *My picture
was in the paper.* Mein Foto war in der
Zeitung.

3 (*painting*)
das Gemälde (PL die Gemälde) ◊ *a
famous picture* ein berühmtes Gemälde

♦**to paint a picture of something** etwas
malen

♦**the pictures** (*cinema*) das Kino ◊ *Shall we
go to the pictures?* Sollen wir ins Kino
gehen?

picture messaging NOUN
das Picture Messaging

picturesque ADJECTIVE
malerisch

pie NOUN

1 (*savoury*)
die Pastete

2 (*sweet*)
der Obstkuchen (PL die Obstkuchen)

♦**an apple pie** ein gedeckter Apfelkuchen

piece NOUN
das Stück (PL die Stücke) ◊ *A small piece,
please.* Ein kleines Stück, bitte.

♦**a piece of furniture** ein Möbelstück NEUT

♦**a piece of advice** ein Ratschlag MASC

pier NOUN
der Pier (PL die Piere)

pierced ADJECTIVE

1 durchstochen ◊ *I've got pierced ears.*
Ich habe durchstochene Ohrläppchen.

2 gepierct ◊ *She's got a pierced nose.*
Sie hat eine gepiercte Nase.

piercing ADJECTIVE
durchdringend (*cry*)

pig NOUN
das Schwein (PL die Schweine)

pigeon NOUN
die Taube

piggyback NOUN

♦**to give somebody a piggyback**
jemanden huckepack nehmen

piggy bank NOUN
das Sparschwein (PL die Sparschweine)

pigtail NOUN
der Zopf (PL die Zöpfe)

pile NOUN

1 (*tidy*)
der Stapel (PL die Stapel)

2 (*untidy*)
der Haufen (PL die Haufen)

piles PL NOUN
die Hämorriden PL

pile-up NOUN
der Auffahrunfall (PL die Auffahrunfälle)

pill NOUN
die Pille

♦**to be on the pill** die Pille nehmen

P

pillar NOUN
die Säule
pillar box NOUN
der Briefkasten (PL die Briefkästen)
pillow NOUN
das Kopfkissen (PL die Kopfkissen)
pilot NOUN
der Pilot (GEN des Piloten, PL die Piloten)
die Pilotin
◊ *He's a pilot.* Er ist Pilot.
pimple NOUN
der Pickel (PL die Pickel)
pin NOUN
die Stecknadel
♦ **I've got pins and needles in my foot.**
Mein Fuß ist eingeschlafen.
PIN NOUN (= *personal identification number*)
die PIN-Nummer
pinafore NOUN
die Schürze
pinball NOUN
der Flipper (PL die Flipper)
♦ **to play pinball** flippern
♦ **a pinball machine** ein Flipper
to **pinch** VERB
⓵ kneifen (IMPERFECT kniff, PERFECT hat gekniffen) ◊ *He pinched me!* Er hat mich gekniffen!
⓶ klauen (*informal: steal*) ◊ *Who's pinched my pen?* Wer hat meinen Schreiber geklaut?
pine NOUN
die Kiefer ◊ *a pine table* ein Kieferntisch MASC
pineapple NOUN
die Ananas (PL die Ananas)
pink ADJECTIVE
rosa
rosa is invariable.
◊ *a pink shirt* ein rosa Hemd
pint NOUN
das Pint (PL die Pints)

ⓘ *In Germany measurements are in litres and centilitres. A pint is about 0.6 litres. German people don't drink pints of beer, they are more likely to order* **ein großes Bier.**

♦ **to have a pint** ein Bier trinken ◊ *He's gone out for a pint.* Er ist ein Bier trinken gegangen.
pipe NOUN
⓵ (*for water, gas*)
das Rohr (PL die Rohre) ◊ *The pipes froze.* Die Rohre sind eingefroren.
⓶ (*for smoking*)
die Pfeife ◊ *He smokes a pipe.* Er raucht Pfeife.
♦ **the pipes** (*bagpipes*) der Dudelsack SING
◊ *He plays the pipes.* Er spielt Dudelsack.
pirate NOUN

der Pirat (GEN des Piraten, PL die Piraten)
pirated ADJECTIVE
♦ **a pirated video** ein Raubvideo NEUT
Pisces SING NOUN
die Fische MASC PL ◊ *I'm Pisces.* Ich bin Fisch.
pissed ADJECTIVE
besoffen (*informal*)
pissed off ADJECTIVE
♦ **I'm pissed off with him.** Ich hab die Schnauze voll von ihm. (*rude*)
pistol NOUN
die Pistole
pitch NOUN
see also **pitch** VERB
der Platz (GEN des Platzes, PL die Plätze)
◊ *a football pitch* ein Fußballplatz
to **pitch** VERB
see also **pitch** NOUN
aufschlagen (*tent*) (PRESENT schlägt auf, IMPERFECT schlug auf, PERFECT hat aufgeschlagen) ◊ *We pitched our tent near the beach.* Wir haben unser Zelt in der Nähe des Strandes aufgeschlagen.
pity NOUN
see also **pity** VERB
das Mitleid
♦ **What a pity!** Wie schade!
to **pity** VERB
see also **pity** NOUN
bemitleiden (PERFECT hat bemitleidet)
pizza NOUN
die Pizza (PL die Pizzas)
place NOUN
see also **place** VERB
⓵ (*location*)
der Ort (PL die Orte) ◊ *It's a quiet place.* Es ist ein ruhiger Ort. ◊ *There are a lot of interesting places to visit.* Es gibt viele interessante Orte zu besuchen.
⓶ (*space*)
der Platz (GEN des Platzes, PL die Plätze) ◊ *a parking place* ein Parkplatz ◊ *a university place* ein Studienplatz
♦ **to change places** die Plätze tauschen
◊ *Tamsin, change places with Christine!* Tamsin, tausch die Plätze mit Christine!
♦ **to take place** stattfinden
♦ **at your place** bei dir ◊ *Shall we meet at your place?* Sollen wir uns bei dir treffen?
♦ **to my place** zu mir ◊ *Do you want to come round to my place?* Willst du noch zu mir mitkommen?
to **place** VERB
see also **place** NOUN
legen ◊ *He placed his hand on hers.* Er legte seine Hand auf ihre.
♦ **He was placed third.** Er wurde Dritter.
plaid ADJECTIVE
kariert ◊ *a plaid shirt* ein kariertes Hemd
plain NOUN
see also **plain** ADJECTIVE

die <u>Ebene</u>

plain ADJECTIVE, ADVERB

see also **plain** NOUN

[1] <u>einfarbig</u> (*self-coloured*) ◊ *a plain carpet* ein einfarbiger Teppich
[2] <u>einfach</u> (*not fancy*) ◊ *a plain white blouse* eine einfache weiße Bluse

plain chocolate NOUN
die <u>bittere Schokolade</u>

plait NOUN
der <u>Zopf</u> (PL die Zöpfe) ◊ *She wears her hair in a plait.* Sie trägt einen Zopf.

plan NOUN

see also **plan** VERB

der <u>Plan</u> (PL die Pläne) ◊ *What are your plans for the holidays?* Welche Ferienpläne habt ihr? ◊ *to make plans* Pläne machen ◊ *a plan of the campsite* ein Plan des Zeltplatzes
♦ **Everything went according to plan.** Alles lief nach Plan.
♦ **my essay plan** das Konzept für meinen Aufsatz

to **plan** VERB

see also **plan** NOUN

<u>planen</u> ◊ *We're planning a trip to Germany.* Wir planen eine Reise nach Deutschland. ◊ *Plan your revision carefully.* Plant eure Stoffwiederholung sorgfältig.
♦ **to plan to do something** vorhaben, etwas zu tun ◊ *I'm planning to get a job in the holidays.* Ich habe vor, mir einen Ferienjob zu suchen.

plane NOUN
das <u>Flugzeug</u> (PL die Flugzeuge) ◊ *by plane* mit dem Flugzeug

planet NOUN
der <u>Planet</u> (GEN des Planeten, PL die Planeten)

planning NOUN
die <u>Planung</u> ◊ *family planning* die Familienplanung
♦ **The trip needs careful planning.** Die Reise muss sorgfältig geplant werden.

plant NOUN

see also **plant** VERB

[1] die <u>Pflanze</u> ◊ *to water the plants* die Pflanzen gießen
[2] die <u>Fabrik</u> (*factory*)

to **plant** VERB

see also **plant** NOUN

<u>pflanzen</u>

plant pot NOUN
der <u>Blumentopf</u> (PL die Blumentöpfe)

plaque NOUN
[1] die <u>Gedenktafel</u> (*to famous person, event*)
[2] der <u>Zahnbelag</u> (*on teeth*)

plaster NOUN
[1] (*sticking plaster*)

das <u>Pflaster</u> (PL die Pflaster) ◊ *Have you got a plaster, by any chance?* Hast du zufälligerweise ein Pflaster?
[2] (*for fracture*)
der <u>Gips</u> (GEN des Gipses, PL die Gipse) ◊ *Her leg's in plaster.* Sie hat das Bein in Gips.

plastic NOUN

see also **plastic** ADJECTIVE

das <u>Plastik</u> ◊ *It's made of plastic.* Es ist aus Plastik.

plastic ADJECTIVE

see also **plastic** NOUN

aus Plastik ◊ *a plastic mac* ein Regenmantel aus Plastik
♦ **a plastic bag** eine Plastiktüte

plate NOUN
der <u>Teller</u> (*for food*) (PL die Teller)

platform NOUN
[1] (*at station*)
der <u>Bahnsteig</u> (PL die Bahnsteige) ◊ *on platform seven* auf Bahnsteig sieben
[2] (*for performers*)
das <u>Podium</u> (PL die Podien)

play NOUN

see also **play** VERB

das <u>Stück</u> (PL die Stücke) ◊ *a play by Shakespeare* ein Stück von Shakespeare ◊ *to put on a play* ein Stück aufführen

to **play** VERB

see also **play** NOUN

[1] <u>spielen</u> ◊ *He's playing with his friends.* Er spielt mit seinen Freunden. ◊ *What sort of music do they play?* Welche Art von Musik spielen sie? ◊ *I play hockey.* Ich spiele Hockey. ◊ *I play the guitar.* Ich spiele Gitarre. ◊ *She's always playing that record.* Sie spielt dauernd diese Platte.
[2] <u>spielen gegen</u> (*against person, team*) ◊ *Germany will play Scotland next month.* Deutschland spielt nächsten Monat gegen Schottland.

to **play down** VERB
<u>herunterspielen</u> (PERFECT hat heruntergespielt) ◊ *He tried to play down his illness.* Er versuchte, die Schwere seiner Krankheit herunterzuspielen.

player NOUN
der <u>Spieler</u> (PL die Spieler)
die <u>Spielerin</u>
◊ *a football player* ein Fußballspieler

playful ADJECTIVE
<u>verspielt</u>

playground NOUN
[1] (*at school*)
der <u>Schulhof</u> (PL die Schulhöfe)
[2] (*in park*)
der <u>Spielplatz</u> (GEN des Spielplatzes, PL die Spielplätze)

playgroup NOUN
die <u>Spielgruppe</u>

P

playing card NOUN
die Spielkarte

playing field NOUN
der Sportplatz (GEN des Sportplatzes, PL die Sportplätze)

playtime NOUN
die Pause

to **play up** VERB
♦ **The engine's playing up again.** Der Motor macht schon wieder Schwierigkeiten.

playwright NOUN
der Dramatiker (PL die Dramatiker)
die Dramatikerin

pleasant ADJECTIVE
angenehm

please EXCLAMATION
bitte ◊ *Two coffees, please.* Zwei Kaffee bitte.

pleased ADJECTIVE
1 erfreut (*happy*) ◊ *My mother's not going to be very pleased.* Meine Mutter wird nicht sehr erfreut sein.
2 zufrieden (*satisfied*) ◊ *It's beautiful, she'll be pleased with it.* Es ist wunderschön, sie wird damit sehr zufrieden sein.
♦ **to be pleased about something** sich über etwas freuen ◊ *Are you pleased about the exam results?* Freust du dich über die Prüfungsergebnisse?
♦ **Pleased to meet you!** Angenehm!

pleasure NOUN
das Vergnügen (PL die Vergnügen) ◊ *I read for pleasure.* Ich lese zum Vergnügen.

plenty NOUN
mehr als genug ◊ *I've got plenty.* Ich habe mehr als genug. ◊ *That's plenty, thanks.* Danke, das ist mehr als genug.
♦ **I've got plenty to do.** Ich habe viel zu tun.
♦ **plenty of (1)** viele ◊ *There were plenty of opportunities.* Es gab viele Möglichkeiten.
♦ **plenty of (2)** (*more than enough*) genügend ◊ *I've got plenty of money.* Ich habe genügend Geld. ◊ *We've got plenty of time.* Wir haben genügend Zeit.

pliers PL NOUN
die Zange SING
♦ **a pair of pliers** eine Zange

plot NOUN
see also **plot** VERB
1 die Handlung (*of story, play*)
2 die Verschwörung (*against somebody*) ◊ *a plot against the president* eine Verschwörung gegen den Präsidenten
♦ **a plot of land** ein Stück Land NEUT
♦ **a vegetable plot** ein Gemüsebeet NEUT

to **plot** VERB
see also **plot** NOUN
planen ◊ *They were plotting to kill him.* Sie planten, ihn zu töten.

plough NOUN
see also **plough** VERB
der Pflug (PL die Pflüge)

to **plough** VERB
see also **plough** NOUN
pflügen

plug NOUN
1 (*electrical*)
der Stecker (PL die Stecker) ◊ *The plug is faulty.* Der Stecker ist kaputt.
2 (*for sink*)
der Stöpsel (PL die Stöpsel)

to **plug in** VERB
einstecken (PERFECT hat eingesteckt) ◊ *Is it plugged in?* Ist es eingesteckt?

plum NOUN
die Pflaume ◊ *plum jam* die Pflaumenmarmelade

plumber NOUN
der Klempner (PL die Klempner)
die Klempnerin
◊ *He's a plumber.* Er ist Klempner.

plump ADJECTIVE
rundlich

to **plunge** VERB
tauchen

plural NOUN
der Plural (PL die Plurale)

plus PREPOSITION, ADJECTIVE
plus ◊ *Four plus three equals seven.* Vier plus drei macht sieben. ◊ *I got a B plus.* Ich habe eine Zwei plus bekommen.

> ⓘ *In Germany, grades are given from 1 to 6, with 1 being the best.*

♦ **three children plus a dog** drei Kinder und ein Hund

p.m. ABBREVIATION
♦ **at eight p.m.** um acht Uhr abends

> ⓘ *In Germany times are often given using the 24-hour clock.*

◊ *at two p.m.* um vierzehn Uhr

pneumonia NOUN
die Lungenentzündung

poached ADJECTIVE
♦ **a poached egg** ein verlorenes Ei NEUT

pocket NOUN
die Tasche
♦ **pocket money** das Taschengeld ◊ *eight pounds a week pocket money* acht Pfund Taschengeld pro Woche

pocket calculator NOUN
der Taschenrechner (PL die Taschenrechner)

poem NOUN
das Gedicht (PL die Gedichte)

poet NOUN
der Dichter (PL die Dichter)
die Dichterin

poetry NOUN
die <u>Gedichte</u> NEUT PL ◊ *to write poetry*
Gedichte schreiben

point NOUN
see also **point** VERB
1 (*spot, score*)
der <u>Punkt</u> (PL die Punkte) ◊ *a point on the horizon* ein Punkt am Horizont ◊ *They scored five points.* Sie machten fünf Punkte.
2 (*comment*)
die <u>Bemerkung</u> ◊ *He made some interesting points.* Er machte ein paar interessante Bemerkungen.
3 (*tip*)
die <u>Spitze</u> ◊ *a pencil with a sharp point* ein Bleistift mit einer scharfen Spitze
4 (*in time*)
der <u>Zeitpunkt</u> ◊ *At that point, our team was three one up.* Zu dem Zeitpunkt lag unsere Mannschaft mit drei zu eins in Führung.
♦ **a point of view** ein Gesichtspunkt MASC
♦ **to get the point** begreifen ◊ *Sorry, I don't get the point.* Entschuldigung, ich begreife das nicht.
♦ **That's a good point!** Da hast du recht.
♦ **There's no point.** Das hat keinen Wert. ◊ *There's no point in waiting.* Es hat keinen Wert zu warten.
♦ **What's the point?** Wozu? ◊ *What's the point of leaving now?* Wozu jetzt gehen?
♦ **Punctuality isn't my strong point.** Pünktlichkeit ist nicht meine Stärke.
♦ **two point five (2.5)** zwei Komma fünf (2,5)

to **point** VERB
see also **point** NOUN
mit dem Finger zeigen ◊ *Don't point!* Man zeigt nicht mit dem Finger!
♦ **to point at somebody** auf jemanden zeigen ◊ *She pointed at Anne.* Sie zeigte auf Anne.
♦ **to point a gun at somebody** auf jemanden mit der Waffe zielen
♦ **to point something out (1)** (*show*) auf etwas zeigen ◊ *The guide pointed out Big Ben to us.* Unser Führer zeigte auf Big Ben.
♦ **to point something out (2)** (*mention*) auf etwas hinweisen ◊ *I should point out that ...* Ich möchte darauf hinweisen, dass ...

pointless ADJECTIVE
<u>nutzlos</u> ◊ *It's pointless to argue.* Es ist nutzlos zu streiten.

poison NOUN
see also **poison** VERB
das <u>Gift</u> (PL die Gifte)

to **poison** VERB
see also **poison** NOUN
<u>vergiften</u> (PERFECT hat vergiftet)

poisonous ADJECTIVE
giftig

to **poke** VERB
♦ **He poked me in the eye.** Er stieß mir ins Auge.

poker NOUN
das <u>Poker</u> ◊ *I play poker.* Ich spiele Poker.

Poland NOUN
<u>Polen</u> NEUT
♦ **from Poland** aus Polen
♦ **to Poland** nach Polen

polar bear NOUN
der <u>Eisbär</u> (GEN des Eisbären, PL die Eisbären)

Pole NOUN
(*Polish person*)
der <u>Pole</u> (GEN des Polen, PL die Polen)
die <u>Polin</u>

pole NOUN
der <u>Mast</u> (PL die Masten) ◊ *a telegraph pole* ein Telegrafenmast
♦ **a tent pole** eine Zeltstange
♦ **a ski pole** ein Skistock MASC
♦ **the North Pole** der Nordpol
♦ **the South Pole** der Südpol

pole vault NOUN
das <u>Stabhochspringen</u>

police PL NOUN
die <u>Polizei</u> ◊ *We called the police.* Wir haben die Polizei gerufen.
*Note that **police** is used with a plural verb and **Polizei** with a singular verb.*
◊ *The police haven't arrived yet.* Die Polizei ist noch nicht da.
♦ **a police car** ein Polizeiwagen MASC
♦ **a police station** ein Polizeirevier NEUT

policeman NOUN
der <u>Polizist</u> (GEN des Polizisten, PL die Polizisten) ◊ *He's a policeman.* Er ist Polizist.

policewoman NOUN
die <u>Polizistin</u> ◊ *She's a policewoman.* Sie ist Polizistin.

polio NOUN
die <u>Kinderlähmung</u>

Polish ADJECTIVE
see also **Polish** NOUN
polnisch
♦ **He's Polish.** Er ist Pole.
♦ **She's Polish.** Sie ist Polin.

Polish NOUN
see also **Polish** ADJECTIVE
das <u>Polnisch</u> (*language*) (GEN des Polnischen)

polish NOUN
see also **polish** VERB
1 (*for shoes*)
die <u>Schuhcreme</u> (PL die Schuhcremes)
2 (*for furniture*)
die <u>Politur</u>

to **polish** VERB
see also **polish** NOUN

P

☞

[1] (*shoes*)
eincremen (PERFECT hat eingecremt)
[2] (*glass, furniture*)
polieren (PERFECT hat poliert)
polite ADJECTIVE
höflich
politely ADVERB
höflich
politeness NOUN
die Höflichkeit
political ADJECTIVE
politisch
politician NOUN
der Politiker (PL die Politiker)
die Politikerin
politics PL NOUN
die Politik ◊ *I'm not interested in politics.*
Ich interessiere mich nicht für Politik.
poll NOUN
die Umfrage ◊ *A recent poll revealed
that ...* Eine Umfrage ergab vor Kurzem,
dass ...
pollen NOUN
der Pollen (PL die Pollen)
to **pollute** VERB
verschmutzen (PERFECT hat verschmutzt)
polluted ADJECTIVE
verschmutzt
pollution NOUN
die Umweltverschmutzung
◆ **air pollution** die Luftverschmutzung
polo-necked sweater NOUN
der Rollkragenpullover (PL die
Rollkragenpullover)
polo shirt NOUN
das Polohemd (PL die Polohemden)
polythene bag NOUN
die Plastiktüte
pond NOUN
der Teich (PL die Teiche) ◊ *We've got a
pond in our garden.* Wir haben einen
Teich im Garten.
pony NOUN
das Pony (PL die Ponys)
ponytail NOUN
der Pferdeschwanz (GEN des
Pferdeschwanzes, PL die Pferdeschwänze)
◊ *He's got a ponytail.* Er hat einen
Pferdeschwanz.
pony trekking NOUN
◆ **to go pony trekking** Pony reiten gehen
poodle NOUN
der Pudel (PL die Pudel)
pool NOUN
[1] (*puddle*)
die Pfütze
[2] (*pond*)
der Teich (PL die Teiche)
[3] (*for swimming*)
das Schwimmbecken (PL die
Schwimmbecken)
[4] (*game*)

das Poolbillard ◊ *Shall we have a game
of pool?* Sollen wir eine Partie Poolbillard
spielen?
◆ **the pools** (*football*) das Toto ◊ *to do the
pools* Toto spielen
poor ADJECTIVE
[1] arm ◊ *a poor family* eine arme Familie
◊ *They are poorer than we are.* Sie sind
ärmer als wir. ◊ *Poor David, he's very
unlucky!* Der arme David, er hat wirklich
kein Glück!
◆ **the poor** die Armen MASC PL
[2] schlecht (*bad*) ◊ *a poor mark* eine
schlechte Note
poorly ADJECTIVE
◆ **She's poorly.** Es geht ihr schlecht.
pop ADJECTIVE
◆ **pop music** die Popmusik
◆ **a pop star** ein Popstar MASC
◆ **a pop group** eine Popgruppe
◆ **a pop song** ein Popsong MASC
to **pop in** VERB
vorbeikommen (IMPERFECT kam vorbei,
PERFECT ist vorbeigekommen)
to **pop out** VERB
kurz weggehen (IMPERFECT ging weg,
PERFECT ist weggegangen) ◊ *I'm just
popping out for an hour.* Ich gehe nur
mal kurz für eine Stunde weg.
to **pop round** VERB
◆ **I'm just popping round to John's.** Ich
gehe nur mal kurz zu John.
popcorn NOUN
das Popcorn
pope NOUN
der Papst (PL die Päpste)
poppy NOUN
der Mohn
Popsicle ® NOUN [US]
das Eis am Stiel (GEN des Eises am Stiel,
PL die Eis am Stiel)
popular ADJECTIVE
beliebt ◊ *She's a very popular girl.* Sie
ist sehr beliebt.
population NOUN
die Bevölkerung
porch NOUN
die Veranda (PL die Veranden)
pork NOUN
das Schweinefleisch ◊ *I don't eat pork.*
Ich esse kein Schweinefleisch.
◆ **a pork chop** ein Schweinekotelett NEUT
porn NOUN
see also **porn** ADJECTIVE
die Pornografie
porn ADJECTIVE
see also **porn** NOUN
◆ **a porn film** ein Pornofilm MASC
◆ **a porn mag** ein Pornoheft NEUT
pornographic ADJECTIVE
pornografisch ◊ *a pornographic
magazine* eine pornografische Zeitschrift

pornography NOUN
die Pornografie

porridge NOUN
der Haferbrei

port NOUN
[1] (*harbour*)
der Hafen (PL die Häfen)
[2] (*wine*)
der Portwein ◊ *a glass of port* ein Glas Portwein

portable ADJECTIVE
tragbar ◊ *a portable TV* ein tragbarer Fernseher

porter NOUN
[1] (*in hotel*)
der Portier (PL die Portiers)
[2] (*at station*)
der Gepäckträger (PL die Gepäckträger)

portion NOUN
die Portion ◊ *a large portion of chips* eine große Portion Pommes frites

portrait NOUN
das Porträt (PL die Porträts)

Portugal NOUN
Portugal NEUT
♦ **from Portugal** aus Portugal
♦ **to Portugal** nach Portugal

Portuguese ADJECTIVE

see also **Portuguese** NOUN

portugiesisch
♦ **She's Portuguese.** Sie ist Portugiesin.

Portuguese NOUN

see also **Portuguese** ADJECTIVE

[1] (*person*)
der Portugiese (GEN des Portugiesen, PL die Portugiesen)
die Portugiesin
[2] (*language*)
das Portugiesisch (GEN des Portugiesischen)

posh ADJECTIVE
vornehm ◊ *a posh hotel* ein vornehmes Hotel

position NOUN
die Stellung ◊ *an uncomfortable position* eine unbequeme Stellung

positive ADJECTIVE
[1] positiv (*good*) ◊ *a positive attitude* eine positive Einstellung
[2] ganz sicher (*sure*) ◊ *I'm positive.* Ich bin ganz sicher.

to **possess** VERB
besitzen (IMPERFECT besaß, PERFECT hat besessen)

possession NOUN
♦ **Have you got all your possessions?** Hast du all deine Sachen?

possibility NOUN
die Möglichkeit ◊ *It's a possibility.* Das ist eine Möglichkeit.

possible ADJECTIVE

möglich ◊ *as soon as possible* sobald wie möglich

possibly ADVERB
vielleicht (*perhaps*) ◊ *Are you coming to the party? – Possibly.* Kommst du zur Party? – Vielleicht.
♦ **... if you possibly can.** ... wenn du irgend kannst.
♦ **I can't possibly come.** Ich kann unmöglich kommen.

post NOUN

see also **post** VERB

[1] (*letters*)
die Post ◊ *Is there any post for me?* Ist Post für mich da?
[2] (*pole*)
der Pfosten (PL die Pfosten) ◊ *The ball hit the post.* Der Ball traf den Pfosten.

to **post** VERB

see also **post** NOUN

aufgeben (PRESENT gibt auf, IMPERFECT gab auf, PERFECT hat aufgegeben) ◊ *I've got some cards to post.* Ich muss ein paar Karten aufgeben.

postage NOUN
das Porto (PL die Portos)

postbox NOUN
der Briefkasten (PL die Briefkästen)

postcard NOUN
die Postkarte

postcode NOUN
die Postleitzahl

> ⓘ German postcodes consist of a 5-figure number which precedes the name of the city.

poster NOUN
[1] das Poster (PL die Poster) ◊ *I've got posters on my bedroom walls.* Ich habe in meinem Zimmer Poster an den Wänden.
[2] (*advertising*)
das Plakat (PL die Plakate) ◊ *There are posters all over town.* In der ganzen Stadt hängen Plakate.

postman NOUN
der Briefträger (PL die Briefträger) ◊ *He's a postman.* Er ist Briefträger.

postmark NOUN
der Stempel (PL die Stempel)

post office NOUN
das Postamt (PL die Postämter)
◊ *Where's the post office, please?* Wo ist das Postamt, bitte?
♦ **She works for the post office.** Sie arbeitet bei der Post.

to **postpone** VERB
verschieben (IMPERFECT verschob, PERFECT hat verschoben) ◊ *The match has been postponed.* Das Spiel wurde verschoben.

postwoman NOUN

P

die Briefträgerin ◊ *She's a postwoman.*
Sie ist Briefträgerin.

pot NOUN
1 der Topf (PL die Töpfe) ◊ *a pot of jam*
ein Marmeladentopf
2 (*for hot drinks*)
die Kanne
3 (*marijuana*)
das Gras ◊ *to smoke pot* Gras rauchen
♦ **the pots and pans** Töpfe und Pfannen

potato NOUN
die Kartoffel ◊ *a baked potato* eine
gebackene Kartoffel ◊ *potato salad* der
Kartoffelsalat
♦ **mashed potatoes** der Kartoffelbrei
♦ **potato chips** die Kartoffelchips MASC PL

potential NOUN
see also **potential** ADJECTIVE
♦ **He has great potential.** Er ist sehr
vielversprechend.

potential ADJECTIVE
see also **potential** NOUN
möglich ◊ *a potential problem* ein
mögliches Problem

pothole NOUN
das Schlagloch (*in road*) (PL die
Schlaglöcher)

pot plant NOUN
die Topfpflanze

pottery NOUN
die Keramik

pound NOUN
see also **pound** VERB
das Pfund (*weight, money*) (PL die Pfunde
or Pfund)

When talking about an amount of money
or specifying a quantity of something
use the plural form **Pfund**.

◊ *two pounds of carrots* zwei Pfund
Karotten ◊ *How many euros do you get
for a pound?* Wie viel Euro bekommt
man für ein Pfund? ◊ *a pound coin* eine
Pfundmünze

to **pound** VERB
see also **pound** NOUN
pochen ◊ *My heart was pounding.* Mein
Herz hat gepocht.

to **pour** VERB
gießen (*liquid*) (IMPERFECT goss, PERFECT hat
gegossen) ◊ *She poured some water into
the pan.* Sie goss etwas Wasser in den
Topf.
♦ **She poured him a drink.** Sie goss ihm
einen Drink ein.
♦ **Shall I pour you a cup of tea?** Soll ich
Ihnen eine Tasse Tee einschenken?
♦ **It's pouring.** Es gießt.
♦ **in the pouring rain** im strömenden
Regen

poverty NOUN
die Armut

powder NOUN

1 das Pulver
2 (*face powder*)
der Puder (PL die Puder)

power NOUN
1 (*electricity*)
der Strom ◊ *The power's off. Es gibt
keinen Strom.*
♦ **a power cut** ein Stromausfall MASC
♦ **a power point** eine Steckdose
♦ **a power station** ein Kraftwerk NEUT
2 (*energy*)
die Energie ◊ *nuclear power* die
Kernenergie ◊ *solar power* die
Sonnenenergie
3 (*authority*)
die Macht (PL die Mächte) ◊ *to be in
power* an der Macht sein

powerful ADJECTIVE
1 mächtig ◊ *a powerful man* ein
mächtiger Mann
2 kräftig (*physically*)
3 leistungsstark (*machine*)

practical ADJECTIVE
praktisch ◊ *a practical suggestion* ein
praktischer Vorschlag ◊ *She's very
practical.* Sie ist sehr praktisch.

practically ADVERB
praktisch ◊ *It's practically impossible. Es
ist praktisch unmöglich.*

practice NOUN
1 das Training (*for sport*) ◊ *football
practice* das Fußballtraining
2 die Übung ◊ *You need more practice.*
Du brauchst mehr Übung.
♦ **I've got to do my piano practice.** Ich
muss Klavier üben.
♦ **It's normal practice in our school.** Das ist
in unserer Schule so üblich.
♦ **in practice** in der Praxis
♦ **a medical practice** eine Arztpraxis

to **practise** VERB
1 (*music, hobby, language*)
üben ◊ *I ought to practise more.* Ich
sollte mehr üben. ◊ *I practise the flute
every evening.* Ich übe jeden Abend
Flöte. ◊ *I practised my German when we
were on holiday.* Ich habe in den Ferien
mein Deutsch geübt.
2 (*sport*)
trainieren (PERFECT hat trainiert) ◊ *The
team practises on Thursdays.* Die
Mannschaft trainiert donnerstags. ◊ *I
don't practise enough.* Ich trainiere nicht
genug.

practising ADJECTIVE
praktizierend ◊ *She's a practising
Catholic.* Sie ist praktizierende Katholikin.

to **praise** VERB
loben ◊ *The teacher praised her work.*
Der Lehrer lobte ihre Arbeit.

pram NOUN
der Kinderwagen (PL die Kinderwagen)

prawn NOUN

die Garnele

prawn cocktail NOUN
der Krabbencocktail (PL die Krabbencocktails)

to **pray** VERB
beten ◊ to pray for something für etwas beten

prayer NOUN
das Gebet (PL die Gebete)

precaution NOUN
die Vorsichtsmaßnahme ◊ to take precautions Vorsichtsmaßnahmen treffen

preceding ADJECTIVE
vorherig

precinct NOUN
♦a shopping precinct ein Einkaufsviertel NEUT
♦a pedestrian precinct eine Fußgängerzone

precious ADJECTIVE
kostbar

precise ADJECTIVE
genau ◊ at that precise moment genau in diesem Augenblick

precisely ADVERB
genau ◊ Precisely! Genau!
♦at ten o'clock precisely um Punkt zehn Uhr

to **predict** VERB
vorhersagen (PERFECT hat vorhergesagt)

predictable ADJECTIVE
vorhersehbar

prefect NOUN

> *ⓘ* German schools do not have prefects.

♦My sister's a prefect. Meine Schwester ist im letzten Schuljahr und führt die Aufsicht bei den Jüngeren.

to **prefer** VERB
lieber mögen (PRESENT mag lieber, IMPERFECT mochte lieber, PERFECT hat lieber gemocht) ◊ Which would you prefer? Was magst du lieber? ◊ I prefer German to chemistry. Ich mag Deutsch lieber als Chemie.
♦I preferred the first version. Die erste Version hat mir besser gefallen.

preference NOUN
die Vorliebe ◊ his preference for detective stories seine Vorliebe für Kriminalromane

pregnant ADJECTIVE
schwanger ◊ She's six months pregnant. Sie ist im siebten Monat schwanger.

prehistoric ADJECTIVE
prähistorisch

prejudice NOUN

prawn cocktail → Presbyterian

[1] das Vorurteil (PL die Vorurteile) ◊ That's just a prejudice. Das ist ein Vorurteil.
[2] die Vorurteile NEUT PL ◊ There's a lot of racial prejudice. Es gibt viele Rassenvorurteile.

prejudiced ADJECTIVE
voreingenommen
♦to be prejudiced against somebody gegen jemanden voreingenommen sein

premature ADJECTIVE
verfrüht
♦a premature baby eine Frühgeburt

Premier League NOUN
die erste Liga ◊ in the Premier League in der ersten Liga

> *ⓘ* The **Premier League** is similar to the German **Bundesliga**.

premises PL NOUN
die Geschäftsräume MASC PL ◊ They're moving to new premises. Sie ziehen in neue Geschäftsräume um.

premonition NOUN
die Vorahnung

preoccupied ADJECTIVE
♦He's very preoccupied with his exams at the moment. Er denkt im Moment nur an seine Prüfungen.

prep NOUN
die Hausaufgaben FEM PL (homework) ◊ history prep die Hausaufgaben in Geschichte

preparation NOUN
die Vorbereitung

to **prepare** VERB
vorbereiten (PERFECT hat vorbereitet) ◊ She has to prepare lessons in the evening. Sie muss abends Stunden vorbereiten.
♦to prepare for something Vorbereitungen für etwas treffen ◊ We're preparing for our skiing holiday. Wir treffen Vorbereitungen für unseren Skiurlaub.

prepared ADJECTIVE
♦to be prepared to do something bereit sein, etwas zu tun ◊ I'm prepared to help you. Ich bin bereit, dir zu helfen.

prep school NOUN
die private Grundschule

Presbyterian NOUN
see also **Presbyterian** ADJECTIVE
der Presbyterianer (PL die Presbyterianer)
die Presbyterianerin
◊ She is a Presbyterian. Sie ist Presbyterianerin.

Presbyterian ADJECTIVE
see also **Presbyterian** NOUN
presbyterianisch

P

to **prescribe** VERB
verschreiben (*medicine*) (IMPERFECT
verschrieb, PERFECT hat verschrieben)
◊ *He prescribed me a course of
antibiotics.* Er hat mir eine Antibiotikakur
verschrieben.

prescription NOUN
das Rezept (PL die Rezepte) ◊ *You can't
get it without a prescription.* Das
bekommt man nicht ohne Rezept.

presence NOUN
die Anwesenheit
♦ **presence of mind** die Geistesgegenwart

present ADJECTIVE
see also **present** NOUN, VERB
[1] anwesend (*in attendance*) ◊ *He wasn't
present at the meeting.* Er war bei der
Besprechung nicht anwesend.
[2] gegenwärtig (*current*) ◊ *the present
situation* die gegenwärtige Situation
♦ **the present tense** die Gegenwart

present NOUN
see also **present** ADJECTIVE, VERB
[1] (*gift*)
das Geschenk (PL die Geschenke) ◊ *I'm
going to buy presents.* Ich kaufe
Geschenke.
♦ **to give somebody a present** jemandem
etwas schenken
[2] (*time*)
die Gegenwart ◊ *She was living in the
past not the present.* Sie lebte in der
Vergangenheit, nicht in der Gegenwart.
♦ **up to the present** bis heute
♦ **for the present** momentan
♦ **at present** im Augenblick
♦ **the present tense** das Präsens

to **present** VERB
see also **present** ADJECTIVE, NOUN
♦ **to present somebody with something**
(*prize, medal*) jemandem etwas verleihen

presenter NOUN
(*on TV*)
der Moderator (PL die Moderatoren)
die Moderatorin

presently ADVERB
[1] sofort (*soon*) ◊ *You'll feel better
presently.* Sie werden sich sofort besser
fühlen.
[2] im Moment (*at present*) ◊ *They're
presently on tour.* Sie sind im Moment
auf Tournee.

president NOUN
der Präsident (GEN des Präsidenten, PL die
Präsidenten)
die Präsidentin

press NOUN
see also **press** VERB
die Presse
♦ **a press conference** eine Pressekonferenz

to **press** VERB
see also **press** NOUN

[1] drücken ◊ *Don't press too hard!* Nicht
zu fest drücken!
[2] treten auf +ACC (PRESENT tritt auf, IMPERFECT
trat, PERFECT hat getreten) ◊ *He pressed the
accelerator.* Er trat aufs Gaspedal.

pressed ADJECTIVE
♦ **We are pressed for time.** Wir haben
wenig Zeit.

press-up NOUN
der Liegestütz (GEN des Liegestützes, PL
die Liegestütze) ◊ *I do twenty press-ups
every morning.* Ich mache jeden Morgen
zwanzig Liegestütze.

pressure NOUN
see also **pressure** VERB
der Druck ◊ *He's under a lot of pressure
at work.* Er steht unter viel Druck bei
seiner Arbeit.
♦ **a pressure group (1)** (*small-scale, local*)
eine Bürgerinitiative
♦ **a pressure group (2)** (*large-scale, more
political*) eine Pressuregroup

to **pressure** VERB
see also **pressure** NOUN
Druck ausüben auf +ACC (PERFECT hat Druck
ausgeübt) ◊ *My parents are pressuring
me.* Meine Eltern üben Druck auf mich
aus.

prestige NOUN
das Ansehen

prestigious ADJECTIVE
angesehen

presumably ADVERB
vermutlich

to **presume** VERB
annehmen (PRESENT nimmt an, IMPERFECT
nahm an, PERFECT hat angenommen) ◊ *I
presume so.* Das nehme ich an.

to **pretend** VERB
♦ **to pretend to do something** so tun, als
ob man etwas täte
Note that **als ob** is followed by the
subjunctive.
◊ *He pretended to be asleep.* Er tat so,
als ob er schliefe.

pretty ADJECTIVE, ADVERB
[1] hübsch ◊ *She's very pretty.* Sie ist
sehr hübsch.
[2] ziemlich (*rather*) ◊ *That film was pretty
bad.* Der Film war ziemlich schlecht.
♦ **It's pretty much the same.** Das ist mehr
oder weniger dasselbe.

to **prevent** VERB
verhindern (PERFECT hat verhindert)
♦ **to prevent somebody from doing
something** jemanden davon abhalten,
etwas zu tun ◊ *They tried to prevent us
from smoking.* Sie haben versucht, uns
vom Rauchen abzuhalten.

previous ADJECTIVE
vorherig

previously ADVERB

früher

prey NOUN
die Beute
♦ **a bird of prey** ein Raubvogel MASC

price NOUN
der Preis (GEN des Preises, PL die Preise)

price list NOUN
die Preisliste

to **prick** VERB
stechen (PRESENT sticht, IMPERFECT stach, PERFECT hat gestochen) ◊ *I've pricked my finger.* Ich habe mir in den Finger gestochen.

pride NOUN
der Stolz (GEN des Stolzes)

priest NOUN
der Priester (PL die Priester) ◊ *He's a priest.* Er ist Priester.

primarily ADVERB
vor allem

primary ADJECTIVE
hauptsächlich

primary school NOUN
die Grundschule

> ❶ *Children in Germany begin* **Grundschule** *at the age of 6. The* **Grundschule** *provides primary education in school years 1 to 4.*

◊ *She's still at primary school.* Sie ist noch in der Grundschule.

prime minister NOUN
der Premierminister (PL die Premierminister)
die Premierministerin

primitive ADJECTIVE
primitiv

prince NOUN
der Prinz (GEN des Prinzen, PL die Prinzen) ◊ *the Prince of Wales* der Prinz von Wales

princess NOUN
die Prinzessin ◊ *Princess Anne* Prinzessin Anne

principal ADJECTIVE
| see also **principal** NOUN |
♦ **the principal reason** der Hauptgrund
♦ **my principal concern** mein Hauptanliegen NEUT

principal NOUN
| see also **principal** ADJECTIVE |
(*of college*)
der Direktor (PL die Direktoren)
die Direktorin

principle NOUN
das Prinzip (PL die Prinzipien)
♦ **on principle** aus Prinzip

print NOUN
① (*photo*)
der Abzug (PL die Abzüge) ◊ *colour prints* Farbabzüge

② (*letters*)
die Schrift
♦ **in small print** klein gedruckt

③ (*fingerprint*)
der Fingerabdruck (PL die Fingerabdrücke)

④ (*picture*)
der Kunstdruck (PL die Kunstdrucke) ◊ *a framed print* ein gerahmter Kunstdruck

printer NOUN
der Drucker (*machine*) (PL die Drucker)

printout NOUN
der Ausdruck (PL die Ausdrucke)

priority NOUN
die Priorität

prison NOUN
das Gefängnis (GEN des Gefängnisses, PL die Gefängnisse)
♦ **in prison** im Gefängnis

prisoner NOUN
der Gefangene (GEN des Gefangenen, PL die Gefangenen)
die Gefangene (GEN der Gefangenen) ◊ *a prisoner* (*man*) ein Gefangener

prison officer NOUN
der Gefängniswärter (PL die Gefängniswärter)
die Gefängniswärterin

privacy NOUN
das Privatleben ◊ *an invasion of my privacy* ein Eingriff in mein Privatleben

private ADJECTIVE
privat
♦ **a private school** eine Privatschule
♦ **private property** das Privateigentum
♦ **"private"** (*on envelope*) "persönlich"
♦ **a private bathroom** ein eigenes Badezimmer
♦ **I have private lessons.** Ich bekomme Nachhilfestunden.

to **privatize** VERB
privatisieren (PERFECT hat privatisiert)

privilege NOUN
das Privileg (PL die Privilegien)

prize NOUN
der Preis (GEN des Preises, PL die Preise) ◊ *to win a prize* einen Preis gewinnen

prize-giving NOUN
die Preisverleihung

prizewinner NOUN
der Preisträger (PL die Preisträger)
die Preisträgerin

pro NOUN
der Profi (PL die Profis)
> *der Profi* is also used for women.
◊ *This was her first year as a pro.* Dies war ihr erstes Jahr als Profi.
♦ **the pros and cons** das Für und Wider ◊ *We weighed up the pros and cons.* Wir haben das Für und Wider abgewogen.

probability NOUN
die Wahrscheinlichkeit

probable ADJECTIVE

P

☞

wahrscheinlich

probably ADVERB
wahrscheinlich ◊ *probably not*
wahrscheinlich nicht

problem NOUN
das Problem (PL die Probleme) ◊ *No problem!* Kein Problem!

proceeds PL NOUN
der Erlös SING (GEN des Erlöses, PL die Erlöse)

process NOUN
der Prozess (GEN des Prozesses, PL die Prozesse) ◊ *the peace process* der Friedensprozess
♦ **to be in the process of doing something** gerade dabei sein, etwas zu tun ◊ *We're in the process of painting the kitchen.* Wir sind gerade dabei, die Küche zu streichen.

procession NOUN
die Prozession (*religious*)

to **produce** VERB
1 (*manufacture*)
herstellen (PERFECT hat hergestellt)
2 (*play, show*)
inszenieren (PERFECT hat inszeniert)
3 (*film*)
produzieren (PERFECT hat produziert)

producer NOUN
1 (*of play, show*)
der Regisseur (PL die Regisseure)
die Regisseurin
2 (*of film*)
der Produzent (GEN des Produzenten, PL die Produzenten)
die Produzentin

product NOUN
das Produkt (PL die Produkte)

production NOUN
1 die Produktion ◊ *They're increasing production of luxury models.* Sie erhöhen die Produktion der Luxusmodelle.
2 die Inszenierung (*play, show*) ◊ *a production of "Hamlet"* eine Hamletinszenierung

profession NOUN
der Beruf (PL die Berufe)

professional NOUN
see also **professional** ADJECTIVE
der Profi (PL die Profis)
der Profi is also used for women.
◊ *She now plays as a professional.* Sie spielt jetzt als Profi.

professional ADJECTIVE
see also **professional** NOUN
professionell (*player*) ◊ *a very professional piece of work* eine sehr professionelle Arbeit
♦ **a professional musician** ein Berufsmusiker MASC

professionally ADVERB

♦ **She sings professionally.** Sie ist Sängerin von Beruf.

professor NOUN
der Professor (PL die Professoren)
die Professorin
♦ **He's the German professor.** Er hat den Lehrstuhl für Deutsch inne.

profit NOUN
der Gewinn (PL die Gewinne)

profitable ADJECTIVE
gewinnbringend

program NOUN
see also **program** VERB
das Programm (PL die Programme) ◊ *a computer program* ein Computerprogramm

to **program** VERB
see also **program** NOUN
programmieren (PERFECT hat programmiert) ◊ *to program a computer* einen Computer programmieren

programme NOUN
das Programm (PL die Programme)

programmer NOUN
der Programmierer (PL die Programmierer)
die Programmiererin
◊ *She's a programmer.* Sie ist Programmiererin.

programming NOUN
das Programmieren

progress NOUN
der Fortschritt (PL die Fortschritte)
◊ *You're making progress!* Du machst Fortschritte!

to **prohibit** VERB
verbieten (IMPERFECT verbat, PERFECT hat verboten) ◊ *Smoking is prohibited.* Das Rauchen ist verboten.

project NOUN
1 (*plan*)
das Projekt (PL die Projekte)
2 (*at school*)
das Referat (PL die Referate) ◊ *I'm doing a project on education in Germany.* Ich schreibe ein Referat über das deutsche Schulwesen.

projector NOUN
der Projektor (PL die Projektoren)

promenade NOUN
die Strandpromenade

promise NOUN
see also **promise** VERB
das Versprechen (PL die Versprechen)
◊ *You didn't keep your promise.* Du hast dein Versprechen nicht gehalten.
♦ **That's a promise!** Versprochen!

to **promise** VERB
see also **promise** NOUN
versprechen (PRESENT verspricht, IMPERFECT versprach, PERFECT hat versprochen) ◊ *She promised to write.* Sie hat versprochen

zu schreiben. ◊ *I'll write, I promise!* Ich schreibe, das verspreche ich!

promising ADJECTIVE
vielversprechend

to **promote** VERB
♦ **to be promoted** befördert werden ◊ *She was promoted after six months.* Sie wurde nach sechs Monaten befördert.

promotion NOUN
[1] die Beförderung (*in job*)
[2] die Werbung (*advertising*)

prompt ADJECTIVE, ADVERB
schnell ◊ *a prompt reply* eine schnelle Antwort
♦ **at eight o'clock prompt** genau um acht Uhr

promptly ADVERB
pünktlich ◊ *We left promptly at seven.* Wir sind pünktlich um sieben gegangen.

pronoun NOUN
das Pronomen (PL die Pronomen)

to **pronounce** VERB
aussprechen (PRESENT spricht aus, IMPERFECT sprach aus, PERFECT hat ausgesprochen) ◊ *How do you pronounce that word?* Wie spricht man das Wort aus?

pronunciation NOUN
die Aussprache

proof NOUN
der Beweis (GEN des Beweises, PL die Beweise)

proper ADJECTIVE
[1] echt (*genuine*) ◊ *proper German bread* echtes deutsches Brot
[2] ordentlich (*decent*) ◊ *We didn't have a proper lunch, just sandwiches.* Wir hatten kein ordentliches Mittagessen, nur belegte Brote. ◊ *It's difficult to get a proper job.* Es ist schwierig, einen ordentlichen Job zu bekommen. ◊ *We need proper training.* Wir brauchen eine ordentliche Ausbildung.
[3] richtig (*appropriate*) ◊ *You have to have the proper equipment.* Sie brauchen die richtige Ausrüstung.
♦ **If you had come at the proper time ...** Wenn du zur rechten Zeit gekommen wärst ...

properly ADVERB
[1] richtig (*correctly*) ◊ *You're not doing it properly.* Du machst das nicht richtig.
[2] anständig (*appropriately*) ◊ *Dress properly for your interview.* Zieh dich zum Vorstellungsgespräch anständig an.

property NOUN
das Eigentum
♦ **"private property"** "Privateigentum"
♦ **stolen property** das Diebesgut

proportional ADJECTIVE
♦ **proportional representation** das Verhältniswahlrecht

proposal NOUN

der Vorschlag (*suggestion*) (PL die Vorschläge)

to **propose** VERB
vorschlagen (PRESENT schlägt vor, IMPERFECT schlug vor, PERFECT hat vorgeschlagen) ◊ *I propose a new plan.* Ich schlage einen neuen Plan vor.
♦ **to propose to do something** vorhaben, etwas zu tun ◊ *What do you propose to do?* Was haben Sie zu tun vor?
♦ **to propose to somebody** (*for marriage*) jemandem einen Heiratsantrag machen ◊ *He proposed to her at the restaurant.* Er hat ihr im Restaurant einen Heiratsantrag gemacht.

to **prosecute** VERB
strafrechtlich verfolgen (PERFECT hat verfolgt) ◊ *They were prosecuted for murder.* Sie wurden wegen Mordes strafrechtlich verfolgt.
♦ **"Shoplifters will be prosecuted"** "Jeder Diebstahl wird zur Anzeige gebracht"

prospect NOUN
die Aussicht ◊ *It'll improve my career prospects.* Das wird meine Berufsaussichten verbessern.
Be careful not to translate **prospect** *by* **Prospekt**.

prospectus NOUN
das Lehrprogramm (*for school, university*) (PL die Lehrprogramme)

prostitute NOUN
die Prostituierte (GEN der Prostituierten)
♦ **a male prostitute** ein Prostituierter

to **protect** VERB
schützen

protection NOUN
der Schutz (GEN des Schutzes)

protein NOUN
das Protein (PL die Proteine)

protest NOUN
see also **protest** VERB
der Protest (PL die Proteste) ◊ *He ignored their protests.* Er hat ihre Proteste ignoriert. ◊ *a protest march* ein Protestmarsch MASC

to **protest** VERB
see also **protest** NOUN
protestieren (PERFECT hat protestiert)

Protestant NOUN
see also **Protestant** ADJECTIVE
der Protestant (GEN des Protestanten, PL die Protestanten)
die Protestantin
◊ *She's a Protestant.* Sie ist Protestantin.

Protestant ADJECTIVE
see also **Protestant** NOUN
protestantisch ◊ *a Protestant church* eine protestantische Kirche

protester NOUN
der Demonstrant (GEN des Demonstranten, PL die Demonstranten)
die Demonstrantin

proud ADJECTIVE

stolz ◊ *Her parents are proud of her.* Ihre Eltern sind stolz auf sie.

to **prove** VERB

beweisen (IMPERFECT bewies, PERFECT hat bewiesen) ◊ *The police couldn't prove it.* Die Polizei konnte es nicht beweisen.

proverb NOUN

das Sprichwort (PL die Sprichwörter)

to **provide** VERB

stellen ◊ *We'll provide the food if you see to the drinks.* Wir stellen das Essen, wenn ihr euch um die Getränke kümmert.

♦ **to provide somebody with something** jemandem etwas zur Verfügung stellen ◊ *They provided us with maps.* Sie haben uns Karten zur Verfügung gestellt.

to **provide for** VERB

versorgen (PERFECT hat versorgt) ◊ *He can't provide for his family any more.* Er kann seine Familie nicht mehr versorgen.

provided CONJUNCTION

vorausgesetzt, dass ◊ *He'll play in the next match provided he's fit.* Er spielt im nächsten Spiel, vorausgesetzt, dass er fit ist.

provisional ADJECTIVE

vorläufig

prowler NOUN

der Herumtreiber (PL die Herumtreiber) die Herumtreiberin

prune NOUN

die Backpflaume

pseudonym NOUN

das Pseudonym (PL die Pseudonyme)

psychiatrist NOUN

der Psychiater (PL die Psychiater) die Psychiaterin

◊ *She's a psychiatrist.* Sie ist Psychiaterin.

psychoanalyst NOUN

der Psychoanalytiker (PL die Psychoanalytiker) die Psychoanalytikerin

psychological ADJECTIVE

psychologisch

psychologist NOUN

der Psychologe (GEN des Psychologen, PL die Psychologen) die Psychologin

◊ *He's a psychologist.* Er ist Psychologe.

psychology NOUN

die Psychologie

PTO ABBREVIATION (= *please turn over*)

b. w. (= bitte wenden)

pub NOUN

die Kneipe

public NOUN

see also **public** ADJECTIVE

die Öffentlichkeit ◊ *open to the public* der Öffentlichkeit zugänglich

♦ **in public** in der Öffentlichkeit

public ADJECTIVE

see also **public** NOUN

öffentlich ◊ *public opinion* die öffentliche Meinung

♦ **a public holiday** ein gesetzlicher Feiertag

♦ **the public address system** die Lautsprecheranlage

publican NOUN

der Gastwirt die Gastwirtin

◊ *He's a publican.* Er ist Gastwirt.

publicity NOUN

die Publicity

public school NOUN

die Privatschule

public transport NOUN

die öffentlichen Verkehrsmittel NEUT PL

> ℹ️ Almost all German cities operate an integrated public transport system; you buy a single ticket which is valid on all buses, trams and light railway vehicles in a particular zone. You can buy a weekly **Wochenkarte**, monthly **Monatskarte** or yearly **Jahreskarte**.

to **publish** VERB

veröffentlichen (PERFECT hat veröffentlicht)

publisher NOUN

der Verlag (*company*) (PL die Verlage)

pudding NOUN

der Nachtisch ◊ *What's for pudding?* Was gibt's zum Nachtisch?

♦ **rice pudding** der Milchreis

♦ **black pudding** die Blutwurst

puddle NOUN

die Pfütze

puff pastry NOUN

der Blätterteig

to **pull** VERB

ziehen (IMPERFECT zog, PERFECT hat gezogen) ◊ *Pull!* Zieh!

♦ **He pulled the trigger.** Er drückte ab.

♦ **to pull a muscle** sich einen Muskel zerren ◊ *I pulled a muscle when I was training.* Ich habe mir beim Training einen Muskel gezerrt.

♦ **You're pulling my leg!** Du willst mich wohl auf den Arm nehmen! (*informal*)

♦ **to pull down** abreißen

♦ **to pull out (1)** (*tooth, weed*) herausziehen

♦ **to pull out (2)** (*car*) ausscheren ◊ *The car pulled out to overtake.* Das Auto scherte aus, um zu überholen.

♦ **to pull out (3)** (*withdraw*) aussteigen ◊ *She pulled out of the tournament.* Sie ist aus dem Turnier ausgestiegen.

♦ **to pull through** (*survive*) durchkommen ◊ *They think he'll pull through.* Sie meinen, er kommt durch.

♦ **to pull up** (*car*)

anhalten ◊ *A black car pulled up beside me.* Ein schwarzes Auto hielt neben mir an.

pullover NOUN
der Pullover (PL die Pullover)

pulse NOUN
der Puls (GEN des Pulses, PL die Pulse)
◊ *The nurse felt his pulse.* Die Schwester fühlte ihm den Puls.

pulses PL NOUN
die Hülsenfrüchte FEM PL

pump NOUN

see also **pump** VERB

1 die Pumpe ◊ *a bicycle pump* eine Fahrradpumpe
♦ **a petrol pump** eine Zapfsäule
2 (*shoe*)
der Sportschuh (PL die Sportschuhe)

to **pump** VERB

see also **pump** NOUN

pumpen
♦ **to pump up** (*tyre*) aufpumpen

pumpkin NOUN
der Kürbis (GEN des Kürbisses, PL die Kürbisse)

punch NOUN

see also **punch** VERB

1 (*blow*)
der Schlag (PL die Schläge) ◊ *Tyson went down on the third punch.* Beim dritten Schlag ging Tyson zu Boden.
2 (*drink*)
der Punsch

to **punch** VERB

see also **punch** NOUN

1 (*hit*)
schlagen (PRESENT schlägt, IMPERFECT schlug, PERFECT hat geschlagen) ◊ *He punched me!* Er hat mich geschlagen!
2 (*in ticket machine*)
entwerten (PERFECT hat entwertet) ◊ *Punch your ticket before you get on the train.* Entwerten Sie Ihre Fahrkarte, bevor Sie in den Zug steigen.
3 (*by ticket inspector*)
knipsen ◊ *He forgot to punch my ticket.* Er hat vergessen, meine Fahrkarte zu knipsen.

punch-up NOUN
die Schlägerei (*informal*)

punctual ADJECTIVE
pünktlich

punctuation NOUN
die Zeichensetzung

puncture NOUN
die Reifenpanne ◊ *to have a puncture* eine Reifenpanne haben

to **punish** VERB
bestrafen (PERFECT hat bestraft) ◊ *The teacher punished him for forgetting to do his homework.* Der Lehrer bestrafte ihn,

weil er vergessen hatte, seine Hausaufgaben zu machen.

punishment NOUN
die Strafe

punk NOUN
(*person*)
der Punker (PL die Punker)
die Punkerin
♦ **a punk rock band** eine Punkband

pupil NOUN
der Schüler (PL die Schüler)
die Schülerin

puppet NOUN
die Marionette

puppy NOUN
der junge Hund (PL die jungen Hunde)

to **purchase** VERB
erwerben (PRESENT erwirbt, IMPERFECT erwarb, PERFECT hat erworben)

pure ADJECTIVE
rein ◊ *pure orange juice* reiner Orangensaft
♦ **He's doing pure maths.** Er macht rein theoretische Mathematik.

purple ADJECTIVE
violett

purpose NOUN
der Zweck (PL die Zwecke) ◊ *What is the purpose of these changes?* Welchen Zweck haben diese Veränderungen?
♦ **his purpose in life** sein Lebensinhalt
♦ **on purpose** absichtlich ◊ *He did it on purpose.* Er hat es absichtlich getan.

to **purr** VERB
schnurren

purse NOUN
1 (*for money*)
der Geldbeutel (PL die Geldbeutel)
2 (*handbag*)
die Handtasche

to **pursue** VERB
verfolgen (PERFECT hat verfolgt)

pursuit NOUN
die Aktivität ◊ *outdoor pursuits* Aktivitäten im Freien

push NOUN

see also **push** VERB

♦ **to give somebody a push** jemanden stoßen ◊ *He gave me a push.* Er hat mich gestoßen.

to **push** VERB

see also **push** NOUN

1 drücken (*button*)
2 drängeln ◊ *Don't push!* Nicht drängeln!
♦ **to push somebody to do something** jemanden drängen, etwas zu tun ◊ *My parents are pushing me to go to university.* Meine Eltern drängen mich zu studieren.
♦ **to push drugs** mit Drogen handeln

P

☞

◆ **to push around** herumkommandieren ◊ *He likes pushing people around.* Er kommandiert die Leute gern herum.
◆ **Push off!** Hau ab! (*informal*)
◆ **I pushed my way through.** Ich drängelte mich durch.

pushchair NOUN
der <u>Sportwagen</u> (PL die Sportwagen)

pusher NOUN
(*of drugs*)
der <u>Drogenhändler</u> (PL die Drogenhändler)
die <u>Drogenhändlerin</u>

push-up NOUN
der <u>Liegestütz</u> (GEN des Liegestützes, PL die Liegestütze) ◊ *I do twenty push-ups every morning.* Ich mache jeden Morgen zwanzig Liegestütze.

to **put** VERB
> Use **legen** when you're putting something down flat, use **stellen** when you're standing something upright.

1 <u>legen</u> ◊ *Where shall I put my things?* Wohin soll ich meine Sachen legen? ◊ *She's putting the baby to bed.* Sie legt das Baby ins Bett.
2 <u>stellen</u> ◊ *Put the vase on the table.* Stell die Vase auf den Tisch.
◆ **Don't forget to put your name on the paper.** Vergiss nicht, deinen Namen auf das Papier zu schreiben.

to **put aside** VERB
<u>zurücklegen</u> (PERFECT hat zurückgelegt) ◊ *Can you put this aside for me till tomorrow?* Können Sie mir das bis morgen zurücklegen?

to **put away** VERB
<u>wegräumen</u> (PERFECT hat weggeräumt) ◊ *Can you put away the dishes, please?* Kannst du bitte das Geschirr wegräumen?

to **put back** VERB
1 <u>zurücklegen</u> (PERFECT hat zurückgelegt) ◊ *Put it back when you've finished with it.* Leg es zurück, wenn du es nicht mehr brauchst.
2 <u>zurückstellen</u> (PERFECT hat zurückgestellt) ◊ *to put the clock back* die Uhr zurückstellen ◊ *Put the milk back in the fridge.* Stell die Milch in den Kühlschrank zurück.

to **put down** VERB
1 <u>abstellen</u> (PERFECT hat abgestellt) ◊ *I'll put these bags down for a minute.* Ich stelle diese Taschen für eine Minute ab.
2 (*in writing*)
<u>aufschreiben</u> (IMPERFECT schrieb auf, PERFECT hat aufgeschrieben) ◊ *I've put down a few ideas.* Ich habe ein paar Ideen aufgeschrieben.
◆ **to have an animal put down** ein Tier einschläfern lassen ◊ *We had to have our*

old dog put down. Wir mussten unseren alten Hund einschläfern lassen.

to **put forward** VERB
<u>vorstellen</u> (PERFECT hat vorgestellt) ◊ *to put the clock forward* die Uhr vorstellen

to **put in** VERB
<u>einbauen</u> (*install*) (PERFECT hat eingebaut) ◊ *We're going to get central heating put in.* Wir werden eine Zentralheizung einbauen lassen.
◆ **He has put in a lot of work on this project.** Er hat viel Arbeit in dieses Projekt gesteckt.

to **put off** VERB
1 (*switch off*)
<u>ausmachen</u> (PERFECT hat ausgemacht) ◊ *Shall I put the light off?* Soll ich das Licht ausmachen?
2 (*postpone*)
<u>verschieben</u> (IMPERFECT verschob, PERFECT hat verschoben) ◊ *I keep putting it off.* Ich verschiebe es dauernd.
3 (*distract*)
<u>stören</u> ◊ *Stop putting me off!* Hör auf, mich zu stören!
4 (*discourage*)
<u>entmutigen</u> (PERFECT hat entmutigt) ◊ *He's not easily put off.* Er lässt sich nicht so schnell entmutigen.

to **put on** VERB
1 (*clothes*)
<u>anziehen</u> (IMPERFECT zog an, PERFECT hat angezogen) ◊ *I'll put my coat on.* Ich ziehe mir den Mantel an.
2 (*lipstick*)
<u>auftragen</u> (PRESENT trägt auf, IMPERFECT trug auf, PERFECT hat aufgetragen)
3 (*record*)
<u>auflegen</u> (PERFECT hat aufgelegt)
4 (*light, heater, TV*)
<u>anmachen</u> (PERFECT hat angemacht) ◊ *Shall I put the heater on?* Soll ich den Heizofen anmachen?
5 (*play, show*)
<u>aufführen</u> (PERFECT hat aufgeführt) ◊ *We're putting on "Bugsy Malone".* Wir führen "Bugsy Malone" auf.
6 <u>aufstellen</u> (PERFECT hat aufgestellt) ◊ *I'll put the potatoes on.* Ich stelle die Kartoffeln auf.
◆ **to put on weight** zunehmen ◊ *He's put on a lot of weight.* Er hat viel zugenommen.

to **put out** VERB
1 (*light, cigarette*)
<u>ausmachen</u> (PERFECT hat ausgemacht) ◊ *Put the light out.* Mach das Licht aus.
2 (*fire*)
<u>löschen</u> ◊ *It took them five hours to put out the fire.* Sie haben fünf Stunden gebraucht, um das Feuer zu löschen.

to **put through** VERB

verbinden (IMPERFECT verband, PERFECT hat verbunden) ◊ *Can you put me through to the manager?* Können Sie mich mit dem Geschäftsführer verbinden?
♦ **I'm putting you through.** Ich verbinde.

to **put up** VERB
1 (*pin up*)
aufhängen (PERFECT hat aufgehängt) ◊ *The poster's great. I'll put it up in my room.* Das Poster ist toll. Ich hänge es bei mir im Zimmer auf.
2 (*tent*)
aufschlagen (PRESENT schlägt auf, IMPERFECT schlug auf, PERFECT hat aufgeschlagen) ◊ *We put up our tent in a field.* Wir haben unser Zelt auf einem Feld aufgeschlagen.
3 (*price*)
erhöhen (PERFECT hat erhöht) ◊ *They've put up the price.* Sie haben den Preis erhöht.
4 (*accommodate*)
übernachten lassen (PRESENT lässt übernachten, IMPERFECT ließ übernachten, PERFECT hat übernachten lassen) ◊ *My friend will put me up for the night.* Mein Freund lässt mich bei sich übernachten.

♦ **to put one's hand up** sich melden ◊ *If you have any questions, put up your hand.* Wenn ihr Fragen habt, dann meldet euch.
♦ **to put up with something** sich etwas gefallen lassen ◊ *I'm not going to put up with it any longer.* Ich lasse mir das nicht länger gefallen.

puzzle NOUN
das Puzzle (*jigsaw*) (PL die Puzzles)
puzzled ADJECTIVE
verdutzt ◊ *You look puzzled!* Du siehst verdutzt aus!
puzzling ADJECTIVE
rätselhaft
pyjamas PL NOUN
der Schlafanzug (PL die Schlafanzüge)
◊ *my pyjamas* mein Schlafanzug
♦ **a pair of pyjamas** ein Schlafanzug
♦ **a pyjama top** ein Schlafanzugoberteil NEUT
pyramid NOUN
die Pyramide
Pyrenees PL NOUN
♦ **the Pyrenees** die Pyrenäen PL

P

Q

quaint ADJECTIVE
malerisch (*house, village*)

qualification NOUN
die Qualifikation ◊ *vocational qualifications* die beruflichen Qualifikationen
♦ **to leave school without any qualifications** die Schule ohne einen Abschluss verlassen

qualified ADJECTIVE
ausgebildet ◊ *a qualified driving instructor* ein ausgebildeter Fahrlehrer ◊ *a qualified nurse* eine ausgebildete Krankenschwester

to **qualify** VERB
① (*for job*)
seinen Abschluss machen ◊ *She qualified as a teacher last year.* Sie hat letztes Jahr ihren Abschluss als Lehrerin gemacht.
② (*in competition*)
sich qualifizieren (PERFECT hat sich qualifiziert) ◊ *Our team didn't qualify.* Unsere Mannschaft konnte sich nicht qualifizieren.

quality NOUN
① die Qualität ◊ *a good quality of life* eine gute Lebensqualität
♦ **good-quality ingredients** qualitativ hochwertige Zutaten
② die Eigenschaft (*of person*) ◊ *She's got lots of good qualities.* Sie hat viele gute Eigenschaften.

quantity NOUN
die Menge

quarantine NOUN
die Quarantäne ◊ *in quarantine* in Quarantäne

quarrel NOUN
see also **quarrel** VERB
der Streit (PL die Streite)

to **quarrel** VERB
see also **quarrel** NOUN
sich streiten (IMPERFECT stritt sich, PERFECT hat sich gestritten)

quarry NOUN
der Steinbruch (*for stone*) (PL die Steinbrüche)

quarter NOUN
das Viertel (PL die Viertel) ◊ *three quarters* drei Viertel ◊ *a quarter of an hour* eine viertel Stunde
♦ **three quarters of an hour** eine Dreiviertelstunde
♦ **a quarter past ten** Viertel nach zehn
♦ **a quarter to eleven** Viertel vor elf

quarter final NOUN
das Viertelfinale (PL die Viertelfinale)

quartet NOUN
das Quartett (PL die Quartette) ◊ *a string quartet* ein Streichquartett

quay NOUN
der Kai (PL die Kais)

queasy ADJECTIVE
♦ **I'm feeling queasy.** Mir ist schlecht.

queen NOUN
① die Königin ◊ *Queen Elizabeth* Königin Elisabeth
② die Dame (*playing card*) ◊ *the queen of hearts* die Herzdame
♦ **the Queen Mother** die Königinmutter

query NOUN
see also **query** VERB
die Frage

to **query** VERB
see also **query** NOUN
infrage stellen ◊ *No one queried my decision.* Niemand hat meine Entscheidung infrage gestellt.
♦ **They queried the bill.** Sie reklamierten die Rechnung.

question NOUN
see also **question** VERB
die Frage ◊ *That's a difficult question.* Das ist eine schwierige Frage.
♦ **Can I ask a question?** Kann ich etwas fragen?
♦ **It's out of the question.** Das kommt nicht infrage.

to **question** VERB
see also **question** NOUN
befragen (PERFECT hat befragt)
♦ **He was questioned by the police.** Die Polizei hat ihn vernommen.

question mark NOUN
das Fragezeichen (PL die Fragezeichen)

questionnaire NOUN
der Fragebogen (PL die Fragebögen)

queue NOUN
see also **queue** VERB
die Schlange

to **queue** VERB
see also **queue** NOUN
Schlange stehen (IMPERFECT stand Schlange, PERFECT hat Schlange gestanden) ◊ *We had to queue for an hour.* Wir mussten eine Stunde lang Schlange stehen.
♦ **to queue for something** für etwas anstehen ◊ *We had to queue for tickets.* Wir mussten für Karten anstehen.

quick ADJECTIVE, ADVERB
schnell ◊ *a quick lunch* ein schnelles Mittagessen ◊ *Quick, phone the police!* Schnell, rufen Sie die Polizei! ◊ *It's*

quicker by train. Mit dem Zug geht es schneller.
- **Be quick!** Beeil dich!
- **She's a quick learner.** Sie lernt schnell.

quickly ADVERB
schnell ◊ *It was all over very quickly.* Es war alles sehr schnell vorbei.

quiet ADJECTIVE
[1] ruhig (*not talkative, peaceful*) ◊ *You're very quiet today.* Du bist heute sehr ruhig. ◊ *a quiet little town* eine ruhige, kleine Stadt
[2] leise (*not noisy*) ◊ *The engine's very quiet.* Der Motor ist sehr leise.
- **Be quiet!** Sei still!
- **Quiet!** Ruhe!

quietly ADVERB
leise ◊ *He quietly opened the door.* Er öffnete leise die Tür.

quilt NOUN
die Steppdecke (*duvet*)

to **quit** VERB
[1] aufgeben (PRESENT gibt auf, IMPERFECT gab auf, PERFECT hat aufgegeben) ◊ *I quit my job last week.* Ich habe meine Stelle letzte Woche aufgegeben.
[2] aufhören ◊ *I quit smoking.* Ich habe mit dem Rauchen aufgehört.

quite ADVERB
[1] ziemlich (*rather*) ◊ *It's quite warm today.* Heute ist es ziemlich warm. ◊ *I've been there quite a lot.* Ich war schon ziemlich oft da. ◊ *quite a lot of money* ziemlich viel Geld ◊ *There were quite a few people there.* Es waren ziemlich viele Leute da. ◊ *It costs quite a lot to go abroad.* Es ist ziemlich teuer, ins Ausland zu fahren. ◊ *It's quite a long way.* Es ist ziemlich weit.
- **It was quite a shock.** Es war ein ziemlicher Schock.
- **I quite liked the film, but ...** Der Film hat mir ganz gut gefallen, aber ...
[2] ganz (*entirely*) ◊ *I'm not quite sure.* Ich bin mir nicht ganz sicher. ◊ *It's not quite the same.* Das ist nicht ganz das Gleiche.
- **quite good** ganz gut

quiz NOUN
das Quiz (GEN des Quiz, PL die Quiz)

quota NOUN
die Quote

quotation NOUN
das Zitat (PL die Zitate) ◊ *a quotation from Shakespeare* ein Shakespearezitat

quotation marks PL NOUN
die Anführungszeichen PL

quote NOUN

> see also **quote** VERB

das Zitat (PL die Zitate) ◊ *a Shakespeare quote* ein Shakespearezitat
- **quotes** (*quotation marks*) die Anführungszeichen ◊ *in quotes* in Anführungszeichen

to **quote** VERB

> see also **quote** NOUN

zitieren (PERFECT hat zitiert)

Q

R

rabbi NOUN
der Rabbiner (PL die Rabbiner)

rabbit NOUN
das Kaninchen (PL die Kaninchen) ◊ *a
rabbit hutch* ein Kaninchenstall MASC

rabies SING NOUN
die Tollwut
♦ **a dog with rabies** ein tollwütiger Hund

race NOUN
see also **race** VERB
1 (*sport*)
das Rennen (PL die Rennen) ◊ *a cycle
race* ein Radrennen
2 (*species*)
die Rasse ◊ *the human race* die
Menschheit
♦ **race relations** Rassenbeziehungen FEM PL

to **race** VERB
see also **race** NOUN
1 rennen (IMPERFECT rannte, PERFECT ist
gerannt) ◊ *We raced to catch the bus.*
Wir sind gerannt, um den Bus zu
erreichen.
2 (*have a race*)
um die Wette laufen mit (PRESENT läuft
um die Wette, IMPERFECT lief um die Wette,
PERFECT ist um die Wette gelaufen) ◊ *I'll
race you!* Ich laufe mit dir um die Wette!

racecourse NOUN
die Pferderennbahn

racehorse NOUN
das Rennpferd (PL die Rennpferde)

racer NOUN
das Rennrad (*bike*) (PL die Rennräder)

racetrack NOUN
die Rennbahn

racial ADJECTIVE
♦ **racial discrimination** die
Rassendiskriminierung

racing car NOUN
der Rennwagen (PL die Rennwagen)

racing driver NOUN
der Rennfahrer (PL die Rennfahrer)
die Rennfahrerin

racism NOUN
der Rassismus (GEN des Rassismus)

racist ADJECTIVE
see also **racist** NOUN
rassistisch
♦ **He's racist.** Er ist ein Rassist.

racist NOUN
see also **racist** ADJECTIVE
der Rassist (GEN des Rassisten, PL die
Rassisten)
die Rassistin

rack NOUN
der Gepäckträger (*for luggage*) (PL die
Gepäckträger)

racket NOUN
1 (*for sport*)
der Schläger (PL die Schläger) ◊ *my
tennis racket* mein Tennisschläger
2 (*noise*)
der Krach ◊ *They're making a terrible
racket.* Sie machen einen furchtbaren
Krach.

racquet NOUN
der Schläger (PL die Schläger)

radar NOUN
das Radar

radiation NOUN
die Strahlung

radiator NOUN
der Heizkörper (PL die Heizkörper)

radio NOUN
das Radio (PL die Radios)
♦ **on the radio** im Radio
♦ **a radio station** ein Rundfunksender
MASC

radioactive ADJECTIVE
radioaktiv

radio cassette NOUN
der Radiorekorder (PL die Radiorekorder)

radio-controlled ADJECTIVE
ferngesteuert (*model plane, car*)

radish NOUN
1 (*small red*)
das Radieschen (PL die Radieschen)
2 (*long white*)
der Rettich (PL die Rettiche)

RAF NOUN (= Royal Air Force)
die britische Luftwaffe ◊ *He's in the
RAF.* Er ist bei der britischen Luftwaffe.

raffle NOUN
die Tombola (PL die Tombolas) ◊ *a raffle
ticket* ein Tombolalos NEUT

raft NOUN
das Floß (GEN des Floßes, PL die Flöße)

rag NOUN
der Lumpen (PL die Lumpen) ◊ *dressed
in rags* in Lumpen gekleidet
♦ **a piece of rag** ein Lappen MASC

rage NOUN
die Wut ◊ *mad with rage* wild vor Wut
♦ **to be in a rage** wütend sein ◊ *She was in
a rage.* Sie war wütend.
♦ **It's all the rage.** Es ist große Mode.

raid NOUN
see also **raid** VERB
1 (*burglary*)
der Überfall (PL die Überfälle) ◊ *There
was a bank raid near my house.* Es gab
einen Banküberfall in der Nähe meines
Hauses.
2 die Razzia (PL die Razzien) ◊ *a police
raid* eine Polizeirazzia

to **raid** VERB

> see also **raid** NOUN

eine Razzia machen in +DAT (police) ◊ The police raided a club in Soho. Die Polizei machte in einem Klub in Soho eine Razzia.

rail NOUN

1 (on stairs, bridge, balcony)
das Geländer (PL die Geländer)
2 (on railway line)
die Schiene
♦ **by rail** mit dem Zug

railcard NOUN
die Bahncard ® (PL die Bahncards)

railroad NOUN US
die Eisenbahn
♦ **a railroad station** ein Bahnhof MASC

railway NOUN
die Eisenbahn ◊ the privatization of the railways die Privatisierung der Eisenbahn
♦ **a railway line** eine Eisenbahnlinie
♦ **a railway station** ein Bahnhof MASC

rain NOUN

> see also **rain** VERB

der Regen ◊ in the rain im Regen

to **rain** VERB

> see also **rain** NOUN

regnen ◊ It rains a lot here. Hier regnet es viel.
♦ **It's raining.** Es regnet.

rainbow NOUN
der Regenbogen (PL die Regenbogen)

raincoat NOUN
der Regenmantel (PL die Regenmäntel)

rainfall NOUN
der Niederschlag (PL die Niederschläge)

rainforest NOUN
der Regenwald (PL die Regenwälder)

rainy ADJECTIVE
regnerisch

to **raise** VERB

1 (lift)
hochheben (IMPERFECT hob hoch, PERFECT hat hochgehoben) ◊ He raised his hand. Er hob die Hand hoch.
2 (improve)
heben (IMPERFECT hob, PERFECT hat gehoben) ◊ They want to raise standards in schools. Sie wollen das Niveau in den Schulen heben.
♦ **to raise money** Spenden sammeln ◊ The school is raising money for a new gym. Die Schule sammelt Spenden für eine neue Turnhalle.

raisin NOUN
die Rosine

rake NOUN
der Rechen (PL die Rechen)

rally NOUN

1 (of people)
die Kundgebung
2 (sport)

die Rallye (PL die Rallyes) ◊ a rally driver ein Rallyefahrer MASC
3 (in tennis)
der Ballwechsel (PL die Ballwechsel)

Ramadan NOUN
der Ramadan

ramble NOUN
die Wanderung ◊ to go for a ramble eine Wanderung machen

rambler NOUN
der Wanderer (PL die Wanderer)
die Wanderin

ramp NOUN
die Rampe (for wheelchairs)

ran VERB see **run**

ranch NOUN
die Ranch (PL die Ranches)

random ADJECTIVE
♦ **a random selection** eine Zufallsauswahl
♦ **at random** aufs Geratewohl ◊ We picked the number at random. Wir haben die Nummer aufs Geratewohl ausgewählt.

rang VERB see **ring**

range NOUN

> see also **range** VERB

die Auswahl ◊ There's a wide range of colours. Es gibt eine große Auswahl an Farben.
♦ **a range of subjects** verschiedene Themen ◊ We study a range of subjects. Wir studieren verschiedene Themen.
♦ **a mountain range** eine Bergkette

to **range** VERB

> see also **range** NOUN

♦ **to range from ... to** gehen von ... bis ◊ Temperatures in summer range from twenty to thirty-five degrees. Die Temperaturen im Sommer gehen von zwanzig bis fünfunddreißig Grad.
♦ **Tickets range from two to twenty pounds.** Karten kosten von zwei bis zwanzig Pfund.

rank NOUN

> see also **rank** VERB

♦ **a taxi rank** ein Taxistand MASC

to **rank** VERB

> see also **rank** NOUN

rangieren (PERFECT hat rangiert) ◊ He's ranked third in the United States. Er rangiert in den Vereinigten Staaten an dritter Stelle.

ransom NOUN
das Lösegeld (PL die Lösegelder)

rap NOUN
der Rap (music)

rape NOUN

> see also **rape** VERB

die Vergewaltigung

to **rape** VERB

> see also **rape** NOUN

vergewaltigen (PERFECT hat vergewaltigt)

rapids PL NOUN

R

die <u>Stromschnellen</u> FEM PL

rapist NOUN
der <u>Vergewaltiger</u> (PL die Vergewaltiger)

rare ADJECTIVE
[1] <u>selten</u> (*unusual*) ◊ *a rare plant* eine seltene Pflanze
[2] <u>blutig</u> (*steak*)

rash NOUN
der <u>Ausschlag</u> (PL die Ausschläge) ◊ *I've got a rash on my chest.* Ich habe einen Ausschlag auf der Brust.

rasher NOUN
♦**an egg and two rashers of bacon** ein Ei und zwei Streifen Speck

raspberry NOUN
die <u>Himbeere</u> ◊ *raspberry jam* die Himbeermarmelade

rat NOUN
die <u>Ratte</u>

rate NOUN
see also **rate** VERB
[1] (*price*)
der <u>Preis</u> (GEN des Preises, PL die Preise)
◊ *There are reduced rates for students.* Studenten bekommen ermäßigte Preise.
[2] (*level*)
die <u>Rate</u> ◊ *the divorce rate* die Scheidungsrate
♦**a high rate of interest** ein hoher Zinssatz

to **rate** VERB
see also **rate** NOUN
<u>einschätzen</u> (PERFECT hat eingeschätzt)
◊ *He was rated the best.* Man schätzte ihn als den Besten ein.

rather ADVERB
<u>ziemlich</u> ◊ *I was rather disappointed.* Ich war ziemlich enttäuscht. ◊ *Twenty pounds! That's rather a lot!* Zwanzig Pfund! Das ist aber ziemlich viel!
♦**rather a lot of** ziemlich viel ◊ *I've got rather a lot of work to do.* Ich habe ziemlich viel Arbeit.
♦**rather than** statt ◊ *We decided to camp, rather than stay at a hotel.* Wir haben beschlossen zu zelten statt im Hotel zu übernachten.
♦**I'd rather ...** Ich würde lieber ... ◊ *I'd rather stay in tonight.* Ich würde heute Abend lieber zu Hause bleiben. ◊ *Would you like a sweet? – I'd rather have an apple.* Möchtest du ein Bonbon? – Ich hätte lieber einen Apfel.

rattle NOUN
die <u>Rassel</u> (*for baby*)

rattlesnake NOUN
die <u>Klapperschlange</u>

to **rave** VERB
see also **rave** NOUN
<u>schwärmen</u> ◊ *They raved about the film.* Sie schwärmten von dem Film.

rave NOUN
see also **rave** VERB
die <u>Raveparty</u> (*party*) (PL die Ravepartys)
♦**rave music** die Ravemusik

raven NOUN
der <u>Rabe</u> (GEN des Raben, PL die Raben)

ravenous ADJECTIVE
♦**to be ravenous** einen Riesenhunger haben ◊ *I'm ravenous!* Ich habe einen Riesenhunger!

raving ADVERB
♦**raving mad** total verrückt (*informal*)

raw ADJECTIVE
<u>roh</u> (*food*)
♦**raw materials** die Rohstoffe MASC PL

razor NOUN
der <u>Rasierapparat</u> (PL die Rasierapparate)
♦**a razor blade** eine Rasierklinge

RE NOUN (= *religious education*)
der <u>Religionsunterricht</u>

reach NOUN
see also **reach** VERB
♦**out of reach** außer Reichweite ◊ *The light switch was out of reach.* Der Lichtschalter war außer Reichweite.
♦**within easy reach** leicht zu erreichen
◊ *The hotel is within easy reach of the town centre.* Das Hotel ist vom Stadtzentrum leicht zu erreichen.

to **reach** VERB
see also **reach** NOUN
[1] <u>ankommen in</u> +DAT (IMPERFECT kam an, PERFECT ist angekommen) ◊ *We reached the hotel at ten o'clock.* Wir sind um zehn Uhr im Hotel angekommen.
♦**We hope to reach the final.** Wir wollen ins Endspiel kommen.
[2] (*decision*)
<u>treffen</u> (PRESENT trifft, IMPERFECT traf, PERFECT hat getroffen) ◊ *Eventually they reached a decision.* Sie haben schließlich eine Entscheidung getroffen.
♦**He reached for his gun.** Er griff nach seiner Pistole.

to **react** VERB
<u>reagieren</u> (PERFECT hat reagiert)

reaction NOUN
die <u>Reaktion</u>

reactor NOUN
der <u>Reaktor</u> (PL die Reaktoren) ◊ *a nuclear reactor* ein Kernreaktor

to **read** VERB
<u>lesen</u> (PRESENT liest, IMPERFECT las, PERFECT hat gelesen) ◊ *I don't read much.* Ich lese nicht viel. ◊ *Have you read "Animal Farm"?* Hast du "Die Farm der Tiere" gelesen? ◊ *Read the text out loud.* Lies den Text laut.

reader NOUN
(*person*)
der <u>Leser</u> (PL die Leser)
die <u>Leserin</u>

readily ADVERB

bereitwillig ◊ *She readily agreed.* Sie stimmte bereitwillig zu.

reading NOUN
das <u>Lesen</u> ◊ *Reading is one of my hobbies.* Lesen ist eines meiner Hobbies.

ready ADJECTIVE
<u>fertig</u> ◊ *She's nearly ready.* Sie ist fast fertig.
♦ **He's always ready to help.** Er ist immer bereit zu helfen.
♦ **a ready meal** ein Fertiggericht NEUT
♦ **to get ready** sich fertig machen ◊ *She's getting ready to go out.* Sie macht sich zum Ausgehen fertig.
♦ **to get something ready** etwas machen

real ADJECTIVE
[1] <u>echt</u> (*not fake*) ◊ *He wasn't a real policeman.* Er war kein echter Polizist. ◊ *It's real leather.* Es ist echtes Leder.
[2] <u>wirklich</u> ◊ *Her real name is Cordelia.* Ihr wirklicher Name ist Cordelia. ◊ *in real life* im wirklichen Leben
♦ **It was a real nightmare.** Es war wirklich ein Albtraum.

realistic ADJECTIVE
<u>realistisch</u>

reality NOUN
die <u>Wirklichkeit</u>

reality TV NOUN
das <u>Reality TV</u>

to **realize** VERB
♦ **to realize that ...** bemerken, dass ... ◊ *We realized that something was wrong.* Wir bemerkten, dass irgendetwas nicht stimmte.

really ADVERB
<u>wirklich</u> ◊ *She's really nice.* Sie ist wirklich nett. ◊ *I'm learning Italian. – Really?* Ich lerne Italienisch. – Wirklich? ◊ *Do you really think so?* Meinst du wirklich?
♦ **Do you want to go? – Not really.** Willst du gehen? – Eigentlich nicht.

realtor NOUN US
der <u>Immobilienhändler</u> (PL die Immobilienhändler)
die <u>Immobilienhändlerin</u>

rear ADJECTIVE
see also **rear** NOUN
<u>hintere</u> ◊ *the rear windows* die hinteren Fenster
♦ **the rear wheel** das Hinterrad

rear NOUN
see also **rear** ADJECTIVE
das <u>hintere Ende</u> (PL die hinteren Enden) ◊ *at the rear of the train* am hinteren Ende des Zuges

reason NOUN
der <u>Grund</u> (PL die Gründe) ◊ *There's no reason to think that ...* Es gibt keinen Grund zu meinen, dass ...
♦ **for security reasons** aus Sicherheitsgründen

♦ **That was the main reason I went.** Das war der Hauptgrund, warum ich gegangen bin.

reasonable ADJECTIVE
[1] <u>vernünftig</u> (*sensible*) ◊ *Be reasonable!* Sei vernünftig!
[2] <u>ganz ordentlich</u> (*not bad*) ◊ *He wrote a reasonable essay.* Er hat einen ganz ordentlichen Aufsatz geschrieben.

reasonably ADVERB
<u>ziemlich</u> ◊ *The team played reasonably well.* Die Mannschaft hat ziemlich gut gespielt.
♦ **reasonably priced accommodation** preiswerte Unterbringung

to **reassure** VERB
<u>beruhigen</u> (PERFECT hat beruhigt)

reassuring ADJECTIVE
<u>beruhigend</u>

rebel NOUN
see also **rebel** VERB
der <u>Rebell</u> (PL die Rebellen)
die <u>Rebellin</u>

to **rebel** VERB
see also **rebel** NOUN
<u>rebellieren</u> (PERFECT hat rebelliert)

rebellious ADJECTIVE
<u>aufmüpfig</u>

receipt NOUN
die <u>Quittung</u>

to **receive** VERB
<u>erhalten</u> (PRESENT erhält, IMPERFECT erhielt, PERFECT hat erhalten)

receiver NOUN
der <u>Hörer</u> (*of phone*) (PL die Hörer) ◊ *to pick up the receiver* den Hörer abnehmen

recent ADJECTIVE
<u>neueste</u> ◊ *the recent developments in ...* die neuesten Entwicklungen in ...
♦ **in recent years** in den letzten Jahren

recently ADVERB
<u>in letzter Zeit</u> ◊ *I've been doing a lot of training recently.* Ich habe in letzter Zeit viel trainiert.

reception NOUN
[1] (*in hotel*)
die <u>Rezeption</u> ◊ *Please leave your key at reception.* Bitte geben Sie Ihren Schlüssel an der Rezeption ab.
[2] (*party*)
der <u>Empfang</u> (PL die Empfänge) ◊ *The reception will be at a big hotel.* Der Empfang findet in einem großen Hotel statt.

receptionist NOUN
der <u>Empfangschef</u> (PL die Empfangschefs)
die <u>Empfangsdame</u>

recession NOUN
die <u>Rezession</u>

recipe NOUN
das <u>Rezept</u> (PL die Rezepte)

R

to **reckon** VERB

meinen ◊ *What do you reckon?* Was meinst du?

reclining ADJECTIVE

♦ **a reclining seat** ein Liegesitz MASC

recognizable ADJECTIVE

1 wieder zu erkennen ◊ *He was scarcely recognizable after the accident.* Er war nach dem Unfall kaum wieder zu erkennen.

2 erkennbar (*noticeable*) ◊ *There was a recognizable improvement in his work.* Seine Arbeit hat erkennbare Fortschritte gemacht.

to **recognize** VERB

erkennen (IMPERFECT erkannte, PERFECT hat erkannt) ◊ *You'll recognize me by my red hair.* Du wirst mich an meinen roten Haaren erkennen.

to **recommend** VERB

empfehlen (PRESENT empfiehlt, IMPERFECT empfahl, PERFECT hat empfohlen) ◊ *What do you recommend?* Was können Sie empfehlen?

to **reconsider** VERB

♦ **to reconsider something** sich etwas noch einmal überlegen ◊ *I think you should reconsider your decision.* Ich denke, du solltest dir die Entscheidung noch einmal überlegen.

record NOUN

see also **record** VERB

1 (*recording*)

die Schallplatte ◊ *my favourite record* meine Lieblingsschallplatte

2 (*sport*)

der Rekord (PL die Rekorde) ◊ *the world record* der Weltrekord

♦ **in record time** in Rekordzeit ◊ *She finished the job in record time.* Sie war in Rekordzeit mit der Arbeit fertig.

♦ **He's got a criminal record.** Er ist vorbestraft.

♦ **records** (*of police, hospital*) die Akten ◊ *I'll check in the records.* Ich sehe in den Akten nach.

♦ **There is no record of your booking.** Ihre Buchung ist nirgends belegt.

to **record** VERB

see also **record** NOUN

aufnehmen (*on film, tape*) (PRESENT nimmt auf, IMPERFECT nahm auf, PERFECT hat aufgenommen) ◊ *They've just recorded their new album.* Sie haben eben ihr neues Album aufgenommen.

recorded delivery NOUN

♦ **to send something recorded delivery** etwas per Einschreiben senden

recorder NOUN

die Blockflöte (*instrument*) ◊ *She plays the recorder.* Sie spielt Blockflöte.

♦ **a cassette recorder** ein Kassettenrekorder

MASC

♦ **a video recorder** ein Videorekorder MASC

recording NOUN

die Aufnahme

record player NOUN

der Plattenspieler (PL die Plattenspieler)

to **recover** VERB

sich erholen (PERFECT hat sich erholt) ◊ *He's recovering from a knee injury.* Er erholt sich von einer Knieverletzung.

recovery NOUN

die Erholung

♦ **Best wishes for a speedy recovery!** Gute Besserung!

rectangle NOUN

das Rechteck (PL die Rechtecke)

rectangular ADJECTIVE

rechteckig

to **recycle** VERB

wiederverwerten (PERFECT hat wiederverwertet)

recycling NOUN

das Recycling

red ADJECTIVE

rot ◊ *a red rose* eine rote Rose ◊ *red meat* rotes Fleisch ◊ *Peter's got red hair.* Peter hat rote Haare.

♦ **to go through a red light** bei Rot über die Ampel fahren

Red Cross NOUN

das Rote Kreuz

redcurrant NOUN

die Rote Johannisbeere

to **redecorate** VERB

renovieren (PERFECT hat renoviert)

red-haired ADJECTIVE

rothaarig

red-handed ADJECTIVE

♦ **to catch somebody red-handed** jemanden auf frischer Tat ertappen ◊ *He was caught red-handed.* Er wurde auf frischer Tat ertappt.

redhead NOUN

der Rothaarige (GEN des Rothaarigen, PL die Rothaarigen)

die Rothaarige (GEN der Rothaarigen) ◊ *a redhead* (*man*) ein Rothaariger

to **redo** VERB

noch einmal machen

to **reduce** VERB

ermäßigen (PERFECT hat ermäßigt) ◊ *at a reduced price* zu ermäßigtem Preis

♦ **"reduce speed now"** "Geschwindigkeit verringern"

reduction NOUN

der Nachlass (GEN des Nachlasses, PL die Nachlässe) ◊ *a five per cent reduction* ein Nachlass von fünf Prozent

♦ **"Huge reductions!"** "Stark reduzierte Preise!"

redundancy NOUN

die Entlassung ◊ *There were fifty*
redundancies. Es gab fünfzig
Entlassungen.
♦ **his redundancy payment** seine
Abfindung
redundant ADJECTIVE
♦ **to be made redundant** entlassen werden
◊ *He was made redundant yesterday.* Er
wurde gestern entlassen.
reed NOUN
das Schilf (*plant*)
reel NOUN
die Spule (*of thread*)
to **refer** VERB
♦ **to refer to** anspielen auf +ACC ◊ *What are*
you referring to? Auf was spielst du an?
referee NOUN
der Schiedsrichter (PL die Schiedsrichter)
die Schiedsrichterin
reference NOUN
das Arbeitszeugnis (*for job application*)
(GEN des Arbeitszeugnisses, PL die
Arbeitszeugnisse) ◊ *Would you*
please give me a reference? Können
Sie mir bitte ein Arbeitszeugnis
geben?
♦ **With reference to your letter of ...** Mit
Bezug auf Ihren Brief vom ...
♦ **a reference book** ein Nachschlagewerk
NEUT
to **refill** VERB
nachfüllen (PERFECT hat nachgefüllt) ◊ *He*
refilled my glass. Er füllte mein Glas
nach.
refinery NOUN
die Raffinerie
to **reflect** VERB
reflektieren (*light, image*) (PERFECT hat
reflektiert)
reflection NOUN
das Spiegelbild (*in mirror*) (PL die
Spiegelbilder)
reflex NOUN
der Reflex (GEN des Reflexes, PL die
Reflexe)
reflexive ADJECTIVE
reflexiv ◊ *a reflexive verb* ein reflexives
Verb
refresher course NOUN
der Wiederholungskurs (GEN des
Wiederholungskurses, PL die
Wiederholungskurse)
refreshing ADJECTIVE
erfrischend
refreshments PL NOUN
die Erfrischungen FEM PL
refrigerator NOUN
der Kühlschrank (PL die Kühlschränke)
to **refuel** VERB
auftanken (PERFECT hat aufgetankt) ◊ *Our*
plane refuelled in Boston. Unser
Flugzeug hat in Boston aufgetankt.
refuge NOUN

die Zuflucht
refugee NOUN
der Flüchtling (PL die Flüchtlinge)
der Flüchtling is also used for women.
refund NOUN
see also **refund** VERB
die Rückvergütung
to **refund** VERB
see also **refund** NOUN
zurückerstatten (PERFECT hat
zurückerstattet)
refusal NOUN
die Weigerung
to **refuse** VERB
see also **refuse** NOUN
sich weigern
refuse NOUN
see also **refuse** VERB
der Müll
♦ **refuse collection** die Müllabfuhr
to **regain** VERB
♦ **to regain consciousness** wieder zu
Bewusstsein kommen
regard NOUN
see also **regard** VERB
♦ **Give my regards to Alice.** Grüße an
Alice.
♦ **Martin sends his regards.** Martin lässt
grüßen.
♦ **"with kind regards"** "mit freundlichen
Grüßen"
to **regard** VERB
see also **regard** NOUN
♦ **to regard something as** etwas betrachten
als
♦ **as regards ...** was ... betrifft ◊ *As regards*
offensive weapons ... Was
Angriffswaffen betrifft, ...
regarding PREPOSITION
betreffend ◊ *the laws regarding the*
export of animals die Gesetze den Export
von Tieren betreffend
♦ **Regarding John, ...** Was John betrifft, ...
regardless ADVERB
trotzdem ◊ *to carry on regardless*
trotzdem weitermachen
regiment NOUN
das Regiment (PL die Regimenter)
region NOUN
die Gegend
regional ADJECTIVE
regional
register NOUN
see also **register** VERB
das Klassenbuch (*in school*) (PL die
Klassenbücher)
to **register** VERB
see also **register** NOUN
sich einschreiben (*at school, college*)
(IMPERFECT schrieb sich ein, PERFECT hat sich
eingeschrieben)
registered ADJECTIVE

R

☞

◆ **a registered letter** ein eingeschriebener Brief

registration NOUN

1 (*in school*)

der Namensaufruf (PL die Namensaufrufe)

2 (*of car*)

das polizeiliche Kennzeichen (PL die polizeilichen Kennzeichen)

regret NOUN

> see also **regret** VERB

das Bedauern

◆ **I've got no regrets.** Ich bedaure nichts.

to **regret** VERB

> see also **regret** NOUN

bedauern (PERFECT hat bedauert) ◊ *Give me the money or you'll regret it!* Gib mir das Geld oder du wirst es bedauern!

◆ **to regret doing something** es bedauern, etwas getan zu haben ◊ *I regretted having said that.* Ich habe bedauert, dass ich das gesagt habe.

regular ADJECTIVE

1 regelmäßig ◊ *at regular intervals* in regelmäßigen Abständen ◊ *a regular verb* ein regelmäßiges Verb

◆ **to take regular exercise** regelmäßig Sport machen

2 normal (*average*) ◊ *a regular portion of fries* eine normale Portion Pommes frites

regularly ADVERB

regelmäßig

regulation NOUN

die Bestimmung

rehearsal NOUN

die Probe

to **rehearse** VERB

proben

rein NOUN

der Zügel (PL die Zügel) ◊ *the reins* die Zügel

reindeer NOUN

das Rentier (PL die Rentiere)

to **reject** VERB

verwerfen (*idea, suggestion*) (PRESENT verwirft, IMPERFECT verwarf, PERFECT hat verworfen) ◊ *We rejected that idea straight away.* Wir haben die Idee sofort verworfen.

◆ **I applied but they rejected me.** Ich habe mich beworben, wurde aber abgelehnt.

relapse NOUN

der Rückfall (PL die Rückfälle) ◊ *to have a relapse* einen Rückfall haben

related ADJECTIVE

verwandt (*people*) ◊ *Are you related to her?* Bist du mit ihr verwandt? ◊ *We're related.* Wir sind miteinander verwandt.

◆ **The two events were not related.** Es bestand kein Zusammenhang zwischen den beiden Ereignissen.

relation NOUN

1 (*person*)

der Verwandte (GEN des Verwandten, PL die Verwandten)

die Verwandte (GEN der Verwandten) ◊ *He's a distant relation.* Er ist ein entfernter Verwandter. ◊ *I've got relations in London.* Ich habe Verwandte in London. ◊ *my close relations* meine engsten Verwandten

2 (*connection*)

der Bezug (PL die Bezüge) ◊ *It has no relation to reality.* Es hat keinen Bezug zur Wirklichkeit.

◆ **in relation to** verglichen mit

relationship NOUN

die Beziehung ◊ *We have a good relationship.* Wir haben eine gute Beziehung. ◊ *I'm not in a relationship at the moment.* Ich habe im Moment keine Beziehung.

relative NOUN

der Verwandte (GEN des Verwandten, PL die Verwandten)

die Verwandte (GEN der Verwandten) ◊ *a relative* (*man*) ein Verwandter ◊ *my close relatives* meine engsten Verwandten

◆ **all her relatives** ihre ganze Verwandtschaft

relatively ADVERB

relativ

to **relax** VERB

sich entspannen (PERFECT hat sich entspannt) ◊ *I relax listening to music.* Ich entspanne mich beim Musikhören.

◆ **Relax! Everything's fine.** Immer mit der Ruhe! Alles ist in Ordnung.

relaxation NOUN

die Entspannung ◊ *I don't have much time for relaxation.* Ich habe nicht viel Zeit für Entspannung.

relaxed ADJECTIVE

entspannt

relaxing ADJECTIVE

entspannend ◊ *I find cooking relaxing.* Ich finde Kochen entspannend.

relay NOUN

◆ **a relay race** ein Staffellauf MASC

to **release** VERB

> see also **release** NOUN

1 (*prisoner*)

freilassen (PRESENT lässt frei, IMPERFECT ließ frei, PERFECT hat freigelassen)

2 (*report, news*)

veröffentlichen (PERFECT hat veröffentlicht)

3 (*record, video*)

herausbringen (IMPERFECT brachte heraus, PERFECT hat herausgebracht)

release NOUN

> see also **release** VERB

die Freilassung (*from prison*) ◊ *the release of Nelson Mandela* die Freilassung Nelson Mandelas

◆ **the band's latest release** die neueste Platte der Band

relegated ADJECTIVE
abgestiegen (*sport*) ◊ *Our team was relegated.* Unsere Mannschaft ist abgestiegen.

relevant ADJECTIVE
entsprechend (*documents*)
◆ **That's not relevant.** Das ist nicht relevant.
◆ **to be relevant to something** einen Bezug zu etwas haben ◊ *Education should be relevant to real life.* Die Ausbildung sollte einen Bezug zum wirklichen Leben haben.

reliable ADJECTIVE
zuverlässig ◊ *a reliable car* ein zuverlässiges Auto ◊ *He's not very reliable.* Er ist nicht sehr zuverlässig.

relief NOUN
die Erleichterung ◊ *That's a relief!* Das ist eine Erleichterung!

to **relieve** VERB
lindern ◊ *This injection will relieve the pain.* Diese Spritze wird den Schmerz lindern.

relieved ADJECTIVE
erleichtert ◊ *I was relieved to hear ...* Ich war erleichtert zu hören ...

religion NOUN
die Religion ◊ *What religion are you?* Welche Religion hast du?

religious ADJECTIVE
religiös ◊ *I'm not religious.* Ich bin nicht religiös.
◆ **my religious beliefs** mein Glaube MASC

reluctant ADJECTIVE
◆ **to be reluctant to do something** etwas nur ungern tun ◊ *They were reluctant to help us.* Sie haben uns nur ungern geholfen.

reluctantly ADVERB
ungern ◊ *She reluctantly accepted.* Sie hat ungern angenommen.

to **rely on** VERB
sich verlassen auf +ACC (PRESENT verlässt sich, IMPERFECT verließ sich, PERFECT hat sich verlassen) ◊ *I'm relying on you.* Ich verlasse mich auf dich.

to **remain** VERB
bleiben (IMPERFECT blieb, PERFECT ist geblieben)
◆ **to remain silent** schweigen

remaining ADJECTIVE
restlich ◊ *the remaining ingredients* die restlichen Zutaten

remains PL NOUN
die Reste MASC PL ◊ *the remains of the picnic* die Reste des Picknicks
◆ **human remains** die menschlichen Überreste
◆ **Roman remains** römische Ruinen

remake NOUN
das Remake (*of film*) (PL die Remakes)

remark NOUN
die Bemerkung

remarkable ADJECTIVE
bemerkenswert

remarkably ADVERB
bemerkenswert

to **remarry** VERB
wieder heiraten ◊ *She remarried three years ago.* Sie hat vor drei Jahren wieder geheiratet.

remedy NOUN
das Mittel (PL die Mittel) ◊ *a good remedy for a sore throat* ein gutes Mittel gegen Halsschmerzen

to **remember** VERB
sich erinnern (PERFECT hat sich erinnert) ◊ *I can't remember his name.* Ich kann mich nicht an seinen Namen erinnern. ◊ *I don't remember.* Ich erinnere mich nicht.
In German you often say "don't forget" rather than **remember** *when reminding somebody about something.*
◊ *Remember your passport!* Vergiss deinen Pass nicht! ◊ *Remember to write your name on the form.* Vergiss nicht, deinen Namen auf das Formular zu schreiben.

Remembrance Day NOUN
der Volkstrauertag ◊ *on Remembrance Day* am Volkstrauertag

to **remind** VERB
erinnern (PERFECT hat erinnert) ◊ *It reminds me of Scotland.* Es erinnert mich an Schottland. ◊ *I'll remind you tomorrow.* Ich werde dich morgen daran erinnern. ◊ *Remind me to speak to Daniel.* Erinnere mich, dass ich mit Daniel sprechen will.

remorse NOUN
die Reue ◊ *He showed no remorse.* Er zeigte keine Reue.

remote ADJECTIVE
abgelegen ◊ *a remote village* ein abgelegenes Dorf

remote control NOUN
die Fernbedienung

remotely ADVERB
entfernt ◊ *There was nobody remotely resembling this description.* Niemand sah dieser Beschreibung auch nur entfernt ähnlich.
◆ **I suppose it is remotely possible that ...** Ich denke, es it gerade eben noch möglich, dass ...

removable ADJECTIVE
abnehmbar

removal NOUN
der Umzug (*from house*) (PL die Umzüge)
◆ **a removal van** ein Möbelwagen MASC

to **remove** VERB

R

rendezvous → reptile

entfernen (PERFECT hat entfernt) ◊ *Did you remove the stain?* Hast du den Fleck entfernt?

rendezvous NOUN
das Treffen (PL die Treffen)

to **renew** VERB
verlängern lassen (*passport, licence*) (PRESENT lässt verlängern, IMPERFECT ließ verlängern, PERFECT hat verlängern lassen) ◊ *You'll need to renew your passport.* Du musst deinen Pass verlängern lassen.
♦ **to renew a contract** einen Vertrag verlängern

renewable ADJECTIVE
erneuerbar (*energy, resource, passport*)

to **renovate** VERB
renovieren (PERFECT hat renoviert) ◊ *The building's been renovated.* Das Gebäude ist renoviert worden.

renowned ADJECTIVE
berühmt

rent NOUN
see also **rent** VERB
die Miete
*Be careful not to translate **rent** by **Rente**.*

to **rent** VERB
see also **rent** NOUN
mieten ◊ *We rented a car.* Wir haben ein Auto gemietet.

rental NOUN
die Miete ◊ *Car rental is included in the price.* Die Automiete ist im Preis inbegriffen.

rental car NOUN US
der Mietwagen (PL die Mietwagen)

to **reorganize** VERB
umorganisieren (PERFECT hat umorganisiert)

rep NOUN (= *representative*)
der Vertreter (PL die Vertreter)
die Vertreterin

repaid VERB see **repay**

to **repair** VERB
see also **repair** NOUN
reparieren (PERFECT hat repariert)
♦ **to get something repaired** etwas reparieren lassen ◊ *I got the washing machine repaired.* Ich habe die Waschmaschine reparieren lassen.

repair NOUN
see also **repair** VERB
die Reparatur

to **repay** VERB
zurückzahlen (*money*) (PERFECT hat zurückgezahlt)

repayment NOUN
die Rückzahlung

to **repeat** VERB
see also **repeat** NOUN
wiederholen (PERFECT hat wiederholt)

repeat NOUN
see also **repeat** VERB

die Wiederholung ◊ *There are too many repeats on TV.* Es gibt zu viele Wiederholungen im Fernsehen.

repeatedly ADVERB
wiederholt

repellent NOUN
♦ **insect repellent** das Insektenschutzmittel

repetitive ADJECTIVE
monoton (*movement, work*)

to **replace** VERB
ersetzen (PERFECT hat ersetzt)

replay NOUN
see also **replay** VERB
♦ **There will be a replay on Friday.** Das Spiel wird am Freitag wiederholt.

to **replay** VERB
see also **replay** NOUN
wiederholen (*match*) (PERFECT hat wiederholt)

replica NOUN
die Kopie

reply NOUN
see also **reply** VERB
die Antwort

to **reply** VERB
see also **reply** NOUN
antworten

report NOUN
see also **report** VERB
1 (*of event*)
der Bericht (PL die Berichte) ◊ *a report in the paper* ein Zeitungsbericht
2 (*at school*)
das Zeugnis (GEN des Zeugnisses, PL die Zeugnisse) ◊ *I got a good report this year.* Ich habe in diesem Jahr ein gutes Zeugnis.
♦ **report card** das Zeugnis

to **report** VERB
see also **report** NOUN
1 melden ◊ *I reported the theft to the police.* Ich habe den Diebstahl bei der Polizei gemeldet.
2 sich melden ◊ *Report to reception when you arrive.* Melden Sie sich bei Ihrer Ankunft am Empfang.

reporter NOUN
der Reporter (PL die Reporter)
die Reporterin
◊ *She'd like to be a reporter.* Sie möchte gern Reporterin werden.

to **represent** VERB
vertreten (*person*) (PRESENT vertritt, IMPERFECT vertrat, PERFECT hat vertreten) ◊ *my lawyer represented me in court.* Mein Anwalt hat mich vor Gericht vertreten.

representative ADJECTIVE
repräsentativ

reproduction NOUN
die Reproduktion

reptile NOUN
das Reptil (PL die Reptilien)

republic NOUN
die Republik

repulsive ADJECTIVE
abstoßend

reputable ADJECTIVE
angesehen

reputation NOUN
der Ruf

request NOUN
see also **request** VERB
die Bitte

to **request** VERB
see also **request** NOUN
bitten um (IMPERFECT bat, PERFECT hat gebeten) ◊ He requested information. Er bat um Informationen.

to **require** VERB
erfordern (PERFECT hat erfordert) ◊ Her job requires a lot of patience. Ihre Arbeit erfordert viel Geduld.

requirement NOUN
die Voraussetzung ◊ What are the requirements for the job? Was sind die Voraussetzungen für diese Arbeit?
♦ entry requirements (for university) die Aufnahmebedingungen

resat VERB see **resit**

to **rescue** VERB
see also **rescue** NOUN
retten

rescue NOUN
see also **rescue** VERB
die Rettung ◊ a rescue operation eine Rettungsaktion
♦ a mountain rescue team ein Team der Bergwacht
♦ the rescue services der Rettungsdienst SING
♦ to come to somebody's rescue jemandem zu Hilfe kommen ◊ He came to my rescue. Er kam mir zu Hilfe.

research NOUN
die Forschung (experimental) ◊ He's doing research. Er ist in der Forschung tätig.
♦ Research has shown that ... Forschungen haben ergeben, dass ...
♦ She's doing some research in the library. Sie sammelt in der Bibliothek Material.

resemblance NOUN
die Ähnlichkeit

to **resent** VERB
übel nehmen (PRESENT nimmt übel, IMPERFECT nahm übel, PERFECT hat übel genommen) ◊ I really resent your criticism. Ich nehme Ihnen Ihre Kritik wirklich übel.
♦ I resent being dependent on her. Ich ärgere mich darüber, von ihr abhängig zu sein.

resentful ADJECTIVE
verärgert ◊ He was resentful at the way they had been treated. Er war verärgert darüber, wie man sie behandelt hatte.

reservation NOUN
[1] die Reservierung (at restaurant)
♦ I'd like to make a reservation for this evening. Ich möchte für heute Abend einen Tisch reservieren.
[2] die Buchung (for journey, at hotel)
♦ I've got a reservation for two nights. Ich habe für zwei Nächte gebucht.

reserve NOUN
see also **reserve** VERB
[1] (place)
das Schutzgebiet (PL die Schutzgebiete)
◊ a nature reserve ein Naturschutzgebiet
[2] (person)
der Reservespieler (PL die Reservespieler)
die Reservespielerin
◊ She was reserve in the game last Saturday. Sie war beim Spiel letzten Samstag Reservespielerin.

to **reserve** VERB
see also **reserve** NOUN
reservieren (PERFECT hat reserviert) ◊ I'd like to reserve a table for tomorrow evening. Ich möchte für morgen Abend einen Tisch reservieren.

reserved ADJECTIVE
reserviert ◊ a reserved seat ein reservierter Platz ◊ He's quite reserved. Er ist ziemlich reserviert.

reservoir NOUN
das Reservoir (PL die Reservoire)

resident NOUN
der Bewohner (PL die Bewohner)
die Bewohnerin

residential ADJECTIVE
♦ a residential area ein Wohngebiet NEUT

to **resign** VERB
[1] zurücktreten (PRESENT tritt zurück, IMPERFECT trat zurück, PERFECT ist zurückgetreten) ◊ The foreign minister has resigned. Der Außenminister ist zurückgetreten.
[2] (employee)
kündigen ◊ She resigned to take up a post abroad. Sie kündigte, um einen Posten im Ausland zu übernehmen.

resistance NOUN
der Widerstand (PL die Widerstände)

to **resit** VERB
wiederholen (PERFECT hat wiederholt)
◊ I'm resitting the exam in December. Ich wiederhole die Prüfung im Dezember.

resolution NOUN
der Beschluss (decision) (GEN des Beschlusses, PL die Beschlüsse)
♦ Have you made any New Year's resolutions? Hast du zum neuen Jahr gute Vorsätze gefasst?

R

resort NOUN

der Badeort (at seaside) (PL die Badeorte)
◊ It's a resort on the Costa del Sol. Es ist
ein Badeort an der Costa del Sol.

♦ **a ski resort** ein Skiort

♦ **as a last resort** als letzter Ausweg

resources PL NOUN

die Mittel NEUT PL (financial) ◊ We do not
have the resources to build a new
swimming pool. Wir haben nicht die
Mittel, um ein neues Schwimmbad zu
bauen.

♦ **natural resources** Bodenschätze MASC PL

respect NOUN

see also **respect** VERB

der Respekt

to **respect** VERB

see also **respect** NOUN

respektieren (PERFECT hat respektiert)

respectable ADJECTIVE

[1] anständig ◊ respectable people
anständige Leute PL

[2] ordentlich (standard, marks)

respectively ADVERB

beziehungsweise ◊ Britain and
Germany were third and fourth
respectively. Großbritannien und
Deutschland belegten den dritten
beziehungsweise vierten Platz.

responsibility NOUN

die Verantwortung

responsible ADJECTIVE

[1] verantwortlich ◊ to be responsible
for something für etwas verantwortlich
sein

♦ **It's a responsible job.** Es ist ein
verantwortungsvoller Posten.

[2] verantwortungsbewusst (mature)
◊ You should be more responsible. Du
solltest verantwortungsbewusster sein.

rest NOUN

see also **rest** VERB

[1] (relaxation)

die Pause ◊ five minutes' rest eine
fünfminütige Pause

♦ **to have a rest** sich ausruhen ◊ We
stopped to have a rest. Wir haben
haltgemacht, um uns auszuruhen.

[2] (remainder)

der Rest (PL die Reste) ◊ I'll do the rest.
Ich mache den Rest. ◊ the rest of the
money der Rest des Geldes

♦ **the rest of them** die anderen ◊ The rest
of them went swimming. Die anderen
sind schwimmen gegangen.

to **rest** VERB

see also **rest** NOUN

[1] (relax)

sich ausruhen (PERFECT hat sich
ausgeruht) ◊ She's resting in her room.
Sie ruht sich in ihrem Zimmer aus.

[2] (not overstrain)

schonen ◊ He has to rest his knee. Er
muss sein Knie schonen.

[3] (lean)

lehnen ◊ I rested my bike against the
window. Ich habe mein Fahrrad ans
Fenster gelehnt.

restaurant NOUN

das Restaurant (PL die Restaurants) ◊ We
don't often go to restaurants. Wir gehen
nicht oft ins Restaurant.

♦ **a restaurant car** ein Speisewagen MASC

restful ADJECTIVE

ruhig

restless ADJECTIVE

unruhig

restoration NOUN

die Restauration

to **restore** VERB

restaurieren (building, picture) (PERFECT hat
restauriert)

to **restrict** VERB

beschränken (PERFECT hat beschränkt)

rest room NOUN US

die Toilette

result NOUN

das Ergebnis (GEN des Ergebnisses, PL die
Ergebnisse) ◊ my exam results meine
Prüfungsergebnisse

♦ **What was the result? — One nil.** Wie ist
das Spiel ausgegangen? – Eins zu null.

résumé NOUN US

[1] die Zusammenfassung ◊ a résumé of
her speech eine Zusammenfassung ihrer
Rede

[2] (CV)

der Lebenslauf (PL die Lebensläufe)

to **retire** VERB

in Rente gehen (IMPERFECT ging in Rente,
PERFECT ist in Rente gegangen) ◊ He retired
last year. Er ist letztes Jahr in Rente
gegangen.

retired ADJECTIVE

im Ruhestand ◊ She's retired. Sie ist im
Ruhestand. ◊ a retired teacher ein Lehrer
im Ruhestand

retirement NOUN

der Ruhestand

to **retrace** VERB

♦ **to retrace one's steps** zurückgehen ◊ I
retraced my steps. Ich bin
zurückgegangen.

return NOUN

see also **return** VERB

[1] die Rückkehr ◊ after our return nach
unserer Rückkehr

♦ **the return journey** die Rückfahrt

♦ **a return match** ein Rückspiel NEUT

[2] die Rückfahrkarte (ticket) ◊ A return to
Freiburg, please. Eine Rückfahrkarte nach
Freiburg, bitte.

♦ **in return** dafür ◊ ... and I help her in
return ... und dafür helfe ich ihr

♦ **in return for** für

♦ **Many happy returns!** Herzlichen
Glückwunsch zum Geburtstag!

to **return** VERB

> see also **return** NOUN

[1] (*come back*)
zurückkommen (IMPERFECT kam zurück,
PERFECT ist zurückgekommen) ◊ *I've just
returned from holiday.* Ich bin gerade
aus den Ferien zurückgekommen.

♦ **to return home** wieder nach Hause
kommen

[2] (*go back*)
zurückkehren (PERFECT ist zurückgekehrt)
◊ *He returned to Germany the following
year.* Er ist im Jahr danach nach
Deutschland zurückgekehrt.

[3] (*give back*)
zurückgeben (PRESENT gibt zurück, IMPERFECT
gab zurück, PERFECT hat zurückgegeben)
◊ *She borrows my things and doesn't
return them.* Sie leiht sich meine
Sachen aus und gibt sie dann nicht
zurück.

reunion NOUN
das Treffen (PL die Treffen)

to **reuse** VERB
wiederverwenden (PERFECT hat
wiederverwendet)

to **reveal** VERB
ans Licht bringen (*truth, facts*) (IMPERFECT
brachte ans Licht, PERFECT hat ans Licht
gebracht) ◊ *The survey reveals that too
many people are overweight.* Die
Untersuchung bringt ans Licht, dass zu
viele Menschen Übergewicht
haben.

♦ **She refused to reveal the whereabouts
of her daughter.** Sie weigerte sich, den
Aufenthaltsort ihrer Tochter
preiszugeben.

♦ **It was revealed that ...** Es wurde bekannt
gegeben, dass ...

revenge NOUN
die Rache ◊ *in revenge* aus Rache

♦ **to take revenge** sich rächen ◊ *They
planned to take revenge on him.* Sie
haben geplant, sich an ihm zu rächen.

to **reverse** VERB

> see also **reverse** ADJECTIVE

rückwärtsfahren (*car*) (PRESENT fährt
rückwärts, IMPERFECT fuhr rückwärts, PERFECT
ist rückwärtsgefahren) ◊ *He reversed
without looking.* Er fuhr rückwärts ohne
zu sehen.

♦ **to reverse the charges** (*telephone*) ein R-
Gespräch führen ◊ *I'd like to make a
reverse charge call to Britain.* Ich möchte
gern ein R-Gespräch nach
Großbritannien führen.

reverse ADJECTIVE

> see also **reverse** VERB

umgekehrt ◊ *in reverse order* in
umgekehrter Reihenfolge

♦ **in reverse gear** im Rückwärtsgang

review NOUN
[1] die Überprüfung (*of policy, salary*)
[2] die Prüfung (*of subject*)

♦ **to be under review** überprüft werden

to **revise** VERB
den Stoff wiederholen

♦ **I haven't started revising yet.** Ich habe
noch nicht angefangen, den Stoff zu
wiederholen.

♦ **I've revised my opinion.** Ich habe meine
Meinung geändert.

revision NOUN
die Wiederholung des Stoffes

♦ **Have you done a lot of revision?** Hast du
schon viel Stoff wiederholt?

to **revive** VERB
wiederbeleben (PERFECT hat wiederbelebt)
◊ *The nurses tried to revive him.*
Die Schwestern versuchten, ihn
wiederzubeleben.

revolting ADJECTIVE
ekelhaft

revolution NOUN
die Revolution ◊ *the French Revolution*
die Französische Revolution

revolutionary ADJECTIVE
revolutionär

revolver NOUN
der Revolver (PL die Revolver)

reward NOUN
die Belohnung

rewarding ADJECTIVE
dankbar ◊ *a rewarding job* eine
dankbare Arbeit

to **rewind** VERB
zurückspulen (PERFECT hat zurückgespult)
◊ *to rewind a cassette* eine Kassette
zurückspulen

rheumatism NOUN
das Rheuma

Rhine NOUN
der Rhein

rhinoceros NOUN
das Nashorn (PL die Nashörner)

rhubarb NOUN
der Rhabarber ◊ *a rhubarb tart* ein
Rhabarberkuchen

rhythm NOUN
der Rhythmus (GEN des Rhythmus, PL die
Rhythmen)

rib NOUN
die Rippe

ribbon NOUN
das Band (PL die Bänder)

rice NOUN
der Reis

♦ **rice pudding** der Milchreis

rich ADJECTIVE
reich

♦ **the rich** die Reichen MASC PL

to **rid** VERB

R

♦ **to get rid of** loswerden ◊ *I want to get rid of some old clothes.* Ich will ein paar alte Kleider loswerden.

ride NOUN

see also **ride** VERB

♦ **to go for a ride (1)** (*on horse*) reiten gehen
♦ **to go for a ride (2)** (*on bike*) mit dem Fahrrad fahren
♦ **We went for a bike ride.** Wir haben eine Fahrt mit dem Fahrrad gemacht.
♦ **It's a short bus ride to the town centre.** Die Stadtmitte ist nur eine kurze Busfahrt entfernt.

to **ride** VERB

see also **ride** NOUN

reiten (*on horse*) (IMPERFECT ritt, PERFECT ist geritten) ◊ *I'm learning to ride.* Ich lerne reiten.
♦ **to ride a bike** Fahrrad fahren ◊ *Can you ride a bike?* Kannst du Fahrrad fahren?

rider NOUN

1 (*on horse*)
der Reiter (PL die Reiter)
die Reiterin
◊ *She's a good rider.* Sie ist eine gute Reiterin.
2 (*on bike*)
der Fahrradfahrer (PL die Fahrradfahrer)
die Fahrradfahrerin

ridiculous ADJECTIVE

lächerlich ◊ *Don't be ridiculous!* Mach dich nicht lächerlich!

riding NOUN

das Reiten
♦ **to go riding** reiten gehen
♦ **a riding school** eine Reitschule

rifle NOUN

das Gewehr (PL die Gewehre) ◊ *a hunting rifle* ein Jagdgewehr

rig NOUN

♦ **an oil rig** eine Bohrinsel

right ADJECTIVE, ADVERB

see also **right** NOUN

There are several ways of translating **right**. *Scan the examples to find one that is similar to what you want to say.*

1 richtig (*correct, suitable*) ◊ *the right answer* die richtige Antwort ◊ *Am I pronouncing it right?* Spreche ich das richtig aus? ◊ *It isn't the right size.* Es ist nicht die richtige Größe. ◊ *We're on the right train.* Wir sind im richtigen Zug. ◊ *It's not right to behave like that.* Es ist nicht richtig, sich so zu benehmen.
♦ **Is this the right road for Hamburg?** Sind wir hier richtig nach Hamburg?
♦ **I think you did the right thing.** Ich glaube, du hast das Richtige getan.
♦ **to be right (1)** (*person*) recht haben ◊ *You were right!* Du hattest recht!
♦ **to be right (2)** (*statement, opinion*) richtig sein ◊ *That's right!* Das ist richtig!

2 genau (*accurate*) ◊ *Do you have the right time?* Haben Sie die genaue Zeit?
3 rechte (*not left*) ◊ *the right foot* der rechte Fuß ◊ *my right arm* mein rechter Arm ◊ *your right hand* deine rechte Hand ◊ *her right eye* ihr rechtes Auge
4 rechts (*turn*) ◊ *Turn right at the traffic lights.* Biegen Sie an der Ampel rechts ab.
♦ **Look right!** Sehen Sie nach rechts!
♦ **Right! Let's get started.** Okay! Fangen wir an.
♦ **right away** sofort ◊ *I'll do it right away.* Ich mache es sofort.

right NOUN

see also **right** ADJECTIVE

1 das Recht (PL die Rechte) ◊ *You've got no right to do that.* Du hast kein Recht, das zu tun.
2 (*not left*)
die rechte Seite
♦ **on the right** rechts ◊ *Remember to drive on the right.* Vergiss nicht, rechts zu fahren.
♦ **right of way** die Vorfahrt ◊ *We had right of way.* Wir hatten Vorfahrt.

right-hand ADJECTIVE

♦ **the right-hand side** die rechte Seite
♦ **It's on the right-hand side.** Es liegt rechts.

right-handed ADJECTIVE

rechtshändig

rightly ADVERB

richtig ◊ *If I remember rightly, his name was Jeremy.* Wenn ich mich richtig erinnere, hieß er Jeremy. ◊ *She rightly decided that he was lying.* Sie kam zu dem richtigen Schluss, dass er log.

rim NOUN

der Rand (PL die Ränder) ◊ *glasses with wire rims* eine Brille mit Metallrand

ring NOUN

see also **ring** VERB

1 der Ring (PL die Ringe) ◊ *a gold ring* ein goldener Ring ◊ *a diamond ring* ein Diamantring
♦ **a wedding ring** ein Ehering
2 (*circle*)
der Kreis (GEN des Kreises, PL die Kreise) ◊ *to stand in a ring* im Kreis stehen
3 (*of bell*)
das Klingeln
♦ **There's a ring at the door.** Es klingelt.
♦ **to give somebody a ring** jemanden anrufen ◊ *I'll give you a ring this evening.* Ich rufe dich heute Abend an.

to **ring** VERB

see also **ring** NOUN

1 anrufen (IMPERFECT rief an, PERFECT hat angerufen) ◊ *Your mother rang this morning.* Deine Mutter hat heute früh angerufen.

♦ **to ring somebody** jemanden anrufen ◊ *I'll ring you tomorrow morning.* Ich rufe dich morgen früh an.

♦ **to ring somebody up** jemanden anrufen 2 klingeln ◊ *The phone's ringing.* Das Telefon klingelt.

♦ **to ring the bell** (*doorbell*) klingeln ◊ *I rang the bell three times.* Ich habe dreimal geklingelt.

♦ **to ring back** zurückrufen ◊ *I'll ring back later.* Ich rufe später zurück.

ring binder NOUN
das Ringheft (PL die Ringhefte)

ring road NOUN
die Ringstraße

ringtone NOUN
der Klingelton (PL die Klingeltöne)

rink NOUN
1 die Eisbahn (*for ice-skating*)
2 die Rollschuhbahn (*for roller-skating*)

to **rinse** VERB
spülen

riot NOUN
see also **riot** VERB
die Krawalle MASC PL

to **riot** VERB
see also **riot** NOUN
randalieren (PERFECT hat randaliert)

to **rip** VERB
zerreißen (IMPERFECT zerriss, PERFECT hat zerrissen) ◊ *I've ripped my jeans.* Ich habe meine Jeans zerrissen. ◊ *My skirt's ripped.* Mein Rock ist zerrissen.

to **rip off** VERB
ausnehmen (*informal*) (PRESENT nimmt aus, IMPERFECT nahm aus, PERFECT hat ausgenommen) ◊ *The hotel ripped us off.* Das Hotel hat uns ausgenommen.

to **rip up** VERB
zerreißen (IMPERFECT zerriss, PERFECT hat zerrissen)

ripe ADJECTIVE
reif

rip-off NOUN
♦ **It's a rip-off!** Das ist Nepp! (*informal*)

rise NOUN
see also **rise** VERB
1 (*in prices, temperature*)
der Anstieg (PL die Anstiege) ◊ *a sudden rise in temperature* ein plötzlicher Temperaturanstieg
2 (*pay rise*)
die Gehaltserhöhung

to **rise** VERB
see also **rise** NOUN
1 (*increase*)
steigen (IMPERFECT stieg, PERFECT ist gestiegen) ◊ *Prices are rising.* Die Preise steigen.
2 aufgehen (IMPERFECT ging auf, PERFECT ist aufgegangen) ◊ *The sun rises early in June.* Die Sonne geht im Juni früh auf.

riser NOUN
♦ **to be an early riser** ein Frühaufsteher sein

risk NOUN
see also **risk** VERB
das Risiko (PL die Risiken)
♦ **to take risks** Risiken eingehen ◊ *I don't want to take risks.* Ich möchte kein Risiko eingehen.
♦ **It's at your own risk.** Auf eigene Gefahr.

to **risk** VERB
see also **risk** NOUN
riskieren (PERFECT hat riskiert) ◊ *You risk getting a fine.* Du riskierst einen Strafzettel. ◊ *I wouldn't risk it if I were you.* Das würde ich an deiner Stelle nicht riskieren.

risky ADJECTIVE
gefährlich

rival NOUN
see also **rival** ADJECTIVE
der Rivale (GEN des Rivalen, PL die Rivalen)
die Rivalin

rival ADJECTIVE
see also **rival** NOUN
rivalisierend ◊ *a rival gang* eine rivalisierende Bande
♦ **a rival company** ein Konkurrenzunternehmen NEUT

rivalry NOUN
die Rivalität (*between towns, schools*)

river NOUN
der Fluss (GEN des Flusses, PL die Flüsse)
♦ **the river Rhine** der Rhein

Riviera NOUN
die Riviera ◊ *the Italian Riviera* die italienische Riviera
♦ **the French Riviera** die Côte d'Azur

road NOUN
die Straße ◊ *There's a lot of traffic on the roads.* Es herrscht viel Verkehr auf den Straßen.
♦ **They live across the road.** Sie wohnen gegenüber.

road map NOUN
die Straßenkarte

road rage NOUN
die Aggressivität im Straßenverkehr

road sign NOUN
das Verkehrsschild (PL die Verkehrsschilder)

roadworks PL NOUN
die Bauarbeiten FEM PL

roast ADJECTIVE
♦ **roast chicken** das Brathähnchen
♦ **roast potatoes** die Bratkartoffeln
♦ **roast pork** der Schweinebraten
♦ **roast beef** der Rindsbraten

to **rob** VERB

R

♦**to rob somebody** jemanden berauben ◊ *I've been robbed.* Ich bin beraubt worden.

♦**to rob a bank** eine Bank ausrauben

♦**to rob somebody of something** jemandem etwas rauben ◊ *He was robbed of his wallet.* Man hat ihm seine Brieftasche geraubt.

robber NOUN
der Räuber (PL die Räuber)
die Räuberin

♦**a bank robber** ein Bankräuber

robbery NOUN
der Raub (PL die Raube)

♦**a bank robbery** ein Bankraub

♦**armed robbery** der bewaffnete Raubüberfall

robin NOUN
das Rotkehlchen (PL die Rotkehlchen)

robot NOUN
der Roboter (PL die Roboter)

rock NOUN
see also **rock** VERB
1 (*substance*)
der Fels (GEN des Fels) ◊ *They tunnelled through the rock.* Sie gruben einen Tunnel durch den Fels.
2 (*boulder*)
der Felsbrocken (PL die Felsbrocken) ◊ *I sat on a rock.* Ich saß auf einem Felsbrocken.
3 (*stone*)
der Stein (PL die Steine) ◊ *The crowd started to throw rocks.* Die Menge fing an, Steine zu werfen.
4 (*music*)
der Rock ◊ *a rock concert* ein Rockkonzert ◊ *He's a rock star.* Er ist ein Rockstar.
5 (*sweet*)
die Zuckerstange ◊ *a stick of rock* eine Zuckerstange

♦**rock and roll** der Rock 'n' Roll

to **rock** VERB
see also **rock** NOUN
erschüttern (PERFECT hat erschüttert) ◊ *The explosion rocked the building.* Die Explosion erschütterte das Gebäude.

rockery NOUN
der Steingarten (PL die Steingärten)

rocket NOUN
die Rakete (*firework, spacecraft*)

rocking chair NOUN
der Schaukelstuhl (PL die Schaukelstühle)

rocking horse NOUN
das Schaukelpferd (PL die Schaukelpferde)

rod NOUN
die Angel (*for fishing*)

rode VERB *see* **ride**

role NOUN
die Rolle

role play NOUN
das Rollenspiel (PL die Rollenspiele) ◊ *to do a role play* ein Rollenspiel machen

roll NOUN
see also **roll** VERB
1 die Rolle ◊ *a roll of tape* eine Rolle Klebstreifen ◊ *a toilet roll* eine Rolle Toilettenpapier
2 (*bread*)
das Brötchen (PL die Brötchen)

to **roll** VERB
see also **roll** NOUN
rollen

♦**to roll out the pastry** den Teig ausrollen

roll call NOUN
der Namensaufruf (PL die Namensaufrufe)

roller NOUN
die Walze

Rollerblade ® NOUN
der Rollerblade ® (PL die Rollerblades)

roller coaster NOUN
die Achterbahn

roller skates PL NOUN
die Rollschuhe MASC PL

roller-skating NOUN
das Rollschuhlaufen

♦**to go roller-skating** Rollschuh laufen

rolling pin NOUN
das Nudelholz (PL die Nudelhölzer)

Roman ADJECTIVE, NOUN
römisch (*ancient*) ◊ *a Roman villa* eine römische Villa ◊ *the Roman empire* das Römische Reich

♦**the Romans** die Römer MASC PL

Roman Catholic NOUN
der Katholik (GEN des Katholiken, PL die Katholiken)
die Katholikin
◊ *He's a Roman Catholic.* Er ist Katholik.

romance NOUN
1 (*novels*)
der Liebesroman (PL die Liebesromane) ◊ *I read a lot of romances.* Ich lese viele Liebesromane.
2 (*glamour*)
der romantische Zauber ◊ *the romance of Venice* der romantische Zauber von Venedig

♦**a holiday romance** ein Ferienflirt MASC

Romania NOUN
Rumänien NEUT

♦**from Romania** aus Rumänien

♦**to Romania** nach Rumänien

Romanian ADJECTIVE
rumänisch

romantic ADJECTIVE
romantisch

roof NOUN
das Dach (PL die Dächer)

roof rack NOUN
der Dachträger (PL die Dachträger)

room NOUN

1 das <u>Zimmer</u> (PL die Zimmer) ◊ *the biggest room in the house* das größte Zimmer des Hauses ◊ *She's in her room.* Sie ist in ihrem Zimmer. ◊ *the music room* das Musikzimmer
♦ **a single room** ein Einzelzimmer
♦ **a double room** ein Doppelzimmer
2 (*space*)
der <u>Platz</u> (GEN des Platzes) ◊ *There's no room for that box.* Es ist kein Platz für diese Schachtel.

roommate NOUN
der <u>Zimmergenosse</u> (GEN des Zimmergenossen, PL die Zimmergenossen)
die <u>Zimmergenossin</u>

root NOUN
die <u>Wurzel</u>

rope NOUN
das <u>Seil</u> (PL die Seile)

rose VERB *see* **rise**

rose NOUN
die <u>Rose</u> (*flower*)

to **rot** VERB
<u>verfaulen</u> (PERFECT ist verfault)

rotten ADJECTIVE
<u>faulig</u> (*decayed*) ◊ *a rotten apple* ein fauliger Apfel
♦ **rotten weather** das Mistwetter (*informal*)
♦ **That's a rotten thing to do.** Das ist gemein.
♦ **to feel rotten** sich mies fühlen *informal*

rough ADJECTIVE
1 <u>rau</u> ◊ *My hands are rough.* Meine Hände sind rau. ◊ *It's a rough area.* Das ist eine raue Gegend.
2 <u>hart</u> (*game*) ◊ *Rugby's a rough sport.* Rugby ist ein harter Sport.
3 <u>stürmisch</u> (*water*) ◊ *The sea was rough.* Das Meer war stürmisch.
4 <u>ungefähr</u> ◊ *I've got a rough idea.* Ich habe eine ungefähre Vorstellung.
♦ **to feel rough** sich nicht wohlfühlen ◊ *I feel rough.* Ich fühle mich nicht wohl.

roughly ADVERB
<u>ungefähr</u> ◊ *It weighs roughly twenty kilos.* Es wiegt ungefähr zwanzig Kilo.

round ADJECTIVE, ADVERB, PREPOSITION
see also **round** NOUN
1 <u>rund</u> ◊ *a round table* ein runder Tisch
2 <u>um</u> (*around*) ◊ *We were sitting round the table.* Wir saßen um den Tisch herum. ◊ *She wore a scarf round her neck.* Sie trug einen Schal um den Hals.
♦ **It's just round the corner.** (*very near*) Es ist gleich um die Ecke.
♦ **to go round to somebody's house** bei jemandem vorbeigehen ◊ *I went round to my friend's house.* Ich bin bei meiner Freundin vorbeigegangen.
♦ **to have a look round** sich umsehen ◊ *We're going to have a look round.* Wir möchten uns umsehen.

♦ **to go round a museum** sich ein Museum ansehen ◊ *I went round the local museum.* Ich habe mir das örtliche Museum angesehen.
♦ **round here** hier in der Gegend ◊ *Is there a chemist's round here?* Gibt es hier in der Gegend eine Apotheke? ◊ *He lives round here.* Er wohnt hier in der Gegend.
♦ **all round** ringsherum ◊ *There were vineyards all round.* Ringsherum waren Weinberge.
♦ **all year round** das ganze Jahr über
♦ **round about** (*roughly*) etwa ◊ *It costs round about a hundred pounds.* Es kostet etwa hundert Pfund. ◊ *round about eight o'clock* etwa um acht Uhr

round NOUN
see also **round** ADJECTIVE
die <u>Runde</u> (*of tournament, boxing match*) ◊ *a round of golf* eine Runde Golf
♦ **a round of drinks** eine Runde ◊ *He bought a round of drinks.* Er hat eine Runde ausgegeben.

roundabout NOUN
1 (*at junction*)
der <u>Kreisverkehr</u> (PL die Kreisverkehre)
2 (*at funfair*)
das <u>Karussell</u> (PL die Karussells)

rounders SING NOUN
der <u>Schlagball</u>

round trip NOUN US
die <u>Hin- und Rückfahrt</u>
♦ **a round-trip ticket** eine Rückfahrkarte

route NOUN
die <u>Route</u> ◊ *We're planning our route.* Wir planen unsere Route.

routine NOUN
die <u>Routine</u>

row (1) NOUN
see also **row** VERB AND **row (2)** NOUN
die <u>Reihe</u> ◊ *a row of houses* eine Reihe Häuser ◊ *Our seats are in the front row.* Unsere Plätze sind in der ersten Reihe.
♦ **five times in a row** fünfmal hintereinander

row (2) NOUN
see also **row** VERB AND **row (1)** NOUN
1 (*noise*)
der <u>Krach</u> ◊ *What's that terrible row?* Was ist das für ein furchtbarer Krach?
2 (*quarrel*)
der <u>Streit</u> (PL die Streite) ◊ *They've had a row.* Sie haben Streit gehabt.
♦ **to have a row** Streit haben ◊ *They've had a row.* Sie haben Streit gehabt.

to **row** VERB
see also **row (1)** NOUN AND **row (2)** NOUN
<u>rudern</u> ◊ *We took turns to row.* Wir haben abwechselnd gerudert.

rowboat NOUN US
das <u>Ruderboot</u> (PL die Ruderboote)

rowing NOUN
das <u>Rudern</u> (*sport*) ◊ *My hobby is rowing.* Rudern ist mein Hobby.

R

♦ **a rowing boat** ein Ruderboot NEUT

royal ADJECTIVE
königlich ◊ *the royal family* die königliche Familie

to **rub** VERB
1 (*stain*)
reiben (IMPERFECT rieb, PERFECT hat gerieben)
2 (*part of body*)
sich reiben ◊ *Don't rub your eyes!* Reib dir nicht die Augen!
♦ **I rubbed myself dry with a towel.** Ich rieb mich mit einem Handtuch trocken.
♦ **to rub something out** etwas ausradieren

rubber NOUN
1 der Gummi (PL die Gummis) ◊ *rubber soles* die Gummisohlen
2 (*eraser*)
der Radiergummi (PL die Radiergummis) ◊ *Can I borrow your rubber?* Kann ich deinen Radiergummi ausleihen?
♦ **a rubber band** ein Gummiband NEUT

rubbish NOUN
see also **rubbish** ADJECTIVE
1 der Müll (*refuse*) ◊ *When do they collect the rubbish?* Wann wird der Müll abgeholt?
2 der Krempel (*junk*) ◊ *They sell a lot of rubbish at the market.* Sie verkaufen eine Menge Krempel auf dem Markt.
3 der Unsinn (*nonsense*) ◊ *Don't talk rubbish!* Red keinen Unsinn!
♦ **That's a load of rubbish!** Das ist doch Unsinn! (*informal*)
♦ **This magazine is rubbish!** Die Zeitschrift ist Schrott! (*informal*)
♦ **a rubbish bin** ein Mülleimer MASC
♦ **a rubbish dump** eine Müllkippe

rubbish ADJECTIVE
see also **rubbish** NOUN
miserabel (*informal*) ◊ *They're a rubbish team!* Sie sind eine miserable Mannschaft!

rucksack NOUN
der Rucksack (PL die Rucksäcke)

rude ADJECTIVE
1 unhöflich (*impolite*) ◊ *It's rude to interrupt.* Es ist unhöflich dazwischenzureden. ◊ *He was very rude to me.* Er war sehr unhöflich zu mir.
2 unanständig (*offensive*) ◊ *a rude joke* ein unanständiger Witz
♦ **a rude word** ein Schimpfwort NEUT

rug NOUN
1 der Teppich (PL die Teppiche) ◊ *a Persian rug* ein Perserteppich
2 (*blanket*)
die Decke ◊ *a tartan rug* eine karierte Decke

rugby NOUN
das Rugby ◊ *I play rugby.* Ich spiele Rugby.

ruin NOUN
see also **ruin** VERB

die Ruine ◊ *the ruins of the castle* die Ruine der Burg
♦ **My life is in ruins.** Mein Leben ist ruiniert.

to **ruin** VERB
see also **ruin** NOUN
ruinieren (PERFECT hat ruiniert) ◊ *You'll ruin your shoes.* Du ruinierst dir deine Schuhe. ◊ *That's far too expensive. You are ruining me!* Das ist viel zu teuer. Du ruinierst mich noch!
♦ **It ruined our holiday.** Es hat uns den Urlaub verdorben.

rule NOUN
see also **rule** VERB
1 die Regel ◊ *the rules of grammar* die Grammatikregeln
♦ **as a rule** in der Regel
2 die Vorschrift (*regulation*) ◊ *It's against the rules.* Das ist gegen die Vorschriften.

to **rule** VERB
see also **rule** NOUN
regieren (PERFECT hat regiert)

to **rule out** VERB
ausschließen (*possibility*) (IMPERFECT schloss aus, PERFECT hat ausgeschlossen)

ruler NOUN
das Lineal (PL die Lineale) ◊ *Can I borrow your ruler?* Kann ich dein Lineal ausleihen?

rum NOUN
der Rum

rumour NOUN
das Gerücht (PL die Gerüchte) ◊ *It's just a rumour.* Es ist nur ein Gerücht.

rump steak NOUN
das Rumpsteak (PL die Rumpsteaks)

run NOUN
see also **run** VERB
der Lauf (*in cricket*) (PL die Läufe) ◊ *to score a run* einen Lauf machen
♦ **to go for a run** einen Dauerlauf machen ◊ *I go for a run every morning.* Ich mache jeden Morgen einen Dauerlauf.
♦ **I did a ten-kilometre run.** Ich bin zehn Kilometer gelaufen.
♦ **on the run** auf der Flucht ◊ *The criminals are still on the run.* Die Verbrecher sind noch auf der Flucht.
♦ **in the long run** auf Dauer

to **run** VERB
see also **run** NOUN
1 laufen (PRESENT läuft, IMPERFECT lief, PERFECT ist gelaufen) ◊ *I ran five kilometres.* Ich bin fünf Kilometer gelaufen.
♦ **to run a marathon** an einem Marathonlauf teilnehmen
2 (*manage*)
leiten ◊ *He runs a large company.* Er leitet ein großes Unternehmen.
3 (*organize*)
veranstalten (PERFECT hat veranstaltet) ◊ *They run music courses in the*

holidays. Sie veranstalten Musikkurse
während der Ferien.

4 (*water*)
laufen ◊ *Don't leave the tap running.*
Lass das Wasser nicht laufen.

♦ **to run a bath** ein Bad einlaufen lassen

5 (*by car*)
fahren (PRESENT fährt, IMPERFECT fuhr, PERFECT
hat gefahren) ◊ *I can run you to the
station.* Ich kann dich zum Bahnhof
fahren.

♦ **to run away** weglaufen ◊ *They ran away
before the police came.* Sie sind
weggelaufen, bevor die Polizei kam.

♦ **Time is running out.** Die Zeit wird knapp.

♦ **We ran out of money.** Uns ist das Geld
ausgegangen.

♦ **to run somebody over** jemanden
überfahren

♦ **to get run over** überfahren werden ◊ *Be
careful, or you'll get run over!* Pass auf,
sonst wirst du überfahren!

rung VERB *see* **ring**

runner NOUN
der Läufer (PL die Läufer)
die Läuferin

runner beans PL NOUN
die Stangenbohnen FEM PL

runner-up NOUN
der Zweite (GEN des Zweiten, PL die
Zweiten)
die Zweite (GEN der Zweiten)

running NOUN
das Laufen ◊ *Running is my favourite
sport.* Laufen ist mein Lieblingssport.

run-up NOUN
♦ **in the run-up to Christmas** in der Zeit vor
Weihnachten

runway NOUN
die Startbahn

rural ADJECTIVE
ländlich

rush NOUN
see also **rush** VERB
die Eile

♦ **in a rush** in Eile

to **rush** VERB
see also **rush** NOUN

1 (*run*)
rennen (IMPERFECT rannte, PERFECT ist
gerannt) ◊ *Everyone rushed outside.* Alle
rannten hinaus.

2 (*hurry*)
sich beeilen (PERFECT hat sich beeilt)
◊ *There's no need to rush.* Wir brauchen
uns nicht zu beeilen.

rush hour NOUN
die Hauptverkehrszeit ◊ *in the rush hour*
in der Hauptverkehrszeit

rusk NOUN
der Zwieback (PL die Zwiebacke)

Russia NOUN
Russland NEUT

♦ **from Russia** aus Russland

♦ **to Russia** nach Russland

Russian ADJECTIVE
see also **Russian** NOUN
russisch

♦ **He's Russian.** Er ist Russe.

♦ **She's Russian.** Sie ist Russin.

Russian NOUN
see also **Russian** ADJECTIVE

1 (*person*)
der Russe (GEN des Russen, PL die
Russen)
die Russin

2 (*language*)
das Russisch (GEN des Russischen)

rust NOUN
der Rost

rusty ADJECTIVE
rostig ◊ *a rusty bike* ein rostiges Fahrrad

♦ **My German is very rusty.** Mein Deutsch
ist ziemlich eingerostet.

ruthless ADJECTIVE
rücksichtslos

rye NOUN
der Roggen

♦ **rye bread** das Roggenbrot

R

S

Sabbath NOUN
1 (*Christian*)
der Sonntag (PL die Sonntage)
2 (*Jewish*)
der Sabbat (PL die Sabbate)
sack NOUN
see also **sack** VERB
der Sack (PL die Säcke)
♦ **to get the sack** gefeuert werden
to **sack** VERB
see also **sack** NOUN
♦ **to sack somebody** jemanden feuern ◊ *He was sacked.* Er wurde gefeuert.
sacred ADJECTIVE
heilig
sacrifice NOUN
das Opfer (PL die Opfer)
sad ADJECTIVE
traurig
saddle NOUN
der Sattel (PL die Sättel)
saddlebag NOUN
die Satteltasche
sadly ADVERB
1 traurig ◊ *"She's gone," he said sadly.* "Sie ist weg", sagte er traurig.
2 leider (*unfortunately*) ◊ *Sadly, it was too late.* Leider war es zu spät.
safe NOUN
see also **safe** ADJECTIVE
der Safe (PL die Safes) ◊ *She put the money in the safe.* Sie tat das Geld in den Safe.
safe ADJECTIVE
see also **safe** NOUN
1 sicher ◊ *Don't worry, it's perfectly safe.* Mach dir keine Sorgen, es ist völlig sicher. ◊ *This car isn't safe.* Das Auto ist nicht sicher.
2 in Sicherheit (*out of danger*) ◊ *You're safe now.* Sie sind jetzt in Sicherheit.
♦ **to feel safe** sich sicher fühlen
♦ **safe sex** Safer Sex
safety NOUN
die Sicherheit
♦ **a safety belt** ein Sicherheitsgurt MASC
♦ **a safety pin** eine Sicherheitsnadel
Sagittarius NOUN
der Schütze (GEN des Schützen) ◊ *I'm Sagittarius.* Ich bin Schütze.
Sahara NOUN
♦ **the Sahara Desert** die Wüste Sahara
said VERB *see* say
sail NOUN
see also **sail** VERB
das Segel (PL die Segel)
to **sail** VERB
see also **sail** NOUN

1 (*travel*)
segeln (PERFECT ist gesegelt)
2 (*set off*)
abfahren (PRESENT fährt ab, IMPERFECT fuhr ab, PERFECT ist abgefahren) ◊ *The boat sails at eight o'clock.* Das Schiff fährt um acht Uhr ab.
sailing NOUN
das Segeln ◊ *His hobby is sailing.* Segeln ist sein Hobby.
♦ **to go sailing** segeln gehen
♦ **a sailing boat** ein Segelboot NEUT
♦ **a sailing ship** ein Segelschiff NEUT
sailor NOUN
der Matrose (GEN des Matrosen, PL die Matrosen)
die Matrosin
◊ *He's a sailor.* Er ist Matrose.
saint NOUN
der Heilige (GEN des Heiligen, PL die Heiligen)
die Heilige (GEN der Heiligen) ◊ *a saint* (*man*) ein Heiliger
sake NOUN
♦ **for the sake of** um ... willen ◊ *for the sake of your parents* um deiner Eltern willen
salad NOUN
der Salat (PL die Salate)
♦ **salad cream** die Salatmayonnaise
♦ **salad dressing** die Salatsoße
salami NOUN
die Salami (GEN der Salami, PL die Salamis)
salary NOUN
das Gehalt (PL die Gehälter)
sale NOUN
der Schlussverkauf (*end of season reductions*) (PL die Schlussverkäufe) ◊ *There's a sale on at Harrods.* Bei Harrods ist Schlussverkauf.
♦ **on sale** erhältlich
♦ **"for sale"** "zu verkaufen"
sales assistant NOUN
der Verkäufer (PL die Verkäufer)
die Verkäuferin
◊ *She's a sales assistant.* Sie ist Verkäuferin.
salesman NOUN
1 (*sales rep*)
der Vertreter (PL die Vertreter) ◊ *He's a salesman.* Er ist Vertreter.
♦ **a double-glazing salesman** ein Vertreter für Doppelfenster
2 (*sales assistant*)
der Verkäufer (PL die Verkäufer)
sales rep NOUN
der Vertreter (PL die Vertreter)

die <u>Vertreterin</u>

saleswoman NOUN
  [1] die <u>Vertreterin</u> (*sales rep*) ◊ *She's a
saleswoman.* Sie ist Vertreterin.
  [2] die <u>Verkäuferin</u> (*sales assistant*)

salmon NOUN
  der <u>Lachs</u> (GEN des Lachses, PL die
Lachse)

salon NOUN
  der <u>Salon</u> (PL die Salons) ◊ *a hair salon*
ein Friseursalon ◊ *a beauty salon* ein
Kosmetiksalon

saloon car NOUN
  die <u>Limousine</u>

salt NOUN
  das <u>Salz</u> (GEN des Salzes, PL die Salze)

salty ADJECTIVE
  <u>salzig</u>

to **salute** VERB
  <u>grüßen</u>

Salvation Army NOUN
  die <u>Heilsarmee</u>

same ADJECTIVE
  <u>gleiche</u> ◊ *The same coat is cheaper
elsewhere.* Der gleiche Mantel ist
anderswo billiger. ◊ *He asked me the
same question.* Er hat mir die gleiche
Frage gestellt. ◊ *I have the same car.* Ich
habe das gleiche Auto. ◊ *We obviously
have the same problems.* Wir haben
offensichtlich die gleichen Probleme.
  ◆ **at the same time** zur gleichen Zeit
  ◆ **It's not the same.** Das ist nicht das
Gleiche.
  ◆ **They're exactly the same.** Sie sind genau
gleich.

sample NOUN
  die <u>Probe</u> ◊ *a free sample of perfume*
eine kostenlose Parfümprobe

sand NOUN
  der <u>Sand</u>

sandal NOUN
  die <u>Sandale</u> ◊ *a pair of sandals* ein Paar
Sandalen

sand castle NOUN
  die <u>Sandburg</u>

sandwich NOUN
  das <u>belegte Brot</u> (PL die belegten Brote)
  ◆ **a cheese sandwich** ein Käsebrot

sang VERB *see* **sing**

sanitary napkin NOUN US
  die <u>Damenbinde</u>

sanitary towel NOUN
  die <u>Damenbinde</u>

sank VERB *see* **sink**

Santa Claus NOUN
  der <u>Weihnachtsmann</u> (PL die
Weihnachtsmänner)

sarcastic ADJECTIVE
  <u>sarkastisch</u>

sardine NOUN
  die <u>Sardine</u>

sat VERB *see* **sit**

satchel NOUN
  der <u>Schulranzen</u> (PL die Schulranzen)

satellite NOUN
  der <u>Satellit</u> (GEN des Satelliten, PL die
Satelliten)
  ◆ **a satellite dish** eine Satellitenschüssel
  ◆ **satellite television** das
Satellitenfernsehen

satisfactory ADJECTIVE
  <u>befriedigend</u>

satisfied ADJECTIVE
  <u>zufrieden</u>

Saturday NOUN
  der <u>Samstag</u> (PL die Samstage) ◊ *on
Saturday* am Samstag ◊ *every Saturday*
jeden Samstag ◊ *last Saturday* letzten
Samstag ◊ *next Saturday* nächsten
Samstag
  ◆ **on Saturdays** samstags
  ◆ **I've got a Saturday job.** Ich habe einen
Samstagsjob.

sauce NOUN
  die <u>Soße</u>

saucepan NOUN
  der <u>Kochtopf</u> (PL die Kochtöpfe)

saucer NOUN
  die <u>Untertasse</u>

Saudi Arabia NOUN
  <u>Saudi-Arabien</u> NEUT
  ◆ **to Saudi Arabia** nach Saudi-Arabien

sauna NOUN
  die <u>Sauna</u> (PL die Saunas)

sausage NOUN
  die <u>Wurst</u> (PL die Würste)
  ◆ **a sausage roll** eine Wurst im Blätterteig

to **save** VERB
  [1] <u>sparen</u> (*money, time*) ◊ *I've saved fifty
pounds already.* Ich habe schon fünfzig
Pfund gespart. ◊ *I saved twenty pounds
by waiting for the sales.* Ich habe
zwanzig Pfund gespart, weil ich bis zum
Schlussverkauf gewartet habe. ◊ *We took
a taxi to save time.* Wir haben ein Taxi
genommen, um Zeit zu sparen.
  [2] <u>retten</u> (*rescue*) ◊ *Luckily, all the
passengers were saved.* Zum Glück
wurden alle Passagiere gerettet.
  [3] <u>sichern</u> (*on computer*) ◊ *I saved the file
onto a diskette.* Ich habe die Datei auf
Diskette gesichert.
  ◆ **to save up** sparen ◊ *I'm saving up for a
new bike.* Ich spare für ein neues
Fahrrad.

savings PL NOUN
  die <u>Ersparnisse</u> FEM PL ◊ *She spent all her
savings on a computer.* Sie gab all ihre
Ersparnisse für einen Computer aus.

savoury ADJECTIVE
  <u>pikant</u> (*spicy*)

saw VERB *see* **see**

saw NOUN
  die <u>Säge</u>

S

sax NOUN

das <u>Saxofon</u> (PL die Saxofone) ◊ *I play the sax.* Ich spiele Saxofon.

saxophone NOUN

das <u>Saxofon</u> (PL die Saxofone) ◊ *I play the saxophone.* Ich spiele Saxofon.

to **say** VERB

<u>sagen</u> ◊ *What did he say?* Was hat er gesagt? ◊ *Did you hear what she said?* Hast du gehört, was sie gesagt hat? ◊ *Could you say that again?* Können Sie das noch einmal sagen?

♦ **That goes without saying.** Das ist selbstverständlich.

saying NOUN

die <u>Redensart</u> ◊ *It's just a saying.* Das ist so eine Redensart.

scale NOUN

1 (*of map*)

der <u>Maßstab</u> (PL die Maßstäbe) ◊ *a large-scale map* eine Karte großen Maßstabs

2 (*size, extent*)

das <u>Ausmaß</u> (GEN des Ausmaßes, PL die Ausmaße) ◊ *a disaster on a massive scale* eine Katastrophe von riesigem Ausmaß

3 (*in music*)

die <u>Tonleiter</u>

scales PL NOUN

die <u>Waage</u> SING (*in kitchen, shop*)

♦ **bathroom scales** die Personenwaage

scampi PL NOUN

die <u>Scampi</u> PL

scandal NOUN

1 (*outrage*)

der <u>Skandal</u> (PL die Skandale) ◊ *It caused a scandal.* Es hat einen Skandal verursacht.

2 (*gossip*)

der <u>Tratsch</u> ◊ *It's just scandal.* Das ist nur Tratsch.

Scandinavia NOUN

<u>Skandinavien</u> NEUT

♦ **from Scandinavia** aus Skandinavien

♦ **to Scandinavia** nach Skandinavien

Scandinavian ADJECTIVE

<u>skandinavisch</u>

♦ **He's Scandinavian.** Er ist Skandinavier.

scar NOUN

die <u>Narbe</u>

scarce ADJECTIVE

1 <u>knapp</u> ◊ *scarce resources* knappe Geldmittel

2 <u>rar</u> ◊ *Jobs are scarce.* Jobs sind rar.

scarcely ADVERB

<u>kaum</u> ◊ *I scarcely knew him.* Ich kannte ihn kaum.

scare NOUN

see also **scare** VERB

der <u>Schrecken</u> (PL die Schrecken)

♦ **a bomb scare** ein Bombenalarm MASC

to **scare** VERB

see also **scare** NOUN

♦ **to scare somebody** jemandem Angst machen ◊ *He scares me.* Er macht mir Angst.

scarecrow NOUN

die <u>Vogelscheuche</u>

scared ADJECTIVE

♦ **to be scared** Angst haben ◊ *I was scared stiff.* Ich hatte furchtbar Angst.

♦ **to be scared of** Angst haben vor ◊ *Are you scared of him?* Hast du vor ihm Angst?

scarf NOUN

1 (*long*)

der <u>Schal</u> (PL die Schals)

2 (*square*)

das <u>Halstuch</u> (PL die Halstücher)

scary ADJECTIVE

<u>furchterregend</u> ◊ *It was really scary.* Es war wirklich Furcht erregend.

scene NOUN

1 (*place*)

der <u>Ort</u> (PL die Orte) ◊ *The police were soon on the scene.* Die Polizei war schnell vor Ort. ◊ *the scene of the crime* der Ort des Verbrechens

2 (*event, sight*)

das <u>Spektakel</u> (PL die Spektakel) ◊ *It was an amazing scene.* Es war ein erstaunliches Spektakel.

♦ **to make a scene** eine Szene machen

scenery NOUN

die <u>Landschaft</u> (*landscape*)

scent NOUN

der <u>Duft</u> (*perfume*) (PL die Düfte)

schedule NOUN

das <u>Programm</u> (PL die Programme) ◊ *a busy schedule* ein volles Programm

♦ **on schedule** planmäßig

♦ **to be behind schedule** Verspätung haben

scheduled flight NOUN

der <u>Linienflug</u> (PL die Linienflüge)

scheme NOUN

1 (*idea*)

der <u>Plan</u> (PL die Pläne) ◊ *a crazy scheme he dreamed up* ein völlig verrückter Plan, den er sich ausgedacht hat

2 (*project*)

das <u>Projekt</u> (PL die Projekte) ◊ *a council road-widening scheme* ein Straßenverbreiterungsprojekt der Gemeinde

scholarship NOUN

das <u>Stipendium</u> (PL die Stipendien)

school NOUN

die <u>Schule</u>

♦ **to go to school** in die Schule gehen

schoolbook NOUN

das <u>Schulbuch</u> (PL die Schulbücher)

schoolboy NOUN

der Schuljunge (GEN des Schuljungen, PL
die Schuljungen)
schoolchildren NOUN
die Schulkinder NEUT PL
schoolgirl NOUN
das Schulmädchen (PL die
Schulmädchen)
science NOUN
die Wissenschaft
science fiction NOUN
die Science-Fiction
scientific ADJECTIVE
wissenschaftlich
scientist NOUN
der Wissenschaftler (PL die
Wissenschaftler)
die Wissenschaftlerin
◊ *She's a scientist.* Sie ist
Wissenschaftlerin.
♦ **He trained as a scientist.** Er hat eine
wissenschaftliche Ausbildung.
scissors PL NOUN
die Schere ◊ *a pair of scissors* eine
Schere
to **scoff** VERB
futtern (*informal: eat*) ◊ *My brother
scoffed all the sandwiches.* Mein Bruder
hat alle Brote gefuttert.
scooter NOUN
[1] der Motorroller (PL die Motorroller)
[2] (*child's toy*)
der Roller (PL die Roller)
score NOUN
see also **score** VERB
der Spielstand (PL die Spielstände)
♦ **What's the score?** Wie steht das Spiel?
♦ **The score was three nil.** Es stand drei zu
null.
to **score** VERB
see also **score** NOUN
[1] (*goal*)
schießen (IMPERFECT schoss, PERFECT hat
geschossen) ◊ *to score a goal* ein Tor
schießen
[2] (*point*)
machen ◊ *to score six out of ten* sechs
von zehn Punkten machen
[3] (*keep score*)
zählen ◊ *Who's going to score?* Wer
zählt?
Scorpio NOUN
der Skorpion ◊ *I'm Scorpio.* Ich bin
Skorpion.
Scot NOUN
der Schotte (GEN des Schotten, PL die
Schotten)
die Schottin
Scotch tape ® NOUN US
der Tesafilm ®
Scotland NOUN
Schottland NEUT
♦ **from Scotland** aus Schottland
♦ **in Scotland** in Schottland

♦ **to Scotland** nach Schottland
Scots ADJECTIVE
schottisch ◊ *a Scots accent* ein
schottischer Akzent
Scotsman NOUN
der Schotte (GEN des Schotten, PL die
Schotten)
Scotswoman NOUN
die Schottin
Scottish ADJECTIVE
schottisch ◊ *a Scottish accent* ein
schottischer Akzent
♦ **He's Scottish.** Er ist Schotte.
♦ **She's Scottish.** Sie ist Schottin.
scout NOUN
der Pfadfinder (PL die Pfadfinder) ◊ *I'm in
the Scouts.* Ich bin bei den Pfadfindern.
♦ **girl scout** die Pfadfinderin
scrambled eggs PL NOUN
die Rühreier NEUT PL
scrap NOUN
see also **scrap** VERB
[1] das Stück (PL die Stücke) ◊ *a scrap of
paper* ein Stück Papier
[2] (*fight*)
die Schlägerei
♦ **scrap iron** das Alteisen
to **scrap** VERB
see also **scrap** NOUN
verwerfen (*plan, idea*) (PRESENT verwirft,
IMPERFECT verwarf, PERFECT hat verworfen)
◊ *In the end the plan was scrapped.* Am
Ende wurde der Plan verworfen.
scrapbook NOUN
das Album (PL die Alben)
to **scratch** VERB
see also **scratch** NOUN
kratzen ◊ *Stop scratching!* Hör auf zu
kratzen!
scratch NOUN
see also **scratch** VERB
(*on skin*)
der Kratzer (PL die Kratzer)
♦ **to start from scratch** von vorn anfangen
scream NOUN
see also **scream** VERB
der Schrei (PL die Schreie)
to **scream** VERB
see also **scream** NOUN
schreien (IMPERFECT schrie, PERFECT hat
geschrien)
screen NOUN
[1] (*cinema*)
die Leinwand (PL die Leinwände)
[2] (*television, computer*)
der Bildschirm (PL die Bildschirme) ◊ *An
error message appeared on the screen.*
Auf dem Bildschirm erschien eine
Fehlermeldung.
screen saver NOUN
der Bildschirmschoner (PL die
Bildschirmschoner)

S

screw NOUN
die Schraube

screwdriver NOUN
der Schraubenzieher (PL die Schraubenzieher)

to **scribble** VERB
kritzeln

to **scrub** VERB
schrubben ◊ *He scrubbed the floor.* Er schrubbte den Boden.

sculpture NOUN
die Skulptur

sea NOUN
das Meer (PL die Meere)

seafood NOUN
die Meeresfrüchte FEM PL ◊ *I don't like seafood.* Ich mag Meeresfrüchte nicht.

seagull NOUN
die Möwe

seal NOUN
see also **seal** VERB
1 (*animal*)
der Seehund (PL die Seehunde)
2 (*on container*)
das Siegel (PL die Siegel)

to **seal** VERB
see also **seal** NOUN
1 (*container*)
versiegeln (PERFECT hat versiegelt)
2 (*letter*)
zukleben (PERFECT hat zugeklebt)

seaman NOUN
der Seemann (PL die Seeleute)

to **search** VERB
see also **search** NOUN
durchsuchen (PERFECT hat durchsucht)
◊ *They searched the woods for her.* Sie haben den Wald nach ihr durchsucht.
♦ **to search for something** nach etwas suchen ◊ *He was searching for gold.* Er suchte nach Gold.

search NOUN
see also **search** VERB
die Suche

search engine NOUN
die Suchmaschine (*Internet*)

search party NOUN
der Suchtrupp (PL die Suchtrupps)

seashore NOUN
der Strand (PL die Strände) ◊ *on the seashore* am Strand

seasick ADJECTIVE
seekrank ◊ *to be seasick* seekrank sein

seaside NOUN
♦ **at the seaside** am Meer
♦ **We're going to the seaside.** Wir fahren ans Meer.

season NOUN
die Jahreszeit ◊ *What's your favourite season?* Welche Jahreszeit hast du am liebsten?

♦ **out of season** außerhalb der Saison ◊ *It's cheaper to go there out of season.* Es ist billiger, wenn man außerhalb der Saison dorthin fährt.
♦ **during the holiday season** während der Ferienzeit
♦ **a season ticket** eine Dauerkarte

seat NOUN
der Platz (GEN des Platzes, PL die Plätze)

seat belt NOUN
der Sicherheitsgurt (PL die Sicherheitsgurte)
♦ **You should fasten your seat belt.** Du solltest dich anschnallen.

sea water NOUN
das Meerwasser

seaweed NOUN
die Alge

second ADJECTIVE
see also **second** NOUN
zweite ◊ *the second man from the right* der zweite Mann von rechts ◊ *her second husband* ihr zweiter Mann ◊ *on the second page* auf der zweiten Seite ◊ *my second child* mein zweites Kind
♦ **to come second** (*in race*) Zweiter werden ◊ *She came second.* Sie wurde Zweite.
♦ **the second of August** der zweite August

second NOUN
see also **second** ADJECTIVE
die Sekunde ◊ *It'll only take a second.* Es dauert nur eine Sekunde.

secondary school NOUN
1 das Gymnasium (PL die Gymnasien)
2 die Realschule

> ℹ️ Germans always specify the type of secondary school. **Gymnasium** takes nine years and leads to **Abitur**, **Realschule** takes six years and leads to **mittlere Reife**.

second-class ADJECTIVE, ADVERB
1 zweiter Klasse (*ticket, compartment*)
◊ *to travel second-class* zweiter Klasse fahren
2 normal (*stamp, letter*)

> ℹ️ In Germany there is no first-class or second-class post. However, letters cost more to send than postcards, so you have to remember to say what you are sending when buying stamps. There is also an express service.

◊ *to send something second-class* etwas mit normaler Post schicken

second-hand ADJECTIVE
gebraucht
♦ **a second-hand car** ein Gebrauchtwagen MASC

secondly ADVERB

zweitens ◊ firstly ... secondly ... erstens ... zweitens ...

secret ADJECTIVE

see also **secret** NOUN

geheim ◊ a secret mission eine geheime Mission

secret NOUN

see also **secret** ADJECTIVE

das Geheimnis (GEN des Geheimnisses, PL die Geheimnisse) ◊ It's a secret. Es ist ein Geheimnis. ◊ Can you keep a secret? Kannst du ein Geheimnis für dich behalten?

♦ **in secret** heimlich

secretary NOUN

der Sekretär (PL die Sekretäre)

die Sekretärin

◊ She's a secretary. Sie ist Sekretärin.

secretly ADVERB

heimlich

section NOUN

[1] der Teil (PL die Teile) ◊ I passed the written section of the exam very easily. Ich habe den schriftlichen Teil der Prüfung leicht bestanden.

[2] (in shop)

die Abteilung ◊ the food section die Lebensmittelabteilung

security NOUN

die Sicherheit ◊ They are trying to improve airport security. Man versucht, die Sicherheit auf den Flughäfen zu erhöhen.

♦ **to have no job security** keinen sicheren Job haben

♦ **a security guard** ein Sicherheitsbeamter

security guard NOUN

der Wächter (PL die Wächter)

die Wächterin

♦ **She's a security guard.** Sie ist beim Sicherheitsdienst.

sedan NOUN US

die Limousine

to **see** VERB

sehen (PRESENT sieht, IMPERFECT sah, PERFECT hat gesehen) ◊ I can't see. Ich kann nichts sehen. ◊ I saw him yesterday. Ich habe ihn gestern gesehen. ◊ Have you seen him? Hast du ihn gesehen?

♦ **See you!** Tschüs! (informal)

♦ **See you soon!** Bis bald!

♦ **to see to something** sich um etwas kümmern ◊ The window's stuck. Can you see to it please? Das Fenster klemmt. Kannst du dich bitte darum kümmern?

seed NOUN

der Samen (PL die Samen)

♦ **sunflower seeds** Sonnenblumenkerne MASC PL

to **seem** VERB

scheinen (IMPERFECT schien, PERFECT hat geschienen) ◊ The shop seemed to be closed. Das Geschäft schien geschlossen

zu haben. ◊ That seems like a good idea. Das scheint eine gute Idee zu sein.

♦ **She seems tired.** Sie wirkt müde.

♦ **It seems that ...** Es sieht so aus, dass ... ◊ It seems she's getting married. Es sieht so aus, dass sie heiratet.

♦ **There seems to be a problem.** Anscheinend gibt's ein Problem.

seen VERB see **see**

seesaw NOUN

die Wippe

see-through ADJECTIVE

durchsichtig

seldom ADVERB

selten

to **select** VERB

auswählen (PERFECT hat ausgewählt)

selection NOUN

die Auswahl

self-assured ADJECTIVE

selbstsicher ◊ He's very self-assured. Er ist sehr selbstsicher.

self-catering ADJECTIVE

♦ **a self-catering apartment** eine Wohnung für Selbstversorger

self-centred ADJECTIVE

egozentrisch

self-confidence NOUN

das Selbstvertrauen ◊ He hasn't got much self-confidence. Er hat nicht viel Selbstvertrauen.

self-conscious ADJECTIVE

gehemmt

self-contained ADJECTIVE

♦ **a self-contained flat** eine separate Wohnung

self-control NOUN

die Selbstbeherrschung

self-defence NOUN

die Selbstverteidigung ◊ self-defence classes der Selbstverteidigungskurs

♦ **She killed him in self-defence.** Sie hat ihn in Notwehr getötet.

self-discipline NOUN

die Selbstdisziplin

self-employed ADJECTIVE

♦ **to be self-employed** selbstständig sein ◊ He's self-employed. Er ist selbstständig.

♦ **the self-employed** die Selbstständigen MASC PL

selfish ADJECTIVE

egoistisch ◊ Don't be so selfish. Sei nicht so egoistisch.

self-respect NOUN

die Selbstachtung

self-service ADJECTIVE

♦ **It's self-service.** (café, shop) Da ist Selbstbedienung.

♦ **a self-service restaurant** ein Selbstbedienungsrestaurant NEUT

to **sell** VERB

S

verkaufen (PERFECT hat verkauft) ◊ *He sold
it to me.* Er hat es mir verkauft.
♦ **to sell off** verkaufen
♦ **The tickets are all sold out.** Alle Karten
sind ausverkauft.
♦ **The tickets sold out in three hours.** Die
Karten waren in drei Stunden
ausverkauft.
sell-by date NOUN
das Verfallsdatum (PL die Verfallsdaten)
selling price NOUN
der Verkaufspreis (GEN des
Verkaufspreises, PL die Verkaufspreise)
Sellotape ® NOUN
der Tesafilm ®
semi NOUN
die Doppelhaushälfte ◊ *We live in a
semi.* Wir wohnen in einer
Doppelhaushälfte.
semicircle NOUN
der Halbkreis (GEN des Halbkreises, PL die
Halbkreise)
semicolon NOUN
der Strichpunkt (PL die Strichpunkte)
semi-detached house NOUN
die Doppelhaushälfte ◊ *We live in a
semi-detached house.* Wir wohnen in
einer Doppelhaushälfte.
semi-final NOUN
das Halbfinale (PL die Halbfinale)
semi-skimmed milk NOUN
die fettarme Milch
to **send** VERB
schicken ◊ *She sent me a birthday card.*
Sie hat mir eine Geburtstagskarte
geschickt.
♦ **to send back** zurückschicken
♦ **to send off (1)** (*goods, letter*) abschicken
♦ **to send off (2)** (*in sports match*) vom Platz
schicken ◊ *He was sent off.* Er wurde
vom Platz geschickt.
♦ **to send off for something (1)** (*free*) etwas
kommen lassen ◊ *I've sent off for a
brochure.* Ich habe mir eine Broschüre
kommen lassen.
♦ **to send off for something (2)** (*paid for*)
bestellen ◊ *She sent off for a book.* Sie
hat ein Buch bestellt.
♦ **to send out** verschicken
sender NOUN
der Absender (PL die Absender)
die Absenderin
senior ADJECTIVE
leitend ◊ *senior management* die
leitenden Angestellten
♦ **senior school** die weiterführende Schule
♦ **senior pupils** die Oberstufenschüler
senior citizen NOUN
der Senior (PL die Senioren)
die Seniorin
sensational ADJECTIVE
sensationell
sense NOUN

1 (*faculty*)
der Sinn (PL die Sinne) ◊ *the five senses*
die fünf Sinne ◊ *the sixth sense* der
sechste Sinn
♦ **the sense of touch** der Tastsinn
♦ **the sense of smell** der Geschmacksinn
♦ **sense of humour** der Sinn für Humor
◊ *He's got no sense of humour.* Er hat
keinen Sinn für Humor.
2 (*wisdom*)
der Verstand
♦ **Use your common sense!** Benutze
deinen gesunden Menschenverstand!
♦ **It makes sense.** Das macht Sinn.
♦ **It doesn't make sense.** Das macht keinen
Sinn.
senseless ADJECTIVE
sinnlos
sensible ADJECTIVE
vernünftig ◊ *Be sensible!* Sei vernünftig!
◊ *It would be sensible to check first.* Es
wäre vernünftig, zuerst nachzusehen.
*Be careful not to translate **sensible** by
sensibel.*
sensitive ADJECTIVE
sensibel ◊ *She's very sensitive.* Sie ist
sehr sensibel.
sensuous ADJECTIVE
sinnlich
sent VERB *see* **send**
sentence NOUN
see also **sentence** VERB
1 der Satz (GEN des Satzes, PL die Sätze)
◊ *What does this sentence mean?* Was
bedeutet dieser Satz?
2 (*judgment*)
das Urteil (PL die Urteile) ◊ *The court will
pass sentence tomorrow.* Das Gericht
wird morgen das Urteil verkünden.
3 (*punishment*)
die Strafe ◊ *the death sentence* die
Todesstrafe
♦ **He got a life sentence.** Er hat
lebenslänglich bekommen.
to **sentence** VERB
see also **sentence** NOUN
verurteilen (PERFECT hat verurteilt) ◊ *to
sentence somebody to life imprisonment*
jemanden zu einer lebenslangen
Gefängnisstrafe verurteilen ◊ *to sentence
somebody to death* jemanden zum Tode
verurteilen
sentimental ADJECTIVE
sentimental
separate ADJECTIVE
see also **separate** VERB
getrennt ◊ *The children have separate
rooms.* Die Kinder haben getrennte
Zimmer.
♦ **I wrote it on a separate sheet.** Ich habe
es auf ein extra Blatt geschrieben.
♦ **on separate occasions** bei verschiedenen
Gelegenheiten

♦ **on two separate occasions** zweimal
to **separate** VERB
  see also **separate** ADJECTIVE
  1 trennen
  2 sich trennen (married couple)
separately ADVERB
  extra
separation NOUN
  die Trennung
September NOUN
  der September ◊ in September im September
sequel NOUN
  die Fortsetzung (book, film)
sequence NOUN
  1 die Reihenfolge ◊ in the correct sequence in der richtigen Reihenfolge
  ♦ **in sequence** der Reihenfolge nach
  ♦ **a sequence of events** eine Folge von Ereignissen
  2 die Sequenz (in film)
sergeant NOUN
  1 (army)
  der Feldwebel (PL die Feldwebel)
  die Feldwebelin
  2 (police)
  der Polizeimeister (PL die Polizeimeister)
  die Polizeimeisterin
serial NOUN
  die Fernsehserie
series SING NOUN
  1 die Sendereihe ◊ a TV series eine Sendereihe im Fernsehen
  2 die Reihe (of numbers)
serious ADJECTIVE
  1 ernst ◊ You look very serious. Du siehst sehr ernst aus.
  ♦ **Are you serious?** Ist das dein Ernst?
  2 schwer (illness, mistake)
  Be careful not to translate **serious** by seriös.
seriously ADVERB
  im Ernst ◊ No, but seriously ... Nein, aber im Ernst ...
  ♦ **to take somebody seriously** jemanden ernst nehmen
  ♦ **seriously injured** schwer verletzt
  ♦ **Seriously?** Im Ernst?
sermon NOUN
  die Predigt
servant NOUN
  der Diener (PL die Diener)
  die Dienerin
to **serve** VERB
  see also **serve** NOUN
  1 servieren (PERFECT hat serviert) ◊ Dinner is served. Das Essen ist serviert.
  2 aufschlagen (PRESENT schlägt auf, IMPERFECT schlug auf, PERFECT hat aufgeschlagen) ◊ It's Agassi's turn to serve. Agassi schlägt auf.
  3 (prison sentence)

absitzen (IMPERFECT saß ab, PERFECT hat abgesessen)
♦ **to serve time** im Gefängnis sein
♦ **It serves you right.** Das geschieht dir recht.
serve NOUN
  see also **serve** VERB
  der Aufschlag (tennis) (PL die Aufschläge)
  ♦ **It's your serve.** Du hast Aufschlag.
server NOUN
  der Server (computer) (PL die Server)
to **service** VERB
  see also **service** NOUN
  überholen (car, washing machine) (PERFECT hat überholt)
service NOUN
  see also **service** VERB
  1 die Bedienung ◊ Service is included. Die Bedienung ist inklusive.
  2 (of car)
  die Inspektion
  3 (church service)
  der Gottesdienst (PL die Gottesdienste)
  ♦ **the Fire Service** die Feuerwehr
  ♦ **the armed services** die Streitkräfte
service area NOUN
  die Raststätte
service charge NOUN
  die Bedienung ◊ There's no service charge. Die Bedienung wird nicht extra berechnet.
serviceman NOUN
  der Militärangehörige (GEN des Militärangehörigen, PL die Militärangehörigen) ◊ a serviceman ein Militärangehöriger
  ♦ **He's a serviceman.** Er ist beim Militär.
service station NOUN
  die Tankstelle
serviette NOUN
  die Serviette
session NOUN
  die Sitzung
set NOUN
  see also **set** VERB
  der Satz (GEN des Satzes, PL die Sätze) ◊ a set of keys ein Satz Schlüssel ◊ Becker won the set. (tennis) Becker hat den Satz gewonnen.
  ♦ **a chess set** ein Schachspiel NEUT
  ♦ **a train set** eine Spielzeugeisenbahn
to **set** VERB
  see also **set** NOUN
  1 (alarm clock)
  stellen ◊ I set the alarm for seven o'clock. Ich habe den Wecker auf sieben Uhr gestellt.
  2 (record)
  aufstellen (PERFECT hat aufgestellt) ◊ The world record was set last year. Der

S

Weltrekord wurde letztes Jahr aufgestellt.

3 (*sun*)

<u>untergehen</u> (IMPERFECT ging unter, PERFECT ist untergegangen) ◊ *The sun was setting*. Die Sonne ging unter.

◆ **The film is set in Morocco.** Der Film spielt in Marokko.

◆ **to set off** aufbrechen ◊ *We set off for London at nine o'clock*. Wir sind um neun Uhr nach London aufgebrochen.

◆ **to set out** aufbrechen ◊ *We set out for London at nine o'clock*. Wir sind um neun Uhr nach London aufgebrochen.

◆ **to set the table** den Tisch decken

settee NOUN

das <u>Sofa</u> (PL die Sofas)

to **settle** VERB

1 (*problem*)

<u>lösen</u>

2 (*argument*)

<u>beilegen</u> (PERFECT hat beigelegt)

◆ **to settle an account** eine Rechnung begleichen

◆ **to settle down** (*calm down*) ruhiger werden

◆ **Settle down!** Beruhige dich!

◆ **to settle in** sich einleben

◆ **to settle on something** sich für etwas entscheiden ◊ *I've finally settled on Crete for my holidays*. Ich habe mich endlich dafür entschieden, nach Kreta in Urlaub zu fahren.

seven NUMBER

<u>sieben</u> ◊ *She's seven*. Sie ist sieben.

seventeen NUMBER

<u>siebzehn</u> ◊ *He's seventeen*. Er ist siebzehn.

seventeenth ADJECTIVE

<u>siebzehnte</u>

◆ **the seventeenth of August** der siebzehnte August

seventh ADJECTIVE

<u>siebte</u> ◊ *the seventh floor* der siebte Stock

◆ **the seventh of August** der siebte August

seventy NUMBER

<u>siebzig</u> ◊ *She's seventy*. Sie ist siebzig.

several ADJECTIVE, PRONOUN

<u>einige</u> ◊ *several schools* einige Schulen ◊ *several of them* einige von ihnen

to **sew** VERB

<u>nähen</u>

◆ **to sew up** (*tear*) flicken

sewing NOUN

das <u>Nähen</u>

◆ **I like sewing.** Ich nähe gern.

◆ **a sewing machine** eine Nähmaschine

sewn VERB *see* **sew**

sex NOUN

das <u>Geschlecht</u> (PL die Geschlechter)

◆ **to have sex with somebody** mit jemandem Verkehr haben

◆ **sex education** der Aufklärungsunterricht

sexism NOUN

der <u>Sexismus</u> (GEN des Sexismus)

sexist ADJECTIVE

<u>sexistisch</u>

sexual ADJECTIVE

<u>sexuell</u> ◊ *sexual harassment* die sexuelle Belästigung

◆ **sexual discrimination** die Diskriminierung aufgrund des Geschlechts

sexuality NOUN

die <u>Sexualität</u>

sexy ADJECTIVE

<u>sexy</u>

shabby ADJECTIVE

<u>schäbig</u>

shade NOUN

1 der <u>Schatten</u> (PL die Schatten) ◊ *It was thirty degrees in the shade*. Es waren dreißig Grad im Schatten.

2 (*colour*)

der <u>Ton</u> (PL die Töne) ◊ *a shade of blue* ein Blauton

shadow NOUN

der <u>Schatten</u> (PL die Schatten)

to **shake** VERB

1 <u>ausschütteln</u> (PERFECT hat ausgeschüttelt) ◊ *She shook the rug*. Sie hat den Teppich ausgeschüttelt.

2 <u>schütteln</u> ◊ *She shook the bottle*. Sie hat die Flasche geschüttelt.

3 (*tremble*)

<u>zittern</u> ◊ *He was shaking with fear*. Er zitterte vor Angst.

◆ **to shake one's head** (*in refusal*) den Kopf schütteln

◆ **to shake hands with somebody** jemandem die Hand geben ◊ *They shook hands*. Sie gaben sich die Hand.

shaken ADJECTIVE

<u>mitgenommen</u> ◊ *I was feeling a bit shaken*. Ich war etwas mitgenommen.

shaky ADJECTIVE

<u>zittrig</u> (*hand, voice*)

shall VERB

◆ **Shall I shut the window?** Soll ich das Fenster zumachen?

◆ **Shall we ask him to come with us?** Sollen wir ihn fragen, ob er mitkommt?

shallow ADJECTIVE

<u>flach</u> (*water, pool*)

shambles SING NOUN

das <u>Chaos</u> (GEN des Chaos) ◊ *It's a complete shambles*. Es ist ein völliges Chaos.

shame NOUN

die <u>Schande</u> ◊ *The shame of it!* Diese Schande!

◆ **What a shame!** Wie schade!

◆ **It's a shame that ...** Es ist schade, dass ... ◊ *It's a shame he isn't here*. Es ist schade, dass er nicht da ist.

shampoo NOUN
das <u>Shampoo</u> (PL die Shampoos) ◊ *a bottle of shampoo* eine Flasche Shampoo
shandy NOUN
das <u>Bier mit Limonade</u>

> **ⓘ** *shandy* is also called **das Alsterwasser** in North Germany and **der Radler** in South Germany.

shan't = shall not
shape NOUN
die <u>Form</u>
share NOUN
see also **share** VERB
[1] (*in company*)
die <u>Aktie</u> ◊ *They've got shares in British Telecom.* Sie haben Aktien der British Telecom.
[2] (*portion*)
der <u>Anteil</u> (PL die Anteile)
to **share** VERB
see also **share** NOUN
<u>teilen</u> ◊ *to share a room with somebody* ein Zimmer mit jemandem teilen
♦ **to share out** verteilen ◊ *They shared the sweets out among the children.* Sie haben die Bonbons unter den Kindern verteilt.
shark NOUN
der <u>Hai</u> (PL die Haie)
sharp ADJECTIVE
[1] <u>scharf</u> (*razor, knife*) ◊ *I need a sharper knife.* Ich brauche ein schärferes Messer.
[2] <u>spitz</u> (*spike, point*)
[3] <u>gescheit</u> (*clever*) ◊ *She's very sharp.* Sie ist sehr gescheit.
♦ **at two o'clock sharp** Punkt zwei Uhr
to **shave** VERB
<u>sich rasieren</u> (*have a shave*) (PERFECT hat sich rasiert)
♦ **to shave one's legs** sich die Beine rasieren ◊ *I don't shave my legs.* Ich rasiere mir die Beine nicht.
shaver NOUN
♦ **an electric shaver** ein Elektrorasierer MASC
shaving cream NOUN
die <u>Rasiercreme</u> (PL die Rasiercremes)
shaving foam NOUN
der <u>Rasierschaum</u>
she PRONOUN
<u>sie</u> ◊ *She's very nice.* Sie ist sehr nett.
shed NOUN
der <u>Schuppen</u> (PL die Schuppen)
she'd = she had, = she would
sheep NOUN
das <u>Schaf</u> (PL die Schafe) ◊ *Dozens of sheep were blocking the road.* Dutzende von Schafen haben die Straße versperrt.
sheepdog NOUN
der <u>Schäferhund</u> (PL die Schäferhunde)
sheer ADJECTIVE

rein ◊ *It's sheer greed.* Das ist die reine Gier.
sheet NOUN
das <u>Leintuch</u> (*on bed*) (PL die Leintücher)
♦ **a sheet of paper** ein Blatt Papier NEUT
shelf NOUN
das <u>Regal</u> (PL die Regale)
shell NOUN
[1] die <u>Muschel</u> (*on beach*)
[2] die <u>Schale</u> (*of egg, nut*)
[3] die <u>Granate</u> (*explosive*)
she'll = she will
shellfish NOUN
das <u>Schalentier</u> (PL die Schalentiere)
shell suit NOUN
der <u>Jogginganzug</u> (PL die Jogginganzüge)
shelter NOUN
♦ **to take shelter** sich unterstellen ◊ *They took shelter beneath a bridge.* Sie stellten sich unter eine Brücke unter.
♦ **a bus shelter** eine überdachte Bushaltestelle
shelves PL NOUN see **shelf**
shepherd NOUN
der <u>Schäfer</u> (PL die Schäfer)
die <u>Schäferin</u>
sheriff NOUN
der <u>Sheriff</u> (PL die Sheriffs)
sherry NOUN
der <u>Sherry</u> (PL die Sherrys)
she's = she is, = she has
Shetland Islands PL NOUN
die <u>Shetlandinseln</u> FEM PL
shield NOUN
der <u>Schild</u> (PL die Schilde)
shift NOUN
see also **shift** VERB
die <u>Schicht</u> ◊ *His shift starts at eight o'clock.* Seine Schicht fängt um acht Uhr an. ◊ *the night shift* die Nachtschicht
♦ **to do shift work** Schicht arbeiten
to **shift** VERB
see also **shift** NOUN
<u>verschieben</u> (*move*) (IMPERFECT verschob, PERFECT hat verschoben) ◊ *I couldn't shift the wardrobe on my own.* Ich konnte den Schrank nicht allein verschieben.
♦ **Shift yourself!** jetzt aber los!
shifty ADJECTIVE
[1] <u>zwielichtig</u> (*person*) ◊ *He looked shifty.* Er sah zwielichtig aus.
[2] <u>unstet</u> (*eyes*)
shin NOUN
das <u>Schienbein</u> (PL die Schienbeine)
to **shine** VERB
<u>scheinen</u> (IMPERFECT schien, PERFECT hat geschienen) ◊ *The sun was shining.* Die Sonne schien.
shiny ADJECTIVE
<u>glänzend</u>

S

ship NOUN
das Schiff (PL die Schiffe)
shipbuilding NOUN
der Schiffbau
shipwreck NOUN
der Schiffbruch (accident) (PL die Schiffbrüche)
shipwrecked ADJECTIVE
♦ **to be shipwrecked** Schiffbruch erleiden
shipyard NOUN
die Werft
shirt NOUN
1 (man's)
das Hemd (PL die Hemden)
2 (woman's)
die Bluse
to **shiver** VERB
zittern
shock NOUN
see also **shock** VERB
der Schock (PL die Schocks)
♦ **to get a shock (1)** (surprise) einen Schock bekommen
♦ **to get a shock (2)** (electric) einen Schlag bekommen
♦ **an electric shock** ein elektrischer Schlag
to **shock** VERB
see also **shock** NOUN
schockieren (upset) (PERFECT hat schockiert) ◊ They were shocked by the tragedy. Sie waren über die Tragödie schockiert. ◊ Nothing shocks me any more. Mich schockiert nichts mehr.
shocked ADJECTIVE
schockiert ◊ He'll be shocked if you say that. Wenn du das sagst, wird er schockiert sein.
shocking ADJECTIVE
schockierend ◊ It's shocking! Es ist schockierend! ◊ a shocking waste eine schockierende Verschwendung
shoe NOUN
der Schuh (PL die Schuhe)
shoelace NOUN
der Schnürsenkel (PL die Schnürsenkel)
shoe polish NOUN
die Schuhcreme (PL die Schuhcremes)
shoe shop NOUN
das Schuhgeschäft (PL die Schuhgeschäfte)
shone VERB see **shine**
shook VERB see **shake**
to **shoot** VERB
1 (gun, in football)
schießen (IMPERFECT schoss, PERFECT hat geschossen) ◊ Don't shoot! Nicht schießen!
♦ **to shoot at somebody** auf jemanden schießen

♦ **He was shot in the leg.** (wounded) Er wurde ins Bein getroffen.
♦ **to shoot an arrow** einen Pfeil abschießen
2 (kill)
erschießen (IMPERFECT erschoss, PERFECT hat erschossen) ◊ He was shot by a sniper. Er wurde von einem Heckenschützen erschossen.
♦ **to shoot oneself** (dead) sich erschießen ◊ He shot himself with a revolver. Er erschoss sich mit einem Revolver.
3 (film)
drehen ◊ The film was shot in Prague. Der Film wurde in Prag gedreht.
shooting NOUN
1 die Schüsse MASC PL ◊ They heard shooting. Sie hörten Schüsse.
♦ **a shooting** eine Schießerei
2 die Jagd (hunting) ◊ to go shooting auf die Jagd gehen
shop NOUN
das Geschäft (PL die Geschäfte) ◊ a sports shop ein Sportgeschäft
shop assistant NOUN
der Verkäufer (PL die Verkäufer)
die Verkäuferin
◊ She's a shop assistant. Sie ist Verkäuferin.
shopkeeper NOUN
der Ladenbesitzer (PL die Ladenbesitzer)
die Ladenbesitzerin
◊ He's a shopkeeper. Er ist Ladenbesitzer.
shoplifting NOUN
der Ladendiebstahl (PL die Ladendiebstähle)
shopping NOUN
die Einkäufe MASC PL (purchases) ◊ Can you get the shopping from the car? Kannst du die Einkäufe aus dem Auto holen?
♦ **I love shopping.** Ich gehe gern einkaufen.
♦ **to go shopping** einkaufen gehen
♦ **a shopping bag** eine Einkaufstasche
♦ **a shopping centre** ein Einkaufszentrum NEUT
shop window NOUN
das Schaufenster (PL die Schaufenster)
shore NOUN
die Küste
♦ **on shore** an Land
short ADJECTIVE
1 kurz ◊ a short skirt ein kurzer Rock ◊ short hair kurze Haare ◊ a short break eine kurze Pause ◊ a short walk ein kurzer Spaziergang
♦ **too short** zu kurz ◊ It was a great holiday, but too short. Es waren tolle Ferien, nur zu kurz.
2 klein (person) ◊ She's quite short. Sie ist ziemlich klein.

- **to be short of something** knapp an
  etwas sein ◊ *I'm short of money.* Ich bin
  knapp an Geld.
- **In short, the answer's no.** Kurz, die
  Antwort ist nein.
- **at short notice** kurzfristig

shortage NOUN
   der Mangel ◊ *a water shortage* ein
   Wassermangel

short cut NOUN
   die Abkürzung ◊ *I took a short cut.* Ich
   habe eine Abkürzung genommen.

shorthand NOUN
   das Steno

shortly ADVERB
   1 bald ◊ *He'll be arriving shortly.* Er
   kommt bald.
   2 kurz ◊ *shortly after the accident* kurz
   nach dem Unfall

shorts PL NOUN
   die Shorts PL ◊ *a pair of shorts* ein Paar
   Shorts

short-sighted ADJECTIVE
   kurzsichtig

short story NOUN
   die Kurzgeschichte

shot VERB *see* **shoot**

shot NOUN
   1 (*gunshot*)
   der Schuss (GEN des Schusses, PL die
   Schüsse)
   2 (*photo*)
   das Foto (PL die Fotos) ◊ *a shot of
   Edinburgh Castle* ein Foto des
   Edinburgher Schlosses
   3 (*injection*)
   die Spritze

shotgun NOUN
   die Flinte

should VERB
   sollen ◊ *You should take more exercise.*
   Du solltest mehr Sport machen.
- **He should be there by now.** Er müsste
  jetzt da sein.
- **That shouldn't be too hard.** Das dürfte
  nicht zu schwer sein.
- **I should have told you before.** Ich hätte
  es dir vorher sagen sollen.
  *When **should** means "would" use **würde**.*
- **I should go if I were you.** Ich würde
  gehen, wenn ich du wäre.
- **I should be so lucky!** Das wäre zu schön!

shoulder NOUN
   die Schulter
- **a shoulder bag** eine Umhängetasche

shouldn't = **should not**

to **shout** VERB
   │ *see also* **shout** NOUN │
   schreien (IMPERFECT schrie, PERFECT hat
   geschrien) ◊ *Don't shout!* Schrei doch
   nicht so! ◊ *"Go away!" he shouted.* "Geh
   weg!" schrie er.

shout NOUN
   │ *see also* **shout** VERB │
   der Schrei (PL die Schreie)

shovel NOUN
   die Schaufel

show NOUN
   │ *see also* **show** VERB │
   1 (*performance*)
   die Show (PL die Shows)
   2 (*programme*)
   die Sendung
   3 (*exhibition*)
   die Ausstellung

to **show** VERB
   │ *see also* **show** NOUN │
   1 zeigen
- **to show somebody something**
  jemandem etwas zeigen ◊ *Have I shown
  you my new trainers?* Habe ich dir meine
  neuen Turnschuhe schon gezeigt?
  2 beweisen (IMPERFECT bewies, PERFECT hat
  bewiesen) ◊ *She showed great courage.*
  Sie hat großen Mut bewiesen.
- **It shows.** Das sieht man. ◊ *I've never
  been riding before. – It shows.* Ich bin
  noch nie geritten. – Das sieht man.
- **to show off** angeben (*informal*)
- **to show up** (*turn up*) aufkreuzen ◊ *He
  showed up late as usual.* Er kreuzte wie
  immer zu spät auf.

shower NOUN
   1 die Dusche
- **to have a shower** duschen
  2 (*of rain*)
  der Schauer (PL die Schauer)

showerproof ADJECTIVE
   regendicht

showing NOUN
   die Vorführung (*of film*)

shown VERB *see* **show**

show-off NOUN
   der Angeber (PL die Angeber)
   die Angeberin

shrank VERB *see* **shrink**

to **shriek** VERB
   kreischen

shrimps PL NOUN
   die Krabben FEM PL

to **shrink** VERB
   einlaufen (*clothes, fabric*) (PRESENT läuft
   ein, IMPERFECT lief ein, PERFECT ist
   eingelaufen)

Shrove Tuesday NOUN
   der Fastnachtsdienstag

to **shrug** VERB
- **He shrugged his shoulders.** Er zuckte mit
  den Schultern.

shrunk VERB *see* **shrink**

to **shudder** VERB
   sich schütteln

to **shuffle** VERB
- **to shuffle the cards** die Karten mischen

S

to **shut** VERB
   zumachen (PERFECT hat zugemacht)
   ◊ *What time do you shut?* Wann machen
   Sie zu? ◊ *What time do the shops shut?*
   Wann machen die Geschäfte zu?
   ◆ **to shut down** schließen ◊ *The cinema*
   shut down last year. Das Kino hat letztes
   Jahr geschlossen.
   ◆ **to shut up (1)** (*close*) verschließen
   ◆ **to shut up (2)** (*be quiet*) den Mund halten
   ◊ *Shut up!* Halt den Mund!
shutters PL NOUN
   die Fensterläden MASC PL
shuttle NOUN
   ☐1 (*plane*)
   das Pendelflugzeug (PL die
   Pendelflugzeuge)
   ☐2 (*train*)
   der Pendelzug (PL die Pendelzüge)
   ☐3 (*bus*)
   der Pendelbus (GEN des Pendelbusses, PL
   die Pendelbusse)
shuttlecock NOUN
   der Federball (*badminton*) (PL die
   Federbälle)
shy ADJECTIVE
   schüchtern
Sicily NOUN
   Sizilien NEUT
   ◆ **from Sicily** aus Sizilien
   ◆ **to Sicily** nach Sizilien
sick ADJECTIVE
   ☐1 krank (*ill*) ◊ *He was sick for four days.*
   Er war vier Tage krank.
   ☐2 übel (*joke, humour*) ◊ *That's really sick!*
   Das war wirklich übel!
   ◆ **to be sick** (*vomit*) sich übergeben
   ◆ **I feel sick.** Mir ist schlecht.
   ◆ **to be sick of something** etwas leid sein
   ◊ *I'm sick of your jokes.* Ich bin deine
   Witze leid.
sickening ADJECTIVE
   ekelhaft
sick leave NOUN
   ◆ **to be on sick leave** krankgeschrieben
   sein ◊ *Rudi's been on sick leave for three*
   weeks now. Rudi ist seit drei Wochen
   krankgeschrieben.
sickness NOUN
   die Krankheit
sick note NOUN
   ☐1 (*from parents*)
   die Entschuldigung
   ☐2 (*from doctor*)
   das ärztliche Attest (PL die ärztlichen
   Atteste)
sick pay NOUN
   die Bezahlung im Krankheitsfall
side NOUN
   ☐1 die Seite ◊ *He was driving on the*
   wrong side of the road. Er fuhr auf der
   falschen Straßenseite. ◊ *He's on my side.*
   Er ist auf meiner Seite.

◆ **side by side** nebeneinander
◆ **the side entrance** der Seiteneingang
◆ **to take sides** Partei ergreifen ◊ *She*
always takes your side. Sie ergreift
immer für dich Partei.
   ☐2 (*edge*)
   der Rand (PL die Ränder) ◊ *by the side of*
   the road am Straßenrand
   ☐3 (*of pool, river*)
   das Ufer (PL die Ufer) ◊ *by the side of the*
   lake am Ufer des Sees
sideboard NOUN
   die Anrichte
side effect NOUN
   der Nebeneffekt (PL die Nebeneffekte)
side street NOUN
   die Seitenstraße
sidewalk NOUN US
   der Bürgersteig (PL die Bürgersteige)
sideways ADVERB
   ☐1 von der Seite (*look*)
   ☐2 zur Seite (*move, be facing*)
   ◆ **sideways on** von der Seite
sieve NOUN
   das Sieb (PL die Siebe)
sigh NOUN
   | see also **sigh** VERB |
   der Seufzer (PL die Seufzer)
to **sigh** VERB
   | see also **sigh** NOUN |
   seufzen
sight NOUN
   der Anblick ◊ *It was an amazing sight.*
   Es war ein irrer Anblick.
   ◆ **in sight** in Sicht
   ◆ **out of sight** nicht zu sehen
   ◆ **to have poor sight** schlechte Augen
   haben
   ◆ **to know somebody by sight** jemanden
   vom Sehen kennen
   ◆ **the sights** (*tourist spots*) die
   Sehenswürdigkeiten ◊ *to see the sights*
   of London sich die Sehenswürdigkeiten
   von London ansehen
sightseeing NOUN
   das Sightseeing
   ◆ **to go sightseeing** Sightseeing machen
sign NOUN
   | see also **sign** VERB |
   ☐1 (*notice*)
   das Schild (PL die Schilder) ◊ *There was*
   a big sign saying "private". Da war ein
   großes Schild, auf dem "privat" stand.
   ◆ **a road sign** ein Verkehrsschild
   ☐2 (*gesture, indication*)
   das Zeichen (PL die Zeichen) ◊ *There's no*
   sign of improvement. Es gibt kein
   Zeichen einer Besserung.
   ◆ **What sign are you?** (*star sign*) Was für ein
   Sternzeichen sind Sie?
to **sign** VERB
   | see also **sign** NOUN |

unterschreiben (IMPERFECT unterschrieb, PERFECT hat unterschrieben)
- **to sign on (1)** (*as unemployed*) sich arbeitslos melden
- **to sign on (2)** (*for course*) sich einschreiben

signal NOUN
> see also **signal** VERB

das Signal (PL die Signale)

to **signal** VERB
> see also **signal** NOUN

- **to signal to somebody** jemandem ein Zeichen geben

signalman NOUN
der Stellwerkswärter (PL die Stellwerkswärter)
die Stellwerkswärterin

signature NOUN
die Unterschrift

significance NOUN
die Bedeutung

significant ADJECTIVE
bedeutend

sign language NOUN
die Zeichensprache

signpost NOUN
der Wegweiser (PL die Wegweiser)

silence NOUN
die Stille ◊ *There was absolute silence.* Es herrschte absolute Stille.

silent ADJECTIVE
still

silicon chip NOUN
der Siliciumchip (PL die Siliciumchips)

silk NOUN
> see also **silk** ADJECTIVE

die Seide

silk ADJECTIVE
> see also **silk** NOUN

seiden ◊ *a silk scarf* ein seidener Schal

silky ADJECTIVE
seidig

silly ADJECTIVE
dumm ◊ *That's the silliest excuse I've ever heard.* Das ist die dümmste Ausrede, die ich je gehört habe.

silver NOUN
das Silber ◊ *a silver medal* eine Silbermedaille

similar ADJECTIVE
ähnlich ◊ *My sister is very similar to me in that respect.* Meine Schwester ist mir in der Hinsicht sehr ähnlich.

simple ADJECTIVE
1 einfach ◊ *It's very simple.* Das ist sehr einfach.
2 einfältig (*simple-minded*) ◊ *He's a bit simple.* Er ist etwas einfältig.

simply ADVERB
einfach ◊ *It's simply not possible.* Es ist einfach nicht möglich.

simultaneous ADJECTIVE

gleichzeitig

sin NOUN
> see also **sin** VERB

die Sünde

to **sin** VERB
> see also **sin** NOUN

sündigen

since PREPOSITION, ADVERB, CONJUNCTION
1 seit ◊ *since Christmas* seit Weihnachten ◊ *I haven't seen her since she left.* Ich habe sie nicht gesehen, seit sie weggezogen ist.
- **since then** seither ◊ *I haven't seen him since then.* Ich habe ihn seither nicht gesehen.
- **ever since** seitdem
2 da (*because*) ◊ *Since you're tired, let's stay at home.* Da du müde bist, bleiben wir doch zu Hause.

sincere ADJECTIVE
aufrichtig

sincerely ADVERB
- **Yours sincerely ...** Mit freundlichen Grüßen ...

to **sing** VERB
singen (IMPERFECT sang, PERFECT hat gesungen) ◊ *He sang out of tune.* Er hat falsch gesungen. ◊ *Have you ever sung this tune before?* Hast du die Melodie schon mal gesungen?

singer NOUN
der Sänger (PL die Sänger)
die Sängerin

singing NOUN
das Singen

single ADJECTIVE
> see also **single** NOUN

alleinstehend (*unmarried*)
- **a single room** ein Einzelzimmer NEUT
- **not a single thing** absolut nichts

single NOUN
> see also **single** ADJECTIVE

1 (*ticket*)
die einfache Fahrkarte ◊ *A single to Bonn, please.* Eine einfache Fahrkarte nach Bonn, bitte.
2 (*record*)
die Single (PL die Singles)
- **a CD single** eine CD-Single

single parent NOUN
- **She's a single parent.** Sie ist alleinerziehende Mutter.
- **a single parent family** eine Einelternteilfamilie

singles PL NOUN
das Einzel (*in tennis*) SING (PL die Einzel) ◊ *the women's singles* das Dameneinzel

singular NOUN
der Singular (PL die Singulare) ◊ *in the singular* im Singular

sinister ADJECTIVE
unheimlich

S

sink NOUN

see also **sink** VERB

die Spüle

to **sink** VERB

see also **sink** NOUN

sinken (IMPERFECT sank, PERFECT ist gesunken)

sir NOUN

In German no form of address is normally used apart from **Sie**.
◊ *Would you like to order, Sir?* Möchten Sie bestellen?

♦ **Yes sir.** Ja.

siren NOUN

die Sirene

sister NOUN

die Schwester ◊ *my little sister* meine kleine Schwester ◊ *I wanted to speak to the sister on the ward.* Ich wollte die Stationsschwester sprechen.

sister-in-law NOUN

die Schwägerin

to **sit** VERB

1 (*be sitting*)

sitzen (IMPERFECT saß, PERFECT hat gesessen)
◊ *She was sitting on the floor.* Sie saß auf dem Boden.

2 (*sit down*)

sich setzen ◊ *Sit on that chair.* Setz dich auf den Stuhl.

♦ **to sit down** sich setzen

♦ **to be sitting** sitzen

♦ **to sit an exam** eine Prüfung machen

sitcom NOUN

die Situationskomödie

site NOUN

1 die Stätte ◊ *an archaeological site* eine archäologische Stätte

♦ **the site of the accident** der Unfallort

2 (*campsite*)

der Campingplatz (GEN des Campingplatzes, PL die Campingplätze)

♦ **a building site** eine Baustelle

sitting room NOUN

das Wohnzimmer (PL die Wohnzimmer)

situated ADJECTIVE

♦ **to be situated** liegen ◊ *The village is situated on the side of the hill.* Das Dorf liegt am Berghang.

situation NOUN

die Situation

six NUMBER

sechs ◊ *He's six.* Er ist sechs.

sixteen NUMBER

sechzehn ◊ *He's sixteen.* Er ist sechzehn.

sixteenth ADJECTIVE

sechzehnte

♦ **the sixteenth of August** der sechzehnte August

sixth ADJECTIVE

sechste ◊ *the sixth floor* der sechste Stock

♦ **the sixth of August** der sechste August

sixty NUMBER

sechzig ◊ *She's sixty.* Sie ist sechzig.

size NOUN

> 🛈 *Germany uses the European system for clothing and shoe sizes.*

1 die Größe (*of object, clothing*) ◊ *What size do you take?* Welche Größe haben Sie?

♦ **I'm a size ten.** Ich habe Größe achtunddreißig.

2 die Schuhgröße (*of shoes*)

♦ **I take size six.** Ich habe Schuhgröße neununddreißig.

to **skate** VERB

1 (*ice-skate*)

Schlittschuh laufen (PRESENT läuft Schlittschuh, IMPERFECT lief Schlittschuh, PERFECT ist Schlittschuh gelaufen)

2 (*roller-skate*)

Rollschuh laufen (PRESENT läuft Rollschuh, IMPERFECT lief Rollschuh, PERFECT ist Rollschuh gelaufen)

skateboard NOUN

das Skateboard (PL die Skateboards)

skateboarding NOUN

das Skateboardfahren

♦ **to go skateboarding** Skateboard fahren

skates PL NOUN

1 die Schlittschuhe MASC PL

2 die Rollschuhe MASC PL (*roller skates*)

skating NOUN

1 das Schlittschuhlaufen

♦ **to go skating** Schlittschuh laufen

♦ **a skating rink** eine Eisbahn

2 das Rollschuhlaufen (*roller-skating*)

♦ **to go skating** Rollschuh laufen

♦ **a skating rink** eine Rollschuhbahn

skeleton NOUN

das Skelett (PL die Skelette)

sketch NOUN

see also **sketch** VERB

die Skizze (*drawing*)

to **sketch** VERB

see also **sketch** NOUN

skizzieren (PERFECT hat skizziert)

to **ski** VERB

see also **ski** NOUN

Ski fahren (PRESENT fährt Ski, IMPERFECT fuhr Ski, PERFECT ist Ski gefahren) ◊ *Can you ski?* Kannst du Ski fahren?

ski NOUN

see also **ski** VERB

der Ski (PL die Skier)

♦ **ski boots** die Skistiefel

♦ **a ski lift** ein Skilift MASC

♦ **ski pants** die Skihose SING

♦ **a ski pole** ein Skistock MASC

♦ **a ski slope** eine Skipiste

♦ **a ski suit** ein Skianzug MASC

to **skid** VERB

schleudern (PERFECT ist geschleudert)

skier NOUN
der Skifahrer (PL die Skifahrer)
die Skifahrerin

skiing NOUN
das Skifahren
♦ **to go skiing** Ski fahren
♦ **to go on a skiing holiday** in den Skiurlaub fahren

skilful ADJECTIVE
geschickt

skill NOUN
das Können ◊ *It requires a lot of skill.* Es verlangt viel Können.

skilled ADJECTIVE
♦ **a skilled worker** ein Facharbeiter MASC

skimmed milk NOUN
die Magermilch

skimpy ADJECTIVE
knapp (*clothes*)

skin NOUN
die Haut (PL die Häute)
♦ **skin cancer** der Hautkrebs

skinhead NOUN
der Skinhead (PL die Skinheads)
der Skinhead is also used for women.

skinny ADJECTIVE
mager

skin-tight ADJECTIVE
hauteng

skip NOUN
see also **skip** VERB
der Container (*container*) (PL die Container)

to **skip** VERB
see also **skip** NOUN
1 (*with rope*)
seilspringen (PERFECT ist seilgesprungen)
2 auslassen (PRESENT lässt aus, IMPERFECT ließ aus, PERFECT hat ausgelassen) ◊ *to skip a meal* eine Mahlzeit auslassen
♦ **I skipped the maths lesson.** Ich habe die Mathestunde geschwänzt.

skirt NOUN
der Rock (PL die Röcke)

skittles SING NOUN
das Kegeln
♦ **to play skittles** kegeln

to **skive** VERB
faulenzen (*be lazy*)
♦ **to skive off** schwänzen (*informal*) ◊ *to skive off school* die Schule schwänzen

skull NOUN
der Schädel (PL die Schädel)

sky NOUN
der Himmel (PL die Himmel)

skyscraper NOUN
der Wolkenkratzer (PL die Wolkenkratzer)

slack ADJECTIVE
1 locker (*rope*)
2 nachlässig (*person*)

to **slag off** VERB
♦ **to slag somebody off** über jemanden herziehen (*informal*) ◊ *She's always slagging me off.* Sie zieht dauernd über mich her.

to **slam** VERB
zuknallen (PERFECT hat/ist zugeknallt)
*For the perfect tense use **haben** when the verb has an object and **sein** when there is no object.*
◊ *The door slammed.* Die Tür ist zugeknallt. ◊ *She slammed the door.* Sie hat die Tür zugeknallt.

slang NOUN
der Slang (PL die Slangs)

slap NOUN
see also **slap** VERB
die Ohrfeige

to **slap** VERB
see also **slap** NOUN
♦ **to slap somebody** jemandem einen Klaps geben ◊ *She slapped him.* Sie gab ihm einen Klaps.

slate NOUN
1 der Schiefer (PL die Schiefer)
2 (*for roof*)
der Schieferziegel (PL die Schieferziegel)

sledge NOUN
der Schlitten (PL die Schlitten)

sledging NOUN
♦ **to go sledging** Schlitten fahren

sleep NOUN
see also **sleep** VERB
der Schlaf ◊ *I need some sleep.* Ich brauche Schlaf.
♦ **to go to sleep** einschlafen

to **sleep** VERB
see also **sleep** NOUN
schlafen (PRESENT schläft, IMPERFECT schlief, PERFECT hat geschlafen) ◊ *I couldn't sleep last night.* Ich konnte heute Nacht nicht schlafen.
♦ **to sleep with somebody** mit jemandem schlafen
♦ **to sleep together** miteinander schlafen
♦ **to sleep around** mit jedem schlafen
♦ **to sleep in** verschlafen

sleeping bag NOUN
der Schlafsack (PL die Schlafsäcke)

sleeping car NOUN
der Schlafwagen (PL die Schlafwagen)

sleeping pill NOUN
die Schlaftablette

sleepy ADJECTIVE
schläfrig
♦ **to feel sleepy** schläfrig sein ◊ *I was feeling sleepy.* Ich war schläfrig.
♦ **a sleepy little village** ein verschlafenes kleines Dorf

sleet NOUN
see also **sleet** VERB
der Schneeregen

to **sleet** VERB

S

☞

see also **sleet** NOUN

♦**It's sleeting.** Es fällt Schneeregen.

sleeve NOUN

[1] der Ärmel (PL die Ärmel) ◊ *long sleeves* lange Ärmel ◊ *short sleeves* kurze Ärmel

[2] (*record sleeve*)
die Hülle

sleigh NOUN

der Pferdeschlitten (PL die Pferdeschlitten)

slept VERB *see* **sleep**

slice NOUN

see also **slice** VERB

die Scheibe

to **slice** VERB

see also **slice** NOUN

aufschneiden (IMPERFECT schnitt auf, PERFECT hat aufgeschnitten)

slick NOUN

♦**an oil slick** ein Ölteppich MASC

slide NOUN

see also **slide** VERB

[1] (*in playground*)
die Rutschbahn

[2] (*photo*)
das Dia (PL die Dias)

[3] (*hair slide*)
die Klemme

to **slide** VERB

see also **slide** NOUN

rutschen (PERFECT ist gerutscht)

slight ADJECTIVE

klein ◊ *a slight problem* ein kleines Problem ◊ *a slight improvement* eine kleine Verbesserung

slightly ADVERB

etwas

slim ADJECTIVE

see also **slim** VERB

schlank

to **slim** VERB

see also **slim** ADJECTIVE

abnehmen (*be on a diet*) (PRESENT nimmt ab, IMPERFECT nahm ab, PERFECT hat abgenommen) ◊ *I'm slimming.* Ich nehme gerade ab.

sling NOUN

die Schlinge ◊ *She had her arm in a sling.* Sie hatte den Arm in der Schlinge.

slip NOUN

see also **slip** VERB

[1] (*mistake*)
der Schnitzer (PL die Schnitzer)

[2] (*underskirt*)
der Unterrock (PL die Unterröcke)

♦**a slip of paper** ein Zettel MASC

♦**a slip of the tongue** ein Versprecher MASC

to **slip** VERB

see also **slip** NOUN

ausrutschen (PERFECT ist ausgerutscht)
◊ *He slipped on the ice.* Er ist auf dem Eis ausgerutscht.

♦**to slip up** (*make a mistake*) einen Fehler machen

slipper NOUN

der Hausschuh (PL die Hausschuhe) ◊ *a pair of slippers* ein Paar Hausschuhe

slippery ADJECTIVE

glatt

slip-up NOUN

der Schnitzer (PL die Schnitzer)

♦**There's been a slip-up.** Da ist etwas schiefgelaufen.

slope NOUN

der Abhang (PL die Abhänge)

sloppy ADJECTIVE

schlampig

slot NOUN

der Schlitz (GEN des Schlitzes, PL die Schlitze)

slot machine NOUN

[1] (*for gambling*)
der Geldspielautomat (GEN des Geldspielautomaten, PL die Geldspielautomaten)

[2] (*vending machine*)
der Automat (GEN des Automaten, PL die Automaten)

slow ADJECTIVE, ADVERB

langsam ◊ *He's a bit slow.* Er ist etwas langsam.

♦**to go slow (1)** (*person*) langsam gehen

♦**to go slow (2)** (*car*) langsam fahren
◊ *Drive slower!* Fahr langsamer!

♦**My watch is slow.** Meine Uhr geht nach.

to **slow down** VERB

verlangsamen (PERFECT hat verlangsamt)

slowly ADVERB

langsam

slug NOUN

die Nacktschnecke (*animal*)

slum NOUN

der Slum (PL die Slums)

slush NOUN

der Matsch

sly ADJECTIVE

gerissen (*person*)

♦**a sly smile** ein verschmitztes Lächeln

smack NOUN

see also **smack** VERB

der Klaps (*slap*) (GEN des Klapses, PL die Klapse)

to **smack** VERB

see also **smack** NOUN

♦**to smack somebody** jemandem einen Klaps geben ◊ *She smacked him.* Sie gab ihm einen Klaps.

small ADJECTIVE

klein

♦**small change** das Kleingeld

Be careful not to translate **small** *by* **schmal**.

smart ADJECTIVE
1 schick (*elegant*)
2 intelligent (*clever*) ◊ *a smart idea* eine intelligente Idee

smart phone NOUN
das Smartphone (PL die Smartphones)

smash NOUN
see also **smash** VERB
der Zusammenstoß (GEN des Zusammenstoßes, PL die Zusammenstöße)

to **smash** VERB
see also **smash** NOUN
1 (*break*)
kaputt machen (PERFECT hat kaputt gemacht) ◊ *I've smashed my watch.* Ich habe meine Uhr kaputt gemacht.
2 (*get broken*)
zerbrechen (PRESENT zerbricht, IMPERFECT zerbrach, PERFECT ist zerbrochen) ◊ *The glass smashed into tiny pieces.* Das Glas zerbrach in winzige Scherben.

smashing ADJECTIVE
klasse (*informal*) ◊ *I think he's smashing.* Ich finde, er ist klasse.
klasse is invariable.
◊ *a smashing film* ein klasse Film

smell NOUN
see also **smell** VERB
der Geruch (PL die Gerüche)
♦ **the sense of smell** der Geruchsinn

to **smell** VERB
see also **smell** NOUN
1 stinken (IMPERFECT stank, PERFECT hat gestunken) ◊ *That old dog really smells!* Der alte Hund stinkt!
♦ **to smell of something** nach etwas riechen ◊ *It smells of petrol.* Es riecht nach Benzin.
2 (*detect*)
riechen (IMPERFECT roch, PERFECT hat gerochen) ◊ *I can't smell anything.* Ich kann nichts riechen.

smelly ADJECTIVE
stinkend
♦ **He's got smelly feet.** Seine Füße stinken.

smelt VERB *see* **smell**

smile NOUN
see also **smile** VERB
das Lächeln

to **smile** VERB
see also **smile** NOUN
lächeln

smiley NOUN
das Smiley (PL die Smileys)

smoke NOUN
see also **smoke** VERB
der Rauch

to **smoke** VERB
see also **smoke** NOUN
rauchen ◊ *I don't smoke.* Ich rauche

nicht. ◊ *He smokes cigars.* Er raucht Zigarren.

smoker NOUN
der Raucher (PL die Raucher)
die Raucherin

smoking NOUN
das Rauchen ◊ *to give up smoking* mit dem Rauchen aufhören ◊ *Smoking is bad for you.* Rauchen schadet der Gesundheit.
♦ **"no smoking"** "Rauchen verboten"

smooth ADJECTIVE
1 glatt (*surface*)
2 aalglatt (*person*)

smug ADJECTIVE
selbstgefällig ◊ *He's grown smugger since getting promotion.* Seit seiner Beförderung ist er selbstgefälliger geworden.

to **smuggle** VERB
schmuggeln

smuggler NOUN
der Schmuggler (PL die Schmuggler)
die Schmugglerin

smuggling NOUN
das Schmuggeln

smutty ADJECTIVE
schmutzig ◊ *a smutty story* eine schmutzige Geschichte

snack NOUN
der Snack (PL die Snacks) ◊ *to have a snack* einen Snack zu sich nehmen

snack bar NOUN
die Imbissstube

snail NOUN
die Schnecke

snake NOUN
die Schlange

to **snap** VERB
brechen (*break*) (PRESENT bricht, IMPERFECT brach, PERFECT ist gebrochen) ◊ *The branch snapped.* Der Zweig brach.
♦ **to snap one's fingers** mit dem Finger schnipsen

snapshot NOUN
das Foto (PL die Fotos)

to **snarl** VERB
knurren (*animal*)

to **snatch** VERB
♦ **to snatch something from somebody** jemandem etwas entreißen ◊ *He snatched the keys from my hand.* Er riss mir die Schlüssel aus der Hand.
♦ **My bag was snatched.** Man hat mir meine Handtasche entrissen.

to **sneak** VERB
♦ **to sneak in** sich hineinschleichen
♦ **to sneak out** sich hinausschleichen
♦ **to sneak up on somebody** an jemanden heranschleichen

to **sneeze** VERB
niesen

S

to **sniff** VERB

[1] schniefen ◊ *Stop sniffing!* Hör auf zu schniefen!

[2] schnüffeln an +DAT ◊ *The dog sniffed my hand.* Der Hund schnüffelte an meiner Hand.

♦ **to sniff glue** schnüffeln

snob NOUN

der Snob (PL die Snobs)

der Snob is also used for women.

◊ *She is such a snob.* Sie ist ein furchtbarer Snob.

snooker NOUN

das Snooker ◊ *to play snooker* Snooker spielen

snooze NOUN

das Nickerchen (PL die Nickerchen) ◊ *to have a snooze* ein Nickerchen machen

to **snore** VERB

schnarchen

snow NOUN

see also **snow** VERB

der Schnee

to **snow** VERB

see also **snow** NOUN

schneien ◊ *It's snowing.* Es schneit.

snowball NOUN

der Schneeball (PL die Schneebälle)

snowflake NOUN

die Schneeflocke

snowman NOUN

der Schneemann (PL die Schneemänner)

◊ *to build a snowman* einen Schneemann machen

SO CONJUNCTION, ADVERB

[1] also ◊ *The shop was closed, so I went home.* Das Geschäft war zu, also ging ich nach Hause. ◊ *It rained, so I got wet.* Es hat geregnet, also bin ich nass geworden. ◊ *So, have you always lived in London?* Also, hast du schon immer in London gewohnt?

♦ **So what?** Na und?

[2] so ◊ *It was so heavy!* Es war so schwer! ◊ *It's not so heavy!* Es ist nicht so schwer! ◊ *He was talking so fast I couldn't understand.* Er hat so schnell geredet, dass ich nichts verstanden habe. ◊ *How's your father? – Not so good.* Wie geht's deinem Vater? – Nicht so gut. ◊ *He's like his sister but not so clever.* Er ist wie seine Schwester, aber nicht so klug.

♦ **so much** (*a lot*) so sehr ◊ *I love you so much.* Ich liebe dich so sehr!

♦ **so much ...** so viel ... ◊ *I've got so much work.* Ich habe so viel Arbeit.

♦ **so many ...** so viele ... ◊ *I've got so many things to do today.* Ich muss heute so viele Dinge erledigen.

♦ **so do I** ich auch ◊ *I love horses. – So do I.* Ich mag Pferde. – Ich auch.

♦ **so have we** wir auch ◊ *I've been to Germany twice. – So have we.* Ich war schon zweimal in Deutschland. – Wir auch.

♦ **I think so.** Ich glaube schon.

♦ **I hope so.** Hoffentlich.

♦ **That's not so.** Das ist nicht so.

♦ **so far** bis jetzt ◊ *It's been easy so far.* Bis jetzt war es einfach.

♦ **so far so good** so weit, so gut

♦ **ten or so people** so etwa zehn Leute

♦ **at five o'clock or so** so gegen fünf Uhr

to **soak** VERB

einweichen (PERFECT hat eingeweicht)

soaked ADJECTIVE

völlig durchnässt ◊ *By the time we got back we were soaked.* Bis wir zu Hause waren, waren wir völlig durchnässt.

soaking ADJECTIVE

völlig durchnässt ◊ *By the time we got back we were soaking.* Bis wir zu Hause waren, waren wir völlig durchnässt.

♦ **soaking wet** patschnass ◊ *Your shoes are soaking wet.* Deine Schuhe sind patschnass.

soap NOUN

die Seife

soap opera NOUN

die Seifenoper

soap powder NOUN

das Waschpulver (PL die Waschpulver)

to **sob** VERB

schluchzen ◊ *She was sobbing.* Sie schluchzte.

sober ADJECTIVE

nüchtern

to **sober up** VERB

nüchtern werden (PRESENT wird nüchtern, IMPERFECT wurde nüchtern, PERFECT ist nüchtern geworden)

soccer NOUN

der Fußball ◊ *to play soccer* Fußball spielen

♦ **a soccer player** ein Fußballspieler MASC

social ADJECTIVE

sozial ◊ *social problems* soziale Probleme

♦ **a social class** eine gesellschaftliche Schicht

♦ **I have a good social life.** Ich komme viel unter Leute.

socialism NOUN

der Sozialismus (GEN des Sozialismus)

socialist ADJECTIVE

see also **socialist** NOUN

sozialistisch

socialist NOUN

see also **socialist** ADJECTIVE

der Sozialist (GEN des Sozialisten, PL die Sozialisten)

die Sozialistin

◊ *She's a Socialist.* Sie ist Sozialistin.

social security NOUN

[1] die Sozialhilfe (*money*)

♦ **to be on social security** Sozialhilfe bekommen

[2] die Sozialversicherung (*organization*)

social worker NOUN

der Sozialarbeiter (PL die Sozialarbeiter)

die Sozialarbeiterin

◊ *She's a social worker.* Sie ist Sozialarbeiterin.

society NOUN

[1] die Gesellschaft ◊ *We live in a multicultural society.* Wir leben in einer multikulturellen Gesellschaft.

[2] der Verein (PL die Vereine) ◊ *the Royal Society for the Prevention of Cruelty to Animals* der Tierschutzverein

♦ **a drama society** eine Theatergruppe

sociology NOUN

die Soziologie

sock NOUN

die Socke

socket NOUN

die Steckdose

soda NOUN

das Sodawasser (*soda water*) (PL die Sodawasser)

soda pop NOUN US

die Limo (PL die Limos)

sofa NOUN

das Sofa (PL die Sofas)

soft ADJECTIVE

weich

♦ **soft cheese** der Weichkäse

♦ **to be soft on somebody** (*be kind to*) nachsichtig mit jemandem sein

♦ **a soft drink** ein alkoholfreies Getränk

♦ **soft drugs** weiche Drogen

♦ **a soft option** eine bequeme Lösung

software NOUN

die Software

soggy ADJECTIVE

[1] nass (*soaked*) ◊ *a soggy tissue* ein nasses Taschentuch

[2] weich (*not crisp*) ◊ *soggy chips* weiche Pommes frites

soil NOUN

der Boden (PL die Böden)

solar ADJECTIVE

♦ **solar eclipse** die Sonnenfinsternis

solar power NOUN

die Sonnenenergie

sold VERB *see* **sell**

soldier NOUN

der Soldat (GEN des Soldaten, PL die Soldaten)

die Soldatin

◊ *He's a soldier.* Er ist Soldat.

solicitor NOUN

[1] (*for lawsuits*)

der Rechtsanwalt (PL die Rechtsanwälte)

die Rechtsanwältin

◊ *He's a solicitor.* Er ist Rechtsanwalt.

[2] (*for property, wills*)

der Notar (PL die Notare)

die Notarin

◊ *She's a solicitor.* Sie ist Notarin.

solid ADJECTIVE

[1] stabil ◊ *a solid wall* eine stabile Wand

[2] massiv ◊ *solid gold* massives Gold

♦ **for three hours solid** drei geschlagene Stunden lang

solo NOUN

das Solo (PL die Soli) ◊ *a guitar solo* ein Gitarrensolo

solution NOUN

die Lösung

to **solve** VERB

lösen

some ADJECTIVE, PRONOUN

[1] ein paar

Use **ein paar** *with plural nouns.*

◊ *I've got some nice pictures of you.* Ich habe ein paar nette Bilder von dir. ◊ *I only sold some of them.* Ich habe nur ein paar verkauft.

♦ **Some people say that ...** Manche Leute sagen, dass ...

♦ **some day** eines Tages

♦ **some day next week** irgendwann nächste Woche

[2] einige (*some but not all*) ◊ *Are these mushrooms poisonous? – Only some.* Sind diese Pilze giftig? – Nur einige.

♦ **I only took some of it.** Ich habe nur etwas davon genommen.

♦ **I'm going to buy some stamps. Do you want some too?** Ich kaufe Briefmarken. Willst du auch welche?

♦ **Would you like some coffee? – No thanks, I've got some.** Möchten Sie Kaffee? – Nein danke, ich habe schon welchen.

some is frequently not translated.

◊ *Would you like some bread?* Möchtest du Brot? ◊ *Have you got some mineral water?* Haben Sie Mineralwasser?

somebody PRONOUN

jemand ◊ *Somebody stole my bag.* Jemand hat meine Tasche gestohlen.

somehow ADVERB

irgendwie ◊ *I'll do it somehow.* Ich mache es irgendwie. ◊ *Somehow I don't think he believed me.* Irgendwie hat er mir anscheinend nicht geglaubt.

someone PRONOUN

jemand ◊ *Someone stole my bag.* Jemand hat meine Tasche gestohlen.

something PRONOUN

etwas ◊ *something special* etwas Besonderes ◊ *Wear something warm.* Zieh etwas Warmes an.

♦ **That's really something!** Das ist echt toll!

♦ **It cost a hundred pounds, or something like that.** Es kostete hundert Pfund, oder so in der Gegend.

S

☞

♦ **His name is Phil or something.** Er heißt Phil oder so ähnlich.

sometime ADVERB

mal ◊ *You must come and see us sometime.* Du musst uns mal besuchen.

♦ **sometime last month** irgendwann letzten Monat

sometimes ADVERB

manchmal ◊ *Sometimes I think she hates me.* Manchmal denke ich, sie hasst mich.

somewhere ADVERB

irgendwo ◊ *I've left my keys somewhere.* Ich habe irgendwo meine Schlüssel liegen lassen. ◊ *I'd like to go on holiday, somewhere sunny.* Ich würde gern in Ferien fahren, irgendwo in die Sonne.

son NOUN

der Sohn (PL die Söhne)

song NOUN

das Lied (PL die Lieder)

son-in-law NOUN

der Schwiegersohn (PL die Schwiegersöhne)

soon ADVERB

bald ◊ *very soon* sehr bald

♦ **soon afterwards** kurz danach

♦ **as soon as possible** sobald wie möglich

sooner ADVERB

früher ◊ *Can't you come a bit sooner?* Kannst du nicht etwas früher kommen?

♦ **sooner or later** früher oder später

soot NOUN

der Ruß

soppy ADJECTIVE

sentimental

soprano NOUN

der Sopran (PL die Soprane)

sorcerer NOUN

der böse Zauberer (PL die bösen Zauberer)

sore ADJECTIVE

see also **sore** NOUN

♦ **It's sore.** Es tut weh.

♦ **That's a sore point.** Das ist ein wunder Punkt.

sore NOUN

see also **sore** ADJECTIVE

die Wunde

sorry ADJECTIVE

♦ **I'm really sorry.** Es tut mir wirklich leid. ◊ *I'm sorry, I haven't got any change.* Es tut mir leid, aber ich habe kein Kleingeld. ◊ *I'm sorry I'm late.* Es tut mir leid, dass ich zu spät komme. ◊ *I'm sorry about the noise.* Es tut mir leid wegen des Lärms. ◊ *You'll be sorry!* Das wird dir leidtun!

♦ **Sorry!** Entschuldigung!

♦ **Sorry?** Wie bitte?

♦ **I feel sorry for her.** Sie tut mir leid.

sort NOUN

die Art ◊ *There are different sorts of mushrooms.* Es gibt verschiedene Arten von Pilzen.

♦ **what sort of ... (1)** was für ein ... ◊ *What sort of cake is that?* Was für ein Kuchen ist das? ◊ *What sort of bike have you got?* Was für ein Fahrrad hast du?

♦ **what sort of ... (2)** was für eine ... ◊ *What sort of school do you go to?* In was für eine Schule gehst du?

to **sort out** VERB

[1] (*objects*)

sortieren (PERFECT hat sortiert)

[2] (*problems*)

lösen

so-so ADVERB

so lala (*informal*) ◊ *How are you feeling?* – *So-so.* Wie geht's dir? – So lala.

soul NOUN

[1] die Seele (*spirit*)

[2] der Soul (*music*)

sound NOUN

see also **sound** VERB, ADJECTIVE

[1] (*noise*)

das Geräusch (PL die Geräusche)

♦ **Don't make a sound!** Still!

♦ **I hear the sound of footsteps.** Ich höre Schritte.

[2] die Lautstärke ◊ *Can I turn the sound down?* Kann ich die Lautstärke runterdrehen?

to **sound** VERB

see also **sound** NOUN, ADJECTIVE

klingen (IMPERFECT klang, PERFECT hat geklungen) ◊ *That sounds interesting.* Das klingt interessant.

♦ **It sounds as if she's doing well at school.** Allem Anschein nach ist sie gut in der Schule.

♦ **That sounds like a good idea.** Das scheint eine gute Idee zu sein.

sound ADJECTIVE, ADVERB

see also **sound** NOUN, VERB

gut ◊ *That's sound advice.* Das ist ein guter Rat.

♦ **to be sound asleep** fest schlafen

soundtrack NOUN

der Soundtrack (PL die Soundtracks)

soup NOUN

die Suppe ◊ *vegetable soup* die Gemüsesuppe

sour ADJECTIVE

sauer

south ADJECTIVE, ADVERB

see also **south** NOUN

♦ **the south coast** die Südküste

♦ **a south wind** ein Südwind MASC

nach Süden ◊ *We were travelling south.* Wir sind nach Süden gefahren.

♦ **south of** südlich von ◊ *It's south of London.* Es liegt südlich von London.

south NOUN

see also **south** ADJECTIVE

der Süden ◊ *in the south* im Süden
♦ **in the South of Germany** in Süddeutschland
South Africa NOUN
Südafrika NEUT
♦ **from South Africa** aus Südafrika
♦ **to South Africa** nach Südafrika
South America NOUN
Südamerika NEUT
♦ **from South America** aus Südamerika
♦ **to South America** nach Südamerika
South American NOUN
see also **South American** ADJECTIVE
der Südamerikaner (PL die Südamerikaner)
die Südamerikanerin
South American ADJECTIVE
see also **South American** NOUN
südamerikanisch
southbound ADJECTIVE
in Richtung Süden ◊ *Southbound traffic is moving very slowly.* Der Verkehr in Richtung Süden kommt nur sehr langsam voran.
southeast NOUN
der Südosten
♦ **southeast England** Südostengland NEUT
southern ADJECTIVE
südlich ◊ *the southern part of the island* der südliche Teil der Insel
♦ **Southern England** Südengland NEUT
South Pole NOUN
der Südpol
South Wales NOUN
Südwales NEUT
♦ **to South Wales** nach Südwales
southwest NOUN
der Südwesten
♦ **southwest Germany** Südwestdeutschland NEUT
souvenir NOUN
das Souvenir (PL die Souvenirs) ◊ *a souvenir shop* ein Souvenirgeschäft
soya NOUN
die Soja
soy sauce NOUN
die Sojasoße
space NOUN
[1] der Platz (GEN des Platzes) ◊ *There isn't enough space.* Es ist nicht genug Platz da.
♦ **a parking space** ein Parkplatz
[2] (*outer space*)
der Raum
spacecraft NOUN
das Raumschiff (PL die Raumschiffe)
spade NOUN
der Spaten (PL die Spaten)
♦ **spades** (*in cards*) das Pik ◊ *the ace of spades* das Pikass
Spain NOUN
Spanien NEUT

♦ **from Spain** aus Spanien
♦ **in Spain** in Spanien
♦ **to Spain** nach Spanien
Spaniard NOUN
der Spanier (PL die Spanier)
die Spanierin
spaniel NOUN
der Spaniel (PL die Spaniel)
Spanish ADJECTIVE
see also **Spanish** NOUN
spanisch
♦ **He's Spanish.** Er ist Spanier.
♦ **She's Spanish.** Sie ist Spanierin.
Spanish NOUN
see also **Spanish** ADJECTIVE
das Spanisch (*language*) (GEN des Spanischen)
♦ **the Spanish** die Spanier MASC PL
to **spank** VERB
♦ **to spank somebody** jemandem den Hintern versohlen
spanner NOUN
der Schraubenschlüssel (PL die Schraubenschlüssel)
to **spare** VERB
see also **spare** ADJECTIVE, NOUN
♦ **Can you spare a moment?** Hast du mal einen Moment Zeit?
♦ **I can't spare the time.** Ich habe die Zeit nicht.
♦ **There's no room to spare.** Es ist kein Platz übrig.
♦ **We arrived with time to spare.** Wir waren zu früh da.
*Be careful not to translate **to spare** by sparen.*
spare NOUN
see also **spare** ADJECTIVE, VERB
das Ersatzteil (PL die Ersatzteile)
♦ **I've lost my key. – Have you got a spare?** Ich habe meinen Schlüssel verloren. – Hast du einen Ersatzschlüssel?
spare ADJECTIVE
see also **spare** VERB, NOUN
♦ **spare batteries** die Ersatzbatterien FEM PL
♦ **a spare part** ein Ersatzteil NEUT
♦ **a spare room** ein Gästezimmer NEUT
♦ **spare time** die Freizeit ◊ *What do you do in your spare time?* Was machen Sie in Ihrer Freizeit?
♦ **spare wheel** das Reserverad
sparkling ADJECTIVE
mit Kohlensäure (*water*)
♦ **sparkling wine** der Sekt
sparrow NOUN
der Spatz (GEN des Spatzen, PL die Spatzen)
spat VERB see **spit**
to **speak** VERB
sprechen (PRESENT spricht, IMPERFECT sprach, PERFECT hat gesprochen) ◊ *Do you speak English?* Sprechen Sie Englisch?

S

☞

◆ **to speak to somebody** mit jemandem reden ◊ *Have you spoken to him?* Hast du mit ihm geredet? ◊ *She spoke to him about it.* Sie hat mit ihm darüber geredet.

◆ **spoken German** gesprochenes Deutsch

to **speak up** VERB
lauter sprechen (PRESENT spricht, IMPERFECT sprach, PERFECT hat gesprochen) ◊ *You'll need to speak up, we can't hear you.* Sie müssen etwas lauter sprechen, wir können Sie nicht hören.

speaker NOUN
☐1 (*loudspeaker*)
der Lautsprecher (PL die Lautsprecher)
☐2 (*in debate*)
der Redner (PL die Redner)
die Rednerin

special ADJECTIVE
besondere ◊ *a special occasion* ein besonderer Anlass

specialist NOUN
der Fachmann (PL die Fachleute)
die Fachfrau

speciality NOUN
die Spezialität

to **specialize** VERB
sich spezialisieren (PERFECT hat sich spezialisiert) ◊ *We specialize in skiing equipment.* Wir haben uns auf Skiausrüstung spezialisiert.

specially ADVERB
☐1 besonders ◊ *It can be very cold here, specially in winter.* Es kann hier sehr kalt werden, besonders im Winter.
☐2 speziell ◊ *It's specially designed for teenagers.* Das ist speziell für Teenager gedacht.

◆ **not specially** nicht besonders ◊ *Do you like opera? – Not specially.* Magst du Opern? – Nicht besonders.

species SING NOUN
die Art

specific ADJECTIVE
☐1 speziell (*particular*) ◊ *certain specific issues* gewisse spezielle Fragen
☐2 genau (*precise*) ◊ *Could you be more specific?* Könnten Sie sich etwas genauer ausdrücken?

specifically ADVERB
☐1 extra ◊ *It's specifically designed for teenagers.* Es ist extra für Teenager gedacht.
☐2 genau ◊ *in Britain, or more specifically in England* in Großbritannien, oder genauer gesagt in England ◊ *I specifically said that ...* Ich habe ganz genau gesagt, dass ...

specs PL NOUN
die Brille SING ◊ *a pair of specs* eine Brille

spectacles PL NOUN
die Brille SING ◊ *a pair of spectacles* eine Brille

spectacular ADJECTIVE

spektakulär

spectator NOUN
der Zuschauer (PL die Zuschauer)
die Zuschauerin

speech NOUN
die Rede ◊ *to make a speech* eine Rede halten

speechless ADJECTIVE
sprachlos ◊ *speechless with admiration* sprachlos vor Bewunderung ◊ *I was speechless.* Ich war sprachlos.

speed NOUN
☐1 der Gang (PL die Gänge)
◆ **a three-speed bike** ein Dreigangrad NEUT
☐2 die Geschwindigkeit ◊ *at top speed* mit Höchstgeschwindigkeit
◆ **to speed up** schneller werden

speedboat NOUN
das Schnellboot (PL die Schnellboote)

speeding NOUN
das zu schnelle Fahren ◊ *He was fined for speeding.* Er hat wegen zu schnellen Fahrens einen Strafzettel bekommen.

speed limit NOUN
die Geschwindigkeitsbegrenzung ◊ *to break the speed limit* die Geschwindigkeitsbegrenzung überschreiten

speedometer NOUN
der Tachometer (PL die Tachometer)

to **spell** VERB
see also **spell** NOUN
☐1 (*in writing*)
schreiben (IMPERFECT schrieb, PERFECT hat geschrieben) ◊ *How do you spell that?* Wie schreibt man das?
☐2 (*out loud*)
buchstabieren (PERFECT hat buchstabiert) ◊ *Can you spell that please?* Können Sie das bitte buchstabieren?

◆ **I can't spell.** Ich kann keine Rechtschreibung.

spell NOUN
see also **spell** VERB
◆ **to cast a spell on somebody** jemanden verhexen
◆ **to be under somebody's spell** von jemandem wie verzaubert sein

spelling NOUN
die Rechtschreibung ◊ *My spelling is terrible.* Meine Rechtschreibung ist furchtbar.

◆ **a spelling mistake** ein Rechtschreibfehler MASC

spelt VERB see **spell**

to **spend** VERB
☐1 (*money*)
ausgeben (PRESENT gibt aus, IMPERFECT gab aus, PERFECT hat ausgegeben)
☐2 (*time*)
verbringen (IMPERFECT verbrachte, PERFECT hat verbracht) ◊ *He spent a month in*

Italy. Er verbrachte einen Monat in Italien.

Be careful not to translate **to spend** *by* **spenden.**

spice NOUN
das Gewürz (GEN des Gewürzes, PL die Gewürze)

spicy ADJECTIVE
scharf ◊ *Indian food's much spicier than German food.* Indisches Essen ist viel schärfer als deutsches.

spider NOUN
die Spinne

to **spill** VERB
verschütten (*tip over*) (PERFECT hat verschüttet) ◊ *He spilled his coffee over his trousers.* Er hat den Kaffee auf seine Hose verschüttet.
♦ **to get spilt** verschüttet werden

spinach NOUN
der Spinat

spin drier NOUN
die Schleuder

spine NOUN
das Rückgrat (PL die Rückgrate)

spinster NOUN
die unverheiratete Frau

spire NOUN
der Kirchturm (PL die Kirchtürme)

spirit NOUN
[1] der Mut (*courage*)
[2] die Energie (*energy*)
♦ **to be in good spirits** gut gelaunt sein

spirits PL NOUN
die Spirituosen PL

spiritual ADJECTIVE
geistlich ◊ *the spiritual leader of Tibet* der geistliche Führer Tibets

to **spit** VERB
spucken
♦ **to spit something out** etwas ausspucken
♦ **It's spitting.** Es tröpfelt.

spite NOUN
| see also **spite** VERB |

♦ **in spite of** trotz ◊ *in spite of the bad weather* trotz des schlechten Wetters
♦ **out of spite** aus Gehässigkeit

to **spite** VERB
| see also **spite** NOUN |

ärgern ◊ *He just did it to spite me.* Er tat es nur, um mich zu ärgern.

spiteful ADJECTIVE
[1] gemein (*action*)
[2] gehässig (*person*)

to **splash** VERB
| see also **splash** NOUN |

bespritzen (PERFECT hat bespritzt)
◊ *Careful! Don't splash me!* Vorsicht! Bespritz mich nicht!

splash NOUN
| see also **splash** VERB |

der Platsch ◊ *I heard a splash.* Ich hörte einen Platsch.
♦ **a splash of colour** ein Farbfleck MASC

splendid ADJECTIVE
wunderbar

splint NOUN
die Schiene

splinter NOUN
der Splitter (PL die Splitter)

to **split** VERB
[1] zerteilen (PERFECT hat zerteilt) ◊ *He split the wood with an axe.* Er zerteilte das Holz mit einer Axt.
[2] zerbrechen (PRESENT zerbricht, IMPERFECT zerbrach, PERFECT ist zerbrochen) ◊ *The ship hit a rock and split in two.* Das Schiff lief auf einen Fels auf und zerbrach in zwei Teile.
[3] (*divide up*)
teilen ◊ *They decided to split the profits.* Sie haben beschlossen, den Gewinn zu teilen.
♦ **to split up (1)** (*couple*) sich trennen
♦ **to split up (2)** (*group*) sich auflösen

to **spoil** VERB
[1] verderben (PRESENT verdirbt, IMPERFECT verdarb, PERFECT hat verdorben) ◊ *It spoiled our evening.* Es hat uns den Abend verdorben.
[2] (*child*)
verwöhnen (PERFECT hat verwöhnt)

spoiled ADJECTIVE
verwöhnt ◊ *a spoiled child* ein verwöhntes Kind

spoilsport NOUN
der Spielverderber (PL die Spielverderber)
die Spielverderberin

spoilt ADJECTIVE
verwöhnt ◊ *a spoilt child* ein verwöhntes Kind

spoilt VERB *see* **spoil**

spoke VERB *see* **speak**

spoke NOUN
die Speiche (*of wheel*)

spoken VERB *see* **speak**

spokesman NOUN
der Sprecher (PL die Sprecher)

spokeswoman NOUN
die Sprecherin

sponge NOUN
der Schwamm (PL die Schwämme)
♦ **a sponge bag** ein Kulturbeutel MASC
♦ **a sponge cake** ein Rührkuchen MASC

sponsor NOUN
| see also **sponsor** VERB |

der Sponsor (PL die Sponsoren)
die Sponsorin

to **sponsor** VERB
| see also **sponsor** NOUN |

sponsern ◊ *The festival was sponsored by ...* Das Festival wurde gesponsert

S

☞

von ...

spontaneous ADJECTIVE
spontan

spooky ADJECTIVE
1 gruselig (*eerie*) ◊ *a spooky story* eine gruselige Geschichte
2 komisch (*strange*) ◊ *a spooky coincidence* ein komischer Zufall

spoon NOUN
der Löffel (PL die Löffel) ◊ *a spoon of sugar* ein Löffel Zucker

spoonful NOUN
♦ *a spoonful of soup* ein Löffel Suppe

sport NOUN
der Sport ◊ *What's your favourite sport?* Was ist dein Lieblingssport?
♦ *a sports bag* eine Sporttasche
♦ *a sports car* ein Sportwagen MASC
♦ *a sports jacket* eine Sportjacke
♦ *Go on, be a sport!* Nun komm schon, sei kein Frosch!

sportsman NOUN
der Sportler (PL die Sportler)

sportswear NOUN
die Sportkleidung

sportswoman NOUN
die Sportlerin

sporty ADJECTIVE
sportlich ◊ *I'm not very sporty.* Ich bin nicht besonders sportlich.

spot NOUN
see also **spot** VERB
1 (*mark*)
der Fleck (PL die Flecke) ◊ *There's a spot of blood on your shirt.* Du hast einen Blutfleck auf dem Hemd.
2 (*in pattern*)
der Punkt (PL die Punkte) ◊ *a red dress with white spots* ein rotes Kleid mit weißen Punkten
3 (*pimple*)
der Pickel (PL die Pickel) ◊ *I've got a big spot on my chin.* Ich habe einen großen Pickel am Kinn.
4 (*place*)
der Platz (GEN des Platzes, PL die Plätze) ◊ *It's a lovely spot for a picnic.* Es ist ein herrlicher Platz für ein Picknick.
♦ *on the spot (1)* (*immediately*) sofort ◊ *They gave her the job on the spot.* Sie haben ihr den Job sofort gegeben.
♦ *on the spot (2)* (*at the same place*) an Ort und Stelle ◊ *Luckily they were able to mend the car on the spot.* Zum Glück konnten sie das Auto an Ort und Stelle reparieren.

to **spot** VERB
see also **spot** NOUN
entdecken (PERFECT hat entdeckt) ◊ *I spotted a mistake.* Ich habe einen Fehler entdeckt.

spotless ADJECTIVE
makellos

spotlight NOUN
das Scheinwerferlicht

spotty ADJECTIVE
pickelig (*pimply*)

spouse NOUN
der Ehemann (PL die Ehemänner)
die Ehefrau

to **sprain** VERB
see also **sprain** NOUN
♦ *I've sprained my ankle.* Ich habe mir den Fuß verstaucht.

sprain NOUN
see also **sprain** VERB
die Verstauchung ◊ *It's just a sprain.* Es ist nur eine Verstauchung.

spray NOUN
see also **spray** VERB
das Spray (PL die Sprays) ◊ *hair spray* das Haarspray

to **spray** VERB
see also **spray** NOUN
sprühen ◊ *to spray perfume on one's hand* sich Parfüm auf die Hand sprühen ◊ *Somebody had sprayed graffiti on the wall.* Irgendjemand hatte Graffiti auf die Wand gesprüht.

spread NOUN
see also **spread** VERB
♦ *cheese spread* der Streichkäse
♦ *chocolate spread* der Schokoladenaufstrich

to **spread** VERB
see also **spread** NOUN
1 streichen (IMPERFECT strich, PERFECT hat gestrichen) ◊ *to spread butter on a slice of bread* Butter auf eine Scheibe Brot streichen
2 (*disease, news*)
sich verbreiten (PERFECT hat sich verbreitet) ◊ *The news spread rapidly.* Die Nachricht verbreitete sich schnell.
♦ *to spread out* (*people*) sich verteilen ◊ *The soldiers spread out across the field.* Die Soldaten verteilten sich über das Feld.

spreadsheet NOUN
die Tabellenkalkulation (*computer program*)

spring NOUN
1 (*season*)
der Frühling (PL die Frühlinge) ◊ *in spring* im Frühling
2 (*metal coil*)
die Feder
3 (*water hole*)
die Quelle

spring-cleaning NOUN
der Frühjahrsputz (GEN des Frühjahrsputzes)

springtime NOUN

das Frühjahr (PL die Frühjahre) ◊ *in springtime* im Frühjahr

sprinkler NOUN
der Rasensprenger (for lawn) (PL die Rasensprenger)

sprint NOUN
see also **sprint** VERB
der Sprint (PL die Sprints)
♦ **a hundred-metre sprint** ein Einhundertmeterlauf MASC

to **sprint** VERB
see also **sprint** NOUN
rennen (IMPERFECT rannte, PERFECT ist gerannt) ◊ *She sprinted for the bus.* Sie rannte, um den Bus zu erreichen.

sprinter NOUN
der Sprinter (PL die Sprinter)
die Sprinterin

sprouts PL NOUN
♦ **Brussels sprouts** der Rosenkohl SING

spy NOUN
see also **spy** VERB
der Spion (PL die Spione)
die Spionin

to **spy** VERB
see also **spy** NOUN
♦ **to spy on somebody** jemandem nachspionieren ◊ *She's spying on me.* Sie spioniert mir nach.

spying NOUN
die Spionage

to **squabble** VERB
sich kabbeln ◊ *Stop squabbling!* Hört auf, euch zu kabbeln!

square NOUN
see also **square** ADJECTIVE
[1] das Quadrat (PL die Quadrate) ◊ *a square and a triangle* ein Quadrat und ein Dreieck
[2] der Platz (GEN des Platzes, PL die Plätze) ◊ *the town square* der Rathausplatz

square ADJECTIVE
see also **square** NOUN
♦ **two square metres** zwei Quadratmeter
♦ **It's two metres square.** Es misst zwei mal zwei Meter.

squash NOUN
see also **squash** VERB
das Squash (sport) ◊ *I play squash.* Ich spiele Squash.
♦ **a squash court** ein Squashcourt MASC
♦ **a squash racket** ein Squashschläger MASC
♦ **orange squash** der Orangensaft

to **squash** VERB
see also **squash** NOUN
zerdrücken (PERFECT hat zerdrückt) ◊ *You're squashing me.* Du zerdrückst mich.

to **squeak** VERB
[1] quieksen (mouse, child)
[2] quietschen (creak)

to **squeeze** VERB
[1] pressen (fruit, toothpaste)
[2] drücken (hand, arm) ◊ *to squeeze somebody's arm* jemandem den Arm drücken
♦ **to squeeze into tight jeans** sich in enge Jeans quetschen

to **squint** VERB
see also **squint** NOUN
schielen

squint NOUN
see also **squint** VERB
♦ **He has a squint.** Er schielt.

squirrel NOUN
das Eichhörnchen (PL die Eichhörnchen)

to **stab** VERB
♦ **to stab somebody (1)** (wound) jemanden mit dem Messer verletzen
♦ **to stab somebody (2)** (kill) jemanden erstechen

stable NOUN
see also **stable** ADJECTIVE
der Stall (PL die Ställe)

stable ADJECTIVE
see also **stable** NOUN
stabil ◊ *a stable relationship* eine stabile Beziehung

stack NOUN
der Stapel (PL die Stapel) ◊ *a stack of books* ein Stapel Bücher

stadium NOUN
das Stadion (PL die Stadien)

staff NOUN
[1] die Belegschaft (in company)
[2] die Lehrerschaft (in school)

stage NOUN
[1] (in plays)
die Bühne
[2] (for speeches, lectures)
das Podium (PL die Podien)
♦ **at this stage (1)** an diesem Punkt ◊ *at this stage in the negotiations* an diesem Punkt der Verhandlungen
♦ **at this stage (2)** im Augenblick ◊ *At this stage, it's too early to comment.* Im Augenblick ist es zu früh, etwas dazu zu sagen.
♦ **to do something in stages** etwas in Etappen machen

to **stagger** VERB
taumeln (PERFECT ist getaumelt)

stain NOUN
see also **stain** VERB
der Fleck (PL die Flecke)

to **stain** VERB
see also **stain** NOUN
beflecken (PERFECT hat befleckt)

stainless steel NOUN
der Edelstahl

stain remover NOUN
der Fleckenentferner (PL die Fleckenentferner)

S

stair NOUN
die <u>Stufe</u> (step)
staircase NOUN
die <u>Treppe</u>
stairs PL NOUN
die <u>Treppe</u> SING
stale ADJECTIVE
altbacken (bread)
stalemate NOUN
das <u>Patt</u> (in chess) (PL die Patts)
stall NOUN
der <u>Stand</u> (PL die Stände) ◊ He's got a market stall. Er hat einen Marktstand.
◆ **the stalls** (in cinema, theatre) das Parkett SING
stamina NOUN
das <u>Durchhaltevermögen</u>
stammer NOUN
das <u>Stottern</u>
◆ **He's got a stammer.** Er stottert.
to **stamp** VERB
| see also **stamp** NOUN |
abstempeln (passport) (PERFECT hat abgestempelt)
◆ **to stamp one's foot** mit dem Fuß aufstampfen
stamp NOUN
| see also **stamp** VERB |
1 die <u>Briefmarke</u> ◊ My hobby is stamp collecting. Briefmarkensammeln ist mein Hobby. ◊ a stamp album ein Briefmarkenalbum ◊ a stamp collection eine Briefmarkensammlung
2 (rubber stamp)
der <u>Stempel</u> (PL die Stempel)
stamped ADJECTIVE
◆ **a stamped addressed envelope** ein frankierter und adressierter Rückumschlag
to **stand** VERB
1 (be standing)
stehen (IMPERFECT stand, PERFECT hat gestanden) ◊ He was standing by the door. Er stand an der Tür.
2 (stand up)
aufstehen (PERFECT ist aufgestanden)
3 (tolerate, withstand)
aushalten (PRESENT hält aus, IMPERFECT hielt aus, PERFECT hat ausgehalten) ◊ I can't stand all this noise. Ich halte diesen Lärm nicht aus.
◆ **to stand for (1)** (be short for) stehen für ◊ "BT" stands for "British Telecom". "BT" steht für "British Telecom".
◆ **to stand for (2)** (tolerate) dulden ◊ I won't stand for it! Ich dulde das nicht!
◆ **to stand in for somebody** jemanden vertreten
◆ **to stand out** herausragen
◆ **to stand up** (get up) aufstehen
◆ **to stand up for** eintreten für ◊ Stand up for your rights! Tretet für eure Rechte ein!

standard ADJECTIVE
| see also **standard** NOUN |
normal ◊ the standard procedure die normale Vorgehensweise
◆ **standard German** das Hochdeutsch
◆ **standard equipment** die Standardausrüstung
standard NOUN
| see also **standard** ADJECTIVE |
das <u>Niveau</u> (PL die Niveaus) ◊ The standard is very high. Das Niveau ist sehr hoch.
◆ **the standard of living** der Lebensstandard
◆ **She's got high standards.** Sie hat hohe Ansprüche.
stand-by ticket NOUN
das <u>Stand-by-Ticket</u> (PL die Stand-by-Tickets)
standpoint NOUN
der <u>Standpunkt</u> (PL die Standpunkte)
stands PL NOUN
die <u>Tribüne</u> SING (at sports ground)
stank VERB see **stink**
staple NOUN
| see also **staple** VERB |
die <u>Heftklammer</u>
to **staple** VERB
| see also **staple** NOUN |
zusammenheften (PERFECT hat zusammengeheftet)
stapler NOUN
die <u>Heftmaschine</u>
star NOUN
| see also **star** VERB |
1 (in sky)
der <u>Stern</u> (PL die Sterne)
2 (celebrity)
der <u>Star</u> (PL die Stars)
der Star is also used for women.
◊ She's a TV star. Sie ist ein Fernsehstar.
◆ **the stars** (horoscope) die Sterne
to **star** VERB
| see also **star** NOUN |
die <u>Hauptrolle spielen</u> ◊ The film stars Glenda Jackson. Glenda Jackson spielt in dem Film die Hauptrolle.
◆ **... starring Johnny Depp** ... mit Johnny Depp in der Hauptrolle
to **stare** VERB
◆ **to stare at something** etwas anstarren
stark ADVERB
◆ **stark naked** splitternackt
start NOUN
| see also **start** VERB |
1 der <u>Anfang</u> (PL die Anfänge) ◊ It's not much, but it's a start. Es ist nicht viel, aber es ist immerhin ein Anfang.
◆ **Shall we make a start on the washing-up?** Sollen wir den Abwasch in Angriff nehmen?
2 (of race)

der <u>Start</u> (PL die Starts)

to **start** VERB

> see also **start** NOUN

[1] <u>anfangen</u> (PRESENT fängt an, IMPERFECT fing an, PERFECT hat angefangen) ◊ *What time does it start?* Wann fängt es an?

♦ **to start doing something** anfangen, etwas zu tun ◊ *I started learning German three years ago.* Ich habe vor drei Jahren angefangen, Deutsch zu lernen.

[2] (*organization*)
<u>gründen</u> ◊ *He wants to start his own business.* Er möchte ein eigenes Geschäft gründen.

[3] (*campaign*)
<u>ins Leben rufen</u> (IMPERFECT rief ins Leben, PERFECT hat ins Leben gerufen) ◊ *She started a campaign against drugs.* Sie hat eine Kampagne gegen Drogen ins Leben gerufen.

[4] (*car*)
<u>anlassen</u> (PRESENT lässt an, IMPERFECT ließ an, PERFECT hat angelassen) ◊ *He couldn't start the car.* Er konnte das Auto nicht anlassen.

♦ **The car wouldn't start.** Das Auto ist nicht angesprungen.

♦ **to start off** (*leave*) aufbrechen ◊ *We started off first thing in the morning.* Wir sind frühmorgens aufgebrochen.

starter NOUN
die <u>Vorspeise</u> (*first course*)

to **starve** VERB
<u>verhungern</u> (*die*) (PERFECT ist verhungert) ◊ *People were literally starving.* Die Menschen sind förmlich verhungert.

♦ **I'm starving!** Ich bin am Verhungern!

♦ **They starved us in prison.** Sie ließen uns im Gefängnis hungern.

state NOUN

> see also **state** VERB

[1] der <u>Zustand</u> (PL die Zustände)

♦ **He was in a real state.** (*upset*) Er ist fast durchgedreht.

[2] (*government*)
der <u>Staat</u>

♦ **the States** (*USA*) die Staaten ◊ *in the States* in den Staaten

to **state** VERB

> see also **state** NOUN

[1] (*say*)
<u>erklären</u> (PERFECT hat erklärt) ◊ *He stated his intention to resign.* Er erklärte seine Absicht zurückzutreten.

[2] (*give*)
<u>angeben</u> (PRESENT gibt an, IMPERFECT gab an, PERFECT hat angegeben) ◊ *Please state your name and address.* Geben Sie bitte Ihren Namen und Ihre Adresse an.

stately home NOUN
das <u>Schloss</u> (GEN des Schlosses, PL die Schlösser)

statement NOUN

die <u>Erklärung</u>

station NOUN
(*railway*)
der <u>Bahnhof</u> (PL die Bahnhöfe)

♦ **the bus station** der Busbahnhof

♦ **a police station** eine Polizeiwache

♦ **a radio station** ein Rundfunksender MASC

stationer's NOUN
das <u>Schreibwarengeschäft</u> (PL die Schreibwarengeschäfte)

station wagon NOUN [US]
der <u>Kombiwagen</u> (PL die Kombiwagen)

statue NOUN
die <u>Statue</u>

to **stay** VERB

> see also **stay** NOUN

[1] (*remain*)
<u>bleiben</u> (IMPERFECT blieb, PERFECT ist geblieben) ◊ *Stay here!* Bleiben Sie hier!

♦ **to stay in** (*not go out*) zu Hause bleiben

♦ **to stay up** aufbleiben ◊ *We stayed up till midnight.* Wir sind bis um Mitternacht aufgeblieben.

[2] (*spend the night*)
<u>übernachten</u> (PERFECT hat übernachtet) ◊ *to stay with friends* bei Freunden übernachten

♦ **Where are you staying?** Wo wohnen Sie?

♦ **to stay the night** über Nacht bleiben

♦ **We stayed in Belgium for a few days.** Wir waren ein paar Tage in Belgien.

stay NOUN

> see also **stay** VERB

der <u>Aufenthalt</u> (PL die Aufenthalte) ◊ *my stay in Germany* mein Aufenthalt in Deutschland

steady ADJECTIVE

[1] <u>stetig</u> ◊ *steady progress* stetiger Fortschritt

[2] <u>fest</u> ◊ *a steady job* eine feste Arbeit

[3] <u>ruhig</u> (*voice, hand*)

[4] <u>solide</u> (*person*)

♦ **a steady boyfriend** ein fester Freund

♦ **a steady girlfriend** eine feste Freundin

♦ **Steady on!** Immer mit der Ruhe!

steak NOUN
das <u>Steak</u> (*beef*) (PL die Steaks) ◊ *steak and chips* Steak mit Pommes frites

to **steal** VERB
<u>stehlen</u> (PRESENT stiehlt, IMPERFECT stahl, PERFECT hat gestohlen)

steam NOUN
der <u>Dampf</u> (PL die Dämpfe) ◊ *a steam engine* eine Dampflokomotive

steel NOUN
der <u>Stahl</u> ◊ *a steel door* eine Stahltür

steep ADJECTIVE
<u>steil</u> (*slope*)

steeple NOUN
der <u>Kirchturm</u> (PL die Kirchtürme)

steering wheel NOUN
das <u>Lenkrad</u> (PL die Lenkräder)

S

step NOUN

see also **step** VERB

1 (*pace*)

der <u>Schritt</u> (PL die Schritte) ◊ *He took a step forward.* Er machte einen Schritt nach vorn.

2 (*stair*)

die <u>Stufe</u> ◊ *She tripped over the step.* Sie stolperte über die Stufe.

to **step** VERB

see also **step** NOUN

♦ **to step aside** zur Seite treten ◊ *She stepped aside to let him pass.* Sie trat zur Seite, um ihn vorbeizulassen.

♦ **to step back** zurücktreten

stepbrother NOUN

der <u>Stiefbruder</u> (PL die Stiefbrüder)

stepdaughter NOUN

die <u>Stieftochter</u> (PL die Stieftöchter)

stepfather NOUN

der <u>Stiefvater</u> (PL die Stiefväter)

stepladder NOUN

die <u>Trittleiter</u>

stepmother NOUN

die <u>Stiefmutter</u> (PL die Stiefmütter)

stepsister NOUN

die <u>Stiefschwester</u>

stepson NOUN

der <u>Stiefsohn</u> (PL die Stiefsöhne)

stereo NOUN

die <u>Stereoanlage</u>

sterling ADJECTIVE

♦ **five pounds sterling** fünf britische Pfund

stew NOUN

der <u>Eintopf</u> (PL die Eintöpfe)

steward NOUN

der <u>Steward</u> (PL die Stewards)

stewardess NOUN

die <u>Stewardess</u> (PL die Stewardessen)

stick NOUN

see also **stick** VERB

der <u>Stock</u> (PL die Stöcke)

to **stick** VERB

see also **stick** NOUN

<u>kleben</u> (*with adhesive*)

♦ **I can't stick it any longer.** Ich halte das nicht mehr aus.

to **stick out** VERB

<u>herausstrecken</u> (PERFECT hat herausgestreckt) ◊ *The little girl stuck out her tongue.* Das kleine Mädchen streckte seine Zunge heraus.

sticker NOUN

der <u>Aufkleber</u> (PL die Aufkleber)

stick insect NOUN

die <u>Gespenstheuschrecke</u> (PL die Gespenstheuschrecken)

sticky ADJECTIVE

<u>klebrig</u> ◊ *to have sticky hands* klebrige Hände haben

♦ **a sticky label** ein Aufkleber MASC

stiff ADJECTIVE, ADVERB

<u>steif</u> (*rigid*)

♦ **to have a stiff neck** einen steifen Hals haben

♦ **to feel stiff (1)** steif sein ◊ *I feel stiff after the long journey.* Ich bin nach der langen Reise ganz steif.

♦ **to feel stiff (2)** Muskelkater haben ◊ *I feel stiff after playing football yesterday.* Ich habe gestern Fußball gespielt und habe jetzt Muskelkater.

♦ **to be bored stiff** sich zu Tode langweilen

♦ **to be frozen stiff** total durchgefroren sein

♦ **to be scared stiff** furchtbare Angst haben

still ADVERB

see also **still** ADJECTIVE

1 <u>immer noch</u> ◊ *I still haven't finished.* Ich bin immer noch nicht fertig. ◊ *Are you still in bed?* Bist du immer noch im Bett?

♦ **better still** noch besser

2 <u>trotzdem</u> (*even so*) ◊ *She knows I don't like it, but she still does it.* Sie weiß, dass ich das nicht mag, sie macht es aber trotzdem.

3 <u>immerhin</u> (*after all*) ◊ *Still, it's the thought that counts.* Es war immerhin gut gemeint.

still ADJECTIVE

see also **still** ADVERB

<u>still</u> ◊ *Keep still!* Halt still!

sting NOUN

see also **sting** VERB

der <u>Stich</u> (PL die Stiche) ◊ *a wasp sting* ein Wespenstich

to **sting** VERB

see also **sting** NOUN

<u>stechen</u> (PRESENT sticht, IMPERFECT stach, PERFECT hat gestochen) ◊ *I've been stung.* Ich bin gestochen worden.

stingy ADJECTIVE

<u>geizig</u>

to **stink** VERB

see also **stink** NOUN

<u>stinken</u> (IMPERFECT stank, PERFECT hat gestunken) ◊ *It stinks!* Es stinkt!

stink NOUN

see also **stink** VERB

der <u>Gestank</u>

to **stir** VERB

<u>umrühren</u> (PERFECT hat umgerührt)

to **stitch** VERB

see also **stitch** NOUN

<u>nähen</u> (*cloth*)

stitch NOUN

see also **stitch** VERB

der <u>Stich</u> (PL die Stiche) ◊ *I had five stitches.* Ich wurde mit fünf Stichen genäht.

stock NOUN

see also **stock** VERB

1 (*supply*)

der <u>Vorrat</u> (PL die Vorräte)

2 (*in shop*)

das <u>Lager</u> (PL die Lager) ◊ *in stock* auf
Lager
♦ **out of stock** ausverkauft
[3] die <u>Brühe</u> ◊ *chicken stock* die
Hühnerbrühe

to **stock** VERB
> *see also* **stock** NOUN

<u>führen</u> (*have in stock*) ◊ *Do you stock
camping stoves?* Führen Sie
Campingkocher?
♦ **to stock up** sich eindecken ◊ *We stocked
up with food.* Wir deckten uns mit
Lebensmitteln ein.

stock cube NOUN
der <u>Brühwürfel</u> (PL die Brühwürfel)

stocking NOUN
der <u>Strumpf</u> (PL die Strümpfe)

stole, stolen VERB *see* **steal**

stomach NOUN
[1] der <u>Magen</u> (PL die Mägen) ◊ *on a full
stomach* mit vollem Magen
[2] der <u>Bauch</u> (PL die Bäuche) ◊ *to lie on
one's stomach* auf dem Bauch liegen

stomachache NOUN
♦ **to have a stomachache** Bauchschmerzen
haben

stone NOUN
der <u>Stein</u> (*rock*) (PL die Steine) ◊ *a stone
wall* eine Steinmauer ◊ *a peach stone* ein
Pfirsichstein

> ℹ️ In Germany weight is expressed in
> kilos. A stone is about 6.3 kg.

◊ *I weigh eight stone.* Ich wiege fünfzig
Kilo.

stood VERB *see* **stand**

stool NOUN
der <u>Hocker</u> (PL die Hocker)

to **stop** VERB
> *see also* **stop** NOUN

[1] <u>aufhören</u> (PERFECT hat aufgehört) ◊ *He
stopped crying.* Er hörte auf zu weinen.
◊ *I think the rain's going to stop.* Ich
glaube, es hört auf zu regnen. ◊ *You
should stop smoking.* Du solltest
aufhören zu rauchen.
♦ **to stop somebody doing something**
jemanden daran hindern, etwas zu tun
♦ **Stop it!** Hör auf!
[2] (*bus, train, car*)
<u>halten</u> (PRESENT hält, IMPERFECT hielt, PERFECT
hat gehalten) ◊ *The bus doesn't stop
here.* Der Bus hält hier nicht.
[3] <u>stoppen</u> ◊ *a campaign to stop whaling*
eine Kampagne, um den Walfang zu
stoppen
♦ **Stop!** Halt!

stop NOUN
> *see also* **stop** VERB

die <u>Haltestelle</u> ◊ *a bus stop* eine
Bushaltestelle

♦ **This is my stop.** Ich muss jetzt
aussteigen.

stopwatch NOUN
die <u>Stoppuhr</u>

store NOUN
> *see also* **store** VERB

[1] (*shop*)
das <u>Geschäft</u> (PL die Geschäfte) ◊ *a
furniture store* ein Möbelgeschäft
[2] (*stock, storeroom*)
das <u>Lager</u> (PL die Lager)

to **store** VERB
> *see also* **store** NOUN

[1] <u>lagern</u> ◊ *They store potatoes in the
cellar.* Sie lagern Kartoffeln im Keller.
[2] <u>speichern</u> (*information*)

storey NOUN
der <u>Stock</u> (PL die Stock) ◊ *the first storey*
der erste Stock ◊ *on the first storey* im
ersten Stock
♦ **a three-storey building** ein dreistöckiges
Gebäude

storm NOUN
[1] (*gale*)
der <u>Sturm</u> (PL die Stürme)
[2] (*thunderstorm*)
das <u>Gewitter</u> (PL die Gewitter)

stormy ADJECTIVE
<u>stürmisch</u>

story NOUN
die <u>Geschichte</u>

stove NOUN
[1] (*in kitchen*)
der <u>Herd</u> (PL die Herde)
[2] (*camping stove*)
der <u>Kocher</u> (PL die Kocher)

straight ADJECTIVE
[1] <u>gerade</u> ◊ *a straight line* eine gerade
Linie
[2] <u>glatt</u> ◊ *straight hair* glatte Haare
[3] <u>normal</u> (*heterosexual*)
♦ **straight away** sofort
♦ **straight on** geradeaus

straightforward ADJECTIVE
<u>einfach</u>

strain NOUN
> *see also* **strain** VERB

die <u>Anstrengung</u> (*stress*)
♦ **It was a strain.** Es war anstrengend.

to **strain** VERB
> *see also* **strain** NOUN

<u>sich verrenken</u> (PERFECT hat sich verrenkt)
◊ *I strained my back.* Ich habe mir den
Rücken verrenkt.
♦ **I strained a muscle.** Ich habe mir einen
Muskel gezerrt.

strained ADJECTIVE
♦ **a strained muscle** eine Muskelzerrung

stranded ADJECTIVE
♦ **We were stranded.** Wir saßen fest.

strange ADJECTIVE

S

☞

sonderbar ◊ *That's strange!* Das ist sonderbar!

stranger NOUN
der <u>Fremde</u> (GEN des Fremden, PL die Fremden)
die <u>Fremde</u> (GEN der Fremden) ◊ *a stranger (man)* ein Fremder
♦ **Don't talk to strangers.** Sprich nicht mit fremden Menschen.
♦ **I'm a stranger here.** Ich bin hier fremd.

to **strangle** VERB
<u>erwürgen</u> (PERFECT hat erwürgt)

strap NOUN
1 (*of bag, camera, shoe, suitcase*)
der <u>Riemen</u> (PL die Riemen)
2 (*of bra, dress*)
der <u>Träger</u> (PL die Träger)
3 (*of watch*)
das <u>Armband</u> (PL die Armbänder)

straw NOUN
das <u>Stroh</u>
♦ **That's the last straw!** Jetzt reicht's aber!

strawberry NOUN
die <u>Erdbeere</u> ◊ *strawberry jam* die Erdbeermarmelade

stray NOUN
♦ **a stray cat** eine streunende Katze

stream NOUN
der <u>Bach</u> (PL die Bäche)

street NOUN
die <u>Straße</u> ◊ *in the street* auf der Straße

streetcar NOUN US
die <u>Straßenbahn</u>

streetlamp NOUN
die <u>Straßenlampe</u>

street plan NOUN
der <u>Stadtplan</u> (PL die Stadtpläne)

streetwise ADJECTIVE
<u>gewieft</u> (*informal*)

strength NOUN
die <u>Kraft</u> (PL die Kräfte)

to **stress** VERB
see also **stress** NOUN

<u>betonen</u> (PERFECT hat betont) ◊ *I would like to stress that ...* Ich möchte betonen, dass ...

stress NOUN
see also **stress** VERB

der <u>Stress</u> (GEN des Stresses)

to **stretch** VERB
1 (*person, animal*)
<u>sich strecken</u> ◊ *The dog woke up and stretched.* Der Hund wachte auf und streckte sich.
2 (*get bigger*)
<u>ausleiern</u> (PERFECT ist ausgeleiert) ◊ *My sweater stretched when I washed it.* Mein Pullover ist in der Wäsche ausgeleiert.
3 (*stretch out*)
<u>spannen</u> ◊ *They stretched a rope*

between the trees. Sie spannten ein Seil zwischen den Bäumen.
♦ **to stretch out one's arms** die Arme ausbreiten

stretcher NOUN
die <u>Trage</u>

stretchy ADJECTIVE
<u>elastisch</u>

strict ADJECTIVE
<u>streng</u>

strike NOUN
see also **strike** VERB

der <u>Streik</u> (PL die Streiks)
♦ **to be on strike** streiken
♦ **to go on strike** in den Streik treten

to **strike** VERB
see also **strike** NOUN

1 <u>schlagen</u> (PRESENT schlägt, IMPERFECT schlug, PERFECT hat geschlagen) ◊ *The clock struck three.* Die Uhr schlug drei.
◊ *She struck him across the mouth.* Sie schlug ihm auf den Mund.
2 (*go on strike*)
<u>streiken</u>
♦ **to strike a match** ein Streichholz anzünden

striker NOUN
1 (*person on strike*)
der <u>Streikende</u> (GEN des Streikenden, PL die Streikenden)
die <u>Streikende</u> (GEN der Streikenden)
2 (*footballer*)
der <u>Torschütze</u> (GEN des Torschützen, PL die Torschützen)

striking ADJECTIVE
1 <u>streikend</u> (*on strike*) ◊ *striking miners* die streikenden Bergarbeiter
2 <u>auffällig</u> (*noticeable*) ◊ *a striking difference* ein auffälliger Unterschied

string NOUN
1 die <u>Schnur</u> (PL die Schnüre)
♦ **a piece of string** eine Schnur
2 (*of violin, guitar*)
die <u>Saite</u>

to **strip** VERB
see also **strip** NOUN

<u>sich ausziehen</u> (*get undressed*) (IMPERFECT zog sich aus, PERFECT hat sich ausgezogen)

strip NOUN
see also **strip** VERB

der <u>Streifen</u> (PL die Streifen)
♦ **a strip cartoon** ein Comicstrip MASC

stripe NOUN
der <u>Streifen</u> (PL die Streifen)

striped ADJECTIVE
<u>gestreift</u> ◊ *a striped skirt* ein gestreifter Rock

strip mall NOUN US
die <u>Einkaufsmeile</u>

stripper NOUN
der <u>Stripper</u> (PL die Stripper)
die <u>Stripperin</u>

stripy ADJECTIVE
gestreift ◊ *a stripy shirt* ein gestreiftes Hemd

to **stroke** VERB
see also **stroke** NOUN
streicheln

stroke NOUN
see also **stroke** VERB
der Schlag (PL die Schläge) ◊ *to have a stroke* einen Schlag bekommen

stroll NOUN
♦ **to go for a stroll** einen Spaziergang machen

stroller NOUN US
der Sportwagen (for child) (PL die Sportwagen)

strong ADJECTIVE
stark ◊ *She's very strong.* Sie ist sehr stark. ◊ *Gerry is stronger than Robert.* Gerry ist stärker als Robert.

strongly ADVERB
dringend ◊ *We strongly recommend that ...* Wir empfehlen dringend, dass ...
♦ **He smelt strongly of tobacco.** Er roch stark nach Tabak.
♦ **strongly built** solide gebaut
♦ **I don't feel strongly about it.** Das ist mir ziemlich egal.

struck VERB *see* **strike**

to **struggle** VERB
see also **struggle** NOUN
sich wehren (physically) ◊ *He struggled, but he couldn't escape.* Er wehrte sich, aber er konnte sich nicht befreien.
♦ **to struggle to do something (1)** (fight) kämpfen, um etwas zu tun ◊ *He struggled to get custody of his daughter.* Er kämpfte, um das Sorgerecht für seine Tochter zu bekommen.
♦ **to struggle to do something (2)** (have difficulty) Mühe haben, etwas zu tun ◊ *She struggled to pay her phone bill.* Sie hatte Mühe, ihre Telefonrechnung zu bezahlen.

struggle NOUN
see also **struggle** VERB
der Kampf (for independence, equality) (PL die Kämpfe) ◊ *It was a struggle.* Es war ein Kampf.

stub NOUN
die Kippe (of cigarette)

stubborn ADJECTIVE
stur

to **stub out** VERB
ausdrücken (PERFECT hat ausgedrückt) ◊ *He stubbed out the cigarette.* Er drückte die Zigarette aus.

stuck VERB *see* **stick**

stuck ADJECTIVE
♦ **It's stuck.** Es klemmt.

♦ **to get stuck** stecken bleiben ◊ *We got stuck in a traffic jam.* Wir sind im Stau stecken geblieben.

stuck-up ADJECTIVE
hochnäsig (informal)

stud NOUN
1 (earring)
der Ohrstecker (PL die Ohrstecker)
2 (on football boots)
der Stollen (PL die Stollen)

student NOUN
der Student (GEN des Studenten, PL die Studenten)
die Studentin

studio NOUN
das Studio (PL die Studios) ◊ *a TV studio* ein Fernsehstudio
♦ **a studio flat** eine Einzimmerwohnung

to **study** VERB
1 (at university)
studieren (PERFECT hat studiert) ◊ *I plan to study biology.* Ich habe vor, Biologie zu studieren.
2 (do homework)
lernen ◊ *I've got to study tonight.* Ich muss heute Abend lernen.

stuff NOUN
1 die Sachen FEM PL (things) ◊ *There's some stuff on the table for you.* Auf dem Tisch stehen Sachen für dich.
2 das Zeug (possessions) ◊ *Have you got all your stuff?* Hast du all dein Zeug?

stuffy ADJECTIVE
stickig (room) ◊ *It's really stuffy in here.* Hier drin ist es wirklich stickig.

to **stumble** VERB
stolpern (PERFECT ist gestolpert)

stung VERB *see* **sting**

stunk VERB *see* **stink**

stunned ADJECTIVE
sprachlos (amazed) ◊ *I was stunned.* Ich war sprachlos.

stunning ADJECTIVE
umwerfend

stunt NOUN
der Stunt (in film) (PL die Stunts)

stuntman NOUN
der Stuntman (PL die Stuntmen)

stupid ADJECTIVE
blöd ◊ *a stupid joke* ein blöder Witz
♦ **Me, go jogging? Don't be stupid!** Ich und joggen? Du spinnst wohl!

to **stutter** VERB
see also **stutter** NOUN
stottern

stutter NOUN
see also **stutter** VERB
♦ **He's got a stutter.** Er stottert.

style NOUN
der Stil (PL die Stile) ◊ *That's not his style.* Das ist nicht sein Stil.

subject NOUN

S

1 das Thema (PL die Themen) ◇ *The subject of my project was the Internet.* Das Thema meines Referats war das Internet.
2 (*at school*)
das Fach (PL die Fächer) ◇ *What's your favourite subject?* Was ist dein Lieblingsfach?

subjunctive NOUN
der Konjunktiv

submarine NOUN
das U-Boot (PL die U-Boote)

subscription NOUN
das Abonnement (*to paper, magazine*) (PL die Abonnements)
♦ **to take out a subscription to something** etwas abonnieren

subsequently ADVERB
später

to **subsidize** VERB
subventionieren (PERFECT hat subventioniert)

subsidy NOUN
die Subvention

substance NOUN
die Substanz

substitute NOUN
see also **substitute** VERB
(*player*)
der Ersatzspieler (PL die Ersatzspieler)
die Ersatzspielerin

to **substitute** VERB
see also **substitute** NOUN
ersetzen (PERFECT hat ersetzt) ◇ *to substitute wine for beer* Bier durch Wein ersetzen

subtitled ADJECTIVE
mit Untertiteln

subtitles PL NOUN
die Untertitel MASC PL ◇ *an English film with German subtitles* ein englischer Film mit deutschen Untertiteln

subtle ADJECTIVE
fein ◇ *a subtle difference* ein feiner Unterschied

to **subtract** VERB
abziehen (IMPERFECT zog ab, PERFECT hat abgezogen) ◇ *to subtract three from five* drei von fünf abziehen

suburb NOUN
die Vorstadt (PL die Vorstädte) ◇ *a suburb of Berlin* eine Vorstadt von Berlin ◇ *They live in the suburbs.* Sie wohnen in der Vorstadt.

suburban ADJECTIVE
♦ **a suburban train** eine S-Bahn

subway NOUN
1 die Unterführung (*underpass*)
2 die U-Bahn (*underground*)

to **succeed** VERB
Erfolg haben (PRESENT hat Erfolg, IMPERFECT hatte Erfolg, PERFECT hat Erfolg gehabt)

◇ *He succeeded in his plan.* Er hatte mit seinem Plan Erfolg.
♦ **I succeeded in convincing him.** Es ist mir gelungen, ihn zu überzeugen.

success NOUN
der Erfolg (PL die Erfolge) ◇ *The play was a great success.* Das Stück war ein großer Erfolg.

successful ADJECTIVE
erfolgreich ◇ *a successful attempt* ein erfolgreicher Versuch ◇ *He's a successful businessman.* Er ist ein erfolgreicher Geschäftsmann.
♦ **to be successful in doing something** etwas mit Erfolg tun

successfully ADVERB
mit Erfolg

successive ADJECTIVE
♦ **on four successive occasions** viermal hintereinander

such ADJECTIVE, ADVERB
so ◇ *such nice people* so nette Leute ◇ *such a long journey* eine so lange Reise
♦ **such a lot of (1)** (*so much*) so viel ◇ *such a lot of work* so viel Arbeit
♦ **such a lot of (2)** (*so many*) so viele ◇ *such a lot of mistakes* so viele Fehler
♦ **such as** (*like*) wie zum Beispiel ◇ *hot countries, such as India* heiße Länder, wie zum Beispiel Indien
♦ **not as such** nicht eigentlich ◇ *He's not an expert as such, but ...* Er ist nicht eigentlich ein Experte, aber ...
♦ **There's no such thing.** So was gibt es nicht. ◇ *There's no such thing as the yeti.* So was wie den Yeti gibt es nicht.

such-and-such ADJECTIVE
der und der ◇ *such-and-such a place* der und der Ort
die und die
◇ *such-and-such a time* die und die Zeit
das und das
◇ *such-and-such a problem* das und das Problem

to **suck** VERB
lutschen (*sweets*) ◇ *to suck one's thumb* am Daumen lutschen

sudden ADJECTIVE
plötzlich ◇ *a sudden change* eine plötzliche Änderung
♦ **all of a sudden** plötzlich

suddenly ADVERB
plötzlich ◇ *Suddenly, the door opened.* Plötzlich ging die Tür auf.

suede NOUN
das Wildleder ◇ *a suede jacket* eine Wildlederjacke

to **suffer** VERB
leiden (IMPERFECT litt, PERFECT hat gelitten) ◇ *She was really suffering.* Sie hat wirklich gelitten.

♦ **to suffer from a disease** an einer Krankheit leiden

to **suffocate** VERB
ersticken (PERFECT ist erstickt)

sugar NOUN
der Zucker (PL die Zucker)

to **suggest** VERB
vorschlagen (PRESENT schlägt vor, IMPERFECT schlug vor, PERFECT hat vorgeschlagen) ◊ *I suggested they set off early.* Ich habe vorgeschlagen, dass sie früh aufbrechen sollen.

suggestion NOUN
der Vorschlag (PL die Vorschläge)

suicide NOUN
der Selbstmord (PL die Selbstmorde)
◊ *to commit suicide* Selbstmord begehen

suicide bomber NOUN
der Selbstmordattentäter (PL die Selbstmordattentäter)
die Selbstmordattentäterin

suicide bombing NOUN
das Selbstmordattentat (PL die Selbstmordattentate)

suit NOUN
see also **suit** VERB
1 (*man's*)
der Anzug (PL die Anzüge)
2 (*woman's*)
das Kostüm (PL die Kostüme)

to **suit** VERB
see also **suit** NOUN
1 (*be convenient for*)
passen ◊ *What time would suit you?* Welche Zeit würde Ihnen passen? ◊ *That suits me fine.* Das passt mir gut.
♦ **Suit yourself!** Wie du willst!
2 (*look good on*)
stehen (IMPERFECT stand, PERFECT hat gestanden) ◊ *That dress really suits you.* Das Kleid steht dir wirklich.

suitable ADJECTIVE
1 passend ◊ *a suitable time* eine passende Zeit
2 angemessen (*clothes*) ◊ *suitable clothing* angemessene Kleidung

suitcase NOUN
der Koffer (PL die Koffer)

suite NOUN
die Suite (*of rooms*)
♦ **a bedroom suite** eine Schlafzimmereinrichtung

to **sulk** VERB
schmollen

sulky ADJECTIVE
beleidigt

sultana NOUN
die Sultanine

sum NOUN
1 das Rechnen (*calculation*)
♦ **She's good at sums.** Sie kann gut rechnen.

2 die Summe (*amount*) ◊ *a sum of money* eine Geldsumme

to **sum up** VERB
zusammenfassen (PERFECT hat zusammengefasst)

to **summarize** VERB
zusammenfassen (PERFECT hat zusammengefasst)

summary NOUN
die Zusammenfassung

summer NOUN
der Sommer (PL die Sommer) ◊ *in summer* im Sommer
♦ **summer clothes** die Sommerkleidung SING
♦ **the summer holidays** die Sommerferien

summertime NOUN
der Sommer (PL die Sommer) ◊ *in summertime* im Sommer

summit NOUN
der Gipfel (PL die Gipfel)

sun NOUN
die Sonne ◊ *in the sun* in der Sonne

to **sunbathe** VERB
sonnenbaden (PERFECT hat sonnengebadet)

sunblock NOUN
das Sonnenschutzmittel (PL die Sonnenschutzmittel)

sunburn NOUN
der Sonnenbrand (PL die Sonnenbrände)

sunburnt ADJECTIVE
♦ **I got sunburnt.** Ich habe einen Sonnenbrand bekommen.

Sunday NOUN
der Sonntag (PL die Sonntage) ◊ *every Sunday* jeden Sonntag ◊ *last Sunday* letzten Sonntag ◊ *next Sunday* nächsten Sonntag ◊ *on Sunday* am Sonntag
♦ **on Sundays** sonntags

Sunday school NOUN
die Sonntagsschule

sunflower NOUN
die Sonnenblume

sung VERB see **sing**

sunglasses PL NOUN
die Sonnenbrille SING ◊ *a pair of sunglasses* eine Sonnenbrille

sunk VERB see **sink**

sunlight NOUN
das Sonnenlicht

sunny ADJECTIVE
sonnig ◊ *a sunny morning* ein sonniger Morgen
♦ **It's sunny.** Die Sonne scheint.

sunrise NOUN
der Sonnenaufgang (PL die Sonnenaufgänge)

sunroof NOUN
das Schiebedach (PL die Schiebedächer)

sunscreen NOUN
die Sonnenschutzcreme (PL die Sonnenschutzcremes)

S

sunset NOUN
der Sonnenuntergang (PL die Sonnenuntergänge)

sunshine NOUN
der Sonnenschein

sunstroke NOUN
der Hitzschlag (PL die Hitzschläge) ◊ *to get sunstroke* einen Hitzschlag bekommen

suntan NOUN
◆ **to have a suntan** braun sein
◆ **suntan lotion** die Sonnenmilch
◆ **suntan oil** das Sonnenöl

super ADJECTIVE
klasse

klasse is invariable.

◊ *a super film* ein klasse Film

superb ADJECTIVE
großartig

supermarket NOUN
der Supermarkt (PL die Supermärkte)

supernatural ADJECTIVE
übernatürlich

superstitious ADJECTIVE
abergläubisch

to **supervise** VERB
beaufsichtigen (PERFECT hat beaufsichtigt)

supervisor NOUN
[1] (*in factory*)
der Vorarbeiter (PL die Vorarbeiter)
die Vorarbeiterin
[2] (*in department store*)
der Abteilungsleiter (PL die Abteilungsleiter)
die Abteilungsleiterin

supper NOUN
das Abendessen (PL die Abendessen)

supplement NOUN
[1] (*of newspaper, magazine*)
die Beilage
[2] (*money*)
der Zuschlag (PL die Zuschläge)

supplies PL NOUN
die Vorräte MASC PL (*food*)

to **supply** VERB
see also **supply** NOUN
[1] liefern (*goods, material*) ◊ *The farm supplied us with food.* Der Bauernhof lieferte uns die Lebensmittel.
[2] stellen (*put at somebody's disposal*) ◊ *The centre supplied them with all the necessary equipment.* Das Zentrum hat ihnen die ganze notwendige Ausrüstung gestellt.

supply NOUN
see also **supply** VERB
der Vorrat (PL die Vorräte) ◊ *a supply of paper* ein Papiervorrat
◆ **the water supply** (*to town*) die Wasserversorgung

supply teacher NOUN
der Aushilfslehrer (PL die Aushilfslehrer)
die Aushilfslehrerin

to **support** VERB
see also **support** NOUN
[1] unterstützen (PERFECT hat unterstützt) ◊ *My mum has always supported me.* Meine Mutti hat mich immer unterstützt.
◆ **What team do you support?** Für welche Mannschaft bist du?
[2] (*financially*)
sorgen für ◊ *She had to support five children on her own.* Sie musste allein für ihre fünf Kinder sorgen.

support NOUN
see also **support** VERB
die Unterstützung (*backing*)

supporter NOUN
[1] der Fan (PL die Fans)

der Fan is also used for women.

◊ *a Liverpool supporter* ein Liverpool-Fan
[2] der Anhänger (PL die Anhänger)
die Anhängerin
◊ *She's a supporter of the Labour Party.* Sie ist Anhängerin der Labour-Party.

to **suppose** VERB
annehmen (PRESENT nimmt an, IMPERFECT nahm an, PERFECT hat angenommen) ◊ *I suppose he's late.* Ich nehme an, er kommt zu spät. ◊ *Suppose you won the lottery.* Nimm mal an, du gewinnst im Lotto. ◊ *I suppose so.* Das nehme ich an.
◆ **to be supposed to do something** etwas tun sollen ◊ *You're supposed to go straight home after school.* Du solltest nach der Schule sofort nach Hause gehen.
◆ **You're supposed to show your passport.** Sie müssen Ihren Pass zeigen.

supposing CONJUNCTION
angenommen ◊ *Supposing you won the lottery ...* Angenommen, du gewinnst im Lotto ...

surcharge NOUN
der Zuschlag (PL die Zuschläge)

sure ADJECTIVE
sicher ◊ *Are you sure?* Bist du sicher?
◆ **Sure!** Klar!
◆ **to make sure that ...** sich vergewissern, dass ... ◊ *I'm going to make sure the door's locked.* Ich werde mich vergewissern, dass die Tür abgeschlossen ist.

surely ADVERB
sicherlich ◊ *Surely you've been to London?* Du warst doch sicherlich schon in London? ◊ *The shops are closed on Sundays, surely?* Die Geschäfte sind sonntags doch sicherlich zu, oder?

surf NOUN
see also **surf** VERB
die Brandung

to **surf** VERB
see also **surf** NOUN

surfen (PERFECT hat gesurft)
♦ **to surf the Net** im Internet surfen
surface NOUN
die Oberfläche
surfboard NOUN
das Surfbrett (PL die Surfbretter)
surfing NOUN
das Surfen
♦ **to go surfing** surfen gehen
surgeon NOUN
der Chirurg (GEN des Chirurgen, PL die Chirurgen)
die Chirurgin
◊ *She's a surgeon.* Sie ist Chirurgin.
surgery NOUN
die Arztpraxis (*doctor's surgery*) (PL die Arztpraxen)
♦ **surgery hours** die Sprechstunden
surname NOUN
der Nachname (GEN des Nachnamens, PL die Nachnamen)
surprise NOUN
die Überraschung
surprised ADJECTIVE
überrascht ◊ *I was surprised to see him.* Ich war überrascht, ihn zu sehen.
surprising ADJECTIVE
überraschend
to **surrender** VERB
sich ergeben (PRESENT ergibt sich, IMPERFECT ergab sich, PERFECT hat sich ergeben)
surrogate mother NOUN
die Leihmutter (PL die Leihmütter)
to **surround** VERB
umstellen (PERFECT hat umstellt) ◊ *The police surrounded the house.* Die Polizei hat das Haus umstellt. ◊ *You're surrounded!* Sie sind umstellt!
♦ **surrounded by** umgeben von ◊ *The house is surrounded by trees.* Das Haus ist von Bäumen umgeben.
surroundings PL NOUN
die Umgebung SING ◊ *a hotel in beautiful surroundings* ein Hotel in wunderschöner Umgebung
survey NOUN
die Umfrage (*research*)
surveyor NOUN
[1] (*of buildings*)
der Gebäudesachverständige (GEN des Gebäudesachverständigen, PL die Gebäudesachverständigen)
die Gebäudesachverständige (GEN der Gebäudesachverständigen) ◊ *a surveyor (man)* ein Gebäudesachverständiger
[2] (*of land*)
der Landvermesser (PL die Landvermesser)
die Landvermesserin
to **survive** VERB
überleben (PERFECT hat überlebt)
survivor NOUN

der Überlebende (GEN des Überlebenden, PL die Überlebenden)
die Überlebende (GEN der Überlebenden)
◊ *There were no survivors.* Es gab keine Überlebenden.
to **suspect** VERB
see also **suspect** NOUN
verdächtigen (PERFECT hat verdächtigt)
suspect NOUN
see also **suspect** VERB
der Verdächtige (GEN des Verdächtigen, PL die Verdächtigen)
die Verdächtige (GEN der Verdächtigen)
◊ *a suspect (man)* ein Verdächtiger
to **suspend** VERB
[1] (*from school*)
verweisen (IMPERFECT verwies, PERFECT hat verwiesen) ◊ *He was suspended.* Er wurde von der Schule verwiesen.
[2] (*from team*)
sperren
[3] (*from job*)
suspendieren (PERFECT hat suspendiert)
suspender NOUN US
[1] (*for stockings*)
der Strumpfhalter (PL die Strumpfhalter)
♦ **suspenders** (*braces*) US
[2] die Hosenträger MASC PL
suspense NOUN
[1] die Ungewissheit (*waiting*) ◊ *The suspense was terrible.* Die Ungewissheit war furchtbar.
[2] die Spannung (*in story*)
♦ **a film with lots of suspense** ein sehr spannender Film
suspension NOUN
[1] (*from school*)
der Ausschluss (GEN des Ausschlusses, PL die Ausschlüsse)
[2] (*from team*)
die Sperre
[3] (*from job*)
die Suspendierung
suspicious ADJECTIVE
[1] argwöhnisch ◊ *He was suspicious at first.* Zuerst war er argwöhnisch.
[2] verdächtig (*suspicious-looking*) ◊ *a suspicious person* eine verdächtige Person
to **swallow** VERB
schlucken
swam VERB *see* **swim**
swan NOUN
der Schwan (PL die Schwäne)
to **swap** VERB
tauschen ◊ *Do you want to swap?* Willst du tauschen?
♦ **to swap a stamp for a coin** eine Briefmarke für eine Münze eintauschen
to **swat** VERB
totschlagen (PRESENT schlägt tot, IMPERFECT schlug tot, PERFECT hat totgeschlagen)
to **sway** VERB

S

☞

schwanken

to **swear** VERB
1 (*make an oath*)
schwören (IMPERFECT schwor, PERFECT hat geschworen)
2 (*curse*)
fluchen

swearword NOUN
der Kraftausdruck (PL die Kraftausdrücke)

sweat NOUN
| see also **sweat** VERB |
der Schweiß (GEN des Schweißes)

to **sweat** VERB
| see also **sweat** NOUN |
schwitzen

sweater NOUN
der Pullover (PL die Pullover)

sweaty ADJECTIVE
1 verschwitzt (*person, face*) ◊ *I'm all sweaty.* Ich bin ganz verschwitzt.
2 feucht (*hands*)

Swede NOUN
(*person*)
der Schwede (GEN des Schweden, PL die Schweden)
die Schwedin

swede NOUN
die Steckrübe (*vegetable*)

Sweden NOUN
Schweden NEUT
♦ **from Sweden** aus Schweden
♦ **to Sweden** nach Schweden

Swedish ADJECTIVE
| see also **Swedish** NOUN |
schwedisch
♦ **He's Swedish.** Er ist Schwede.
♦ **She's Swedish.** Sie ist Schwedin.

Swedish NOUN
| see also **Swedish** ADJECTIVE |
das Schwedisch (*language*) (GEN des Schwedischen)

to **sweep** VERB
fegen ◊ *to sweep the floor* den Boden fegen

sweet NOUN
| see also **sweet** ADJECTIVE |
1 (*candy*)
das Bonbon (PL die Bonbons) ◊ *a bag of sweets* eine Tüte Bonbons
2 (*pudding*)
der Nachtisch ◊ *What sweet did you have?* Was für einen Nachtisch hattest du?

sweet ADJECTIVE
| see also **sweet** NOUN |
1 süß ◊ *Isn't she sweet?* Ist sie nicht süß?
2 nett (*kind*) ◊ *That was really sweet of you.* Das war wirklich nett von dir.
♦ **sweet and sour pork** Schweinefleisch süß-sauer

sweetcorn NOUN
der Mais

sweltering ADJECTIVE
♦ **It was sweltering.** Es war eine Bruthitze.

swept VERB *see* **sweep**

to **swerve** VERB
ausscheren (PERFECT ist ausgeschert) ◊ *He swerved to avoid the cyclist.* Er scherte aus, um dem Fahrradfahrer auszuweichen.

swim NOUN
| see also **swim** VERB |
♦ **to go for a swim** schwimmen gehen

to **swim** VERB
| see also **swim** NOUN |
schwimmen (IMPERFECT schwamm, PERFECT ist geschwommen) ◊ *Can you swim?* Kannst du schwimmen? ◊ *She swam across the river.* Sie schwamm über den Fluss.

swimmer NOUN
der Schwimmer (PL die Schwimmer)
die Schwimmerin
◊ *She's a good swimmer.* Sie ist eine gute Schwimmerin.

swimming NOUN
das Schwimmen
♦ **to go swimming** schwimmen gehen
♦ **Do you like swimming?** Schwimmst du gern?
♦ **a swimming cap** eine Bademütze
♦ **a swimming costume** ein Badeanzug MASC
♦ **a swimming pool** ein Schwimmbad NEUT
♦ **swimming trunks** die Badehose SING ◊ *a pair of swimming trunks* eine Badehose

swimsuit NOUN
der Badeanzug (PL die Badeanzüge)

swing NOUN
| see also **swing** VERB |
die Schaukel (*in playground, garden*)

to **swing** VERB
| see also **swing** NOUN |
schaukeln

Swiss ADJECTIVE
| see also **Swiss** NOUN |
Schweizer ◊ *I like Swiss cheese.* Ich mag Schweizer Käse.
♦ **Andreas is Swiss.** Andreas ist Schweizer.
♦ **Claudie is Swiss.** Claudie ist Schweizerin.

Swiss NOUN
| see also **Swiss** ADJECTIVE |
(*person*)
der Schweizer (PL die Schweizer)
die Schweizerin
♦ **the Swiss** die Schweizer

switch NOUN
| see also **switch** VERB |
der Schalter (*for light, radio etc*) (PL die Schalter)

to **switch** VERB

see also **switch** NOUN

tauschen ◊ *to switch A for B* A gegen B tauschen

to **switch off** VERB
ausschalten (PERFECT hat ausgeschaltet)

to **switch on** VERB
anschalten (PERFECT hat angeschaltet)

Switzerland NOUN
die Schweiz (GEN der Schweiz)

Note that the definite article is used in German for countries which are feminine.

♦ **from Switzerland** aus der Schweiz
♦ **in Switzerland** in der Schweiz
♦ **to Switzerland** in die Schweiz

swollen ADJECTIVE
geschwollen (*arm, leg*)

to **swop** VERB
tauschen ◊ *Do you want to swop?* Willst du tauschen?
♦ **to swop a stamp for a coin** eine Briefmarke für eine Münze eintauschen

sword NOUN
das Schwert (PL die Schwerter)

swore VERB *see* **swear**

sworn VERB *see* **swear**

to **swot** VERB

see also **swot** NOUN

pauken (*informal*) ◊ *I'll have to swot for the maths exam.* Ich muss für die Matheprüfung pauken.

swot NOUN

see also **swot** VERB

der Streber (PL die Streber) (*informal*)
die Streberin

swum VERB *see* **swim**

swung VERB *see* **swing**

syllabus NOUN
der Lehrplan (PL die Lehrpläne) ◊ *on the syllabus* auf dem Lehrplan

symbol NOUN
das Symbol (PL die Symbole)

sympathetic ADJECTIVE
verständnisvoll

Be careful not to translate **sympathetic** *by* **sympathisch**.

to **sympathize** VERB
♦ **to sympathize with somebody** (*pity*) Mitgefühl mit jemandem haben

sympathy NOUN
das Mitleid

symptom NOUN
das Symptom

syringe NOUN
die Spritze

system NOUN
das System (PL die Systeme)

S

T

table NOUN
der Tisch (PL die Tische) ◊ *to lay the table* den Tisch decken

tablecloth NOUN
die Tischdecke

tablespoon NOUN
der Esslöffel (PL die Esslöffel) ◊ *a tablespoon of sugar* ein Esslöffel Zucker

tablespoonful NOUN
♦**a tablespoonful of sugar** ein Esslöffel Zucker

tablet NOUN
die Tablette

table tennis NOUN
das Tischtennis (GEN des Tischtennis) ◊ *to play table tennis* Tischtennis spielen

tabloid NOUN
das Boulevardblatt (PL die Boulevardblätter)

tackle NOUN
~~see also **tackle** VERB~~
der Angriff (*in sport*) (PL die Angriffe)
♦**fishing tackle** das Angelzeug

to **tackle** VERB
~~see also **tackle** NOUN~~
angreifen (*in sport*) (IMPERFECT griff an, PERFECT hat angegriffen)
♦**to tackle a problem** ein Problem angehen

tact NOUN
der Takt

tactful ADJECTIVE
taktvoll

tactics PL NOUN
die Taktik SING

tactless ADJECTIVE
taktlos

tadpole NOUN
die Kaulquappe

tag NOUN
das Etikett (*label*) (PL die Etiketts)

tail NOUN
der Schwanz (GEN des Schwanzes, PL die Schwänze)
♦**Heads or tails?** Kopf oder Zahl?

tailor NOUN
der Schneider (PL die Schneider)
die Schneiderin
◊ *He's a tailor.* Er ist Schneider.

to **take** VERB
[1] nehmen (PRESENT nimmt, IMPERFECT nahm, PERFECT hat genommen) ◊ *He took a plate from the cupboard.* Er nahm einen Teller aus dem Schrank. ◊ *We took a taxi.* Wir haben ein Taxi genommen.

[2] (*take along*)
mitnehmen (PRESENT nimmt mit, IMPERFECT nahm mit, PERFECT hat mitgenommen)
◊ *Are you taking your new camera?* Nimmst du deinen neuen Fotoapparat mit? ◊ *Don't take anything valuable with you.* Nehmen Sie nichts Wertvolles mit. ◊ *He goes to London every week, but he never takes me.* Er fährt jede Woche nach London, aber er nimmt mich nie mit. ◊ *Do you take your exercise books home?* Nehmt ihr eure Hefte mit nach Hause?

[3] (*to a certain place*)
bringen (IMPERFECT brachte, PERFECT hat gebracht) ◊ *She always takes her son to school.* Sie bringt ihren Sohn immer zur Schule. ◊ *I'm going to take my coat to the cleaner's.* Ich bringe meinen Mantel in die Reinigung.

[4] (*require*)
brauchen ◊ *She always takes hours to get ready.* Sie braucht immer Stunden, bis sie fertig ist. ◊ *It takes five people to do this job.* Für diese Arbeit braucht man fünf Leute. ◊ *That takes a lot of courage.* Dazu braucht man viel Mut.
♦**It takes a lot of money to do that.** Das kostet viel Geld.

[5] (*last*)
dauern ◊ *The journey took three hours.* Die Fahrt dauerte drei Stunden. ◊ *It won't take long.* Das dauert nicht lange.

[6] (*tolerate*)
ertragen (PRESENT erträgt, IMPERFECT ertrug, PERFECT hat ertragen) ◊ *He can't take being criticized.* Er kann es nicht ertragen, kritisiert zu werden.

[7] (*exam, test, subject*)
machen ◊ *Have you taken your driving test yet?* Hast du deine Fahrprüfung schon gemacht? ◊ *I decided to take German instead of French.* Ich habe beschlossen, Deutsch statt Französisch zu machen.

to **take after** VERB
nachschlagen (PRESENT schlägt nach, IMPERFECT schlug nach, PERFECT hat nachgeschlagen) ◊ *She takes after her mother.* Sie schlägt ihrer Mutter nach.

to **take apart** VERB
♦**to take something apart** etwas auseinandernehmen

to **take away** VERB
[1] (*object*)
wegnehmen (PRESENT nimmt weg, IMPERFECT nahm weg, PERFECT hat weggenommen)
[2] (*person*)

wegbringen (IMPERFECT brachte weg, PERFECT hat weggebracht)
♦ **hot meals to take away** warme Mahlzeiten zum Mitnehmen

to **take back** VERB
zurückbringen (IMPERFECT brachte zurück, PERFECT hat zurückgebracht) ◊ *I took it back to the shop.* Ich habe es in den Laden zurückgebracht.
♦ **I take it all back!** Ich nehme alles zurück!

to **take down** VERB
herunternehmen (PRESENT nimmt herunter, IMPERFECT nahm herunter, PERFECT hat heruntergenommen) ◊ *She took down the painting.* Sie nahm das Gemälde herunter.

to **take in** VERB
verstehen (*understand*) (IMPERFECT verstand, PERFECT hat verstanden) ◊ *I didn't really take it in.* Ich habe das nicht richtig verstanden.

to **take off** VERB
1 (*plane*)
abfliegen (IMPERFECT flog ab, PERFECT ist abgeflogen) ◊ *The plane took off twenty minutes late.* Das Flugzeug ist mit zwanzig Minuten Verspätung abgeflogen.
2 (*clothes*)
ausziehen (IMPERFECT zog aus, PERFECT hat ausgezogen) ◊ *Take your coat off.* Zieh den Mantel aus.

to **take out** VERB
herausnehmen (*from container, pocket*) (PRESENT nimmt heraus, IMPERFECT nahm heraus, PERFECT hat herausgenommen)
♦ **He took her out to the theatre.** Er führte sie ins Theater aus.

to **take over** VERB
übernehmen (PRESENT übernimmt, IMPERFECT übernahm, PERFECT hat übernommen) ◊ *I'll take over now.* Ich übernehme jetzt.
♦ **to take over from somebody** jemanden ablösen ◊ *Mr Jones has taken over from Mr Smith as headteacher.* Herr Jones hat Herrn Smith als Direktor abgelöst.

takeaway NOUN
1 (*meal*)
das Essen zum Mitnehmen (PL die Essen zum Mitnehmen)
2 (*shop*)
die Imbissstube ◊ *a Chinese takeaway* eine chinesische Imbissstube

takeoff NOUN
der Abflug (*of plane*) (PL die Abflüge)

talcum powder NOUN
der Puder (PL die Puder)

tale NOUN
die Geschichte (*story*)

talent NOUN

das Talent (PL die Talente) ◊ *She's got lots of talent.* Sie hat sehr viel Talent.
♦ **to have a talent for something** eine Begabung für etwas haben
♦ **He's got a real talent for languages.** Er ist wirklich sprachbegabt.

talented ADJECTIVE
begabt

talk NOUN
see also **talk** VERB
1 (*speech*)
der Vortrag (PL die Vorträge) ◊ *She gave a talk on rock climbing.* Sie hielt einen Vortrag über das Klettern.
2 (*conversation*)
das Gespräch (PL die Gespräche) ◊ *We had a long talk about her problems.* Wir hatten ein langes Gespräch über ihre Probleme.
♦ **I had a talk with my Mum about it.** Ich habe mit meiner Mutti darüber gesprochen.
3 (*gossip*)
das Gerede ◊ *It's just talk.* Das ist nur Gerede.

to **talk** VERB
see also **talk** NOUN
reden ◊ *We talked about the weather.* Wir haben über das Wetter geredet.
♦ **to talk something over with somebody** etwas mit jemandem besprechen

talkative ADJECTIVE
redselig

tall ADJECTIVE
1 groß (*person, tree*) ◊ *They've cut down the tallest tree in the park.* Sie haben den größten Baum im Park gefällt. ◊ *He's two metres tall.* Er ist zwei Meter groß.
2 hoch (*building*)
Before a noun or after an article, use hohe.
◊ *a very tall building* ein sehr hohes Gebäude

tame ADJECTIVE
zahm (*animal*)

tampon NOUN
der Tampon (PL die Tampons)

tan NOUN
♦ **She's got an amazing tan.** Sie ist erstaunlich braun.

tangerine NOUN
die Mandarine

tank NOUN
1 (*for water, petrol*)
der Tank (PL die Tanks)
2 (*military*)
der Panzer (PL die Panzer)
♦ **a fish tank** ein Aquarium NEUT

tanker NOUN
1 (*ship*)
der Tanker (PL die Tanker) ◊ *an oil tanker* ein Öltanker
2 (*truck*)

T

☞

der <u>Tankwagen</u> (PL die Tankwagen) ◊ *a petrol tanker* ein Benzintankwagen

tap NOUN
☐1 (*water tap*)
der <u>Wasserhahn</u> (PL die Wasserhähne)
☐2 (*gentle blow*)
der <u>Klaps</u> (PL die Klapse)

tap-dancing NOUN
das <u>Stepptanzen</u>
♦ **I do tap-dancing.** Ich mache Stepptanz.

to **tape** VERB
> see also **tape** NOUN

<u>aufnehmen</u> (*record*) (PRESENT nimmt auf, IMPERFECT nahm auf, PERFECT hat aufgenommen) ◊ *Did you tape that film last night?* Hast du den Film gestern Abend aufgenommen?

tape NOUN
> see also **tape** VERB

☐1 die <u>Kassette</u> ◊ *a tape of Sinead O'Connor* eine Kassette von Sinead O'Connor
☐2 (*sticky tape*)
der <u>Klebstreifen</u> (PL die Klebstreifen)

tape deck NOUN
das <u>Kassettendeck</u> (PL die Kassettendecks)

tape measure NOUN
das <u>Maßband</u> (PL die Maßbänder)

tape recorder NOUN
der <u>Kassettenrekorder</u> (PL die Kassettenrekorder)

target NOUN
das <u>Ziel</u> (PL die Ziele)

tarmac NOUN
der <u>Asphalt</u> (*on road*)

tart NOUN
der <u>Kuchen</u> (PL die Kuchen) ◊ *an apple tart* ein Apfelkuchen

tartan ADJECTIVE
im <u>Schottenkaro</u> ◊ *a tartan scarf* ein Schal im Schottenkaro

task NOUN
die <u>Aufgabe</u>

taste NOUN
> see also **taste** VERB

der <u>Geschmack</u> (PL die Geschmäcke)
◊ *It's got a really strange taste.* Es hat einen sehr eigenartigen Geschmack.
◊ *She has good taste.* Sie hat einen guten Geschmack.
♦ **a joke in bad taste** ein geschmackloser Witz
♦ **Would you like a taste?** Möchtest du mal probieren?

to **taste** VERB
> see also **taste** NOUN

☐1 <u>probieren</u> (PERFECT hat probiert)
◊ *Would you like to taste it?* Möchtest du mal probieren?

☐2 <u>schmecken</u> ◊ *You can taste the garlic in it.* Man kann den Knoblauch schmecken.
♦ **to taste of something** nach etwas schmecken ◊ *It tastes of fish.* Es schmeckt nach Fisch.

tasteful ADJECTIVE
<u>geschmackvoll</u>

tasteless ADJECTIVE
☐1 <u>fade</u> (*food*)
☐2 <u>geschmacklos</u> (*in bad taste*) ◊ *a tasteless picture* ein geschmackloses Bild
◊ *a tasteless remark* eine geschmacklose Bemerkung

tasty ADJECTIVE
<u>schmackhaft</u>

tattoo NOUN
die <u>Tätowierung</u>

taught VERB *see* **teach**

Taurus NOUN
der <u>Stier</u> ◊ *I'm Taurus.* Ich bin Stier.

tax NOUN
die <u>Steuer</u> (*on goods, income*)

taxi NOUN
das <u>Taxi</u> (PL die Taxis) ◊ *a taxi driver* ein Taxifahrer

taxi rank NOUN
der <u>Taxistand</u> (PL die Taxistände)

TB NOUN (= *tuberculosis*)
die <u>TB</u> (= Tuberkulose)

tea NOUN
☐1 der <u>Tee</u> (PL die Tees) ◊ *a cup of tea* eine Tasse Tee

> ⓘ Usually, tea is not drunk with milk and sugar in Germany, but is served with lemon, and is referred to as **Schwarztee**. Fruit teas and herbal teas are also very widespread.

♦ **a tea bag** ein Teebeutel MASC
☐2 (*evening meal*)
das <u>Abendessen</u> (PL die Abendessen)
◊ *We were having tea.* Wir saßen beim Abendessen.

to **teach** VERB
☐1 <u>beibringen</u> (IMPERFECT brachte bei, PERFECT hat beigebracht) ◊ *My sister taught me to swim.* Meine Schwester hat mir das Schwimmen beigebracht.
♦ **That'll teach you!** Das wird dir eine Lehre sein!
☐2 (*in school*)
<u>unterrichten</u> (PERFECT hat unterrichtet)
◊ *She teaches physics.* Sie unterrichtet Physik.

teacher NOUN
der <u>Lehrer</u> (PL die Lehrer)
die <u>Lehrerin</u>
◊ *a maths teacher* ein Mathelehrer
◊ *She's a teacher.* Sie ist Lehrerin. ◊ *He's a primary school teacher.* Er ist Grundschullehrer.

teacher's pet NOUN
Lehrers Schätzchen NEUT ◊ *She's
teacher's pet.* Sie ist Lehrers Schätzchen.

tea cloth NOUN
das Geschirrtuch (PL die Geschirrtücher)

team NOUN
die Mannschaft ◊ *a football team* eine
Fußballmannschaft ◊ *She was in my
team.* Sie war in meiner Mannschaft.

teapot NOUN
die Teekanne

tear NOUN
| see also **tear** VERB |
die Träne ◊ *She was in tears.* Sie war in
Tränen aufgelöst.

to **tear** VERB
| see also **tear** NOUN |
zerreißen (IMPERFECT zerriss, PERFECT hat/ist
zerrissen) ◊ *Be careful or you'll tear the
page.* Vorsicht, sonst zerreißt du die
Seite.
*For the perfect tense use **haben** when
the verb has an object and **sein** when
there is no object.*
◊ *You've torn your shirt.* Du hast dein
Hemd zerrissen. ◊ *Your shirt is torn.* Dein
Hemd ist zerrissen. ◊ *It won't tear, it's
very strong.* Es zerreißt nicht, es ist sehr
stark.
♦ **to tear up** zerreißen ◊ *He tore up the
letter.* Er zerriss den Brief.

tear gas NOUN
das Tränengas (GEN des Tränengases)

to **tease** VERB
[1] quälen (*unkindly*) ◊ *Stop teasing that
poor animal!* Hör auf, das arme Tier zu
quälen!
[2] necken (*jokingly*) ◊ *He's teasing you.*
Er neckt dich nur.
♦ **I was only teasing.** Ich habe nur einen
Scherz gemacht.

teaspoon NOUN
der Teelöffel (PL die Teelöffel) ◊ *a
teaspoon of sugar* ein Teelöffel Zucker

teaspoonful NOUN
♦ **a teaspoonful of sugar** ein Teelöffel
Zucker

teatime NOUN
die Abendessenszeit (*in evening*) ◊ *It was
nearly teatime.* Es war fast
Abendessenszeit.
♦ **Teatime!** Abendessen!

tea towel NOUN
das Geschirrtuch (PL die Geschirrtücher)

technical ADJECTIVE
technisch
♦ **a technical college** eine Fachhochschule

technician NOUN
der Techniker (PL die Techniker)
die Technikerin

technique NOUN
die Technik

techno NOUN

der Techno (*music*)

technological ADJECTIVE
technologisch

technology NOUN
die Technologie

teddy bear NOUN
der Teddybär (GEN des Teddybären, PL die
Teddybären)

teenage ADJECTIVE
[1] für Teenager ◊ *a teenage magazine*
eine Zeitschrift für Teenager
[2] heranwachsend (*boys, girls*) ◊ *She has
two teenage daughters.* Sie hat zwei
heranwachsende Töchter.

teenager NOUN
der Teenager (PL die Teenager)
der Teenager is also used for girls.

teens PL NOUN
♦ **She's in her teens.** Sie ist ein Teenager.

tee-shirt NOUN
das T-Shirt (PL die T-Shirts)

teeth PL NOUN *see* **tooth**

to **teethe** VERB
zahnen

teetotal ADJECTIVE
♦ **I'm teetotal.** Ich trinke keinen Alkohol.

telecommunications PL NOUN
die Nachrichtentechnik SING

teleconferencing NOUN
die Telekonferenzen PL

telephone NOUN
das Telefon (PL die Telefone) ◊ *on the
telephone* am Telefon
♦ **a telephone box** eine Telefonzelle
♦ **a telephone call** ein Anruf MASC
♦ **the telephone directory** das Telefonbuch
♦ **a telephone number** eine
Telefonnummer

telesales SING NOUN
der Telefonverkauf (PL die
Telefonverkäufe)

telescope NOUN
das Teleskop (PL die Teleskope)

television NOUN
das Fernsehen
♦ **on television** im Fernsehen
♦ **a television programme** eine
Fernsehsendung

to **tell** VERB
sagen
♦ **to tell somebody something** jemandem
etwas sagen ◊ *Did you tell your mother?*
Hast du es deiner Mutter gesagt? ◊ *I told
him that I was going on holiday.* Ich habe
ihm gesagt, dass ich in Urlaub fahre.
♦ **to tell somebody to do something**
jemandem sagen, er solle etwas tun ◊ *He
told me to wait a moment.* Er sagte mir,
ich solle einen Moment warten.
♦ **to tell lies** lügen
♦ **to tell a story** eine Geschichte erzählen
♦ **I can't tell the difference between them.**
Ich kann sie nicht unterscheiden.

T

to **tell off** VERB
schimpfen

telly NOUN
der Fernseher (PL die Fernseher)
♦ **to watch telly** fernsehen
♦ **on telly** im Fernsehen

temper NOUN
♦ **to be in a temper** wütend sein
♦ **to lose one's temper** wütend werden ◊ *I lost my temper.* Ich bin wütend geworden.
♦ **He's got a terrible temper.** Er ist furchtbar jähzornig.

temperature NOUN
die Temperatur (*of oven, water, person*)
♦ **The temperature was thirty degrees.** Es waren dreißig Grad.
♦ **to have a temperature** Fieber haben

temple NOUN
der Tempel (PL die Tempel)

temporary ADJECTIVE
vorläufig

to **tempt** VERB
in Versuchung führen ◊ *to tempt somebody to do something* jemanden in Versuchung führen, etwas zu tun
♦ **I'm very tempted!** Das reizt mich sehr!

temptation NOUN
die Versuchung

tempting ADJECTIVE
verlockend

ten NUMBER
zehn ◊ *She's ten.* Sie ist zehn.

tenant NOUN
der Mieter (PL die Mieter)
die Mieterin

tender ADJECTIVE
1 zärtlich (*loving*)
2 empfindlich ◊ *The wound is still tender.* Die wunde Stelle ist noch immer empfindlich.

to **tend to** VERB
♦ **to tend to do something** dazu neigen, etwas zu tun ◊ *He tends to arrive late.* Er neigt dazu, zu spät zu kommen.

tennis NOUN
das Tennis (GEN des Tennis) ◊ *Do you play tennis?* Spielst du Tennis?
♦ **a tennis ball** ein Tennisball MASC
♦ **a tennis court** ein Tennisplatz MASC
♦ **a tennis racket** ein Tennisschläger MASC

tennis player NOUN
der Tennisspieler (PL die Tennisspieler)
die Tennisspielerin
◊ *He's a tennis player.* Er ist Tennisspieler.

tenor NOUN
der Tenor (PL die Tenöre)

tenpin bowling NOUN
das Bowling
♦ **to go tenpin bowling** Bowling spielen

tense ADJECTIVE
see also **tense** NOUN
angespannt ◊ *a tense situation* eine angespannte Situation

tense NOUN
see also **tense** ADJECTIVE
♦ **the present tense** das Präsens
♦ **the future tense** das Futur

tension NOUN
die Spannung

tent NOUN
das Zelt (PL die Zelte)
♦ **a tent peg** ein Hering MASC
♦ **a tent pole** eine Zeltstange

tenth ADJECTIVE
zehnte ◊ *the tenth floor* der zehnte Stock
♦ **the tenth of August** der zehnte August

term NOUN
das Trimester (*at school*) (PL die Trimester)

ⓘ *In Germany the school and university year is divided into two semesters rather than three terms.*

♦ **to come to terms with something** sich mit etwas abfinden

terminal ADJECTIVE
see also **terminal** NOUN
unheilbar (*illness, patient*)

terminal NOUN
see also **terminal** ADJECTIVE
das Terminal (*of computer*) (PL die Terminals)
♦ **an oil terminal** ein Ölterminal MASC
♦ **an air terminal** ein Terminal MASC

terminally ADVERB
♦ **to be terminally ill** unheilbar krank sein

terrace NOUN
1 die Terrasse (*patio*)
2 die Häuserreihe (*row of houses*)
♦ **the terraces** (*at stadium*) die Ränge

terraced ADJECTIVE
♦ **a terraced house** ein Reihenhaus NEUT

terrible ADJECTIVE
furchtbar ◊ *My German is terrible.* Mein Deutsch ist furchtbar.

terribly ADVERB
furchtbar ◊ *He suffered terribly.* Er litt furchtbar. ◊ *I'm terribly sorry.* Es tut mir furchtbar leid.

terrier NOUN
der Terrier (PL die Terrier)

terrific ADJECTIVE
super (*wonderful*)
super is invariable.
◊ *That's terrific!* Das ist super! ◊ *You look terrific!* Du siehst super aus!

terrified ADJECTIVE
♦ **I was terrified!** Ich hatte furchtbare Angst!

terrorism NOUN
der Terrorismus (GEN des Terrorismus)

terrorist NOUN
der Terrorist (GEN des Terroristen, PL die Terroristen)
die Terroristin
♦ **a terrorist attack** ein Terrorangriff MASC

test NOUN
see also **test** VERB
1 (*at school*)
die Arbeit ◊ *I've got a test tomorrow.* Ich schreibe morgen eine Arbeit.
2 (*trial, check*)
der Test (PL die Tests) ◊ *nuclear tests* Atomtests
3 (*medical*)
die Untersuchung ◊ *a blood test* eine Blutuntersuchung
♦ **driving test** die Fahrprüfung

to **test** VERB
see also **test** NOUN
1 probieren (PERFECT hat probiert)
♦ **to test something out** etwas ausprobieren
2 (*class*)
abfragen (PERFECT hat abgefragt)
◊ *He tested us on the new vocabulary.* Er hat uns die neuen Wörter abgefragt.
♦ **She was tested for drugs.** Man hat bei ihr ein Drogentest gemacht.

test tube NOUN
das Reagenzglas (GEN des Reagenzglases, PL die Reagenzgläser)

tetanus NOUN
der Tetanus (GEN des Tetanus) ◊ *a tetanus injection* eine Tetanusspritze

text NOUN
see also **text** VERB
die SMS-Nachrichte (*text message*) (PL die SMS-Nachrichten)

to **text** VERB
see also **text** NOUN
eine SMS schicken ◊ *I'll text you when I get there.* Ich schicke dir eine SMS, wenn ich da bin.

text message NOUN
die SMS(-Nachricht) (PL die SMS(-Nachrichten)

text messaging NOUN
das Versenden von SMS-Nachrichten

textbook NOUN
das Lehrbuch (PL die Lehrbücher)
♦ **a German textbook** ein Deutschbuch

textiles PL NOUN
die Textilien FEM PL

Thames NOUN
die Themse

than CONJUNCTION
als ◊ *She's taller than me.* Sie ist größer als ich. ◊ *I've got more books than him.* Ich habe mehr Bücher als er. ◊ *more than ten years* mehr als zehn Jahre ◊ *more than once* mehr als einmal

to **thank** VERB
sich bedanken bei (PERFECT hat sich bedankt) ◊ *Don't forget to thank them.* Vergiss nicht, dich bei ihnen zu bedanken.
♦ **thank you** danke
♦ **thank you very much** vielen Dank

thanks EXCLAMATION
danke
♦ **thanks to** dank ◊ *Thanks to him, everything went OK.* Dank ihm ging alles gut.

that ADJECTIVE, PRONOUN, CONJUNCTION
1 dieser ◊ *that man* dieser Mann
diese ◊ *that woman* diese Frau
dieses ◊ *that book* dieses Buch
♦ **that one (1)** (*masculine*) der da ◊ *This man? – No, that one.* Dieser Mann? – Nein, der da.
♦ **that one (2)** (*feminine*) die da ◊ *This woman? – No, that one.* Diese Frau? – Nein, die da.
♦ **that one (3)** (*neuter*) das da ◊ *This book? – No, that one.* Dieses Buch? – Nein, das da.
2 das ◊ *Did you see that?* Hast du das gesehen? ◊ *What's that?* Was ist das? ◊ *Who's that?* Wer ist das? ◊ *Is that you?* Bist du das?
♦ **That's ...** Das ist ... ◊ *That's my German teacher.* Das ist meine Deutschlehrerin.
♦ **That's what he said.** Das hat er gesagt.

In relative clauses use der, die or das, depending on the gender of the noun that refers to.

3 der ◊ *the man that saw us* der Mann, der uns sah
die ◊ *the woman that saw us* die Frau, die uns sah
das ◊ *the child that saw us* das Kind, das uns sah
die ◊ *the people that helped us* die Leute, die uns geholfen haben
4 dass ◊ *He thought that Henry was ill.* Er dachte, dass Henry krank war. ◊ *I know that she likes chocolate.* Ich weiß, dass sie Schokolade mag.
5 so ◊ *It was that big.* Es war so groß. ◊ *It's about that high.* Es ist etwa so hoch.

thatched ADJECTIVE
strohgedeckt

the ARTICLE

Use der with a masculine noun, die with a feminine noun, and das with a neuter noun. For plural nouns always use die.

1 der ◊ *the boy* der Junge
die ◊ *the orange* die Orange
das ◊ *the girl* das Mädchen
2 die ◊ *the children* die Kinder

theatre NOUN
das Theater (PL die Theater)

theft NOUN
der Diebstahl (PL die Diebstähle)

their ADJECTIVE

T

☞

ihr ◊ *their father* ihr Vater ◊ *their mother* ihre Mutter ◊ *their child* ihr Kind ◊ *their parents* ihre Eltern

*Do not use **ihr** with parts of the body.*

◊ *They can't bend their arms.* Sie können die Arme nicht bewegen.

theirs PRONOUN

1 ihrer ◊ *This is our computer, not theirs.* Das ist unser Computer, nicht ihrer.

ihre ◊ *It's not our garage, it's theirs.* Das ist nicht unsere Garage, sondern ihre.

ihres ◊ *It's not our car, it's theirs.* Das ist nicht unser Auto, sondern ihres.

2 ihre ◊ *These are not our ideas, they're theirs.* Das sind nicht unsere Ideen, sondern ihre.

◆ **Is this theirs?** Gehört das ihnen? ◊ *This car is theirs.* Das Auto gehört ihnen. ◊ *Whose is this? – It's theirs.* Wem gehört das? – Ihnen.

them PRONOUN

1 sie ◊ *I didn't see them.* Ich habe sie nicht gesehen.

*Use **sie** after prepositions which take the accusative.*

◊ *It's for them.* Es ist für sie.

2 ihnen

*Use **ihnen** when **them** means to them.*

◊ *I gave them some brochures.* Ich habe ihnen ein paar Broschüren gegeben. ◊ *I told them the truth.* Ich habe ihnen die Wahrheit gesagt.

*Use **ihnen** after prepositions which take the dative.*

◊ *Ann and Sophie came. Graham was with them.* Ann und Sophie sind gekommen. Graham war bei ihnen.

theme NOUN

das Thema (PL die Themen)

themselves PRONOUN

1 sich ◊ *Did they hurt themselves?* Haben sie sich verletzt?

2 selbst ◊ *They did it themselves.* Sie haben es selbst gemacht.

then ADVERB, CONJUNCTION

1 dann ◊ *I get dressed. Then I have breakfast.* Ich ziehe mich an. Dann frühstücke ich. ◊ *My pen's run out. – Use a pencil then!* Mein Kugelschreiber ist leer. – Dann nimm einen Bleistift!

2 damals (*at that time*) ◊ *There was no electricity then.* Damals gab es keinen Strom.

◆ **now and then** ab und zu ◊ *Do you play chess? – Now and then.* Spielst du Schach? – Ab und zu.

◆ **By then it was too late.** Da war es schon zu spät.

therapy NOUN

die Therapie

there ADVERB

*Use **dort** when something is in a fixed position, **dorthin** when there is movement involved.*

1 dort ◊ *Can you see that house there?* Siehst du das Haus dort? ◊ *Berlin? I've never been there.* Berlin? Ich war noch nie dort.

◆ **over there** dort drüben
◆ **in there** dort drin
◆ **on there** darauf
◆ **up there** dort oben
◆ **down there** dort unten

2 dorthin ◊ *Put it there, on the table.* Stell's dorthin, auf den Tisch. ◊ *He went there on Friday.* Er ging am Freitag dorthin.

◆ **There he is!** Da ist er ja!
◆ **There is ... (1)** Es ist ... ◊ *There's a factory near my house.* In der Nähe von meinem Haus ist eine Fabrik.
◆ **There is ... (2)** Es gibt ... ◊ *There is a lot of poverty in the world.* Es gibt viel Armut auf der Welt.
◆ **There are ... (1)** Es sind ... ◊ *There are five people in my family.* In meiner Familie sind fünf Leute.
◆ **There are ... (2)** Es gibt ... ◊ *There are many schools in this city.* In dieser Stadt gibt es viele Schulen.
◆ **There has been an accident.** Es hat einen Unfall gegeben.

therefore ADVERB

deshalb

there's = there is = there has

thermometer NOUN

das Thermometer (PL die Thermometer)

Thermos ® NOUN

die Thermosflasche ®

these ADJECTIVE, PRONOUN

1 die ◊ *these shoes* die Schuhe

◆ **THESE shoes** diese Schuhe hier

2 die hier ◊ *I want these!* Ich möchte die hier! ◊ *I'm looking for some sandals. Can I try these?* Ich suche Sandalen. Kann ich die hier anprobieren?

they PRONOUN

sie ◊ *Are there any tickets left? – No, they're all sold.* Gibt es noch Karten? – Nein, sie sind schon alle verkauft. ◊ *Do you like those shoes? – No, they're horrible.* Gefallen dir die Schuhe? – Nein, sie sind furchtbar.

◆ **They say that ...** Man sagt, dass ...

they'd = they had, = they would
they'll = they will
they're = they are
they've = they have

thick ADJECTIVE

1 dick (*not thin*) ◊ *The walls are one metre thick.* Die Wände sind einen Meter dick.

2 dumm (*stupid*)

thief NOUN
der Dieb (PL die Diebe)
die Diebin

thigh NOUN
der Schenkel

thin ADJECTIVE
dünn

thing NOUN
das Ding (PL die Dinge) ◊ *beautiful things*
schöne Dinge ◊ *What's that thing called?*
Wie heißt das Ding da?
♦ **my things** (*belongings*) meine Sachen
♦ **You poor thing!** (1) (*man*) Du Armer!
♦ **You poor thing!** (2) (*woman*) Du Arme!

to **think** VERB
1 denken (IMPERFECT dachte, PERFECT hat
gedacht) ◊ *I think you're wrong.* Ich
denke, du hast unrecht. ◊ *What are you
thinking about?* Woran denkst du?
♦ **What do you think about the death
penalty?** Was halten Sie von der
Todesstrafe?
2 glauben ◊ *I don't think I can come to
the party.* Ich glaube nicht, dass ich zur
Party kommen kann.
♦ **I think so.** Ich glaube schon.
♦ **I don't think so.** Ich glaube nicht.
3 (*spend time thinking*)
nachdenken (PERFECT hat nachgedacht)
◊ *Think carefully before you reply.*
Denk gut nach, bevor du antwortest.
◊ *I'll think about it.* Ich denke darüber
nach.
4 (*imagine*)
sich vorstellen (PERFECT hat sich
vorgestellt) ◊ *Think what life would be
like without cars.* Stell dir vor, wie es
wäre, wenn es keine Autos gäbe.
♦ **I'll think it over.** Ich werde es mir
überlegen.

third ADJECTIVE
see also **third** NOUN
dritte ◊ *the third day* der dritte Tag ◊ *the
third time* das dritte Mal
♦ **He came third.** Er wurde Dritter.
♦ **the third of August** der dritte August

third NOUN
see also **third** ADJECTIVE
das Drittel (PL die Drittel) ◊ *a third
of the population* ein Drittel der
Bevölkerung

thirdly ADVERB
drittens

Third World NOUN
die Dritte Welt

thirst NOUN
der Durst

thirsty ADJECTIVE
♦ **to be thirsty** Durst haben ◊ *Are you
thirsty?* Hast du Durst?

thirteen NUMBER
dreizehn ◊ *I'm thirteen.* Ich bin dreizehn.

thirteenth ADJECTIVE
dreizehnte
♦ **the thirteenth of August** der dreizehnte
August

thirty NUMBER
dreißig ◊ *She's thirty.* Sie ist dreißig.

this ADJECTIVE, PRONOUN
1 dieser ◊ *this man* dieser Mann
diese ◊ *this woman* diese Frau
dieses ◊ *this child* dieses Kind
♦ **this one (1)** (*masculine*) der hier ◊ *That
man over there? – No, this one.* Der
Mann dort? – Nein, der hier.
♦ **this one (2)** (*feminine*) die hier ◊ *That
woman over there? – No, this one.* Die
Frau dort? – Nein, die hier.
♦ **this one (3)** (*neuter*) das hier ◊ *I don't like
that picture over there, I prefer this one.*
Das Bild dort gefällt mir nicht, das hier
gefällt mir besser.
2 das ◊ *You see this?* Siehst du das?
◊ *What's this?* Was ist das? ◊ *This is my
mother.* (*introduction*) Das ist meine
Mutter.
♦ **This is Gavin speaking.** (*on the phone*)
Hier spricht Gavin.

thistle NOUN
die Distel

thorough ADJECTIVE
gründlich ◊ *She's very thorough.* Sie ist
sehr gründlich.

thoroughly ADVERB
gründlich (*examine*)

those ADJECTIVE, PRONOUN
1 diese ◊ *those shoes* diese Schuhe
♦ **THOSE shoes** diese Schuhe dort
2 die da ◊ *I want those!* Ich möchte die
da! ◊ *I'm looking for some sandals. Can I
try those?* Ich suche Sandalen. Kann ich
die da anprobieren?

though CONJUNCTION, ADVERB
obwohl ◊ *It's warm outside, though it's
raining.* Es ist warm draußen, obwohl es
regnet.
♦ **He's a nice person, though he's
not very clever.** Er ist ein netter Mensch,
auch wenn er nicht besonders klug
ist.

thought VERB see **think**

thought NOUN
der Gedanke (*idea*) (GEN des Gedankens,
PL die Gedanken) ◊ *I've just had a
thought.* Mir ist eben ein Gedanke
gekommen.
♦ **It was a nice thought, thank you.** Das
war nett, vielen Dank.
♦ **It's the thought that counts.** Es war gut
gemeint.

thoughtful ADJECTIVE
1 nachdenklich (*deep in thought*) ◊ *You
look thoughtful.* Du siehst nachdenklich
aus.
2 aufmerksam (*considerate*) ◊ *She's very
thoughtful.* Sie ist sehr aufmerksam.

T

thoughtless ADJECTIVE
gedankenlos

thousand NUMBER
♦ **a thousand** eintausend ◊ *a thousand euros* eintausend Euro
♦ **two thousand pounds** zweitausend Pfund
♦ **thousands of people** Tausende von Menschen

thousandth ADJECTIVE
tausendste

thread NOUN
der Faden (PL die Fäden)

threat NOUN
die Drohung

to **threaten** VERB
drohen ◊ *He threatened me.* Er hat mir gedroht. ◊ *to threaten to do something* drohen, etwas zu tun

three NUMBER
drei ◊ *She's three.* Sie ist drei.

three-dimensional ADJECTIVE
dreidimensional

three-piece suite NOUN
die dreiteilige Polstergarnitur

threw VERB *see* **throw**

thrifty ADJECTIVE
sparsam

thrill NOUN
der Reiz (*excitement*) (GEN des Reizes, PL die Reize)
♦ **It was a great thrill.** Es war sehr aufregend.

thrilled ADJECTIVE
♦ **I was thrilled.** (*pleased*) Ich habe mich unheimlich gefreut.

thriller NOUN
der Thriller (PL die Thriller)

thrilling ADJECTIVE
spannend

throat NOUN
der Hals (GEN des Halses, PL die Hälse)
♦ **to have a sore throat** Halsweh haben

to **throb** VERB
♦ **a throbbing pain** ein pochender Schmerz
♦ **My arm's throbbing.** Mir pocht es im Arm.

throne NOUN
der Thron (PL die Throne)

through PREPOSITION, ADJECTIVE, ADVERB
durch ◊ *through the window* durch das Fenster ◊ *to go through Birmingham* durch Birmingham fahren ◊ *to go through a tunnel* durch einen Tunnel fahren
♦ **I know her through my sister.** Ich kenne sie über meine Schwester.
♦ **The window was dirty and I couldn't see through.** Das Fenster war schmutzig, und ich konnte nicht durchsehen.

♦ **a through train** ein durchgehender Zug
♦ **"no through road"** "keine Durchfahrt"

throughout PREPOSITION
♦ **throughout Britain** in ganz Großbritannien
♦ **throughout the year** das ganze Jahr über

to **throw** VERB
werfen (PRESENT wirft, IMPERFECT warf, PERFECT hat geworfen) ◊ *He threw the ball to me.* Er warf mir den Ball zu.
♦ **to throw a party** eine Party machen
♦ **That really threw him.** Das hat ihn aus der Fassung gebracht.
♦ **to throw away (1)** (*rubbish*) wegwerfen
♦ **to throw away (2)** (*chance*) vergeben
♦ **to throw out (1)** (*throw away*) wegwerfen
♦ **to throw out (2)** (*person*) rauswerfen ◊ *I threw him out.* Ich habe ihn rausgeworfen.
♦ **to throw up** sich übergeben

thug NOUN
der Schlägertyp (PL die Schlägertypen)

thumb NOUN
der Daumen (PL die Daumen)

thumb tack NOUN US
die Reißzwecke

to **thump** VERB
♦ **to thump somebody** jemandem eine verpassen (*informal*) ◊ *I thumped him.* Ich habe ihm eine verpasst.

thunder NOUN
der Donner (PL die Donner)

thunderstorm NOUN
das Gewitter (PL die Gewitter)

thundery ADJECTIVE
gewitterig

Thursday NOUN
der Donnerstag (PL die Donnerstage)
◊ *on Thursday* am Donnerstag
◊ *every Thursday* jeden Donnerstag
◊ *last Thursday* letzten Donnerstag ◊ *next Thursday* nächsten Donnerstag
♦ **on Thursdays** donnerstags

thyme NOUN
der Thymian (PL die Thymiane)

tick NOUN
see also **tick** VERB
1 (*mark*)
das Häkchen (PL die Häkchen)
2 (*of clock*)
das Ticken
♦ **in a tick** in einer Sekunde

to **tick** VERB
see also **tick** NOUN
1 ankreuzen (PERFECT hat angekreuzt)
◊ *Tick the appropriate box.* Kreuzen Sie das entsprechende Kästchen an.
2 (*clock*)
ticken
♦ **to tick off (1)** (*on list*) abhaken

♦ **to tick off (2)** (*scold*) ausschimpfen

ticket NOUN
1 (*for bus, tube, train*)
die <u>Fahrkarte</u> ◊ *an underground ticket*
eine Fahrkarte für die U-Bahn
2 (*for plane*)
das <u>Ticket</u> (PL die Tickets)
3 (*for theatre, concert, cinema, museum*)
die <u>Eintrittskarte</u>
♦ **a parking ticket** ein Strafzettel MASC

ticket inspector NOUN
der <u>Fahrscheinkontrolleur</u> (PL die
Fahrscheinkontrolleure)
die <u>Fahrscheinkontrolleurin</u>

ticket office NOUN
1 (*for travel*)
der <u>Fahrkartenschalter</u> (PL die
Fahrkartenschalter)
2 (*for theatre, cinema*)
die <u>Kasse</u>

to **tickle** VERB
<u>kitzeln</u>

ticklish ADJECTIVE
<u>kitzlig</u> ◊ *Are you ticklish?* Bist du kitzlig?

tide NOUN
♦ **high tide** die Flut
♦ **low tide** die Ebbe

tidy ADJECTIVE
see also **tidy** VERB
<u>ordentlich</u> ◊ *Your room is very tidy.* Dein
Zimmer ist sehr ordentlich. ◊ *She's very
tidy.* Sie ist sehr ordentlich.

to **tidy** VERB
see also **tidy** ADJECTIVE
<u>aufräumen</u> (PERFECT hat aufgeräumt) ◊ *Go
and tidy your room.* Geh und räum dein
Zimmer auf.
♦ **to tidy up** aufräumen ◊ *Don't forget to
tidy up afterwards.* Vergesst nicht,
nachher aufzuräumen.

tie NOUN
see also **tie** VERB
die <u>Krawatte</u> (*necktie*)
♦ **It was a tie.** (*in sport*) Es gab ein
Unentschieden.

to **tie** VERB
see also **tie** NOUN
1 (*ribbon, shoelaces*)
<u>zubinden</u> (IMPERFECT band zu, PERFECT hat
zugebunden)
♦ **I tied a knot in the rope.** Ich machte
einen Knoten in das Seil.
2 (*in sport*)
<u>unentschieden spielen</u>
♦ **They tied three all.** Sie haben drei zu drei
gespielt.
♦ **to tie up (1)** (*parcel*) zuschnüren
♦ **to tie up (2)** (*dog, boat*) anbinden
♦ **to tie up (3)** (*prisoner*) fesseln

tiger NOUN
der <u>Tiger</u> (PL die Tiger)

tight ADJECTIVE

1 <u>eng</u> (*tight-fitting*) ◊ *tight jeans* enge
Jeans
2 <u>zu eng</u> (*too tight*) ◊ *This dress is a bit
tight.* Das Kleid ist etwas zu eng.

to **tighten** VERB
1 (*rope*)
<u>spannen</u>
2 (*screw*)
<u>anziehen</u> (IMPERFECT zog an, PERFECT hat
angezogen)

tightly ADVERB
<u>fest</u> (*hold*)

tights PL NOUN
die <u>Strumpfhose</u> SING ◊ *a pair of tights*
eine Strumpfhose

tile NOUN
1 (*on roof*)
der <u>Dachziegel</u> (PL die Dachziegel)
2 (*on wall, floor*)
die <u>Fliese</u>

tiled ADJECTIVE
1 <u>gekachelt</u> (*wall*)
2 <u>mit Fliesen ausgelegt</u> (*floor, room*)
♦ **a tiled roof** ein Ziegeldach NEUT

till NOUN
see also **till** PREPOSITION
die <u>Kasse</u>

till PREPOSITION, CONJUNCTION
see also **till** NOUN
1 <u>bis</u> ◊ *I waited till ten o'clock.* Ich habe
bis zehn Uhr gewartet.
♦ **till now** bis jetzt
♦ **till then** bis dann
2 <u>vor</u>
*Use vor if the sentence you want to
translate contains a negative such as
"not" or "never".*
◊ *It won't be ready till next week.* Vor
nächster Woche wird es nicht fertig.
◊ *Till last year I'd never been to
Germany.* Vor letztem Jahr war ich nie in
Deutschland.

time NOUN
1 die <u>Zeit</u> ◊ *It's time to get up.* Es ist Zeit
zum Aufstehen. ◊ *It was two o'clock,
German time.* Es war zwei Uhr, deutsche
Zeit. ◊ *I'm sorry, I haven't got time.* Ich
habe leider keine Zeit.
♦ **What time is it?** Wie viel Uhr ist es?
♦ **What time do you get up?** Um wie viel
Uhr stehst du auf?
♦ **on time** pünktlich ◊ *He never arrives on
time.* Er kommt nie pünktlich.
♦ **from time to time** von Zeit zu Zeit
♦ **in time** rechtzeitig ◊ *We arrived in time
for lunch.* Wir kamen rechtzeitig zum
Mittagessen.
♦ **just in time** gerade noch rechtzeitig
♦ **in no time** im Nu ◊ *It was ready in no
time.* Es war im Nu fertig.
2 (*moment*)

T

der <u>Moment</u> (PL die Momente) ◊ *This isn't a good time to ask him.* Das ist kein guter Moment, um ihn zu fragen.

♦**for the time being** momentan

③ (*occasion*)

das <u>Mal</u> (PL die Male) ◊ *next time* nächstes Mal

♦**this time** diesmal

♦**two at a time** jeweils zwei

♦**How many times?** Wie oft?

♦**at times** manchmal

♦**a long time** lange ◊ *Have you lived here for a long time?* Wohnst du schon lange hier?

♦**in a week's time** in einer Woche ◊ *I'll come back in a month's time.* Ich komme in einem Monat wieder.

♦**Come and see us any time.** Besuchen sie uns, wann Sie wollen.

♦**to have a good time** sich amüsieren ◊ *Did you have a good time?* Habt ihr euch amüsiert?

♦**Two times two is four.** Zwei mal zwei ist vier.

time bomb NOUN
die <u>Zeitbombe</u>

time off NOUN
die <u>Freizeit</u>

timer NOUN
① (*time switch*)
die <u>Schaltuhr</u>
② (*for cooking*)
der <u>Kurzzeitmesser</u> (PL die Kurzzeitmesser)
♦**an egg timer** eine Eieruhr

time-share NOUN
das <u>Timesharing-Appartement</u> (PL die Timesharing-Appartements)

timetable NOUN
① (*for train, bus*)
der <u>Fahrplan</u> (PL dIe Fahrpläne)
② (*at school*)
der <u>Stundenplan</u> (PL die Stundenpläne)

time zone NOUN
die <u>Zeitzone</u>

tin NOUN
① die <u>Dose</u> ◊ *a tin of beans* eine Dose Bohnen ◊ *a biscuit tin* eine Keksdose
② das <u>Zinn</u> (*type of metal*)

tinned ADJECTIVE
in <u>Dosen</u> (*food*) ◊ *tinned peaches* Pfirsiche in Dosen

tin opener NOUN
der <u>Dosenöffner</u> (PL die Dosenöffner)

tinsel NOUN
die <u>Rauschgoldgirlande</u>

tinted ADJECTIVE
getönt (*spectacles, glass*)

tiny ADJECTIVE
winzig

tip NOUN
see also **tip** VERB
① (*money*)

das <u>Trinkgeld</u> (PL die Trinkgelder) ◊ *Shall I give him a tip?* Soll ich ihm ein Trinkgeld geben?
② (*advice*)
der <u>Tipp</u> (PL die Tipps) ◊ *a useful tip* ein guter Tipp
③ (*end*)
die <u>Spitze</u>

♦**It's on the tip of my tongue.** Es liegt mir auf der Zunge.

♦**a rubbish tip** eine Müllkippe

♦**This place is a complete tip!** Was für ein Saustall! (*informal*)

to **tip** VERB
see also **tip** NOUN

♦**to tip somebody** jemandem ein Trinkgeld geben ◊ *He tipped the taxi driver generously.* Er gab dem Taxifahrer ein großzügiges Trinkgeld.

tipsy ADJECTIVE
beschwipst ◊ *I'm feeling a bit tipsy.* Ich bin etwas beschwipst.

tiptoe NOUN
♦**on tiptoe** auf Zehenspitzen

tired ADJECTIVE
müde ◊ *I'm tired.* Ich bin müde.
♦**to be tired of something** etwas leid sein

tiring ADJECTIVE
ermüdend

tissue NOUN
das <u>Papiertaschentuch</u> (PL die Papiertaschentücher) ◊ *Have you got a tissue?* Hast du ein Papiertaschentuch?

title NOUN
der <u>Titel</u> (PL die Titel)

title role NOUN
die <u>Titelrolle</u>

to PREPOSITION
① <u>nach</u> ◊ *to go to Munich* nach München fahren ◊ *We went to Italy.* Wir sind nach Italien gefahren. ◊ *the train to London* der Zug nach London ◊ *the road to Edinburgh* die Straße nach Edinburgh ◊ *to the left* nach links

♦**I've never been to Munich.** Ich war noch nie in München.

② <u>in</u> ◊ *to go to school* in die Schule gehen ◊ *to go to the theatre* ins Theater gehen

③ <u>zu</u>

*Use **zu** when you talk about going to a particular place or person.*

◊ *We drove to the station.* Wir fuhren zum Bahnhof. ◊ *to go to the doctor's* zum Arzt gehen ◊ *to go to the baker's* zum Bäcker gehen ◊ *Let's go to Anne's house.* Lass uns zu Anne nach Hause gehen.

♦**a letter to his mother** ein Brief an seine Mutter

♦**It's hard to say.** Es ist schwer zu sagen.

♦**It's easy to criticize.** Es ist leicht zu kritisieren.

♦**something to drink** etwas zu trinken

[4] bis (*as far as, until*) ◊ *to count to ten* bis zehn zählen ◊ *It's ninety kilometres to the border.* Es sind neunzig Kilometer bis zur Grenze.

♦**from ... to ...** to ... bis ◊ *from nine o'clock to half past three* von neun bis halb vier

♦**ten to nine** zehn vor neun

Use the dative when you say or give something to somebody.

◊ *Give it to me!* Gib es mir! ◊ *That's what he said to me.* Das ist, was er zu mir gesagt hat. ◊ *We said goodbye to the neighbours.* Wir sagten den Nachbarn Auf Wiedersehen. ◊ *I sold it to a friend.* Ich habe es einem Freund verkauft.

♦**to talk to somebody** mit jemandem reden

When to is used with the infinitive, it is often not translated.

◊ *I'd like to go.* Ich würde gern gehen. ◊ *I don't want to see him.* Ich möchte ihn nicht sehen.

[5] um ... zu (*in order to*)

um ... zu is used with the infinitive.

◊ *I did it to help you.* Ich tat es, um dir zu helfen. ◊ *She's too young to go to school.* Sie ist noch zu jung, um in die Schule zu gehen.

♦**the key to the front door** der Schlüssel für die Haustür

♦**the answer to the question** die Antwort auf die Frage

toad NOUN
die Kröte

toadstool NOUN
der Giftpilz (GEN des Giftpilzes, PL die Giftpilze)

toast NOUN
[1] der Toast (PL die Toasts) ◊ *a piece of toast* eine Scheibe Toast
[2] (*speech*)
der Trinkspruch (PL die Trinksprüche) ◊ *to drink a toast to somebody* einen Trinkspruch auf jemanden ausbringen

toaster NOUN
der Toaster (PL die Toaster)

toastie NOUN
der Toast (PL die Toasts) ◊ *a cheese toastie* ein Käsetoast

tobacco NOUN
der Tabak

tobacconist's NOUN
der Tabakladen (PL die Tabakläden)

toboggan NOUN
der Schlitten (PL die Schlitten)

tobogganing NOUN
♦**to go tobogganing** Schlitten fahren

today ADVERB
heute ◊ *What did you do today?* Was hast du heute gemacht?

toddler NOUN
das Kleinkind (PL die Kleinkinder)

toe NOUN
der Zeh (PL die Zehen) ◊ *my big toe* mein großer Zeh

toffee NOUN
der Karamell

together ADVERB
[1] zusammen ◊ *Are they still together?* Sind sie noch zusammen?
[2] gleichzeitig (*at the same time*) ◊ *Don't all speak together!* Redet nicht alle gleichzeitig!

♦**together with** (*with person*) zusammen mit

toilet NOUN
die Toilette

toilet paper NOUN
das Toilettenpapier

toiletries PL NOUN
die Toilettenartikel MASC PL

toilet roll NOUN
die Rolle Toilettenpapier

token NOUN
♦**a gift token** ein Geschenkgutschein MASC

told VERB *see* **tell**

tolerant ADJECTIVE
tolerant

toll NOUN
die Benutzungsgebühr (*on bridge, motorway*)

tomato NOUN
die Tomate ◊ *tomato soup* die Tomatensuppe

tomboy NOUN
der Wildfang ◊ *She's a real tomboy.* Sie ist ein echter Wildfang.

tomorrow ADVERB
morgen ◊ *tomorrow morning* morgen früh ◊ *tomorrow night* morgen Abend
♦**the day after tomorrow** übermorgen

ton NOUN
die Tonne ◊ *That old bike weighs a ton.* Das alte Fahrrad wiegt ja eine Tonne.

tongue NOUN
die Zunge
♦**to say something tongue in cheek** etwas nicht so ernst meinen

tonic NOUN
das Tonic (*tonic water*) (PL die Tonics)
♦**a gin and tonic** ein Gin Tonic

tonight ADVERB
[1] heute Abend (*this evening*) ◊ *Are you going out tonight?* Gehst du heute Abend aus?
[2] heute Nacht (*during the night*) ◊ *I'll sleep well tonight.* Ich werde heute Nacht gut schlafen.

tonsillitis NOUN
die Mandelentzündung ◊ *She's got tonsillitis.* Sie hat eine Mandelentzündung.

tonsils PL NOUN

T

die <u>Mandeln</u> FEM PL

too ADVERB, ADJECTIVE
1 <u>auch</u> (as well) ◊ My sister came too.
Meine Schwester ist auch mitgekommen.
2 <u>zu</u> (excessively) ◊ The water's too hot.
Das Wasser ist zu heiß. ◊ We arrived too
late. Wir sind zu spät gekommen.
◆ **too much** zu viel ◊ too much noise zu
viel Lärm ◊ At Christmas we always eat
too much. Zu Weihnachten essen wir
immer zu viel. ◊ Seventy euros? That's
too much. Siebzig Euro? Das ist zu viel.
◆ **too many** zu viele ◊ too many
hamburgers zu viele Hamburger
◆ **Too bad!** Da kann man nichts machen!

took VERB see **take**

tool NOUN
das <u>Werkzeug</u> (PL die Werkzeuge)
◆ **a tool box** ein Werkzeugkasten MASC

tooth NOUN
der <u>Zahn</u> (PL die Zähne)

toothache NOUN
die <u>Zahnschmerzen</u> MASC PL ◊ to have
toothache Zahnschmerzen haben

toothbrush NOUN
die <u>Zahnbürste</u>

toothpaste NOUN
die <u>Zahnpasta</u> (PL die Zahnpasten)

top NOUN

see also **top** ADJECTIVE

1 (of tree)
die <u>Spitze</u>
2 (of mountain)
der <u>Gipfel</u> (PL die Gipfel)
3 (of garment)
das <u>Oberteil</u> (PL die Oberteile) ◊ a bikini
top ein Bikinioberteil
4 (of table)
das <u>Kopfende</u> (PL die Kopfenden)
5 (of box, jar)
der <u>Deckel</u> (PL die Deckel)
6 (of bottle)
der <u>Verschluss</u> (GEN des Verschlusses, PL
die Verschlüsse)
◆ **at the top of the page** oben auf der Seite
◆ **to reach the top of the ladder** oben auf
der Leiter ankommen
◆ **on top of** (on) oben auf ◊ on top of the
cupboard oben auf dem Schrank
◆ **There's a surcharge on top of that.** Es
kommt noch ein Zuschlag dazu.
◆ **from top to bottom** von oben bis unten
◊ I searched the house from top to
bottom. Ich habe das Haus von oben bis
unten durchsucht.

top ADJECTIVE

see also **top** NOUN

<u>erstklassig</u> (first-class) ◊ a top hotel ein
erstklassiges Hotel
◆ **a top surgeon** ein Spitzenchirurg MASC
◆ **a top model** (fashion) ein Topmodel NEUT

◆ **He always gets top marks in German.** Er
bekommt in Deutsch immer
Spitzennoten.
◆ **the top floor** der oberste Stock ◊ on the
top floor im obersten Stock

topic NOUN
das <u>Thema</u> (PL die Themen) ◊ The essay
can be on any topic. Der Aufsatz kann
über ein beliebiges Thema sein.

topical ADJECTIVE
<u>aktuell</u> ◊ a topical issue ein aktuelles
Problem

topless ADJECTIVE, ADVERB
<u>oben ohne</u> ◊ to go topless oben ohne
gehen

top-secret ADJECTIVE
<u>streng geheim</u> ◊ top-secret documents
streng geheime Dokumente

torch NOUN
die <u>Taschenlampe</u>

tore, torn VERB see **tear**

tortoise NOUN
die <u>Schildkröte</u>

torture NOUN

see also **torture** VERB

die <u>Folter</u>
◆ **It was pure torture.** Es war die Hölle.
(informal)

to **torture** VERB

see also **torture** NOUN

<u>quälen</u> ◊ Stop torturing that poor
animal! Hör auf, das arme Tier zu
quälen!

Tory ADJECTIVE

see also **Tory** NOUN

<u>konservativ</u> ◊ the Tory government die
konservative Regierung

Tory NOUN

see also **Tory** ADJECTIVE

der <u>Konservative</u> (GEN des
Konservativen, PL die Konservativen)
die <u>Konservative</u> (GEN der Konservativen)
◊ a Tory (man) ein Konservativer
◆ **the Tories** die Konservativen

to **toss** VERB
◆ **to toss pancakes** Pfannkuchen in der Luft
wenden
◆ **Shall we toss for it?** Sollen wir eine
Münze werfen?

total ADJECTIVE

see also **total** NOUN

<u>gesamt</u> ◊ the total amount der gesamte
Betrag

total NOUN

see also **total** ADJECTIVE

1 die <u>Gesamtmenge</u> (amount)
2 die <u>Endsumme</u> (money, figures)
◆ **the grand total** die Gesamtsumme

totally ADVERB
<u>völlig</u> ◊ He's totally useless. Er ist völlig
unfähig.

touch NOUN

see also **touch** VERB

+ **to get in touch with somebody** sich mit jemandem in Verbindung setzen
+ **to keep in touch with somebody** mit jemandem in Verbindung bleiben
+ **Keep in touch!** Lass von dir hören!
+ **to lose touch** sich aus den Augen verlieren
+ **to lose touch with somebody** jemanden aus den Augen verlieren

to **touch** VERB

see also **touch** NOUN

berühren (PERFECT hat berührt)
+ **"Do not touch"** "Nicht berühren"
+ **Don't touch that!** Fass das nicht an!

touchdown NOUN
die Landung

touched ADJECTIVE
gerührt ◊ *I was really touched.* Ich war wirklich gerührt.

touching ADJECTIVE
rührend

touchline NOUN
die Seitenlinie

touchy ADJECTIVE
empfindlich ◊ *She's a bit touchy.* Sie ist etwas empfindlich.

tough ADJECTIVE
[1] hart ◊ *It was tough, but I managed OK.* Es war hart, aber ich habe es geschafft. ◊ *It's a tough job.* Das ist eine harte Arbeit. ◊ *He thinks he's a tough guy.* Er meint, er sei ein harter Bursche.
[2] zäh (*meat*) ◊ *The meat's tough.* Das Fleisch ist zäh.
[3] fest (*strong*) ◊ *tough leather gloves* feste Lederhandschuhe
+ **Tough luck!** Das ist Pech!

toupee NOUN
das Toupet (PL die Toupets)

tour NOUN

see also **tour** VERB

[1] die Besichtigung (*of town, museum*)
+ **We went on a tour of the city.** Wir haben die Stadt besichtigt.
+ **a guided tour** eine Führung
+ **a package tour** eine Pauschalreise
[2] die Tournee (*by singer, group*) ◊ *on tour* auf Tournee ◊ *to go on tour* auf Tournee gehen

to **tour** VERB

see also **tour** NOUN

+ **Sting's touring Europe.** Sting ist auf Europatournee.

tour guide NOUN
der Reiseleiter (PL die Reiseleiter)
die Reiseleiterin

tourism NOUN
der Tourismus (GEN des Tourismus)

tourist NOUN
der Tourist (GEN des Touristen, PL die Touristen)

die Touristin
+ **tourist information office** das Verkehrsbüro

tournament NOUN
das Turnier (PL die Turniere)

tour operator NOUN
der Reiseveranstalter (PL die Reiseveranstalter)

towards PREPOSITION
[1] auf ... zu (*in the direction of*) ◊ *He came towards me.* Er kam auf mich zu.
[2] gegenüber (*of attitude*) ◊ *my feelings towards him* meine Empfindungen ihm gegenüber

towel NOUN
das Handtuch (PL die Handtücher)

tower NOUN
der Turm (PL die Türme)
+ **a tower block** ein Hochhaus NEUT

town NOUN
die Stadt (PL die Städte)
+ **a town plan** ein Stadtplan MASC
+ **the town centre** die Stadtmitte
+ **the town hall** das Rathaus

tow truck NOUN US
der Abschleppwagen (PL die Abschleppwagen)

toy NOUN
das Spielzeug (PL die Spielzeuge)
+ **a toy shop** ein Spielwarengeschäft NEUT
+ **a toy car** ein Spielzeugauto NEUT

trace NOUN

see also **trace** VERB

die Spur ◊ *There was no trace of the robbers.* Es gab keine Spur von den Räubern.

to **trace** VERB

see also **trace** NOUN

nachziehen (*draw*) (IMPERFECT zog nach, PERFECT hat nachgezogen)

tracing paper NOUN
das Pauspapier

track NOUN
[1] (*dirt road*)
der Pfad (PL die Pfade)
[2] (*railway line*)
das Gleis (GEN des Gleises, PL die Gleise)
[3] (*in sport*)
die Rennbahn ◊ *two laps of the track* zwei Runden der Rennbahn
[4] (*song*)
das Stück (PL die Stücke) ◊ *This is my favourite track.* Das ist mein Lieblingsstück.
[5] (*trail*)
die Spur ◊ *They followed the tracks for miles.* Sie folgten der Spur meilenweit.

to **track down** VERB
+ **to track somebody down** jemanden finden ◊ *The police never tracked down the killer.* Die Polizei hat den Mörder nie gefunden.

tracksuit NOUN

T

der Jogginganzug (PL die Jogginganzüge)

tractor NOUN
der Traktor (PL die Traktoren)

trade NOUN
das Handwerk (*skill, job*) ◊ *to learn a trade* ein Handwerk erlernen

trade union NOUN
die Gewerkschaft

> ⓘ *Unions in Germany are organized within the* **Deutscher Gewerkschaftsbund (DGB)**.

trade unionist NOUN
der Gewerkschafter (PL die Gewerkschafter)
die Gewerkschafterin

tradition NOUN
die Tradition

traditional ADJECTIVE
traditionell

traffic NOUN
der Verkehr ◊ *The traffic was terrible.* Es war furchtbar viel Verkehr.

traffic circle NOUN US
der Kreisverkehr (PL die Kreisverkehre)

traffic jam NOUN
der Stau (PL die Staus)

traffic lights PL NOUN
die Ampel SING

traffic warden NOUN
[1] (*man*)
der Hilfspolizist (GEN des Hilfspolizisten, PL die Hilfspolizisten)
[2] (*woman*)
die Politesse

tragedy NOUN
die Tragödie

tragic ADJECTIVE
tragisch

trailer NOUN
[1] (*vehicle*)
der Anhänger (PL die Anhänger)
[2] (*caravan*)
der Wohnwagen (PL die Wohnwagen)
[3] (*advert for film*)
die Vorschau

train NOUN
> see also **train** VERB

der Zug (PL die Züge)

to **train** VERB
> see also **train** NOUN

trainieren (*sport*) (PERFECT hat trainiert)
◊ *to train for a race* für ein Rennen trainieren
♦ **to train as a teacher** eine Lehrerausbildung machen
♦ **to train an animal to do something** ein Tier dressieren, etwas zu tun

trained ADJECTIVE
gelernt ◊ *She's a trained nurse.* Sie ist gelernte Krankenschwester.

trainee NOUN
[1] (*in profession*)
der Praktikant (GEN des Praktikanten, PL die Praktikanten)
die Praktikantin
◊ *She's a trainee.* Sie ist Praktikantin.
[2] (*apprentice*)
der Lehrling (PL die Lehrlinge)
> *der Lehrling* is also used for women.

◊ *She's a trainee plumber.* Sie ist Klempnerlehrling.

trainer NOUN
[1] (*sports coach*)
der Trainer (PL die Trainer)
die Trainerin
[2] (*of animals*)
der Dresseur (PL die Dresseure)
die Dresseuse

trainers PL NOUN
die Turnschuhe MASC PL ◊ *a pair of trainers* ein Paar Turnschuhe

training NOUN
[1] die Ausbildung ◊ *a training course* ein Ausbildungskurs MASC
[2] (*sport*)
das Training (PL die Trainings)

tram NOUN
die Straßenbahn

tramp NOUN
der Landstreicher (PL die Landstreicher)
die Landstreicherin

trampoline NOUN
das Trampolin (PL die Trampoline)

tranquillizer NOUN
das Beruhigungsmittel (PL die Beruhigungsmittel) ◊ *She's on tranquillizers.* Sie nimmt Beruhigungsmittel.

transfer NOUN
das Abziehbild (*sticker*) (PL die Abziehbilder)

transfusion NOUN
die Transfusion

transistor NOUN
der Transistor (PL die Transistoren)

transit lounge NOUN
die Transithalle

to **translate** VERB
übersetzen (PERFECT hat übersetzt) ◊ *to translate something into English* etwas ins Englische übersetzen

translation NOUN
die Übersetzung

translator NOUN
der Übersetzer (PL die Übersetzer)
die Übersetzerin
◊ *Anita's a translator.* Anita ist Übersetzerin.

transparent ADJECTIVE
durchsichtig

transplant NOUN
die Transplantation ◊ *a heart transplant* eine Herztransplantation

transport NOUN

> see also **transport** VERB

der Transport (PL die Transporte)
◊ the transport of goods der Warentransport

to **transport** VERB

> see also **transport** NOUN

transportieren (PERFECT hat transportiert)

trap NOUN
die Falle

trash NOUN US
der Müll

trash can NOUN US
der Mülleimer (PL die Mülleimer)

trashy ADJECTIVE
schlecht ◊ a really trashy film ein wirklich schlechter Film

traumatic ADJECTIVE
traumatisch ◊ It was a traumatic experience. Es war ein traumatisches Erlebnis.

travel NOUN

> see also **travel** VERB

das Reisen

to **travel** VERB

> see also **travel** NOUN

reisen (PERFECT ist gereist) ◊ I prefer to travel by train. Ich reise lieber mit dem Zug.
♦ I'd like to travel round the world. Ich würde gern eine Weltreise machen.
♦ We travelled over eight hundred kilometres. Wir haben über achthundert Kilometer zurückgelegt.
♦ News travels fast! Neuigkeiten sprechen sich schnell herum!

travel agency NOUN
das Reisebüro (PL die Reisebüros)

travel agent NOUN
der Reisebürokaufmann (PL die Reisebürokaufleute)
die Reisebürokauffrau
◊ She's a travel agent. Sie ist Reisebürokauffrau.
♦ at the travel agent's im Reisebüro

traveller NOUN
[1] (on bus, train)
der Fahrgast (PL die Fahrgäste)
der Fahrgast is also used for women.
[2] (on plane)
der Passagier (PL die Passagiere)
die Passagierin

traveller's cheque NOUN
der Reisescheck (PL die Reiseschecks)

travelling NOUN
♦ I love travelling. Ich reise sehr gern.

travel sickness NOUN
die Reisekrankheit

tray NOUN
das Tablett (PL die Tabletts)

to **tread** VERB

treten (PRESENT tritt, IMPERFECT trat, PERFECT ist getreten) ◊ to tread on something auf etwas treten ◊ He trod on her foot. Er ist ihr auf den Fuß getreten.

treasure NOUN
der Schatz (GEN des Schatzes, PL die Schätze)

treat NOUN

> see also **treat** VERB

[1] (present)
das Geschenk (PL die Geschenke)
[2] (food)
der Leckerbissen (PL die Leckerbissen)
♦ to give somebody a treat jemandem eine besondere Freude machen

to **treat** VERB

> see also **treat** NOUN

behandeln (well, badly) (PERFECT hat behandelt)
♦ to treat somebody to something jemandem etwas spendieren ◊ He treated us to an ice cream. Er hat uns ein Eis spendiert.

treatment NOUN
die Behandlung

to **treble** VERB
sich verdreifachen (PERFECT hat sich verdreifacht) ◊ The cost of living has trebled. Die Lebenshaltungskosten haben sich verdreifacht.

tree NOUN
der Baum (PL die Bäume)

to **tremble** VERB
zittern

tremendous ADJECTIVE
[1] fantastisch ◊ Gordon is a tremendous person. Gordon ist fantastisch.
[2] gewaltig ◊ a tremendous success ein gewaltiger Erfolg

trend NOUN
der Trend (fashion) (PL die Trends)

trendy ADJECTIVE
modisch

trial NOUN
der Prozess (in court) (GEN des Prozesses, PL die Prozesse)

triangle NOUN
das Dreieck (PL die Dreiecke)

tribe NOUN
der Stamm (PL die Stämme)

trick NOUN

> see also **trick** VERB

[1] der Streich (PL die Streiche) ◊ to play a trick on somebody jemandem einen Streich spielen
[2] (knack)
der Trick (PL die Tricks) ◊ It's not easy: there's a trick to it. Das ist nicht leicht: Da ist ein Trick dabei.

to **trick** VERB

> see also **trick** NOUN

♦ to trick somebody jemanden reinlegen

tricky ADJECTIVE

T

knifflig

tricycle NOUN
das Dreirad (PL die Dreiräder)

trifle NOUN
(*dessert*)
das Trifle (PL die Trifles)

to **trim** VERB
see also **trim** NOUN
1 (*hair*)
schneiden (IMPERFECT schnitt, PERFECT hat geschnitten)
2 stutzen ◊ *He trimmed his moustache.* Er stutzte seinen Schnurrbart.
3 (*grass*)
mähen

trim NOUN
see also **trim** VERB
◆**to have a trim** sich die Haare schneiden lassen ◊ *You need a trim.* Du solltest dir die Haare schneiden lassen.

trip NOUN
see also **trip** VERB
die Reise ◊ *to go on a trip* eine Reise machen ◊ *Have a good trip!* Gute Reise!
◆**a day trip** ein Tagesausflug MASC

to **trip** VERB
see also **trip** NOUN
stolpern (*stumble*) (PERFECT ist gestolpert)

triple ADJECTIVE
dreifach

triplets PL NOUN
die Drillinge MASC PL

trivial ADJECTIVE
trivial

trod, trodden VERB *see* **tread**

trolley NOUN
1 (*for shopping*)
der Einkaufswagen (PL die Einkaufswagen)
2 (*for luggage*)
der Kofferkuli (PL die Kofferkulis)

trombone NOUN
die Posaune ◊ *I play the trombone.* Ich spiele Posaune.

troops PL NOUN
die Truppen FEM PL ◊ *British troops* die britischen Truppen

trophy NOUN
.die Trophäe ◊ *to win a trophy* eine Trophäe gewinnen

tropical ADJECTIVE
tropisch ◊ *tropical plants* tropische Pflanzen
◆**The weather was tropical.** Es war tropisch heiß.

to **trot** VERB
traben (PERFECT ist getrabt)

trouble NOUN
das Problem (PL die Probleme) ◊ *The trouble is, it's too expensive.* Das Problem ist, dass es zu teuer ist.

◆**What's the trouble?** Wo ist das Problem?
◆**to be in trouble** in Schwierigkeiten sein
◆**stomach trouble** die Magenbeschwerden FEM PL
◆**to take a lot of trouble over something** sich mit etwas viel Mühe geben ◊ *I took a lot of trouble over that project.* Ich habe mir mit dem Referat viel Mühe gegeben.
◆**Don't worry, it's no trouble.** Keine Sorge, das macht keine Mühe.

troublemaker NOUN
der Unruhestifter (PL die Unruhestifter)
die Unruhestifterin

trousers PL NOUN
die Hose SING ◊ *a pair of trousers* eine Hose

trout NOUN
die Forelle

truant NOUN
◆**to play truant** die Schule schwänzen

truck NOUN
der Lastwagen (PL die Lastwagen)
◆**He's a truck driver.** Er ist Lastwagenfahrer.

trucker NOUN US
der Lastwagenfahrer (*driver*) (PL die Lastwagenfahrer)

true ADJECTIVE
wahr ◊ *true love* wahre Liebe ◊ *That's true.* Das ist wahr.
◆**to come true** wahr werden ◊ *I hope my dream will come true.* Ich hoffe, mein Traum wird wahr.

trumpet NOUN
die Trompete ◊ *She plays the trumpet.* Sie spielt Trompete.

trunk NOUN
1 (*of tree*)
der Stamm (PL die Stämme)
2 (*of elephant*)
der Rüssel (PL die Rüssel)
3 (*luggage*)
der Schrankkoffer (PL die Schrankkoffer)
4 (*boot of car*)
der Kofferraum (PL die Kofferräume)

trunks PL NOUN
◆**swimming trunks** die Badehose SING ◊ *a pair of trunks* eine Badehose

trust NOUN
see also **trust** VERB
das Vertrauen ◊ *to have trust in somebody* Vertrauen zu jemandem haben

to **trust** VERB
see also **trust** NOUN
◆**to trust somebody** jemandem vertrauen ◊ *Don't you trust me?* Vertraust du mir nicht?
◆**Trust me!** Glaub mir!

trusting ADJECTIVE
vertrauensvoll

truth NOUN
die Wahrheit

truthful ADJECTIVE
ehrlich

try NOUN
see also **try** VERB
der Versuch (PL die Versuche) ◊ *his third
try* sein dritter Versuch
♦ **to have a try** es versuchen ◊ *I'll have a
try.* Ich werd's versuchen.
♦ **It's worth a try.** Der Versuch lohnt sich.
♦ **to give something a try** etwas versuchen

to **try** VERB
see also **try** NOUN
1 (*attempt*)
versuchen (PERFECT hat versucht) ◊ *to try
to do something* versuchen, etwas zu tun
♦ **to try again** es noch einmal versuchen
2 (*taste*)
probieren (PERFECT hat probiert) ◊ *Would
you like to try some?* Möchtest du etwas
probieren?
♦ **to try on** (*clothes*) anprobieren
♦ **to try something out** etwas
ausprobieren

T-shirt NOUN
das T-Shirt (PL die T-Shirts)

tube NOUN
die Tube
♦ **the Tube** (*underground*) die U-Bahn

tuberculosis NOUN
die Tuberkulose

Tuesday NOUN
der Dienstag (PL die Dienstage) ◊ *on
Tuesday* am Dienstag ◊ *every Tuesday*
jeden Dienstag ◊ *last Tuesday* letzten
Dienstag ◊ *next Tuesday* nächsten
Dienstag
♦ **on Tuesdays** dienstags

tug of war NOUN
das Tauziehen

tuition NOUN
1 der Unterricht
♦ **extra tuition** die Nachhilfestunden FEM PL
◊ *She receives extra tuition.* Sie
bekommt Nachhilfestunden.
2 die Studiengebühren FEM PL (*tuition
fees*)

tulip NOUN
die Tulpe

tumble dryer NOUN
der Wäschetrockner (PL die
Wäschetrockner)

tummy NOUN
der Bauch (PL die Bäuche) ◊ *I've got a
sore tummy.* Ich habe Bauchschmerzen.

tuna NOUN
der Thunfisch (PL die Thunfische)

tune NOUN
die Melodie (*melody*)
♦ **to play in tune** richtig spielen
♦ **to sing out of tune** falsch singen

Tunisia NOUN
Tunesien NEUT

♦ **in Tunisia** in Tunesien

tunnel NOUN
der Tunnel (PL die Tunnel)
♦ **the Tunnel** (*Chunnel*) der Kanaltunnel

Turk NOUN
der Türke (GEN des Türken, PL die Türken)
die Türkin

Turkey NOUN
die Türkei
*Note that the definite article is used in
German for countries which are
feminine.*
♦ **from Turkey** aus der Türkei
♦ **in Turkey** in der Türkei
♦ **to Turkey** in die Türkei

turkey NOUN
der Truthahn (PL die Truthähne)

Turkish ADJECTIVE
see also **Turkish** NOUN
türkisch

Turkish NOUN
see also **Turkish** ADJECTIVE
das Türkische (*language*) (GEN des
Türkischen)

turn NOUN
see also **turn** VERB
die Abbiegung (*in road*)
♦ **"no left turn"** "links abbiegen verboten"
♦ **Whose turn is it?** Wer ist an der Reihe?
♦ **It's my turn!** Ich bin an der Reihe!

to **turn** VERB
see also **turn** NOUN
1 abbiegen (IMPERFECT bog ab, PERFECT ist
abgebogen) ◊ *Turn right at the lights.*
Biegen Sie an der Ampel rechts ab.
2 (*become*)
werden (PRESENT wird, IMPERFECT wurde,
PERFECT ist geworden) ◊ *to turn red* rot
werden
♦ **to turn into something** sich in etwas
verwandeln ◊ *The frog turned into a
prince.* Der Frosch verwandelte sich in
einen Prinzen.

to **turn back** VERB
umkehren (PERFECT ist umgekehrt) ◊ *We
turned back.* Wir sind umgekehrt.

to **turn down** VERB
1 (*offer*)
ablehnen (PERFECT hat abgelehnt)
2 (*radio, TV*)
leiser stellen
3 (*heating*)
herunterdrehen (PERFECT hat
heruntergedreht)

to **turn off** VERB
1 (*light, radio*)
ausmachen (PERFECT hat ausgemacht)
2 (*tap*)
zudrehen (PERFECT hat zugedreht)
3 (*engine*)
ausschalten (PERFECT hat ausgeschaltet)

to **turn on** VERB
1 (*light, radio*)

T

anmachen (PERFECT hat angemacht)

2 (*tap*)

aufdrehen (PERFECT hat aufgedreht)

3 (*engine*)

anlassen (PRESENT lässt an, IMPERFECT ließ an, PERFECT hat angelassen)

to **turn out** VERB

♦ **It turned out to be a mistake.** Es stellte sich heraus, dass das ein Fehler war.

♦ **It turned out that she was right.** Es stellte sich heraus, dass sie recht hatte.

to **turn round** VERB

1 (*car*)

umkehren (PERFECT ist umgekehrt) ◊ *At the end of the street we turned round.* Am Ende der Straße kehrten wir um.

2 (*person*)

sich umdrehen (PERFECT hat sich umgedreht) ◊ *I turned round.* Ich drehte mich um.

to **turn up** VERB

1 (*arrive*)

aufkreuzen (PERFECT ist aufgekreuzt)

2 (*heater*)

höherstellen

3 (*radio, TV*)

lauter machen

turning NOUN

♦ **It's the third turning on the left.** Es ist die dritte Straße links.

♦ **We took the wrong turning.** Wir sind falsch abgebogen.

turnip NOUN

die Steckrübe

turquoise ADJECTIVE

türkis (*colour*)

turtle NOUN

die Meeresschildkröte

tutor NOUN

(*private teacher*)

der Lehrer (PL die Lehrer)

die Lehrerin

tuxedo NOUN US

der Smoking (PL die Smokings)

TV NOUN

das Fernsehen

tweezers PL NOUN

die Pinzette SING ◊ *a pair of tweezers* eine Pinzette

twelfth ADJECTIVE

zwölfte ◊ *the twelfth floor* der zwölfte Stock

♦ **the twelfth of August** der zwölfte August

twelve NUMBER

zwölf ◊ *She's twelve.* Sie ist zwölf. ◊ *at twelve o'clock* um zwölf Uhr

twentieth ADJECTIVE

zwanzigste

♦ **the twentieth of August** der zwanzigste August

twenty NUMBER

zwanzig ◊ *He's twenty.* Er ist zwanzig.

twice ADVERB

zweimal

♦ **twice as much** doppelt so viel ◊ *He gets twice as much pocket money as me.* Er bekommt doppelt so viel Taschengeld wie ich.

twin NOUN

der Zwilling (PL die Zwillinge)

der Zwilling is also used for women.

♦ **my twin brother** mein Zwillingsbruder MASC

♦ **her twin sister** ihre Zwillingsschwester

♦ **identical twins** eineiige Zwillinge

♦ **a twin room** ein Doppelzimmer mit zwei Betten

twinned ADJECTIVE

♦ **Oxford is twinned with Bonn.** Oxford und Bonn sind Partnerstädte.

to **twist** VERB

1 (*bend*)

biegen (IMPERFECT bog, PERFECT hat gebogen)

♦ **I've twisted my ankle.** Ich habe mir den Fuß vertreten.

2 (*distort*)

verdrehen (PERFECT hat verdreht) ◊ *You're twisting my words.* Sie verdrehen meine Worte.

twit NOUN

der Trottel (*informal*) (PL die Trottel)

der Trottel is also used for women.

two NUMBER

zwei ◊ *She's two.* Sie ist zwei.

type NOUN

see also **type** VERB

die Art ◊ *What type of camera have you got?* Welche Art von Fotoapparat hast du?

to **type** VERB

see also **type** NOUN

Schreibmaschine schreiben (IMPERFECT schrieb Schreibmaschine, PERFECT hat Schreibmaschine geschrieben) ◊ *Can you type?* Kannst du Schreibmaschine schreiben?

♦ **to type a letter** einen Brief tippen

typewriter NOUN

die Schreibmaschine

typical ADJECTIVE

typisch ◊ *That's just typical!* Das ist typisch!

tyre NOUN

der Reifen (PL die Reifen) ◊ *the tyre pressure* der Reifendruck

U

UFO NOUN (= *unidentified flying object*)
das UFO (PL die UFOs) (= unbekanntes
Flugobjekt)

ugh EXCLAMATION
igitt

ugly ADJECTIVE
hässlich

UK NOUN (= *United Kingdom*)
das Vereinigte Königreich
♦ **from the UK** aus dem Vereinigten
Königreich
♦ **in the UK** im Vereinigten Königreich
♦ **to the UK** in das Vereinigte Königreich

ulcer NOUN
das Geschwür (PL die Geschwüre)

Ulster NOUN
Ulster NEUT
♦ **from Ulster** aus Ulster
♦ **in Ulster** in Ulster
♦ **to Ulster** nach Ulster

ultimate ADJECTIVE
äußerste ◊ *the ultimate challenge* die
äußerste Herausforderung
♦ **It was the ultimate adventure.** Das war
das große Abenteuer.

ultimately ADVERB
schließlich ◊ *Ultimately, it's your
decision.* Schließlich ist es deine
Entscheidung.

umbrella NOUN
1 der Regenschirm (PL die
Regenschirme)
2 (*for sun*)
der Sonnenschirm (PL die
Sonnenschirme)

umlaut NOUN
der Umlaut ◊ *The plural of 'Haus' is
written with an umlaut.* Der Plural von
"Haus" wird mit Umlaut gebildet.
♦ **a umlaut** ä
♦ **o umlaut** ö
♦ **u umlaut** ü

umpire NOUN
der Schiedsrichter (PL die Schiedsrichter)
die Schiedsrichterin

UN NOUN (= *United Nations*)
die UN PL

unable ADJECTIVE
♦ **to be unable to do something** etwas
nicht tun können ◊ *I was unable to come.*
Ich konnte nicht kommen.

unacceptable ADJECTIVE
unannehmbar

unanimous ADJECTIVE
einstimmig ◊ *a unanimous decision* ein
einstimmiger Beschluss

unavoidable ADJECTIVE
unvermeidlich

unaware ADJECTIVE
♦ **to be unaware (1)** (*not know about*) nichts
wissen ◊ *I was unaware of the
regulations.* Ich wusste nichts von den
Bestimmungen.
♦ **to be unaware (2)** (*not notice*) nicht
merken ◊ *She was unaware that she was
being filmed.* Sie merkte nicht, dass sie
gefilmt wurde.

unbearable ADJECTIVE
unerträglich

unbeatable ADJECTIVE
unschlagbar

unbelievable ADJECTIVE
unglaublich

unborn ADJECTIVE
ungeboren ◊ *the unborn child* das
ungeborene Kind

unbreakable ADJECTIVE
unzerbrechlich

uncanny ADJECTIVE
unheimlich ◊ *That's uncanny!* Das ist
unheimlich!
♦ **an uncanny resemblance to** eine
verblüffende Ähnlichkeit mit

uncertain ADJECTIVE
ungewiss ◊ *The future is uncertain.* Die
Zukunft ist ungewiss.
♦ **to be uncertain about something** sich
über etwas nicht im Klaren sein ◊ *I'm
uncertain about her plans.* Ich bin mir
über ihre Pläne nicht im Klaren.

uncivilized ADJECTIVE
unzivilisiert

uncle NOUN
der Onkel (PL die Onkel)

uncomfortable ADJECTIVE
unbequem ◊ *The seats are rather
uncomfortable.* Die Sitze sind ziemlich
unbequem.

unconscious ADJECTIVE
bewusstlos

uncontrollable ADJECTIVE
unkontrollierbar

unconventional ADJECTIVE
unkonventionell

under PREPOSITION
unter

*Use the accusative to express movement
or a change of place. Use the dative
when there is no change of place.*

◊ *The ball rolled under the table.* Der Ball
rollte unter den Tisch. ◊ *The cat's under
the table.* Die Katze ist unter dem Tisch.
◊ *children under ten* Kinder unter zehn
♦ **under there** da drunter ◊ *What's under
there?* Was ist da drunter?

♦ **under twenty people** weniger als zwanzig Leute

underage ADJECTIVE
minderjährig

undercover ADJECTIVE, ADVERB

♦ **an undercover agent** (*secret agent*) ein Geheimagent MASC

♦ **She was working undercover.** Sie führte verdeckte Ermittlungen durch.

underdog NOUN
der Underdog (PL die Underdogs)
◊ *Arsenal were the underdogs on this occasion.* Arsenal waren diesmal die Underdogs.

to **underestimate** VERB
unterschätzen (PERFECT hat unterschätzt)
◊ *I underestimated her.* Ich habe sie unterschätzt.

to **undergo** VERB
sich unterziehen (*operation*) (IMPERFECT unterzog sich, PERFECT hat sich unterzogen)

underground ADJECTIVE, ADVERB

see also **underground** NOUN

[1] unterirdisch ◊ *underground water pipes* unterirdische Wasserrohre

♦ **an underground car park** eine Tiefgarage

[2] unter der Erde ◊ *Moles live underground.* Maulwürfe leben unter der Erde.

underground NOUN

see also **underground** ADJECTIVE

die U-Bahn ◊ *Is there an underground in Bonn?* Gibt es in Bonn eine U-Bahn?

to **underline** VERB
unterstreichen (IMPERFECT unterstrich, PERFECT hat unterstrichen)

underneath PREPOSITION, ADVERB

[1] unter

Use the accusative to express movement or a change of place. Use the dative when there is no change of place.

◊ *I put it underneath that pile.* Ich habe es unter diesen Stapel gelegt. ◊ *It was hidden underneath the carpet.* Es war unter dem Teppich versteckt.

[2] darunter ◊ *I got out of the car and looked underneath.* Ich stieg aus dem Auto aus und sah darunter.

underpaid ADJECTIVE
unterbezahlt ◊ *I'm underpaid.* Ich bin unterbezahlt.

underpants PL NOUN
die Unterhose SING ◊ *a pair of underpants* eine Unterhose

underpass NOUN
die Unterführung

undershirt NOUN US
das Unterhemd (PL die Unterhemden)

underskirt NOUN
der Unterrock (PL die Unterröcke)

to **understand** VERB

verstehen (IMPERFECT verstand, PERFECT hat verstanden) ◊ *Do you understand?* Verstehst du? ◊ *I don't understand this word.* Ich verstehe dieses Wort nicht. ◊ *Is that understood?* Ist das verstanden?

understanding ADJECTIVE
verständnisvoll ◊ *She's very understanding.* Sie ist sehr verständnisvoll.

understood VERB see **understand**

undertaker NOUN
der Beerdigungsunternehmer (PL die Beerdigungsunternehmer)
die Beerdigungsunternehmerin

underwater ADJECTIVE, ADVERB
unter Wasser ◊ *This sequence was filmed underwater.* Diese Sequenz wurde unter Wasser gefilmt.

♦ **an underwater camera** eine Unterwasserkamera

underwear NOUN
die Unterwäsche

underwent VERB see **undergo**

to **undo** VERB
aufmachen (PERFECT hat aufgemacht)

to **undress** VERB
sich ausziehen (*get undressed*) (IMPERFECT zog sich aus, PERFECT hat sich ausgezogen) ◊ *The doctor told me to get undressed.* Der Arzt bat mich, mich auszuziehen.

uneconomic ADJECTIVE
unrentabel

unemployed ADJECTIVE
arbeitslos ◊ *He's unemployed.* Er ist arbeitslos. ◊ *He's been unemployed for a year.* Er ist seit einem Jahr arbeitslos.

♦ **the unemployed** die Arbeitslosen MASC PL

unemployment NOUN
die Arbeitslosigkeit

unexpected ADJECTIVE
unerwartet ◊ *an unexpected visitor* ein unerwarteter Gast

unexpectedly ADVERB
überraschend ◊ *They arrived unexpectedly.* Sie sind überraschend gekommen.

unfair ADJECTIVE
unfair ◊ *It's unfair to girls.* Es ist Mädchen gegenüber unfair.

unfamiliar ADJECTIVE
unbekannt ◊ *I heard an unfamiliar voice.* Ich hörte eine unbekannte Stimme.

unfashionable ADJECTIVE
unmodern

unfit ADJECTIVE
nicht fit ◊ *I'm rather unfit at the moment.* Ich bin im Moment nicht sehr fit.

to **unfold** VERB
auseinanderfalten (PERFECT hat auseinandergefaltet) ◊ *She unfolded the map.* Sie faltete die Karte auseinander.

unforgettable ADJECTIVE
<u>unvergesslich</u>

unfortunately ADVERB
<u>leider</u> ◊ *Unfortunately, I arrived late.* Ich bin leider zu spät gekommen.

unfriendly ADJECTIVE
<u>unfreundlich</u> ◊ *The waiters are a bit unfriendly.* Die Kellner sind etwas unfreundlich.

ungrateful ADJECTIVE
<u>undankbar</u>

unhappy ADJECTIVE
<u>unglücklich</u> ◊ *He was very unhappy as a child.* Er war als Kind sehr unglücklich.
◊ *to look unhappy* unglücklich aussehen

unhealthy ADJECTIVE
<u>ungesund</u>

uni NOUN
die <u>Uni</u> (PL die Unis) ◊ *to go to uni* zur Uni gehen

uniform NOUN
die <u>Uniform</u> ◊ *the school uniform* die Schuluniform

> ❶ School uniforms are virtually nonexistent in Germany.

uninhabited ADJECTIVE
<u>unbewohnt</u>

union NOUN
die <u>Gewerkschaft</u> (*trade union*)

Union Jack NOUN
die <u>britische Flagge</u>

unique ADJECTIVE
<u>einzigartig</u>

unit NOUN
die <u>Einheit</u> ◊ *a unit of measurement* eine Maßeinheit
♦ **a kitchen unit** ein Kücheneinbauschrank MASC

United Kingdom NOUN
das <u>Vereinigte Königreich</u>
♦ **from the United Kingdom** aus dem Vereinigten Königreich
♦ **in the United Kingdom** im Vereinigten Königreich
♦ **to the United Kingdom** in das Vereinigte Königreich

United Nations PL NOUN
die <u>Vereinten Nationen</u> FEM PL

United States NOUN
die <u>Vereinigten Staaten</u> MASC PL
♦ **from the United States** aus den Vereinigten Staaten
♦ **in the United States** in den Vereinigten Staaten
♦ **to the United States** in die Vereinigten Staaten

universe NOUN
das <u>Universum</u>

university NOUN
die <u>Universität</u> ◊ *Do you want to go to university?* Möchtest du auf die Universität gehen? ◊ *Lancaster University* die Universität von Lancaster
♦ **She's at university.** Sie studiert.

unleaded petrol NOUN
das <u>bleifreie Benzin</u>

unless CONJUNCTION
<u>es sei denn</u> ◊ *unless he leaves* es sei denn, er geht ◊ *I won't come unless you phone me.* Ich komme nicht, es sei denn, du rufst an.

unlike PREPOSITION
<u>im Gegensatz zu</u> ◊ *Unlike him, I really enjoy flying.* Im Gegensatz zu ihm fliege ich wirklich gern.

unlikely ADJECTIVE
<u>unwahrscheinlich</u> ◊ *It's possible, but unlikely.* Es ist möglich, aber unwahrscheinlich.

unlisted ADJECTIVE US
♦ **to have an unlisted number** nicht im Telefonbuch stehen

to **unload** VERB
<u>ausladen</u> (PRESENT lädt aus, IMPERFECT lud aus, PERFECT hat ausgeladen) ◊ *We unloaded the car.* Wir haben das Auto ausgeladen.
♦ **The lorries go there to unload.** Die Lastwagen fahren dorthin um abzuladen.

to **unlock** VERB
<u>aufschließen</u> (IMPERFECT schloss auf, PERFECT hat aufgeschlossen) ◊ *He unlocked the door of the car.* Er schloss die Autotür auf.

unlucky ADJECTIVE
♦ **to be unlucky (1)** (*number, object*) Unglück bringen ◊ *They say thirteen is an unlucky number.* Es heißt, dass die Zahl dreizehn Unglück bringt.
♦ **to be unlucky (2)** (*person*) kein Glück haben ◊ *Did you win? – No, I was unlucky.* Hast du gewonnen? – Nein, ich habe kein Glück gehabt.

unmarried ADJECTIVE
<u>unverheiratet</u> (*person*) ◊ *an unmarried couple* ein unverheiratetes Paar
♦ **an unmarried mother** eine ledige Mutter

unnatural ADJECTIVE
<u>unnatürlich</u>

unnecessary ADJECTIVE
<u>unnötig</u>

unofficial ADJECTIVE
1 <u>inoffiziell</u> (*meeting, leader*)
2 <u>wild</u> (*strike*)

to **unpack** VERB
<u>auspacken</u> (*clothes, case*) (PERFECT hat ausgepackt) ◊ *I went to my room to unpack.* Ich ging auf mein Zimmer, um auszupacken.

unpleasant ADJECTIVE
<u>unangenehm</u>

U

to **unplug** VERB
  ausstecken (PERFECT hat ausgesteckt)
  ◇ *She unplugged the TV.* Sie hat den
  Fernseher ausgesteckt.

unpopular ADJECTIVE
  unbeliebt

unpredictable ADJECTIVE
  unvorhersehbar (*event*)

unreal ADJECTIVE
  unglaublich (*incredible*) ◇ *It was unreal!*
  Es war unglaublich!

unrealistic ADJECTIVE
  unrealistisch

unreasonable ADJECTIVE
  unmöglich ◇ *Her attitude was
  completely unreasonable.* Ihre Haltung
  war völlig unmöglich.

unreliable ADJECTIVE
  unzuverlässig ◇ *He's completely
  unreliable.* Er ist total unzuverlässig.

to **unroll** VERB
  aufrollen (PERFECT hat aufgerollt)

unsatisfactory ADJECTIVE
  unbefriedigend

to **unscrew** VERB
  aufschrauben (PERFECT hat aufgeschraubt)
  ◇ *She unscrewed the top of the bottle.*
  Sie schraubte den Flaschenverschluss
  auf.

unshaven ADJECTIVE
  unrasiert

unskilled ADJECTIVE
  ungelernt ◇ *an unskilled worker* ein
  ungelernter Arbeiter

unstable ADJECTIVE
  1 nicht stabil (*object*)
  2 labil (*person*)

unsteady ADJECTIVE
  unsicher (*walk, voice*)
  ♦ **He was unsteady on his feet.** Er war
  wackelig auf den Beinen.

unsuccessful ADJECTIVE
  erfolglos (*attempt*) ◇ *an unsuccessful
  artist* ein erfolgloser Künstler
  ♦ **to be unsuccessful in doing something**
  keinen Erfolg bei etwas haben ◇ *He was
  unsuccessful in getting a job.* Er hatte bei
  der Arbeitssuche keinen Erfolg.

unsuitable ADJECTIVE
  ungeeignet (*clothes, equipment*)

untidy ADJECTIVE
  unordentlich

to **untie** VERB
  1 (*knot, parcel*)
  aufmachen (PERFECT hat aufgemacht)
  2 (*animal*)
  losbinden (IMPERFECT band los, PERFECT hat
  losgebunden)

until PREPOSITION, CONJUNCTION
  1 bis ◇ *I waited until ten o'clock.* Ich
  habe bis zehn Uhr gewartet.

♦ **until now** bis jetzt ◇ *It's never been a
  problem until now.* Es war bis jetzt nie
  ein Problem.

♦ **until then** bis dahin ◇ *Until then I'd never
  been to Germany.* Bis dahin war ich noch
  nie in Deutschland gewesen.

  2 vor

Use **vor** if the sentence you want to
translate contains a negative, such as
"not" or "never".

  ◇ *It won't be ready until next week.* Es
  wird nicht vor nächster Woche fertig
  sein. ◇ *Until last year I'd never been to
  Germany.* Vor letztem Jahr war ich noch
  nie in Deutschland.

unusual ADJECTIVE
  ungewöhnlich ◇ *an unusual shape* eine
  ungewöhnliche Form ◇ *It's unusual to
  get snow at this time of year.* Es ist
  ungewöhnlich, dass es um diese
  Jahreszeit schneit.

unwilling ADJECTIVE
  ♦ **to be unwilling to do something** nicht
  gewillt sein, etwas zu tun ◇ *He was
  unwilling to help me.* Er war nicht
  gewillt, mir zu helfen.

to **unwind** VERB
  sich entspannen (*relax*) (PERFECT hat sich
  entspannt)

unwise ADJECTIVE
  unklug (*person*) ◇ *That was rather
  unwise of you.* Das war ziemlich unklug
  von dir.

unwound VERB *see* **unwind**

to **unwrap** VERB
  auspacken (PERFECT hat ausgepackt)
  ◇ *After the meal we unwrapped the
  presents.* Nach dem Essen haben wir die
  Geschenke ausgepackt.

up PREPOSITION, ADVERB
  auf

Use the accusative to express movement
or a change of place. Use the dative
when there is no change of place.
  ◇ *He drove me up the hill.* Er hat mich
  den Berg hinaufgefahren. ◇ *the chapel
  up on the hill* die Kapelle auf dem Berg
  ♦ **up here** hier oben
  ♦ **up there** dort oben
  ♦ **up north** oben im Norden
  ♦ **to be up** (*out of bed*) auf sein ◇ *We were
  up at six.* Wir waren um sechs Uhr auf.
  ◇ *He's not up yet.* Er ist noch nicht auf.
  ♦ **What's up?** Was gibt's?
  ♦ **What's up with her?** Was ist los mit ihr?
  ♦ **to get up** (*in the morning*) aufstehen
  ◇ *What time do you get up?* Um wie viel
  Uhr stehst du auf?
  ♦ **to go up (1)** hinauffahren ◇ *The bus went
  up the hill.* Der Bus ist den Berg
  hinaufgefahren.

♦**to go up (2)** (*on foot*) hinaufgehen ◊ *We went up the hill.* Wir sind den Berg hinaufgegangen.

♦**to go up to somebody** auf jemanden zugehen

♦**She came up to me.** Sie kam auf mich zu.

♦**up to** (*as far as*) bis ◊ *to count up to fifty* bis fünfzig zählen ◊ *up to three hours* bis zu drei Stunden ◊ *up to now* bis jetzt

♦**It's up to you.** Das ist dir überlassen.

For other expressions with up, see the verbs go, come, put, turn etc.

upbringing NOUN
die Erziehung

uphill ADVERB
bergauf

upper sixth NOUN
♦**the upper sixth** die dreizehnte Klasse ◊ *She's in the upper sixth.* Sie ist in der dreizehnten Klasse.

upright ADJECTIVE
♦**to stand upright** aufrecht stehen

upset NOUN
see also **upset** ADJECTIVE, VERB
♦**a stomach upset** eine Magenverstimmung

upset ADJECTIVE
see also **upset** NOUN, VERB
1 gekränkt (*hurt*) ◊ *She was upset when he said that.* Sie fühlte sich gekränkt, als er das sagte.
2 betrübt (*sad*) ◊ *I was very upset when my father died.* Ich war sehr betrübt, als mein Vater starb.
♦**an upset stomach** eine Magenverstimmung

to **upset** VERB
see also **upset** NOUN, ADJECTIVE
aufregen (PERFECT hat aufgeregt) ◊ *Don't say anything to upset her!* Sag nichts, was sie aufregen könnte.

upside down ADVERB
verkehrt herum ◊ *That painting is upside down.* Das Bild ist verkehrt herum.

upstairs ADVERB
oben ◊ *Where's your coat? – It's upstairs.* Wo ist dein Mantel? – Er ist oben.
♦**the people upstairs** die Leute von oben
♦**to go upstairs** hinaufgehen

uptight ADJECTIVE
nervös (*nervous*) ◊ *She's really uptight.* Sie ist echt nervös.

up-to-date ADJECTIVE
1 modern (*car, stereo*)
2 aktuell (*information*) ◊ *an up-to-date timetable* ein aktueller Fahrplan
♦**to bring something up to date** etwas auf den neuesten Stand bringen

♦**to keep somebody up to date** jemanden auf dem Laufenden halten

upwards ADVERB
hinauf ◊ *to look upwards* hinaufsehen

urgent ADJECTIVE
dringend ◊ *Is it urgent?* Ist es dringend?

urine NOUN
der Urin

US SING NOUN
die USA PL
♦**from the US** aus den USA
♦**in the US** in den USA
♦**to the US** in die USA

us PRONOUN
uns ◊ *They saw us.* Sie haben uns gesehen. ◊ *They gave us a map.* Sie gaben uns eine Karte.
♦**Who is it? – It's us!** Wer ist da? – Wir sind's!

USA NOUN
die USA PL
♦**from the USA** aus den USA
♦**in the USA** in den USA
♦**to the USA** in die USA

use NOUN
see also **use** VERB
♦**It's no use.** Es hat keinen Zweck. ◊ *It's no use shouting, she's deaf.* Es hat keinen Zweck zu brüllen, sie ist taub. ◊ *It's no use, I can't do it.* Es hat keinen Zweck, ich kann's nicht.
♦**to make use of something** etwas benützen

to **use** VERB
see also **use** NOUN
benützen (PERFECT hat benützt) ◊ *Can we use a dictionary in the exam?* Können wir in der Prüfung ein Wörterbuch benützen?
♦**Can I use your phone?** Kann ich mal telefonieren?
♦**to use the toilet** auf die Toilette gehen
♦**to use up** aufbrauchen ◊ *We've used up all the paint.* Ich habe die ganze Farbe aufgebraucht.
♦**I used to live in London.** Ich habe früher mal in London gelebt.
♦**I used not to like maths, but now ...** Früher habe ich Mathe nicht gemocht, aber jetzt ...
♦**to be used to something** an etwas gewöhnt sein ◊ *He wasn't used to driving on the right.* Er war nicht daran gewöhnt, rechts zu fahren. ◊ *Don't worry, I'm used to it.* Keine Sorge, ich bin daran gewöhnt.
♦**a used car** ein Gebrauchtwagen MASC

useful ADJECTIVE
nützlich

useless ADJECTIVE
nutzlos ◊ *This map is just useless.* Diese Karte ist echt nutzlos.
♦**You're useless!** Du bist zu nichts zu gebrauchen!

U

♦ **It's useless asking her!** Es ist zwecklos,
sie zu fragen!
user NOUN
der <u>Benutzer</u> (PL die Benutzer)
die <u>Benutzerin</u>
user-friendly ADJECTIVE
<u>benutzerfreundlich</u>
usual ADJECTIVE
<u>üblich</u> ◊ *as usual* wie üblich
usually ADVERB

<u>normalerweise</u> ◊ *I usually get to school
at about half past eight.* Ich bin
normalerweise um halb neun in der
Schule.
utility room NOUN
der <u>Abstellraum</u> (PL die Abstellräume)
U-turn NOUN
die <u>Wende</u>
♦ **to do a U-turn** wenden
♦ **"No U-turns"** "Wenden verboten"

V

vacancy NOUN
1 (job)
die freie Stelle
2 (room in hotel)
das freie Zimmer (PL die freien Zimmer)
♦ "Vacancies" "Zimmer frei"
♦ "No vacancies" "Belegt"

vacant ADJECTIVE
1 frei (seat, job)
2 leer stehend (building)
3 leer (look) ◊ There was a vacant look in her face. Sie hatte einen leeren Blick.

vacation NOUN US
1 (from school)
die Ferien PL ◊ They went on vacation to Mexico. Sie haben in Mexiko Ferien gemacht.
2 (from work)
der Urlaub (PL die Urlaube) ◊ I have thirty days' vacation a year. Ich habe dreißig Tage Urlaub im Jahr.

to **vaccinate** VERB
impfen

to **vacuum** VERB
staubsaugen (IMPERFECT staubsaugte, PERFECT hat gestaubsaugt) ◊ to vacuum the hall den Flur staubsaugen

vacuum cleaner NOUN
der Staubsauger (PL die Staubsauger)

vagina NOUN
die Vagina (PL die Vaginen)

vague ADJECTIVE
vage

vain ADJECTIVE
eitel ◊ He's so vain! Er ist so eitel!
♦ in vain umsonst

Valentine card NOUN
die Valentinskarte

> *i* Germans celebrate Valentine's Day by giving flowers rather than sending cards.

Valentine's Day NOUN
der Valentinstag (PL die Valentinstage)

valid ADJECTIVE
gültig ◊ This ticket is valid for three months. Dieser Fahrschein ist drei Monate lang gültig.

valley NOUN
das Tal (PL die Täler)

valuable ADJECTIVE
wertvoll ◊ a valuable picture ein wertvolles Bild ◊ valuable help wertvolle Hilfe

valuables PL NOUN

die Wertsachen FEM PL ◊ Don't take any valuables with you. Nehmen Sie keine Wertsachen mit.

value NOUN
der Wert (PL die Werte)

van NOUN
der Lieferwagen (PL die Lieferwagen)

vandal NOUN
der Vandale (GEN des Vandalen, PL die Vandalen)
die Vandalin

vandalism NOUN
der Vandalismus (GEN des Vandalismus)

to **vandalize** VERB
mutwillig zerstören (PERFECT hat mutwillig zerstört)

vanilla NOUN
die Vanille
♦ vanilla ice cream das Vanilleeis

to **vanish** VERB
verschwinden (IMPERFECT verschwand, PERFECT ist verschwunden)

variable ADJECTIVE
wechselhaft (mood, weather)

varied ADJECTIVE
abwechslungsreich ◊ a varied diet eine abwechslungsreiche Kost ◊ a varied life ein abwechslungsreiches Leben
♦ a varied selection eine reichhaltige Auswahl

variety NOUN
1 die Abwechslung ◊ She likes variety in her life. Sie hat gern Abwechslung im Leben.
2 die Sorte (kind) ◊ a new variety of rose eine neue Rosensorte
♦ a variety of books eine Vielzahl von Büchern

various ADJECTIVE
verschieden ◊ We visited various villages in the area. Wir haben verschiedene Dörfer in der Gegend besucht.

to **vary** VERB
schwanken ◊ It varies between two and four per cent. Es schwankt zwischen zwei und vier Prozent.
♦ It varies. Das ist unterschiedlich.

vase NOUN
die Vase

VAT NOUN (= value added tax)
die Mehrwertsteuer

VCR NOUN (= video cassette recorder)
der Videorekorder (PL die Videorekorder)

VDU NOUN (= visual display unit)
der Bildschirm (PL die Bildschirme)

veal NOUN
das Kalbfleisch

vegan NOUN
der Veganer (PL die Veganer)
die Veganerin
◇ *I'm a vegan.* Ich bin Veganerin.
vegetable NOUN
die Gemüsesorte
♦ **vegetables** das Gemüse SING
♦ **vegetable soup** die Gemüsesuppe
vegetarian ADJECTIVE

see also **vegetarian** NOUN

vegetarisch ◇ *vegetarian lasagne* die
vegetarische Lasagne
♦ **He's vegetarian.** Er ist Vegetarier.
vegetarian NOUN

see also **vegetarian** ADJECTIVE

der Vegetarier (PL die Vegetarier)
die Vegetarierin
◇ *She's a vegetarian.* Sie ist Vegetarierin.
vehicle NOUN
das Fahrzeug (PL die Fahrzeuge)
vein NOUN
die Vene
velvet NOUN
der Samt
vending machine NOUN
der Automat (GEN des Automaten, PL die
Automaten)
Venetian blind NOUN
die Jalousie
verb NOUN
das Verb (PL die Verben)
verdict NOUN
das Urteil (PL die Urteile)
vertical ADJECTIVE
senkrecht
vertigo NOUN
das Schwindelgefühl
♦ **He had an attack of vertigo.** Ihm wurde
schwindlig.
very ADVERB
sehr ◇ *very tall* sehr groß ◇ *not very
interesting* nicht sehr interessant
♦ **very much (1)** sehr viel ◇ *He didn't eat
very much.* Er hat nicht sehr viel
gegessen.
♦ **very much (2)** (*like, love, respect*) sehr ◇ *I
love her very much.* Ich liebe sie sehr.
♦ **Thank you very much.** Vielen Dank.
vest NOUN
[1] das Unterhemd (PL die Unterhemden)
[2] (*waistcoat*)
die Weste
vet NOUN
der Tierarzt (GEN des Tierarztes, PL die
Tierärzte)
die Tierärztin
◇ *She's a vet.* Sie ist Tierärztin.
via PREPOSITION
über ◇ *We went to Munich via Ulm.* Wir
sind über Ulm nach München gefahren.
vicar NOUN
der Pastor (PL die Pastoren)

die Pastorin
◇ *He's a vicar.* Er ist Pastor.
vice NOUN
der Schraubstock (*for holding things*) (PL
die Schraubstöcke)
vice versa ADVERB
umgekehrt
vicious ADJECTIVE
[1] brutal ◇ *a vicious attack* ein brutaler
Überfall
[2] bissig (*dog*)
[3] bösartig (*person*)
♦ **a vicious circle** ein Teufelskreis MASC
victim NOUN
das Opfer (PL die Opfer) ◇ *He was the
victim of a mugging.* Er wurde das Opfer
eines Straßenüberfalls.
victory NOUN
der Sieg (PL die Siege)
to **video** VERB

see also **video** NOUN

auf Video aufnehmen (PRESENT nimmt auf
Video auf, IMPERFECT nahm auf Video auf,
PERFECT hat auf Video aufgenommen)
video NOUN

see also **video** VERB

[1] (*film*)
das Video (PL die Videos) ◇ *to watch a
video* ein Video ansehen ◇ *a video of my
family on holiday* ein Video von meiner
Familie in den Ferien ◇ *It's out on video.*
Das gibt's als Video. ◇ *She lent me a
video.* Sie hat mir ein Video geliehen.
[2] (*video recorder*)
der Videorekorder (PL die Videorekorder)
◇ *Have you got a video?* Habt ihr einen
Videorekorder?
♦ **a video camera** eine Videokamera
♦ **a video cassette** eine Videokassette
♦ **a video game** ein Videospiel NEUT ◇ *He
likes playing video games.* Er spielt gern
Videospiele.
♦ **a video recorder** ein Videorekorder
♦ **a video shop** eine Videothek
Vienna NOUN
Wien NEUT
♦ **to Vienna** nach Wien
Vietnamese NOUN

see also **Vietnamese** ADJECTIVE

der Vietnamese (PL die Vietnamesen)
die Vietnamesin
Vietnamese ADJECTIVE

see also **Vietnamese** NOUN

vietnamesisch
view NOUN
[1] die Aussicht ◇ *There's an amazing
view.* Man hat dort eine tolle Aussicht.
[2] die Meinung (*opinion*) ◇ *in my view*
meiner Meinung nach
viewer NOUN
der Fernsehzuschauer (PL die
Fernsehzuschauer)
die Fernsehzuschauerin

viewpoint NOUN
der Standpunkt (PL die Standpunkte)
vile ADJECTIVE
ekelhaft (*smell, food*)
villa NOUN
die Villa (PL die Villen)
village NOUN
das Dorf (PL die Dörfer)
villain NOUN
1 (*criminal*)
der Verbrecher (PL die Verbrecher)
die Verbrecherin
2 (*in film*)
der Bösewicht (PL die Bösewichte)
vine NOUN
die Weinrebe
vinegar NOUN
der Essig
vineyard NOUN
der Weinberg (PL die Weinberge)
viola NOUN
die Bratsche ◊ *I play the viola.* Ich spiele
Bratsche.
violence NOUN
die Gewalt
violent ADJECTIVE
1 gewalttätig (*person, film*)
♦ **a violent crime** ein Gewaltverbrechen
NEUT
2 gewaltig (*explosion*)
violin NOUN
die Geige ◊ *I play the violin.* Ich spiele
Geige.
violinist NOUN
der Geigenspieler (PL die Geigenspieler)
die Geigenspielerin
virgin NOUN
die Jungfrau ◊ *to be a virgin* Jungfrau
sein
Virgo NOUN
die Jungfrau ◊ *I'm Virgo.* Ich bin
Jungfrau.
virtual reality NOUN
die virtuelle Realität
virus NOUN
das Virus (GEN des Virus, PL die Viren)
visa NOUN
das Visum (PL die Visa)
visible ADJECTIVE
sichtbar
visit NOUN
see also **visit** VERB
1 der Besuch (PL die Besuche) ◊ *my last
visit to my grandmother* mein letzter
Besuch bei meiner Großmutter
2 (*to country*)
der Aufenthalt (PL die Aufenthalte) ◊ *Did
you enjoy your visit to Germany?* Hat
euer Deutschlandaufenthalt Spaß
gemacht?
to **visit** VERB
see also **visit** NOUN

1 (*person*)
besuchen (PERFECT hat besucht)
2 (*place*)
besichtigen (PERFECT hat besichtigt)
◊ *We'd like to visit the castle.* Wir würden
gern die Burg besichtigen.
visitor NOUN
der Besucher (PL die Besucher)
die Besucherin
♦ **to have a visitor** Besuch haben
visual ADJECTIVE
visuell
to **visualize** VERB
sich vorstellen (PERFECT hat sich
vorgestellt) ◊ *I tried to visualize his face.*
Ich versuchte, mir sein Gesicht
vorzustellen.
vital ADJECTIVE
äußerst wichtig ◊ *It's vital for you to
take these tablets.* Es ist äußerst wichtig,
dass du diese Tabletten nimmst.
♦ **of vital importance** äußerst wichtig
vitamin NOUN
das Vitamin (PL die Vitamine)
vivid ADJECTIVE
lebhaft ◊ *to have a vivid imagination*
eine lebhafte Fantasie haben
vocabulary NOUN
der Wortschatz (GEN des Wortschatzes, PL
die Wortschätze)
vocational ADJECTIVE
beruflich ◊ *vocational training* die
berufliche Ausbildung
♦ **a vocational college** eine Berufsschule
vodka NOUN
der Wodka (PL die Wodkas)
voice NOUN
die Stimme
voice mail NOUN
die Voicemail
volcano NOUN
der Vulkan (PL die Vulkane)
volleyball NOUN
der Volleyball ◊ *to play volleyball*
Volleyball spielen
volt NOUN
das Volt (GEN des Volt, PL die Volt)
voltage NOUN
die Spannung
voluntary ADJECTIVE
freiwillig (*contribution, statement*)
♦ **to do voluntary work** ehrenamtlich tätig
sein
volunteer NOUN
see also **volunteer** VERB
der Freiwillige (GEN des Freiwilligen, PL
die Freiwilligen)
die Freiwillige (GEN der Freiwilligen) ◊ *a
volunteer (man)* ein Freiwilliger
to **volunteer** VERB
see also **volunteer** NOUN

V

◆**to volunteer to do something** sich
freiwillig melden, etwas zu tun

to **vomit** VERB
sich übergeben (PRESENT übergibt sich,
IMPERFECT übergab sich, PERFECT hat sich
übergeben)

vote NOUN
see also **vote** VERB
die Stimme

to **vote** VERB
see also **vote** NOUN

wählen ◇ *to vote Labour* Labour wählen
◆**to vote for somebody** für jemanden
stimmen ◇ *I voted for Bill Clinton.* Ich
habe für Bill Clinton gestimmt.

voucher NOUN
der Gutschein (PL die Gutscheine) ◇ *a gift
voucher* ein Geschenkgutschein

vowel NOUN
der Vokal (PL die Vokale)

vulgar ADJECTIVE
vulgär

W

wafer NOUN
die <u>Waffel</u>

wage NOUN
der <u>Lohn</u> (PL die Löhne) ◊ *He collected his wages.* Er hat seinen Lohn abgeholt.

waist NOUN
die <u>Taille</u>

waistcoat NOUN
die <u>Weste</u>

to **wait** VERB
<u>warten</u>
♦ **to wait for something** auf etwas warten ◊ *We were waiting for the bus.* Wir haben auf den Bus gewartet.
♦ **to wait for somebody** auf jemanden warten ◊ *I'll wait for you.* Ich warte auf dich. ◊ *Wait for me!* Warte auf mich!
♦ **Wait a minute!** Einen Augenblick!
♦ **to keep somebody waiting** jemanden warten lassen ◊ *They kept us waiting for hours.* Sie haben uns stundenlang warten lassen.
♦ **I can't wait for the holidays.** Ich kann die Ferien kaum erwarten.
♦ **I can't wait to see him again.** Ich kann's kaum erwarten, bis ich ihn wiedersehe.

to **wait up** VERB
<u>aufbleiben</u> (IMPERFECT blieb auf, PERFECT ist aufgeblieben) ◊ *My mum always waits up till I get in.* Meine Mutti bleibt immer auf, bis ich nach Hause komme.

waiter NOUN
der <u>Kellner</u> (PL die Kellner)

waiting list NOUN
die <u>Warteliste</u>

waiting room NOUN
das <u>Wartezimmer</u> (PL die Wartezimmer)

waitress NOUN
die <u>Kellnerin</u>

to **wake up** VERB
<u>aufwachen</u> (PERFECT ist aufgewacht) ◊ *I woke up at six o'clock.* Ich bin um sechs Uhr aufgewacht.
♦ **to wake somebody up** jemanden wecken ◊ *Would you wake me up at seven o'clock?* Könntest du mich um sieben Uhr wecken?

Wales NOUN
<u>Wales</u> NEUT ◊ *the Prince of Wales* der Prinz von Wales
♦ **from Wales** aus Wales
♦ **in Wales** in Wales
♦ **to Wales** nach Wales

to **walk** VERB
see also **walk** NOUN

[1] <u>gehen</u> (IMPERFECT ging, PERFECT ist gegangen) ◊ *He walks fast.* Er geht schnell.

[2] (*go on foot*)
<u>zu Fuß gehen</u> ◊ *Are you walking or going by bus?* Geht ihr zu Fuß oder nehmt ihr den Bus? ◊ *We walked ten kilometres.* Wir sind zehn Kilometer zu Fuß gegangen.
♦ **to walk the dog** mit dem Hund spazieren gehen

walk NOUN
see also **walk** VERB
der <u>Spaziergang</u> (PL die Spaziergänge) ◊ *to go for a walk* einen Spaziergang machen
♦ **It's ten minutes' walk from here.** Von hier ist es zehn Minuten zu Fuß.

walkie-talkie NOUN
das <u>Walkie-Talkie</u> (PL die Walkie-Talkies)

walking NOUN
das <u>Wandern</u>
♦ **I did some walking in the Alps last summer.** Ich bin letzten Sommer in den Alpen gewandert.

walking stick NOUN
der <u>Spazierstock</u> (PL die Spazierstöcke)

Walkman ® NOUN
der <u>Walkman</u> ® (PL die Walkmen)

wall NOUN
[1] die <u>Mauer</u> ◊ *There is a wall round the property.* Um das Grundstück ist eine Mauer.
[2] die <u>Wand</u> (PL die Wände) ◊ *They have lots of pictures on the wall.* Sie haben viele Bilder an der Wand.

wallet NOUN
die <u>Brieftasche</u>

wallpaper NOUN
die <u>Tapete</u>

walnut NOUN
die <u>Walnuss</u> (PL die Walnüsse)

to **wander** VERB
♦ **to wander around** herumlaufen ◊ *I just wandered around for a while.* Ich bin einfach eine Zeit lang herumgelaufen.

to **want** VERB
<u>möchten</u> (PRESENT mag, IMPERFECT mochte, PERFECT hat gemocht) ◊ *Do you want some cake?* Möchtest du Kuchen?
♦ **to want to do something** etwas tun wollen ◊ *I want to go to the cinema.* Ich will ins Kino gehen. ◊ *What do you want to do tomorrow?* Was willst du morgen machen?

war NOUN
der <u>Krieg</u> (PL die Kriege)

ward NOUN
der <u>Krankensaal</u> (*room in hospital*) (PL die Krankensäle)

warden NOUN
(of youth hostel)
der Herbergsvater (man) (PL die Herbergsväter)
die Herbergsmutter (woman) (PL die Herbergsmütter)

wardrobe NOUN
der Kleiderschrank (piece of furniture) (PL die Kleiderschränke)

warehouse NOUN
das Lagerhaus (GEN des Lagerhauses, PL die Lagerhäuser)

warm ADJECTIVE
[1] warm ◊ warm water warmes Wasser
◊ It's warm in here. Hier drin ist es warm.
◊ It's warmer in the kitchen. In der Küche ist es wärmer.

> When you talk about a person being **warm**, you use the impersonal construction.

◊ I'm warm. Mir ist warm. ◊ I'm too warm. Mir ist zu warm.
[2] herzlich ◊ a warm welcome ein herzlicher Empfang
◆ to warm up (1) (for sport) sich aufwärmen
◆ to warm up (2) (food) aufwärmen ◊ I'll warm up some lasagne for you. Ich wärme dir etwas Lasagne auf.
◆ to warm over aufwärmen

to **warn** VERB
warnen ◊ Well, I warned you! Ich habe dich ja gewarnt.
◆ to warn somebody not to do something jemanden davor warnen, etwas zu tun
◊ He warned me not to go there. Er warnte mich davor, dort hinzugehen.

warning NOUN
die Warnung

Warsaw NOUN
Warschau NEUT
◆ to Warsaw nach Warschau

wart NOUN
die Warze

was VERB see be

wash NOUN
see also **wash** VERB
◆ to have a wash sich waschen ◊ I had a wash. Ich habe mich gewaschen.
◆ to give something a wash etwas waschen ◊ He gave the car a wash. Er hat das Auto gewaschen.

to **wash** VERB
see also **wash** NOUN
[1] waschen (PRESENT wäscht, IMPERFECT wusch, PERFECT hat gewaschen) ◊ to wash something etwas waschen
[2] (have a wash)
sich waschen ◊ Every morning I get up, wash and get dressed. Jeden Morgen stehe ich auf, wasche mich und ziehe mich an.

◆ to wash one's hands sich die Hände waschen ◊ Where can I wash my hands? Wo kann ich mir die Hände waschen?
◆ to wash one's hair sich die Haare waschen ◊ You should wash your hair. Du solltest dir die Haare waschen.
◆ to wash up abwaschen

washbasin NOUN
das Waschbecken (PL die Waschbecken)

washcloth NOUN US
der Waschlappen (PL die Waschlappen)

washing NOUN
die Wäsche (clothes)
◆ Have you got any washing? Hast du etwas zu waschen?
◆ to do the washing Wäsche waschen

washing machine NOUN
die Waschmaschine

washing powder NOUN
das Waschpulver (PL die Waschpulver)

washing-up NOUN
der Abwasch ◊ to do the washing-up den Abwasch machen

washing-up liquid NOUN
das Spülmittel (PL die Spülmittel)

wasn't = was not

wasp NOUN
die Wespe

waste NOUN
see also **waste** VERB
[1] die Verschwendung ◊ It's such a waste! Es ist so eine Verschwendung!
◊ It's a waste of time. Es ist Zeitverschwendung!
[2] der Müll (rubbish) ◊ nuclear waste der Atommüll

to **waste** VERB
see also **waste** NOUN
verschwenden (PERFECT hat verschwendet) ◊ I don't like wasting money. Ich verschwende nicht gerne Geld. ◊ There's no time to waste. Wir haben keine Zeit zu verschwenden.

wastepaper basket NOUN
der Papierkorb (PL die Papierkörbe)

watch NOUN
see also **watch** VERB
die Uhr

to **watch** VERB
see also **watch** NOUN
[1] (film, video)
ansehen (PRESENT sieht an, IMPERFECT sah an, PERFECT hat angesehen) ◊ Did you watch that film last night? Hast du dir gestern Abend den Film angesehen?
◆ to watch television fernsehen
[2] zusehen (PRESENT sieht zu, IMPERFECT sah zu, PERFECT hat zugesehen) ◊ Watch me! Sieh mir zu!
[3] (keep a watch on)
beobachten (PERFECT hat beobachtet)
◊ The police were watching the house. Die Polizei beobachtete das Haus.

◆ **to watch out** aufpassen
◆ **Watch out!** Pass auf!

water NOUN
> see also **water** VERB

das <u>Wasser</u> (PL die Wasser)

to **water** VERB
> see also **water** NOUN

[1] (*plant*)
<u>gießen</u> (IMPERFECT goss, PERFECT hat gegossen) ◊ *He was watering his tulips.* Er goss seine Tulpen.
[2] (*garden*)
<u>sprengen</u> ◊ *We should water the lawn.* Wir sollten den Rasen sprengen.

waterfall NOUN
der <u>Wasserfall</u> (PL die Wasserfälle)

watering can NOUN
die <u>Gießkanne</u>

watermelon NOUN
die <u>Wassermelone</u>

waterproof ADJECTIVE
<u>wasserdicht</u> ◊ *Is this jacket waterproof?* Ist die Jacke wasserdicht?

water-skiing NOUN
das <u>Wasserskifahren</u>
◆ **to go water-skiing** Wasserski fahren

wave NOUN
> see also **wave** VERB

die <u>Welle</u> (*in water*)
◆ **We gave him a wave.** Wir haben ihm zugewinkt.

to **wave** VERB
> see also **wave** NOUN

<u>winken</u>
◆ **to wave at somebody** jemandem zuwinken ◊ *I waved at my friend.* Ich winkte meinem Freund zu.
◆ **to wave goodbye** zum Abschied winken ◊ *I waved her goodbye.* Ich habe ihr zum Abschied gewinkt.

wavy ADJECTIVE
<u>wellig</u> ◊ *wavy hair* welliges Haar

wax NOUN
das <u>Wachs</u> (GEN des Wachses)

way NOUN
[1] die <u>Art und Weise</u> (*manner*) ◊ *That's no way to talk to your mother!* Das ist keine Art und Weise, mit deiner Mutter zu reden!
◆ **She looked at me in a strange way.** Sie sah mich sonderbar an.
◆ **This book tells you the right way to do it.** Dieses Buch erklärt, wie man es machen muss.
◆ **You're doing it the wrong way.** Du machst das falsch.
◆ **In a way you're right.** In gewisser Weise hast du recht.
◆ **a way of life** eine Art zu leben
[2] der <u>Weg</u> (*route*) ◊ *I don't know the way.* Ich kenne den Weg nicht.
◆ **on the way** unterwegs ◊ *We stopped for lunch on the way.* Wir haben unterwegs

angehalten und zu Mittag gegessen.
◊ *He's on his way.* Er ist unterwegs.
◆ **It's a long way.** Es ist weit. ◊ *Berlin is a long way from London.* Berlin ist weit von London entfernt.
◆ **Which way is it?** In welcher Richtung ist es?
◆ **The supermarket is this way.** Zum Supermarkt geht es in diese Richtung.
◆ **Do you know the way to the hotel?** Wissen Sie, wie man zum Hotel kommt?
◆ **"way in"** "Eingang"
◆ **"way out"** "Ausgang"
◆ **by the way** ... übrigens ...

we PRONOUN
<u>wir</u> ◊ *We're staying here for a week.* Wir sind eine Woche lang hier.

weak ADJECTIVE
<u>schwach</u> ◊ *Maths is my weakest subject.* In Mathe bin ich am schwächsten.

wealthy ADJECTIVE
<u>reich</u>

weapon NOUN
die <u>Waffe</u>

to **wear** VERB
<u>tragen</u> (*clothes*) (PRESENT trägt, IMPERFECT trug, PERFECT hat getragen) ◊ *She was wearing a hat.* Sie trug einen Hut. ◊ *She was wearing black.* Sie trug Schwarz.

weather NOUN
das <u>Wetter</u> ◊ *What was the weather like?* Wie war das Wetter? ◊ *The weather was lovely.* Das Wetter war herrlich.

weather forecast NOUN
die <u>Wettervorhersage</u>

Web NOUN
◆ **the Web** das Web

webmaster NOUN
der <u>Webmaster</u> (PL die Webmaster)
die <u>Webmasterin</u>

web page NOUN
die <u>Webseite</u>

website NOUN
die <u>Website</u> (PL die Websites)

webzine NOUN
das <u>Web-Magazin</u> (PL die Web-Magazine)

we'd = we had, = we would

wedding NOUN
die <u>Hochzeit</u>
◆ **wedding anniversary** der Hochzeitstag
◆ **wedding dress** das Brautkleid
◆ **wedding ring** der Ehering

Wednesday NOUN
der <u>Mittwoch</u> (PL die Mittwoche) ◊ *on Wednesday* am Mittwoch ◊ *every Wednesday* jeden Mittwoch ◊ *last Wednesday* letzten Mittwoch ◊ *next Wednesday* nächsten Mittwoch
◆ **on Wednesdays** mittwochs

weed NOUN

☞

das <u>Unkraut</u> ◊ *The garden's full of weeds.* Der Garten ist voller Unkraut.

week NOUN

die <u>Woche</u> ◊ *last week* letzte Woche ◊ *every week* jede Woche ◊ *next week* nächste Woche ◊ *in a week's time* in einer Woche

◆ **a week on Friday** Freitag in einer Woche

weekday NOUN

◆ **on weekdays** werktags

weekend NOUN

das <u>Wochenende</u> (PL die Wochenenden) ◊ *at the weekend* am Wochenende ◊ *at weekends* am Wochenende ◊ *last weekend* letztes Wochenende ◊ *next weekend* nächstes Wochenende

to **weigh** VERB

<u>wiegen</u> (IMPERFECT **wog**, PERFECT **hat gewogen**) ◊ *How much do you weigh?* Wie viel wiegst du? ◊ *First, weigh the flour.* Wiegen Sie zuerst das Mehl.

◆ **to weigh oneself** sich wiegen

weight NOUN

das <u>Gewicht</u> (PL die Gewichte)

◆ **to lose weight** abnehmen

◆ **to put on weight** zunehmen

weightlifter NOUN

der <u>Gewichtheber</u> (PL die Gewichtheber)

weightlifting NOUN

das <u>Gewichtheben</u>

weird ADJECTIVE

<u>sonderbar</u>

welcome NOUN

see also **welcome** VERB

◆ **They gave her a warm welcome.** Sie haben sie herzlich empfangen.

◆ **Welcome!** Herzlich willkommen! ◊ *Welcome to Germany!* Herzlich willkommen in Deutschland!

to **welcome** VERB

see also **welcome** NOUN

◆ **to welcome somebody** jemanden begrüßen

◆ **Thank you! – You're welcome!** Danke! – Bitte!

well ADJECTIVE, ADVERB

see also **well** NOUN

1 <u>gut</u> ◊ *You did that really well.* Das hast du wirklich gut gemacht.

◆ **to do well** gut sein ◊ *She's doing really well at school.* Sie ist wirklich gut in der Schule.

◆ **to be well** (*in good health*) gesund sein ◊ *I'm not very well at the moment.* Ich bin im Moment nicht gesund.

◆ **Get well soon!** Gute Besserung!

◆ **Well done!** Gut gemacht!

2 <u>na ja</u> ◊ *It's enormous! Well, quite big anyway.* Es ist riesig! Na ja, jedenfalls ziemlich groß.

◆ **as well** auch ◊ *We worked hard, but we had some fun as well.* Wir haben hart gearbeitet, aber auch Spaß

gehabt.

well NOUN

see also **well** ADJECTIVE

der <u>Brunnen</u> (PL die Brunnen)

we'll = **we will**

well-behaved ADJECTIVE

<u>artig</u>

well-dressed ADJECTIVE

<u>gut angezogen</u>

wellingtons PL NOUN

die <u>Gummistiefel</u> MASC PL

well-known ADJECTIVE

<u>bekannt</u> ◊ *a well-known film star* ein bekannter Filmstar

well-off ADJECTIVE

<u>gut situiert</u>

Welsh ADJECTIVE

see also **Welsh** NOUN

<u>walisisch</u>

◆ **He's Welsh.** Er ist Waliser.

◆ **She's Welsh.** Sie ist Waliserin.

◆ **Welsh people** die Waliser MASC PL

Welsh NOUN

see also **Welsh** ADJECTIVE

das <u>Walisisch</u> (*language*) (GEN des Walisischen)

Welshman NOUN

der <u>Waliser</u> (PL die Waliser)

Welshwoman NOUN

die <u>Waliserin</u>

went VERB *see* **go**

were VERB *see* **be**

we're = **we are**

weren't = **were not**

west NOUN

see also **west** ADJECTIVE

der <u>Westen</u> ◊ *in the west* im Westen

west ADJECTIVE, ADVERB

see also **west** NOUN

◆ **the west coast** die Westküste

◆ **a west wind** ein Westwind MASC

<u>nach Westen</u> ◊ *We were travelling west.* Wir fuhren nach Westen.

◆ **west of** westlich von ◊ *Stroud is west of Oxford.* Stroud liegt westlich von Oxford.

◆ **the West Country** der Südwesten Englands

western NOUN

see also **western** ADJECTIVE

der <u>Western</u> (*film*) (GEN des Western, PL die Western)

western ADJECTIVE

see also **western** NOUN

<u>westlich</u>

◆ **the western part of the island** der westliche Teil der Insel

◆ **Western Europe** Westeuropa NEUT

West Indian ADJECTIVE

see also **West Indian** NOUN

<u>westindisch</u>

◆ **He's West Indian.** Er ist aus Westindien.

West Indian NOUN

> see also **West Indian** ADJECTIVE

(*person*)
der Westinder (PL die Westinder)
die Westinderin

West Indies PL NOUN
die Westindischen Inseln FEM PL
♦ **in the West Indies** auf den
Westindischen Inseln

wet ADJECTIVE
nass ◊ *wet clothes* nasse Kleider ◊ *to get wet* nass werden
♦ **wet weather** regnerisches Wetter
♦ **dripping wet** klatschnass
♦ **It was wet all week.** Es hat die ganze
Woche geregnet.

wet suit NOUN
der Neoprenanzug (PL die
Neoprenanzüge)

we've = **we have**

whale NOUN
der Wal (PL die Wale)

what ADJECTIVE, PRONOUN
[1] was ◊ *What are you doing?* Was tust
du? ◊ *What did you say?* Was hast du
gesagt? ◊ *What is it?* Was ist das?
◊ *What's the matter?* Was ist los?
◊ *What happened?* Was ist passiert?
◊ *I saw what happened.* Ich habe
gesehen, was passiert ist. ◊ *I heard
what he said.* Ich habe gehört, was er
gesagt hat.
♦ **What?** Was?
[2] welcher ◊ *What hat do you like best?*
Welcher Hut gefällt dir am besten?
welche ◊ *What colour is it?* Welche
Farbe hat es?
welches ◊ *What book do you want?*
Welches Buch möchten Sie?
welche ◊ *What subjects are you
studying?* Welche Fächer studierst du?
♦ **What's the capital of Finland?** Wie heißt
die Hauptstadt von Finnland?
♦ **What a mess!** So ein Chaos!

wheat NOUN
der Weizen

wheel NOUN
das Rad (PL die Räder) ◊ *the steering
wheel* das Lenkrad

wheelchair NOUN
der Rollstuhl (PL die Rollstühle)

when ADVERB, CONJUNCTION
[1] wann ◊ *When did he go?* Wann ist er
gegangen?
[2] als ◊ *She was reading when I came in.*
Sie las, als ich hereinkam.

where ADVERB, CONJUNCTION
wo ◊ *Where's Emma today?* Wo ist
Emma heute? ◊ *Where do you live?* Wo
wohnst du? ◊ *a shop where you can buy
gardening tools* ein Geschäft, wo man
Gartengeräte kaufen kann
♦ **Where are you from?** Woher sind Sie?

♦ **Where are you going?** Wohin gehst du?
> *Be careful not to translate **where** by **wer**.*

whether CONJUNCTION
ob ◊ *I don't know whether to go or not.*
Ich weiß nicht, ob ich gehen soll oder
nicht.

which ADJECTIVE, PRONOUN
[1] welcher ◊ *Which coat do you like
better?* Welcher Mantel gefällt dir
besser?
welche ◊ *Which CD did you buy?* Welche
CD hast du gekauft?
welches ◊ *Which book do you want?*
Welches Buch willst du?
welche ◊ *Which shoes should I wear?*
Welche Schuhe soll ich anziehen?
> *When asking **which one** use **welcher** or
welche or **welches**, depending on
whether the noun is masculine, feminine
or neuter.*
♦ **I know his brother. – Which one?** Ich
kenne seinen Bruder. – Welchen?
♦ **I know his sister. – Which one?** Ich kenne
seine Schwester. – Welche?
♦ **I took one of your books. – Which one?**
Ich habe eines deiner Bücher
genommen. – Welches?
♦ **Which would you like?** Welches
möchtest du?
♦ **Which of these are yours?** Welche davon
gehören dir?
> *In relative clauses use **der**, **die** or **das**,
depending on the gender of the noun
which refers to.*
[2] der ◊ *the film which is on now* der
Film, der gerade läuft
die ◊ *the CD which is playing now* die
CD, die gerade läuft
das ◊ *the book which I am reading* das
Buch, das ich lese
die ◊ *the sweets which I ate* die
Süßigkeiten, die ich gegessen habe

while CONJUNCTION

> see also **while** NOUN

während ◊ *You hold the torch while I
look inside.* Halt du die Taschenlampe,
während ich hineinsehe. ◊ *Isobel is very
dynamic, while Kay is more laid-back.*
Isobel ist sehr dynamisch, während Kay
eher lässig ist.

while NOUN

> see also **while** CONJUNCTION

die Weile ◊ *after a while* nach einer
Weile
♦ **a while ago** vor einer Weile ◊ *He was
here a while ago.* Er war vor einer Weile
hier.
♦ **for a while** eine Zeit lang ◊ *I lived in
London for a while.* Ich habe eine Zeit
lang in London gelebt.
♦ **quite a while** ziemlich lange ◊ *That
happened quite a while ago.* Das ist
schon ziemlich lange her. ◊ *I haven't*

W

☞

seen him for quite a while. Ich habe ihn schon ziemlich lange nicht mehr gesehen.

whip NOUN

> see also **whip** VERB

die Peitsche

to **whip** VERB

> see also **whip** NOUN

[1] peitschen ◊ *She whipped her horse.* Sie peitschte ihr Pferd.

[2] (*eggs*)

schlagen (PRESENT schlägt, IMPERFECT schlug, PERFECT hat geschlagen)

whipped cream NOUN

die Schlagsahne

whisk NOUN

der Schneebesen (PL die Schneebesen)

whiskers PL NOUN

die Schnurrhaare NEUT PL

whisky NOUN

der Whisky (PL die Whiskys)

to **whisper** VERB

flüstern

whistle NOUN

> see also **whistle** VERB

die Pfeife

♦ **The referee blew his whistle.** Der Schiedsrichter hat gepfiffen.

to **whistle** VERB

> see also **whistle** NOUN

pfeifen (IMPERFECT pfiff, PERFECT hat gepfiffen)

white ADJECTIVE

weiß ◊ *He's got white hair.* Er hat weiße Haare.

♦ **white wine** der Weißwein

♦ **white bread** das Weißbrot

♦ **white coffee** der Kaffee mit Milch

♦ **a white man** ein Weißer

♦ **a white woman** eine Weiße

♦ **white people** die Weißen MASC PL

Whitsun NOUN

das Pfingsten (GEN des Pfingsten, PL die Pfingsten)

who PRONOUN

[1] wer ◊ *Who said that?* Wer hat das gesagt? ◊ *Who is Lafontaine?* Wer ist Lafontaine?

> *In relative clauses use **der**, **die** or **das**, depending on the gender of the noun **who** refers to.*

[2] der ◊ *the man who saw us* der Mann, der uns gesehen hat ◊ *the man who we saw* der Mann, den wir gesehen haben

die ◊ *the woman who saw us* die Frau, die uns gesehen hat ◊ *the woman who we saw* die Frau, die wir gesehen haben

das ◊ *the child who saw us* das Kind, das uns gesehen hat ◊ *the child who we saw* das Kind, das wir gesehen haben

die ◊ *the people who saw us* die Leute, die uns gesehen haben

> *Be careful not to translate **who** by **wo**.*

whole ADJECTIVE

> see also **whole** NOUN

ganz ◊ *the whole class* die ganze Klasse ◊ *the whole afternoon* den ganzen Nachmittag ◊ *the whole world* die ganze Welt

whole NOUN

> see also **whole** ADJECTIVE

♦ **The whole of Wales was affected.** Ganz Wales war davon betroffen.

♦ **on the whole** im Großen und Ganzen

wholemeal ADJECTIVE

♦ **wholemeal bread** das Vollkornbrot

♦ **wholemeal flour** das Vollkornmehl

wholewheat ADJECTIVE US

♦ **wholewheat bread** das Vollkornbrot

whom PRONOUN

wen ◊ *Whom did you see?* Wen hast du gesehen?

♦ **the man to whom I spoke** der Mann, mit dem ich gesprochen habe

♦ **the woman to whom I spoke** die Frau, mit der ich gesprochen habe

whose PRONOUN, ADJECTIVE

wessen ◊ *Whose book is this?* Wessen Buch ist das?

♦ **Whose is this?** Wem gehört das?

♦ **I know whose it is.** Ich weiß, wem das gehört.

♦ **the man whose picture was in the paper** der Mann, dessen Bild in der Zeitung war

♦ **the woman whose picture was in the paper** die Frau, deren Bild in der Zeitung war

♦ **the girl whose picture was in the paper** das Mädchen, dessen Bild in der Zeitung war

why ADVERB

warum ◊ *Why did you do that?* Warum hast du das getan? ◊ *Tell me why.* Sag mir warum. ◊ *I've never been to Germany. – Why not?* Ich war noch nie in Deutschland. – Warum nicht? ◊ *All right, why not?* Also gut, warum auch nicht?

♦ **That's why he did it.** Deshalb hat er es getan.

wicked ADJECTIVE

[1] böse (*evil*)

[2] geil (*informal: really great*)

wicket NOUN

das Mal (*stumps*) (PL die Male)

wide ADJECTIVE, ADVERB

breit ◊ *a wide road* eine breite Straße

♦ **wide open** weit offen ◊ *The door was wide open.* Die Tür stand weit offen. ◊ *The windows were wide open.* Die Fenster waren weit offen.

♦ **wide awake** hellwach

widow NOUN
die Witwe ◊ *She's a widow.* Sie ist
Witwe.

widower NOUN
der Witwer (PL die Witwer) ◊ *He's a
widower.* Er ist Witwer.

width NOUN
die Breite

wife NOUN
die Frau ◊ *She's his wife.* Sie ist seine
Frau.

wig NOUN
die Perücke

wild ADJECTIVE
1 wild ◊ *a wild animal* ein wildes
Tier
2 verrückt (*crazy*) ◊ *She's a bit wild.* Sie
ist ein bisschen verrückt.

wild card NOUN
die Wildcard (PL die Wildcards)

wildlife NOUN
die Tierwelt ◊ *I'm interested in
wildlife.* Ich interessiere mich für die
Tierwelt.

will NOUN
  see also **will** VERB
das Testament (PL die Testamente) ◊ *He
left me some money in his will.* Er
hat mir in seinem Testament Geld
vermacht.
♦ **He came of his own free will.** Er ist
freiwillig gekommen.

will VERB
  see also **will** NOUN

*In German the present tense is often
used to express somebody's intention to
do something.*

◊ *I'll show you your room.* Ich zeige
Ihnen Ihr Zimmer. ◊ *I'll give you a hand.*
Ich helfe dir.
♦ **Will you help me?** Hilfst du mir?
♦ **Will you wash up? – No, I won't.**
Wäschst du ab? – Nein.

*Use the German future tense when
referring to the more distant future.*

◊ *I will come back one day.* Ich werde
eines Tages zurückkommen. ◊ *It
won't take long.* Es wird nicht lange
dauern.
♦ **That will be the postman.** Das wird der
Briefträger sein.
♦ **Will you be quiet!** Werdet ihr wohl still
sein!

willing ADJECTIVE
♦ **to be willing to do something** bereit
sein, etwas zu tun

to **win** VERB
  see also **win** NOUN
gewinnen (IMPERFECT gewann, PERFECT hat
gewonnen) ◊ *Did you win?* Hast du
gewonnen?
♦ **to win a prize** einen Preis bekommen

win NOUN
  see also **win** VERB
der Sieg (PL die Siege)

to **wind** VERB
  see also **wind** NOUN
1 wickeln (*rope, wool, wire*) ◊ *He wound
the rope round the tree.* Er wickelte das
Seil um den Baum.
2 sich schlängeln (*river, path*) ◊ *The
road winds through the valley.* Die
Straße schlängelt sich durch das
Tal.

wind NOUN
  see also **wind** VERB
der Wind (PL die Winde) ◊ *There was
a strong wind.* Es wehte ein starker
Wind.
♦ **a wind instrument** ein Blasinstrument
NEUT
♦ **wind power** die Windkraft

windmill NOUN
die Windmühle

window NOUN
das Fenster (PL die Fenster) ◊ *to break a
window* ein Fenster kaputt machen
◊ *a broken window* ein kaputtes
Fenster
♦ **a shop window** ein Schaufenster

windscreen NOUN
die Windschutzscheibe

windscreen wiper NOUN
der Scheibenwischer (PL die
Scheibenwischer)

windshield NOUN US
die Windschutzscheibe

windshield wiper NOUN US
der Scheibenwischer (PL die
Scheibenwischer)

windy ADJECTIVE
windig (*place*) ◊ *It's windy.* Es ist windig.

wine NOUN
der Wein (PL die Weine) ◊ *a bottle of
wine* eine Flasche Wein ◊ *a glass of wine*
ein Glas Wein
♦ **white wine** der Weißwein
♦ **red wine** der Rotwein
♦ **a wine bar** eine Weinstube
♦ **a wine glass** ein Weinglas NEUT
♦ **the wine list** die Getränkekarte

wing NOUN
der Flügel (PL die Flügel)

to **wink** VERB
♦ **to wink at somebody** jemandem
zublinzeln ◊ *He winked at me.* Er hat mir
zugeblinzelt.

winner NOUN
der Sieger (PL die Sieger)
die Siegerin

winning ADJECTIVE
♦ **the winning team** die Siegermannschaft
♦ **the winning goal** das entscheidende
Tor

winter NOUN

W

der Winter (PL die Winter) ◊ *in winter* im Winter

winter sports PL NOUN
der Wintersport SING

to **wipe** VERB
abwischen (PERFECT hat abgewischt)
♦ **to wipe one's feet** sich die Füße abstreifen ◊ *Wipe your feet!* Streif dir die Füße ab!
♦ **to wipe up** aufwischen

wire NOUN
der Draht (PL die Drähte)

wisdom tooth NOUN
der Weisheitszahn (PL die Weisheitszähne)

wise ADJECTIVE
weise

to **wish** VERB
see also **wish** NOUN

♦ **to wish for something** sich etwas wünschen ◊ *What more could I wish for?* Was mehr könnte ich mir wünschen?
♦ **to wish to do something** etwas tun möchten ◊ *I wish to make a complaint.* Ich möchte mich beschweren.
♦ **I wish you were here!** Ich wünschte, du wärst da!
♦ **I wish you'd told me!** Wenn du mir das doch nur gesagt hättest!

wish NOUN
see also **wish** VERB

der Wunsch (PL die Wünsche)
♦ **to make a wish** sich etwas wünschen ◊ *You can make a wish.* Du darfst dir etwas wünschen.
♦ **"best wishes"** (*on greetings card*) "Alles Gute"
♦ **"with best wishes, Kathy"** "alles Liebe, Kathy"

wit NOUN
der geistreiche Humor (*humour*)

with PREPOSITION
1 mit ◊ *Come with me.* Komm mit mir.
◊ *a woman with blue eyes* eine Frau mit blauen Augen
♦ **Fill the jug with water.** Tu Wasser in den Krug.
♦ **He walks with a stick.** Er geht am Stock.
2 bei (*at the home of*) ◊ *We stayed with friends.* Wir haben bei Freunden übernachtet.
3 vor ◊ *green with envy* grün vor Neid
◊ *to shake with fear* vor Angst zittern

within PREPOSITION
♦ **The shops are within easy reach.** Die Geschäfte sind schnell zu erreichen.
♦ **within the week** innerhalb dieser Woche

without PREPOSITION
ohne ◊ *without a coat* ohne einen Mantel
◊ *without speaking* ohne etwas zu sagen

witness NOUN
der Zeuge (GEN des Zeugen, PL die Zeugen)

die Zeugin
◊ *There were no witnesses.* Es gab keine Zeugen.
♦ **witness box** der Zeugenstand
♦ **witness stand** der Zeugenstand

witty ADJECTIVE
geistreich

wives PL NOUN see **wife**

woke up VERB see **wake up**

woken up VERB see **wake up**

wolf NOUN
der Wolf (PL die Wölfe)

woman NOUN
die Frau
♦ **a woman doctor** eine Ärztin

won VERB see **win**

to **wonder** VERB
sich fragen ◊ *I wonder why she said that.* Ich frage mich, warum sie das gesagt hat. ◊ *I wonder what that means.* Ich frage mich, was das bedeutet.
♦ **I wonder where Caroline is.** Wo Caroline wohl ist?

wonderful ADJECTIVE
wunderbar

won't = **will not**

wood NOUN
1 (*timber*)
das Holz (PL die Hölzer) ◊ *It's made of wood.* Es ist aus Holz.
2 (*forest*)
der Wald (PL die Wälder) ◊ *We went for a walk in the wood.* Wir sind im Wald spazieren gegangen.

wooden ADJECTIVE
hölzern
♦ **a wooden chair** ein Holzstuhl MASC

woodwork NOUN
das Schreinern ◊ *Dieter's hobby is woodwork.* Schreinern ist Dieters Hobby.

wool NOUN
die Wolle ◊ *It's made of wool.* Es ist aus Wolle.

word NOUN
das Wort (PL die Wörter) ◊ *a difficult word* ein schwieriges Wort
♦ **What's the word for "shop" in German?** Wie heißt "shop" auf Deutsch?
♦ **in other words** in anderen Worten
♦ **to have a word with somebody** mit jemandem reden
♦ **the words** (*lyrics*) der Text SING ◊ *I really like the words of this song.* Der Text dieses Liedes gefällt mir wirklich gut.

word processing NOUN
die Textverarbeitung

word processor NOUN
das Textverarbeitungssystem (PL die Textverarbeitungssysteme)

wore VERB see **wear**

work NOUN
see also **work** VERB

die <u>Arbeit</u> ◊ *She's looking for work.* Sie sucht Arbeit. ◊ *He's at work at the moment.* Er ist zur Zeit bei der Arbeit. ◊ *It's hard work.* Das ist harte Arbeit.
♦ **to be off work** (*sick*) krank sein
♦ **He's out of work.** Er ist arbeitslos.

to **work** VERB
⸢see also **work** NOUN⸥

[1] (*person*)
<u>arbeiten</u> ◊ *She works in a shop.* Sie arbeitet in einem Laden. ◊ *to work hard* hart arbeiten

[2] (*machine, plan*)
<u>funktionieren</u> (PERFECT hat funktioniert) ◊ *The heating isn't working.* Die Heizung funktioniert nicht. ◊ *My plan worked perfectly.* Mein Plan hat prima funktioniert.

♦ **to work out (1)** (*exercise*) trainieren ◊ *I work out twice a week.* Ich trainiere zweimal pro Woche.
♦ **to work out (2)** (*turn out*) klappen ◊ *In the end it worked out really well.* Am Ende hat es richtig gut geklappt.
♦ **to work something out** (*figure out*) auf etwas kommen ◊ *I just couldn't work it out.* Ich bin einfach nicht darauf gekommen.
♦ **It works out at ten pounds each.** Das macht für jeden zehn Pfund.

worker NOUN
der <u>Arbeiter</u> (PL die Arbeiter)
die <u>Arbeiterin</u>
◊ *He's a factory worker.* Er ist Fabrikarbeiter.
♦ **She's a good worker.** Sie macht gute Arbeit.

work experience NOUN
das <u>Praktikum</u> (PL die Praktika) ◊ *I'm going to do work experience in a factory.* Ich mache ein Praktikum in einer Fabrik.

working-class ADJECTIVE
der <u>Arbeiterklasse</u> ◊ *a working-class family* eine Familie der Arbeiterklasse

workman NOUN
der <u>Arbeiter</u> (PL die Arbeiter)

works NOUN
das <u>Werk</u> (*factory*) (PL die Werke)

worksheet NOUN
das <u>Arbeitsblatt</u> (PL die Arbeitsblätter)

workshop NOUN
die <u>Werkstatt</u> (PL die Werkstätten)
♦ **a drama workshop** ein Theaterworkshop MASC

workspace NOUN
der <u>Arbeitsplatz</u> (GEN des Arbeitsplatzes, PL die Arbeitsplätze)

workstation NOUN
der <u>Arbeitsplatzcomputer</u> (PL die Arbeitsplatzcomputer)

world NOUN
die <u>Welt</u>

♦ **He's the world champion.** Er ist der Weltmeister.

World Wide Web NOUN
♦ **the World Wide Web** das World Wide Web

worm NOUN
der <u>Wurm</u> (PL die Würmer)

worn VERB *see* **wear**

worn ADJECTIVE
<u>abgenutzt</u> ◊ *The carpet is a bit worn.* Der Teppich ist etwas abgenutzt.
♦ **worn out** (*tired*) erschöpft

worried ADJECTIVE
<u>besorgt</u> ◊ *She's very worried.* Sie ist sehr besorgt.
♦ **to be worried about something** sich wegen etwas Sorgen machen ◊ *I'm worried about the exam.* Ich mache mir wegen der Prüfung Sorgen.
♦ **to look worried** besorgt aussehen ◊ *She looks a bit worried.* Sie sieht etwas besorgt aus.

to **worry** VERB
<u>sich Sorgen machen</u> ◊ *You worry too much.* Du machst dir zu viele Sorgen.
♦ **Don't worry!** Keine Sorge!

worse ADJECTIVE, ADVERB
<u>schlechter</u> ◊ *My results were bad, but his were even worse.* Meine Noten waren schlecht, aber seine waren noch schlechter. ◊ *I'm feeling worse.* Mir geht es schlechter.
♦ **It was even worse than that.** Es war sogar noch schlimmer.

to **worship** VERB
<u>anbeten</u> (PERFECT hat angebetet) ◊ *He worships his girlfriend.* Er betet seine Freundin an.

worst ADJECTIVE
⸢see also **worst** NOUN⸥

♦ **the worst (1)** der schlechteste ◊ *the worst student in the class* der schlechteste Schüler der Klasse
♦ **the worst (2)** die schlechteste ◊ *He got the worst mark in the whole class.* Er hat von der ganzen Klasse die schlechteste Note bekommen.
♦ **the worst (3)** das schlechteste ◊ *the worst report I've ever had* das schlechteste Zeugnis, das ich je hatte
♦ **my worst enemy** mein schlimmster Feind
♦ **Maths is my worst subject.** In Mathe bin ich am schlechtesten.

worst NOUN
⸢see also **worst** ADJECTIVE⸥

das <u>Schlimmste</u> (GEN des Schlimmsten) ◊ *The worst of it is that …* Das Schlimmste daran ist, dass …
♦ **at worst** schlimmstenfalls
♦ **if the worst comes to the worst** schlimmstenfalls

worth ADJECTIVE

W

♦**to be worth** wert sein ◊ *It's worth a lot of money.* Es ist sehr viel Geld wert. ◊ *How much is it worth?* Wie viel ist das wert?

♦**It's worth it.** Das lohnt sich. ◊ *Is it worth it?* Lohnt es sich? ◊ *It's not worth it.* Das lohnt sich nicht.

would VERB

♦**Would you like ...?** Möchtest du ...? ◊ *Would you like a biscuit?* Möchtest du einen Keks? ◊ *Would you like to go and see a film?* Möchtest du ins Kino gehen?

♦**Would you close the door please?** Würden Sie bitte die Tür zumachen?

♦**I'd like ...** Ich würde gern ... ◊ *I'd like to go to America.* Ich würde gern nach Amerika fahren.

♦**Shall we go and see a film? – Yes, I'd like that.** Sollen wir ins Kino gehen? – Au ja!

♦**I said I would do it.** Ich sagte, ich würde es tun.

♦**If you asked him he'd do it.** Wenn du ihn fragen würdest, würde er es tun.

♦**If you had asked him he would have done it.** Wenn du ihn gefragt hättest, hätte er es getan.

wouldn't = **would not**

wound VERB *see* **wind**

to **wound** VERB

see also **wound** NOUN

verwunden (PERFECT hat verwundet) ◊ *He was wounded in the leg.* Er wurde am Bein verwundet.

wound NOUN

see also **wound** VERB

die Wunde

to **wrap** VERB

einpacken (PERFECT hat eingepackt) ◊ *She's wrapping her Christmas presents.* Sie packt ihre Weihnachtsgeschenke ein.

♦**Can you wrap it for me please?** (*in shop*) Können Sie es mir bitte in Geschenkpapier einpacken?

♦**to wrap up** einpacken

wrapping paper NOUN

das Geschenkpapier

wreck NOUN

see also **wreck** VERB

das Wrack (PL die Wracks) ◊ *That car is a wreck!* Das Auto ist ein Wrack. ◊ *After the exam I was a complete wreck.* Nach der Prüfung war ich ein totales Wrack.

to **wreck** VERB

see also **wreck** NOUN

1 (*building*)

zerstören (PERFECT hat zerstört) ◊ *The explosion wrecked the whole house.* Die Explosion hat das ganze Haus zerstört.

2 (*car*)

kaputt fahren (PRESENT fährt kaputt, IMPERFECT fuhr kaputt, PERFECT hat kaputt gefahren)◊ *He's wrecked his car.* Er hat sein Auto kaputt gefahren.

3 (*plan, holiday*)

verderben (PRESENT verdirbt, IMPERFECT verdarb, PERFECT hat verdorben) ◊ *Our trip was wrecked by bad weather.* Das schlechte Wetter hat uns den Ausflug verdorben.

wreckage NOUN

1 (*of vehicle*)

das Wrack (PL die Wracks)

2 (*of building*)

die Trümmer PL

wrestler NOUN

der Ringer (PL die Ringer)

die Ringerin

wrestling NOUN

das Ringen ◊ *His hobby is wrestling.* Ringen ist sein Hobby.

wrinkled ADJECTIVE

faltig

wrist NOUN

das Handgelenk (PL die Handgelenke)

to **write** VERB

schreiben (IMPERFECT schrieb, PERFECT hat geschrieben) ◊ *to write a letter* einen Brief schreiben

♦**to write to somebody** jemandem schreiben ◊ *I'm going to write to her in German.* Ich werde ihr auf Deutsch schreiben.

♦**to write down** aufschreiben ◊ *I wrote down the address.* Ich habe die Adresse aufgeschrieben. ◊ *Can you write it down for me, please?* Können Sie es mir bitte aufschreiben?

writer NOUN

der Schriftsteller (PL die Schriftsteller)

die Schriftstellerin

◊ *She's a writer.* Sie ist Schriftstellerin.

writing NOUN

die Schrift ◊ *I can't read your writing.* Ich kann deine Schrift nicht lesen.

♦**in writing** schriftlich

written VERB *see* **write**

wrong ADJECTIVE, ADVERB

1 falsch (*incorrect*) ◊ *The information they gave us was wrong.* Die Information, die sie uns gegeben haben, war falsch. ◊ *the wrong answer* die falsche Antwort

♦**You've got the wrong number.** Sie haben sich verwählt.

2 unrecht (*morally bad*) ◊ *I think fox hunting is wrong.* Ich meine, dass Fuchsjagden unrecht sind.

♦**to be wrong** (*mistaken*) unrecht haben ◊ *You're wrong about that.* Sie haben da unrecht.

♦**to do something wrong** etwas falsch machen ◊ *You've done it wrong.* Du hast das falsch gemacht. ◊ *Have I done something wrong?* Habe ich etwas falsch gemacht?

♦**to go wrong** (*plan*) schiefgehen ◊ *The robbery went wrong and they got caught.* Der Überfall ist schiefgegangen, und man hat sie gefasst.

♦**What's wrong?** Was ist los?

♦**What's wrong with her?** Was ist mit ihr los?

wrote VERB *see* **write**

WWW ABBREVIATION (= *World Wide Web*)

♦**the WWW** das WWW

W

X

Xmas NOUN (= *Christmas*)
Weihnachten NEUT

to **X-ray** VERB
see also **X-ray** NOUN
röntgen ◊ *They X-rayed my arm.* Sie haben meinen Arm geröntgt.

X-ray NOUN
see also **X-ray** VERB
die Röntgenaufnahme
♦ **to have an X-ray** geröntgt werden

Y

yacht NOUN
[1] (*sailing boat*)
das <u>Segelboot</u> (PL die Segelboote)
[2] (*luxury motorboat*)
die <u>Jacht</u>

yard NOUN
der <u>Hof</u> (*of building*) (PL die Höfe) ◊ *in the yard* auf dem Hof

to **yawn** VERB
<u>gähnen</u>

year NOUN
das <u>Jahr</u> (PL die Jahre) ◊ *last year* letztes Jahr ◊ *next year* nächstes Jahr ◊ *to be fifteen years old* fünfzehn Jahre alt sein
♦ **an eight-year-old child** ein achtjähriges Kind

> ❶ In Germany secondary schools, years are counted from the **fünfte Klasse** (youngest) to the **dreizehnte Klasse** (oldest).

◊ *the first year* die fünfte Klasse ◊ *the fifth year* die neunte Klasse ◊ *She's in the fifth year.* Sie ist in der neunten Klasse.
♦ **He's a first-year.** Er ist in der fünften Klasse.

to **yell** VERB
<u>schreien</u> (IMPERFECT schrie, PERFECT hat geschrien)

yellow ADJECTIVE
<u>gelb</u>

yes ADVERB
[1] <u>ja</u> ◊ *Do you like it? – Yes.* Gefällt es dir? – Ja. ◊ *Would you like a cup of tea? – Yes please.* Möchtest du eine Tasse Tee? – Ja bitte.
[2] <u>doch</u>
> Use **doch** to contradict a negative statement or question.

◊ *Don't you like it? – Yes!* Gefällt es dir nicht? – Doch! ◊ *You're not Swiss, are you? – Yes I am!* Sie sind nicht Schweizer, oder? – Doch, ich bin Schweizer. ◊ *That's not true. – Yes it is!* Das ist nicht wahr. – Doch!

yesterday ADVERB
<u>gestern</u> ◊ *yesterday morning* gestern früh ◊ *yesterday afternoon* gestern Nachmittag ◊ *yesterday evening* gestern Abend ◊ *all day yesterday* gestern den ganzen Tag
♦ **the day before yesterday** vorgestern

yet ADVERB
[1] <u>noch</u> ◊ *It has yet to be proved that ...* Es muss noch bewiesen werden, dass ...

[2] <u>schon</u> (*in questions*) ◊ *Has the murderer been caught yet?* Ist der Mörder schon gefasst worden?
♦ **not yet** noch nicht ◊ *It's not finished yet.* Es ist noch nicht fertig.
♦ **not as yet** noch nicht ◊ *There's no news as yet.* Es gibt noch keine Nachricht.
♦ **Have you finished yet?** Bist du fertig?

yield EXCLAMATION [US]
<u>Vorfahrt achten</u> (*on road sign*)

yob NOUN
der <u>Rowdy</u> (PL die Rowdys)

yoghurt NOUN
der <u>Joghurt</u> (PL die Joghurt)

yolk NOUN
das <u>Eigelb</u> (PL die Eigelbe)

you PRONOUN
> *Only use* **du** *when speaking to one person, and when the person is your own age or younger. Use* **ihr** *for several people of your own age or younger. If in doubt use the polite form* **Sie**.

[1] <u>Sie</u> (*polite form, singular and plural*) ◊ *Do you like football?* Mögen Sie Fußball? ◊ *Can I help you?* Kann ich Ihnen behilflich sein? ◊ *I saw you yesterday.* Ich habe Sie gestern gesehen. ◊ *It's for you.* Das ist für Sie.
[2] <u>du</u> (*familiar singular*) ◊ *Do you like football?* Magst du Fußball? ◊ *She's younger than you.* Sie ist jünger als du. ◊ *I know you.* Ich kenne dich. ◊ *I gave it you.* Ich habe es dir gegeben. ◊ *It's for you.* Es ist für dich. ◊ *I'll come with you.* Ich komme mit dir mit.
[3] <u>ihr</u> (*familiar plural*) ◊ *Do you two like football?* Mögt ihr beiden Fußball? ◊ *I told you to be quiet.* Ich habe euch gesagt, ihr sollt still sein. ◊ *This is for you two.* Es ist für euch beide. ◊ *Can I come with you?* Kann ich mit euch mitkommen?

young ADJECTIVE
<u>jung</u> ◊ *young people* junge Leute

younger ADJECTIVE
<u>jünger</u> ◊ *He's younger than me.* Er ist jünger als ich. ◊ *my younger brother* mein jüngerer Bruder ◊ *my younger sister* meine jüngere Schwester

youngest ADJECTIVE
<u>jüngste</u> ◊ *his youngest brother* sein jüngster Bruder ◊ *She's the youngest.* Sie ist die Jüngste.

your ADJECTIVE
> *Only use* **dein** *when speaking to one person, and when the person is your own age or younger. For several people of your own age or younger use* **euer**. *If in doubt use the polite form* **Ihr**.

Y

1 Ihr (*polite form, singular and plural*)
◇ *your father* Ihr Vater ◇ *your mother*
Ihre Mutter ◇ *your house* Ihr Haus ◇ *your
seats* Ihre Plätze
2 dein (*familiar singular*) ◇ *your brother*
dein Bruder ◇ *your sister* deine
Schwester ◇ *your book* dein Buch ◇ *your
parents* deine Eltern
3 euer (*familiar plural*) ◇ *your father* euer
Vater ◇ *your mother* eure Mutter ◇ *your
car* euer Auto ◇ *your teachers* eure
Lehrer

> *Do not use Ihr, dein or euer with parts of
> the body.*
> ◇ *Would you like to wash your hands?*
> Möchten Sie sich die Hände waschen?
> ◇ *Do you want to wash your hair?*
> Möchtest du dir die Haare waschen?
> ◇ *You two, go upstairs and brush your
> teeth.* Ihr beide geht nach oben und putzt
> euch die Zähne.

yours PRONOUN

> *Only use deiner/deine/deines when
> talking to one person of your own age or
> younger. Use euer/eure/eures when
> talking to several people of your own
> age or younger. If in doubt use the polite
> form Ihrer/Ihre/Ihres.*

1 (*polite form, singular and plural*)
Ihrer ◇ *That's a nice coat. Is it yours?* Das
ist ein hübscher Mantel. Ist es Ihrer?
Ihre ◇ *What a pretty jacket. Is it yours?*
Was für eine hübsche Jacke. Ist das
Ihre?
Ihres ◇ *I like that car. Is it yours?* Das
Auto gefällt mir. Ist es Ihres?
Ihre ◇ *my parents and yours* meine
Eltern und Ihre
♦ **Is this yours?** Gehört das Ihnen? ◇ *This
book is yours.* Das Buch gehört Ihnen.
♦ **Yours sincerely,** ... Mit freundlichen
Grüßen ...
2 (*familiar singular*)
deiner ◇ *I've lost my pen. Can I use
yours?* Ich habe meinen Schreiber
verlegt. Kann ich deinen benützen?
deine ◇ *Nice jacket. Is it yours?* Hübsche
Jacke. Ist das deine?
deines ◇ *I like that car. Is it yours?* Das
Auto gefällt mir. Ist das deines?
deine ◇ *my parents and yours* meine
Eltern und deine ◇ *My hands are dirty,
yours are clean.* Meine Hände sind
schmutzig, deine sind sauber.
♦ **Is this yours?** Gehört das dir? ◇ *This
book is yours.* Das Buch gehört dir.
◇ *Whose is this? – It's yours.* Wem gehört

das? – Es gehört dir.
3 (*familiar plural*)
euer ◇ *My computer is broken. Can I use
yours?* Mein Computer ist kaputt. Kann
ich euren benutzen?
eure ◇ *I haven't got a typewriter. Can I
use yours?* Ich habe keine
Schreibmaschine. Kann ich eure
benutzen?
eures ◇ *Our house is bigger than yours.*
Unser Haus ist größer als eures.
eure ◇ *our parents and yours* unsere
Eltern und eure
♦ **Is this yours?** Gehört das euch? ◇ *These
books are yours.* Diese Bücher gehören
euch. ◇ *Whose is it? – It's yours.* Wem
gehört das? – Es gehört euch.

yourself PRONOUN

> *Only use dich/dir when talking to one
> person of your own age or younger. If in
> doubt use the polite form sich.*

1 sich (*polite form*) ◇ *Have you hurt
yourself?* Haben Sie sich verletzt? ◇ *Tell
me about yourself!* Erzählen Sie etwas
von sich!
2 dich (*familiar form*) ◇ *Have you hurt
yourself?* Hast du dich verletzt?
3 dir (*familiar form*) ◇ *Tell me about
yourself!* Erzähl mir etwas von dir! ◇ *If
you are not happy with yourself ...* Wenn
du mit dir selbst nicht zufrieden bist ...
4 selbst
♦ **Do it yourself! (1)** Machen Sie es selbst!
♦ **Do it yourself! (2)** Mach's selbst!

yourselves PRONOUN

> *Only use euch when talking to people of
> your own age or younger. If in doubt use
> the polite form sich.*

1 sich (*polite form*) ◇ *Did you enjoy
yourselves?* Haben Sie sich amüsiert?
2 euch (*familiar form*) ◇ *Did you enjoy
yourselves?* Habt ihr euch amüsiert?
3 selbst
♦ **Did you make it yourselves? (1)** Haben
Sie es selbst gemacht?
♦ **Did you make it yourselves? (2)** Habt ihr
es selbst gemacht?

youth club NOUN
das Jugendzentrum (PL die
Jugendzentren)
youth hostel NOUN
die Jugendherberge
Yugoslavia NOUN
Jugoslawien NEUT
♦ **in the former Yugoslavia** im ehemaligen
Jugoslawien

Z

zany ADJECTIVE
irre komisch ◊ *a zany film* ein irre komischer Film

zebra NOUN
das Zebra (PL die Zebras)

zebra crossing NOUN
der Zebrastreifen (PL die Zebrastreifen)

zero NOUN
die Null

Zimbabwe NOUN
Simbabwe NEUT ◊ *in Zimbabwe* in Simbabwe

Zimmer frame ® NOUN
der Gehapparat (PL die Gehapparate)

zip NOUN
der Reißverschluss (GEN des Reißverschlusses, PL die Reißverschlüsse)

zip code NOUN US
die Postleitzahl

zip drive NOUN
das Zip-Laufwerk (PL die Zip-Laufwerke)

zipper NOUN US
der Reißverschluss (GEN des Reißverschlusses, PL die Reißverschlüsse)

zit NOUN
der Pickel (PL die Pickel)

zodiac NOUN
der Tierkreis (GEN des Tierkreises)
♦ **the signs of the zodiac** die Sternzeichen

zone NOUN
die Zone

zoo NOUN
der Zoo (PL die Zoos)

zoom lens NOUN
das Zoomobjektiv (PL die Zoomobjektive)

zucchini PL NOUN US
die Zucchini PL

LIST OF NEW GERMAN SPELLINGS

▶ GERMAN SPELLING REFORM

In July 1996 all German-speaking countries signed a declaration concerning the reform of German spelling, with the result that a number of new spelling rules were established. These new German spelling rules are now taught in all schools, and are widely used throughout the German-speaking world. In the dictionary we have shown the new spellings where they occur as headwords on the German-English side or as translations on the English-German side. In addition, where the old spelling of a word does not come immediately before or after the new spelling in the dictionary text, the old spelling has been shown in its alphabetical position and a reference has been given to tell you where you can find the new spelling and its translation e.g. **rauh** is cross-referred to **rau**. Of course, you will still come across old spellings in other texts, so to help you recognize them, we have given here a list of new spellings, together with the corresponding old spellings. Words appearing in the dictionary which were previously spelt as one word, and which are now spelt as two words, or vice versa e.g. **freihalten – frei halten, leid tun – leidtun** have also been included in this list.

NEW	OLD	NEW	OLD
Abend	abend	Esskastanie	Eßkastanie
Abfluss	Abfluß	Esslöffel	Eßlöffel
Abschlussprüfung	Abschlußprüfung	esst	eßt
allzu oft	allzuoft	Esszimmer	Eßzimmer
allzu viel	allzuviel	Fairness	Fairneß
Anlass	Anlaß	Fass	Faß
Anschluss	Anschluß	Fitnesszentrum	Fitneßzentrum
Ass	As	floss	floß
auf sein	aufsein	Fluss	Fluß
aufschlussreich	aufschlußreich	Flüsschen	Flüßchen
Ausschluss	Ausschluß	Flussufer	Flußufer
Ausschuss	Ausschuß	föhnen	fönen
aus sein	aussein	frei halten	freihalten
Balletttänzer	Ballettänzer	frisst	frißt
Balletttänzerin	Ballettänzerin	Gebiss	Gebiß
Bass	Baß	gefangen nehmen	gefangennehmen
beiseitelassen	beiseite lassen	gefasst	gefaßt
beiseitelegen	beiseite legen	geheim halten	geheimhalten
beiseiteschaffen	beiseite schaffen	gemusst	gemußt
Beschluss	Beschluß	genau genommen	genaugenommen
bewusst	bewußt	genoss	genoß
bewusstlos	bewußtlos	Genuss	Genuß
Bewusstlosigkeit	Bewußtlosigkeit	genüsslich	genüßlich
Bewusstsein	Bewußtsein	gernhaben	gern haben
biss	biß	geschrien	geschrien/geschrieen
Biss	Biß	gewiss	gewiß
bisschen	bißchen	Gewissheit	Gewißheit
blass	blaß	gewusst	gewußt
Brennnessel	Brennessel	goss	goß
Cashewnuss	Cashewnuß	grässlich	gräßlich
dabei sein	dabeisein	Gräuel	Greuel
da sein	dasein	Grundriss	Grundriß
dass	daß	Haselnuss	Haselnuß
durchnässt	durchnäßt	Hass	Haß
Einfluss	Einfluß	hässlich	häßlich
Engpass	Engpaß	Hexenschuss	Hexenschuß
entlässt	entläßt	Imbiss	Imbiß
Entschluss	Entschluß	Imbisshalle	Imbißhalle
Erdgeschoss	Erdgeschoß	Imbissstand	Imbißstand
Erdnuss	Erdnuß	Imbissstube	Imbißstube
Erdnussbutter	Erdnußbutter	iss	iß
essbar	eßbar	isst	ißt

GERMAN SPELLING REFORM

Känguru → **so wenig**

NEW	OLD	NEW	OLD
Känguru	Känguruh	nass	naß
Karamell	Karamel	Nebenfluss	Nebenfluß
Karamellbonbon	Karamelbonbon	nummerieren	numerieren
Kokosnuss	Kokosnuß	Nuss	Nuß
Kompass	Kompaß	Obergeschoss	Obergeschoß
Kompromiss	Kompromiß	Ölmessstab	Ölmeßstab
Kontrabass	Kontrabaß	Pass	Paß
Kuss	Kuß	Passkontrolle	Paßkontrolle
lässt	läßt	Passwort	Paßwort
leidtun	leid tun	patschnass	patschnaß
Messgerät	Meßgerät	pflichtbewusst	pflichtbewußt
missbilligen	mißbilligen	Prozess	Prozeß
Missbrauch	Mißbrauch	Rad fahren	radfahren
missbrauchen	mißbrauchen	Rassenhass	Rassenhaß
Misserfolg	Mißerfolg	rau	rauh
Missgeschick	Mißgeschick	Regenguss	Regenguß
misshandeln	mißhandeln	Reisepass	Reisepaß
misslang	mißlang	Reißverschluss	Reißverschluß
misslingen	mißlingen	riss	riß
misslingt	mißlingt	Riss	Riß
misslungen	mißlungen	Rollladen	Rolladen
missmutig	mißmutig	Rosskastanie	Roßkastanie
misst	mißt	Russland	Rußland
misstrauen	mißtrauen	Schifffahrt	Schiffahrt
Misstrauen	Mißtrauen	Schikoree/Chicorée	Chicorée
misstrauisch	mißtrauisch	schiss	schiß
Missverständnis	Mißverständnis	schloss	schloß
missverstehen	mißverstehen	Schloss	Schloß
Mopp	Mop	Schluss	Schluß
muss	muß	Schlussverkauf	Schlußverkauf
musst	mußt	schmiss	schmiß
müsst	müßt	schnäuzen	schneuzen
musste	mußte	Schnellimbiss	Schnellimbiß
müsste	müßte	schoss	schoß
mussten	mußten	Schuss	Schuß
müssten	müßten	Schusswaffe	Schußwaffe
musstest	mußtest	selbstbewusst	selbstbewußt
müsstest	müßtest	selbstständig/selbständig	selbständig
musstet	mußtet	Sommerschlussverkauf	Sommerschlußverkauf
müsstet	müßtet	so viel	soviel
Nachlass	Nachlaß	so weit	soweit
Nacht	nacht	so wenig	sowenig

NEW	OLD
spazieren fahren	spazierenfahren
spazieren gehen	spazierengehen
Stewardess	Stewardeß
Stress	Streß
Tipp	Tip
tollpatschig	tolpatschig
Trugschluss	Trugschluß
tschüss	tschüs
Tunfisch/Thunfisch	Thunfisch
Überdruss	Überdruß
Überschuss	Überschuß
Umriss	Umriß
unbewusst	unbewußt
ungewiss	ungewiß
Ungewissheit	Ungewißheit
Universitätsabschluss	Universitätsabschluß
unmissverständlich	unmißverständlich
Unterbewusstsein	Unterbewußtsein
Untergeschoss	Untergeschoß
unvergesslich	unvergeßlich

NEW	OLD
verantwortungsbewusst	verantwortungsbewußt
vergesslich	vergeßlich
Vergissmeinnicht	Vergißmeinnicht
vergisst	vergißt
verschliss	verschliß
Verschluss	Verschluß
Vorhängeschloss	Vorhängeschloß
Walnuss	Walnuß
wie viel	wieviel
wisst	wißt
wusste	wußte
wussten	wußten
wusstest	wußtest
wusstet	wußtet
Zuckerguss	Zuckerguß
zugutekommen	zugute kommen
Zungenkuss	Zungenkuß
zu viel	zuviel
zu wenig	zuwenig